Carl Wilhelm Eduard Nägelsbach, Samuel Ralph Asbury

The book of the prophet Jeremiah

Carl Wilhelm Eduard Nägelsbach, Samuel Ralph Asbury
The book of the prophet Jeremiah
ISBN/EAN: 9783337103484
Printed in Europe, USA, Canada, Australia, Japan
Cover: Foto ©Lupo / pixelio.de

More available books at **www.hansebooks.com**

A

COMMENTARY

ON THE

HOLY SCRIPTURES:

CRITICAL, DOCTRINAL AND HOMILETICAL,

WITH SPECIAL REFERENCE TO MINISTERS AND STUDENTS.

BY

JOHN PETER LANGE, D.D.

IN CONNECTION WITH A NUMBER OF EMINENT EUROPEAN DIVINES.

TRANSLATED FROM THE GERMAN, REVISED, ENLARGED, AND EDITED

BY

PHILIP SCHAFF, D.D.

ASSISTED BY AMERICAN SCHOLARS OF VARIOUS EVANGELICAL DENOMINATIONS.

VOL. XII. OF THE OLD TESTAMENT: CONTAINING JEREMIAH AND LAMENTATIONS.

NEW YORK:
CHARLES SCRIBNER'S SONS,
1899

THE BOOK
OF THE
PROPHET JEREMIAH.

THEOLOGICALLY AND HOMILETICALLY EXPOUNDED

BY

Dr. C. W. EDUARD NAEGELSBACH,

PASTOR IN BAYREUTH, BAVARIA.

TRANSLATED, ENLARGED, AND EDITED

BY

SAMUEL RALPH ASBURY,

RECTOR OF TRINITY CHURCH, MOORESTOWN, N. J.

NEW YORK:
CHARLES SCRIBNER'S SONS,
1899

ENTERED, according to Act of Congress, in the year 1870, by
CHARLES SCRIBNER,
In the Clerk's Office of the District Court of the United States for the Southern District of New York.

PREFACE BY THE GENERAL EDITOR.

JEREMIAH was the most prominent personage in a period of deepest distress and humiliation of the Jewish theocracy. He witnessed one by one the departure of all prospects of a reformation and deliverance from impending national ruin. Profoundly sympathizing with the calamities of his people and country, he is emphatically the prophet of sorrow and affliction. The first quotation from him in the New Testament is " a voice of lamentation and weeping and great mourning" (Matt. ii. 17, 18). In his holy grief over Jerusalem and his bitter persecutions he resembles the life of Christ. Should he, instead of David, be the author of the xxii. Psalm, as HITZIG plausibly conjectures, the resemblance would even be more striking; but the superscription is against it. Standing alone in a hostile world, fearless and immovable, he delivered for forty years his mournful warnings and searching rebukes, dashed the false hopes of his deluded people to the ground, counselled submission instead of resistance, denounced the unfaithful priests and false prophets, and thus brought upon himself the charge of treachery and desertion; yet in the midst of gloom and darkness he held fast to trust in Jehovah, and in the stormy sunset of prophecy he beheld the dawn of a brighter day of a new covenant of the gospel written on the heart (xxxi. 31). He is therefore the prophet of the dispensation of the Spirit (Hebr. viii. 13; x. 16, 17). The character and temper of Jeremiah is reflected in his strongly subjective, tender, affecting, elegiac style, which combines the truth of history with the deepest pathos of poetry. It is the language of holy grief and sorrow. Even his prose is " more poetical than poetry, because of its own exceeding tragical simplicity." Jeremiah has proved a sympathizing companion and comforter in seasons of individual suffering and national calamity from the first destruction of Jerusalem down to the siege of Paris in our own day.

The elaborate Commentary on Jeremiah and the Lamentations, which appeared in 1868, as a part of Dr. LANGE's *Bibel-werk*, was prepared by Dr. C. W. EDWARD NAEGELSBACH, pastor in Bayreuth, Bavaria, the author of a Hebrew Grammar, of several small monographs, and important articles in HERZOG's *Theol. Encyclopædia*.

The Commentary on the Book of the Prophet Jeremiah was translated by the Rev. SAMUEL R. ASBURY, Rector of Trinity Church, Moorestown, N. J.

The Commentary on the Lamentations was translated by the Rev. WM. H. HORNBLOWER, D.D., of Paterson, N. J.

Considerable additions, amounting to 147 pages, were made in both works, especially the latter.* Dr. HORNBLOWER justly dissents from Dr. NAEGELSBACH's opinion concerning the authorship of the *Lamentations*, and defends the old tradition which assigns it to Jeremiah.

* The German Commentary on Jeremiah has 401 (xxii. and 379), that on Lamentations 94 (xvii. and 77), both 495 pages. The English edition has 446 pages on the Book of Jeremiah, 196 on Lamentations, in all 642 pages.

i

PREFACE BY THE GENERAL EDITOR.

In justice to the German author, I extract from his Preface what he says concerning his views on Biblical criticism:

"With reference to the critical principles I have adopted I ought perhaps to say something. There is inconsiderate criticism; there is also inconsiderate hostility to criticism. Between these two I have endeavored to preserve the golden mean. The absolute integrity of the received text cannot be maintained, and indeed is now held by none. But once granting that the original has undergone corruptions, and the right of criticism is admitted in principle. Of this right, however, a very unrighteous use may be made, as is the case whenever criticism sets itself in opposition to the spirit in which a work was produced. Such criticism may possibly hit the truth, it may discover errors, which the eye of love and reverence has failed to observe. It has done undeniable service in this regard. But this effect is accidental and exceptional, not necessary and universal. Criticism proceeding from adverse opinions will do more to render the good and genuine suspicious than to purify it from spurious elements. We must correct it, not with a denial of its right *per se*, but on the one hand with a rejection of the principles which govern the application of this right, and on the other with a rigid examination of the objective results. In the latter respect it is important, above all, not to confound the eternal truth with human traditional conceptions thereof. The eternal truth is not prejudiced, even though an interpolation or a lacuna may be discovered here and there in a canonical book. Did such discoveries inflict a vital injury, care would have been taken that not a single variation should creep into the sacred archives. But such variations do exist in number; there are, as we have said, unquestionable distortions of the original text of greater or less extent. It is thus seen that the Almighty was not concerned at a little dust, a slight rent, or a small piece of patchwork, affixed by an unhallowed hand, on the hem of the majestic garment of His holy oracles. There is always enough of the unassailable sacred text remaining intact, which to some may be a 'fountain of living water,' to others the 'sword of the Spirit.' Now would it be of any advantage to the good cause if we admitted no critical suspicion, but warded off every such attack at *any* price? Would it be well—would it be right—to ward off such attacks by artificial expedients? We should thus be in danger of defending the truth, consciously or unconsciously, with lies, so that the good cause would be rather injured than subserved. For thus we should undermine the citadel we were defending; we should induce in our readers the conviction that we were acting on the principle that 'the end justifies the means,' and were anxious not so much for truth as for victory. I have from the first guarded, for God's and my conscience' sake, against such unspiritual knight-errantry.

"And yet I consider that there is great advantage in criticism exercised with conscientious care. In the first place, the good cause is thus spared the miserable *testimonium paupertatis* to which a paltry fear of criticism exposes it, and it receives a *testimonium opulentiæ*, that is, we thus testify that we know the cause we espouse to stand on an impregnable basis and to be able to withstand every trial of critical fire. In the second place, we afford to ourselves a *testimonium honestatis*, that is, we cause it to be understood that we have to do with the truth, and will contend for it only with honorable means. In the third place, if the unquestionable, but relatively insignificant, corruptions do no harm, still a knowledge of the correct text is, directly for exegesis and indirectly for doctrinal theology, always of some importance. In the fourth and last place, a right exercise of criticism is an exemplification of the ἡλικία τοῦ πληρώματος τοῦ Χριστοῦ (Eph. iv. 13) and the αἰσθητήρια γεγυμνασμένα πρὸς διάκρισιν καλοῦ τε καὶ κακοῦ (Heb. v. 14)."

PHILIP SCHAFF.

New York, 40 *Bible House, April*, 1871.

THE

PROPHET JEREMIAH.

INTRODUCTION.

§ 1. THE HISTORICAL BACKGROUND OF JEREMIAH'S PROPHETIC LABORS.

The Old Testament theocracy in its external relations suffered two disastrous shocks ; the destruction by Nebuchadnezzar and that by Titus. Both culminated in the demolition of the temple and the holy city, and the carrying away of the people. Each of the two catastrophes had its prophet: the latter, as definitive, forming the first act of the judgment—Christ, the Judge, Himself (Matth. xxiv.): the former, the prophet Jeremiah.

It is however noteworthy that Jeremiah began his dirge at a time when the sick nation appeared to have been healed. The abomination of apostasy reached its acme in the act of Manasseh, the son of Hezekiah (2 Kings xxi 1–17), who placed idols and idol-altars in the temple, dedicated to the exclusive worship of Jehovah. After the short reign of his like-minded son Amon (2 Kings xxi. 18–25) Josiah ascended the throne of Judea, a prince of whom the book of Kings declares (xxiii. 25) that neither before him nor after him was there a king like him, who turned to the Lord with his whole heart, according to all the law of Moses. This pious king cleansed the land from all the abominations of idolatry, and restored the worship of Jehovah with a completeness which had not before existed (vers. 22-24, *etc.*). Unfortunately, notwithstanding his earnestness and good-will, Josiah's reform was only partial. The good soil was wanting for the seed, and hence his reformation was but a sowing among thorns. He had cleansed the land but not the hearts of the people (Jer. iv. 1-4. HERZOG, *Real-Enc.* XII. *S.* 227) and after his death the weeds shot forth again in full luxuriance. From its geographical position the theocracy was placed between two great powers, that of Egypt on the South, that of Assyria on the North. Assyria was about to succumb beneath the heavy blows of the Babylonians and Medes, and Pharaoh Necho, King of Egypt, regarded this as a favorable opportunity to conquer Syria. If he succeeded in this, Judea would be surrounded and in constant danger of being overpowered by him. Josiah attempted to repel P. Necho, and made the independence of Syria the final object of his policy (see NIEBUHR, *Ass. u. Bab. S.* 364). But he was defeated and slain at Megiddo, and Necho conquered Syria as far as the Euphrates. (2 Kings xxiv. 7). In the meantime Nineveh had fallen, B. C. 606. Nabopolassar, king of Babylon, sent the army thus set at liberty, under the command of his son Nebuchadnezzar, against the Egyptians, with whom a decisive and victorious battle was fought at Carchemish B. C. 605-4 In the same year his father died, and the youthful conqueror mounted the Babylonian throne. In Judea, after Josiah's death, the people had elected king not the eldest but second [surviving] son, Jehoahaz, probably fearing the despotic character of Jehoiakim. But Jehoahaz did not prove to be a good sovereign. He did that which was evil in the sight of the Lord, according to all that his fathers had done (2 Kings xxiii. 32). In Riblah, where he had probably gone to treat with Necho, he was taken prisoner, and was afterwards carried away as captive to Egypt, since Necho did not

1

desire a ruler in Jerusalem, who would pursue a national policy (2 Kings xxiii. 32, 34; Jer. xxii. 10-12). Jehoiakim was appointed by the Egyptian king in his place, and thus, as the creature of the latter, laid under obligation to serve him. The fears entertained as to his character were realized. He ruled despotically; his love of splendid architecture leading him to oppress the people severely (Jer. xxii. 13 sqq.); he shed much innocent blood, (ver. 17) and served idols like the ungodly kings before him. The overthrow of the Egyptian power in consequence of the battle of Carchemish involved his fall also. Although Nebuchadnezzar did not immediately take possession of Judea, his father's death necessitating his hasty return to Babylon, his supremacy over Syria and Egypt was secured. It was four years after the battle, in the eighth year of Jehoiakim, that he took Judea and Jerusalem (2 Kings xxiv. 1). The circumstance that the book of Kings makes no mention of the battle of Carchemish indicates that this made no perceptible difference in the condition of the kingdom of Judea. If Nebuchadnezzar had then invaded Judea, besieged and taken Jerusalem, and carried off prisoners and booty, it would certainly have been mentioned. The book of Jeremiah also contains no trace of Judea having then come into the actual possession of the Chaldeans. Jeremiah is always exhorting to submission. Jehoiakim reigns undisturbed in his fourth and fifth year at Jerusalem (comp. Jer. xxv. and xxxvi.) The fasting mentioned in xxxvi. 9, may as well have been occasioned by a danger threatening from a distance as any other,—least probably by the burden of a foreign rule then weighing on the people, since there is not a syllable intimating such an occasion. I therefore agree with those, who assume with Josephus (*Antiq.* X. 6, 1) that Nebuchadnezzar took Jerusalem for the first time in the eighth year of Jehoiakim. Comp. DUNCKER, *Gesch. d. Alterth.*, I. *S.* 825, on the other side FR. R. HASSE, *De Prima Neb. adv. Hierosol. expeditione*, Bonn., 1856. NIEBUHR, *Ass. u. Bab.*, *S.* 370, 373 sq. NIEBUHR seems to me to make too much of the passage, Dan. i. 1, 2, as well as of a notice in the *Seder Olam Rabba, c.* 24, and on the other hand too little of the testimony of the book of Kings and of Jeremiah. But however this may be, Jehoiakim, as well as the large majority of the people, took no heed to Jeremiah's exhortation to submit willingly to Nebuchadnezzar, and the consequence was that they were compelled to do so (2 Kings xxiv. 1). Three years afterwards Jehoiakim again revolted. A Chaldean army, with auxiliaries from Syria, Moab, and Ammon, reduced the rebellious people again to submission. At this juncture Jehoiakim lost his life, but whether in consequence of the capture of the city (JOSEPHUS *Antiq.* X. 6, 3, speaks of a voluntary admission of the Chaldeans into the city) or being taken prisoner outside the walls (so VAIHINGER in HERZOG, *Real-Enc.* VI. *S.* 790, as it appears, on the basis of Ezek. xix. 8 sq.) is uncertain. According to the book of Kings the Chaldeans do not appear to have taken the city immediately after the death of Jehoiakim, for his son Jehoiachin succeeded by right of inheritance, not by the will of the Babylonian monarch. As heir to his father's obligations he is indeed made war upon and punished, but not so severely as Zedekiah (comp. 2 Kings xxiv. 15; and xxv. 27 sq., with xxv. 6 sq.; Jer. lii. 9-11). Whether the siege of Jerusalem began before Jehoiakim's death or after cannot be ascertained; certainly not long after, for Jehoiachin (who had also reigned in a manner displeasing to Jehovah) only three months after his accession to the throne, had to yield to the besieging forces of Nebuchadnezzar. The latter carried him, his family, the princes, the soldiers, and the smiths, all who could make or bear arms, captives to Babylon. (2 Kings xxiv. 14 sq.). This was the first deportation, and did not attain its object of rendering the people incapable of resistance. Nebuchadnezzar seems not to have been aware of the amazing tenacity of the Jewish character, or he would have done then what he was obliged to do afterwards. He allowed the kingdom of Judah to remain, but appointed a king of his own choice, Mattaniah, the youngest son of Josiah. He, like Eliakim, had to change his name, and perhaps with reference to the promise given in xxiii. 5, (יהוָה צִדְקֵנוּ) assumed that of צִדְקִיָּהוּ. This sounds like mockery when we read the actual history of this king. He was not indeed inaccessible to better feelings, and seems to have been by no means so barbarous and cruel as Jehoiakim, but he was weak, and from dread of his too powerful nobles permitted every kind of transgression of the laws of Jehovah and injustice towards His prophet. The whole fanatical national party of the Jews, supported by a number of false prophets, united to induce him to break his oath of allegiance to the king of Babylon (Jer. xxiii. 9), and an impulse to this from without also was not wanting. In Zedekiah's fourth year ambassadors came

§ 1. THE HISTORICAL BACKGROUND OF JEREMIAH'S PROPHET LABORS.

from Tyre, Sidon, Ammon, Moab, and Edom (Jer. xxvii.) to consult together concerning a united revolt against the Babylonian rule. Then indeed Jeremiah appears to have stayed the revolt. The same year Zedekiah made a journey to Babylon to do homage (Jer. li. 59 sqq.), on which occasion by a strange turn Jeremiah gave to the king's marshall his great prophecy *against* Babylon, that he might read it to his master on the banks of the Euphrates, and then sink it in the stream. But scarcely had the Jews received intelligence that Pharaoh Hophra, grandson of Necho, who ascended the throne B. C. 589, was preparing to make war on Babylon than they thought themselves strong enough to venture on a revolt. But Nebuchadnezzar was not to be trifled with. Quickly, before the Egyptians could come up, he appeared with his army before Jerusalem, in the ninth year of Zedekiah (B. C. 588). He was indeed compelled by the approach of the Egyptian army to raise the siege, but he succeeded in repulsing the Egyptians, and Jerusalem was at once invested and sorely pressed. After being devastated by famine and pestilence, the city was taken in the 11th year of Zedekiah. The king fled with a part of his army, but was overtaken in the plain of Jericho, brought before Nebuchadnezzar at Riblah, in the land of Hamath, and after his children and the captive princes of Judah had been slain in his presence, his eyes were put out. He was then laden with chains, and carried to Babylon, where he remained in prison till his death (Jer. lii. 11; 2 Kings xxv. 7). Yet it appears that towards the end his imprisonment was less rigorous, and that he was honorably interred (Jer. xxxiv. 1–5). A month after the capture of the city, in the 4th month of the 9th year of Zedekiah, came Nebuzaradan, the captain of Nebuchadnezzar's guard, to Jerusalem, and caused the city and temple to be completely destroyed, and the people carried away. A few of the common people only remained in the country, over whom Gedaliah, the son of Ahikam, was appointed governor. Concerning him see the article by OEHLER in HERZOG's *Real-Enc.*, IV. *S.* 699. To his care Jeremiah, who was given his option, and preferred to remain in the country, was committed. Gedaliah was however soon afterward murdered by a certain Ishmael, a descendant of the royal family, at the instigation of Baalis, King of Ammon. The remaining Jews feared the vengeance of the Chaldeans, and although Jeremiah promised them safety and exemption from punishment if they stayed in the country, they removed with their wives and children and whole possessions to Egypt, whither the prophet was compelled to follow them. In Egypt they appear to have settled in different places (xliv. 1) and to have continued the worship of the queen of heaven (the Moabitish goddess, Astarte, see on vii. 18). At a festival of this deity, for which all the Jews in Egypt assembled in Pathros (upper Egypt) Jeremiah for the last time raised his prophetic voice in warning and rebuke. From an intimation of the approaching death of Pharaoh Hophra, which he gave to his countrymen, as a prophetic sign, and which we can only regard as shortly preceding the death of that monarch, we may infer that he continued his prophetic labors till towards the year B. C. 570.

If now we survey at a glance the whole character of the historical position in which Jeremiah was placed, we see in him the herald of the first precursory catastrophe of the external theocracy. At the same time he had also a mission to Babylon, the power which was appointed, after Egypt and Assyria, to engulf the theocracy, and thus in a certain sense to be the first universal monarchy. He was first to prepare the way for the divine mission of this power as the instrument of judgment on the theocracy, and then to announce its appointed judgment, after a brief respite of seventy years, and the redemption of the theocracy. This he could do only in the form of that perspective fore-shortening, which is peculiar to prophetic pictures of the future, and which has to be rectified by the fulfilment. Thus we may say that Jeremiah stands at that epoch in universal history, at which the first precursory judgment is inflicted by worldly power on the kingdom of God, and here he has to announce to both judgment and redemption; to the kingdom of God first judgment and afterwards redemption, to the world first victory and glory, but afterwards judgment (chaps. l. li.).

§ 2. THE PERSON AND MINISTRY OF JEREMIAH.

The name יִרְמְיָהוּ (abbreviated and later form יִרְמְיָה xxvii. 1; xxviii. 5, 10, 11, 15; xxix. 1; Dan. ix. 2) is not, with Jerome and many since (comp. NEUMANN, *Jer. v. Anat.* I., *S.* 8), to be derived from יָרַם *a rad.* יָרַם=רוּם with the meaning of *elatio, elatus, Domini*, but (according to many analogies יִרְחִיָה, יִפְדְיָה, יִבְנְיָה, etc.) from רָמָה and the only possible meaning is *Jova jacit, projicit, dejicit* or *ejicit* (see HENGSTENBERG, *Christology*, *Edinb. Transl.* II. p. 362). It is probable, as HENGSTENBERG supposes, that the name is based on the passage Exod. xv. 1 (אָשִׁירָה לַיהוָֹה כִּי רָכְבוּ רָמָה בַיָּם).

As to his origin, Jeremiah is called (i. 1) "a son of Hilkiah, of the priests who were at Anathoth, in the land of Benjamin." From this it is seen that he was of the sacerdotal race. It is possible, but cannot be proved, that his father was the same with that high-priest Hilkiah, who, in the 15th year of Josiah, found the book of the law in the temple (2 Kings xxii. 3 sq.), as maintained by CLEM. ALEX., JEROME, THEODORET, KIMCHI, ABARBANEL, EICHHORN, VON BOHLEN, and UMBREIT. Comp. NEUMANN, *Commentar. S.* 16 sqq. [HENDERSON: "The opinion that his father, Hilkiah, was the high priest of that name who discovered the book of the law, can only have originated in the identity of name: for if that exalted official had been his father, he could not have failed to be designated by the appellative הַכֹּהֵן הַגָּדוֹל, *the high priest*, or at least הַכֹּהֵן, *the priest*, by way of eminence; whereas, he is merely spoken of as belonging to the priests who resided at Anathoth."—S. R. A.]

Anathoth, the birth-place of our prophet, is mentioned Josh. xxi. 28; 1 Kings ii. 26; Isa. x. 30; 1 Chron. vii. 60; Neh. ii. 32. In the Talmud the place is called עֲנָת in which we may perceive the transition to the present Anâta, which, according to ROBINSON (*Bibl. Res.* II. 109, comp. *Zeitschr. f. d. K. d. Morgenl.* II. *S.* 354 f.; TOBLER, *Topog.* II. *S.* 395; RITTER [*Palestine*, GAGE'S *Transl.* IV. 217; STANLEY, *Sinai and Pal.*, p. 212. THOMSON, *The Land and the Book*, II. 548.—S. R. A.]), is situated about three miles to the north-east of Jerusalem. This agrees pretty accurately with the statement of EUSEBIUS (*Onomast, s. v.*) and of JEROME (on i. 1; xi. 21; xxxii. 7), according to which Anathoth was three Roman miles, and of JOSEPHUS (*Antiquities*, X. 7, 3), according to which it was twenty Roman stadia distant from Jerusalem.

According to i. 6, Jeremiah was called to the prophetic office while still young, and according to i. 2; xxv. 3, in the thirteenth year of Josiah, therefore B. C. 627. This was the time in which Josiah had commenced his work of reformation (2 Chron. xxxiv. 3), and also that in which the overthrow of Syria by the united forces of the Medes and Babylonians was impending. Jeremiah thus appeared at a moment when the chief internal and external enemies of the theocracy, idolatry and Assyria, had been sensibly checked. Apparently excellent auspices for the success of his ministry! But it is noteworthy that in his book we do not find the trace of an allusion to these two circumstances. From xi. 21 it is probable that Jeremiah prophesied for a while in his native place, but afterwards we find him fixed in Jerusalem, where, in the temple (*e. g.*, vii. 2, xxvi. 1 sq.), in the gates of the city (xvii. 19), in prison (xxxii. 2), in the king's house (xxii. 1; xxxvii. 17), and in other places (xviii. 1; xix. 1), by word, by writing (xxix. 1; xxxvi. 2), and by signs (xviii. 1; xix. 1; xxvii. 2), he proclaims the word of the Lord. The first twenty-two years of his ministry flow by without any special personal experiences, and the quintessence only of his life at that time is preserved in the earlier prophetic sections. The year 605-4 however forms a turning point in the prophet's career. This was the year of the battle of Carchemish and the succession of Nebuchadnezzar to the throne, two facts which involve a new epoch in history, the founding of the Babylonian universal monarchy, and its subjugation of the Jewish theocracy. Jeremiah had long before, even in the commencement of his labors (i. 13), prophesied evil to the theocracy from a people coming from the north, but he had not said that these people were the Chaldeans. It has been much debated what nation Jeremiah understood by these enemies to be expected from the north, and in recent times the view has been almost universal that they were the Scythians (see *Comm.* on i. 14), but it is plain that the prophet did not himself know the name of the enemies announced by him. If he knew, why should he not have named them? He names them first in that most important prophetic discourse (ch. xxv.), which may properly be regarded as central to, and presenting in outline, the whole of his prophecies. The highly important events of that year had manifestly given the external historical occasion to this extension of the prophet's vision. Although Nebuchadnezzar did not invade

§ 2. THE PERSON AND MINISTRY OF JEREMIAH.

Judea till four years later, yet the facts of his victory over the Egyptians and his accession to the throne furnished to the prophet sufficient support for a prophetic programme, which he proposed for the next seventy years, and which ran thus: "Since ye, inhabitants of Jerusalem and Judea, to whom I have proclaimed the word of the Lord for twenty-three years from the thirteenth year of Josiah, would not hear, ye shall be given into the hands of Nebuchadnezzar, king of Babylon, and not ye only, but Egypt, Uz, the Philistines, the Phœnicians, Edom, Moab, Ammon, the Arabians, Elamites and Medes (xxv. 19–25). Resistance to this instrument of God will not avail, but lead to greater misery (xxvii. 8). Hence the only remedy for entire overthrow will be voluntary submission. Those who yield will at least be allowed to inhabit the land and cultivate it (xxvii. 11). For seventy years all these nations will serve the king of Babylon, but at the expiration of this period the king and the land of the Chaldeans will themselves be visited (xxv. 11 sq. with xxvii. 7; xxix. 11), and Israel will be freed from their dominion."

This is the great prophetic programme which Jeremiah proposed in the fourth year of Jehoiakim for the *next* seventy years; for it is evident that he reckons the seventy years from this epoch. Though he does not expressly say so, it is plain from this circumstance that from this moment he regards the supremacy of Nebuchadnezzar, with remarkable distinctness, as a *fait accompli*. Though it was not so outwardly, it was so according to the inner reality known only to the prophet. To him the victory at Carchemish seemed the principle, which, as the manifestation of a divine purpose, infallibly involved all the subsequent successes of that prince. Hence it was settled in his mind that from the moment of victory at Carchemish, Nebuchadnezzar, if not *de facto*, yet *de jure*, and moreover *de jure divino*, was lord and ruler of all the nations mentioned in xxv. 11 sqq. (See the *Comm.* on xxv. 1–11).

In the same year Jeremiah received the command of the Lord to write out his prophecies, which is evidence that his prophetic labors were about to close. The twenty-fifth chapter and the chapters pertaining to it are the kernel and centre of his prophecies. Having reached this point, they were ripe and ready to be committed to writing, and at the same time a final assault was to be made on the hard hearts of the people by the powerful impression of all the discourses combined into a single whole (xxxvi. 3, 7). This object was attained with respect neither to the people nor their leaders. At this time indeed Jeremiah had many patrons among the princes, and the majority seem to have been well disposed toward him. For when, after hearing the great discourse (ch. vii.—x.), priests, prophets and people threatened Jeremiah with death, the princes brought the people over to their side, and took the prophet into their protection from the priests and prophets (xxvi. 8, 16). And when the existence of Jeremiah's writing was communicated to Jehoiakim, who, according to xxvi. 22, had, before this, caused the prophet Urijah to be brought from Egypt and executed, the princes instructed Jeremiah and Baruch to hide themselves, without doubt, on the correct presumption that the king would cause them to be apprehended. After reading the book, the king did indeed give the order for their apprehension, "but the Lord hid them" (xxxvi. 26). The writing and reading of the collected discourses passed over without the desired effect, though the destruction of the book produced a slight feeling of respectful awe in some of the princes. The catastrophe took place. Jehoiakim and Jehoiachin came to the miserable end predicted. Jeremiah's period of suffering began in the reign of the feeble Zedekiah. The princes who had taken him under their protection from the priests and prophets, now appear to be his bitterest enemies. They seem to have regarded his constant exhortation to submit to the Chaldeans as in the highest degree dangerous and treasonable (xxxviii. 4). DUNCKER (*Gesch. d. Alterth.* I. *S.* 831) is disposed to think that they were right. But he forgets that the Jews persevered in their opposition with impenitent, criminal and superstitious obstinacy (vii. 4), and that Jeremiah rebuked not their patriotism, but their ungodliness. Once indeed it seemed as though they would enter on the path of obedience to the commands of their God, when, in accordance with the law, they proclaimed the emancipation of the Hebrew slaves (xxxiv. 8). But their conscientiousness was only apparent: it was to subserve the interest of defence, and when, in consequence of the temporary withdrawal of the Chaldeans, this interest seemed less important, the emancipation was revoked. About this time Jeremiah was apprehended on a false pretext (xxxvii. 11), beaten and kept in close confinement until the city was taken. The king indeed was compelled repeatedly to seek counsel from the despised and hated prophet (xxxvii. 17; xxxviii. 11 sq.), but the weak monarch could accomplish nothing against the will of his nobles, who cherished the fiercest resentment toward the prophet who had humbled so severely their carnal disposition of pride and stubbornness. Since Jeremiah, even in prison, persisted in proclaiming the decree of the Lord that Jerusalem must be given up to its enemies, and that he only would escape with his life, who should surrender himself to the Chaldeans, they caused him to be thrown into a pit full of slime, from which he was rescued only through the intercession of a royal eunuch, Ebed-melech, the Cushite (xxxviii. 1-13). This was the lowest point in the personal sufferings of Jeremiah. How fearful they were, is evident from the representation of ch. xxxviii., which, though uncomplaining, is all the more eloquent from its silence. It is highly significant that it is just in this most terrible period of the prophet's life, and in the midst of the immediate preparation for the entire destruction of the theocracy, that we find the glorious prophecy of THE LORD OUR RIGHTEOUSNESS (ch. xxxiii.). In the deepest affliction the Lord here also bestows the highest consolation.

Finally, in the 11th year of Zedekiah Jerusalem was taken. There seems to be a double account of the fate of the prophet at this juncture. According to xxxix. 11-14, Jeremiah appears to have been liberated at Jerusalem, while according to xl. 1 sqq., he was first dragged in chains to Rama and then set at liberty. Yet the contradiction is only apparent, for if after he had been *declared* free by the commander he remained among the people (וַיֵּשֶׁב בְּתוֹךְ הָעָם, xxxix. 14) he might in the confusion have been treated like the rest by the common soldiers After his liberation Jeremiah betook himself to Mizpah, to Gedaliah, the governor appointed by Nebuchadnezzar (xl. 1-6), but the latter being soon after murdered, the people compelled the prophet to accompany them to Egypt, although he had most emphatically advised against their course, as displeasing to Jehovah (xli. 17; xliii. 7). The Jews settled first in Tahpanhes [a strong boundary-city on the Tanitic or Pelusian branch of the Nile. HEND.] Here and again in Pathros, ten years later, Egypt heard the voice of the prophet admonishing and rebuking his people (xliii. 8-13; xliv.). This is the last that we learn of Jeremiah from biblical sources. Further we have only traditions concerning him. Neither the time, place nor manner of his death is known. It may be inferred that he lived to a great age, from the fact that he was still alive about the year B. C. 570 (see § 1). It is a common assumption that at the time of his call in the thirteenth year of Josiah, he was twenty years old (i. 6, נַעַר), so that in 586, the year of the fall of Jerusalem, he was 61, and 16 years after was 77. But this calculation, resting on a mere assumption, is only problematic. With respect to the place and manner of his death, the tradition of the fathers, which has been adopted by the Romish church and fixed in the *Martyrologium Romanum* 1 May, is that he was stoned by the people at Tahpanhes (*a populo lapidibus obrutus apud Taphnas occubuit, ibique sepultus est*). Comp. TERTULLIAN *Scorp.* 8, *coll. c. Marcion*, 6, in which latter passage he says: "*nulla morte virum constat neque cædc peremtum.*" HIERON. *adv. Jovin* 2, 37; EPIPHAN. περὶ τῶν προφητῶν, etc. *Opp. II., pag.* 239. According to another Jewish tradition, Nebuchadnezzar having subdued Egypt in the 27th year of his reign, took Jeremiah and Baruch with him to Babylon (*Seder Olam Rabba, c.* 26).

Greatly persecuted during his life-time, Jeremiah was as greatly honored by his fellow-countrymen after his death. It was natural that the prophecies relating to the captivity should become in an eminent degree the objects of reverence and study to the captive Jews. Comp. Dan. ix. 2; 2 Chron. xxxvi. 21; Ezra i. 1. The destruction of the holy city and the captivity were themselves the most brilliant justification of the formerly despised and hated prophet. As it not rarely happens in such cases, a complete revolution gradually took place in the estimate of the prophet. His person was transfigured into a purely ideal character; multitudes of marvellous legends contributed to his glorification (2 Macc. ii. 1; xv. 12-16. Comp. HERZOG, *Real-Enc.* VII. *S.* 245) and to his countrymen he appeared so much the greatest of all the prophets that they called him ὁ προφήτης (in which sense also Deut. xviii. 15 was interpreted) and believed that he would return at the end of days. Allusions to this belief are found even in the New Testament, Matt. xvi. 14; John i. 21; *coll.* vi. 14; vii. 40. Comp Wisd. xlix. 6-8.—CARPZOV *Introd.* P. III. C. 3, § 2; FABRICIUS, *Codex pseudep. V. T.* p. 1110 sqq.; BERTHOLDT, *Christol. Jud.* § 15, pp. 61-67 and his *Einl.* IV. *S.* 1415 sq.; DE WETTE, *Bibl. Dogmatik,* § 197.—Concerning an apocryphal Jeremiah in the Hebrew language, from which the quotation Matt.

§ 2. THE PERSON AND MINISTRY OF JEREMIAH.

xxvii. 9, is alleged to have been made, see FABRIC., p. 1103, etc.; HERZOG, *Real-Enc.* XII. *S.* 314. For a very full synopsis of the material relating to this subject, see NEUMANN, *Jer. v. Anat. Einl.* I. *S.* 67.—On the supposed influence of Jeremiah on Grecian philosophy, see especially GHISLERUS, *In proph. Jerem Comment. I. Præf. cap.* 5.

From this historical sketch it may be perceived under what difficult external conditions Jeremiah had to exercise his prophetic office. If we compare with these his mental constitution, the task appears still more arduous. By nature of a mild and timid disposition, more of a John than a Peter, a Baptist or an Elijah, he had yet to conduct a life and death struggle against powerful and imbittered foes. The deep degradation of his people in the carnal lust of idolatry and their almost inconceivable presuming on the privileges of the chosen race, and the seemingly indestructible safeguard of the הֵיכַל יְהוָה (vii. 4), and in consequence their stiff-necked refusal to obey the Lord's command to submit to the Chaldeans as the only means of escape—all this Jeremiah had to combat. And as though he did not suffer enough from the enmity of his own people he was also obliged to denounce, with threatening words and signs, the judgments of the Lord on foreign nations (chapters xxv., xxvii.; xlvi.-li.). Thus on all sides arose fearful hatred and likewise fearful scorn of the prophet, who on his part was impelled by no other motive than a most hearty love for his people, which in the hour of his deepest affliction he never renounced (comp. viii. 21 sq.), on which account he is called in the second book of Maccabees, φιλάδελφος and πολλὰ προσευχόμενος περὶ τοῦ λαοῦ καὶ τῆς ἁγίας πόλεως (xv. 14), and by GREGORY NAZIANZ. (*Orat.* X.) συμπαθέστατος τῶν προφητῶν. Comp. GHISLER, *Præf. Cap.* 1. His life was exposed to constant danger, his honor to constant insult (xi. 21; xx. 7-10; xxxviii. 4; Lam. iii. 14). Like a second Job he curses the day of his birth (xx. 15), and longs to be free from the office, which he accepted only with fear and trembling (xx. 9*). But the consciousness of his vocation leaves him no rest. "But it was in my heart as a burning fire shut up in my bones, and I was weary with forbearing and I could not." Comp. HERZOG, (*Real-Enc.* XVII. *S.* 628, 634). But the Lord's strength was mighty in his weakness. "For behold I have made thee this day a defenced city and an iron pillar and brazen walls against the whole land" (i. 18). He needed this the more since he was deprived of all human aid. He had not even a fellow-prophet to stand by him, at least not in the time of his greatest distress. For of the prophets contemporary with him, Zephaniah and the prophetess Huldah (2 Kings xxii. 14; 2 Chron. xxxiv. 22) lived in the reign of Josiah, Habakkuk and Urijah (xxvi. 20) in the reign of Jehoiakim, that is, in the first and calmer period of his ministry. Ezekiel and Daniel indeed survived with him the great catastrophe, but they lived at a distance, themselves already in exile. Jeremiah could derive no support from them.

It has been correctly inferred from xvi. 2 that our prophet was unmarried, and his *virginitas* has therefore been extolled, especially by JEROME, in his *Præfatio* and *Comm.* on chap. xxiii. We read that here and there among the people, and in earlier times among the princes (xxvi. 16, 24; xxxvi. 19), a favorable disposition towards him was manifested; even King Zedekiah was secretly inclined to favor him, and besides these he may have had many friends, as Baruch (chap. xlv.) and his brother, Seraiah (li. 59), the royal eunuch, Ebedmelech (xxxviii. 7 sq.), and Ahikam, the son of Shaphan, with his son Gedaliah (xxvi. 24; xxxix. 14; xl. 5), but what were these to the hostility with which he was persecuted by the great mass of the proud princes, prophets, priests, and the people led by them! We see Jeremiah standing alone in the midst of that great catastrophe which forms the lowest point in the history of the Old Testament theocracy and resisting the attacks of ungodly power, not in the strength of natural ability, but wholly in the strength of Him who had chosen him, against his will, to the prophetic office. We behold here "the servant of God," as represented in the sphere of a prophet's personality, on the highest stage of his Old Testament history. He was the type, not of John the Baptist (as HENGSTENBERG, *Christol. Eng. Tr.* II., p. 362), but of Christ, the Lord, Himself. I do not mean this in the sense of the older theologians (comp. NEUM. *S.* 28, *etc.*, and GHISLER, cap. 1. *etc.*, "*Jerem. Christum præfiguravit vitæ puritate, innocentia, sanctitate, ærumnarum perpessione,*

---

* ISIDOR of Pelusium has therefore correctly styled him, πολυπαθέστατος τῶν προφητῶν (*Epistl. Lib.* I., *Epist.* 238) Comp. GHISLER.

consignatione doctrinæ suæ per proprii sanguinis effusionem") for the points of resemblance which they trace are not specific, but in the sense that Jeremiah and Christ stand at two corresponding epochs in history, as their divine witnesses and heralds, their inner resemblance being also manifested outwardly, as when (xi. 19) Jeremiah calls himself a sheep brought to the slaughter, when he weeps over Jerusalem (xi. 1; xiii. 17; xiv. 17), and when again our Lord, at the crowning point of His life, utters the opening words of Psalm xxii., the composition of which by Jeremiah is opposed by nothing but **the** superscription. Comp. also HILLER, *Neues System aller Vorbilder J. Christi*, 1858, *S.* 522.

§ 3. THE LITERARY CHARACTER OF JEREMIAH.

The peculiarities of his person and official work are fully reflected in the literary character of our prophet. Jeremiah as an author is like a brazen wall, and at the same time like soft wax. Brazen, since no power on earth could induce him to alter the tenor of his proclamation; but soft, in that we feel that a man of gentle disposition and broken heart has given utterance to these powerful words. His style is wanting in the noble, bold conciseness and concentration which we so much admire in the older prophets, Isaiah and Hosea. His periods are long, the development verbose. Even when he quotes the language of others, he does it in such a way that it is robbed of all that is harsh or incisive, and moulded over, as it were, into a milder form. "*Sæpius complura epitheta adduntur et difficiliora vel audaciora aut fusius explicantur aut formis statæ Jeremiæ usitatioribus receptis in speciem leviorem abeunt,*" says KUEPER (*Jer. libr. ss. interpr.*, p. xiv.). The same peculiarity is displayed in the prophet's logic. While he maintains his fundamental thoughts with such undeviating monotony that the contents of his discourses seem almost meagre, yet on the other hand there is such luxuriance in the development that the unity and the consecutiveness of the thoughts seem to suffer. For one is not deduced logically from another, but we see, as it were, a series of *tableaux* pass before us, of which each presents the same stage and the same persons, but in the most various groupings (see my work *Der Proph. Jer. u. Bab. S.* 32, etc.). This peculiarity of his logic refutes the objection which has been made and constantly repeated, that Jeremiah springs analogically from one thing to another ("*non ad certum quendam ordinem res dispositæ sunt et descriptæ, sed libere ab una sententia transitur ad alteram,*" MAURER). The transitions are frequently abrupt, but there is still a logical progression, and the repetitions are a necessary feature of the tableauesque style. There is, however, another kind of repetition very frequent in Jeremiah:—he not only quotes himself very often (there is a table of these self-quotations in my work, *S.* 128, *etc.*), but he likes also to introduce the sayings of others. Jeremiah is especially at home in the Pentateuch, and most of all in Deuteronomy. (Comp. KUEPER, *ut supra*, and KÖNIG, *Alttest. Studien 2 Theil: das Deuteronomium u. d. Prophet Jeremia*). It is on account of this reproduction of the thoughts of others that he has been reproached with a want of originality (see KNOBEL, *Prophetismus der Hebræer* II., *S.* 367). But this is as true as that he was deficient in poetry. In power he is certainly not equal to Isaiah. But he is not wanting in originality, for who could say that he has himself produced nothing or only an insignificant amount? To lose himself in his predecessors is necessary even for the most original author. As to a deficiency in poetry I point to UMBREIT, who says (*Prakt. Comm. S.* XV.): "The most spiritual and therefore the greatest poet of the desert and of suffering is certainly Jeremiah. But we have maintained yet more than this, having boldly asserted that of all the prophets his genius is the most poetical." I fully subscribe to this judgment. For assuredly universal sympathy and deep and pure emotion are the qualities of a poet, and we undoubtedly find these elements of poetic inspiration, in the highest degree, in the finely-strung nature of Jeremiah. The circumstances of his life caused his emotions to be predominantly sad, hence in the whole range of human composition there is scarcely a poetical expression of sorrow so thrilling as that of this prophet (viii. 23, *Eng. Bib.* ix. 1): "O that my head were waters, and mine eyes a fountain of tears, that I might weep day and night for the slain of the daughter of my people" UMBREIT remarks (*S.* XIV., *etc.*) that these words form the portrait of the prophet, and BENDEMANN, in painting his celebrated picture, seems really to have had this passage especially in view.

It cannot be denied that, in *form*, Jeremiah, though not discarding art altogether, has far less polish than ISAIAH. JEROME refers to this in his *Præfatio:* "*Jeremias propheta sermone quidem apud Hebræcs Isaia et Hosia et quibusdam aliis prophetis videtur esse rusticior. Sed sensibus par est, quippe qui eodem spiritu prophetaverit. Porro simplicitas eloquii a loco ei, in quo natus est, accidit. Fait enim Anatotites.*" This charge of rusticity has, however, been exaggerated. Let us also regard the counter-testimony in the word "*sensibus par est,*" and which is given still more strongly in expressions like that of SIXTUS SENENSIS (in GHISLER, *Kap.* III., *etc.*), "*sermone quidem inculto et pæne subrustico, sed sensuum majestati sublimo*"—and of CUNÆUS (*De rep. Hebr.* III. 7), "*Jeremias omnis majestas posita in verborum neglectu est, adeo illum decet rustica dictio.*" Finally, in respect to language, it may be remarked that the influence of the Aramaic idiom on Jeremiah may be detected, but not in the degree usually supposed. Comp. KNOBEL, *Jeremias Chaldaizans dissert.* Vratisl., 1831; HAEVERNICK, *Einl.* I. 1, *S.* 231 sq.; STAEHELIN, *Spez. Einl. in die kan. Büch. des A. T.,* S. 279 sq.; comp. UMBREIT, *S.* XV..*Anm.,* etc.

§ 4. THE BOOK OF THE PROPHET.

1. Concerning its origin, the book itself gives us some, but not complete, information. According to xxxvi. 2, Jeremiah, in the fourth year of Jehoiakim, dictated to Baruch the discourses which had then been delivered. In the fifth year of Jehoiakim (xxxvi. 9) the writing was finished and publicly read. Jehoiakim burned it, upon which the prophet was commanded to re-write it, and this time it was severer than before. This writing consisted of prophecies which had been spoken in denunciation and threatening against Israel. Historical and consolatory passages, with prophecies against foreign nations, were excluded. This is clear both from the object of the writing (comp. *Comm.* on xxxvi. 7) and the fate to which Jehoiakim consigned it (xxxvi. 23). When the second transcription was finished, we are not informed, but it is evident from i. 3, "It came [the word of the Lord to Jeremiah] unto the end of the eleventh year of Zedekiah, unto the carrying away of Jerusalem captive in the fifth month," that it was after the destruction of the city and the deportation of the people. For the superscription, i. 1–3, is suitable only for a writing which contains nothing of later date than the period mentioned. But the book does contain prophecies relating to the time subsequent to this epoch, which even pertain to the residence of the prophet in Egypt toward the close of his life. If now it is possible that Jeremiah, during the two months that he spent with Gedaliah in Mizpah (comp. on i. 2 sq.), or perhaps still better (on account of the allusions to the journey to Egypt in ii. 16, 36), on the way to Egypt, or in Egypt itself, continued the writing begun in the fourth year of Jehoiakim to the time mentioned in i. 3, and concluded it, it follows that this writing forms the main body of the book, written and edited by the prophet himself, to which the superscription, i. 1-3, refers. The subsequent portions of the book, though the genuine production of Jeremiah, were added by a later editor, who did not venture to alter the original title, though it was no longer suitable.

Thus it is evident, as it seems to me, that the present form and arrangement are not those of Jeremiah, for he would certainly have given the whole a title corresponding to its contents. Some other circumstances, to be mentioned hereafter, also favor this view.

2. As to the arrangement or plan of the book, as we have it, it has been accused of endless confusion,* and the most various theories have been broached to account for this confusion. Compare, to name only the most eminent, EICHHORN, in the *Repert. für biblische u. morgenländ. Lit. Th.* 1, *S.* 141; *Einleit.* III. *S.* 157, etc.; BERTHOLDT, *Einl.* IV. *S.* 1457; MOVERS, *De utriusque recensionis ratic. Jer. indole et origine.* Hamb., 1837; HITZIG, *Comm.. S.* XII. ff.; then the attempts of EWALD, UMBREIT (in their commentaries), HAEVERNICK (*Einl.* II. 2, *S.* 206 ff.), KEIL (who follows HAEVERNICK almost entirely, *Einl., S.* 252 ff.), SCHMIEDER (in GERLACH's *Bibelwerk*), STAEHELIN (on the principle at the basis of the arrangement of Jeremiah's prophecies, in the *Zeitschr. der deutsch morgenl. Gesellsch,* 1849; *Heft* 2 and 3, *S* 216 ff.; and in

---

* Even LUTHER (Preface to the prophet Jeremiah) says: "We often find some of the first part in the following chapter, which happened before that in the previous chapter, which looks as though Jeremiah did not arrange these books himself, but that they were composed piecemeal from his discourses, and compiled in a book. We must not trouble ourselves about the order, or allow the want of order to hinder us."

his *Spez Einl. in die kan. Bücher des A. T.*, 1862, *S.* 260 ff.); NEUMANN (*Comm S.* 81 ff. and *S.* 111. ff.). In my opinion, the case is not so bad as represented, but a reasonable arrangement will at once present itself, if we only take the following points into consideration. 1. In general, the principle of chronological order is followed, but admitting, in some cases, a certain order of subjects, which is sometimes suggested by external occasions (comp. ch. xxi. 1-7). 2. With respect to the chronological order in particular, we have a safe guide in the fact that before the fourth year of Jehoiakim, viz., before the battle of Carchemish and Nebuchadnezzar's accession to the throne, Jeremiah never mentions the latter or the Chaldeans, while after this time he presents them constantly in all his discourses as appointed by God to be the instrument of His judgments on Israel and the nations. Until shortly before the battle of Carchemish, Assyria was at war with the Medes and Babylonians, and it was undecided which of the three would obtain the supremacy. After the fall of Nineveh and the defeat of Pharaoh Necho, the star of Nebuchadnezzar rose above the horizon like an all-prevailing sun. Jeremiah now knew definitely that the people coming from the North (i. 13, *etc.*) were the Chaldeans under Nebuchadnezzar, and he could no longer speak to the people without counselling submission as the only means of safety. I think, then, that I may lay down this canon distinctly, that all parts of the book in which the threatening enemies are spoken of generally, without mention of Nebuchadnezzar or the Chaldeans, belong to the period before the fourth year of Jehoiakim, viz., before the time represented in ch. xxv. as that of Jeremiah's first acquaintance with them; while all the portions in which Nebuchadnezzar and the Chaldeans are named belong to the subsequent period; so that a passage which mentions the Chaldeans and is yet dated in the beginning of the reign of Jehoiakim (ch. xxvii.), may be safely regarded as bearing a false superscription, as likewise one that is dated in the reign of Zedekiah, and does not mention the Chaldeans (xlix. 34 sqq.). In the first place, it is quite clear that our Hebrew recension, omitting chapters l. and lii. as introduction and conclusion, falls into two principal divisions: 1. The portions relating to the theocracy (ch. ii.—xlv.). 2. The prophecies against the nations (ch. xlvi.—li.). Chapter xlv., the promise given to the writer of the book, the faithful Baruch, is to be regarded (as it is by KEIL) as an appendix to the first division. To attach this chapter to the second division, as HAEVERNICK does, is entirely unsuitable. The first division may evidently be divided again into two subdivisions, the collection of discourses, with appendices, ch. ii.—xxxv., and the historical portions, ch. xxxvi.—xliv. In speaking of a collection of discourses, it should be remarked that, according to the intention of the arranger of the book, we must not always understand by a discourse one which forms a rhetorical unit, but also a complexus of rhetorical and historical passages, if in its fundamental thought, its form or its chronology, it presents a connected whole. In this sense our collection contains eleven (or ten) discourses, the beginning of each of which is designated by a superscription (comp. iii. 6; vii. 1; xi. 1, *etc.*). The first two pertain to the reign of Josiah (ch. ii. and iii.—vi.). It is natural that in the earliest period the proportionally smallest amount of matter should be committed to writing, so that in the passages mentioned, especially in ch. ii., only the quintessence of the discourses of the earliest period is given. The third discourse pertains to the reign of Jehoiakim (ch. vii.—x.). These two, ch. iii.—vi. and ch. vii.—x., are distinguished from the rest by their length, and may therefore, with ch. xxv., which is inferior in length, but far superior in importance, be designated as the principal discourses. Ch. xi.—xiii., which also pertain to the reign of Jehoiakim, have a common title, but only ch. xi. and xii. form a rhetorical whole. For ch. xiii. is entirely independent, though of the same date with the preceding, and on account of its brevity, added as an appendix. The fifth discourse, though somewhat inferior to the second and third, is still one of the most important. It belongs to the period before the fourth year of Jehoiakim. The passage xvii. 19-27 is related to the fifth discourse as ch. xiii. to the fourth. I regret that by an oversight I have not designated them in the same way in the text. The seventh discourse is an account of two symbolical occurrences, to which is appended that of a personal experience and the outburst of feeling thus occasioned. Although these occurrences belong to different periods, before and after the fourth year of Jehoiakim, they are brought together because both symbols are derived from pottery and on account of the unity of the subjects. All is here brought into connection which the prophet spoke at different times against the false shepherds of the people (kings and prophets). The opening passage (xxi. 1-7)

§ 4. THE BOOK OF THE PROPHET.

though in general, as *oratio contra regem*, not altogether unsuitable for this place, is doubtless placed here chiefly on account of the name Pashur, which it has in common with the preceding The transitional words (xxi. 11-14) seem also to be a fragment which is subjoined here not altogether appropriately. But in what follows we have a well-ordered series of denunciations against the evil kings of Judah. The first, in which no name is mentioned, seems to stand first as a collective admonition, though the king addressed in ver. 2 can be no other than Jehoiakim (xxii. 1-9). The second is a prophecy relating to the person of Jehoahaz. It is of earlier date than that which precedes it, and is evidently an interpolation (xxii. 10-12). The third is directed against Jehoiakim by name (xxii. 13-23). The fourth relates to Jehoiachin (xxii. 24-30). As a foil to these dark pictures of the kings of the present, the prophet, by an antithesis reminding us of ch. iii., gives us a bright picture of the King of the Messianic future (xxiii. 1-8). The second part of the main discourse (xxiii. 9-40) is an earnest rebuke of the false prophets. The conclusion is formed by ch. xxiv., a vision which the prophet had in the reign of Zedekiah, and which is added here evidently in order that the fourth bad king Jeremiah had lived to see might not fail to receive his appropriate denunciation. The ninth discourse is that highly important one which Jeremiah pronounced in the fourth year of Jehoiakim after the great catastrophe which made an epoch in the prophet's ministry, the battle of Carchemish and the succession of Nebuchadnezzar. To this are attached a series of three historical appendices, of which the first falls before the fourth year of Jehoiakim, the second in the fourth year of Zedekiah, the third somewhat earlier than the preceding. All three appendices, however, relate to the conflict of the *true* prophet (it should be noted, however, that Jeremiah is called הַנָּבִיא for the first time in xxv. 2) with the false prophets. Here also is a pre-arranged antithesis. Ch. xxvi. standing before ch. xxvii. and xxviii. has a clear chronological basis, while ch. xxix., which in time is somewhat earlier than ch. xxvii. and xxviii. coming after them, has a topical basis, since thus the prophet's conflict with the false prophets at home is first shown, and then his conflict with those at a distance. The tenth passage occupies an independent סֵפֶר, *viz.*, the book of consolation, which consists of two discourses, with a double appendix. Ch. xxx. and xxxi., originally written specially, and not as a part of the first writing, ch. xxxvi. 2-10, form a rhetorical unit, certainly contemporary with ch. iii.—vi., and therefore pertaining to the reign of Josiah. The second consolatory discourse consists of two separate passages, which, however, are most closely connected. The first relates to the purchase of a field which, at the command of the Lord, Jeremiah made while confined in the court of the prison, at the time of his greatest affliction. The second is connected with the demolition of many houses in Jerusalem for defensive purposes. On this double, gloomy background the prophet presents the most glorious Messianic salvation. It is not, as I have already said, a connected discourse; in ch. xxxii. we have first the account of the purchase of land, then the prayer expressing the prophet's astonishment, then the Lord's consolatory promises. Ch. xxxiii. is, however, from beginning to end, a connected prophetic discourse.

This book of consolation is followed in chaps. xxxiv. and xxxv. by a double appendix, the second half of which (xxxiv. 8—xxxv. 19) itself consists of two independent parts. The short passage xxxiv. 1-7 is only a more exact account of the occurrence narrated in xxxii. 1-5, in consequence of which Jeremiah was confined in the court of the prison, and therefore refers only to the contents of chaps. xxxii. and xxxiii. The two facts however which are related in xxxiv. 8-22, and xxxv. 1-19, are to be regarded as an appendix to the whole collection. For they show by a striking example, the accomplished but immediately revoked emancipation of the Hebrew slaves, how entirely indisposed the people of Israel were to obey the commands of their God, while a contrast to this shameful disobedience is given in the example of affecting obedience afforded by the Rechabites to the command of their *earthly* progenitor. We thus see that the arrangement is by no means without plan, and may in general have been made by the prophet himself. Only the mere juxtaposition of xxi. 1-7 for the sake of the name Pashur, and the insertion of the heterogeneous passage xxi. 11-14 in this place, seem to betray a different hand.

With chap xxxvi. begins the second subdivision of the first main division. Historical passages follow each other in chronological order, which have for their subject partly personal experiences of the prophet, and partly the history of the fatal catastrophe of the theocracy in general. There is no difficulty here. Chap. xlv., as already remarked, is an appendix to the first main division. The second part contains the prophecies against foreign nations in an order to which there is nothing to object (xlvi.—li.). Chap. lii. finally forms the conclusion, which is not from the prophet himself.

The following table may serve to facilitate a review:

I. THE INTRODUCTION, CHAP. I.

II. FIRST DIVISION, CHAPS. II.—XLIV.

PASSAGES RELATING TO THE THEOCRACY, WITH AN APPENDIX. CHAP. XLV.

A. FIRST SUBDIVISION.

The collection of discourses, chaps. ii.-xxxiii.
With appendices, Chaps. xxxiv. and xxxv.

1. First discourse, chap. ii.
2. Second discourse, chaps. iii.—vi.
3. Third discourse, chaps. vii.—x.
4. Fourth discourse, chaps. xi. and xii. with appendix, chap. xiii.
5. Fifth discourse, chaps xiv.—xvii. 18.
6. Sixth discourse, chap. xvii. 19-27.
7. Seventh discourse, chaps. xviii.—xx. (the symbols taken from pottery).
8. Eighth discourse, chaps. xxi.—xxiv.
9. Ninth discourse, chap. xxv. With three appendices, chaps xxvi.—xxix.
10. The book of consolation, consisting of
    a. the tenth discourse, chaps. xxx. and xxxi.
    b. the eleventh discourse, chaps. xxxii. and xxxiii. With an appendix, chap. xxxiv. 1-7.
11. Historical appendix to the collection—the disobedience of Israel offset by the obedience of the Rechabites, chaps. xxxiv. 8—xxxv. 19.

B. SECOND SUBDIVISION.

Historical presentation of the most important events from the fourth year of Jehoiakim to the close of the prophet's ministry, chaps. xxxvi.—xliv.

1. Events before the fall of Jerusalem, chaps. xxxvi.—xxxviii.
2. Events after the fall of Jerusalem, chaps. xxxix.—xliv.

Appendix to First Division, ch. xlv. The promise made to Baruch.

III. SECOND DIVISION.

THE PROPHECIES AGAINST FOREIGN NATIONS. CHAPS. XLVI.—LI.

1. Against Egypt, I., chap. xlvi. 2-12.
2. Against Egypt, II., chap. xlvi. 13-26. With an appendix, chap. xlvi. 27-28.
3. Against the Philistines, chap. xlvii.
4. Against Moab, chap. xlviii.
5. Against Ammon, chap. xlix. 1-6.
6. Against Edom, chap. xlix. 7-22.
7. Against Damascus, chap. xlix. 23-27.
8. Against the Arabians, chap. xlix. 28-33.
9. Against Elam, chap. xlix. 34-39.
10. Against Babylon, chap. l. li.

IV. CONCLUSION, CHAP. LII.

3. The relation of the Masoretic text to the Alexandrian translation. It may here be premised that Jeremiah, closing his labors and probably his life in Egypt, was on this account especially honored by the Jews residing there. They regarded him as peculiarly their own, the Egyptian prophet. (Comp. *Chron. Pasch.* p. 156; FABRICIUS, in the *Cod. pseudepigr.* V. T. p

§ 4. THE BOOK OF THE PROPHET.

1108; *Apocr. N. T.* p. 1111; HAEVERNICK, *Einl.* I. 1, *S.* 45, II. 2, *S.* 259; HERZOG, *Real-Enc.* VII. *S.* 255.) He was therefore diligently studied, and it is not improbable, as FABRICIUS says "*Codices græcæ versionis jam privata quorundam Apocryphis se delectantium studio interpolati, jam librariorum oscitantia manci fraudi beato Martyri fuerunt.*" The difference between our Masoretic text and the Alexandrian version is twofold—in matter and in form. The former extends through the whole book, and consists of innumerable discrepancies, which sometimes affect single letters, syllables and words, sometimes whole verses. The difference in form consists in a different arrangement from xxv. 15 onwards, the LXX. introducing here (but in a different sequence) the prophecies against the nations, so that all in the Hebrew text from xxv. 15 to ch. xlv. is deferred to make room for these prophecies, and since in the LXX. these extend from xxv. 15 to ch. xxxi. it follows that what in the Hebrew is from xxv. 15 to ch. xlv. is in the Greek ch. xxxi.—li. It should be remarked that the LXX. does not treat ch. xlv. of the Hebrew as an independent chapter, but as part of ch. li.—vers. 31-35. The following little table will exhibit the discrepancies more clearly:

LXX.			Masor.
xxv. 15 sqq.	The prophecy against	Elam,	xlix. 34 sqq.
xxvi.	"	" Egypt,	xlvi.
xxvii. 28.	"	" Babylon,	l.—li.
xxix. 1-7.	"	" the Philistines.	xlvii. 1-7.
xxix. 7-22.	"	" Edom,	xlix. 7-22.
xxx. 1-5.	"	" Ammon,	xlix. 1-6.
xxx. 6-11.	"	" Kedar,	xlix. 28-33.
xxx. 12-16.	"	" Damascus,	xlix. 23-27.
xxxi.	"	" Moab,	xlviii.
xxxii.	.	. . .	xxv. 15-38.
xxxiii.—li.	.	. . .	xxvi.—xlv.
lii.	.	. . .	lii.

I was formerly of opinion that these two kinds of difference were to be judged alike, and were to be traced, not to a divergence of Hebrew MSS., but entirely to the ignorance, carelessness or caprice of the editor. I have now changed my view in so far that I am convinced that the case is not the same with the difference in form as with that in matter. The different order is certainly founded on a divergence in the Hebrew originals. If we had no other testimony to this than the text of the LXX., so far as this is the conscious and intended production of its author, this testimony would certainly be worthless. But in the first place, the Hebrew text is itself a witness, and secondly, we have in the LXX. an involuntary and impartial testimony. I believe that in the *Comm.* on xxv. 12-14; xxvii. 1; xlix. 34, and in the introduction to the prophecies against the nations, I have furnished proof that these verses (xxv. 12-14) presuppose the existence in their immediate vicinity of the כֹּפֶר עַל הַגּוֹיִם or rather that ch. xxv. belongs to this ספר. I think I have shown that the peculiar expression τὰ Αἰλάμ at the close of xxv. 13 (LXX.), and the absence of xxvii 1 in the LXX., with the strange chronology of xlix. 34, are evidence that the prophecies against the nations must at one time have had their place immediately after ch. xxv. and before ch. xxvii. This τὰ Αἰλάμ shows that the superscription of the prophecies against Elam originally read like the rest, xlvi. 2; xlviii. 1; xlix. 1, 7. 23, 28, לְעֵילָם. The peculiar postscript to the prophecy in the LXX., however, which is no other than the missing verse xxvii. 1, proves that the Alexandrian translator had an original text before him in which the prophecies against the nations stood before ch. xxvii, and in such wise that the prophecy against Elam was the last, as at present in the Masoretic text. But how is it that the present Masoretic text of the prophecies against Elam no longer bears the old simple inscription לעילם but likewise the words transposed from xxvii. 1? I believe that it can be explained only in this way—that two originals were before the Alexandrian translator, of which one had the prophecies against the nations in the old place; the other agreed with the present Masoretic recension. The translator must have been guided by both. He adhered to the older recension so far as to retain its arrangement on the whole (altering only the sequence of the prophecies against the nations in detail). From this he adopted the position of ch. xxvii. ver. 1 immediately after the prophecy against Elam, while from the later text he took the περὶ Αἰλάμ (אֶל־עֵילָם Hebr.). The misplacement of the prophecies against the nations must therefore have taken place before the preparation of the Alexandrian version. Its originator must have first overlooked xxvii 1, and then altered it into an inscription for the prophecy against Elam, and he must also have put ch. xxvi. in its present place. Since in the LXX. the superscription of ch. xxvii. is still wanting, it is possible, nay, probable, that it was wanting in the later Hebrew copy of the translator. The present verse, xxvii. 1, of the Hebrew text, with the wrong name of Jehoiakim, would then be a later supplement. On the occasion of this error, comp. remarks on xxvii. 1.

As to the difference in matter between the Alexandrian version and the Hebrew text, I still retain the conviction which I expressed in my work, *Der proph. Jer. u. Bab.*, and in HERZOG, *Real-Enc.* VI. S. 488, that the far greater part of the discrepancies are to be explained, not by a difference in the original text, but by the caprice, ignorance or carelessness of the translator. Proof of this in detail may be seen in the earlier editions of DE WETTE's *Introduction*, in KUEPER, *Jer. libr. ss. interpr. atque vindex*, p. 177; in HAEVERNICK, *Einl.* II. 2, S 250; in WICHELHAUS, *De Jeremiae versione Alexandrina*, 1847, p. 67; in my work, *Jer. u. Bab* S. 86; but especially in GRAF. (*Commentar.* S. XL. sqq.), who, as it seems to me, by a thoroughly impartial and careful investigation, has brought the matter to a conclusion. The arguments in favor of the LXX. still adduced in the later edition of BLEEK's *Einleitung* (1865, S. 491) possess no validity.

4. The integrity of the text has been relatively but little questioned. With respect to some passages, I have been unable to avoid the suspicion of an interpolation. The chief of these are the following: x. 1-16; xv. 11-14; xxv. 12-14; xxx. 23, 24; xxxix. 1-14; li. 15-19. Ch. lii. even according to the editor, is not to be regarded as written by Jeremiah, as follows from the statement in li. 64, "Thus far the words of Jeremiah." I formerly regarded the passage l. 43-46 as also interpolated, but, on closer examination, am convinced of the erroneousness of this view. In reference to other passages (especially ch. xxx.—xxxiii. l. li.), on renewed investigation, I am perfectly satisfied of their authenticity. Though Jeremiah was one of the most read of the prophets, his text has been handed down to us, on the whole, pure and unadulterated.

5. The book of Jeremiah occupies in the Canon the second place among the major prophets, after Isaiah and before Ezekiel. This position, being the historical one, is the most natural. MELITO, of Sardis, and ORIGEN (in EUSEB. *Hist. Eccl.* IV. 26 and VI. 25) in their lists of the Jewish canon make Jeremiah follow Isaiah, though between Jeremiah and Ezekiel the former inserts the twelve minor prophets and Daniel, the latter (omitting the twelve minor prophets altogether) only Daniel. But according to the Talmud, (*Tractate Baba batra Fol.* 14, b) the order was:—*Regum libri, Jeremias, Ezechiel, Jesajas, duodecim prophetarum volumen.* And ELIAS LEVITA (in *Masoret hammasoret Praef.* III.) testifies that this is the order in the German and French MSS. This Talmudic divergence from the natural order appears to have a genuine Talmudic reason. Since Jeremiah treats only of *desolatio*, Ezekiel first of *desolatio* and then of *consolatio*, Isaiah only of *consolatio*, they wished, as the tract *Baba batra* informs us, to connect *desolationem cum desolatione* and *consolationem cum consolatione.* For further particulars see ROSENMUELLER, *Schol. Proleg. in Jerem.* p. 27; HERZOG, *Real-Enc.* VII. S. 253; NEUMANN, *Comm. Einl.* S. 10; DELITZSCH, *Comm. zu Jes.* S. XXII.

§ 5. LITERATURE.

Of the church-fathers THEODORET and EPHREM SYRUS wrote complete commentaries on Jeremiah. A commentary by the latter in Syriac is still extant (*Tom.* II. of the Roman Edition of PETRUS BENEDICTUS, 1740). JEROME commented on the first thirty-three chapters only. From ORIGEN we have only homilies. The edition of LOMMATZSCH gives nineteen in Greek, two in the Latin translation of JEROME and some fragments. According to CASSIODORUS (*Lib. Inst. Div.* cap. III.) there were forty-five homilies, which were also known to RHABANUS MAURUS (according to a passage in his *Praefat. in Jerem.*). Comp. LOMMATZSCH, *Prolegg. in Tom.*

XV., of his edition. GHISLERUS gives a catena of the Greek and Latin fathers in his commentary, of which hereafter.

Of Rabbinical commentaries the principal are those of RASCHI, DAVID KIMCHI, ABARBANEL and SOLOMON BEN MELECH.

There are Roman Catholic commentaries by RHABANUS MAURUS, RUPERT VON DEUTZ, THOMAS AQUINAS, ALBERTUS MAGNUS; by JOACHIM FLORIS, *Comm. in Jer.*, Venice, 1525, and Cologne, 1577 (comp. GIESELER. [*Church History*, Philada. Ed. II., p. 300], *etc., etc.*, and NEANDER, [Boston, Tr. IV. p. 291]); FRANC. ZICHEMIUS, Cologne, 1559; HECTOR PINTUS, Leyden, 1561, 1584 and 1590: ANDREAS CAPELLA, Tarracona, 1586; PETRUS FIGUEIRO, Leyden, 1598; CHRISTOF. DE CASTRO (Jesuit), Paris, 1609; CASP. SANCTIUS (Jesuit), Leyden, 1618: BENED. MANDINA, *In pr. Jer. expositiones, Neap.*, 1620; MICHAEL GHISLERUS, *In Jer. Commentarii cum catena PP. græcorum et comm. in Lamentt. et Baruch*, Leyden, 1623. (This is the most complete commentary, and the most distinguished for patristic learning, that we have on Jeremiah, but heavy and with a Romish bias; comp. FABRIC., *Biblioth. gr. ed. Harl. III.*, p. 734).

By Protestant theologians we have the following commentaries:—ZWINGLI, *Complanatio Jeremiæ*, Zürich, 1531, *etc.*; MART. BUCER, *Complanationes Jer. proph.*, Zürich, 1531; OECO-LAMPADIUS, *In Jeremiam proph. comment. libri tres*, Strasburg, 1533; BUGENHAGEN, *Adnotationes in Jerem.*, Wittenberg, 1546; CALVIN, *Prælectiones in Jerem.*, Geneva, 1563, etc. (notes, of lectures); VICTORIN STRIGEL, *Conciones Jeremiæ proph. ad ebr. veritatem recognita*, etc. Leipzig, 1566; LUCAS OSIANDER, *Jes. Jer. et Thr. Jerem.*, Tübingen, 1578; HUGO BROUGHTON, *Comment. in Jerem. prophetiam et Lamentationes*, Geneva, 1606; AMANDUS POLANUS (Prof. in Basle), *Comment. in Jerem. et exegesis in Threnos*, Basle, 1608; PISCATOR, Herborn, 1614; JOH. HULSEMANN, *In Jerem. et Threnos comment. posthumus*, etc., Rudolstadt, 1663; JOH. FÖRSTER, *Comment. in Proph. Jeremiam.*, Wittenb., 1672 and 1699; SEB. SCHMIDT, *Comm. in librum prophetarum Jeremiæ*, Strasburg, 1685; JACOB ALTING (Prof. in Gröningen, *ob.*, 1697), *Comment. in Jerem.* Amsterdam, 1688; ELBERT NOORDBECK (Pastor in Workum), *Bekoopte Uitlegginge van de prophetie Jeremie*, Franeker, 1701; J. FRIEDRICH BURSCHER, *Versuch einer kurzen Erläuterung des propheten Jeremiä*, etc., with a preface by CHR. A. CRUSIUS, Leipzig, 1756; HERMANN VENEMA, *Comment. ad librum prophetiarum Jeremiæ*, Leuwarden, 1765; CHRIST. GOTTFR. STRUENSEE, *Neue Uebersetzung der Weissagung Jeremiæ*, etc., Halberstadt, 1777; (the last volume of STRUENSEE'S *Translations of the Prophets*); JOH. DAV. MICHAELIS, *Observationes philolog. et crit. in Jeremiæ vaticinia et Threnos*, ed. *Schleussner*, Göttingen, 1793; CHRIST. FR. SCHNURRER, *Observationes ad vaticinia Jeremiæ*, Tübingen, 1793 to 1794; A. FR. W. LEISTE, *Observationes in vatt. Jer. aliquot locos*, Göttingen, 1794, and extended in POTT and RUPERTI, *Sylloge Commentt. Theologg*, Vol. II., Helmst., 1801; HENSLER, *Bemerkungen über Stellen in Jerem. Weiss.*, Leipzig, 1805; EICHHORN, *Die hebr. Propheten*, 1816-19; GAAB, J. F. (Prelate in Tübingen), *Erklärung schwererer Stellen in den Weissagungen Jeremia's*, Tübingen, 1824; TACONIS ROORDÆ, *Commentarii in aliquot Jeremiæ loca*, Gröningen, 1824; DAHLER, *Jérémie traduit sur le texte original, accompagné de notes*, Strasburg, 1825; ROSENMUELLER, *Scholien*, 1826; MAURER, 1833; EWALD, *Die Propheten des alten Bundes*, 1840; HITZIG (part of his *Kurzgefasste exeget. Handbuch über das A. T.*), 1841, *2te Aufl.* 1866; and his *Die Proph. Büch des A. T. übersetzt*, Leipzig, 1854; UMBREIT, *Praktischer Commentar*, 1842; WILHELM NEUMANN, *Jeremias von Anatot, die Weissag. und Klagelieder ausgelegt*, Leipzig, 1856-8; CARL HEINRICH GRAF, Prof. in the *Landeschule* at Meissen, *Der Proph. Jeremia erklärt*, Leipzig, 1862; ERNST MEIER, Prof. in Tubingen, *Die proph. Bücher des A. T. übersetzt und erläutert*, Stuttgard, 1863. Comp. with respect to the literature, CARPZOV, *Introd. ad V. Test.*, edit. III. p. 169 sqq.; DE WETTE. *Einl. 6 Aufl. S.* 298; ROSENMUELLER, *Scholien* I. *S.* 32.

[Works in English:—WILL. LOWTH, *Commentary upon the Prophecy and Lamentations of Jeremiah*, London, 1718; BENJ. BLAYNEY, *Jeremiah and Lamentations; A new translation with notes*, etc., Edinb, 2d ed., 1810; Translation of CALVIN'S *Commentary*, 5 vols., Edinburgh, 1850; HENDERSON, *The Book of the Prophet Jeremiah*, etc., London, 1851, Andover, 1868; NOYES, *New Translation of the Hebrew Prophets*, Boston, 4th ed., 1868; DAVIDSON, *Introduction to the Old Testament*, London, 1863; CH. WORDSWORTH, *Jeremiah, Lamentations and*

Ezekiel, with Notes and Introductions, London, 1869; H. COWLES, *Jeremiah and Lamentations, with Notes*, New York, 1869.—S. R. A.]

The following works may serve as critical aids and for the exhibition of the prophet's character:—Dr. MICH. WEBER, *Intempestiva lectionis emendandæ cura e Jeremia illustrata* (4 Programme), Wittenb., 1785, '88 and '94; J. ANDR. MICH. NAGEL, *Dissert in var. lectt. 25 capp. priorum Jer. ex. duobus Codd. MSS. hebr. desumtas*, Altorf, 1772; JOH. JAC. GUILCHER, *Observv. criticæ in quædam Jer. loca.* in the *Symbolis Haganis*, Cl. I; G. L. SPOHN, *Jer. vates e versione Judæorum Alex. emendatus*, Leipzig, 1824; KUEPER, *Jeremias libr. Sacrorum interpres atque vindex* Berlin, 1837; MOVERS, *De utriusque recensionis vatt. Jer. indole et origine*, Hamburg, 1837; KÖSTER, *Die Propheten des A. u. N. B.*, Leipzig, 1838; J. L. KÖNIG, *Alttest Studien*, 2 Heft. *das Deuteronomium u. d. Proph. Jeremia*, Berlin, 1839; RÖDIGER, *Art. " Jeremia" in Ersch u. Gruber's Encykl.*, Sect. II., Bd., 15; CASPARI, *Jer. ein Zeuge f. d. Aechtheit v. Jes. 34, etc., in der Zeitschr. f Luth. Theol. u. Kirche*, 1843; WICHELHAUS, *De Jer. versione Alexandrina*, Halle, 1847; NAEGELSBACH, *Der Prophet Jeremias und Babylon*, Erlangen, 1850; *Idem. Art. " Jeremia" in* HERZOG's *Real-Enc.*; NIEMEYER, *Charakteristik der Bibel, Bd. V. S. 472*; Roos, *Fuss-stapfen des Glaubens Abrahams*, edited by W. F. Roos, 1838, II., *S.* 281 ff.; SACK, *Apologetik, S.* 272, ff.; HENGSTENBERG, *Christologie, Aufl. II.*, Bd. II., *S.* 399 ff.; E. MEIER, *Gesch , d. poet. Nat-Lit. der Hebr.*, 1856, *S.* 385 ff.; REINKE, *Die Messian. Weissagungen bei den grossen und kleinen Proph. d. A. B.*, Giessen, 1859-61; A. KÖHLER, *Die Wirksamkeit des Pr. Jer. während des Verfalls des jüd. Staats*, in *Beweiss des Glaubens*. [A. P. STANLEY, *Jewish Church*, 2d series, 2d Ed., London, 1866.; MILMAN, *History of the Jews*, Vol. I., London. 1863; ISAAC TAYLOR, *Spirit of Hebrew Poetry*, pp. 277, 8, New York, 1863; The Articles in SMITH's and KITTO's *Biblical Cyclopædias*.—S. R. A.]

The following practical works may also be mentioned:—HEINR. BULLINGER, *In Jer. Sermonem primum (6 primis capp. comprehensum) conciones 26*, Zürich, 1557; NIK. LUDW. COUNT ZINZENDORF, *Jeremias ein Prediger der Gerechtigkeit* [" Jeremiah, A Preacher of Righteousness"] reprinted from the second edition, Berlin, 1830; HEIM and HOFFMANN, *Die vier grossen Propheten erbaulich ausgelegt aus den Schriften der Reformatoren*, Stuttgart, 1839; *Biblische Summarien* (known under the name of " *Würtembergische Summarien*"), newly edited by the Christian Union in North Germany, Halle, 1848; J. DIEDRICH, *Die Propheten Jeremia und Ezechiel kurz erklärt*, Neu-Ruppin, 1863; E. HÖCHSTETTER *Zwölf Gleichnisse aus dem Propheten Jeremia*, Kirchheim U. T., 1865; [MAURICE, *The Prophets and Kings of the Old Testament*, Cambridge, 1863; and the commentaries of T. SCOTT and MATTHEW HENRY. —S. R. A.]

I may also mention the peculiar, long-vanished Literature of a branch of the *theologia prophetica*, which set itself to the task of proving the *Locos Communes* of dogmatic theology by the prophets. This was done either by naming the *locos* contained in each passage, at the close of it (thus SEB. SCHMIDT, in his commentary, at the close of each chapter, evolves two *locos* from almost every verse); or by arranging the prophetic utterances according to the scheme of the dogmatic *loci*. Thus *ex. gr.* PHILIP HAILBRUNNER (Prof. in Lauingen) in his work, *" Jer. proph. monumenta in locos communes theologicos digesta*," Lauingen, 1586, enumerates 28 *locos*, comprising under each the appropriate passages from the prophet in a Latin translation. The same course is taken by JOH. HEINRICH MAJUS, Prof. in Giessen, who, besides a *Theologia prophetica ex selectionibus V. T. oraculis secundum seriem locorum theolog. dispositis*, Frankfort, a. M. 1710, edited a similarly composed *Theologia Davidis, Theologia Jesajana* and *Theologia Jeremiana* (the complete title is: *Theol. Jeremiana ex Jeremiæ vaticiniis et lamentationibus juxta articulos fidei ordine per theses collecta, Disput. Resp. Bened. Henr. Thering.*, Giessen, 1703).

THE
PROPHET JEREMIAH.

1. THE INTRODUCTION.

CHAPTER I.

1. *The Superscription.*

1. 1-3.*

1 The words of Jeremiah, the son of Hilkiah, [one] of the priests that *were* [LXX.,
2 dwelt] in Anathoth in the land of Benjamin, To whom the word of the Lord
  [Jehovah] came [was communicated][1] in the days of Josiah, the son of Amon,
3 king of Judah, in the thirteenth year of his reign. It came also in the days of
  Jehoiakim, the son of Josiah, king of Judah, unto the end of the eleventh year
  of Zedekiah, the son of Josiah, king of Judah, unto the carrying away of Jerusalem
  captive in the fifth month.

TEXTUAL AND GRAMMATICAL.

* [The text of the common English Version will be retained in the prose portions of the book, with occasional corrections, included in brackets; but a new rendering of the poetical portions will be given, founded on a comparison of the German and English Versions with the Hebrew.—S. R. A.]
1 Ver. 2.—[HENDERSON: was communicated.]

EXEGETICAL AND CRITICAL.

Ver. 1. **The words of Jeremiah ... Benjamin.** We find a similar commencement in the prophetical book of Amos (i. 1) and in the Song of Solomon (i. 1). Etymologically דָּבָר might certainly be rendered *historia Jeremiæ* (DE WETTE), compare דִּבְרֵי יְמֵי so frequent in the book of Kings (1 Kings xi. 41; xiv. 19, 29, *etc.*). Since, however, this book is not historic, but prophetic, since the prophet's work consisted essentially in preaching, since the other prophetic books bear inscriptions denoting discourses (כְּשַׁר. דָּבָר) or visions (חֲזוֹן), and since finally the historical narratives contained in the book are also the words of Jeremiah (so STAHELIN, *ad h. l.*), it is more correct to take דָּבָר in the sense of "words," which it certainly has in Song of Sol. i. 1. Concerning the name, origin and birthplace of the prophet, see the Introduction. Besides Jeremiah (and Nathan, 1 Kings iv. 5, *Vide* THOLUCK, *Die Proph. und ihre Weiss. S.* 20, *u.* 32), the prophet Ezekiel (i. 3; comp. Jos. *Ant.* X 5, 1), and most probably Zechariah (i. 1; comp. KÖHLER, *Sacharja, S.* 9), were of sacerdotal origin. No special traces of his priestly descent

are found in the book of our prophet, unless we reckon as such his accurate knowledge of the Law, especially Deuteronomy, of which the exposition will furnish proofs in great number.

Vers. 2 and 3. **To whom .... in the fifth month.** The subject of **came** in ver. 3 is *word of Jehovah*, repeated from ver. 2. CHR. B. MICHAELIS falsely renders in the *Hallesche Bibel: idemque etiam fuit propheta.* As regards the chronological statements in vers. 2 and 3, it should first be noticed that the two kings Jehoahaz and Jehoiakim are passed over, without doubt because each of them reigned only three months. Since Jeremiah labored from the thirteenth year of Josiah, consequently eighteen years under Josiah, and eleven years each under Jehoiakim and Zedekiah, he ministered altogether, including the six months under the two kings omitted, forty years in the midst of the theocracy. How long afterwards he labored, cannot be ascertained with any certainty. Comp. Introduction and remarks on xliv. 29. Since the book, as we have it, contains not only those words of Jehovah which were communicated to the prophet before the fifth month of the eleventh year of Zedekiah, but others of later date (ch. xl.—xliv.), this inscription does not comport with its present extent. According to xxxvi. 32, in place of the writing

17

destroyed by Zedekiah, Jeremiah prepared another, which was twice as large as the first. When he completed the second roll, we are not told. After the destruction of Jerusalem in the fifth month of the eleventh year of Zedekiah, Jeremiah remained more than two months longer in the country (comp. xli. 1; xlii. 7). During this time, or perhaps after his arrival in Egypt (comp. rems. on ii. 16, 36), he may have continued his writing till the time mentioned, and provided it with the present inscription, vers. 1–3. Comp. EWALD, *Die Propheten des A. B.* II, S. 15. We have the contents of this writing in our present book, though not in the same order. On this point see the Introduction.

HOMILETICAL AND PRACTICAL.

ORIGEN, in his first homily on Jeremiah, regards the chronological statements of the inscription as a proof of the long-suffering of God. He says, § 3, "God had pronounced judgment against Jerusalem for its sins, and it was condemned to captivity. But as the time approaches, the compassionate God sends this prophet under the third king before the captivity. For the long-suffering God wished to grant them a respite, and Jeremiah was to prophesy, so to speak, the day before the captivity, as a preacher of repentance, in order that the cause of the captivity might be removed." ["Dr. LIGHTFOOT observes that as Moses was so long with the people as a teacher in the wilderness, till they entered into their own land, Jeremiah was so long to their own land a teacher before they went into the wilderness of the heathen." M. HENRY.—S. R. A.]

2. *The Call of the Prophet by Word and Vision* (i. 4–19).

a. His choice, call and aggressive destination

CHAP. I. 4–10.

4, 5 Then the word of the Lord [Jehovah] came unto me,[1] saying, Before I formed thee in the belly[2] I knew thee; and before thou camest forth out of the womb I sanctified [separated] thee, *and* I ordained thee a prophet unto the nations.
6 Then said I [But I said], Ah,[3] Lord God! [Jehovah] behold, I cannot speak: for
7 I am a child. But the Lord [Jehovah] said unto me, Say not, I am a child: for thou shalt go to[4] all that [wherever] I shall send thee, and whatsoever I command
8 thee thou shalt speak. Be not afraid of their faces: for I am with thee to deliver
9 thee, saith the Lord [Jehovah]. Then the Lord [Jehovah] put forth his hand
10 and touched my mouth. And the Lord [Jehovah] said unto me, Behold, I have put my words into thy mouth. See, I have this day set thee over the nations and over the kingdoms, to root out and to pull down [extirpate and exterminate] and to destroy and to throw down, to build and to plant.

TEXTUAL AND GRAMMATICAL.

[1] Ver. 4.—Cod. 1092, DE ROSSI, Cod. D. Mosc., LXX., Vatic., THEODORET in Cod. Monac., ORIGEN, read אֵלַי, misled by the previous context.
[2] Ver. 5.—Since the 3d pers. masc. imperf. of a strong verb with the suffix ךָ requires the short o in the last root-syllable (EWALD, *Ausf. Lehrb.* § 251, b), the Masoretes, deriving אֶצָּרְךָ from צָרַר, read אֶצָרְךָ with the marginal note יָתִיר ו. But the form comes from יָצַר (with the meaning "to form," Exod. xxxii. 11; 1 Kings vii. 15), and the Chethibh is therefore to be pronounced אֶצָּרְךָ.
[3] Ver. 6.—LXX. ὁ ὤν (δέσποτα κύριε), which SPOHN supposes to have arisen from ܐ by the fault of the transcriber; but from the peculiarity of this translation, which would presuppose a derivative from הָיָה (Exod. iii. 14), we may judge it to have been the original.
[4] Ver. 7.—The preposition עַל might not unfitly in this connection be rendered "against" (MAURER), yet elsewhere עַל after הָלַךְ differs little in meaning from אֶל, 1 Sam. xv. 20; ii. 11; comp. Neh. vi. 17 and rems. on x 1

EXEGETICAL AND CRITICAL.

Ver. 5. **Before I formed thee ... to the nations.** Observe the progress of thought in the three clauses of this verse—1. Before I *formed* thee, I *knew* thee: the Divine idea in eternity lies back of the creative act in time. Comp. Ps. cxxxix 15. 2. Before thou *camest forth* from the womb, I *sanctified* thee: the instrument prepared in accordance with the Divine idea is set apart for the sacred service. Comp. Isa. xlv. 4; xlix. 1; Acts ix. 15; Rom. i. 1; Gal. i. 15; Luke i. 15. 3. I *ordained* thee a *prophet* to the nations: it is expressly stated in what this sacred service consists: Jeremiah is to proclaim the word of the Lord as a prophet, not to one nation only, but to the nations generally.

Ver. 6. **Then said I...... I am a child.** Jeremiah perceives directly the difficulty and danger of this Divine commission. He therefore pleads his inability to speak on account of his youth. By a similar plea Moses seeks to escape the Divine legation, Exod. iii. 11; iv. 10. 13; but Jonah flees from before the Lord, i. 3.—Many expositors suppose that Jeremiah was then twenty years of age, but no definite age is designated by נַעַר. The Rabbins understand by this term a boy to his fourteenth year. See BUXTORF, *Lex. Chald. Talm. sub voce.* MAURER more correctly concludes from the long continuance of the prophet's ministry (vers. 2 and 3, coll. xl. 1; xliii. 8), that he could not then have passed his twenty-fifth year.

Ver. 7. **But Jehovah said unto me, say not... thou shalt speak.** Jehovah rebuts the objection of Jeremiah at the outset, not by the promise of His assistance, but by a categorical declaration of His will. He is to go where he is sent, and speak what he is commanded. כֹּל in itself might be taken in a personal sense (πρὸς πάντας, LXX.). But since the following אֶת כֹּל is certainly to be regarded as neuter, and as the neutral signification, being the more general, includes the other, the former is to be preferred =*wherever*. We should also expect עֲלֵיהֶם after the verb, and from its absence conclude that אֲשֶׁר is intended for an adverb of place=whither (Zech. vi. 10).

Ver. 8. **Be not afraid ... saith Jehovah. Their faces** refers to the persons indicated *implicite* in the word **wherever,** ver. 7. Here first the Lord removes Jeremiah's scruples by the promise of His protection and assistance. So with Moses, Exod. iii. 12; iv. 15; comp. Ezek. ii. 6; Josh. i. 5; vii. 9; Judges vi. 16; Matth. x. 18-20; xxviii. 20; Luke xxi. 17; Acts xviii. 9, 10.

Ver. 9. **Then Jehovah put forth his hand .... into thy mouth.** The opposition of the prophet is now broken down. The Lord was too strong for him. Comp. xx. 7; 1 Cor. ix. 10.— So the Lord now proceeds to the solemn act of inauguration. In this we distinguish two points: (*a*) the communication of the necessary ability, ver. 9; (*b*) the conferring of the commission and privileges of the office. Both indicate a vigorous offensive attitude of the prophet, which corresponds to an equally strong defensive position, vers. 18 and 19. The first consists in the symbolical act of touching the lips. We call this act symbolical in so far as the touching of the lips and the words spoken were the visible and audible manifestation of a still deeper spiritual transaction. The Lord cannot literally have put His words in the prophet's mouth: He can only have given him the charism of which the words were the necessary result. "*Attactus oris signum est notans efficaciam spiritus sancti, quippe qui digitus Dei sit, aperiens labia ministrorum verbi,* Ps. li. 13, 14, 17; Luc xxi. 15" (FÖRSTER). The transaction is, however, to be regarded as an historical objective fact, though occurring outside the sphere of physical or bodily life, and therefore as ἐν πνεύματι, or a vision. Comp. DRECHSLER on Isa. vi. 7. We thus avoid a double error. First, that which apprehends the transaction as purely subjective: "as the moment when the presentiment first flashed clearly through the soul of Jeremiah, that his prophetic calling was of Divine appointment" (EWALD, *Die Proph. des A. B.* II. *S.* 26). Secondly, that according to which the transaction took place in the sphere of physical or corporeal existence. So STARKE, who, actually says that the "Son of God, in pre-intimation of His blessed incarnation, appeared to Jeremiah in a human form." —This touching of the lips occurs several times, but always with a different meaning. In Isa. vi. 6 it is for the purpose of expiation, in Dan. x. 16 for the purpose of strengthening. Here in Jeremiah it is the outward form of *inspiratio* (ἐμπνευσις). For the expression "I have put my word in thy mouth" (comp. almost the same expression in Isaiah li. 16) is, on the one hand, an explanation of the act of touching the lips, on the other the designation of that operation on the human spirit by virtue of which "holy men of God spake as they were moved by the Holy Ghost" (2 Pet. i. 21). From the following verse moreover we perceive that the prophet was prepared not only for speaking, but for acting, or, that his words were to be at the same time deeds, real exhibitions of power.

Ver. 10. **See, I have this day .. to build and to plant.** These words represent the second part of the act of inauguration, the conferring of authority and of the commission. Authority is at the same time power. The prophet is not only formally authorized, but rendered physically capable. He is first authorized and empowered to act vigorously in the offensive. הִפְקַדְתִּיךָ I have set thee as a פָּקִיד, *i. e.,* overseer, administrator (ἐπίσκοπος, οἰκονόμος), consequently as my *officer* over the nations and kingdoms, which are my dominion and property. In הִפְקִיד is also included the idea of official plenipotence, which forms the legal basis of the prophet's ministry. The sphere in which this ministry is to be exercised is "the nations and the kingdoms." These are not designated more exactly, but the definite article and the plural denote that not only the kingdom of Judah, but all the nations and kingdoms are meant which were then present on the arena of history. They are enumerated xxv. 17-26. The commission which the prophet received with respect to them has two sides—a positive and a negative. First, he is to extirpate and exterminate (we may thus express the alliteration), to destroy and to throw down, but then also to build and to plant. The first he does by prophesying the Divine judgment, the second by the promise of Divine mercy and grace. נָטַע corresponding to נָטַשׁ is used of plants (xii. 14 sqq.: xxiv. 6: xlv. 4) בָּנָה corresponding to בָּנָה, of buildings (xxxix. 8; lii. 14; Ezek. xxvi. 9, 12). It is noteworthy that the negative side is expressed by four verbs, the positive by only two. With this the contents of the book correspond, as owing to the moral condition of the times, it contains more threatenings and rebukes than promises of grace. It is full of the former with respect to Israel. The latter are found with respect to the theocracy, besides in many scattered passages, especially in ch. xxx.-xxxiii. With respect to the heathen nations both are found especially in ch xlvi.-li. It is understood that the prophet was not actually to destroy and to build, but only by word, which as spoken by God involves the certainty of the accomplishment. Analogous modes of expression are found in Gen. xlix. 6; Isa. vi. 10; Ezek. xxxii. 18: xliii. 3; Hos. vi. 5. Rev. xi. 5.—Comp. Jer. v. 14; xxiii. 29.

DOCTRINAL AND ETHICAL.

1. There is a *vocatio immediata*, which is however restricted to the bearers of the prophetic and apostolic office. We know of no prophet who was chosen and called by man to be a prophet. Aaron and Elisha are only apparent exceptions. Comp. Exod. iv. 14-16, 27; 1 Kings xix. 16. The apostles also were all called immediately by our Lord: Matt. iv. 18-22; x. 1; John i. 37; Acts ix.; Gal. i. 1, 11 sqq. Since then this *vocatio immediata* or *extraordinaria* is for those servants and instruments, of which the Lord will make use "*ad fundandam ecclesiam*," all those who wish to bear office in the church already founded must be called thereto *rite*, *i. e.* by the human organ authorized for this purpose. (*Conf. August., Art. XIV.*) Comp. BUDDE, *Instit. theol. dogm. L. V.*, cap. IV., § 4.—TURRETIN. *Inst. theol. elencht*, Loc. XVIII., Quæst. 23.

2. The free creative act of the personal God, who prepares and forms His instruments according to His idea even in the womb, contradicts both the mechanical idea of development, and a one-sided traducianism.—It is simply remarked, that Catholic theologians (see CORN. A LAPIDE), in order to obtain analogies for the immaculate conception of the Virgin Mary, would conclude from ver. 5 that Jeremiah was conceived without original sin. NEUMANN understands הקדשתיך of a communication of the Holy Ghost to Jeremiah even before his birth. Comp. on the other hand HOFMANN, *Schriftbeweis*, 1, S. 65. ["קדש does not primarily signify to be pure or holy, but to be separated from a common to some special purpose. The idea of purity, whether physical, ceremonial or moral, was originated by that of such separation. When, therefore, Jehovah declares that He had sanctified the prophet before his birth, the meaning is not that He had cleansed him from the pollution of original sin, or that He had regenerated him by His Spirit, as some have imagined, but that He had separated him in His eternal counsel to the work in which he was to be engaged." HENDERSON. So CALVIN. —"In this respect, as in many others, Jeremiah, who was sanctified from his mother's womb, and was *known*, *i. e. loved*, by God before he was conceived and was made a prophet to the Nations, was a figure of Christ, who was loved by the Father from the beginning . . . . and who was the Prophet of all Nations . . . . (see S. JEROME here and comp. S. CYPRIAN c. *Judæos*, 1. 21; S. AMBROSE, *in Ps*. 43, and ORIGEN *Homil*. 1, in Jer.). S. JEROME says: "*Certe nullum puto sanctiorem Jeremia, qui virgo propheta, sanctificatusque in utero, ipso nomine præfigurat Dominum Salvatorem*.' S. JEROME (who is regarded as a saint and as a great doctor of the church, by the Church of Rome) could not have written these words *if* he had known anything of the dogma of the Immaculate Conception (*i. e.* of the original sinlessness) of the Blessed Virgin, which is now enforced by the Church of Rome as an article of faith necessary to everlasting salvation." WORDSWORTH.—S. R. A.]

3. The divine call involves, 1. with respect to the called, (*a*) the duty, to discharge the commission received without shyness or fear of man, and without regard to his own weakness, (*b*) the privilege of the divine protection and assistance, and of certain success in his work; 2. with respect to those for whose sake the divine commission is given, (*a*) the duty of believing obedience, (*b*) the certain prospect of the realization of the threatenings or promises addressed to them.—ZINZENDORF ("*Jeremiah a preacher of righteousness*," S. 5 of the Berlin Ed. of 1830) remarks on ver. 10: "A general promise which is addressed not to court preachers and general superintendents and such like only, in their extended dioceses, but city and village pastors may *a majori ad minus*, safely conclude that it will apply also to their rooting out and pulling down, building and planting. Only [be] faithful! only faithful!"—I note that some have sought to derive from ver. 9 a proof of verbal inspiration, hence STARKE remarks: "Those sin against the Holy Ghost Himself who attribute to Jeremiah a rude style and solecisms, as ABARBANEL, JEROME, CUNÆUS (*De Rep. ebr*. III., 7) have done,"—further that POPE INNOCENT III., founded on ver. 10 his claim to the primacy over civil rulers. Comp. *Decret. L. I. Tit*. 33. *cap. sollicite* (FÖRSTER).

HOMILETICAL AND PRACTICAL.

1. This passage may be suitably employed on the tenth Sunday after Trinity. It is also especially adapted to Ordination and Installation sermons.

2. The Lord never allows His Church to lack the strength which time and place demand. He need not seek this or wait for it. He makes it. As the Lord elsewhere chose that which was foolish, weak and base in the sight of the world (1 Cor. i. 19-29; Matt. xi. 25; John vii. 48; Jas. ii. 5), so now he chooses one who to himself and others appears too young. It is not always the greybeard that is wanted (FÖRSTER). When God gives office He gives also understanding.—It would be presumptuous to begin a great work in one's own strength. It is natural that in view of a great and difficult task one should at first be afraid. (AMBROSE, *De officiis ministrorum*, 1.66: "*Moyses et Hieremias, electi a Domino, ut oracul e Dei prædicarent populo, quod poterant per gratiam, excusabant per verecundiam*.") But it would also be wrong if from pusillanimous despondency or love of ease, one should take no heed to an evident call of God.

"Mark, O my soul, God's word to thee.
And go at Christ's command,
Where'er He draws thee hasten on,
When He detains thee, stand," *etc*.

"The word and glory, Lord divine,
Not ours, O Christ, but all are Thine,

Grant then Thy gracious aid to those,
Who sweetly on Thy word repose."
(Vid. SALNEKKER, in the hymn, "Abide with us, Lord Jesus Christ," etc., ver. 7).—Since the cause is not ours, but the Lord's, and we have not undertaken it in our own strength, but in obedience to His command, it devolves upon the Lord to protect His cause and His servant.— Where one receives an office from the Lord and conducts it according to the Lord's purpose and in His Spirit, there the Lord Himself is present with shield and spear, that is, with weapons of defence and offence.—The word of the Lord even in the mouth of the humblest of His servants, is a hammer which breaks the rock in pieces, and no rock is too hard or too high for it.—The work in the vineyard of the Lord. It must 1. be performed by men, whom the Lord prepares and sends. It is 2. a difficult and dangerous work. But 3. rich in success and reward.—The office to which the Lord appoints is 1. for the purpose of accomplishing His will.—needs, 2. the means which the Lord Himself provides.

3. STARKE:—"He who is called by the Lord to the office of preacher becomes indeed a sacrifice and instrument of God, in that he regards only God's will and command, and must without exception and without self-conceit do and proclaim that which the Lord commands him to do and preach.—Since the anger of God against sin and the punishment which will certainly follow has to be declared to whole kingdoms, a preacher must set their sins and the anger of God awakened thereby, before governors as well as subjects, the high as well as the low.—A teacher in view of gross corruption must not proceed softly; he must break down, root out, pull up and destroy.—When a teacher has by the Law destroyed the kingdom of Satan in the hearts of men, he must seek to build up the kingdom of Christ therein by the Gospel."

["*Propheta nascitur non fit*—*A man is not educated unto a prophet, but originally formed for the office.*—Samuel declared a message from God to Eli when he was a little child. Note, God can, when He pleases, make children prophets and ordain *strength out of the mouths of babes and sucklings.*—If God do not deliver His ministers from trouble, it is to the same effect if He support them under their trouble.—Earthly princes are not wont to go along with their ambassadors, but God goes along with those whom He sends." HENRY.—"You need not fear their *faces*—the thing that timid young men are most wont to fear. Think only that the Lord God is with you, and let His presence be your joy and strength." COWLES.—Nothing can sustain the prophet in His outward and inward conflicts but the assurance of his divine calling.—MAURICE says: "If Jeremiah had fancied that he was a prophet because there was in him a certain aptitude for uttering divine discourses and foreseeing calamities, who can tell the weariness and loathing which he would have felt for his task when it led to no seeming result, except the dislike of all against or for whom it was exercised,—still more when the powers and graces which were supposed to be the qualifications for it, became consciously feeble."—S. R. A.]

b. The Visions, Rehearsal and Programme.

CHAP. I. 11-16.

11 Moreover the word of the Lord [Jehovah] came unto me, saying, Jeremiah,
12 what seest thou? And I said, I see a [wakeful] rod of an almond tree. Then said the Lord [Jehovah] unto me, Thou hast well [rightly] seen, for I will hasten
13 [be wakeful (Germ., *wacker*) concerning] my word, to perform it. And the word of the Lord [Jehovah] came unto me the [a] second time, saying, What seest thou? And I said, I see a seething [boiling] pot, and the face thereof is
14 toward [from] the north. Then the Lord [Jehovah] said unto me, Out of the north an evil [calamity] shall break forth upon all the inhabitants of the land.
15 For lo, I will call all the families of the kingdoms of the north, saith the Lord [Jehovah]; and they shall come, and they shall set every one his throne [seat] at the entering of the gates of Jerusalem, and against all the walls thereof round
16 about, and against all the cities of Judah. And I will utter my judgments against them[1] touching [for] all their wickedness, who[2] [because they] have forsaken me, and have burned[3] incense [sacrifice] unto other gods, and worshipped the works[4] of their own hands.

TEXTUAL AND GRAMMATICAL.

[1] Ver. 16.—The form אוֹתָם for אֹתָם is frequent in Jeremiah, ii. 35; iv. 12; xii. 1. Comp. NAEGELSB. *Gr.* § 55, 3, *Anm.*
[2] Ver. 16.—אֲשֶׁר before יְעָזְבֻנִי refers to the suffix in בְּרָעָתָם, and since it is to be regarded as explicative, introducing a

more particular definition of רָעָה, we may translate it by: that, that namely. Moreover רָעָה here refers to the same expression in ver. 14.

³ Ver. 16.—יִקְטְרוּ. This Piel is frequently synonymous with the Hiphil הִקְטִיר. (Comp. 1 Kings iii. 3; xi. 8 with xxii. 44; 2 Kings xxii. 17 with 2 Chron. xxiv. 25 Chethibh) in the wider sense of *offering* in general. (Comp. GRAF *in loc.*)—That Jeremiah also uses the Piel in the wider sense seems to follow from the fact that he uses it almost exclusively,—every where indeed with the exception of two places (xxxii. 18; xlviii. 35), where it was proper to use the official *terminus technicus*. But it is not clear whether the Piel in Jeremiah has the wider meaning, in consequence of a grammatical confusion of the Hiphil with the Piel, or of a rhetorical *denominatio a potiore*.

⁴ Ver. 16.—מַעֲשֵׂי, the plural, is found again only xliv. 8, the singular xxv. 6, 7; xxxii. 30; 2 Kings xxii. 17; coll. 2 Chron. xxxiv. 25.

EXEGETICAL AND CRITICAL.

In general this section is the continuation of Jeremiah's induction into the prophetic office, commenced in the previous section. This continuation consists in this, that the Lord at once causes the prophet to make a little trial or exercise in prophetic vision, in which he shows him not only the *manner*, but the main *purport* of the prophetic vision and announcement, *i. e.* the programme in outline of his prophetic ministry. The two sections thus stand in the closest reciprocal relation. Whether we are to assume an interval of time between them, is not clear from the text, which however does not forbid the supposition of a very brief interim.

Ver. 11. **Moreover . . . rod of an almond tree.** The question, "What seest thou?" is found not only here, in ver. 13 and xxiv. 3, but also in Amos vii. 8; viii. 2; Zech. iv. 2; v. 2. It is the object of the inquirer to assure himself that the person addressed has rightly seen, which thus presupposes a certain difficulty, as well as importance, in seeing correctly. Apart from the objective difficulty of always perceiving the object shown, which we meet with, *ex. gr.*, in Amos viii. 2; Zech. v. 2; the subjective ability of beholding visions, the seeing power of the inner eye, as it were, had to be tested. שָׁקֵד is the almond (Gen. xliii. 11; Num. xvii. 8; Eccles. xii. 5). The word comes from שָׁקַד, *vigilavit*. What the cock is among domestic animals the almond is among trees. It awakes first from the sleep of winter: "*floret omnium prima mense Januario, Martio vero poma maturat,*" says PLINY, *Hist. Nat.* L. XVI. c. 25.—The LXX have βακτηρίαν καρυΐνην, *baculum nuceum*. It is questionable whether by this they wished to designate a nut-tree-staff (with a hint at the sweet kernel in a bitter shell, as THEODORET and AMBROSE suppose, the latter in *Epist. ad Marcellinam sororem*, the 41st in the Bened. Ed.). For, according to HERACLITUS EPHESIUS (κάρυα ἐκάλουν καὶ τὰς ἀμυγδάλας, etc.), HESYCHIUS (καρύας· ἀμυγδάλας καὶ κασσάνους) and others (see DRUSIUS *ad h. l. cfr.* PASSOW: κάρυον, *every kind of nut*), βακτηρία καρυΐνη may also mean an almond-tree-staff, as the LXX also translate Gen. xxx. 37, לוּז by ῥάβδος καρυΐνη (לוּז is however the proper word in Hebrew and the dialects for almond-tree. See ARNOLD in HERZOG, *Real-Enc.*, Art. *Mandelbaum*), and in Gen. xliii. 11, at least the *Cod. Vatic* has κάρυα for שְׁקֵדִים, while the *Cod. Alex.* renders this word by ἀμύγδαλα.—But although the language allows the meaning of "almond" for שָׁקֵד, it has not been universally admitted here. BUGENHAGEN, *ex. gr.* translates *baculum alacrem* or *virgam vigilantem*,

and expressly excludes the idea of an almond tree. For in another reference he makes this remarkable declaration; "*Qui in hebraico nunc superstitiosius sua puncta (quæ tamen sciunt olim non fuisse) sequuntur, faciunt hoc loco: baculum amygdalinum. Sed si hoc placet ipsis, cur non postea faciunt etiam sic: bene vidisti, quia ego amygdalabor ad verbum meum*" Most commentators admit the idea of "almond-tree" in שָׁקֵד, they differ only in this that some express this idea in the translation as that which is in reality the only one befitting the word, while the others for the sake of the similarity with the following שֹׁקֵד prefer the radical signification (*vigilare*). The latter again are distinguished into those who take שֹׁקֵד=שָׁקֵד in the substantive sense, "watchman" (so CALVIN: *baculus vigilis*; (ECOLAMPAD.: the watchman club), and those who retain the adjectival signification (*vigilans, alacer*).—The endeavor to recommend the latter meaning by the explanation, "*virga vigilans pro minaci, incumbente, instar destricti gladii vibrata*" (ZWINGLI) is wrecked on the difficulty of a rod alone, without an arm to raise it or an object over which it is held, being recognized as *vigilans*. If on the other hand the staff be recognized by the prophet as an almond-tree staff, not only is this explicable but the subsequent explanation is connected easily and naturally with the idea of an almond-tree. EWALD has made the thought clear by the translation: A watch-staff of elder, for I will watch, etc.—THEODORET says, long-suffering is a sleep (Ps. xliv. 24; lxxviii. 65); watchfulness for vengeance an awaking. That He will not sleepily delay, but will be fresh and watchful to own by speedy fulfilment the word spoken by the mouth of His prophet,—this is what God says to the fearful, hesitating Jeremiah for his comfort and encouragement. But is מַקֵּל a branch with twigs and leaves, or a stick stripped of leaves, such as is used for walking with or striking? Many, like STARKE and ROSENMUELLER, favor the former view. They appeal to the circumstance that otherwise the staff would not be recognized as from an almond-tree. Others, as KIMCHI, VATABLE, SEB. SCHMID, VENEMA, GAAB, decide for the latter, being only not agreed whether the staff is to be understood as being a pilgrim's staff, a shepherd's staff, or a stick for beating. I accept the latter view, and take the staff to be a threatening rod of castigation, for the following reasons: 1 Although GESENIUS and FUERST derive מַקֵּל from the root בקל which in Ethiopic, Arabic and Syriac has the meaning of "to sprout, shoot forth," the word in Hebrew never has the signification of a fresh, green, leafy branch (not even in Jeremiah

CHAP. I. 11-16.

xlviii. 17, which passage is adduced by FUERST), but always that of a stick or staff, and therefore agrees at least in signification with *baculus*, βακτηρία. The Hebrew expressions for a fresh branch are מַטֶּה (Ezek. xix. 11 sqq.), שׁוֹט, עָנָף, עָבוֹת. סְעִיף. 2. The connection requires that an instrument of chastisement be meant. The expositors have pointed with justice to the climax: rod—boiling pot. "*Qui noluerint percutiente virga emendari, mittentur in ollam æneam atque succensam,*" says JEROME. But a leafy branch is not an instrument of punishment.—The objection that the prophet would not then be in a condition to recognize the staff as from an almond-tree is unfounded. He might be able to do this even if we had reason to suppose that a dry almond tree was shown him. To distinguish between different kinds of dry wood is not difficult for a half-informed man. We must imagine a staff stripped indeed of leaves and adapted for striking, but yet fresh, unbarked and sappy. Since it is just in its being fresh and full of sap that the point lies, we may certainly presume that it was an almond rod in this stage that was shown to the prophet. Perhaps the recognition was facilitated by the circumstance that the vision occurred at a time when the sap had just commenced to flow in the almond tree.

Ver. 12. **Then said Jehovah . . . to perform it.** VENEMA remarks on this verse: "*Visum eo tendit, ut propheta experimentum suæ aptitudinis ad munus propheticum cuperet.—Bene vidisti: capax ergo es visionum propheticarum.*" There seems to be some truth in this. In the other passages where the formula, **What seest thou?** occurs it is without the **Thou hast well seen** of confirmation. When it is here said to Jeremiah his first vision there is certainly something encouraging in the fact, and it may not incorrectly be referred to the apprehension of incapacity expressed by the prophet in ver. 6. At the same time it corroborates what has been remarked on שָׁקֵד. If it were a leafy twig, **thou hast well seen** appears to be superfluous, for there would have been no skill in distinguishing it—**I will be wakeful,** etc. Comp. xxxi. 28, where the Lord refers expressly to this passage. The paronomasia is the same as between קֵרן and קֹף (Am. viii. 2).—Observe that we have דָּבָר and not דֶּבֶר. The word which the prophet has to proclaim is that of God, who will not allow His own word to be dishonoured. The prophet need not be anxious either about its impression on the hearts of men or about the verification of his threatenings and promises; both will verify themselves. Comp. Heb. ii. 1; Isa. lv. 11.

Ver. 13. **And the word . . . from the north.** This second vision is closely related to the first, both as to form and matter, we are therefore not to suppose a long pause between them. In form this vision is like the first, but in matter it forms a climax, since, as already remarked, the boiling pot in relation to the simple rod of castigation appears to be an emblem of an extreme fury of anger. There is also a progress here, in that the second vision, with the explanation attached, plainly expresses *why, how* and *by whom* the judgment should be inflicted upon Judah. Thus far vers. 13-16 present an outline of the whole prophecy of Jeremiah, for the whole book is no more than a development of the great thought here expressed: Judgment upon Judah by a people coming from the north; and the consolatory portions are but exceptions, like single rays of light in the prevailing darkness of the picture.—**A boiling pot,** etc. Etymologically it is a pot *blown upon*, i. e., a pot brought to boiling by blowing the fire. Comp. נָפוּחַ רוּחַ Job xli. 11. The idea of BRENZ, that סִיר is here to be taken as = *spina* (*spina, quæ in die iræ Domini ab igne hujus succenditur*) is refuted by the singular. We should then expect סִירִים. Comp. Isa. xxxiv. 13; Hos. ii. 8; Nah. i. 10; Eccles. vii. 6, in which place the word is used in both meanings. The seething pot is an emblem among the Arabs of warlike fury. Comp. ROSENMUELLER, *ad. h. l.* Most expositors understand by the pot here the theocracy. The Chaldeans are then the fire inflamed to a violent heat, which boils the Jews in the pot (comp. Ezek. xi. 3, 7, 11; xxii. 20), and that which foams over is the inhabitants driven out of the holy land. So, *ex. gr.*, says (ECOLAMPADIUS: "*Hierusalem ollæ vel lebeti comparatur (ussgesotten Haffen) in qua carnales homines per ignem coquantur, ut quasi spuma ebulliantur per fervorem.*" But they have been led by the general similarity of these passages in Ezekiel to overlook the difference. There the pot, with the flesh in it and that which is to come out of it, as well as the fire, are expressly distinguished from each other. In reference to our passage VENEMA has correctly remarked: "*Nihil hic de igne, nihil de folle et sufflatione attunde orta; simpliciter memoratur olla sufflata, quæ est olla in tumorem erecta et effervescens.*" And the prophet certainly *sees* nothing more than a pot boiling and foaming from the north. So that this itself is presented as the instrument of the severer punishment, and therefore symbolizes the Chaldeans. So BUGENHAGEN ("*olla malum per Chaldæos et Assyrios Judæis paratum*"), VENEMA ("*olla representat regnum Chaldæum sub Nebucadnezare et vasta molimina coquens, et summe sese efferens, simul iratum et ad omnia absorbenda paratum*"). With the opposite view of the pot is closely connected the incorrect interpretation of פָּנָיו כִּפְנֵי צָפוֹנָה. If we understand by the pot the Jewish people, and imagine this placed over a burning fire, which, though not expressly mentioned, we assume to be the Chaldeans, then it is natural to view פָּנָיו as the side of the pot turned towards the fire. But it is not the side turned towards the fire, but towards the prophet. For in the first place in the vision there is no fire, so that פָּנָיו could denote only the front of the pot, supposing it had one. It would, secondly, be difficult to show that the pot (or kettle, as some translate) had a side which could be expressly marked as the front. Thirdly, if the opposite view were correct we should read אֶל פְּנֵי צ not צ כִּפְנֵי. For the prophet certainly sees the pot from his standpoint as in the north. If now we say that the pot was placed against a fire burning on its northern side, the prophet from his southern standpoint would certainly be unable to see the side towards the fire. I know that frequently in Hebrew the *terminus a quo* is put where we should use the *terminus in quo* or *in quem* (comp. NAEGELSB. *Heb. Gram.*, 2d Ed., S. 228), but this mode of expression is applicable only when the object in question presents itself from just that point, at which it is according to our conception of it or towards which it is moving. In the present case, however, the side turned away from the prophet and not visible to him would be designated as that which is presenting itself to him (from the north). We therefore take פָּנִים as the side turned towards and displayed to the prophet, whence according to a frequent idiom (comp. Num. viii. 2; Ex. xxviii. 25; Ex. xl. 44) it is designated as the face of the pot, and on this account also no further emphasis is to be laid on it. It is merely the visible side as opposed to the invisible; and we therefore translate simply "and it looks from the north." The *He locale* in צָפוֹנָה, as in several cases after prepositions, does not serve to indicate the direction more definitely, Isa. xv. 10, 21,

מִבָּבֶלָה and מִבָּבֶל Jer. xxvii. 16, but here as in

לַיְלָה appears to have lost its significance as a particle and to be in transition to a mere phonetic substantive termination.

Ver. 14. **Then Jehovah said . . . the inhabitants of the land.** *From the north* is a general and indefinite expression, and it remains so to the prophet until a great historical event renders it sharply defined. Until the battle of Carchemish a people from the north only is spoken of (iv. 6; vi. 1, 22; x. 22), after the battle this people appears distinctly as the Chaldeans under Nebuchadnezzar (xxv. 9, *etc*). This settles the question whether by this northern nation the Chaldeans or Scythians were meant. All the older expositors held the former view. After EICHHORN's example (*Heb. Proph.* II. 9), VON BOHLEN (*Gen.* S. 166), DAHLER (*Jérémie* II. 81), EWALD (*Proph. d. A. B.* 1, S. 361, 373; II., S. 9; *Gesch. Isr.* III. 392), BERTHEAU (*Gesch. d. Isr.* S. 361), HITZIG and others in general, as RÖSCH says (*Zeitschr. d. morg. Ges.* XV., S. 536) "pretty nearly all exegetical authorities," maintain the latter. Without wishing to oppose that which ADOLPH STRAUSS (*Vatt. Zephanjie*, S. XV.), THOLUCK (*Die Proph. u. ihre Weiss*., S. 94), and GRAF (*D. proph. Jer. erklärt*, S. 16) have urged in favor of the older view, especially from the circumstance that the incursion of the Scythians was made at least five years before the public appearance of our prophet, I am still of opinion, that Jeremiah could have had neither the Scythians, nor the Chaldeans, nor any other people definitely in mind. He saw only this much, that a northern people would visit Judah as the rod of divine discipline. What people this would be, or rather what people **all the families of the kingdoms of the earth** would unite under their leadership, he knew not. He learned this first, as we have said, from the decisive turn given by the battle of Carchemish. We shall see when we come to consider the respective passages that where he characterizes this unknown people more particularly (comp. iv. 11; v. 15; vi. 22; x. 22; xiii. 20) his description suits the Chaldeans, and that afterwards when he names them (ch. xxv.) he is not conscious of correcting an error. Comp. GRAF, S. 17, *etc*.—We thus come to the question, how can Jeremiah call the Chaldeans a northern people, since Babylon lay to the east or southeast of Palestine? We are not to expect an exact localization here, since, as we have said, Jeremiah has no definite people in view. The origin of the Chaldeans in the Koordish mountains (J. D. MICHAELIS), the extension of the Babylonian kingdom to the north and the connection with it of the Medes and Assyrians (ECOLAMPADIUS, GROTIUS, and others) are not to be urged as reasons for this expression of the prophet. He knows only that they will come against Jerusalem from the north over Dan and the mountains of Ephraim (iv. 15; viii. 16). At the same time it was determined that these enemies belonged to the dominion not of a southern, but of a (in relation to this) northern empire, for which reason, after he had recognized the Chaldeans, the prophet does not cease to designate them as coming from the north; xxv. 9, coll. Ezek. xxvi. 7.—**Shall break forth,** *etc.* Vers. 14-16 contain the interpretation of the second vision, ver. 14 giving its general import. פָּתַח is used only of the opening of a closed gate, but metaleptically of the dismission or exclusion of what was enclosed by it, whether *in bonam partem, ex. gr.* of prisoners (Isa. li. 14: Job xii. 14), or *in malum partem* of a calamity, as here. ZWINGLI remarks on this passage: "*hac metalepsi 'aperiri pro prodire' non temere utuntur Latini, sed pro 'prodere' frequentius.*" [HENDERSON: "Though more to the east than to the north of Judea, the Hebrews always represent the Babylonians as living in, or coming from, the north, partly because they usually appropriated the term east to Arabia Deserta, stretching from Palestine to the Euphrates, and partly because that people, not being able to cross the desert, had to take a northern route when they came against the Hebrews, and always entered their country by the northern frontier." —S. R. A.]

Ver. 15. **For lo . . . the cities of Judah.** In this verse the general idea רָעָה is more exactly defined. The calamity will consist in this that the Lord will call all the kingdoms of the north against Judah. But *all* is not to be emphasized. It is only meant that the (in relation to Egypt) northern empire will come with its whole force upon Judah. The expression "and they shall set every one his throne," *etc.*, is very variously explained. CALVIN understands it as the arrangement for a permanent residence ("*ut consideant tanquam domi suae*") which is entirely unsuited to the connection. Others understand by the *throne* the seat of the general, from which orders are issued as well as judgments. The latter have been referred either to the hostile soldiers (so, *ex. gr.*, SEB. SCHMID), or to Judah (STARKE, J. D. MICHAELIS, "*describuntur ut assessores ejus judicii, quod v. seq. informatur*"). The reference to the hostile soldiery does not agree with the context, the reference to Judah is in so far unsuited that a throne for the purpose of judging a city, is set not before the gates, but within the conquered city. I therefore concur with VENEMA, ROSENMUELLER, MAURER and others in the view, that the seat here is only a seat for sitting upon, and that to sit down before a city is simply to besiege it, as in Latin *obsidere*, and as the French say *mettre le siége devant une ville*. The phrase אִישׁ כִּסְאוֹ expresses that Jerusalem will be surrounded by many such seats. They will be set especially before the gates of Jerusalem (פֶּתַח prepositive, as Gen. xviii. 1; xix. 11, *etc.*) because it is the metropolis and because the siege is directed against the gates, as the approaches to it. From the principal stations before the gates of the capital the attack may be directed not only against the walls of Jerusalem, but against the other cities of the land.

Ver. 16. **And I will utter... their own hands.** These words designate the visitation threatened in the preceding verses as a divine judgment, and name also the guilt which has brought such a judgment upon Judah. The expression בְּ אֶת דָּבָר מִשְׁפָּטִים signifies to *discuss rights* with any one, *i. e.* to *dispute* (*causam agere*) between those who have equal rights (Jer. xii. 1), and partly as a judge with the accused (iv. 12; xxxix. 5). The expression here has the suffix of a definite person, which signifies that the case is not one of reciprocal rights, but entirely of the rights of the Lord, for the infraction of which the people are here called to account. This discussion of the Lord with the people is not to take place in words, but by the judgment announced in the previous verses. ["The idea conveyed by the LXX is somewhat different, and I believe that it is what the original words mean, λαλήσω πρὸς αὐτοὺς μετὰ κρίσεως—I will speak to them with judgment. The original literally is, 'I will speak my judgments to them;' that is, I will not speak words but judgments.—The verse may be thus rendered—'And I will speak *by* my judgments unto them,' *etc.*" CALVIN'S *Comm.* I., 58. *Tr's note.*—S. R. A.]

DOCTRINAL AND ETHICAL.

1. In form both of these visions are *objective* symbols, in distinction from *verbal* symbols (parables, tropes, *etc.*) and from types. The prophetic element is essential to the latter, but not to symbols. The almond-tree staff is only an objective expression of the truth that the Lord is early awake to verify His truth. The seething pot also is only an actual representation of the judgment which is threatening Judah. The circumstance that this is future is not essential. While the type represents a future fact the symbol is only the emblematic expression of a speech, and may refer to the present, the past or the future.—It may be remarked that the older theologians used the expression *theologia symbolica* in a triple sense, (*a*) = *theologia mystica*, *kabbalistica* (comp. BUDDE, *Inst. Dogm.* p. 186), (*b*) = theology of the confessions or creeds, (*c*) as correlative to *revelatio symbolica, i. e.* revelation imparted by bodily signs, in opposition to *revelatio simplex*, which passes internally from spirit to spirit (comp. BUDDE *S.* 25, *etc.*, and STARKE, *in loc.*).—Concerning the Biblical symbols, comp. ZÖCKLER, *Theologia naturalis, S.* 200. [FAIRBAIRN'S *Typology, passim.* "Here is a beautiful type of the Resurrection, especially the Resurrection of Christ. '*Virga Aaron quæ putabatur emortua, in Resurrectione Domini floruit*' (S. JEROME)." WORDSWORTH.—S. R. A.]

2. It may be asked whether the *alacritas, vigilantia, assiduitas, diligentia Dei* does not claim to be regarded as a special quality in opposition to the *somnolentia, inertia, pigritia* of men. The answer must be in the negative. In the conception of the absolute Spirit, who is at the same time the absolute life, the material basis is given for this *vigilantia* or *diligentia* as truly as holiness, love, faithfulness, wisdom serve for the formal (ethical and intellectual) basis: He that keepeth Israel neither slumbers nor sleeps. Ps. cxxi. 4.

3. The justice of God demands the satisfaction of His wounded honor (Isa. xlii. 8). The divine wisdom in connection with omniscience selects the instruments and fixes the time and manner of the judgment.

HOMILETICAL AND PRACTICAL.

1. [On ver. 12. "Prophets have need of good eyes; and those that *see* well shall be commended, and not those only that *speak* well." M. HENRY. —S. R. A.]

God's justice is, 1. long-suffering: at first it uses only the rod (Rom. ii. 4); 2. recompensing zealously and severely: when the gentle chastisement is without result, it becomes a consuming fire (Ex. xx. 5; Ps. vii. 12; Heb. x. 31). [AMBROSE on Ps. xxxviii., quoted by WORDSWORTH.—S. R. A.]

2. [On ver. 16. MAURICE:—"We perceive as much from the words of the prophet as from the history, that this idolatry has now become deep and radical.—The state of mind which was latent in them and which they brought forth into full, conscious activity, is represented as an apostate state; not so much an adoption of false gods as a denial of the true. There is a great practical difference between the frivolous, heartless taste for foreign novelties, which was denounced by the earlier prophets, and the utter incapacity for acknowledging a God not appealing to the senses, which Jeremiah discovers in his contemporaries. He boldly sets up the faith of the heathen as a lesson to the Israelites, ii. 10, 11."—S. R. A.]

c. Repetition of the Commission and Promise as the basis of the impregnable defensive position of the Prophet.

I. 17–19.

17   Thou therefore gird up thy loins, and arise and speak unto them all that I [shall] command thee: be not dismayed [confounded] at their faces, lest I con-
18   found thee before them. For, behold, I have made [make] thee this day a defenced city, and an iron pillar and brazen walls[1] against the whole land, against[2] the kings of Judah, against[2] the princes thereof, against[2] the priests thereof and
19   against[2] the people of the land. And they shall [may] fight against thee, but they shall not prevail against thee; for I am with thee, saith the LORD [Jehovah], to deliver thee.

TEXTUAL AND GRAMMATICAL.

[1] Ver. 18.—[HENDERSON: "Instead of the plural חֹמוֹת, walls, the singular חֹמָה, wall, is found in twelve of DE ROSSI'S MSS.; it has been originally in seven more, and is now in two by correction. It is likewise in five ancient editions, and occurs in the defective form without the Vau in a great number of MSS. and editions. The LXX., Targ., Syr. and Vulg. all read in the singular. This form further commends itself on the ground of its being the less usual, but at the same time more appropriate in application to a singular subject."—S. R. A.]

[2] Ver. 18.—לְ is a feebler continuation of עַל. Comp. iii. 17; Ps. xxxiii. 28. NAEGELSB. Gram. ? 112, 8.

EXEGETICAL AND CRITICAL.

In these concluding verses the general purport of section (a) is first repeated: ver. 17 from speak to faces, and the conclusion of ver 19, reproducing the conclusion of vers. 7 and 8. On the basis of this promise (comp. For I am with thee, ver. 19), however, the prophet is assured, in antithesis to the *offensive* position commanded in vers. 9 and 10, of an equally strong *defensive* position, and this is the new and characteristic element of this concluding section.

Ver. 17. **Thou therefore ... before them.** A summons to set vigorously to work. The servant of God must be neither cowardly nor slothful. The expression, "gird up the loins," is frequently used in a proper as well as in a figurative sense; 1 Kings xviii. 46; 2 Kings iv. 29; ix. 1; Job xxxviii. 3; Eccles. xxxi. 17; Luke xii. 35; Eph. vi. 14; 1 Pet. i. 13.—**Be not dismayed** forms a climax in relation to **Be not afraid**, ver. 8, as in Deut. i. 21; Josh. x. 25.—תֵּחַת and אַחְתְּךָ מִפְּנֵיהֶם and לִפְנֵיהֶם correspond. [This play upon words may be expressed in English thus: "Be not dumbfounded before them, lest thou be confounded before them."—S. R. A.] Many commentators have hesitated at rendering the Hiphil of חָתַת in the primary sense of "*frangere*, to break to pieces." They have thought the threatening would be too severe. "*erigendus erat animus persuasione incolumitatis non minis ac metu frangendus,*" says SCHNURRER. They therefore take either פֶּן in a reduced and grammatically inadmissible sense (BUGENHAGEN; *quasi te terream*; STARKE, "I should terrify thee;" GROTIUS: *nec enim timere te faciam*;

SCHNURRER supplies לֵאמֹר = *putans concessurum me esse, ut tibi sit pereundem*), or they understand the verb in the meaning which certainly pertains to the word, "to make afraid." But what sense is there in this rendering: "Be not afraid before them, lest I make thee afraid before them"? (ECOLAMP., MAURER, EWALD). If the prophet was afraid before his enemies he did not need to be rendered still more so. I take חָתַת, with most commentators, in the sense *frangere, conterere,* which it has in the radical signification of the Kal.—*to be broken in pieces, crushed* (see FUERST), and which is undoubtedly has in such passages as Isa. ix. 3. The threatening is not too severe. Comp. 1 Cor. ix. 16, " For though I preach the Gospel, I have nothing to glory of: for necessity is laid upon me; yea, woe is unto me, if I preach not the gospel." From this we see that the inward pressure which a man of God feels in consequence of the divine operation is very strong. He who should resist this divine impulse, like Jonah, would be crushed by it. And it would be the just punishment of that faint-hearted disdain, which would reject such high honor from a miserable fear of man.

Ver. 18. **For behold ... the people of the land.** I is emphatic in antithesis to **thou,** ver. 17. Thou gird up thy loins and do thy part, I will do mine, to protect thee. In the words "a defenced city and an iron pillar and brazen wall," the prophet is assured that for the difficult offensive commission which is given him he will receive a sufficient defensive equipment. Offence and defence stand in exact relation to each other. Reference is afterwards made to this promise, in xv. 20, 21. Comp. Ps. cv. 15.—On the subject-matter comp. Matt. x. 18, 19.—**people of the land.** This expression occurs frequently in the sense of "the common people": xxxiv. 19; xxxvii. 2; xliv. 21; lii. 6; Ezek. vii. 27, &c. It is the basis of the later Rabbinical usage according to which it signifies the "unlearned and ignorant" (Acts iv. 13) comp. BUXTORF. *Lex Rabb.* s. v. עַם.

Ver. 19. **And they shall fight ... to deliver thee.** יְכֹל with לְ in the sense of *prævalere*, Gen. xxxii. 26; 1 Sam. xvii. 9; Obad. 7; Jer. xxxviii. 22.—**For I am with thee,** comp. ver. 8.

DOCTRINAL AND ETHICAL.

1. It is fundamentally the same sin, to labor in the Lord's vineyard without a calling, and not to be willing to labor when one has been called, for in both cases a man seeks his own, not that which is God's.
2. "He who fears nothing and hopes nothing may preach the truth. He who is unequal to either of these two will act more wisely for his own repose and more honorably for the truth, if he keep silence."—DR. LEIDEMIT.
3. Behold I send you forth as lambs among wolves. Luke x. 3; Matt. x. 16 sqq. God's strength is made perfect in weakness. 2 Cor. xii. 9.
4. Fear not those who kill the body, but are not able to kill the soul. Rather fear Him who can destroy both soul and body in hell. Matt. x. 28. God is no respecter of persons. Rom. ii. 11; Eph. vi. 9; 1 Pet. i. 17.

HOMILETICAL AND PRACTICAL.

1. Duty and privilege of the servants of God. 1. Their duty: (*a*) always to have their loins girded, (*b*) to proclaim without fear of man whatever the Lord commands. 2. Their privilege: —through the power of God to be obliged to yield to no power on earth. 2. The Lord's requirements and promise to His servants. 1. The requirement, (*a*) to be always ready for His service, (*b*) to accomplish that which is bidden without delay. 2. The promise: (*a*) that the Lord will be with them, (*b*) that no earthly power will conquer them. [M. HENRY: "He must be quick—*Arise,* and lose no time; he must be busy—*Arise, and speak unto them,* in season, out of season; he must be bold—*Be not dismayed at their faces.*—In a word he must be faithful; it is required of ambassadors that they be so. In two things he must be faithful. 1. He must speak *all* that he is charged with. He must forget nothing —Every word of God is weighty. He must conceal nothing for fear of offending. 2. He must *speak to all* that he is *charged against.* Two reasons why he should do this. 1. Because he had reason to fear the wrath of God, if he should be false. 2. Because he had no reason to fear the wrath of man, if he were faithful."—S. R. A.]

II. FIRST DIVISION.

The Passages relating to the Theocracy, Chaps. II.—XLIV.

(WITH AN APPENDIX, CHAP. XLV.)

FIRST SUBDIVISION.

The Collection of Discourses, with Appendices, Chaps. II.—XXXV.

1. *The First Discourse.*

CHAPTER II.

This chapter contains an independent discourse; it does not, as GRAF supposes, form, with chap. iii.-vi., a connected whole. For, as we shall show, chap. iii. *begins a discourse clearly arranged and complete in itself, which would not bear any addition either at the beginning or at the close. The present discourse is of very general import, and contains probably only the quintessence of several discourses made before those in* chap. iii.-vi., *since it is scarcely probable that in the course of nearly two decades Jeremiah only addressed this short discourse, besides* chap. iii.-vi., *to the people. The position at the beginning, the style, the non-mention of the Chaldeans* (comp. rems. on xxv. 1), *besides the command "Go and cry in the ears of Jerusalem"* (ver. 2), *and an intimation probably to be referred to the time of Josiah* (ver. 35, see the Comm.), *all point to the commencement of Jeremiah's prophetic ministry. This seems to be contradicted by some not obscure allusions to the flight of the remaining Jews to Egypt* (vers. 16, 36 and 37; coll. chaps. xlii.–xliv). *But since Jeremiah, as was remarked on* i. 2, *probably did not finish the second writing out of his book till after the destruction of Jerusalem* (xxxvi. 32), *possibly not till his arrival in Egypt, it is possible that he then added to this earliest discourse some allusions to the eventful journey to Egypt. He may have added them to this discourse for the reason that it contained some passages, the connection and purport of which especially invited such allusions to the emigration to Egypt. Compare* ver. 15, *the predicted devastation so exactly corresponding to the result, and* ver. 33, *the mention of the religio-political errors of the people.*

After the introduction (vers. 1-3), *the ever-recurring theme of complaint and threatening is treated in four tableaux or acts, the particular contents of which may be designated as follows:*

 1. *Israel's infidelity in the light of the fidelity of Jehovah and the heathen* (vers. 4-13).
 2. *Israel's punishment and its cause* (vers. 14-19).
 3. *The lust of idolatry: deeply rooted, outwardly insolent, false at last* (vers. 20-28).
 4. *Whose is the guilt?* (vers. 29-37).

The Introduction.

II. 1-3.

1. And the word of Jehovah came also unto me, saying,
2. Go and cry in the ears of Jerusalem, saying,
   Thus saith Jehovah ; I remember of thee,
   The kindness of thy youth,
   The love of thine espousals,
   When thou wentest after me in the desert,
   In a land that was not sown.
3. Israel is a sanctuary unto Jehovah,
   The first-fruits of his produce:
   All who devour him¹ incur guilt;
   Calamity will come upon them, saith Jehovah.

TEXTUAL AND GRAMMATICAL.

¹ Ver. 3.—For תְּבוּאָתֹה (Comp. NAEGELSB. Gram. § 93, Anm.) some Codd. read תְּבוּאָתוֹ. It would be natural to pronounce the consonants תְּבוּאָתֹה which has been also done by J. D. MICHAELIS who refers the word to זְרוּעָה אֶרֶץ לֹא ver. 2, but the reference of the suffix to Jehovah is demanded by the connection.

EXEGETICAL AND CRITICAL.

These words form the introduction both to the first discourse and at the same time to the whole of Jeremiah's prophetic announcements. Indeed, it may be said that they contain the thought, which reaches far beyond the prophecies of Jeremiah, and lies at the foundation of the entire history of the theocracy, that notwithstanding the revolts on the one side and the punishments on the other, love is the key-note of the relation between God and Israel, and the Lord's inalienable property.

Vers. 1 and 2. **And the word ... not sown.** —It is probable that in the opening words of ver. 2 Jeremiah received the command to leave Anathoth and go to Jerusalem as the scene of his prophetic labors. For here only is the audience, to which he was to address himself, designated thus briefly by the word "Jerusalem." Everywhere else the address reads differently. Comp. xvii. 19; xix. 3; xxxv. 13.—**I remember of thee.** The expression occurs *in malam partem* Ps. lxxix. 8; cxxxvii. 7; Neh. vi. 14; xiii. 29: *in bonam partem* Ps. xcviii. 3; cvi. 45; cxxxii. 1; Neh. v. 19; xiii. 22, 31. In any case *of thee* contains an emphasis which should not be overlooked in the exposition.—**The kindness of thy youth.** The commentators dispute whether the kindness and love of God toward the people or that of the people toward God is meant. In behalf of the former view it is urged, (1) that in the following context the people is described as rebellious from the first, and (2) that with this the historical representation of the Pentateuch and other declarations of Old Testament passages accord. (Comp. especially Hos. xi. 1; Ezek. xvi.) To the first argument it may be objected that these verses form the introduction not to the second chapter only, but to the whole book, and although the greater part of this consists of threatenings, or rather *because* it does so, the prophet places the assurance of God's unchangeable fidelity in the foreground. Though Israel may have always sinned, yet originally he was united to God in love, and this fundamental relation is eternal and inviolable. Comp. Rom. xi. It cannot then be disputed that the infidelity of Israel was of an early date (comp. **from of old**, ver. 20) going back to the pilgrimage through the desert (the golden calf, and even prior to this, the murmuring of the people, Exod. xv. 24; xvi. 2; xvii. 2), but it must nevertheless be maintained that the acceptance by Israel of the privileges offered by the Lord, when He sent Moses, and the people trustingly followed him into the Red Sea and the wilderness, is to be regarded as the binding of an inviolable and perpetual covenant. Compare the short and significant, "and the people believed," Exod. iv. 31, with Gen. xv. 6, "and he believed in Jehovah"; Rom. iv. 3; Gal. iii. 6. To this also point many prophetic declarations, *ex. gr.* Hos. xi. 1: "When Israel was a child, then I loved him, and called my son out of Egypt." The period in the youth of Israel at which the Lord loved the people was that in which He brought them out of Egypt. For immediately afterwards (ver. 2), it is said of them that they sacrificed to Baalim, and burned incense to graven images. But *then*, in that important moment, when the Lord delivered Israel from the encircling power of Egypt, displaying His might so grandly, He concluded a covenant of love with Israel; they must therefore then have not only been found worthy of love, but have reciprocated His love. How sweet and precious Israel's love then was to Him is expressed by Hosea in the splendid image of the early figs, which the pilgrim finds in the desert, Hos. ix. 10. So, says the Lord, He found Israel in the wilderness, but alas! He has to add, "they went to Baalpeor, and separated themselves unto their shame." The objections are then unfounded which have been raised to the rendering of verses 2 and 3 in the sense of Israel's love for God, and other arguments speak positively in its favor, viz. (1) לְךָ זָכַרְתִּי. This dative has everywhere the sense of a reckoning to one's account in a good or bad sense. (See the passages cited above.) But since this is not possible here in a bad sense, for the kindness and love of the past are remembered only as good, it can be meant only in a good sense. If, now, Israel has a balance with Jehovah in an active sense, he (Israel) must have done something,—performed some service. It might be said that this service is in allowing himself to be loved, but this is himself to love. We are thus brought again to this point, that Israel in that opening period of his existence turned to the Lord with such love that, though of momentary duration, it sufficed to found an everlasting covenant and imperishable remembrance of its glory. We may also take חֶסֶד in the sense of "the kindness of a maiden towards her master," being justified in doing so by passages like Hos. vi. 4, 6. Indeed, in view of Isa. xl. 6, it might not appear unsuitable to recognize in חֶסֶד the element of loveableness, gracefulness, which in itself is connected with the idea of love and grace, and etymologically in *gratia*, χάρις, grace;

(2) the words לֶכְתֵּךְ אַחֲרַי favor this interpretation, since they represent Israel, a pilgrim through the desert, walking in the foot-prints of the Lord. Some indeed would understand these words as denoting, not the obedient following of the people, but the gracious precedence of the divine Leader. This interpretation, however, is arbitrary. The text expresses only the idea of following, or pushing after; we are not justified in exchanging this idea for another. (3). The third verse is manifestly in favor of Israel. When it is said (GRAF, *S.* 23), "It should be so, but how it became entirely otherwise is shown in what follows," we reply, it has not become otherwise; but on this point we shall say more presently.

Ver. 3. Israel . . . come upon them.—Though in the words remember of thee it is implied that the kindness and love of the espousals are now only an object of remembrance, a lost joy, yet the third verse declares what a permanent relation was the result of that transient one, an indelible character having been impressed upon the people by that sometime connection with their Lord. They thus became a sanctuary of Jehovah, separate from the *profanum vulgus* of the nations. This thought is further expressed by a beautiful image: Israel is related to the Gentiles as the first fruits sanctified unto the Lord are to the multitude of common wild fruits, and as profane foys were forbidden to eat the former (Exod. xxiii. 19; Num. xv. 20, sq.; xviii. 12; Deut. xxvi. 1; comp. Lev. xxii. 16–26), so will guilt be upon those who touch the sacred first-fruits in the field of humanity. In accord with this image are x. 25: 1 7; Ps. xiv. 4; lxxix. 7.—**All who devour,** *etc.* The instruments of discipline though chosen by the Lord Himself, by the manner in which they execute their commission, bring guilt upon themselves and call for the vengeance of Jehovah, as is especially set forth in reference to Babylon. Hab. i. 11; Jer. l. 11; xv. 23, 28; li. 5 (N. B.), 8, 11, 24.

DOCTRINAL AND ETHICAL.

1. Although in xxxi. 32 Jeremiah represents the covenant made with Israel at the exodus from Egypt as the worse because broken by them, and that a new one in the future, to be kept faithfully by the people, would be opposed to it (comp. xxxii. 40; l. 5; Isa. lv. 3), and although in Rom. xi. 28 ("as touching the election beloved for the fathers' sake") the steadfastness of God is founded entirely on the promise given by Him and on the worth of the fathers in His sight, it is yet evident from our passage that the entering into covenant relation by Israel at the Exodus was not without significance. Though the covenant does not rest positively and in principle on that acceptance, yet this latter appears to be the negative condition *sine qua non*. Had Israel decidedly rejected Moses, had they refused to follow him into the wilderness, the promise given to the fathers would have been nullified. But if we should say that the people were obliged to believe in and follow Moses, we should injure the law of freedom, and endanger the moral value of human personality as well as the glory of God.

2. Every important historical appearance has its paradise or golden age. It is thus with humanity in general, with Israel, with the Christian Church (Acts ii. 41–iv. 37), with the Reformation, so also with single churches (Gal. iv. 14), and with individual Christians. This period of first, nuptial love does not, however, usually continue long, comp. Rev. ii. 4.

3. As Israel is called the firstling among the nations, so Christians are called the firstlings of His creatures, being regenerated by the word of truth (James i. 18, comp. WIESINGER *in loc.*, Rev. xiv. 5), in whom first that life-principle is active which is to renew heaven and earth. (Isa. lxv. 17; lxvi. 22; Rev. xxi. 1; 2 Pet. iii. 13). And since Israel as the firstling of the nations is called the sanctuary of God, so Christians by virtue of that principle, implanted in them by word and sacrament, of true, divine, eternal life, without regard to their subjective constitution are ἅγιοι, ἡγιασμένοι (1 Cor. i. 2; Acts xx. 32, etc.), the community of the saints, in antithesis to the *homo communis*, *i. e.* natural, earthly, profane humanity. Thus as the firstling Israel cannot be devoured by its enemies, so likewise with the Church (community of the saints), Matt. xvi. 18; Luke xxi. 17; Matt. xxviii. 20; Rev. xii. 5, *etc.*

4. ZINZENDORF: "*Jeremiah a preacher of Righteousness*," (*S*. 148). "Behold this maiden who is here described! Listen to her leaders, Moses and Aaron! Consider the rods with which she has been beaten and that unbelief and disobedience swept all but two away in the desert, and compare that with the words, 'I remember still that we were together in the wilderness.' *quasi re bene gesta;* and with the others which we heard before from Moses: 'Happy art thou, O Israel: who is like unto thee, O people saved by Jehovah,' Deut. xxxiii. 29). The cause is to be found in this. 'Thou followedst me.'"

5. IDEM (*S.* 150): "In the application to the people it is useful and well to show them that

they also were once a maiden who 'followed' partly in the beginnings of the Gospel (see Acts iv. 4), partly in the beginnings of the Reformation. There is an important trace of this in the letter of Luther to the Elector Johann Friedrich. So it then appeared. Likewise in the earlier ages of the Church, even so late as last century, since certainly in the sermons of an Arndt, a Joh. Gerhard, a Selnecker, a Martin Heger, a Scriver, a Spener, a Schade, the people still made quite another figure, and had not only another form, but certainly also a different feeling."

HOMILETICAL AND PRACTICAL.

1. The period of first love (in a spiritual sense). (1) In experience extremely precious. (2) In duration relatively brief. (3) In effect a source of everlasting blessing.—2. The nuptial state of Christ's Church in its stages. (1) The first stage, first love, (2) second stage, alienation, (3) third stage, return.—3. The covenant of Christ with His Church, (1) its ground, election, (2) its condition, faith, (3) its promise, the Church an indestructible sanctuary.

---

2. *The Infidelity of Israel viewed in the light of the Fidelity of Jehovah and of the Heathen.*

II. 4–18.

4 Hear ye the word of Jehovah, O house of Jacob!
  And all the families of the house of Israel!
5 Thus saith Jehovah, What injustice have your fathers found in me,
  That they went far from[1] me,
  And followed vacuity and became vacuous?
6 They said not: Where is Jehovah?
  Who brought us up from the land of Egypt,
  Who led us through the wilderness,
  A land of deserts and pits,
  A land of drought and the shadow of death,
  A land which no man traversed,
  And where no man dwelt?
7 And I brought you into the garden-[*literally*, Carmel-] land
  To eat its fruit and its goodliness ;
  But ye came and defiled my land,
  And made my heritage an abomination.
8 The priests said not, Where is Jehovah?
  And those that handle the law knew me not;
  The shepherds also rebelled against me,
  And the prophets prophesied by Baal,
  And followed those that cannot profit.
9 Wherefore I will reckon with you, saith Jehovah,
  And with your children's children will I reckon.
10 For pass over to the isles [*or* countries] of Chittim, and see,
  And send to Kedar, and well consider,
  And see if there has been anything like this.
11 Has a people changed[2] gods, which yet are no gods?
  But my people has changed its glory for that which cannot profit.
12 Be ye astonished, O ye heavens! at this,
  Be ye horrified, utterly amazed [*lit.*, shudder and be withered away]; saith Jehovah.
13 For my people have committed two evils :
  Me they have forsaken, the fountain of living waters,
  To hew out for themselves cisterns,
  Broken cisterns that hold no water.

TEXTUAL AND GRAMMATICAL.

¹ Ver. 5.—בְּעִיר [from upon=from near]. Comp. Gen. xxxii. 12; Exod. xxxv. 22; Jer. iii. 18; Am. iii. 15. The Hebrew loves to consider that as cumulation, which we represent as association.
² Ver. 11.—The form הֵימִיר seems to require the root כָּר, which occurs besides only in Hithpael, Isa. lxi. 6. Since the form הֵמִיר follows directly afterwards, the present form may have originated in a mere oversight, as OLSHAUSEN supposes (§ 39 f.; 255 e. i.)

EXEGETICAL AND CRITICAL.

The conduct of Israel is compared (*a*) with the conduct of Jehovah towards him (vers. 4-9) (*b*), with the conduct of the heathen nations towards their gods (vers. 10-13.)

Ver. 4. **Hear ye ... house of Israel.** Although the reformation of Josiah extended over the rest of the kingdom of Israel (2 Kings xxiii. 15-20; 2 Chron. xxxiv. 33), and although some from the tribes of Israel were present at divine service in Jerusalem (2 Chron. xxxv. 18), the expression used here is too comprehensive to designate these only; it includes the whole nation. Comp. Isa. xlvi. 3; Jer. xxxi. 1.—Jeremiah addresses himself not only to those who are actually present, but to an ideal audience: to the whole people of Israel of all times and places, to all those whose common fathers had incurred the guilt reproved in the following verses, and bequeathed it to their descendants. Comp. the address to a still greater circle of ideal hearers, Deut. xxxii. 1; Isa. i. 2; Mic. i. 2; vi. 1, 2.

Ver. 5. **Thus saith ... vacuous.** Observe the gradation: your fathers, you (vers. 7 and 9), your children's children; an historical survey which proceeds from the conduct of the fathers in the past and present, to the fate of the children in the future. The prophet by beginning with "the fathers," shows that Israel's ingratitude and disobedience was of ancient date. Moreover, these fathers were not those of any definite period, and therefore not as KIMCHI supposes, those who have lived since the entrance into the promised land. Could those who had accompanied the journey through the desert indeed speak thus?—The expression "What iniquity have your fathers found in me?" is an exhibition of the condescending love of God, who speaks just as though He were under obligation to Israel, and they had a right to call Him to account. Comp. Mic. vi. 3; Isa. v. 3. THEODORET: οὐ γὰρ ὡς κριτής κρίνει, ἀλλ' ὡς ὑπεύθυνος ἀπολογίαν προσφέρει, καὶ ἐλεγχθῆναι βούλεται εἴτε πράξαι δέον οὐκ ἔπραξε.—**Followed vacuity and became vacuous.** הֶבֶל are the idols (x. 15; xiv. 22; Deut. xxxii. 21, *etc.*). He who devotes himself to that which is nothing and vanity, becomes himself vain. LXX. ἐματαιώθησαν, which phrase seems to be a reminiscence in Rom. i. 21. The words are found reproduced verbatim in 2 Kings xvii. 15.

Ver. 6. **They said not ... no man dwelt.** —Comp. ver. 8. To ask "where is Jehovah?" is to ask after Him, to seek Him. To ask after Him implies that He is forgotten or lightly esteemed. **A land of deserts** עֲרָבָה, comp. l. 12; li. 43. שׁוּחָה, comp. xviii. 20; Prov. xxii. 16; xxiii. 27. They are pits or holes in which man and beast sink. Comp. ROSENMUELLER, *ad loc.*—**Shadow of death.** Ps. xxiii. 4; Job iii. 5; xxviii. 3; Isa. ix. 1; Am. v. 8. [For a similar description of the Arabian desert, see ROBINSON, *Bibl. Res.*, II., 502.—S. R. A.]

Ver. 7. **And I brought you ... an abomination.**—וָאָבִיא resumes the address of Jehovah from ver. 5. On the subject-matter compare Deut. viii. If כַּרְמֶל stood here in a merely appellative signification, the article would be either superfluous or insufficient. We should expect either merely כַּרְמֶל (or fruitful land, or כַּרְמֶל הַזֹּאת (in *this* fruitful land) for Palestine cannot be called *the* fruitful land κατ' ἐξοχήν, since there are many others more fruitful. To ascribe a demonstrative signification to the article is not allowable, since it has this only in formulas like הַפַּעַם הַיּוֹם. I believe, therefore, that the Prophet here intended Carmel for a proper name, with a hint, however, at the appellative meaning. So the Vulgate: *in terram Carmeli.* Carmel, in this reference, is contrasted with the desert, as a mountain with the plain, as a fertile cultivated land of forests, vineyards, gardens, and fields, with the desert sand, as a place of springs with the land of drought. Comp. JEROME on iv. 26.—**And its goodliness.** This addition is not superfluous. The Vau is here the climactic *and indeed*, Gen. iv. 4.—**But ye came.** After that has been enumerated which the Lord did for the people, we are told what the people did against their Lord. Herein a comparison is instituted between the conduct of Jehovah and the conduct of the people.

Ver. 8. **The priests said not ... that cannot profit.** That which in ver. 6 was laid on as a reproach upon all, is now declared specially of the priests. It was their especial duty to seek and inquire after the Lord, comp. דָּרַשׁ, Jer. x. 21; Ps. ix. 11; xxxiv. 5; שָׁאַל, Judges i. 1; xxviii. 5; 1 Sam. xxii. 13; Josh ix. 14.—**Who handle the law**, not those who decide legal cases, but those who handle the book of the law. We see that the handling is intended in this external sense from the contrast, **knew me not.** Comp. xviii. 18; Ezek. vii. 26; Mal. ii. 7.— The shepherds ought to keep the flock well together and lead it, and how can they do this when they are themselves in rebellion against the chief shepherd? Comp. x. 21; xiii. 10; xxiii. 1; l. 6.—**By Baal** (xxiii. 13) or *through* Baal, that is, through the influence and inspiration of Baal. It is opposed to "in the name of Jehovah" xi. 21; xiv. 15; xxvi. 9, 20. Remark the antithesis: They would be prophets, and yet are the organs of falsehood, they would be leaders, yet themselves go astray. The imperfect יֵעָלוּ is used of a permanent quality. Comp. NAEGELSB.

Gr., § 87 d. There appears, moreover, in this expression, to be an allusion to בְּלִיַּעַל (comp. especially בַּל יוֹעִילוּ Isa. xliv. 9), perhaps also to לֹא אֱלֹהִים, comp. also 1 Sam. xii. 21.

Ver. 9. **Wherefore ... will I reckon.**—The comparison of Israel's conduct in the past and present, with that of Jehovah, results so much to the disadvantage of the former, that in the future, remote as well as proximate, only רִיב *litigatio* is to be expected. Jehovah will now prosecute His claims. Isa. iii. 13; lvii. 16; coll. Ps. ciii. 9.

Ver. 10. **For pass over ... anything like this.** Ver. 9 divides the two halves of the strophe, belonging to both, as the statement of the result. It is affixed to the first half by means of לָכֵן, and prefixed to the second by כִּי. Comp. Am. v. 10-12.—**Chittim.** The word כִּתִּים or כִּתִּיִּים occurs eight times in the Old Testament: Gen. x. 4 (1 Chron. i. 7), Num. xxiv. 24; Isa. xxiii. 1, 12; Jer. ii. 10; Ezek. xxvii. 6; Dan. xi. 30. Comp. 1 Macc. i. 1; viii. 5. It is acknowledged that it denotes primarily the inhabitants of the "islands of the Eastern Mediterranean" (KNOBEL on Gen. x. 4). The name seems to have been given by way of preference to the island of Cyprus, the ancient capital of which was Citium, (HERZOG, *Real-Enc.*, III. *S*, 215). We have, therefore, translated אִי "islands" in preference to "coasts."
It is evident that Chittim, in a wider sense, denoted Greece, and even the North-western coasts of the Mediterranean in general, since according to Dan. xi. 30, Antiochus Epiphanes was attacked by ships from Chittim, according to 1 Macc. i. 1, Alexander the Great, and according to viii. 5, Perseus came from Chittim [pronounced Kittim]. The Chittæans are here the representatives of the West, Kedar of the East. For Kedar, according to Gen. xxv. 13, is a son of Ishmael; Jer. xlix. 28, Kedar is reckoned with the men of the East, בְּנֵי קֶדֶם. They are a pastoral people inhabiting the Arabian desert (Isa. xxi. 13-17; xlii. 11; lx. 7; Ezek. xxvii. 21; Ps. cxx. 5; Song of Sol. i. 5). The Rabbins designate the Arabians generally by Kedar. לְשׁוֹן קֵדָר is the Arabic language. Comp. KNOBEL on Gen. xxv. 13. BUXTORF, *Lex. Talm. et Rabb.* p. 1976.
—**If,** הֵן in the conditional sense as *ex. gr.* Exod. iv. 1; viii. 22; Isa. liv. 15; Jer. iii. 1. Hence it may also be used as an interrogative particle, like אִם (comp. *si* in French). It never occurs in this sense, however, except in this passage. The passages, Job xii. 14; xxiii. 8, which FUERST adduces, may be otherwise explained.

Ver. 11 **Has a people ... cannot profit.**—**But my people has changed,** comp. Am. viii. 7.—**Which cannot profit.** The idols are meant, comp. rem. on ver. 8,—xvi. 19; Hab. ii. 18.—This is the second comparison unfavorable to Israel which is instituted in this strophe. The heathen nations who have good reason to change their gods do not, but Israel, whose preeminence over all other nations is founded in their possession of the true God, exchanges Him for vain idols.

Ver. 12. **Be ye astonished ... saith Jehovah.** The greatness of the crime can be estimated by none so well as the over-arching heavens, which can behold and compare all that takes place. Comp. Deut. xxxii. 1; Isa. i. 2. חָרַב, *to be dry, stiff*, is found here only in the sense of *to be amazed*. The imperative with o, corresponds to the intransitive signification: transitive חָרְבוּ, Jer. l. 27.

Ver. 13. **For my people ... water.** The two evils are a negative and a positive. The Lord, the fountain of living waters, who offered Himself to them, they have forsaken, and leaky cisterns they have dug, comp. xvii. 13. In the physical sense the phrase is used in Gen. xxvi. 19; "a well of springing water."—**Fountain of living water**; Ps. xxxvi. 10; Prov. x. 11; xiii. 14; xvi. 22. Ὕδωρ ζῶν, John iv. 10; vii. 37 sqq.—The repetition of בֹּארוֹת, *cisterns*, reminds us of Gen. xiv. 10. Leaky wells are cisterns dug in the ground, which, having cracks in them will not retain the collected rain-water. לֹא יָכִלוּ reminds us in sense and sound of לֹא יוֹעִילוּ, ver 8.

DOCTRINAL AND ETHICAL.

1. God's love is "meek and lowly of heart," Matth. xi. 29, comp. 1 Cor. xiii. 4. It is not a love which desires only to receive. It will take, but only on the ground of that which it has given. But since in giving it has done its duty, in taking it demands its rights. It would reap where it has sowed, and not let the devil reap what God has sowed, Isa. xlii. 8; xlviii. 11. Comp. Matth. xxv. 14-30.

2. Only the true is the real. Falsehood is mere appearance, and all that is based on falsehood, is only an apparent life. It disappears in the fire of judgment, Ps. lxii. 11; cxv. 9; cxxxii. 18.

3. When God tells us, I am doing this for thee, what art thou doing for me? we cannot answer Him one for a thousand. Every sin is at the same time the basest ingratitude towards the greatest benefactor and the most disgraceful rebellion against the truest, most gracious and wisest Lord.

4. Since priests, pastors, and prophets, who have been regularly inducted into office may be deceivers, it is necessary to try the spirits according to the criterion given in 1 John iv. 1 sqq.

5. As we read here that the heathen adhere more faithfully to their false gods than Israel to the true God, so is it generally confirmed by experience that men, as a rule, pursue a bad cause with more zeal, devotion and wisdom, than a good one. Comp. the case of the unrighteous steward; Luke xvi. 1-8; 1 Kings xviii. 27, 28; Jer. iv. 22.

6. "His people, the nation on which He has bestowed the true religion, have the fountain, they can obtain water without difficulty, as much as they want, but they choose in preference means difficult, new, insufficient, deceptive, rejected on trial and even in daily experience, rather than be willing to do as they should. Hence come the works of supererogation, the many ceremonies, vows, ecclesiastical regula-

tions, which unquestionably are twice as difficult as to follow the Saviour, and have no promise for this life or for the life to come. . . . The sin is twofold: (1) they do not obey the Lord. (2) They will labor tooth and nail, if only they may not obey Him." ZINZENDORF, ut sup., S. 162.

HOMILETICAL AND PRACTICAL.

1. On ii. 4 sqq. The ingratitude of man towards God: (1) It is not to be laid to the charge of God (2). It consists in this, that men (a) forget the divine benefits, (b) they adhere to idols (both coarse and refined), (3). It does not remain unpunished.
2. On ver. 12. ["These strongest terms in the language show how intensely amazed all the holy in heaven are at the monstrous folly of human sinning. That when men might have the infinite God for their Friend, they choose to have Him their enemy; that when they might have Him their exhaustless portion of unmeasured and eternal good, they spurn Him away and set themselves to the fruitless task of making some ruinous substitute: this is beyond measure amazing! Verily, sin is a mockery of human reason! It defies all the counsels of prudence and good sense, and glories only in its own shame and madness:" COWLES.—S. R. A].
3. On ver. 13. All hunger and thirst is a desire for nourishment by those elements which are necessary to life. This brings us to the question:

What can quench the thirst of the soul?
1. It cannot be quenched by drawing from the broken cisterns of earthly good.
2. It can be quenched only by drawing from the fountain of life, from which the soul originally sprang, even from God.
4. On ii. 13. "Our double sin. It consists in this, that we (1) have forsaken the Lord, the living fountain, and (2) have dug for ourselves cisterns which hold no water." GENZKEN, Epistelpredigten, 1853.—"How is it that the Lord has to say, they have forsaken me, the living spring? It arises from this, that the hewn cisterns please us better. The creature attracts us so powerfully, all that is below has such an influence on the wavering heart, that it is drawn away from the living spring, and finds the cistern-water of this world more to its taste than the living water, the living God and His word." HOCHSTETTER. "Twelve Parables from the prophet Jer.," 1865, S. 6, sq. [" This may be applied to every sinner: qui relicto fonte fodit sibi cisternas rimosas; and to heretics: qui purum doctrinæ fontem in Scripturis et Ecclesia Dei deserunt et fodiunt sibi cisternas cœnosas falsorum dogmatum (S. IRENÆUS, III. 40; S. CYPRIAN, Ep. 40; A. LAPIDE). Comp. Ecclus. xxi. 13, 14, and Bp. SANDERSON, I. 361." WORDSWORTH. Comp. THOMSON, The Land and the Book, I. 443.—S. R. A.]
5. Those who have forsaken the true God, the Creator of all, and serve false gods, are worthy that all creatures should refuse them service. Deut. xxviii. 23. STARKE.

3. *Israel's Punishment and its Cause.*

II. 14–19.

14 Was Israel a slave? Was he a house-born (slave)?
    Why then is he become a spoil?
15 The young lions roar over him,
    They raise their voice,
    And they made his land desolate:
    His cities were burned up[1] without an inhabitant.[2]
16 Even the children of Noph and Tahpanhes[3]
    Will depasture the crown of thy head.
17 Did not thy forsaking[4] of Jehovah, thy God, procure thee this,
    At the time when he was leading thee[5] in the way?
18 And now what hast thou to do[6] in the way to Egypt,
    To drink the water of the Black river [Nile]?
    And what hast thou to do in the way to Assyria,
    To drink the water of THE river [Euphrates]?
19 Thine own wickedness shall correct thee,
    And thine apostasies shall punish thee,
    That thou mayest know and see[7] how evil and bitter it is,
    That thou hast forsaken Jehovah thy God,
    And that[8] the fear of me[9] is not in thee,
    Saith the Lord Jehovah of Hosts.

TEXTUAL AND GRAMMATICAL.

¹ Ver. 15.—The Keri נֶתְנוּ is an unnecessary correction by the Masoretes, who here as in xxii. 6, regarded the plural as necessary with עָרָי. But the singular may be used, in accordance with the capacity of the 3d Per. Fem. Sing., to involve an ideal plural. NAEGELSB. *Gr.,* § 105, 4, 6. EWALD, § 317, a. Whether נִצְּתָה is derived from נָצָה (comp. EWALD, § 140, a.

FUERST, s. v. יָצַת) צוּת) *to kindle* (OLSHAUSEN regards it as a derivative from a root פָּן, *Lehrb. d. Hebr. Spr., S.* 591), or נָצָה *to destroy* (iv. 7; ix. 11; Isa. xxxvii. 26; 2 Kings xix. 25) is undecided.

² Ver. 15.—מִבְּלִי יֹשֵׁב. מִן is not to be taken as causal but local = *away from without*. Comp. iv. 7; ix. 9, 10, 11. There are two negatives: *without no inhabitant*. GESEN., § 152, 2.

³ Ver. 16.—The reading תַּחְפַּנְחֵס for תַּחְפַּנְחֵס (*vide* Jer. xliii. 7, 8, 9; xliv. 1; xlvi. 14, תַּחְפַּנְחֵס; Ezek. xxx. 18 תְּחַפְנְחֵס) is probably no more than an ancient clerical error.

⁴ Ver. 17.—The Infinitive, in accordance with its abstract signification, is regarded as feminine, and therefore has the predicate in the fem. (comp. 1 Sam. xviii. 23) as for the same reason it frequently assumes a fem. termination, *ex. gr.* גֶּשֶׁת, שְׂנֵאָה, etc. Comp. NAEGELSB. *Gr.,* § 22, *Anm.* 3.

⁵ Ver. 17.—בְּעֵת מוֹלִיכֵךְ, we should expect הוֹלִיכֵךְ. The participle is used in a somewhat unusual manner, as *concretum pro abstracto*.

⁶ Ver. 18.—The construction is not the same as in the formula מַה לִּי וָלָךְ, for this means: What have I and thou in common? The construction here, without the Vau, expresses only having to do with, having reference to. Comp. Ps. l. 16; Hos. xiv. 9.

⁷ Ver. 19.—וְרָאִי. The intended consequences are represented as a command. Comp. Ps. cxxvii. 5; Gen. xx. 7; xli. 2; Ruth i. 9; EWALD, § 347, a. NAEGELSB. *Gr.,* § 90, 2.

⁸ Ver. 19.—וְלֹא פָחַדְתִּי אֵלַי is to be regarded as *one* conception, and as the subject, co-ordinate with עָזְבֵךְ to the predicate רַע וָמָר. Comp. v. 7; Isa. x. 15; xxxi. 8. This passage moreover has this specialty, that besides the negation, the proposition with the suffix also pertains to the *one* conception.

⁹ Ver. 19.—פַחְדָּתִי might be taken in an objective sense like כִּרְאֹבֶן, Gen. ix. 2 (comp. NAEGELSB. *Gr.,* § 64, 4)—*timor mei.* אֵל would then have to be taken as a fortified לְ as it in fact occurs, *ex. gr.,* after verbs like נָתַן (Exod. xxv. 16) נִגְלָה (Isa. xiv. 10) (1 Sam. ii. 27). But the suffix may also be regarded as the genitive of subject = *terror, quem injicio.* Then the construction would be entirely like that in Job xxxi. 23, פַּחַד אֵל and אֵל would be taken in its proper sense: my fear enters not into thee. The latter view seems to me the more correct, because in this the preposition receives its full significance.

EXEGETICAL AND CRITICAL.

In a new picture the prophet sees Israel in the form of slaves, evil entreated and dragged away by enemies, their land desolated, their cities destroyed. He asks the question: Why is this? The answer is: This is the consequence of their revolt from Jehovah, and their devotion to their idols.

Ver. 14. **Was Israel a slave?... become a spoil?** Who is the interrogator? God, the people, the prophet, or some other? Not the people; for this condition of misery is still future, perceived only prophetically, therefore still hidden from the people. It would then also read עָרָיו אֶרֶץ. God also is not the questioner, for He it is who is asked, and who answers, (vers. 17, 18). A third person at a distance cannot be the interrogator, since the subject of inquiry being still future is not known by him. The prophet only can be the questioner. He perceives prophetically the future calamitous condition of his people, and he implores from God a disclosure concerning it.—As to the import of the question, it cannot possibly be regarded as requiring an affirmative answer, as HITZIG supposes, explaining the meaning: "for is not Israel the servant of God or son of the house?" For, 1. We must then read הֲלֹא; 2. We must then have יהוה עֶבֶד or עַבְדִּי; 3. לִיד בַּיִת never signifies the son of the house, but always the house-born slave in opposition to one who is

bought. Gen. xiv. 14; xvii. 12, 13, 23, 27; Lev. xxii. 11.—The question must then be one requiring a negative answer; Israel is not a purchased slave but one born in the house. But how then could he be left like a mere thing for a spoil to the enemy? How far this has taken place is shown in the following verse.

Ver. 15. **The young lions roar... without an inhabitant.** This is the condition of Israel which the prophet sees with prophetic glance, and from which it seems to proceed that Israel has ceased to be God's son (comp. Ex. iv. 22; Deut. xxvi. 18; xxxii. 9 sqq.). עָלָיו GRAF renders =*against him,* because the lion only *growls* (הִנָּה Isa. xxxi. 4) over prey that is slain. Strange! As though the lion could not roar for joy and from a desire for more, *etc.* Comp. Am. iii. 4. The connection requires the sense of "over," since Israel appears to have already become a prey; his land is wasted, his cities destroyed. On this account the inquiry is made, whether then he is a slave and no longer Jehovah's first-born son. The imperfect יְשַׁאֲגוּ denotes that the fact is not yet an objective reality but still pertains to the subjective conception of the prophet. What further follows is nevertheless represented as present or past. Comp. NAEGELSB., *Gr.,* § 84, h.

Ver. 16. **Even the children of Noph... thy head.**—נֹף (Isa. xix. 13; Jer. xliv. 1; xlvi. 14, 19; Ezek. xxx. 13, 16) or מֹף (only in Hos. ix. 6: both forms are explained by the Egyptian

Mon-nufi, see Arnold in HERZOG *Real-Enc.* Art. *Memphis*), is the Hebrew name for Memphis, the ancient capital of lower Egypt. Tahpanhes (Δάφναι Πηλούσιαι, Herod. II. 30. Τάονας not Τάφναι, LXX. Jer. xliii 8, 9; xliv. 1), was a fortified border city to the east. In these two cities especially, the Jews who fled to Egypt after the murder of Gedaliah, appear to have settled (xliii. 7; xliv. 1: xlvi. 14).—**Depasture the crown**, *etc.* Triple explanation: 1. The LXX and translations dependent upon it appear to have read יִרְעוּךְ or יְעָרוּךְ. For they translate ἐγνωσάν σε καὶ κατέπαιξάν σε (the latter probably κατὰ σύνεσιν). The Vulgate also has *constupraverunt te usque ad verticem*. 2. Most expositors up to the time of the Reformation follow the Peschito version in translating *affligent*, *contundent*, *conterent*. They derive the word from רָעַע *confregit*. 3. The only grammatically admissible derivation from רָעָה *pascere*, *depascere* is found first (according to SED. SCHMIDT) in LUTHER (but not in his translation). He is followed by most of the modern commentators. But it is decidedly wrong to take the imperfect here in the past sense, as GRAF does. If a definite, past fact, *viz.*, the incursion of Shishak (1 Kings xiv. 25 sq.) were alluded to, we should have the perfect here. For there is no occasion to render this act of depasturing as taking place in the past (comp. NAEGELSB. *Gr.*, § 87, 3). We are rather led by the mention of Noph and Tahpanhes to the conclusion that something in the future, resulting from the residence of the Jews in the places named (xliii. 7; xliv. 1) is alluded to. We read in xlii. 15-22, that Jeremiah predicted complete destruction to the Jews who were proposing to flee from the vengeance of Nebuchadnezzar into Egypt. Particularly in xliv. 12 he insists that the last remnant of the fugitives in Egypt would be destroyed (ver. 14, "none of the remnant of Judah, which are gone into the land of Judah to sojourn there, shall escape or remain"). To this I refer the depasturing of the crown. The last and only covering, the natural covering of the hair, shall be taken from Judah, he shall be made entirely bald, that is, he shall be entirely swept away: "and they shall all be consumed," xliv. 12. ["The hair of the head being held in high estimation among the Hebrews, baldness was regarded as ignominious and humbling." HENDERSON.—S. R. A.] In the meantime I confess that the definite mention by name of these places is remarkable. The prophet has hitherto mentioned no names. As was shown above on i. 44 sqq., he does not yet know what nation is appointed for the accomplishment of the divine judgment on Judah. Why, when he is ignorant of the northern enemy, should he know so exactly the southern, who in comparison with the former is of almost no importance? Although I cannot agree with EWALD that vers. 14-17 did not originally belong here, since if we divide correctly, there is no break in the connection, yet ver. 16 may possibly be an addition which the prophet himself made when writing out his book the second time (xxxvi 32), after the destruction of Jerusalem, in Palestine or in Egypt. (Comp. Comm. on i. 3 and ii. 36, and the Introduction to chapter ii). ["I render it,

'The children of Noph and Tahpanhes have *pastured down* the crown of thy head.'—Memphis and Daphne, distinguished cities of Egypt, are here put for Egypt herself. Jehoiakim made a league with Egypt, but was subjected to severe and shameful taxation. Such a process of shaving, taxation and consequent disgrace our passage forcibly describes." COWLES.—S. R. A.]

Ver 17. **Did not thy . . . leading thee in the way?** The fate of the people described in vers. 14-16, so directly contradictory to the filial relation, is explained by their revolt from Jehovah. Comp. iv. 18.—**This**, is without doubt the object, **forsaking**, the subject. As here the leader is put for the leading, so elsewhere the proclaimer for the message (Isa. xli. 27), the destroyer for the destruction (Exod, xii. 13), the shooter for the shot (Gen. xxi. 16), the retractor for the retraction (Gen. xxxviii. 29). Comp. NAEGLSB. *Gr.*, § 50, 2; 61, 2 b, and below, ver. 25 בְּיָתֵן and the remarks thereon.—The expression **leading thee** points back to **led thee**, ver. 6. It is not then God's leading in general which is meant, but His leading through the desert, the rather, as the following verse shows that their forsaking of Him was not confined to the time of their pilgrimage. ["Most of the moderns take זאת to be the nominative to the verb and in opposition to עָזְבֵךְ and render: 'Is it not this that hath procured it to thee,—thy forsaking,' *etc.*; but the common rendering seems more appropriate, as it includes both the agent and the act, charging directly on the former the guilt contracted by the latter.—By *the way* is meant the right way, the way of the Lord; and the leading of the Jews therein denotes the whole of the moral training which they enjoyed under the Mosaic dispensation. In spite of every motive to the contrary, they forsook Jehovah as the object of their fear and confidence." HENDERSON.—S. R. A.]

Ver. 18. **And now what hast thou to do in the way to Egypt . . . to drink the water of the river?** וְעַתָּה is in antithesis to בְּעֵת מוֹלִיכֵךְ ver. 17. The latter points to the ancient time, the former to the present. **The way to Egypt** according to the analogy of Am. viii. 14, is not the Egyptian idol-worship. We see this from the statement of its object,—to drink the water of Shihor. The sense is, what will the way to Egypt (or Assyria) avail thee, which thou takest in order to drink the water of the Nile, &c.: that is, to draw from this source power and re-invigoration, *i. e.* to procure help in Egypt (or Assyria)? Here the question arises, whether the facts experienced by the prophet were the occasion of this mode of expression. Josiah so far from seeking to obtain help from the Egyptians lost his life in contending against them (2 Ki. xxiii. 29; 2 Chron. xxxv. 20). He did not undertake this contest as an ally of Assyria, for his object undoubtedly was to prevent these powers from encountering each other. Comp. the Article *"Josia"* in HERZOG, *Real-Enc*.—Subsequently, indeed (Jer. xxxvii. 5; comp. 2 Ki. xxiv. 20, and Jer. xliii.), we find Jeremiah's contemporaries laying claim to aid from Egypt, but at the same time the northern empire, by which we must understand Assyria, was the enemy which menaced them. Hence it appears that Jeremiah does not here, as in ver. 16 and probably also in ver. 3, allude to definite facts of recent date, but that he has in view only in general the propensity repeatedly manifested in the later history of Israel since Phul to seek help from the two heathen empires between which it was placed, instead of from Jehovah. In this period Egypt and Assyria are, as it were, two poles, which are always mentioned together in a stereotyped form in the most various connections. (Hos. xi. 11; Isa. vii. 28; x. 24; xix. 23 sqq.; xxvii. 13; lii. 4; Ezek. xxxi.) Particularly the seeking aid from Egypt and Assyria is a reproach made both by the older prophets (Hos. vii. 11. "They call to Egypt, they go to Assyria," xii. 2, comp. xi. 5) by his contemporaries (Ezek. xvi. 26 sqq.; xxiii. 2) and by Jeremiah himself elsewhere (Lam. v. 6). There is therefore no reason here for the inquiry whether by Assyria Jeremiah meant Babylon, for he has really, at least in the first intention, the true Assyria in mind.—שִׁחוֹר here as in Isa. xxiii. 3 is the Nile. The name signifies "the black, black-water" (Leyrer, Art. *Sichor* in HERZOG *R.-Enc.*); hence, also, among the Greeks and Romans the name Μέλας, Melo, from the black mud of the Nile (Comp. Servius on Virg. Georg. IV. 288 sqq. Æn. I. 745, IV. 246). נְהַר the Euphrates, as in Gen. xxxi. 21; Exod. xxiii. 31; Numb. xxii. 5, &c.

Ver. 19. **Thine own wickedness shall correct thee . . . Jehovah of hosts.** There is here a reference to vers. 17, 18. The wickedness described in these verses will correct Israel, that is, will produce the effects portrayed in vers. 14–16, and this correction will lead Israel to shameful but yet wholesome knowledge.— **Apostasies** (מְשֻׁבָה) is a word used especially by Jeremiah. Except in this book it occurs in only three passages (Prov. i. 32; Hos. xi. 7; xiv. 5), the plural only in Jer. iii. 22; v. 6; xiv. 7. With this the train of thought in this strophe seems to conclude. It begins with astonishment at the desolate condition of the people (ver. 14 to ver. 16), then explains why it must be so (vers. 17, 18), and finally designates salutary knowledge as the intended effect of this severe discipline (ver. 19). The full form, "Saith the Lord," &c., seems to denote the close of a section. The following strophe, though an independent tableau, is closely connected with the preceding, opening a deeper insight into the source of the apostasy described in vers. 17–19.

---

3. *The lust of idolatry: deeply rooted, outwardly insolent, false at last.*

II. 20–28.

20 For from of old thou hast broken thy yoke,[1]
   Thou hast burst thy bonds,
   And hast said, I will not serve.
   For upon every high hill
   And under every green tree
   Thou stretchest thyself as a harlot.
21 And yet I had planted thee a noble[2] vine,
   It was wholly of genuine seed.[3]
   But how art thou changed[4] with respect to me
   Into bastards of a strange vine!
22 For though thou wash thyself with alkali
   And take thee much of the soap,
   Yet thine iniquity is a stain before me,
   Saith the Lord Jehovah.
23 How canst thou then say: I am not polluted,
   I have not followed the Baalim.
   Look at thy way in the valley!
   Know what thou hast done!
   A she camel, young, fast, involving her courses;
24 A wild she-ass,[5] accustomed to the desert;
   In the desire of her soul she gasps for air,
   Her leaping,[6] who can repel it?
   All, who seek her, become not weary;
   In her month they find her.

CHAP. II. 20-28.   87

25 Guard thy foot from the loss of shoe,
   And thy throat¹ from thirst!
   But thou sayest: In vain! No!
26 For I love strangers, and after them I will go.
   As a thief is ashamed when caught,
   So the house of Israel is put to shame,
   They, their kings, their princes, their priests, their prophets:
27 Who say to a block, My father thou!
   And to a stone, Thou hast begotten me.⁸
   For they turn to me the back and not the face,
   But in the time of their calamity
   They say, Up and deliver us!
28 But where are thy gods which thou madest for thyself?
   Let them arise, if they can save thee in the time of thy trouble.
   For as many as thy cities
   Are thy gods, O Judah!

TEXTUAL AND GRAMMATICAL.

¹ Ver. 20.—The Masoretes take שְׁבַרְתִּי and נְתַקְתִּי as in the first person. So, also, the Chaldee and Syriac versions and most of the Jewish expositors. As עֲבֹד, then, does not give a good meaning, unless with the Syriac, we arbitrarily assume the false gods to be objects of service, the Keri reads אֶעֱבוֹר which must then be taken in the sense—*transgredi verbum divinum*. But neither does עָבַר occur in this sense without an accusative of the object, nor does this explanation suit the following ing בָּ.—The Masoretic punctuation is therefore erroneous, and the words are to be punctuated as 2nd Pers. Fem. according to the analogy of ver. 33; iii. 4, 5; iv. 19; xiii. 21; xxii. 23; xlvi. 11; Ezek. xvi. 18, 20, 22, 31, 33, 43, 44, 47, 51, etc. Comp. on this form EWALD, § 190 c; OLSHAUSEN, § 226, b; 232, b; and NAEGELSB, *Gr.* § 21.   *Anm.* 3.

² Ver. 21.—שֹׂרֵק only here and in Isai. v. 2. The fem. form שֹׂרֵקָה Gen. xlix. 11.

³ Ver. 21.—אֱמֶת זֶרַע literally: seed of truth, *i. e. genuine* seed, (Comp. Prov. xi. 18), opposed to גֶּפֶן נָכְרִיָּה.

⁴ Ver. 21.—סוּר. The passive participial form (Comp. EWALD, § 149, f) occurs, except here, only in the fem. form סוֹרָה (Isai. xlix. 21) and as Keri, Jer. xvii. 13. (Chethibh יָסוּר.) The meaning is not doubtful,—*anomalous, alienated, bastard.*

⁵ Ver. 24.—Instead of פֶּרֶה, many editions read פָּרָא, which we usually find elsewhere, Gen. xvi. 12; Job vi. 5; xi. 12; xxxix. 5; Hos. viii. 9.—It is clear that the female is meant, both from the connection and the construction of the following sentence. The masc. stands in לְמֹד and נַפְשָׁהּ, under the immediate influence of the form פֶּרֶא, but further on, the gender, which the prophet has in mind, comes to light, hence, שְׁאָפָה, etc.—The Masoretes would incorrectly read נַפְשָׁהּ. The Hebrew language is much freer with respect to gender, number, and person than our modern languages. Comp. NAEGELSB, *Gr.* § 60, 4. Comp. xiv. 6.

⁶ Ver. 24.—תַּאֲנָתָהּ is also an ἅπ. λεγ.—There is a double root אנה: I. *respirare, suspirare, ejulare* (Isai. iii. 26; xix. 8), from which the substantive forms אֲנִיָּה וַאֲנִיָּה (groan, and groaning, Isai. xxix. 2; Lam. ii. 5) are derived. From this derivation we obtain for תַּאֲנָה the meaning of deep breathing, snorting, catching for air, which is usually a symptom of excited passions. II. Kal inus. Piel.—a meeting, to prepare to meet (Exod. xxi. 12); Pual, to be made to meet, *occurrere* (Ps. xci. 10; Prov. xii. 21); Hithp. to prepare a meeting for one's self, to seek occasion (2 Ki. v. 7).—From this root is derived תַּאֲנָת (Comp. תֹּאֲנָה, Judges xiv. 4) encounter, *occursus*. Etymologically both are possible. The connection favors the latter view.

⁷ Ver. 25.—The Chethibh גּוֹרְנֵךְ is an anomaly which is by no means to be traced back to a form גּוֹרֶן for גָּרוֹן as עָשֵׁק (xxi. 12) for עָשׁוֹק (xxii. 3), but as frequently (xvii. 23; xxvii. 1; xxix. 23; xxxii. 23) through an oversight, a displacement of the *mater lectionis* seems to have occurred. See on xvii. 23.

⁸ Ver. 27.—יְלִדְתָּנִי. So according to xv. 10 the Chethibh is to be spoken. The Keri יְלִדְתָּנוּ is occasioned by אֹמְרִים, but needlessly, for the sing. may be used collectively. Those who pronounce יְלִדְתָּנִי overlook the fact that אֶת precedes, and that this second member is doubtless intended to designate the part of the mother. Wood my father,—a stone my mother!

EXEGETICAL AND CRITICAL.

Israel's propensity to idolatry is ancient (ver. 20), deeply rooted (vers. 21, 22), yet at the same time betraying itself outwardly by the most passionate behaviour (vers. 23-25), but finally causing deep shame on account of the nothingness of its objects (vers. 26-28). The connection with the previous strophe is this, that here the *forsaking of Jehovah* (ver. 17), and the *wickedness* and *apostasies* (ver. 19), are more particularly explained.

The כִּי is, therefore, to be regarded as explicative.

Ver. 20. **For from of old . . . as a harlot.** עוֹלָם here as frequently (comp. Isa. xlii. 14; xlvi. 9; lxiii. 16; Ps. xxiv. 7, *etc.*), is used of inconceivable duration.—Israel is compared with wild refractory draught cattle ('a bullock untrained,' xxxi. 18; a 'backsliding heifer,' Hos. iv. 16), because they refuse the discipline and guidance of the Lord (comp. v. 5; Prov. ii. 3), and are obstinate in carrying out their own carnal will.

—I will not serve. The second כִּי is also explicative. It forms the transition to the explanation of the imagery employed in Hemist. a.—**Every high hill**, etc., a frequent designation of the places especially sacred to the worship of nature. Comp. 1 Kings xiv. 23; 2 Kings xvi. 4; xvii. 10; Isa. lvii. 5; Jer. iii. 6, 13; xvii. 2; Ezek. vi. 13.—**Stretchest thyself**. צֹעָה occurs only in Isa. li. 14 of one who is bound and thus bent crooked, in Isa. lxiii. 1 of the strong man, who bends proudly backwards; Jer. xlviii. 12 of the vessel, which we bend over in order to pour from it. Hence it seems to be used in the sense of παρακλίνεσθαι or *inclinari* of the bending of the body in a woman who lies with a man. Comp. בָּרִיחַ of the man, in Job xxxi. 10.

Ver. 21. **And yet I had planted thee .. strange vine.**—And I stands in strong antithesis to thou, ver. 20.—The antithesis is similar, which Isaiah sets forth between the vineyard for which all has been done, and the proprietor, whose hope is disappointed, Isa. v. 1 sqq. Comp. Ps. lxxx. 9 sqq.—That we are not to translate (with EWALD): "I have planted thee *with* noble vines," as in Isa. v. 2, is clear from the identity of the object of נְטַעְתִּיךְ with the subject of נֶהְפַּכְתְּ.—**Noble vine**, properly reddish from שָׂרַק *splendere, subrubicundum esse*, comp. Isa. xi. 8; Zech. i. 8, and KOEHLER, *ad loc.*— That the red wine was considered the nobler, may be inferred from the fact that it was prescribed for the feast of the Passover. See LIGHTFOOT, *Hor. Hebr.* p. 478.—**But how art thou changed**, etc. It is not inadmissible to regard סוּרֵי as the accusative, as GRAF, HITZIG, and others suppose. The mere accusative frequently stands in apposition with the object, (or in passive construction with the subject, where we use a preposition of motion, and the Hebrew more commonly uses לְ, comp. יוֹם לַיְלָה הֶחֱשִׁיךְ), Am. v. 8; vi. 11; Isa. xxviii. 38; xxxvii. 26. See NAEGELSB., *Gr.* § 69, 3.—The absence of the article before נָכְרִיָּה is certainly abnormal, but not without example: xxii. 26; Isa. xxxvii. 4, 17; 2 Sam. vi. 3. See NAEGELSB. *Gr.* § 78, 2. *Anm.*

Ver. 22. **For though thou wash thyself ... thy iniquity is a stain before me.** כִּי is causal. Israel is to be compared with degenerate vines; their depravation, therefore, is essential, since it cannot be removed by outward means.—This figure of speech is based on the work of the fuller. For simple washing is רָחַץ; כָּבַס properly *to tread, to stamp*, is the technical expression for the work of the fuller. Hence, also, we have Piel here, comp. NAEGELSB., *Gr.* § 41, 2; 61, 2, c. תְּכַבְּסִי is, therefore, properly, *even if thou doest the work of a fuller*, comp. Mal. iii. 2. The reflexive meaning is implied by the connection, and is sufficiently indicated by the following לָךְ.—נֶתֶר *nitrum*, is a mineral, בְּרִית (בֹּר among the Greeks and Romans, also called *nitrum*) is a vegetable alkali. The former is obtained from water, the latter from the soap-plant. Comp. WINER, R. B. W., s. v. *Laugensalz*. [THOMSON, *The Land and the Book*, II. pp. 302, 303.— S. R. A.]—נִכְתָּם is an ἅπαξ λεγόμενον. Some

commentators render it (=כָּתַב) "ingrained, indelibly engraven is thy guilt." Some render, "hidden, laid up," others; "spotted, dirty, a stain." The last meaning, which is certified by the dialects (Aram. כְּתְמָא *macula*, כְּתִים *maculosus*) is also required by the connection. Comp. Ps. li. 3, 9.

Ver. 23. **How canst thou then say ? ... involving her courses.** The prophet has in mind an assertion actually made and often repeated by his contemporaries. This is the sense of the imperfect. comp. NAEGELSB., *Gr.* § 87, c.— **Thy way in the valley**, בַּגַּיְא must mean a definite valley, since hills, and not valleys were the places usually appropriated by the Israelites to idolatrous worship. In the vicinity of Jerusalem there was, however, a valley celebrated as a place of worship; the vale of Hinnom (vii. 31; xxix. 2, 6; xxxii. 35; Josh. xv. 8; 2 Kings xxiii. 10).—That the valley might be called absolutely הַגַּיְא is seen from the fact that the gate leading to it was called absolutely שַׁעַר הַגַּיְא (2 Chron. xxvi. 9; Neh. ii. 13, 15), comp. RAUMER, *Palästina*, 4 Aufl. *S.* 291.—**A she-camel**, etc., בִּכְרָה and פָּרָה stand in apposition to the subject of the preceding sentence, *viz.*, Israel. The former is feminine of בֶּכֶר (Isa. lx. 6), camel-foal. The (unused) root בָּכַר signifies "to be early there," hence בְּכוֹר—בָּכַּר. מְשָׂרֶכֶת is found here only as a verb. It means to "weave, cross, involve." Hence שְׂרוֹךְ shoestring, Gen. xiv. 23; Isa. v. 27.

Ver. 24. **A wild she-ass ... they find her**. It is clear that the female is meant both from the connection and the construction of the following sentence:—**Accustomed to the desert**, (Job xxiv. 5; xxxix. 5), therefore, in general shy, wild and unconfined.—**All who seek her**, etc. Since they meet her half-way, there is no need to weary themselves with seeking her. In her month, (that is, in her period of heat, they find her. This is the natural rendering. Other artificial explanations are found in J. D. MICHAELIS, *Obsv.*, p. 17, und in ROSENMUELLER, *ad h. loc.*

Ver. 25. **Guard thy foot ... after them I will go.** As a further proof of the intensity of this proneness to idolatry (vers. 21 and 22), the prophet adduces the answer of the people to all warnings against it, their decided declaration that they would not relinquish it. The words of admonition, "Guard," etc., are not to be regarded as spoken by commission from the Lord. The figure of passionate running is continued, but man is now understood as the subject.—The construction is that of the concrete for the abstract. Comp. 1 Sam. xv. 23, where it reads "hath rejected thee from king," while afterwards it is, "hath rejected thee from being king," ver. 26 and viii. 7; in xvi. 1, it is "from reigning." Comp. further ver. 17 and 1 Kings xv. 13; Ezek. xvi. 41.—יֵחַם is not of the same gender as רַגְלִי, being feminine, but this variation is of no account. See remark on ver. 24.—We might as well translate: "Hold back thy foot, to be somewhat unshod," as in Ps. lxxiii. 2, נָטָיוּ רַגְלָי means *inclinatum aliquid sunt pedes mei.*—On the general subject, comp. xxxi. 10; Prov. i. 15.— As to the import of the warning, we are certainly not to take רגל with SCHNURRER, ROSENMUELLER and others, as in Gen. xlix. 10; Deut. xxviii. 57; Ezek. xvi. 25 in the sense of *crura et pudenda*, and the *discalceatio* as *denudatio*. The prophet would merely say, 'Cease from thy mad running after idols, from which nothing accrues to thee, but wounded feet and a dry throat, *i. e.*, bitter injury instead of the expected advantage.'— נואש) Part. Niph., from יאש (comp. 1 Sam. xxvii. 1; Job vi. 26; Isa. lvii. 10; Jer. xviii. 12) = *desperatum*, *perditum*. The sense is: the warning is in vain. לוא No! as in Gen. xlii. 10; Numb. xxii. 30, *etc.*—The following verses portray the contrast between the passionate striving of Israel after the favor of their gods, and the results thereof.

Vers. 26 and 27. **As a thief... deliver us.** Comp. Exod. xxii. 1, 6, 7. The thief is ashamed not merely because he is caught in his wickedness, but because at the moment of discovery he makes a ridiculous figure. Israel also plays this ridiculous part when the "poodle's heart" is displayed.—**Put to shame.** Comp. vi. 15; viii. 9,

12 —**Who say,** אמרים, apposition to the *nomen determinatum* without the article, as frequently in the later books. See NAEGELSB., *Gr.* § 97, 2 n.— **For they turn to me the back,** *etc.* This period to the end of ver. 28. shows in three clauses the shameful character of idol-worship: (*a*) they turn their back on me; (*b*) in the time of calamity I am yet to help them; (*c*) I cannot then do so, but must direct them to their gods. These, however, are nowhere to be found, though as numerous as the cities in Israel.

Ver. 28. **But where are thy gods.—O Judah!** This inquiry is made of the idolaters as a punishment for their having previously made it in scorn of the faithful, comp. Ps. xlii. 4, 11; lxxix. 10; cxv. 2.—**If they can save.** We are reminded of Deut. xxxii. 37, 38. See KUEPER, *S.* 6. Comp. xi. 12. The indirect interrogative sentence is best understood as dependent on a verb to be supplied: *let us see?* **For as many as the cities,** *etc.*, is repeated verbatim in xi. 13. כי is causal. One would think they could save thee, since they are so numerous. The close of this strophe corresponds to the close of the preceding, (ver. 19).

---

5. *Whose is the guilt?*

II. 29–37.

29   Why do you contend against Me?
    Ye have, all of you, offended against Me, saith **Jehovah.**
30   In vain have I smitten your children,
    Chastisement they have not accepted.
    Your sword has devoured your prophets
    Like a ravening lion.
31   O ye generation! see the word of Jehovah:
    Have I been a desert, O Israel?
    Or a land of deepest night?[1]
    Why do my people say: We ramble,[2]
    No more will we come to thee?
32   Can a virgin forget her ornaments?—
    A bride her girdle?
    But my people have forgotten Me days without number.
33   How well trimmest thou thy way to seek love intrigue!
    Therefore also to wickedness thou hast accustomed[3] thy **ways.**
34   Even on thy skirts [wings] has been found
    The blood of the souls of poor innocents.
    Not at the place of burglary have I found it,
    But on all these.
35   Yet thou sayest,[4] I am innocent,[5]
    Surely His anger is turned from me.
    Behold, I enter into judgment with thee concerning this,
    That thou sayest: I have not sinned.
36   How goest thou asunder[6] much in changes of thy ways?
    Even by Egypt shalt thou be put to shame,
    As thou hast been put to shame by Assyria.

37 Also from thence⁷ wilt thou go forth, thy hands on thy head,
   For Jehovah rejects thy supports,
   And thou wilt have no success with them.

TEXTUAL AND GRAMMATICAL.

¹ Ver. 31.—כָּאְפֵלְיָה is ἅπαξ λεγ. Composed of כָּאְפֵל and יָה = caligo Jovæ, as שַׁלְהֶבֶתְ־יָה = God's flame (of love) Cant. viii. 6. יָה serves to enhance the force of the expression according to the analogy of אֵל הַרְרֵי "great deep," Ps. xxxvi. 6. תַּרְדֵּמַת ‸ 1 Sam. xxvi. 12, חֶרְדַּת אֵל 1 Sam. xiv. 15.—יָה is also punctuated יָֽה in connections, ex. gr., xxvii. 1, etc. The Masoretes have given two accents to the whole word in the text, because they were uncertain as to the etymology of the syllable יָה and consequently as to its accentuation. Kimchi found כָּאְפֵלְיָה in some codices, which Ewald also accepts and translates simply "darkness" ad form. מַכְלֵנִת viii. 18, coll. עֲלִילְיָה פְלִילְיָה.

² Ver. 31.—רַדְנוּ. רוּד only in Gen. xxvii. 40; Ps. lv. 3; Hos. xii. 1. Radical signification vagari. We are not with Rosenmueller to translate vagabimur. The perfect is used expressly to designate an accomplished fact.

³ Ver. 33.—לְמִדְבָּר. On this form comp. rem. on ver. 20.—On the double accusative comp. Ewald, § 283, c; Naegelsb. Gr., § 69, 2, c.
⁴ Ver. 35.—כִּי before a direct address, as frequently, ex.gr., Josh. ii. 24; 1 Sam. x. 19. Comp. Naegelsb. Gr., § 109, 1, a.
⁵ Ver. 35.—נִקֵּיתִי Niph. Comp. Num. v. 28, 31.

⁶ Ver. 36.—תֵּזְלִי contracted from הֵאָזְלִי as אָהַב from אָהַב (Prov. viii. 17), אַחֵר from אָאְחֵר (Gen. xxxii. 5), comp. Naegelsb. Gr., § 10, II., Anm.
⁷ Ver. 37.—זֶה Masc. referring to the people. Comp. Naegelsb. Gr., § 60, 3, Anm.

EXEGETICAL AND CRITICAL.

As in the beginning of the discourse (ver. 5), the prophet proceeds on the ground, that Israel's revolt cannot be excused by any neglect on the part of Jehovah, but Israel is alone to blame (ver. 20). The Lord has allowed nothing to fail: neither discipline (Ver. 30), nor the necessaries of life (ver. 31), not even ornament and splendor (ver. 32). But the people have shown a taste and fitness only for the service of idols (ver. 33 a). The consequence is two-fold: (1) deep moral corruption (ver. 33 b-34) which at the same time affords the most striking proof of the rebellion of the people, which they boldly deny (ver. 35); (2) the shame of the people resulting from their political and religious wanderings (vers. 36, 37).

Ver. 29. Why do you contend ... saith Jehovah. Israel's propensity to complain of the Lord was displayed even in the wilderness at Meribah (Exod. xvii. 2, 3, 7), and that Jeremiah's contemporaries manifested the same disposition is evident from v. 19; xiii. 22; xvi. 10. Not I, saith the Lord, towards you have failed, but you towards Me, even all of you. Comp. ver. 26.—The following verses enumerate what the Lord has done for Israel. Three things are mentioned; first, discipline.

Ver. 30. In vain ... ravening lion— לַשָּׁוְא in vain, used only by Jeremiah among the prophets, iv. 30; vi. 29; xlvi. 11. Comp. besides, Exod. xx. 7; Deut. v. 11; Ps. xxiv. 4; cxxxix. 20.—אֶת־בְּנֵיכֶם cannot be taken in a proper sense = your young men, as Hitzig maintains, for Jehovah's blows were upon the whole people. When we reflect that the persons smitten by the Lord are those, who instead of accepting chastisement, slay God's servants, and further, that these same are afterwards, ver. 31, addressed as generation, and previously, in ver. 28, as Judah, there can be no doubt that the prophet has here in view the abstract communities, the people being designated as their children. Comp. v. 7; Lev. xix. 18; Joel iv. 6; Zech. ix. 13.—The smiting had not the intended effect (comp. v. 3) but was answered by the murder of the prophets, 1 Ki. xviii. 4, 13; 2 Chron. xxiv. 20 sqq. Comp. Matth. xxiii. 35, 37; Luke xi. 47, etc.—The second fact, with which the charge is indignantly repelled, is Jehovah's liberal provision for all the wants of the people.

Ver. 31. O ye generation ... come to thee? The first words of this verse are attached by Jerome and Maurer to the preceding verse: tanquam leo vastator est hæc vestra ætas. But the beginning of the following sentence is then altogether too bald. It is better to take them as in the vocative, and the subject of the following verb. On the article with the vocative, comp. Ewald, § 327, a; Naegelsb. Gr., § 71, Anm. 4.—It is disputed whether דּוֹר is to be taken in the sense of "age, generation" (Ewald: "The present people") or in the sense of "race, kind, breed." It is not clear why the generation then living should be rendered so expressly prominent. דּוֹר does not occur again, at least not alone in a bad sense. But from passages like vii. 29; Deut. i. 35; xxxii. 5; Ps. lxxviii. 8; Prov. xxx. 11 it is evident that the word is at any rate capable of such a determinatio in malam partem.—רְאוּ See, comp. ver. 19, is a stronger הִנֵּה. The word of the Lord is held before them with the demand that they regard it. —Desert, i. e., barren land, where no bodily nourishment or necessaries are found.—Here follows the third point, which the Lord has not neglected; glory and adornment. He is Himself His people's highest glory, Israel's crown of glory is He (Gen. ix. 27; Isa. xxviii. 5). But they have forgotten this emblem of royalty, which causes them to rank above all other nations. The Lord is however Israel's jewel as her husband. This is the thought which suggests the figure in ver. 32.

Ver. 32. Can a virgin forget ... without number? קִשֻּׁרִים besides only in Isa. iii. 20. Comp. Isa. xlix. 18. Is it a girdle or a fillet? Drechsler on Isa. l. c. translates "a small girdle of fine material," which unites both meanings.—The failure then is not in this, that the Lord has forgotten to make provision for the adornment of His bride, but that the bride has forgotten to make use of the ornament. Comp. xviii. 14.—**Days without number.** Comp. of old. ver. 20.

Ver. 33. **How well trimmest thou . . . accustomed thy ways.** הֵיטִבְתְּ cannot here be rendered in the sense of *bonum simulare*, *exornare*, as many of the ancients rendered, because then the following לְבַקֵּשׁ אַהֲבָה does not afford a suitable meaning. It is therefore necessary to take it in the sense of *scite instituere* (MAURER) according to the analogy of vii. 3; Isa. xxiii. 16; Deut. ix. 21, *etc.* Observe the contrast: (; people in criminal frivolity forget Jehovah, their highest glory, but with the greatest diligence employ means and ways to procure illicit love (with foreign nations and their idols). The effects of this are shown in what follows.—לָכֵן is neither = *but*, as DE WETTE proposes, nor = לָהֵן (VENEMA, DATHE: *ut confirmes malitiam, assuefacis vias tuas*), but simply = therefore, thus, in this way.—**To wickedness.** The article before רָעוֹת (comp. iii. 5) is general. Israel has accustomed his ways not to particular wickedness, but to wickedness in general, to wickedness of every kind.—לִמֵּד to teach, to accustom, as לִמֵּד, ver. 24. In meaning the expression is coincident with that in xiii. 23, "accustomed to do evil."—On the subject-matter, comp. Rom. i. 24 sqq.—In what follows the statement is verified by an instance.

Ver. 34. **Even on thy wings ... on all these.** The גַּם here resumes the גַּם in ver. 33 *b*. The special fact is introduced by the same particle as the general statement. In German "*nämlich*" [*videlicet*, namely] would be used. כָּנָף is used here, as frequently of the skirts, (wings) of a coat, 1 Sam. xxiv. 6; Hagg. ii. 12; Zech. viii. 23, *etc.*—**Has been found.** The plural נִמְצָאוּ is explained thus, (1) an ideal plural is contained in דָּם, namely, the idea of innocent blood, in which sense דָּמִים is usually employed (the sing. *ex. gr.* Jer. xix. 4; Lam. iv. 13). The same construction in Ezek. xxii. 13, comp. NAEGELSB. *Gr.*, § 61, 2, c. (2) with connected subjects the predicate may be governed in number by the main grammatical or logical idea. So also here the conception of the multiplicity of what has been stained by blood may have determined the number of the predicate. Comp. NAEGELSB. *Gr.*, § 105, 6.—**Not at the place,** *etc.* בְּמַחְתֶּרֶת occurs only in Exod. xxii. 1 (2), and our passage may be explained by this. "If a thief be found breaking up (or at the place of burglary) and he be smitten and die, he (the doer) shall incur no guilt." Jeremiah alludes to this both in words and sense. The Lord has found the blood of the murdered (and we may here understand the blood of the prophets, ver 30) not in the place of the crime committed by them. In this case their murderers would accord-

ing to the law quoted above, be without guilt. But he says, "On all these have I found it." These words have given much trouble to the commentators. Disregarding the circumstance that the LXX, the Syriac and Arabic translations instead of אֵלֶה read אַלָּה, and therefore translate ἐπὶ πάσῃ δρυΐ or *sub quacunque arbore*, and that JEROME combines the two renderings: "*in omnibus istis quæ supra memoravi, sive sub quercu*," having in mind the often denounced hill-worship (comp. ver. 20),—omitting those interpretations which are based on a wrong reading we mention only three proposed by eminent modern commentators: (1) EWALD translates after ABARBANEL, "not in the murderer's den found I it, but on all these, *viz.*, summits." The objection to this is, that the word does not signify "den of murderers," and that the reference to Exod. xxii. 1 (2) is wholly ignored. (2) VENEMA, DATHE, VOGEL, GAAB, MAURER, UMBREIT and others attach the final clause to the next verse and take עַל in the sense of "notwithstanding—notwithstanding all this (thou sayest)." This rendering leaves both the כִּי and the *Vau cons.* before תֹּאמְרִי without any satisfactory explanation. (3) GRAF: "not for the sake of a crime didst thou kill the poor ones, but on account of all this," *i. e.* because they stood in the way of thy harlotry and opposed thy revolt. But it must be objected to this that we cannot say, "not at the breaking in hast thou met them (GRAF takes מְצָאתִים as 2d person), but on account of all this." For here the verb "met" does not suit the second clause of the sentence. We should have to supply a suitable verb "hast thou killed them," which would be arbitrary, because the author, if he had this verb in mind, could not have omitted it. The whole question seems to me to turn on the correct rendering of מַחְתֶּרֶת, namely, not as burglary in general, but the place of burglary. It is well known that substantives with מ (*Mem loci*) have this meaning, EWALD, § 160 *b*.—In the original passage Exod. xxii. 1, we may indeed translate "at the breaking in," but in the text, where it is not the seizure of the thief, but the subsequent discovery of blood-stains, which is spoken of, the *place* of burglary must be meant. Traces of blood are subsequently discovered, not at a burglary, but at the place where the surprised thief was wounded. If this is the correct rendering of this word, the final clause must also designate a place. If we consider that in the first clause the Lord has rebuked Israel for the murder of the innocents, it is appropriate that in the second He should bring a proof of this heavy charge. This proof is afforded in this way;—the Lord says He found the blood of the slain not in places where they had committed burglary, but on the persons of those He addresses. Thus "on all these" refers back certainly to **thy skirts**, but only indirectly. אֵלֶּה refers primarily to persons. We may suppose that the prophet pointed with his hand to his hearers.—In spite of this flagrant proof of guilt, Israel is so bold as to continue to maintain his innocence, and dares even to boast that the divine anger is already turned away from him.

Ver. 35. **Yet thou sayest ... not sinned.**
אַךְ שָׁב. The translation of the LXX., ἀποστραφήσεται and of the Vulgate, *aversatur* would suit very well in the connection, if it were grammatically justifiable. As the words read they make declaration of a fact, not a wish. אַךְ=nothing but, only, *i. e.* sure, certain. Comp. Gen. xxvi. 9; xxix. 14, *etc.*—To what historical fact this erroneous assumption of Israel refers, it is difficult to say; perhaps to the narrative of 2 Ki. xxiii. 26 (observe also the resemblance of the words). Josiah's reforms might have given rise to the idea that the wrath of the Lord formerly threatened (comp. 2 Ki. xxii. 17) was now turned away from Judah. The people are here assured that this was not the case, because the reform was more outward than inward (at least among the masses).—**I enter into judgment.** Comp. i. 16; xxv. 31. He who denies the sin he has committed adds to his guilt and provokes a new manifestation of the divine judgment.

Vers. 36 and 37. **How goest thou? ... no success with them.** אַל (in Aramaic אֲזַל frequently = הָלַךְ) has in Hebrew throughout the meaning of to melt, dissolve, go asunder. So of yielding to a misfortune (Prov. xx. 14), of the flowing away of water (Job xiv. 11), of the running out of the means of subsistence (1 Sam. ix. 7), of the disappearance of power (Deut. xxxii. 36). The infinitive לֵאזִל designates not the end but the mode of the going asunder: *quid diffluis mutando viam?* The לְ is the particle of the *Infin. modalis.* Comp. NAEGELSB, *Gr.*, § 95, *e*. On the meaning comp. iii. 13.—As vers. 34 and 35 are dependent on ver. 33 *b*, so vers. 36 and 37 on 33 *a*. The inquiry, "how trimmest thou thy ways?" is resumed here more definitely.—In respect to the historical bearing of the passage, as we have already remarked on ver. 18, it is not known that Josiah ever sought aid from the Egyptians. From the time of Jehoiakim, who was an Egyptian vassal (2 Kings xxiii. 33 sqq.), much aid was continually sought. To this ver. 36 may refer. The expression "also from thence wilt thou go forth," seems even to imply a residence in Egypt. Comp. on ver. 16. As was remarked on this passage we admit the possibility of Jeremiah's having made this addition on the completion of his second writing. Comp. GRAF, *ad loc.*—זוֹ Masc. referring to the people. Comp. NAEGELSB. *Gr.* § 60, 3, *Anm.*—It appears as if the story of Tamar and Absalom hovered before the prophet's mind. Comp. KUEPER, *S.* 55; 2 Sam. xiii. 19, "*Est ibi nostra manus, in qua nos parte dolemus*" (BUGENHAGEN).

DOCTRINAL AND ETHICAL.

1. On ii. 14: "Whoever makes himself a servant of sin makes himself also a servant of punishment, for sticks and cudgels are for a bad servant. *Malitiæ comes individua est miseria.*" CRAMER.

2. On ii. 14: "*Peccatum ex hominibus liberis facit miserrimos servos: ex filiis Dei mancipia diaboli.*" SEB. SCHMIDT.—"Is then Israel a servant or a bondman? So that get him who may, except the one father, whose son he is, he may starve him? A noble question to lead the soul to reflect what it is; a subject on which Joh. Arndt much labored and in which Fr. Richter of Halle lived altogether. He wrote a book on the exceeding nobility of the soul. . . . . We can also form an idea from his poems, 'The soul is born to enjoy, something that is divine,'—'How bright the Christian's inner life.'—'O how happy are the souls,' *etc.*, how important this subject was to him. And it is a great subject even if we leave aside all exaggerated mystical or still more loftily conceived ideas. It is enough that we are 'His workmanship, created in Christ Jesus unto good works.' We must indeed be ashamed, and a preacher may well grieve his whole life long (as Spener is said to have done), that our glory is so departed." ZINZENDORF.

3. On ver. 17: Sin is the destruction of a people, Prov. xiv. 34. But the Lord is not willing that any be lost but that all should come to repentance (2 Pet. iii. 9). He therefore chastises them, not to destroy them, but by bodily sufferings to save the soul (1 Pet. iv. 1).

4. On ver. 15: "The sins of men, especially of God's people, strengthen the arm of their enemies, encourage them to their hurt (Judith v. 22)." STARKE.

5. On ver. 16: "If God wishes to chastise His people He usually employs the ungodly for this purpose (Deut. xxviii. 49, 50)." IDEM.

6. On ver. 16: "It often happens that those redound to the injury and destruction of the ungodly, from whom they have promised themselves the greatest help (Judges xv. 3)." IDEM.

7. On ver. 17: What a man soweth that will he also reap (Gal. vi. 7). They sow wind and reap the whirlwind (Hos. viii. 1). "What they've done, that they've won." BULLINGER. Comp. Micah vii. 9.

8. On ver. 19: "*Sanitatis initium immo dimidium est agnoscere morbum.*" SEB. SCHMIDT.

"*O si ista videremus
Quantum flere deberemus.*" THOM. AQUINAS.

9. On ver. 20: Although the Lord's yoke is easy (Matt. xi. 29), it seems intolerable to our flesh, and we would rather sacrifice our children to Moloch and cut ourselves with knives and lancets (1 Kings xviii. 28) than bow to the chastisement of the Spirit and renounce carnal freedom.

10. On ver. 21: "*Peccata tam contra sanam hominis naturam sunt quam labruscæ contra naturam bonæ vitis.*" SEB. SCHMIDT.

11. On ver. 24: Whatever comes from God's hand is good and welcome. Man was originally כָּלֹה זֶרַע אֱמֶת. He bore no principle of corruption within him. This came from without. Hence such depravity has become possible [actual, S. R. A.], as on its side renders necessary a complete remoulding (regeneration) of man.

12. On ver. 22: "We see in nature that affected beauties, which are intended either to hide deformities or give new adornments not proper to the person, only render one uglier than before." ZINZENDORF.

13. On ver. 25: ["The passage suggests that

in many cases the plea of despair is not half honest. The heart takes it up simply as an apology for rushing madly and headlong into sin To quiet conscience and to seem to lend some ear to reason, men try and even pretend to think there is no longer any hope from God, and hence that they may as well get all the good from sin they can while they can get any." Cowles.—S. R. A.]

14. On ver. 26: "It often occurs in the office of a preacher that he sees poor humanity in its nakedness. He must be on his guard that he use his victory with moderation and in such a way that the souls ashamed may see more hearty love and compassion than tyranny and assumption.... There ought not to be mere Hildebrands or mere Henry Fourths; a village schoolmaster may also show to one of his scholars that he is more concerned about his own authority than the pupil's salvation; and this has no better effect on the youth than his penance in the court at Canossa had on the Emperor Henry IV." ZINZENDORF.

15. On ver. 28. Necessity teaches prayer. Necessity compels men to cast away all false props and to stay themselves on Him, who alone endures everlastingly. Yet this may be done with insincerity, merely for outward advantage. Then will God say: He who will not serve Me, but will only serve himself with Me, has nothing to hope from Me. He may serve himself with those whom only he wishes to serve.

16. On ver. 30: MICH. GHISLERUS, in his commentary, discusses the question at length:—In how far it may be said that the Lord has smitten Israel *in vain*, since the means which God uses always correspond exactly to the end in view, and therefore the application of means without the attainment of the object is inconceivable. He answers in the words of PETRUS A FIGUEIRA: "*Dicitur autem Deus frustra percussisse quantum ad finem extrinsecum, qui erat emendatio percussorum, non quantum ad internum, qui erat ipsemet. Ideo enim percutiebat etiam eos, quos sciebat non recepturos disciplinam nec emendationem, ut omnibus se bonum medicum, bonumque parentem demonstraret, utpote omnia faciendo ad ægrotorum sanitatem et filiorum disciplinam necessaria. Atque quoad hunc finem non frustra percussit, sed finem consecutus est.*" GHISLERUS more correctly distinguishes between a *percussio gratiæ* and a *percussio justitiæ*, the former for salvation, the latter for judgment. We must, indeed, say that the strokes of God are relatively, but not absolutely in vain. If they do not attain the end of conversion, they show at least that God has done His part, which is the meaning also of this passage; and they serve for "a testimony against them." Comp. Gal. iii. 4.

17. On ver. 30. In order that the divine chastisement may have the desired result, it is necessary that man enter into the divine purpose, *i. e.*, that he understand what God would say to him, and whereto He would move him, and that he also hear and obey. This is to accept the chastisement. To accept chastisement is a sign of wisdom (Prov. viii. 10; xix. 20), while not to accept it is a sign of folly (Prov. i. 7; iii. 11, 12; v. 12, 23; xiii. 18; xv. 32. Comp. Ps. l. 17; Isa. i. 5).

18. On "Ye generation," ver. 31. "That is not to be denied, which Paul says to the Cretans, they are altogether κακὰ θηρία. This applies sometimes to whole nations, sometimes to certain cities and places. Servants of Christ, who have fallen in such places where their hearers are of a bad sort, experience it indeed." ZINZENDORF.—On "Have I been a desert." *etc.* "Where God bestows most benefits, there He receives the least gratitude." FOERSTER.

19. On ver. 32. The children of this world are wiser in their generation than the children of light (Luke xvi. 8).—A virgin who forgets her bridal ornaments might be compared to the foolish virgins who forgot their oil (Matth. xxv. 1), nay, she is even worse than these.

20. On ver. 33, *a*. Not only zealous, but clever and inventive is man in evil, but lazy and unskilful for good; comp. iv. 22.

21. On ver. 33, *b*. Φθείρουσιν ἤδη χρηστὰ ὁμιλίαι κακαί (1 Cor. xv. 33). Every man is as his God. Everything, which is called a god, is inimical to the true God, therefore also to the absolute idea of the True and the Good. All kinds of idolatry, therefore, whether gross or refined, must demoralize men.

22. On ver. 35, *a*. Men frequently from obstinacy and pride will not confess their sins. Comp. 1 John i. 8. But ZINZENDORF (*Pred. d. Ger. S.*, 184) remarks with justice on this passage: "It is not so absolutely obstinacy and wickedness, hypocrisy, dogmatism; but men really come by many sins in such a way that they do not know them. As that savage at Copenhagen who killed his comrade and was severely wounded, thought that he should die for such a legitimate cause (for the other had insulted him)."

23. On vers. 36 and 37. "*Serus post pœnam luctus. Sero sapiunt Phryges, si tamen vere sapiant, non sero supiunt.*" SEB. SCHMIDT.

HOMILETICAL AND PRACTICAL.

1. On ver. 14–19. Israel's slavery an emblem of the universal human slavery of sin: (1) In both it is not original. (2) In both cases it is self-incurred. (3) In both it is severely punished. (4) In both the punishment is the means of salvation. [1. "The nature of sin; it is *forsaking the Lord* as our God. 2. The cause of sin; it is because *His fear is not in us*. 3. The malignity of sin, *it is an evil thing and a bitter*. 4. The fatal consequences of sin. 5. The use and application of all this—*repent of thy sin.*" HENRY.—S. R. A.].

2. On ver. 17. Penitential sermon: on a retrospect of the past three things are manifest. (1) The goodness of God who sought to lead us in the right way. (2) Our disobedience, in forsaking the Lord our God. (3) God's justice, in not allowing our rebellion to go unpunished.

3. On ver. 19. The evils of the present time are (1), The consequences of sin (not natural necessity, not chance, not the effect of an overpowering evil influence), (2) Means of salvation from sin, since by them we learn that (*a*) sin is ruinous deception, (*b*) godliness is life and salvation.

4. On ver. 20. The endeavor to cast off the yoke of God is (1) an ancient one (the angels,

the apostasy, Israel), (2) a ruinous one; for (a) it deprives us of true freedom: (b) it renders us the servants of powers hostile to God and destructive to ourselves.

5. On vers. 21-25. The sinful corruption of humanity is (1) not original, but (2) very deep. (3) It cannot be denied away; (4) it cannot be removed by external means.

6. On vers. 26-28. How ruinous a course it is to trust in a creature: (1) who on account of his weakness leaves us disgracefully in the lurch: (2) we thus insult God and lose His help.

7. On vers. 29-32. When man quarrels with God, the fault is always on the side of man (Ps. li. 6). For (1) God chastises us, but we do not obey: (2) He bestows on us the necessaries of life, but we do not thank Him; (3) He makes us partakers of the highest glory, but we reject it with disdain.

8. On ver. 31. "Have I been a desert," etc., there is extant a homily of Origen on this text, the third of his homilies on Jeremiah. His fundamental thought is, God is a desert to none. This is true (1) in reference to all men (comp. Matth. v. 45) (a) in a bodily, (b) in a spiritual regard. For He was always a fruitful land to Israel, (a) when He blessed them and punished the heathen, (b) when He blessed the heathen and punished them, (c) even when He allowed the church of Christ to pass from the Jews to the heathen.—["An unjust imputation repelled by Jehovah. To an ingenuous mind God never appears so irresistible as when He addresses His creatures in the language of tender expostulation. Christians treat God as a wilderness (1) when they are reluctant to serve Him, (2) when they seek their happiness in the world. The ground of complaint is in them, not in God." PAYSON.—S. R. A.]

9. On ver 32. "What is the adornment of clothes compared with the imperishable adornment of the righteousness of Christ! Food for moths and worms, and nothing more. Shall such a perishable adornment be so dear to thy heart that thou never forgettest to put it on when thou art going out, or when thou preparest thyself for church on Sunday: but the imperishable adornment be so unimportant that thou art ever forgetting it, even though so frequently spoken to concerning it? No, be followers of the apostle Paul, Phil. iii." HOCHSTETTER. "Twelve Parables from the prophet Jeremiah," S. 9.

10. On ver. 35. Obstinate impenitence. (1) It is blind to its own guilt. (2) It blasphemes God, accusing Him of unjust anger. (3) It will not escape just punishment.

THE SECOND DISCOURSE.

(CHAPTERS III.–VI.)

This discourse, according to iii. 6, belongs to the reign of Josiah, and moreover, according to iii. 4, 10; iv. 1 to the period of his reformation, which occupied from the twelfth to the eighteenth year of his reign. (2 Chron. xxxiv. 3, 8; xxxv. 19). Since Jeremiah began his ministry in the 13th year of Josiah, this discourse pertains to the period from the 13th to the 18th year of Josiah, consequently to the commencement of his ministry. Its position at the beginning of the book corresponds, therefore, entirely to the historical date of its composition.

The discourse falls into two main divisions and a conclusion. It may be arranged as follows:—

I. FIRST MAIN DIVISION (CHAPTER III. 1.—IV. 4.)

The Call to Return, שׁוּב.

1. *Basis:—Notwithstanding Deut. xxiv. 1-4, a return is possible,* iii. 1-5.
2. *The call to return in the past,* iii. 6-10.
3. *The call to return in the future,* iii. 11-25.
4. *The call to return in the present,* iv. 1-4.

II. SECOND MAIN DIVISION (CHAPTER IV. 5.—VI. 26.)

Threatening of Punishment on Account of their Neglect to Return.

1. *Description of the judgment to be expected,* iv. 5-31.
2. *Proof of its justice by an enumeration of causes,* chap. v.
3. *Recapitulation, consisting of a combination of the call to return, the announcement of punishment, and the ground of punishment,* vi. 1-26.

III. CONCLUSION.—OBJECT AND EFFECT OF THE DISCOURSE, (CHAPTER VI. 27-30).

CHAP. III. 1–5.   45

FIRST DIVISION (CHAPTER III. 1—IV. 4).

The Call to Return, שׁוּב.

1. *Basis:—Notwithstanding* Deut. xxiv. 1-4, *a return is possible.*

III. 1-5.

1 .... therefore, if a man dismiss his wife,
And she go from him and become another man's,
Will he return to her again?
Would not such a land be desecrated?
But thou hast whored it with many paramours,
YET RETURN TO ME, saith Jehovah.
2 Raise thine eyes to the hills[1] and see;
Where hast thou not been lain with?[2]
By the roads thou satest for them like an Arab in the desert,
And desecratedst the land by thy whoredom[3] and wickedness.
3 And the showers were withheld,
And there came no latter rain:
But thou hadst the brow of a harlot,
And wouldst not be ashamed.
4 Hast thou not henceforth cried[4] to me, my Father!
Thou, the companion of my youth!
5 Will he then everlastingly mark,[5]
And always bear a grudge?
Behold, thus didst thou speak,
And didst the evil and didst prevail.[6]

TEXTUAL AND GRAMMATICAL.

[1] Ver. 2.—[Literally "bare heights" as HITZIG renders. BLAYNEY incorrectly translates "open plains."—S. R. A.]
[2] Ver. 2.— לֹא שֻׁגַּלְתְּ *Per verecundiam* the Masoretes always put for this the corresponding form from שָׁכַב Deut. xxviii. 30; Isa. xiii. 16; Zech. xiv. 2. [" A few MSS. and the Soncin. Edition also exhibit שְׁכַבְתְּ."—HENDERSON].
[3] Ver. 2.—וּנְתֻיִךְ a plural formation like חֲנֻיִים, which occurs besides only in Num. xiv. 33, analogous to תְּנוּנֹתִים frequent in Ezekiel, ch. xvi. (vers. 15, 22, *etc.*), and ch. xxii. (vers. 7, 8, *etc.*). Comp. NAEGELSB. *Gr.*, § 48, 4.
[4] Ver. 4.—On the form קָרָאתִי and דִּבַּרְתִּי, comp. rem. on ii. 20.
[5] Ver. 5.—To יִנְטֹר and יִשְׁמֹר suppl. אַף. Comp. ver. 12; Ps. ciii. 9.
[6] Ver. 5.—On the form וַתּוּכָל (for וַתּוּכְלִי). Comp. EWALD, § 191 *b*. [NOTES translates this line, "but doest evil with all thy might," but comp. EXEG. rem.—S. R. A.]

EXEGETICAL AND CRITICAL.

That these verses belong not to chapter ii. but to the following discourse, and indeed form its basis, is evident from the following reasons: 1. The fundamental thought of the previous strophe was that Israel had incurred misfortune not by Jehovah's fault but by his own. 2. It is shown in ch. iii. 6–11 that hitherto neither Israel nor Judah has been obedient to the call "return." In vers. 12-25 it is shown that in the distant future they will obey this call; in ch. iv.—vi. that if the people do not obey the call made to them now, in the *present*, they must expect severe punishment, to be inflicted by a people from the North. Since then the basis of the thought developed in iii. 1-5 is that the return of apostate Israel is brought into connection with the regulation of the Mosaic law, according to which a woman who had been divorced and married to another man, could not return to her former husband, it is manifest that ch. iii. 1-5 attach themselves to what follows, and not to the previous section. That לֵאמֹר in ver. 1 does not militate against this, will be shown immediately, and that this strophe serves as the basis of what follows will be clear from the explanation of וְשׁוֹב.

Ver. 1. . . . **therefore: If a man dismiss his wife . . . yet return to me, saith Jehovah.**

The various explanations of לֵאמֹר may be divided into two classes. 1. The LXX. and the translations and commentaries which follow it, (of the later Comm. also GULCHERUS in *Symb. Hagan., Cl. 1, Fasc.* 1) omit it altogether. The character of the LXX. renders it probable that this omission was founded not on MS. evidence, but in mere caprice. 2. It is connected with the preceding, *viz.*, מֵאָס, ii. 37, by KIMCHI, ABAR-

BANEL, LUTHER, BUGENHAGEN, ŒCOLAMPADIUS, VATABLE. TREMELLI, MUENSTER, STARKE, MAURER and HITZIG. It is opposed to this connection, (a) that the contents of this verse are as heterogeneous with the previous verse as they are homogeneous with the following, as already shown; (b) that לֵאמֹר is separated from מֵאִם by a sentence, so that it would be intolerably harsh to connect them. 3. Most commentators explain it by the aid of an ellipsis before לֵאמֹר, supplying יֹאמַר, " וַיֹּאמֶר לִי יֵשׁ אָמְרוּ; so the Vulgate and the Roman Catholic divines; also RASCHI, ZWINGLI, BULLINGER, SEB. SCHMIDT, DE WETTE, ROSENMUELLER, etc. But all these supplementations are arbitrary and unexampled. An idea, on which לֵאמֹר depends as a more particular definition, would no more be unexpressed in Hebrew, than one before "therefore" in English. To render this clear we have begun the translation of this verse thus ".. therefore." The passages Josh. xxii. 11; Jud. xvi. 2; Isa. ix. 8; xliv. 28 are indeed quoted as analogous. But in the passages in Joshua and Isaiah, the idea which serves as a point of support is not wanting, though only implied (comp. NAEGELSB. § 95, e). The passage in Judges might be appealed to if a corruption of the text were not very much to be suspected. 3. CALVIN and VENEMA seek to render לֵאמֹר in such a sense that it need not depend on the foregoing. CALVIN translates indeed dicendo, but would take this in the sense of par manière de dire or of posito casu. VENEMA modifies this interpretation, rendering "if it is said," and regarding it as the antecedent to which "saith Jehovah" at the close of the verse, corresponds:—" If it is said, Will a man return? etc.—yet saith Jehovah, thou hast been lewd, yet return to Me." But leaving out of account that לֵאמֹר would then be superfluous, this absolute use of it is quite undemonstrable. 5. J. D. MICHAELIS, EWALD and GRAF acknowledge that this isolated לֵאמֹר is a grammatical anomaly, and therefore declare the text to be corrupt. They assume that either before לֵאמֹר a formula like וַיְהִי דְבַר " אֵלַי has dropped out, or that the date in ver. 6, after which לֵאמֹר contrary to rule, is wanting, should be transposed to this place. The latter would seem to be the most probable. [HENDERSON renders Further, which seems to be an evasion of the difficulty. The English Editor of CALVIN suggests that לְ be rendered according to, "According to what is said," but as WORDSWORTH notes, this phrase is the universal formula for introducing a message from God; and he therefore regards it as used by the prophet to intimate that what he is uttering is a quotation from the law of the Lord. COWLES renders "Saying" and connects it with the preceding context. BLAYNEY, "whilst thou sayest." NOYES, "it is said,"—S. R. A.]—הֵן is here, as frequently, used in a hypothetical sense, comp. Exod. iv. 1; viii. 22; Levit. xxv. 20; Isa. liv. 15. The following contains a partial verbal reference to Deut. xxiv. 1-4, where it is said, that a woman who has been divorced and married again, cannot when released from her second marriage by separation or death, again become the wife of her first husband, since this would be an abomination before the Lord, and increase the moral corruption of the land. חָנֵף in an intransitive sense (comp. טָמֵא Levit. xviii. 25) as in Isa. xxiv. 5; Ps. cvi. 38 = *profanari*, to be desecrated. The LXX. reads οὐ μιανθήσεται ἡ γυνὴ ἐκείνη; probably in connection with the previous translation μὴ ἀνηκάμψει πρὸς αὐτόν; which change without doubt was intended to render this sentence accordant with the subsequent application (return to me). The Syrohexapla translation however follows the Hebrew, and GRABE in his edition reads ἡ γῆ. So also SPOHN. Both are certainly wrong.—וְגוּ with accus. of the person is found also in Ezek. xvi. 28. Most of the ancients (with the exception of the LXX. ἀνέκαμπες, Ar. *et revertereris?* THEODOR. *ἐπανήξεις*, VICTOR. PRESB., πῶς ἐπιστρέφεις πρός με); render וְשׁוֹב אֵלַי as imperative; the modernus (MAURER, HITZIG, EWALD, UMBREIT, NEUMANN, GRAF) as interrogative. I decidedly regard the first as correct. As I have shown above it is the fundamental idea of the whole discourse that Israel is to return to his Lord. The adherents of the more recent interpretation also find themselves compelled, to avoid contradiction, to take the question not as a negation but as expressing wonder, which is not logically admissible; for why should the Lord wonder concerning that which, according to what follows, is His definite wish? The *vau* is therefore to be taken as adversative—" although in accordance with legal regulations, I ought not to receive you, yet I say, Return to me." The appeal to the passage in the law belongs to the domain rather of prophetic rhetoric than of morals; for the command refers to a physical relation, which does exist between Jehovah and His people. If however we interpret this relation spiritually, we prove too much, for every sin is spiritual adultery. When it was remarked above that this strophe forms the introductory basis of the discourse, it was meant that in this strophe, (a) an apparent hindrance, (b) a false presumption is removed which might stand in the way of a true return. The apparent hindrance is the legal regulation which is removed by an authoritative decree (vers. 1-3 a). The false presumption is that pseudo-conversion, which took place under Josiah, and which consisted in this, that the people sought to deceive themselves and others with fine words, which their deeds proved to be lies (vers. 3 b.-5).

Ver. 2. **Raise thine eyes . . . and wickedness.** These words furnish the actual proof of "thou hast played the harlot," etc., ver. 1.—**Hills.** Comp. "high mountain," Isa. xiii. 2. *Mons culmine planus, silva non contectus.*

Ver. 3. **And the showers were withheld . . . wouldest not be ashamed.** The first hemistich refutes the objection that Israel committed this wickedness unreproved, comp. ii. 30. The divine displeasure was rendered palpable by the withholding of the necessary rain (v. 25;

coll. iv. 18; ii. 19), but Israel refused to be brought by this chastisement to perceive, confess and repent of his sin. With the boldness of a harlot who not only does not confess that she has done wickedly, but does it besides as though she had a claim to the recognition of her services,— with such boldness does Israel speak in a confident and affectionate tone to the Lord, and even ventures on a gentle reproach for undeserved severity. While ver. 2 expresses a subordinate thought which merely defines more particularly a point in ver. 1, and to which ver. 3 *a* is attached as a corollary, vers. 4, 5 express the second main thought of the strophe, to which ver. 3, *b* serves as a transition.

Ver. 4. **Hast thou not henceforth cried to me** . . . **the companion of my youth?**— **Henceforth** appears to refer to the time when the people recognized the divine anger in the withholding of the rain, for then they at once became, at least in words, friendly and officious. But it is not equivalent to מֵאָז from times of old. We are thus led to conjecture that the three facts, withholding of rain, hypocritical conversion of the people, and this prophecy, were contemporaneous. This is also confirmed by a comparison of the dates in i. 2 and 2 Chron. xxxiv. 3. According to the latter passage Josiah began in the twelfth year of his reign "to purge Judah and Jerusalem," while according to Jer. i. 2, our prophet commenced his ministry in the 13th year of Josiah. Now, since according to iii. 6, the present discourse belongs at any rate to the time of Josiah, and from its position and contents, probably to the beginning of Jeremiah's prophetic labors, the prophet doubtless, as CHR. B. MICHAELIS, ROSENMUELLER, HITZIG and GRAF, have also perceived, describes in vers. 4 and 5 the conduct of the people in the time of Josiah's reformation, to which there is also a very distinct allusion in ver. 10. The prophet, therefore, says **henceforth**, because really even at the time when he proclaimed this divine message, such voices were still heard from the midst of the people. We need not, therefore, render it in the sense of *haud ita pridem*, nor **shall cry**, in the future. On **companion of my youth**, comp. Prov. ii. 17.

Ver. 5. **Will he then everlastingly mark?** . . . **prevail.** In these words of the first hemistich is a slight reproach. It is as though Israel's misfortune was due to the pertinacious anger of Jehovah.—The sense of the second half of the verse is this:—the acts of the people are in contradiction to their words, that the latter were not honestly meant, but were false and deceptive. Observe the antithesis of **saidst** and **didst.** Comp. a similar want of uprightness on the part of the people, ii. 35.—וַתּוּכָל **didst prevail,** is here used as in xx. 7, 9. Comp. Gen. xxxii. 28; 1 Sam. xxvi. 25; 1 Kings xxii. 22. It is strange here that the preceding verbs do not appear to involve the idea of effort, as is the case in the other passages and as the meaning of יָכֹל (to be grown, to be able, to set through) seems to require. But leaving out of account that עָשֹׂה and יָכֹל following one another, seem to have a sort of proverbial character (comp. 1 Sam. xxvi. 25), it is evident that the idea of a struggle lies at the basis of the antithesis mentioned, and **didst prevail** intimates that the struggle will be decided in favor of the evil.

DOCTRINAL AND ETHICAL.

1. That a man live a second time with a woman whom he has divorced, and who has been the wife of another man, is regarded as an abomination which corrupts the land. In what does this abomination consist? Not that the woman has previously been the wife of another, for then a divorced woman is not permitted to marry the second time, and all marriages of widows would be an abomination. In this case then the abomination must consist in this, that the man takes back a woman who had first been his wife, but afterwards another's. Not the series A+B+C, etc., is forbidden, but the series A+B+A. But why is this? MICHAELIS, (*Mos. Rechte.*, 1 S. 241, 2), after his manner seeks the *ratio legis* in this, that if the re-marriage were permitted, the second husband's life would not be safe, should the old love be revived, or that the chastity of the woman would not be safe, her feminine modesty not being easily able to resist the advances of one to whom she had formerly yielded. But this is superficial talk. The matter must lie deeper than this, and be founded in the laws of a higher corporeality, which are still far too little known to us. It is remarkable that according to the Koran (Sur. II., 226), a man is at liberty to take back a divorced wife only in case she has been in the meantime the wife of another man. Comp. MICHAELIS, *Mos. Rechte.*, I. S. 237.

2. " *Quodlibet igitur studendum unicuique est, ut evitetur peccatum sicut fornicatio, quia per peccatum quodlibet quædam cum aliqua creaturarum admittitur fornicatio, per quam membra Christi fiunt membra iniquitatis, duoque fiunt in carne una.*" GHISLERUS.

3. "How great is the goodness of God, when the sinner wilfully thrusts Him away from him, yet God receives him again into His favor when he truly repents! Ezek. xviii. 21, 22." STARKE.

4. " *Revertere ad me et mundaberis, reparaberis, si confundaris tibi et refundaris mihi.*" AUGUSTIN. *contra Faustum*, I. 15, i. f.

5. "The feeling of need to call God Father and beseech Him to save, is not an infallible sign of true penitence, Isa. xxvi. 16." STARKE.

HOMILETICAL AND PRACTICAL.

The mercy of God to sinners is,—1. On the one side endless (the prohibition of re-marriage with a former wife, who has been married to another, —the sinner is not dismissed, but is voluntarily apostate, sin is not a conjugal, but an adulterous relation,—still the Lord is ready to receive the sinner back); 2. On the other hand limited, in so far that it is connected strictly with the fulfilment of a condition (not a hypocritical return with fine words, but only sincere, earnest return, with fruits meet for repentance, can render us partakers of His grace).

2. The call to return in the Past.

III. 6–10.*

6   The LORD [Jehovah] said also unto me in the days of Josiah the king, Hast thou seen that which backsliding² Israel hath done? She hath gone up upon every
7   high mountain and under every green tree, and there hath played the harlot. And I said after she had done all these things, Turn thou unto me! But she returned not. And her treacherous sister [Faithless, her sister] Judah saw it.
8   And I saw, when for all the causes whereby backsliding Israel committed adultery I had put her away, and given her a bill of divorce;³ yet her treacherous⁴ sis-
9   ter Judah feared not, but went and played the harlot also. And it came to pass⁵ through the lightness [correctly: cry] of her whoredom, that she defiled the land,⁶
10 and committed adultery with stones and with stocks [wood]. And yet for [notwithstanding] all this her treacherous sister Judah hath not turned to me with her whole heart, but feignedly [hypocritically; *lit.* in falsehood] saith the Lord [Jehovah].

TEXTUAL AND GRAMMATICAL.

* [As this passage presents no signs of poetry I have followed BLAYNEY, NOYES, and HENDERSON in giving it the form of prose. UMBREIT prints it in parallelisms, while WORDSWORTH renders not only those verses but the whole chapter as prose.—S. R. A.]
² Ver. 6.—מְשֻׁבָה rejection, revolt, apostacy, the abstract for the concrete; comp. NAEGELSB. *Gr.*, ¿ 19, 1. The word in this sense is peculiar to this chapter; comp. viii. 11, 12. Comp. also viii. 5.
³ Ver. 8.—כְּרִיתֻתֶיהָ. The plural here only, comp. Deut. xxiv. 1, 3; Isa. l. 1.
⁴ Ver. 8.—בָּגוֹדָה is related to בָּגוֹדָה בְּנוֹדָה as שׁוּבָב (vers. 14, 22) to מְשֻׁבָה. On the form comp. NAEGELSB. *Gr.*, ¿ 47, 1; EWALD, ¿ 188, *b.*
⁵ Ver. 9.—וַיְהִי here as in 1 Sam. xiii. 22: xxv. 20, and elsewhere, stands for וְהָיָה. Comp. NAEGELSB. *Gr.*, ¿ 83, 7, *Anm.*
⁶ Ver. 9.—וַתֶּחֱנַף אֶת־הָאָרֶץ, a frequent paratactic construction. Comp. וַתֵּלֶד וַיִּפְגַּשׁ, Gen. xxii. 24. Comp. NAEGELSB. *Gr.*, ¿ 87, 7; ¿ 111, 1 *b*.

EXEGETICAL AND CRITICAL.

The theme of this strophe is "Return unto Me" (ver. 7, comp. ver. 10). It is however shown how this call hitherto, in the past, has been heeded, or rather *not* heeded, by Israel and Judah. The main regard of the prophet is naturally directed to Judah. Israel serves only as a foil; on the background of the transgression of Israel, which should have served for a warning to Judah, the sin of the latter stands out still more glaringly.

Ver. 6. **And Jehovah . . . played the harlot.** If as cannot be disputed there is a close connection between this strophe and the preceding, it is evident that this inscription is not in place. For it would indicate the beginning of a larger section, while here, on the contrary, there is intimate connection. The greater section begins at ver. 1. The isolated and puzzling לֵאמֹר requires a sentence before it, where then this inscription belongs. The reason of its transposition from ver. 1 may be, as GRAF supposes, that ver. 10 contains an evident allusion to the reformation of Josiah. But he overlooks the fact that such an allusion is contained also in vers. 4 and 5.—**Upon every high moun-**tain. Comp. ver. 13; ii. 20.—וַתֵּרֶא. If this is not the 2d Pers. Fem., which would be possible only by a violent change of person, the formation is to be explained either according to the analogy of תִּשְׁקֹט (Jer. xlvii. 7) as an Aramaism (comp. EWALD, ¿ 191, *c*, and *Anm.*) or according to the analogy of תֵּפְחִי (Jer. xviii. 23) as a לה- formation with prominence of the radical Yod (comp. EWALD, ¿ 224, *c*). OLSHAUSEN (*S.* 510, *Anm.*) at once assumes an error.

Ver. 7. **And I said . . . sister Judah saw it.** It is not necessary, with GRAF and others to take וָאֹמַר in the sense of "I thought," and תָּשׁוּב as 3d Pers., since the Lord not only thought this but really said it to Israel. This "Return to Me" is the underlying theme of all prophetic admonition (Jer. xxxi. 20). In this passage it is emphatic. It points back to the **Yet return to me** in ver. 1, and with the following **returned not** represents the main thought of the section. In form תָּשׁוּב is like תּוּכַל in ver. 5—**And Faithless, her sister Judah.** To take בָּגוֹדָה as *subst. abstr.* corresponding to מְשֻׁבָה = faithlessness, would form a fine parallelism; but we should then expect בְּגוֹדָה. The form קָטוּל

with firm א (בְּגוֹד) even or בְּיִרְדָה only here and in ver. 10) designates everywhere else only *con creta*. Comp. EWALD, § 152, 6. The position of the word and the absence of the article seem to intimate that it is intended for a proper name, and we have therefore written it with an initial capital.—The Keri וְהֵרֵא is unnecessary. וְהֵרָאָה does not indeed occur elsewhere, but נֵרְאָה does (1 Sam. xvii. 42; 2 Ki. v. 21; Job xlii. 16; Ezek. xviii. 14, Keri, 28); and וַיֵּרָאֶה (1 Sam. x. 14) leaving out of account the analogous forms of other verbs, *ex. gr.* וְהֶעֱשָׂה, Jer. xxxii. 20; xxxvi. 5, 26, *etc.*—The question whether it is to be translated "and Judah saw it," or whether the object seen is contained in the following sentence beginning with כִּי depends on the other, whether the following וָאֵרֶא is genuine and original.

Ver. 8. (And I saw) . . . played the harlot also. The construction: "I saw, that I, because she played the harlot, had dismissed Israel, and I gave her a bill of divorce, and Judah feared not," is not so devoid of meaning, as GRAF supposes, if we change the paratactic mode of expression into the syntactic. The main object of saw is feared not. All that lies between has the force of a parenthetical clause of adversative signification: "And I saw, that, although I had dismissed Israel, and given her a bill of divorce, yet Judah feared not." Comp. NAEGELSB. *Gr.*, § 111, 1, *Anm*. But at all events the connection of verses 7 and 8 is interrupted in a very awkward way by And I saw. Verse 7 concludes in this way, that Judah had seen how Israel had not returned at the call of Jehovah, and then ver. 8 designates as the object of the divine seeing what, according to the conclusion of the whole course of thought, vers. 8 *b*, 9, 10, must be the object seen by Judah. For the prophet draws a parallel between the behaviour of Israel and of Judah. Israel, first apostate, is called to repent, but returns not and is rejected. Judah sees this and—also does not return. It is evidently in this connection very essential that Judah should have perceived not only the impenitence of Israel, but also the punishment he thus incurred. The very sight of this destructive judgment should have brought Judah to sincere repentance. Judah's seeing the impenitence, but not the judgment, the latter being ascribed to the Lord, introduces an inappropriate element into the connection, although we cannot say that an incorrect idea would be thus originated. If however we omit the words, and I saw. we have a perfectly clear and satisfactory connection. The critical authorities indeed give no safe support to its rejection. Only JEROME omits the word, but whether on MS. evidence, may be questioned. He is followed by LUTHER in his translation, and GULCHER. *Symb. Hag.*, C. 1. Fasc. 1. The LXX. Chaldee and Arabic versions certainly found it in their copies of the original. But the Syriac appears to have read וְחֵרָא, the same word twice, and this EWALD regards as the correct reading.—If וָאֵרֶא is an error it is at any rate a very ancient one. According to the rule of preferring the more difficult reading, it is certainly safer to retain it, al-

though it is easy to conceive a reason for its insertion. If we strike it out, the words "her sister Judah saw" belong to the following sentence, and the second hemistich of ver. 7 consists merely of the words "But she returned not." The brevity of this clause may have been the occasion of connecting the words "and Faithless," *etc.*, with ver. 7, but then it became necessary to introduce a verb in the beginning of ver. 8, as וָאֵרֶא or וְהֵרָא.—For all the causes. עַל־כָּל before אֹדוֹת and אֲשֶׁר after it, are found here only. Elsewhere אֹדוֹת is always connected with a following genitive (Gen. xxi. 11, 25; xxvi. 32. Exod. xviii. 8) or with suffixes (Josh. xiv. 6) עַל expresses the multitude of the adulteries (hence GRAF suitably translates "alldieweilen" = for all the causes). אֲשֶׁר is rendered necessary to the connection of אֹדוֹת with a finite verb. As a relative particle in the widest sense, (Comp. NAEGELSB. *Gr.*, § 80, 1) it involves here the meaning of *eo quod*, thereby that, (on the ground of all the occasions that have been afforded thereby, that, *etc.*)

Ver. 9. And it came to pass . . . with wood. קַל is elsewhere always written *plene*. On account of this unusual defective manner of writing the ancient translations seem to have derived the word from קָלַל; for the Vulgate translates "*facilitate fornicationis suæ contaminavit terram;* LXX. καὶ ἐγένετο εἰς οὐδὲν ἡ πορνεία αὐτῆς. Arab., "*fuit fornicatio ejus cum nihilo;*" Chald. "*levia videbantur idola in oculis ejus.*"— But this defective manner of writing is not a sufficient reason for departing from the primary meaning (comp. Gen. xxvii. 22), nor is this in itself doubtful. Only we must not take קַל in the sense of "report" (Gen. xlv. 16), but the prophet means to say that so far as the land extends, so far also whoredom with idols, as a heaven-crying sin, defiles the land (comp. Gen. iv. 10). It may not be objected to this, that the cry for the vengeance of heaven does not defile the land, for this cry is not an immediate, but a mediate provocation of the divine justice; that is, by their very impudent appearance (this is their cry), their sin challenges the justice of God.—As to the construction with the accusative, we need neither to read וַתְּחַנֵּף with EWALD, nor to strike out אֶת with GRAF. For the intransitive verb may be taken in a passive sense, and accordingly, as the passive, may have an accusative of the proximate object which may be regarded as dependent on an ideal transitive. חָנֵף *is to be desecrated* (comp. FUERST), therefore properly rendered *et profanatum est terram*. This *profanatum est* is, however, properly no more than *profanare* in a passive-perfect statement; *et factum est profanare terram*. Comp. יְרֵא אֶת־הַדָּבָר (2 Sam. xi. 25; coll. 1 Sam. viii. 6: See NAEGELSB. *Gr.*, § 69, *Anm*. 1; § 100, 2.) Certainly תֶּחֱנַף הָאָרֶץ may also be said (Ps. cvi. 38.)

Ver. 10. Further, but hypocritically, saith Jehovah. —If we should refer the words "Further," *etc.*, *to* what immediately precedes, they would retain no meaning, for it is absurd to say that Judah in spite of her idolatry had yet not repented. They refer rather to ver. 8, a, where it was said that the Lord had repudiated Israel. On this account a double accusative thought is added; (1) "feared not," etc., ver. 8 b.; (2) "notwithstanding all this," ver. 10. Although Judah had witnessed the punishment of Israel, she did two things: first, she continued the whoredom of idolatry, and then sought to appease Jehovah by a hypocritical conversion, by which the prophet apparently alludes to the reformation of Josiah, which was entered on in earnest by the king, but not by the people.

DOCTRINAL AND ETHICAL.

1. God in His judgments has in view not merely those who are primarily affected by them, but those who witness them also. If the latter do not allow themselves thus to be warned, their guilt increases just in the proportion that the judgment might have been an impulse and a help to repentance. Comp. 2 Kings xvii. 18; Prov. xxviii. 14; 1 Cor. x. 6, 11; 2 Pet. ii. 4-6, (ὑπόδειγμα μελλόντων ἀσεβεῖν τεθεικώς, ver. 6.)

2. "Blessed is he who is rendered wise by the losses of others." CRAMER. Comp. Jer. xviii. 5-8; Zech. i. 3.

3. GHISLERUS remarks that the present passage has been frequently interpreted allegorically. Thus the Abbot JOACHIM DE FLORE (ob. 1202, Commentary on Jeremiah, printed at Venice, 1525, and Cologne, 1577), interprets it of the Greek and Roman church (comp. HERZOG's Real-Enc., VI. S., 713). NICOLAUS DE LYRA interpreted it of the rich monastic orders, and the mendicant friars; Cardinal HUGO (de St. Caro, one of the inquisitors of the Abbot Joachim, ob. 1263), of the "illiterati et sæculares pravi," and of the "improbi religiosorum et clericorum et literatorum."

4. ORIGEN also treats of this passage (iii. 6-10) in his fourth homily on Jeremiah (in JEROME it is the fourteenth). He understands by Israel, the whole Jewish people, and by Judah, the Gentile church which, in spite of the judgments inflicted on Israel before their eyes, had in the course of time fallen into many sins and errors.

5. EPHREM SYRUS emphasizes the encouragement contained in ver. 7 ("Return to me"), when he says (Tom. 1. In threnis de div. retributione, according to GHISLER.), "O miseranda anima quousque torpescis et de salute animum despondes? Quam veniam in die judicii assequeris, quum salvator per prophetam exclamet dicens: ad me revertere!"

6. On ver. 10. Though the reform of Josiah was only a pseudo-revival, it furnishes us with the means of judging how deep a genuine revival must go. If thy right eye offend thee, pluck it out and cast it from thee (Matth. v. 29; xviii. 8, 9; Mark ix. 43-48).

HOMILETICAL AND PRACTICAL.

1. The severity and the goodness of God in His dealings with the Jewish nation (Rom. xi. 22): (1) His severity in His judgments upon Israel; (2) His goodness in His constantly repeated invitations to return (ver. 7.)

2. The difference between false and true repentance. (1) False repentance; (a) its ground—servile fear; (b) its effect—external reform. (2) True repentance; (a) its ground—love to God; (b) its effect—honest fruits of sanctification.

---

3. *The call to Return in the Future* (iii. **11-25.**)

a. How and whom God will call.

III. 11-17.

11 And Jehovah said to me, Apostasy Israel
    Has justified her soul before Faithless Judah.
12 Go and cry these words to the north, and say,
    Return[1] Apostasy Israel, saith Jehovah.
    I will not lower my face[2] against you,
    For I am merciful, saith Jehovah,
    I do not bear a grudge for ever.[3]
13 Only acknowledge thy sin,
    That thou hast transgressed against the Lord thy God,
    And hast run hither and thither to the strangers under **every green tree**,
    And ye have not heeded my voice, saith Jehovah.
14 Return, apostate children, saith Jehovah,
    For I am your husband[4] and take you one from a **city**,
    And two from a tribe and bring you towards Zion.
15 And give you pastors after my heart,
    And they shall pasture you with understanding[5] and judgment.[6]

CHAP. III. 11–17.   51

16 And it shall come to pass, when ye shall multiply,
    And spread in the land in those days, saith Jehovah,
    It will no more be said, Ark of the covenant of Jehovah!
    And it will no more come to mind,¹
    Nor will they remember it or esteem it;
    Also they will not make it again
17 At that time Jerusalem will be called Jehovah's throne,
    And all the nations shall gather to it,
    To the name of Jehovah, to Jerusalem,
    And will no more follow the perverseness of their evil heart.

TEXTUAL AND GRAMMATICAL.

¹ [Ver. 11.—BLAYNEY, NOYES and HENDERSON, render vers. 11, 12 as prose.—S. R. A.]
² [Ver. 12.—HENDERSON renders: I will not continue to frown upon you.—NOYES: I will not turn a frowning face upon you.—S. R. A.]
³ Ver. 12.—שׁוּבָה, apart from the assonant מְשֻׁבָה the paragogic *He* is never attached to forms with vowel terminations.
Comp. NAEGELSB. *Gr.* § 23, *Anm.* 5
⁴ [Ver. 14.—HITZIG, UMBREIT and others, translate "lord, master." HENDERSON and NOYES follow DE WETTE, GESENIUS and others in rendering "I have rejected you." NOYES also renders, "yet will I receive you again."—S. R. A.].
⁵ Ver. 15.—רעה *nom. verbale.* Comp. Exod. ii. 4; Isa. xi. 9; xxviii. 9.
⁶ Ver. 15.—הַשְׁכֵּל *Inf. abs.,* with substantive meaning as Prov. i. 3; xxi. 16; Dan. i. 17. On the *acc. adverb.* Comp.
NAEGELSB. *Gr.*, § 70, k.
⁷ Ver. 16.—זָכַר. The Kal with בְּ here only; the Hiphil is so construed in Ps. xx. 8; Am. vi. 10; Isa. xlviii. 1, analogously to the construction of *verba sentiendi* with בְּ. Comp. NAEGELSB. *Gr.*, § 112, 5, a. On יַעֲלֶה עַל־לֵב. Comp. li. 50; Isa. lxv. 17.

EXEGETICAL AND CRITICAL.

The purport of this and the following strophe points evidently to the future. We find the call שׁוּבָה, here also, addressed in the first instance to the Israel of the ten tribes, then to the whole people; but he who calls has the consciousness, that no longer, as hitherto, is he preaching to deaf ears. The times are changed. Israel repents, and a period opens before him of unanticipated outward and spiritual glory. The prophet comprises in his view first the past and the future, then the present, for the same reason that he treats of the present so much more at length: he has the present Israel most at heart; it is his object to subordinate the Past and the Future as means. Before, therefore, he enters in detail into the present condition of things, he seeks by brief and significant intimations concerning the past and future, to make an impression on the hearts of his hearers.

Ver. 11. **And Jehovah ... Judah.** It results from the preceding section that Judah, besides the aids afforded by the temple and the legitimate royalty, had also the example of Israel before her as a powerful impulse to amendment. The consequence of leaving these advantages unemployed, is that Israel appears more righteous than Judah. Comp. Ezek. xvi. 51, 52, the reverse of the expression, κατακρίνειν, Matth. xii. 41, coll. ver. 27. This point, favorable to Israel, serves the prophet as a point of support for a consolatory prophecy which is addressed primarily to Israel.

Ver. 12. **Go and cry these words towards the north ... I do not bear a grudge for ever.—Go and cry,** comp. ii. 2.—**Towards the north.** Comp. ver. 18. The prophet is to cry towards the north because Israel was carried captive into Assyria, towards the north. Comp. xvi. 15; xxiii. 8; xxxi. 8.—**Lower my face,** comp. Gen. iv. 5, 6. The expression denotes that lowering of the countenance, which is accompanied by the look which Homer portrays in the expression ὑπόδρα ἰδών.—**Bear a grudge,** comp. ver. 5.

Ver. 13. **Only acknowledge ... heeded my voice.** The only condition of the grace promised in ver. 12 is acknowledgment of sin. The prophet of course means that fruitful acknowledgment which includes corresponding action, comp. Luke xii. 10, 11.—וּתְפַזְּרִי, comp. ii. 23, 25, 36 (תִּלִּי) [*lit.* scattered (thy ways)].

Ver. 14. **Return ... towards Zion.** The old call in a new form. No longer **Apostasy** Israel is addressed (so Israel alone is called, comp. ver. 6), but **apostate children.** This not only sounds more comprehensive, but seems besides in ver. 22, to be the common designation of both halves of the people. Observe further, that the following strophe, ver. 18, begins at once with the declaration that Judah and Israel would come together. This seems to be the performance of the command given them in ver. 14. Finally in vers. 14 and 17, the possession of Zion and Jerusalem is spoken of. Should Judah be excluded from this possession? Evidently then the prophet in vers. 11-13, turns first to Israel, who had the preference, because less was given him; but, although he does not expressly name Judah, wishing to excite her to emulation by the promise of salvation apparently addressed to Israel alone (comp. παραζηλοῦν, Rom. xi. 14), yet in substance the pictures of the two kingdoms in the prophetic perspective, pass imperceptibly into one another, vers. 14-17. This strophe is thus preliminary to the following, in which the union of Israel and Judah is the fundamental idea.—**For I am your husband,** etc., בַּעַל (as *verb. denom.* = to be Lord, possessor, especially a spouse, to take a wife), is certainly elsewhere construed with an accusative (Isa. xxvi. 13; liv. 1; lxii. 4), or with לְ (1 Chron. iv. 22). But the construction with בְּ is possible, because the verbs of ruling (comp. Gen. iii. 16; Deut. xv. 6; Judges viii. 22) are thus connected. The explanation of KIMCHI, SCHLEUSSNER, SCHNURRER and others, who would take בָּעַל here as in xxxi. 32, according to the doubtful analogy of the Arabic (See HENGSTENBERG, Christol., II., S. 416), in the meaning "to be disgusted, to disdain," is admissible neither here nor in xxxi., 32 (vide ad loc), and the less in this place, that we are obliged to take בְּ in the sense of although. It is also grammatically incorrect to take בָּעַלְתִּי in the sense of the future, as some do, following the example of the LXX. (κατακυριεύσω ὑμῶν). Rather does the Lord ground His promise of blessing on the fact that He is Israel's husband, and has never ceased and never will cease to be so. Comp. the remarks on ii. 1-3.—**One from a city**, etc. EICHHORN, EWALD, GRAF understand this: "and even if so few fulfil the condition of true return," (named in ver. 13). But to the ear it would then be definitely stated that only a few would return. We should then also expect the antithesis of בֵּית אָבוֹת, מָטֶּה or שֵׁבֶט. The expressions **city** and **tribe** (comp. Gen. x. 5; xii. 3; Ps. xxii. 28; xcvi. 7), intimate rather that the prophet has the cities and tribes of the heathen in view. He would evidently indicate the great scattering of Israel, cast out among the heathen, and would say that great as this scattering was, if ez. gr., there were only one Jew in a city, or only two in a whole nation; yet these members of the holy family, almost vanishing amid the mass of the heathen, should not be forgotten. Thus also KIMCHI and ROSENMUELLER. [NOYES and HENDERSON.]

Ver. 15. **And give you pastors ... understanding and judgment**. The promise that Israel shall be gathered out of his dispersion (ver. 14) contains an allusion to the final period, and this point is now brought out more clearly. Pastors after God's heart can be those only, who are no longer as hitherto (comp. Hos. viii. 4), governed inwardly or outwardly by the spirit of the world, but who allow themselves to be guided by the Spirit of God alone, and are therefore fit instruments for the realization of God's kingdom upon earth. There is here an unmistakable allusion to David, the man after God's own heart (1 Sam. xiii. 14; Acts xiii. 22), and at the same time the representative of the idea of God's kingdom in its earthly realization (2 Sam. vii.), as well as to Solomon, who next after David, prayed for and received wisdom and judgment from God (2 Chron. i. 10, 11). The explanation of the older commentators, who understand by the pastors, Zerubbabel, Joshua, Ezra, or the Apostles and their successors, may have this much of truth in it that the return under Zerubbabel or the Christian Church may be numbered among the beginnings of the fulfillment of this promise. At any rate we must understand spiritual as well as worldly pastors (ποιμένες λαῶν). Comp. x. 21; xxiii. 4; Ezek. xxxiv. 23; John x. 1.

Vers. 16 and 17. **And it shall come to pass ... evil heart**. These verses portray in a few but expressive traits the character of that future epoch. Its characteristic feature will be this, that in the place of a merely representative there will be a real and therefore, extensively and intensively, an infinitely active presence of God. The pastors of understanding and judgment will bring about a period of prosperity to which it is an essential element, that Israel from the little heap, which according to ver. 14 it will be on its return to the land, will become so to numbers a respectable nation. Comp. xxiii. 3, 4; Isa. xlix. 18-21; liv. 1-3. As in the beginning of the human race, as the basis of all further steps towards the attainment of its destiny, the command was given to be fruitful and multiply (פְּרוּ וּרְבוּ, Gen. i. 28; ix. 1), of which we are reminded by the sound of the words here (הרבו ופרותם), and as the family of Jacob in Egypt had first to develop into a great people before it could be the receptacle of the fundamental revelation of the kingdom, so according to this passage the Israel of the future is first to become numerous, in order to be fitted for the concluding and perfected revelation of the kingdom.—**In those days**. Though connected with the preceding by the accents, which make a pause at נְאֻם יְהֹוָה, these words belong, at any rate in meaning to **it will no more be said**. They correspond to בְּ as tum to a previous quando.—**Ark**, etc., is not the accusative of the object dependent on **say**, but an exclamation; and the latter word, therefore, is not to name, to mention, but to say, to speak. The word "ark of the covenant" will no more be heard, because the thing itself and every thought of it will have disappeared. The ark will not be an object of desire or remembrance. In consequence of this it will no more be looked for or sought, as something that is missed (1 Sam. xx. 6; xxv. 15; Isa. xxxiv. 16; 1 Chron. xiii. 3) and still less prepared anew.—**Will not make it**. LUTHER: they will no longer sacrifice there, but עָשָׂה occurs in this meaning without an object-accusative only at a very late period (2 Ki. xvii. 32), and it is not credible that the prophet should designate this important idea by an expression so easily misunderstood. The Chaldee, RASCHI, GROTIUS and others render "and it shall no more take place," but they differ among themselves in reference to what shall no more take place. They thus resort to arbitrary supplementations (the taking of the ark into battle 1 Sam. iv. 11; ea quae nunc in bello fieri solent; the previously stated). The only natural subject is **ark**.—**Jehovah's throne**. The period when the ark is lacking, described in ver. 16, does not represent a retrograde but a progressive interval. What the ark has hitherto been to Jerusalem (Exod. xxv. 18-22; Numb. vii. 89; Ps. lxxx. 2; xcix. 1) Jerusalem is now to be in relation to the nations. All Jerusalem is now to be the throne of the Lord. The prophet's glance penetrates to the remotest distance, without distinguishing the progressive stages into which the final period itself is divided. While thus this prophecy on one hand reminds us of Micah iv. (coll. Isa. ii. 2 sqq.; Zech. viii. 20; Jer. xxxi. 6. Comp. CASP. *Micah der Morasth. S.* 453), on the other hand it reminds us of Rev. xxi.—The declaration of this passage that Jerusalem itself will be the throne of God is covered by the declaration of the Apocalypse that the New Jerusalem will be the tabernacle of God with men (xxi. 3) as the earth was in the beginning (Gen. iii.), and as the glory of Melchisedek consists in his being the representative of that original relation to God. Comp. the article in HERZOG, *Real-Enc.* on Melchisedek, IX., *S.* 303. Comp. also Ezek. xlviii. 35; Joel iv. 17. The correspondence of the Jerusalem of this passage with the New Jerusalem is further intimated by what is said in Rev. xxi. 22, 23, That the latter will have no temple, neither sun nor moon, but all these the Lord Himself will be to it. The analogy of this declaration with that in Jeremiah concerning the absence of the ark is strikingly evident. Comp. THOLUCK, *Die Propheten und ihre Weiss. S.* 154 and 194.—This analogy is finally confirmed by the declaration that all the heathen will assemble in the name of God at Jerusalem, for a similar declaration is made in Revelation, on the basis of many prophetic passages (Isa. lx.; lxvi. 18 sqq.; Zech. xiv. 16; Zeph. iii. 9, 10; comp. Rom. ix. 24-26; x. 18-20) of the New Jerusalem in xxi. 24, 26.—**To the name.** The expression is supported by the passages Exod. xx. 21; Deut. xii. 5, 11: coll. 1 Kings viii. 16 sqq.; 2 Chron. vi. 5 sqq., where even the first earthly sanctuary is designated as the residence of the name of Jehovah. As the preposition אֶל designates the direction in space, so לְ before שֵׁם designates the object of the coming; to Jerusalem, however, cannot be the bare repetition of the idea in it (HITZIG) any more than the addition of a later hand, for it renders the sense more difficult, instead of more easy, on which account the absence of the word in the LXX and the Syriac is evidently due to the critics. We can regard it only with HENGSTEN-BERG as the more exact definition of שָׁם לְ, before which אֲשֶׁר is to be supplied. It has then a causative sense; not Jerusalem is the object of the assembling of the nations, but the name of the Lord, which belongs to Jerusalem, and Jerusalem only in so far as the name of the Lord was inseparably connected with it.—**And will no more follow,** *etc.* The expression שְׁרִרוּת לִבָּם is found on the basis of Deut. xxix. 18, also in Ps. lxxxi. 13, and in Jer. vii. 24; ix. 13; xi. 8; xiii. 10; xvi. 12; xviii. 12; xxiii. 17—in all these places of Israel. It has nothing in itself which requires this limitation, it may therefore be used also in a wider sense, so that the heathen, in so far as Jerusalem is also their centre, may be reckoned together with Israel. All then, Israel and the heathen, will finally lose their stony heart and receive a heart soft and filled with the Spirit (Ezek. xi. 19; xxxvi. 26), and not outwardly only but with the whole heart will they be subject to the Lord and His kingdom.—If we once more look over this strophe we are struck above all by the sublimely rapt progress of the prophet's discourse from the circumstances of the present to the remotest future. The prophet proceeds from the comparison of the Judah of the present with the Israel in a certain sense belonging already to the past. Thus comparison issues favorably to Israel. Thus a prophecy is called forth which sets in prospect before Israel the highest material and spiritual prosperity. With this two questions are connected. Since the realization of this prosperity is connected with the condition of Israel's conversion, the question arises, Will this conversion take place? and when? The prophetic gaze can in the inconceivably distant ages perceive no element of religious or political restoration in the Israel of the ten tribes, as these are in fact unknown even to the present day. It must then be reserved for the final period (אַחֲרִית הַיָּמִים Mic. iv. 1) to bring back the lost ten tribes to the light,—the light of knowledge and of salvation. But here another question also arises, Will not Judah also participate in this light of knowledge and salvation? These two questions then: What will become of Judah? and How is it as to the conversion required in ver. 13? still wait for a solution. We may indeed read this solution from ver. 14 between the lines. But the sublime haste of the prophet's flight hindered him from giving it in express words; he adds it therefore in the following strophe.

(Special dissertations on this passage by LOS-CANUS, Frankfort, 1720; ZICKLER, Jena, 1747; FRISCHMUTH, Jena).

DOCTRINAL AND ETHICAL.

1. ["Here is a great deal of Gospel in these verses, both that which was always gospel, God's readiness to pardon sin, and to receive and entertain returning, repenting sinners, and those blessings which were in a special manner reserved for gospel-times, the forming and founding of the gospel-church by bringing into it the *children of God* that were scattered abroad, the superseding of the ceremonial law, and the uniting of Jews and Gentiles, typified by the uniting of Israel and Judah in their return out of captivity." HENRY.—S. R. A.]

b. Supplement of the preceding, stating more exactly who is called and how the call is received.

III. 18–25.

18 In that day the house of Judah and the house of Israel shall walk together,
And shall come with each other from the north country
Into the land which I have given your fathers for an inheritance.
19 And I said: How will I put thee among the children,
And give thee a pleasant land,
The most glorious inheritance among the nations!
And further I said, My Father thou wilt call me,[1]
And wilt not turn away behind me.
20 But! Was ever a woman faithless to her lover,
So were you faithless towards me,
O house of Israel, saith Jehovah.
21 A cry is heard on the hills,
The weeping supplication of the children of Israel;
That they have perverted their way,
Have forgotten Jehovah, their God.
22 Return, ye apostate children,
I will heal[2] your apostasies!
Behold, we come[3] to thee,
For thou art Jehovah, our God.
23 As certainly as hills are false,
Mountains an empty sound,[4]
So certain is the salvation of Israel
With Jehovah our God.
24 Shame however hath devoured the gains of our fathers from our youth,
Their sheep and their oxen,
Their sons and their daughters.
25 Let us lie in our shame,
And our disgrace cover us,
That we have sinned against Jehovah our God,
We and our fathers from our youth to this day,
And have not heeded the voice of Jehovah our God.

TEXTUAL AND GRAMMATICAL.

[1] Ver. 19.—The Masoretes would read תִּקְרָאִי and תָּשׁוּבִי on account of אָשִׁיתֵךְ and לָךְ, but unnecessarily. ["The Keri are found in the text of upwards of thirty MSS., and in some of the earlier editions, and would seem to deserve the preference, on the ground of אָב in the singular occurring immediately before. The LXX., Arab., and Syr., however, have read הַקָּרָא the present textual reading." HENDERSON.—S. R. A.]

[2] Ver. 22.—On the exchange of the forms לֹא and לֹה comp. EWALD, § 142, c; 198, b; OLSHAUSEN, § 233.—In reference to אַף and רָפָה comp. Jer. vi. 14, coll. viii. 11; xix. 11; li. 9. The Masoretes approve of the Chethibh here, while they correct it in xix. 11, because here the vowel pronunciation is correct (1 Pers. with *He parag.*) but not in xix. 11.

[3] Ver. 22.—אָתָנוּ instead of אֲנַחְנוּ (Comp. NAEGELSB. *Gr.* § 10, 11, *Anm.* from אָת, comp. Isa. xxi. 12), and this instead of אֲנִי; comp. OLSHAUSEN, § 233 b; EWALD, § 198, b.

[4] Ver. 23.—["On the authority of thirty-six MSS. and others in the margin, two early editions, the LXX., Arab., Hexaplar, Syr., the Peshito, Aq., Symm., Vulg. הָכִין should be pointed הָכוּן in the construct." HENDERSON. In the rendering HENDERSON and NOYES follow the A. V.; BLAYNEY has "Surely hills are lies, the tumult of mountains;" HITZIG, "for a deception from the hills is the host of mountains;" UMBREIT, "Verily! a lie is become from the hills, the tumult of the mountains."—S. R. A.]

EXEGETICAL AND CRITICAL.

This strophe evidently consists of two parts, of which the first (ver. 18-19) treats of the participation of Judah in the prosperity promised to Israel, the second (vers. 20-25) of the conversion of both as one which satisfies all demands.

Vers. 18. **In that day** **an inheritance.** Reference to the last strophe. Comp. **at that time** ver. 17.—**together,** in the sense of heaping so that those are designated as *upon* one another,

CHAP. III. 18–25.   55

of whom we should speak as *together, with each other*, is frequent: Gen. xxviii. 9; xxxii. 12; Exod. xii. 9; xxxv. 22; Amos iii. 15; Job xxxviii. 32. We see also that על is to be regarded as a preposition from the following sentences where their coming in company is manifestly the result of their meeting together. The promise of a reunion of the exiles from Judah and Jerusalem, and their return in company to the land of their fathers is found also,—to mention only the principal passages, in Hos. ii. 2: Isa. xi. 11; Jer. xxx. and xxxi.; l. 4, 5; Ezek. xxxvii. 15–17.—It forms an essential element in the glorious picture of the future, which prophecy presents by the announcement of a glorious restoration of Israel to Canaan after long humiliation and dispersion. To the original passages Levit. xxvi. 42–45; Deut. xxx. 1–10; xxxii. 36-43 follows a long series of prophetic declarations, of which the most important are Ps. lxxii.; Isai. ii. 2-4; iv. 2-6; ix. 1-6; Chap. xxiv. sqq; lx. sqq; Jer. xxix. 10-14; xxx.,-xxxiii.; Ezek. xxxiv. 23-25; Joel iv. 16; Am. ix. 8; Ob. 17-21; Mic. iv. 5; Zeph. iii. 14-20; Zech. ii. 4, sqq. viii. 7 sqq; ix. 9 sqq. x. 8 sqq.—Comp. AUBERLEN, *der proph. Daniel*, S. 391 sqq.— HEBART, *The Second Visible Coming of Christ*, (*Die Zweite*, etc. Erlangen. 1850. S. 70, 84, etc.)

Ver. 19. **And I said ... behind me.** If above, in the concluding remark on the preceding strophe, we have correctly defined its relation to vers. 18-25, it follows that ver. 18 does not belong to the foregoing, and that vers. 19 and 20 are not connected as thesis and antithesis, as most modern commentators would have it. The reasons for this view are the following: (1) ver. 18 seems then entirely isolated. GRAF says: "Only in passing is a glance cast in this verse at the final destiny of Judah." But the destiny of Judah demands more than a passing glance. Either an elucidation concerning the fate of Judah must be interwoven with the contents of the preceding discourse, or Judah must be spoken of in appropriate measure in a special section. (2) According to the view which I combat, there is a hiatus between verses 18 and 19. With ver. 19, the discourse proceeds to an entirely new subject, the relation of which to the preceding can be designated neither by a separative nor by a connective particle. The Vau before אנכי accordingly appears not only superfluous, but interruptive. (3) If vers. 19 and 20 are so connected that the former declares the expectation cherished by Jehovah, the latter the sad non-fulfilment of this expectation, the discourse makes a spring from ver. 20 to ver. 21 which could not be more abrupt. No one would then expect the delightful continuation of the discourse after ver. 20. Suddenly and without preparation we are met by the description of Israel's penitence. In short, verses 19 and 20 do not then at all agree with what follows, and since they are equally severed from what precedes, they appear to be a wholly needless and interruptive interpolation. It will therefore be correct to attach ver. 19 closely to ver. 18, as a short but satisfactory description of the condition of the entire Israelitish people after their return to the land of their fathers. In the form of an objection, which is subsequently removed, ver. 20 then forms an appropriate transition to the second subject, concerning which, as remarked above, the prophet had to pronounce in this strophe. The emphatic אנכי, "I," on the one hand forms an antithesis to Israel an Judah in ver. 18, and on the other brings out the importance of the promise here given—Not a *man*, but *I*, Jehovah, declare this. אמרתי is neither future, as *ex. gr.* SEB. SCHMIDT supposes, nor is it a narrative preterite, so as to refer to a definite event in the past, as *ex. gr.*, ABARBANEL reads, referring it to the exodus from Egypt. It simply presents this declaration of God as an accomplished fact. It asserts that there is a divine decree of the afterwards designated import. But thus this import is absolutely guaranteed, for the Lord's word is true, and what He says is certain (Ps. xxxiii. 4). The strange addition, γένοιτο κύριε, which the LXX. make after καὶ ἐγὼ εἶπα, may be explained by the circumstance, as we may gather from THEODORET, that they understood כנא not of God but of the prophet, and since **I put thee among the children** could not possibly be uttered by the prophet, they supplied him with words *ex propriis*.— The explanation of this expression of reception among the children, agrees well with that view of the connection which has been rejected by us, although it is still strange even according to this view, that ver. 20 should pass over to another picture. We should expect that the Israelites, in view of the gracious purpose of God expressed in ver. 19, would be designated as disobedient children (comp. Isai. i. 2), and not as a faithless spouse. We render the expression with the CHALDEE, BUGENHAGEN, LUTHER, CLARIUS, GROTIUS, SCHMIDT, VENEMA, HITZIG in the sense of bestowing a rich paternal benediction. On the importance of such benediction, compare the remarks on ver. 16; KUEPER (S. 9), calls this a *benedictio vere theocratica*. Israel and Judah, according to ver. 14, having returned in small numbers must before all become a numerous people. The promise in ver. 16, made primarily to Israel, is here presented to the view of both.—VENEMA mentions, that they say also in Dutch, *jemant in kinderen setten*. Comp בְּשִׁית בֵּין in *salute ponere*, Ps. xii. 6.—**a pleasant land.** Comp. Ps. cvi. 24; Zech. vii. 14.—**a most glorious inheritance.** It is a question whether to derive צבאות from בוא or from צבי. Both are grammatically possible. Comp. NAEGELSB. *Gr. S.* 106; (OLSHAUSEN, § 145, 6; EWALD, § 186 e; § 55, e. Comp. צְבָאִים (Gazelles) 1 Chron. xii. 8; and צְבָאוֹת (in the same meaning) Song of Sol. ii. 7; iii. 5.—It is of no account that the form occurs elsewhere only as St. constr. from צָבָא (Exod. xii. 41; 1 Kings ii. 5), and that צְבִי in the sense of *decus* does not occur elsewhere in the plural, since for the sake of a play upon words the prophet might employ an unusual expression. The juxtaposition of the singular and plural to form a climax, is also, as is well known, not infrequent; Eccles. i. 2; Ezek. xvi. 7. Comp. NAEGELSB. *Gr.* § 61, 3. The decision is the more difficult since the meaning in both cases is the same (MAURER). Most commentators preferring the more normal form decide in favor of the derivation from צְבָא. Yet I would prefer the derivation from צְבִי. Since the juxtaposition of צְבָאוֹת צְבִי seems more pregnant and forcible than the flat and tautological צְבָאוֹת גּוֹיִם. Besides which the Holy Land is elsewhere called אֶרֶץ צְבִי, Ezek. xx. 6, 15; Dan. xi. 16, 41.—וָאֹמַר we translate: "And further I said," for from the first divine decree flows a second of this import, that Israel will not only receive but show himself worthy of receiving. That which Israel spoke before (ver. 4) in hypocritical pretence, will be presented in the future, which the Prophet has in view, in glorious reality.

Ver. 20. **But! Was ever woman faithless to her lover?... O house of Israel! saith Jehovah.** In these words the Lord Himself raises a protest against the promise given to Judah and Israel in verses 18 and 19. How shall such glory be imparted to this people, who have hitherto been distinguished only for their infidelity? אָכֵן is taken by many, ex. gr. FUERST (*Handwb. s. v.*) EWALD, (*Lehrb. S.* 273,) in a relative signification=*so as, entirely so as*. But there is no example of this meaning and it is not necessary that there should be here a particle of contingency or comparison. (Comp. Isai. lv. 9; coll. vers. 10, 11). We therefore take אָכֵן (which like אַךְ may from the meaning "*tantum*, only" obtain an affirmative as well as a restrictive sense) here=*but, however*, which meaning it undoubtedly has in Ps. xxxi. 23; lxxxii. 7; Isai. xlix. 4; Zeph. iii. 7. Since the prophet in this strophe has in view the period of re-united Israel, **Israel or house of Israel** is to be taken in these verses to 4, 2, not in the restricted sense of ver. 6 sqq. but in the wider sense mentioned. (Comp. Isai. i. 3, etc.)

Ver. 21. **A cry is heard on the hills.... forgotten Jehovah, their God.** With dramatic vividness the penitent people are now brought forward to refute the exception taken in ver. 20, in such a way that ver. 21 designates their appearance in general outlines, ver. 22 the call to the people to repent, repeated from ver. 14; and in the following verses it is shown by the *verba ipsissima* of the people, how they responded to this call.—**On the hills.** These high places which had formerly been the seats of wickedness (see ver. 2) are now the scenes of penitence, comp. vii. 29.

Ver. 22. **Return, ye apostate children... for thou art Jehovah, our God.** The same call as in ver. 14, from which we see that this passage is closely connected with that. The question; Will the people respond to the call? there obtruded itself. Here it is satisfactorily answered. It might be asked why the words "Return, etc," do not come before ver. 21. But this verse is only to describe the disposition of the people towards repentance, their general penitence. Israel was indeed formerly "faithless" (ver. 20), but now they acknowledge their sin and are able to obey the call, should it again be heard as before (ver 22, a) in a manner well-pleasing to God. (ver. 22, b-25)—**I will heal**, etc. The thought is from Hos. xiv. 5. In the connection of **heal** with the plural it seems to

be implied that the Lord will both pardon the single acts, and remove the evil root.

Ver. 23. **As certainly as the hills are false... Jehovah, our God.** Without *Dagesh forte* in נִּבְעוֹת would mean the priests' caps, since the word occurs in this sense only; Exod. xxix. 9; xxviii. 40; xxxix. 28; Levit. viii. 13. But what have these to do here? The Masoretes have therefore punctuated the ב with *Dag. forte*, in order thus to secure the meaning of "hills." Now the explanation of the כ prepares new difficulties. The ancient translators ignore this כ altogether, and yet take the rest in the sense of *colles*. The later commentators (if they do not with LUD. DE DIEU take הָרִים =*offerre, i. e. victimas*) either supply כְּ before הָרִים or alter הָמוֹן into הָמוֹן. Besides this they differ very widely in determining the meaning of הָמוֹן.— It seems to me that the prophet understood the word מִגְּבָעוֹת in the sense of "hills," and chose it for the sake of its secondary meaning. Although the word occurs in the Old Testament only in the sense of "priests' caps," yet "hills" was the original meaning from which the other was developed, the word being transferred on account of the hill-like shape of the caps. Now as *ex. gr.* the word for weapon in German (*Gewehr*) has gradually assumed the meaning of musket, but might be used in its original and more general sense in a manner intelligible to every German, so here the prophet has employed a word restricted by usage to a special meaning, in its original signification in such a way that at the same time he intended an allusion to the secondary sense. Not the hills are the deceivers, but the priests, of whom Elijah on this account slew a great number (1 Kings xviii. 40). In הָמוֹן which means *tumultus, strepitus*, there may be an allusion to the bacchanalian noise of the unchaste idol-worship. Comp. Am. v. 23—לַשֶּׁקֶר like לַשָּׁוְא has become an adverb and signifies *false, deceptive, useless*. (Levit. v. 24; xix. 12; 1 Sam. xxv. 21; Jer. v. 2; vii. 9; viii. 8; xxvii. 15; Zech. v. 4; Mal. iii. 5). אָכֵן is taken by the commentators both times in the affirmative sense. (iv. 10; viii. 8). It appears to me that this doubling includes also the idea of reciprocal relation (comp. פֶּה־בְּפֶה): as certainly as the hills are vanity and nothing, so certainly is Israel's salvation in Jehovah, their God.

Ver. 24. **Shame, however.. their sons and their daughters.** Not merely as vanity and nothing, but as positively injurious are the idols opposed to the real saving power of Jehovah. The Vau at the beginning of this verse corresponds especially to the last clause of ver. 23, as containing the main thought, and is accordingly adversative=*however*, as Hos. xi. 1. From 11, 13; Hos. ix. 10 we see that בֹּשֶׁת is here placed in parallelism with בַּעַל. KIMCHI remarks that in ancient names composed with בֹּשֶׁת the place of this word is afterwards supplied by בַּעַל. Hence for אִישׁ־בֹּשֶׁת 2 Sam. ii. 8; אֶשְׁבַּעַל 1 Chron. viii. 33. For יְרֻבַּעַל Judges vi. 32

CHAP. III. 18-25.   57

ירבשֶׁת 2 Sam. xi. 21. From all this we see that the abstract בֹשֶׁת is to be regarded primarily as an ironical synonym of בַּעַל, the chief deity. From what, however, is ascribed in this passage to בֹשֶׁת the prophet cannot have had merely Baal in mind but also the other idols. All these have from the youth not of the speaker, but of the people generally (comp. the golden calf, Exod. xxxii., and Baal Peor, Num. xxv.), devoured the substance of the fathers, in part immediately by sacrifices which were not due to them as to the Lord, in part mediately by the judgments which such apostasy brought upon the people.
Ver. 25. **Let us lie . . . the voice of Jehovah, our God.** As vers. 22-24 contain acknowledgment and confession, so ver. 25 contains shame and sorrow. As the penitent seats himself in dust and ashes (Job xlii. 6; Dan. ix. 3), so they casting themselves down in the feeling of their shame, would lie before the Lord, and as the penitent clothes himself in sackcloth (1 Kings xxi. 27: 2 Kings vi. 30; xix. 1, 2,) or veils his face (Exod. iii 6; 2 Sam. xv. 30), so would they, deeply feeling their disgrace, hide their countenance before the Lord (comp. the publican, Luke xviii. 13). The entire guilt which the people had incurred from their youth up (ii. 2; Hos. xi. 1) is according to the scale of Ps. xxxii. 5, to be expiated.

DOCTRINAL AND ETHICAL.

1. On ver. 21. Although Paul in Gal. vi. 4, 5, says that every one should prove his own work, that he may have praise in himself and not in another, and that every one will have his own burden, yet we read on the other hand that the people of Nineveh and the Queen of Sheba will in the day of judgment condemn the γενεά of Christ's contemporaries (Matt. xii. 41, 42; comp. ver. 27; 11, 21, etc.). The apparent contradiction is dispelled when we consider that Paul in the Epistle to the Galatians urges the absolute standard against those who desire to find in the faults of others a mantle for their own, that is, that every one will be judged above all and essentially according to that which he is in and of himself. Christ Himself, however, in the passages cited applies the relative standard to those who, in the blindness of their pride, believe themselves beyond comparison better than all others. To these it is said that a comparison may certainly be made, but that it will result to their disadvantage, since the guilt which they have incurred, notwithstanding the most favorable circumstances, will serve for a ground of mitigation for others, who have sinned in less favorable circumstances, (ἀνεκτότερον ἔσται, Matt. xi. 22, 24).

2. "*Erubesce Sidon, ait mare. Quasi enim per vocem maris ad verecundiam Sidon adducitur, quando per comparationem vitæ sæcularium atque in hoc mundo fluctuantium ejus, qui munitus et quasi stabilis cernitur, vita reprobatur.*" Gregor M. in Isidor. Hisp. *Vide* GHISLER. *S.* 289.

3. On vers. 12, 13. The grace of God is an open door to every one through which the finger of penitence, 1 John i. 8-10. "*Erranti medicina confessio—Cessat vindicta divina, si confessio præcurrat humana.*" AMBROS.

4. GHISLERUS. "*Deus sol hominis et homo sol Dei. Quod Deus sit sol hominis, indicatur eo, quod peccatores metaphora designati sint aquilonis. Ut enim ab aquilone sol sensibilis, ita a peccatoribus Deus, sol justitiæ longe est. Quod antem homo quodammodo sit et Dei sol, indicat ipsemet Deus, dum ait: reverttre aversatrix Israel et non avertam faciem meam a vobis (Vulg.). Significat enim ad hominem se habere ut heliotropium ad solem; convertente homine se ad Deum, convertit statim et se Deus ad illum; eoque non se avertente, nec Deus faciem suam ab illo avertit.*"

5. On ver. 14. "God in proof of his mercy keeps his covenant, which men have broken by their sins, as strictly and securely, as though they had never broken it. Ezek. xviii. 22." STARKE.

6. On ver. 15. *Donatur, fato non decidit arbore mysta.*

A teacher true never falls from a tree,
But comes by divine authority.

M. G. ALDRECHT. *Hierarch. Eccl. Cap.* 10.

7. On ver. 16. "The ceremonial law and custom must have an end, and the ark of the covenant, as only a shadow of good things to come, must also cease to be (Heb. x. 1). It is therefore only a rabbinical fiction, that people still derive consolation from the second book of Maccabees (ii. 5), as though the ark of the covenant were somewhere in a mountain and would eventually be found, for the true ark of the covenant, which is found again, is Jesus Christ, the true Messiah typified by the Ark." CRAMER. The manner in which Jeremiah here speaks of the ark of the covenant is moreover so extraordinary that we may apply to it the words of Matthew xvi. 17. Flesh and blood have not revealed it unto thee, but my Father in heaven. The ark at that time in the reign of Josiah was again regarded with the greatest reverence (comp. 2 Chron. xxxv. 3; III. Esd. i. 3, 4). What a divinely lofty and distant view must the prophet have had to be able to treat the ark as he here does, as something of small account!

8. The view that this prophecy was fulfilled by the return under Zerubbabel and Ezra is opposed by the fact (1), that not even the whole of Judah, not to speak of the whole of Israel then returned (of the latter a few at most: comp. HERZOG *Real-Enc.* XIV. *S.* 773; I. *S.* 651); (2), that not even Judah had then returned to the Lord, not to speak of the conversion of the heathen. Its fulfilment by the founding of the Christian church is contradicted by the fact, (1) that the reunion of Judah and Israel had not yet taken place, the latter people must still be regarded as unknown (comp. HERZOG, *Real-Enc.* I. *S.* 651; XVII. *S.* 284): (2) that Israel in general has rejected the Lord and refused to enter the Christian church (comp. Rom. xi.-xii.): (3) that the heathen have indeed begun to turn to the name of the Lord and to the Jerusalem that is above (Gal. iv. 26), but that this has taken place neither in such measure nor in such a manner that we can recognize in it the complete fulfilment of that which this passage declares of the conversion of all nations and the removal of their hardness of heart. We must therefore still wait for the complete fulfilment of this prophecy. The argument

of BERTHEAU in his essay, "The Old Testament prophecies of Israel's imperial glory in his own land," ("*Die Alttest., Weiss, etc.*" *In Jahrb. f. deutsche Theol.* IV. 2, 4; V. 3,) which he urges from the point of view that many prophecies remain unfulfilled, because men on their part have not fulfilled the required conditions, is not applicable here, for in ver. 20, sqq., it is expressly said that Israel will comply most satisfactorily with the single condition imposed by the Lord. (ver. 13).

9. On vers. 18 and 19. As the separation of the kingdom of Israel from the kingdom of Judah may be regarded as the type of the denominational divisions in Christendom, so the reunion here promised may be regarded as a type of all true union. This must always rest on a double, negative and positive, basis: (1) on the fundamental return of both from the false ground on which they have been standing (typified by the common exit of both tribes from the north country, the land of captivity): (2) on unreserved sincere devotion to the Lord, who is for both the only source of life and truth, (typified in the words "My father, wilt thou call me, etc." ver. 19). The result of this will be a condition of glorious prosperity in the church (typified in the first clause of ver. 19).

10. On vers. 20-25. The peculiarities of true penitence meet us plainly in this section: it proceeds from the inmost heart (the weeping supplication of the people, ver. 21, as well as their deep shame evince this, ver. 25). It is free from all false penitence, which proceeds merely from the feeling of the disadvantageous consequences of wickedness. Its principle is rather sorrow at having grieved God by the rejection of His holy love. This is intimated by the second clause of ver. 21. True penitence, finally, is made known by the honest fruits of repentance. These are here set forth in the words "I will heal your apostasies" ver. 22, and by the detestation of evil, and yearning for the Lord, which are expressed in vers. 24, 25.

HOMILETICAL AND PRACTICAL.

1. On ver. 11. "To what reflections should the declaration of Scripture give rise, that the divine judgment is determined by the comparison of men with each other? 1. We should reflect that it is impossible for us to institute this comparison with perfect justice ourselves. 2. We should therefore draw from comparison with others occasion neither for despair nor false comfort. 3. We should rather allow this comparison to be a motive to severe self-discipline.

2 On ver. 12. Reformation sermon by LOHE (7 *Predigten*. Nürnberg, 1834, *S.* 49). 1. The reformation was a return; 2. a return is necessary now; 3. it is now possible.

3. On verses 12 and 13, *God's call to repentance*, (a) its ground (I am merciful); (b) its object (to obtain grace); (c) its condition (acknowledge thy sin).

4. On ver. 15. (Text for an installation sermon). The evangelical pastorate; (a) its standard, (after my heart); (b) its task, (to feed them with doctrine and wisdom).

5. On vers. 16 and 17. The true worship of God. (John iv. 21-24). 1. It is not connected with any outward forms or ceremonies. 2. It consists, (a) in the direction of the inmost heart to God (assembling at the throne of the Lord), (b) in the evidence of this direction of the heart in a holy walk (to walk no more according to the thoughts of the wicked heart).

6. On vers. 18 and 19. The conditions of true union, 1. common return from sin and error (Judah and Israel come together from the north), 2. common return to the source of life and truth (the inheritance of the fathers—dear father!—will not depart from me).

7. On vers. 21 and 22. How does a nation worthily keep the yearly fast? 1. When it humbles itself before God in hearty repentance of its sins. 2. When it believingly hears the call of the Father of eternal grace. 3. When it heartily returns to the Lord, its God.—From an anon. sermon.

8. Vers. 21-25 (Text for a penitential discourse) True repentance. 1. Its form (crying and weeping, ver. 21). 2. Its subject—primary, forgetting God (ver. 21) and sinning against Him (ver. 25)—secondary, the destruction come upon us in consequence of the deception of sin, (ver. 23, sqq.). 3. Its object (salvation in God).—Comp. the fifth homily of Origen on Jer. iii. 21-iv. 8.—On ver. 22. Comp. the Confirmation Sermon of Dr. F. Arndt in his work, "The Christian's pilgrimage through Life" ("*Der Christen Pilgerfahrt*," etc. Halle, 1865) on the subject. "The gracious hours of life at and after confirmation."

---

4. *The call to return in the Present.*

IV. 1-4.

1   If thou returnest, O Israel, saith Jehovah,
    Return unto Me.
    And if thou puttest away thine abominations **out of my sight,**
    Then waver not,[1]
2   But swear 'As Jehovah liveth!'
    In truth and justice and righteousness,

CHAP. IV. 1-4.   59

So that the nations bless themselves in him,¹
And boast of him.
3 For thus saith Jehovah to the men of Judah and Jerusalem,
Break up your fallow-ground³
And sow not among thorns.
4 Circumcise yourselves to the Lord,
And take away the foreskin of your heart,
Ye men of Judah and inhabitants of Jerusalem;
Lest my fury break forth like fire,
And burn, and there be no quencher,—
On account of the wickedness of your doings.

TEXTUAL AND GRAMMATICAL.

¹ Ver. 1.—[BLAYNEY renders "thou shalt not be removed from before me." MOVERS and HITZIG also connect the words "out of my sight" with what follows: neque a facie mea oberraveris. HENDERSON and NOYES following DE WETTE, have "Thou shalt not be a fugitive (wanderer)." UMBREIT renders as in the text.—S. R. A].
² Ver. 2.—וְהִתְבָּרְכוּ בוֹ The Perfect with Vau consec., expresses intended result. Comp. NAEGELSB. Gr. §. 84, h. sqq. [The usual rendering is the simple future].
³ Ver. 3.—[BLAYNEY renders well "Break up your ground in tillage." The German Commentators have Brechet euch Neubruch for which we have no exact equivalent.—S. R. A].

EXEGETICAL AND CRITICAL.

The fundamental thought of the whole discourse (RETURN) is distinctly stamped on the head of this section. True and honest conversion is the indispensable condition of present life. All that the prophet has previously said, partly in severe rebuke, partly in friendly invitation, was to serve as an exhortation to procure an entrance into this life. If the people do not heed this exhortation, they fall inevitably under the just judgment of God.

Ver. 1. If thou returnest .. waver not. These words point back to iii. 7 and 10. The call "Return to me" according to iii. 7, had been addressed to Israel in vain. Judah on the other hand, according to iii. 10, had been obedient to the call "Return," but not to the "to me," for their return was not hearty but hypocritical. We have shown above that by this is meant the reform of Josiah. A hypocritical return is the same as one which is not to the Lord, for the hypocrite avoids indeed the forms in which his sins have hitherto been manifested, but he does not turn positively with his heart to the Lord. The Lord does not therefore allow the conversion occasioned by the reformation under Josiah to be regarded as unto Him. And hence the prophet thus addresses the people: if you would answer the call "Return to me" (iii. 7), it must not be done by a return "with falsehood" which is no return to me at all, but by such a conversion as may be truly thus designated.—Comp. Hos. vi. 14. An example of such a conversion, "not unto the Lord" is also the reformation of Jehu, 2 Kings ix. x. Comp. especially 2 Kings x. 31. In the reformation of Josiah, Judah did outwardly put away their abominations from God's sight (2 Kings xxiii. 4 sqq.) but they were far from directing their hearts fixedly and alone to God. Instead of this they wavered, wishing partly to serve the Lord and partly also their idols. Comp. Zeph. i. 5. How ambiguous the conduct of the people must then have been is clear from 2 Kings xxii. 14 sqq.; xxiii. 25–27; 2 Chron. xxxiv. 22–28. Comp. HERZOG, Real-Enc. VII. 36.—In translating נוּד by "waver"

I appeal to the radical signification of the word, "to oscillate," by virtue of which it is used of the waving of a reed (2 Kings xiv. 15), the flapping of wings (Ps. xi. 1; Prov. xxvi. 2), of the wandering of a fugitive (Gen. iv. 12) and of the shaking of the head, (Jer. xviii. 16; Ps. xliv. 15). From the meaning of commiserari which it has in several places (Jer. xvi. 5; xlviii. 17, etc.) it is evident that the word is also capable of being transferred to the sphere of spiritual relations.

Ver. 2. But swear . . . and boast of him. In swearing by Jehovah in truth, justice and righteousness is included not only that they swear the truth (Lev. xix. 12; Num. xxx. 3; Jer. v. 2 coll. Matt. v. 33) but also that they swear by Jehovah alone and not also by idols, as according to Zeph. i. 5. they then did. To refer בּוֹ to Israel, and then to assume either a change of person or a quotation from Gen. xviii. 18, (coll. xii. 3; xxii. 18; xxvi. 4; xxviii. 14) or to read בָּךְ (as ez. gr. E. MEIER) is arbitrary. The reference to God is perfectly justified by the connection. The moral course of Israel is to win over the heathen to God, who is the source of that power by which they pursue this course (1 Pet. iii. 1, 2), as on the other hand the sin of Israel is designated as causing the heathen to blaspheme (Rom. ii. 24, coll. Ezek. xxxvi. 20, 23). As in Isai. lxv. 16, so also here הִתְבָּרֵךְ בּוֹ signifies to recognize God as the source of all blessing, and therefore to seek all blessing only through him. "And boast of him," refers to the possession of the desired blessing. For they justly boast in a dispenser of blessing, who causes those who bless themselves in his name to appear really blessed. Comp. Isai. xli. 16; Jer. ix. 22, 23; Ps. xxxiv. 3; cv. 3.

Ver. 3. For thus saith Jehovah . . . sow not among thorns. כִּי here is not causative but explicative. The words return unto Me, waver not and swear by Jehovah in truth are so explained in what follows as to show plainly that the prophet has in view the hypocritical half-heartedness with which the people submitted to the reformation of Josiah. Break up your fallow-ground is from Hos. x. 12. Israel is not to sow on the unemployed field of his heart, but to break it up, as is done with wild land, which is cleansed from weeds only by deep and repeated ploughing. It was just in this that the people failed in Josiah's reformation. It was a sowing among thorns. Comp. Luke viii. 7. Ver. 4. **Circumcise yourselves to the Lord .. your doings.** Circumcision to the Lord is opposed to that which is done only in accordance with outward ordinance or custom. The latter is done merely on the body, the former on the heart also, of which sin is the real defiling foreskin. Comp. Levit. xxvi. 41; Jer. ix. 25, coll. Exod. vi. 12 (iv. 10); Jer. vi. 13. The expression "take away the foreskin of your heart" is a reminiscence from Deut. x. 16; xxx. 6. Comp. KUEPER, S. 10.—**Men of Judah and inhabitants of Jerusalem**, a frequent formula in Jeremiah (Comp. xi. 2, 12; xvii. 20; xviii. 11; xxv. 2; xxxv. 17, etc.) in which a certain prerogative of the citizens of Jerusalem is recognizable. Comp. viii. 1; xiii. 13; xix. 3.—**My fury**, etc. Comp. Am. v. 6; Jer. vii. 20.—The words **on account of the wickedness**, etc. (coll. xxi. 22; xxiii. 2; xxvi. 3; xliv. 22) are from Deut. xxviii. 20. The prophet in these words prepares the way for the transition to the second main division. Israel obeys not the call, the fury of the Lord must therefore break forth. The manner in which this will take place is described in section second.

DOCTRINAL AND ETHICAL.

1. On ver. 1. Mere turning from earthly things without positive returning to God, the pole of the soul, is not true repentance. So long as the prodigal son, after the loss of all earthly goods, had not formed the resolution of returning to his father, he was not yet in a penitent condition. A man, who should denounce this or that sin, but yet not devote himself wholly and decidedly to God, would thus give no guarantee of the genuineness or permanence of his conversion. Comp. what is said of following Jesus, Matt. xix. 16; Luke ix. 59 sqq. For repentance to be honest, it must have the right object, i. e. it must be towards God.—CRAMER.
2. On ver. 2. Swearing by Jehovah involves the acknowledgment of His deity. For no one would swear by Him who was not convinced that He is the witness of truth and the avenger of falsehood. But when one swears by others he robs God of His glory and gives it to idols: Isa. xlii. 8.
3. On ver. 3. Rooting out weeds from the field of the heart is the most difficult part of repentance. Many would receive the gospel gladly if they were permitted to leave the thorns and sow the seed of the gospel among them. Comp. Matt. vi. 24; 1 Ki. xviii. 21.
4. On ver. 4. We Christians also know of a double circumcision, a bodily and a spiritual, which however are not related to each other, as the bodily and spiritual circumcision of Judaism. For according to Col. ii. 11 baptism corresponds to conversion as the περιτομὴ ἀχειροποιητός, as the ἀπέκδυσις τοῦ σώματος τῆς σαρκός. Thus the sacrament of baptism is the spiritual and bodily basis of the περιτομὴ τῆς καρδίας, which is spoken of in Phil. iii. 3, coll. Rom. ii. 29; vi. 1 sqq.

HOMILETICAL AND PRACTICAL.

1. ORIGEN treats this passage in his peculiar style in his fifth homily on Jeremiah. Vide S. 149 and 164 sqq., ed. LOMMATZSCH.
2. On ver. 3. "We Christians also, like the Jews, love to sow under the hedges. We allow the divine word to be strewn on the field of our heart, we hear and read God's word on week-days and Sundays, but we also allow the thickets of evil passions and sinful habits to grow on."—HOCHSTETTER, 12 *Parables* (12 *Gleichnisse*, etc., S. 10).
3. True repentance consists (a) in decided turning away from evil (not sowing among the thorns but breaking up new ground); (b) in decided turning to God (positive devotion to God alone, ver. 1, so that He alone is served and worshipped, ver. 2).

SECOND DIVISION

CHAP. IV. V.–VI. 26.

Threatening of punishment for neglecting to return.

The call, "return" was unheeded. The prophet therefore now proceeds to announce the punishment. He does this in three sections: in the first (chap. iv.) *he announces the approaching calamity; in the second* (chap. v.) *he shows particularly its causes in the moral corruption of the people; in the third* (chap. vi. 1–26) *he recapitulates the main thought of the discourse, adding to the repeated proof of the incorrigibility of the people, a repeated admonition and a threatening of still severer judgments*

Description of the expected judgment (CHAP. iv. 5–31).

1. *This is described as future under a triple emblem* (iv. 5–18).

a. The first emblem: the Lion.

IV. 5–10.

5 Declare it in Judah and publish it in Jerusalem,
And speak—and blow the trumpet in the land,
Cry with a loud voice and say:
Assemble yourselves, that we may go into the fortified cities.
6 Raise banners towards Zion,
Flee! stand not!
For I am bringing calamity from the North,
And great destruction.
7 A lion cometh up from his thicket,¹
And a destroyer of nations hath broken up.
He is come forth from his place
To make thy land a desert:
Thy cities shall be desolate,²—without inhabitant.
8 For this gird on sackcloth, lament and howl!
For the heat of Jehovah's anger hath not turned from us.
9 And it shall come to pass in that day, saith Jehovah,
The heart of the king shall fail and the heart of the princes,
The priests shall be amazed and the prophets full of horror.
10 And I said: Ah Lord Jehovah,
Surely thou hast prepared³ deception for this people and Jerusalem,
Saying: "ye shall have peace,"
And yet the sword reacheth even to the soul.⁴

TEXTUAL AND GRAMMATICAL.

¹ Ver. 7.—סֻבְּכוֹ with *Dag. forte,* to emphasize the sharpening from סְבָךְ (EWALD, § 255, d.) or סֹבֶךְ (OLSHAUSEN, § 155, b.) The word is ἅπαξ λεγ. Comp. the related forms from סָבַךְ Isai. ix. 17; x. 34; Gen. xxii. 13; Ps. lxiv. 5.

² Ver. 7.—הִצָּֽיְתָה is certainly Kal from נָצָה, which must here be taken in an intransitive sense. Comp. ix. 11; Isai. xxxvii. 26; 2 Kings xix. 25.

³ Ver. 10.—הִשֵּׁאתָ with לְ as in xxix. 8; 2 Kings xviii. 29.

⁴ Ver. 10.—[*Or* even to the life, as HENDERSON, *etc.*—S. R. A.]

EXEGETICAL AND CRITICAL.

Ver. 5. **Declare it in Judah ... fortified cities.** The prophet speaks, and indeed as the mouth of God. This is seen from the 'אנכ, "I." Ver. 6. The persons addressed are primarily those who dwell on the border, who are to inform those in the interior, even as far as the capital, of the invasion of the enemy. That which is declared is not the command to blow the trumpet, and to cry "assemble," *etc.* For why should not those first addressed themselves at once cry to their next neighbors, "assemble," *etc.?* Accordingly all that comes after the general sentence, "declare—Jerusalem," is only introductory to "assemble." Thus it is evident that the Chethib יִתְקְעוּ is not incorrect, and the Keri, which is followed by the ancient commentators and many MSS. is therefore unnecessary. "Assemble," *etc.*, should have come after the first אִכְרוּ. But the prophet (1) according to well-known linguistic usage adds an accompanying circumstance paratactically, (2) he distributes the command to cry into three parts, of which the two first refer to the form, the last to the contents.—On the construction comp. xiii. 18; 1 Sam. ii. 3; NAEGELSD. *Gr.* § 95, g. *Anm.*

Ver. 6. **Raise banners towards Zion** . . . **great destruction.** The signal is to be so arranged that it will indicate to the inhabitants the direction of flight. הֵעִיז only in the Hiphil =*to fly to* (Exod. ix. 19), and to make flight, *i. e.* to flee (thus only besides here in vi. 1; Isa. x. 31).—**From the north** points back to i. 13, 14. Compare the remarks there made.

Ver. 7. **A lion cometh up** . . . **without inhabitants.** The enemy is here represented by the emblem of a lion as in xlix. 19; l. 44, 17. —**Without inhabitant.** Comp. ii. 15, and the remarks thereon.

Ver. 8. **For this gird on** . . . **turned from us.** This last sentence points back to ii. 35. The people had expected a return of God to graciousness on the ground of their hypocritical return under Josiah.

Ver. 9. **And it shall come to pass** . . . **full of horror.** After the prophet in ver. 8 has summoned them to general lamentation, he describes the effect of the calamity on those who are called by their position to provide means and ways of defence; they are helpless, and lose their presence of mind. לֵב in the sense of *understanding, ex. gr.* Prov. xxviii. 26; xv. 32; Hos. iv. 11; vii. 11; Jer. v. 21. Comp. DELITZSCH, *Psychol.* IV., § 12.—**Shall be amazed.** Comp. Ezek. iv. 17; Job xvii. 9; xviii. 20.

Ver. 10. **And I said** . . . **even to the soul.** The prophet here declares what impression was made by the denunciatory prophecy upon himself, after he had previously in ver. 9 described the impression which its fulfilment will make on the chiefs of the people. This denunciatory prophecy does not at all harmonize with that earlier and exceedingly glorious one in ch. iii. 12-25. This was correctly perceived by JEROME, who says: "*Quia supra dixerat: in illo tempore vocabunt Jerusalem solium Dei*, etc. (iii. 17), *et nunc dicit: peribit cor regis* (ver. 9), *turbatur propheta et in se Deum putat esse mentitum; nec intelligit, illud multa post tempora repromissum, hoc autem vicino futurum tempore.*"—Following the example of THEODORET very many commentators refer **prepared deception** to the false prophets, coll. 1 Kings xxii. 22. But is it conceivable that a true prophet like Jeremiah would have traced back false prophecy so directly to the Lord? Comparison with 1 Pet. i. 11 renders it conceivable that Jeremiah may himself have been deceived as to the difference of the times.

---

b. The Second Emblem: the Tempest.

IV. 11–13.

11 About this time it will be said to this people and Jerusalem,
   A hot wind of the bare heights in the deserts
   Comes thence against the daughters of my people—
   Not to winnow and not to cleanse.
12 With full cheeks comes a wind to me from those.
   Now will I also contend with them.
13 Behold, as clouds he ascends,
   And as the stormwinds his chariots,
   Swifter than eagles are his horses.
   Woe to us, for we are destroyed!

EXEGETICAL AND CRITICAL.

Ver. 11. **About this time** . . . **not to cleanse.** As the invasion of the lion-like enemy, so also the approach of the destructive desert-wind is to be announced in Jerusalem. The prophet alludes to the custom of signalizing those who are threatened by a hurricane or flood. דֶּרֶךְ (*Acc. loci.* xxxix. 4) seems also to point to this. צַח (besides here also in Isa. xviii. 4; xxxii. 4; Song of Sol. v. 10) if we compare the words radically related to it (צָחָה Isa. v. 13; צְחִיחָה Ps. lxviii. 7; צְחִיחִים Neh. iv. 7; צַחְצָחוֹת Isa. lviii. 11), appears to unite the meanings *calidus, candidus, aridus,* and to designate the brilliant clearness of the air heated by the hot-wind. So JEROME (*ventus urens*), AQUILA (*ventus fulgoris*), SYMMACHUS (*v. æstus*). On the position of צַח between the *nomen regens* and *rectum,* comp. NAEGELSD. *Gr.,* § 63, 4 f.—**Bare** heights. Comp. iii. 2, 21. The bare rocky mountains of the eastern desert are meant, over which the dry, hot east wind blows (קָדִים the "wind of the wilderness," Jer. xiii. 24). Comp. WINER, R-B-W., s. v. Winde. The expression is found also in xii. 12.—**Not to winnow,** etc. It is not one of the winds, which is favorable to human industry, but a hostile, destructive wind.

Ver. 12. **With full cheeks . . . contend with them.** כְּלֹא here is fundamentally the same as in ver. 5 and xii. 6. The idea of "full" we are accustomed to apply to wind only as expressed in the translation. As **hot wind** denotes the quality so **full** denotes the quantity—**from those** refers to **bare heights.** The Lord says, **the wind comes to me,** because it is in His service. לְ is *Dat. commodi.*—**I also** refers to ii. 5, 29. The prophet of Israel according to these passages really contended with the Lord. Comp. the remarks on ii. 29. The sense is this: after they have presumed to contend with the Lord (or, to use His pretended fault as a pretext of revolt, comp. xliv. 18), He contends with them, *i. e.* He punishes them, and His instrument is he, who is understood by the wind. Comp. i. 16.

Ver. 13. **Behold as clouds . . . we are destroyed.** The prophet still retains his emblem in the region of the air, but he modifies it. The total impression of the hostile masses is now compared with threatening storm-clouds, the chariots in the rapidity of their motion and power of their impetus are like the storm-blast, the riders are like swift eagles. The prophet seems to have had Hab. i. 8 generally in mind. Comp. KUEPER, *S.* 76.

---

c. The Third Emblem: the Keepers.

IV. 14–18.

14 Wash thy heart from wickedness, Jerusalem,
   In order that thou mayest be delivered.
   How long do tny sinful thoughts tarry within thee?
15 For a loud call sounds from Dan,
   A message of misfortune from Mount Ephraim.
16 Announce it to the nations!
   Behold, call it out over Jerusalem:
   Watchmen [Besiegers] are coming from a distant land,
   They raised their cry over the cities of Judah.
17 For like keepers of a field are they over her from all sides,
   For against me hath she rebelled, saith Jehovah.
18 Thy walk and thy works bring this upon thee;
   This is thy wickedness, that a bitter thing (comes upon thee),
   That it reaches even to thine heart.

EXEGETICAL AND CRITICAL.

The first emblem was from the animal kingdom, the second from the region of the air, the third is taken from the sphere of human life. The third appeals most strongly to the moral consciousness of the people; this calamity is held up before them as the punishment of their sin, and acknowledgment and renunciation of this as the only means of escape.

Ver. 14. **Wash thy heart . . . tarry within thee?**—**Wash** [Cleanse]. Comp. ii. 22.—Comp. the beginning and end of the strophe; the idea of **wickedness** forms the frame-work.

It is quite unnecessary to take הָלִין, with VATABLE and others, as causative. Comp. NAEGELSB. *Gr.* § 105, 4 *b.* אָוֶן from אָנָה in the sense of *sin,* while אָוֶן, ver. 15, means *calamity.* Comp. Gen. xxxv. 18; Deut. xxvi. 14; Ps. lv. 4.

Ver. 15. **For a loud call . . . Ephraim.** It is high time to comply with the admonition contained in ver. 14 (comp. "how long," *etc.*), for the news is already received of the approach of the avenger. The prophet's mention of Dan and Mount Ephraim is a confirmation of the view expressed concerning **from the north** in i. 14. Comp. the remarks there made.

Vers. 16 and 17. **Announce it to the nations . . . saith Jehovah.** הַזְכִּירוּ verbally: cause כִּי to the nations, that is, cause that those reflecting upon it are deeply impressed by the significance of the fact. From the meaning, to penetrate, to bore in (comp. FUERST, *Handwb.*), is developed the meaning of *to remember,* which is the common one, *to consider, to reflect* (Lam. i. 9; Ps. ciii. 14; Job vii. 7). This call to the nations is made only incidentally, not with a friendly purpose, but only to denote the greatness and importance of the event. The invasion of this enemy is something so great that it cannot be cried out loud enough, and this the rather since the nations round about Israel are implicated with them. Comp. ch. xxv.—It is therefore unnecessary to follow HITZIG as he follows the LXX. KIMCHI and others, in taking ל =from or E. MEIER and others in rendering גוים = tribes (of Israel).—The business of watchmen, keepers of a field, is usually to protect from robbery and violence. But the prophet has such keepers in mind who do not remove their gaze from him to whom it is directed, as, ex. gr., those who beset a fox, a weasel or a polecat, so that the animal may either perish in his hole or be killed when he comes out. In short the prophet here means the same thing as he expressed in i. 15 by setting seats before the gates. Comp. 2 Sam. xi. 16, שְׁמוֹר אֶל־הָעִיר; Jer. v. 6; vi. 25.—These raised their cry, etc. It is announced to Jerusalem, that the cry of these keepers has already sounded over the other cities of Judah. Jerusalem alone is still in the power of the enemy. Hence it is also said in ver. 17 that they are over her from all sides.—As in the beginning of the strophe, ver. 14, the exhortation to repentance as the only means of escape is prominent, so in ver. 17 b and ver. 18 is ungodliness as the self-inflicted cause of the punitive judgments.

Ver. 18. **Thy walk and thy works ... reaches even to thy heart.** Comp. ii. 19.— Both this parallel passage and the parallelism in the verse itself prove that hemistich 2 is a subjective sentence (comp. NAEGELSB. Gr. § 109, 1). The two sentences with **for** represent the subject, **this thy wickedness** is the predicate. The bitter thing which comes upon thee is nothing more than thine own wickedness, here developing its own true nature.—The conclusion of the strophe reminds us of ver. 10, and in such a way as to show that the prophet intended a similarity in diversity.

---

2. *The Prophet Hears and Sees the Enemy Present.*

IV. 19-26.

19 My bowels, my bowels! Cramp[1] in the chambers[2] of the heart!
    My heart palpitates! I cannot be silent,
    For the trumpet's sound thou hearest,[3] my soul,
    The cry of battle.
20 Blow upon blow is reported,
    For desolated is the whole land;
    Suddenly my huts are desolated,
    In a twinkling my tents.
21 How long shall I see the banner,
    Hear the sound of the trumpet?
22 For my people are foolish, they know me not;
    Silly children are they and undiscerning:
    They are wise to do evil,
    But doing good they understand not.
23 I look at the earth and behold—desolation and emptiness!
    And up towards heaven, and its light is gone.
24 I look at the mountains and behold they quake,[4]
    And all the hills are shaken.
25 I look and behold, man is gone,
    And all the birds of heaven are fled.
26 I look and behold, the fertile field has become a waste,
    And all its cities are desolated[5]—
    Before Jehovah, before the fury of his anger.

TEXTUAL AND GRAMMATICAL.

[1] Ver. 19.—אוֹחוּלָה. The form of the Chethibh אוֹחִילָה is a grammatical anomaly and therefore certainly incorrect. The Keri reads אוֹחִילָה. This however would mean: *I wait, expect* (2 Sam. xviii. 14; Mic. vii. 7), which does not well suit the connection. The reading אָחִילָה or אָחֻלָה which is expressed in the LXX, and is found in very many MSS. and editions (STEPH., JOS. ATHIAS, *Bibl. Mant.*) should therefore be preferred. חוּל (or חִיל, comp. FUERST, s. v.) is *to twist one's self, to quiver with pain*, grief or terror. Comp. v. 3; Ezek. xxx. 16.—As to the construction we may (a) divide after מֵעַי, אֲחוּלָה לִבִּי קִי בִי הוֹכָהֵל (so GRAF, or (b) after כְּיָי, הוֹכָה־לִי אֲחוּלָה אָחֵרֵשׁ (see HITZIG, E. MEIER), (c) מֵעַי, לִבִּי, אָחֵרֵשׁ לִבִּי. I would give the preference to the last division, since חוּל declared of קִירוֹת־לֵב (the expression here

only) designates very appropriately the *cramp* of the heart, while לֵב הוֹמֶה evidently denotes the *palpitation* of the heart. The cohortative form in אָחוּלָה as in אַשְׁמִיעָה, ver. 21, is not to be insisted on. Comp. NAEGELSB. *Gr.* § 69, 3 *a*.
² Ver. 19.—קִירוֹת is the accusative of more exact definition. Comp. NAEGELSB. *Gr.* § 70 f.
³ Ver. 19.—שָׁמַעַתְּ, 2 Pers. fem. Comp. ii. 20, 33; iii. 4, 5. EWALD, HITZIG, E. MEIER, read with the Cod. Regiomont. 1. שִׁמְעַת, which is unnecessary. [Comp. GREEN'S *Heb. Gr.* § 86, *b*.]
⁴ Ver. 24.—עָשִׂים. On the absence of the subject comp. NAEGELSB. *Gr.* § 97, 1, *a Anm*.
⁵ Ver. 26.—נִצְּתוּ Niph. from נָתַץ. Comp. Nah. i. 6. LXX.: ἐμπεπυρισμέναι, confounded with יָצְתוּ, ix. 9.

EXEGETICAL AND CRITICAL.

This entire strophe describes the desolation of the country from the standpoint of the *present*. The prophet places himself in spirit in that mournful future, and describes in the liveliest colors what he hears, sees and feels, as one who is present.
Ver. 19. **My bowels . . . cry of battle.** LXX.: τὴν κοιλίαν μου ἀλγῶ. So also the authors of the Syro-Hexapla. HITZIG has "my belly." The prophet in these and the following verses describes in a most drastic style the physical sensation which is produced by the immediate perception of the calamity.—Passages related in subject are Isa. xvi. 11; xxi. 2-4; Jer. xlviii. 36.—**I cannot be silent** (comp. Hab. i. 13: Job xli. 4) expresses that the prophet would relieve the inward pain, which he has just described, by speech. He does this by enumerating the occurrences which have so excited him.—The expression: **hearest thou, my soul**, seems to intimate that the prophet heard it not with the outward but the inward ear.
Ver. 20. **Blow upon blow is reported . . . my tents.** The exposition, which, following the Chaldee and Syriac, takes נקרא for נקרה (destruction meets destruction) is not correct, because the prophet in vers. 20 and 21 mentions what he *hears*, while in ver. 23 sqq. he relates what he *sees*. If, moreover, we consider that the prophet is here speaking of messages or signals, which *report* disasters, we see that the existence of a middle point is presupposed, to which these reports of misfortune proceed. We shall not then err, if we refer ver. 20 to the laying waste of the country surrounding the capital.
Ver. 21. **How long shall I . . . trumpet.** הַנֵּס the signal, ver. 6. Although this is *seen* it is mentioned among the things which the prophet *hears* because it also brings news, or a message.

Ver. 22. **For my people are foolish . . they understand not.** This verse contains the answer to the question of the prophet, *how long?* Still long, is the answer of course, for the people are still as they were. So KIMCHI.—With Hemist. 2 comp. ii. 8; Mic. vii. 3.
Vers. 23-26. **I look at the earth . . . fury of his anger.** רָאִיתִי four times repeated shows plainly that the prophet would here render expressly prominent what he has seen, in antithesis to vers. 19 and 20, where he narrates what he has heard. But there is also a climax in the progress from the one to the other. While that which the prophet *hears* is only the herald and preliminary stage of the main catastrophe, in vers. 23-26 he portrays the condition of the country after the occurrence of this catastrophe. In spirit he beholds in the place of the once so fruitful land a dismal waste, over which the heavens veil themselves in mourning, and with which even lifeless and unintelligent creatures sympathize.—Ver. 23, reminds us of Gen. i. 2, 14, and therefore presupposes the existence of this passage. The land has, as it were, returned to chaos. Comp. Isa. xxxiv. 11.—**The fruitful field a waste** [lit., *the* Carmel *the* desert], a free reminiscence from Isa. xxxii. 15; xxix. 17. That **Carmel** here denotes not the mountain, but the fruitful field (comp. ii. 7), follows (*a*) from the connection, which declares the desolation not of a small strip, but of the whole country, (*b*) from **all its cities**, which evidently cannot be referred to that single mountain but only to the whole land. The article before **Carmel** and **waste** has a general significance, not *a* waste, but *the* waste had the fruitful field become, that is, the genus **Carmel** had passed over into the genus **desert**. Comp. NAEGELSB. *Gr.* § 71, 4.—**Before**, *etc*. Comp. xxiii. 9; xxv. 37.—On the general subject compare Joel ii. 10; iv. 15; Nah. i. 5; Isa. xiii. 10, 13; Ps. xviii. 8.

---

8. *The Judgment is Irrevocably Determined, but it aims not at Absolute Destruction.*

IV. 27–31.

27 For thus hath Jehovah spoken:
 The whole land shall be waste,
 But I will not utterly make an end of it.
28 For this the whole land keeps lamenting,
 And the heaven above wears the garment of mourning;
 For this namely, that I have spoken and determined,¹
 And I repent not, nor draw back from it.
5

29 Before the tumult of the horsemen and archers
The whole city is fled,
They are in their hiding-places, up on the rocks;
The whole city is abandoned, not an inhabitant therein.
30 But thou, destroyed one,[2] what art thou doing?
That thou clothest thyself in purple,
That thou puttest on cloth of gold,
That thou rendest thine eyes with paint?
In vain dost thou beautify thyself;
Thy lovers despise thee, they seek thy soul.
31 For I hear a cry like that of a parturient,[3]
The call of anguish, like one who bears for the first time:
The voice of the daughter of Zion,
Who panteth and spreadeth forth her hands:
Woe is me, for my soul succumbs[4] to the murderers!

TEXTUAL AND GRAMMATICAL.

[1] Ver. 28.—E. MEIER reads יִפָּתַח ? instead of וּפֹתַח. But the Masoretic reading being the more difficult has the presumption of genuineness.
[2] Ver. 30.—[NOYES translates correctly ad sensum, "destined to perish."—S. R. A.]
[3] Ver. 31.—חוֹלָה, Part. like בּוֹסִים in Zech. x. 5, קוֹמִים in 2 Ki. xvi. 7, etc. FUERST s. v. חוּל; EWALD, § 151, 6.
[4] Ver. 31.—[HENDERSON: My soul fainteth because of murderers; NOYES, more freely: I am dying of murderers.—S. R. A.]

EXEGETICAL AND CRITICAL.

The theme of this strophe is contained in ver. 27. This has two parts: 1. The destruction is founded in an irrevocable divine decree. This is the main point which is expressed still more emphatically, vers. 28, 29, and in ver. 30, etc., placed in the light of a contrast (what can Israel's feeble attempts effect in opposition to the divine counsel?). 2. The second point, "but I will not utterly make an end," is briefly stated and not further discussed, but is for this purpose twice repeated in the course of the prophecy, v. 10, 18.

Ver. 27. **For thus hath Jehovah spoken ... make an end of it.** The certainty of the statement in the previous strophe is found in the fact that Jehovah has thus spoken.—**I will not utterly**, etc., is, as we have said, a briefly stated parenthetical thought, which is only to give a correct limitation to the declaration of the first clause. Comp. Levit. xxvi. 44.

Ver. 28. **For this the whole land keeps lamenting ... draw back from it.** Comp. Hos. iv. 3, whence the words הָאָבֶל הָא are taken.—**This** refers to the following **I have spoken.** The mourning posture of the earth and heavens mentioned in ver. 23 sqq. is here designated as the result of a divine decree. Not by chance, nor by the power of idols, did it take place, but by the power of the Lord. It should moreover be remarked that this strophe forms the transition to the following section, in which also the cause of the judgment is spoken of, but in another sense. While here only the immediate cause, the *causa efficiens*, of the calamity is mentioned, the prophet in what follows goes more deeply into the matter and designates the corruption of the people as the immediate, deepest provocative cause.—**That** is a repetition of **for**

this. LXX., διότι ἐλάλησα καὶ οὐ μετανοήσω, ὥρμησα καὶ οὐκ ἀποστρέψω ἀπ' αὐτῆς. We must first take **spoken** independently. Then the external announcement which is made to men through the prophet, is set over against the inner cause, which has a positive (**determined**) and a negative side (**repent not**). The last point is designated also by **nor draw back from it**, in order that the prophet may connect this declaration of God with the same made by Israel (iii. 7 sqq.; iv. 1).

Ver. 29. **Before the tumult ... not an inhabitant therein.** This verse seems to interrupt the connection. Yet it may be justified as a brief and condensed description of the calamity which has been described at length in the previous strophes, and only hinted at in ver. 28. We might regard it as the explanation of **from it,** with which ver. 28 closes. On the neutral rendering of this *Vide* NAEGELSB. *Gr.*, § 60, 6 b.—It is not necessary to render (with GRAF and others) כָּל־הָעִיר=**every city.** It is, as the rule requires, the *whole* city. But the prophet understands the whole city, supposing this to be the general fate of all the cities. This collective rendering explains also **therein** in the plural.—עָבִים are obscure hiding-places. בְּפִים comp. Job xxx. 6.

Ver. 30. **But thou, destroyed one ... seek thy soul.** שָׁדוּד (comp. נְטוּיֵ רָגֶל, Ps. lxxiii. 2, *inclinatum aliquid pedes mei*) is to be rendered as neuter: Thou, as good as destroyed, a thing devoted to destruction. The expression is contemptuous. *Vide* NAEGELSB. *Gr.*, § 60, 4. [GREEN's *Gr.*, § 275, 5].—It can neither mean: *if thou art destroyed*, for then Israel can no more paint; nor: *if thou shalt be attacked*, for the word does not mean *to attack.* (Comp. שָׁדֻדָה Ps. cxxxvii. 8). The prophet has in view the present attempts of Israel to procure assistance by coquetting with foreign nations (comp. ii. 18, 36, 37), which are foolish in opposition to the decree of Jehovah, solemnly announced in ver. 28, according to which Israel is already destroyed. — **Thine eyes with paint.** The effect of paint is to make the eyes look not only more fiery, but larger. Comp. Henzon's *Real-Enc.*, *Art. Schminke.* XIII. *S.* 607 [Smith, *Dict.* II., 657]. — 2 Kings ix. 30; Ezek. xxiii. 40.

Ver. 31. **For I hear a cry ... my soul succumbs to the murderers.**—For refers to seek thy soul. On this account Israel cries: Wo is me, I succumb to the murderers. 31 *b.*— לִי הֹפֵעַ *constr. prægnans* ; my soul is weary, *i. e.* as one who succumbs to murderers. Comp. Naegelsb. *Gr.*, § 112, 7. [Green, 156, 1].

DOCTRINAL AND ETHICAL.

1. On ver. 10. It is not here a matter for consideration, how God may be said to deceive men (comp. 1 Kings xxii. 20; Job xii. 24; 2 Thess. ii. 11), for it was only the opinion of the prophet, who here interrupts the discourse revealed to him by the expression of a subjective view, just as Paul in 1 Cor. vii. 10, 12, 25, 40, inserts his view of the λόγος κυρίου.

2. On ver. 14. Aristotle (*De partibus animal.* II. 4) and Pliny (*Hist. nat.* XI. 37) remark that the heart alone of all the internal organs will not bear any injury. The latter says "*solum cor viscerum vitiis non maceratur, nec supplicia vitæ trahit; læsumque mortem illico affert.*" The heart also in a spiritual sense will not bear the least injury, as the fall shows. Yet though every sin is a death-germ, a poison, yet all poison is not equally rapid in its effects. Bernhard of Clairvaux says in his *Sermo de triplici genere cogitationum nostrarum* (*sub fin.*) as follows: "*Et primum quidem genus cogitationum otiosarum scil. ad rem non pertinentium lutum est, sed lutum simplex, id est non inhærens, nec fœtens, nisi forte diutius immoretur in nobis, et per incuriam ac negligentiam nostram in alterum genus cogitationum vertatur, quod quotidie experimur. Dum enim otiosa tamquam minima spernimus, ad turpia atque inhonesta dilabimur. Secundum vero cogitationum genus non lutum simplex, sed viscosum ac limosum est. Num tertium quidem sic cavendum est, non tamquam lutum aut limus, sed tamquam immundissimum ac fœtidissimum cœnum.*" He explains what he understands by this *tertium genus* in the words: "*Dico autem cogitationes illas immundas penitus et fœtidas, quæ ad luxuriam, ad invidiam et vanam gloriam pertinent, cæteraque vitia detestanda.*"—He further says of the conflicts with sinful thoughts: "*Quid ergo agendum, cum limosa cogitatio mentem subierit? Plane exclamandum nobis est cum sancto Jacobo: Ruben, primogenito meus, non crescas, ascendisti enim cubile patris tui* (Gen. xlix. 3). *Ruben enim carnalis atque sanguinea illius modi concupiscentia est, quæ tunc cubile nostrum ascendit, cum non solum memoriam tangit cogitatione, sed et ipsum voluntatis stratum ingreditur et polluit prava cogitatione.*" Ghisler.

3. On ver. 22. (They are wise to do evil, but do not understand well-doing.) The Israelites are here designated as children of the world, for it is the manner of the world to be wise in worldly matters, but foolish in spiritual, as our Lord says (Luke xvi. 8) the children of this world are wiser in their own generation than the children of light in theirs, and Paul (1 Cor. ii. 14) says the natural man perceiveth nothing of the Spirit of God, for it is foolishness to him, and he cannot know it, for it must be spiritually discerned.—The blind man understands nothing about color. Every one is at home in his own element. But this is the greatest misery that the world knows, that man, the image of God, is not at home in His house, but in the Devil's, and that the greatest labor the world knows, scarcely suffices to bring him back into his Father's house.

4. On ver. 27. How wonderfully do the anger and love of God here touch! How proportionate appear both! How is one the limit of the other! God does not so love that He cannot be angry; and He is not so angry that He cannot love. He leaves room for His anger in order that justice may be preserved and the sinner reformed. Thus His anger is also guided by love, yea, in a certain sense it is a manifestation of love. Comp. Schöberlein, *Grundlehren des Heils, S.* 50, 51. "Anger is the energy of love towards the sinner, the expression, namely, of its pain, that he himself has become untrue to his better self, and he who cannot be angry has no hearty love for this true I of another. . . . For the very reason that God in holy self-preservation places Himself in opposition to him, man is not really forsaken of God, but love is still with him in the might of its anger." Jer. x. 24; xxx. 11; xlvi. 28; Isai. xxvii. 8.

HOMILETICAL AND PRACTICAL.

1. The first eight verses of this chapter are part of the text of the fifth homily of Origen (the whole text is Jer. iii. 21—iv. 8).

2. Förster remarks: "*ex versu* 31 *haberi potest concio in funere mulieris, quæ in partu, vel post partum obiit.*"

3. True repentance is 1. a true return from evil (not a sowing among remaining thorns, not a merely external circumcision, but a circumcision of the heart and removal of abominations); 2. a true return to God (right and holy swearing, as a symptom of right and holy disposition); 3. a source of blessing for ourselves and others (thou shalt not be exiled—the heathen shall be blessed in thee).

4. On ver. 10. Warning against false peace. This is 1. a lie, for men say there is peace when the sword reaches even to the soul; 2. a misfortune, for it will disappoint the heart of those who cherish it.

5. On ver. 22. Since Scripture distinguishes a wisdom that is from above from a wisdom that is from below (James iii. 13-18), the question arises, wherein consists the difference between the two? 1. The wisdom from below is a wisdom in evil doing (*a.* unbelief, *b.* destruction, *a.* of self, *β.* of others—consequently absolute folly); Wisdom from above is wisdom in well-doing (*a.* faith, *b.* observing God's word in love—consequently blessing).

II. Demonstration of the justice of the judgments by the enumeration of their causes.

(Chap. V. 1–31.)

The prophet enumerates these by first denouncing the universal corruption, especially in reference to the want of אֱמוּנָה. *Vers. 1–6 he shows that truth and faith have entirely disappeared from public life;* vers. *7–9 that* אֱמוּנָה *is wanting in conjugal relations;* vers. *10–18 that none of this is any longer found in the sense of faith in God;* vers. *19–24 he describes the idolatry resulting from unbelief;* vers. *25–29 the deception and rude violence connected therewith;* vers. *30, 31 finally he comprises all in a brief survey, in which the main points of this sad condition are set forth. The section contains six strophes of unequal length.*

1. Universal want of truth and faith in public life.

V. 1–6.

1 Run through the lanes of Jerusalem and see,
   And ascertain and search in her streets,
   Whether ye find one, whether there be one,
   Who doeth right and asketh after truth—
   And I will pardon her.
2 And though they say "As Jehovah liveth,"
   Even thus they swear falsely.
3 Jehovah, thine eyes, look they not for fidelity?
   Thou hast smitten them, but it pained them not.
   Thou destroyedst them,—they refused to receive correction;
   They made their faces harder than a rock,
   They refused to return.
4 And I said: These are only the poor!
   They are stultified![1]
   For they know not the way of Jehovah,
   The judgment of their God.
5 I will go[2] to the great and speak with them,
   For they know the way of Jehovah,
   The judgment of their God.
   Yet they have broken the yoke among them,
   They have torn asunder the cords.
6 Therefore the lion from the forest slayeth them,
   The wolf of the deserts[3] rendeth them,[4]
   The leopard lurks by their cities;
   Every one who goes out is torn in pieces;
   For many are their misdeeds, great their apostasies.[5]

TEXTUAL AND GRAMMATICAL.

[1] Ver. 4.—נוֹאֲלוּ from אוּל used only in Niphal. Num. xii. 11; Isai. xix. 13; l. 36. The meaning is to become אֱוִיל, fools, to be stultified, to act foolishly.

[2] Ver. 5.—אֵלְכָה לִּי, Comp. NAEGELSB. *Gr.* §112, 5 *b*.

[3] Ver. 5.—[DE WETTE, HENDERSON, NOYES render: an evening-wolf; BLAYNEY has: a wolf of the plains.—S. R. A.]

[4] Ver. 6.—שְׁדָדָם for שֹׁדְדָם (Prov. xi. 3, Keri). Comp. EWALD, §251, *c.;* OLSHAUSEN, §243, *a.* [GREEN, *Gr.* §141, 1.].

[5] Ver. 6.—[BLAYNEY, NOYES, HENDERSON render: their apostasies (rebellions) are increased.—S. R. A.]

EXEGETICAL AND CRITICAL.

Ver. 1. **Run through the lanes** ... **I will pardon her.** This verse contains the theme not merely of this strophe, but in a certain degree of the whole chapter. For the statements here of the universality of the corruption apply not only to the moral deficiency which is denounced in this strophe, but to all the sins of the people afterward enumerated. And in the second place the lack of honesty is the root of all the rest.—

Run through, comp. Am. viii. 12; Zech. iv. 10.—**her streets,** comp. Gen. xviii. 23 sqq.—**right—truth.** Since the prophet uses these two words in conjunction with each other, since in ver. 2 the unreliableness of the oath sworn in Jerusalem forms the contrast to the *truth* demanded, since further this moral deficiency is first designated as the most striking, manifesting itself in all the lanes and streets of the city, this being followed in the ensuing strophes by the more special sins against *truth*, we must understand the former word of "right, justice" (comp. Gen. xviii. 19; Exod. xxiii. 6; Job viii. 3) as the basis of all trade and intercourse, the guarantee of all security of life and property, but the latter as "truth and faith," without which no public life can exist. The asker after truth cannot be he, who seeks it in *others*, for why should he in such a deficiency? but one who seeks it for its own sake, that he may have it and practise it himself.

Ver. 2. **And though they say.... swear falsely.** There may have been many different kinds of swearing in use (comp. Matth. v. 34 sqq.). The formula "חַי was at any rate regarded as the most sacred and binding. But even the oath thus made was broken.—לָכֵן. The passages which are adduced for the meaning "nevertheless, yet" (Isai. vii. 14; x. 24; xxvii. 9) are uncertain. We must therefore retain the original meaning (in reference to such a condition, this being the case)=*even thus*. The expression of identity;—an oath by Jehovah and a false oath are with them the same thing.

Ver. 3. **Jehovah, thine eyes.. refused to return.** The explanation of HITZIG (are not thine eyes true, reliable, do they not see correctly? Ps. xvii. 2) does not suit the connection. What ground would the prophet have for opposing such a supposition, as that the Lord had erred? It is evidently declared that the Lord seeks *truth*, in contrast with the declaration in ver. 1 that among the Israelites none asks after truth. After in ver. 2 he had shown by a striking example, to what a degree truth and faith were lacking in this people, he shows in ver. 3 how contrary this was to the will of the Lord. For (*a*) the Lord seeks אֱמוּנָה, (as to the sense comp. Ps. liii. 3; as to the construction the לְ here is used after a verb of motion to be supplied, as it frequently is, after such actual verbs, instead of אֶל, where the idea not of "into" but of "up to" is to be expressed; 1 Sam. x. 26; 2 Sam. xix. 9; Ruth i. 8, *etc.*); (*b*) the Lord has sought by severe and manifold chastisements to bring the people to אֱמוּנָה, but in vain. Comp. ii. 29 sqq. From which it is clear how the Lord regarded this quality. It is on this account that this idea stands at the head of this section, as its fundamental thought, as will also be seen in the ensuing explanation of the single strophes.—**In they refused to return** we have the fundamental thought of the entire discourse (see on iii. 1 sqq.).

Ver. 4. **And I said: these are only the poor ... the judgment of their God.** The prophet interrupts his address to the people by communicating an objection which he himself made to the Lord. It is thus presupposed that the prophet was not at the moment of speaking first made acquainted with the judgment of the Lord concerning the moral condition of the people, as contained in vers. 1-3, but that he was previously aware of the divine purpose, so that he had time to go and make investigations among the higher circles of the people, the result of which he presents in ver. 5. **These are only the poor; poor** is the subject, **these** is the predicate: it is only the poor to which the previous description applies.

Ver. 5. **I will go to the great.. torn asunder the cords.—With them.** Comp. i. 16; ii. 35; iv. 12.—**Yet they.** The particle אַךְ stands here also in a restrictive sense. It is as though the prophet would say: I also really went; only the success did not meet my expectation, they had, *etc.* Comp. Deut. xviii. 20; 1 Sam. xxix. 9.—The great were the worst. They had burst all bands asunder. Comp. ii. 20.

Ver. 6. **Therefore the lion ... great their apostasies.** The prophetic perfect—the prophet beholds the future as though it were past. Comp. NAEGELSB. *Gr.* § 84, g.—**The wolf of the deserts.** There are two explanations of this. 1. The Chald., Vulg., Syr., after Hab. i. 8; Zeph. iii. 3 render the evening-wolf (coll. Ps. civ. 20). To this is opposed (*a*) the parallelism with **from the forest,** (*b*) the plural; since this never occurs elsewhere as the plural of עֶרֶב, nor is it at all here in place. Therefore most commentators take (2) עֲרָבוֹת as the plural of עֲרָבָה, *the steppe, desert: the desert-wolf.*—**For many,** comp. xxx. 13, 14.—On the subject-matter comp. Exod. xxvi. 22.

---

2. Their infidelity in marriage, in marriage with Jehovah as in human marriages.

V. 7-9.

7   What reason[1] have I to pardon[2] thee?
    Thy children leave me and swear by that which is no God.
    And I bound them in allegiance,[3]
    But they committed adultery
    And rushed[4] into the harlot's house.

8 Fat stallions,[5] dissolute are they;
Every one neighs after his neighbour's wife.
9 Should I not punish such as these? saith Jehovah;
Or should not my soul avenge itself on a people like this?

TEXTUAL AND GRAMMATICAL.

[1] Ver. 7.—לָוֹת אֵי can only mean grammatically: in reference to what? why? [GREEN, *Gr.*, § 75, 2.]—לָמָּה comp. NAEGELSB. *Gr.*, § 17, 3; § 53, 1; EWALD, § 326, *a*. OLSHAUSEN, 222, *e*. [GREEN, § 231, 4. *a*].

[2] Ver. 7.—אֲסָלוֹחַ (for which the Keri has אֶסְלַח as in ver. 1) certainly did not, as HITZIG supposes, arise from לִסְלוֹחַ, but the ancient form (ROSENM.) is retained as being the more solemn (NEUMANN). Comp. OLSH. § 238, *a*. *Anm.* [GREEN, *Gr.*, § 125, 1].

[3] Ver. 7.—אוֹתָם אַשְׁבִּיעַ וָ. Many Codices and Editions, as given by DE ROSSI, read אַשְׂבִּיעַ. By far the majority of the translators and commentators follow this reading: LXX., Vulg., Chald., Syr., Arab., JEROME, THEODORET, RASCHI, KIMCHI, LUTHER, CALVIN, BUGENHAGEN, OECOLAMP., FÖRSTER, SEB. SCHMIDT, MUENSTER, GROTIUS, VENEMA, the English Bible, J, D. MICHAELIS, ROSENMUELLER, EWALD, UMBREIT, MEIER. The former reading is adopted, after the example of some of the Rabbins, only by ZWINGLI, CH. B. MICHAELIS, GAAB (=*earnest petition, adjurare*,) HITZIG (divine assistance in human marriage) MAURER, NEUMANN (*and I made them swear*: namely, *falsely*—a judgment of obduracy. Jer. vi. 9), GRAF. [BLAYNEY, NOYES and HENDERSON follows the former. HENDERSON; though I supplied them abundantly.—S. R. A.]

[4] Ver. 7.—יִתְגֹּדָדוּ for which the LXX. and Codd. 578, 575 read, according to DE ROSSI יִתְגֹּרָרוּ, κατελύοντο, *diversabantur* is used as in Mic. iv. 14 in the sense of: to penetrate sharply, to rush in, which comes easily from the radical meaning *incidere*. [Others render: gather.]

[5] Ver. 8.—Chethibh מוּזָנִים, Keri מְיֻזָּנִים; the former Hoph. from יָזַן, the latter Pual from יָזַן. Neither of these roots occurs in Hebrew. The form of the Keri can be brought only by a wide and circuitous process to afford a tolerable meaning: יָזַן is regarded as the primitive root of אָזַן (*to weigh*, hence מֹאזְנַיִם); the Part. Pual would then—*weighed*:—it is however taken as—*provided with* ponderibus (*strong genitals*), probe vasati.—It is simpler to retain the Chethibh. יָזַן from which מוּזָן, *cibus, alimentum* (Gen. xlv. 23; 1 Chron. xi. 23) has also in the dialects the sense of *nourish* (comp. Dan. iv. 9), סוּסִים מוּזָנִים are therefore well-nourished, fat horses. The word is perhaps chosen in allusion to זוֹנָה. מַשְׁכִּים has been variously explained (=מַשְׁפִּים by the Rabbins; מַשְׂכִּים, *trahentes, i. e., genitalia, emissarii*, by Jerome, the Chald., etc.; Ewald reads מַשְׂכִּים which according to the Arabic is said to denote "lewd," etc.). The simplest derivation is that from שָׂכָה which indeed does not occur in Hebrew, but yet seems assured by the dialects and by שָׁגָה in the sense "to err, to rove" (ii. 23). So most of the recent commentators.

EXEGETICAL AND CRITICAL.

1. **What reason .. into the harlot's house.** This strophe is an exact parallel to the preceding. As the beginning of the first strophe (ver. 1) presupposes a request for forgiveness, so does ver. 7. There it was: when you find one, who asks after truth, I will pardon. Here it is: How can I pardon? Thy children have forsaken me. There the chief reason for not pardoning was the lack of truth in public life. Here, indeed, the word אֱמוּנָה is not mentioned, but the substance is the same, only in a different, more restricted sphere. The breach of conjugal fidelity, first in a theocratic and then in a human sense, is also a proof of the lack of fidelity. As finally ver. 6 ends with a threatening of punishment, so does ver. 7. The three, 7-9, thus form a whole, complete in themselves, a tableau after the usual type of the strophes of this prophet.—**and swore**, etc., corresponds exactly to ver. 2. There their breach of fidelity was rebuked, because they swore *falsely* by Jehovah,—here, because they swore by those who were no gods (comp. ii. 11; Deut. xxxii. 17, 21).—**And I bound them**, etc. I believe that the difficulty in this sentence is solved if we transpose the paratactic mode of speech into the syntactic: *and although* I had allowed them to swear (had bound them) by oath and allegiance) yet they committed adultery. The form of the word does not contradict this view, as GRAF supposes. We must not, however, think that this allowing to swear refers to the restoration of the Jehovah-cultus, effected by Josiah's reformation. For although that refor-

mation, begun in the 12th year of Josiah, and ended in the 18th (2 Chron. xxxiv. 3, 8), as frequently remarked, did not result in an honest return, yet it is not to be supposed that Jeremiah, during the period to which this discourse certainly belongs, had to complain of public idolatry. In saying "thy children have forsaken me and sworn by no gods" the prophet has in view not the events of that period, but of the whole past history of the people. In the course of this history, from the Exodus onward, it often enough happened that the people fell into idolatry, and were received again by the Lord into covenant with Him. Comp. *e. g.*, the repeated apostasies in the wilderness (Exod. xxxii.; Numb. xxv.), and the renewal of the covenant in Arboth Moab (Deut. xxix. 1); further, the continuance of the idolatrous cult, even after the capture of the Holy Land, and the repetition of the covenant under Joshua (Josh. xxiv. 13, sqq). With reference to this and other facts of the past (*e. g.*, 1 Sam. vii.; 1 Kings xviii.): Jeremiah may well say: "thy children forsook me . . . and I let them swear, and they committed adultery," etc., which according to our syntactic mode of expression is equivalent to: "although after their apostasy, to guard against another, I bound them by oath and allegiance, yet still again they committed adultery." Comp on this paratactic mode of expression the remarks on iii. 8 and NAEGELSBACH *Gr.*, § 111, 1, *Anm.* This explanation combines these advantages, that (*a*) it is supported by the more difficult and critically, more secure reading,—(*b*) it agrees with the grammar, and (*c*) with the connection. For in the latter respect it is clear that the prophet very suitably opposes the idol-oaths to the Jehovah-oath, and thus develops a chain of proofs of the faithfulness of God, and the unfaithfulness of the people, which place the latter in the clearest light.— **Rush into the harlot's house.** That these words have a double sense, passing imperceptibly from the religious to the physical sphere of thought, is evident from a comparison of what precedes and follows. The justification of this mode of expression is found in the well-known commingling of unchastity with the idolatrous nature-worship. Comp. HERZOG, *Real-Enc.*, Artt. *Astarte* and *Baal* [SMITH, *Dict.* I., 123, 145].— The *harlot's houses* are accordingly, if not exclusively yet preferentially the idol-temples, so far as these were at the same time places of spiritual and carnal adultery. Comp. HERZOG 1. 199.

Ver. 9. **Should I not punish . . . such a people as this.** This verse is repeated, ver. 29 and ch. ix. 8. As already remarked, its contents denote the conclusion of a strophe.

3. The Treachery of Unbelief.

V. 10–18.

10 Scale her walls[1] and destroy,
But make not utterly an end of her!
Hew off her branches,
For they are not Jehovah's.
11 For they have been faithless towards me,
House of Israel and house of Judah, saith Jehovah.
12 They have denied Jehovah, and said:
"He is not—and calamity will not come upon us;
Nor sword and famine shall we behold.
13 And the prophets are become wind
And the word is not in them:
So will it happen to *them*."[2]
14 Therefore thus saith Jehovah, the God of hosts:
Because ye speak this word,
Behold, I make my word fire in thy mouth,
And this people wood, and it shall devour them.
15 Behold, I bring upon you a people from afar,
O house of Israel, saith Jehovah.
A mighty nation it is, an ancient nation it is,
A nation whose language thou knowest not,
And understandest not what it speaketh.
16 Its quiver is like an open sepulchre,—
They are all heroes—
17 And it devours thy harvest and thy bread.
They devour thy sons and thy daughters,—
It devours thy sheep and thy cattle;
It devours thy vine and thy fig-tree,—
It destroys thy fortified cities,
In which thou trustest, with the sword.
18 But even in these days, saith Jehovah,
I will not make an utter end of you.

TEXTUAL AND GRAMMATICAL.

[1] Ver. 10.—שָׁרוֹת (not to be confounded with שָׁרוֹת, *waves*, Ezek. xxvii. 25) occurs here only. עָל denotes the idea of "walls" in general, as in Hemistich 2, of the walls of a vineyard (comp. Isai. v.). A wall is elsewhere שׁוּר Pl. שׁוּרוֹת, which moreover occurs only in Job xxiv. 11. The Plural שָׁרוֹת is formed like כִּים from יוֹם, רָאשִׁים from רֹאשׁ, עָרִים from עִיר (comp. OLSH. § 151, *Anm.*). עָלָה with בְּ is not, as HITZIG asserts, to mount *on* something. The idea of the preposition is most variously modified by the connection, so that it denotes *into* (1 Kings xii. 18; 2 Kings xix. 28; Jer. xlviii. 18); *upon* (Deut. v. 5) *through, over* (Ezek. xiii. 5) *etc.* To read with E. MEIER שְׁדֵרוֹתֶיהָ is therefore unnecessary and already forbidden by עָלוּ.

※ Ver. 13.—["This sentence is left out in the LXX, the Syriac and the Arabic, but retained by the Vulg.: *Hæc ergo eveníent illis*—These things shall therefore come to them. This meaning the original will hardly bear. The reference seems to be to the prophet's becoming wind, being so proved by the event." Note by Eng. Ed. of CALVIN.—S. R. A.]

EXEGETICAL AND CRITICAL.

That these verses form a strophe is seen not only from the unity of the contents, but also from the concordance of the commencement and the close. The whole strophe is only a picture in detail of the brief sketch in ver. 10 a, "destroy, but not utterly."—It is further evident that the fundamental thought of the strophe depends on ver. 1; that the people are wanting in אֱמוּנָה is clear from the fact that they deny Jehovah, and consequently do not believe the word of His prophets.

Ver. 10. **Scale her walls . . . for they are not Jehovah's.** The image of a vine in an unwalled vineyard suggests the expression.—The phrase **for they are not Jehovah's** involves the idea of depravation. Comp. ii. 21.

Ver. 11. **For they have been faithless toward me . . . saith Jehovah.** The threatening of punishment repeated in a new form follows the fundamental declaration "Israel has been faithless towards the Lord." The prophet says this of both kingdoms, though the kingdom of Israel was no longer in existence. We see that he still has always in view the entire past history of the people. Comp. the remarks on וְאַשְׁרִיעַ at ver. 7.—**Faithless** (comp. iii. 7 sqq.) is evidently in antithesis to **truth**, vers. 1 and 3. It is a word of general signification, and would not in itself afford a new, specific element. It is therefore more particularly defined in what follows.

Ver. 12. **They have denied Jehovah . . . shall we behold.** It is here declared that they injured the **truth** in such a manner by their faithlessness, that they virtually denied the existence of Jehovah.—**have denied**, Josh. xxiv. 27; Isai. lix. 13. Comp. Prov. xxx. 9. The sense of this is explained unmistakably by **He is not.** If Jehovah is not, there is no possibility of a judgment to be effected by Him.

Ver. 13. **And the prophets . . . so will it happen to them.** It is the necessary consequence of Jehovah's non-existence that the word prophesied in His name is regarded as nothing, or as wind. When it is said, the prophets are become wind, the reference is of course not to their persons, but only to their prophetic ministry: *qua* prophets they will prove to be mere windbags. הַדִּבֵּר might certainly be rendered as a finite verb (comp. Hos. i. 2) and the article with the signification of *Nota relationis* (Gen. xxi. 3; Isai. lvi. 3; Josh. x. 24; 1 Chron. xxvi. 28; xxix. 17; EWALD, § 331 *b*; NAEGELSB. *Gr.*, § 71, 5, *Anm*. 3). [GREEN'S *Gr.* § 245, 5 *b*.] The sense would then be: he who speaks is not in them, that is, what they say, they say entirely of themselves. But דִּבֵּר might also be a nominal form (*ad f.* פֶּקַח) although this does not occur elsewhere. (*Vid.* FUERST, *s. v.*). The meaning would then be: *the speaker, the prophetic spirit*. The LXX.: λόγος κυρίου. Both are grammatically possible, the sense in both cases

being the same.—**So will it happen to them.** As they threaten us, so may it happen to themselves; let their empty threatening fall back upon themselves.

Ver. 14. **Therefore thus saith Jehovah . . . and it shall devour them.** Provoked by the bold declaration of unbelief in the word of the prophet, vers. 12, 13, the Lord here puts in the mouth of His prophet an emphatic repetition of the denunciatory prophecy, which from i. 13 onwards forms the focus of his prophetic announcement for the proximate future. Because Israel will not believe the word of the prophet, this word is to be equipped with the highest energy of a real active force. Comp. i. 9, 10.—The sudden change of person in **in thy mouth** should not offend. Comp. ver. 19, and NAEGELSB. *Gr.*, § 101, 2 *Anm*.

Vers. 15–17. **Behold I bring upon you . . . with the sword.** This passage has its root in Deut. xxviii. 49 sqq. Comp. Isai. v. 26; Hab. i. 6; Am. vi. 14; *Vid*. KUEPER, *S*. 12, *etc*.—**from afar.** Comp. iv. 16.—**House of Israel** is here used as a common name, ii. 26; iii. 20, 21, 23; iv. 1, *etc*.—The prophet heaps all the predicates on the people appointed to inflict the punishment which might cause them to appear terrible in the highest degree to the Israelites; they are coming from a distance, all sympathetic disposition to spare is therefore distant from their hearts; they are an ancient people (אֵיתָן of streams = unconquerable, ever-flowing, Deut. xxi. 4; Ps. lxxiv. 15,—of rocks, mountains, mountain-fastnesses = firmly founded, immovable, Numb. xxiv. 21; Mic. vi. 2; Jer. xlix. 19—designates firmly-rooted, impregnable power;—גּוֹי מֵעוֹלָם designates ancient nobility and the hard-hearted and ruthless pride called forth by it); further, they speak a foreign, unintelligible language (from Deut. xxviii. 49): their quiver is on account of its form compared with an open grave—that the quiver has not a receptive but an aggressive relation may have been overlooked by the poet.—All the necessaries of life will be devoured by the enemy (the devouring of the children seems to be based on a reminiscence of Deut. xxviii. 53, where, however, it is said, that the Israelites will devour the flesh of their own children. Comp. KUEPER, *S*. 12, 13;—moreover the prophet may have taken אָכַל in the more general sense, (comp. x. 25);—the fortified cities, in which Israel trusted (Deut. xxviii. 52) shall be destroyed (Mal. i. 4) with the power of the sword (*sword* as in the phrase "fire and sword" being employed for warlike implements generally, comp. Lev. xxvi. 6).—What people it is which is called to accomplish this, the prophet is not yet aware. Comp. the remarks above on i. 13 sqq. If he had known the name of the people, why should he not have mentioned it? To think of the Scythians because they once made an incursion through Palestine, because there is a Scythopolis in the valley of the Jordan (comp. HERZOG, *Real-Enc.* XIV. *S*. 170), is absurd. We can at most suppose that the prophet borrowed from the Scythian invasion some tints for the coloring of his picture. Moreover the whole description applies also to the Babylonians. These especially, according to Gen. x. and xi., might be regarded as an ancient people, even if we assume from Isai. xxiii. 13 that the Chaldeans were a younger branch grafted into the old stock. [HENDERSON:—"The antiquity ascribed to the invaders has special respect to the Chaldeans, a nation originally inhabiting the Carduchian mountains and the northern parts of Mesopotamia, but who had immigrated into the Babylonian territory, where they had a settlement allotted them: and being, like all mountaineers, distinguished for their bravery, doubtless composed the most formidable part of the invading army. See my comment on Isai. xxiii. 13. From its being affirmed that the Jews would not understand the language of this people, it follows that after they left their original abodes, they must have retained their native tongue, which was in all probability the mother of the present Kurdish,—a language totally different from any of Semitic origin, but showing much affinity with the ancient Persic."—S. R. A.]

Ver. 18. **But even in those days ... an utter end of you.** Comp. iv. 27 and ver. 10, and the remarks on the latter passage.—**Make an end** is decidedly connected with the accusative, Nah. i. 8; Neh. ix. 31;—with בְּ Jer. xxx. 11; xlvi. 28—decidedly with אֵת="with" in this passage;—when it occurs elsewhere: Jer. xxx. 11; xlvi. 28; Ezek. xi. 13; xx. 17; Zeph. i. 18; it is uncertain whether אֵת is a *Nota Accus.* or a preposition.

4. Infidelity from blindness of heart and ingratitude.

V. 19–24.

19 And it shall come to pass, when ye say:
For what cause doth Jehovah our God all these things to us?—
So shalt thou say to them:
As ye have forsaken me, and served strange gods in your land,
So shall ye serve strangers in a land that is not yours.
20 Announce it in the house of Jacob,
And publish it in Judah:
21 Now hear it, ye people, foolish and without understanding,
Who have eyes and see not, ears and hear not!
22 Will ye still not fear me? saith Jehovah,
Or will ye not tremble before me,
Who have placed the sand for a boundary to the sea,
As an everlasting barrier, which it will not pass?
And though they rage, they can do nothing,—
And though they roar, its waves, they come not over it!
23 But this people have an apostate and rebellious heart;
They have revolted and are gone.
24 And say not in their hearts:
We will fear Jehovah, our God,
Who giveth rain, the early and the latter rain in its season,
Who secureth to us the weeks as harvest-tide.

EXEGETICAL AND CRITICAL.

The main object of this section (chap. v.) is to present before the people the *causes* of this punitive judgment, as is especially evident in the beginning of this strophe. For the question (ver. 19): Why doth the Lord all this to us? would then refer to the whole, if vers. 14 to 17 did not present the principal object in the prophetic perspective. This question is therefore only a turn, in order to proceed to the main purpose of the section from another side. As, however, according to ver. 1–3, the lack of אֱמוּנָה is the chief cause of the judgment, so also in this strophe it is only a new species of this which is adduced: apostasy to the idols in consequence of mad blindness, which recognizes not Jehovah as the Almighty Creator, and hence denies Him the thanks which are due to Him as the Author of the most precious gifts of nature. The strophe falls into two parts: 1. Cause of the punitive judgment, ver. 19 (forsaking of Jehovah and idolatry); 2. Cause of this forsaking a double one: (*a*) being without heart (vers. 20–22); (*b*) an apostate and rebellious heart (vers. 23 and 24).

Ver. 19. **And it shall come to pass** ...

that is not yours.—On the change of the person (הָאֹמְרוּ—וְאָמְרָה) *vide supra*, on ver. 14. Vers. 20 and 21. **Announce it in the house of Jacob ... ears and hear not.—House of** Jacob frequently designates the whole people (*e. g.*, in Numb. xxiii. 7; Deut. xxxii. 9; Jer. x. 25; Am. vi. 7), but here, as elsewhere (*e. g.* Isai. ix. 7; xvii. 4; Mic. i. 5), the kingdom of Israel, partly for the sake of the antithesis to Judah, partly on account of vers. 11 and 15. This in reality exists no longer as such, but ideally it is still ever present to the spirit of the prophet, and indeed with the more justice since its constituent parts were still in existence, though as *membra disjecta*. Observe that in chap. iii. Jeremiah sharply and emphatically distinguishes Israel and Judah, because he is speaking of the past and the distant future; in ch. iv. he uses in ver. 1 the conjoint appellation, but in what follows, having the present in view he turns to Judah and Jerusalem only (vers. 3, 4, 5, 6, 10, 11, 14, 16, 31); in ch. v. he still addresses Jerusalem in ver. 1, but in what follows (vers. 11, 15) the entirety of the people is more prominent in his mind, quite naturally, since he has to present the causes of the judgment predicted by him, which carry him back into the remote past. He could not then possibly restrict what he says in ver. 21 sqq. to Judah, for it all applies with equal force to Israel.—**Foolish and without understanding.** Comp. iv. 22; Hos. vii. 11. **Have eyes,** *etc.* Comp. Deut. xxix. 3; Isai. vi. 9, 10; Ezek. xii. 2. The apostasy of the people is here explained by their spiritual blindness and dulness generally, and this appears to have come upon them, because notwithstanding the grand displays of His power they had witnessed, they feared not the Lord.

Ver. 22. **Will ye still not fear me ... they come not over it.** From the connection the prophet cannot intend an exhortation, but only the confirmation of a fact. It is thus not so much: *Will ye not fear me then?* as: *Ye fear me not therefore.*—The wide ocean with the immense body of its waves is an emblem of the wildest and most irresistible force of nature. And yet the Lord is strong enough to control this violence. Comp. Job xxxviii. 8-11; Ps. xxxiii. 7; Prov. viii. 29. [The sea is also an emblem of the world, and its waves of the turbulence of the nations, which are yet under divine control. Comp. Ps. xciii. 3, 4. HENGSTENBERG on John vi. 16-21.—S. R. A.]—**They rage,** comp. xlvi. 7, 8; 2 Sam. xxii. 8; Ps. xviii. 8; subject—**its waves.—Can do nothing.** Comp. iii. 5; xx. 11; Isai. xvi. 12; Job xxxi. 23

Ver. 23. **But this people ... are gone.** How can a people be impelled by the greatness of God's works to fear Him, who are not moved to such fear by His goodness? He whom the love of God wins not, is not won by His omnipotence, for the former is the stronger. The connection is therefore this, that vers. 23 and 24 introduce a new element of their unfaithful disposition, which has at the same time a causal relation to that which was previously mentioned in vers. 21, 22. The Vau in וְלָעָם is adversative: I ask, *Will ye still not fear?* but to this question I can obtain no satisfactory answer, because this people is both **apostate** and **rebellious.**—These last named predicates are stronger than those in ver. 21, for those were negative, while these are positive. They are not only insensible and dull, but positively hostile. They *can* not—and what is worse—they *will* not. There is no occasion in the text to take **and are gone** as forming a climax (comp. Judges iv. 24; Gen. iii. 8). It rather corresponds to **have revolted** as its positive side: they break *loose* from the Lord and go *away* into the unmeasured distance, whithersoever their heart impels them.

Ver. 24. **And say not in their hearts ... as harvest-tide.—We will fear [Let us fear—** HENDERSON] corresponds to the **not fear me,** ver. 22: neither the grandeur nor the kindness of God's works move them to fear Jehovah.—The rain is an emblem of blessing. Comp. iii. 3.—גֶּשֶׁם is the general term, as we may perceive from Lev. xxvi. 4 (וְנָתַתִּי גִשְׁמֵיכֶם בְּעִתָּם). The double Vau before יוֹרֶה (early rain, October to December) and מַלְקוֹשׁ (the latter rain, in the spring, before the harvest) is disjunctive=*et—et.* Comp. NAEGELSB. *Gr.* § 110, 3. The Masoretes, not understanding this, would strike out the first Vau, but unnecessarily.—**Secureth.** The fruitfulness of the year depends on the regularity of the rainy seasons. Comp. Deut. xi. 14; 1 Sam. xii. 17, 18; RAUMER, *Paläst.* 4 *Aufl. S.* 90—[*Vid.* LIGHTFOOT, XII. p. 71].—**The weeks as harvest-tide** are the seven weeks of harvest from Easter to Whitsuntide [Passover to Pentecost] (Exod. xxiii. 16; xxxiv. 22; Numb. xxviii. 26; Deut. xvi. 9, 10, 16). They are called thus because the beginning marks the close of the (principal) harvest was determined by the two festivals as by fixed boundary-lines. The חֻקּוֹת קָצִיר (**harvest-tide**) correspond to the חָק־עוֹלָם (**everlasting barrier**), ver. 22.

---

5. Infidelity as deceit and violence.

V. 25-29.

25 Your transgressions hindered such things,
    Your sins withheld the good from you.
26 For godless [men] are found among my people;
    They lurk, like fowlers crouch;

They set traps, they catch men.
27 As a cage is full of birds
   So are their houses full of unrighteous wealth.
   Therefrom they are become great and rich.
28 They are fat, they shine, they overflow with iniquities:
   In justice they settle not the affairs of the orphan, and prosecute them;
   And the rights of the poor they procure not.
29 Should I not punish such, saith Jehovah,
   Should not my soul avenge itself on a nation like this?

EXEGETICAL AND CRITICAL.

Ver. 25 is closely connected with the previous strophe, but in such wise that it evidently does not belong to it, but conducts to a new passage. It involves in a certain measure a contradiction to the preceding. While in ver. 24 it was declared: *they say not, let us fear the Lord, who gives us rain*, etc., it is here said that Jehovah had *not given* them rain because of the sins of the people. And these sins are now so specified in what follows, that we see the prophet would confirm by new facts the fundamental thought of the section that אכונה has departed from Israel. Moreover the end here reverts to the beginning. For when he here speaks of the ruling of the כרמה, and of the unrighteousness of those in power it is evident that the phrase "any one doing right or seeking truth," in ver. 1, is hovering before his mind. Ver. 29 shows by its identity with ver. 9, that it is the conclusion of the strophe, and thus in its structure this strophe entirely resembles that in vers. 7-9, which likewise begins and ends with a reference to the divine judgment.

Ver. 25. **Your transgressions . . . from you.** Comp. iii. 3; iv. 18. When the prophet here, as in iii. 3, refers to the withholding of the rain as past, he certainly had definite facts in view (*e. g.*, 1 Kings xvii.; Am. iv. sqq.) and would intimate that the Lord not merely *will* punish, but already *has* punished, by which a guarantee is afforded of the infliction of the expected judgment.

Ver. 26. **For godless men are found . . .** they catch men. יָשׁוּר is to be regarded as impersonal: *it is lurked*. Comp. Naegelsb. *Gr.*, § 101, 2.—כְּשַׂךְ יְקוּשִׁים. Comp. Naegelsb. *Gr.*, § 95, 2. [Green's *Gr.*, § 139, 2.—S. R. A.] (בְּעֶבֶר כּוּפָה) Prov. x. 25).—מַשְׁחִית, *destroyer* generally (Exod. xii. 13; Ezek. xxi. 36), here specially, on account of הָרַע, destructive snares.

Ver. 27. **As a cage is full of birds . . . become great and rich.** כְּרֻמָּה is evidently the antithesis of אֱמוּנָה. At the same time the word is to be taken as *abstr. pro concr.=res fraude partae*, as עָמָל Ps. cv. 4; Eccles. ii. 19; comp. Naegelsb. *Gr.*, § 59, 1. From riches gained by deceit is developed violent injustice.

Vers. 28 and 29. **They are fat . . . nation like this.** Being fat is not all:. luxury produces lust, it runs over like a seething pot, and that with iniquities [matters of wickedness: Henderson] דִּבְרֵי־רָע involving the ideas of *res* and *verbum*) which are afterwards enumerated. עָבַר is construed as a verb of fulness with the accusative, like הָלַךְ, Joel iv. 18. Comp. Naegelsb. *Gr.*, § 69, 2, a.—**They settle not.** Comp. Ps. x. 18; xliii. 2; Gen. xxx. 5; Jer. xxii. 16.—**and prosecute them,** might certainly be rendered grammatically=*that they prosper* [Henderson]. But then the plural is strange and the sense is flat. Therefore it is better to regard it as the positive side of **settle not** = and they carry them through.—Ver. 29, comp. ver. 9.

---

6. Comprehensive conclusion.

V. 30, 31.

30 Fear and horror have happened in the land;
31 The prophets prophesy falsely,
   And the priests rule by their hand,[1]
   And my people love to have it so:
   But what will they do when the end of the song comes?

TEXTUAL AND GRAMMATICAL.

[1] Ver. 31.—[" The LXX. and the *Vulgate* have 'And the priests have applauded with their own hands,' and the *Targum* 'And the priests have blessed their hands.' Both mean the same thing ;] though the words are different ; and Blayney [and Boothroyd] gives the same meaning. 'And the priests have concurred with them.' Houbigant says the words [? really are] 'And the priests go down according to their hands;' that is, he adds, ' the priests go which way the [? ...]

the priests are directed by them.'—When followed by עַל as here, the preposition never means according to, as HORSLEY renders it, but ever, upon, toward or against, and mostly 'upon.' See Ex. ix. 9; Numb. iv. 9; Ps. vii. 10; lxxii. 8. Therefore the literal rendering is this. 'And the priests have descended upon their hands.' An idiomatic expression, which seems to mean, that the priests assisted the prophets, according to what is expressed by the *Targum*, etc. Note by Eng. ed. of CALVIN, I. p. 309.—S. R. A.]

EXEGETICAL AND CRITICAL.

These verses express the result of the examination instituted by the prophet into the moral condition of the people, *viz.*, that it was horribly bad in all ranks of life. While ver. 30 has reference to the entire section, ver. 31 refers especially to vers. 4 and 5.

Ver. 30. **Fear ... in the land.**—Fear. Comp. Deut. xxviii. 37; 2 Kings xxii. 19; Jer. xix. 8; xxv. 9, *etc*.—**horror**, a horrible thing, xxiii. 14. Comp. xviii. 13; Hos. vi. 10.

Ver. 31. **The prophets ... when the end of the song comes.** The prophets are first mentioned as the medium of all knowledge which determines to action. Comp. xx. 6; xxix. 9. The priests ought to have been a corrective to the misleading of the prophets, comp. Mal. ii. 7; Ezek. vii. 26. Instead of this they made profit by them.—עַל־יְדֵי or עַל־יְרֵי apart from its local signification, is a priestly *terminus technicus*, which means *ad latus* = under inspection, by appointment (1 Chron. vi. 16; xxv. 2, 3, 6; 2 Chron. xvii. 15, 17; xxiii. 18; xxix. 27; Ezr. iii. 10). So here. For an instance of such corrupting influence exercised by the prophets on the priests, see Jer. xxix. 24-32.—The corruption of the priests and prophets should in the last instance be rebuked by the sound sense of the people. But no. The people love to have it so. They do not cause a reaction but co-operate.—**When the end of the song comes,** or in reference to its end. The fem. suff. must be regarded as mental (ver. 20, comp. NAEGELSB. *Gr.*, § 60, 6 *b*) and to be referred in general to the totality of the condition described by the prophet. The sense is: What will you do when the present condition enters upon its last stage of development, or as we say, when the end of the song comes? Comp. Isai. x. 3; Hos. ix. 5. [LIGHTFOOT, XII. p. 550.—S. R. A.]

DOCTRINAL AND ETHICAL.

1. On ver. 1. "The wicked world has in the pious and believing a noble treasure and defence" (Gen. xviii. 32); LANGE.—Even Zoar is preserved for the sake of Lot, (Gen. xix. 20 sqq.)— Comp. Isai. xxxvii. 35.—GHISLERUS reminds us of a story which Pliny relates (vol. xxxv. cap. 10) of King Demetrius, who retired from the city of Rhodium, because he could not take it on its only accessible side without destroying some celebrated paintings of Protogenes.

2. ZINZENDORF here relates (*S.* 198) a story of M. Joh. Christoph Schwedler, *ob.* 1730. "Once when in the church at Wiese (Silesia) they were singing before the communion 'I will say to thee Farewell,' at the words 'Thy sinful, wicked living, pleases me not at all,' such an Elias-like zeal seized upon him, that raising his voice above the organ and the choral of a thousand voices, he cried out in tones of thunder, 'For God's sake what are you singing? What

does not please you? The Lord Jesus does not please you. To him ye must say : Thou pleasest us not, then you would speak the truth ; but you do say, the world.'—When now all, convicted by their consciences, sat there in grief and tears, and few knew how this happened to them, he said: 'Now, if it be thus as it should be, let him to whomsoever your sinful life has become offensive, confess it in the name of the Lord,' whereupon this verse was wept rather than sung."

3. On ver. 3. ORIGEN says in his sixth homily, of which the text is Jer. v. 3-5, "If now thou wilt that the beams of God's eye rest upon thee, embrace the virtues. So will it be with thee according to this 'the eyes of the Lord look for faith.' And if thou art such an one that the eyes of the Lord shine upon thee, then wilt thou say, 'the light of thy countenance rose upon us, O Lord,' Ps. iv. 7."—" He asks for returns and that too in *cash*. This is the fund to which he applies and on which he depends. Words are of no value to him. But just this is the complaint: Faith is rare among the children of men (Ps. xii. 2); 'it is not every man's possession,' as it is there said. In these days preachers might exclaim with Isaiah: who believes? (Isai. liii. 1). And Abraham pleads with the Lord for Sodom on condition of five righteous persons being found in it (Gen. xviii)." ZINZENDORF.—" *Ecce verbera desuper et flagella non desunt, et trepidatio nulla, nulla formido est. Quid si non intercederet rebus humanis vel ista censura?*" CYPRIAN. *ad Demetrianum.*—"*Haud grave est plagis affici, sed plaga melioremnonfieri gravissimum est.*" GREGOR. NAZIANZ.

4. On vers. 4 and 5. "A preacher has no more miserable and ignorant hearers than the respectable. While they are spelling their way back to the cross, and are getting so far as to know how to learn that we are saved alone by the grace of the Lord Jesus, till we get them so far as to understand that the command of the New Test. is to believe, and all that morality can lug about for eighty years is gone with a word : Son, be of good courage, thy sins are forgiven thee,— the *ignorant* would have been able to do it thrice. Enough has been said to show that a teacher greatly deceives himself, if he seeks among the respectable that comfort in his office, which he does not meet with among the common people." ZINZENDORF. *S.* 12, 13. Comp. *S.* 65, 66 ; 1 Cor. i. 26, 27.

5. On ver. 13. "*Yes, the prophets are gossips.* How does this sound and whence comes the saying? It sounds somewhat distinguished, and a teacher may draw it upon himself. Almost the whole body has incurred this, that they are reckoned with afterwards, and because after their discourse one has been able to do away with it by head work, he has finally come to the conclusion : the pastors are gossips ; and the precious treasure of the public testimony is much calumniated. Whoever is grieved on account of the teachers, let him reflect that this arises not so much from the fault of the hearers as of the

teachers. I will assure him: As soon as the words of the Lord become fire in his mouth, the hearers become wood, and criticism is at an end, and feeling comes and *savor* comes, be it unto life or unto death. From that time the preacher is in earnest, and laughter is forbidden by the hearers themselves." ZINZENDORF, *S.* 13, 14.

6. On ver. 15 sqq. "The prophet takes his direction from God's unchangeable calendar, as it was composed by Moses: Deut. xxviii. 49. Therefore he could well prognosticate how it would terminate with his disobedient people. It is of use, that we diligently peruse such an ever-enduring calendar, and ever have it before our eyes. For it is more certain than all other prognostications can be." CRAMER.

7. On vers. 21, 22. "*Hear, ye mad people, that have no understanding! Will ye not fear me?* This is a glorious discovery of the omnipotence and majesty of God. If, however, men see one, they see all; but they have no ears to hear until the whole is changed. But that men are so secure and think not of Him who allows them to live so securely, this is indeed an insane business." ZINZENDORF, *S.* 202.

8. On ver. 24. "O man, as often as thou puttest bread into thy mouth, reflect, that God by this means of nourishment would bring thee to Himself. Cling not also to carnal bread, but let thy immortal soul be satisfied by God." STARKE.

9. [On ver. 25. "This passage is worthy of special note: for God's paternal favor does not so continually shine forth in our daily sustenance, but that many clouds intercept our view. Hence it is, that ungodly men think that the years are now barren, and then fruitful through mere chance. We indeed see nothing so regulated in every respect in the world, that the goodness of God can be seen without clouds and obstructions: but we do not consider whence this confusion proceeds, even because we obstruct God's access to us, so that His beneficence does not reach us. We throw heaven and earth into confusion by our sins. For were we in right order as to our obedience to God, doubtless all the elements would be conformable, and we should thus observe in the world an angelic harmony. But as our lusts tumultuate against God, as we stir up war daily, and provoke Him by our pride, perverseness and obstinacy, it must needs be that all things, above and below, should be in disorder, that the heavens should at one time appear cloudy, and that continuous rains should at another time destroy the produce of the earth, and that nothing should be unmixed and unstained in the world. This confusion then, in all the elements, is to be ascribed to our sins: and this is what is meant by the prophet. Though indeed the reproof was then addressed to the Jews, we may yet gather hence a lesson of general instruction." CALVIN. —S. R. A.]

10. On ver. 28. ZINZENDORF remarks on the words "and they prosper" that the chief cause of the condemnation of the rich man (Luke vi. 19 sqq.) was that he was prospered in all things in this world. He consequently received his good things in this life and fared sumptuously every day. Comp. Ps. xxxvii. 35; Luke vi. 25; Jas. v. 1 sqq.

11. On ver. 28. "It would be better for one to have the Turkish emperor with all his army for an enemy than a poor widow with her fatherless orphans. For the widow's tears are water which rises above all the mountains and then falls again and washes away all her enemies into hell." LUTHER. Comp. Wisd. xxxv. 18-21.

12. On ver. 31. "*My people like it so.* Like sought, like found. The people wish to have false preachers and get them, and a blind man leads the blind until both fall into the ditch, Luke vi. 39." CRAMER.—"How will it be at last? We finally become as accustomed to disorder as disorderly people, and the more everything goes to ruin, the less concerned are we. There is, perhaps, however, still an uncompromising servant or old friend of our Father, who is constantly repeating the little word to us: How will it be? How will it end at last? This is the peculiar office of the teacher, and nobody likes to hear him." ZINZENDORF, *S.* 203.

HOMILETICAL AND PRACTICAL.

1. On ver. 3. **Lord, thine eyes look for faith.** Why does God impose faith as the only condition of salvation? 1. Because faith gives the greatest glory to God. 2. Because it is at the same time the easiest and most difficult exercise of the human heart. For (*a*) to believe, *i. e.*, to accept God's grace as a free gift, every one is, and must be, able to do. (*b*) He who can do it, has vanquished himself at the *one* point and won all.

2. [On ver. 4. "All sin proceeds from some misapprehension of God. (1) Skeptical humor as to God's particular Providence, and inspection over all events. (2) Disbelief that He is concerned about the moral good or evil actions of men. (3) Abuse of the doctrine of God's foreordination, and (4) of His mercy. But (1) God's mercy will not interfere with His justice. (2) The execution will be no less severe than the threatening. (3) God will not accept less than He requires in the Gospel." DR. S. CLARKE.— S. R. A.]

3. On ver. 11. Obstinate unbelief. 1. Its nature: it denies God and therefore despises (*a*) God's word, (*b*) those who proclaim it. 2. Its punishment: the tables are turned; (*a*) the unbeliever, before fire, now becomes wood, (*b*) the word of God, before regarded as wood, becomes fire.

4. On ver. 19. **Why doth the Lord our God all these things to us?** Three answers to this one question: 1. John xiii. 7, What I do, thou knowest not now, *etc.* 2. Matth. xx. 15, Is it not lawful for me to do what I will? *etc.* 3. James i. 12. Blessed is the man that endureth temptation, *etc.* FLOREY, 1863.

5. On vers. 21, 24. Of the fear of God. 1. Motives from without, (*a*) God's displays of power, (*b*) His displays of grace. 2. Inner conditions: (*a*) That we *open* our eyes and ears, (*b*) that we *allow* ourselves to be impelled by that which we see and hear.

6. On ver. 24. (Harvest [Thanksgiving] sermon). The harvest-blessing: 1. From whom it comes. 2. To whom it leads.

7. On ver. 24. It is the Lord who faithfully guards the harvest forces. This truth calls for

1. humility and trust in the sowing of earthly seed; 2. confidence in working in this world; 3. hope in the interment of bodies in the earth. V. D. TRENK, Gesetz und Zeugniss (Law and Testimony), Apr. 1860, S. 226.
8. On ver. 24. The call which the present year's harvest makes on the hearts of men. It is, Fear the Lord. For 1, without Him all labor and toil is in vain; 2. He does not allow Himself to be interfered with in His government; 3. He gives and blesses without respect to our deserts and in spite of our sins. FLOREY, 1863.
9. On vers. 30 and 31. A cry of warning in a period of universal apostasy. 1. The condition of the people is shocking and abominable, for (a) the leaders of the people misguide them, (b) the people wish to be misled. 2. The consequences correspond to the guilt (comp. vers. 25, 14 sqq., 6).

III. Recapitulation, consisting of a combination of the points already presented: the call to return, announcement of punishment and its reasons.

(CHAP. VI. 1–26).

1. *Exhortation to flee from Jerusalem.*

VI. 1–8.

1 Flee, ye children of Benjamin, out of Jerusalem,
And in Blow (Tekoa) blow the trumpet,
And over the vineyard (Beth-hakkerem) erect the signal,[2]
For calamity threatens from the north and great ruin.
2 Thou art like the meadow, the tenderly cared for,
O daughter of Zion.
3 Against her shall come shepherds and their flocks
And pitch their tents against her round about,
And depasture each his spot.
4 Sanctify war against her!
"Arise, let us go up at noon!
Wo to us, for the day has turned,
For the shadows of evening are lengthening.
5 Arise, and let us go up in the night
And destroy her palaces!"
6 For thus saith Jehovah Zebaoth,
Fell her trees,[3] and raise a rampart[4] against Jerusalem!
She is the city of which it is ascertained
That nothing but rude violence is found in her.
7 As a spring[5] poureth forth its waters
So she poureth forth her wickedness.
Injustice and desolation are heard of in her,
Sickness and wounds are continually before Me.
8 Be warned, O Jerusalem, lest my soul be forced from thee,
Lest I make thee desolate, a land uninhabited.

TEXTUAL AND GRAMMATICAL.

[1] Ver. 1.—["It is singular that the SEPT. render this in ch. iv. 6, 'Haste ye,' and here 'Be ye strong.' The *Targum* renders it 'migrate' or, remove ye. The idea of assembling it never has.—Where BLAYNEY got the phrase, 'Retire in a body' it is difficult to say." Ed. of CALVIN.—S. R. A.]

[2] Ver. 1.—["The word has no connection with 'fire,' as mentioned in our version, which has been derived from the Rabbins. BLAYNEY's rendering is 'light up a fire—beacon,' but the words admit of no such meaning." Ed. of CALVIN.—S. R. A.]

[3] Ver. 6.—עֵצָהּ is not to be regarded as a fem. collective form (comp. הָנָה) which does not occur elsewhere, but ה is the suffix without mappik, as frequently (Exod. ix. 18; Num. xv. 28; Ps. xlviii. 14; Ew. § 247, d; OLSH. § 40, c; NAEGELSB. § 44, 4. *Anm.*) The LXX. Vulg. Syr. and several Codd. in De Rossi also express the suffix.

[4] Ver. 6.—שָׁפַךְ כְּרָלָה is the standing mode of expression, so much so that כְּלָלָה occurs only in this connection, 2 Sam. xx. 15; 2 Ki. xix. 32; Isai. xxxvii. 33; Ezek. iv. 2; xvii. 17; xxi. 27; xxvi. 8; Dan. xi. 15.

[5] Ver. 7.—It is probable that בוֹר here stands for בְּאֵר, as the Masoretes suppose to have happened, *vice versa*, in 2 Sam.

xxiii. 15, 16, 20. This is also proved by the fem. suffix in הָמִיךְ. For בּוֹר, pit is masc., while בְּאֵר is fem. This change of gender between the noun and the suffix is probably also the ground of the Keri רִיב, which does not occur elsewhere. On the construction comp. v. 16, and NAEGELSB. *Gr.*, § 95, 2.

EXEGETICAL AND CRITICAL.

That vers. 1-8 form a strophe is seen partly from their close connection (ver. 6 traces the undertaking of the besiegers to a divine command), partly from the fact that the eight verses contain the complete cycle of the fundamental thought of the prophet, announcement of judgment, statement of reasons (vers. 6 and 7) and call to reform (ver. 8). At the same time however a climax is evident on a comparison with the preceding context. For the prophet here sees the judgment upon Jerusalem so near its accomplishment that he already earnestly admonishes to flight those who live to the south of this city.

Ver. 1. **Flee, ye children of Benjamin . . great ruin.—Flee**, comp. iv. 6.—**Children [sons] of Benjamin** is explained without doubt by the circumstance that Benjaminites formed a part (probably the principal part. Comp. GRAF, WINER, *R. W. B.*, *s. v.*, Jerusalem) of the inhabitants of Jerusalem. According to the original settlement of boundaries (Josh. xv. 8; xviii. 16) Jerusalem belonged entirely to Benjamin. But even before David's time it was inhabited by Judeans (Josh. xv. 63) and Benjaminites (Judg. i. 21). Since David's time, being the capital of the whole country, it also belonged to the whole people (comp. RAUMER, *Paläst. S.* 339) and doubtless had inhabitants from all the tribes, which would not however exclude Judeans and Benjaminites from forming the bulk of the population. Jeremiah's mentioning only the latter may be explained by the fact that he himself was of the tribe of Benjamin (i. 1).—**From [from the midst]** is an antithesis to **towards Zion**, iv. 6. While there they were called upon to flee *to* Jerusalem, where at first they would find safety, now they are exhorted to flee *from* Jerusalem.—תִּקְעוּ (to blow, blow, Germ. *stossen, Stoss.* Comp. the place named *Stoss* in Appenzell, Switz.) is mentioned partly for the sake of the paronomasia and partly because it is a prominent point to the south of Jerusalem; for after the capital, the bulwark of the South, has fallen, this also is threatened and must think of flight. Tekoa lay 9 to 12 m. p. south from Jerusalem. It is mentioned in 1 Sam. xiv. 2; Am. i. 1, etc. JEROME says on this passage, "*Thecuam quoque viculum esse in monte situm, et 12 millibus ab Hierosolymis separatum quotidie oculis cernimus.*" According to Robinson (II. 406) [THOMSON, *The Land and the Book*, II. p. 424] the place is still called Tekua, and is situated on a mountain covered with ruins.—For a similar paronomasia *Vid.* Mic. i. 10 sqq.—בֵּית־הַכֶּרֶם is mentioned only here and in Neh. iii. 14. JEROME testifies that it was a considerable elevation, near to Tekoa.—According to POCOCKE it is the Frank mountain, "an insulated, lofty cone." Comp. RAUMER, *Paläst., S.* 223. [ROBINSON, *Bibl. Res.* II., pp. 174, 182-184. RITTER, *Geog.* III., p. 96.—S. R. A.] מַשְׂאֵת from its radical meaning

of *elatio* obtains a variety of derivative significations. See the Lexicons. Here as in Judg. xx. 38, 40, it denotes the sign raised high aloft, (elsewhere נֵס).—**For calamity**, comp. iv. 6.

Ver. 2. **Thou art like the meadow . . . daughter of Zion.** The passage is difficult, and has been very variously explained. נָוָה is taken in the sense of "meadow" (LUTHER, NEUMANN); *habitatrix* (VENEMA); shepherdess (SEB. SCHMIDT). Most commentators render it = נָאוָה (Song of Sol. ii. 14; iv. 3; vi. 3) *pulchra, formosa.* הַמְעֻנָּגָה from עָנַג *delicate vixit* (Pual here only) is without doubt = *delicate habita,* which is always well cared for, spared, never roughly handled, comp. הָעֲנֻגָּה Deut. xxviii. 56; Isai. xlvii. 1.—דִּמִּיתִי 1. *assimilavi* (Vulg., KIMCHI, ABARB., PAGN., TREMELL., PISCATOR, etc.); 2. *similis facta es* (Syr.); 3. *similis sum* (SEB. SCHMIDT); 4. *periisti mihi* (VENEMA); 5. as fair and luxurious have I *imagined* the daughter of Zion (derived from the meaning "to compare," comp. Song of Sol. ii. 17; viii. 14; FUERST); 6. the fair and luxurious—I mean the daughter of Zion—to her come, *etc.* (EWALD, MEIER); 7. I make still (NEUMANN), exterminate (so most recent commentators). The connection requires without doubt the meaning of gay, well-tended and well-preserved meadow. For after, in ver. 1, a grievous calamity in general is set in immediate prospect before Jerusalem, we see from ver. 3 more particularly that this calamity will consist in a visitation of rough shepherds, who will ruthlessly depasture and desolate Jerusalem with their flocks. In contrast with its later condition, Jerusalem before its desolation can be represented under no more suitable figure than that of a meadow well-preserved and tended by its owner with special predilection. נָוָה designates not only a visitation generally, but also a pastoral visitation in particular (*caula cum pascuo,* FUERST), as is clear from Job viii. 6; coll. Zeph. ii. 6. Comp. נְאוֹת Jer. ix. 9; xxiii. 10; xxv. 36. דָּמָה is indisputably = *similis fuit* (Ps. lxxxix. 7; cii. 7; cxliv. 4, *etc.*) It is usually construed with לְ (see the passages cited) or with אֶל (Ezek. xxxi. 8). But that it may also have the subject compared, without a preposition, in the nominative is seen from Ezek. xxxii. 2, where it reads כְּפִיר גּוֹיִם נִדְמֵיתָ, *i. e.*, a lion among the nations art thou compared. Comp. Isai. xxxviii. 13. The meanings of Niphal and Kal *intrans.* here, as frequently, coincide. The construction is explained thus, that דָּמָה נִדְמָה properly signify: to be as a comparison, as a thing compared; Egypt is (in Ezek. l. c.) compared; *i. e.*, by way of comparison, figuratively designates, a lion. Israel (in this passage) is a figure or comparison a meadow—דִּמִּיתִי I take as the Syriac did, according to the frequent usage in Jeremiah (comp. on ii. 20) as 2 Pers. Fem.—The Masoretes have not added in the Keri the regular form here as in the other passages, which may be explained by the circumstance that they took דכית as the 1st person. The article before נָוֶה is generic as in iv. 25; comp. NAEGELSB., § 71, 4, a.—ו before הֲמִיעֶנָּה is epexegetical = and indeed, comp. NAEGELSB. Gr., § 111, 1 a.

Ver. 3. **Against her shall come shepherds . . . each his spot.** The enemies are compared with shepherds, who break in with flocks and ruthlessly depasture and tread down. Comp. Mic. v. 4, 5.—**And pitch their tents,** etc., comp. i. 15.—יָד side, place, spot. Comp. Lev. ii. 17; Deut. xxiii. 13; Isai. lvi. 5.

Ver. 4. **Sanctify war against her . . the shadows of evening are lengthening.**—**Sanctify** as in Joel iv. 9; Mic. iii. 5; Zeph. i. 7; Jer. xxii. 7; li. 27. The expression refers to the solemn ceremonies attending the proclamation and commencement of war. Comp. Ezek. xxi. 26 sqq.—This and the following are calls made from the midst of the enemy.—The expressions exhibit the zeal of the enemy with dramatic liveliness. This zeal is so great that the unfavorable time of the day even cannot detain them. At noon, when the heat usually compels all to rest they depart, and when the evening comes they deplore it, but instead of going to rest prepare at once for the assault.—**Has turned.** Comp. Ps. xc. 9, [all our days turn away].

Ver. 5. **Arise, and let us go up . . . destroy her palaces.** אַרְמְנוֹת is translated by SCHNURRER and EWALD, here and in ix. 20, by *lofty buildings*, in order to comprise the fortifications. But here, as frequently, the expression denotes the final object, the completion of the work of destruction. Comp. Jer. xvii. 27; Am. i. 4.

Ver. 6. **For thus saith Jehovah . . found in her.** The besieging of Jerusalem by its enemies is not a baseless, vain undertaking. It rests on a double, solid ground: 1. Immediately on a divine command (כִּרְתוּ); 2. mediately on the ungodliness of Israel, which provokes the vengeance of Jehovah (עֻשְׁק וגו to ver. 7, fin.) —**Fell her trees** is evidently an allusion to Deut. xx. 19, 20, where it is commanded that Israel when they besiege a city, are not to cut down all the trees for the purposes of the siege (walls and machines.—Comp. WINER, *R. W. B.*, and HERZOG *Real-Enc.* Art. *Festungen*). Here the enemy is commanded to do the exact contrary. Thus it is rendered evident how savage the enemy is and what Israel has to expect. The latter are so ungodly that the enemy is excused from those considerations which are imposed on the Israelites themselves in war. If this passage is thus based on Deut. xx. 19, 20, we are then justified in regarding כִּרְתוּ עֵצָה as a verbal reminiscence.—The following sentence is construed in three ways: 1. *Hæc illa urbs—punitur quantaquanta est—oppressio in ea*; 2. *hæc est urbs in quam animadvertitur,—tota illa oppressio in ea*; 3. *urbs ista—oppressio est, quod non est nisi oppressio in ea.*—Of these interpretations the first must be unconditionally rejected, for כָּלֹה is as unnecessary with הָפְקַד, as it is necessary to what follows. The second is the

most generally adopted. But the abrupt הָפְקַד is flat: we expect a stronger word and the imperfect, since the visitation is impending. I therefore prefer the third interpretation, adopted by ABARBANEL and SED. SCHMIDT. Since פָּקַד=*explorare* (comp. Ps. xvii. 18; Job vii. 18) הָפְקַד may well mean *exploratum est.* This agrees excellently with what follows: that their inward part is full of thoughts of violence is confirmed by the fact that they well forth these like a spring its waters; the *cry* thereof is *heard*, the effects thereof are *visible* (ver. 7). Levit. v. 23 also evidently hovered before the mind of the prophet. Since there only besides the Hophal occurs, though with another meaning; so there also is found the idea of עֹשֶׁק. For the restoration is there alluded to of that which any one has appropriated by violence (עֹשֶׁק) or by illegal retention of property entrusted to him. Though the thought in general is a very different one, yet a comparison of this passage explains (*a*) why the prophet here designates the sin of Israel as עֹשֶׁק (*b*) the choice of the singular word הָפְקַד; also (*c*) the article in הָעִיר is satisfactorily explained, if the prophet refers to a former utterance. כָּלֹה עֹשֶׁק בְּקִרְבָּהּ is a *confusio duarum constructionum,* עֹשֶׁק כָּלֹה and כָּלָה בְּקִרְבָּהּ.

Ver. 7. **As a spring . . . . continually before me.**—The Inf. הָקִיר points to a root קוּר, from which besides only קִרְתִי (2 Kings xix. 24; Isai. xxxvii. 25). The following הַקָּרָה presupposes a root קָרַר, from which no verbal form occurs in the Old Test. Yet by virtue of the relationship of the verbs עו and עי it not rarely happens that the same word derives forms from both conjugations. Comp. EWALD, § 114, *a.*—The interpretation is difficult of הֵקֵר הַקָּרָה and בּוֹר. קוּר means: to dig (2 Kings xix. 24), but קָרַר means (after קֹר, מִקְרָה, coldness, קַר fresh), *to be cold, fresh.* The meaning *to pour forth* therefore seems to suit neither the one nor the other of these two roots. Hence after the example of the LXX. and JEROME many commentators have interpreted the passage thus: "As the cisterns keep their water cool, so Jerusalem keeps its wickedness constantly fresh" (GRAF). This rendering seems to be supported by בּוֹר meaning not *spring,* but *pit, cistern.* I cannot nevertheless regard this explanation as correct; for 1. the connection is opposed to it, according to our explanation, but also aside from this **are heard of** and **before me** afterwards require the meaning of *to bring forth, reveal.* 2. Although the root קוּר in the single passage where it occurs has the meaning *to dig,* yet even in this place it is used of digging for water, and must include a reference to springing water, while the only noun derived from it is מָקוֹר, which certainly does not denote a pit or cistern, but a spring or fountain, since, as it is generally used only in a poetic and figurative sense (comp. fountain of blood, Levit. xii. 7; xx. 18; fountain of tears, Jer. viii. 23) it expresses the idea of a spring in its highest and most original sense. Accordingly the meaning of to *spring*, to *pour forth*, is certainly not ascribed to קִיר without reason. As to בּוֹר, it certainly does in itself denote a pit or cistern. But in the later books it also designates a pit, in which water is springing, a well-spring (*puteus*): Prov. v. 15; Eccles. xii. 6.—**Injustice and desolation** [Violence and spoil] is a standing formula: xx. 18; Ezek. xlv. 9; Am. iii. 10; coll. Hab. i. 3—are heard (comp. Isai. lx. 18) and the following **before me** are explained by the preceding **poureth forth**, as all three members of the sentence afford proof of the fact ascertained, ver. 6.—In are con- tinually before me there is a climax; not only are deeds of violence heard of, but their most palpable effects are continually being witnessed. Ver. 8. **Be warned, O Jerusalem... a land uninhabited.** Here also as above (iii. 1, 7, 12-22; iv. 1, 3, 4, 14, *etc.*) the prophet uses the threatening of punishment as a support for a call to repentance. The Lord's heart is still towards Jerusalem, though it is to be feared that it will be alienated from the stiff-necked, impenitent people. תִּקַּע from יָקַע (to be thrust away, to turn away) occurs only in the imperfect, while the perfect forms are formed from נָקַע. Comp. Ezek. xxiii. 17, 18.

---

2. *The prophet is compelled by an inward pressure to announce the judgment of extermination, notwithstanding the unwillingness to hear on account of the universal horrible corruption.*

VI. 9–15.

9   Thus saith Jehovah Zebaoth:
    They shall glean the remnant of Israel as a vine.
    Turn again and again thine hand[1] as a grape-gatherer to the baskets.
10 To[2] whom shall I speak and testify, that they may hear?
    Behold their ear is uncircumcised, and they cannot hearken.
    Behold the word of Jehovah is a mockery to them;
    They have no delight in it.
11 But I am full of the fury of Jehovah,
    I cannot longer restrain myself.[3]
    Pour out over the child in the street
    And over the company of youths together;
    For both man and wife shall be taken,
    The aged with him that is full of days.
12 And their houses shall come to others,
    Fields and wives together,
    For I will stretch out my hand against the inhabitants of the land,
    Saith Jehovah.
13 For from the least to the greatest all are given to covetousness,
    And from the prophet to the priest they practice deceit.
14 And healed the hurt of the daughter[4] of my people most slightly,
    Saying : Peace, Peace! And there is no peace.
15 They are put to shame,[5] for they wrought abominations,
    Yet they blush not, nor[7] know how to be ashamed.[8]
    Therefore will they fall with them that fall.
    At the time that I visit them, they will be overthrown,
    Saith Jehovah.

TEXTUAL AND GRAMMATICAL.

[1] Ver. 9.—הָשֵׁב יָדְךָ. It is quite unnecessary with Hitzig and Graf to explain the suffix ךָ by the reduplication of the following כ (in כְּבוֹצֵר). The discourse is rather dramatically vivid as in vers. 3-6.—הָשֵׁב is to turn back as the grape-gatherer does his hand with respect to the basket, therefore=to turn again and again.

[2] Ver. 10.—עַל here as frequently in Jer. (comp. xix. 15; xxv. 2; xxvi. 15; xxvii. 19; xxviii. 8; xliv. 20) has almost the meaning of אֶל, except that here the proximate idea of hostility may be detected in it.

[3] Ver. 11.—[Henderson: I am weary of containing it; the A. V. better: I am weary of holding in.] Comp. Isai. i. 14; Jer. ix. 4; xv. 6.

[4] Ver. 14.—["בַּת, *daughter*, is omitted in thirty-eight MSS. and twenty-four printed editions. The combination

בַּת עַמִּי, *the daughter of my people*, however, meaning the people themselves, is not foreign to Jeremiah. See chap. viii. 21, 22." HENDERSON.—S. R. A.]

⁵ Ver. 14.—עַל־נְקַלָּה comp. עַל־שֶׁקֶר (Lev. v. 22), עַל־יֶתֶר (Ps. xxxi. 24).

⁶ Ver. 15.—[HENDERSON translates: They ought to have been ashamed. He says: "Verbs in Heb. express sometimes, not the action, but the duty or obligation to perform it. Comp. אֲשֶׁר לֹא־יֵעָשׂוּ, *which ought not to be* done, Gen. xx. 9. אִבְרָא שְׁקִי, *should keep*, Mal. ii. 7."—S. R. A.]

⁷ Ver. 15.—לֹא־גַם גַם־לֹא—=neither—nor. Comp. NAEGELSB. *Gr.* § 110, 3.

⁸ Ver. 15.—הַכְּלִים elsewhere Niph. (viii. 12; xxxi. 19). The Hiphil here as in הוֹבִישׁ.

EXEGETICAL AND CRITICAL.

This strophe reproduces with some modification one side of the fundamental thought of the discourse: under a new figure (that of gleaning) the prophet announces the entire destruction of the people (ver. 9). Here however the thought occurs to him that he is really speaking in vain, because nobody wishes to hear him (ver. 10). This objection is removed by the fact that the prophet cannot be silent. He therefore gives free course to the prophetic impulse to pour out upon the *whole* people the fulness of the divine wrath (vers. 11, 12), which they have so richly deserved by their sins, (pre-eminently of covetousness, deceit and shamelessness, vers. 13-15).

Ver. 9. **Thus saith Jehovah . . . to the baskets.** Not hastily but carefully is the divine judgment executed: thorough work is done, as in gleaning (Isai. xxiv. 13; Ob. 5; Jer. xlix. 9). These words seem also to refer to a precept of the Law, namely, to that which expressly forbade the Israelites to glean (Levit. xix. 10; Deut. xxiv. 21). The case is the same here as with **Fell her trees,** ver. 6. This gleaning does not of course contradict what was said in iv. 27; v. 10, 18.—**I will not utterly make an end.** Even in gleaning something may be left. Comp. Isai. vi. 11 sqq.; Zech. xiii. 8, 9.—כַּלּוֹת here only. EWALD, HITZIG, GRAF, MEIER, appealing to וְלָלִים Isai. xviii. 5 coll. תַּלְתַּלִּים Song of Sol. v. 11, כְּנִצָּנִים Song of Sol. vii. 9, would give it the meaning of "branches, tendrils," which they also regard as favored by the connection, since הָשִׁיב יָד denotes to turn the hand against any one with a hostile intention (comp. Am. i. 8; Isai. i. 25; Ps. lxxxi. 15). But in the first place the plucking of grapes is not a hostile act, but a kindness to the vine. Secondly, the connection requires the idea of repetition, so that the phrase must not be taken in the sense of the passages cited, but much more according to the analogy of Ps. lxxii. 10; 2 Kings iii. 4; xvii. 3; as *to turn back again and again.* Thirdly, the mention of the basket portrays much more vividly the fate of the grapes than the mention of the branch would; for the former sets before us the grapes as definitively separated from the vine. Fourthly, the linguistic relations are in favor of the rendering "basket," for the word most nearly related, כֹּל, decidedly has this meaning (Gen. xl. 16. 17; Levit. xxix. 3).

Ver. 10. **To whom shall I speak . . . delight in it.** After in ver. 9 he has presented to their view the extremity to which they would be reduced, the objection occurs to the prophet that all his speaking is in vain.—**Uncircumcised** is used in the Old Test. of the ear in this place only. In the New Test. comp. Acts vii. 51. Of the heart, Levit. xxvi. 41; Deut. x. 16; Jer. ix. 25; Ezek. xliv. 7, 9. Of the lips, Exod. vi. 12, 30. We see from **and they cannot hearken** that it designates a substantial incapability, which, however, is guilty, as hardness of heart and perversity. **A mockery,** comp. xx. 7, 8.

Ver. 11. **But I am full of the fury . . . full of days.** The objection raised in ver. 10 is removed by the impossibility of keeping silence. On the subject comp. xx. 9.—The prophet feels as though the Lord's fury were his own, and he is so full of it that it is with him as in Matth. xii. 34 [out of the abundance of the heart, etc.].— **Pour,** *etc.* The change of the person is here just as in **Turn,** *etc.,* ver. 9. The Lord, whose fury he cannot restrain, calls to him to pour it out. With EWALD then to change to שְׁפוֹךְ is quite unnecessary. The fury shall be poured over the whole people, irrespective of sex or age. Comp. xviii. 21; Lam. ii. 21.—On **company of youth** comp. **xv. 17.**—יַלְדֵּי is to be taken in the wider sense= to be caught, comp. Josh. vii. 15.—זָקֵן is the aged man without respect to his vigor, the man "full of days" is he who is superannuated and decrepit.

Vers. 12, 13. **And their houses . . . practice deceit.** Comp. viii. 10 sqq.—נָסַבּוּ as in 1 Kings ii. 15; Numb. xxxvi. 7, 8. The prophet seems to be thinking of this latter passage in the same antithetical way, as of the passages from the Law in vers. 6 and 9. Comp. also Deut. xxviii. 30.—**I will stretch.** Comp. xv. 6.—In ver. 13 begins a repeated enumeration of the sins of the people as forming a motive for the fury described in ver. 11. The faults of covetousness, deceit and wantonness which smothered shame, are here rendered prominent. It seems as though the prophet as in ch. v. has still in mind the antithesis of אֱמוּנָה.—**given to covetousness.** The prophet seems to have thought of Isai. lvi. 11. Comp. KUEPER, *S.* 144. The same expression also in Prov. i. 19; xv. 27; Hab. ii. 9; Ezek. xxii. 27.

Ver. 14. **And healed the hurt . . no peace.** This is the deceit, or at least one and a very important kind of deceit, which the priests and prophets practised, that they designated (as was certainly to their material interest) the course adopted by the people and the princes as true and saving. Comp. xiv. 14 sqq.; xxiii. 9-40; xxvii. 14, 15; xxviii 1-10 —**healed** is intended ironically. The aorist denotes that they have done this hitherto.—**And there is no peace.** Comp. Mic. iii. 5; Ezek. xiii. 10 and *supra,* iv. 10.

Ver. 15. **They are put to shame .. will be overthrown, saith Jehovah.** הוֹבִישׁ (comp. viii. 9; x. 14, *etc.*) means likewise to make a shameful figure, as הֵשִׁין, to make fat, *i. e.*, to become fat, הִלְבִּין, to bring forth whiteness, *i. e.*, to become white. Comp. NAEGELSB. *Gr.* § 18, 3. —They are put to shame, says the prophet, because those false predictions of peace have already been frequently falsified. And this could not be otherwise, since their prophecy was an abomination. The Lord therefore in respect to them does just the contrary of that which He does in respect of true prophecy (i. 12).—But notwithstanding this, that they were put to shame, yet they were not ashamed.—**Not know how** reminds us of Isai. lvi. 11.—**fall with them**, *etc.* When the victims of their false guidance fall, they will not, as they have hoped, escape scotfree, but will be overthrown. Comp. the expression in li. 49.

3. *Because Israel would not hear the prophet announces to all lands and nations the impending judgment, to be executed by a people from the north.*

VI. 16-26.

16 Thus has Jehovah spoken:
 Stand in the ways[1] and look around
 And inquire for[2] the paths of ancient times,
 Which is the way of salvation ;[3]
 And walk therein and find a resting place[4] for your souls!
 But they said : We will not walk therein.
17 Then I set[5] watchmen over you, saying:
 " Hearken to the sound of the trumpet !"
 But they said : We will not hearken thereto.
18 Therefore hear, ye nations,
 And know, O congregation, what is among them.
19 Hear, O earth ! Behold I bring evil upon this **people,**
 The fruit of their counsels.
 For they have not heeded my words,
 And my law—they despised it.[6]
20 To what purpose should incense come to me from **Sheba,**
 And the sweet cane from a far country ?
 Your burnt offerings are not grateful to me,
 And your sacrifices are not pleasant to me.
21 Therefore thus saith Jehovah :
 Behold I lay stumbling-blocks against the people,
 And the fathers and sons together shall fall over them ;
 The inhabitant and his companion shall perish.[7]
22 Thus saith Jehovah : Behold, a people comes from the **north country,**
 And a great nation arises from the ends of the earth.
23 Bow and lance they bear,
 Cruel are they and have no mercy.
 Their voice roars like the sea,
 And they ride upon horses,
 Equipped as a man for war, against thee, thou daughter of **Zion.**
24 We have heard the report of them ; feeble are our **hands,**
 Anguish has seized us, and trembling as a parturient.
25 Go not forth into the field, nor walk in the way,
 For the sword of the enemy[8]—fear on every side.
26 Daughter of my people, gird thee in sackcloth,
 And wallow thyself in ashes.
 Make mourning as for an only son—bitter lamentation ;
 For suddenly will the destroyer come upon us.

TEXTUAL AND GRAMMATICAL.

¹ Ver. 16.—עָמְדוּ עַל־דְּרָכִים comp. iii. 2; Isai. xlix. 9, where likewise the article is wanting. In iii. 2 the words שָׁפִים, אֶרֶץ are also without the article, although in meaning they are definite. Comp. GESEN. § 109; NAEGELSB. Gr. § 71, 3.

² Ver. 16.—דֶּרֶךְ הַטּוֹב (via boni, not bona, on account of the following בָּהּ). Comp. Ps. cxxxix. 24.

³ Ver. 16.—שְׁאַל with לְ, Gen. xxvi. 7; xxxii. 30.

⁴ Ver. 16.—מָצְאוּ. Comp. NAEGELSB. Gr. § 90, 2.—מַרְגּוֹעַ. Comp. Matth. xi. 29.

⁵ Ver. 17.—וְהִקְשִׁיבוּ. The perfect is abnormal, and is a sign of the later idiom. Comp. EWALD, § 343, c. 2.

⁶ Ver. 19.—On the construction comp. NAEGELSB. Gr. § 88, 7, c, et supra, iii. 9.

⁷ Ver. 21.—For יֹאבֵדוּ the Keri has וְאָבְדוּ because the Masoretes connected וְרָעַ שָׁבֶן as the subject with כֶּשֶׁל, which is however unnecessary and unjustifiable.

⁸ Ver. 25.—To translate : the enemy hath a sword [as HENDERSON] is very flat. Better חֶרֶב (אֲשֶׁר) לְאֹיֵב, and as subject co-ordinate with the following מָגוֹר [for the sword of the enemy and fear are, etc.]. Comp. NAEGELSB. Gr. § 67, 2.

EXEGETICAL AND CRITICAL.

This last strophe of the discourse forms two parts. In the first part (vers. 16-20) the prophet shows the *genesis* of the calamity. The Lord had at first kindly directed Israel in the right way (ver. 16), but when they had refused to walk in it, He had solemnly threatened them with His punishment (ver. 17). Since they regarded not this also, He turns now with His announcement of punishment to all nations, calling them as it were to witness to the justice of His cause (vers. 18, 19). He refutes a nugatory objection of Israel's (ver. 20). In the second part the merited destruction is announced to the people of Israel directly (vers. 21-26), first in general (ver. 21), then its execution is described in detail (vers. 22-25), so that (a) the nation from the North is again mentioned as the instrument of this execution, with more particular features; (b) the experience of the punishment is presented in the words of the suffering people. Finally the prophet calls upon the people to do that which alone remains to them, namely, to humble themselves in deepest mourning.

Ver. 16. **Thus has Jehovah spoken . . . we will not walk therein.** אָמַר compared with the progress of time in ver. 17 sqq. is to be regarded as preterite.—As the absence of the article is not to be pressed, we translate: stand in *the ways, i. e.*, not in any or some, but in all. They are to compare by examination all the ways (דֶּרֶךְ here as in Ps. cxxxix. 24; Am. viii. 14 = religion, *cultus*). A criterion is at the same time given them, by which to recognize the right way, *viz.*, antiquity. The oldest is the true religion. Let them examine the different religious of the primitive period, in order to find the oldest among the old ways, which is then the way of good or well-being.

Ver. 17. **Then I set watchmen over you . . . we will not hearken thereto.—Watchmen,** used frequently by the prophet for seers and warners. Comp. Ezek. iii. 17; xxxiii. 7; coll. Isai. xxi. 11, 12; Jer. xxxi. 6.—**Hearken to the sound,** *etc.* Observe the climax: after Israel had rejected the friendly admonition in ver. 16, the prophets standing on the walls before watchmen must strike wholesome terror into their hearts by sounding the trumpet of their denunciatory prophecies. But even this is in vain.

The words **hearken,** *etc.*, may be regarded as spoken by Jehovah or by the prophets themselves; for even the latter might admonish the Israelites to respect the warning, which they brought to them. Yet this admonition certainly seems more appropriate in the mouth of Jehovah. Comp. ii. 25.

Ver. 18. **Therefore hear, ye nations . . . what is among them.** After the Lord had found among the Israelites a hearing neither for friendly admonition nor for severe warning, He turns to the other nations, in order that *they* may learn Jehovah's judgment on His people and its true motives.—Concerning עֵדָה opinions are much divided. According to the connection and the unquestioned Masoretic reading it can mean neither *testimony* (Aqu.) nor *troop* (HITZIG) nor *congregation* in the sense of the Israelites, for an address to the whole or a part of the Israelite nation would form a most violent interruption in the parallelism and connection. I do not see why it should not denote the totality of the heathen nations, united as it were into a grand jury. It is true, no passage can be produced, where עֵדָה has exactly this meaning, but it is a word of such general signification, that it may fairly have this sense. For if in Judg. xiv. 8 it signifies a *swarm* of bees, in Job xv. 34 and Ps. xxii. 16 an *assembly* of the wicked, and in Numb. xvi. 5, the company of Korah, no one can say that it may not in certain circumstances be used of the assembly of the heathen. Since now according to the idea of the connection previously stated, the prophet turns in ver. 18 right diligently to the heathen, *because Israel would not hear him,* עֵדָה can denote no other than the *totality* of the heathen in antithesis to the *single* nations, who were addressed as גּוֹיִם; thus *singuli et omnes.* At the same time it is not improbable, that עֵדָה (comp. הָעִיר *ad judicium citare,* Jer. xlix. 19; l. 44) might also designate a "*judicialis conventus*" (so VENEMA, ROSENM., J. D. MICH.)—The phrase אֶת־אֲשֶׁר־בָּם is also variously interpreted. Some (LEISTE, ROSENM.) translate : *quæ in iis fiam,* which presupposes an impossible ellipsis; EWALD would read פֶּה instead of בָּם. GRAF changes into וְדְעוּ־אֲשֶׁר הֵעִידוֹתִי בָּם. I find no difficulty in the text, as it exists. The heathen assembled, as it were for a jury, are first to know what thoughts Israel cherishes within. For this purpose a glance into their heart is afforded them by what is said in vers. 16 and 17. On the basis of this state of the facts it is then disclosed to them in ver. 19, what the Lord will bring as a punishment upon Israel. In **I bring evil upon, upon** is in antithesis to **among** in ver. 18.

Ver. 19. **Hear, O earth!** . . **they despised it.**—**Hear,** *etc.,* forms a climax in relation to ver. 18: the whole earth is called to witness. Comp. Deut. xxxii. 1 (coll. xxx. 19; xxxi. 28); Mic. i. 2; vi. 1, 2; Isai. i. 2. After the Lord has granted a glance into the heart of Israel, He shows the punishment which is the result of this inward condition, and which is therefore designated as **the fruit of their counsels** (comp. ii. 19 ; iv. 18).

Ver. 20. **To what purpose should incense** . . . **are not pleasant to me.** לְבוֹנָה the aromatic resin of a tree not yet definitely ascertained. Comp. Exod. xxx. 31; Levit. ii. 1, *etc.* ; Isai. lx. 6; HERZOG, *Real-Enc.* XVII. S. 602; XII. S. 504.—שְׁבָא (not to be confounded with כְּבָא, *i. e.,* Meroe) is the tribe and home of the Sabeans in Southern Arabia. Comp. Isai. lx. 6; Ezek. xxvii. 22; Joel iv. 8; Ps. lxxii. 15.— קָנֶה הַטּוֹב, comp. Exod. xxx. 23 (קְנֵה בֹשֶׂם); Isai. xliii. 24; Ezek. xxvii. 19; Song of Sol. iv. 14 = calamus, the root of which was used in the preparation of the anointing oil. Vid. WINER, *R. W. B.,* Art. *Kalamus.*—In these words the Lord meets an objection of the Israelites to the effect that they had not failed in outward worship. The sense of the reply coincides with 1 Sam. xv. 22; Mic. vi. 8; Isai. i. 11 sqq.; Ps. 1. 8 sqq.; li. 18, *etc.*—The juxtaposition of עוֹלוֹת and זְבָחִים is also found in several of the passages mentioned, comp. Jer. vii. 21; DRECHSLER, *Jes.* I. S. 68.

Ver. 21. **Therefore thus saith Jehovah** . . . **and his companion shall perish.** After the refutation of the vain objection in ver. 20 the prophet turns again to the people of Israel. He seems to presuppose that the people excited to jealousy by vers. 18 and 19, (comp. Rom. xi. 14) in opposition to their former disinclination even to hear the Lord, yet at least answer him. The answer is indeed worth nothing, and therefore now follows a direct announcement of judgment, addressed to the Israelites themselves, first, in this verse 21, in *general.*—**Stumbling-blocks.** Comp. Isai. viii. 14; Ezek. iii. 20.

Ver. 22. **Thus saith Jehovah** . . **ends of the earth.** This and the following verses specify the calamity announced generally in ver. 21. For the third time the executioner is mentioned as **a mighty nation from the North.** (Comp. iv. 6 sqq.; v. 15 sqq.)—The passage repeated and applied to Babylon in l. 41-43.— יִרְכְּתֵי אֶרֶץ *extrema terrae.* Comp. Isai. xiv. 13, 15; Jer. xxv. 32; xxxi. 8, *etc.*

Ver. 23. **Bows and lances they bear** . . . **against thee, thou daughter of Zion.** Comp. Hab. i. 7.—**Like the sea.** Comp Isai. v. 30; xvii. 12; xxiv. 14.—On the question what nation, see the remarks above on i. 14.—**Equipped as a man for war.** The singular attaching to **cruel are they.** On the change of number, comp. EWALD, § 317, *b.* **As a man** can neither denote *one* man, nor a *hero.* Rather do **equipped and against thee** (as the accents also denote) belong together and **as a man for war** declares how this preparation is made; not as a woman for peaceful labor, but as a man for war, is the enemy equipped against Zion.

Vers. 24 and 25. **We have heard the report** . . . **fear on every side.** A description of the feeling which Israel experiences on the incursion of the enemy, so that vers. 22, 23 on the one hand, and vers. 24 and 25 on the other correspond to each other as objective and subjective, or as cause and effect.—**Anguish.** Comp. iv. 31; xlix. 24; l. 43.—**Trembling as,** *etc.* Comp. Ps. xlviii. 8; Mic. iv. 9; Jer. xxii. 23; l. 43.—Ver. 25 is also related to ver. 24 as the effect to the cause: the not venturing out of Jerusalem is the consequence of what has been heard. The personification of Jerusalem as a woman lies at the basis of the forms תֵּלְכִי־תֵצְאִי for which the way is prepared by **as a parturient,** and continued by **daughter of my people** ver. 26.—**Fear on every side,** Ps. xxxi. 14; Jer. xx. 3, 10; xlvi. 5; xlix. 29; Lam. ii. 22; see especially remarks on xx. 10.

Ver. 26. **Daughter of my people** . . **come upon us.**—**Gird thee,** *etc.,* comp. iv. 8,—**wallow,** comp. xxv. 34; Mic. i. 10; Ezek. xxvii. 30. —**Mourning,** *etc.* Comp. Am. viii. 10; Zech. xii. 10.—**Bitter lamentation.** Comp. xxxi. 15; Hos. xii. 15.—The prophet in conclusion advises Jerusalem to do the only thing that remains to her; repent in sackcloth and ashes (comp. Isai. lviii. 5; Jer. xxv. 34; Ezek. xxvii. 30; Dan. ix. 3) and deep, sincere mourning. For their sins or their destruction? Doubtless for both. For the former is occasioned by penitence, the latter by inevitable destruction. Penitence and mourning can no longer ward off the destruction (as might have been possible before, comp. iv. 1-4; xiv. 6, 8). The prophet indeed expresses this in the words "for suddenly will the destroyer come upon us." But though the calamity cannot be warded off by penitence and mourning it may yet be thus mitigated, and the way may be thus prepared for subsequent restoration.

4. Conclusion: object and result of the Discourse.

VI. 27–30.

27 I have set thee a prover[1] among my people, the ore,[2]
   That thou mayest know and prove their way.
28 They are all arch traitors,[3] slanderers[4]—brass and iron;
   Profligate are they all![5]
29 The bellows glows,[6] out of its fire comes—lead;
   In vain one[7] melts and melts,
   The base[8] are not separated.
30 Reprobate silver they are called,
   For Jehovah *has reprobated* them.

TEXTUAL AND GRAMMATICAL.

[1] Ver. 27.—בָּחוֹן (on the form comp. EWALD, § 152, b) [GREEN'S *Gr.* § 185, 2, c] occurs here only. It is=בַּחַן (xi. 20; xvii. 10).

[2] Ver. 27.—מִבְצָר, DURELL, GAAB, MAURER, HITZIG=כִּבְצָר, *i. e., without gold*, בֶּצֶר being equivalent to בֶּצֶר (Job xxxvi. 19) and כ unreduplicated as in כְּבָצִיר (Judges viii. 2). EWALD, MEIER would punctuate מְבַצֵּר (*Separator*) [HENDERSON : an explorer]. Yet both are unnecessary, if we take מִבְצָר itself in the meaning of בֶּצֶר (Job xxii. 24) בֶּצֶר (Job xxxvi. 19) בְּצוּר (Job xxii. 24) as also כָּתָב is used as of like meaning with כָּתַב (2 Chron. xxxv. 4), מִשְׁקָל with מֶשֶׁק (Gen. xv. 2, 3 ; Zeph. ii. 9), מִשְׁפָּט with שָׁפַט (Exod. vi. 6 ; vii. 4, etc.), מִשְׁקָל with שָׁקַל (according to its radical meaning), etc. כְּבָצָר would accordingly=בְּצָר, *abscissum*, a piece, in the sense of a piece of ore cut off (comp. FUERST, s. v. בֶּצֶר and מִבְצָר). I would however prefer not to make כְּבָצָר dependent on בָּחוֹן, from which it is remotely, but on עַמִּי, with which it is immediately connected. The construction is then as in דַּרְכֵּךְ זִמָּה (Ezek. xvi. 27), הַכְלִתוֹ חוֹב (Ezek. xviii. 7). Comp. NAEGELSB. *Gr.* § 63, 4, g.

[3] Ver. 28.—סוֹרְרִים is so expressed by the Vulg., Syr., Chald. and Aquila that it is evident they read שָׂרֵי, which is also actually found in Cod. Regiom. I. and II. as well as in 22 Codd. of KENNICOTT and in 18 of DE ROSSI. This reading may have been occasioned by the unusual construction and the similarity of the passages Isai. i. 23; Hos. ix. 15. The construction is however not unusual in this, as substantives are not rarely thus connected. Comp. הֲבֵל הַבָּלִים, יֶגַע עֲבָדִים etc. *Vid.* NAEGELSB. *Gr.* § 61, 3.—כָּרֵי moreover may be (comp. סַר וְזָעֵף, 1 Kings xx. 43; xxi. 4) Part. Kal from סָרַר, so that from this form a double Part. Kal would be formed. [HENDERSON: desperate revolters.]

[4] Ver. 28.—הֹלְכֵי רָכִיל. Comp. ix. 3; Ezek. xxii. 9. On the construction *Vid.* NAEGELSB. *Gr.* § 70, b. [HENDERSON renders: conversant with destruction.—S. R. A.]

[5] Ver. 28.—מַשְׁחִיתִים. Comp. Isai. i. 4 (on the direct causative signification of the Hiphil—*to do a pernicious thing.* *Vid.* NAEGELSB. *Gr.* § 18, 3).

[6] Ver. 29.—נָחַר Niph: from חָרַר (so most of the older translators and commentators) can mean only: the bellows is on fire, is red hot (HITZIG). This meaning is required by the connection, for it is to be declared, that an extreme degree of heat was applied, which is here denoted by the burning of the bellows. But even this degree of heat has extracted nothing from the ore but—lead. The other explanation from נָחַר (*anhelat*) is indeed well founded on the nominal forms נְחָרָה נַחַר, נָחִיר, but it gives an unsatisfactory sense; for it is not declared generally that the bellows works, but that it has done its best. The Chethibh must be pronounced בְּאֵשְׁתָם and presupposes a noun אֶשָׁה, which does not occur, but is formed quite normally. [HENDERSON: נָחַר may either be the root of the verb, *to snort*, and designed in this place to express the sound produced by the violent blowing of the bellows; or it may be the Niphal of חָרַר, *to burn*. The former best suits the connection. Thus MICHAELIS, ROSENMUELLER, DAHLER, DE WETTE, SCHULZ and UMBREIT.—S. R. A.]

[7] Ver. 29.—צָרַף צָרוֹף. The third plur. sing. is employed to denote an independent subject—*one*. Comp. NAEGELSB. *Gr.* § 101, 2, b.

[8] Ver. 29.—רָעִים never denotes the dross directly.

EXEGETICAL AND CRITICAL.

The prophet's sermon by no means aimed at a general conversion, it was rather to serve only as a touch-stone. By it a separating process was to be instituted, by which it would be decided which was good and which base metal (ver. 27). Unfortunately the great mass proved to be common brass (ver. 28). In the smelting-process also (past and future) the same result is presented. In two further figures which express essentially the same thing, the Lord compares Israel with a piece of ore, which in the fire produces lead, and again with one which contains silver, but unhappily so mixed, that the base cannot be separated from the true metal (vers. 29 and 30).

Ver. 27. **I have set.... their way.** The people are denominated the ore, because their value is to be ascertained by the process of assaying. The term (מְצָרֵף) is also doubtless chosen with reference to i. 18, where it is used of the prophet [a fortified (tried) city]. The nation is also tried, not as a fortress, but as ore which is yet to be proved.

Ver. 28. **They are ... all.—Slanderers.** The prophet here as elsewhere (comp. remarks on vers. 13 sqq.), in thus particularizing appears to have had the eighth commandment in mind. Comp. LUTHER'S explanation: to betray, to backbite, or to make an evil report.—**Brass and iron.** These words state, still figuratively, the result of the proving, ver. 27: the ore contains not gold or silver, but only base metal.

Ver. 29. **The bellows glows... separated.** The bellows *glows* or *is on fire*. This refers of course to Israel: *their* fire is the fire in which they are melted, the fire of affliction, both of the past, the present and the future. Even the severest trials of affliction can produce from this people nothing but lead. It is seen that the prophet proceeds to a related figure, as immediately afterwards he also makes application of a third. The first figure represents the prophet as a trier of metals, who first takes the rough ore in hand in order mineralogically to distinguish its constituent parts. In the second figure the ore is exposed to fire, in order in this way to ascertain its metallic value. The result is lead. I find accordingly that the Keri כָּתֵם אֲשֶׁר, however explained, is an entirely necessary alteration.—In what follows the prophet makes use of a third figure. Israel is here definitely presented as silver ore. But in the smelting-places it appears that the silver is so mingled with the stone that the production of clear pure silver is impossible. Israel therefore remains—refuse, impure silver, which, as unfit for noble uses, the Lord rejects.—**base** [wicked]. The prophet passes from the figurative to the literal mode of speaking.

Ver. 30. **Reprobate silver... Jehovah has reprobated them.**—The conclusion is sad. But this reprobate silver is not Israel in general, but only the Israel of the present time. Comp. iii. 11-25; iv. 27; v. 10, 18.

DOCTRINAL AND ETHICAL.

1. On ver. 1 sqq. "It is very difficult to believe the preaching of God's anger and punishment, for we look at the powerful assistance, the watchmen, the towers and fortresses, and trust in them. But fortresses here, fortresses there! These cannot withstand human force, let alone the calamity which comes from God Himself." CRAMER.

[On ver. 2. M. HENRY: "The more we indulge ourselves in the pleasures of this life, the more we disfit ourselves for the troubles of this life." On ver. 4. "It is good to see how the counsel and decree of God are pursued and executed in the devices and designs of men, even theirs that know Him not, Isai. x. 6, 7."—S. R. A.]

2. On ver. 6. "This is the strongest and most dangerous mining-powder of cities and fortresses, when sin, shame, vice and wantonness get the upper hand. For instance, Sodom and Gomorrah." CRAMER.

3. On ver. 7. "Sin cries, rises and stinks up to heaven, so that God and the angels are obliged to shut mouth, nose and ears. Compare Gen. xviii. 20; Jon. i. 2." FÖRSTER.

4. On ver. 9. "God has two kinds of vintage: one is in grace, when He plucks His glorious grapes, the fruits of good works, and says: 'Destroy it not, for there is a blessing in it' (Isai. lxv. 8). But where He finds only poisonous berries (Isai. v. 2) and is as one who gleans in the vineyard (Mic. v. 14) He employs other vintagers with iron gloves, and presses them out in His anger (Rev. xiv. 20) till neither stem nor stalk is left." CRAMER.

5. On ver. 10. "Patience! Perhaps it is not long since the preaching was begun. But in the beginning it is just so with one. When one year or forty accustomed to office, things are more tractable, God grant, not too comfortable. We must tell our story with a simple heart, as it is. We must be violent enough to gain a hearing. This joyful, honest, ever-enduring testimony of the truth, which is in us, will excite attention in time, and moreover never returns void (Isai. lv. 11)." ZINZENDORF.

6. On vers. 10, 11. "Draw off thy shoes, for the place whereon thou standest is holy ground, Exod. iii. 5. Moses, Elijah, Elisha, David, the prophet before the altar at Bethel, our Jeremiah in particular, and Paul, the evangelical Apostle, used the severest and most feeling methods against the mockers of their religion in the least and the greatest, and it is evident that God will not allow Himself to be mocked. Freely as the heart is treated, and little the violence that God does to it, yet the creature is often cut short when it comes to testifying. For there is a great difference between respect and love. Love is a grace, but respect is in accordance with a creature's nature; it is imbued in every one. For the devil himself, if his hands are bound in the least (as then more is granted him than any other), when it comes to respect—must 'tremble' (Jas. ii. 19). The Lord teach the witnesses the right measure, that their threatenings and the feelings of men suitably concur, and that it may be with every witness for religion as with John, whom King Herod feared and heard him." ZINZENDORF.

7. On ver. 14. How beautiful are the feet of them that announce true peace! (Isa. lii. 7; Nah. ii. 1.) In like measure destructive are the feet of those who preach false peace. The latter are Satan, who transforms himself into an angel of light (2 Cor. xi. 14).

8. On ver. 16. "There are two kinds of *patres*. Some are the ancients, some the young. Of the young fathers Asaph says (Ps. lxxviii. 8): that they were not as their fathers, a stubborn and rebellious generation (comp. Ezek. xx. 18). But as regards the ancient, original fathers, Abraham, Isaac, Jacob, Moses, David, the Evangelists, Apostles and such like, these are the true fathers, who preserve God's word for us, that by means of it we may follow them, and ask after the

former ways. Thus we go right and safely." CRAMER.

9. On ver. 16. *"Hic arripiunt Papicolæ semitas antiquas, indeque nobis persuadere conantur, ut et nos semitas antiquas quæramus, i. e., ut religione Lutherana valere jussa nos adjungamus ecclesiæ papisticæ, quam omnium antiquissimam nusquam non superbe jactitant. Sed nos ipsis* 1. *obvertimus illud Ignatii: nobis vera antiquitas est* Jesus Christus, *cui nolle obedire manifestum est exitium.* 2. *Argumentum, quod isthinc consarcinare satagunt, hunc in modum invertimus: ea ecclesia pro vera habenda, quæ omnium antiquissima. Atqui nostra—est antiquissima. Cœpit enim mox ab initio mundi in Paradiso cum Protevangelio* (Gen. iii. 15, coll. xv. 6): *Romanensium vero ecclesia, sicut ipsi haud diffitentur, circa a Chr.* 606 *cœpit. Ergo.*" FÖRSTER.

10. On ver. 16. "Those are the honest knaves, who tell the prophet to his face: we will not do it (Jer. xliv. 16). But such the Lord will honestly punish. For the servant, who knew his Lord's will and did it not, shall suffer double stripes (Luke xii. 47)." CRAMER.

11. [CALVIN: On ver. 19. "We may learn from this passage that nothing is more abominable in the sight of God than the contempt of divine truth: for His majesty, which shines forth in His word, is thereby trampled under foot; and further, it is an extreme ingratitude in men when God Himself invites them to salvation, wilfully to seek their own ruin and to reject His favor." On ver. 20. "And we see at this day, that men cannot be rightly taught, except we carry on war against that external splendor with which they will have God to be satisfied. As then men deceive themselves with such trifles, it is necessary to show that all those things which hypocrites obtrude on God, without sincerity of heart, are frivolous trumperies."—S. R. A.]

12. On ver. 27 sqq. "When goldsmiths wish to purify the silver, they add lead to it. When preachers would try their hearers, they must apply the law. The fire is God's word (Jer. xxiii. 29), the bellows the Holy Spirit in the mouth of the teacher, the metals the hearers, of which some are objectionable, others are unobjectionable." CRAMER.

13. On ver. 27. As Christ is called a sign which shall be spoken against, that the thoughts of many hearts may be revealed (Luke ii. 34, 35), the power dwells in His word generally to compel men to separation and decision. For no one can remain neutral towards Him long. He is a touchstone which makes manifest the real condition of the heart, whether the man is of God or not of God, Heb. iv. 12; John viii. 47.

HOMILETICAL AND PRACTICAL.

1. Vers. 6-8 may serve for the text of an exhortation to repentance. On the punitive justice of God. 1. With what it threatens us. 2. Why it threatens us. 3. How this threatening can be averted.

2. On vers. 6 and 7. "We find such fountains of evil in our own perverted hearts. Original sin is the true fountain of evil, from which from childhood up much water of obstinacy, disobedience, indolence, envy, falsehood is poured forth. And such water flows every year more abundantly. Soon also flows the water of vanity, of impurity and excess, of reviling and cursing. How does man help himself? Either he will not allow others to observe what wickedness comes from his heart, and hides his sins, or he is himself grieved that so much sin flows from his heart, and begins to stop the flow, *i. e.,* he makes good resolves and proposes no more to commit the old sins. But lo! the streams break forth again, and the fountain of a depraved heart ceases not to flow. Again others allow the stream free course and pollute the city and the country with their sins, as the Jewish people did. Where is help to be found against this fountain of a depraved heart? In the fountain of which Zechariah prophesies, xiii. 1." HOCHSTETTER, 12 *Parables from the proph. Jer., S.* 12, 13.

3. [TILLOTSON on ver. 8. 1. The infinite goodness and patience of God towards a sinful people, and His great unwillingness to bring ruin upon them. 2. The only proper and effectual means to prevent the misery and ruin of a sinful people. 3. The miserable case and condition of a people when God takes off His affection from them."—S. R. A.]

4. On vers. 11, 12. The double trouble of a preacher of the truth. 1. From without, (*a*) indisposition to hear, (*b*) scorn. 2. From within, irresistible necessity of announcing the word of the Lord.

5. On vers. 13-15. Warning against false prophets: 1. Their course: they teach false worship, *i. e.,* they lead not to God but away from Him, by (*a*) being silent as to the real inconvenient truth, (*b*) putting the conscience to sleep by a falsehood. 2. Their motive: covetousness, selfishness (ver. 13). 3. Their end: they are put to shame (ver. 15).

6. On ver. 14. [CHALMERS: "The evils of false security. 1. It is not based on the mercy offered by God. 2. It casts an aspersion on the character of God. 3. It is hostile to the cause of practical righteousness."—SPURGEON: "I have heard of a city missionary who kept a record of two thousand persons who were supposed to be on their death-bed but recovered, and whom he should have put down as converted persons, had they died; and how many do you think lived a Christian life afterwards out of the two thousand? Not two. Positively he could only find one who was found to live afterwards in the fear of God. Is it not horrible that when men and women come to die they should cry, 'Comfort, comfort!' and that hence their friends conclude that they are children of God, while after all they have no right to consolation, but are intruders on the enclosed grounds of the blessed God?" —S. R. A.]

7. On ver. 15. [SOUTH: "Shamelessness in sin the certain forerunner of destruction. 1. How shame is more effectual than law. 2. How men cast off shame. 3. The several degrees of shamelessness. 4. Reasons why shamelessness is so destructive. 5. The destruction by which it procures the sinner's ruin."—S. R. A.]

8. On ver. 16. Which is the good way? That which has 1, the right starting-point (the one, unalterable, ancient truth); 2 the right ending (rest for the soul). [DOOLITTLE has a sermon with this text on the theme, "Popery a novelty," and CALAMY has two on the Trinity!—S. R. A.]

CHAP. VII. 1-7.

9. On ver. 16. New Year's Sermon. What does a retrospect of the ways of the past year show us? 1. That they have been under God's wondrous guidance; 2. that they were intended to be only ways of salvation for our soul; 3. that we have often said, we will not walk in them; 4. that we should care best for our salvation, if we would henceforth walk in the good ways of God. FLOREY, 1863.
10. On vers. 18-21. The righteous judgments of God. 1. They do not shun publicity, but rather appeal to the moral sense of the whole world. 2. They bring upon men their merited recompense. 3. They can be averted, not by outward worship, but by honest submission to God's word (vers. 19, 20).
11. On vers. 27-30. The word of truth a touchstone for the human heart. 1. The good are attracted by it; 2. the bad turn away and are rejected.

3. THE THIRD DISCOURSE.

CHAPS. VII.—X.

The time of this discourse may be determined pretty accurately, since ch. xxvi. gives us information concerning the historical circumstances in which the discourse was delivered. We learn from it that in the beginning of the reign of Jehoiakim Jeremiah received from Jehovah the commission to place himself in the fore-court of the temple, and to announce to all the Jews who had come to worship (comp. xxvi. 2 with vii. 2) that if they continued to act in opposition to the repeated admonitions of the prophets (xxvi. 5, and vii. 13, 25) the Lord would make the temple like Shiloh, (comp. xxvi. 3-13 with vii. 8-14). Since the enemies who are to execute this judgment are still designated generally as a people coming from the North (comp. viii. 16), and not yet definitely as the Chaldeans, the discourse must have been delivered before the fourth year of Jehoiakim. Comp. infra on xxv. 1. The place which the discourse occupies in the book is therefore in accordance with the principle of chronological arrangement.
The contents of the discourse may be distinguished as follows:

Main thought: Indictment of the people on account of their three prevailing vices, with threatening of punishment.

I. FIRST CHARGE.

1. HYPOCRITICAL MINGLING OF THE WORSHIP OF JEHOVAH WITH IDOLATRY, AND OTHER MORAL ABOMINATIONS.

VII. 1—VIII. 3.

1. *Fundamental: the fundamental requirement and promise,* vii. 1-7.
2. *Their demoralizing trust in the outward temple-service. Admonitory reference to Shiloh,* vii. 8-15.
3. *The hypocrisy of the worship of Jehovah, boasted of in ver. 4 sqq. is evinced by the idolatry practised elsewhere. Thus the nation is provoking a severe and inevitable judgment,* vii. 16-20.
4. *Refutation of the objection that the Lord Himself commanded the outward temple-service,* vii. 21-28.
5. *The abomination of idolatry in the highest degree a most evident proof of the hypocrisy of the people. Beginning of retribution,* vii. 29-34.
6. *The fulfilment of retribution corresponding to the idol abominations,* viii. 1-3.

II. SECOND CHARGE.

THEIR RUINOUS PERSISTENCE IN EVIL.

VIII. 4-23.

7. *Their stiff-necked impenitence and its punishment,* viii. 4-12.
8. *Further portrayal of the visitation announced in* ver. 12, viii. 13-17.
9. *Continuation: The visitation ends with the carrying away captive of Israel, to the inexpressible grief of the people and the prophet,* viii. 18-23.

III. THIRD CHARGE.

THE GENERAL ENTIRE ABSENCE OF TRUTH AND FAITH.

IX. 1-21.

10. *Description of the prevailing deceit,* ix. 1-8.
11. *First punishment: Desolation of the land and dispersion of the people,* ix. 9-15.
12. *Second punishment: Death snatching away an innumerable sacrifice,* ix. 16-21.

IV. CONCLUSION.

IX. 22-25 ; X. 16-25.

13. *The only means of escape and the reason why it is not used,* ix. 22-25.
14. *The beginning of the end of retribution : Command to the people to retire ; Lament of the desolated land ; last watch-cry of the prophet : the enemy is here,* x. 17-22.
15. *Consolatory glance into the future,* x. 23-25.

I. FIRST CHARGE.

THE HYPOCRITICAL MINGLING OF THE SERVICE OF JEHOVAH WITH IDOLATRY AND OTHER MORAL ABOMINATIONS.

VII. 1—VIII. 3.

1. *Fundamental: the fundamental requirement and promise.*

VII. 1-7.

1 The word which came to Jeremiah from Jehovah, saying:
2 Stand in the gate of the house of Jehovah
   And proclaim there this word, and say:
   Hear the word of Jehovah, all ye of Judah,
   Who have entered at these gates to worship Jehovah.
3 Thus saith Jehovah Zebaoth, the God of Israel ;
   Amend your ways and your doings,
   So will I cause you to dwell[1] in this place.
4 Trust[2] not to[3] those lying words :
   " The Lord's temple, the Lord's temple, the Lord's temple is this."[4]
5 But amend your ways and your doings !
   If ye execute judgment between every man and his neighbor,
6 Oppress not stranger, orphan and widow,
   And shed not innocent blood in this place,
   And go not after other gods to your destruction;
7 So will I cause you to dwell in this place,
   In the land which I gave to your fathers,
   From everlasting to everlasting.[5]

TEXTUAL AND GRAMMATICAL.

[1] Ver. 3.—["The Piel or intensive form of the verb must here have a continuative force, or it must have a permissive signification. There is no example of the simple signification *to dwell* attaching to this conjugation, so that the rendering of the Vulgate, which BLAYNEY adopts : *I will dwell with you* is not sustained; comp. ver. 12." HENDERSON.—S. R. A.]
[2] Ver. 4.—לָכֶם after תִּבְטְחוּ (comp. ver. 8) is *Dat. ethicus.* Comp. 2 Ki. xviii. 21, 24; Cant. ii. 17 ; NAEGELSB. *Gr.* § 112, 5, b.
[3] Ver. 4.—אֶל־דִּבְרֵי. More frequently בָּטַח is followed by בְּ or עַל (vers. 8, 14) but אֶל is not unfrequent, Jud. xx. 36 ; 3 Ki. xviii. 22 ; Isai. xxxvi. 7, *etc.*
[4] Ver. 4.—[Lit. ; are these].
[5] Ver. 7.—[Or : forever and ever].

EXEGETICAL AND CRITICAL.

The prophet begins with friendly admonition and promise. In ver. 3 he briefly states in advance the fundamental requirement and promise. Vers. 4-7 continue the theme by opposing to false confidence in the apparently infallible objective guarantee of salvation in the possession of the outward temple (ver. 4) exhortation to positive (ver. 5) and negative (ver. 6) fulfilment of the true subjective condition of salvation, after which however the promise, which includes all further salvation for Israel, is repeated more at length. We easily recognize in this strophe the outlines of the whole discourse, for these exhortations correspond, if not in order in contents, exactly with the following exhortations and threatenings, the latter having also for their subject pseudo-worship of Jehovah, idolatry, impenitence, falsehood, deceit, violence, and finally exile.

Vers. 1, 2. **The word which came ... to worship Jehovah.** A similar introductory formula is found in xi. 1 ; xviii. 1 ; xxi. 1 ; xxv. 1 ; xxx. 1 ; xxxii. 1 ; xxxiv. 1 ; xxxv. 1 ; xl. 1 ; xliv. 1.—**In the gate of the house.** If we compare xxvi. 2, where the historical particulars

CHAP. VII. 1-7.

relating to this discourse are given, we see that Jeremiah delivered it in the fore-court (comp. xix. 14). Further information is derived from xxxvi. 1C, where it is said that Baruch read the book of the words of Jeremiah "in the chamber of Gemariah, in the *higher* court, at the entrance of the new gate." Now since this new gate is the same under which the princes called Jeremiah to account for this very discourse (xxvi. 10), it is highly probable that the gate spoken of was not that which formed the main eastern entrance of the outer court (Ezek. xi. 1), but one of the gates which led from the outer into the inner or upper court. From this point the prophet could view the whole assembly of the people in the outer court, as well as the gates leading from without into it.—**All ye of Judah**. A great festival to Jehovah must have brought the whole people together, for they had not sunk into that state of entire alienation, which, *ex. gr.* prevailed under Manasseh, when they no longer worshipped the God of their fathers (2 Kings xxi. 2), but now they served other gods together with Him (ver. 6).

Ver. 3. **Thus saith Jehovah . . . dwell in this place**. These words express as to form the theme of the strophe, but at the same time also as to matter the positive main thought of the whole discourse, which however retires in what follows for the reason stated in vers. 24-28.—דֶּרֶךְ **ways** and מַעֲלָל **doings** are distinguished like *habitus* and *actus*, the former denoting the inward inclination or disposition of the heart (comp. v. 16), the latter the outward fruits in the life (iv. 13; xviii. 11; xxvi. 13; xxxii. 19).—**Cause to dwell**. Comp. Numb. xiv. 30.—**This place**. The temple is meant primarily as the centre of the theocracy. Comp. ver. 6, where the desecration of the holy places by the shedding of innocent blood is emphasized (2 Kings xxi. 16; xxiv. 4; Matth. xxiii. 35), and then ver. 7, where *this place* and the land are distinguished, and ver. 13, where מָקוֹם is distinguished from Shiloh and taken in the more restricted sense of the holy places of worship.

Ver. 4. **Trust not . . . temple is this**. An example of similar threefold repetition is found in xxii. 29; Isai. vi. 3 coll. 2 Sam. xix. 1. For the sense comp. Mic. iii. 11.—הֵמָּה. Without this word הֵיכָל would be the subject, and the only meaning would be: *templum est*, *i. e.*, we have God's temple. With this word הֵיכָל is predicate, and the former the subject, and the difference in the sense is this, that it is not the existence, the possession of the temple generally, which is declared, but the concrete objects, to which the predicate applies, are indicated. We must therefore render this הֵמָּה δεικτικῶς. The plural has been variously explained. The Chaldee refers the threefold repetition to the three main forms of worship and their appearance thrice in the year; JOSEPH KIMCHI to the three divisions of the temple-building (court, sanctuary and holy of holies); MENOCHIUS (*Vid.* NEUMANN, *S.* 439) to the Jewish nation itself, coll. 1 Cor. iii. 16, 17; VENEMA and others to the temple and priests, and with reference to אַתָּה־הוּא (Ps. cii. 28) finds also in הֵמָּה the meaning of continuance and immutability.—In a purely linguistic view הֵמָּה would apply best to the people, and the thought, that the people as the temple of God were safe from all danger to themselves or the sanctuary, would suit the connection. But the mention of the sanctuary at Shiloh (vers. 12 and 14) requires that in ver. 4 also the temple-edifice be referred to. Comp. especially ver. 14.—Nothing further then remains but to refer הֵמָּה to the various parts of the temple; not merely the three divisions of the edifice proper, but also the other parts—walls, gates, courts, halls, *etc*. Still however the plural is remarkable, and a satisfactory explanation of it a *desideratum*. At any rate we perceive that it was a prevalent delusion among the people that the temple could not be destroyed, because it was Jehovah's. Three times is this emphatically repeated. And by the temple all else seemed to be secured. NEUMANN rightly calls attention to the circumstance that the people make use of the prouder expression הֵיכָל only, while the prophet speaks only of בַּיִת."

Vers. 5-7. **But amend your ways . . from everlasting to everlasting**. Not the outward temple with its service ensures the favor of Jehovah, but the service, which is offered in His temple by sanctified hearts and which manifests itself in works of righteousness. That such works as are here (vers. 5 and 6) enumerated pertain especially to the Old Testament "righteousness," which is opposed not to grace but to violent unrighteousness, is proved by many passages: Ps. v. vii. ix. x. xi. xii. xv. xvii.; Jer. x. 24, 25; xxii. 3-17; Isai. i. 17, *etc*. Comp. OETLOFF on the idea of צֶדֶק, *etc.*, in RUDELB.U.GUER. 1860, III. *S.* 403.—The אֶל before תִּשְׁפְּכוּ is quite abnormal, and there is no other instance of it. GRAF correctly supposes that it owes its origin to the similarly sounding sentence, xxii. 3.—**To your destruction**. Comp. xxv. 7.—**From everlasting** (comp. ver. 25) belongs to **dwell**. Israel is to inhabit the land given to the fathers, from the original epoch (vi. 16; Ps. xxiv. 7) at which they took possession of it even to the remotest future. Comp. on **xxv. 5**.

2. *Demoralizing trust in the outward temple-service. Admonitory reference to Shiloh.*

VII. 8-15.

8 Behold, ye trust in such lying words to your hurt.
9 To steal, murder, commit adultery,[1]
   Swear falsely and burn incense to Baal,
   And follow other gods which ye know not,—
10 And then ye come[2] and stand before me in this house,
   Which is called by my name: and say:
   We are delivered—to do all these abominations?
11 Is then this house which bears my name
   Become a den of robbers in your eyes?
   Behold! even I have seen it, saith Jehovah.
12 For go now to my place which was in Shiloh
   Where I caused my name to dwell at the first,
   And see what I have done to it
   On account of the wickedness of my people Israel!
13 And now, because ye do all these works, saith Jehovah,
   And I spoke to you most urgently,[3] but ye heard not.—
   I called to you, but ye gave no answer,—
14 Therefore I do to the house which bears my name
   In which ye put your trust,
   And the place which I gave to you and your fathers,
   As I did to Shiloh.
15 And I cast you out from my presence,
   As I cast out all your brethren,
   The whole seed of Ephraim.

TEXTUAL AND GRAMMATICAL.

[1] Ver. 9.—Similar infinitive constructions are found in Isai. xxi. 5; xxii. 13; lix. 4; Hos. iv. 2. Comp. NAEGELSB. *Gr.* 92, 2 b.
[2] Ver. 10.—On the transition from the infinitive to the finite verb, comp. NAEGELSB. *Gr.* § 99, 3.
[3] Ver. 13.—הַשְׁכֵּם. Comp. ver. 25; xxix. 19; and NAEGELSB. *Gr.* § 93 f. [GREEN, *Gr.* § 282].

EXEGETICAL AND CRITICAL.

Vers. 8-11 state that Israel did not follow the exhortation given in ver. 3 sqq., but regarded the external place of grace as though it were a spot where one only needed to present himself in order to be delivered from all the evil consequences of sin,—so that the sanctuary was misused and became a den of robbers. The Lord dispels this allusion as to the infallible power to save of the supposed irrevocably chosen place of grace by pointing to Shiloh: as it is with this, so will it be with the temple and Jerusalem (vers. 12-15).

Ver. 8. **Behold, ye trust . . . to your hurt.** The statement corresponds to the warning in ver. 4, and affirms that this was not heeded by Israel. "To your hurt" depends on "trust." It is a *litotes*. The delusion causes injury in a twofold way, by demoralizing the people and thus rendering them ripe for the divine judgment. Comp. Isai. xliv. 10.

Ver. 9. **To steal, murder . . . which ye know not.** These words in connection with vers. 10, 11, designate the first effect of that hurtful confidence. The people, considering salvation as unconditionally guaranteed by the temple, fall into the delusion, that presence in the temple is sufficient to procure absolution after the practice of the most heinous abominations and license for new crimes, by which course the temple is turned into a place of security and concealment for robbers. The question expresses indignant amazement: What? Steal, murder, commit adultery, *etc.*? Such wickedness ye do, and then ye come, *etc.*—**Incense to Baal,** comp. xi. 13, 17.—**And follow other gods which ye know not** is taken verbatim from Deut. xi. 28; coll. xiii. 14. Comp. xix. 4; xlix. 3.

Ver. 10. **And then ye come . . . all these abominations?** The question is continued to וַנִּצַּלְנוּ, for it is this which is the object of the divine indignation, that the people can unite such moral contrasts.—**Stand before me.** The expression has the collateral idea of *serving*; comp. Deut. x. 8; 1 Kings i. 2; xvii. 1; xviii. 15; 2 Kings iii. 14; iv. xl. 10; Ezek. xliv. 15, *etc.*—**Which is called by my name.** This expression corresponds to put my name upon (*nomen indere, imponere*), Numb. vi. 27; 1 Kings ix. 3, 5; comp. Exod. iii. 18; v. 3; Deut. xii. 5, 11; xxviii. 10; 2 Sam. xii. 28; Jer. vii. 30; xxxii. 34; xxxiv. 15.—**We are delivered.** The people regard their standing before God, their service in the temple as an unfailing means of removing all their guilt in a convenient external manner. The word therefore means: *we are saved*, freed from all the guilt and punishment of sin. Comp. Luke iii. 8.—Many commentators take לְמַעַן as=*because*: because ye have done these abominations? (ironical.) Others=*although*. The language will allow neither. It is the secondary object of their temple-service which is indicated. The primary, immediate object is expressed in נִצַּלְנוּ: they wish to purify themselves from their guilt. But as they do not use the right means for this, so also they are not actuated by the right motive,—it is not that they may henceforward hate and abandon their sin, but that like a sow they may return with the more gusto to their wallowing in the mire (2 Pet. ii. 22).

Ver. 11. **Is then this house . . saith Jehovah.** In these words the prophet discovers to the people the very heart of their proceeding: with such usage the temple is not a place of salvation, but a refuge for robbers where they purify themselves from the blood and filth of their evil deeds, so as to be the readier for new ones.— **Even I.** This perception is confirmed ironically, but in a double sense. First by this word, secondly by act. In so far namely as the Lord treats the sanctuary at Jerusalem like that at Shiloh, He causes it to be understood that He regards it as a nest of robbers. That first point results from the evident reference of **I have seen it** to **in your eyes**, the second from the following **For**, ver. 12.

Ver. 12. **For go now . . my people Israel.** In these words it is explained how far the Lord actually regards the temple as a den of robbers: we learn that He will treat it as He did Shiloh. **For** is accordingly to be referred not to ver. 12 only, but to all that follows. The prophet thus shows the second calamitous effect (ver. 8) of those lying words (ver. 4). — **To my place.** This denotes the place as such, the spot on which the sanctuary stood, not the latter itself. On this spot nothing more was now to be seen of the sacred dwellings and vessels which once adorned it. A proof is thus furnished that when the Lord has once selected a place for His dwelling upon earth He is not irrevocably bound to this place to all eternity. Whether the city of Shiloh was then destroyed or not, and whether some ruins of the former sanctuary remained to testify of its previous existence, is a matter of indifference. Shiloh was still standing in the reign of Jeroboam I. (1 Kings xi. 20; xii. 15; xiv. 2) and Jeremiah mentions it as though it were still in existence (xli. 5). Comp. GRAF, *ad loc.*—HERZOG's *Real-Encyc.* XIV. S. 369. ["Dr. ROBINSON found its ruins under the name of *Seilun* on his way from Jerusalem to Shechem." HENDERSON.]

Vers. 13-15. **And now, because ye do . . . the whole seed of Ephraim.** The apodosis begins with ver. 14. With respect to the transition from the infinitive to the finite verb, see GRAMMATICAL rems. on ver. 9.— הֲשָׁבֵם. Comp. ver. 25; xxix. 19; and NAEGELSBACH, *Gr.* § 93, *f* [GREEN's *Gr.* § 282].—**The place.** The prophet cannot mean the whole country, any more than in vers. 3, 6, 7. As in ver. 12, it is the spot on which the house stands. This spot of earth is the hallowed and hallowing centre of the whole country, on which all other dwelling-places are founded. Comp. Exod. iii. 5.—For Ephraim as a designation of the ten tribes *vide* Hos. iv. 17; Isai. vii. 2, *etc.*

---

3. *The hypocrisy of the worship of Jehovah, boasted of in ver. 4 sqq., is evinced by the idolatry practised elsewhere. Thus the nation is provoking a severe and inevitable judgment.*

VII. 16-20.

16 And as to thee, pray not for this people,
    And make not a cry and supplication for them,
    Nor intercede with me; for I will not hear thee.
17 Seest thou not what they are doing
    In the cities of Judah and in the streets of Jerusalem?
18 The children gather wood and the fathers kindle the fire,
    And the women knead the dough, to make cakes for the queen of the heavens,
    And pour out libations to other gods, to aggrieve me.
19 Do they aggrieve me? saith Jehovah.
    Do they not themselves to their own shame?
20 Therefore thus saith the Lord Jehovah:
    Behold, my anger and my fury is poured out in this place,
    On the men and the cattle,
    And on the trees of the field and the fruits of the land,
    That it may burn and not be extinguished.

EXEGETICAL AND CRITICAL.

How fixedly the judgment announced in vers. 14, 15 is determined upon by Jehovah, is evinced by this, that the prophet is forbidden to interpose with any plea (ver. 16). The motive of this seemingly harsh decree is indicated by reference to the idolatry still in full course in the cities of Judah and Jerusalem, and which forms a gloomy offset to that pseudo-Jehovah-worship mentioned in ver. 4. This idolatry may be directed primarily against Jehovah, but it will prove at last self-destructive to Israel (vers. 19, 20).

Ver. 16. **And as to thee I will... not hear thee.** JEROME remarks that "*sanctorum preces Dei iræ possunt resistere,* Ex. xxxii. 10 sq.; Ps. cvi. 30; Numb. xvi. 46 sq." Comp. 1 John v. 16— רִנָּה with תְּפִלָּה is frequent, *ex. gr.,* Ps. xvii. 1; 1 Kings viii. 28, *etc.*—This verse is repeated xi. 14; xiv. 11.

Vers. 17 and 18. **Seest thou not what they are doing ... to aggrieve me.** The motive of the severe prohibition in ver. 16.—**The queen of the heavens** is mentioned besides only in xliv. 17, 18, 19, 25. The form, which in Hebrew indeed has general analogies (*ez. gr.* גְּבֶרֶת) but does not otherwise occur, bespeaks the foreign origin of the phrase as of the thing. The expression "heaven's-queen" points to the worship of the stars, and indeed the moon as the feminine potence (together with the sun as the masculine) appears not seldom under this name. It is called by APULEIUS (*Metaph.* XI. init.) directly *regina cœli,* and in HORACE (*Carm. Secul.* 35) we find the words: *Siderum regina bicornis audi Luna puellas.* For more on this subject consult ABR. CALOV. *Diss. de Selenolatria Viteb.* 1680 (also in *Thes. theol. philol.,* Vol. 1. p. 808 sqq.). To the further question, what deity is represented by the moon, we can only answer that since it, as the female principle of fructification, corresponds to the sun-god Baal as the male principle, the feminine deity corresponding to Baal, *i. e.,* Astarte, must be represented by the moon. HERODIAN (V. 6, 10) says expressly, Οὐρανίαν Φοίνικες Ἀστροάρχην (Græcism for Astarte) ὀνομάζουσι, σελήνην εἶναι θέλοντες. Comp. HEROD. III. 8.—On the Carthaginian inscriptions (*Insc. Karth.* 8), חַמְלֶכֶת (=מַלְכֶּת), חֵן, *i. e.,* the Νηΐθ, Τανάϊς, the Asiatic, originally Egyptian ARTEMIS appears as the feminine opposite of בַּעַל חַפֻּן, בַּעַל חַפֻּן. This is certainly no longer the original Phœnician Astarte, but a later modification with unchaste cultus, and probably admixture of star-worship. Comp. 2 Kings xxi. 3; xxiii. 4; Jer. xix. 13.— Comp. CREUZER, *Symbol.* II. *Kap.* 4, § 1, 2, 3, 6; *Appendix on the Carthag. religion,* § 3. For the less recent literature on this passage consult ROSENMUELLER.—The כַּוָּנִים (xliv. 19) are probably the Egyptian confection *Neideh* (*Vid.* HITZIG *ad hoc l.* and FUERST *H. W. B. s. v.* כַּוָּן). According to the לְהַעֲצִבָה, xliv. 19, it is not improbable that the cakes were in the form of a moon; compare the cakes offered to Artemis as the moon-god in Athens under the name of σελήναι (*Vid.* GRAF *ad loc.*).—On the heathen custom of celebrating the new moon with fires kindled in the streets and sweet cakes, comp. SPENCER, *De Legg. Hebr. ritual.* L. III. Diss. IV. *Cap.* 3.—The etymology of כֵּן is uncertain. It is most probably derived from כּוּן, *to prepare.* Is it not perhaps connected with כִּי (Am. v. 26)? With this adoration of the queen of heaven may have been connected as a later remnant the worship of the Collyridians, who existed in Arabia in the 4th century, and gave divine honors to the Virgin Mary, offering her little cakes of bread (κολλυρίς), *Vid.* EPIPH. *Hær.* 79.—**And pour out libations.** The infinitive here may certainly depend on the (לְ) before **make** (עֲשׂוֹת) (comp. NAEGELSB. *Gr.* § 112, 8). But it must also be remarked that the Inf. הַסֵּךְ is used by Jeremiah in a very peculiar manner absolutely: xix. 13; xiv. 19 (where the לְ perhaps from oversight stands instead of in vers. 17 and 18). At any rate it designates the drink-offerings pertaining to the meat-offering of cakes.

Vers. 19 and 20. **Do they aggrieve me?... that it may burn and not be extinguished.** —On **aggrieve** comp. Ezek. xxxii. 9.—**themselves.** אֹתָם reciprocal (comp. NAEGELSB. *Gr.* § 81, *b*).—**fury is poured out** (comp. Nah. i. 6). —**In this place.** The divine anger is poured out immediately *in* the centre of the Theocracy (אֵל) and from thence immediately over the whole land (עַל).

---

4. *Refutation of the objection that the Lord Himself commanded the outward temple service.*

VII. 21–28.

21 Thus saith Jehovah Zebaoth, the God of Israel:
    Take your burnt offerings with the sin offerings and eat flesh.
22 For I spoke not with your fathers in the day that I brought[1] them out of Egypt,
    Nor commanded them concerning burnt offerings and slain offerings.
23 But this I commanded them: "Hearken to my voice,
    That I may be your God, and you my people,

And walk in all the ways that I command you,
That it may be well with you."
24 But they hearkened not, nor inclined their ear,
And walked after their own counsels [2]—
In the hardness of their evil heart,
And turned to the back and not to the face.[3]
25 From the day that your fathers went out of the land of **Egypt**,
To this day I send you all my servants,
The prophets, zealously and unremittingly.
26 But they hearkened not to me, nor inclined their ear.
But they stiffened their neck and acted more wickedly than their fathers.
27 And though thou speakest to them all these words,
Yet will they not hearken unto thee;
And though thou callest to them,
Yet will they not answer thee.
28 Therefore shalt thou say unto them:
This is the people that has not hearkened
To the voice of Jehovah, their God,
Nor accepted chastisement.
Truth is vanished and eradicated from their mouth.

TEXTUAL AND GRAMMATICAL.

[1] Ver. 22.—["A vast number of MSS., three of the early editions, and all the versions read, with the Keri, הוֹצִיאִי instead of הוֹצִיא." HENDERSON.—S. R. A.]

[2] Ver. 24.— בְּמֹעֲצוֹת is *stat. absol.* and therefore not co-ordinated with the following שְׁרִרוּת, but the following sentence forms a sort of opposition to it: They walked in counsels!—in hardness of their heart. Comp. NAEGELSB. *Gram.* § 66.

[3] Ver. 24.—[BLAYNEY, UMBREIT, HENDERSON render: and went (drew, turned) backward, and not forward. NOYES and HITZIG: turned the back and not the face.—S. R. A.]

EXEGETICAL AND CRITICAL.

The hypocritical people might appeal to the fact that their outward temple service was in accordance with the precepts of the Law. To this however it is opposed, that from the beginning the Lord directed His chief regard not to external worship, but to the obedience of the heart, and to this gave the promise of prosperity (vers. 21-23). But the people never observed this requirement of the Lord, though He caused it to be repeated often and urgently by the prophets (vers. 24-26). They will close their ears even to the exhortation of Jeremiah, and thus call down upon themselves the judgment of incorrigibility (vers. 27, 28).

Ver. 21. **Thus saith Jehovah . . . and eat flesh. — Take**, סְפוּ (comp. Isai. xxix. 1), may be derived from סָכַף or סָפָה. (Comp. Isai. xxx. 1: Numb. xxxii. 14). The primary idea seems to be "to scrape, scratch, sweep," from which are derived the meanings both of *to sweep up* or *together* (comp. also Deut. xxxii. 23) and *to scrape off* (Isai. vii. 20) and *sweep away* (Ps. xl. 15). עַל also stands after the word in the passages cited. Comp. iii. 18.—**And eat flesh**, an expression of contempt: throw all your sacrifices and burnt-offerings together and devour them as meat. Comp. vi. 20.

Vers. 22 and 23. **For I spoke not . . . . may be well with you**. When the Rabbins emphasize **in the day**, *etc*, or when others appealing to Levit. i. 2, *etc.* find in this passage an indication of the voluntariness of the offerings, or at least of the view that only voluntary offerings are here spoken of, GRAF is certainly right in designating such points as subtleties. But to find in the passage a proof that Jeremiah was ignorant of any legal enactments with respect to sacrifices at the time of the Exodus, since in his time the middle books of the Pentateuch, which owed their origin to Ezra, were not in existence, as GRAF does, following HITZIG and others (comp. especially his latest work. *On the historical books of the Old Test.*, Leipzig, 1866), is a proceeding for which there is no ground either in those books, in the writings of the preëxilic prophets generally (comp. only *ex. gr.*, Am. iv. 5 with Levit. vii. 13; Hos. iv. 7-9 with Levit. vi. 18; xxvi. 26), or in this particular passage. For it is indeed true that the words that **I may be your God and you my people** (the substance of which is found in Exod. vi. 7 coll. Deut. xxix. 12) are a verbal quotation from the certainly peculiar 26th chapter of Leviticus (ver. 12), that the next line likewise resembles almost word for word Deut. v. 33 (the expression **in all the ways** occurs in this sense only in this passage of Deut.), finally that **that it may be well with you** also is exclusively Deuteronomic (v. 16, 26; vi. 18; xii. 25, 28; xxii. 27). But (1.) the book of Deuteronomy presupposes the preceding books of the Pentateuch and cannot be understood without them. Thus it is explained that precepts relating to the sacrifices do not here occur except in a summary (Deut. xii. 6, 11, 13, 14, 27) or modified form, according to the circumstances (comp. Deut. xii. 15 with Levit. xvii. 2 sqq.). (2) If this passage is to be understood in a literal sense, as by HITZIG and GRAF, the prophet would declare not only something incredible in itself, but also what would be in the highest degree prejudicial to the assumed post-exilic composition of the middle books of the Pentateuch. For how could these place the origin of the sacrificial enactments in the period of the exodus, if prophetic utterances like this and Am. v. 25 expressly contradict it? (3) As in Exod. xvi. 8 the words "Your murmurings are not against us, but against Jehovah," declare not that the Israelites did not murmur at all against Moses and Aaron (which is expressly maintained in ver. 2), but only that the sin of murmuring against Moses and Aaron vanished in comparison with the sin which they committed in their murmuring against the Lord Himself,—as Hos. vi. 6 likewise denies pleasure in sacrifices not absolutely but only relatively, in so far that it does not enter into comparison with the pleasure of the Lord in true piety (comp. Gen. xxxii. 29; lv. 8; 1 Sam. viii 7)—so also in this passage the negation has a rhetorical, not a logical significance (comp. WINER, Gramm. N. T. Sprachidioms § 58, 7). Thus those commentators are right who find here this meaning, that the whole of the enactments relating to sacrifices do not enter into consideration in comparison with the importance of the moral Law. Comp. the parallel passages:— Isa. v. 11; lviii. 8 sqq.; lxvi. 3; 1 Sam. xv. 22; Mic. vi. 6-8; Ps. xl. 7 sqq.; Ps. l.; Ps. li. 18, 19; Prov. xxi. 27; Matt. ix. 13. The expression: I will be your God and ye shall be my people, is found with special frequency in Jeremiah: xi. 4; xxiv. 7; xxx. 22; xxxi. 1, 33; xxxii. 38. Almost as frequently in Ezekiel: xi. 20; xiv. 10; xxxvi. 28; xxxvii. 23, 27. Twice also in Zechariah: ii. 15; viii. 8.

Ver. 24. **But they hearkened not . . . back not face.—In the hardness of their heart,** comp. Deut. xxix. 18; Jer. iii. 17.—In general comp. xi. 8; Ps. lxxxi. 13.—ויהי לאחור וגו׳. Comp. ii. 27. Literally:—they came to the back and not to the face, viz., from the standpoint of Jehovah. Comp. NAEGELSB. Gr., § 69, 3, as to the substantives *back* and *face* taking the place of adjectives or participles.

Vers. 25, 26. **From the day . . . more wickedly than their fathers.**—לְמִן comp. ver. 7.—וָאֶשְׁלַח. Vau constr. after a definition of time. Comp. NAEGELSB. Gr., § 88, 7.—Comp. xi. 7; xxv. 4; xxvi. 5; xxix. 19; xxxv. 15; xliv. 4.—Alone יוֹם never means "daily." But with an infinitive construction it represents the idea "day" in the same sense as הַשְׁכֵּם the idea "early," *i. e.,* the sending has taken place day by day, daily and always early, *i. e.*, not sleepily, dilatorily, but diligently and unremittingly, comp. besides Gr. § 93, b.—On ver. 26 comp. Deut. x. 16; Jer. xvii. 23; xix. 15.

Vers. 27, 28. **And though thou speakest to them . . . from their mouth.** There is a reason here for וגו׳. Although the word is also used of Israel without a bad side-meaning (comp. Exod. xix. 6; Josh. iii. 17; iv. 1; x. 3), yet we never find יהוה וגו׳, but always עַם וגו׳ is therefore chosen here to designate Israel as a common, profane nation. Comp. Isa. i. 4.—The prophet is to pronounce the judgment of incorrigibility on Israel as the basis of the announcement of judgment which comes afterwards. On אֱמוּנָה comp. v. 3, and the entire chapter. Truth or fidelity, is substantially lost: it is therefore no longer in their mouth. The prophet alludes to what was said in ver. 4: even though they take the words upon their lips, these are but empty sounds. For he whose heart is empty can avail nothing with his mouth.

---

5. *The abomination of idolatry in the highest degree a most evident proof of the hypocrisy of the people. Beginning of retribution.*

VII. 29–34.

29 Shear off thy hair and cast it away,
And raise on the heights a wailing,
For Jehovah hath rejected and forsaken the generation of his wrath.
30 For the children of Judah have done that which is evil in my sight, saith Jehovah.
They have set their abominations in the house,
Which bears my name, to pollute it.
31 And they have built the high places of Tophet,
Which is in the valley of Ben-Hinnom.
To burn their sons and daughters in the fire;
Which I commanded not, neither did it come into my mind.
32 Therefore behold! the days are coming, saith Jehovah,
That it will no more be called Tophet and vale Ben-Hinnom,
But the valley of slaughter:
And they will bury in Tophet, because there is no room.

33 And the carcases of this people shall be for food
To the birds of heaven and the beasts of earth,
And there will be none to scare them away.
34 And I will cause to cease from this city of Judah,
And from the streets of Jerusalem,
The voice of gladness and the voice of joy,
The voice of the bridegroom and the voice of the bride;
For the land shall become a desolation.

EXEGETICAL AND CRITICAL.

How little the appeal of the Israelites to the chosen place of mercy, and to their observance of the ritual, could help them (ver. 29) the prophet shows by setting forth their desecration of the sanctuary by Baal-worship, and their infraction of the Law by abominable practices which were directly forbidden in it (vers. 30, 31). Thus it is rendered most clearly manifest what shameful hypocrisy was concealed under the Jehovah-worship boasted of in ver. 4.

The rejection consequently announced in ver. 29 will consist in this, that the places in the vale of Hinnom hitherto considered sacred will be places of slaughter and burial, and that still a large number of unburied corpses will afford food for the beasts; the further consequence of which will be, that the land, bereft of its inhabitants, will become a barren waste (vers. 31-34).

Ver. 29. **Shear off thy hair . . . generation of his wrath.** נֵזֶר is properly *crown:* here it is used of the hair as the natural adornment of the head, comp. Numb. vi. 19. The cutting off of the hair was a sign of mourning, xvi. 6; xlviii. 37; Isa. xv. 2; Mic. i. 16, etc. Comp. HERZOG, *Real-Enc.* XVI., S. 363. [HENDERSON:—"Jerusalem is here addressed under the image of a female, who, in the depth of her grief for the loss of her children, deprives her head of its chief ornament, and betakes herself to the hills to bewail her bereavement." HENRY after BLAYNEY:—"The word is peculiar to the hair of the Nazarites, which was the badge and token of their dedication to God, and it is called their crown. Jerusalem had been a city, which was a Nazarite to God, but must now *cut off her hair*, must be profaned, degraded and separated from God, as she had been separated to Him. It is time for those who have lost their holiness to lay aside their joy."—S. R. A.]—On the feminine form in נָטַשְׁתְּ etc. Comp. NAEGELSB. *Gr.*, § 60, 7.—**On the heights.** Comp. iii. 21; ix. 9.—**generation of his wrath.** Comp. Isa. x. 6; Prov. xxii. 8.

Ver. 30. **For the children of Judah . . . to pollute it.**—in my sight, does not depend on **have done,** but on **that which is evil.** Comp. Jud. iii. 7, 12, etc., and NAEGELSB. *Gr.*, § 112, 5 b, (where moreover we must understand in the *physical* sense [Isa. xiv. 16] as distinguished from the *spiritual* sense, Gen. xxviii. 8, etc).—**Their abominations.** That Jeremiah refers to the abominable practices of Manasseh (2 Kings xxi. 4-7) has been fully proved by GRAF. I will only add that Jehoiakim represents the relapse into the principle forsaken by Josiah, and that this explains why responsibility for the sins of Manasseh is attributed to him and his contemporaries (2 Kings xxiv. 3; Jer. xv. 4), on which account also in this passage the abominations are spoken of as though they had been committed by Jehoiakim himself. This passage is repeated in xxxii. 34.

Ver. 31. **And they have built . . . come into my mind.** בָּמוֹת is not merely high places, but in a derivative sense every place of worship erected for idolatrous service, or every building for that purpose, as is proved by passages like 2 Kings xxiii. 15, where the בָּמָה is distinguished from the altar in it, and is *burnt,*—Ezek. xvi. 16, where high places are mentioned as composed of garments. Here also they are not the altars alone, but the places of worship with the altars. There appear to have been several such places in Tophet, this being intimated by the expression תָּפְתֵּ הַטְּפָאִים Jer. xix. 13. Tophet, as is well known, was a place in the valley of Ben-Hinnom, where the horrible sacrifices of children (comp. SELDEN, *De Diis Syr. Syntagm.* I. 6) were offered to Baal (xix. 5—with which Molech, xxxii. 35, is parallel, comp. Levit. xviii. 21 ; xx. 2-5; 1 Kings xi. 7; 2 Kings xxiii. 10). But the derivation of the word is uncertain. Some (LORSBACH, GESEN., HITZIG, EWALD, FUERST, and others) appeal to Isa. xxx. 33 in favor of the rendering *place of burning*, deriving it from תָּפָה= שָׁוָה *to burn.* Others (WINER, BÖTTCHER, GRAF, PRESSEL) finding their support in Job xvii. 6, give the word the meaning of *sputum, abomination, horror*, from the Chaldee תּוּף=*to spew out.* HOFMANN (in *Weiss. u. Erf.*, II., 125) suggests the not improbable derivation from תָּפָה and gives it the meaning of *pit.* A decision on this point is as difficult as with reference to the vale Ben-Hinnom. The situation of this valley is indeed fixed, as it is certain it was to the south of Jerusalem, but the views are various as to its exact location. Comp. HERZOG, *Real-Enc.,* IV. S. 710.—There is not perfect agreement even as to the name of the valley, the ancients regarding Hinnom as a proper name, of the moderns some deriving it from נָהַם (by transposition=the valley of wailing, so HITZIG and GRAF), and others from אִנֵּה=יָנָה (with the same meaning, so BÖTTCHER, *De Inf.,* I. S. 82, 83). Were the valley only the vale of Hinnom, as in Josh. xv. 8; xviii. 16; Neh. xi. 30, or the vale Beni-Hinnom (as in 2 Kings xxiii. 10 only, Chethibh) the appellative signification would have much in its favor. But as the name *Vale Ben-Hinnom* is the most frequent and certainly the original (Josh. xv. 8; xviii. 16; Jer. vii. 31, 32; xix. 2, 6; 2 Chr. xxviii. 3; xxxiii. 6), the derivations given above are very insecure, and it is most advisable to retain the old interpretation.—**To burn.** Two passages coincide with this almost word for word: xix. 5 and xxxii. 35. In the latter passage, instead of this expression, we find *to cause to pass through*, which shows that it is not to be understood literally as Maimonides and other Jewish commentators suppose, but as an euphemism.—The words *which I commanded not* repeated in all three passages (comp. iii. 16), intimate that this custom was relatively a new one. Although the worship of Molech (the Ammonitish) is attributed even to Solomon (1 Kings xi. 7), yet the abomination of burning children was first introduced into Judah by Ahaz (2 Kings xvi. 3). Comp. MOVERS, *Phœn.* I., *S.* 327 sqq.— In the Pentateuch this cult was forbidden, Deut. xii. 30; xviii. 10.

Vers. 32-34. **Therefore behold! the days are coming . . . a desolation.** The place of worship, held sacred by the idolatrous Jews, but in fact desecrated, shall even for them be forever polluted. That this would be accomplished by a massacre on the spot, is not stated in the text. This would not have polluted it forever, as we read of Josiah that he polluted the places of idolatrous worship either by the burning of human bones (2 Ki. xxiii. 16, 20) or by filling them up with these (ver. 14) or the reverse, by strewing the ashes of the idols on the graves (ver. 6). At any rate he must have defiled Tophet (ver. 10) and other places (vers. 8, 13) in the same way. Here then also the pollution is caused by the interment, and the name "valley of slaughter" is connected with it only in so far that the vale is used as a place of burial only in consequence of the want of room, resulting from the great slaughter (comp. xix. 11; Ezek. ix. 7). But even thus a great number of corpses will remain unburied, which will be food for beasts (comp. Deut. xxviii. 26, whence ver. 33 is taken verbatim, and Jer. xvi. 4; xix. 7; xxxiv. 20).—**None to scare**, *etc.* Comp. Levit. xxvi. 6; Deut. xxviii. 26; Mic. iv. 4; Nah. ii. 12; Zeph. iii. 14; Jer. xxx. 10; xlvi. 27. The further result of the slaughter is depopulation, the cessation of every sign of normal human existence, complete desolation of the land. (xvi. 9; xxv. 10, 11, coll. xxxiii. 11). [HENDERSON:—"In ver. 34, reference is made to the joyous processions in which the bride and bridegroom are led through the streets, accompanied by bands of singers and musicians, which are common in many parts of the East, and even among the Jews in some parts of Europe. See my Biblical Researches and Travels in Russia, p. 217."—S. R. A.]

---

6. *Fulfilment of retribution corresponding to the idol-abominations.*

VIII. 1–3.

1   At this time, saith Jehovah, they shall bring[1]
    The bones of the kings of Judah and the bones of his princes,
    And the bones of the priests and the bones of the prophets,
    And the bones of the citizens of Jerusalem out of their graves,
2   And they shall spread them out to the sun,
    And to the moon, and to all the host of heaven,
    Which they loved and which they served and followed,
    And which they sought and worshipped;
    They shall not be gathered, nor buried;
    They shall be dung on the surface of the earth.
3   And the whole remnant of the survivors of this wicked race
    Shall prefer[2] death to life in all places of the survivors[3],
    Whither I have driven them, saith Jehovah Zebaoth.

TEXTUAL AND GRAMMATICAL.

[1] Ver. 1.—Instead of וְיֹצִיאוּ the Masoretes would omit the ו, as they perceived that neither as consecutive nor as copulative is it in place, while in accordance with the constant usage we should expect it to be followed by the perfect. Comp. NAEGELSB. *Gr.*, § 89. Yet in such cases the imperfect with *Vau copulat.* is not without example; comp. Exod. xii. 3.

[2] Ver. 3.—וְנִבְחַר comp. Prov. xxi. 3. NAEGELSB. *Gr.*, § 100, 4.

[3] Ver. 3.—הַנִּשְׁאָרִים. If we do not with HITZIG and GRAF reject this word as resting on a clerical error, we must explain it with MAURER and DE WETTE as the repetition of the noun instead of the pronoun, so that the article stands before the construct state in an emphatic almost pronominal signification; in all *those* places. Comp. NAEGELSB. *Gr.*, § 71, 5 *Anm.*

EXEGETICAL AND CRITICAL.

It is clear from the contents that this strophe is closely connected with the preceding. Death is to come in a new form, as it were, in those who are already dead. The bones of the buried shall be disinterred and strewed in the face of the stars, their powerless deities, shall become stinking ordure (vers. 1, 2). And the surviving remnant will long for death as a benefit (ver. 3).

Vers. 1, 2. **At this time, saith Jehovah ..**

surface of the earth. Of the motive of the disinterment the prophet says nothing. He had certainly no idea of its being the search for booty (JEROME, HITZIG, [HENDERSON]). He has in mind only the punitive justice of God.—**His** before princes is to be referred to the kings, *viz.*, the princes of each king or kingdom, or of the crown. Comp. xxiv. 8; xxv. 19; xxxiv. 21. We should have expected in reference to Judah *their* princes, as in Isai. iii. 4; Hos. vii. 16; ix. 15.—**Spread them out.** Observe the irony. The stars look powerlessly down on the bones of their worshippers—while these send up a stench!—**Gathered.** Comp. xvi. 4; xxv. 33.—For the subject-matter compare 2 Sam. xxi. 12 sqq.

Ver. 3. **And the whole remnant .. saith Jehovah.** The discourse concludes with a parting glance at the survivors, who are the most unfortunate of all. Comp. xxv. 26.—On the subject-matter comp. xxiv. 8 sqq.

DOCTRINAL AND ETHICAL.

1. On vii. 1. The exhortation which Jeremiah here addresses to his contemporaries is, as CHRYSOSTOM remarks, substantially the same as that of John the Baptist to the Jews of his time: "Bring forth therefore fruits—meet for repentance, and begin not to say within yourselves, we have Abraham to our father; for I say unto you that God is able of these stones to raise up children unto Abraham." But there is a difference between trusting in descent from Abraham, and in the stone Sanctuary at Jerusalem. For as the tabernacle and the sanctuary at Shiloh have disappeared, so the temple built by Solomon and the ark of the covenant itself; and even the temple re-erected without the ark was destroyed a second time by Titus and not rebuilt, though according to the testimony of Josephus (*Bell. Jud.* VI. 2, 1) the mad resistance of the Jews was chiefly based on the idea that Jerusalem being the city of God was in no danger of destruction. Now while the sacred places and buildings for worship, from the tabernacle to the temple of Herod, were destroyed, never to be re-built (comp. iii. 16 עוֹד יֵעָשֶׂה לֹא) the descent from Abraham, in spite of all temporary reversions, retains its eternal significance, as the Apostle Paul shows in Rom. xi., where he says, "If the first fruit be holy, the lump is also holy, and if the root be holy so are the branches. ... If some of the branches have been broken off on account of unbelief, yet they may be grafted in again. ... For according to the Gospel, he says, I regard them as enemies, but according to the election, they are beloved for the fathers' sake. For the gifts and calling of God are without repentance." If now to trust in descent from Abraham is in so far foolish and unjustifiable, as it does not prevent partial destruction of the nation, to trust in the outward sanctuary, constructed of earthly material, is still less justifiable, for this has no guarantee of continuance; it may indeed suffer total destruction without endangering the foundations of the theocracy. Just as unjustifiable as this confidence of the Jews in an earthly sanctuary as the chosen place of divine presence and blessing is every analo-gous confidence of the Christian church in a real or supposed divinely chosen earthly substratum of tokens of blessing, whether it be a place, office or race. All the places consecrated by the presence of the Lord and the ministry of His apostles have been destroyed and given up to the abomination of desolation: Jerusalem with the Mt. of Olives and Golgotha, Bethlehem, Nazareth, the whole of Palestine, Asia Minor and Greece, became Christian and yet fell a prey to the crescent. All the less may Rome count on perpetuity, since the chair of Peter rests not on divine but on arbitrary human institution. So also the legitimate ruling families of Europe, who so fondly imagine, that they are irrevocably chosen, should never forget that the Lord not only appoints but deposes kings. (Comp. Dan. iv. 32; v. 21).

2. PETRUS GALATINUS (*de Arc. cath.* ver. v. 10) remarks (according to GHISLER.) that some Rabbins refer the lying word of the thrice repeated הֵיכָל to the false hope of those who suppose that a third temple will yet be built. But this hope is not a false one. It certainly will not be realized in the erection of a third sanctuary of stone but in that spiritual body of which we must regard Ezekiel's temple as the type. Comp. BALMER-RINCK, on the prophet Ezekiel's vision of the temple, Basel, 1858, and my review of this work in *Deut. Rep.* 1860, H. III. S. 151, 2. This is not of course to say that the thrice repeated word does not really refer to the third temple.

3 "If God has not His temple and abode in the heart, that (*viz.*, that thou hast an outward temple or house of God) will avail thee nothing." Mic. iii. 11, 12. STARKE.

4. "The words 'this is the Lord's temple' might properly be written on the hearts of believers," 1 Cor. iii. 16; Gen. xxviii. 17. STARKE.

5. "It is a heathenish delusion and false confidence to suppose that God is bound to any place or spot, as the Trojans thought because they had the temple of Pallas in their city it could not be taken, and in the present day the manner of the Papists is to bind Christ to Rome and the chair of Peter, and then defiantly maintain 'I shall never be moved' (Ps. x. 6). For, they say, the ship of Peter may sink a little, but not altogether. Then the only point that is deficient is this, that they are not the ship of Peter, but rather an East Indianman with a cargo of Indian apes and such like foreign merchandize, pearls, purple, silk, brass, iron, silver, gold, incense, lead, that they may carry on simony and make merchandize of religion, and deceive the whole world (Rev. xviii. 11 sqq.)." CRAMER.

6. On vii. 9–11. Necessary as the doctrine of the church is in the organic system of Christian doctrine it may become dangerous, if the church is regarded one-sidedly as an objectively saving-institution, and the subjective conditions of its operation are undervalued. For then it is regarded as alone necessary to salvation, and not only in the sense that this virtue is ascribed exclusively to *one* particular church in opposition to another, but also in the sense of supposing that the church alone, as an objective institution, is the means of salvation, a man needing to do nothing more than to enter into a passive rela-

tion to the church, *i. e.*, without conscious resistance (*obex*). From this alone saving church there is but one step to the infallibly saving, *i. e.*, to that, of which a passive member cannot be lost, however much he may steal, murder, commit adultery, swear falsely, *etc.* Where this ruinous delusion prevails men enter the church, perform the ceremonies, wipe their mouths, and say *salvi sumus* (נִצַּלְנוּ). But thus the church of Christ becomes a den of robbers.

7. On vii. 16. "This may serve to comfort you, for God thus testifies to the power of prayer, that it would stand in His way so that He could not go on. Therefore He had first of all to forbid the prophet from praying. Thus also He says to Moses (Exod. xxxii. 10) 'Let Me alone that My wrath may burn against them.' So much may a believing prayer accomplish." CRAMER.

8. On vii. 22, 23. In Ps. li. 16, 17, we read "For thou desirest not sacrifice; else would I give it: thou delightest not in burnt-offering. The sacrifices of God are a broken spirit: a broken and a contrite heart, O God, thou wilt not despise." Had sacrifices and burnt-offerings been positively displeasing to God, He would have forbidden them. But they must have been pleasing to Him even as types of the sacrifice on Golgotha. They displease Him only when He is to accept them instead of a broken and contrite heart. The sacrifices have thus a two-fold significance; objectively as types, and in so far as God beholds in every sacrifice that of Christ, they are pleasing to Him—subjectively, as the offering of man. But when in this relation God is to be satisfied with the fat and blood of an animal instead of the spiritual *oblatio cordis*, the sacrifice is displeasing. Thus as the sacrifice is on the one hand pleasing, on the other displeasing, Jeremiah might say that God did not speak of sacrifices, though on the other hand it is admitted, that He did speak of them.

9. On vii. 26. "It is an evil consolation, and one of the greatest exercises of the witnesses, when they are treated with such indifference, that they are not opposed, but also receive no real attention. Then is Satan most firmly seated, and his business best established when he has induced such a state of indifference. Phlegm in religion, patience in hearers (a sign that they are inured to blows) is an incurable evil. So long as they are calumniated, persecuted, mocked, the witnesses still have a handle. But the time, when one preaches and no one rises, is a miserable epoch for the ministry. Yet it must be endured, for it is either not general or a teacher is usually free. For because the Lord 'spews out of His mouth' such men and such times of lethargy are heralds of the overflowing of the divine judgments, and especially of the removal of the candlestick from its place, there is generally a new period for the teachers, and they become elsewhere a *great nation* (Exod. xxxii. 10)." ZINZENDORF.

10. On vii. 33. "*Charitati Christianæ et legi naturæ consentaneum est, ut hominum cadavera terra obruantur, unde Augustinus (De Civ. D. 1. 13); non contemnenda et abjicienda sunt corpora justorum et fidelium, quibus tanquam organis et casis suis ad omnia bona opera spiritus sanctus fuit usus.*" FÖRSTER.

HOMILETICAL AND PRACTICAL.

1. On vii. 1-3. [HENRY:—"Note: (1) Even those that profess religion have need to be preached to, as well as those that are *without*. (2) It is desirable to have opportunity of preaching to many together. Wisdom chooses to cry *in the chief place of concourse*, and as Jeremiah here, *in the opening of the gates*, the temple gates. (3) When we are going to worship God, we have need to be admonished to *worship Him in the Spirit, and to have no confidence in the flesh*. Phil. iii. 3."—S. R. A.]

2. On vii. 3-7. The doctrine of the Church. 1. The church externally or as an external ordinance. 1. What is this external ordinance? (Word, sacrament, office). 2. How far is this external ordinance necessary? 3. What reasons have we to be on our guard respecting it? (ver. 4. It may be overestimated).—II. The church internally. 1. It is essentially a community of saints and true believers. ("*Congregatio sanctorum et vere credentium.*" *Conf. Aug. Art.* VIII.) 2. Its existence is manifested, *a.* in the holy walk of its members (vers. 3, 5, 6); *b.* in the blessings of the Divine presence (vers. 3 and 7).

3. On vii. 8. [HENRY:—"The privileges of a *form of godliness* are often the pride and confidence of those that are strangers and enemies to the *power* of it. It is common for those that are *furthest* from God to boast themselves most of their being *near to the church*."—S. R. A.]

4. On vii. 8-15. An earnest warning against merely external ecclesiasticism. I. Its essence is: false confidence in the unconditional saving efficacy of a supposed or real sanctuary (vers. 8, 10). II. Its consequences are: 1. Demoralization (vers. 9, 10). 2. Desecration of the holy (ver. 11). 3. Destruction of the offenders (vers. 12-15).

5. On vii. 16. On Intercession. 1. When it is not in place (compare this verse with 1 John v. 16). 2. When it is in place. 3. What it can accomplish. [HENRY:—"See here (1). That God's prophets are *praying* men. (2). That God's praying prophets have a great interest in heaven, how little soever they have on earth. (3). It is an ill omen for a people when God restrains the spirits of His ministers and people from praying for them. (4). Those that will not regard good ministers' preaching cannot expect any benefit by their praying. If you will not hear us when we speak *from God to you*, God will not hear us when we speak *to Him for you*."—S. R. A.]

6. On vii. 18. [HENRY:—"Let us be instructed even by this bad example in the service of our God. (1) Let us honor Him with our substance. (2). Let us not decline the hardest service, nor disdain to stoop to the meanest, for *none shall kindle a fire on God's altar for naught*. (3). Let us bring up our children in the acts of devotion; let them, as they are capable, be employed in doing something toward the keeping up of religious exercises."—S. R. A.]

7. On vii. 22, 23. Of the true service of God. 1. Its nature (1) not outward ceremonies, but (2) walk according to the divine commands. II. Its reward. (I will be your God, that it may be well with you).

8. On vii. 24-29. Of disobedience to God's word. I. Its cause is, (1) not neglect on the part of God to make known His word to men (ver. 25). (2) Not the imperfect performance of his duties by the preacher (ver. 27) but (3) the hardness of men's hearts, who (a) walk only after the thoughts of their heart, and therefore (b) do not hear, do not believe, (ver. 28) do not wish to improve. II. Its consequence is (1) increasing moral corruption (vers. 24, 26) and (2) rejection on the part of God (ver. 29).

9. On vii. 25-28. The sad characteristics of an unbelieving epoch. 1. Contempt of the preaching of the divine word. 2. Stiff-neckedness in respect to the visitations of divine chastisement. 3. Increase of wickedness in spite of all the warnings of the past. (LIC. CLAUSS).—When is a people ripe for destruction? 1. When it despises the visitations of divine grace (ver. 25).

2. When it hardens itself in unbelief against God's word and voice (vers. 26 and 27). 3. When in spite of the divine judgment it departs the more into sin (vers. 26, 28).—The people Israel a warning example for the present race in view of the prevailing unbelief of the times. Their example is admonitory, 1. with respect to their ingratitude for God's gracious visitations; 2. with respect to their opposition to the true friends of the nation ; 3. with respect to their frivolity in view of inevitable destruction. (DR. GR.)—Let the remembrance of our calling serve to awaken us. To this end let us consider, 1. What is our calling ? 2. How does the Lord call us ? 3. How long does He call us ? 4. How have we answered Him ? 5. What will be the end of our calling ? (Z.—: *Gesetz u. Zeugniss, Juni.* 1860, *S.* 339).

II. SECOND CHARGE: THEIR RUINOUS PERSISTENCE IN EVIL.

VIII. 4-23.

1. *Their stiff-necked impenitence and its punishment.*

VIII. 4-12.

4 And say to them: Thus saith Jehovah:
Do men[1] fall and rise not up again?
Or does one turn away and not return again?
5 Why then does this people, Jerusalem,
Turn away[2] with a perpetual[3] apostacy ?
They hold fast to error,[4] wish not to return.
6 I inclined myself and listened:
They speak that which is worth nothing.
There is none who repents of his wickedness
And who says: what have I done ?
They are all[5] turned away in their courses,
Like a mad[6] stallion in the battle.
7 Even the stork in the air knoweth his seasons,
The turtle-dove, swallow and crane keep the time of their coming,
But my people know not the judgment of Jehovah.
8 How say ye then, We are wise,
And the law of Jehovah is with us?
Behold ! surely the lying style of the writer has brought forth only lies.
9 The wise men are put to shame,
Confounded and taken are they.
Behold ! they have despised Jehovah's word,
What wisdom,[7] however, is among them?
10 Therefore[8] will I give their wives to others,
Their fields to the conquerors,
For from the least to the greatest they are all bent on gain;
From the prophet to the priest they all practise deceit,
11 And healed the hurt of the daughter of my people most slightly,
Saying, Peace, peace ! when there is no peace.

12 They are put to shame, for they have committed abomination;
Yet they blush not, nor understand to be ashamed.
Therefore shall they fall with the falling,
At the time of their visitation will they be overthrown,
Saith Jehovah.

TEXTUAL AND GRAMMATICAL.

¹ Ver. 4.—הֵיפַּל. The indefinite subject in Hebrew may be expressed as here by the 3d pers. of the plural or of the singular. Comp. NAEGELSB. Gr., § 101, 2.—On the disjunctive question comp. Gr. § 107, 4. [BLAYNEY, NOYES, UMBREIT, etc. render as in the text: HENDERSON has: Shall they fall; but incorrectly, for as HITZIG says, the Jews cannot be the subject in ver. 4.—S. R. A.]
² Ver. 5.—שׁוֹבְבָה (not שׁוֹבֵבָה, xxxi. 21; xlix. 4, nor שׁוֹבָב, iii. 14. 22) is to be regarded according to EWALD, § 188 b, as a verbal form, and in a directly causative sense = to make a turn. Comp. rems. on xxxi. 21.—THIS PEOPLE is not in the relation of a genitive to the following JERUSALEM, as is evinced by the form, but the latter is in simple apposition to the former. Comp. NAEGELSB. Gr. § 66. [HENDERSON: this people of Jerusalem].
³ Ver. 5.—נִצַּח (adject. denomin. ad formam דָּבָר. עַר. Comp. N. Gr., § 42, a, S. 87) is an ἅπ. λεγ. The meaning is derived from נֶצַח perfectio, absolutio = perfectus, absolutus.
⁴ Ver. 5.—הַרְבִּית (comp. xiv. 14, Keri; xxiii. 26; Zeph. iii. 13; Ps. cxix. 118) must here according to the connection be rendered in a passive sense = error.
⁵ Ver. 6.—כֻּלֹּה is literally: its entirety. From the singular suffix we perceive that the nation is regarded as a single individual. EWALD, § 286, e.
⁶ Ver. 6.—שׁוֹטֵף used originally of streaming water (comp. Isai. xxx. 28; lxvi. 12; Ezek. xiii. 11, 13); in the transferred sense of the running of a horse here only (comp. effuso cursu, fuga effusior in Livy). [All the English translations render: as a horse rushes into the battle.—S. R. A.]
⁷ Ver. 9.—חָכְמַת־מָה [lit.: the wisdom of what]? sapientia cujus? Comp. xliv. 28; Gen. xxiv. 33; NAEGELSB. Gr., § 65, 2, b.
⁸ Ver. 9.—["The LXX. omit these three verses with the exception of the first two lines of the 10th. The repetitious character of many parts of the book of Jeremiah leaves no reason to doubt that the repetition here of chap. vi. 12-15 is genuine. Theodotion and the Hexaplar Syriac supply the omission of the LXX." HENDERSON.—S. R. A.]

EXEGETICAL AND CRITICAL.

The second point in the charge concerns the impenitent obduracy with which the people, true to their often censured character (comp. Exod. xxxii. 9: xxxiii. 3, 5; xxxiv. 9; Deut. ix. 6, 13; x. 16; xxxi. 27 coll. Jer. v. 3; Isai. xlviii. 4; Ezek. ii. 4; iii. 7) persist in the perverse course they have adopted (vers. 4-7). To be sure they will not admit that they have adopted a false course. They maintain on the contrary (comp. vii. 21 sqq.) that they are in the right way, because they are not lacking in instruction or knowledge of the law of God (ver. 8). But the prophet does not allow this to pass. He traces their imagined wisdom to the deception of their false leaders, of whom he predicts that with their pseudo-sophy they must be put to shame (ver. 9), and then he again announces to all in the words of a former discourse the judgment of God for their manifold wickedness (vers. 10-12). This strophe contains the main thought of this chapter, i. e., of the second part. The two following strophes describe only the particular features of the punishment.

Vers. 4, 5. And say to them .. wish not to return. The simple introduction by and say shows that what follows is closely connected with the preceding. The meaning of שׁוּב is here, the first time to turn, to make any kind of a turn (comp. Josh. xix. 12, etc.), the second time to return.—It is evident that the prophet had hoped that Israel would have returned in view of his previous representations. No one who falls remains lying on the ground, and no one perseveres in the course he has taken without turning to one side or another, how then is it that Israel so obstinately persists in his perverse ways?

The answer is given in ver. 6. By the manner in which the prophet emphasizes the idea of turning we are forcibly reminded of iii. 1-4; iv.—Wish not to return, comp. v. 3; Hos. xi. 5. Ver. 6. I inclined myself ... stallion in the battle. It is best to regard this as an answer to the question why? in ver. 5. In order to be able to give the Lord a correct answer, the prophet listens. For thus he may be able to learn the true secret thoughts of their hearts. The information he thus obtains is not comforting; from their speeches he learns only the radically corrupt condition of their hearts, closed against all knowledge of the right. Hence their obduracy.—They do not speak that which is right, i. e., they not only are silent with respect to the right, but they speak that which is not right, which is false. Comp. Gen. xlii. 11, 19, 31, 33, 34, and Exod. x. 29; 2 Ki. vii. 9; Prov. xv. 7; Isai. xvi. 6; Jer. xxiii. 10; xlviii. 30.—Their conduct corresponds to their words: there is none who repents.—שׁוּב stands in opposition to the שׁוּב desired in vers. 4 and 5, with a certain irony: they are not wanting in שׁוּב turn, but they practise it only in the sense se avertere. This they certainly pursue with the greatest ardor. They turn away in their entirety.—in their courses. The plural form is explained by the collective idea of the noun, to which all refers. This plural gives a satisfactory sense, and it is therefore unnecessary to alter it as the Keri does according to xxiii. 10. As to the meaning: the word in 2 Sam. xviii. 27 has the meaning of violent running, hunting, chasing. This meaning is suitable to Jer. xxii. 17; xxiii. 10, and is also demanded by the connection here. They turn them in this sense, that with violent haste they pursue their chosen path.

Ver. 7. Even the stork .. the judgment

of Jehovah. What חָסִידָה is, is very uncertain, since the distinctive marks mentioned in Old Testament passages (Levit. xi. 19: Deut. xiv. 18; Ps. civ. 17; Job xxxix. 13; Zech. v. 9) suit several birds, on which account (apart from the fact that the LXX. translate sometimes ἔποψ, sometimes ἐρωδιός or πελεκάν, the Targumists and Talmudists חֲוָרִיתָא חֲוָרְתָּא milvus albus, vide BUXTORF, Lex. Chald., p. 528) modern commentators are divided between "heron" (So BOCHART, GESEN., ROSENM., FUERST in his concordance, EWALD, MEIER, and others) and "stork" (WINER, FUENST Lex., GRAF and others). Since the derivation from חָסִיד pius is the most natural and the designation of the stork as avis pia is very general (comp. ἀντιπελαργεῖν, although in single cases the filial piety of the heron is also celebrated, ÆLIAN, Anim. III. 23), I give my preference in this instance to the meaning *stork*. —הוֹר is the turtle-dove. That it is migratory in the East (comp. the American migratory pigeon) may be inferred also from Song of Sol. ii. 11, 12. Comp. WINER, R. W. B. s. v. וְסוּס וְעָגוּר. The meaning of these words is uncertain. Both words occur besides only in Isai. xxxviii. 14.— There it reads כְּסוּס עָגוּר כֵּן אֲצַפְצֵף. There the asyndeton is in favor of rendering עָגוּר as the predicate or in apposition to סוּס, but in the present passage the וְ is opposed to it. Neither the dialects nor the early translators and commentators afford us any secure *data*. In order to deal fairly with both passages, we must take one of the two words in a sense which would allow it to be rendered both as in opposition and as an independent word, as, for example, we may say *felis leo* or *felis et leo*. Perhaps סוּס (for which the Keri and Palestinian could read סִי) is an onomatopoeticum or imitation of the natural sound (Venetian *Zysilia* = swallow. *Vide* ROSENM.) and in this sense the name of the genus and species at the same time (comp. *felis-felis*). At any rate the prophet wishes to say that the irrational animals punctually obey the natural law which prescribes their return into a certain country, while Israel seems not even to know the rule instituted by Jehovah for their moral action.—**But my people.** Comp. Isai. i. 3; Jer. v. 4, 5.

Ver. 8. **How say ye then . . . only lies.** To the charge at the close of ver. 7 the prophet supposes the people to reply: **We are wise,** etc.; just as what is said in vii. 21 sqq., presupposes an appeal of the people to their observance of the ceremonial law, so here also the assertion is put into their mouth that they were well instructed in the law. It may be inquired whether חֲכָמִים is here used in a general sense, or whether it contains an allusion to those who from the age of Solomon constituted a particular class of the supporters and promoters of culture by the side of the priests and prophets. (Comp. BRUCH, *Weisheits-Lehre der Hebräer*, Strassb., 1851, *S.* 48). Jeremiah himself (xviii. 18) names *wise men* together with priests and prophets. But Ezekiel in the parallel passage vii. 26, uses *elders* for *wise men*, and generally it might be difficult to prove that in Jeremiah and elsewhere, (especially in Prov. i. 6; xiii. 20; xv. 12; xxii. 17; xxiii. 24), they appear as a special class and not rather as specially gifted men of every class and calling, as Solomon also was a חָכָם, and with him men of the priestly and levitical orders (1 Ki. v. 9-11). Observe also that it is said not: *wise men are among us*, but, **wise men are we.**— That תּוֹרָה must designate the Torah in the sense of the Pentateuch cannot be maintained, for the word occurs frequently in a more general signification, *ex. gr.*, Isai. ii. 3; viii. 16. Certainly the word would have to be rendered in the narrower sense if hemistich 2 were to be translated: truly (אָכֵן comp. iii. 23; iv. 10) the lying style of the scribes has *made it* a lie. But on the other hand 1, to supply the suffix is not a matter of course, as it must be if the want of the suffix (which is certainly frequent, comp. NAEGELSU. *Gr.*, § 78, 2, *Anm.*) is to appear justified. 2, סֹפְרִים, *scribes* in the sense of those who spin a web of human inventions around the word of God is of later date. Ezra, as is well known, was the first סֹפֵר (comp. Ezra vii. 6, 11) but not in a bad sense, for the evil practices of the scribes were only a corruption of the praiseworthy labors commenced by him (comp. HERZOG, *R.-Enc.* XIII. *S.* 733, etc.) Since the verb עָשָׂה is decidedly used in an absolute sense = *to make, to work*, (Exod. v. 9; xxxi. 4; 1 Ki. v. 30; xx. 40; Ruth ii. 19; Prov. xiii. 16; xxxi. 13) this passage can mean only: *behold! he has worked for a lie, i. e.*, has done lying work, the pen of the scribe has produced lies. Scribes indeed occur almost up to the time of Jeremiah only as Stateofficials (Judges v. 14; 2 Sam. viii. 17; **xx.** 25; 2 Ki. xii. 11; xix. 2, etc.), but Baruch also is called a *scribe* (Jer. xxxvi. 26, 32), and since the canonical writings set before us the picture of a literary activity in a good sense, why may they not also have given us one in a bad sense? False prophets labored with their word in opposition to the word of the true prophets, why might they not do the same with their writings? Jeremiah here presupposes a literary activity which designated its productions as the directions of Jehovah, but not in truth. For what was thus written in the name of Jehovah, and doubtless with an appeal to the law, was human invention and lies. Comp. Isai. x. 1.

Ver. 9. **The wise men are put to shame . . what wisdom however is among them?** The prophet for every "abuse of the name of God" declares the divine punishment. They are put to shame with their *teaching* and *prophecy*. The false scribes had evidently flattered the people and promised them good days to come. (Comp. *infra* ver. 11, and vi. 14; xxiii. 9; Ezek. xiii.). The contrary, says Jeremiah, will be the case, to their shame and their hurt.—**Put to shame,** comp. on ii. 26.—The **wise** here are not identical with those to whom the predicate *wise* is applied in ver. 8. For while the latter refers to all Israel, the former refers only to the *scribes*. These are called *wise men*, not because they formed a special class, but because they boasted of special insight into religious things.— **Confounded,** etc. Comp. xlviii. 1; l. 2. Because they have despised the word of the Lord and substituted their own wisdom, it will come to the light that they know nothing.

Vers. 10-12. **Therefore will I give their wives . . . saith Jehovah.** These verses refer not to the false prophets alone but to all those previously mentioned in common. They announce both to the whole people, who were addressed in vers. 4-7, and to their perverse leaders, to whom vers. 8 and 9 refer, their common, public, and outwardly palpable punishment, and in so far form the necessary conclusion of the strophe. This announcement is made in the form of a quotation, these three verses being a repetition of vi. 12-15. As it is the leaders of the people, the priests and prophets who are there spoken of (vi. 13-15), the verses suit this place very well, particularly as ver. 11, **and healed,** etc., so well proves the shaming of the false prophets (ver. 9). But nevertheless we see that this passage is a quotation and is not here in its original position. For ver. 10 is a contracted form of vi. 12, 13. Here also the sequence of thought is not quite correct, the causal כִּי following the illative particle לָכֵן. But that a copyist did not transpose the passages, but the prophet himself repeated with freedom his former utterance, is seen from the little alterations which betray a reproduction from memory as well as the hand of an author making free use of his own property, in vers. 10, 11, 12 (comp. x. 15; xi. 23; xxiii. 12, etc.). On the repetitions in Jeremiah see the table in NAEGELSB.: *Jer. u. Bab. S.* 128.—Comp. besides the excellent refutation of HITZIG's view as to the interpolation of this passage in GRAF, *S.* 185.

---

2. *Further portrayal of the visitation announced in* ver.

VIII. 13-17.

13 I will sweep[1] them utterly away, saith Jehovah.
   There were no grapes on the vine,
   No figs on the fig-tree,
   The land was withered.—
   So I gave to them[2] those who shall overrun them.
14 "What is then the ground on which we remain?
   Assemble, let us go into the fortified cities and perish[3] there?
   For Jehovah, our God, has allowed us to perish
   And given us water of poison to drink;
   For we have sinned against Jehovah.
15 We hoped[4] for blessing but no good came—
   For a time of healing,[5] and behold terror!"
16 From Dan is heard the snorting of his horses,
   At the sound of the neighing of his stallions the whole earth trembles.
   And they came and devoured the land and what was in it,
   The city and those that dwelt therein.
17 For behold, I send among you serpents,
   Basilisks, against which no charm avails,—
   These shall bite you, saith Jehovah.

TEXTUAL AND GRAMMATICAL.

[1] Ver. 13.—אָסֹף from אָסַף, אֲסִיפָם from סוּף *desinere,* Hiph. *finem imponere, consumere.* As in סוּף at the same time the idea of storm is contained (comp. סוּפָה, *procella*) this compound evidently signifies *to sweep away in a storm.* The connection of two verbs, having roots of different or similar sound, in this construction frequently occurs. Comp. xlviii. 9; Isai. xxviii. 28, and especially Zeph. i. 2, 3; where we find the same connection as in this passage (NAEGELSB. *Gr.,* § 93, *d.* *Anm.*) The Hiph. הֹסֵף occurs only in these three passages.

[2] Ver. 13.—The ancient rendering, occurring in the Chaldee and Syriac: *and I recompensed to them that which they transgressed,* is harsh and opposed especially by the difficulty of thus satisfactorily explaining the suffix.—The explanation preferred by most modern commentators: and I give them up to those who come over them—has against it, (1) that אֶתֵּן must be made into אֶתֵּן which besides is not a normal construction, comp. the remarks on יָצַע ver. 1; (2) that לָהֶם must be translated not "*to them*" but "to those," (3) that the suffix must be supplied to אֶתֵּן, which, as was remarked on שָׁעַט, can only take place where this supplementation is a matter of course.

[3] Ver. 14.—וְנִדְּמָה. This form follows the Aramaic formation with reduplication of the first radical. Comp. יִתֹּמּוּ Deut. xxxiv. 8; יְדֹךְ Ps. xxxi. 78; Job xxix. 21. Comp. NAEGELSB. *Gr.,* § 31, *Anm.* OLSH. § 243, *d.*

[4] Ver. 15.—קַוֵּה *Inf. abs.* Comp. NAEGELSB. *Gr.,* § 92, 2, *b.*

[5] Ver. 15.—מַרְפֵּה instead of מַרְפֵּא. Comp. ver. 11.

CHAP. VIII. 13-17. 105

EXEGETICAL AND CRITICAL.

This strophe is entirely occupied with the further portrayal of the visitation which is announced in ver. 12. The object of the discourse, the visitation, appears under various images, according to the use of literal or figurative language. The speakers are also changed several times. First the Lord announces that He will sweep them away in the storm as unfruitful withered plants. Then they must themselves announce that they wish to flee into the fortified cities but without the hope of escape. For they themselves feel and express that they bear their death within them, as it were, the Lord Himself having grown them poison-water as a punishment for their sins, and instead of healing they find (in the cities) only terror. (Vers. 14, 15). For they already perceive the approach of the enemy from the North (ver. 16 a), which the prophet confirms, describing in blunt words the sad end as already begun (ver. 16 b). At last the Lord Himself again speaks, and returning to the figurative mode of speech compares the threatening enemies with serpents of the poisonous kind, for whose bite there is no remedy (ver. 17).

Ver. 13. **I will sweep them . . . overrun them.** In what follows the motive of this punishment is presented. Israel is an unfruitful vine and fig-tree, a withered branch. The same figure in Ps. i. 3; Jer. xvii. 7; Isai. i. 30; v. 2; Mic. vii. 1; Luke xiii. 8.—I regard the words **I will sweep them utterly away** as a general statement of what follows. In this the Lord Himself accounts for the genesis of this declaration. He relates that he instituted an investigation, the result of which was that Israel was like an unfruitful, withered tree. In consequence of this He determined that they should be swept away by a storm: then I gave to them those who shall overrun them. (Comp. Isai. viii. 8; Dan. xi. 10, and Jer. v. 22; xxiii. 9). In **overrun** is evidently an allusion to **whirlwind**, to which **sweep** points, and the verse forms a sort of circle, the end returning to the beginning. The plural *overrun* intimates that in reality a number of persons would represent this storm. Comp. ver. 16.—The certainly peculiar expression וָאֶתֵּן for *then I appointed for them, hung over them*, is explained by supposing that the prophet intended a play upon the words הַתְּאֵנָ֖ים.

Vers. 14, 15. **What is then the ground on which we remain ? . . . and behold terror.** The people themselves relate how that which was determined in the secret counsels of Providence was actually carried out. The prophet portrays how the people, seized by the foreboding of threatening destruction, felt themselves insecure in their abodes, and concluded to flee to the fortified cities: עַל־מָה causal = *why?* Comp. ix. 11; Job xiii. 14. Yet I would take עַל at the same time as local: on what? on what insecure ground are we sitting? I endeavored to express this double sense in the translation.—**Assemble.** etc., taken verbatim from iv. 5. The people thus do something to which the Lord had previously summoned them by His prophet, but to follow this advice now will not avail, since they so long openly transgressed the holy will of God, as revealed in His law. In all their measures for flight they have this consciousness: there is no help, we are already lost.—**And perish there.** Not to be saved, but only to perish somewhat later, to obtain a little respite, do they flee to the cities.—**For Jehovah**, *etc.* They know that their destruction is already determined upon, and that they bear death, as it were, in their bodies into the cities. This is the sense of **given us water of poison,** *etc.* Comp. ix. 14; xxiii. 15, and xxv. 15, 17; Lam. iii. 15; Ps. lx. 5. On רֹאשׁ comp. WINER, *R. W. B.*, s. v. *Gift.*—Vain therefore is also the hope, which they still maintain, because every man hopes while he lives. This passage is repeated in xiv. 19.

Ver. 16. **From Dan . . that dwelt therein.** Hemistich *a* states the cause of the *terror*, again referring to a former declaration (iv. 16; vi. 22, 23). It appears that these words belong still to the speech of the Israelites, at least these may thus speak, since the words contain only the description of what was then perceived. But hemistich *b* describes the future as though it had already taken place. This could be done only by the prophet; וַיָּבֹאוּ וַיֹּאכְלוּ are therefore prophetic aorists. Comp. NAEGELSB. *Gr.* § 88, 5. [GREEN'S *Gr.* § 262, 4.—S. R. A.]—The prophet interposes with **and they came,** *etc.*, to say that the *terror* was not an empty one, but that the enemy thus announced had really come. The singular suffixes refer to the enemy represented as a *single* person. Comp. iv. 13.—אַבִּירָיו of horses, xlvii. 3; l. 11.

Ver. 17. **For behold, I send . . . saith Jehovah.** The discourse is now again figurative and Jehovah speaks Himself, as in the beginning of the strophe, ver. 13. We might compare a strophe like this with the variations of a musical theme. The more frequently the theme changes its form, the more impression does it make, the more ways of entrance are opened to it. That this verse has the character of a conclusion is seen, (*a*) from the return to the beginning. (*b*) from the climax, which is expressed in the figure of serpents inaccessible to all charms. This contains the idea of the most intensive destruction, excluding all possibility of healing. Since this is the main thought of the verse כִּי is best referred to ver. 16, *b.*:—Thus is it, for, *etc.* The Lord Himself confirms the words of the prophet. This verse has moreover a striking resemblance to Gen. xlix. 17, and it would not be impossible that the prophet, reminded by the mention of Dan of the prophecy concerning him, makes use of the images there employed for his description of the enemy coming from Dan.—צִפְעֹנִי (Isai. xi. 8; lix. 5; Prov. xxiii. 32) and יָעֵף (Isai. xiv. 29) so called probably *a sibilardo* (so GESEN. THES., FUERST, DRECHSLER) are regarded by most modern commentators, following in this Aquila and the Vulgate (the LXX. vary) as the basilisk, a small. exceedingly poisonous kind of viper. On **no charm,** *etc.*, comp. Ps. lviii. 5, 6, [4, 5].

3. *Continuation: The visitation ends with the carrying away captive of Israel, to the inexpressible grief of the people and of the prophet.*

VIII. 18–23.

18 O my comfort¹ in the sorrow!
My heart within me is faint.
19 Hark! a cry of my people from distant² lands:
"Is Jehovah not in Zion, or her king not in her?"
"Why have they provoked me to anger with their images,
With their foreign vanities?"
20 "The harvest is past, the fruit-gathering is over,
And we are not saved!"
21 For the wound of the daughter of my people am I wounded,³
I go mourning; horror hath seized me.
22 Is there no balsam in Gilead?
Is there no physician there?
Why then proceeds not the healing of the daughter of my people?
23 O that mine head were waters,⁴
And mine eye a fountain of tears,
That I might weep day and night
For the slain of the daughter of my people!

TEXTUAL AND GRAMMATICAL.

¹ Ver. 18.—מַבְלִיגִיתִי is ἅπαξ λεγ.—The radix בָּלַג *illuminate, beam upon*, (in Arabic of the rising sun) occurs only in Hiphil: Am. v. 9; Ps. xxxix. 13; Job ix. 27; x. 20. It is formed like כְּרִבִּית (multitude, fulness, increase, Levit. xxiii. 37), מְרִעִית (*pastio*, flock, Jer. xxiii. 1), מַשְׂבִּית (copy, Numb. xxxiii. 52). Comp. Olsh. § 218, a. The meaning is therefore: beaming, enlightening, exhilaration. [Henderson renders: my exhilaration within me is sorrow. Noyes, with a better sense: O where is consolation for my sorrow?—S. R. A.] The construction with עַל (comp. Am. v. 9) appears to be founded on the radical meaning, O beam on sorrow! The suffix of the first person refers to the whole, which is to be regarded as a single conception, in like manner as in בַּחֲסִי עוֹ, הַרְבֵּךְ יָפָה, comp. Naegelsb. *Gr.*, § 63, 4, *g*. According to the Keri, and even according to the Chethibh of several codices of Kennicott and De Rossi we should read בְּלִי נִיתִ׳ in two words, which reading the LXX. seem to follow (καὶ δύξονται ὑμᾶς ἀνίατα μετ' ὀδύνης) yet without its being possible to give to this נִיתִ׳ a satisfactory meaning. For many other explanations, comp. Rosenmueller.
² Ver. 19.—The form כְּרֻחֻקִּים is found besides only in Isd. xxxiii. 17.
³ Ver. 21.—הָשְׁבָּר Hoph. here only. The Niph. in this sense is frequent, *ex. gr.*, Jer. xxiii. 9.
⁴ [Ver. 23.—In the A. V. this verse is ix. 1, but not in the Hebrew.—S. R. A.]

EXEGETICAL AND CRITICAL.

This strophe, in which the nameless grief of the prophet at the destruction of his people is expressed in simple but highly poetical words, serves for the elucidation and completion of the previous one. In that the manner of the destruction, which the Northern enemy was to inflict, was not distinctly designated; at the most ver. 13 contained a dim intimation of a threatening captivity. That this will be the punishment of the people, is now distinctly expressed in this strophe. In deep sorrow (ver. 18), the prophet tells us that he has heard from distant lands the mournful question of his people, whether Jehovah is no longer in Zion (ver. 19, *a*). To this the answer of the Lord is: This is the punishment of idolatry (ver. 19, *b*).—New lamentation of the people: respite after respite and no salvation! (Ver. 20).—Finally the wailing of the prophet: the cause of his sorrow is the misery of his people (ver. 21) being hopeless (ver. 22), wherefore nothing remains for the prophet but to bewail this misery with endless weeping (ver. 23). Observe also in this strophe the dramatic character of the change in persons.
Ver. 18. **O my comfort . . . is faint**. Comp. the Text. and Gram. rems.—In the words **within me** is contained the idea of the *heavy* heart, which is felt as an oppression or burden. Comp. Ps. xlii. 6, 7, 12; xliii. 5; cxli. 4; coll. xxxix. 4; Lam. i. 20.
Ver. 19. **Hark! a cry . . foreign vanities**. The prophet beholds Israel in exile. Their eyes are still turned towards Zion as the chosen abode of the God of Israel (comp. Ps. xiv. 7; xx. 3; cxxviii. 5; cxxxiv. 3; Isai. xxxvii. 32, *etc*.) but it appears that He has forsaken it. Comp. Mic. iv. 9.—This painful question is answered by the Lord Himself, who continues and accounts for this impression. The expression *provoked to anger*

with their images reminds us of Deut. xxxii. 21; 1 Ki. xvi. 13, 26. Comp. Jer. xiv. 22; Ps. xxxi. 7.

Ver. 20. **The harvest is passed ... not saved.** Period after period elapses without help coming (comp. Isai. lix. 9). Without observing ver. 19, *a*, or the time when this discourse was composed, most of the ancient commentators refer these words to the vain expectation of Egyptian help, which presupposes 2 Ki. xxiv. 1; or to that which is expressly announced in Jer. xxxvii. 5. On the other hand SCHNURRER correctly remarks that the expression has somewhat of a proverbial character. Even those who are in exile still hope, as is also intimated in ver. 19 *b*, but still in vain.

Vers. 21, 22. **For the wound .. the daughter of my people.—I go mourning.** Comp. iv. 28; xiv. 2. The prophet is inwardly broken, and to this corresponds his outward appearance. —The prophet tells us in ver. 22 why the wound of his people causes him so much pain: it is not only a very dangerous one, as is clear from all that precedes, but also, which is the worst, no one heals it. It is as though Gilead no longer possessed any balsam, or any man skilful in the application of it, though the balsam was especially, according to Pliny (*Hist. Nat.*, XII. 54) exclusively, to be found in Palestine. The question: "Is there no balsam," *etc.*, has then the meaning: Is Israel wanting in that which was given to him in preference to all other nations? It is plain that the prophet here alludes to the relation of Israel to Jehovah, as the peculiar "glory of the land." (Gen. xliii. 11, song = best fruits, of the land). Whether יְרִי is precisely the resin of the balsam-plant, which elsewhere is called בֹּשֶׂם, בֶּשֶׂם, or בָּשָׂם, is uncertain. Comp. WINER, *R. W. B.* s. v. *Balsam*. It is mentioned as a remedy also in Jer. xlvi. 11; li. 8. as an article of commerce, Gen. xliii. 11; Ezek. xxvii. 17.—**Is there no physician there?** GRAF would not refer **there** to Gilead, because it is not known that physicians were fetched from thence. But we may well suppose that in the land of the balsam the use of it was best understood. The prophet therefore wishes only to say: Is there then in Israel, where the true *medicina salutis* is found, no one who understands how to make the application of it? He silently answers this question in the negative, and gives the reason for it in what follows.—**The healing.** The same expression in xxx. 17; xxxiii. 6; 2 Chron. xxiv. 13; Neh. iv. 1. Comp. Isa. lviii. 8. The expression "bandage" does not suit in all these passages, but "healing" does everywhere. Comp. ROSENM. *ad loc.*

Ver. 23. **O that mine head ... daughter of my people.** The poetry of suffering is presented most touchingly in these brief but thrilling words. It is the wish of the prophet that the whole interior of his head might dissolve into water, so that his eyes might be inexhaustible fountains of tears. For all he can do is to weep, and this is his only comfort.

DOCTRINAL AND ETHICAL.

1. On ver. 4. "In this consists our human blindness in spiritual matters, that he who has fallen cannot imagine he has fallen, he who errs will not be convinced that he errs. For the natural man receiveth not the things of the Spirit of God: for they are foolishness unto him, 1 Cor ii. 14." CRAMER.—"*Labi humanum est, resurgere Christianum, nolle resurgere diabolicum.*" FÖRSTER.

2. On ver. 5. "The people will still go astray more and more, they hold so fast to their false worship that they will not be turned away, and this because they have no proper place: because they have the service of God in reserve only *au pis aller*, it does not so much concern them whether they lie or steal, whether they go right or wrong, they do not wish to go anywhere." ZINZENDORF.

3. On ver. 7. "God opens to us the book of nature not only that we may behold as in a mirror the divine wisdom and omnipotence, but that we may also take thence good examples of discipline and improvement. Isa. i. 3; Prov. vi. 6. For if we behold such examples in nature we ought surely to be ashamed that irrational creatures are so willing and obedient, and do that for which they are created, but we men (who were made in His image and sealed with the Holy Ghost on the day of redemption) are so opposed, rebellious and disobedient to Him. This will certainly, in the case of no amendment, lead to a devilish bad ending." CRAMER.

4. On ver. 5. "*Manifeste docet nos, malitiam non esse opus naturæ, sed voluntatis* (προαιρέσεως)." THEODORET.

5. On ver. 7. "CHRYSOSTOM, *homil de Turture seu de virtute: turturem dicit omnem castam ecclesiam, hirundinem vero Joannem hominum amatorem, ciconiam autem eloquentissimum Paulum, ecclesiæ organum.*" GHISLERUS.

6. On ver. 8. "Jeremiah finds some of those also among us, who (according to this description of the theologians of his country) either deduce propositions from the Scriptures which a child may see are not so, or make up sentences and bring them to the people, and when they are asked: Where is that in the Bible? reply unabashed: O there is much in the Bible that is no longer applicable! or, All that is true is not in the Bible." ZINZENDORF.

7. On ver. 9. GHISLERI's here remarks that the *concionatores bene prædicantes sed male operantes* are put to shame and judged by the progress in wisdom and virtue of their hearers. He adduces a passage from the 18th Sermon of Bernard on the Song of Solomon, where it is said that the preacher should be *concha* not *canalis*. "*Hic pæne simul et recipit et refundit; illa vero donec impleatur exspectat, et sic quod superabundat sine suo damno communicat.*"

8. On ver. 13. Compare here Luke xiii. 6 sqq. and the New Year's hymn of RAMBACH, "One year after another comes," especially ver. 3. "Hew down, said He, the barren tree." *etc.*

9. On ver. 14. "Despair is the last point to which God in His just judgments allows the godless to fall (Matt. xxvii. 4, 5). Despairing men know indeed God's just judgment concerning them, but not so that they are penitent for their sins (Gen. iv. 13, 14)." STARKE.

10. On ver. 16. In accordance with the view widely extended among the church fathers and

supported by Gen. xlix. 17 (see DELITZSCH *ad. h. l.*), that the Antichrist should proceed from Dan (comp. also Levit. xxiv. 11 and the supposed origin of Judas Iscariot from the tribe of Dan). IRENÆUS (*Adv. Hær.* V. 30) remarks on this passage: "*Jeremias non solum subitaneum Antichristi adventum sed et tribum, ex quo veniet, manifestavit dicens; ex Dan audiemus vocem velocitatis equorum ejus, etc. Et propter hoc non adnumeratur tribus hæc in Apocalypsi* (vii. 5-8) *cum his quæ salvantur.*"

11. On ver. 16. "As the snorting of the horses sounded long before in the ears of the prophet, so shall the voice of Christ forever sound in our ears: 'Arise ye dead and come to judgment.'" CRAMER.

12. On ver. 17. "*Frustra ad Deum preces fundunt adversus serpentem antiquum qui Dei præcepta contemserint.*" GHISLERUS.

13. On ver. 21. "Our connection with those who hear us continually is so full, so intimate, so tender, no one can understand it who has not experienced it. We get love, we get somewhat from the heart, which was broken for its enemies, and which could cry even on the cross: Father, forgive them, they know not what they do." ZINZENDORF.

14. On ver. 22. "A pastor of a separatistic spirit cannot make many things whole, and it will be better for him to testify in earnest for the building up of those whom he would rather see pulled down.—He who will help his religion must regard it not as a *Babylon*, but as a broken *Zion*, and this from his heart; then he asks for salve and help, then he mourns for the hurt of Joseph." ZINZENDORF.

15. On ver. 22. "*Non solum in præsenti loco, sed et in multis aliis testimoniis scripturarum invenimus resinam Galaad pro pænitentia poni atque medicamine, mirarique nunc Deum, quare vulnera Jerusalem nequaquam curata sint, et necdum cicatrices obduxerint cutem, eo quod non sint prophetæ nec sacerdotes, quorum debeant curari medicamine.*" JEROME.

16. On ver. 23. The tears of Jeremiah are a prelude and type of the tears which the Lord wept over Jerusalem. Luke xix. 41. As the blood of Abel cried to heaven so do these tears, and it is here first truly manifest how ruinous it is for men when the servants of God exercise their office among them not with joy but with sighs (Heb. xiii. 17).

HOMILETICAL AND PRACTICAL.

1. On vers. 4-9. An earnest admonition to all who know that they are walking in perverse ways. They are admonished 1. to uprightness. They are (*a*) not to palliate their sins, (*b*) least of all to palliate them by a false interpretation of the divine word, either *a.* themselves or *β.* allow others to do it (vers. 8, 9).—2. To speedy return, for (*a*) he who returns betimes may be helped (ver. 4 the falling, the erring, ver. 7 the migratory birds); (*b*) but he who wilfully persists goes to ruin (ver. 6, the mad stallion). [HENRY: Those who persist in sin oppose 1. the dictates of reason (vers 4 and 5), 2. the dictates of conscience (ver. 6), 3. the dictates of Providence (the judgment of the Lord, ver. 7), 4. the dictates of the written word (vers. 8 and 9).— S. R. A.]

2. On vers. 4-7. God's complaint of the impenitence of His people. 1. How far this applies to us; 2. what should awaken us to repentance: 3. what true repentance is. BRANDT. *Epistelpredigten.*

3. On vers. 10-13. Signs of the decline and fall of a nation. 1. Avarice reigns. 2. Priests and prophets teaching false worship, hush up and deceive the people with false comfort. Deacon HAUBER, in PALMER's *Casual-Reden. 2te Folge.* I. Stuttgardt, 1860.

4. On vers. 18-23. In times of great distress in the church this text gives us occasion to consider I. Zion's complaint. This is 1. (in its subject) (*a*) general (ver. 19, *a*), (*b*) special, of the true servants of the church (vers. 21, 23): 2. (in its object) directed (*a*) to being (for the moment) forsaken (ver. 19 *b*), (*b*) to the delay of help (ver. 20). II. Zion's guilt (ver. 19 *b*). III. Zion's salvation. This is conditioned (*a*) by the presence of the true means of salvation (word and sacraments), (*b*) by the true application of the same.

5. On vers. 20-22. The question of the divine word in our harvest-complaint and the answer of the divine word to our harvest-question. 1. Our harvest-complaint runs thus: the harvest is past, the summer is ended and no help is come to us. Then God's word asks thee: (*a*) What is at fault? Is it not thy sin? (*b*) Is it really true that there was no help for thee? 2. Our harvest question runs: Is there then no salve in Gilead? Or is there no physician there? Why then is not the daughter of my people healed? To this the word of God answers: (*a*) O yes, salve and physician are there. The salve is the word of the fathers and the physician is thy Lord. (*b*) It is because the salve and the physician are not employed that our people are not healed. FLOREY, 1862.

6. [On ver. 20. 1. Every person who still remains in sin may at the close of the year usefully adopt this lamentation. 2. A season of religious revival is also eminently a time of harvest, and such as lose this season may usefully adopt his lamentation. 3. Another situation to which this melancholy reflection is peculiarly liable is that of a dying sinner. DWIGHT—"There is in this text I. The acknowledgment of opportunity. II. The confession of neglect. III. The anticipation of doom." J. W. W.—S. R. A.]

7. [On ver. 22. I. Sin prevails as a disease. It is (*a*) hereditary, (*b*) pervading, (*c*) vital and inveterate, (*d*) deceitful, (*e*) often painful, (*f*) mortal. II. There is a physician. III. How then does this condition exist? Because men are (*a*) insensible of need, (*b*) disposed to procrastinate, (*c*) will not take the remedy simply. DR. A. THOMSON, *of Edinburgh.*—S. R. A.]

8. [On ver. 23. "The same word in Hebrew signifies both the eye and a fountain, as if in this land of sorrows our eyes were designed rather for weeping than seeing." HENRY.—S. R. A.]

III. THIRD CHARGE: THE GENERAL ENTIRE ABSENCE OF TRUTH AND FAITH.

IX. 1–21.

1. *Description of the prevailing deceit.*

IX. 1–8.

1 O that I had¹ in the desert a travellers' lodge,
 That I might leave my people and go from them:
 For they are all adulterers, a gang of knaves,
2 And bend² their tongue as their bow of deceit;
 And not by truth do they prevail in the land,
 But proceed from wickedness to wickedness:
 But Me they knew not, saith Jehovah.
3 Guard ye every one against his neighbor,
 And trust no brother;
 For every brother practices deceit,
 And every neighbor slanders.
4 One overreaches³ another, and truth they speak not;
 They taught their tongues to speak lies,
 And weary themselves to commit iniquity.⁴
5 Thy habitation is in the midst of deceit;⁵
 And through deceit they refuse to know Me, saith Jehovah.
6 Therefore thus saith Jehovah Zebaoth:
 Behold, I melt them and try them;
 For how should I act in view of the daughter of my people?
7 A deadly arrow⁶ is their tongue, they speak deceit;
 With the mouth they speak⁷ to their neighbor peaceably,
 But in the heart⁸ they lay snares.
8 Should I not visit them for such things? saith Jehovah,
 Or should not my soul avenge itself on a people like this?

TEXTUAL AND GRAMMATICAL.

¹ Ver. 1.—מִי־יִתְּנֵנִי. Comp. Ps. lv. 7, and NAEGELSB. *Gr.*, § 78.
² Ver. 2.—The Masoretes punctuate וַיִּדְרְכוּ (the form like וַיִּבְקַע 1 Sam. xiv. 22; xxxi. 2; תֶהְבְּרֶן Job xix. 3) probably because they regarded the Hiphil as causative. But for various reasons (*Vid.* EXEG. AND CRIT.) it is better with HITZIG, GRAF and MEIER to suppose that the reading, which corresponds to the consonants, וַיִּדְרְכוּ is the original and correct.
³ Ver. 4.—יְהָתֵלּוּ. Comp. הִהְתַלְתֶּם Job xiii. 9, and יְהָתֵל 1 Ki. xviii. 27. The forms may be Piel from הָתַל or Hiphil from הָלַל. Comp. OLSH. § 257. EWALD, § 127, *d*.
⁴ Ver. 4.—הַעֲוֵה (iii. 21) *Inf. constr.*, as הַיֹּה Ezek. xxi. 15, חֲבִי Hos. vi. 9.—Comp. EWALD, § 238, *c*; OLSHAUSEN, § 191, *b*.
⁵ Ver. 5.—GRAF has rightly declared against the alteration of the text, while EWALD, appealing to the LXX., proposes נִלְאוּ שֶׁב תּוֹךְ בְּתוֹךְ מִרְמָה בְּמִרְמָה. The infinitive שֶׁבֶת is frequently used with suffixes; Ps. xxvii. 4; cxxxix. 2; 1 Ki. viii. 30; Ruth ii. 7, *etc.*
⁶ Ver. 7.—Instead of the Chethibh שׁוֹחֵט *jugulans*, throttling, killing, the Keri would read שָׁחוּט which elsewhere occurs only with זָהָב (1 Kings x. 16, 17; 2 Chron. ix. 15) and seems to denote gold beaten thin. Although from this the meaning "pointed" may be derived, which is also expressed by the Syriac and Chaldee, yet it is better to adhere to the reading of the text and to translate, a deadly murderous arrow.
⁷ Ver. 7.—דִבֶּר. The change of number is analogous to the frequently occurring change of person. Comp. *Gram.* § 101, *Anm.*
⁸ Ver. 8.—אָרְבּוֹ. The suffix is most naturally referred to the subject like that of בְּקִרְבּוֹ ver. 8. *Vide* v. 9, 29.

EXEGETICAL AND CRITICAL.

As the main thought of the preceding chapter was contained in vers. 4–9 so the main thought of the present is found in vers. 1–8. The rest is added as a sequel. As in ch. viii. the stiff-necked impenitence of Israel is censured, so here (as the third charge) their falseness in every relation. The two following strophes (vers. 9–15 and vers.

16-21) relate to the punishment threatened by God. In vers. 1-8 the prophet portrays the want of fidelity and trust, the falseness, malicious desire to defame, which was prevalent among his contemporaries (vers. 1-5) and which would compel the Lord to subject them to the punishment of a severe melting and refining process. (vers. 6-8).

Ver. 1. **O that I had in the desert . . . a gang of knaves.** On travellers' lodge comp. xiv. 8. Living with his godless countrymen is so intolerable to the prophet that he would prefer the scanty protection of a tent erected in the desert to his present residence. [HENDERSON supposes the discomfort of a caravanserai to be alluded to.—S. R. A.]—**Adulterers.** The violation of conjugal fidelity or of the fidelity due to a neighbor by the invasion of his conjugal rights was censured by the prophet in the second discourse, in the passage where he reproaches the Israelites with their violations of faith, v. 7, 8.—בֹּגֵד, he who acts secretly (Vide, FUERST) who deals in falsehood, deceit and treachery in general. This reproach also is found in ver. 11.

Ver. 2. **And bend their tongue . . . saith Jehovah.** The imperfect with Vau consecutive here designates not a single act, but oft recurring acts, from which this course is to be understood as habitual; this case is therefore to be numbered among those in which the imperfect with Vau consec. is used to designate a permanent quality. Comp. NAEGELSB. Gr., § 88, 9.— According to the Masoretes we must read: they caused their tongue to tread the bow of deceit. In this way the tongue would not be compared to a bow, (which might appear unsuitable to the Masoretes), but to an archer, and the bow would then be a purely ideal conception, a figure for the means and instrument of the intellectual activity connected with the tongue. But this would be a very artificial mode of expression. Since the tongue is elsewhere compared with a sword, (Ps. lvii. 4; lxiv. 3) and an arrow (infra ver. 7) it may also be compared with a bow and in Ps. lxiv. 3 this is the fundamental conception.—**bow** is used as a simile in apposition with tongue. Comp. Ps. xxii. 13; xi. 1. NAEGELSB. Gr., § 72, 4.—**Deceit** may according to the sense be referred either to bend or bow, but on account of its position it is better to refer it to the latter. On the construction comp. NAEGELSB. Gr., § 63, 4, g.—**And not by truth.** The prophet has especially the rulers in view. Comp. Ps. xii. 4, לָאֱמוּנָה different from v. 3; ל here indicates the norm as in לַמִּשְׁפָּט, לַמִּצְעָר Vid. NAEGELSB. Gr., § 112, 5, b.—On **wickedness to wickedness.** Comp. xxv. 32.

Ver. 3. **Guard ye . . slanders.** Comp. Mic. vii. 5, 6.—On **every brother**, etc. Comp. NAE-

GELSB. Gr., § 82, 1.—עָקֹב יַעְקֹב. Since this verb in Kal occurs besides only in Gen. xxvii. 36 and Hos. xii. 4, both times of Jacob (it is found in Piel in Job xxxvii. 4) it is certainly probable that the prophet, speaking here of the deceit practised by one brother towards another, had this early instance in view (Gen. xxv. 29 sqq.; xxvii. 35).—רָכִיל יַהֲלֹךְ go about for tale-bearing. Vide supra vi. 28.

Ver. 4. **One overreaches another . . . to commit iniquity.—They taught.** Comp. ii. 33. The Niphal of לָאָה signifies elsewhere "to be weary, disgusted with a thing" (vi. 11; xv. 6; xx. 9). This meaning does not suit here. The connection requires the meaning to weary one's self. Comp. Gen. xix. 11; Isai. xvi. 12.

Ver. 5. **Thy habitation . . saith Jehovah.** The verse has this object, to describe the relation of the deceitful race to the prophet and to Jehovah. They surround the prophet so that he dwells as the only honest man among deceivers (comp. Ps. cxx.); from the Lord however they turn away, the lying spirit rules them in such wise (comp. Gen. xxvii. 35; xxxiv. 13) that they know nothing of God and desire not to know Him. (Comp. v. 3).

Ver. 6. **Therefore . . daughter of my people.** A corruption so deeply rooted and so widely extended can be removed only by a process of entire melting, which will certainly be grievous but will also refine. Comp. vi. 27, etc.—אֵיךְ has by no means always a negative sense, (as for example Gen. xliv. 34, quomodo ascenderem? i. e., non ascendam) but as often a decidedly positive meaning, ver. 18, 2 Sam. i. 25, 27; how do ye advise me? 1 Kings xii. 6. So the Lord here asks, how He should act, if not as already indicated? He would say, there is nothing else remaining but to do this.—After מִפְּנֵי to supply רָעַת, with reference to iv. 4; vii. 12, appears to me unnecessary, for מִפְּנֵי is used in a causative sense even immediately before names of persons. Comp. iv. 26; xxiii. 9. In both these passages it is also evinced by an explanatory addition that it is to be taken in a causative sense.

Vers. 7, 8. **A deadly arrow . . . on a people like this.** It might appear strange that the prophet, after he had properly concluded with ver. 6, should repeat the main point of the charge. But he evidently intended to conclude with the words repeated from v. 9, 20, in order to indicate by this conclusion that he had the section of his former discourse, so closely related to this, (ch. 5) in view. The words of the eighth verse could not however follow immediately on ver. 6. The words **them for such things** would thus obtain a false reference. The prophet was therefore compelled again to mention the sins of the people.

2. *First punishment: Desolation of the land and dispersion of the people.*

IX. 9-15.

9 On the mountains let me raise a weeping and wailing,
And on the pastures of the desert a lamentation,
For they are desolated, without a man to pass through them;
And hear no longer the lowing of the cattle.
From the fowl of the heavens to the beast they are fled—gone!
10 And I will make Jerusalem a heap of stones,
The dwelling of jackals;
And the cities of Judah I will make desolate
Without an inhabitant,
11 Who is the man who is wise and understands this?
And who is he to whom the mouth of Jehovah has spoken,
That he may declare such things?
Why was the land destroyed
And laid waste as a desert without a man to pass through it?
12 And Jehovah said:
Because they have forsaken My law which I set before them,
And have not heard My voice, nor walked according to it;
13 But walked after the perversity of their heart,
And after the Baalim which their fathers have taught them;
14 Therefore thus saith Jehovah Zebaoth, God of Israel:
Behold! I give to them, this nation,
Wormwood to eat and poison water to drink.
15 And I scatter them among nations
Whom neither they nor their fathers have known;
And send after them the sword till I extirpate them.

EXEGETICAL AND CRITICAL.

The preceding strophe contained the main thought of the chapter; description of the want of truth and faith among the people. As already remarked, to this are attached two additional strophes, which are occupied with the judgment provoked by that moral corruption. The connection of this strophe with the preceding is effected by vers. 6 and 8, declaring how the Lord would try and purify the people and avenge Himself upon them. Verses 9 and 10 describe accordingly the desolation of the land ordained as a punishment; vers. 11-13 again set forth the main causes of the moral corruption (ver. 12 negatively, ver. 13 positively); vers. 14 and 15 show us the fate of the inhabitants driven from the lands, and serve therefore to supplement the figure contained in verses 9 and 10.

Vers. 9, 10. **On the mountains ... make desolate without an inhabitant.** עַל may grammatically and according to the connection designate both the place and the object. Comp. in the latter reference ix. 17; Ezek. xxvi. 17; Am. v. 1. Yet it would be flat and prosaic to restrict עַל to the object. The poetic liveliness of the style requires us to refer it to the place (comp. iii. 21) and the object at the same time. —נִצְּתוּ properly *they are burnt, singed*, and then generally *desolated*. Comp. ver. 11 and the remark on ii. 15. Compare besides xlvi. 19; 2 Kings xxii. 13, 17; Neh. i. 3; ii. 17.—**Without a man**, *etc.* Comp. ver. 11, Zeph. iii. 6; Ezek. xxxiii. 28.—**fled**, *etc.* Comp. iv. 25; I. 3. —**And I will make**, *etc.* Sudden change of subject. Jehovah Himself announces that not only the country but the cities, Jerusalem before all, shall be desolated.—**heap of stones**. Comp. li. 37.—מְעוֹן (comp. x. 22; xlix. 33; Isai. xxxiv. 13; xxxv. 7; xliii. 20) and אִיִּים (Isai. xiii. 22) both mean **jackals.** Comp. GES. THES. S. 30, 1457, 1511.—**Make desolate**. Comp. ii. 15; iv. 17; xxxiii. 10; xlvi 19; li. 29, *etc.*

Vers. 11-13. **Who is the man ... have taught them.** These three verses present the motive of the prospective desolation. It might be supposed that after what was said in vers. 1-8 this question would be superfluous. But we must not lose sight of the tableauesque character of Jeremiah's style. Thus this strophe, besides the new elements contained in vers. 9 and 10, 14 and 15, presents also the old elements in a modified form. The real root of this moral corruption is here indicated, *viz.*, that Israel had turned from the Lord and to idols.—**Who is he**, *etc.* These words remind us of Hos. xiv. 9. It is only the wise man who knows, only he to whom the Lord has spoken, who tells the truth. The prophet presupposes that the correct knowledge of the true cause of the destruction (ver. 9) is not such an easy matter. The unspiritual sense seeks the cause everywhere but where it is really to be found. To it external accidental circumstances are at fault. To seek the reason in themselves, in the perversity of their own hearts, does not occur to the foolish Israelites. Hence it is that not Israel but the Lord answers in ver. 12. Among Israel there was none so wise as to know the reason. The Lord is obliged to declare it.— **This** and the suffix in **such things** point back to vers. 8 and 9;—**to whom** expresses in the form of a direct question in what relation that which was previously said is to be understood. It is knowledge of the reason, namely, which is treated of.—נְצָתָה֙ points back to נִצְּתוּ֙, ver. 9, and is to be taken in the same sense.—Allusions to passages in Deuteronomy are here frequent. Comp. Deut. iv. 8; xi. 32; xxviii. 15; Jer. xxvi. 4; xliv. 10.—**According to it** refers back to **my law**. In ver. 12 the negative reason for the judgment coming upon the land is stated: in ver. 13 the positive. —**Walked**. Comp. iii. 17; vii. 24; Deut. xxix. 18.—**Baalim**. Comp. ii. 8, 23; Deut. iv. 3.—On **taught** comp. xii. 16; Deut. xi. 19.

Vers. 14, 15. **Therefore thus saith Jehovah ... extirpate them**.—With **therefore** the prophet proceeds to the statement of the consequences, naming first the consequences which the sins mentioned in vers. 12, 13 will bring upon the *men*, and afterwards those mentioned vers. 9, 10, on the *land*. —לַעֲנָה and רֹאשׁ occur together in Deut. xxix. 17; Am. vi. 12; Lam. iii. 19. Wormwood was considered poisonous by the ancients, but in the biblical use it is its bitterness which is prominent. Comp. Am. v. 7; Prov. v. 4; Lam. iii. 15.—On **poison-water**, comp. viii. 14. Our words are repeated, xxiii. 15. — **To them, this nation**. The anticipation of a noun by a pronoun is frequent in Jeremiah: xxvii. 8; xxxi. 2; xli. 2, 3; xliii. 11; xlvii. 44; li. 56. Comp. EWALD, § 309, c., NAEGELSB. *Gr.*, § 77, 2.— **neither they nor their fathers**, *etc*. Comp. Deut. xxviii. 36, 64; Lev. xxvi. 33; Jer. xvi. 13; xvii. 4. That **till I extirpate them** is not to be understood absolutely, is seen from passages like iv. 27; v. 10, 18 coll. Lev. xxvi. 44.

---

3. *Second Punishment: death snatches away an innumerable sacrifice.*

IX. 16-21.

16 Thus saith Jehovah Zebaoth : Consider ye,
And call for mourning women,¹ that they may come,²
And send for the skilful ones, that they appear;
17 And hasten, and raise a wailing³ over us,
That our eyes may run⁴ with tears,
And our eyelids overflow with water.
18 For—loud wailing is heard from Zion :
"How are we spoiled! We are greatly confounded;
For we have forsaken the land,
For they have thrown down our dwellings."
19 Hear then, ye women, the word of Jehovah,
And let your ear receive the word of his mouth,
And teach your daughters⁵ a song of lamentation,
And [teach ye] one another a dirge!
20 For death cometh in through our windows,
It enters into our palaces,
To exterminate the child from the street,
The youths from the free places.
21 [Speak : Thus saith Jehovah :]
And the carcases of men fall like dung⁶ on the field,
And like sheaves behind the reaper
When there is none to gather them.

TEXTUAL AND GRAMMATICAL.

¹ Ver. 16.—מְקוֹנְנוֹת here only. Comp. besides Ezek. xxxii. 16, and WINER, *R. W. B.*, art. *Leichen*.

² Ver. 16.—תְּבוֹאֶינָה, Ps. xlv. 17; 1 Sam. x. 7 (Chethibh)—תְּבוֹאנָה is the more frequent form, comp. *ex. gr.*, Gen. xxx. 38; 1 Kings iii. 16; Isa. xlviii. 3.

CHAP. IX. 16–21.   113

³ Ver. 17.—וְתִשֶּׂנָה (the same form in Ruth i. 14; Zech. v. 9) for הַשֶּׂאנָה (Ruth i. 9) for which also תִּשֶּׂאנָה (Ezek. xxiii. 49). Comp. Olsh., § 239; Gesen., § 74: *Anm*. 4.
⁴ Ver. 17.—וְתֵרַדְנָה designates the intended effect. Comp. Naegelsb. *Gr*., § 89, 3, *b*. 2.—On the accusative construction. Comp. xiv. 17; Lam. iii. 48; Joel iv. 18; N. *Gr*., § 69, 2 *a*.
⁵ Ver. 19.—On the suffix in אוֹנְכֶם and בְּנוֹתֵיכֶם, comp. Naegelsb. *Gr*., § 60, 5. [Green, *Gr*, § 220, 1 *b*.]
⁶ Ver. 21.—דְּבַר occurs only in the passages, Ps. lxxxiii. 11; Jer. viii. 2; xvi. 4; xxv. 33, and in figurative language.

EXEGETICAL AND CRITICAL.

In connection with the close of the preceding strophe, the prophet sets forth another element of the punishment, viz., the fruitful harvest, which the sword would yield. He does this by even now calling for the mourning-women to lament over the *future* destruction of Zion and the dispersion of the people (vers. 16-18): but not content with this, he also calls upon all other women, as by divine command, to instruct their daughters and one another in the art of wailing, for death will summon his victims in masses.

Vers. 16, 17. **Consider ye . . . overflow with water.—Consider** is emphatic (comp. ii. 10; xxiii. 20; xxx. 24) for what is required is something unusual. Usually mourning-women are called to weep over those who are already dead, and therefore others than those who call them. Here they are to raise their wailing over those very persons who call them, and over their future destruction. — **Skilful.** Since wailing does not require wisdom in the higher sense, and as the expression "wise women" is not proved to be a technical term for mourning-women (as *sage femme* for midwife), the word must denote only those who are skilful, experienced, in general, comp. x. 9, and "skilful of lamentation," Am. v. 16. [Comp. also Matt. ix. 23, and Thomson, *The Land and the Book*, I., p. 146.—S. R. A.]

Vers. 18, 19. **For loud wailing . . . a dirge.** The prophet feigns a kind of vision: the Israelites perceive, not with their bodily but spiritual ear, a loud wailing. This is future, and it is they who wail. The subject of lamentation is: we are destroyed (iv. 13), put to shame (li. 51), have been obliged to forsake the land, because the enemy has thrown down our dwellings. So I render, with Raschi, Rosenmuller, Graf and others, since שָׁלַךְ is not merely to throw away, but also to throw to the ground (Job xviii. 17; Ezek. xix. 12), and of the throwing down of a dwelling is expressly used in Dan. viii. 11.— **Hear them.** The second כִּי introduces a second reason for the wailing commanded in ver. 18. Ver. 18 speaks only of destruction and exile in general. But dirges presuppose particular cases of death. Therefore in vers. 19, 20 it is added, that the destruction and deportation will result in the death of many. This is introduced in this way: the mourning-women in the divine commission are further commanded to instruct not only their daughters, but also the other women in the art of wailing, for on account of the unusual number of deaths, a much larger number of mourners than usual will be required. The wailing of ver. 17 is not to be raised, therefore, because the women received the command contained in ver. 19, but because they received this command for the reason given in vers. 20, 21.

Vers. 20, 21. **For death cometh in . . . when there is none to gather them.** Death will not, as an enemy lurking without, attack those only who venture out to him, but will assault the people, penetrating into all their houses to fetch his sacrifices. The figure is like that in Joel ii. 9.—**From the street.** While death strangles the children and youths in the houses, he has at the same time taken them from the street and the places.—The words **speak, thus saith Jehovah,** are very disturbing. They interrupt the close connection, which according to the sense and the construction there is between **and the carcases,** *etc*., and ver. 20; they are wanting in the LXX., and the whole manner of expression is foreign to Jeremiah. For the imperative דַּבֵּר does not occur once in Jeremiah, either in the addresses of God to the prophet or elsewhere, and Jeremiah never says כֹּה־נְאֻם. He also never places נְאֻם־י׳ before, but always after the beginning, like the Latin *inquam*, or at the close of the address.—**And the carcases,** *etc*. These words we read in 2 Kings ix. 37 of the corpse of Jezebel. Comp. Ps. lxxxiii. 11; Jer. viii. 2; xvi. 4; xxv. 33.—The stricken will lie like sheaves behind the reaper, but there is to be this difference, that while the sheaves are collected and taken home, the dead bodies will lie in the field unregarded. Compare the figure of the sheaves, Mic. iv. 12.

DOCTRINAL AND ETHICAL.

1. On ver. 1. **O that I had in the desert,** *etc*. "So it sounds here and there when the servant of the Lord comes from confession, from church, from the sick, from pastoral visitation, on the great fast-day, on the third festival-day, on almost every Sunday afternoon. A beautiful character of a witness when he needs nothing but a little spot in the desert, no improvement, no great management, when it is not necessary to say, 'Alas, my heart is whelmed with grief! and whence can I obtain relief?' When no one sits by him who presses upon him. The desert was to retain Jeremiah in connection with his people. He wished there to *weep* for them." Zinzendorf.

2. On ver. 2. "**They proceed from one wickedness to another**—punished with the sins, which are suspended over them . . . . a poor sold people who know not how to raise their ransom-money. We must tell them, and tell them again, whence it is to be fetched." Zinzendorf.

3. On ver. 3. "**Guard ye every one against his friend, and trust not even his brother.** This is the *Hobbesii jus naturæ.*" Zinzendorf. "*Hoc loco utendum est in tempore persecutionis et angustiæ, quando aut rara, aut nulla fides est; quando nec fratri, nec proximo credendum est, et inimici hominis domestici ejus, quando juxta evangelium tradet pater filium et filius patrem, et dividentur duo in tres et tres in duo* (Matt. x. 34 sqq.)" Jerome.

8

4. On ver. 4. "*Laborant homines loqui menda-cium, nam veritatem tota facilitate loquerentur. Ille enim laborat, qui fingit quod dixit. Nam qui verum vult dicere non laborat. Ipsa veritas sine labore loquitur. Ipsum mendacium hominum est labor laboriorum ipsorum* (Ps. vii. 14)," AUGUSTIN., *Enarr. in Ps.* cxxxix. [HENRY:—"They are wearied with their sinful pursuits, but not weary of them. The service of sin is a perfect drudgery; men run themselves out of breath in it; and put themselves to a great deal of toil to damn their own souls."—S. R. A.]

5. On ver. 11. "We are not to search with culpable curiosity into the causes of divine judgment which God has hidden from us. But if God Himself discovers them to us, we should ponder them well and apply them as best we may (vi. 17, 18)." STARKE.

6. On ver. 11. It is always an important part of true wisdom to recognize the object of the divine chastisement. At Jericho (Josh. vii.) it was made known by an extraordinary revelation that the ban of sacrilege was resting upon Israel, and the lot further brought to light the author of the crime. But this mode of revelation is not the usual one. When punishment is the direct and immediate consequence of sin, *ex. gr.*, when sickness follows on dissipation, and poverty on laziness and negligence, then every one who wishes, may easily see, whither the chastisement tends. But often the connection between sin and punishment is more remote and secret, although it is never an artificial and arbitrary, but always an organic and necessary one. Then is the time, in all humility and honesty to examine one's self in order to learn "why the land is laid waste."

HOMILETICAL AND PRACTICAL.

1. On vers. 1-6. This text might serve as a foundation in cases where a preacher has occasion to speak to his congregation on separation from the world, *etc.* He might especially draw from it arguments *in favor* of such separation. Comp. Rev. ii. 2, οὐ δύνῃ βαστάσαι κακούς.—As a counterpoise might be applied, Heb. xii. 3; 2 Tim. ii. 24.—A servant of the Lord is to be ἀνεξίκακος and ἀλεξίκακος.

2. On ver. 3. On the various stages in the condition of security. 1. Of evil rising into act. 2 Of rising from one sin to another. BRANDT: *Altes und Neues in extemporirb. Entwürfen*, Nürnberg, 1829, 1, 2.

3. On vers. 7-9. The double object of the divine judgments. 1. Restoration of the right (ver. 9). 2. Improvement of men (ver. 7, to melt and try).

4. On vers. 12-16. On the connection of temporal evil with our sins. Such a connection (1) undoubtedly exists, and should be (2) recognized and (3) announced by us (that is, not passed over in silence, but openly expresssed).

5. On vers. 20 and 21 (to be used in times when death snatches many away). Death as a destroying angel: 1. Who sends him; 2. Wherefore he is sent: 3. How we may protect ourselves against him.

IV. CONCLUSION: (IX. 22-25; X. 17-25.)

1. *The only means of escape, and the reason why it is not used.*

IX. 22-25.

22 Thus saith Jehovah:
    Let not the wise man glory in his wisdom,
    Nor let the strong man glory in his strength,
    Nor let the rich man glory in his riches.
23 But let him that glorieth glory[1] in this,
    To be wise[2] and to know me—
    That I am Jehovah—who exercise mercy,
    Judgment and righteousness on the earth;
    For in these do I delight, saith Jehovah.
24 Behold! the days are coming, saith Jehovah,
    That I will punish every circumcision in foreskin:[3]
25 Egypt and Judah and Edom, and the children of Ammon and Moab,
    And all with shorn hair [-corners] who dwell in the desert;
    For all the people are uncircumcised,
    The whole house of Israel is uncircumcised at heart.

TEXTUAL AND GRAMMATICAL.

[1] Ver. 23.—הִתְהַלֵּל. Comp. NAEGELSB. *Gr.*, § 101, 2 c.

[2] Ver. 23.—הַשְׂכֵּל. The preposition is omitted, as frequently: Isa. xlviii. 16; xxviii. 6; lxi. 7. Comp. N. *Gr.*, § 72, 2; 112, 8.

[3] Ver. 24.—[A. V.: The circumcised with the uncircumcised.]

EXEGETICAL AND CRITICAL.

The prophet introduces the concluding part of his discourse with a general moral reflection, the object of which is to present the only means of escape from such fearfully threatening dangers, viz., a living and truly productive knowledge of the Lord (vers. 22, 23). Unfortunately the prophet is at the close of the strophe (vers. 24, 25) compelled to acknowledge the mournful fact that such a true knowledge of God by the people Israel was not to be expected, since they were a people of uncircumcised heart, and were therefore, notwithstanding their bodily circumcision, essentially like the uncircumcised heathen nations. From this it is evident that the passage (vers. 22-25) can be dispensed with neither from the inner connection nor the connection with the preceding context, and we should not therefore be justified in regarding it (with GRAF) as a later addition.

Vers. 22, 23. **Let not the wise man... delight.** As the things in which they are not to glory, wisdom, strength (power), riches, are certainly mentioned, because they appear above all to the natural man as the most desirable, comp. 1 Kings i. 13, where in substance these three ideas are placed in juxtaposition, with 2 Chron. ix. 22; Job xii. 13. But at the same time the prophet has doubtless in view actual circumstances and declarations previously made by him. The inclination of his hearers presumptuously to boast of external carnal advantages was censured by him in the seventh chapter (comp. vers. 4, 8, 10, 14, 24, 26, 28); that the Jews gloried in their wisdom is expressly stated in vii. 8, 9. The mention of strength seems to point back to v. 2, and **riches** remind us of v. 26-28. The wisdom in which they are not to glory is not that which is called "better than strength" in Eccles. ix. 16, and which is essentially identical with that recommended in ver. 23, but it is worldly wisdom, which though it boast of enjoying divine direction, in truth rejects the word of God, and is therefore put to shame (viii. 8, 9,) against which also a warning is given in Prov. iii. 5, in the words, "Trust in Jehovah with all thine heart, but on thine own understanding rely thou not."—**Strength** is both physical strength (Ps. cxlvii. 10, Job xxxix. 19) and power (2 Kings x. 34, xx. 20.)—Every man must have something in which to glory, i. e., which he esteems as his highest blessing and honor (without self-esteem) comp. Isai. li. 16; 1 Cor. i. 31; 2 Cor. x. 17.— **Me must depend on knows** alone, or also **on to be wise** (understand) (Ps. lxiv. 10; cvi. 7.) I prefer the latter. **Wise** then does not, as GRAF assumes, contradict the beginning of ver. 22, but only opposes the true to the false wisdom. **For in these**, etc., is not the fundamental statement, but the explanation of the general אֵת. Comp. NAEGELSB. Gr § 109, 1 a.—God is to be known as the eternally existent, therefore the only true God, who exercises mercy, judgment and righteousness on the earth. There is an antithesis here to **strength**, etc., ver. 22 (ix. 2; v. 26 sqq.) But he who has learned to *know* the Lord as such, acts accordingly. Mercy is not in opposition to justice and righteousness as sometimes in Christian usage, but mercy is the root of righteousness, i. e, the disposition which does not with brute force trample upon the poor and weak, but with kindness and love secures to them their rights, and thus blessing and salvation. Comp. rems. on vii. 5, 6. Ps. cxlv. 17.

Vers. 24, 25. **Behold! the days are coming... uncircumcised at heart.** All here primarily depends on the explanation of the expression בְּעָרְלָה מוּל = **circumcision in foreskin.** The explanations *all circumcised on the foreskin* (LXX. and Vulg.) and *all the circumcised, together with those who have the foreskin* (TREMELL., PISC., ROSENM.) neither suit the connection, nor can they be justified grammatically. The explanation of HITZIG, GRAF, [HENDERSON, NOYES, BLAYNEY,] according to which *circumcised in foreskin* is equivalent to *uncircumcised* (HITZIG compares "a knife without a handle and to which the blade is wanting") imputes nonsense to the prophet. Grammatically the words can mean only: to circumcise in foreskin, i. e., circumcision, which is yet connected only with the foreskin, therefore no true circumcision. In favor of this explanation is 1. That the prophet mentions Judah among these nations. If it cannot be denied of this nation, that its circumcision was connected with the foreskin, the same must apply, though in a different sense, to the others. 2. If the prophet wished to mention only absolutely *uncircumcised* nations, why has he mentioned particularly these? He might then have omitted Judah, and mentioned all others in preference to these. The selection is evidently intentional. All these nations are either notoriously or—on account of their affinity of race with Israel—at least probably circumcised. The former was the case with the Egyptians (Herod. II. 36, 104). If circumcision was practiced only among the higher castes of the Egyptians (WINER, R. W. B. Art. "*Beschneidung*") this would be another reason for the prophet to reckon the nation generally among the "circumcised in foreskin." The קְצוּצֵי פֵאָה were undoubtedly circumcised. For it is evident from xxv. 23; xlix. 28, 32, that by this phrase Arabian tribes, especially the Kedarenes, are understood, of which Herodotus (III. 8) reports that they περιτρόκαλα κείρονται, περιξυροῦντες τοὺς κροτάφους which was forbidden to the Jews (Levit. xix. 27; xxi. 5). The Kedarenes, however, were descended from Ishmael (Gen. xxv. 13; comp. HERZOG, R-Enc. 1, S. 463) who was circumcised by Abraham (Gen. xvii. 23) and among whose descendants the practice of this rite is continued even to this day, not by order of Mohammed (the Koran nowhere enjoins circumcision, comp. MICHAELIS, *Mos. Recht.* § 184) but as an ancient sacred custom. If now it cannot also be proved of the Edomites, Ammonites and Moabites (Gen. xix. 37, 38) that they had circumcision (John Hyrcanus gave the Edomites the alternative either of abandoning their country or accepting circumcision, and they chose the latter. JOSEPH. *Antiqu.* XIII. 9, 1) yet Jeremiah must have *reckoned* them among the circumcised. Whether he erred in this or not is another question. There is of course the possibility that the usage may have prevailed at his time among them also and afterwards declined, as even among the Israelites this law was by no means always punctually followed (Josh. v. 2, sqq. Comp. HERZOG. *R-Enc.* II. *S.* 108).—In short the juxtaposition of Judah and two other undoubtedly circumcised nations with three whose circumcision on account of their origin is possible and indeed highly probable, but not proved, shows that according to the intention of the prophet the expression (מול כערלה) is to be taken in the sense, which as we have shown above, is alone grammatically admissible.—With this also accords the causal sentence "for all the nations," etc. It is entirely unnecessary to regard the article as a retrospective pronoun—all *these* nations. The prophet really wishes to say that all the nations of the heathens are uncircumcised, from which however it follows that those previously mentioned are so. If these are uncircumcised in spite of a circumcision, which from the standpoint of the theocracy must appear an unjustifiable imitation of the sacred sign of the covenant, and the whole house of Israel, including Judah, is uncircumcised of heart, it is explained why the Lord named Judah's and the other nations' circumcision—in foreskin. From this it further results that an improvement of Judah in the sense of ver. 23 is not to be expected, whence finally it follows that Judah is exposed to the judgment of the Lord as well as those other nations.

DOCTRINAL AND ETHICAL.

1. On ix. 22, 23. "Paul says, He that glorieth, let him glory in the Lord (2 Cor. x. 17), and Jesus, This is life eternal that they might know Thee that Thou art the only true God and Jesus Christ, whom Thou hast sent (John xvii. 3). This is to glory, as though one should say, God be praised, I am right well and sound. To be sound in the faith is to have the knowledge of Jesus Christ, to maintain it, to grow in it. This is to prosper. To be silent concerning grace from humility is an affectation. To make a great noise of good works as our own, is ridiculous. For grace produces them, the power of God dwelling in us. We do nothing and should do nothing if it were not left to us; but the work of God in us, that we believe, is not to be passed over in silence, moroseness, and ingratitude. What a noise do the humble saints in the Revelation make of their grace, freedom, priesthood, royal dignity, victory, redemption (chap. iv., v., vii., xii., xiv., xv., xvii, xix.). There is also nothing any longer secret when we bear His name on our forehead. O that the whole earth were full of our glorying in the Lord! 'O that we were able, our songs so high to raise, That all the country round, might echo with His praise.' The world and false theology recommend in this respect a certain silence, which shows that they do not know which is their proper power. And against them it is best to contend *realiter* by manifestation of the Spirit and of power. Let your light so shine before men that they may glorify the Father in heaven (Matt. v. 16)." ZINZENDORF.

2. On ix. 23. "*Qui fideliter et obedienter vivit,*

non de ipsa obedientia tamquam de suo non accepto bono extollatur, sed qui gloriatur, in Domine glorietur. In ullo enim gloriandum, quando nostrum nihil sit." AUGUSTIN: *De bono Persever.* Cap. xiv. 7. Comp. HILARIUS, *Enarr in* Ps. lii. 3.
3. On ix. 23. "*Qui gloriatur, in Domine glorietur. Hoc est Christum pascere, hoc est Christo pascere, in Christo pascere, præter Christum sibi non pascere.*" AUGUSTIN: *De Pastoribus.* Cap. xiii. 9.
4. On ix. 23. "*Videte quomodo nobis abstulit gloriam, ut daret gloriam; abstulit nostrum ut daret suum; abstulit inanem, ut daret plenam; abstulit nutantem, ut daret solidam.*" ANSELM. *Comment. in* 1 Cor. i. 31.
5. On ix. 24, 25. "Like brothers, like caps. If the circumcised and uncircumcised are alike good and pious, they will not unfairly be punished in like manner." CRAMER.
6. On ix. 24, 25. "A clear testimony that the holy sacraments procure nothing *per opus operatum*, for the work's sake. For the Jews were indeed circumcised in the flesh, but this was to be a sign to them of righteousness, that they should be spiritually circumcised in faith and good works. But since such spiritual circumcision did not follow, and they remained uncircumcised at heart, the other fleshly circumcision helped them not, but redounded instead to their sin." CRAMER.

HOMILETICAL AND PRACTICAL.

1. On vers. 22, 23. (LUTHER, vers. 23, 24). The Christian's highest and true glory. It consists in 1. Believing in the Lord; 2. Living in the Lord; 3. Working for the Lord; 4. Suffering for the Lord's sake. (FLOREY: *Trost und Mahnung an Graben*, I. Bändchen, *S.* 151).
2. On vers. 22, 23. The true knowledge of God 1. Its nature (not dead science, but living experience); 2. its fruit, *a.* the highest blessing (mercy, justice and righteousness in Jesus Christ); *b.* the highest honor (he who has it will not be put to shame as he who glories in the flesh).
3. On ver. 22. [Eng. Vers. Ver. 23. BP. BULL:—Examples of the folly of glorying (or trusting) in wisdom, might or riches:—Solomon, Samson and Ahab.—S. R. A].
4. On ver. 23. [Eng. Vers. ver. 24. ABP. TILLOTSON:—1. The wisest and surest reasonings in religion are grounded on the unquestionable perfections of the divine nature (*ex. gr.* belief in Divine Providence and veracity). 2. The nature of God is the true idea and pattern of perfection and happiness.—S. R. A.].
5. On ver. 23. "The Christian's self-glorying. 1. Evil self-glorying keep far from thee; 2. If thou wilt glory, glorify thyself in the Lord." *Gezetz. u. Zeugniss,* 1860, Jan.
6. On vers. 25, 26. Circumcision as a figure of the relation of man to God. 1. The three stages of circumcision, uncircumcised, outwardly circumcised, truly circumcised, correspond to the three stages of being without God, serving God outwardly, serving God in spirit and in truth. 2. As external circumcision without that of the heart is equivalent to uncircumcision, so the outward service of God without the inward is equivalent to no service at all.

LATER ADDITION: WARNING AGAINST IDOLATRY.

X. 1-17.

a. The nothingness of idols.

X. 1-5.¹

1 Hear the word, which Jehovah has spoken to you,² house of Israel!
2 Thus saith Jehovah: To the way of the heathen accustom³ yourselves not,
  And be not affrighted at the signs of Heaven, because the heathen are affrighted at them;
3 For the institutions of the nations—breath are they!
  For as a forest tree have they been cut out,—
  For the work⁴ of the hands of the artificer, with an axe.⁵
4 With gold and silver they adorn it,
  With nails and hammers they fasten them, that it totter not.
5 They are as the pillars in a cucumber-field and speak not;
  They must be borne,⁶ for they walk not.
  Fear them not, for they do no harm,
  But also to do good is not in their power.⁷

TEXTUAL AND GRAMMATICAL.

¹ MOVERS (*De Utr. Rec. Jer.* p. 43) was the first to deny the authenticity of the section x. 1-16. After careful examination I have come to the following result: 1. That the passage breaks the connection cannot be doubted. For ix. 22-25 and x. 17-25 joined to each other form an appropriate, orderly, progressive conclusion to the great discourse of the prophet. Comp. the introductory remarks on ix. 22-25 and x. 17-25. This warning against idolatry to those who had just been rebuked for the most wanton idolatrous abominations (vii. 17 sqq.; 30 sqq.) is exceedingly surprising, particularly as the expression, "accustom yourselves not," ver. 2, presupposes either a nation unspotted by idolatry or a nation purified from it, which however exposes itself to new temptations. The view of J. D. MICHAELIS and KUEPER, that the ten tribes already carried away into Assyria are here addressed (on account of "house of Israel," ver. 1), is no improvement, for the interruption of the connection still remains. When KEIL (*Einl. S.* 256) says that the section affords only the foundation to that which Jeremiah has said in ix. 22-25 on the glorying of Israel and his equality with the uncircumcised heathen, and that the deeper ground of their idolatry is thus discovered to the people and the necessity of their being scattered among the heathen (ix. 15) proved, one might almost suppose that he had not read the passage with the necessary attention, for there is not a trace of reproach which would be thus brought upon Israel: throughout there is not a word on the inner spiritual condition of the people. At most we should conclude from ver. 2 that this was presupposed to be a good one. All which KEIL designates as the object of this passage has been given by the prophet in part long before, and in part in vers. 24 and 25, for the uncircumcised heart is indeed the deepest ground of all the inner and outer corruption which the prophet so deeply bewails.—2. As to the language, I find in the first three verses some traces of Jeremiah's idiom, but not so decisively as to feel compelled on their account to admit Jeremiah to be the author. The formula (הַדָּבָר אֲשֶׁר דִּבֶּר is certainly Jeremiah's (comp. xlv. 1; xlvi. 13; l. 1), but in Jeremiah it stands only at the commencement of the larger sections. In the midst of the context, as here, it is striking, the more so as it is further extended by שִׁמְעוּ.—לְמַד is nowhere else, even in Jeremiah, construed with אֶל, but with עַל (xiii. 21), though very frequently he uses עַל and אֶל as synonymous (comp. on עֲלֵיכֶם ver. 1) wherefore also GRAF on xiii. 21 supposes that עַל in this passage is written "as so frequently" for אֶל.—The verb חָתַת (ver. 2) occurs in the Old Test. 55 times, in Jeremiah 20 times, from which it is clear that relatively it is used most frequently in this prophet.—חֻקּוֹת (ver. 3) is the more usual form in Jer.; besides here it is found 5 times (v. 24; xxxi. 35; xxxiii. 25; xliv. 10, 23), חֻקִּים only twice (xxxi. 36 and xxxii. 11, here perhaps after Deut. v. 28. But the first form is as much used as the latter.—בְּאַיִן (ver. 6) is a current word in Jer., but used so absolutely, simply as a negation, it is found neither in Jer. nor elsewhere. Comp. the exposition. עֵת פְּקֻדָּתָם, ver. 15, is the only expression which would speak decidedly in favor of the Jer. authorship, if the possibility of imitation were excluded. (Comp. Jer. viii. 12; xlvi. 21; l. 27 and שְׁנַת פְּ xi. 23; xxiii. 12; xlviii. 44). Apart from these few forms which correspond to Jeremiah's usage, without being exclusively his or being raised above the suspicion of imitation, there are a relatively large number of expressions, which are in part ἅπαξ λεγόμενα, on which however we lay no stress (the Pi. פָּאָה ver. 4; יָאֲתָה ver. 7; בְּאַחַת in the meaning *und* ver. 8; יְכַלּוּ *ibid.*; אֵת אֱלֹהִים ver. 10; תַּעְתֻּעִים ver. 15) and in part do not occur elsewhere in Jer., but take the place of other usual expressions. To these belong מַרְקוֹעַ ver. 9; לְבוּשׁ ver. 4; אַרְגָּמָן, תְּכֵלֶת ver. 9 (Jer. uses for the latter בְּגֶד xii. 1; xxxvi. 24; xli. 5; xliii. 12; כַּד xiii. 25); הֶבֶל ver. 12; תְּבוּנָה ibid.; נֹטֶה שָׁמַיִם (the latter expression Job ix. 8; Isa. xl. 22; xlii. 5; xliv. 24; xlv. 12; li. 13; lxvi. 12; Ps. civ. 2; Zech. xii. 2); נְשִׂאִים (comp. on the other hand Ps. cxxxv. 7) מָרָק and מָטָר ver. 13; הֶבֶל ver. 14; (Jer. always says פְּסִיל viii. 19; l. 38; li. 47, 52), נֶסֶךְ in the sense of מַסֵּכָה ver. 14 (נֶסֶךְ in Jer. is always *libatio*, vii. 18; xix. 3; xxxii. 29; xliv. 17 sqq.), חֵלֶק and שֵׁבֶט ver. 16.

From all this might well proceed some suspicion as to the authenticity of the passage vers. 1-16. In opposition to MOVERS, HITZIG and DE WETTE, GRAF has fully shown that the supposed Isaiah II. could not be the author (*S.* 171 *Anm.*), although many relations are not to be denied. Who was the author and when and by whom the addition was made can scarcely be ascertained.

² Ver. 1.—עַל in עֲלֵיכֶם is used here, as frequently in Jeremiah, as synonymous with אֶל (comp. the exchange of the two in xi. 2; xviii. 11; xxiii. 35; xxv. 2; xxvii. 19; xxxvi. 31; xliv. 20; besides xxv. 1; xxvi. 15; xxxv. 15; xlii. 19 coll. Hos. xii. 11).

³ Ver. 2.—לָמַד with אֶל here only. But it is found in xiii. 21 with the synonymous עַל. Comp. GRAF on this passage. —With לְ and the following subst., Deut. iv. 10; xiv. 23; xvii. 19; Ps. xviii. 35; cxliv. 1. With לְ and the following inf., Deut. xviii 9; Isa. xlviii. 17; Jer. xii. 16; Ezek. xix. 3, 6; Ps. cxliii. 10.

⁴ Ver. 3.—כְּרָתֻהוּ is the accusative of the object. Comp. 1 Kings xviii. 32: " he built the stones to an altar." (NAEGELSB. *Gr.* § 69, 3).—As כָּרַת denotes not to hew but only to fell, the object designated is not the immediate but remote end of the activity.

⁵ Ver. 3.—מַעֲצָד is found only in Isa. xliv. 12 in a similar connection. The connection and the dialects are both in favor of the meaning of *axe*. In Arabic the corresponding word designates a cutting instrument. Comp. Aram. חֲצַד *metere*. The prefix מ may depend on מַעֲשֵׂה or on בְּרָתוֹ, or on both. The latter is the more probable since in fact the axe is the instrument which serves for felling and hewing. Comp. Isa. xliv. 14.

⁶ Ver. 5.—יִנָּשׂוּא for יִנָּשְׂאוּ, Comp. EWALD, § 194 *b*; OLSH. § 38 *b*, *Anm. g*; 265 *s*.

⁷ Ver. 5.—אוֹתָם for אֶתְהֶם. Comp. rems. on f. 16.

EXEGETICAL AND CRITICAL.

According to ver. 2 the object of this passage is to warn Israel from the worship of idols. In this behalf first the nothingness of idols, the dead work of men, is shown (vers. 1-5). Then the incomparable greatness of Jehovah and in contrast with the origin of the idol images His overwhelmingly impressive self-existence and power, in view of which the adoration of empty idols appears disgraceful folly, are set forth as the source of all great phenomena in nature and history (vers. 6-16).

Vers. 1, 2. **Hear the word . . . affrighted at them.** דֶּרֶךְ, **way.** Comp. v. 4, 5. It is simply religion, *cultus*. On this account and from what follows (ver. 3 sqq.) the "signs of the heaven" cannot be passing and chance signs, be they constellations (HITZIG), or comets, darkness, *etc.* (ROSENM., GRAF), but only permanent signs which are connected with permanent worship, and **affrighted** is to be understood not of the momentary impression excited by an extraordinary phenomenon, but only of the constant religious terror manifesting itself in the ordinary worship (comp. Mal. ii. 5. and פַּחַד, Gen. xxxi. 42, 53). Were we to take **affrighted** in the former sense it would signify either an emphasis on the point of terror: ye may feel joy at favorable signs but ye are not to be terrified at supposed unfavorable signs—which would be a contradiction and at the same time confirm the superstition—or it would be: ye are not to conceive of the signs of heaven as under the influence of higher powers and therefore indifferent to human life, which would be a warning against astrology not in correspondence with the connection. In accordance with the subsequent warning against the worship of images idolatry only can be here spoken of, which renders not merely the extraordinary, but above all the ordinary signs of the heavens the object of adoration. The expression "signs" would refer less to the destination determined by the stars, Gen. i. 14, than to the ancient constellations (Job ix. 9), as whose signs appear the stars which form them (comp. the twelve signs of the Zodiac,

2 Kings xxiii. 5).—**Because the heathen,** *etc.*, is not the argument of the author against idolatry—this does not come till ver. 13—but a statement of the reason, from the soul of the Israelites, why this service has so much that is seductive for them. This causal sentence corresponds to "accustom yourselves not." The learning and becoming accustomed is the effect of the example. How dangerous this was to the Israelites we learn from the warnings: Exod. xxiii. 24, 32, 33; Lev. xviii. 3; Deut. vii. 1 sqq. Comp. Judges ii. and iii.—כִּי here=because. Comp. NAEGELSB. *Gr.* § 110, 1.

Ver. 3. **For the institutions of the nations . . . with an axe.**—The institutions, *etc.*, stand in antithesis to the ordinances of Jehovah, Lev. xviii. 3, 4.—**Breath are they** [lit.: is it]. The singular of the pronoun appears to involve a contemptuous collective sense=all that trash. Comp. ver. 8; EWALD, § 319, *c*; Josh. xiii. 14.—The nothingness of the deities which are here identified with the idol-images, is clear from their origin. If we trace the origin of the idol we find that the artificer found it as a tree standing among others in the forest, and has adapted to his purpose cut it down.—On the subject in **cut out** comp. NAEGELSB. *Gr.* § 101, 2 *b*. As to the object it is formally undefined, but from the connection is clearly recognizable as the idol.—Second stage: the forest tree becomes a work of art in the hands of an artificer and by the aid of an axe.

Ver. 4. **With gold and silver . . . that it totter not.** Third stage: adornment with precious metals (Isa. xxx. 20; xl. 19). Fourth stage: fastening on the place of exhibition (Isa. xli. 7).—**Fasten them.** Observe the change of number. (Comp. NAEGELSB. *Gr.* § 105, 7, *Anm. 2*). With these words the construction passes into the plural. Comp. ver. 5. The subject of פִּיק is ideal, namely the idea of the fastened derived from יְתַקְּעוּם.—Comp. xlvi. 6, 7.

Ver. 5. **They are as the pillars . . . is not in their power.**—**Pillars in a cucumber field.** JEROME: *in similitudinem palmæ fabricata sunt.* Syr.; *tanquam palmæ sunt erectæ*, in which תֹּמֶר is taken according to analogy from תָּמָר

and Judges iv. 5, but מקשה is very freely translated. Others, following KIMCHI's example take תִּ֫מְרָה=תֹּ֫מֶר, columna (Joel iii. 3; Song of Sol. iii. 6) and תְּמוּרִים (Jer. xxxi. 21); כִּפְשׂוֹת however =turned work (Exod. xxv. 18; xxxi ..; xxxvii. 7, 17, 22; Numb. viii. 4; x. 2 coll. Isa. iii. 24). The comparison is strange. More satisfactory is the explanation proposed by MOVERS, FUERST (*H. W. B.*, *S.* 781), GRAF, according to which

כְּקֹשָׁה, as in Isa. i. 8, signifies a cucumber field and תֹּמֶר the scarecrows, or more correctly the priapus-pillars erected as such. These priapus-pillars are elsewhere ridiculed as useless watch-guards (comp. Epist. Jerem. ver. 70: ὥσπερ ἐν σικυηράτῳ προβασκάνιον οὐδὲν φυλάσσον οὕτως εἰσὶν οἱ θεοὶ αὐτῶν. Comp. PASSOW, *s. v.*, προβασκάνιον, SELDEN *de Diis Syriis*, p. 300).—**They must be borne.** Comp. Isa. xlvi. 7.

---

b. The idols contrasted with **Jehovah.**

X. 6–16.

6   None is like Thee,[1] O Jehovah!
    Great art Thou, and great is Thy name in might.
7   Who should not fear Thee, Thou King of nations?
    For unto Thee is it due.[2]
    For among all the wise men of the nations,
    And in all their dominion there is none like Thee.
8   But altogether they are stupid[3] and become fools:[4]
    Vain instruction! It is wood![5]
9   Silver plates are brought from Tarshish and gold from **Uphaz.**
    The work of the smith and the hands of the smelter;
    Blue and red purple is their raiment,
    Artists' work are they all.
10 But Jehovah is truly God,
    He is a living God, and an everlasting King:
    Before His anger the earth trembleth,
    And the nations cannot endure His wrath.
11 *Ye shall therefore say unto them: The gods,
    Which have not made heaven and earth,[6]
    Shall vanish away from the earth under the heaven.*
12 Who made the earth by His power,
    Established the world by His wisdom,
    And by His understanding spread out the heavens.
13 At the sound of His voice a heaving of waters in the heavens,
    He bringeth up vapors from the ends of the earth;
    He produceth lightnings with the rain,
    And bringeth the wind out of His storehouses.
14 Stupid are all men there without understanding;
    All the founders of idol-images are put to shame,
    For a lie is their casting, and there is no spirit in them.
15 For they are vapour and work of deceit;[7]
    In the time of their visitation they perish.
16 Not like these is the portion of Jacob;
    For He forms all things and Israel is the stock of His inheritance:
    Jehovah Zebaoth is His name.

TEXTUAL AND GRAMMATICAL.

[1] Ver. 6.—בְּמוֹךָ מֵאֵין is remarkable. VENEMA supposes a transposition of the מ from אוֹתָם at the close of ver. 5, as hypothesis to which we can have recourse only in extreme cases, especially as the initial and final מ are different in form. NEUMANN would take כְּאֵין in a causal sense, but I. it would be scarcely appropriate to designate the Lord as great merely in mparison with other great ones: 2. כִּי must also then be taken as causal in ver. 7. NEUMANN indeed does this, but thus he obtains only a linguistic monstrosity, which condemns itself and also his rendering of the word. HITZIG would

read מֵאֵין, as in xxx. 7, and with similarity of thought we should certainly expect similarity of expression. But might we not just as well require אָן to be read in xxx. 7, as in this place? The expression, *from whence* Thy like? is at least quite unusual. In this sense we elsewhere always find כְּ (Deut. iii. 24; iv. 7; 2 Sam. xxii. 32; 2 Kings xviii. 35; Ps. xviii. 32; lxxvii. 14; Mic. vii. 18 and the passages adduced by HITZIG himself Ps. xxxv. 10; lxxi. 19) while אַיִן or אַיֵּה occurs only in an ironical negative sense (*ex. gr.* Ps. xlii. 4; lxxix. 10; cxv. 2; Jer. ii. 27), or in the sense of earnest search (Jer. ii. 6, 8; 2 Kings ii. 14), but מֵאַיִן never occurs in that sense.—אָן occurs frequently in Jeremiah, more frequently than in any other author of the Old Testament.—The preposition כְּ is in this connection used evidently sometimes in a causal sense (vii. 32; xix. 11; Isa. l. 2; Ezek. xxxv. 8), but mostly in a negative sense=away from, without. Two negatives thus united do not make an affirmative, but strengthen the negation. Comp. NAEGELSB. *Gr.*, § 106, 5; GESEN. § 152, 2. Everywhere, however, except here, כְּ depends on a preceding verb or noun, and indeed for the most part mediately, so that the preposition is to be considered as depending on an idea of existence (*constructio praegnans*) latent in the verb (or noun). Comp. Isa. vi. 11; Jer. iv. 7; xx. 9; xxxii. 43; xxxiii. 10, 12; xxxiv. 22; xliv. 22; xlvi. 19; xlvii. 9; ii. 20, 37; Ezek. xxxiii. 28; Zeph. ii. 5; iii. 6. In Jer. v. 9 only is this idea of existence explicitly present.—That in this place מֵאַיִן stands so abruptly is very remarkable and contrary to the usage of Jeremiah.

² Ver. 7.—יֶאֱתָה from אָתָה (which occurs only in this single form and place) = אֶרֶץ, *decorum, consentaneum fuit*, Isai. lii. 7; Ps. xciii. 5; Song of Sol. i. 10. On the feminine in the impersonal sense, comp. NAEGELSB. *Gr.* § 60, 6, b.

³ Ver. 8.—יִבְעֲרוּ comp. vers. 14 and 21. Elsewhere occur only the participial forms בֹּעֲרִים (Ps. xciv. 8; Ezek. xxi. 36) and נִבְעָרָה (Isai. xix. 11). The meaning, according to the analogy of בַּעַר, בְּעִיר =*bardum, stolidum esse*.

⁴ Ver. 8.—יִכְסָלוּ. The verb here only—meaning (comp. כְּסִיל כָּסַל) *stultum, stupidum esse*.

⁵ Ver. 8.—[BLAYNEY renders: the very word itself being a rebuker of vanities; NOYES better: Most vain is their confidence; it is wood—with the note, "Lit. *their doctrine, their instruction*: i. e., that in which they are taught to confide." HENDERSON has: The tree itself is a reproof of vanities.—S. R. A.]

⁶ Ver. 11.—אַרְקָא is a harsher form of אֶרֶץ. Comp. FUERST, *H. W. B.* 1, S. 142. BUXTORF, *Lex. Chald.* p. 228. אֱלָהּ is again Hebrew and is referred by the LXX. to שְׁמַיִא but by most commentators to אֱלָהַיָּא.

⁷ Ver. 14.—מַעֲשֵׂה תַּעְתֻּעִים. The noun here only, the verb Gen. xxvii. 12; 2 Chron. xxxvi. 16.

EXEGETICAL AND CRITICAL.

Vers. 6 and 7 contain the theme of the strophe: Jehovah is the highest, there is none like Him, all the world should fear Him. It is stupidity which opposes this truth, says ver. 8. The impropriety of this opposition is proved by the exposition of what idols really are. On the other hand the right of Jehovah maintained in ver. 7 is proved by the exposition of His attributes and works, vers. 10, 12, 13. From this exposition it is evident how well-founded on the one hand is the judgment pronounced against this opposition (vers. 14, 15), and on the other hand the justice of Jehovah and the welfare of the people who serve Him. (ver. 16.)

Vers. 6 and 7, **None is like thee . . . none like thee.—In might** is to be referred both to **Thou** and **Thy name**. Since the latter in relation to the former can designate only the name in the objective sense, the renown, glory, in **might** is equivalent to *in manifestation of might,* comp. xvi. 21.—**Who should not** negative expression for the positive,—all must fear Thee.—**For among all.** SEB. SCHMIDT here rightly calls attention to the fact that בְּ here is to be regarded as local not partitive, because otherwise God would be compared with men: among all the wise men and in the whole circuit of their dominion, therefore in the whole domain of their wisdom and might, no God is found like unto Jehovah. Comp. CASPARI, *Micha der Morastite*, S. 13 ff.

Ver. 8. **But altogether . . . it is wood.** That which really is does not correspond to that which ought to be. The entirety of the heathen (בְּאַחַת =*und*, Targum Jon. בַּחֲדָא; the meaning *in one* contradicts the connection) feareth not the Lord, as it becomes them. This is to say, they are stupid as brutes.—**Vain instruction!** It is wood! If with GRAF we should construe these words like 3 *a*, we should develop the meaning that wood is wooden. But since this could not possibly be meant in the figurative sense, in which we use the word wooden, we should be obliged to take it literally, which, however we interpreted מוּסָר, would yield only nonsense. Accordingly עֵץ cannot be the predicate of מוּסָר. We must therefore regard the latter as a declaration made absolutely, with pregnant brevity, an exclamation which represents a sentence.—Since the radical meaning of הֶבֶל is breath, *vanitas*, we are perfectly justified by passages like Eccles. i. 2; v. 6; xii. 8, in taking the plural in this sense, although an adhesion to the derived meaning (idols) may certainly be contained in the words מוּסַר ה is therefore=*institutio vanitatum*, in the double sense of vain instruction and that which treats of vanities. At the same time the author may have had in mind an opposition to the "chastisement of Jehovah" (מוּסַר) (Deut. xi. 2; Prov. iii. 11; Job v. 17).—Whatever also in idol doctrine is declared great and glorious of the idols is all vain lies and deceit. For the idol is wood! This points back to ver. 3, and at the same time declares in contradiction of what follows, that, though the idols may be ornamented with precious metals and material, the heart is still always wood. הוּא is used here, as in ver. 3, collectively with a contemptuous side-meaning.

Ver. 9. **Silver plates are brought . . . artists' work are they all.** כֶּסֶף מְרֻקָּע beaten silver, therefore silver plates, comp. Gen. i. 6-8; Numb. xvii. 3, 4. I do not think that these and the following words are to be regarded as a continuation of **It is wood or are brought**, as forming a relative sentence. For ver. 8 compared with vers. 3, 4, is evidently intended to express that the idol is wood, a common material, and that the more precious metals, *etc.* are only the shell which covers the base kernel. The thought therefore that the idol is wood, silver and gold is remote from the connection. For what object silver and gold are brought from a great distance is not expressly stated, but is understood from the context, and especially from ver. 4.—Tartessus in Spain is mentioned as producing silver in Ezek. xxvii. 12.—The name אוּפָז occurs besides only in Dan. x. 5, where כֶּתֶם אוּפָז is spoken of. There are three views with respect to it: 1. Uphaz is designated as a real locality, and BOCHART (*Phaleg*. II. 27], supposes it to be Tabrobana (Ceylon) where according to Ptolemy (VII. 4) there was a river and harbor Phasis; (HITZIG and FUERST, *H. W. B. S.* 37) a place in Yemen (comp. Usal, Gen. x. 27; Ophir, Sheba, Ps. xlv. 10; 1 Chron. xxix. 4; Ps. lxxii. 15); in which case Uphaz may be regarded either as a synonym of אוֹפִיר = אוּפָז and פָז *i. e.* gold coast, or = Vipaça (Hyphasis); 2. Uphaz is regarded as incorrectly written for אוֹפִיר. So the Chaldee and Syriac, Theodoret and many of the moderns; 3. מְאוּפָז is taken to be identical with מוּפָז *purgatum* (Part. Hoph. from פוז 1 Kings x. 18, *Vid.* FUERST, *Conc. p.* 895). But since, 1. The hypothesis of a scriptural error is opposed to the critical principle of preferring the more difficult reading; 2. Tartessus is designated only as a land of silver never of gold (with the exception of the general and later passage, Macc. viii. 3); 3. The East is elsewhere generally represented as the home of gold (comp. Havila, Gen. ii. 11, 12; Ophir, Sheba, *ut supra*)—and finally, 4. The connection of the passage requires the thought that the materials of the idols were brought from the most distant and opposite places. I am in favor of regarding Uphaz as a definite locality to be sought in the East, although it is not possible now to determine its position more exactly.— **The work of the smith is** in apposition with **silver and gold.**—תְּכֵלֶת blue, אַרְגָּמָן red purple, comp. Exod. xxvi. 31, 36; xxvii. 16; xxviii. 8, 15, 33.—**Artists'** [lit. skilful ones] comp. ix. 16; Isai. xl. 20.

Ver. 10. **But Jehovah...endure his wrath** In contrast to the merely imaginary deity of the idols, Jehovah is designated as the true God (אֱמֶת) in apposition, comp. NAEGELSB. *Gr.* § 66) in contrast to their lifelessness as the living (חַיִּים) adject. comp. ii. 13; the plural as in Deut. v. 23; 1 Sam. xvii. 26; Jer. xxiii. 36 coll.: Josh. xxiv. 19; Isai. xxxvii. 4, 17. *Vide* NAEGELSB. *Gr.* § 105, 4, *a*) in contrast to their powerlessness finally as the eternal governor (comp. Exod. xv. 18; Ps. x. 16; lxvi. 7; xciii. 1 sqq.; xcvii. 1). Before such a mighty God the earth trembles (Exod. xix. 16 sqq.; Ps. lxviii. 9; xcvii. 5; Nah. i. 5) and the nations are not in a condition to hold or to bear the fulness of His anger (the figure is that of a vessel which is burst by the liquid poured into it. Matt. ix. 17; comp. Jer. ii. 13).

Ver. 11. **Ye shall therefore say . . . under the heaven.** HOUBIGANT, VENEMA, DATHE, BLAYNEY, DÖDERLEIN, ROSENMUELLER, MAURER, EWALD, GRAF, [HENDERSON—S. R. A.] and others declare this verse to be a gloss which has crept into the text. Even NEUMANN (*S.* 549 *Anm.*) inclines to this view. I must also decide in its favor. For 1. Since we must suspect the authenticity of vers. 1-10, 12-16, we have no interest in maintaining that of this verse, but a reason is afforded for the insertion of the verse just here. To the marginal gloss of a second a third might have added a second gloss in a foreign language. He would not have ventured to make such an irrelevant addition to the text of the prophet. Both glosses have in later times been unjustifiably admitted into the text. Jeremiah would certainly not have interrupted a Hebrew discourse by a Chaldee interpolation, when he elsewhere never uses this language, not even in the letter to the exiles, ch. xxix. The reasons which have been adduced in favor of their authenticity are specious only. They may be found in NEUMANN, *S.* 547, sqq. [*Vide* also Eng. Trans. of Calvin, II. p. 31, *n.*—S. R. A.]. 2. The verse breaks the connection in the most abrupt manner. Ver. 12 is by this verse suspended in the air, while without it, ver. 12 is connected quite regularly with ver. 10. The assumption of a parenthesis also (J. D. MICHAELIS) does not avail. For then the verse must be a necessary, not interruptive supplement to ver. 10, or preparation for ver. 12, neither of which is the case.

Ver. 12. **Who made the earth . . . the heavens—Who made** (עֹשֶׂה) is in apposition to the main idea of ver. 10: Jehovah Elohim. The absence of the article before such a participle standing in apposition after a *Nom. determ.* is frequent. Comp. ii. 27 ; Ps. ix. 12; civ. 2-4; Zech. xii. 1. *Vide* NAEGELSB. *Gr.* § 97, 2, *a*.— The contents of vers. 12 and 13 serve by the enumeration of facts as a confirmation of ver. 11, comp. ch. xxvii. 5; xxxi. 17.—**established,** *etc.* comp. Ps. lxv. 7; lxxxix. 12; xciii. 1.— **spread out,** *etc.* comp. civ. 2; Isai. xl. 22; xliv. 24; li. 13; Zech. xii. 1.

Ver. 13. **At the sound . . . . storehouses.** This verse, with the exception of the beginning is found in Ps. cxxxv. 7.—**Sound of his voice.** It is not necessary with EWALD to take this for לְתִתּוֹ קוֹל, or with MAURER for קוֹלֹת לְתֵת, or with HITZIG to make הֲמוֹן depend on תִּתּוֹ as the object. For the words mean simply *ad vocem, quam edit.* We are not then to take נָתַן in the general sense (on the noise which His giving makes) but in the special sense which lies at the root of the expression נָתַן בְּקוֹל (xii. 8; Ps. xlvi. 7 ; lxviii. 34) *i. e.,* "to make a noise, sound *with the voice.*" That the thunder is meant is evident from the context. Thunder, lightning, clouds, rain and storm are mentioned as the essential constituents of a tempest, comp. xi. 16.

Vers. 14 and 15. **Stupid are all . . . they perish.** In contrast to the living power of God the vanity of the idols is again set forth. While before Jehovah, when He arises, all trembles and is afraid, the worshippers of idols are by these merely—put to shame. The two members of ver. 14 *a*, stand in the relation of explicative, not of synonymous parallelism. The second is the explanation and more exact definition of the first. A change of reading therefore (אָדָם) into (חָכָם)

or of the usual meaning of the word (רָעָה=*arte factum*, idol-image) is unnecessary. בָּעַר we take in the explicative sense=to appear stupid, to prove so, comp. Isai. xix. 11; EWALD, § 123, b. קִדְעָה without insight, comp. NAEGELSB. Gr. § 112, 5, d.—Men appear in the entire nakedness of their stupidity, in so far as they are put to shame by their idols, which are not God, but dead castings.—**Work of deceit.** The sense is: a work by which they themselves are stultified and put to shame who make it.

Ver. 16. **Not like these . . . is his name.** The worshippers of Jehovah are yet again comprised with the idolaters, Jehovah is opposed to the idols, and the whole force of the demonstration is concentrated into the significant name of the true God. The first hemistich falls into two members. 1. *Not like these is the portion of Jacob.* The expression **portion of Jacob** reminds us of Deut. xxxii. 9; Ps. xvi. 5. Observe how by this expression Jehovah and His servants are aptly comprised together. 2. Again the first sentence has a double basis: as former of all things Jehovah is not like the idols, and as those who have this God for their portion and inheritance the Israelites are not like the heathen.—**Stock of his inheritance.** Comp. Deut. iv. 20; Ps. lxxiv. 2.—On the relation of this passage to Ii. 19, and of the Hebrew original of the Alexandrian translation, consult NAEGELSB. *Jeremia u. Bab. S.* 93, 131.

---

2. *Beginning of the end of the retribution: Command to the people to retire; Lament of the desolated land; last watch-cry of the Prophet: the enemy is here!*

X. 17-22.[1]

17 Pick up thy bundle[2] from the earth, thou that sittest[3] in distress!
18 For thus saith Jehovah: Behold!
   I sling away the inhabitants of this land at this once,
   And bring them into straits, that they may find it so.
19 Wo is me for my hurt! My wound is incurable.[4]
   But I say: this is now my suffering and I will bear it.
20 My tent is laid waste and all my cords are broken.[5]
   My children forsake me and are never here.
   There is none to pitch my tent and set up my curtains,
21 For the pastors are become stupid and seek not Jehovah.
   Hence they have effected nothing prudent and their whole flock is dispersed.
22 Hark, a message comes and great tumult out of the north country,
   That the cities of Judah are to become a desolation,
   For the habitation of jackals.

TEXTUAL AND GRAMMATICAL.

[1] This strophe apart from the general relationship which it bears to chh. vii. ix., also has many particular points of connection with this passage, especially with viii. 13 sqq. Comp. ver. 17 with viii. 14— קוֹלֵעַ, ver. 18 with הִשְׁלַכְתִּי vii. 15.— שִׁבְרִי ver. 19 with viii. 21.— צֹאנִי ver. 20 with עֲרָבִי ix. 18.— מֵאֶרֶץ צָפוֹן ver. 22 with viii. 16.— לְשׂוּם וְגוֹ ver. 22 with vii. 34; ix. 10.
[2] Ver. 17.— כִּנְעָה (ἅπ λεγ) from בָּנָה= the bowed together, twisted together, pack, bundle. On אָסַף comp. OLSH. § 234, b, Isai. xlvii. 2.
[3] Ver. 17.—The Keri יֹשֶׁבֶת is superfluous. Comp. xxii. 23; Gen. xlix. 11; Hos. x. 11; OLSH. § 123, d.: NAEGELSB. Gr. § 2, 1. On the construct state before prepositions, comp. *Ib.* § 63, 4 c. [HENDERSON renders: O inhabitress of the siege.]
[4] Ver. 19.— נַחְלָה (OLSHAUS. § 266, a). Comp. xiv. 17; xxx. 12. [HENDERSON: My stroke is grievous.]
[5] Ver. 20.—[HENDERSON: all my tent pins are plucked up, but without reason.—S. R. A.]

EXEGETICAL AND CRITICAL.

After by ix. 25 it is affirmed that the last and only means of safety is despised the prophet now in vers. 17 and 18 addresses a command to the people to remove into exile. The now desolated land is hereupon introduced as lamenting its misfortune and its causes (vers. 19-21). At last the prophet announces, as a herald or watchman on the lookout, that the enemy (long predicted and called to execute judgment) is present (ver. 22).

Ver. 17. **Pick up thy bundle . . . distress.** It is the prophet who speaks.— מֵאֶרֶץ= from the earth, away from the ground, for here we have to do not with the retirement of the possessors from the country, but only of the hasty gathering up of the few effects, which a poor exile might take with him. The word "bundle" has therefore a contemptuous side-meaning.—**In distress.** The prophet speaks this of the people already severely distressed by the enemy in the cities whither they have fled, viii. 14. Comp. xix 9; lii. 5.

Ver. 18. **For thus saith Jehovah . . . may find it so.** Jehovah Himself is now introduced as speaking, to give a reason for the command in ver. 17.—Since the time of the Judges the people had often been oppressed by foreign enemies *within* their borders, now they are to be dragged far away into banishment, comp. Isa. xxii. 17 — **That they may find it so.** לִמְצֹא יִמְצָאוּ. This expression, which has been very variously interpreted is explained most easily by remembering, *a.* its relation to **bring into straits**, *b.* the ease of supplying the indefinite object "it" (NAEGELSB. *Gr.*, § 78, 2 *Anm.*), *c.* the close connection of the ideas "to find" and "to know." With respect to the latter, I refer especially to Eccles. viii. 17 (and I saw that man cannot *find* all God's work, that is done under the sun; though a man labor to seek [it], yet he finds it not, and though a wise man think to *know* [it], yet can he not *find* it). Comp. also Jer. xvi. 21.—He who is driven into straits must go whither he is driven. So God by affliction drives Israel into such straits that they must find, *i. e.*, know what it is above all necessary and desirable for them to know, that great "it," namely, which though unnamed, is well understood. Chap. Isa. xliii. 20; Hos. ix. 7.

Vers. 19 and 20. **Wo is me . . . set up my curtains.** That both these verses are the words of the country personified, is seen from "my children," etc., in ver. 20, for neither the prophet says this, nor the people, who are identical with the children and not forsaken, but forsaking.—**And I say.** In these words also we have a proof that the land is the speaker. For the words express no consciousness of guilt, but a comfort, which the innocent land alone could find, in the fact that a calamity is laid upon it, which must be borne. At the same time we perceive in these words the first gleam of hope in a future deliverance. For men speak thus composedly only when they know that they will not have to bear perpetual but only transient suffering. Comp. v. 4. Also the suffixes of the 1st Pers. in ver. 20 are in favor of the land as the speaker.—**Forsake me.** Comp. Gen. xliv. 4; Numb. xxxv. 26; NAEGELSB. *Gr.*, § 70, *b.*

Ver. 21. **For the pastors are become stupid . . . dispersed.** The land is the speaker: 1. on account of בְּ; 2. because the metaphor of pastoral life is continued; 3. because in the mouth of the land this statement does not appear as the repetition of things which have been already frequently said, but as it were a confirmatory testimony from an impartial witness.—**Become stupid.** Comp. ver. 8,—**effect nothing prudent.** The meaning is to effect that which is prudent, sensible and in so far also prosperous, comp. xx. 11; Prov. xvii. 8.

Ver. 22. **Hark, a message . . . jackal.**— These words are, as it were, a last watch-call and signal which denotes (comp. i. 14; iv. 6; vi. 1, 22; viii. 16) that the enemy so frequently announced is present.—**For a habitation**, comp. ix. 10.

---

3. Consolatory glance into the future.

X. 23–25.

23 I know, Jehovah, that not to man belongs his way,
    It is not in man that walketh to direct his steps.[1]
24 Correct me, Jehovah, but only as it is just,
    Not in thine anger, lest thou bring me to nothing.
25 Pour out thy wrath on the nations that know thee not,
    And on the nations that call not on thy name ;
    For they have devoured Jacob, yea they consumed **and destroyed him,**
    And his pasture have they laid waste.

TEXTUAL AND GRAMMATICAL.

[1] Ver. 23.—וְהָכִין. From the LXX. (οὐδὶ ἀνὴρ πορεύσεται καὶ κατορθώσει πορείαν αὐτοῦ) and the Vulgate (*nec viri est, ut ambulet et dirigat gressus suos*), we might conclude that they read הֵלֵךְ וְהָכֵן, if we might assume any exactness in these translations, and if it were not evident from the Chaldee (וּמְהַתְקֵן) רָאזֵל *qui ambalat et dirigit*), and the Syriac, that they also read דֶרֶךְ. It is impossible to justify the Van grammatically, when it stands before the Infinitive. Even EWALD has accomplished nothing by reference to § 344, *a*. GAAB, by transposing the Van, would read הֲלֹכוֹ, which is an equally unusual construction, and gives a feeble sense. The easiest way would be to read לְחָכְיָ, if the very facility of this reading did not stand in its way. The general meaning is clear, but we must abandon for the present an exact determination of the word.

EXEGETICAL AND CRITICAL.

These verses form a very appropriate conclusion. They involve an honest confession of sin in view of the numerous charges of the discourse. To the threatenings of punishment, however, corresponds the petition to punish not too severely, not in anger, but to pour out the fury on the heathen nations; the basis of which petition is the theocratic hope that Israel cannot be wholly rejected, but there must in the future be a day of grace for them, and vengeance on their enemies. The prophet must be regarded as the speaker, but as speaking not in his own name, but in that of the people.

Ver. 23. I know . . . his steps. Man has not the power to determine how and where he will go. Comp. Ps. xxxvii. 23; Prov. xvi. 1, 9; xix. 21.—הֵלֵךְ is taken by HITZIG=perishable, mortal. And the word, according to passages like Ps. xxxix. 14; lviii. 9; cix. 23; Job xix. 10, cannot be denied this meaning. But since the most natural sense: it is not for man, *so long as he walks*, to determine his course—seems equally appropriate, the word may be regarded as having a double sense, or, as uniting both these meanings.

Vers. 24 and 25. Correct me . . . and his pasture have they laid waste. In ver. 23 the thought is implicitly contained that Israel had wished in his own strength to walk in his own way contrary to the will of God. He now sees how greatly he has sinned and submits to the necessary and merited punishment, praying only for the utmost possible mildness and forbearance. The final conversion and re-acceptance of the people is thus set forth as prospective.—As is just, comp. xxx. 11; xlvi. 28. As was remarked on vii. 5; ix. 23, justice in the Old Testament is not opposed to grace, but to brutal violence. The antithesis of צֶדֶק is not to הֶסֶד, but to חָמָס the violence (עָשַׁק) exercised toward the poor, the stranger, orphan and widow. In contrast to this he who consciously maintains the straight line of justice appears fairly disposed and mild, not making his subjective desires his law, but submitting himself to the objective law. Accordingly this **as it is just**, which evidently has its antithesis in the following: **in thine anger**, also involves the idea of mildness, because justice in contrast to that anger which is its own law, and respects no other, appears like mildness. It must be granted that this dualistic conception of God as just towards Israel, but wrathful towards the heathen, is not that of the New Testament. That it is the genuine Old Testament view is shown by passages like Ps. vi. 2; xxxviii. 2; lxxix. (where in vers. 6 and 7 our ver. 24 is reproduced); cxxxvii. 8. Observe, moreover, how the prophet here turns the tables. To Israel, now being severely punished, he presents the prospect of grace, but before the heathen, who are now God's instruments in the punishment of Israel, is complete destruction. Comp. Isa. xlvii. 6; Hab. i. 11; iii. 8-12, and Jer. l. and li., especially l. 40 sqq.—The repetition and accumulation of verbs in 25 *b*, is to portray graphically the rage of the enemies, comp. li. 34.

DOCTRINAL AND ETHICAL.

1. On ver. 6. There cannot be two highest Beings, or there would be none. In the idea of the Absolute is involved that of uniqueness. Polytheism has therefore no highest Being in the absolute sense. Where, however, traces of such are found, polytheism is about either to rise to monotheism (comp. FRIEDRICH NAEGELSBACH, *nachhom. Theol. S.* 140), or to dissolve into pantheism.

2. **Who shall not fear thee?** *etc.*, ver. 7, GHISLERUS remarks: "*S. Remigius, Episc. Rhemensis ex hoc loco probat, multos ex gentibus credidisse et placuisse Deo, additque in hoc multo magis dici Deum gentium, quoniam multo plures credunt in eum ex gentibus, quam ex Judæis.*" Comp. Rom. ii. 14, 15, and THOLUCK *ad h. l.*—John i. 4 (λόγος σπερματικός).

3. AUGUSTINE remarks on the Infinity of God, *de Trin.*, V. 1. "*Intelligimus Deum sine qualitate bonum, sine quantitate magnum, sine indigentia creatorem, sine situ præsentem, sine habitu omnia continentem, sine loco ubique totum, sine tempore sempiternum, sine ulla sui mutatione mutabilia facientem nihilque patientem.*"

4. On ver. 10. In hemist. *a*, a proof of the Trinity has been repeatedly found. So *ex. gr.*, HAILBRUNNER (*Jer. proph. monumenta in locos comm. Theol. digesta*, Lauingen, 1586, page 38), FÜRSTER (*S.* 61), and among the moderns NEUMANN (*S.* 547). The latter says . . . "the passage affords a sure testimony of the trinitarian view of God in the Old Testament; the truth of the Spirit, the life of the Father, the kingdom of the Son, comprising in themselves the fulness of all emanations of the divine existence in opposition to heathen superstition." But against this it may be urged that in opposition to the multiplicity of idols the author had to set forth not the trinity, but the unity of the divine nature, as he has done in vers. 6 and 7, and that his purpose here (ver. 10) is merely to contrast the false gods with the true, the dead with the living, the powerless with the Almighty. That the contrast is exhibited in three points, we are not indeed to regard as accidental, but to explain it rather by the general significance of the number three, than by the purpose of intimating the Trinity.

5. On ver. 14: "*All men are fools. Ye fools and blind*, says our Saviour (Matt. xxiii). Such a word, spoken in season takes hold and produces conviction; but it must be administered with spirit and fire; for if it is only human words to men, they will make a quarrel out of them." ZINZENDORF.

6. On ver. 14 (**A lie is their casting**). This applies not only to the idols which men make of earthly materials, but to all self-made idols of the heart. The carnal mind, which tends downwards, feels annoyed by the nearness of God, and seeks therefore at all times to escape from it. But since man cannot do without God, he makes himself a god or gods, as he wants them. Whether these gods are visible and palpable images, or the abstract forms of speculation, the words of the text always apply to them; they are a lie, and there is no spirit in them. Accordingly there is heathenism enough in the

CHAP. X. 23-25.   125

midst of Christianity, and it may be asked, which is worse, the new or the old?
7. On ver. 16. What perfect historical reality and personality is here! A creator of the universe stands before us, one therefore, who has called all things into existence by His free, personal will, and who at the same time as the living personal Head of all the spirits governing the world is infinitely exalted above every limited local deity. But at the same time the relation of this Deity to the world is not an abstract and general, but a living and personal relation. For this God primarily holds immediate personal intercourse with one nation of the earth, as a father with his son, and He is this nation's greatest treasure and inalienable property, as on the other hand the nation belongs to Him as the object of His free personal election, which none may dispute or annul.
8. On ver. 19 (**I must bear it**). "I pray all teachers for God's sake, that they reflect and err not, that they do not, in order to retain their living, repeat these words of Jeremiah, and cover up their laziness, ill-success, frivolity, their own unfruitfulness and selfishness, with the excuse, 'this is my plague.' O no, what we should call a plague is burdens of a hundred-weight, from which we long to be freed, which crush us almost to death; persons from whom we would flee as a bird from a cage; a pressure under which we are martyred with shame, and yet have no permission to depart. These lead one finally, after many struggles and cries unto the Lord for his dismission, and after an answer of absolute denial, to say in calmness: I believe this is now my plague, and I must bear it." ZINZENDORF.
9. On ver. 20. "The jealousy of the Saviour is so strict, that He will have His children directed to Him (Isa. xlv. 11), and the idea of the pastoral office with which some good teachers are infected, of regarding and treating souls as *their* souls, sheep as *their* sheep, children as *their* children, is in the highest degree opposed to His will. Hence He often, for a just judgment, does not allow their joy in souls to last, but lets them see and conclude more of their decline and less of their success, than there really is. For He will not give His glory to another, and the teachers are not Christ, but sent by Him, *before Him*." ZINZENDORF.
10. On ver. 21. "As sheep must either starve or be led to filthy and poisonous pasture, if their shepherds are fools, who do not know how to manage sheep, so is this much more the case in the spiritual pastorate." CRAMER.
11. On ver. 23. "The steps of every man are ordered by the Lord, what man understands His way? (Prov. xx. 24). And every man's way is right in his own eyes, but the Lord alone maketh the hearts certain (Prov. xxi. 2). Therefore we must pray: Lord, make known to me the way in which I should walk, for after Thee is my desire. Teach me to do Thy will, for Thou art my God; let Thy good Spirit guide me in a plain path (Ps. cxliii. 8-10)." CRAMER.
12. On ver. 23. "*Certum est, nos velle, cum volumus, sed ille facit, ut velimus bonum, de quo dictum est, quod praeparatur voluntas a Domino* (Prov. viii. 35 sec. Sept.) *Certum est, nos facere, cum facimus, sed ille facit, ut faciamus praebendo vires efficacissimas voluntati, qui dixit; faciam ut in justifi-*

cationibus meis ambuletis et judicia mea observetis (Ezek. xxxvi. 26, 27)." AUGUSTIN. *De grat. et lib. arbitr.* Cap. 16.
13. On ver. 24. "There is a beautiful distinction between the suffering and punishment of the pious and the ungodly, which consists *in modo et in fine*. For when God chastises the pious He does it not with anger and fury, but as a discreet and kind father or teacher may discipline his son and disciple, without ill-humor. Thus also God does with His children. He does it, not that He may bring them to nothing, but that they may not esteem themselves innocent (xxx. 11). On the other hand he makes an end of the ungodly, and they must drink up the dregs (Ps. lxxv. 8)." CRAMER.
14. On ver. 25. "*Quaeri potest hic, an contra infideles, ut hodie sunt Turcae et Judaei, orandum? Orandum est contra eos et pro iis.* Contra eos, *quatenus persequuntur ecclesiam.* pro iis, *quatenus ecclesiam non persequuntur, ut convertantur, quemadmodum fit in Lituania;* forgive our enemies, persecutors and slanderers, and turn their hearts." FÖRSTER.

HOMILETICAL AND PRACTICAL.

1. [On ver. 7. SAURIN:—Fear may be 1. Terror. 2. A disposition to render God all the worship He requires, to submit to all the laws He imposes, to conceive all the emotions of admiration, devotedness and love, which the eminence of His perfections demands. 3. A disposition which considers Him as alone possessing all that can contribute to our happiness and misery. In the last sense (which is meant here) God is the only object of fear; for 1. God is a being whose will is self-efficient; 2. the only being who can act immediately on spiritual souls; 3. the only being who can make all creatures concur in His designs."—S. R. A.]
2. On ver. 10. There are three main forms of idolatry: 1. Polytheism, which does not deny the predicates of deity, but attributes them to false subjects.—2. Pantheism, which denies the subjects and the predicates.—3. Deism, which confesses the subject but denies the predicates.— These errors are opposed in ver. 10, from which we derive the theme:—The Scriptural doctrine of God in opposition to the errors of idolatry.— This teaches us to know God, 1. as the *true, real* God in opposition to those who attribute the divine properties to imaginary false gods; 2. as the *living* God in opposition to those who represent God as a mere all-pervading force; 3. as the eternal *King*, in opposition to those who represent God only as a transient work-master, and not as the ever active ruler of the world.
3. There is a homily of Origen (Hom. VIII. ed. LOMMATZSCH) on vers. 12-14. in which by the earth be understands the body, by תֵּבֵל (οἰκουμένη) the soul, by the heavens the spirit. The clouds (mist) ver. 13 from the ends of the earth are the saints whom God has chosen from the least of the earth.
4. On vers. 14-16. It is manifest that the task of religion is not to make God, but to receive Him, who is, in faith. Every manufactured god is an idol, be it a visible one made with hands, or an invisible one made only in thought. The latter kind of idolatry is alas! very prevalent

among us Christians. For a warning against such ruinous heresies, and for the confirmation of our faith in the God, whom as Christians we ought to serve, we institute on the basis of the text, a comparison between the manufactured gods and the God, of whom the Scriptures teach us. I. The manufactured gods, 1. are deceit, *etc.*, vers. 14, *b;* 15, *a.* 2. They perish when they are visited (in the day of divine judgment upon them they vanish into nothing). 3. Those who made them are with all their skill put to shame. II. The God, of whom the Holy Scriptures teach us. 1. He is not a lifeless deceptive image, for He has created all things, the visible and the invisible (Jehovah Zebaoth). 2. Being the source of all life He cannot perish. 3. Those who serve Him are not put to shame, for He is their treasure, as they again are His heritage (He is not only infinitely exalted above time and space, but infinitely near us, His children).

5. On ver. 10. From these words of the prophet we may learn what it is in great affliction and sorrow of heart to *bow under the mighty hand of God.* It is 1, that a man recognize the suffering as *his* suffering, *i. e.*, (*a*) as that which he has himself prepared, (*b*) as that which *is right for him, i. e.*, not too heavy and not too light, but exactly corresponding to its beneficent purpose; 2, that they suffer willingly, (*a*) in patience, (*b*) in hope.

6 On ver. 23. Theme: Man proposes, God disposes. This is 1, a humbling of our pride, 2, a strong support of our hope.

NOTE.—FÖRSTER remarks that these words may serve for the text of a *concio valedictoria*.

7. On ver. 25. Theme: How we should behave under the chastisements of God. 1. We should humbly submit to them as necessary and wholesome means of improvement. 2. We should be certain that they will not then transgress those bounds nor proceed to our destruction.

4. FOURTH DISCOURSE.

(CHAPTERS XI.—XII.)

WITH AN APPENDIX. CHAP. XIII.

The three chapters **xi.-xiii.** *are headed in common by a longer superscription* (**xi.** 1) *such as those with which Jeremiah is accustomed to introduce the greater sections. A similar one occurs again in* xiv. 1. *But* chaps. **xi.** *and* **xii.** *only form a connected whole, as will hereafter be shown. In the passage* xii. 14, *where the prophet speaks of the wicked neighbors by which the inheritance of Israel was assailed, an allusion has been found to the event reported in* 2 Kings xxiv. 2 *and the time of composition of this discourse determined accordingly.* (So DAHLER, MAURER, HITZIG, UMBREIT, GRAF). *The discourse would accordingly pertain to the end of the reign of Jehoiakim. But in this case Jeremiah must have named the Chaldeans as the instruments of punishment, as he does without exception in all the discourses delivered after the battle of Carchemish. The fact that the Chaldeans are not mentioned is a sure sign that the discourse was delivered before the date mentioned, which falls in the fourth year of Jehoiakim* (xxv. 1 ; xlvi. 2). *Since now in the lifetime of Josiah a violation of covenant in the degree with which the people are reproached in* xi. 9-13 *(observe especially* ver. 13) *is not to be thought of, and the three months' reign of Jehoahaz is scarcely worth consideration, we are referred to the first years of Jehoiakim, consequently the same period to which the preceding discourse* (ch. vii. 10) *belongs. If what is said in* xii. 9 *sqq. of wicked neighbors has some reference to* 2 Kings xxiv. 2 *it can only be that we may perceive in the latter the at least partial fulfilment of the former. Comp. the comments on* xii. 14.—Ch. xiii. *is not connected with* chaps. xi. *and* xii. *It forms a well-compacted whole, the time and origin of which may be perceived partly from its silence with respect to the Chaldeans, and partly from what is said concerning the pride of the king. It must likewise belong to the first years of Jehoiakim. Comp. the preliminary remarks on* ch. xiii. *The principle of chronological arrangement is here also perceptible.*

That xii. 7-17 *is not a later addition, as* MAURER, HITZIG *and* GRAF *suppose, is evident, as it seems to me, from the structure of the whole.*

The fundamental thought of the discourse is:

The contrast of the covenant and conspiracy.

(בְּרִית and קֶשֶׁר.)

1. *Reminder of the recent renewal under Josiah of the covenant between Jehovah and the people,* xi. 1-8.
2. *First stage of the conspiracy ; entire Israel, instead of keeping the covenant with Jehovah, conspires against Him,* xi. 9-13.
3. *Punishment of the conspiracy an inevitable, severe judgment,* xi. 14-17. (*Appendix to the previous strophe*).
4. *Second stage of the conspiracy: the plot of the Anatotites,* xi. 18-23.
5. *Third stage of the conspiracy: the plot in the prophet's own family,* xii. 1-6.
6. *The conspiracy of Israel punished by the conspiracy of the neighbors against them,* xii. 7-13.
7. *Solution of all antitheses by the final union of all in the Lord,* xii. 14-17.

CHAPTER XI.

1. *Reminder of the recent renewal under Josiah of the Covenant between Jehovah and the people.*

XI. 1–8.

1 The word which came to Jeremiah from Jehovah, saying:
2 Hear ye the words of this covenant,
And speak ye to the men of Judah,
And to the inhabitants of Jerusalem.
3 And say to them : Thus saith Jehovah, the God of Israel:
Cursed[1] be the man who hears not the words of this covenant,
4 Which I commanded to your fathers
In the day that I brought them forth out of the land of Egypt,
And out of the iron furnace, saying,
Hearken ye unto my voice and do them [my commands]
According to all that which I command you ;
So shall ye be my people and I will be your God ;
5 To perform the oath which I swore to your fathers ;
To give them a land flowing with milk and honey, as it is this day.
And I said, Amen, Jehovah!
6 And Jehovah said unto me,
Proclaim all these words in the city of Judah
And in the streets of Jerusalem, saying,
Hear ye the words of this covenant and do them !
7 For I testified to your fathers on the day[2]
That I brought them out of the land of Egypt,
Even to this day urgently and unceasingly :
Hearken ye unto my voice!
8 But they hearkened not, nor inclined their ear,
And went, every man in the hardness of his wicked heart ;
And I brought upon them all the words of this covenant,
Which I commanded them to keep ; but they kept them not.

TEXTUAL AND GRAMMATICAL.

[1] Ver. 3.—וְ֙ אָר֔וּר ver. 3, and the corresponding אָ֣ם, ver. 5, remind us of Deut. xxvii. 15 sqq., especially ver. 26.— IRON FURNACE is found only in Deut. iv. 20 and (as a quotation) in 1 Ki. viii. 51. וְ הָיָ֤ה is not exclusively yet especially peculiar to Deut., since besides Gen. xliii. 3 ; Exod. xix. 21, 22 it occurs in the Pentateuch only Deut. iv. 26 ; viii. 19 ; xxx. 10; xxxi. 28 ; xxxii. 46.—שְׁרִי֣רוּת ver. 8, is found in the Pentateuch only in Deut. xxix. 18. Also the expressions *so shall ye be my people*, ver. 4, and *a land flowing, etc.*, are not indeed peculiar to, but very common in Deuteronomy. (Comp. in reference to the former Exod. vi. 7 ; Levit. xxvi. 12 ; and Deut. iv. 20 ; vii. 6 ; xiv. 2 ; xxvi. 18; xxix. 9 ; xxix. 12,—in reference to the latter Exod. iii. 8, 17, and Deut. vi. 3 ; xi. 9 ; xxvi. 9, 15 ; xxvii. 3 ; xxxi. 20).

[2] Ver. 7.—בְּי֣וֹם we should expect כַּיּוֹם. The former is perhaps occasioned by בְּי֣וֹם, ver. 4.

EXEGETICAL AND CRITICAL.

This strophe forms the basis of the discourse. It must therefore, to be understood, be rendered in closest connection with what follows. It relates how the Lord once (in the 18th year of king Josiah, 2 Kings xxii.), after the discovery of the book of the law, admonished to the observance of the covenant formed between him and their fathers, and especially according to the standard of the 5th book of the Torah, both on the whole (vers. 1-5) and particulars (*i. e.*, by repeated proclamation in the cities of Judah and streets of Jerusalem, vers. 6-8) indicating both the blessed consequences of covenant-fidelity (vers. 4 and 5) and the ruinous consequences of infidelity (ver. 8). In so far as ver. 10 relates the breach of the covenant so expressly enjoined in this strophe it is seen that this injunction must have been made previously, that therefore this strophe gives a representation of a past fact. But so far as the strophe reports only this inculcation of the covenant it is clear that it points to something later than its redintegration.

Vers. 1 and 2. **The word which came . . . and to the inhabitants of Jerusalem.** The superscription is like vii. 1.—**Hear,** *etc*. Since, as previously remarked, what follows is to be regarded as the narrative of a fact which occurred in former times, **hear** does not refer to the contents of the word proclaimed in ver. 1, but of an earlier word. Ver. 1 refers therefore to the whole discourse, and before **hear** is to be supplied an introductory formula leading back to the real time of this inculcation of the covenant. The subject of **hear** is most probably according to ver. 6, the people of Judah and Jerusalem. The words stand at the head as a general call of awakening and admonition. וְדִבַּרְתָּם, LXX., καὶ λαλήσεις, which recommends the reading וְדִבַּרְתָּה. But according to the reading of the text it is the priests, elders and prophets, who in 2 Kings xxii. 1; 2 Chron. xxxiv. 29, are expressly mentioned as participating in the covenant. There are as it were three concentric circles. The smallest represents Jeremiah, who would bring home to the people the importance of keeping the covenant. But it cannot be denied that the want of an express designation of the subject is remarkable. Perhaps the brevity of the expression may be thus explained that the prophet wished to give mere hints, knowing that these would be sufficient to recall to the memory of his hearers the former more extended discourses.—**The words of this covenant.** The pronoun this designates the covenant as one before their eyes and well-known. Comp. this passage with 2 Kings xxii. and xxiii.; 2 Chron. xxxiv. (Vid., especially 2 Kings xxiii. 3, coll. xxii. 13; xxiii. 2; 2 Chron. xxxiv. 30), and there can be no doubt that by the words **this covenant** in vers. 2, 3, 6, 8, is meant that, the archives of which were contained in the book found by Hezekiah. The expression is found besides only in Deut. (v. 3; xxix. 13). The expression, words of the covenant, besides 2 Kings xxiii. 2; 2 Chron. xxxiv. 30, is found only Deut. xxviii. 69; xxix. 8, and in Jer. xxxiv. 18. This passage also (to anticipate) contains several references from which it follows that the covenant-record, which both Jeremiah in this passage and the authors of the books of Kings and Chronicles (2 Kings xx. and xxiii.; 2 Chron. xxxiv.) have in view, is to be understood at least primarily and especially to be Deuteronomy.— **Men of Judah.** Comp. rems. on iv. 4. On the exchange of אֶל and עַל, see rems. on x. 1.

Vers. 3–5. **And say to them . . . Amen, Jehovah!** Jeremiah receives the special commission to present before the people the importance of keeping the covenant; cursing and blessing being dependent on it. While in vers. 3, 5, the discourse seems to be addressed to the whole of the people, it turns in vers. 6-8, to the particular portions. Further, while the prophet in vers. 3-5 holds before the people the divine curse and blessing, he seeks in vers. 6-8 to make an impression on them by pointing to the fulfilment of the curse already taken place on their disobedient fathers.—**In the day,** etc. Comp. vii. 22; xxxiv. 13.—The pronoun **them** is to be referred to the plural conception of *commands* implied in **according to all**, comp. NAEGELSB. Gr., § 61, 1.—**To perform the oath.** In order to realize the existence of the oath, comp. Deut. viii. 18, coll.; xxvii. 26.—**Amen, Jehovah is,** as remarked, a quotation from Deut. xxvii. 15 sqq. The prophet gives it to be understood by this *Amen*, that he has understood the allusion contained in **cursed**, ver. 3.

Vers. 6-8. **And Jehovah said unto me . . . but they kept them not.** The prophet here reads the commission given him in the 18th year of Josiah, to make known the words of the covenant by reading them not only in the central sanctuary (comp. 2 Kings xxiii. 1-3), but also by repeated readings in the cities of Judah and the streets of Jerusalem. The prophet may have accompanied king Josiah on his circuit, which is spoken of in 2 Kings xxiii. 15-20. Since it was the making known of a written document, the proclamation is most probably meant in the sense of reading, as קְרָא generally signifies to read aloud; comp. 2 Kings xxii. 8, 10, 16; xxiii. 2; Jer. xxxvi. 6, 8, 10, 13, *etc.*—**For I testified.** Comp. Ps. l. 7, and the previously cited passages of Deut.—**urgently.** Comp. vii. 13, 25. —**But they hearkened not.** Comp. vii. 24.— hardness. Comp. rems. on iii. 17.

---

2. *Entire Israel, instead of keeping the covenant with Jehovah, enters into conspiracy against Him.*

XI. 9–13.

9 And Jehovah said unto me,
  A conspiracy is found among the men of Judah,
  And among the citizens of Jerusalem.
10 They are returned to the sins of their fathers,
  Who scorned to hear my words;
  And are gone after other gods, to serve them.
  The house of Israel, and the house of Judah
  Have broken the covenant which I made with their fathers.
11 Therefore thus saith Jehovah, Behold!
  I bring upon them evil, from which they cannot escape;
  And they will cry to me, but I will not hear them.
12 And the cities of Judah and citizens of Jerusalem shall go,
  And cry to the gods to which they burn incense,
  But help them—this they will not at the time of their calamity.

13 For as the number of thy cities are thy gods, O Judah!
And as the number of the streets in Jerusalem
Have ye set up altars of shame,
Even altars to burn incense unto Baal.

EXEGETICAL AND CRITICAL.

The Lord has made a covenant with the people, but when the people are regarded now (at the time when Jeremiah thus speaks), there is no longer any trace of it (the covenant made in the reign of Josiah) to be found, but only conspiracy. The prophet shows the existence of such a conspiracy in three stages: 1, in the entire people of Israel (vers. 9, 10); 2, among the people of Anathoth (vers. 18-23); 3, in the prophet's own family (xii. 1-6).—In this strophe the existence of such conspiracy among the people in general is just stated (vers. 9 and 10), then its punishment is announced, (ver. 11) which will be of such a nature that the gods will be unable to deliver from it (ver. 12), though Judah and Jerusalem worship so large a number of them (ver. 13).

Vers. 9 and 10. **A conspiracy is found ... which I made with their fathers.** On is found (נִמְצָא), comp. ii. 34; v. 26. שֶׁקֶר=conspiracy against the rightful Lord, in opposition to the covenant (בְּרִית) which is in accordance with right and duty. In such conspiracies the time of the kings was especially rife (comp. 1 Kings xvi. 20; 2 Kings xii. 20: xiv. 19; xv. 15, 30; xvii. 4), as generally a disposition to conspire is attributed to the Jews (comp. DRECHSLER on Isa. viii. 12; Acts xxiii. 12 sqq.).—The expression שָׁבוּ presupposes the covenant mentioned in ver. 1 sqq., and proves that this section is to be regarded as a reminder of a past fact.— **House of Israel,** etc. A comprehensive survey: not merely Judah and Jerusalem (ver. 9), but Israel and Judah have broken the covenant.

Vers. 11-13. **Therefore thus saith Jehovah ... to burn incense to Baal.** Announcement of punishment.—For gives the reason and explanation of the declaration of ver. 12, that Israel will take refuge with the idols. This may happen because they have idols in numbers, and offer to them numerous acts of worship.—**as the number.** Comp. ii. 28. —**altars of shame.** Comp. rems. on iii. 24; Hos. ix. 10

---

3. *The punishment of the conspiracy is an inevitable and severe judgment.*

XI. 14-17.

14 Therefore pray not thou for this people,
Nor raise for them crying and supplication;
For I hear not, if they cry unto me on account of their calamity.
15 What has my beloved to do in my house?
To practise it—the enormity?
Will crying and holy flesh take away from thee thy hurt?[1]
Then mayest thou exult!
16 "Green olive-tree, splendid with goodly fruit,"
Thus did Jehovah call thy name.
Amid rattling thunder he set fire to it;
And they broke—its branches.
17 And Jehovah Zebaoth, who planted thee,
Hath pronounced evil against thee
"On account of the wickedness of the house of Israel and the house of Judah
Which they practised to their own hurt,[2]
Provoking me and burning incense to Baal."[3]

TEXTUAL AND GRAMMATICAL.

[1] Ver. 15.—The text here is certainly corrupt; 1. because, as it reads at present, it affords no intelligible meaning; 2, because the ancient translations indicate other readings. הָרַבִּים especially is unintelligible, whether we connect it with what goes before or after. The LXX. translate μὴ εὐχαὶ καὶ κρέα ἅγια ἀφελοῦσιν ἀπὸ σοῦ τὰς κακίας σου. They seem then to have read הֲנְדָרִים as some suppose, or more probably הָרַבִּים (BUXTORF, MAURER, GRAF). This latter word, indeed, occurs only in Ps. xxx.i. 7 in the expression פֶּלֶס רָבִי: but since the word is formed quite regularly (comp. חֹק, רָב, יָד, etc.) the plural רָבִים (instead of רַבִּים, which elsewhere is certainly the form exclusively used; comp. OLSEN., §156), being analogous to the forms רִבִּי, חִין, etc., since further נֶגֶד, also vii. 16; xi. 14; xiv. 12, coll. Ps. xvii. 1; 1 Ki. viii. 28, etc., signifies *supplication, prayer,* and is translated in xi. 14; xiv. 12 by the LXX. δέησις, since finally the idea of "beseeching, crying," corresponds exactly to קָרָא. I regard it as most probable that רָבִים was the original word in this place, but that the

word, either purposely, because it does not occur elsewhere, or by mistake, was changed into the slightly differing form רבים. If the question begins with הרגים, the following ו in וּבְשַׂר is entirely in place.—בְּשַׂר־קֹדֶשׁ is found also in Hagg. ii. 12 of the flesh of sacrifice, and seems here especially to indicate the *Holocausta* or burnt-offerings, in which the flesh of the animal is burnt (Levit. i). The following word is also are scarcely intelligible without an alteration of the text. We, therefore, after the example of many commentators, either render רָבִּים as Hiph., like רָבִיב I. 9, 2. *Vide in loc.*), or read יַעֲבֹרוּ. We connect כִּי after הָרַע (LXX., EWALD, MEIER, *etc*), and obtain the sense, *Will thy prayers and sacrifices take away thy wickedness* (רָעָה has the double sense=sin and punishment) *from thee?* The thought then corresponds exactly to the close of ver. 14.

[BLAYNEY renders: Shall vows and holy flesh be allowed to come from thee? When thou art malignant, shalt thou then rejoice? NOYES and HENDERSON, adhering to the text, render, the former: While many pollute it with wickedness?—The holy flesh shall pass away from thee. For when thou doest evil, thou rejoicest; the latter: Committing as she doth the manifold enormity? And the holy flesh hath passed away from thee, *etc*. It seems, however, strained to render this expression "pass away" of their sacrifices being unacceptable to God.—S. R. A.]

² Ver. 17.—[HENDERSON: Which they committed against themselves.]

¹ Ver. 17.—On the infinitives לְהַכְעִיסֵנִי, לְקַטֵּר. Comp. NAEGELSB. *Gr.*, § 95, *e*.

EXEGETICAL AND CRITICAL.

This section is closely attached to the preceding as an appendix. In ver. 11 it was said that a punishment of Israel was determined upon, which they could not escape. For neither will the Lord hear their cries, nor the idols be able to help them.—The thought **I hear not** (ver. 11 *b*), is further explained in this strophe: 1. The Lord will not even hear the prophet (ver. 14 *a*); 2, nor the people (ver. 14 *b*) even though they offer prayers and sacrifices in His temple (ver. 15). Although the Lord even acknowledges Israel to be a beautiful olive-tree which He Himself planted, yet He must adhere to His determination to punish on account of the wickedness which Israel has practised (vers. 16 and 17).

Vers. 14 and 15. **Therefore pray not thou . . . then mayest thou exult.** At first the Lord explains that the intercession of the prophet will be of no avail in the same words as in vii. 16 coll. xiv. 11. He then says that the people's own supplication to avert the calamity will be in vain. This he elucidates in ver. 14, by showing that this beseeching, though offered in the temple and with sacrifices, is only a deceptive mask, under which is hidden the object of continuing in sin. יְדִיד is not Jehovah nor the prophet, but the people, this being imperatively demanded by the sense of the question. What has my beloved to do in my house? can be asked only of such a beloved, whose appearance in the house of the Lord is not welcome. This can be Israel alone, who, although in themselves and originally the beloved of Jehovah, have yet been so estranged from Him, that the question may be fairly asked, what this faithless beloved (now ironically so called) has to do in the house of the Lord? The expression appears to be based on Deut. xxxiii. 12, where Benjamin, in evident allusion to his dwelling in the vicinity of the national sanctuary, is called the beloved of Jehovah. Comp. besides Isa. v. 1 : Ps. lx. 7; cviii. 7 ; cxxvii. 2.—The answer to the question is: **To practise it . . . the enormity.** As to the construction of these words, the anticipation of the object by a pronoun is nothing unusual. Comp. xxvii. 8; li. 56; 1 Sam. ix. 13; NAEGELSB., *Gr.*, § 77, 2.—But why this anticipation here? It presupposes that the object has been already mentioned, or is generally known. Now this הַמְזִמָּתָה, by which not any wickedness, but in accordance with the question, the hypocritical pseudo-worship of Jehovah is to be understood, has not been mentioned in the discourse hitherto. But in rhetorical vivacity the prophet presupposes as known, that which, now as before, deeply troubles him, and which by the initial words of the verse he has indicated with sufficient plainness. The thought and the expression recall unmistakably (as MAURER remarks) vii. 10: "and then ye come and stand before me in the house which bears my name, and say, we are hidden—to do all these abominations." As here (vii. 10) the head of the wickedness is found in this, that Israel regard the temple-service as a sort of sow-washing (2 Pet. ii. 22), to which they betake themselves, not to purify themselves thoroughly, but only to make room for fresh filth, so in this passage the prophet says that Israel has nothing to do in the house of the Lord, but "to do it, the wickedness," namely, that described in chap. vii . which, under the appearance of wishing to be freed from sin, only hides the object of more completely committing it. Accordingly הַמְזִמָּתָה is here to be taken in the sense in which it most frequently occurs, *viz.*, in that of evil design, of purposed, conscious wickedness (Ps. x. 2 ; xxi. 12; cxxxix. 20; Job xxi. 27, *etc.*). The more full-sounding form (comp. OLSH. § 133) has a rhetorical reason, as also the rarer suffix forms following כִּי. This double form, (which does not occur elsewhere in Jeremiah) may both in itself and in its accumulation, be for the purpose of rhetorical effect and more particularly that of irony. With this agrees the distinctly ironical expression, **then mayest thou exult,** which bears reference to **what has my beloved?** *etc.*, that is, to the manner in which the proud and secure people appeared in the temple. Not now, the prophet means to say, but then may you exult, when your prayers and sacrifices have helped you.

Vers. 16 and 17. **Green olive-tree . . . incense to Baal.** The occasion of the thought, prayers. *etc.* would not avert thy calamity. This will be on this account, *viz.*, that the Lord, though He acknowledges Israel to be a beautiful olive-tree, planted by Himself, has determined to destroy him. The parable of the olive-tree in reference to Israel is found also in Ps. lii. 10 [8]; Isa. xvii. 6; xxiv. 13; Hos. xiv. 6.— **Amid rattling** (לְקוֹל) comp. on x. 13.—הֲמוּלָה synonymous with הָכוֹן, besides only in Ezek. i. 24. The prophet compares the catastrophe threatening Israel to a tempest.—**Set fire,** *etc.*, comp. xvii. 27; xxi.

14; xliii. 12; xlix. 27; l. 32; Am. i. 14.—**They broke**. Since an intransitive meaning of the original word cannot be proved, we must regard as the subject either (by a rapid transition from figure to reality) the enemies, or it is to be derived from another root רעע, the radical meaning of which is *tumultuari, agitari, concitari* (comp. FUERST, *H. W. B.* and *Concord. s. v.*) The former is to be preferred, since fire is not followed by a mere shaking but a breaking of branches. —**And Jehovah Zebaoth**, *etc*. If in and **they broke** we perceived a partial transition into the sphere of reality (namely, in respect to the subject), here we perceive the transition to be complete. It is declared in plain words that the Lord has pronounced the judgment of condemnation on Israel, (xix. 15; xxvi. 19). In the word **planted** only, which contains a corroborative point, as it traces not only the name but also the existence of the beautiful olive tree to God (comp. ii. 21) is the figure still retained. On **practised to their own hurt**, comp. vii. 19; xliv. 3.

---

2. *Second stage of the conspiracy: the plot of the Anathothites.*

XI. 18-23.

18 And Jehovah instructed me and I learned.
   Then didst thou show me their doings.
19 But I was as a tame sheep, that is led to the slaughter,
   And remarked not, that they had had thoughts concerning **me**:
   "Let us destroy the tree with its fruit,
   And extirpate him from the land of the living,
   That his name may no more be mentioned."
20 But Jehovah Zebaoth judges with justice;
   He tries the reins and heart.
   I shall see thy vengeance on them,
   For on thee have I devolved my cause.
21 Therefore this saith Jehovah of the men of **Anathoth**,
   Who sought after thy life, saying:
   "Prophesy not in the name of Jehovah,
   That thou die not[1] by our hand"—
22 Therefore thus saith Jehovah Zebaoth:
   Behold, I visit them,
   The young men shall die by the sword;
   Their sons and their daughters shall die of famine.
23 And there shall be no remnant of them,
   For I will bring calamity on the men of Anathoth
   In the year of their visitation.[2]

TEXTUAL AND GRAMMATICAL.

[1] Ver. 21.—On the construction of וְלֹא תָמוּת comp. NAEGELSB. *Gr.*, § 89, 3 *b*.

[2] Ver. 22.—שְׁנַת פְּ׳ is not the accusative of the object but of the time. Comp. x. 15 בְּעֵת פְּקֻדָּתָם [HENDERSON renders it as the former: the year, *etc.*—S. R. A.]

EXEGETICAL AND CRITICAL.

The prophet here also evidently speaks of a conspiracy, and of one which existed in a narrower circle (the city of Anathoth). Ver. 18 opens with the declaration that in what follows a fact will be communicated, of which the prophet received intelligence only from the Lord. In ver. 19 it is stated that this fact consisted in a plot against the life of the prophet. In ver. 20 the prophet expresses his hope that the Lord will avenge him. Vers. 21-23 announce the vengeance of the Lord in response.

Vers. 18 and 19. **And Jehovah instructed me ... no more be mentioned**. The connection with 1 shows that the following verses are closely connected with the preceding. The construction in ver. 18 *a* is like **xx.** 7 *a*. By **instructed me** the prophet gives the Lord the glory and preintimates at the same time that it was something secret.—**Their doings** declares that this consisted in an act of wicked men.— **Tame**, comp. iii. 4; 2 Sam. xii. 3. [HENDERSON:—A lamb that has been tamed so as to be familiar and play with children. One such is commonly to be found in the house of the Arab. —S. R. A.]—**With its fruit**. HITZIG would read בְּלֵחוֹ *in its lap* (comp. Deut. xxxiv. 7; Ezek. xxi. 3) because לֶחֶם signifies corn, not the fruit of a tree. But the idea of the product afforded by the tree such as serves for food is here essential. Comp. ver. 21 b. Since, as it is acknowledged לחם originally meant food in general (comp. Gen. xlvii. 12; Isai. lxv. 25; Job xxviii. 5; Prov. xxvii. 27) we here also understand by it the edible product of the tree. This is certainly the fruit in opposition to the sap, wood, leaves, etc. On בְּ = cum comp. NAEGELSB. Gr. § 112, 5, a.

Vers. 20-23. **But Jehovah Zebaoth .. in the year of their visitation.** Ver. 20 is repeated almost verbatim in xx. 12 coll. xvii. 10.

—**Tries.** The prophet appeals for a confirmation of his innocence to the omniscient God.—גְּלִיתִ. The form according to Piel, from גָּלָה. The connection however requires the meaning "to shove, to roll," which is also favored by the analogy of the passages, Ps. xxii. 9; xxxvii. 5; Prov xvi. 3, comp. EWALD, § 121, a. —**prophesy not.** Comp. Am. ii. 12; vii. 13. Doubtless the plot was to perform the unnecessary threatening. —In ver. 22 the introductory formula is repeated after the interruption.—**I will bring calamity,** comp. xix. 15; xxiii. 12.

---

5. *Third stage of the conspiracy: the plot in the prophet's own family.*

XII. 1-6.

1   Thou maintainest justice, O Jehovah, when I plead with thee.
   Only on matters of judgment will I speak with thee.
   Why is the way of the wicked prosperous?
   Why do all live in peace, who practise knavery?
2 Thou hast planted them and they have taken root;
   They grow up, they also bear fruit:
   Thou art near in their mouth, but far from their reins.
3 But thou, O Jehovah, knowest me,
   Regard me and prove my heart towards thee:[1]
   Pluck them out as sheep to the slaughter,
   And set them apart for the day of execution.
4 How long shall the land mourn,
   And the green of the whole plain wither?
   From the wickedness of those who dwell in it,
   Beast and bird are consumed;[2]
   For they say, he shall not see our end.
5 If thou hast run with footmen and they wearied thee,
   How mayest thou contend[3] with the horses?
   And in a land of peace thou wast secure,
   But how wilt thou do in the pride of Jordan?
6 For even thy brethren and the house of thy father,
   Even they have practised knavery towards thee;
   Even they with a loud cry[4] have pursued thee.
   Trust them not when they speak good to thee.

TEXTUAL AND GRAMMATICAL.

[1] Ver. 3.—אֹתְךָ depends on לִבִּי. The meaning is as in 2 Sam. xvi. 17; Zech. vii. 9.

[2] Ver. 4.—סָפְתָה. On the construction comp. NAEGELSB. Gr., § 105, 4 b.

[3] Ver. 5.—הִתְחָרָה Tiphel. Comp. xxii. 15; GESEN. § 55, 5; EWALD, § 122 a; OLSH. § 255 a.

[4] Ver. 6.—מָלֵא as adverb (Nah. i. 10) = plene, plena voce. Comp. iv. 5, 12.

EXEGETICAL AND CRITICAL.

This strophe attaches itself closely to the preceding, proving conspiracy even in the narrowest circle, in the family of the prophet, where it was the least to be expected. After the prophet had given the Lord to understand his dissatisfaction that the ungodly, of whom ch. xi. treats, still pursue their course in safety (vers. 1, 2) and after he has expressed the hope of his justification and their destruction (ver. 3) the more confidently, these people infect the air, as it were, with the poisonous breath of their unbelief, and render the land uninhabitable (ver. 4), the Lord answers him: If even the enmity of

those at a distance is so intolerable, what wilt thou do when the members of thine own family treacherously waylay thee (vers. 5 and 6)?
Vers. 1-3. **Thou maintainest justice . . . day of execution.** The prophet (compare Jonah before Nineveh) has waited in vain for the performance of the threatenings pronounced in xi. 11-21, *etc.* He now ventures to speak to the Lord concerning it. He knows that the Lord will maintain the right (comp. Ps. li. 6; Job ix. 2, 3 sqq.; xxxix. 32; Rom. iii. 4; ix. 20) he will only therefore inquire into His judgments (i. 16; iv. 12) in order to receive illumination. On אַךְ comp. v. 5. **Bring forth fruit,** reference to xi 17, 18. Comp. Ps. xxxvii. 35. —**Near,** *etc.* Refutation of the objection that these people serve Jehovah. It is only lip-service, while their hearts are alienated (Isai. xxix. 13; Matth. xv. 8). The prophet on the other hand can appeal for the rectitude of his disposition to the knowledge of the Searcher of hearts, whom, moreover, for the sake of perfect satisfaction, he invites to a renewed observation and trial of his heart.—**Pluck them out.** On the subject matter comp. Job xxi. 27 sqq.; Ps. vii., ix., x., xi., lxxiii.; Mal. iii. 13 sqq., *etc.*—נתק comp. vi. 29. —**set them apart.** Comp. vi. 4; xxii. 7; li. 27; Isai. xiii. 3. In the words **pluck them**, *etc.*, Jeremiah has expressed what in his opinion is to be done to the ungodly (comp. Ps. xlix. 15 sqq.) In what follows he supports this opinion from another point of view.
Ver. 4. **How long shall the land mourn . . . not see our end.** In this verse a contradiction has been found to the preceding, and HITZIG would therefore strike out the verse here and insert it at xiv. 1-9. But GRAF correctly remarks that the wicked (ver. 1) also appear as guilty in the curse of barrenness, as this calamity is ever regarded as a divine punishment (iii. 3; v. 24, 25; xiv. 2 sqq.; xxiii. 10; Hos. iv. 3). I add to this, that it is not single wicked individuals who are designated as the authors of the adversity of all their fellow-citizens, but that the "inhabitants of the land," the men generally (as in fact in xi. 9 the whole population is accused) are considered guilty of the destruction of innocent irrational creatures. 2. That by the sentence **for they say,** *etc.*, their unbelieving scorn of the divine word proclaimed by the prophet is especially represented as the cause of this curse which has come upon the whole land. When in ver. 1 it is said "the way of the ungodly is prosperous; all they live in peace who practise knavery," this is to be understood relatively. In the midst of the national calamity it is comparatively still well with them.—**We shall not see.** The subject must be the prophet. אַחֲרִית is the last, extreme end, the final fate (comp Isai. xlvi. 10). When they say that the prophet will not see their extremity, their final fate, they mean that they will survive him, that he will perish before them. Comp. on the subject v. 18. [HENDERSON:—"I take this to be impersonal: *No one shall see our end;* that is, it shall not be realized, we shall not be destroyed. The worldly Jews flattered themselves that they might securely pursue their ungodly course, disbelieving all the predictions of calamity uttered by the prophet."—S. R. A.]

Vers. 5 and 6. **If thou hast run with the footmen . . when they speak good to thee.** To the question of the prophet (vers. 1, 2) the Lord makes no other answer than this: the power of the ungodly, of which thou complainest, is not the worst. Still worse is threatening thee, the enmity of the members of thine own family. Here is evidently the point of the climax, begun in xi. 9, the conspiracy of his associates in the nation, the town and the family. The last is the most deplorable.—**In a land,** *etc.* Instead of **wast secure,** בּוֹטֵחַ, HITZIG would read בּוֹרֵחַ *fleeing.* The expression would certainly be more correct. But the structure of the second member is not like that of the first. Here it is not admitted that the prophet has hitherto had an evil experience. The Lord says, thy condition hitherto has been comparatively secure, as of a man who lives in a peaceful country. The attacks previously made left thee in a condition of security compared with what is before thee. It is evident that here there is a climax, the second member of the sentence being stronger than the first.—**Pride of Jordan,** (גְּאוֹן הַ) HITZIG, MEIER, GRAF understand by this the bank of the Jordan overgrown with trees and tall reeds (comp. RAUMER, *Paläst.* IV. *Aufl. S.* 68), which according to Jer. xlix. 19; l. 44; Zech. xi. 3 serves for the residence of lions (comp. KÖHLER, *Sach.* II. *S.* 109). Since nothing is known of inundations of the Jordan as particularly extensive and dangerous, this explanation may be correct, though the expression in itself (comp. Job xxxviii. 11) might certainly be used of inundations. In ver. 6 we perceive the traces of a conspiracy; on the one hand behaviour intended to awaken confidence, on the other בֶּגֶד, treachery which manifests itself in this, that behind the back of him who is threatened (אַחֲרֶיךָ designates absence, removal to such a distance, as to be out of hearing of a call) they loudly cry and agitate against him.—On the subject matter comp. Matth. x. 36; xiii. 57.

6. The conspiracy of Israel punished by the conspiracy of the neighbors against them.

XII. 7–13.

7 I have forsaken my house, repudiated my heritage;
   I have given the desire of my soul into the hands of her enemies.
8 My heritage is become to me as a lion in the forest;
   It has roared against[1] me, therefore have I hated it.
9 Is my heritage to me a parti-colored bird?[2] Birds round about it?
   Go, assemble ye all the beasts of the field,
   Fetch[3] them to devour.
10 Many pastors have destroyed my vineyard.
   They have trodden under foot my ground property,
   Have made the ground property of my desire a barren waste.
11 They[4] have made it a desert, it mourneth towards me as a desert.
   Desolated was the whole land, for there was no one who took it to heart.
12 On all the heights in the desert are come spoilers:
   For Jehovah has a sword, which devours from land's-end to land's-end.
   There is no flesh that can find means to escape.
13 They have sown wheat and reaped thorns;
   They have tormented themselves and will profit nothing:
   So then—ye shall be ashamed of your revenue[5]
   Before the fierceness of Jehovah's wrath.

TEXTUAL AND GRAMMATICAL.

[1] Ver. 8.—The expression נָתַן בְּקוֹל is found also in Ps. xlvi. 7. Comp. rems. on x. 13.

[2] Ver. 9.—[HENDERSON: a speckled bird of prey. NOTES following the LXX.: a rapacious beast, a hyena; BLAYNEY: the ravenous bird Tsebon.—S. R. A.]

[3] Ver. 9.—On הֵתָיוּ as an imperative form comp. OLSH. § 236 b, S. 568.

[4] Ver. 11.—The subject of שָׂמָהּ is formally undetermined (= they, comp. NAEGELSB. Gr., § 101, 1) but from the connection it is the previously mentioned enemies. Observe the play upon words שָׂמָהּ, שְׁמָמָה, שְׁרֵכָה, נְשַׁמָּה, שָׁם. The last is used with reference to שָׂמָהּ, while שָׂמָהּ לִשְׁמָמָה corresponds to לֹא שָׂם עַל־לֵב.

[5] Ver. 13.—It is not necessary to read כִּתְבוּאָתְיהֶם, after the LXX. The change of person need not offend (comp. NAEGELSB. Gr., § 101, Anm.) nor the emphatic Vau before the imperative (comp. rems. on ii. 19).

EXEGETICAL AND CRITICAL.

As the undertakings of the conspirators against the prophet were virtually against the Lord also, so the prophet's action is a symbol of the judgment which the Lord will inflict in larger and severer measure. Therefore what is said in vers. 7 and 8 of abandoning house and heritage applies at the same time to the prophet who leaves his paternal house in Anathoth, and to the Lord who forsakes Israel. The positive punishment, however, which will consist in the combination of many enemies against Israel (vers. 9-11) corresponds exactly to that triple combination against the Lord and His prophet, spoken of in xi. 9—xii. 6.

Vers. 7 and 8. **I have forsaken my house . . . have I hated it.** After what, according to ver. 6, his house has inflicted upon him, nothing is more natural than he should leave it. It is, therefore, a matter of course, to regard the prophet himself as the subject of the verb **have forsaken.** But in the course of the speech it certainly becomes evident that Jehovah is the forsaker and Israel the forsaken house (ver. 9 sqq.). ZWINGLI and BUGENHAGEN regard vers. 7 and 8 as the words of the prophet. The former considers that Jehovah begins to speak at "Go." I am of opinion, as already remarked, that the words are to be understood as having a double reference. The prophet declares that he has forsaken his father's house in Anathoth, that he has abandoned his heritage, his beloved, to the hands of those, who from enmity towards its possessors would abuse it. Yea, he has been compelled to hate and shun his heritage, since it has become hostile to him, and no longer affords him any security. He, whose life the inmates of the house were seeking, was most threatened in the very house, which he was inhabiting with them. He therefore says that his heritage has become to him as a lion, which one meets in the forest; and that he does not fear the lion without reason, is seen from the fact that it has roared against him, in which is an evident allusion to "with a loud cry have pursued thee," ver. 6. At the same time, as all the commentators recognize, these words are perfectly applicable to Jehovah. The point of connection is this, that the inimical relation of the prophet and his house is only a symptom of the enmity which Israel, as an entire nation, cherish towards the Lord their God. Hence it results, that the *perfects* in this entire passage are not altogether *prophetic* perfects. For they are based on the fact that the prophet is obliged to speak of that which has occurred between himself and his house as of past facts. He cannot, *ex. gr.*, speak otherwise in vers. 7 and 8, than I *have* forsaken, repudiated, given, hated. But since this, at the same time, refers to Jehovah, these *in so far* still future facts are expressed by præterites, which yields the meaning that the action of the prophet as emblematical includes the action of Jehovah. Hence it is, that in accordance with the main fact in vers. 7 and 8, the whole discourse is presented as in past time. In so far as the words of ver. 7 refer to Jehovah, we may apply **my house** to the temple (comp. vii. 2-10, *etc.*), and **my heritage** to the people of Israel (comp. Deut. xxxii. 9), while **the desire of my soul** (יְדִדוּת, *ἄπ. λεγ.*, comp. xi. 15; Ps. lxxxiv. 2) refers to the whole.

Ver. 9. **Is my heritage . . . to devour.—** That עַיִט is a bird of prey, or collectively, birds of prey, is placed beyond doubt by Gen. xv. 11; Isa. xviii. 6; Ezek. xxxix. 4; Job xxviii. 7. This meaning is therefore assured for this passage and Isa. xlvi. 11.—צְבֻעַ, according to צְבָעִים, Judges v. 30 (comp. Aram. עֲבַע *tingere*) can signify only the *colored, variegated*, as, from Jerome and the Syriac downwards, most of the commentators translate it: this parti-colored bird, which appears in their midst, is attacked by the other birds. Comp. the vouchers in Hitzig —לִי **to me**, is not equivalent to *in relation to me*, but merely expresses interest (*Dat. ethicus*). Whether the ה in the second הַעַיִט is an article or interrogative is doubtful. Grammatically the latter is preferable, but the former accords best with the sense. Olshausen, ¿ 100, 1, maintains that it is grammatically admissible. Taken as a question, it expresses astonishment (comp. vii. 9).—**Go** is affirmative and confirmatory: yea, not only the birds, all birds (*i. e.*, all nations) shall fall upon the heritage of the Lord.

Ver. 10. **Many pastors . . . a barren waste.** The same matter in a new form. Comp. vi. 3; Mic. v. 4, 5. —**The ground property of my desire**, comp. iii. 19.

Vers. 11 and 12. **They have made it a desert . . . find means to escape.** Not only the inhabited country, but the plains which serve for pasturage with their hills (comp. iii. 2, 21; xiv. 6), are laid waste, so that the devouring sword has swept through the whole land from one end to the other (comp. vi. 25; xxv. 29, xlvi. 10, 14).

Ver. 13. **They have sown wheat . . . Jehovah's wrath.** Total result:—No harvest, labor is vain,—weakness, shame. The thought is not, what a man soweth that shall he reap, but what a man soweth he shall *not* reap, the harvest shall fail, all the labor expended shall be lost. Of course it is a material harvest alone which is spoken of, comp. Deut. xxviii. 30 sqq.; Isa. lxv. 21, 22; lxii. 8.—On **tormented themselves**, comp. x. 19: Ezek. xxxiv. 4, 21.—On profit comp. Isa. xlviii. 17.

---

7. Solution of all antitheses by the final union of all in the Lord.

XII. 14-17.

14   Thus saith Jehovah against all my neighbors,[1] the wicked,
    Who attacked the inheritance which I gave to Israel, my people, to possess:
    Behold I pluck them forth out of their land,
    And the house of Judah I will pluck forth out of their midst.
15   And it shall come to pass, after I have plucked them out,
    I will again have compassion upon them,
    And bring them back[2] every man to his heritage and every man to his land.
16   And it shall come to pass, if they learn the way of my people,
    To swear by my name ' Jehovah liveth,'
    As they have taught my people to swear by Baal:
    Then shall they be built in the midst of my people.
17   But if they hear not, I will utterly pluck up
    And destroy such a nation, saith Jehovah.

TEXTUAL AND GRAMMATICAL.

[1] Ver. 14.—שְׁכֵנַי, transition to the first person, as in xiv. 15. The connection with the preceding strophe is unmistakable. Comp. נַחֲלָה and נָתַשׁ with נָחֲלָה and נָטַשׁ, ver. 7, sqq.

[2] Ver. 15.—On וּ אָשׁוּב. Comp. Naegelsb. *Gr.*, § 95, *g.*, *Anm.*

EXEGETICAL AND CRITICAL.

Even in these concluding words the fundamental idea is evidently that of association. The conspiracy of the nations against the covenant people who have conspired against their Lord (xi. 9; xii. 6) has for its first consequence, that the two are associated in punishment (ver. 14). But afterward when they have made common cause in penitence, and turning to the Lord, they are to be equally regarded in their redemption and re-establishment (ver. 16). In this only is there dissimilarity, that in the heathen nations a possibility of disobedience and consequent total destruction is assumed, which is not the case with respect to Israel (ver. 17).

Ver. 14. **Thus saith Jehovah . . . pluck forth out of their midst.** The enemies who, according to ver. 9, combine against Israel, are here seen to be chiefly their neighbors; comp. 2 Kings xxiv. 2, to which passage, however, I refer not as the occasion, but as the, at least, partial fulfilment of our prophecy. The Syrians, Moabites and Ammonites, are here mentioned, and in Ps. cxxxvii. 7 the Edomites also, as auxiliaries of the Chaldees in the work of Judah's destruction.—Judah and the neighboring nations will meet the same fate, because they have both sinned against Jehovah: Judah directly, the others indirectly; for what they did against Judah, was against Judah's God.—**Out of their midst** refers to the geographical position of Judah, and at the same time to ver. 9.—The carrying away of Judah involves their liberation from the attacks of their neighbors. Comp. besides xxv. 15 sqq.

Vers. 15-17. **And it shall come to pass . . . destroy such a nation, saith Jehovah.** Every nation shall be brought back (comp. xlvi. 26; xlviii. 47; xlix. 6, 39), therefore also Israel. Consequently they are alike in this.—The highest and most glorious stage of the association is this, that the nations will be one among themselves and with Judah in the true worship of Jehovah, which is expressed as swearing by His name alone (comp. iv. 2; v. 7; Deut. vi. 13; x. 20). In this is, at the same time, given the unity of God with men; He in them, they in Him (John xvii. 21, 23). It is noteworthy that the nations are to be built (בְּתוֹךְ עַמִּי) **in the midst of my people.** Before *Israel* was in their midst (vers. 7, 9); now *they* are in the midst of Israel. Israel is now not merely the ideal, but the real stock which bears all. (Comp. Rom. xi. 17 sqq.—Isa. xlv. 22 sqq.: lvi. 1 sqq.; lxv. and lxvi.).—In this only a dissimilarity between Israel and the nations comes fairly to light, that the possibility of resistance to the loving purpose of God is presupposed of the latter, but not of the former (comp. xxx. 10, 11).—On **learn the ways,** comp. x. 2; ii. 33.

DOCTRINAL AND ETHICAL.

1. On xi. 3. "The curse of the Law excites anger, but the curse of the covenant abashes. I have seen an atheist tremble at the words 'If any man love not the Lord Jesus Christ, let him be anathema (1 Cor. xvi. 22).' He remarked it himself, and sought to excuse himself by saying 'it was *motus involuntarii.*' But it was the words of the covenant, Thou shalt love." ZINZENDORF.

2. On xi. 5. "*Hic παίδευμα latet et pro ministris verbi, et pro eorum auditoribus. Ministri exemplo prophetæ monentur, ut similem in officio promtitudinem et animi alacritatem Deo probent, quemadmodum etiam de Jesaja legitur.* vi. 8. *Auditores hic docentur, ut de voluntate Dei ex verbo moniti in corde suo dicant; amen, promti et parati ad obedientiam verbo præstandam.*" FÖRSTER.

3. On xi. 14. "Intercession for all men has good reason for it in the love which is due to one's neighbor, and it is also commanded, 1 Tim. ii. 1, 2, but on the part of those who offer it, a certain order is required so that it may be heard (Luke xiii. 8, 9; John ix. 31)." LANGII *Op. bibl.*

4. On xi. 15. "It is a snare to a man to blaspheme the holy, and after that to seek vows [after vows to make inquiry] (Prov. xx. 24). For that is the manner of hypocrites, to offer St. Martin a penny and then steal a horse; and when they have opposed God and His word to the utmost, to turn afterwards to sacrifices, fasting and alms, and wish thus to exculpate themselves." CRAMER.

5. On xi. 16, 17. "God has appointed us to be trees of righteousness, plants of the Lord for His glory (Isa. lxi. 3). He, however, who bringeth not forth good fruit, is hewn down and cast into the fire (Matt. vii. 19)." CRAMER. ["Every sin against God is a sin against ourselves, and so it will be found sooner or later." HENRY.—S. R. A.]

6. On xi. 18. "Although the human heart cannot be fathomed (Jer. xvii. 9), yet nothing can be hidden from God, and He frequently reveals secret counsels, so that they are known and manifest, as in the case of Absalom and Ahithophel (Isa. viii. 10). Therefore do nothing in secret, in the hope that it will remain hidden, for the birds of heaven carry the voice, and the winged repeat it (Eccles. x. 20)." CRAMER.

7. On xi. 20. "The first New Testament vengeance was executed on the cross, when an evil-doer who had mocked at Jesus, cringed on the cross, and asked for a gracious remembrance. The Lamb of God could scarcely wait the time of vengeance: To-day, said He, shalt thou be with Me in Paradise. According to this may the Jeremiahs of our times, the preachers of righteousness, take the measure of their holy desire for vengeance." ZINZENDORF. ["It is a comfort, when we are wronged that we have a God to commit our cause to; and our duty to commit it to Him, with a resolution to acquiesce in His definite sentence; to subscribe and not prescribe to Him." HENRY.—S. R. A.]

8. On xi. 20. "A teacher is advised to say this if he can, 'I have ceased to concern myself about myself.' DR. LUTHER says,

> Once I grasped too many things:—
> None staid; they all had wings:
> But since I've weary grown,
> And all away have thrown,
> Not one from me has flown.
> And do you ask, how can it be thus?—
> Because I've cast my all on Jesus.

Messengers and servants, who concern themselves about their own injuries must have bad masters." ZINZENDORF.

9. On xi. 22. When the people will not endure the rod of Christ's mouth, with which He smites the earth (Isai. xi. 4), *item* His rods Beauty and Bands (Zech. xi. 7), God sends one with the sword to preach, which is followed by the red spice, and then we see what the smooth preachers have effected (Isai. xxx. 10)." CRAMER.

10. On xii. 1. "But can we conceive anything more humane and gracious than our dear Lord? We know beforehand that we are wrong; we do not doubt that He does all well, but it yet oppresses us. We should like to make a clean breast of it. Where shall we find one with whom we could do this? The fly on the wall, the domestic, the child, that comes in our way? Assuredly not! Straight to our Lord, the eternal and living God, with all our ill-humor, doubt, care, scruples! Pour out your heart before Him (Ps. lxii. 8)." ZINZENDORF.

11. On xii. 1-3. "It is a common grievance, to live and experience that the ungodly are prosperous and the godly are unfortunate (Ps. xxxviii. 20; lxxiii. 12; Job xxi. 7; xxxi. 2), against which David wrote the xxxvii. Ps. Have recourse to the testimony that there is another life, when the tables will be turned and the evil will be recompensed with evil and the good with good (Isai. lxv. 13)." CRAMER.

12. On xii. 3. "The prosperity of the ungodly should exhort them to repentance by the long-suffering of God (Rom. ii. 4). But when even this does not avail, there are still people of this world, who have their portion in this life, who fill only their belly (Ps. xvii. 14) and carry nothing away. What profit then is there to them even if they had the whole world, and suffer injury to their souls (Matth. xvi. 26. The rich man in Luke xvi. 23)." CRAMER.

13. On xii. 4. "It is strange that even in the people of God the Epicurean opinion has found acceptance, that God sits idly in the heavens, caring nothing about what goes on below, doing neither that which is good nor that which is evil, (Zeph. i. 12), seeing not what men do (Ezek. viii. 10, ix. 9), and that future things are altogether hidden both from him and his prophet. So powerful is the devil among the children of unbelief." CRAMER.

14. On xii. 4. "*Tales hodie sunt Epicuri de grege porci, quibus sæpe est in ore,* the devil is not so black, hell is not so hot, as the parson in the pulpit makes out. *Sed his historia divitis epulonis occinenda* (Luke xvi). *Nam ibi*—Christ puts forth his hand into hell-fire, snatches a brand out therefrom, and holds it in the face of all Epicureans, as though He would say, Smell, smell, how hot hell-fire is." FÖRSTER.

15. On xii. 5. "I have heard that an able preacher, when he had to deliver a trial sermon for the position of court-preacher, took this text. The exposition is plain. No servant of the Lord should long for more respectable, rich, discreet, sociable hearers. Let every one approve himself thoroughly in all changes, and be sure of his cause and lean not to his own understanding." ZINZENDORF.

16. On xii. 6. "Many must add to this, wife, child, colleague, domestics, and whatever more the Saviour mentions, which may be against a man. One is often offered by his mother to the dear God (*i. e.* dedicated to the pastoral office) but in an altogether different sense; and when he afterwards walks as becomes him, according to the gospel of Christ, those are his bitterest enemies, who hoped that he might comfort them in all their travail, and who not only do not gain anything from his labors as a witness, but must bear the shame and ridicule, that their son, brother, cousin, husband, father, friend, *etc.* will yet render them all unfortunate." ZINZENDORF.

17. On xii. 7, sqq. "They are sweet words and beautiful names with which the Lord baptizes and names His city, and it is so hard for it to be punished by God for its sins that we are long in learning to consider our own account." (Rom. xi. 21). CRAMER.

18. On xii. 7, sqq. "The heart of a believer is God's most cherished abode, but if man corrupt it with wilful sin, God must forsake this house." (Isai. lix. 2). STARKE.

19. On xii. 10, sqq. "A servant of the Lord who should follow on twelve hirelings or wolves may depend on this, that he will find nothing else than a house, a vineyard of the Lord, but a desecrated house, an uprooted vineyard, in which many preparations are needed before he can proceed to his regular work." ZINZENDORF.

20. On xii. 14, sqq. "The Christian church has a triple consolation. 1. That its enemies will be punished; 2. That God again has mercy on it; 3. That it also converts a part of its enemies and gathers them into its little flock of believers." CRAMER.

21. On xii. 16. "Some time since I found in the so-called Herrnhut lot-book for the year 1737 the words in the vision of Isaiah, lix. 17: Thy destroyer and they that made thee waste shall go forth of thee! Under them were these two lines, 'let them rather remain and attach them to us.' This is what Jeremiah says; they may yet come out right.—Paul has confirmed it by his example. Within three days he was a persecutor, a false teacher, a poor sinner, a justified sinner, a witness, an apostle. With joy would I bestow the same happiness on every one of those, whom I at this moment cannot regard otherwise than as the enemies of the cross of Christ." ZINZENDORF.

HOMILETICAL AND PRACTICAL.

1. On xi. 1-10 there is extant a homily of ORIGEN (the 9th in Lommatzsch's ed.) likewise on xi. 18–xii. 9 (the 10th) and on xii. 11–xiii. 1 (the 11th.)

2. FÖRSTER remarks that xi. 19, 20 accords with Matth. xxii. 15 sqq. (XXIII. Sunday after Tr.) and that the persecution of Jeremiah corresponds to the sufferings of the Lord. Likewise that xii. 2 bears relation to Luke xvi. 19 sqq. (I. Sund. after Trin.) and xii. 7 to Acts vi. 8 sqq. (St. Stephen's day, Sunday after Christmas), and to Luke xix. 41 sqq. (X. after Trin.)

3. On x. 16, 17. The divine election is never intended to be a license from all discipline. Indeed when men break the covenant, the Lord interposes with punishment, which may proceed to instantaneous destruction. Surely God's gifts and calling are without repentance. If the

branches cut off abide not in unbelief they shall be graffed in; for God is able to graff them in again. Rom. xi. 23, 29.
4. On xi. 21. That which the people of Anathoth say here to Jeremiah, the people of this world say everywhere and at all times to the preachers of the truth. Comp. 2 Tim. iv. 3, 4. It is important then to preach the word, to be instant in season and out of season; to reprove, rebuke, exhort, with all long-suffering and doctrine (2 Tim. iv. 2).
5. On xii. 5. It is not becoming that we prescribe to God, to what extent He shall lay burdens upon us. Our patience and steadfastness are as elastic and extensible as our faith is firm and rock-like (Petrine, Matth. xvi. 18).
6. On xii. 14-17. When mankind depart from God they lose the bond of unity and of peace. They are divided then into parties, which contend with and exterminate each other. But when these have again united themselves with the Lord, the unity of the members is restored. Therefore there is liberty, equality and fraternity only in the Lord.

CHAPTER XIII.

Since the foregoing discourse is complete in itself, it is not correct to say that ch. xi.-xiii. *form "a whole, one prophetic discourse"* (GRAF, *S.* 174). Chap. xiii. *on the contrary is an independent portion, but contemporaneous with the preceding. For although the cleft in the rock by the river Euphrates involves an obscure intimation of the place of exile, the enemies from the North are still spoken of indefinitely* (comp. on ver. 20). *This portion therefore belongs to the period before the fourth year of Jehoiakim. The reign of Jehoiakim is also indicated in what is said of the pride of the great, and especially of the King,* ver. 12 sqq.—*Comp. on the despotism of Jehoiakim, Comm.* on xvi. 13-19. *As to the purport of this passage—it is a reproof of pride.* Comp. ver. 9, *"I will mar the pride of Judah and the pride of Jerusalem, for it is great;"* ver. 2, *"bottle,"* and the interpretation given of it; ver. 15, *"be not proud;"* ver. 17, *"for your pride;"* ver. 18, *"humble yourselves, sit down."*— *The reproof is however addressed to the people in a threefold gradation—first the pride of the chosen people generally* (ver. 9, *Judah and Jerusalem*) *is rebuked under the figure of a destroyed girdle. This is then done with respect to the particular orders enumerated in ver.* 13, *which are represented under the figure of drunken pitchers breaking each other; finally the prophet humbles the pride of the highest, the king and the king's mother* (ver. 18) *and the form of the concrete mother of the country gradually passes over into the abstract, i. e., ideal, person of the daughter of Zion (Jerusalem,* ver. 27). *There are thus three strophes:*
1. Vers. 1-11. *The entire chosen nation a destroyed girdle.*
2. Vers. 12-17. *The particular orders broken pitchers.*
3. Vers. 18-27. *The father and mother of the country humbled, driven away, insulted.*

1. *The entire chosen nation a destroyed girdle.*

XIII. 1-11.

1 Thus saith the LORD [Jehovah] unto me, Go and get [buy] thee a linen girdle,
2 and put it upon thy loins and put it not in water. So I got [bought, procured] a [the] girdle according to the word of the LORD [Jehovah], and put it on my loins.
3 And the word of the LORD came [was communicated] unto me the second time,
4 saying: Take the girdle that thou hast got [bought, procured], which is upon thy loins, and arise, go to Euphrates [Phrath] and hide it there in a hole [cleft] of the
5 rock. So [And] I went and hid it by Euphrates [in Phrath, *or* on the Phrath] as
6 the LORD [Jehovah had] commanded me. And it came to pass after many days, that the LORD [Jehovah] said unto me, Arise, go to Euphrates [Phrath] and take
7 [fetch] the girdle from thence, which I commanded thee to hide there. Then I went to Euphrates [Phrath] and digged, and took the girdle from the place where I had hid it, and behold, the girdle was marred [spoiled]; it was profitable [good]
8 for nothing. Then the word of the LORD [Jehovah] came unto me, saying:
9 Thus saith Jehovah:
Thus will I spoil the pride of Judah,
And the pride of Jerusalem, which is great.
10 This wicked people, who refused to hear my words,
Who walked in the hardness of their heart,
And went after other gods to serve them and to worship them,
They shall even be as this girdle, which is good for nothing.

11 For as a girdle lies around the loins of a man,
    So have I laid around myself the whole house of Israel,
    And the whole house of Judah, saith Jehovah,
    That they may be to me for a people,
    For a name, for praise, and for beauty ;
    But they hearkened not.

EXEGETICAL AND CRITICAL.

Vers. 1 and 2. **Go and buy thee a girdle . . on my loins.** The reason why the prophet was to buy a *girdle* appears in ver. 11. As of all parts of the clothing the girdle is that which fits most closely, so Israel of all nations is the most closely connected with Jehovah. And as a beautifully ornamented girdle serves to adorn a man (comp. HERZOG, *Real-Enc.*, V. S. 407 ; VII. 717) so the Lord thought to put on Israel as an armament. The prophet was to buy a *linen* girdle without doubt, because the sacred garments of the priests were linen (comp. Exod. xxviii. 40; HERZOG, *R.-Enc.* VII. S. 714) and because Israel was to be a holy, priestly nation (Exod. xix. 6). On the question why the prophet was not to put the girdle in water there has been much debate. GRAF's view that the girdle was to be preserved from the *injurious* effects of the water, and kept new and undamaged, refutes itself. For no damage would be done to a linen girdle by washing, but it would rather be renewed. The prohibition to put the girdle in water evidently presupposes that the prophet would have washed the girdle when it became dirty. But this was not to be done. It was to remain dirty. As a dirty girdle it was to be taken to the Euphrates. Since now the girdle denotes the people, it was thus to be set before their eyes what was impending over them as having become unclean, and yet long borne by the Lord in their filth. So ROSENMULLER and MAURER.

Vers. 3-7. **Take the girdle . . . profitable for nothing.** פְּרָת is in Jeremiah always the Euphrates, xlvi. 2, 6, 10; li. 63, though in ch. xlvi. we always find נְהַר־פְּרָת. Now it is inconceivable that Jeremiah made the long journey to the Euphrates twice "merely to show that a linen girdle is destroyed by lying a long time in the damp." Therefore פְּרָת is said by some to be a water-gap (פְּרָת) near Jerusalem (EWALD), by others an abbreviation of אֶפְרָת (BOCHART, VENEMA, HITZIG), by others again the whole is regarded as merely an allegorical narrative (STAEUDLIN, *Neue Beitr. zur Erl. d. bibl. Proph.* Gött., 1791, *S.* 129 sqq., GRAF). I do not see why the words may not be regarded as historical truth, if only we do not apply the standard of the paltry present to the great past. Was it too much for a prophet to make a long journey in order to set visibly before the eyes of his people their impending fate? There are indeed narratives of such a kind as bear in themselves the necessity of a parabolic interpretation, *ex. gr.* when Jeremiah in xxv. 15 sqq. says that he took the wine cup of fury from the hand of the Lord and caused Jerusalem with all the cities of Judah, Pharaoh and many other kings and princes to drink of it. But where this is not the case we must be on our guard against transferring our standard of the suitable, or of the morally and physically possible to those times. I therefore do not perceive why the account in Hos. i. ; Ezek. iv. 5 is less real than what we read in Jer. xix. 1 sqq. ; xxvii. 2; Isa. xx. 3. And here also Jeremiah may have really made a double journey to the Euphrates for the most palpable warning of his people. But let us not expect that Jeremiah will trouble himself to affirm in many words what great result he accomplished by these journeys. He who relates so simply, without even an exclamation, how he was thrown into the miry pit (ch. xxxviii.) might here also leave it to his readers to estimate the importance of the facts.

[HENDERSON:—"On the authority of the LXX., Vulg. and other ancient versions, it has been taken for granted, that by פְּרָת here the river *Euphrates* is to be understood. That the name is elsewhere employed to designate that river is beyond dispute. Not reckoning the present verse, it occurs fifteen times with this application, but except in three instances, Gen. ii. 14 ; 2 Chron. xxxv. 20 ; Jer. li. 63, it never stands alone, but always has נְהַר, *river*, attached to it. Indeed the same must have taken place Gen. ii. 14 if that word had not been used immediately before פְּרָת, so that this passage ought not to be taken into account. With respect to Jer. li. 63 also, there was no necessity for employing the qualifying noun, as Seraiah is supposed to be at Babylon the time to which reference is there made, consequently in the closest contact with the Euphrates. It seems not a little strange, therefore, that the name should appear not fewer than four times in the present verse without the use of the qualifying term, if that river had really been intended. This circumstance appears to have struck the LXX., whose text, ver. 7, exhibits τὸν Εὐφράτην ποταμόν. EWALD, who rejects the Euphrates, renders the word by *Flussufer* (bank of the river) and thinks that it may be used of fresh or sweet water rivers generally, or that it may express the same as the Arab.

فرضة, a rent in the land formed by water.

I prefer the solution proposed by BOCHART, and adopted by VENEMA, DATHE and HITZIG, that פְּרָת is here only an abbreviation of אֶפְרָת, *Ephrath*, which appears to have been the original name of Bethlehem and its vicinity, and most commonly appears with the paragogic ה–אֶפְרָתָה, *Ephratha*. The aphaeresis of the prosthetic א is not without examples.—The whole extent of the prophetic journey therefore was only about six miles northward of Jerusalem. There at Bethlehem, he was to hide the girdle in a fissure of עֵלָה‎, *the rock*, some well-known rock in the vicinity of that town. Why he was especially sent to that place it is impossible to say, except that it may have been that the use of the term *Prath* might lead the Jews, when the symbolical actions came to be understood by them, to think of the Euphrates, to which they were to be carried away captive, as designated by the same name."—S. R. A.]

Vers. 8-11. **Then the word ... but they hearkened not.** Observe in vers. 9 and 10 the relation of this parable to that which follows, of the pitchers. The girdle signifies the entirety of the people, the pitchers the individuals of all ranks. Hence in ver. 9, "the pride of Judah and Jerusalem," and in ver. 10, "this evil people," is spoken of, while in ver. 13 all ranks are enumerated. The meaning of the destruction of the girdle in the cleft of the rock is declared in vers. 9 and 10: *pride* shall be brought low, the chosen people shall become as a girdle, which is profitable for nothing. And certainly, though there was a partial return from exile, yet with the captivity in Babylon ceased the existence of Israel as an independent State with compact national unity. Observe in ver. 9 the doubling of the strong word גָאוֹן‎, pride, with the addition רַב‎, great. The main thought of the passage is thus emphasized.—In the words, **for a name, for a praise,** *etc.*, there appears to be an allusion to Exod. xxviii. 2, where it is said of the holy garments of Aaron that they should be "for glory and for beauty."

---

2. *The particular orders—broken pitchers.*

XIII. 12-17.

12 Therefore [And] thou shalt speak unto them this word: Thus saith the LORD [Jehovah the] God of Israel, Every bottle [vessel, pitcher] shall be filled with wine; and they shall [will] say unto thee, Do we not certainly know that every
13 bottle [pitcher] shall be filled with wine? Then shalt thou say unto them, Thus saith the Lord [Jehovah]:
Behold, I fill all the inhabitants of this land,
And the kings who sit for David on his throne,
And the priests and the prophets and all the citizens of Jerusalem with drunkenness,
14 And dash them one against another,
And the fathers and sons together, saith Jehovah.
I will not spare, nor have pity, nor be merciful,
So as not to destroy them.
15 Hear ye and attend! Be not high-minded! For Jehovah hath spoken.
16 Give to Jehovah, your God, the glory,
Before he causes darkness,
And your feet stumble on mountains of twilight,
And ye wait for light, but he turneth it[1] into dark shadow,
And change it[2] into cloudy night.
17 But if ye hear it[3] not, my soul will weep in secret for your pride
And mine eyes shall weep sore and run down with tears,[4]
That the flock of Jehovah is carried away captive.

TEXTUAL AND GRAMMATICAL.

[1] Ver. 16.—שָׂמָהּ‎ refers to אוֹר‎, which is used as a feminine besides only in Job xxxvi. 32. Comp. EWALD, § 174 c
[2] Ver. 16.—The Chethibh וְשִׁית‎ for שִׁית‎ is foolish.
[3] Ver. 17.—תִּשְׁמָעוּהָ‎ referable to ver. 15. The feminine suffix in a neuter sense. Comp. NAEGELSB. *Gr.*, § 60, 6 *b*.
[4] Ver. 17.—On the construction, comp. NAEGELSB. *Gr.*, § 60, 2 *a.*; Jer. ix. 17; xiv. 17; Lam. i. 16; iii. 48.

EXEGETICAL AND CRITICAL.

Ver. 12. Announcement of the punitive judgment under a new figure, that of pitchers to be filled, which is not understood by the people. Jehovah explains the figure, vers. 13, 14. Admonition of the prophet to follow the warning of Jehovah, vers. 15-17.

Ver. 12. **Therefore thou shalt speak ... shall be filled with wine.** After the declaration, in the words "they would not hear," ver. 11, that the symbolical action had been unsuccessful, a new attempt is set on foot by a visible parable to make an impression on the people. The first symbolical act was intended to bring the thoughts of God home to the people in an *analytical* way, the new parable takes a *syntheti-*

cal form. The short sentence, "every bottle shall be filled with wine," is set at the head of an obscure, mysterious problem. The people express their understanding of the sentence in the most natural physical sense, but with the silent assumption (we knew *that* before, no one need tell us that. Comp. Gen. xliii. 7) that this interpretation is not satisfactory. The Lord therefore develops His meaning more particularly in what follows.

Vers. 13 and 14. **Then shalt thou say unto them . . . destroy them.** It should first be observed that in the three parts of this discourse (ch. xiii.) there is a climax, in so far as the first part (vers. 9, 10) is addressed to the mass of the people, without distinction of the particular orders, the second part specifies these orders with evident emphasis on the favored classes, the third part applies to the king and the king's mother alone (ver. 18). The prominence of the higher classes in the second part is doubtless connected with the purport of the parable. They are compared with earthen pitchers. [HENDERSON: "These bottles are frequently of a large size. On entering the city of Tiflis, in 1821, the author found the market-place full of such bottles, consisting of the skins of oxen, calves, *etc.*, distended with wine.—It is from this custom that our English word *hogshead* is derived—that term being a corrupt pronunciation of ox-hide."— But HITZIG renders wine-*pitchers, earthen* vessels or pots.—S. R. A.] (Comp. Jer. xlviii. 12; Isa. xxx. 14; Lam. iv. 2). These pitchers are bellied, to a certain extent swollen, but internally they are hollow and empty and moreover of frangible material. They are therefore an excellent emblem of that carnal aristocratic pride to which there is no corresponding inner merit. That this is the prophet's meaning is clear from the emphatically prefixed **Be not high-minded** (אַל־תִּגְבָּהוּ), ver. 15, and from **pride** (גְּוָה), ver. 17.—What a suitable punishment for such men, who are like pitchers, to be filled with wine of intoxication! שִׁכָּרוֹן, **drunkenness**, designates the immediate subjective effect of the wine of fury (comp. xxv. 15; Isa. xxviii. 7; li. 17; Ps. lx. 5), of which the further objective effect is collision and breaking to pieces. The Midianites (Judges vii. 22) and the Philistines (1 Sam. xiv. 20), who exterminated each other, were also seized by a spirit of intoxication. If not in this sense, yet in that of mutual hatred, reciprocal oppression and injury in general, the prophet applies וְנִפַּצְתִּים, **dash them,** to the Israelites. But when a kingdom is divided against itself it cannot stand, Mark iii. 24.—The plural **kings** in ver. 13, intimates that not merely the then reigning king, but several, one after another (as the majority of the kings contemporary with Jeremiah were evil-disposed) were included in this category. The addition, **who sit for David** (comp. xxii. 4), sets forth that very element on which the pride of these kings especially rested. (Comp. 2 Sam. vii.).

Vers. 15 and 17. **Hear ye and attend . . . carried away captive.** The prophet interposes as a mediator with an earnest admonition to observe the divine warning. On **high-minded** comp. the foregoing remarks.—**For Jehovah hath spoken,** *viz.*, every bottle, *etc.*, ver. 12.— **Give glory.** Comp. Josh. vii. 19. It is opposed to **be proud.—Cause darkness.** Comp. Ps. cv. 28; cxxxix. 12. According to the connection it is easiest to regard God as the subject. —**Stumble,** reference to **dash together,** ver. 14.—**Dark mountains** are more than stones of stumbling. The prophet imagines them to be wandering in a mountainous country and in a dark ravine. Comp. Ps. xxiii. 4.—**In secret places.** The prophet will retire from the publicity, in which he has hitherto lived and labored, into solitude, in order that he may give way to his sorrow.—**Weep** in contrast with **drunkenness,** ver. 13: the prophet's eyes will overflow with tears.—**Flock.** Comp. ver. 20; Zech. x. 8. Even the disobedient people continue to be the Lord's flock.

---

3. *The father and mother of the country humbled, driven away, insulted.*

XIII. 18–27.

18 Say to the king and the princes, sit down low,[1]
   For fallen is your chief ornament,[2] your glorious crown!
19 The cities of the south are shut up, and no man openeth them;
   Judah is carried away[3] wholly, carried away completely.[4]
20 Lift up your eyes and see who are coming from the north.
   Where is the flock that was given thee, thy beautiful flock?
21 What wilt thou say, when he sets over thee those,[5]
   Whom thou hast thyself drawn[6] to thee for friends, as chief?[7]
   Will not pangs seize thee as a parturient woman?[8]
22 And if thou sayest in thy heart, why have these things happened to me?—
   For the greatness of thy iniquity are thy skirts discovered,[9]
   Thy heels abused.[10]

23 Will a Cushite change his skin, or a leopard his spots?
Then shall ye also be able to do good, ye accustomed to evil-doing!
24 Therefore I will scatter them as the stubble,[11]
That hasteth away[12] before the wind of the desert.
25 This is thy lot, thy measured[13] portion from me, saith Jehovah,
Because thou didst forget me and trust in falsehood.
26 Therefore I also have discovered thy skirts from before,
That[14] thy shame may be seen:—
27 Thy adulteries and ardent neighings, the enormity of thy unchastity—
On the hills in the field have I seen thy abominations!
Wo to thee, O Jerusalem! Wilt thou not be cleansed—still after how long!

TEXTUAL AND GRAMMATICAL.

[1] Ver. 18.—On the construction comp. NAEGELSB. *Gr.*, § 95, *Anm.*

[2] Ver. 18.—מֵרֹאשׁוֹתֵיכֶם. Thus punctuated the word is found here only. On the derivation comp. OLSH. § 197, *e*, S. 374. The meaning is: that which is found at the head or on the head. (Comp. מַרְגְּלוֹת Ruth iii. 4, 7, 8, 14). Elsewhere we find (occurring only in this form) מְרַאֲשֹׁתָיו, Gen. xxviii. 11, 18; 1 Sam. xix. 13, 16, *etc.*: and (erroneously punctuated) מְרַאֲשֹׁתָיו, 1 Sam. xxvi. 12.—That which is found on the head is the ornament, which is more particularly designated as the crown. On the sing. masc. רֹאשׁ comp. NAEGELSB. *Gr.* § 105, 4 *b*, 3.

[3] Ver. 19.—הָגְלָת. Comp. Lev. xxv. 21; xxvi. 34; 2 Ki. ix. 37 (Chethibh): EWALD, § 194 *a*; OLSH., § 226 *b*, S. 449.

[4] Ver. 19.—שְׁלוֹמִים adjective=שָׁלֵם *integer.* Comp. Am. i. 6, 9.

[5] Ver. 21.—Since there is no nominative to יִפְקֹד, either mentioned or implied, in the connection, it must be either the ideal-general subject (One), or Jehovah, which in sense amounts to the same thing. All the commentators recognize a parenthesis as beginning with וְאַתְּ. But some conclude this with אַתְּ (GAAB), others with עָלַיִךְ (HITZIG, GRAF), others with אַלֻּפִים (EICHHORN, DE WETTE, UMBREIT). It is opposed to the first rendering that then the sense of לִמְרָתָהּ remains indefinite, to the second, that then the parenthesis is either superfluous, if we consider אַלֻּפִּיךְ=עָלַיִךְ, or as incorrectly introduced by it, if עָלַיִךְ is to be considered as=*adversum te* (Vulg., HITZIG). It would then need to be בָּהּ. I therefore agree with those who conclude the parenthesis with אַלֻּפִים. Then וְאַתְּ is sentence of condition with an adversative meaning (comp. NAEGELSB. *Gr.*, § 109, 4 *e*) which in its entirety is to be regarded as the object of יִפְקֹד. The meaning of this verb is that which occurs frequently: *to set, ordain over one* (comp. xv. 3).

[6] Ver. 21.—לִמַּד—to accustom, to train, of beasts (xxxi. 18; Hos. x. 11), of men (x. 2). In the latter passage it is construed with אֶל for which we here have עַל, which prepositions, as frequently remarked, are often used as synonymous by Jeremiah (comp. on x. 2).—The construction with a double accusative is similar to ii. 33, only here it is a double accusative of person, since it is not said: thou teachest them intimacy, but as intimates, which is to be regarded as a prolepsis and to be included in the cases enumerated in NAEGELSB. *Gr.* § 69, 3.

[7] Ver. 21.—לְרֹאשׁ, the thought is the same as in Lam. i. 5.

[8] Ver. 21.—לֵדָה—אֵשֶׁת, *mulier partus;* elsewhere יֹלֵדָה (comp. vi. 24; xxii. 23; xlix. 24), לֵדָה besides only in 2 Ki. xix. 3; Isa. xxxvii. 3; Hos. ix. 11.

[9] Ver. 22.—וְנִגְלוּ. Comp. Nah. iii. 5.

[10] Ver. 22.—The Niph. נֶחְמְסוּ here only. Comp. xxii. 3. The captive driven before the enemy is exposed both to shame and abuse. [HENDERSON: "The reason why the heels are particularly mentioned, seems to be that the sandal was fastened by a strap or thong which came round above the heel to the instep. As the sandal was not so easily removed as the skirt was turned up, hence the appropriate selection of the verb חָמַס, to tear off, or do anything with violence. Both parts of the description literally apply to those who were removed into a state of expatriation by a victorious army."—S. R. A.]

[11] Ver. 24.—קַשׁ stubble. Comp. Ps. lxxxiii. 14; Isa. xli. 2; xlvii. 14.

[12] Ver. 24.—עוֹבֵר לְרוּחַ, literally stubble, which is related to the wind as going along, which runs from the wind. That עָבַר also signifies *discedere, abire, auferri* is seen from passages like Ruth ii. 8; 2 Chron. xviii. 23; Ps. lxxxi. 7; Ezek. xlviii. 14. Comp. כִּי יַעֲבֹר, Isa. xxix. 5.

[13] Ver. 25.—מְנָת־מִדַּיִךְ. In Job xi. 9 also מִדָּה is to be derived from מַד, with the meaning *mensura*=מִדָּה. Comp. OLSH., § 139, S. 268; FUERST., Conc. S. 616, *s. v.*, מַד. Therefore it is not necessary to render מַד here=*upper garment*, with reference to Ruth iii. 15 (coll. Ps. xi. 6; Isa. lxv. 6), [as HITZIG does, declaring that מַד never means *mensura.* HENDERSON: "As the noun is here parallel with גּוֹרָל, *the lot*, which was specially employed in determining portions of land, it seems preferable to explain it of such measurements."—S. R. A.]

[14] Ver. 26.—אֲשֶׁר is causal. Comp. Josh. iv. 23; 1 Ki. viii. 33; Zech. i. 15.

EXEGETICAL AND CRITICAL.

The discourse of the prophet still rising higher, is now addressed to the king and his mother, thus to the heads of the State (comp. on ver 13). He announces humbling of pride (ver. 18), overthrow of power and exile (ver. 19). Enemies from the north (ver. 20), whose friendship was formerly sought, will bring this about to the extreme misery of the subjects (ver. 21), as a punishment for their sins (ver. 22). And since Israel is corrupt to the core, an amelioration on their part is not to be expected (ver. 24), wherefore the Lord must also scatter them to the winds (ver. 24), and as a just punishment of their wickedness (vers. 25-27 a), deliver them up to inconceivable woe (ver. 27 b). The address, which at first has the king and his mother alone in view (vers. 18, 19), passes over gradually more to the latter (vers. 20-22), and at last (since the king's mother may easily be regarded as the mother of the country and representative of the mother-country) to the entirety of the nation (vers. 23-27), the end of the discourse thus returning to the beginning (comp. vers. 9 and 10).

Vers. 18 and 19. **Say to the king ... carried away completely.** — גְּבִירָה is the queen-mother, who had precedence in rank over the many chosen women of the harem. Therefore the book of Kings (with two exceptions) always mentions with the name of the king, that of his mother.—Comp. xxix. 2 ; 1 Kings xv. 12 ; 2 Kings x. 13 (2 Chron. xv. 16).—**Sit down.** Here, also, the prophet attacks worldly pride.—**Of the south.** As the enemy comes from the north, the siege of the cities of the south is a sign that the capital is surrounded, and that flight to the south, is no longer possible. [HENDERSON following HITZIG, more correctly refers this to the complete desertion of the cities,—"the inhabitants having all been carried away into captivity, and not so much as one left to open the gates to a traveler."—S. R. A].

Vers. 20-22. **Lift up your eyes ... thy heels abused.** The circumstance that the princess is mentioned immediately before, and that ver. 20 b appears to refer to the shepherds of the people (the ideal person of the people is represented as wife, mother, daughter, but never as shepherdess), appears to me to indicate that the prophet has made use of the feminine forms שְׂאִי, רְאִי (lift up and see), with primary reference to princess:—**thou hast thyself drawn,** ver. 21, also seems to favor this. For such acts always proceeded especially from the heads of the people, and how powerful the influence of the princesses was, is shown in Maachah, the mother of Asa (1 Kings xv. 13), Jezebel (1 Kings xvi. 31 sqq.), and Athaliah (2 Kings xi.). The sudden change of number is not unusual. Comp. NAEGELSB. Gr., § 105, 7. Anm. 2.—As certainly as the prophet means by *those coming from the north* the same enemies, of which he has already spoken in i. 14, 15; iv. 6, etc., so certain is it also, that he does not know definitely what northern people were meant; comp. remarks on i. 14. Thus it is also declared that this prophecy must have been delivered before the fourth year of Jehoiakim. For from this year (comp. chap. xxv.) Jeremiah knows definitely that the nation is the Chaldeans.—**What wilt thou say,** ver. 21. It having been said of the ruling pair in the previous verse, that they are to lose their flock, it is here added by way of climax, that they will themselves come under the dominion of others, and indeed of those whose friendship might rather have been expected from the previous relations of the kings of Judah towards them. This cannot, indeed, be said of Jehoiakim, for although he had not engaged in direct hostilities against the king of Babylon (his revolt, 2 Kings xxiv. 1, must have taken place after the battle of Carchemish, and therefore long after this prophecy), he was yet a creature of his opponent Pharaoh Nechoh (2 Kings xxiii. 34). But of his predecessors, from Ahaz onward (comp. 2 Kings xvi. 7 sqq.), most of them had entered into more or less intimate relations with the northern empire, partly as seeking aid from it (comp. on ii. 18, 36), partly as introducing among themselves the forms of religion there prevailing (comp. Manasseh, 2 Kings xxi. 3 ; Amon, Ib. xxi. 20 ; Zeph. i. 5 coll. 2 Kings xxiii. 5, 11 sqq.), partly at least like Hezekiah in an apparently innocuous, but really fatal display of courtesy. If with this we take into account the relations of the Jewish kings to Assyria, as well as to Babylon, we are justified, both by the words of this passage, which speaks only generally of אֲלֻפִים מְלַמְּדִים, and the inner unity of those empires (comp. the name Asshur, transferred to the Babylonian and Persian monarchy; 2 Kings xxiii. 29; Ezr. vi. 22).

Vers. 23-27. **Will the Cushite ... after how long!** There might still be a means of escape—Reform. But this is not to be expected, because evil-doing has become the people's second nature. Comp. v. 3; vi. 10, 13-15, 27 sqq.; viii. 4-7; ix. 24, 25.—**Therefore I also.** Ver. 26. The declaration of cause and consequence are entwined after the manner of a chain in vers. 23-27; ver. 23 cause, vers. 24, 25 a, consequence; ver. 25 b, repeated cause; ver. 26, consequence; ver. 27 a, cause again; ver. 27 b, the final consequence. Yet since **I have discovered thy skirts,** evidently points back to ver. 22, where the same is said of the enemy, there is in the words, **Therefore I also,** not merely the antithesis to **thou didst forget me,** ver. 25, but also the thought: whatever the enemy does to thee is done according to my will; I am He who does it.—**From before.** Jeremiah quotes here only Nah. iii. 5, which passage also refers back to Isa. xlvii. 1-3 (comp. KUEPER, S. 136, STRAUSS on *Nahum, S.* 95).—GRAF strangely maintains that עַל־פָּנָיִךְ cannot mean "over thy face;" that the expression never has this meaning. I refer only to 1 Kings xviii. 7, 39. But I also believe that the meaning *face* is not to be insisted upon, but that פָּנֶיהָ here as frequently (comp. i. 13) signifies the fore-part.—**Still after how long!** Jeremiah had maintained in ver. 23 the incorrigibility of the people. From the conclusion of ver. 27 it is seen, that he understands this only of the Israel of the present. In the future, though far distant, he sets forth in prospect the purification of the people, comp. iii. 18 sqq.; xii. 14 sqq.

DOCTRINAL AND ETHICAL.

1. On xiii. 1-11. The Lord has put on Israel as a girdle for His own adornment and for Israel's highest glory. This figure is unquestionably one of the most precious which the Scripture employs to represent the mystery of election. Elsewhere Israel is called Jehovah's inheritance (Deut. iv. 20, vii. 6), His wife and His beloved bride (Hos.

ii. 16 sqq.; Jer. ii. 2), his first-born son (Exod. iv. 22), His servant (Isa. xli. 8), His flock (Jer. xiii. 17), his vineyard (Isa. v. 7), his signet-ring (Hagg. ii. 23. *Vid.* KÖHLER, *S.* 114). Like the last emblem, the girdle also denotes the closest intimacy, indispensable service, a valuable ornament. But great as is the love which the Lord thus shows to Israel in calling them His girdle, as great is the severity with which he declares, that the honor thus received will not save them from destruction. Let every particular Christian church mark this! However closely it may be attached to the Lord, this saves it neither from internal corruption, nor from external judgment. comp. Luke iii. 8, 9. Not this or that particular church, but the whole church only has the promise of infallibility (John xvi. 13) invincibility and permanent existence. (Matt. xvi. 18).

2. On xiii. 17. "This is a good advice. In the words of a hymn, 'when witnesses have sown God's word, they water it with prayer and many thousand tears.' In one hour more grace is drawn by weeping from God the lover of life, who allows Himself to be implored, and who hearkens to the voice of His servants; and hearts, which feel the tears of their lover, are thus brought nearer to their object in a quarter of an hour, than could be accomplished by three sermons . . . 'Everything is born in pain.' . . When ye can do no more, ye witnesses, go and weep and moisten your seed, then you will come again with joy bringing your sheaves with you." ZINZENDORF. *Preces et lacrimæ sunt arma ecclesiæ.*

3. On xiii. 18. "When the enemies are at the gate, the plague in the city or the village, and there is no escape, and human help there is none, then it is of some use for preachers to speak to their princes out of tune; at other times they would be regarded as insolent. . . . Sometimes God's witnesses are clothed with an authority which no one understands, but all feel. Jehoram's visit to Elisha was for the purpose of decapitating him, and a polite conversation was the result, (2 Kings vi. 30 sqq.)" ZINZENDORF.

4. On xiii. 18. "A preacher is not to take court-soup and robes of grace and leave the hare's head unstript, but put salt even into Herod's wounds." FÖRSTER from a sermon of CELICH, 3 *Dom. Adv.*

5. [On ver. 23. "Inveterate habits are justly regarded as a second nature; but being moral in their character, instead of extenuating they aggravate the guilt of those who are the subjects of them. Strong, therefore, as is the physical reference here made, it can with no propriety be employed in support of the physical impossibility of moral reformation." HENDERSON.—"Learned men in our age do not rightly refer to this passage, when they seek to prove that there is no free-will in man; for it is not simply the nature of man which is spoken of here, but the habit that is contracted by long practice. Aristotle, a strong advocate of free will, confesses that it is not in man's power to do right, when he is so immersed in his vices as to have lost a free choice (7 *Lib. Ethicon*) and this also is what experience proves. We hence see that this passage is improperly adduced to prove a sentiment which is yet true and fully confirmed by many passages of Scripture." CALVIN.—S. R. A.]

HOMILETICAL AND PRACTICAL.

1. On xiii. 1-11. "God has cast off His first people, the whole house of Judah and the house of Jerusalem . . God has put on us as a girdle in their stead. For He has not thrown away the girdle and remained naked, but has woven Himself another. This girdle is the church from the heathen. It should know that as God spared not the former, much more will He not spare it, when it sins and is not worthy of God's loins. But he who is joined to the Lord is one spirit (1 Cor. vi. 17) in Christ Jesus, to whom be glory and dominion forever. Amen." ORIGEN, *Hom.* XI. 6.

2. On xiii. 12-17. Exhortation to repentance: *The earthen wine-pitchers of the prophet Jeremiah.* 1. What they signify (the proud yet perishable world); 2. What will be their fate (vers. 14, 17); 3. What is the means of escaping this fate (vers. 15 and 16).

3. [On ver. 17. "Pride the great hindrance to the reception of the word. Pride will not seek 1, the knowledge of God. Pride (*a*) will not brook a rival : (*b*) is unwilling to be taught, (*c*) is unwilling to use the means of knowledge, (*d*) is unwilling to pray ; 2, the favor of God; 3, likeness to God ; 4, communion with God." PAYSON on Ps. x. 14.—S. R. A.]

4. On xiii. 23 sqq. The expression in ver. 23 opens up to us a comfortless perspective. But with God nothing is impossible (Matth. xix. 26). The conclusion of ver. 27 shows us that a purification, though slow and successive is possible, in that we obtain a point of support without ourselves, (Archimedes), and a new principle of life in Christ Jesus. [On ver. 23. I. The great difficulty of reforming vicious habits, or of changing a bad course, arises 1, from the general nature of habits ; 2, from the particular nature of bad habits; 3, the natural and judicial consequences of the great progress and long continuance of a bad course. II. This difficulty is not desperate, but there is some ground of hope and encouragement. 1. There is left even in the worst of men a natural sense of the evil and unreasonableness of sin. 2. Very bad men when they have any thought of becoming better are apt to conceive some good hopes of God's grace and mercy. 3. Who knows what man thoroughly roused and startled may resolve and do ? 4. The grace and assistance of God when sincerely sought is never to be despaired of. TILLOTSON.— S. R. A.]

5. [JER. TAYLOR uses ver. 26 as the text of a sermon on the invalidity of a death-bed repentance.—S. R. A.]

THE FIFTH DISCOURSE.

(Chap. XIV.—XVII. 18).

A fearful drought gives the prophet occasion to offer a hearty and touching intercession for his people. The twice-repeated decisive refusal of his petition, based on the revolt of the people (xiv. 10 coll. iii. 3) compels him to take into view his own situation, rendered exceedingly dangerous in consequence of his prophetic ministry, and then also to present before the people the sad prospect, that from the present calamity which is not spoken of after xiv. 22, there is no hope of escape, but that far worse, even a fearful punitive judgment ending in captivity, is impending.

As to the time of composition no data are furnished by the mention of the drought (comp. rems. on xiv. 1). *That it was before the fourth year of Jehoiakim, and therefore before the decisive turning point in the history of the theocracy and in Jeremiah's prophecies, is evident from the circumstance, already urged, that nowhere in the discourse is the enemy mentioned as known. Twice only and in passages critically suspicious, are the northern iron (*xv. 12*) and the north country as the place of exile (*xvi. 15*) mentioned. On the other hand there are many traces that the discourse cannot have originated long before the fourth year of Jehoiakim or the discourse preserved in ch. xxv. The prophet, when he delivered this discourse, must have been a long time in office. For the hatred against him has become as much deeper as more general (*xv. 10 sqq.*): he is mocked, because the fulfilment of his prophecy is so long delayed (*xvii. 15*): he moreover complains of the endless duration of his sufferings (*xv. 18*), while on the other hand he represents to the Lord that he has obtained universal recognition as a prophet of Jehovah (*xv. 16*). The command not to take a wife (*xvi. 2*) further indicates that the prophet, who at his calling was only a* נַעַר *(i. 6, 7) has in the meantime reached a mature age. The words "this once" also (*xvi. 21*) seem to indicate that the great catastrophe was very near. It is also seen that this discourse must belong to the same period as ch. xiii. Comp. the introduction to the fourth discourse.*

The attempts to ascribe different parts of the discourse to different periods (comp. GRAF, S. 208, 9) *are rendered abortive by the fact that it is a well-compacted whole, as will be seen from the following table of contents.*

FIRST MAIN DIVISION.

THE TWICE REPEATED INTERCESSION OF THE PROPHET CONCERNING THE DROUGHT, AND ITS TWICE REPEATED REJECTION.

XIV. 1—XV. 9.

1. *The first petition,* xiv. 1-9.
2. *The first refusal,* xiv. 10-18.
3. *The second petition,* xiv. 19-22.
4. *The second refusal,* xv. 1-4.
5. *Further portrayal of the sad fate which is impending over the thus rejected nation,* xv. 5-9.

SECOND MAIN DIVISION.

THE CONSEQUENCES OF REFUSAL WITH RESPECT TO THE PERSON OF THE PROPHET AND INSTRUCTION CONCERNING HIS FURTHER COURSE.

XV. 10—XVI. 9.

1. *Complaint and petition of the prophet on account of the consequences of the refusal with respect to his own person,* xv. 10-18.
2. *Tranquilizing and consolatory answer of the Lord,* xv. 19-21.
3. *Instructions how the servant of the Lord should conduct himself among the people on whom the judgment has fallen,* xvi. 1-9.

THIRD MAIN DIVISION.

REASON OF THE REJECTION AND ANNOUNCEMENT OF THE CAPTIVITY.

XVI. 10—XVII. 4.

1. *Idolatry is the cause of the removal into exile,* xvi. 10-15.
2. *More particular description of the removal announced in* xvi. 13, xvi. 16-18.
3. *Refutation of the objection (*xvi. 10*) that the people had committed no sin by their idolatry,* xvi. 19-21.
4. *Refutation of the objection (*xvi. 10*) that the people generally had not served idols,* xvii. 1-4.

CONCLUSION.
XVII. 5–18.

1. *Retrospective glance at the deep roots of the corruption*, xvii. 5-13.
2. *Petition of the prophet for the safety of his person and the honor of his official ministrations*, xvii. 14-18.

FIRST MAIN DIVISION.

THE TWICE REPEATED INTERCESSION OF THE PROPHET CONCERNING THE DROUGHT, AND ITS TWICE RE-PEATED REJECTION. (XIV. 1—XV. 9.)

CHAPTER XIV.
1. *The first petition.*
XIV. 1–9.

1 The word which came to Jeremiah concerning the drought[1]:
2 Judah mourns and her gates are in trouble,
  Covered by mourning[2] even to the earth;
  And the cry of Jerusalem goes up.
3 And their mighty ones have sent their mean ones[3] for water.
  They came to the cisterns, found no water;
  Returned with their vessels empty.
  Ashamed and confounded are they and cover their heads.
4 On account of the ground, which is dismayed, because there was no rain in the land,
  The husbandmen are ashamed and cover their heads.
5 For the hind also in the field has brought forth
  And—forsaken,[4] for there is no green thing there.
6 And the wild asses stand on the high places,
  They gasp for air like the jackals.
  Their eyes have failed, for there is no herb there.
7 Though our sins testify against us, O Jehovah,
  Act[5] for thine own name's sake;
  For many are our apostasies, against thee have we sinned.
8 O thou Hope of Israel, his deliverer in distress;
  Why wilt thou be as a stranger in the land,
  Or as a traveller who pitches (his tent) for the night?
9 Why wilt thou be as a man taken by surprise,[6]
  As a warrior who can give no help?
  Yet thou art in our midst, O Jehovah!
  And we bear thy name; forsake us not![7]

TEXTUAL AND GRAMMATICAL.

[1] Ver. 1.—הבצרות may be the plural of בצרה Jer. xvii. 8, which undoubtedly signifies drought, in case בְּצָרָה Ps. ix. 10; x. 1 is to be otherwise rendered. Comp. עַשְׁתָּרֹת from עַשְׁתֶּרֶת. The plural does not necessarily imply many things, as GRAF supposes. In Hebrew all things which have extension in time or space (comp. שְׁכָבִים, בְּתוּלִים, etc. NAEGELSB. Gr., § 61, 2, e) may be in the plural. The word means a drought, which extends through a plurality of moments (perhaps also of points of space). [HITZIG: The plural stands here *ad designandam diuturnam continuationem siccitatis*, Ch. B. Mich.—S. R. A.]

[2] Ver. 2.—קדרו ל Omst. *pragnans*. Comp. NAEGELSB. Gr., § 112, 7.

[3] Ver. 3.—The form צוּר is found here only, and xlviii. 4 in the Chethibh. Elsewhere צְיֹר.

[4] Ver. 5.—ועזוב, comp. NAEGELSB. Gr., § 92, 2, a; Exod. viii. 11; Gen. xli. 43; Jer. xxxii. 33, 44.

[5] Ver. 7.—On עשה comp. rems. on xviii. 23.

[6] Ver. 9.—נדהם ἅπ. λεγ., since SCHULTENS, is by most commentators derived from the Arabic (*dahama*=to fall upon, surprise).

[7] Ver. 9.—אל־תנחנו literally *ne deponas, dejicias nos* (comp. Num. xix. 9). From this are developed the meanings *relinquere* (Gen. xliii. 33) and *deserere*.

EXEGETICAL AND CRITICAL.

A fearful drought prevails in the land. Proceeding from the whole to the particulars, from the higher to the lower, the prophet shows how the whole of Judah and Jerusalem mourns (ver. 2), how the rulers of the people send out their subjects in vain for water (ver. 3), how the husbandmen also in like distress stand in like consternation. Passing to the beasts he describes how the terrible thirst conquers even the maternal feeling of the hind (ver. 6) and how the wild asses seek the heights in order to obtain some mitigation at least from stronger currents of air (ver. 6). To this the prophet attaches a hearty prayer that the Lord will not have regard only to the acknowledged sins of Israel, but for the sake of His own glory (ver. 7), will no longer act towards His people as a stranger, who *will* not help (ver. 8), or as one who has become powerless and *cannot* help (ver. 9 *a*), but as one who is near, their shield and Father, and who accordingly will not forsake His people (ver. 9 *b*).

Ver. 1. **The word which .. drought.** Contraction of two sentences into one, the predicate of the main sentence having been attracted by the subordinate sentence and become its predicate, so that the subject of the subordinate sentence becomes the predicate. Comp. the same construction xlvi. 1; xlvii. 1; xlix. 34.—Most commentators following the example of Jerome understand this of a future drought, which they believe to be intimated in 2 Kings xxv. 3. The connection is, however, opposed to deferring the drought to the future, as well as that the historical accounts contain no *data* for the determination of any real time.

Vers. 2-4. **Judah mourns ... cover their heads.—Gates** = those assembled in the gates. Comp. Isai. iii. 26; xiv. 31; Ruth iii. 11.—In dark, mourning-attire they seat themselves on the ground. Isai. iii. 26; Jer. viii. 21; Ps. xxxv. 14.—**The cry of Jerusalem goes up,** in contrast to **covered to the earth.**—They do not send their private servants, but as it is a matter of general interest, mean, common people generally.—חתה, **dismayed,** is a relative sentence (comp. Isai. li. 1. NAEGELSB. *Gr.,* § 80, 6, 1). חת, **dismayed,** forms a climax with בוש **ashamed** (comp. FUERST, *H. W. B. s. v.*) and can therefore be used of impersonal objects like the latter. Comp. li. 47; Isai. xxiv. 23; Joel i. 10.—**The husbandmen are ashamed,** *etc.* Comp. Joel i. 11.

Vers. 5 and 6. **For the hind also ... no herb there.** It is not necessary to take 'כ [with HITZIG and HENDERSON.—S. R. A.] in the insecure sense of *Yea.* It is causal: what is said of the distress of the men is confirmed by the distress of the beasts.—**Forsaken.** The hind is celebrated by the ancients for her tender maternal affection (BOCHART, *Hieroz,* P. I., L. III., Cap. 17) to which may be added, that she is said to bring forth with difficulty (comp. Ps. xxix. 9; Job xxxix. 1).—**Like the jackals.** HITZIG and GRAF suppose that jackals cannot be meant here, but that תנים must stand for תני (comp. Ezek. xxix. 3; xxxii. 2) = sea monsters. But I do not see why the open, panting wolf-jaws (the jackal like the wolf belongs to the canine species) should not serve for a comparison in a case like the present. Comp. Job xl. 24.—**Their eyes have failed.** Comp. Job xl. 20; Lam. ii. 11. [HENDERSON:—The wild asses betake themselves to the heights in order to discover some supply. They are very sharp-sighted, and travellers in the desert often avail themselves of their appearance, knowing that there must be herbage and water in the vicinity.—S. R. A.]

Vers. 7-9. **Though our sins .. forsake us not!**—Act for Thy name's sake (comp. ver. 21) *i. e.,* though we cannot ask that thou shouldest interpose actively for our sake, yet do it in behalf of Thine own glory, which is pledged partly for the sake of the election, partly for the sake of Thy renown among other nations. Comp. Num. xiv. 13-16; Deut. v. 28, 29; Ezek. xx. 14; Ps. cix. 21.—**Pitches (his tent).** HITZIG supposes, that the traveller does not trouble himself with a tent. But traveller (ארח) is collective, (comp. ארחה, the caravans). These certainly take tents with them. I do not think therefore that נטה is = to deviate from the way, to turn in (for the night). In this sense סור is elsewhere always used. (Gen. xix. 2; Judges iv. 18; xv. 19, *etc.*) I suppose with the elder commentators אהל, **his tent** (comp. Gen. xii. 8).—**Yet thou art in our midst** (comp. x. 21) *i. e.,* thou art constantly and permanently with us (antithetic to גר ver. 8).—**We bear thy name,** we are called the people of Jehovah. Comp. Exod. v. 3; Deut. xxviii. 10, coll. Jer. vii. 10.

---

e. The First Refusal.

XIV. 10-18.

10 Thus saith Jehovah to this people:
They loved so to wander, their feet they restrained not;
Jehovah moreover hath no pleasure in them;
Now he will remember their guilt and visit their sin.
11 Then said Jehovah unto me:
Pray not on behalf of this people for good.
12 Though they fast, I hearken not to their cry,
And though they offer holocausts and oblations, I have no pleasure in them:
But by the sword, by hunger and pestilence I consume them

13 And I said:
Ah, Lord Jehovah! Behold the prophets say to them,
" Ye will not see the sword, and famine will not come to you,
For I will give you assured peace in this place."
14 And Jehovah said unto me:
The prophets prophesy falsehood in my name,
I have not sent them nor commissioned them,
Nor have I spoken to them;
False vision and divination and nothingness
And the deceit[1] of their heart they prophesy to you.
15 Therefore thus saith Jehovah concerning the prophets,
Who prophesy in my name though I have not sent them,
And who say, There shall be no sword or famine in this land:
By the sword and by famine shall these prophets perish.
16 And the people to whom they prophesy
Shall lie cast out in the streets of Jerusalem,
By reason of the famine and the sword ·
And will have none to bury them,
Them, their wives, their sons and their daughters:
And I pour out over them their wickedness.
17 And thou shalt say to them this word:
Mine eyes shall flow with tears day and night and cease not,
For the virgin daughter of my people[2] is stricken with a grievous stroke,
With a wound very incurable.
18 If I go forth into the field, behold! the slain with the sword,
If I return to the city, behold! the tortures[3] of famine!
For even prophet and priest go into the country and know nothing.

TEXTUAL AND GRAMMATICAL.

[1] Ver. 14.—The forms אֱלִיל and תַּרְמִית here only, everywhere else תַּרְמִית, אֱלִיל.
[2] Ver. 17.—עַ/ בְּ בְּתוּלַת. Comp. NAEGELSB. *Gr.*, § 64, 4; Isa. xxxvii. 22.
[3] Ver. 18.—תַּחֲלוּאֵי, sufferings, torments. Comp. xvi. 4; Deut. xxix. 21; Ps. ciii. 3; 2 Chron. xxi. 19.

EXEGETICAL AND CRITICAL.

The Lord answers the prophet's petition, that in the description of the thirst-stricken beasts he only describes the conduct of the idolatrous people and has thus himself shown the reason why the Lord must punish them (ver. 10). Therefore he (the prophet) may cease his intercession (ver. 11), and the people their ceremonies, for their destruction by famine, sword and pestilence is determined upon (ver. 12). Thereupon the prophet ventures to interpose in behalf of the people from another side. He calls attention to the fact that the prophets have sustained the people in their errors by false promises (ver. 13). Upon this the Lord declares them to be false prophets (ver. 14), and pronounces their destruction (ver. 15). Moreover the same destruction is impending over the people who believe in them (ver. 16), from which it is seen that the prophet has accomplished nothing by his intervention. The wound is incurable (ver. 17); everywhere in the country, as he wanders hither and thither, the prophet meets with death in its most terrible forms. He learns that neither prophet nor priest is any longer in a condition to propitiate the Lord, or avert the calamity from the people (ver. 18).
Ver. 10. **Thus saith Jehovah . . . their**

sin. The commentators mistake the connection of this verse with the preceding, when they overlook, that in כֵּן, **thus**, the Lord refers to the description of the animals tormented with thirst (vers. 5 and 6), and finds in it a description of the passionate, ungovernable lust of the people for idolatry, the true, final cause of the ruin now come upon Israel. As the hind, impelled by her desire for refreshment, abandons her newly born young in order to seek for food, so Israel forsakes the Lord in order to satisfy his lust for idolatry. As the wild-ass runs to the high places, in order there, with wide-open jaws, to drink in at least a cooler breath of air, so Israel pants for idols. We are justified in this interpretation the rather as the prophet has previously used essentially the same emblems of idolatry. In ii. 24 he compared idolatrous Israel with the wild-ass, who (there indeed in the heat of sexual impulse) gasps for breath (comp. xiv. 6). *Wandering* (נוּעַ) is there also censured in the people, as a symptom of their lust for idols, as in those who cannot restrain the foot (comp. ii. 25). In ver. 10 a, then there is a statement of the reason, why He is compelled to refuse, as He does in ver. 10 b, the petition of the prophet (ver. 7 sqq.). This second half of the verse is moreover taken verbatim from Hos. viii. 13; ix. 9.
Vers. 11 and 12. **Then said Jehovah . . .**

I consume them. To this denial the Lord adds by way of climax as before (vii. 16) a prohibition of further intercession, at the same time announcing that the people also will accomplish nothing by the ceremonies of divine worship, which train of thought we found also in xi. 14 sqq.—For good. Comp. Deut. xxviii. 11; xxx. 9; Jer. xxi. 10; xxiv. 5, 6.

Vers. 13–16. And I said . . . pour out over them their wickedness.—Assured peace [lit., peace of truth]. Comp. right seed, ii. 21. So here genuine, lasting, secure prosperity. Comp. Isa. xxxix. 8; Jer. xxxiii. 6. In general comp. vi. 14; iv. 10.—Divination (קֶסֶם) is used here in a bad sense, as almost always, comp. Numb. xxiii. 23; 1 Sam. xv. 23; Ezek. xiii. 6, 23, etc.—With the description, cast out in the streets, comp. viii. 2; xvi. 4; xxv. 33. —I will pour out, etc. Comp. ii. 19; Hos. ix. 15.

Vers. 17 and 18. And thou shalt say to them . . . know nothing. The formula in ver. 17 never introduces greater sections. It occurs verbatim as here only in xiii. 12. Here certainly at the beginning of a strophe. But there is nothing in the tenor of the words to prevent their being used wherever a definite single word is to be marked. Comp. xxviii. 7.—

Let mine eyes, etc. As before (viii. 23; xiii. 17), the prophet here expresses the thought that nothing but weeping is left for him.—Stroke, etc. Comp. x. 19; xxx. 12.—For even prophet, etc. The prophet evidently wishes to say, that he has looked about everywhere, both in the country and the city, but has found only symptoms of irretrievable destruction. This moreover was not only his conclusion, for all the priests and prophets who, like him, had gone into the country, had also learned that there was nothing more to be done, so that it must be said of them: לֹא יָדְעוּ, i. e. non sapiunt (comp. Ps. lxxiii. 22; Job xxxiv. 2), they know nothing.—סָחַר occurs only in Gen. xxxiv. 10, 21; xlii. 34, as a finite verb, is contrasted in these passages with the Accusative and signifies at any rate not simply to go directly out, but (after the manner of business-people) to go hither and thither (commeare, ἐμπορεύεσθαι). Here then at any rate we must suppose a journeying directed to several points. The אֶל is explained by Jerusalem's being considered as the central point from which they went now this way now that way. The omission of the article before אֶרֶץ is not uncommon (comp. on iii. 2.)

3. *The Second Petition.*

XIV. 19–22.

19 Hast thou utterly rejected Judah, or has thy soul disgust at Zion?
    Why then hast thou smitten us and there is no cure for us?
    We hoped for peace but there came nothing good;—
    For a time of healing, and behold terror!
20 We acknowledge, O Jehovah, our wickedness,
    The guilt of our fathers, that we have sinned against thee.
21 Reject us not for thy name's sake;
    Disgrace not the throne of thy glory;
    Hold in remembrance, break not thy covenant with us.
22 Are there then among the vain deities of the heathen rain-dispensers?
    Or will the heaven [itself] give rain?
    Art not thou He, Jehovah, our God?
    And our hope because thou hast made all these things?

EXEGETICAL AND CRITICAL.

The prophet is not easily turned from his intercession. He here begins again the second time. He asks the Lord why He has rejected Judah and Zion (ver. 19). He then adduces three reasons why this cannot be. 1. Israel acknowledges his sins (ver. 20); 2. Jehovah must help for His own glory and for the sake of the covenant (ver. 21); 3. There is no other dispenser of rain and of blessing than He (ver. 22).

Ver. 19. Hast thou utterly . . . terror. קוֹץ repetition from viii. 15.

Vers. 20, 22. We acknowledge . . . made all these things. As in ver. 7, so also here (ver. 20), the prophet supports his petition on the confession of sin. Therefore he likewise adds, in ver. 7, an appeal to the Lord's own honor. Hence he further strengthens his appeal by urging (a) that Zion's destruction would disgrace the throne of the Lord Himself, in so far as Zion in part is the throne of the Lord, and in part conceals Him in its midst (comp. on xvii. 12); (b) he reminds the Lord of the covenant made with Israel, which is to be kept, not to be broken. Comp. xi. 1 sqq.; Lev. xxvi. 11, 12, which passage seems to have been in the prophet's mind.—From ver. 22 we perceive plainly the connection with the first petition, ver. 1 sqq.—**Art not thou He?** אתה is never a simple copula, not even in Eccles. (comp. i. 17 with ii. 13). Here it is demonstrative, *i. e.* referring to the previously mentioned idea of rain-dispenser. Thou alone art He, who art at the same time our God and the object of our hope. God alone is the rain-dispenser, for He has made all things. Comp. Job v. 10; xxxviii. 25, 26.—**For thou hast made** is the basis of **Thou art he;—our God**, *etc.*, is therefore a parenthesis. Comp. NAEGELSB. *Gr.* § 80, 8.—[HENDERSON: "From the commencement of ver. 19 to the end of the chapter the people are introduced as doing what the prophet was forbidden to do on their behalf."—S. R. A.]

CHAPTER XV.

4. *The Second Refusal.*

XV. 1–4.

1 And Jehovah said unto me :
 If Moses and Samuel stood before me,
 Yet my soul is not inclined towards this people :
 Away with them from my presence! Out with them!
2 And if they say to thee: Out whither shall we go ?—
 Then say to them: Thus saith Jehovah:
 He who is for death to death, he for the sword to the sword,
 And he who is for famine to famine, and he for captivity to captivity.
3 And I appoint over them four kinds, saith Jehovah :
 The sword to kill and the dogs to tear,
 The birds of heaven and the beasts of the field to devour and to destroy.
4 And I make them a horror¹ to all kingdoms of the earth,
 On account of Manasseh, the son of Hezekiah, king of Judah,
 And on account of what he did at Jerusalem.

TEXTUAL AND GRAMMATICAL.

¹ Ver. 4.—Here and in Ezek. xxiii. 46 זועה is found without marginal reading, but in Isa. xxviii. 19 the older form זועה. In the other places (besides those quoted in Jeremiah also 2 Chron. xxix. 8), where EWALD (comp. § 53, *b*) would read זועה (scarecrow, sport [of chance]) there is always the Keri זועה. Except in Isa. xxviii. 19, the word occurs only as the designation of the *terminus in quem* after נתן or before היה. The root זוע has both in the Hebrew (it occurs in the Old Test. only in Eccl. xii. 3; Esth. v. 9; Hab. ii. 7) and in the dialects (comp. Dan. v, 19; vi. 27) the meaning of violent motion, commotion. Hence זועה is commotion, quaking, horror.

EXEGETICAL AND CRITICAL.

The second petition is refused with a decisiveness which allows of no repetition and the people are rejected from the presence of the Lord (ver. 1), but not to a definite place, for they are delivered up to destruction in the most various forms (ver. 2), and to destroyers of the most terrible kinds (ver. 3), so that their destruction will excite the horror of all nations; but all this will correspond to the seed of abomination which Manasseh, the son of Hezekiah, scattered in Judah (ver. 4).

Ver. 1. **And Jehovah said ... out with them!** Moses is an intercessor, Exod. xvii. 11 sqq.; xxxii. 11 sqq.; Numb. xvi. 13; Ps. cvi. 23.—Samuel in 1 Sam. vii. 8; viii. 6; xii. 16-23; xv. 11; Ps. xcix. 6; Ecclus. xlvi. 16. Comp. HERTZOG, *Real-Enc.* XIII. *S.* 398.—Noah, Daniel and Job are mentioned in a similar manner in Ezek. xiv. 14; and in later times Jeremiah himself in 2 Macc. xv. 14.—The object of **away**, according to the preceding context, and to **whither shall we go?** ver. 2, can be no other than the people. Vers. 2 and 3. **And if they say ... to destroy.** The question, **whither shall we go?** presupposes the thought of a mere banishment. It is declared in what follows that far worse than this is meant.— **He who is for death.** A fearful destructive blow is to follow, which causes the people to be scattered and drives individuals, without selection or respect of persons, into the hands of the agents of death.—**Death**, with sword, famine and captivity, is evidently the relatively spontaneous death by disease or pestilence (דבר), wherefore the latter word is also used with the other in xiv. 12; Ezek. xiv. 21; xxxiii. 27; comp. Jer. xliii. 11.—Ver. 3 fortifies this judgment of destruction, by declaring it in a certain measure permanent. For and I appoint declares that Israel is to be placed as it were under the jurisdiction of these four destructive forces, as also in Ezek. xiv. 21 it is expressly said that the Lord will send His "four sore judgments—the sword and the famine and the noisome beast and the pestilence," upon Jerusalem.—**Kinds**, מִשְׁפָּחוֹת. Comp. רוּחַ, the four generations, Prov. xxx. 11 sqq. Since the four instruments here mentioned correspond to the four kinds of destruction mentioned in ver. 2, it is evident that ver. 3 bears to ver. 2 not a logical but rhetorical relation. The sword moreover represents the judgment on the living, the three others the judgment on the dead. Comp. xiv. 16; Deut. xxviii. 26.

Ver. 4. **And I make them ... at Jerusalem**. Repetition of the first half of the verse xxiv. 9; xxix. 18; xxxiv. 17. The expression is taken from Deut. xxviii. 25. Concerning Manasseh comp. 2 Kings xxi. 1-17; xxiii. 26; xxiv. 3. The biblical accounts dismiss the long reign of this king with remarkable brevity. We obtain the impression that this is the effect of a certain reluctance to recall this name, which represents the darkest portion of the history of Judah, an epoch which is to be regarded as the concentration and end of all ungodliness.

5. *Further description of the sad fate impending over the rejected nation.*

XV. 5–9.

5 For who will have pity on thee, O Jerusalem?
  Or who will have sympathy for thee?
  Or who will turn aside to wish thee well?
6 Thou hast rejected me, saith Jehovah, [and] wentest backwards.[1]
  Then I stretched out my hand against thee and destroyed thee:
  I was weary of repenting.
7 And I winnowed them out with a fan
  At the gates of the land;
  I orphaned, I destroyed my people,—
  For they had not turned them from their ways.
8 Their widows are become to me more than the sand of the sea.
  I brought them over the mother of the chosen[2] the spoiler at noon-day;
  I caused to fall on her sudden anguish[3] and terror.
9 She who bore seven is exhausted;
  She breathed out her soul [expired];
  Her sun went down while it was yet day;
  She was ashamed and confounded [put to shame];
  But the residue I will give to the sword,
  Before their enemies, saith Jehovah.

TEXTUAL AND GRAMMATICAL.

[1] Ver. 6.—אָחוֹר תֵּלֵכִי. The imperfect is frequently used to designate a fact often repeated in the past. Comp. NAEGELSB. *Gr.*, § 87. f.

[2] Ver. 8.—[A. V. "I have brought upon them against the mother of the young men a spoiler at noon-day;" BOOTHROYD: "against their mother city, a chosen one that spoileth," etc. HENDERSON:—"The words עַל־אֵם בָּחוּר (ver. 8) have been very differently construed. Nor is the difficulty which they present by any means easy of solution, however simple the words may be in themselves. LXX. ἐπὶ μητέρα νεανίσκους. Some compare the phrase אֵם עַל בָּנִים *the mother with her children* [Syr., Arab., C. B. MICH., EWALD, etc.—S. R. A.] but the position of the preposition before and not after אֵם renders such construction untenable. Others take אֵם בָּחוּר to be in the construct state: *the mother of the young man* [CHALD., KIMCHI, J. D. MICH., HITZIG, etc.—S. R. A.] or regarding the nouns as collectives: *the mothers of the young men* [DE WETTE, MAURER, ROSENMUELLER, etc.—S. R. A.] but neither of these affords a suitable sense. JAHCHI, CAPELLUS, CASTALIO, DE DIEU, DOEDERLEIN, EICHHORN, DAHLER, consider אֵם *mother*, to mean *the metropolis*, as 2 Sam. xx. 19, and אַפִּי 2 Sam. viii. 1. The word is thus used on Phœnician coins. Comp. the Arab. ࢴ the Greek μήτηρ; Callin. Fragm., 112; and the Latin *mater*, Flor. iii. 7, 18; Ammian, xvii. 13; GESENIUS, *in voc.* The objection of SCHURRER, that it wants the article, is of little force, as the prophets sometimes omit it for the sake of condensation. See Isai. xxi. 12, and NORDHEIMER'S *Gr.*, II. p. 13, note. This, on the whole, as the text now stands, is the preferable interpretation."—S. R. A.]

[3] Ver. 8—בַּצְהֳרָיִם has the meaning of unusual, unexpected. Comp. vi. 4; Am. viii. 9.—עִיר ἄπ. λεγ. radically related to צוּר, צַר — *coarctatio, angor.*

EXEGETICAL AND CRITICAL.

After the definite refusal in vers. 1-4, the prophet can declare only that there is no further prospect of pity or succor for Jerusalem (ver. 5). The people having rejected the Lord, He rejects them, and will not as before retract this determination (ver. 6). Winnowed out of the country, Israel is bereaved of his men and sons (vers. 7-9 a); and the enemy will come with the sword after the fugitive remnant (ver. 9 b).

Ver. 5. **For who will take pity ... to wish thee well.** From vers. 1-4 it follows with absolute certainty that Jehovah will no longer help, and that therefore Israel is inevitably lost. כִּי, **For,** implies a reference to this thought. No longer any escape! If the Lord will not, who else will have pity on the people? (Isai. li. 19; Nah. iii. 7). Who indeed will even ask how they are? (שְׁאָל לְשָׁלוֹם properly = to ask after one's good health, to greet, Gen. xliii. 27; Exod. xviii. 7; Judges xviii. 15, etc.) The thought seems to be thus implied, that still less will any one do aught for the welfare of the people, or any longer intercede for them as the prophet has done (xiv. 7 sqq.; 19 sqq.).—**Turn aside.** סוּר is here, as frequently, to deviate from the direct, proposed way, in order to turn to some other object, with which, as here, the idea of taking trouble may be connected. Ruth iv. 1; 1 Ki. xx. 39; Exod. iii. 3.

Ver. 6. **Thou hast rejected me ... of repenting.** The reason for the declaration in ver. 5, that Israel is irretrievably lost, is stated in ver. 6, and more particularly in ver. 7 sqq. The reason first given, in ver. 6 a, is objective, it being declared what Israel has done to draw upon himself such a punishment. The words **then I stretched** to **repenting** express the subjective reason, i. e., they declare what facts on the part of the speaker (i. e., of God) are presented as causae efficientes of destruction. The præterite וָאַט, etc., is not strange; as the apostasy is an already accomplished fact, so also is the hostile position which God assumes towards it. The "stretched-out arm," which is so often mentioned as Israel's saving arm (Deut. iv. 34; v. 15; xxvi. 8, etc.), signifies the hostile position of God towards the enemies of the people. Elsewhere the stretching out of the hand frequently designates the declaration of war, or the command to use force; 1 Ki. xiii. 4; Job xv. 25; Isai. v. 25; ix. 11; x. 4; Jer. vi. 12; li. 25; Ezek. vi. 14; xiv. 9. 13, etc.—Perhaps also the assonance of וָאַט to אָתָּה is intended.—**Destroyed thee** is a summary intimation of the import of the gesture **I was weary,** etc., a more particular definition, in so far as it declares that the destruction will no longer be deferred as heretofore by a gracious "repenting." Comp. iv. 28; vi. 11; Isai. i. 14

Vers. 7-9. **And I winnowed them .. before their enemies.** I do not think with Graf that שַׁעֲרֵי הָאָרֶץ is to denote the uttermost lands of the earth. How then could בְּ be used? The preposition retains its proper meaning, if as in Nah. iii. 13 we understand the exits of the land. The Lord winnows so powerfully that as the chaff flies out over the threshing-floor, so Israel flies out through the exits of the land to a distance.— **Had not turned,** etc., is a causal sentence.—In vers. 8 and 9 the prophet uses similar colors to those in xiv. 16, 17. Comp. xi. 22; xvii. 21.— The words אִם בָּחוּר, variously interpreted by the commentators, are most easily explained by the antithesis to the subsequently mentioned יֹלֶדֶת הַשִּׁבְעָה. Even the strongest women, both those who have borne distinguished warriors, and those who have had numerous sons, shall perish. Without insisting on the singular in בָּחוּר I believe that it includes the idea of quality, as שִׁבְעָה does of quantity. (Comp. 1 Sam. ii. 5).—[Henderson:—"By the 'young spoiler' [text 'destroyer'] is meant Nebuchadnezzar II., who, when his father was old and infirm, had part of the Chaldean army committed to him, and after defeating Pharaoh Necho at Carchemish marched forward against Jerusalem and captured it. The attack being made at noon indicates the unexpectedness by which it was characterized, that being the time of day when, owing to intense heat, military operations are carried on with less vigor."—Hitzig: "The description in ver. 8 points to a lost battle; and on this hypothesis all the single features of the picture in vers. 7-9 may be brought into one point of view, so as to present one event. The author then refers to the battle of Megiddo, the more probably (2 Ki. xxiii. 29) as the figure of the sun setting in bright daylight might then be founded on the eclipse which took place in that valley 30th Sept., A. D. 610. (Vid. Thenius on 2 Ki. S. R. A.]—**Breathed,** etc., From Job xxxi. 39 the meaning of the word ex-spirare seems plain. The rendering "to sigh" is too feeble in this connection.—**Her sun,** the sun of her life, and the happiness (comp. Mal. iii. 20; Ps. lxxxiv. 12) which she had in her sons is gone down. בָּאָה as in Gen. xv. 17; 2 Sam. ii. 24; Mic. iii. 6. וּבֹעֲרִי, comp. the previous "at noon-day."—**And confounded.** בוֹשָׁה. The reference to the mother is to be preferred; for the sun itself does not suffer shame, but those who by the setting of the sun are reduced from the condition of an honored mother to the wretched state of a bereaved and childless one. In Isai. xxiv. 23 it is the sun and moon themselves which must pale before a more brilliant star.—**Deliver to the sword.** Comp. Mic. vi. 14.

SECOND MAIN DIVISION.

THE CONSEQUENCES OF THE REFUSAL WITH RESPECT TO THE PERSON OF THE PROPHET AND INSTRUCTIONS CONCERNING HIS FURTHER COURSE (XV. 10—XVI. 9).

1. *Complaint and petition of the prophet on account of the consequences of the refusal with respect to his person.*

XV. 10-18.

10 Wo unto me, my mother, that thou hast borne me,
 A man of strife and a man of contention to the whole land:
 I have not borrowed nor lent, yet all curse me.[1]
11 Jehovah said: Verily, I distress thee[2] for thy good,
 Verily the enemy shall approach thee imploringly[3]
 In the time of calamity and in the time of distress.
12 Will then iron break iron from the north and brass?
13 Thy substance and thy treasures will I give up for spoil, not for hire,[4]
 But on account of all thy sins and in all thy borders.
14 And I take thee[5] with thine enemies into a land that thou knowest not,
 For a fire[6] is kindled in my nostrils which shall burn over you.[6]
15 Thou knowest it, O Jehovah, remember me,
 And visit me, and avenge me of my persecutors;
 Sweep me not away by[7] thy long suffering;
 Know that for thy sake I have suffered reproach.
16 Thy words were offered and I devoured them,
 And thy words[8] were to me the joy and rejoicing of my heart.
 For I bear thy name, O Jehovah, God of Zebaoth.
17 I sat not in the assembly of the joyful, nor was merry.
 Before thy hand I sat solitary, for thou hast filled me with indignation.
18 Why then has my pain become perpetual,[9]
 And my wound helpless,[10] that will not heal?
 Art thou then become to me as a deceitful brook,[11]
 As precarious water?

TEXTUAL AND GRAMMATICAL.

[1] Ver. 10.—כלה מקללוני. This wholly abnormal form (comp. OLSH., § 206 b) which as *forma mixta* has been variously explained, is evidently due, as J. D. MICHAELIS, HITZIG, GRAF, MEIER have recognized, to a wrong division. It should read כֻּלֹּה קִלְלוּנִי. The attraction of the ם to the following word may have been occasioned by the circumstance that the form ending with it is not found elsewhere (similar formation כֻּלָּבֶם Deut. i. 22. Comp. אוֹתָהֶם Ezek. xxiii. 45, 47; אֶתְהֶם Gen. xxxii. 1; xix. 8). The 1st Pers. כֻּלָּהֶם however is found in 2 Sam. xxiii. 6.

[2] Ver. 11.—אִם לֹא שֵׁרוֹתִךָ. The Chethibh may be read שֵׁרוֹתִךָ (who attack thee, anomalous Inf. Kal. from שָׁרַר, as HITZIG), שֵׁרוֹתִךָ (*solvendo te*, ROSENMUELLER), שֵׁרֻגְתָךְ (*initium tuum*, GESEN.), שֵׁרֻגְתָךְ *solutio tua* sc. *erit*, WINER), שֵׁרוֹתָךְ (in different meanings: *confirmabo te* or *exhilarabo te*, J. D. MICHAELIS; *firmabo te*, MAURER, EWALD; I do thee injury, I oppress thee, GESEN., *Thesaur.*, MEIER). The Keri is שֵׁרִיתִךָ Piel from שָׁרָה, which verb occurs besides only in Job xxxvii. 3 (disputed in the latter place) and is said to signify *to loosen* like the Aram. שְׁרָא (comp. Dan. ii. 22; iii. 25; Ezr. v. 2). [So HENDERSON.—S. R. A.] The old translators vacillate and alter arbitrarily. Vulg., Targ., RASCHI, KIMCHI read שְׁאֵרִיתְךָ for שֵׁרִיתְךָ (comp. 1 Chron. xii. 38; OLSH., S. 70 and 412), which they regard as = *reliquiæ tuæ* or *finis tuus* thy remnant, thy exit, for which however אַחֲרִית always stands elsewhere. [A. V.: it shall be well with thy remnant]. I agree with GESENIUS in his *Thesaurus* and MEIER. The *scriptio defect.* is no objection. Comp. *ex. gr.* עֲנָתָךְ Nah. i. 12; לְבַבְתִּנִי Song of Sol. iv. 9. שָׁרַר means *torsit, contorsit*. Hence שֹׁרֵר, *oppressor* (Ps. viii. 3; xxvii. 11; liv. 7), שַׂר cloud (*contortium*) שָׂרָה *torques*, שַׁרְשְׁרָה *catena*. The Lord tells the prophet for his consolation that the oppression will eventuate in favor of his best interests. Comp. ver. 19 sqq., לְטוֹב besides only in xxxii. 39. Elsewhere לְטוֹבָה (xiv. 11; xxi. 10; xxiv. 5, 6; xxxix. 16; xliv. 27).

³ Ver. 11.—יִ הִפָנַיְתִּי בְּ פָּנַע signifies in vii. 16; xxvii. 18; Job xxi. 15; Ruth i. 16 to apply to one, press one with petitions. Accordingly Hiphil here quite regularly = to cause such application, urging, although the Hiph. is elsewhere used in the sense of the Kal. (Isai. liii. 12; lix. 16; Jer. xxxvi. 25).

⁴ Ver. 13.—בְּכִחִיר לֹא. There is probably here a corruption of the text. In the parallel passage xvii. 3 we read after אֶתָן the words בְּמֹתֶיךָ בְּחַטָּאת בְּכָל־נְבוּלֶיךָ. Since now בְּמֹתֶיךָ might very easily become בְּכֹחִיר, especially if we consider the difficulty of this word, it is very natural to perceive in the latter a corruption of the former. The unmeaningness of the sentence then led to the addition of לֹא which is wanting in the LXX. The author of the gloss might also have had in mind passages like Isai. xlv. 13; lii. 3; lv. 1. What occasioned the deviation from xvii. 3 it is difficult to tell. At any rate, if the words are to yield any sense, the first וּ must be rendered by "and indeed" (comp. NAEGELSB. Gr., § 111, 1), and וּבְכָל־נְבוּלֶיךָ be referred to the first section of the verse.

⁵ Ver. 14.—וְהַעֲבַרְתִּי. In xvii. 4 we have וְהַעֲבַדְתִּיךָ, which is also given by the LXX., Syr., Chald. The Hiphil from עָבַר is evidently a corruption, but in the gloss the genuine text, and therefore to be retained, although no commentator has yet been able to give a satisfactory explanation of it. From יָדַעְתִּי לֹא we see that the people (at any rate with the previously mentioned treasures) is regarded as the object.—Comp. ix. 15.

⁶ Ver. 14.—אֵשׁ־כִּי, etc. The words are taken verbatim from Deut. xxxii. 22, while in xvii. 4 we have קְדַחְתֶּם (transit. as in Isai. l. 11; lxiv. 1). For עֲלֵיכֶם we find in xvii. 4 more appropriately עַד־עוֹלָם.

⁷ Ver. 15.—לְ as in לֶאֱמוּנָה, ix. 2; לְפִשְׁעָה, xxx. 11. Comp. Isai. xi. 3; xxxii. 1.

⁸ Ver. 16.—דְּבָרֶיךָ. The Chethibh דְּבָרְךָ is quite impertinent. Comp. NAEGELSB. Gr., § 105, 4 b, 3.

⁹ Ver. 17.—נֶצַח. Subst. (comp. Prov. lxxiv. 3; 1 Chron. xxix. 11) = perpetuitas. Comp. NAEGELSB. Gr., § 74.

¹⁰ Ver. 18.—אֲנוּשָׁה, comp. xxx. 15; Isa. xvii. 11; Mic. i. 9.

¹¹ Ver. 18.—אַכְזָב. Comp. Mic. i. 14. It is the opposite of אֵיתָן נַחַל, Deut. xxi. 4; Am. v. 24. Comp. Exod. xiv. 27.

EXEGETICAL AND CRITICAL.

After a sorrowful lament of the prophet, that without any fault of his, all curse him (ver. 10), follows (if vers. 11-14 are genuine) first a comforting assurance from the Lord, that all will accrue to his advantage and that even his enemies in their distress will turn to him as suppliants (ver. 11); and then a description of this distress: it comes as iron from the North which cannot be broken by other iron or brass (ver. 12); all wealth in all the borders of Israel will be plundered on account of their sin (ver. 13), and the people will be carried away into a strange land in consequence of the violent and inextinguishable anger of Jehovah (ver. 14). In vers. 15-18 follows a further address of the prophet to the Lord, which, by the words "Thou knowest it," may possibly be connected with ver. 12, but may also be connected with ver. 10. The prophet prays the Lord for His gracious interposition, for vengeance on his enemies, for long-suffering forbearance, since he is indeed suffering for God's sake (ver. 15). He grounds his petition further on his willing devotion to the Lord as His instrument (ver. 16), and his having walked worthy of this great honor (ver. 17). In conclusion another lament of the prophet: Why is there then for me no cure, no recreation? (ver. 18).

Ver. 10. **Wo unto me ... all curse me.** Had the intercession of the prophet in ch. xiv. been heard, his lot, in so far as it depended on his countrymen, would have been more agreeable. But now that so stern a refusal has been given he sees the whole fury of the people discharged upon his person. The mention of the calamity of the mother, vers. 8 and 9, reminds the prophet of his own mother, not however to lament on her account, but on his own, that he was ever born. Comp. xx. 14; Job iii. 3; 1 Macc. ii. 7. —Lending and borrowing cause most law-suits. The prophet neither receives loans from others (נֹשֶׁה, Isa. xxiv. 2), which as a bad debtor he did not repay, nor does he himself lend money (נֹשֶׁה בְּ, Deut. xxiv. 11, נֹשֶׁה creditor, exactor, Ps. cix. 11), which as a stern creditor he calls in with rigor.—Observe the contrast between the accusations, which according to ver. 10 were universally raised against the prophet, and the touching petitions, which he, xiv. 7-19, offers for his people. He thus gives a reply to those accusations, which causes their unrighteousness most distinctly to appear.

Ver. 11. **Jehovah said ... in time of distress.** The formula **Jehovah said** (אָמַר י״) thus prefixed is found besides only in Jer. xlvi. 25, and in no other prophet. I cannot agree with GRAF, who in xlvi. 25 would attach it to the preceding context. (Comp. הִנְנִי פֹקֵד). We cannot then say that this position of the formula is a proof of the spuriousness or corruption of the text.—The Lord presents to the prophet's view a second pleasing turn in his affairs: even his opponents, who now press him in a hostile way, shall then be brought to press him with supplications, because they perceive their only salvation to be in his intercession. This is more particularly explained in ver. 12.

Ver. 12. **Will then iron ... brass?** The words are very variously construed. The most simple construction, which agrees well with the context, is to take the first iron, בַרְזֶל, as the nominative, and the two following as in the objective case. Will then iron, i. e. any other iron, brought by men, break the northern iron or brass? That the northern iron is the northern empire (xiii. 20) is clear. The most celebrated iron and steel manufacture among the ancients was that of the Chalybeans in Pontus, of whom Strabo says, οἱ δὲ νῦν Χαλδαῖοι Χάλυβες τὸ παλαιὸν ὀνομάζοντο, XII. p. 826. Comp. J. D. MICHAELIS. Observv. phil. et crit., in Jer., Ed. SCHLEUSNER, p. 136. [Comp. WINER, R.-W.-B., II. S. 512; SMITH, Bibl. Dict., II. p. 1376.—S. R. A.]. It is accordingly quite suitable to represent this northern nation itself under the figure of the strongest iron. The connection with the preceding is this: thine enemies among the people will yet turn to thee as their only refuge, when they have learned their inability to master the northern iron. For the fulfilment see xxxvii. 3; xlii. 2 sqq.

Vers. 13 and 14. **Thy substance ... burn over you.** These verses are evidently intended to give a plainer description of the distress, merely intimated in ver. 11, and briefly and obscurely described in ver. 12. The words are, however, taken from xvii. 3, 4, where they are found in the more original form and proper connection.—**Not for hire.** The thought occurs similarly only in Ps. xliv. 12. In this passage, however, it is the selling of the people, not of their property and treasures, which is spoken of. It is also a question whether in Ps. xliv. 12 the selling is to be understood in a literal sense =thou causest thy people to be sold into slavery by their conquerors at a mean price (comp. Joel iii. 8, 11, 12; VAIHINGER on Ps. xliv. 12). Since now it is doubtful whether the thought that God sells His people for nothing or without return is biblical, and still more doubtful whether it may be said God sells the *treasures* of His people for nothing, the view gains in probability that there is here a corruption of the text. Comp. the TEXTUAL NOTE 4.

Verses 11 and 12 contain in themselves nothing to lead us to doubt their integrity, nor do they in the connection form an incongruous element. Ver. 11 contains a preliminary tranquilization of the prophet, ver. 12 a more particular characterization of the distress intimated in ver. 11, and the reason of **approach imploringly,** *etc.*—**Thou knowest,** in ver. 15, may be connected with ver. 12, in the sense : I cannot indeed conceive how that is possible, but Thou Lord knowest it. For since vers. 11 and 12 contain the words of the Lord to the prophet, "Thou knowest it" cannot be an appeal by the prophet to the divine testimony, but only for the purpose of self-tranquilization. But on the other hand it cannot be denied, that this interruption in the prophet's lament is the more remarkable, as Jeremiah afterwards continues in ver. 15 *as though he had received no consolation* (comp. especially ver. 18) and the consolatory statements of ver. 11 recur in ver. 19 sqq. For these verses also declare that the affliction will accrue to the honor and welfare of the prophet and that the enemies will yet be compelled to apply to him. This is also favored by the perfect appropriateness with which ver. 15 is connected with ver. 10. The prophet had in ver. 10 protested his innocence, for which in ver. 15 he appeals to the Omniscient as a witness. Verses 13 and 14 bear in a much higher degree the stamp of spuriousness. For 1. They prolong in an unnecessary manner (as mere filling out of the portrayal of the previously intimated distress) the interruption of the connection ; 2. They are a mere quotation from xvii. 3, 4 and textually corrupt, with which it accords, that they contain an address to the people which does not suit the connection; 3. The words **Thou knowest.** ver. 15, are then disconnected, for neither can they be referred to the close of ver. 14 nor to vers. 13 and 14 together, since these verses contain neither the words of the prophet, nor anything which appeared incredible to the prophet.

Ver. 15 *a.* **Thou knowest it ... thy longsuffering.** On thou knowest it *vid. supra;* comp. Ps. xl. 10; Ezek. xxxvii. 3.—**And visit me,** פָּקְדֵנִי is frequently used of a gracious visitation of God after a period of disfavor: Gen. xxi. 1; Exod. iii. 16; iv. 31; Ruth i. 16; Ps. viii. 5, 6; Isa. xxiii. 17, *etc.* Comp. Ps. cvi. 4.— **Avenge,** *etc.* וְהִנָּקֶם לִי מֵ properly=avenge Thee for my good upon my enemies. This construction here only. Comp. 1 Sam. xxiv. 13; Numb. xxxi. 2.—**By thy long-suffering.** Since the prophet is not himself conscious of having deserved the divine anger, the long-suffering can be referred only to the enemies: "Suffer not that in consequence of the delay of Thy vengeance I be swept away of my enemies."

Vers. 15 *b*-17. **Know that ... filled with indignation.** In these words the prophet presents the grounds on which he expects help from the Lord. He first prays the Lord to consider that he is suffering for His (the Lord's) sake. Comp. Ps. lxix. 8 (Zeph. iii. 18). He then appeals to the willingness with which he offered himself as the Lord's organ, and his life in accordance with his high calling.—**Thy words,** *etc.* The prophet did not excogitate what he was to proclaim but found it, it was offered to him. The *found* is according to Old Test. usage frequently that which is present of itself in opposition to that which one has produced or procured by his own activity. Comp. Gen. xix. 15; 1 Sam. xxi. 4 ; xxv. 8.—**Devoured.** As in Ezek. ii. 8; iii. 3 coll. Rev. x. 9, 10, he designates by eating the eager complete reception of them into the mind. The commentators refer to PLAUTUS, *Aulul.* III. 6, 1, *nimium lubenter edi sermonem tuum.*—**For I bear,** *etc.* The word of the Lord may then have become the joy of his heart because it effected that "the name of Jehovah was named over him" (comp. rems. on vii. 10), *i. e.* that he was designated as a prophet of Jehovah in opposition to the prophets of the idols (comp. the prophets of Baal, 1 Kings xviii. 19; 2 Kings x. 19). This designation was to him an honorary title of the highest value. But by this it is not excluded that the word of the Lord in itself was already a cause of rejoicing to him.—**I sat not.** The prophet here describes how his life externally had been spent in accordance with the prophetic calling. He had avoided the society of idle, pleasure-seeking men, he had sat in solitude, the feeling of being divinely possessed as well as the sorrow caused by the predominant objects of his vision, *viz.* human sin and divine punishment, rendering him incapable of taking part in the proceedings of the merry.—**Before thy hand.** The expression "hand" designates the divine operation as immediate and irresistible. Comp. Isa. viii. 11; Ezek. iii. 14; viii. 1; xi. 5; xxxvii. 1, *etc.*—**For thou hast filled me,** *etc.* The prophet is filled with indignation and anger by what he beholds in consequence of the divine operation. He cannot possibly be angry with God. Rather is he full of the divine wrath (vi. 11) at the sin of men and at the necessity of punishing them. Moreover we see from ver. 16 that indignation is not the only feeling of the prophet, nor the only reason which detained him from the society of men. He was in part too divinely troubled, in part too joyful in God, to feel at home in such society. [HENDERSON: "The hilarity which the prophet had experienced was not that of the ungodly, who at their festive meetings treated divine things with scorn. With these he had had no fellowship, but because of the faithful communication of his inspired messages he had been expelled from society and made the object of their fiercest indignation. The occurrence of "indignation" with "hand" in this verse has generally induced the supposition that by the latter the afflicting power of God is intended; but it seems more in accordance with the bearing of the connection to regard the expression as designed to convey the idea of powerful divine impulse or prophetical inspiration. Comp. Ezek. i. 3; iii. 14, and frequently. Thus Vatablus, Clarius."—S. R. A.] Ver. 18. **Why then . . . precarious water.** The prophet concludes with an exclamation of hopelessness. After what he could declare of himself in vers. 16 and 17 he thought he had some claim for protection and consolation. But there is no prospect of this. As in despair he therefore inquires, Why is this?—According to the sense the whole verse must be rendered as a question, and **why** therefore be referred to the second section of the verse.—**Precarious.** Comp. Isa. xxxiii. 16. [" On TINDAL's objections to this passage, see WATERLAND, *Scripture Vindicated*, p. 245." WORDSWORTH.—S. R. A.]

2. *The Lord's tranquilizing and consolatory answer.*

XV. 19-21.

19 Therefore thus saith Jehovah:
   If thou return, I will cause thee again to stand before me;[1]
   And if thou bring forth the precious without the base, thou shalt be as my mouth.[2]
   They shall return to thee, but thou shalt not return to them.
20 And I will make thee to this people a brazen wall, a strong one;
   And they will contend against thee, but not prevail over thee;
   For I am with thee to deliver
   And to preserve thee, saith Jehovah.
21 And I preserve thee from the hand of the wicked,
   And redeem thee from the might of the violent.

TEXTUAL AND GRAMMATICAL.

[1] Ver. 19.—וַאֲשִׁיבֶךָ, etc. The construction is like לְךָ יִקְרָאוּ תְּסִיבִי לֹא, Isa. xlvii. 1, 5. Comp. NAEGELSB. *Gr.* § 95, *g, Anm.*

[2] Ver. 19.—כְּפִי, *Kaph veritatis*. Comp. NAEGELSB. *Gr.* § 112, 5 c.

EXEGETICAL AND CRITICAL.

The Lord answers the prophet by promising him anew, together with a mild correction and on the condition of blameless purity, the honor of being permitted to serve Him as His organ (ver. 19 a). He then promises the return to him of his enemies (ver. 19 b), inexpugnable firmness (ver. 20), protection and deliverance from all dangers (ver. 21).

Ver. 19. **Therefore thus . . . return to them.—If thou return.** In these words there is evidently a gentle reproof. In the preceding context, especially ver. 18, the prophet had allowed himself to be carried away into doubt of the fidelity and trustworthiness of the Lord. In this there was an element of alienation from the Lord. Without entering on a confutation or accusing the prophet directly of his departure, he gives him to understand that such a departure has taken place only by the conditional sentence, " If thou return." For turning back presupposes a turning away. Comp. iv. 1.—**To stand before me,** in the sense of mediatorship, which at the same time includes the honor of a servant and of one who stands very near his Lord: xv. 1; xviii. 20; xxxv. 19; xl. 10.—**Bring forth,** etc. From the context such a bringing forth only can be spoken of as on the one hand is opposed to the blameworthy utterances of the prophet in ver. 18, and as on the other hand qualifies him to be the Lord's mouth. הוֹצֵא is therefore to be taken in the sense in which it occurs, *ex. gr.* in Job xv. 13, which passage has in general a remarkable resemblance to the present. Then מִן is *away from, far from, without.* Comp. x. 14 ; Job xi. 15 : xxi. 9. *Vid.* NAEGELSB. *Gr.* § 112, 5 *d.*—**They,** etc. The triumph of a witness of the truth consists in this that his opponents finally agree to his testimony. Comp. Prov. xvi. 7.

Vers. 20 and 21. **And I will . . . violent.**

The Lord confirms the prophet in his office and His promise in the same words in which He had assured him of both in the beginning, i. 18, 19.—**Brazen wall.** ["The Roman Poet felt something of the great truth contained in these divine words, when he said,

'*Hic murus aheneus esto,
Nil conscire sibi, nulla pallescere culpa.*'
(HORAT. I. Epist. i. 60)." WORDSWORTH.—S. R. A.]

CHAPTER XVI.

3. *Instructions as to the conduct of the Lord's servant among the people who have incurred judgment.*

XVI. 1-9.

1   The word of Jehovah came also unto me, saying,
2   Thou shalt not take to thee a wife,
    Nor shalt thou have sons and daughters in this place:
3   For thus saith Jehovah of the sons and of the daughters born in this place,
    And of their mothers that bare them,
    And of their fathers that begat them in this land:
4   Miserable deaths[1] shall they die,
    They shall not be mourned nor buried;
    They shall become dung on the surface of the earth;
    And by sword and famine shall they perish;
    And their carcases shall serve for food to the fowls of heaven and the beasts of the earth.
5   For thus saith Jehovah: Enter not into the house of mourning,[2]
    And go not to bewail them or to commiserate them;
    For I have taken my peace from this people, saith Jehovah,—
    The loving-kindness and the mercy.
6   Both great and small shall die in this land;
    They shall not be buried and men will not mourn them,
    Nor cut themselves, nor make themselves bald for them:
7   Nor will men break bread[3] for them in mourning,
    To console them concerning the dead;
    Nor will they present them the cup of consolation,
    Concerning father or mother.
8   And also thou shalt not go into the house of feasting [*lit.* drinking],
    To sit with them to drink and to eat.
9   For thus saith Jehovah Zebaoth, the God of Israel:
    Behold, I take away from this place before your eyes and in your days,
    The voice of joy and the voice of gladness,
    The voice of the bridegroom and the voice of the bride.

TEXTUAL AND GRAMMATICAL.

[1] Ver. 4.—מְמוֹתֵי תַחֲלֻאִים [*literally*, deaths of diseases], different kinds of death in torment. Comp. Jer. xiv. 18 [the sick (pining) of famine]. מְמוֹת here only and in Ezek. xxviii. 9; comp. כוֹתִי, Ezek. xxviii. 10.

[2] Ver. 5.—בֵּית מַרְזֵחַ. מַרְזֵחַ occurs besides only in Am. vi. 7 (in the construct state, מִרְזַח. Comp. OLSH. § 198, a. b. S. 376, 7), in the latter place with the meaning of jubilation. The root רזח, which does not occur in the Hebrew, has according to the dialects (Arab. *marsih*, *rar rehemens*) the meaning of loud crying, be it for joy or sorrow.

[3] Ver. 7.—פָּרַס interchangeably with פָּרַשׂ (Lam. iv. 4=*frangere, dividere*. With לָהֶם Isa. lviii. 7. Here לָהֶם is wanting, but is found in some codd. of Kennicott. The LXX. and JEROME also express it. At any rate the bread, corresponding to the cup of consolation, is intended, which in Ez. k. xxiv. 17, 22 is called לֶחֶם אֲנָשִׁים; Hos. ix. 4 לֶחֶם אוֹנִים. The suffixes in לְנַחֲכוֹ as in אָבִיו and אִמּוֹ refer to the idea present, not in the words but in the mind of the mourner (Comp. EWALD, § 318 *a*).

EXEGETICAL AND CRITICAL.

The prophet (in xv. 10) had cried to his mother in complaint: Why hast thou borne me? He had explained in ver. 17 that he lived alone and far from all society of cheerful men. The Lord had thereupon in vers. 19-21 consoled him and promised him protection and deliverance. But the great national calamities should nevertheless continue. Hence both the complaint of the prophet in ver. 10 and his separation in ver. 17 are approved. Yea, it is added in confirmation that he is not even to take a wife and beget children (xvi. 2), for these would not escape the universal calamity of death (vers. 3 and 4),—further that he is not to go into any house of mourning or give any token of sympathy in the cases of death, in order to indicate that the dead will remain without burial or mourning;—finally that he is not to go into any house of feasting, in order to indicate that all joy, especially all nuptial rejoicing, will cease.

Vers. 1-4. **The word ... beasts of the earth.** The prohibition to marry is closely connected with the complaint of the prophet in ver. 10: let it not be that thy children charge thee as thou hast charged thy mother. Comp. viii. 2; xxvi. 33.—**With the sword,** comp. xiv. 12, 15; xliv. 12, 27.—**Become food.** Comp. vii. 33; xix. 7; xxxiv. 20.

Vers. 5-7. **For thus saith ... father or mother.** The connection of ver. 4, with ver. 5 sqq., is as follows: the inhabitants shall perish miserably and lie unburied, for it is the command of the Lord that the prophet go into no house of mourning, i. e., it is the divine purpose to decree that punishment of which the command to the prophet is only the outward sign. The ground of this purpose is that God has withdrawn His favor from the people. (**For I have taken,** etc.).—**Commiserate.** Comp. xv. 5; xxii. 10; Job ii. 11; xlii. 11.—**For I have taken.** etc. Comp. Joel ii. 10; iv. 15; Gen. xxx. 23.—**Loving-kindness.** Comp. Hos. ii. 21; Zech. vii. 9.—**Cut. make bald,** customs forbidden by the law (*Vid.* Lev. xix. 28; Deut. xiv. 1), but which were, however, practised. Comp. xli. 5 (xlviii. 37). קָרְחָה [baldness] is mentioned with especial frequency: Isa. xxii. 12; Ezek. vii. 18; Am. viii. 10; Mic. i. 16. Comp. EWALD, *Alterthümer d. V. Isr.* [*Jewish Antiquities*] S. 225; SAALSCHUETZ, *Mos. Recht.*, S. 380.—**They shall not break bread** [A. V., "tear *themselves*." Comp. TEXTUAL NOTES].—**The cup of consolation,** comp. Prov. xxxi. 6, 7.

Vers. 8 and 9. **And also thou shalt not ... voice of the bride.** In this relation also the absence of the prophet is to indicate that joyful festivals are things denied by the Lord.—**Before your eyes.** This calamity will not just come upon a later generation, but upon the present.—**Voice of the bridegroom.** Comp. vii. 34; xxv. 10.

THIRD MAIN DIVISION.

REASON OF THE REJECTION AND ANNOUNCEMENT OF THE CAPTIVITY (XVI. 10—XVII. 4).

1. *Idolatry the cause of the removal into exile.*

XVI. 10-15.

10 And it shall come to pass, when thou shalt shew [declarest to] this people all these words, and they shall say unto thee, Wherefore hath [doth] the LORD [Jehovah] pronounced [denounce] all this great evil against us? or what is our iniquity? or what is our sin that we have committed[1] against the LORD [Jehovah] our God?
11   Then shalt thou say unto them:
    Therefore, because your fathers have forsaken Me. saith Jehovah,
    And went after other gods, and served them and worshipped them,
    And have forsaken me and not kept my law ;
12 And ye have done still worse[2] than your fathers,
    Since ye walk[3] every one according to the hardness of his evil heart,
    That ye hearken not unto me;—
13 Therefore I cast you away out of this land
    Into the land that ye have not known, ye and your fathers ;
    And there ye shall serve the[4] other gods day and night,
    Because[5] I will shew you no favour.[6]
14 Therefore behold, the days come, saith Jehovah,
    When it shall no more be said: As Jehovah liveth,
    Who brought up the children of Israel out of the land of Egypt;

15 But: As Jehovah liveth, Who brought up the children of Israel from the land of the North, And from all lands whither he had driven them: And I bring them back into their land, that I gave to their fathers.

TEXTUAL AND GRAMMATICAL.

1 Ver. 10.—אֲשֶׁר הִטְאָנוּ. The *nota relationis* may be regarded as a pronoun in the accusative, because it is said—הַטְאָה, Exod. xxxii. 31; comp. Lev. iv. 3; Deut. xix. 15.
2 Ver. 12.—וְהַרְעֹתֶם. Comp. NAEGELSB. *Gr.*, § 95, *e*.
3 Ver. 12.—וְהִנְּכֶם, causal sentence. Comp. NAEGELSB, *Gr.*, § 110, 1, *e*.
4 Ver. 13.—The אֶת before אֱלֹהִים in this passage may have this reason, that the word may be regarded as determinate in itself. Comp. NAEGELSD. *Gr.*, § 68, 1. *Anm*. 1.
5 Ver. 13.—אֲשֶׁר־לֹא. אֲשֶׁר is causal here as in xiii. 25. Comp. NAEGELSB. *Gr.*, § 110, 1.
6 Ver. 13.—חֲנִינָה ἅπ. λεγ.

EXEGETICAL AND CRITICAL.

The grounds of the punitive judgment described in the previous context are stated in this way, that the prophet is commanded to answer the people when, assuming an air of innocence, they inquire into those grounds (ver. 10): because your fathers forsook me and served other gods (ver. 11), and ye moreover have done worse (ver. 12), therefore I cast you forth into a strange land, where you may serve those gods; and will show you no more favor (ver. 13). To this are added two verses repeated in xxii. 7, 8, in which it is declared that the oath by Jehovah who brought Israel out of Egypt, will be changed into the oath by Jehovah who brought Israel out of the north country. If these verses are genuine here, their object must be a double one: 1. Confirmation of the threatening pronounced in ver. 13. 2. Mitigation of the harsh utterance at the close of ver. 13, by the prospect of future deliverance. This strophe, moreover, forms the argument of the third division, for the three following strophes serve only to describe more in detail, and to elucidate some points in the first.

Vers. 10-13. **And it shall come to pass . . . shew you no favour.** This mode of speech, *viz.*, the hypothesis of a question of the people and answer to it, is found v. 19; xiii. 22. —**Therefore that your fathers,** *etc.* Comp. vii. 24-28; ix. 11-15; xi. 7, sqq.—**Hardness.** Comp. iii. 17; ix. 13; xviii. 12.—**that ye hearkened not.** Comp. xvii. 23; xviii. 10; xix. 15; xlii. 18.—**Therefore I cast,** *etc.*, comp.

xxii. 26, 28.—**Into the land.** The article is explained by the prophet's reference to what has been already said (xv. 14).—**And ye shall serve.** What was before sin is now punishment. The prophet has in view Deut. iv. 28; xxviii. 36, 64. —**Day and night.** The servants' toil consists in this, that they must attend to their service day and night.—**Because I will shew.** This causal sentence refers not to the first clause of the verse, which is circumstantially founded on the preceding context from ver. 10, but on the second. Because Jehovah has withdrawn His favor, they have to seek help of their idols.

Vers. 14 and 15. **Therefore behold . . . gave to your fathers.** לָכֵן, therefore, at the beginning of ver. 14 is entirely in place. On this very account, because Israel, according to ver. 13, were to be cast away into a foreign land, the form of oath is to be correspondingly altered. Accordingly the purport of vers. 14 and 15 is primarily not consolatory, but sad. It confirms the declaration concerning the captivity. In so far, and because Jeremiah frequently quotes himself, as well as because interruptions of a prophecy of sorrowful import by consolatory prospects also frequently occur (comp. iv. 27; v. 10, 18), these verses may well be genuine here. I **bring back** is then connected with **I cast away** in ver. 13. Moreover that the words, even if transferred by Jeremiah himself, are in their original position in xxiii. 7, is clear from the connection, as well as from "the more peculiar and concrete form of the . ext"(HITZIG) of this passage.

More particular description of the removal announced in xvi. 13.

XVI. 16-18.

16 Behold I send for[1] many fishers,[2] saith Jehovah, who shall fish them.[3]
  After that I send for many hunters, who shall hunt them
  Down from every mountain, and from every hill,
  And from out of the clefts of the rocks.
17 For my eyes overlook all their ways; they are not hidden from me,
  Nor is their iniquity concealed from mine eyes

18 And I recompense the first time double their iniquity and sin,
Because they have desecrated my land with the carcases of their monsters,
And have filled mine inheritance with their abominations.⁴

TEXTUAL AND GRAMMATICAL.

¹ Ver. 16.—לְשָׁלַח ל is used here with the meaning of "to send for, cause to be brought," exactly as in xiv. 3 in the expression שָׁלַח לָמַיִם. It is, therefore, quite a mistake to assume an Aramaism here as in xl. 2 (comp. 2 Chron. xvii. 7; Ezr. viii. 16), or, to refer to entirely different passages, as 1 Kings xx. 7. Even Numb. xxii. 40, cannot be compared.
² Ver. 16.—דָּיָּגִים. The word occurs besides only in Isa. xix. 8 and Ezek. xlvii. 10, in the former place in the form דַּיָּגִים, in the second רוּן, without any proposed alteration of reading in the Keri. In the present passage the Keri probably proceeds from the endeavor to produce uniformity with צַיָּדִים.
³ Ver. 16.—וְרָגוּם ἅπ. λεγ.—FUERST and EWALD (§ 127, a) would explain רָגִין as an abbreviation of הֵרִין. But why should there not be a root with a weak י as middle radical? Comp. NAEGELSB. Gr., § 37; OLSH. § 231 d, S. 486.
⁴ Ver. 18.—As כלא is not construed with בְּ, we must connect with כִּמְלֹאן only וְתוֹעֲבוֹתֵיהֶם (comp. li. 7; xliv. 22).

EXEGETICAL AND CRITICAL.

This strophe serves only to describe more fully the facts announced in ver. 13, **Therefore I cast you,** etc. The deportation is to take place, as it were, according to the rules of art. The enemies are therefore compared to fishermen who fish out a lake, and with hunters who exterminate the wild animals from a hunting-district, even from the most effectual covers (ver. 16). So also the hiding of the Israelites will not avail, for all their ways are so manifest to the Lord that their iniquity lies displayed before His eyes (ver. 17). And so He recompenses to them for the first time double their sin by banishment from the land which they have desecrated by their idolatries. In this it is implied that in case of a second provocation, God's punitive justice will apply a still higher measure than that of double retribution.

Vers. 16-18. **Behold ... abominations.— Many hunters.** The reason why the adjective *many* is used, is that the prophet means to say: then again I send for many, *viz.*, hunters.—**Hunters** is, therefore, epexegetical. That רַבִּים is here used as a numeral (as in Ps. lxxxix. 51; Prov. xxxi. 29; 1 Chron. xxviii. 5; Neh. ix. 28), is less probable. From vers. 17 and 18 it is evident that fisher and hunter were not to bring together the Israelites out of exile, but to drive them out of their own land.—As it follows from בִּי, ver. 17, the figure declares that no conceal-

ment will profit them. As fishers and hunters, who proceed according to the rules of their art, know how to drive out the animals from all their hiding-places, so will the enemies do with the Israelites. The former will see through all the plans and measures of the latter and defeat them, for they are revealed to them by God, before whose sight those measures equally with the sins of Israel lie bare and exposed. Comp. xxiii. 24; xxxii. 19.—רִאשׁוֹנָה, **first time.** [HENDERSON, following HITZIG, *etc.*, renders "previously."—S. R. A.] The explanation according to which this word is referred to ver. 15 (HITZIG, EWALD, UMBREIT), would be perfectly satisfactory if it did not leave unregarded the evidently intended antithesis to מִשְׁנֶה **double.** This explanation can be met satisfactorily without any alteration of the text (as attempted by GRAF, according to Isai. lvi. 7), if we recognize that the prophet assumes the possibility of a second visitation. Then he would say: for this first time double will be recompensed (Isai. lxi. 7; Zech. ix. 12), but in case of repetition a much severer measure will be rendered:—as in reality the second destruction by the Romans was total in comparison with the first merely partial one.
—**Because,** etc. The punishment has an inner relation to the sin: they have desecrated the land and rendered it uninhabitable, they must therefore leave it.

---

3. Refutation of the objection (xvi. 10) that the people had committed no sin by their idolatry.

XVI. 19-21.

19 O Jehovah, my strength and my fortress,
And my refuge in the day of distress!
"To thee will the heathen come from the ends of the earth, and will say:
Falsehood only have our fathers inherited,
Vapour, and there is none among them that profiteth.
20 Should a man make himself gods? And they are not gods!"
21 Therefore behold I teach them this once,
And teach them to know my hand and my might,
And they shall know that my name [is] Jehovah.

CHAP. XVII. 1-4.   161

EXEGETICAL AND CRITICAL.

Having in vers. 14-18 given a confirmation and further description of the judgment threatened in ver. 13, the prophet in the two following strophes, xvi. 19-21, and xvii. 1-4 goes back to xvi. 10, where it is said that the people deny having sinned against Jehovah. This denial may have a double meaning. First it may be intended to declare that it is not a sin to serve other gods, together with Jehovah. Secondly, the meaning may be that the fact itself that Israel served other gods is disputed. To this denial in the first sense the prophet replies by directing his glance into the proximate future, in which the heathen will perceive what Israel has failed to perceive, *viz.*, that the gods are vanity, that Jehovah is alone God, and that therefore idolatry is sin (vers. 19, 20). Now since Israel might and should long ago have perceived that which even the heathen will perceive at last, but did not do so, Jehovah will bring this truth to their knowledge by a thoroughly incisive lesson (ver. 21).

Vers. 19 and 20. **O Jehovah my strength ... not gods.** Since the prophet addresses the Lord as **my strength,** *etc.*, and then says that the heathen, after they have perceived the nothingness of the idols, will all come to this Lord, he includes himself, as it were, together with the heathen, among the believers in Jehovah, but excludes Israel from this communion, until instructed by the judgments they recognize their errors, and obtain the same saving knowledge.—**My strength.** Comp. Ps. xxviii. 7, 8; lix. 17; 2 Sam. xxii. 3.—**Heathen** [*lit.*, nations.—S. R. A.] Even this word shows that it is not the tribes of Israel that are meant. (MEIER).—**Falsehood only.** Comp. x. 14; li. 17.—**Our fathers inherited.** The expression is still stronger than if it had been **we inherited.** The tradition is false from the very beginning.—**Profiteth.** Comp. Isai. xliv. 10; Jer. ii. 8, 11.—**Should a man.** The words of the heathen in which they themselves set forth the vanity of the idols. Manufactured gods are on this very account no gods. The sentence **and they are not gods** is to be taken in a causal sense. Comp. NAEGELSB. *Gr.*, § 109, 4.

Ver. 21. **Therefore behold ... my name Jehovah.** From the connection the prophet's object cannot be to give instruction concerning the future conversion of the heathen. He only wishes, by the good which he says of the heathen, to set the folly of Israel in a clearer light. We are therefore after the sentences "I come to thee," and "the *heathen* will come to thee" to supply: but Israel comes not to thee. There is a reference to this thought in **therefore.** Because Israel has not the knowledge which he might long have had, as well as, or better than the heathen will have it in the future, the Lord will this once impart it to them.—**This once** (comp. x. 18) like **the first time** in ver. 18, refers to the impending first catastrophe of the theocracy by the Chaldeans. Israel is to feel the hand of the Lord, and thus learn to understand the significance of His name. The prophet evidently alludes to Exod. iii. 14. We perceive in what sense the understanding of the name is meant, from the words "I will teach them to know (*i. e.*, to experience, to feel) My hand and My might," in comparison with the expression הֶבֶל, which is used of the idols in ver. 19. By that visitation, namely, will Jehovah manifest Himself as the *Really Existent* (this point from the connection is evidently here brought into the foreground) in opposition to the non-existent deities, and thus bring Israel to the consciousness that he has certainly sinned in worshipping other gods together with Jehovah. Comp. Isai. lii. 6, coll. Jer. xxiii. 27; Exod. vi. 3.

["This passage (xvi. 19—xvii. 14) is appointed as the *Haphtorah*, or Proper Prophetical Lesson, to Lev. xxvi. 3—xxvii. 34, where God declares the vanity of idols, and the blessings of faith, repentance and obedience." WORDSWORTH.—S R. A.]

CHAPTER XVII.

4. *Refutation of the objection* (xvi. 10) *that the people had not generally served idols.*

XVII. 1-4.

1   The sin of Judah is written with an iron stylus,[1]
    Graven with a diamond point on the tablet of their heart,
    On the horns of their altars;
2   As their children remember their altars,
    And their images of Baal[2] by[3] the green trees, by the high hills.
3   My mountain together with[4] the fields,
    Thy substance and all thy treasures will I give up to spoil,
    Thy heights!—for thy sin in all thy borders.
4   And thou shalt withhold thy hand from the inheritance which I have given thee;
    And I cause thee to serve thy enemies in a land that thou knowest not:
    For ye have kindled a fire in my nostrils that shall burn forever.
11

TEXTUAL AND GRAMMATICAL.

1 Ver. 1.—צִפֹּרֶן. This word, which occurs besides only in Deut. xxi. 12 is the nail, *unguis*, but since the finger-nail cannot be used for the engraving of ineffaceable writing, the word must mean a sharp, cutting instrument in general, in correspondence with the fundamental meaning of the root (= *incidere, insculpere*. Comp. Aram. טְפַר).

2 Ver. 2.—[A. V.: their groves; DE WETTE: their Astartes (but comp. EXEGET. *Notes*).—S. R. A.]

3 Ver. 2.—Explanations which render עַל as local = with, together with (אֵל, R. SAL.), or cumulative = *una cum* (SED. SCHMIDT and others) are as unsatisfactory as the reading בְּעָרֵי, which is found in the Chald., Syr., and in 16 Codd. of KENNICOTT and 9 of DE ROSSI.

4 Ver. 3.—בְּ in the midst, but in the sense of accompaniment, together with. Comp. xi. 10; NAEGELSB. *Gr.*, § 112, 5, *a*.

EXEGETICAL AND CRITICAL.

The denial of having sinned against Jehovah (xvi. 10) must mean that the fact of idolatry is denied. Against such a bold and shameless assertion the prophet rises here with visibly increasing indignation. He says that the sin of Judah is certified, and as it were, recorded in the archives, viz. (*a*) in their own conscience, in which the memory of their idolatrous abominations is fixed like an ineffaceable brand, and (*b*) externally, on the horns of the altars, where the blood of the slaughtered children adheres as an equally ineffaceable memorial (ver. 1). These two testimonies were just as deep and inextinguishable to them, the actors present, as to the children the impression of that horrible cult which had snatched away so many from their midst would remain unforgetable. And so deep was this impression, that the mere sight of green trees and high hills was sufficient to refresh it continually (ver. 2). On the basis of the facts thus certified, the prophet repeats the announcement of the divine punishments, which will consist in plunder of substance, desolation of the land, according to the analogy of the year of release, and deportation into an unknown land (vers. 3 and 4).

Vers. 1 and 2.* **The sin of Judah . . high hills.** ORIGEN (*Hom.* XVI. *ed. Lommatzsch.*, *S.* 301), ISID. HISP. (*De Pass. Dom.*, ch. 22). GHISLER (*ad h. l.*) by Judah here understand Judas Iscariot.—**Iron stylus.** Comp. Job xix. 24.—**diamond-point,** שָׁמִיר, which occurs besides, in this sense, only in Ezek. iii. 9; Zech. vii. 12, appears to designate especially the diamond, which serves as a pointed cutting instrument,

---

* The LXX. does not contain verses 1-4. Without doubt Jerome is correct in saying, *forsitan pepercerunt populo suo.* ORIGEN in the *Hexapla* gives under asterisks the following translation, which he found in other translators: Ver. 1. Ἁμαρτία Ἰούδα γέγραπται ἐν γραφείῳ σιδηρῷ, ἐν ὄνυχι ἀδαμαντίνῳ, ἐγκεκολαμμένη ἐπὶ τοῦ στήθους τῆς καρδίας αὐτῶν, καὶ τοῖς κέρασι τῶν θυσιαστηρίων αὐτῶν.
Ver. 2. Ἡνίκα ἀναμνησθῶσιν οἱ υἱοὶ αὐτῶν τὰ θυσιαστήρια αὐτῶν καὶ τὰ ἄλση αὐτῶν ἐπὶ ξύλου δασέος, ἐπὶ βουνῶν μετεώρων, ὀρέων ἐν ἀγωρῷ.
Ver. 3. Ἰσχὺν σου καὶ πάντας θησαυρούς σου εἰς προνομὴν δώσω, τὰ ὑψηλά σου ἐν ἁμαρτίᾳ ἐν πᾶσι τοῖς ὁρίοις σου.
Ver. 4. Καὶ ἀφαιρεθήσεται (al. ἀφαιρεθήσῃ), καὶ ταπεινωθήσεται (al. ταπεινωθήσῃ) ἀπὸ τῆς κληρονομίας σου, ἧς ἔδωκά σοι, καὶ ἀναβιβάσω σε ἐν τοῖς ἐχθροῖς σου ἐν τῇ γῇ ᾗ οὐκ ἔγνως· ὅτι πῦρ ἐγκεκαυσται ἐν τῷ θυμῷ μου, ἕως αἰῶνος καυσθήσεται. Τάδε λέγει κύριος. Thus in MONTFAUCON, *Hexapl. Tom.* II., p. 210.—EUSEBIUS also, *Dem. Ev.* X. 5 (comp. ii. 25), communicates the words, remarking that he found them ἐν τοῖς λοιπῶν ἑρμηνευτῶν ἐκδόσεσιν ὑπὸ μαρτυρίῳ ἀστερίσκων ἐν τοῖς ἀκριβέσι τῶν παρὰ τοῖς Ο. ἀντιγράφοις. DRUSIUS remarks that *in nonnullis codd. graecis et in uno Vaticano leguntur sub asteriscis*.

---

since everywhere else (Isai. v. 9; vii. 23-25; ix. 17; x. 17; xxvii. 4) it is used in the meaning of "thorn." Comp. HERZOG, *Real-Enc.* III., *S.* 642; WINER, *R.-W.-B.* I., *S.* 284.—**On the tablet,** *etc.* Passing momentary events make only a superficial impression. But whatever has exercised a long-continued and intensive activity is deeply graven. In opposition to the assertion (ver. 10) that Israel has not sinned against the Lord, the prophet points to the continuance of idolatry among the people, and the deep, inextinguishable traces, which it has left behind. These are double; of an external and internal sort. Internally is the conscience, the remembrance, the whole spiritual *habitus*, which keeps before Israel the fact of the long practised idolatry. Externally are the idol-altars, with the blood of the children offered upon them, crying towards heaven, which testify of the sin to all the world. It is therefore audacity on the part of the people to pretend that they have forgotten the fact. The expression *write on the table of the heart* is found also in Prov. iii. 3; vii. 3.—**horns of the altars.** That the idol-altars are meant is evident 1, from the plural, for there was but a single altar of Jehovah (J. D. MICHAELIS); 2, from the connection, for Israel's sin was to be read only on the idol-altars, not on the altar of the Lord,—or on the latter only in so far as they had perhaps used it for idolatrous worship (comp. 2 Chron. xv. 3; WINER, *s. v. Brandopferaltar*). The altars in ver. 2 are doubtless also those of the idols, and identical with those mentioned in ver. 1.—On the horns of the altar of burnt offering and the sprinkling of these with the blood of the guilt offering, comp. Exod. xxvii. 2 (coll. Ps. cxviii. 27); xxix. 12; Lev. iv. 18, 25, 30, 34; viii. 15; ix. 9. That the idol-altars also had such horns is clear from Am. iii. 14. Comp. WINER, *R.-W.-B. s. v. Hörner.*—**Their altars,** *lit.*, **your altars.** On the change of person comp. rems. on v. 14; xii. 13.—**remember.** We may reject at the outset the ungrammatical explanations which either take בְּ = לְ (so that their children remember, LUTHER, ZWINGLE, substantially CALVIN) or understand God as the subject of **remember** (SEB. SCHMIDT, CLERICUS, CH. B. MICHAELIS). All these interpretations are at least very harsh, which regard the Jews as the subject, (*ut recordantur filiorum suorum ita altarium, etc., i. e.*, their altars are as dear to their hearts as their children, R. SALOMO, D. KIMCHI, ABARBANEL, DIODATUS, MAURER; remembering their children, they remember also the altars on which they offered them, HITZIG) or which take

CHAP. XVII. 1-4.

בְּ in the sense of *because*, *if*, (JEROME, Chald., Arab., and many later) or which find the apodosis in ver. 3 (EWALD, UMBREIT). Since in ver. 1 there is evidently likewise the idea of a *monumentum*, a record assuring a perpetual remembrance, the reciprocal relation of vers. 1 and 2 is indicated at the outset. There is a third memorial of the sin denied by the Israelites, the testimony of which is the more unexceptionable as it proceeds from the mouth of children (Ps. viii. 3; Matth. xxi. 16): the remembrance by the children of that horrible worship to which so many from their midst fell a sacrifice. The prophet points to an effect of that horrid ritual, which is not indeed elsewhere expressly testified, but is in itself entirely natural. Why should not Moloch have been the terror of the Israelitish children, when there was such real and sad ground for it, as is wanting in other bugbears which terrify the children of the present day?—**Their children** is therefore the subject of remember, and the construction is as *ex. gr.*, v. 26; vi. 7. Comp. NAEGELSB. *Gr.*, § 95, 2.—**Images**, etc. The אֲשֵׁרִים are the masculine images of Baal [not of Astarte, as HENDERSON.—S. R. A.] (comp. 1 Ki. xiv. 23; 2 Ki. xvii. 10; xxiii. 14, etc.) as אֲשֵׁרוֹת are primarily and in general the images corresponding to the female principle of Baal. What was their form is still undecided, also whether they had special relation to the service of Moloch. Should the latter not be the case, yet their relation to the murderous rites of child-sacrifice is beyond a doubt. For children were offered to Baal in all his forms, comp. vii. 31; xix. 5; xxxii. 35. HERZOG, *Real-Enc.* I. S. 638; IX., S. 715.—

By the green trees, עַל־עֵץ. HITZIG and GRAF rightly take עַל here in a causal sense connecting it with **remember**, not with **altars**. If the place was to be designated where the altars and images stood, we cannot conceive why the prophet should write "*on* green trees," and deviate from the stereotyped form of "under every green tree." It is accordingly more probable that it is to express that the mere sight of green trees and high hills awoke in the Israelite children the remembrance of those terrible altars and images.

We can certainly show no passage in which עַל is used, after a verb of remembrance, of that which occasioned the remembrance. But all those passages are analogous in which עַל designates the occasioning circumstances in general, *ex. gr.*, Gen. xxvi. 7, 9; Ps. xliv. 32; 1 Sam. iv. 13. Comp. עַל־מָה, Jer. ix. 11; Job xiii. 14.

Ver. 3. **My mountain . . in all thy borders.** The words הררי בשדה are either connected with the preceding context in various ways (JEROME: *Sacrificantes in agro*; Syr.: *in monti̇bus et in deserto*; Chald.: *Super montes in agro*; Arab.: *in montibus et in agris*; R. SALOMO, ABARBANEL, KIMCHI: *O mons mi, qui in agro es*, as a designation of Jerusalem, to which the previous context is addressed; ZWINGLI: *ut filii recordantur ararum . . . collium, montium et agrorum*; EWALD, MEIER: הַרְרִי בַּשָּׂדֶה as in apposition to בְּבָעוֹת, or with the following, when it is either rendered

as in the vocative, and Zion, as the high place of the country *κατ' ἐξοχήν*, or Israel as sacrificing on mountains, or fleeing to mountains (CALVIN), is understood by it, or it is connected with **thy heights** (LUTHER), or as an accusative with **thy substance** (*montem meum una cum agro . . . dabo*, GESENIUS, GAAB, ROSENMUELLER, UMBREIT). HITZIG calls attention to xviii. 14; xxi. 13, where Zion is designated as צוּר שָׂדַי and צוּר הַמִּישֹׁר. But here the connection is quite different. In this place the prophet would evidently say that all property, movable and immovable, divine and human, dedicated to the service of God and the service of idols will be given up to plunder on account of their intensive (vers. 1, 2), as extensive and universally diffused sin (**in all thy borders**). For this reason also I do not believe that **mountain** is to be rendered as in the vocative. It is rather accusative, dependent on **I will give**, and the explanation already mentioned as that of GESENIUS, GAAB, ROSENMUELLER and UMBREIT, is the correct one. The mountain of the Lord also is desecrated; it therefore, in so far as it contains property that can be so treated, will also, like the fruitful field, be given up to plunder. The prophet says **fields**, because he wishes to designate only the land, which produces substance and treasures, or things that may be plundered. **Thy substance and all**, *etc.*, is a more particular explanation of **my mountain**. It tells us how a mountain and fields can be plundered. *Thy* substance, *thy* treasures have primary reference to **fields**. But that also which the mountain contained belonged in a certain respect to the people, and they were likewise despoiled of it. On the subject comp. xxvii. 16: xxviii. 3; lii. 17 sqq.—**Thy heights** is in antithesis to **my mountain**. Even the sanctuaries dedicated to the idols were to be objects of spoliation. It is clear that **thy heights** is governed by **give**, but its abrupt position is strange. If we could connect exclusively with **for thy sin**, this difficulty would be removed. But not only the high places, but all that has been previously mentioned is given up on account of their sin. SYRUS and the Arabic (MS. Oxon), omit **thy heights** altogether. HITZIG translates "for atonement," comparing Zech. xiv. 17; Deut. xxix. 11, and with respect to the construction, Deut. xxi. 29. But the expression **in all thy borders** would then be quite feeble and superfluous. GRAF after GESENIUS, DE WETTE and others:— Thy heights with the sin cleaving thereto I give up. But was it necessary to guard against the thought that the Lord would give up the heights without the sin, or that He would omit the latter? How is such a separation of the heights and the sin even conceivable? **Thy heights** may then be regarded as an emphatic asyndeton.—**For thy sin.** Comp. Mic. i. 5; 2 Kings xxiv 3.—**In all thy borders.** This addition corresponds exactly to the previously stated extent of the punishment: Since the sin has been universally diffused, so all the possessions in the whole land will be made the means of punishment.

Ver. 4. **And thou shalt . . . forever.** In this verse וכן causes the only difficulty. It has been either entirely passed over (SYRUS, Arab., LUTHER), or explained in a more or less forced manner, as *unfreely* (VATABLE), *by thy iniquity, naked and bare, alone* (so JEROME, on the ground of which EWALD would alter to לְבָד). But it is evident that Jeremiah had in view Deut. xv. 2, 3. This has been recognized by many expositors. Some (*ex. gr.*, SEB. SCHMIDT, ROSENM.) supply, therefore, יָדְךָ from Deut. xv. 2. J. D. MICHAELIS was the first to suppose that יָד alone should be read. GRAF expresses this distinctly, and without doubt correctly. For on the one hand בְּךָ, however interpreted, yields no satisfactory meaning. On the other hand the expression שְׁמֹט יָד כִּי, **withhold thy hand**, *etc.*, corresponds perfectly to the connection. The year of release (comp. Deut. xv. 1-13), so called from the שְׁמִטָּה, the release of the debtor from the oppressive hand of the creditor, coincides with the Sabbatic year (comp. Exod. xxiii. 10, 11; Levit. xxv. 1-7), in which the land is to remain uncultivated (comp. SAALSCHUETZ, *Mos. Recht.*, *S.* 162 ff.; HERZOG, *R-Enc.* XIII., *S.* 204 ff.). The state of desolation, in which the land will be in consequence of the destined exile of the people is in Lev. xxvi. 24, 25 expressly compared with that Sabbatic year, or year of release, and is called the Sabbath-time of the land (שַׁבְּתֹתֶיהָ). In 2 Chron. xxxvi. 21 (comp. 3 Esdr. i. 58) it is expressly set forth that the Babylonian captivity was the fulfilment of the divine word proclaimed by Jeremiah, according to which the land was promised its holiday (שַׁבָּתוֹת). But in no other place than this does Jeremiah intimate this thought. If now it is undoubted that this passage, with reference to Deut. xv. 2 coll. Lev. xxvi. 34, 35, designates the exile as a period of release for the land, we cannot avoid perceiving in בְּךָ an altered form of the יָדְךָ of Deuteronomy. On **I cause thee to serve**, *vide supra*, on xv. 14.—**For ye have kindled,** *etc.* The words are a free quotation from Deut. xxxii. 22, while those in xv. 14, at least in their first part, agree *verbatim* with the original passage.

CONCLUSION (xvii. 5-18).

1. *Retrospective glance at the deep roots of the corruption.*

XVII. 5-13.

5   Thus saith Jehovah: Cursed the man, who trusts in men,
    And makes flesh his arm, and whose heart departs from Jehovah.
6   He will be like one forsaken[1] in the desert
    And will not see when good comes,
    And will dwell in the arid places in the wilderness,
    In a land salt and uninhabited.
7   Blessed the man who trusts in Jehovah,
    And whose confidence Jehovah is!
8   He is like a tree planted by water,
    And which stretches forth[2] its roots to[3] the river,
    And will not fear[4] when the heat comes, and its leaf is green,
    And in the year of drought it will not have care nor cease from **fruit-bearing.**
9   The heart is more deceitful than anything
    And profoundly corrupt   Who can know it?
10 I, Jehovah, search the heart, try the reins,
    Even[5] to give every one according to his way,
    According to the fruit of his doings.
11 A partridge, which fosters without having laid,
    Is he who accumulates riches not by right.
    In the half of his days he will leave them,
    And at his end he will be a fool.
12 O throne of glory, height[6] of beginning, place of our sanctuary!
13 Hope of Israel, Jehovah!
    All who forsake thee are put to shame!
    Those who depart[7] from me must be written in the earth,
    Because they have forsaken the fountain of living water, Jehovah.

TEXTUAL AND GRAMMATICAL.

¹ Ver. 6.—בְּעַרְעָר. The ancient translations all express here, doubtless on the ground of the antithesis in ver. 8, the name of a tree or shrub, while in Ps. cii. where alone the word occurs a second time, they all, in accordance with the context, express the idea of *miser*. Since now עַרְעָר is formed after the analogy of דַּרְדַּר, גַּלְגַּל, זַלְזַל, כְּבָכָב (כּוֹכָב), etc. (comp. OLSH. § 189, *a*; NAEGELSB. *Gr.*, § 42, *a*, *S.* 87), since, further, the corresponding verbal root is given by li. 58 (הִתְעַרְעָר) unquestionably with the meaning *denudare* (comp. Isai. xxiii. 13; xxxii. 11; Hab. iii. 9. מְעֻרְיָה *nuditas*, עֲרִירִי *nudus, solitarius*; Gen. xv. 2; Lev. xx. 20, 21; Jer. xxii. 30), the meaning of "naked, destitute, wretched," is assured also in this passage. [HENDERSON: "I acquiesce in the opinion of Dr. ROBINSON, that it is the same as the Arab.

عرعر *Arar, the juniper-tree* which is found in the vicinity of the Arabah, or the Great Valley, to the south of the Dead Sea. See *Bibl. Res.* II., 506. Thus DE WETTE: *Wachholderbaum*. The same form of the word occurs Ps. cii. 18, where the idea conveyed is that of *naked, destitute*. The point of comparison in the two passages of our prophet is the forlorn appearance of a solitary juniper, deprived of all nourishment in the arid desert."—HITZIG referring to the composition of Ps. cii., after the flight of Jonathan into the desert of Tekoa, and the connection with Jer. xlviii. 6, where also flight is spoken of, decides that the word designates one who has *fled* or been *driven* into the desert, or *one who has come into misfortune as starved or perishing*.—S. R. A.]. On the words in xlviii. 6, בָּעֲרוֹעֵר בַּמִּדְבָּר, comp. rems. there.

² Ver. 8.—יוּבָל ἅπ. λεγ., synonymous with יָבָל, Isai. xxx 25; xliv. 4.

³ Ver. 8.—עַל for אֶל as frequently in Jer. Comp. on x. 1.

⁴ Ver. 8.—וְלֹא יִרְאֶה. The Keri reads יִרְאֶה after ver. 6. The Chethibh should be punctuated יִרָא (Imperf. from יָרֵא), corresponding to יָאֵן, and is at any rate to be preferred; as also the ancient translations express it, with the exception of the Chaldee.

⁵ Ver. 10.—וְלֹתֵת. Comp. xxxii. 19. The Vau, which the ancient translations and many Codd. omit, is not so superfluous as GRAF supposes.

⁶ Ver. 12.—מָרוֹם might grammatically be in the accusative, but as כָּבוֹד appears to be contrasted with בֹּשֶׁת (iii. 24; xl. 13), so does מָרוֹם ה with בָּמוֹת.

⁷ Ver. 13.—יְסוּרַי. The Chethibh יְסוּרַי would be formed like יְרִיב, יְקוּם, יְהוּר (OLSU. § 212). The form יָסוּר as a noun, does not, however, occur elsewhere, and the sudden change of person is strange. The Keri reads יְסוּרַי. The meaning is the same (= those departing from me. Comp. קָמַי, li. 1); the form is likewise a rare one. (Yet comp. ii. 21; Isa. xlix. 21; OLSH. § 172, *b.*) MEIER reads וְסוּרַי.

EXEGETICAL AND CRITICAL.

This long discourse ends with a concluding address in two parts, the first of which relates to general, the second to personal matters. In the first (vers. 5-13) the prophet indicates the most inward and hidden roots of the spiritual and physical corruption of his people. He mentions three chief moral defects, attaching to each the corresponding punishment. At the head he places the perverse disposition, which regards not the Lord, but flesh as the source and treasure of all blessing (ver. 5). The punishment of this sin is mentioned in ver. 6, the shadow being further deepened in vers. 7 and 8 by the contrast there presented. The second radical defect, designated in ver. 9, is the perfidiousness of the heart in connection with its weakness. In consequence of this *habitus*, the human heart is unfathomable to human sight, yet the Lord is in a position to look through and to judge it (ver. 10). Avarice is designated as the third destructive root to which every means is right, to which, however, poverty and shame must follow as a just recompense (ver. 11).—The last two verses express once more in a comprehensive manner, and after a solemn invocation of Jehovah, the judgment of destruction on all those who have forsaken Jehovah, the fountain of living water (vers. 12, 13).

Vers. 5 and 6. **Thus saith Jehovah . . . salt and uninhabited.** The prophet had in the previous context repeatedly designated the Lord as his and Israel's only safety: xiv. 8, 22; xv. 20, 21; xvi. 19. He, however, expressly intimated in xvi. 19, that the Israel of those times was wanting in confidence in this Saviour. Here he renders this sin of unbelief strongly prominent, portraying it according to its positive and its negative side. He mentions the positive side first. Man and flesh designate the totality of all earthly visible forces in antithesis to the spiritual power of the invisible God. It is precisely their visibility which withdraws the carnal mind from the invisible things to be apprehended by faith alone. The mind is first taken captive by things visible. Then having gained a firm footing in these, it breaks loose from the Invisible. It was so in the Fall. This confidence in things visible, however, is idolatry (comp. LUTHER's explanation of the first commandment). Hence the curse may well be an allusion to Deut. xxvii. 15 coll. vi. 28.—**Man and flesh.** (אָדָם and בָּשָׂר) synonymous also in Isa. xxxi. 3 coll. Job x. 4; Ps. lvi. 5. ["The Hebrew language, having three distinct words for *man*, has the advantage over our English in the finer shades of a passage like this, 'cursed is the man (strong man) who trusteth in man (frail man of the earth) who maketh flesh (mere weakness) his arm.'" COWLES.—S. R. A.]—**His arm,** זְרֹעוֹ, the organ for the exhibition of physical force. He who delivers over this function to another, *i. e.* makes him his arm, has him for his assistant, for protection and deliverance. Comp. Isa. xxxiii. 2; Ps. lxxxiii. 9.—**A land salt,** *etc.* Comp. Job xxxix. 6; Ps. cvii. 34.—**Will dwell.** שָׁכַן intransitive, as in ver. 25; xxx. 18; 1. 13, 39; Isa. xiii. 20.

Vers. 7, 8. **Blessed the man . . . fruit**

bearing. We might suppose that these verses were so co-ordinate with the two preceding that the two pairs would constitute an independent, self-contained whole. But then the following verses would be entirely disconnected. I therefore think that verses 7 and 8 are to serve as a foil to the thought expressed in vers. 5, 6, which is shown to be the main thought by its position.— **As a tree.** Comp. Ps. i. 3.—**Drought.** Comp. xiv. 1.

Vers. 9 and 10. **The heart is more deceitful . . . his doings.** Were the hearts of men, and especially of the Israelites, upright and directed to the true and the good, they must agree in word and deed with that which the prophet has declared in vers. 5-8. But there is nothing in the world so deceitful as the human heart, which understands the art thoroughly of pursuing the evil under the appearance of wishing the right (comp. ch. v. and ix. 2-8). This deceitfulness is however only a symptom of the deep depravity, the incurable sickness by which the heart is possessed.—**Deceitful,** עָקֹב. Comp. on ix. 3. The word occurs here only as an adjective with this meaning.—**Corrupt,** אָנֻשׁ. The meaning "desperate" is not contained in the word. It is everywhere = severely sick, incurable (xv. 18; xxx. 12, 15; Isa. xvii. 11; Mic. i. 9; Job xxxiv. 6), full of the deepest pain (ver. 16). No man is in a condition to see through the deceitful hypocrisy of the human heart, but the Lord can do it, and founds on this His knowledge, His strict and righteous judgment. Comp. xi. 20; xii. 3; xx. 12.—**Even to give.** Separating the statement of the object from the fundamental declaration, the word **even** sets forth the independence of the latter. God is not omniscient merely for the purpose of judging, but in His essential nature. Comp. besides comm. on vi. 2.

Ver. 11. **A partridge . . . be a fool.** As the third root of spiritual and bodily corruption the prophet names avarice, which is the root of all evil (1 Tim. vi. 10). The selfish inquire not about the right (comp. v. 1, 26 sqq.; vi. 6, 7; xiii. 8, 10), therefore the blessing of God is also denied them. Lightly come lightly go. Forsaken and put to shame the unrighteous man is at last like the bird, of which it is said that it collects the young of others and fosters them, but is forsaken by them as soon as they perceive that a stranger has usurped a mother's rights over them. The form of comparison is like that in Prov. x. 20; xi. 22; xvi. 24, etc. It is doubtful what bird is to be understood by קֹרֵא. The word is found besides only in 1 Sam. xvi. 20. The ancient translators and most of the Comm. understand the partridge, and the dialects also favor this rendering. Only natural history does not confirm this peculiarity of the partridge. Comp. Winer s. v. Rebhuhn. ["The ancients believed that she stole the eggs of other birds and hatched them as her own. See Epiphan. Physiol. cap. ix.; Isid. Origg. xii. 7." Henderson.—S. R. A.].—**Fosters.** דָּגַר occurs besides only in Isa. xxxiv. 15. It is there expressly distinguished from יָקַב, to hatch, and can mean only the gathering together and cherishing by warmth of the newly hatched young. Winer

quotes inter al. a passage from OLYMPIODORUS: ὁ πέρδιξ * * * τοὺς ἀλλοτρίους προσκαλεῖται νεοττοὺς οἵτινες γνόντες ὕστερον, ὅτι οὐκ εἰσὶν αὐτοῦ, καταλιμπάνουσιν αὐτόν. This agrees admirably with the sense and connection of the passage, though it must still remain undecided whether we have here a real popular opinion existing at the time of Jeremiah, or only one deduced from this passage.—**Shall leave them** refers to the riches. On **fool** comp. x. 8, 14.

Vers. 12 and 13. **O throne of glory . . . Jehovah.** Comprehensive conclusion in the form of a brief but solemn invocation of Jehovah. From **Hope of Israel** it is evident that the words of the prophet were addressed in the last instance to the person of the Lord. But he mentions first the exteriora, which are the places and bearers of His glory: his throne, the place where His throne stands, the sanctuary which surrounds it, for he wishes to set forth distinctly how foolish and criminal it is to do that, which he has censured in vers. 5, 9, 11 and which he afterwards comprises in one word, "forsake the Lord." Israel has given up the truly real and eternal sanctuaries for the miserable high-places of idolatry. I do not therefore hold the view that ver. 12 is addressed to Jehovah Himself, for the reason given by GRAF, that the Lord cannot possibly be called **place of sanctuary.**—**O throne of glory.** Comp. 1 Sam. ii. 8; Isa. xxii. 23; Jer. xiv. 21. The Lord's throne appears in the Old Test. in three degrees. First, Jerusalem is thus named (iii. 17), second, the ark of the covenant (Exod. xxv. 22; Ps. lxxx. 2; xcix. 1), third, the proper, so to speak, and transcendent throne (Isa. vi. 1; Ezek. i. 26; Dan. vii. 9; Ps. ix. 5; xi. 3; xlvii. 9; cx. 1). These three degrees are however so connected, that he who forsakes one does the same to the other. The prophet has primarily in view here, as at any rate in xiv. 21, the visible throne of the Lord.—**Height of beginning.** The idea expressed by מָרוֹם has also several gradations. 1. Mt. Zion is called הַר מְרוֹם יִשְׂרָאֵל, Ezek. xvii. 23; xx. 40 coll. xxxiv. 14; Jer. xxxi. 12. 2. It is very often used to designate the transcendent abode of Jehovah, Isa. xxxiii. 5; lvii. 15; Mic. vi. 6; Jer. xxv. 30; Ps. xciii. 4; lxviii. 19, etc. The expression מֵרֹאשׁוֹן, which occurs here only (comp. מֵרֹאשׁ, Prov. viii. 23) agrees with מָרוֹם in both senses. For that transcendent abode is from the beginning, eternally existing (comp. Ps. xciii. 2), and Zion also as chosen from eternity is in idea the eternal dwelling-place of God. (Comp. Ps. cxxxii. 13, 14 coll. Exod. xv. 17; xx. 24; Deut. v. 12).—**Place of our sanctuary.** Comp. Isa. lx. 13; Dan. viii. 11. Even the sanctuary of Israel (מִקְדָּשׁ) is a double one, an earthly and a heavenly. The former is made according to the type of the latter (Exod. xxv. 8, 9, 40; xxvi. 30). Thus though the expression refers primarily to the earthly sanctuary the heavenly is not excluded. There is no objection to the impersonal rendering of these three substantives in the prophet's addressing words of prayer to them. For that the prophet declares with respect to them: "All who forsake thee are put to shame," would be quite unprejudicial even if "Hope of Israel," etc., did not come between. But the three former are entirely sunk in this last conception, since it is only in and by Jehovah that they have any existence or meaning. Hence also the singular suffix in עָזְבִי. The older commentators render throne of glory as nominative, either taking the first and the last three words together (*solium gloriae excelsum, ab initio locus sanctuarii nostri*, CALVIN), or regarding throne (*thronus, qui est altitudo ab æterno, est locus sanctuarii*, SEB. SCHMIDT), or height (a throne in glory is the height of beginning, the place of our sanctuary, NEUMANN) as the nominative. According to these renderings however it is scarcely possible to find a suitable connection.—Hope of Israel. Comp. xiv. 8; l. 7.—Written in the earth. In the earth (in the dust, Job xiv. 8), where what is written will be speedily effaced, shall those who depart from me be written. The antithesis on the one hand would be to xvii. 1 (the sin in brass, the sinners in dust), on the other hand to the book of life (Exod. xxxii. 32; Ps. lxix. 29; Dan. xii. 1; Mal. iii. 16; Luke x. 20; Phil. iv. 3; Rev. iii. 5; xiii. 8; xvii. 8; xxi. 27). MEIER reads: they vanished away in the land (Job xv. 30), all who are recorded in it (xvii. 1; xxii. 30) that they have forsaken the fountain, etc. This exegesis also is exposed to several objections: 1. that סוּר must be taken in the sense of vanish away: 2. the imperf. יִכָּתֵבוּ. I therefore prefer to adhere to the reading of the Chethibh. The rapid change of person forms no objection to this. Comp. on v. 14; ix. 7; xii. 13; xvii. 1. The Lord then continues in confirmation of the prophet's address. —Fountain, etc. Comp. ii. 13; Ps. xxxvi. 10.

2. *Petition of the prophet for the safety of his person and the honor of his official ministrations.*

XVII. 14-18.

14 Heal me, Jehovah, that I may be healed;
Deliver me that I may be delivered, for thou art my praise!
15 Behold, they say to me: Where is the word of Jehovah? Let it come now.
16 But I have not hastened away from being a pastor after thee;
And the calamitous day I have not desired, thou knowest.
That which went forth from my lips was from thee.
17 Be not[1] a terror to me, my refuge in the day of distress!
18 My persecutors must be put to shame,
But I must not be put to shame;
They must be dismayed, but I must not be dismayed!
Bring[2] upon them the day of calamity,
And doubly[3] with destruction destroy them!

TEXTUAL AND GRAMMATICAL.

[1] Ver. 17.—תִּהְיֵה, comp. EWALD, § 224 c; NAEGELSB. Gr., § 38, Anm. 2.
[2] Ver. 18.—הָבִיא, a rare form instead of הָבֵא, but comp. 1 Sam. xx. 40; OLSH., § 256 b, S. 569.
[3] Ver. 18.—שִׁנָּה (not מִשְׁנֶה) is *accus. modi*. Comp. NAEGELSB. Gr., § 70 g.

EXEGETICAL AND CRITICAL.

The second, personal half of the conclusion. The prophet prays for safety and deliverance for himself (ver. 14). In opposition to the scornful doubt in the fulfilment of his predictions, expressed in ver. 15, he prays on the ground of the fact that he had not hastened into the prophetic office, or declared his own inventions (ver. 16), that the Lord, his refuge, would not be a terror to him or suffer him to be put to shame, but his persecutors, and bring upon them the day of calamity and double destruction (vers. 17, 18).

Ver. 14. Heal me . . . thou art my praise. The prophet begins with a prayer for safety and deliverance in general.—Heal me. Deut. xxxii. 39; Ps. vi. 3; xxx. 3.—My praise, the object of my confident boasting. Comp. Deut. x. 21; Ps. lxxi. 6.

Vers. 15 and 16. Behold, they say . . . was from thee. The prophet resumes the thought in xv. 10, 15-19 (coll. xx. 7-12).—Where, etc. Comp. Isa. v. 19; Ezek. xii. 22 sqq. It is used ironically also in Ps. xlii. 4, 11; lxxix. 10; 2 Kings xviii. 34, *etc*.—On Let it come now, comp. xxviii. 8, 9; Deut. xviii. 21, 22 coll. xiii. 2.—But I have not, *etc*. The prophet would deserve such scorn, if he had taken the word of the Lord into his mouth in his own strength, or deceitfully, as others did, xiv. 14, 15.—But he is not a pseudo-prophet, but a prophet against his will. Comp. i. 6 sqq.: xx. 7.—The words I have not hastened (כִּי לֹא אַצְתִּי) have been variously explained. But all the commentators (when they do not alter the reading, as the Syr., which reads רעה) concur in understanding רעה of the spiritual pastorate. The thought that he had not hastened from the pastoral office or spiritual pasture after Jehovah does not however suit the connection. For he can wish only to defend himself against the imputation of having hurried. It is very remarkable that not a single comm. has yet thought of taking רעה in a physical sense; doubtless because the knowledge of Jeremiah's priestly descent has seemed to preclude the thought of his having been a shepherd. But why may not Jeremiah, who was called as a נביא to the prophetic office, have previously tended his father's sheep? The shepherd's state was rendered sacred to the Israelites by the example of their fathers, and kings as well as prophets had proceeded from it (comp. Am. i. 1; vii. 14 coll. Exod. iii. 1). Moreover the מגרש [pasture, common], which was possessed by every priestly and levitical city (comp. Josh. xxi. and 1 Chron. vi.), was according to Num. xxxv. 4 expressly intended "for the cattle." Anathoth also had its מגרש (Josh. xxi. 18). Comp. HENZOG, R.-Enc. VI. S. 150. How well now it suits the connection if Jer. says: They scorn me as a prophet and yet I did not hurry away from being a shepherd רעה=כרעה כהיות. Comp. ii. 25; xlviii. 2; Ps. lxxxiii. 5; 1 Sam. xv. 23, 26) after thee. —אין=to press, to haste: Exod. v. 13; Josh. x. 13; Prov. xix. 2; xxi. 5; xxviii. 20.—אחריך. Comp. ii. 2; iii. 19. Going after Jehovah is in antithesis to going after the flock (comp. 1 Chr. xvii. 7). [HITZIG: "I have not hastened away not to keep after thee. In אין is the idea of wilfulness, following one's own impulse in any direction. 'I did not struggle away so that I should not be pasturing,' etc. אחריך does not suit the usual rendering of רעה as the trade of the shepherd, but leads to this, that Jahve is the shepherd, leader, and Jeremiah the lamb, Ps. xxiii. 1. Willingly following him (comp. 1 Sam. vii. 2; Numb. xiv. 24) he allowed himself to be fed by Jahve (comp. Prov. x. 21) with words of truth and with revelation, xv. 16." HENDERSON appears to follow HITZIG in this rendering.— WORDSWORTH: "Rather, *I have not hastened backward from being a shepherd* (a prophet) *after thee*. When I was called by Thee, I did not withdraw myself hastily from Thy service (see *Gesen.* 23), but I obeyed Thy call without delay: and *I did not desire the woful day.*"—So also COWLES.—S. R. A.]

And the calamitous day. Comp. rems. on ver. 9. From the connection the prophet can mean only the day of his entrance into the prophetic office. (Comp. xx. 7 sqq.: xv. 10, 11). For he needed not to give the assurance that he did not desire the day of calamity for the whole people. He might indeed have been reproached with loving to prophesy evil, but there is nothing of this in the text.—**Thou knowest.** Comp. xv. 15.—**That which went forth,** etc. That which has gone forth from his lips, since he has been a prophet, God knows and approves, he has nothing then to fear from the criticism of men. Comp. Prov. v. 21; Lam. ii. 19.

Vers. 17 and 18. **Be not a terror . . . destroy them.** The negative petition, comp. ver.

14.—**persecutors,** pursuers. Comp. xv. 15; xx. 11.—**doubly with destruction.** Comp. xvi. 18.

DOCTRINAL AND ETHICAL.

1. On xiv. 7. "*Medicina erranti confessio, qua de re* Ps. xxxii. 3, 4 *et Ambrosius eleganter: Confessio verecunda suffragatur Deo, et pœnam, quam defensione vitare non possumus, pudore revelamus* (*lib. de Joseph., c.* 86), *et alibi idem: Cessat vindicta divina, si confessio præcurat humana. Etsi enim confessio non est causa meritoria remissionis peccatorum, est tamen necessarium quoddam antecedens.*" FÖRSTER.

2. "In earnest and hearty prayer there is a conflict between the spirit and the flesh. The flesh regards the greatness of the sins, and conceives of God as a severe Judge and morose being, who either will not help further or cannot. The spirit, on the other hand, adheres to the *name* of God, *i. e.*, to His promise; he apprehends God by faith as his true comfort and aid, and depends upon Him." CRAMER.

3. On xiv. 9 a. "*Ideo non vult Deus cito dare, ut discas ardentius orare.*" AUGUSTINE.

4. On xiv. 9 b. "*Quia in baptismo nomen Domini, i. e., totius SS. et individuæ Trinitatis super nos quoque invocatum est, eo et ipso nos in fœdus Dei recepti sumus et inde populus Dei salutamur.*" FÖRSTER.

5. On xiv. 10. "So long as the sinner remains unchanged and uncontrite God cannot remove the punishment of the sin (xxvi. 13)." STARKE.— "*Quotidie crescit pœna, quia quotidie crescit et culpa.*" AUGUSTINE.

6. On xiv. 11, 12. ["We further gather from this passage that fasting is not in itself a religious duty or exercise, but that it refers to another end. Except then they who fast have a regard to what is thereby intended—that there may be a greater alacrity in prayer—that it may be an evidence of humility in confessing their sins,—and that they may also strive to subdue all their lusts;—except these things be regarded, fasting becomes a frivolous exercise, nay, a profanation of God's worship, it being only superstitious. We hence see that fastings are not only without benefit except when prayers are added, and those objects which I have stated are regarded, but that they provoke the wrath of God as all superstitions do, for His worship is polluted." CALVIN.—S. R. A.] "Unbelief is a mortal sin, so that by it the good is turned into evil. For fasting or praying is good; but when the man who does it has no faith it becomes sin (Ps. cix. 7)." CRAMER.

7. On xiv. 14. "He who would be a preacher must have a regular appointment. In like form for all parts of divine worship we must have God's word and command for our support. If we have it not all is lost." CRAMER.

8. On xiv. 14 (I have not sent them). "This does not come at all into the account now-a-days; and I do not know, whether to such a preacher, let him have obtained his office as he may, in preaching, absolution, marrying and exorcising, or on any other occasion, when he appeals to his calling before the congregation or against the devil, the thought once occurs, whether he is

truly sent by God. Thus the example of the sons of Sceva (Acts xix. 14, 16) is no longer considered, and it appears that the devil is not yet disposed by such frightful occurrences to interrupt the atheistical carelessness of the teachers." ZINZENDORF.

9. On xiv. 15. "The example of Pashur and others shortly afterwards confirms this discourse. This is an important point. One should however, with that modesty and prudence, which Dr. WIESMANN (Prof. of Theol. in Tübingen), who seems called of God to be a writer of church history, in his *Introd. in Memorabilia historiæ sacræ N. T.* (1731 and 1745) which I could wish were in the hands of all teachers, repeatedly recommends, have regard to this also, when so-called judgments on the wicked are spoken of, that when the Lord in His wisdom and omnipotence exercises justice on such transgressors by temporal judgments, these are often a blessing to them and the yet remaining means of their salvation. It is related that a certain clergyman in a Saxon village, about the year 1730, felt such a judgment upon himself and his careless ministry, and after happy and humble preparation on a usual day of fasting and prayer, presented himself before his church as an example, and exercised on himself what is called church discipline, whereupon he is said to have fallen down dead with the words,

' My sin is deep and very great,
And fills my heart with grief.
O for thy agony and death,
Grant me, I pray, relief.'

He is no doubt more blessed, and his remembrance more honorable, than thousands of others, who are praised by their colleagues in funeral discourses as faithful pastors, and at the same time, or already before, are condemned in the first but invisible judgment as dumb dogs, wolves or hirelings." ZINZENDORF.

10. On xiv. 16. "Although preachers lead their hearers astray, yet the hearers are not thus excused. But when they allow themselves to be led astray, the blind and those who guide them fall together into the ditch (Luke vi. 39)." CRAMER. ["When sinners are overwhelmed with trouble, they must in it see their own wickedness poured upon them. This refers to the wickedness both of the false prophets and the people: the blind lead the blind, and both fall together into the ditch, where they will be miserable comforters one to another." HENRY.—S. R. A.]

11. On xiv. 19. Chrysostom refers to Rom. xi. 1 sqq., where the answer to the prophet's question is to be found.

12. On xiv. 21. "Satan has his seat here and there (Rev. ii. 13). I should like to know why the Saviour may not also have His cathedral. Assuredly He has, and where one stands He knows how to maintain it, and to preserve the honor of the academy." ZINZENDORF.

["Good men lay the credit of religion, and its profession in the world, nearer their hearts than any private interest or concern of their own; and those are powerful pleas in prayer which are fetched from thence, and great supports to faith. We may be sure that God will not *disgrace the throne of His glory*, on earth; nor will He eclipse the glory of His throne by one providence, without soon making it shine forth, and more brightly than before, by another. God will be no loser in His honor in the long run." HENRY.—S. R. A.]

13. On xiv. 22. "Testimony to the omnipotence of God, for His are both counsel and deed (Prov. viii. 14). Use it for consolation in every distress and for the true *apodictica* [demonstration] of all articles of Christian faith, however impossible they may appear." CRAMER.—["The sovereignty of God should *engage*, and His all-sufficiency encourage, our attendance on Him, and our expectations from Him, at all times." HENRY.—"Hence may be learned a useful doctrine—that there is no reason why punishments, which are signs of God's wrath, should discourage us so as to prevent us from venturing to seek pardon from Him; but on the contrary a form of prayer is here prescribed for us; for if we are convinced that we have been chastised by God's hand, we are on this very account encouraged to hope for salvation; for it belongs to Him who wounds to heal, and to Him who kills to restore to life." CALVIN.—S. R. A.]

14. On xv. 1. On the part of the Catholics it is maintained that "*hoc loco refellitur hæreticorum error . . . orationes defunctorum sanctorum nihil prodesse vivis. Contrarium enim potius ex hisce argumentum suggeritur, nempe istiusmodi sanctorum mortuorum orationes et fieri coram Deo solere pro viventibus, et quando viventes ipsi non posuerint ex semet obicem, illas esse iis maxime proficuas.* GHISL. Tom. II. p. 296). To this it is replied on the part of the Protestants. 1. *Enuntiatio isthæc plane est hypothetica.* 2. *Eo tantum spectat, ut si Moses et Samuel in vivis adhuc essent, adeoque in his terris pro populo preces interponerent suas, perinde ut ille,* Ex. xxxii. *hic vero* 1 Sam. vii. (FÖRSTER, S. 86)." He also adds two testimonies of the fathers against the invocation of saints. One from AUGUSTINE, who (*contra Maximin.*, L. 1), calls such invocation *sacrilegium*, the other from EPIPHANIUS who (*Hæres* 2) names it an *error seductorum,* and adds "*non sanctos colimus, sed sanctorum dominum.*"—That the intercession of the living for each other is effective, CRAMER testifies, saying "Intercession is powerful, and is not without fruit, when he who prays and he for whom he prays are of like spirit." Comp. Rom. xv. 30; 2 Cor. i. 11; Eph. vi. 18, 19; 1 Tim. ii. 1, 2; 1 John v. 16. [To the same effect also CALVIN and HENRY.—S. R. A.]

15. On xv. 4 b. "*Scilicet in vulgus manant exempla regentum, utque ducunt lituos, sic mores castra sequuntur.*"—"*Non sic inflectere sensus humanos edicta valent ut vita regentum.*"—" *Qualis rex talis grex.*" FÖRSTER.

16. "God keeps an exact protocol [register] of sins, and visits them to the third and fourth generation." CRAMER. ["See what uncertain comforts children are; and let us therefore rejoice in them as though we rejoiced not." HENRY.—S. R. A.]

17. On xv. 5. "When God abandons us we are abandoned also by the holy angels, and all creatures. For as at court when two eyes are turned away the whole court turns away; so when the Lord turns away all His hosts turn away also." CRAMER.

18. On xv. 7. "God as a faithful husbandman

has all kinds of instruments for cleaning His grain. He has two kinds of besoms and two kinds of winnowing-fan. With one He cleanses, winnows the grain and sweeps the floor, so that the chaff may be separated from the good wheat. This is done by the Fatherly cross. But if this does not avail He takes in hand the besom of destruction." CRAMER.

19. On xv. 10. "The witnesses of Jesus have the name among others of being hard and rough people, from whom they cannot escape without quarreling. It is not only a reproach which Ahab and such like make to Elijah, 'Art thou he that troubleth Israel?' (1 Ki. xix. 17). But even true-hearted people like Obadiah do not thoroughly trust to them; every one has the thought, if they would only behave more gently it would be just as well and make less noise. Meanwhile the poor Elijah is sitting there, knowing not what to do; a Jeremiah laments the day of his birth . . . why am I then such a monster? Why such an apple of discord? What manner have I? How do I speak? 'For when I speak, they are for war' (Ps. cxx. 7). He does not at once remember that they called the master Beelzebub, and persecuted all the prophets before him; that his greatest sin is that he cares for the interests of Jesus in opposition to Satan." ZINZENDORF. [" Even those who are most quiet and peaceable, if they serve God faithfully, are often made *men of strife*. We can but *follow peace;* we have the making only of one side of the bargain, and therefore can but, *as much as in us lies,* live peaceably." HENRY.—S. R. A.]

20. On xv. 10 *b*. (I have neither lent nor borrowed at usury). "My dear Jeremiah! Thou mightest have done that; that is according to the custom of the country, there would be no such noise about that. There is no instance of a preacher being persecuted because he cared for his household. But to take payment in such natural products as human souls, that is ground of distrust, that is going too far, that thou carriest too high, and thou must be more remiss therein, otherwise all will rise up against thee; thou wilt be suspended, removed, imprisoned or in some way made an end of, for that is pure disorder and innovation, that smacks of spiritual revolutionary movements." ZINZENDORF.

21. On xv. 15 *a*. (Thou knowest that for thy sake I have suffered reproach). "This is the only thing that a servant of the Lamb of God should care for, that he does indeed suffer not the least in that he has disguised and disfigured the doctrine of God and his Saviour. . . . It might be wished that no servant of the Lord, especially in small cities and villages, would now and then make a quarrel to relieve the tedium, which will occupy the half of his life, and of which it may be said in the end: *vinco vel vincor, semper ego maculor.*" ZINZENDORF.

22 On xv. 16. "The sovereign sign of a little flock depending on Christ is such a hearty, spiritual tender disposition towards the Holy Scriptures, that they find no greater pleasure than in their simple but heart-searching truths. I, poor child, if I but look into the Bible, am happy for several hours after. I know not what misery I could not alleviate at once with a little Scripture." ZINZENDORF. [On ver. 17. "It is the folly and infirmity of some good people that they lose much of the pleasantness of their religion by the fretfulness and uneasiness of their natural temper, which they humor and indulge instead of mortifying it." HENRY.—S. R. A.]

23. On xv. 19, *a*. (And thou shalt stand before me: [LUTHER: thou shalt remain my preacher]) "Hear ye this, ye servants of the Lord! Ye may be suspended, removed, lose your income and your office, suffer loss of house and home, but ye will again be preachers. This is the word of promise. * * * And if one is dismissed from twelve places, and again gets a new place, he is a preacher to thirteen congregations. For in all the preceding his innocence, his cross, his faith preach more powerfully than if he himself were there." ZINZENDORF.

Note.—On this it may be remarked that in order to be the mouth of the Lord it is not necessary to have a church.

24. On xv. 19 *b*. (Before thou return to them) "We can get no better comfort than this, that our faithful Lord Himself assures us against ourselves. I will make thee so steady, so discreet, so well-founded, so immovable, that, hard as the human heart is, and dead and opposed, yet it will be rather possible that they all yield to thee, than that thou shouldest be feeble or slack and go over to them." ZINZENDORF.

25. On xv. 20. "A preacher must be like a bone, outwardly hard, inwardly full of marrow." FÖRSTER. ["Ministers must take those whom they see to be *precious* into their bosoms, and not *sit alone*, as Jeremiah did, but keep up conversation with those they do good to, and get good by." HENRY.—S. R. A.]

26. On xvi. 2. "It is well-known that in no condition is celibacy attended by so many evils as in that of the clergy and that this condition entails in a certain measure a present necessity of marrying. For if any one needs a helpmeet to be by his side, it is the man who must be sacrificed to so many different men of all classes. But all this must be arranged according to circumstances. Ye preachers! Is it made out that ye marry only for Jesus? . . . that you have the church alone as your object? and that you subject yourselves to all the hardships of this condition with its tribulations only for the profit of many? First, then, examine maturely in your offices, whether there is no word of the Lord, whether circumstances do not show, whether there is not an exception from the rule in your case, that you are to take no wife; whether Paul does not call to you in spirit, 'I would that thou wert as I.' May it not sometimes be said? 'Take no wife at this time or at this place!' or 'Take not another!' How does the matter look on closer examination? The rather, as it is known to the servants of Christ to be no hyperbolical speech, when it is said, 'The minister has slain his thousands, but the minister's wife her ten thousands.' He that loves anything more than Christ is not worthy of Him. If it cannot be cured endure it. But see to it the more, that those who have wives be as those who have them not (1 Cor. vii. 29). Lead your wife in prayer diligently and plainly, as Moses with Zipporah (Exod. iv. 25, Surely a bloody husband art thou to me). If they would not have you dead they

must leave you your Lord. I know not when anything was so pleasing to me as when I saw a certain minister's wife weeping sorely from apprehension that her husband would not endure a certain trial. She saw clearly that he would retain his charge, but she feared the Saviour would make it hard to him." ZINZENDORF.

27. On xvi. 2. "*Ridiculi sunt Papicolæ, qui ex hoc typo articulum religionis suæ de cœlibatu sacerdotum exstruere conantur. Nam* 1. *tota hæc res fuit typica. Typica autem et symbolica theologia non est argumentativa juxta axioma Thomæ.* 2. *Non simpliciter interdicitur conjugium prophetæ in omni loco, sed tantum in hoc loco.*" FÖRSTER.

28. On xvi. 7. This passage (as also Isa. lviii. 7) is used by the Lutheran theologians to prove that *panem frangere* may be equivalent to *panem distribuere*, as also LUTHER translates: "They will not distribute bread among them." This is admitted by the Reformed, who, however, remark that it does not follow from this that *frangere et distribuere* also "*in Sacramento æquipollere, quod esset a particulari ad particulare argumentari.*" Comp. TURRETIN., *Inst. Theol. Elencht. Tom.* III., *p.* 499.

29. On xvi. 8. "When people are desperately bad and will not be told so, they must be regarded as heathen and publicans (Matt. xvii. 18; Tit. iii. 10; 1 Cor. v. 9)." CRAMER.

30. On xvi. 19. "The calling of the heathen is very consolatory. For as children are rejoiced at heart when they see that their parents are greatly honored and obtain renown and praise in all lands, so do all true children of God rejoice when they see that God's name is honored and His glory more widely extended." CRAMER.— This passage is one of those which predict the extension of the true religion among all nations, and are therefore significant as giving impulse and comfort in the work of missions. Comp. Deut. xxxii. 21; Hos. ii. 1, 25; Joel iii. 5; Isa. xlix. 6; lxv. 1: Rom. x. 12 sqq.

31. On xvi. 21. "Nothing can be learned from God without God. God instructs the people by His mouth and His hand, *verbis et verberibus.*" CRAMER.

32. On xvii. 1. "*Scripta est et fides tua, scripta est et culpa tua, sicut Jeremias dixit: scripta est Juda culpa tua graphio ferreo et ungue adamantino. Et scripta est,* inquit, *in pectore et in corde tuo. Ibi igitur culpa est ubi gratia; sed culpa graphio scribitur, gratia spiritu designatur.*" AMBROS. *de Sp. s.* III. 2.

33. On xvii. 1. "The devil is God's ape. For when he sees that God by the writing of His prophets and apostles propagates His works and wonders to posterity, he sets his own pulpiteers to work, who labor with still greater zeal, and write not only with pens and ink, but also with diamonds, that such false religion may have the greater respect and not go down." CRAMER.

34. On xvii. 5.

"O man in human help and favor
Trust not, for all is vanity,
The curse is on it,—happy he,
Who trusts alone in Christ the Saviour."

["When water is blended with fire, both perish: so when one seeks in part to trust in God and in part to trust in men, it is the same as though he wished to mix heaven and earth together, and to throw all things into confusion. It is then to confound the order of nature, when men imagine that they have two objects of trust, and ascribe half their salvation to God and the other half to themselves or to other men." CALVIN.—S. R. A.]

35. On xvii. 5. "A teacher is commanded to be the first to honor the authorities, to pray for them and be subject to them as God's servants... But since the authorities, in all which pertains to the concerns of the soul, have part only as members, there is great occasion for this cursed dependence on flesh . . . when one from the hope of good personal protection . . . gives up the work of the Lord to the powers of the earth. . . . It is true the church is to have foster-parents who are kings. But nevertheless neither kings nor princes are its tutelar deities, much less lords and commanders of the church, but one is our Master, one our Judge, one our King, the Crucified." ZINZENDORF.

36. On xvii. 5. Reformed theologians, *ex. gr.*, LAMBERTUS DANÆUS (*ob.* 1596) have applied this passage in the sense of John vi. 63, in their controversies against the Lutheran doctrine of the Supper. But as CALVIN declared, it is not the flesh of Christ, but only earthly flesh and that *per contemptum* which is here spoken of. Comp. FÖRSTER, *S.* 97.

37. On xvii. 7. "Blessed are those teachers, who have betaken themselves to His protection, who once promised His Church, that even the gates of hell should not prevail against it. . . . Who has ever been put to shame who trusted in Him?" ZINZENDORF.

38. On xvii. 9. "This is a spiritual anatomy of the heart. Examples: Manasseh (2 Chron. xxxiii.); Hezekiah (Isa. xxxviii. 39); the children of Israel (Num. xiv.). *Alii sumus dum lætamur et omnia in vita nobis secundo vento succedunt; alii vero in temporibus calamitosis, ubi quid præter sententiam acciderit.* Comp. Ser. xi. 27." (MS. note in my copy of CRAMER's *Bibel*).

39. On xvii. 9. Νᾶφε καὶ μέμνασο ἀπιστεῖν. This applies with respect to ourselves and others. For the defiant it avails as an extinguisher (Rom. xii. 3); but the despairing may be reassured by it (1 John iii. 19, 20).

40. On xvii. 14. (Thou art my praise)......
"When a teacher confines himself to the praise of the cross and lets all other matters of praise go, which might adorn a theologian of these times, and adheres immovably to this: 'I am determined to know nothing among you but Jesus Christ the crucified' (1 Cor. ii. 2),—amid all the shame of His cross He is victorious over the rest." ZINZENDORF.

41. On xvii. 16. (That which I have preached was right before thee). "It is not difficult to know in these times what is right before the Lord. There is His word; he who adheres to this strictly, knows *in thesi* that he is right . . . . In all this it is the teacher's chief maxim, not to make use of the application without need, but to make the truth so plain in his public discourse, that the hearers *must necessarily make the application to themselves*. . . . 'Thus saying, thou reproachest us also,' said the lawyer (Luke xi. 45). . . . Others went away convicted in their consciences." ZINZENDORF.

42. On xvii. 17. "That is a period which

straitens the hearts of witnesses, when their rock, their protection, their consolation, their trust is a terror to them. But under this we must bow and faithfully endure, and we shall have a peaceable fruit of righteousness. Discipline always ends gloriously." ZINZENDORF.

HOMILETICAL AND PRACTICAL.

On xiv. 7-9. Jeremiah a second Israel, who wrestles with the Lord in prayer. 1. In what the Lord is strong against the prophet: the sin of the people. 2. In what the prophet is strong against the Lord: the Name of the Lord, (a) in itself. This compels him to show that He is not a desperate hero, or giant, who cannot help; (b) in that His name is borne by Israel. Thus the Lord is bound to show Himself as He who is in Israel (not a guest or stranger), and consequently the Comforter and Helper of Israel.—HEIM und HOFFMANN, *The Major Prophets* (Winnenden, 1839). As Daniel (ix. 5) prayed, *We* have sinned and committed iniquity, *etc.*, so Jeremiah took his share in the sin and guilt of his people.—This is true penitence, when one no longer wishes to contend with God in tribulation, but confesses his sin and condemnation, when he sees that if God should treat us according to our misdeeds, He could find no ground for grace. But for His name's sake He can show us favor. He Himself is the cause of the forgiveness of sin.—*Calwer Handbuch* [Manual]. Notwithstanding the ungodliness of the people the prophet may still say, "Thou art among us," because the temple of the Lord and His word were still in the land, and the pious have never all died out. [On xiv. 7-9. "Prayer hath within itself its own reward. The prayer of the prophet consists of confession and petition. 1. Confession fitly begins. It is the testimony of iniquity, and that this iniquity is against God. When we are to encounter any enemy or difficulty, it is sin weakens us. Now confession weakens *it*, takes off the power of accusation, *etc.* 2. Petition: *For Thy name's sake*. This is the unfailing argument which abides always the same and hath always the same force. The children of God are much beholden to their troubles for clear experiences of themselves and God. Though thou art not clear in thy interest as a believer, yet plead thy interest as a sinner, which thou art sure of." LEIGHTON.—S. R. A.]

2. On xiv. 13-16. Against false prophets. 1. They tell the world what it likes to hear (ver. 13); 2. The Lord denies them (ver. 14); 3. The Lord punishes them (ver. 15); 4. The Lord also punishes those who allow themselves to be deceived by them (ver. 16).—*Tüb. Bibelw.*: To enter the preacher's office without divine calling, what an abomination is that! But mark this, ye hirelings! the sentence of condemnation is already pronounced over you (Jer. xxiii. 21; Matt. vii. 15).—OSIANDER *Bibl.*: God avenges the deception of false teachers most severely, if not in this world in the next (Acts xiii. 10, 11).—STARKE: God punishes both deceivers and deceived, the latter cannot then lay all the guilt on the former (xxvii. 45).

3. On xiv. 19-22. The church's distress and consolation. 1. The distress is (a) outward (ver. 19), (b) inward (ver. 20, the reason of the outward, confession). 2. The consolation (a). The Lord's Name. [a] It is called and is One (ver. 22); [β] His glory and that of the church (throne of glory) are one; (b) the Lord's covenant (ver. 21).—What in the present circumstances should be our position towards God? 1. The divine providence, in which we are at present: 2. Our confession, which we make before God: 3. Our petition, which we should address to Him. VOELTER in PALMER'S *Ev. Casual-Reden*. [Occasional Discourses], 4th Ed., 1865.

4. On xv. 16. *Sermon on a Reformation or Bible-Anniversary*. The candlestick of the Gospel has been rejected by more than one church. We therefore pray: Preserve to us Thy word (Ps. cix. 43). 1. Why we thus pray (Thy Word is our hearts' joy and comfort): 2. Why we hope to be heard (for we are named by Thy name).

5. On xv. 19. CASPARI (*Installation-sermon at Munich*, Adv., 1855). These words treat; 1, of the firm endurance; 2, of the holy zeal; 3, of the joyful confidence, with which a preacher of God must come to an evangelical church.

6. Homilies of ORIGEN are extant on xv. 5 and 6; (Hom. XII., Ed. LOMMATZSCH); xv. 10-19 (Hom. XIV.); xv. 10; xvii. 5 (Hom. XV.). [On xv. 20. "I. God's qualification to be an overseer of the church. The metaphor of a wall implies, (1) courage, (2) innocence and integrity, (3) authority. II. The opposition a church-governor will be sure to meet with, (1) by seditious preaching and praying, (2) by railing and libels; (3) perhaps by open force. III. The issue and success of such opposition (they shall not prevail)." SOUTH.—S. R. A.]

7. On xvi. 19-21. *Missionary Sermon*. The true knowledge of God. 1. It is to be had in Christianity (ver. 19, a). 2. It will also make its way to the heathen, for (a) It is God's will that they should be instructed (ver. 21); (b) they are ready to be instructed (ver. 19 b. 20).

8. On xvii. 5-8. The blessing of faith and the curse of unbelief (comp. *Ebal und Gerizim*). 1. Why does the curse come upon the unbeliever? (He departs in his heart from the Lord). 2. Wherein this curse consists (ver. 6). 3. Why must blessing be the portion of the believer? (ver. 7). 4. Wherein this blessing consists (ver. 8).

9. On xvii. 5-8, and xviii. 7-10. SCHLEIERMACHER (*Sermon* on 28 Mar., 1813, in Berlin): We regard the great change (brought about by the events of the period) on the side of our worthiness before God. 1. What in this respect is its peculiar import and true nature. 2. To what we must then feel ourselves summoned.

10. On xvii. 9, 10. The human heart and its judge. 1. The antithesis in the human heart. 2. The impossibility of fathoming it with human eyes. 3. The omniscient God alone sees through it; and 4, judges it with justice. [" The heart is deceitful—it always has some trick or other by which to shuffle off conviction." HENRY.—"It is extremely difficult for sinners to know their hearts. I. What is implied in their knowing their own hearts. 1. It implies a knowledge of their selfishness. 2. Of their desperate incurable wickedness. 3. Of their extreme deceitfulness. II. Why it is so extremely difficult for them to know their own hearts. 1. They are unwilling to know them. 2. Because of the de-

ceitfulness of sin. They love or hate, as they appear friendly or unfriendly to them: (*a*) God, (*b*) Christ, (*c*) good men, (*d*) one another, (*e*) the world, (*f*) their own hearts, (*g*) the means of grace, (*h*) their convictions, (*i*) heaven—Improvement. The only way to know the heart is to inquire whether it loves God or not, *etc.* 2. Saints can more easily ascertain their true character than sinners can. 3. All changes in life are trials of the heart," *etc., etc.* EMMONS.—"I. The human heart exhibits great fraud and treachery. 1. We are changeable by that connection which the soul has with the body. 2. By its connection with external objects by our senses. 3. By its love of novelty and variety. 4. By its hasty resolutions. 5. By its self-love. II. Its excessive malice is seen in history and experience. III. Its deep dissimulation and hypocrisy render it inscrutable. Inferences: 1. We should entertain a sober diffidence of ourselves. 2. We should not be surprised when men use us ill or disappoint us. 3. We should take care and give good principles and a good example to those young persons under our guidance. 4. We should be ready to confess our offences to God. 5. We should bear in mind that we are under the inspection of one who searcheth the hearts," *etc.* JORTIN.—See also two Sermons by JER. TAYLOR. —S. R. A.].

11. RUD. KŒGEL (Court and Cathedral preacher at Berlin, 1865). Sermon on xvii. 9, 19, and Heb. xiii. 9: Two pictures: 1, the unregenerate; 2, the regenerate heart.

12. On xvii. 12, 13. Sermon for the dedication of a church, the anniversary of the Reformation, or on Whitsunday. The church of the Lord. 1. What it is in itself (place of sanctuary, throne of divine glory, house of Him, who is Israel's hope). 2. What it will be (it will ever remain firm, Matt. xvi. 18): 3. What they find who forsake it (ver. 19).

13. On xvii. 14-18. Cry for help of a preacher tempted on account of the truth. 1. The temptation (ver. 15). 2. The demonstration of innocence (ver. 16). 3. The cry for help, (*a*) negative (vers. 17 and 18), (*b*) positive (ver. 19). [On xvii. 14. The penitent's prayer. 1. The words express an earnest desire for salvation. 2. He applies to Almighty God for it. 3. Through the medium of prayer. 4. With confidence that he will be heard. Dr. A. THOMSON of Edinburgh.— S. R. A.].

6. THE SIXTH DISCOURSE.

(CHAP. XVII. 19-27.)

This short passage is closely connected neither with what precedes nor with what follows. Many commentators have, indeed, devised an extensive frame, so as to include this passage in it together with the previous or subsequent context, but these artificial expedients are not satisfactory. The previous discourse is, as shown above, complete in itself, and requires no further addition. The following passages are also as peculiar and independent as this. This forms a small but important and in form a finished whole. Why should not the prophet have addressed short speeches to the people?
As to the date, all is in favor of the reign of Jehoiakim. 1. The state still exists in unenfeebled independence; no trace betrays that the power of the Chaldeans had become predominant, or that they were immediately threatening. 2. The censure of the transgression of so important a command corresponds rather with the times of the godless Jehoiakim, than of the pious Josiah. The great similarity with xxii. 1-5, *which passage indubitably pertains to the reign of Jehoiakim, is in favor of referring this discourse to the same period.* [HENDERSON: *"Eichhorn, Rosenmüller and Maurer, are of opinion that this portion of the chapter belongs to the reign of Jehoiakim, who rapidly undid all the good which had been effected by Josiah, and among other evils encouraged the profanation of the Sabbath, with the due observance of which the prosperity of the State was bound up. The language of the prophet, however, is not objurgatory, as we should have expected, if the profanation in question had actually existed. It is rather that of caution and warning, with a promise of prosperity in case of obedience, and a threatening of destruction to the city in case of disobedience. It would seem, therefore, to belong to the time of Josiah, and to have been delivered in connection with or shortly after his reformation."*
—HITZIG *refers this passage together with chapter* xviii., *to the period of Jeconiah, or that immediately following the death of Jehoiakim.*—S. R. A.]

EXHORTATION TO HALLOW THE SABBATH.

XVII. 19-27.

19 Thus saith the LORD [Jehovah] unto me; Go and stand in the gate of the children of the people,[1] whereby the kings of Judah come in, and by the which they
20 go out, and in all the gates of Jerusalem; And say unto them, Hear ye the word of the LORD [Jehovah], ye kings of Judah and all Judah, and all the inhabitants
21 of Jerusalem that enter in by these gates: Thus saith the LORD [Jehovah]; Take heed ye to yourselves [Care with foresight for your souls],[2] and bear no burden on

22 the Sabbath-day, nor bring it in by the gates of Jerusalem; neither carry forth a burden out of your houses on the Sabbath day, neither do ye any work, but hallow
23 ye the Sabbath-day, as I commanded your fathers. But they obeyed [heard] not, neither inclined their ear, but made their neck stiff, that they might not hear[3] nor
24 receive instruction. And it shall come to pass, if ye diligently hearken unto me, saith the LORD [Jehovah] to bring in no burden through the gates of this city on the Sabbath-day, but hallow the Sabbath day to do [by doing] no work therein;[4]
25 then shall there enter into [through] the gates of this city kings and princes[5] sitting upon [who sit on] the throne of David, riding in chariots and on horses, they and their princes, the men of Judah and the inhabitants of Jerusalem; and this city
26 shall remain [be inhabited] forever. And they shall come from the cities of Judah and from the places about [environs of] Jerusalem and from the land of Benjamin, and from the plains and from the mountains, and from the south, bringing [people who bring] burnt offerings and sacrifices and meat-offerings and incense, and bring-
27 ing sacrifices of praise unto the house of the LORD [Jehovah]. But if ye will not hearken unto me to hallow the Sabbath-day, and not to bear a burden, even entering [or enter] into the gates of Jerusalem on the Sabbath-day; then will I kindle a fire in the [your] gates thereof, and it shall devour the palaces of Jerusalem and it shall not be quenched.

TEXTUAL AND GRAMMATICAL.

[1] Ver. 19.—[HITZIG: Of the common man]. The Chethibh reads בְּנֵי־עָם, but this does not make any difference in the sense. If the absence of the article is not due to an oversight, it may be explained by the later, less exact use of language, of which we repeatedly find traces in Jeremiah (comp. iii. 2; vi. 16; xiv. 18).

[2] Ver. 21.—בְּנַפְשׁוֹתֵיכֶם. The construction is like Mal. ii. 15, 16, בְּרוּחֲכֶם. But בְּ is not =by, per, after verbs of petition or conjuration (by your life not. Vid. GESEN., Thes. III., S. 1443), or=for the sake of (MEIER), but the Niphal involves the meaning of having regard to, observing, and בְּ depends on this. Comp. שָׁכְרוּ־מִי בְּנַעַר, 2 Sam. xviii. 12. That this is the sense of the connection follows plainly from 2 Sam. xx. 10, "took no heed to the sword;" Deut. xxiv. 8, "take heed to the plague." Comp. NAEGELSB. Gr., § 100, 3.

[3] Ver. 23.—שׁוֹמֵעַ [Chethibh, שְׁמוֹעַ] HILLER in Arcano Kri et K'tib. remarks that the Masoretes, when they wished to indicate the Scriptio plena, in order that the difference of their reading might be remarked, set the mater lectionis in another place in the word. So also in ii. 25; ix. 7; xxvii. 1; xxix. 23; xxxii. 23. Comp. the Explicatio lectionum masoret. in the Hebrew Bible of SIMONIS, Halle, 1752.

[4] Ver. 24.—On the form בָּהּ. Comp. EWALD, § 84, b; 247, d. OLSH. § 96, c; 40, h.

[5] Ver. 25.—וְשָׂרִים is strange. GRAF not without reason, assumes an oversight, caused by the frequent juxtaposition of the two words. Comp. xlix. 38; Hos. xiii. 10; 2 Sam. xviii. 5; 1 Chron. xxiv. 6; 2 Chron. xxviii. 21; xxix. 30; xxx. 12; Esth. i. 16, 21, etc.

EXEGETICAL AND CRITICAL.

Jeremiah is to go under the gate of the city and there warn all the people from the king downwards against the desecration of the Sabbath by bearing burdens and laboring as their fathers had done (vers. 18-23). If they would sanctify the Sabbath, their city should remain forever, and their gate should be witnesses of a lively traffic, of importance to the king's house, the city and the temple (vers. 24-26). But if they should continue to desecrate the Sabbath, an inextinguishable fire should consume the gates and palaces of the city (ver. 27). Accordingly three parts may be distinguished in this passage.

Vers. 19-23. **Thus saith Jehovah . . . nor receive instruction.—Go,** etc. Comp. ii. 2; iii. 12; xix. 1.—**Gate of the children of the people.** This gate is mentioned here only. It is, therefore, difficult to determine its position with certainty, as according to VON RAUMER (Paläst., 4th Ed., S. 291), not two interpreters agree as to its position. The first question is whether it was a gate of the city or of the temple. GRAF correctly remarks that, with respect to a gate of the city בֹּא must stand first and יָצָא last (comp. 2 Chron. xxiii. 8). The name בְּנֵי־הָעָם would also be a very strange one for a city gate. The expression occurs with three meanings. 1. It designates the difference between strangers and natives, although in this sense עַם is found in the Old Testament not with the article, but only with suffixes: Gen. xxiii. 11; Judges xiv. 16; Lev. xix. 18; Ezek. iii. 11; Num. xxii. 5; Lev. xx. 17.—2. It designates a difference in rank among the people themselves, and in two degrees, the mass of the people in opposition to the king and the princes (2 Chron. xxxv. 7 coll. 8), and again the commonalty in opposition to the more respectable classes (Jer. xxvi. 23; 2 Kings xxiii. 6).—3. The expression designates the difference between priests and not priests, in which sense it corresponds to our term "laity" (2 Chron. xxxv. 5, 12, 13). It occurs only in the passages cited. Since now nothing is known of a gate of the city through which strangers might not pass, or of one through which only the kings and the dregs of the people, or only the kings and the rest of their subjects to the exclusion of the priests might pass, it follows that the gate must have been a gate of the temple through which only the laity went in and out, since special entrances were reserved for the priests. What gate it was it is difficult to say. The expression was probably not one in general use, but employed only by the priests, since according to the second explanation it included a somewhat dishonorable side-meaning. The rarity of the expression also justifies the conclusion that it was a temporary expression, *i. e.*, in use only in those times, since as is well-known the city-gates of Jerusalem bore successively different names. Comp. RAUMER'S *Paläst. S.* 290, 1.— When in 2 Chron. xxiii. 5, the high-priest Jehoiada posted a third of his people at the שַׁעַר הַיְסוֹד it is natural to suppose that this was the gate through which he expected Athaliah to pass. It is then further probable that this gate was identical with the one mentioned in our passage " whereby the kings of Judah went in and out." [HENDERSON:—" *The gate of the mass of the people* . . was in all probability *the gate of David*, corresponding to what is now called the Jaffa Gate, and was called the 'people's' gate from the circumstance of its being the principal thoroughfare for the tribes in the South, the West, and the North-West."—S. R. A.] That this gate, even were it a gate of the temple, was adapted to the proclamation of this divine message, is evident if we reflect (a), that this gate also might by the purchase and sale of temple-necessaries (comp. Matth. xxi. 12) be the scene of Sabbath-desecrating traffic; (b) that even if this was not the case, at any rate the gate was one which was much frequented, perhaps more than all the rest. —**Not do any work.** Comp. Exod. xii. 16; xx. 8 sqq.; Deut. v. 12 sqq.—The Sabbath was the day of Jehovah (comp. the passages quoted) a *monimentum temporale* for his service, hence the observance of this day stood or fell with the worship of Jehovah.—**But they obeyed not.** The first half of ver. 23 is taken verbatim from vii. 26.—Ver. 23 is parenthetical, suggested by **as I commanded,** *etc.*

Vers. 24-26. **And it shall come** . . . **Jehovah Sitting upon the throne.** Comp. xiii. 13; xxii. 4.—**Shall remain.** Comp. rems. on ver. 6.—**Men of Judah.** Comp. xxxii. 44; xxxiii. 13; coll. Josh. x. 40; Judges i. 9; Deut. i. 7; Zech. vii. 7.—**The plains.** שְׁפֵלָה is the low country between Joppa and Gaza, Josh. ix. 1; xii. 8; xv. 33 sqq.; 1 Kings x. 27; Obad. 19; RAUMER, *Paläst. S.* 51.—**South,** נֶגֶב is the southern, as שְׁפֵלָה the western, מִזְרָח the eastern, הָהָר the northern, parts of the tribe of Judah, separating the two last mentioned. Comp. Josh. xv. 55 sqq.; 2 Sam. xxiv. 7.

Ver. 27. **But if ye will not . . . not be quenched.** The negation before **to bear must** also be referred to **enter.** Comp. ver. 21.— **Will I kindle.** Comp. xxi. 14; xlix. 27; Am. i. 14.

DOCTRINAL AND ETHICAL.

1. On ver. 30. " It is no derogation to the sagacity of a teacher if he directs his public instructions, admonitions and warnings with some special adaptation to the rulers of the country. Only he must guard against offensive or abusive expressions, and see to it that he carefully distinguish between their office and their life, and be sure of his case, that he is not following the motions of nature, but the calling of the Lord. Acts xxiii. 3; 1 Ki. xiv. 7, 8." STARKE.

2. Man in this earthly life needs, besides work, rest also for body and soul. It would be inept to have one rest day for the body and another for the soul. It would be equally so to have more or fewer holidays than God has ordained by sanctification of the Seventh day, whereby He who is the creator of time has at the same time given us the fundamental principles of its division. As the rest of the body is both negative and positive (abstinence from labor and recuperation of forces) so also is that of the soul. The soul is from God, and must on its day of rest be freed from earthly cares and brought into the element of its heavenly origin, as it were into a cleansing and invigorating bath. The observance by Christians of the first, instead of the Seventh day, as a weekly holiday is well founded in the fact that the day of Christ's resurrection is also a day of creation, and so much the more glorious as the new and imperishable world is more glorious than the old and perishable world.

3. "Neglect not church-going. For though the unbelieving heathen thought it a foolish course to spend the day in idleness, yet temporal subsistence will not therefore fail, but rather will the weekly work of other days flourish the more. Matth. vi. 33." CRAMER.

4. [" God did not regard the external rite only, but rather the end, of which He speaks in Ex. xxxi. 13, and in Ezek. xx. 12. In both places He reminds us of the reason why He commanded the Jews to keep holy the Seventh day, and that was that it might be to them a symbol of sanctification. 'I have given My Sabbaths,' He says, 'to you, that ye might know that I am your God who sanctifieth you.' . . And it appears from other places that this command was typical —Christ being the substance. Col. ii. 16." CALVIN.—S. R. A.]

HOMILETICAL AND PRACTICAL.

The weekly holiday as the day of Jehovah and as the day of the Lord. 1. What they have in common. The weekly holiday is in both cases (*a*) a monument of the loving care of our God (*a*) for our body (*β*) for our soul; (*b*) a right of God which forms on our part a holy obligation towards God, ourselves, and our neighbor. 2. The differences. (*a*) The day of Jehovah is founded on the creation of the perishable world ; the day of the Lord is founded on the resurrection of Christ, as of a new, eternal world; (*b*) the observance of the day of Jehovah was only legal, *i. e.*, (*a*) imposed by external compulsion, (*β*) by requirements to be fulfilled by outward observance ;—the observance of the day of the Lord is to be more and more an evangelical one, *i. e.* (*a*) a living, (*b*) a spiritually free one, *i. e.*, satisfying the right as well as the obligation of personality.

[" What blessings God has in store for those who make conscience of Sabbath sanctification. 1. The *court* shall flourish. The honor of the government is the joy of the kingdom, and the support of religion would contribute greatly to both. 2. The *city* shall flourish. Whatever supports religion tends to establish the civil interests of a land. 3. The *country* shall flourish. By this the flourishing of a country may be judged of. What does it do for the honor of God? Those who starve their religion either *are* poor, or are in a fair way to *be* so. 4. The *church* shall flourish. | It is a true observation which some have made, flourishing of all religion run either deep That the streams of all religion run either deep or shallow, according as the banks of the Sabbath, are kept up or neglected." HENRY.—S. R. A.]

THE SEVENTH DISCOURSE.

(CHAPS. XVIII.—XX.)

As these three chapters appear under a common superscription of the longer form, which does not recur till chap. xxi., *they are evidently to be regarded as a connected whole. They have in fact an internal connection, although they cannot by any means be considered as a rhetorical whole, or as a connected discourse. Two historical facts are here set before us, which are internally related, but are different as to time, and probably also as to their original record, to which are also attached both prophetic indications and subjective effusions. The first historical fact is the incident with the potter, related in* ch. xviii. *As in this chapter the impending judgment is still announced in the same general manner as before, the Chaldeans not yet being mentioned as the instrument, it is manifest that it must have been written before the decisive turning-point reported in* ch. xxv., *viz., before the battle of Carchemish in the 4th year of Jehoiakim. On the other hand* chh. xix. *and* xx. *were written after this crisis. For in* xx. 4 *we read "I will give all Judah into the hand of the king of Babylon, and he shall carry them captive into Babylon." Jeremiah does not speak thus till after that decisive battle. It is also noteworthy, that the prophet in* xx. 2 *is called* יִרְמְיָהוּ הַנָּבִיא, *not simply* יִרְמְיָהוּ, *which mode of expression likewise prevails only after the great crisis. (Comp.* xxv. 2; xxviii. 5, 10, 11, 12, 15, *etc.) It follows definitively that* chh. xix. *and* xx. *belong to the time of Jehoiakim from the circumstance that in the reign of Zedekiah, not Pashur, but Zephaniah, the son of Maaseiah, appears to be invested with the dignity of temple-officer (comp.* xxix. 26 coll. xxi. 7; xxxvii. 3; lii. 24), *and moreover as the successor of Jehoiada, which renders the probability that Pashur no longer held this office under Zedekiah so much the greater, especially if we consider that* ch. xxix. *belongs to one of the first years of Zedekiah (see the Introd. to* ch. xxix.) *Pashur, who in* xx. 4 *sqq. is threatened with being carried away captive to Babylon, had most probably met this fate with king Jehoiakim and that numerous company which is spoken of in* xxix. 1 *and* 2 Ki. xxiv. 12-14.—*Notwithstanding therefore that* ch. xviii. *belongs to an earlier period than* chh. xix. *and* xx. *they are placed together because both are based on symbolic actions, of which the productions of pottery form the substratum. In* ch. xviii. *the clay on the potter's wheel first fails, but is then immediately formed anew; in* ch. xix. *the vessel is ready-made, which being poured out is then (irreparably* xix. 11) *broken by the prophet. Both actions are of such a character as to set before the people that the Lord has not only the power but the will to destroy them. Nevertheless there is a great difference between the two actions, the first having a paræ- netic, the second more of a declarative character, as will be shown in the exposition.* GRAF *is of opinion that* xix. 1-13 *was written down at the same time with* ch. xviii., *because the event narrated in* xx. 1 sqq., *is related to the prophecy in* vii. 30 sqq. *as* ch. xxvi. *to* vii. 12, *and since the discourse in* ch. vii. sqq. *belongs to the fourth year of the reign of Jehoiakim, so also the prophecy in* xix. 1-13, *and the event recorded in* xx. 1-6 *must belong to this time. But the latter was not recorded till afterwards, like all the narratives from the life of Jeremiah. The lyrical passage* xx. 7-13 *has no connection with the preceding context. But it may have been composed under the impression of the shameful treatment which Jeremiah had received in the temple, or subsequently in remembrance of this and other persecutions. The five verses,* xx. 14-18, *are said to be an independent fragment, an amplification of* xv. 10, *which was perhaps composed in consequence of the same occurrences, and were put here on this account, or only on account of its agreement with vers.* 7, 8. *To this I have to object;* 1. *It is an unnatural supposition that* xix. 1-13 *was written before* xix. 14-xx. 6. *For both passages are so closely connected that we cannot conceive what could have occasioned the prophet to defer the relation in* xix. 14, *etc., after having recorded the previous facts, together with the prophecy connected with them. The narrative* xix. 14, *etc., was certainly recorded after the prophet had already begun to call himself* הַנָּבִיא, *but only because the prophecy itself belongs to this later period. This is not identical with* vii. 30-34, *and does not therefore belong to the first years of Jehoiakim. The agreement in particular words and phrases corresponds only to the general usage of Jeremiah, to repeat himself frequently and extensively, and in different connections by no means justifies the assumption of identity.* 2. *The passage* xx. 7- 13 *is closely connected with the previous context, as is especially seen in the words* מָגוֹר מִסָּבִיב *(comp. the Comm. on* xx. 10); *it is not however an objective and official word of God, but a memorial of subjective thoughts and feelings, which then moved the prophet, and thus bears to some extent the character of a private record.* 3. *The case is the same with* xx. 14-18. *This passage also is of an entirely subjective and private nature. To strike it out or explain it as only patched on accidentally is to deny* the dualism which must undoubtedly have prevailed in the mind of the prophet. To transpose it from this place and set it before xx. 7 (as EWALD does, in this however opposed by GRAF) would be to disturb the natural course and the clear picture of the inner feelings of the prophet. For it is only too probable that in those troubled times a troubled frame of mind finally became predominant. *I am therefore of opinion that* ch. xviii. *belongs to the period before,* chh. xix. *and* xx. *to the period after, the fourth year of Jehoiakim, that the passages however being of related contents were placed in juxtaposition in the collection of prophecies; further, that* xix. 1—xx. 6 *is to be regarded as a closely connected whole, on which follows as an appendix a subjective effusion of double and contradictory purport, by which however we obtain a true picture of the prophet's then prevailing state of mind.* *The discourse may be divided as follows:—*

THE SYMBOLS OF POTTERY.

FIRST SYMBOL: THE CLAY AND POTTER, CH. XVIII.

1. *The parable of the potter and its interpretation in a negative sense,* xviii. 1-10.
2. *The interpretation of the parable in a positive sense,* xviii. 11-17.
3. *The manner in which the people receive the word of the prophet, and his petition to the Lord for protection from their hostility,* xviii. 18-23.

SECOND SYMBOL:—THE BROKEN VESSEL, CHAPS. XIX. and XX.

1. *The symbolic action and its interpretation,* xix. 1-13.
2. *Opposition and punishment of Pashur,* xix. 14-xx. 6.
3. *Appendix. The prophet's joy and sorrow,* xx. 7-18.
   a. *Through sorrow to joy,* xx. 7-13.
   b. *For the present sorrow only. The prophet curses the day of his birth,* xx. 14-18.

CHAPTERS XVIII. to XX.

THE SYMBOLS OF POTTERY.

FIRST SYMBOL:—THE CLAY AND POTTER.

CHAP. XVIII.

1. *The parable of the potter and its interpretation in the negative sense.*

XVIII. 1-10.

1, 2 The word which came to Jeremiah from the LORD [Jehovah], saying, Arise and go down to the potter's house and there I will cause thee to hear my words.
3 Then I went down to the potter's house, and, behold, he wrought a work on the
4 wheels. And the vessel which he was making[1] of [as] clay[2] was spoiled in the hand of the potter; so he made it again another vessel, as seemed good to the potter to
5 make it. Then the word of the LORD [Jehovah] came to me, saying,
6 Cannot I do to you as this potter does,
O house of Israel? saith Jehovah.
Behold as the clay in the hand of the potter,
So are ye in my hand, O house of Israel!
7 Suddenly I speak against a nation and against a kingdom,
To extirpate and exterminate and to destroy:
8 If now this nation, against which I have spoken, turn from its wickedness,
I repent)[e] the evil which I thought to do unto it.
9 And suddenly I speak concerning a nation and concerning a kingdom,
To build and to plant:
10 If how it does that which is evil[3] in my eyes,
So that it hears not my voice,
I repent of the good wherewith I promised to benefit it.

TEXTUAL AND GRAMMATICAL.

[1] Ver. 4.—וְנִשְׁחַת. The perfects נִשְׁחַת and שָׁב signify that these facts are not to be regarded as co-ordinate points in the course of the narrative, but as further developments of the בִּמְלָאכָה עֹשֶׂה, from which it is not necessary to assume that the word designates more than a single act (HITZIG, GRAF). The form וַיְשַׁב is used (as *cx. gr.,* Gen. xxvi. 17) for the

reason that the word does not contain the main idea, but a subordinate one attached as it were by the preceding perfect. Comp. Gen. xxix. 2 sqq.; Isa. vi. 3; Dan. viii. 4; Ewald, § 342 b; Naegelsb. Gr., § 84, b; § 95 g, Anm.
[3] Ver. 4.—וּ בְחֹמֶר. These words have been unjustly suspected by different translators, transcribers, and commentators. They are not a gloss from ver. 6, but doubtless chosen with reference to this verse. The intention is to set forth prominently the *punctum saliens* by similarity of expression in the historical narrative and the application. The בְּ is to be regarded as *Kaph veritatis*—as clay, i. e., as he is accustomed to do to the clay. Comp. xv. 19; Naegelsb. Gr., § 112, 5, c. [Wordsworth: *As clay* sometimes fails *in* the hand of the potter.—Henderson. בַּחֹמֶר with בְּ instead of כְּ, is found in the text of fifty-eight MSS., has originally been in several more, and is now in five more by correction. It is likewise exhibited in seventeen printed editions, and alone makes sense."—S. R. A.].
[4] Ver. 10.—הָרָעָה. The Masoretes would read הָרָעָה, according to the usage which prevails elsewhere without an exception (comp. Num. xxxii. 13; Jud. ii. 11; iii. 7, 12, *etc.*; 1 Kings xi. 6; xiv. 22; Jer. vii. 30; xxxii. 30, *etc.*). The reading of the Chethibh is, however, evidently occasioned by הַטּוֹבָה after, and וְנִחַמְתִּי before it.

EXEGETICAL AND CRITICAL.

The prophet receives the command to go into the potter's house, to receive there a revelation from the Lord. He obeys and is a witness how the clay is spoiled in the hands of the potter, as he works on the wheel, and how he immediately forms a new vessel out of the clay (vers. 1-4). Hereupon the prophet receives the word of the Lord: As the clay is in the hand of the potter, so is Israel in the hand of the Lord (vers. 5 and 6). As the Lord by penitence and conversion is dissuaded from the accomplishment of His threatenings, so by evil-doing He may be prevented from performing His gracious promises (vers. 7-10).

Vers. 1-4. **The word ... to the potter to make it.** The superscription is like that in vii. 1; xi. 1.—הָאָבְנָיִם, **wheels.** The meaning of the word, which occurs besides only in Exod. i. 16 cannot be doubtful in this passage. With respect however to Exod. i. 16, it was the object of a literary controversy. Comp. Böttcher in Winer's *Zeitsch. f. wiss. Theol., Bd. II.*, H. 1, S. 49 ff.; Rettig, Böttcher u. Redslob, *Stud. u. Krit.*, 1834; Benary, *Berlin, Jahrbb.*, 1841; Ernst Meier, *Stud. u. Krit*, 1842. [For a description and diagram of the wheel, see Gesen. Lex., *s. v.*]—**As seemed good.** Comp. xxvii. 5.

Vers. 5-10. **Then the word ... to benefit it.**—On **as the clay in the hand of the potter** comp. Isa. xxix. 16; xlv. 9; lxiv. 7; Wisd. xv. 7; Ecclus. xxxvi. 13; Rom. ix. 21.— **Suddenly**, vers. 7 and 9, is evidently not to be referred to the proximate verb, but to the main thought, *i. e.*, to the apodosis. The mode of expression is paratactic. In our syntactic mode it would be: Suddenly, if I have spoken against a nation ... and this nation turn, I will repent, *etc.* Comp. Naegelsb. *Gr.*, § 111, 1, *Anm.* Moreover, the word refers evidently to the rapidity with which the potter changes the form of the clay. Observation may be recommended as the best commentator on this passage.—**To extirpate.** Comp. i. 10.—**Against which I spoke** is not to be referred to **wickedness**, but to **nation**.

2. *The interpretation of the parable in the positive sense.*

XVIII. 11-17

11 And now speak indeed[1] to the men of Judah,
  And to[2] the inhabitants [citizens] of Jerusalem, saying,
  Thus saith Jehovah: Behold!
  I frame evil against you, and think thoughts against you:
  Turn ye now, each from his evil way,
  And reform your ways and your works.
12 But they will say: No use![3] but our thoughts we will follow,
  And will practise, each according to the obstinacy[4] of his wicked heart.
13 Therefore thus saith Jehovah:
  Inquire now among the nations, who hath heard the like?
  The virgin Israel hath done a very horrible thing.[5]
14 Ceases[6] from the rock of the field the snow of Lebanon?
  Or do the strong,[7] cool, rippling waters dry up?
15 That my people forgat me and burned incense to vanity,
  And made them stumble in their ways, the ancient paths,[8]
  To walk in roads of an unleveled way,
16 To make their land a desolation,
  An object of everlasting derision?[9]

He who only passes through will be astounded at it,
And will shake his head.[10]
17 Like the east wind will I scatter them before the enemy;
Back not face will I show them in the day of their fall.

TEXTUAL AND GRAMMATICAL.

[1] Ver. 11.—[HENDERSON: I charge thee. BLAYNEY: I pray thee.—S. R. A.]

[2] Ver. 11.—On the change of אֶל to עַל, comp. TEXTUAL NOTE [2] on x. 1.

[3] Ver. 12.—נוֹאָשׁ. Niph. part. of יָאַשׁ, *to despair*. Comp. Comm. on ii. 25. [HENDERSON: It is hopeless. BLAYNEY: It is a thing not to be hope'd.]

[4] Ver. 12.—שְׁרִרוּת. The expression is found here only as the object of עָשָׂה, elsewhere always with בְּ or אַחֲרֵי after הלך (comp. iii. 17; ix. 13; xvi. 12; vii. 24; xi. 8; xiii. 10; xxiii. 17).

[5] Ver. 13.—שְׁעָרֻרִת. This form is found here only. Comp. Hos. vi. 10; Jer. v. 30; xxiii. 14.

[6] Ver. 14.—There is no other instance of the construction in עִי כֵּן עֹזֵב, for עֹזֵב is used transitively even in Gen. xxiv. 27. Should we not perhaps read מִצּוּר instead of מִצּוּר? צוּר is not merely *circumvallatio*, but also *munimentum, arx, turris*. Comp. Hab. ii. 1. GYSEN. *Thes.*, p. 1161.

[7] Ver. 14.—Instead of זָרִים, which certainly affords no satisfactory meaning, the LXX. seems to have read יְדִים, *the proud, splendid*. So also MEIER in comparison with יְדוֹנִים כַּיָּם, Ps. cxxiv. 5. EWALD (and after him GRAF) derives זָרִים from זרר, *to press*. This word, however, signifies *constrinxit, compressit*, and the meaning *to press forth* is a bare assumption. If the word is to be altered, it is then better to agree with MEIER. [" זָרִים from זור, *to compress, straiten*, is descriptive of streams, as contracted within narrow channels, while descending through the gorges and defiles of the rocks. The use of the verb נָזַל, Arab. *nazal*, ﻧﺰل, *discendit loco*, confirms this view." HENDERSON. HITZIG renders "strange," as coming from afar, in the sense of the A. V., and refers to the unknown source of the pool of Siloam, etc.—S. R. A.]

[8] Ver. 15.—The form שְׁבֻגֵל here only in the Chethibh; שְׁבִיל Ps. lxxvii. 20. The word does not recur.

[9] Ver. 16.—שְׁרוּקַת. This form here only; שְׁרִיקַת in Jud. v. 16. In Jeremiah שְׁרֵקַת only occurs elsewhere: xix. 8; xxv. 9, 18; xxix. 18; li. 37.

[10] Ver. 16.—יָנִיד בְּרֹאשׁוֹ. Comp. NAEGELSB. *Gr.*, § 69, 1. *Anm.* 2. The expression occurs here only. Comp. Ps. xliv. 15; xxii. 8; cix. 25.

EXEGETICAL AND CRITICAL.

After it had been shown in vers. 5-10 that the Lord was not bound by His promises with respect to the people, but has as much freedom as the potter with respect to the clay, He now makes the positive application of this parable. He declares what, like a potter, he is about to form, viz., calamity. The expression יֹצֵר, ver. 11, is the only point in which this strophe supports itself on the preceding parable, for in what follows there is no further reference to it. To the brief application and exposition of this word, is attached an exhortation to repentance and reformation (ver. 11 b), to which the people answer with stubborn rejection (ver. 12). On account of this unheard of (ver. 13), and unnatural apostasy (vers. 14, 15), desolation, dispersion and flight are again announced to the people as the divine punishment (vers. 16, 17).

Vers. 11 and 12. **And now speak . . . wicked heart.** — And now introduces the transition, after the basis has been laid for the proper object of the discourse. It has been shown that the Lord can form what He will, it is now positively declared, that He will frame evil.—**I frame** (יֹצֵר). In the transferred sense the word is used also in Isa. xxii. 11; xxxvii. 26; xlvi. 11; Jer. xxxiii. 2.—**Think**. Comp xlix. 30. The words from **turn to way**, are found verbatim in xxv. 5; xxxv. 15. In the last passage is found also the rest of the verse with the exception of דַּרְכֵיכֶם, **your works**. Comp. vii. 3; xxvi. 13.

Vers. 13-17. **Therefore thus . . . day of their fall.** From the peremptory declaration which Israel made in ver. 12, it is concluded that this nation has rendered itself guilty of unfaithfulness, the like of which is found neither in history (ver. 13), nor in nature (ver. 14).—**Inquire now**. Comp. ii. 10, 11.—**Virgin**. Comp. Am. v. 2; Jer. xxxi. 4, 21.—**Ceases**, etc. According to the connection the prophet can only mean to adduce a fact in natural history which forms a parallel to the historical fact that a nation has never forsaken its gods. In general it is plain that he has chosen, as the example from natural history, the perennial connection of the snow on Lebanon, and of the fresh abundant springs, with the שְׂדֵי צוּר. But what is this? Disregarding the various arbitrary and forced explanations, two views may be here considered. According to one it is Mt. Zion, according to the other, Mt. Lebanon itself. It is in favor of the former. 1. That Zion in xvii. 3 appears under the designation שָׂדֶה, and in xxi. 13 as צוּר הַמִּישׁוֹר. 2. That in Ps. cxxxiii. 3 also the dew of Hermon, which descends on Mt. Zion, is spoken of, and in Prov. xxv. 23 it is said: the north wind brings [Eng. Vers.: driveth away] rain. 3. That the expression *snow of Lebanon* intimates that the rock of the plain is not identical with Lebanon. On the other hand it may be objected to this explanation: 1. That a connection between the snow of Lebanon and the springs of Zion is very dubious. In a bold poetical figure the extension of the dew of Hermon over the whole land even to Zion, may be spoken of, but here a fact in natural history is treated of, which must have been familiar to the Israelites, and which must have set before them a clear representation of natural and most intimate union. Now other traces show that the Israelites acknowledged the sea to be the true and proper source of rain and moisture for the land, which it also is in fact (comp. 1 Kings xviii. 44, 45; Luke xii. 54; WINER, R. W. B., s. v., Winde; RAUMER, Paläst. S. 91). Hence in Palestine the rainy winds are the West and South-west, which the Arabs also call the "fathers of the rain." In Prov. xxv. 23 the north-west wind is probably to be understood by רוּחַ צָפוֹן, since the north wind, as with us, is cold, producing frost (Job xxxvii. 9, 10; Ecclus. xliii. 20). 2. In xvii. 3 הררי בשׂדה is a designation of the whole land, for it is not=my mountain set in the plain (as antithesis between mountain and plain) but my mountain together with the plain (antithesis between the sanctuary and the rest of the country inhabited and cultivated by men. Comp. the Comm.). The passage xxi. 13 also does not enter into comparison with this. For there evidently not Mt. Zion, but the house of David, is to be understood, of which it is said that it is like a rock in a valley, eminent above the surrounding level, whereby it is intended to designate, not the topographical position of Zion, but the relation of the king's house to his subjects. 3. That it is not said, Ceases the snow from the rock of the field, from Lebanon? but ceases the snow of Lebanon? etc., is certainly remarkable and in other circumstances would be a strong proof that the prophet wished to distinguish the rock and the mountain. For Lebanon alone presented to them the picture of a snow-capped mountain, and all the snow they had came from it. Add to this, that Lebanon was originally an appellative and signifies albedo (comp. Alpes, which were so called ab albis nivibus) whence there appears to me to be a play upon words in Lebanon: the Lebanon snow and the white snow. The absence of the article favors this, for if Lebanon were regarded merely as a proper name, it would require the article. Comp. NAEGELSB. Gr., § 71, 4 b. [So HENDERSON.—S. R. A.].—In favor of the other view, according to which צוּר שָׂדַי is Lebanon itself, is 1. that the perennial snow of a mountain, like Lebanon, which though in a hot climate is never free from snow, and on which the snow seems to have lost its peculiar quality of disappearing rapidly, is particularly adapted to serve as an emblem of the most faithful adherence. It seems as though TACITUS had this passage in view, when he wrote (Hist. V., 6): "Praecipuum montium Libanum erigit, mirum dictu, tantos inter ardores opacum fidumque nivibus. Idem amnem Jordanem alit funditque." Comp. J. D. MICH., Observ. in Jer., p. 161.—Add to this that 2. the expression used of Lebanon seems particularly appropriate in this connection. For not only may Lebanon be mentioned as an isolated far-looking summit, but especially also as a protecting wall for the plains, which wards off the northerly storms and at the same time mitigates the heat. And is not this "protecting wall of the plains" an excellent emblem of the עוֹלָמִים צוּר, which is spoken of in Isa. xxvi. 4, and of the יִשְׂרָאֵל צוּר, in Isa. xxx. 29? The snow never forsakes the שָׂדַי צוּר, but Israel, changeable as the snow, easily forsakes the עוֹלָמִים צוּר!—Dry up. The meaning of tearing out, uprooting, which נָתַשׁ includes, is not inappropriate if taken in the figurative sense. The change into יִנָּשְׁתוּ [dry up], which perhaps lies at the basis of the old translations, with the exception of the Vulgate, and which is supported on Isa. xix. 5; xli. 17; Jer. li. 30, is therefore unnecessary.—Waters. The wealth of springs on Lebanon is well known. The traveler KORTE assures us that nowhere did he see such large and numerous springs as on Lebanon. Vid. RAUMER, Paläst., S. 30. In Song of Sol. iv. 15 also the rippling waters of Lebanon are used as a comparison. The thought of the prophet is that as the snow covers Lebanon perpetually above, so the flow of waters at its foot is also perpetual. For the snow is the source of the springs. The expression therefore seems to have been chosen purposely to indicate the connection between the snow and the waters of Lebanon. An uprooting of the waters would be caused by the cessation of the snow. Comp. HITZIG on the passage.—Cold (קָרִים, comp. Prov. xxv. 25; xvii. 27) needs no change; the meaning "cold" is perfectly appropriate.—Rippling, נוֹזְלִים, comp. Exod. xv. 8; Isa. xliv. 3; Ps lxxviii. 16; Prov. v. 15; Song of Sol. iv. 15.—That my people, etc. This gives the reason why the questions in vers. 13 and 14 have been put. Since the people have forgotten Him (ii. 32), the Lord looks about to see whether anything similar occurs elsewhere. Comp. Ps. viii. 5.—Made them stumble. The nominative is the collective idea of the idols designated by שָׁוְא, vanity. [HENDERSON: false prophets and idolatrous priests.—S. R. A.] Comp. 2 Chron. xxviii. 23.—When HITZIG and GRAF maintain that the old ways were not good, for even the fathers of the Israelites had sinned from ancient times by idolatry (ii. 32; vii. 25, 26; xi. 10), they forget that the good ways are more ancient than the people of Israel. Even if Israel since the exodus from Egypt had not served the Lord (which after ii. 2 notwithstanding vii. 25 is not to be maintained too unconditionally), yet the way of Jehovah was the way everlasting (vi. 16), and Israel's true and proper way, for their fathers at any rate served the God who from them is called the God of Abraham, Isaac and Jacob, and the fathers' way is de jure that of the children.—To walk, etc., is the immediate and first consequence of the effect designated by made to stumble, while to make . . . a desolation, ver. 16, denotes the mediate consequence.—Like the east wind. Comp. Exod. xiv. 21; Ps. xlviii. 8; Isa. xxvii. 8; Hos. xiii. 15; John iv. 8.—Back, etc. Comp. ii. 27.

§ 8 *The manner in which the people receive the word of the prophet, and his petition to the Lord for protection from their hostility.*

XVIII. 18–23.

18 And they said : Come, let us devise plans against Jeremiah,
   For the law shall not perish from the priest,
   Nor counsel from the wise,
   Nor the word from the prophet.
   Come, and let us smite him with the tongue,
   And give no heed to any of his words.
19 Give thou heed, O Jehovah, to me!
   And listen to the voice of my adversaries.[1]
20 Shall then evil be recompensed for good,
   For they have digged a pit for my soul?
   Remember how I stood before thee to speak good for them,
   And to turn away thy wrath from them.
21 Therefore deliver up their children to famine,
   And give them over to the hands of the sword ;
   And let their wives be childless and widowed,
   But let their men be sacrifices of death,
   Their youths be slain by the sword in battle.
22 Let a cry be heard from their houses,
   When thou bringest the murderous troop suddenly upon them ;
   Because they have digged a pit to take me,
   And laid snares for my feet.
23 But thou, O Jehovah, knowest all their murderous plans against me ;
   Cover not up their iniquity,
   Nor blot out[2] their sin before thy face ;
   That they may be[3] overthrown[4] before thee ;
   And in the time of thy wrath act against them.

TEXTUAL AND GRAMMATICAL.

[1] Ver. 19.—יְרִיבָי. The word is found besides only in Isa. xlix. 25; Ps. xxxv. 1.
[2] Ver. 23.—תֶּמְחִי. Comp. יָנֻת, iii. 6. The form is anomalous for תִּמְחֶה (Neh. xiii. 14). Comp. OLSH. § 257, e, Anm.; EWALD, § 224, c.
[3] Ver. 23.—וְיִהְיוּ. The Chethibh is וְהָיוּ. The Masoretes did not wish the series of jussive or imperative forms to be interrupted.—The word expresses the result. *that they lie overthrown.* Accordingly this sentence concludes the series of negative petitions ; in conclusion follows the positive request : *at the time of thy wrath, etc.* It is evident that the change proposed by the Keri is unnecessary.
[4] Ver. 23.—מֻכְשָׁלִים points back to ver. 15. The form here only. Comp. Ps. ix. 4 ; Jer. vi. 15 ; xx. 11.

EXEGETICAL AND CRITICAL.

Here, as before, the prophet represents his adversaries as answering his faithful admonitions with words of personal enmity. Comp. xi. 19 ; xv. 10 ; xvii. 15. And as in these passages he always prayed that the Lord would avenge him, so here, but in stronger measure. (*Vide infra* DOCTR. AND ETHICAL No. 13, and the EXEGETICAL rems. on xx. 14). After showing the hostile disposition of his opponents, he turns in supplication to the Lord (vers. 19-23). In this prayer he beseeches the Lord to give heed to his and to his adversaries' speeches (ver. 19, and observe above all that they would recompense good with evil, while he has always sought their highest welfare from God (ver. 20). Therefore the Lord may permit death and destruction to come upon those who have digged a pit and laid snares for him (vers. 21 and 22); he is not to forgive these murderous associates their iniquity, but to overthrow them, and let them feel His anger (ver. 23).

Ver. 18. **And they said . . . any of his words.—Let us devise** (נַחְשְׁבָה) as in xi. 19 coll. xviii. 11.—**For the law,** *etc.* The meaning must be: We do not need this Jeremiah, for without him we shall always have priests to instruct us (Mal. ii. 7), wise men to advise us, prophets to proclaim to us the word of the Lord. Comp Comm. on viii. 8-10 ; Ezek. vii. 26. It is

of course presupposed that the instruction, etc. will be in accordance with their views.—**With the tongue.** That these smitings with the tongue (comp. ix. 2, 7; Ps. lxiv. 4, etc.) had the death of the prophet for their object is evident from ver. 23.
Vers. 19-23. **Give thou heed ... act against them.** Observe the antithesis between **Give no heed** in ver. 18 and **give thou heed** in ver. 19.—**Shall then evil.** On the subject-matter comp. xiv. 7-21; 2 Macc. xv. 12-14. In ver. 14 we read: "ὁ φιλάδελφος οὗτός ἐστιν ὁ πολλὰ προσευχόμενος περὶ τοῦ λαοῦ καὶ τῆς ἁγίας πόλεως, Ἱερεμίας ὁ τοῦ θεοῦ προφήτης."—**How I stood.** Comp. xv. 1.—**Into the hands.** This expression is found also in Ps. lxiii. 11; Ezek. xxxv. 5; it is used in the sense of *in potestatem*, which meaning has various gradations. Comp.

2 Kings xii. 12; Job xvi. 21; Jer. xxxiii. 13 with 1 Chron. vi. 16 (into service); 1 Chron. xv. 2, 3, 6; 2 Chron. xxiii. 18; Ezra iii. 10 (in service, under the hands, according to the direction); 2 Chron. xxix. 27 (on the foundation).—**Sacrifices of death.** Comp. Comm. on xv. 2. —**Because,** etc. KIMCHI supposes that the enemies had attempted to administer poison to the prophet; R. SALOMO, with many other Rabbins, that they had accused him of adultery, others of blasphemy. Comp. ver. 18.—**Cover not up.** Comp. Ps. cix. 14; Isa. ii. 9.—**In the time of thy wrath.** Not of grace, *i. e.*, of gracious disposition, but in the moment of wrath, in the Lord to appear and act against them.—**Act,** עָשֵׂה, in the absolute sense, as in xiv. 7; xxix. 12; Dan. xi. 7 coll. viii. 4; xi. 3, 36.

SECOND SYMBOL:—THE BROKEN VESSEL.

CHAPTERS XIX., XX.

1. *The symbolic action and its interpretation.*

XIX. 1-13.

1 Thus saith the LORD [Jehovah], Go and get [buy] a potter's earthen bottle [vessel],¹ and take [some] of the ancients [elders]² of the people, and of the an-
2 cients [elders] of the priests; And go forth into the valley of the Son of Hinnom [valley of Ben-Hinnom], which is by the entry of the east [Potters'] gate,³ and
3 proclaim there the words that I shall tell thee, And say, Hear ye the word of the LORD [Jehovah], O kings of Judah, and inhabitants of Jerusalem: Thus saith the Lord of hosts [Jehovah Zebaoth] the God of Israel, Behold, I will bring evil upon
4 this place, the which whosoever heareth,⁴ his ears shall tingle. Because they have forsaken me, and have estranged⁵ this place, and have burned incense in it to other gods, whom neither they nor their fathers have known, nor the kings of Judah, and
5 have filled this place with the blood of innocents; They have built also the high places of Baal, to burn their sons [children] with fire for burnt offerings unto Baal, which I commanded not, nor spake it, neither came it into my mind.
6 Therefore, behold, the days come, saith the LORD [Jehovah]. that this place shall no more be called Tophet, nor The Valley of the Son of Hinnom [valley of
7 Ben-Hinnom] but The Valley of Slaughter. And I will make void [pour out] the counsel of Judah and Jerusalem in this place; and I will cause them to fall by the sword before their enemies, and by the hands of them that seek their lives; and their carcases will I give to be meat for the fowls of the heaven, and for the
8 beasts of the earth [land]. And I will make this city desolate, and an hissing [a horror of desolation and a derision]; every one that passes thereby [through] shall be astonished and hiss [deride] because of all the plagues thereof.⁶ And I will
9 cause them to eat the flesh of their sons, and the flesh of their daughters, and they shall eat every one the flesh of his friend in the siege and straitness, wherewith their enemies. and they that seek their lives, shall straiten them.⁷
10 Then shalt thou break the bottle [pitcher] in the sight of the men that go with thee.
11 And shalt say unto them, Thus saith the LORD of Hosts [Jehovah Zebaoth], Even so will I break this people and this city, as one breaketh a potter's vessel, that cannot be made whole again; and they shall bury them in Tophet, till [because] there be
12 [is] no place [room] to bury [elsewhere]. Thus will I do unto this place, saith the

LORD [Jehovah], and to the inhabitants thereof, and even make this city as To-
13 phet: and the houses of Jerusalem, and the houses of the kings of Judah, shall be
defiled as the place of Tophet, [because of]⁸ all the houses upon whose roofs they
have burned incense unto all the host of heaven, and have poured out⁹ drink-offerings unto other gods.

TEXTUAL AND GRAMMATICAL.

¹ Ver. 1.—בקבק is found as an appellative in 1 Ki. xiv. 3, and as a proper name in Ezr. ii. 51; Neh. vii. 53, coll. בַּקְבֻּקְיָה, Neh. xi. 17; xii. 9, 25. GESENIUS (*Thes.*, I., p. 232 [*Lex.* s. v.]) derives it from בקק, *evacuavit* (comp. ver. 7), according to the analogy of בְּרָכִים חַרְחַר, etc. So also OLSH. § 190, e. [HITZIG renders: a bottle,—NAEGELSB.: a pitcher,—
from the maker of earthenware.—S. R. A.]—יוֹצֵר חֶרֶשׂ. There is also צְרִי כֶּכֶל, Isa. xliv. 9 coll. liv. 16, 17. חֶרֶשׂ,
synonymous with חֶרֶם, is that which has become dry and rough by heat. (Comp. חֶרֶס, *scabies a scabiendo*, as *Krätze*
from *kratzen* in German), Deut. xxviii. 27, and חֶרֶם, *sun*, in Jud. viii. 13; Job ix. 7; then especially the burnt earthenware:
בְּלִי חֶרֶס, Lev. vi. 21, etc. נִבְלֵי חֶרֶס, Lam. iv. 2.

² Ver. 1.—וּמִזִּקְנֵי. LXX., καὶ ἄξεις ἀπὸ τῶν πρεσβυτέρων, etc. They certainly did not read וְלָקַחְתָּ, but correctly
supplied it from וְקַח, for the prophet was not merely to buy the pitcher, but to take it with him. It is a species of very
bold *constructio praegnans*, the verb to be supplied governing not the preposition present in the sentence, but the preposition
of a second sentence, connected by ן, to which it forms a predicate. (Comp. NAEGELSB. *Gr.*, § 112, 7.

³ Ver. 2.—שַׁעַר הַחַרְסִית. The form חַרְכוּת is not the later, as HITZIG supposes, but חַרְסִית is the only form used
by the Rabbins, and from this both the Keri and the Χαρσείθ (LXX.) or Ἀρσίθ (Aqu., Symm., Theod.) of the Greek translators is to be explained. The Syriac text in the Loudon Polyglot strangely has *Chadsit*.

⁴ Ver. 3.—Comp. 1 Sam. iii. 11; 2 Ki. xxi. 12. As to the construction 1. כָּל־שֹׁמְעָהּ *Partic. absolutum* to be resolved
into a hypothetical sentence. (Comp. Exod. xii. 15; Numb. xxi. 8; NAEGELSB. *Gr.*, § 97, 2 b); 2. אֲשֶׁר is accusative, attracted by שֹׁמְעָהּ; 3. The apodosis on account of the brevity of the sentence is without the connecting Vau. (Comp. Gen.
iv. 15; Ruth i. 16, 17). תְּצַלֶּנָה for תִּצַּלְנָה (so in 1 Sam. iii. 11) according to the Aramaic formation. Comp. EWALD, §
197, a; OLSH., § 243, b, d.

⁵ Ver. 4.—וַיְנַכְּרוּ LXX. ἀπηλλοτρίωσαν: Vulg., *alienum fecerunt*. This rendering accords both with the connection
and the etymology of the word. The latter occurs in Piel besides only in Deut. xxxii. 7; 1 Sam. xxiii. 7; Job xxi. 29;
xxxiv. 19. With the exception of the passages in Job, in which the Piel evidently has the meaning of the Hiphil, the meaning is everywhere appropriate, "to estrange one's self from another."

⁶ Ver. 8.—On the suffix form in כַּבֹּתָהּ comp. NAEGELSB. *Gr.*, § 44, 4 *Anm.* coll. OLSH., § 131, i.

⁷ Ver. 9.—אֲשֶׁר יָצִיקוּ לָהֶם wherewith they procure them distress (Deut. xxviii. 53, 55, 57). אֲשֶׁר is the *Acc. instru-
mentalis* (comp. NAEGELSB. *Gr.*, § 70, i.); הֵצִיק is that Hiphil, which has the substantive idea contained in the verb with
respect to the nearer object (comp. NAEGELSB. *Gr.*, § 69, 1 *Anm.* 2; Judg. xvi. 16; Isai. xxix. 2, 7).

⁸ Ver. 13.—לְכָל. ל is distributive. Comp. Ezek. xliv. 9. NAEGELSB. *Gr.*, § 112, 5 b.

⁹ Ver. 13.—וְהַסֵּךְ. Comp. rems. on vii. 18; xliv. 17 sqq. coll. xxxii. 29. With respect to the construction, comp. NAE-
GELSB. *Gr.*, § 92, 2 a.

EXEGETICAL AND CRITICAL.

The prophet receives the command to buy another pitcher from the potter, and in company
with the elders of the people and priests to betake himself to the valley of Ben-Hinnom, near a
gate, which appears here under the name of the
Potter's gate (vers. 1 and 2). There he is to
proclaim the words which we read in vers. 3-13.
In these words a severe divine judgment is first
proclaimed in general (ver. 3). Then the crimes
are narrated in detail, which the people and the
kings of Judah have committed in this place.
Then the divine punishments are mentioned, of
which the witness and theatre will be the valley
of Ben-Hinnom or Tophet: 1. This will be called
the Valley of Slaughter, (ver. 6), in consequence
of the slaughter, which after the failure of the
plans determined on by the people (here the prophet must have made the gesture of pouring out
of the pitcher), both the enemy will make among
the people, and the people among themselves
(vers. 8-9). 2. The people and city shall be
broken in pieces, which the prophet indicates by
the breaking of the pitcher; Tophet for lack of
room shall become a place of interment, and the
city, with all the houses on whose roofs offerings
have been made to Baal, shall become a place like
the desolate and unclean Tophet (vers. 10-13).

Vers. 1 and 2. **Thus saith . . . I shall tell
thee.** This opening is like that in xvii. 19.—
bottle, Heb. *bakbuk*, is an earthen pitcher with
a long neck. The sound of the word seems to
imitate the noise of water being poured out.—
Comp. the Greek βομβυλός, βομβυλη, and the German *Kutterkrug*.—**Elders of the priests** are
mentioned besides only in Isai. xxxvii. 2 (2 Ki.
xix. 2). Whether they are identical with the
princes or chief of the priests (2 Chron. xxvi.
14; Neh. xii. 7) or only in general the most respectable of the priests is doubtful. Comp. OEHLER,
in HERZOG, *R.-Enc.*, XII. S. 183.—**Valley of
Ben-Hinnom.** Comp. Comm. on vii. 31 coll.
ii. 23.—**By the entry** (פֶּתַח), comp. Gen. xviii.
1; Jul. ix. 35, *etc.* NAEGELSB. *Gr.*, § 70, c.—
Potter's gate. 1. concerning the form, comp.
TEXTUAL NOTES. 2. As to the meaning, (a) some
of the older Rabbins, cited by KIMCHI, who however does not agree with them, are of opinion that

the word is to be derived from חרס sun, and that by the sun-gate is to be understood the eastern gate of the temple, since there was no gate in the city-wall to the South. So also TRENELLIUS, PISCATOR, J. D. MICHAELIS and HITZIG, but they would have the southern gate of the outer court (*a solis æstu sic dictam*) understood to be the nearest way to Tophet. (*b*) The other commentators agree in deriving חַרְסִית from חֶרֶס, *testa*. But opinions greatly differ whether the gate was so called because the potsherds were thrown out there [the Chaldee paraphrast renders: the dung-gate], or because the potters lived in its vicinity, or because the clay-pits were just outside the gate. The last is the view of HOFMANN (*Weiss. u. Erf.* II., S. 124, *etc. Vid.* Comm. on vii. 31). Apart from the etymological signification of the word **Tophet**, which HOFMANN gives, it is in favor of this interpretation that this same place is called in Matth. xxvii. 7 ἀγρὸς τοῦ κεραμέως (observe the generic article). This name decidedly favors the supposition that the place stood in closer relation to pottery than that of a mere depository of potsherds. White clay, a kind of pipe-clay, is also still dug there. Comp. HERZOG, *R.-Enc.*, V. S. 475; RAUMER, *Pal.* S. 306. Finally the choice of an earthen pitcher for the prophetic symbol must have been occasioned by the inner relation which the pitcher bore to the place of the action. If it was merely intended to indicate that death and destruction would come upon Jerusalem even so as to fill Tophet with corpses, the breaking and throwing away of any other object would have answered as well. But Jeremiah is to take an earthen pitcher because Tophet was the place where such vessels were produced, consequently nothing was more natural than to choose for this place of breaking an object to be broken which originated there, in connection with which it is not to be denied that other reasons, as the comparatively easy frangibility, and the climax in relation to ch. xviii. (there transformation, here destruction) may have co-operated. And by all this also it is not disputed that the potters may have lived in the vicinity of the clay-pits, and that the same place may have served at the same time for the deposit of potsherds and other refuse. 3. To what gate otherwise known does the pottery-gate correspond? The name occurs here only. The remark on xvii. 19 is here confirmed that the names of the gates of Jerusalem have been often changed. Many commentators proceed, as we have remarked, on the hypothesis that the city wall had no gates to the South. That this is an error will now scarcely be doubted by any one. Comp. RAUMER, *Pal.*, S. 291. On the southern side of the city were the well-gate [Zion-gate?—S. R. A.] and the dung-gate. Both opened on the Tyropœum, both therefore conducted to Tophet, the former being nearer to this place. But the latter corresponds better to the character of Tophet as an unclean spot, receiving the impurities of the city. Here also the *cloaca Betzo* disembogued. "The site of this gate," says RAUMER, *S.* 352, "is the lowest point of the city, to which all the filth of the city and the ravine of Siloah descends."—[Comp. THOMSON, *The Land and the Book*, II. 497]. A definite conclusion is however not to be reached with respect to things concerning which so much uncertainty still prevails.

Vers. 3-5. **And say . . into my mind.** Here it is not recorded, as in xviii. 3, that the prophet performed the command received in vers. 1, 2, and thereupon in the valley of Hinnom received the revelation contained in vers. 8 sqq. For there (ch. xviii.) the revelation to be received was occasioned by the observations made at the potter's (xviii. 3, 4). There is no similar occasion here, so that ver. 3 proceeds at once to communicate the revelation.—**And say**, reads as though the previous discourse were continued, which cannot be the case on account of **I shall tell.** We shall not err if we attribute the mode of expression here chosen to the written representation.—**Kings of Judah.** Here, as in ver. 4 coll. xiii. 13; xvii. 20 the prophet has in view not only the person of the present king, but the kingdom of Judah generally.—**This place is** here, in accordance with what follows. Tophet.—**They**, *etc.* Comp. ix. 15; xvi. 13; xliv. 3, 21.—**Have filled.** On the verbal form comp. Comm. on xviii. 4.—**Blood of innocents.** According to the connection and Ps. cvi. 37, 38 we must understand this of the blood of the children offered in sacrifice.—Ver. 5 is almost verbatim the same as vii. 31; xxxii. 35. Comp. the remarks on the first of these passages.

Vers. 6-9. **Therefore behold . . . shall straiten them.** After, in vers. 4 and 5, the abominations practised in Tophet have been enumerated, the announcement is now made of the corresponding punishments. This announcement, which appears to be a specification of the summary denunciation in ver. 3 *b*, is made in two stages, of which the first (vers. 6-9) is accompanied by the gesture of pouring out (ver. 7), and the second by the act of breaking (ver. 10).—**The days come**, *etc.*, ver. 6. Comp. Comm. on vii. 32.—**Pour out.** Isai. xxiv. 1; Nah. ii. 3. What is poured out falls to the ground, which is frequently used as a figurative expression for coming to naught. Comp. 1 Sam. iii. 19; 2 Kings x. 10.—**In this place.** Is this the *term. in quo*, or *in quem*? I believe the latter. In Tophet all the counsel of Judah and Jerusalem is to find its tragical end, as this is indeed expressed by the name Valley of Slaughter, and by burying in Tophet (ver. 11) and by becoming like Tophet (ver. 12).—**I will give**, *etc.* Comp. vii. 30; xvi. 4.—**A hissing**, ver. 8. Comp. xviii. 16; xxv. 9, 18; li. 37.—**Every one**, *etc.* Comp. 1 Ki. ix. 8; Jer. xviii. 16; xlix. 17; l. 13.—Ver. 9 is taken entire from Deut. xxviii. 53-55 (Lev. xxvi. 29). Comp. Lam. ii. 20; iv. 10. As historical analogies, comp. 2 Ki. vi. 28, 29. JOSEPH, *Bell. Jud.*, VI. 3, 3-5.

Vers. 10-13. **Then shalt thou break . . . unto other gods.** The second stage of the symbolic action. The progress consists in this, that by the breaking of the pitcher the total ruin of the city and people (therefore not merely of individuals) and by the casting into Tophet its desolation and defilement, or in other words its becoming itself Tophet, is symbolized.—**As one breaketh** (ver. 11). Comp. Comm. on v. 26; vi. 29; viii. 4; x. 3; xii. 11; NAEGELSB. *Gr.*, § 101, 2, *b*.—**Cannot be made whole again.**

Though uttered concerning another object, we find the same words *verbatim* in Deut. xxviii 27, 35.—**And they shall bury**, *etc.* Comp. vii. 32. These words being wanting in the LXX., have been suspected. But they stand in a good connection, and correspond to the casting out, by which the pitcher was not merely broken but buried in Tophet. Consequently by this act Tophet is as it were dedicated to the purposes of a cemetery. Jeremiah says interments will be made in Tophet for want of room. This prophecy may have been fulfilled after the destruction of the city by Nebuchadnezzar (comp. xxxii. 29) though we have no positive statements to this effect. But Tophet, having once become a place of burial, must have accomplished this destination afterwards in a significant manner. It is the ἀγρὸς τοῦ κεραμέως which was bought with the price of blood for the burial-place of pilgrims (Matth. xxvii. 3 sqq.; Acts i. 18, 19). And still at the present day Aceldama is the burial-place of pilgrims dying in Jerusalem; indeed the whole of the valley surrounding Zion on the West and South, on its right side, contains numerous rock sepulchres, a true "Necropolis," says RAUMER. Comp. his *Pal.*, *S.* 306.—Ver. 12. **Thus will I do**, *etc.* The Lord will do to the city as is indicated by the breaking of the pitcher. Thus will Jerusalem become a heap of ruins, and unclean, for the want of room presupposes that even the city itself will be full of corpses. Therefore we find ‍ ‍ before לָתֵת = **and indeed**. Comp. rems. on xvii. 10.—**Shall be defiled**, (הֲטֻמְאִים). [HENDERSON renders: which are polluted, shall be as this place; HITZIG, UMBREIT, NAEGELSBACH: shall be as the place of Tophet,

the unclean, *or* unclean.—S. R. A.]. Since the Hebrew in a much higher degree than our modern languages is capable of *the constructio ad sensum*, since especially an ideal plural is often contained in singular words (comp. 1 Ki. v. 17; 2 Sam. xv. 23. NAEGELSH. *Gr.*, § 105, 2 f.) so the connection of the singular **Tophet** with הַטֻּמְאִים presents in itself no difficulty. Only it is not clear what are the several elements included in the unity of Tophet. HOFMANN and others suppose them to be graves. ... referred above, on vii. 31, to altars. This word is certainly elsewhere used as feminine. But in respect also to gender, the same ideal construction prevails in the Hebrew. (Comp. NAEGELSH. *Gr.*, § 60, 4). It appears to me therefore that the prophet had here the places of worship in view. These he calls unclean both on account of the abominations practised there, and the defilements caused by Josiah, 2 Ki. xxiii. 10. The other renderings (**defiled** as the predicate, **or** as in apposition to **houses** or to **place** or another division of the words: הַפְּתֻה טְמֵאִים) are opposed by such strong grammatical objections, that the remaining uncertainty of our explanation is scarce worth consideration in comparison with them. The houses of Jerusalem will however in this sense be like Tophet, that the place where they now stand, will in the future become as desolate and unclean as it.—**Upon the roofs.** Comp. Zeph. i. 5; 2 Ki. xxiii. 12. J. D. MICHAELIS quotes STRABO (XVI. p. 1131): Ναβαταῖοι (comp. 1 Macc. v. 25; ix. 35) ἥλιον τιμῶσιν ἐπὶ τοῦ δώματος ἱδρυσάμενοι βωμὸν, σπένδοντες ἐν αὐτῷ καθ᾿ ἡμέραν καὶ λιβανίζοντες.

---

2. The opposition and punishment of Pashur.

XIX. 14.—XX. 6.

14 Then came Jeremiah [back] from Tophet, whither the LORD [Jehovah] had sent him to prophesy; and he stood in the court of the LORD's [Jehovah's] house; and
15 said to all the people, Thus saith the LORD of hosts [Jehovah Zebaoth], the God of Israel: Behold, I will bring upon this city and upon all her towns all the evil that I have pronounced against it, because they have hardened their necks, that they might not hear my words.
1 XX. Now Pashur, the son of Immer the priest, who was also chief governor[1] in the house of the LORD, heard [that] Jeremiah prophesied [prophesy] these things.
2 Then Pashur smote Jeremiah the prophet, and put him in the stocks [prison] that were [was] in the high gate of Benjamin, [the Benjamin-gate, the upper] which was
3 by [in] the house of the LORD [Jehovah]. And it came to pass on the morrow that Pashur brought forth Jeremiah out of the stocks [prison]. Then said Jeremiah unto him, The LORD [Jehovah] hath not called thy name Pashur, but Magor-missabib,
4 [" Terror round about "]. For thus saith the LORD [Jehovah], Behold, I will make thee [give thee up] a [to] terror to [for] thyself and to [for] all thy friends: and they shall fall by the sword of their enemies and thine eyes shall behold it: and I will give all Judah into the hand of the king of Babylon, and he shall carry them
5 captive into Babylon, and shall slay them with the sword. Moreover I will deliver all the strength [store][2] of this city, and all the labours [gains] thereof, and all the

precious things thereof, and all the treasures of the kings of Judah will I give into the hand of their enemies, which shall spoil them, and take them, and carry them to
6 Babylon. And thou, Pashur, and all that dwell in thine house shall go into captivity: and thou shalt come to Babylon, and there thou shalt die, and shalt be buried there, thou, and all thy friends, to whom thou hast prophesied lies.

TEXTUAL AND GRAMMATICAL.

¹ Ver. 1.—נָגִיד פָּקִיד וְהוּא. The construction is like עֶשֶׂב רָשָׁא, נְבוֹ אֶל, Comp. NAEGELSB. *Gr.*, §§ 72 and 66.
² Ver. 5.—חֹסֶן = *copia*, store. Comp. Prov. xv. 6; xxvii. 24; Isai. xxxiii. 6; Ezek. xxii. 25.

EXEGETICAL AND CRITICAL.

The prophet betakes himself back from Tophet into the temple, and probably repeats there his predictions of calamity (vers. 14, 15). For this he is struck by Pashur, the governor of the temple, and committed to prison for the night (xx. 1-2). Released from this confinement in the morning, Jeremiah announces to Pashur that the Lord has changed his name to Magor-missabib, for he will be given up a prey to the torments of mortal anguish, his friends shall be slain before his eyes, Judah carried away to Babylon, all its treasures plundered; he himself shall survive all this, and die and be buried in Babylon, the prophet of lies in the midst of those whom he has deceived (vers. 4-6).

Vers. 14, 15. **Then came Jeremiah .. my words.** As these words are closely connected with the previous context וַיָּבֹא, ver. 14, corresponds to יָצָא. In antithesis to יָצָא however בֹּא has always the meaning of *return*. Comp. Numb. xxvii. 17; Deut. xxviii. 6; 1 Chron. xi. 2; Ps. cxxi. 8; cxxvi. 6.—Ver. 15. **Thus saith,** *etc.* It is incredible that Jeremiah spoke only these few words in the temple. He would then have said nothing new, and have given no motive to the evidently increased anger of the temple-governor. We must therefore refer **all that I have pronounced** specially to the words spoken in Tophet, and assume a repetition of these words, in order that the reference might be understood.—**I will bring.** Comp. 2 Sam. v. 2; Mic. i. 15, *etc.* OLSH., § 38, c.; § 208, d. —**All her towns.** Comp. Josh. x. 37, 39; xiii. 17; Jer. xxxiv. 1; Zech. vii. 7.—**Hardened,** *etc.* Comp. xvii. 23; vii. 26.—**That they might not hear.** Comp. xvi. 12; xviii. 10; xlii. 13.

XX. 1-6. **Now Pashur heard... prophesied lies.** According to Ezr. ii. 38; x. 22; Neh. vii. 41, there was a course of priests of the name Pashur. Not of this, however, but of the course named as that of Immer in these passages (comp. 1 Chron. xxiv. 14) was the Pashur of the text. He is not mentioned elsewhere. For though the name frequently occurs (xxi. 1; xxxviii. 1; 1 Chron. ix. 12; Neh. x. 3; xi. 12), none of the individuals designated by it can be regarded as identical with this Pashur. It is at most possible that the father of Gedaliah mentioned in xxxviii. 1 may be the same. Comp. HITZIG, *ad loc.*—**Chief governor.** The expression involves that there were several overseers (comp. JOSEPH. *Antiqq.*, X. 8, 5). Without doubt the temple-watch (comp. WINER, *R.-W.-B*, Art., *Tempel* at the end) was under the orders of the "governor." From a comparison of xxix. 25, 26, with lii. 24, it seems that the temple-governor took the second rank to the high-priest. As the head of the temple-police, Pashur now puts Jeremiah into the מַהְפֶּכֶת. The expression occurs besides only in xxix. 26; 2 Chron. xvi. 10. It is without doubt a contrivance for shutting up in a crooked position (στρεβλωτήριον. Symm. ποδοστράβη). Comp. Acts xvi. 24.—**Gate of Benjamin,** *etc.* From xxxvii. 13; xxxviii. 7, it is evident that there was a city-gate which led into the territory of the tribe of Benjamin, and was therefore called the gate of Benjamin. The one mentioned in the text is expressly distinguished from this as a temple-gate. The same name intimates identity of cause. We must then look for this temple-gate also in the direction of Benjamin, *i. e.*, to the north. The upper gate corresponds to the upper court, forming one of the entrances to it. Whether this upper gate of Benjamin is the same with the new gate, leading to the upper court (xxxvi. 10; xxvi. 10) which, according to 2 Kings xv. 35, was built by Jotham, is questionable. Comp. Ezek. viii. 3; xiv. 5; ix. 2.—**Not called Pashur,** ver. 3. The signification of the name Pashur is very obscure. Most commentators derive the word from the Arabic *pasaha*=*amplius fuit*, and חוּר *circumcirca*. Hence FUERST: *extension*—*around*. Others from פָּשׁ, Lev. xiii. 5, 7, and חוּר, Isa. xxix. 22, as though "the widely extended authority of the man, making all pale" (comp. NEUMANN), were indicated. EWALD renders *Joy* (פָּשׁ or פָּש from שָׂפ, Mal. iii. 20) *around* (as though חוּר were pronounced חוֹל). MEIER: *Spirit of the free* (פָּש as in Job xxxv. 15 =*extension, high spirit, pride*; חוּר=חָר *the noble, the free*). HITZIG and GRAF cannot dispute that Jeremiah had the etymology, obscure as it is to us, in view, for how otherwise can we explain the choice of the name which he gave to the priest? It is certainly natural that Pashur should have some meaning opposed to that of the name Magor-missabib. It is noteworthy that the explanation afterwards given in ver. 4, sqq., corresponds exactly to this name, in so far as Pashur seems to be always surrounded by terrors, but never himself brought to extremity, for he is to die and be buried in Babylon (ver. 6). In this sense the words **thine eyes shall see,** are especially important. For by these the position of a man is designated, who is not himself reached by the most terrible calamity, but is compelled continually to behold how this comes upon others, and therefore does not escape the torture of anxiety. I would therefore neither render לְךָ

thee. after נָתֹן as distributive (xix. 13), nor would I allow it to depend on the latter, but on מָגוֹר, **terror**: *I give thee up to fear for thyself and thy friends*. This is to be the specific punishment of Pashur, that he is not visited by death itself, but by the constant *fear* of death.—**To whom thou hast prophesied lies**. From these concluding words we learn that Pashur was active, not merely as a priest, but also as prophet. But his prophetic office was assumed and false; and his behaviour toward Jeremiah may, in part at least, be thus accounted for.

3. APPENDIX.

Chap. XX. 7-18.

THE PROPHET'S JOY AND SORROW.

This passage contains an outbreak of the deepest sorrow, called forth by the persecutions, whose object Jeremiah was, both in general and specially in the bad treatment just received (xx. 2, 3; comp. xi. 18; xv. 15; xviii. 18 sqq.). The close connection of the passage with the preceding context is evident, as it seems to me from the words Magor-missabib in ver. 10. For the application of this expression to the prophet is certainly most easily explained by the application which he himself had made of it in so pregnant a manner and to so prominent a personage as Pashur. If we further consider that to pass a night in the stocks must have been a fearful torture, and that it was the first time that the prophet had had to suffer bodily ill-treatment, we must admit that the historical epoch was perfectly adapted for the production of such a lamentation. It should, moreover, be observed that there is no superscription or designation of this effusion as " Word of the Lord." From this it follows that the prophet himself ascribes to this passage only a subjective and private character. The passage may be divided into two parts: 1. Vers. 7-13. *Here the prophet rises from his lament on account of the persecution which had come upon him against his will to the expression of the most joyful hope.* 2. Vers. 14-18. *Here the feeling of sorrow, nay of despair, gets the upper hand, and the prophet sinks into a state of the most utter grief and despondency.*

a. Through sorrow to joy.

XX. 7-13.

7 Thou didst persuade me,[1] Jehovah, and I was persuaded:
Thou didst lay hold of me[2] and didst prevail over me.
I am become a derision daily; every one mocketh me.
8 For as often as I speak or cry,[3]
I must cry concerning violence and ill-treatment;
For the word of Jehovah is made to me a scorn and derision the whole **day**.
9 And if I say,[4] I will no more make mention of him,
Nor speak henceforth in his name,
It becomes in my heart like a burning fire, shut up[5] in my bones,
And I weary myself with refraining, and cannot.
10 For I hear the talking of many:
Terror round about! "Announce! We will announce it!"
All who are obligated to be at peace with me watch for my halting:—
" Perhaps he will allow himself to be taken!
Then we will overpower him and take our revenge on him."
11 But Jehovah is with me as a mighty hero;
Therefore my persecutors will stumble and not prevail.
They shall be grievously put to shame, because they have effected **nothing**,
With eternal disgrace, which is not forgotten.
12 But Jehovah Zebaoth tries justly ;[6] he sees reins and heart.
I shall see thy vengeance on them,
For on thee have I devolved my suit.
13 Sing to Jehovah, praise Jehovah,
For he has saved the soul of the poor from the hand of evil doers.

TEXTUAL AND GRAMMATICAL.

¹ Ver. 7.—פִּתִּיתַנִי. The construction is like וַיִּהְוָה הוֹרִיעֵנִי וָאֵדָעָה, xi. 18.
² Ver. 7.—חָזַק, transitive as in 1 Kings xvi. 22; 1 Chron. xxviii. 20.
³ Ver. 8.—According to the Masoretic punctuation, אֶזְעָק is connected as asyndeton with הָמָס וָשֹׁד אֶקְרָא, depending on אֶקְרָא, as an accusative. This punctuation is supported on the fact that the latter phrase frequently occurs in this connection: vi. 7; Am. iii. 10; Ezek. xlv. 9. In itself it would certainly be allowable and more in accordance with the sense to consider the latter sentence as apodosis of the former.
⁴ Ver. 9.—On the form of the conditional sentence, comp. NAEGELSB. Gr., § 85 a, etc.
⁵ Ver.—יָצֹר, being in apposition to אֵשׁ בֹּעֶרֶת, is to be rendered as neuter: *inclusum aliquid*. Comp. NAEGELSB. Gr., § 60, 4.
⁶ Ver. 12.—[HENDERSON: The Trier of the righteous.—S. R. A.]

EXEGETICAL AND CRITICAL.

The prophet first calls to mind that he had not thrust himself into the prophetic office, but undertaken it with reluctance (ver. 7 a). That his objections were well founded is shown by the result, for he has reaped nothing in return for his proclamation of the divine word but scorn and derision (vers. 7 b–8). But when he attempted to divest himself of the prophetic vocation, he found this impossible; there was an impulse from within, which burned like a fire and threatened to consume him unless he were relieved (ver. 9). And yet his ministry did not cease to be ruinous to him. He hears how the words of his prophecy, as "Terror round about" (xx. 3), are turned against him in derision, and used in denunciation of the prophet. Yea, even such as should be well disposed towards him watched curiously to spy out some false step, by which they might obtain the satisfaction of their feeling of revenge (ver. 10). He then consoles himself with the hope that everlasting shame will be the portion of his enemies (ver. 11), and that he will be avenged by God, the true knower of hearts (ver. 12). Finally in the anticipation of being heard, he breaks out into a summons to praise God as the Saviour of the poor (ver. 13).

Vers. 7 and 8. **Thou didst persuade him ... the whole day.** On the subject-matter, comp. i. 5 sqq.

Ver. 9. **And if I say ... and cannot.** The prophet describes his experience, when, having undertaken the prophetic calling, he attempts to escape from it. He had the feeling as if a fire were burning within him, which having no outlet would consume him, to which, therefore, he was obliged to give an outlet by expressing what was inwardly communicated to him. Comp. vi. 11; Am. iii. 8.—**I weary myself.** Comp. ix. 4; xv. 6.

Vers. 10-13. **For I hear ... evil-doers.** כִּי For in ver. 10, cannot possibly refer immediately to ver. 9. It rather presupposes a similar thought to that to which the parallel כִּי in ver. 8 refers, and which is contained in ver. 7 b. We must, therefore, supply after ver. 9 a thought of this kind: since the cause remains, the effect also remains (namely, that indicated in 7 b). How far this is the case, is shown in the following sentence.—**Talk,** דִּבָּה is *fama*, *rumor*, public talk, report (comp. Gen. xxxvii. 2; Num. xiii. 32; xiv. 36, 37; Prov. x. 18; xxv. 10). That it is a secretly circulated, softly whispered rumor, neither follows from the etymology (which is pretty uncertain; comp. FUERST's *Concordance* with his *Lexicon*), nor from the connection of the passage where it occurs. — **Terror,** *etc.* Magor-missabib. The expression occurs in vi. 25; afterwards also in xlvi. 5; xlix. 29 coll. Lam. ii. 22, besides Ps. xxxi. 14. Since the discourse to which vi. 25 belongs, is older than ch. xix. and xx., the prophet did not use the expression in xx. 3 for the first time, but only as a repetition of one previously used. In this passage the expression may be understood as only an ironical quotation. For 1. The form of the expression is not such that it can be designated as a popular form of threatening. מָגוֹר, *magor*, is not only a comparatively rare word, but one which belongs exclusively to poetic and prophetic phraseology; it occurs only eight times in the Old Testament, and except once in Isa. (xxxi. 9 in another connection), only in the formula here used, six times in Jeremiah and in Ps. xxxi. 14. 2. The expression is evidently one peculiar to Jeremiah, as is clear from what has been stated; in addition to which may be remarked, that Ps. xxxi. contains so many elements peculiar to the style of Jeremiah or related to it, that the question whether Jeremiah was not its author is fully justified. As it can scarcely be doubted that those scoffers applied his own phrase to the prophet, it is further in the highest degree probable that they did this from an occasion on which it had been used by the prophet not by the way, but in a pregnant manner. This latter was, however, the case when Jeremiah changed the name of so important a personage as Pashur into Magor-missabib. The question is of subordinate interest in what sense they applied the expression to the prophet; whether it was as a menace against him, or as a reproach for his hostile disposition towards the community. Probably they wished to unite both.—**All who are obligated,** *etc.* Comp. xxii. 22; Ob. 8; Psalm xli. 10.— **Watch for my halting.** צֶלַע in the meaning of "side," according to which "who cover my side" would be in apposition.—**Friends** [literally: men of my peace], from the want of a predicate, gives no sense [though adopted by SCHMID, SCHNURRER, EICHHORN, and GESENIUS]. Doubtless it is, as in Ps. xxxv. 15, *claudicatio*, tottering, making a false step. For שָׁמַר sense of "to watch for, to lie in wait," see Ps lvi. 7; lxxi. 10; Job x. 14; xiii. 27.—**Overpower him.** Comp. i. 19; xv. 20.—**My persecutors.** Comp. xv. 15; xvii. 18.—**Not prevail.** Comp. v. 22; iii. 5 —**Effect nothing.** Comp. Comm. on x. 21.—**Eternal disgrace.** Comp.

xxiii. 40.—**But Jehovah** (ver. 12). Comp. xi. 20.—**Justly**, צַדִּיק might be accusative. But from the parallel with xi. 20, we perceive that it is intended to define more particularly the action predicated. The sense is also more satisfactory, if it is not merely said, *what* the Lord sees, but also *how* He sees it.—**Sing**, *etc.* A hymn of the hopeful man, who by faith possesses that which is still future (Heb. xi. 1).

---

b. **For the present nothing but sorrow: The prophet curses the day of his birth.**

XX. 14-18.

14 Cursed be the day wherein I was begotten!
  Let not the day, wherein my mother bare me, be blessed!
15 Cursed be the man who brought tidings to my father, saying,
  A son is born to thee, a man-child!—making him very glad.
16 And let that man be as the cities which the Lord overthrew without mercy,
  And let him hear the cry in the morning and alarm of war at noontide,
17 Because he slew me not in the womb;
  So that my mother might have been my grave,
  And her womb have remained always gravid.
18 Wherefore came I forth from the womb,
  To see labour and sorrow and my days consumed in shame?

EXEGETICAL AND CRITICAL.

The prophet curses the day of his begetting and the day of his birth (ver. 14). He further curses the man, who brought to his father the first news of his birth (ver. 15). He wishes that this man may be like Sodom and Gomorrah (ver. 16), because he did not kill him in the womb and thus prevent his birth (ver. 17). Finally he breaks out again into a lamentation:—O why must I be born to a life of misery and shame (ver. 18)? Two questions here arise. 1. Is such a cursing in the mouth of a prophet to be justified? 2. Is it in place in this connection immediately after the hopeful words in vers. 11-13? As to the first question, as a preliminary all those arbitrary interpretations are to be rejected, which understand by the day which Jeremiah curses, not the day of his birth, but some other day, especially some future day, as that of the destruction of Jerusalem (as according to Jerome the older Rabbins),—or which suppose that Jeremiah speaks not in his own name, but in the name of others (*perditorum hominum*),—or which suppose that Jeremiah complains here not of external but internal trials, or of the perversity of the people (CALVIN), or that he gives an account of a trial which he had endured previously (in explanation of אָבִי, ver. 13, on account of which אֲשֶׁר אֲבִיךְ or אָמַר is to be supplied before ver. 14. SEB. SCHMIDT). It should be observed that this entire passage from ver. 7 onwards, is not proclaimed by the prophet as a word of Jehovah (Comp. 1 Cor. vii. 25). He gives us merely a true reflex of his human feeling. Who can dispute the possibility of a man like Jeremiah having such temptations of indignation and despair? Is it not human? Do the men of God cease to be men? Think of that man of God, Job, whose words evidently (iii. 3 sqq.) hovered before the mind of the prophet. It is further to be observed, that the cursing is merely a rhetorical form. It has no object. The long past day of his birth is as little an object, to which the curse might really attach itself as the man who announced to the father the birth of his son,—who in reality, probably, never existed. For were men witnesses of confinements? Is it not of purpose that the prophet speaks of a man, and not of a woman? Therefore CHRYSOSTOM says concerning Job: "*in:nimatis facit injuriam*" (GHISL II., S. 523). Finally, however, it must be admitted, as SEB. SCHMIDT sets forth, that it manifests an infirmity on the part of the prophet. FÖRSTER even says: "*Grande hoc et inexcusabile prophetæ peccatum est.*" And indeed the sinfulness of it consists partly in the high degree of impatience and ill-humor, which is here manifested, and partly in the form in which it displays itself. If this may be regarded as rhetorical hyperbole, yet this mode of expression is not New Testament, Christian, evangelical. We find here, too, somewhat of the spirit of the Ben-Hargem, to whom Christ said: Ye know not what manner of spirit ye are of (Luke ix. 55). Comp. the DOCTRINAL AND ETHICAL remarks on xviii. 20. The second question, whether this outbreak of indignation suits the connection, or is supposable as following vers. 11-13, is answered by many in the negative. EWALD even places vers. 14-18 before ver. 7. GRAF regards it as an independent fragment, a further development of xv. 10, which is placed here only on account of its agreement in purport with vers. 7-10. Now it must certainly be admitted that an outbreak of ill-humor such as this, after ver. 13, is in a high degree remarkable. But observe the following points: 1. It is not necessary to suppose that vers. 14-18 contain the expres sion of a state of mind, which followed immediately on that joyous state described in the previous context. There may have been a pause, a transition. None the less does the prophet portray the occurrences in his own mind with perfect correctness. He gives us to understand that his state of comfort did not long continue, but soon made way for its opposite. 2. This arrangement of the psychological tableaux corresponds also to the course of history: the prophet never attained in this life to the enjoyment of outward peace. If he had now and then a moment of rest and of hope, it was soon past. Ver. 18 corresponds only too exactly to the actual tenor of his life.

Ver. 14. **Cursed be the day ... be blessed.** Even R. SALOMO and ABARBANEL, in order to avoid tautology took ילדת in the sense of *beget*. They add that Jeremiah was begotten on the day that Manasseh killed the prophets of the Lord (2 Kings xxi. 16). Moreover comp. xv. 10; Job iii. 3 sqq.

Vers. 15-18. **Cursed be the man ... consumed in shame.** The Rabbins say this man was Pashur.—**Brought tidings** בִּשַּׂר with accusatives of the person, 1 Sam. xxxi. 9; 2 Sam. xviii. 19.—**As the cities,** etc. Allusion to Gen. xix. 25.—**In the morning ... at noontide=** unceasingly, without any breathing pause. Comp. Ps. lv. 18.—In [A. V.: from] **the womb.** מֵרֶחֶם. Comp. Job iii. 11. The preposition מִן, on account of the following sentence, cannot be =*from*—*away*, but is used here in accordance with that idiom, by which the *terminus a quo* is used for the *terminus in quo*, or *in quem*. Comp. מִקֶּדֶם, **eastwards.** Gen. xi. 2. [Eng. Vers. "from the east"—S. R. A.]. גָּס מִפְּרָחָק *he flees into the distance.* Isa. xvii. 13; Prov. vii. 19; NAEGELSB. *Gr.*, § 112, 5 d. The man may be regarded equally well with Jehovah [HENDERSON], as the subject of **slew,** especially if we remember that the whole description is not of a historical but rhetorical character. Comp. Ps. xxxi. 10. ["While destitute of the sublime imagery employed by Job, this passage is not surpassed in pathos; there is a unity and condensation throughout, which heighten its poetical beauty." HENDERSON.—S. R. A.].

DOCTRINAL AND ETHICAL.

1. On xviii. 2. "What is the prophet of God to learn in the house of the potter? How shall this be his Bible or his school? But God chooses the foolish things to confound human wisdom (1 Cor. i. 27)." CRAMER. ["An orator would never choose such an instance for the purpose of making an impression on his audience; still less for the purpose of exhibiting his own skill and liveliness. It must be for business, not for amusement, that such a process is observed."—"What we want in every occupation is some means of preserving the continuity of our thoughts, some resistance to the influences which are continually distracting and dissipating them. But it is especially the student of the events of his own time, of the laws which regulate them, of the issues which are to proceed from them, who has need to be reminded that he is not studying a number of loose disconnected phenomena, but is tracing a principle under different aspects and through different manifestations. A sensible illustration, if we would condescend to avail ourselves of it, would often save us from much vagueness and unreality, as well as from hasty and unsatisfactory conclusions." MAURICE.—S. R. A.]

2. On xviii. 6 sqq. *Omne simile claudicat.* Man is not clay, though he is made of clay (Gen. ii. 7). Consequently in vers. 8 and 10 the moral conditions are mentioned, which by virtue of his personality and freedom must be fulfilled on the part of man, in order that the divine transformation to good or bad may take place. If the clay is spoiled on the wheel, it cannot help it. It is probably only the potter's fault. Nothing then is here symbolized but the omnipotence of God, by virtue of which He can in any given case suppress whole kingdoms and nations, and transform them with the same ease and rapidity as the potter rolls up the spoiled vessel into a ball of clay, and immediately gives it a new form. It would be well for all to convince themselves, by witnessing the process, of the wonderful ease with which the potter forms the clay on the wheel.

3. On xviii. 6-10. "*Cogitet unusquisque peccata sua, et modo illa emendet, cum tempus est. Sit fructuosus dolor, non sit sterilis pœnitudo. Tanquam hoc dicit Deus, ecce indicavi sententiam, sed nondum protuli. Prœdixi non fixi. Quid times, quia dixi? Si mutaveris, mutatur. Nam scriptum est, quod pœnitet Deum. Numquid quomodo hominem sic pœnitet Deum? Nam dictum est: si pœnituerit vos de peccatis vestris, pœnitebit me de omnibus malis, quæ facturus eram vobis. Numquid quasi errantem pœnitet Deum? Sed pœnitentia dicitur in Deo mutatio sententiæ. Non est iniqua, sed justa. Quare justa? Mutatus est reus, mutavit judex sententiam. Noli terreri. Sententia mutata est, non justitia. Justitia integra manet, quia mutato debet parcere, quia justus est. Quomodo pertinaci non parcit, sic mutato parcit.*" AUGUSTIN, *Sermo* 109. *De Tem. ad medium.*

4. On xviii. 6-10. "*Comminationes Dei non intelligendæ sunt absolutæ, sed cum exceptione pœnitentiæ et conditione impœnitentiæ. Promissiones itidem non sunt absolutæ sed circumscriptæ cum conditione obedientiæ, tum exceptione crucis.* God stipulates everywhere for the cross." Comp. Deut. xxviii. FÖRSTER.

5. On xviii. 6-10. "*Præscientia et prædictio Dei non injicit absolutam eventus necessitatem rebus præscitis ac prædictis.*" FÖRSTER.

6. On xviii. 8. "*O felix pœnitentium humilitas! Quam potens es apud omnipotentem.*" BERNARD of Clairvaux.

[On xviii. 8-10. "I apprehend that we shall learn some day that the call to individual repentance, and the promise of individual reformation, has been feeble at one time, productive of turbulent, violent, transitory effects at another, because it has not been part of a call to national repentance, because it has not been connected with a promise of national reformation. We may appeal to men by the terrors of a future state; we may use all the machinery of revivalists to awaken them to a concern for their souls; we may produce in that way a class of religious men who pursue an object which other men do not pursue (scarcely a less selfish, often not a less outward object):—who leave the world to take its own course;—who, when they mingle in it, as in time they must do for the sake of business and gain, adopt again its own maxims, and become less righteous than other men in common affairs, because they consider religion too fine a thing to be brought from the clouds to the earth, while yet they do not recognise a lower principle as binding on them. But we must speak again the ancient language, that God has made a covenant with the nation, and that all citizens are subjects of an unseen and righteous King, if we would have a hearty, inward repentance, which will really bring us back to God; which will turn the hearts of the fathers to the children, and of the children to the fathers; which will go down to the roots of our life, changing it from a self-seeking life into a life of humility and love and cheerful obedience; which will bear fruit upwards, giving nobleness to our policy and literature and art, to the daily routine of what we shall no more dare to call our *secular* existence." MAURICE.—S. R. A.]

7. On xviii. 10. "God writes as it were a reflection in our heart of that which we have to furnish to Him. For God is disposed towards us as we are disposed towards Him. If we do well, He does well to us; if we love Him, He loves us in return; if we forsake Him, He forsakes us. Ps. xviii. 26." CRAMER. ["Sin is the great mischief-maker between God and a people; it forfeits the benefits of His promises, and spoils the success of their prayers. It defeats His kind intentions concerning them (Hos. vii. 1), and baffles their pleasing expectations from Him. It ruins their comforts, prolongs their grievances, brings them into straits, and retards their deliverances. Is. xlix. 1, 2." HENRY.—S. R. A.]

8. On xviii. 12. "Freedom of the Spirit! Who will allow himself to be brought into bondage by the gloomy words of that singular man, Jeremiah? Every one must be able to live according to his own way of thinking." DIEDRICH, *The prophet Jeremiah and Ezekiel briefly expounded.* 1863, *S.* 59.—This is the watchword of impiety in all times. If in truth every one bears the divinity within him, then it is justified. But since every man bears within him only a θεῖόν τι, a divine germ or spark, a point of connection for the objectively divine, and at the same time a point of connection for the diabolical, it is a hellish deception when one supposes he must follow his *ingenium.* For the question is, whether the voice from within is the voice of God or the voice of the devil. Here it is necessary to try ourselves and to open an entrance to the divine sun of life, so that the divine life-germ in us may be strengthened, and enabled to maintain its true authority.

9. On xviii. 14. On the summits of the high mountains, even in tropical countries, the snow does not entirely melt, and therefore the mighty cool springs at their feet never dry up. With those men only does the pure white snow of divine knowledge and godly fear never melt, whose heads are elevated above the steam and vapor of earthly cares and passions, into the pure clear air of heaven. And they it is, from whose bodies flow streams of living water (John vii. 38).

10. On xviii. 18. Consult the treatise of Luther: How a minister should behave when his office is despised?

11. On xviii. 18. (Come and let us smite him with the tongue, *etc.*). "It is indeed uncertain whether this is said by the preachers or by the whole people: but this is certain, that such actions are performed daily by those teachers, who know no other way of stopping the mouth of a servant of Jesus. 'And not give heed to any of his words.' This is *au pis aller.* If we can do him no harm, we will stop our ears, and he shall not convince us." ZINZENDORF.

12. On xviii. 19. (Give heed to me, O Lord). "This takes place in two ways. A teacher is looked at by the eye which is as flames of fire. He is also guided by the same eye, which looks on all lands, to strengthen those whose hearts are towards the Lord. No child can rest more securely in the cradle, while the nurse is looking for any fly that might disturb it, than a servant of the Lord can, to whom God gives heed." ZINZENDORF.

13. On xviii. 20. "It is a pleasing remembrance, when a teacher considers that he has been able to avert divine judgments from his people. It is also an undeniable duty. The spirit of Job, Moses, Jeremiah, Ezra, Nehemiah, Paul in this respect is the true spirit of Jesus Christ. He is a miserable shepherd who can give up his sheep and look on with dry eyes, while the fold is being devastated. Not to mention that teachers are now-a-days, by the salaries which they receive from their congregations, brought into the relation of servitude, and besides the regular obligation of the head are laid under indebtedness, as hospitals and other institutions, to pray for their founders. They give themselves the name of intercessors and thus bind themselves anew to this otherwise universal duty of all teachers." ZINZENDORF. But when the servant of God receives "*odium pro labore, persecutio pro intercessione,*" this is "the world's gratitude and gratuity." FÖRSTER.

14. On xviii. 21-23. With regard to this prayer against his enemies CALVIN remarks, "this vehemence, as it was dictated by the Holy Spirit, is not to be condemned, nor ought it to be made an example of, for it was peculiar to the Prophet to know that they were reprobates." For the prophet, he says, was (1) "endued with the spirit of wisdom and judgment, and (2) zeal also for God's glory so ruled in his heart, that the feelings of the flesh were wholly subdued, or at least brought under subjection; and farther, he pleaded not a private cause.—As all these things fall not to our lot, we ought not indiscriminately to imitate Jeremiah in this prayer: for that would then apply to us which Christ said to His disciples, 'Ye know not what spirit governs you (Luke ix. 55).'" In general the older Comm. agree in this. OECOLAMPADIUS says tersely: "*Subscribit sententiæ divinæ.*" FÖRSTER also says that originally such a prayer is not allowed, but that to the prophet, who by the divine inspiration was certain of the "*obstinata et plane insanabilis malitia*" of his hearers, it was permitted as "*singulare et extraordinarium aliquid.*" The *Hirschberger Bibel* also explains the words as a consignment to the divine judgment, since God

Himself has several times refused to hear prayer in their behalf (xiv. 13, 14), and they themselves could not endure it (ver. 18). *Vide* NEUMANN II. S. 15.—SED. SCHMIDT says plainly, "*Licet hominibus impiis et persecutoribus imprecari malum, modo ejusmodi imprecationes non fiant ex privata vindicta, et conditionatæ sint ad constantem eorum impietatem. Nisi enim ejusmodi imprecationes etiam piis essent licitæ,* propheta non imprecatus esset persecutoribus gravissimam pœnam hanc.*" I believe that it is above all to be observed that Jeremiah does not announce these words (vers. 18-23) as the word of Jehovah. It is a prayer to the Lord, like xx. 7-18. That which was remarked on xx. 14-18, on the Old Testament character of the prayer, applies here also and in a higher degree. For here as there we may set a good share of the harshness to the account of the rhetoric. The standard of judgment may be found in Matt. v. 43. Many ancient Comm. *ex. gr.* JEROME, who regard the suffering prophet as a type of the suffering Saviour, point out the contrast between this prayer of Jeremiah's *against* his enemies and the prayer of Christ *for* His enemies (Luke xxiii. 34). The only parallel adduced from the New Testament is 2 Tim. iv. 4. But there it is ἀποδώσει (according to the correct reading of TISCHENDORF) not ἀποδώῃ (*Text. Rec.*, KNAPP).

15. On xix. 1. "If man were only a Platonic αὐτάνθρωπος, and did not dwell in the flesh, but were pure spirit and soul, as the Schwenkfelder dreamed a man might be, he would not need such visible signs.—But because man consists of body and soul, God uses, together with the Holy Ghost, the word and Sacrament and other signs." CRAMER.

16. On xix. 6-9. Μεγάλων ἀδικημάτων μεγάλαι εἰσὶ τιμωρίαι παρὰ τὸν θεόν. HERODOTUS. *Vide* FÖRSTER, S. 106.

17. On xix. 10, 11. What is more easily broken in pieces than an earthen vessel? Equally easy is it for the hand of the Almighty to break in pieces the kingdoms of men. And if He spared not the kingdom of Judah, whose king was a son of David and the people the chosen nation, shall He spare the kingdoms of the heathen, none of which can point to any prophecy in its behalf, like that which we read in 2 Sam. vii. 16? Comp. Dan. ii. 21; iv. 14, 22, 29; v. 21; Ecclus. x. 4, 8, 10, 14.

18. On xix. 11-13. This prophecy was not completely fulfilled by the destruction of Jerusalem by Nebuchadnezzar. For Jerusalem was restored after this destruction. The second destruction, by the Romans, must then be regarded as the definitive fulfillment. Comp. JEROME *ad loc.* —Tophet was used by the inhabitants of Jerusalem for idolatrous purposes. In consequence, the fires of Tophet set Jerusalem on fire, and again the corpses which filled Jerusalem extended even to Tophet, and by reciprocal calamity Tophet became like Jerusalem and Jerusalem like Tophet.

19. On xx. 1, 2. "Πρώων τέκνα πήματα. *Honores mutant mores.*" FÖRSTER. "*Quod hic fuit tormentum, illic erit ornamentum.*" AUGUSTIN.

20. On xx. 3-6. "Mark, who is the stronger here: Pashur or Jeremiah? For 1. Jeremiah overcomes his sufferings by patience, 2. He is firm in opposition to his enemy and does not allow himself to be terrified by his tyranny, but rebukes him to his face for his sins and lies." CRAMER.

21. On xx. 3-6. Pashur's punishment consists in this, that he will participate in the terrible affliction and be a witness of it, without being able to die.—He is a type of the wandering Jew.

22. On xx. 7-12. The prophet could say with a good conscience that he had not pressed into this office. It was his greatest comfort that the Lord had persuaded and overpowered him, when resisting, and that afterwards the fire within kindled by the Lord compelled him to speak. Thus he at last becomes so joyful, that in the midst of his sufferings he sings a hymn on his deliverance.

Lord Jesus, for Thy work divine,
The glory is not ours, but Thine;
Therefore we pray Thee stand by those,
Who calmly on Thy word repose.

23. On xx. 14-18. "When the saints stumble this serves to us; 1. for doctrine: we see that no man is justified by his own merits; 2. for ἐλεγχος, *i. e.* for the refutation of those, who suppose that there are ἀναμάρτητοι; 3. for ἐπανόρθωσις, if we follow AMBROSE, who called to the emperor Theodosius: '*Si Davidem imitatus es peccantem, imitare etiam pœnitentem;*' 4. for παιδεία, that he who stands take heed that he do not fall; 5. for παρηγορία, that he who has fallen may after their pattern rise again." FÖRSTEN.

24. On xx. 17, 18. "The question is, Does a man do right in wishing himself dead? Answer: He who from impatience wishes himself dead like Job, Elijah, Jonah, Tobias, and here Jeremiah, does wrong, and this is a piece of carnal impatience. But when we think of the wicked world and the dangerous times in which we live and on the other hand of the future joy and glory, and therefore desire with Simeon and Paul to be released, we are not to be blamed." CRAMER.

HOMILETICAL AND PRACTICAL.

1. The 18th homily of ORIGEN has for its text xviii. 1-16 and xx. 1-7. The 19th has xx. 7-12.

2. On xviii. 1-11. Comfort and warning, implied in the fact that the threatenings and promises of the Lord are given only conditionally: 1. The comfort consists in this, that the threatened calamities may be averted by timely repentance. 2. The warning in this, that the promises may be annulled by apostasy.

3. On xviii. 7-10. Comp. the HOMILETICAL on xvii. 5-8.

4. On xviii. 7-11. "How we should be moved by God's judgments and goodness: that each, 1. Should turn from his wickedness; 2. should reform his heart and life." KAPFF, *Passion, Easter and Revival Sermons.* 1866.

5. [On xviii. 12. "The sin, danger and unreasonableness of despair. The devil's chief artifices are to produce either false security and presumption or despair. Despair is 1. sinful, (*a*) in itself, (*b*) because it is the parent of other sins, as is seen in the cases of Cain, Saul, and Judas. 2. It is dangerous. 3. It is groundless, because (*a*) we still enjoy life and the means of

grace, (b) of the long-suffering character of God, (c) of the universality of the scheme of redemption, (d) of the person, character and invitations of Christ, (e) of many instances of final salvation." Payson.—S. R. A.]
6. On xviii. 18-20. Text for a Sermon on the Anniversary of the Reformation. Opposition of the office which has apparent authority to that which has true authority; 1. The basis of the opposition: the assertion of the infallibility of the former office. 2. The mode of the opposition; (a) in not being willing to hear, (b) in the attempt to destroy the latter by violence. 3. The result of the opposition is nugatory, for (a) the Lord hears the voice of the opposers to judge them, (b) He gives heed to His servants to protect them.
7. On xx. 7-13. The trial and comfort of a true minister of the Word; 1. The trial: (a) scorn and derision; (b) actual persecution. 2. The comfort: (a) the Lord put him in office and maintains him in it; (b) that the Lord will interpose for His servants and thus, (1) help His cause to victory, and (2) save their persons.

8. THE EIGHTH DISCOURSE (Against the Wicked Shepherds).

(Chaps. XXI.—XXIV.)

In designating this portion of the book a discourse we do so only a potiori. For neither is it purely of the nature of a discourse, nor does it form one *discourse, i. e., a connected rhetorical whole. The different portions of it, partly of historical, partly of rhetorical character, and pertaining to very different epochs, are however comprised under a common title, such as in Jeremiah is usually prefixed to the greater sections. These portions contain in general the same fundamental thought, viz., that which is stated in the title, "Against wicked Shepherds." By these wicked shepherds are to be understood all the leaders of the people, kings and prophets (and priests, xxiii. 11). The main trunk is formed by the powerful speech against Jehoiakim (xxii. 1-9, 13-23; xxiii. 1-8), which Jeremiah addressed to that violent despot before the gate of his palace, in presence of his court and the people. Around this discourse, enclosing it and interwoven with it, are grouped other portions of similar character. Originally a brief passage (xxi. 11-14) was prefixed to this discourse, on account of its purport, in which it is intimately related to xxii. 3-7 (comp. the Comm. on xxi. 11-14). This passage could not be subjoined after xxii. 9, because here the personal addresses connected with the words spoken to Jehoiakim, xxii. 13-19, had to be inserted, and after xxii. 30, the distance would be too great from the discourse to which it is related, xxii. 3-7. The passage xxi. 1-10 had to be placed before xxi. 11, although as to time the latest in the whole compass of chh. xxi.—xxiv. because in it a Pashur is spoken of. By this it seemed to be connected with ch. xx., in which also a Pashur plays the chief part. XXII. 13-23 followed originally immediately after xxii. 9 (comp. the preliminary remarks to xxii. 13-19). But since there was a brief passage, referring to Shallum-Jehoahaz (xxii. 10-12) the immediate predecessor of Jehoiakim, this had to be placed before xxii. 13. After xxii. 23 the passage referring to Jehoiakim (xxii. 24-30) naturally found its position. The passage xxiii. 1-8 followed finally as the original conclusion of the speech addressed to Jehoiakim, and as a consolatory glance into the future after the dark portraits of the kings of the present. From xxiii. 9-40 follows then the connected discourse against the false prophets. This was by no means delivered on the same day and in the same place as the discourse against Jehoiakim, xxii. 1—xxiii. 8. It may however in general belong to the same period, viz., the first four years of the reign of Jehoiakim, since there is no mention of the Chaldeans, and the reign of Josiah gave much less occasion for such a discourse. Chap. xxiv. finally corresponds to "the punitive judgments on the three predecessors of Zedekiah, and completes the judgment on the corrupt pastors and leaders of the people" (Graf). The reason why this chapter was not inserted immediately after xxii. 30 is that it treats its subject in a form quite peculiar and different from the style of ch. xxii. It would accordingly appear too much like a foreign element after xxii. 30.
If accordingly we cannot speak of this discourse as one properly and logically concatenated, yet we may recognize a certain orderly arrangement of its individual parts. This will be manifest in the following synopsis:—*

AGAINST THE WICKED SHEPHERDS.

Chaps. XXI.—XXIV.

I. Preface, ch. xxi.
    a. *Passage relating to Pashur, as an addition to* ch. xx., xxi. 1-10.
    b. *Transition. Exhortation to the house of David to righteousness,* xxi. 11-14.
II. Main Discourse, chs. xxii. and xxiii.
    Against the wicked kings and prophets.
    1. *Against the wicked kings,* xxii. 1—xxiii. 8.
        a. *The alternative offered the royal house,* xxii. 1-9.
        b. *Prophecy relating to the person of Shallum,* xxii. 10-12.

c. *Prophecy relating to the person of Jehoiakim*, xxii. 13-19.
d. *The consequences to the people*, xxii. 20-23.
e. *Prophecy relating to the person of Jehoiakim*, xxii. 24-30.
   α. *Before the captivity*, xxii. 24-27.
   β. *After the captivity*, xxii. 28-30.
f. *Conclusion and consolation in a glance at the just and the justifier*, xxiii. 1-8.
2. *Against the false prophets*, xxiii. 9-40.
   a. *The blind leaders of the blind*, xxiii. 9-15.
   b. *Warning against deception by the prophets*, xxiii. 16-22.
   c. *The criminal mingling of man's word and God's word*, xxiii. 23-32.
   d. *The criminal use of the word "burden,"* xxiii. 33-40.
III. POSTSCRIPT.
   Supplement to xxii. 13-30: *The fourth king*, xxiv. 1-10.

I. PREFACE.

CHAP. XXI.

a. Passage relating to Pashur, as an addition to ch. xx. (xxi. 1-10).

1. *The king's question and the prophet's consolatory answer*

XXI. 1-7.

1 The word which came unto Jeremiah from the LORD [Jehovah] when king Zedekiah sent unto him Pashur the son of Melchiah, and Zephaniah the son of Maa-
2 seiah [,] the priest, saying, Inquire, I pray thee, of the LORD [Jehovah] for us, for
  Nebuchadrezzar,¹ king of Babylon, maketh war against us; if so be that [perhaps]
  the LORD [Jehovah] will deal with us according to all his wondrous works, that he
3 may go up [withdraw] from us. Then said Jeremiah unto them, Thus shall ye say
4 to Zedekiah: Thus saith the LORD [Jehovah] God of Israel: Behold, I will turn
  back the weapons of war that are in your hands, wherewith ye fight against the king
  of Babylon, and against the Chaldeans, which besiege you without the walls [*or* your
  walls from without] and I will assemble [withdraw] them into the midst of this city.
5 And I myself will fight against you, with an outstretched hand and a strong arm,
6 even in anger and in great fury, and in great wrath. And I will smite the inhabi-
7 tants of this city, both man and beast: they shall die of a great pestilence. And
  afterward, saith the LORD [Jehovah] I will deliver Zedekiah, king of Judah, and
  his servants, and the people, and such as are left² in this city from the pestilence,
  from the sword, and from the famine, into the hand of Nebuchadnezzar, king of Babylon, and into the hand of their enemies, and into the hand of those that seek their
  life: and he shall smite them with the edge of the sword, he shall not spare them,
  neither have pity, nor have mercy.

TEXTUAL AND GRAMMATICAL.

¹ Ver. 2.—On the form of the name נְבוּכַדְרֶאצַּר comp. rems. on xxv. 1.

² Ver. 7.—The וְאֵת here is logically incorrect, since after the general term THE PEOPLE, other survivors are not supposable. The LXX. omits it (και τον λαον καταλειφθέντα). Comp. viii. 3; xxiv. 8; xxxviii. 4; xxxix. 9; xl. 6; xli. 10;
lii. 15.

EXEGETICAL AND CRITICAL.

To the petition of King Zedekiah that the prophet would seek for them the interposition of Jehovah against Nebuchadnezzar (vers. 1, 2), the
prophet answers that the Lord will cause the de-
fenders of the city to retreat before the Chaldeans (vers. 3, 4), yea, will Himself contend
against them with a great pestilence (vers. 5, 6),
and will then surrender the survivors of the
sword, famine and pestilence (among whom will
be the king himself and his servants) to king Nebuchadnezzar, who will slay them without mercy
by the sword (ver. 7).

Vers. 1, 2. **The word which came . . .
withdraw from us.** The beginning is like vii.
1. Comp. *ad hoc loc.*—**Pashur**, the son of Malkiah, is also mentioned in xxxviii. 1.—Zephaniah, the son of Maaseiah, xxix. 25; xxxvii. 3;
lii. 24. Both were priests (Malkiah and Maaseiah are also names of courses of priests, 1
Chron. xxiv. 9-18); the latter כֹּהֵן מִשְׁנֶה the
next after the high-priest (lii. 24). The embassy
was therefore a respectable one.—Zedekiah sent

once again with the same object to the prophet: xxxvii. 3. Comp. also Isai. xxxvii. 2 sqq.—On the relation of time *Vide* Comm. on xxxvii. 23.— **Inquire,** *etc.* The prophet was not merely to ask what will be done, but also to pray that whatever would serve for deliverance may be done, as is evident from **perhaps Jehovah,** *etc.* In xxxvii. 3 it is "*Pray* for us." Comp. xlii. 2.— **That he may go up from us** Comp. 1 Sam. vi. 20; 1 Ki. xv. 19; Jer. xxxvii. 5, 11. The figure of a person thrown down, from whom his vanquisher raises himself, lies at the basis of this expression. [HENDERSON: "The phrase means to recede from the incumbent attitude assumed by a besieging army."—S. R. A.]

Vers. 3-7. **Then said Jeremiah . . . have mercy.** From the words **in the midst of the city** it is evident that the prophet places the line of defence within the walls. Thus the enemy presses the Jews no longer without but within the walls, and certainly the city is then as good as taken. This however is just what the prophet wished them to understand. I believe therefore that **without the walls** is to be referred not to **turn back** nor to **fight,** but to **besiege. —Assemble.** Comp. xvi. 5; Joel ii. 10; iv. 15.— **Outstretched hand.** Comp. Deut. iv. 34; v. 15; xxvi. 8. It should be remarked that everywhere else, with the exception of the formula "and his hand is stretched out still" (Isai. v. 25; ix. 11, 16, 20; x. 4 coll. 1 Chron. xxi. 16), נטויה **outstretched** is the adjective used with זרוע **arm,** and חזקה **mighty,** with יד **hand.—With anger,** *e* Comp. xxxii. 37; Deut. xxix. 27.— **With the edge of the sword.** In Jeremiah here only.—**Not spare them.** Comp. xiii. 14.

2. The only way of escape.

XXI. 8-10.

8 And unto this people thou shalt say, Thus saith the LORD: Behold, I set before
9 you the way of life, and the way of death. He that abideth [remains] in this city
shall die by the sword, and by the famine, and by the pestilence: but he that goeth
out and falleth[1] to the Chaldeans that besiege you, he shall live,[2] and his life shall
10 be unto him for a prey. For I have set my face against this city for evil, and not
for good, saith the LORD [Jehovah], it shall be given into the hand of the king of
Babylon, and he shall burn it with fire.

TEXTUAL AND GRAMMATICAL.

[1] Ver. 9.—וְנָפַל. Comp. NAEGELSB. *Gr.*, § 90, 3.—On לְ. Comp. TEXTUAL on x. 1.

[2] Ver. 9.—The Keri וְחָיָה is here, as in xxxviii. 2, unnecessary. יִחְיֶה, corresponding to יָמוּת in hemistich *a*, is more correct.

EXEGETICAL AND CRITICAL.

It is announced to the people that the life and death of individuals depends on whether they give themselves up to the Chaldeans or not (vers. 8, 9), for the destruction of the city by Nebuchadnezzar is irrevocably determined upon, (ver. 10). These words are closely connected both in form and in matter with the previous context. It is entirely appropriate that the prophet after having informed the ruler what the result of his military operations would be, announces also to the people or to individuals, what is alone left them to do for their escape. GRAF is correct in saying (p. 259), that the summons contained in vers. 8-10 could not have been addressed to the king's embassy. Nevertheless their form and purport testify to their having been addressed to the people contemporaneously with that answer to the king. It is not opposed to this that Jeremiah gave the same advice repeatedly on other occasions. (Comp. xxvii. 11, 17).

Vers. 8-10. **And unto this people . . burn it with fire.—Unto this people,** *etc.*, corresponds to **and thus shall ye say to Zedekiah** in ver. 3, but not as being a part of the answer given to the king. But after the application, ver. 2, had been received by the prophet, a triple divine word was communicated to him. It is not expressly declared that this was the case, but this is the natural and necessary presupposition to the prophetic declarations, communicated in vers. 3-7, 8-10, 11-14.—**I set before you,** *etc.* The prophet evidently has in mind Deut. xi. 26, 27: xxx. 15, 19.—**He that remains,** *etc.* Comp. xxxviii. 2 and the Introd. to the 8th discourse. It is evident that to the prophet the will of God was of more importance than that which according to the limited view of man is required by the honor and interest of his country, so that by obedience to the former this honor and interest are best secured.—**Falleth to the Chaldeans.** Comp. xxxii. 13, 14; xxxix. 9.—**I have set my face** (ver. 10). Comp. xxiv. 6; xliv. 11.— **Shall be given.** Comp. xxxii. 29; xxxiv. 2, 22; xxxvii. 8, 10; xxxviii. 18, 23; xxxix. 8.

b. Transition: Exhortation to the house of David to Righteousness.

XXI. 11–14.

11   And touching [to] the house of the king of Judah, *say*, Hear ye the word of the
12 LORD [Jehovah]; O house of David, thus saith the LORD [Jehovah]. Execute
   judgment [judge righteously][1] in the [every][2] morning, and deliver him that is
   spoiled out of the hand of the oppressor, lest my fury go out like fire, and burn that
13 none can quench it, because of the evil of your doings.[3] Behold, I am against thee,
   O inhabitant of the valley, and rock of the plain, saith the LORD [Jehovah]; which
   say, Who shall come down[4] against us? or who shall enter into our [refuges] ha-
14 bitations? But I will punish you according to the fruit of your doings, saith the
   LORD [Jehovah]; and I will kindle a fire in the forest thereof, and it shall devour
   all things round about it.

TEXTUAL AND GRAMMATICAL.

[1] Ver. 12.—The expression רִין מִשְׁפָּט is found here only: Elsewhere דִּין דִּין (Jer. v. 28; xxii. 16; xxx. 13, *etc.*) מִשְׁפָּט is at the same time accusative of object and of mode, and as the latter involves the meaning of בְּמֵישָׁרִים (Ps. ix. 9; xcvi. 10) or בְּצֶדֶק (Ps. lxxii. 2).

[2] Ver. 12.—לַבֹּקֶר. ל is distributive. Comp. NAEGELSB. *Gr.*, § 112, 5 *b*. As here, in Ps. lix. 17; Am. iv. 4. Comp. also 1 Chron. ix. 27; Ps. lxxiii. 14; ci. 8; Isai. xxxiii. 2; Lam. iii. 23.

[3] Ver. 12.—Instead of הֶם the Keri has the second person as in iv. 4. The change of person however occurs so frequently, that the alteration appears unnecessary. Comp. v. 14; xii. 13; xvii. 13; NAEGELSB. *Gr.*, § 101, *Anm.*

[4] Ver. 13.—יֵחַת. On the form comp. OLSH., *S.* 503.

EXEGETICAL AND CRITICAL.

The royal family is appealed to in warning to exercise righteousness, that the anger of the Lord may not burn inextinguishably (vers. 11 and 12). Afterward, the non-fulfilment of this condition being presupposed, the judgment of destruction is proclaimed to the "rock of the plain," which is defiant in its inapproachability (vers. 13, 14). This passage cannot be contemporary with the two preceding: it must be of older date. For, 1. At the date to which xxi. 1-7 belongs, such an admonition and conditional threatening is no longer in place. In vers. 4-7 his own destruction and that of the nation is unconditionally announced to Zedekiah. 2. The stubbornness also, which is expressed in ver. 13, contradicts the despondency, with which Zedekiah humbles himself in ver. 2. 3. It is strange that after the king, ver. 3, the house of the king should again be specially addressed, since the king is included in the latter, and the exhortation to "judge righteously" applies above all to the king. Should it be said that in vers. 11-14 actual conversion is presented before the king as the only way of escape, it is contradicted by the whole situation and the character of vers. 1-10. Such proposals belong to an earlier stage, which in Judea, at the time of his embassy, was long past. We are referred by the connection of this passage with xxiii. 3-9 (on which comp. the Comm. *ad loc.*) entirely to the times of Jehoiakim. The text forms the transition to this discourse of reproof, addressed to the king. Certainly, according to the view of the compiler, this section must have been regarded as closely connected with the preceding, for **and to the house**, *etc.*, in ver. 11, is grounded on **thou shalt say** in ver. 8.

Vers. 11, 12. **And to the house . . . evil of your doings.** The division of vers. 11 and 12 is awkward. The house of the king is in the narrower sense himself with his family, in a wider sense the entire court (comp. 1 Ki. iv. 6; xvi. 9, *etc.*). Here the house of the king is intended in the narrower sense 1, because afterwards the phrase "house of David" is used instead; 2, because judging was one of the chief functions of a king, which he could transfer to a substitute only in cases of necessity. (2 Ki. xv. 5 coll. 1 Sam. viii. 5, 6, 20; 2 Sam. xv. 2 sqq.; 1 Ki. iii. 16 sqq.; vi. 26; vii. 7; viii. 3-5).

Vers. 13, 14. **Behold I am against thee . . . round about it.** If these verses are not supposed to be attached to the preceding without any inner connection, by **rock of the plain** (צוּר הַמִּישֹׁר) can be understood only the house of David. The house of David was addressed in ver. 12. Ver. 13 presupposes a negative answer of the person addressed, on which the address continues: "Behold I am," *etc.* XXII. 6-9 is indeed referred to, and it is maintained that here as there the destruction of the city appears to be the punishment for the sin of the royal family. But the sentence **which say**, *etc.*, would represent the destruction of the city as the punishment of the obstinate security of the citizens. It remains either to regard vers. 13 and 14 as a disconnected addition, or to understand by צוּר הַמִּישׁר the royal family. According to this rendering עֵמֶק, **valley,** and מִישׁר, **plain,** are to be taken not in the local but figurative meaning. (Comp. rems. on xviii. 14). The royal family is compared to a rock rising in the midst of a plain. עֵמֶק is low land, *regio depressa et longe lateque patens* (GES., *Thes.*) comp. Job xxxix. 10, 21; Ps. lxv. 14. Comp. also בִּקְעָה Gen. xi. 2.—**Rock of the plain** defines more particularly in what sense the royal family can be designated as inhabiting the lowland; it is there enthroned as an elevation dominating all the rest. The inhabitants of this rock regard themselves as very secure. They compare themselves with beasts, which in their lairs or hiding-places are well-concealed. [HENDERSON: "By *the valley* is meant the Tyropœon, running down between Mount Zion and Mount Moriah, and by the *rock of the plain* Mount Zion, so called from its rapid ascent on the South-west, which renders its brow in this direction apparently more lofty than any other point connected with the city (Robinson I., 389).—S. R. A].—**Come down.** The prophet has in mind the image of a bird darting down upon its prey. Since the following, **and who shall come down** evidently indicate attacks by land, by these two figures the thought is expressed of a position secure on all sides.—**I am against thee,** comp. xxiii. 30-32; l. 31; li. 25 —**But I will punish you.** A formula especially frequent in Jeremiah, ix. 24; xxiii. 34; xxx. 20, *etc.*—**According to the fruit.** Comp. xvii. 10.—**And I will kindle a fire.** Comp. Am. i. 14; Jer. xvii. 27; xliii. 12; xlix. 27; l. 32.— **In the forest thereof. Thereof** refers to **inhabitant,** ver. 13. It is apparent that the prophet retains the conception of wild beasts of the forest. Comp. xxii. 7.—Our view of the passage is confirmed by the parallel given in xxii. 1-9. Comp. especially ver. 6, and the Comm. *ad loc.*

II. MAIN DISCOURSE.

CHAPS. XXII. and XXIII.

AGAINST THE WICKED KINGS AND PROPHETS.

1. *Against the wicked kings,* (xxii. 1-xxiii. 8).

   a. The alternative offered the royal house.

XXII. 1-9.

1 Thus saith the LORD [Jehovah]: Go down to the house of the king of Judah,
2 and speak there this word. And say, Hear the word of the LORD [Jehovah], O king of Judah, that sittest upon the throne of David, thou, and thy servants, and
3 thy people that enter in by these gates. Thus saith the LORD [Jehovah]:
  Execute judgment and righteousness,
  And rescue him that is plundered out of the hand of the oppressor,[1]
  Strangers, orphans and widows oppress not, nor be violent towards **them,**
  And innocent blood shed **not in** this place.
4 For if ye indeed do thus,
  Then through the gates of this house,
  Kings, sitting for David on his throne,
  Shall enter in chariots and on horses,
  He, his ministers[2] and his people.
5 But if ye hearken not to these words,
  I have sworn by myself, saith Jehovah,
  That this house shall become a desolation.
6 For thus saith Jehovah concerning the house of the king of **Judah:**
  Gilead art thou to me, summit of Lebanon!
  Surely a wilderness will I make thee,
  Cities uninhabited.
7 And I consecrate against thee destroyers,
  The man and his weapons,
  Who shall fell thy choice cedars,
  And cast them into the fire.

8 And many nations shall go by this city and say one to another,
Why has Jehovah done thus to this great city?
9 And they shall say:
Because they forsook the covenant of Jehovah their God,
And worshipped other gods and served them.

TEXTUAL AND GRAMMATICAL.

¹ Ver. 3.—קֹשֵׁעַ, if not written by mistake for עָשׁוּק, occurs here only. It is formed like גָּדוֹל, meaning *oppressor*.
² Ver. 4.—[" A great number of MSS. and two of the earliest editions, read עֲבָדָיו *his servants*, or ministers, according to the Keri." HENDERSON.—S. R. A.]

EXEGETICAL AND CRITICAL.

The prophet receives the command to go down to the king's house and to deliver to the king and his servants, and to the people, the following divine message (vers. 1, 2); if they would practice justice and righteousness (ver. 3), kings of David's line should possess the throne in royal power and glory (ver. 4); if not, the king's house should be made desolate (ver. 5). For though hitherto like Gilead and Lebanon, it is to be devastated (ver. 6). Destroyers shall come and shall fell the cedars and cast them into the fire (ver. 7), so that afterwards it shall be asked in astonishment, why such a great calamity has come upon the city (ver. 8). To which no other answer can be given than that they forsook the covenant of the Lord and served idols (ver. 9).—As to the relation of these verses to the preceding (xxi. 11-14), the former appear almost only like an extension of the latter. Not only is the fundamental thought the same, but even in details there is great, in part verbal, agreement. The admonition which forms the basis, is found in xxi. 12 and xxii. 3, partly with the same words, only in the latter passage somewhat extended (comp. the second half of ver. 3). As to the promises and threatenings based on the admonition, the form of the alternative is not found in xxi. 11-14, for here the idea of non-fulfilment reigns exclusively. But in the form in which the punishment is announced there are great similarities; both times the royal house is compared with a wooded height, the wood of which will be consumed by fire. Since now repetitions occur so frequently in Jeremiah, there is nothing against the supposition that we have here before us two utterances, related in form and purport because they proceed from the same historical situation. That this situation was in the reign of Jehoiakim and before the crisis of the battle of Carchemish appears to me to admit of no doubt. For 1. there is no mention of the Chaldeans; 2. the king addressed is warned against despotic acts of violence. This warning corresponds neither to the character of Josiah nor to that of Jehoahaz, who was most probably elected by the people, because he was supposed to be free from despotic inclinations, and besides he reigned only three months. The warning, however, corresponds entirely to the character of Jehoiakim, who is also afterwards reproved for such acts of violence (vers. 13-17). 3. Jehoiakim is in vers. 13-15 especially reproached with his lust for building, which he gratified by despotic means. His cedar palace

was a monument of this. Jeremiah is to go down to this proud house (ver. 1 coll. ver. 23), and announce to him the judgment of fire (ver. 7). It follows that 1. the section 1-9 refers to Jehoiakim; 2. it is closely connected with vers. 13-23.
Vers. 1-5. **Thus saith . . . become a desolation.—Go down.** Out from the temple. Comp. xxvi. 10; xxxvi. 12 coll. xviii. 2.—**Thou**, etc. Not the king alone, but his servants, and the people also are to hear the word of the Lord. All are to co-operate in complying with the admonition, as they will all be affected by the consequences.—**Execute judgment and righteousness.** Comp. vii. 6; xxi. 12; Ezek. xxii. 6, 7; xlv. 9.—**The stranger.** Comp. Exod. xxii. 20, 21.—**For if ye will**, etc. Comp. vii. 5.—**There shall enter.** Comp. xvii. 25 coll. xiii. 13.—**But if ye will not hear.** Comp. xvii. 27.—**I swear by myself.** Comp. Gen. xxii. 16; Isa. xlv. 23; Jer. xlix. 13.
Vers. 6-9. **For thus . . . and served them.** Gilead, which taken in its wider meaning, comprises Bashan (comp. V. RAUMER, *Palästina, S.* 229, sqq.), is a type of luxuriant fertility, especially with respect to pasturage. Comp. Num. xxxii. 1; Mic. vii. 14; Jer. l. 19.—Lebanon, the far-reaching, adorned with cedars, is also frequently elsewhere an emblem of the lofty and splendid: Isa. ii. 13; x. 33, 34; xxxv. 2; lx. 13; Hos. xiv. 6-8; Zech. xi. 1, 2.—The figures of blessing and exultation are applied to the house of David, not on account of its present prosperity, for this does not exist, nor only on account of its former prosperity,—under David and Solomon—for this is a secondary consideration with the Lord. From the words **to me** we perceive that the Lord has here in view rather the significance of the Davidic house, which He has most at heart, its universal and transcendent mission (2 Sam. vii.). For this reason we must not translate: *Thou wast to me*, but *Thou art to me*. The comparison with Lebanon is one of the points of coincidence with xxi. 31. Although the royal house of Judah thus stands before the Lord in such ideal glory, He will make it in outward form a desolation and ruin (comp. Isa. liii. 1-5). —On uninhabited comp. Comm. on ii. 15. But why **cities** in the plural? Evidently because the prophet wished to intimate that the judgment on the king's house will be declared in the desolation of the land and the destruction of the cities, especially the capital (ver. 8). It follows that ver. 6 stands to ver. 5 in the relation of more particular explanation, that **for**, ver. 6, is therefore to be regarded as an explicative. For not only the reason but the manner of the

desolation is more particularly defined in vers. 6-9.—**Consecrated.** It is commanded by God and therefore a holy war. Comp. rems. on vi. 4. Therefore both the warriors and their weapons are designated as holy.—**They shall fall,** *etc.* The house of David is still regarded as a wooded mountain (comp. xi. 14). At the same time the remembrance of the cedar palaces (ver. 23; 2 Sam. vii. 2, 7; 1 Chron. xvii. 1, 6; 1 Ki. vii. 2) seems to prevail.—**Cast them.** Comp xxi. 12, 14.—Vers. 8, 9. The prophet has Deut. xxix. 23 sqq. in mind. Comp. also 1 Kings ix. 8, 9.

b. Prophecy relating to the person of Shallum.

XXII. 10–12.

10 Weep ye not for the dead, neither bemoan him:
  Weep, weep rather for him that goeth away;
  For never shall he return, nor see his native land.
11 For thus saith Jehovah concerning Shallum,
  The son of Josiah, the king of Judah, who reigned instead of his father,
  And who is gone away from this place:
  He will not return thither.
12 For in the place whither they have carried him captive he will die,
  And will see this land no more.

EXEGETICAL AND CRITICAL.

That these words were really spoken at the historical epoch to which they correspond (therefore neither earlier nor later) is felt if we weigh the terrible violence of the suffering, which, notwithstanding its brevity, is expressed in it. Jeremiah could speak thus only when it was necessary to give expression, and—a corrective, to the universal mourning at the loss of the noble king Josiah, which was as it were repeated in their horror at the captivity of his successor. Three months after his father's death (2 Ki. xxiii. 31-34), Jehoahaz was taken by Pharaoh Necho as a prisoner to Egypt. The sorrow was still lively at the death of his father. Now came this new misfortune. Many might hope for Jehoahaz: he is still young, he will survive and return. Jeremiah cuts off these hopes. There is more cause, he says, to mourn for Jehoahaz than for Josiah. The dead is more fortunate than the living. He intimates that he will perish miserably in captivity. This utterance is one of the oldest in the book.

Vers. 10-12. **Weep ye not . . this land no more.** The absence of the article with לְכָה may possibly be ascribed to the freedom which Jeremiah allows himself in the use of the article. Comp. rems. on iii. 2; vi. 16; xiv. 18; xvii. 19 (Chethibh). It is however also possible that הַמֵּת, **dead,** may not express so definite a thought as הֹלֵךְ, **going away,** because the dead are mourned in general, but those who go away only when their departure is such as it was in this concrete case, which is indicated by the definite article. On the subject-matter comp. viii. 3.—**Concerning Shallum.** אֶל after *Verbis dicendi* or *audi-* *endi*=of, concerning: Gen. xx. 2; 1 Sam. iv. 19; 2 Ki. xix. 9, 32, *etc.* Comp. NAEGELSB. *Gr.*, S. 227.—It is beyond a doubt that this Shallum is Jehoahaz, the son of that Josiah who fell at Megiddo (2 Ki. xxiii. 29), but it is uncertain why he is here named Shallum. The passage 1 Chron. iii. 15, where four sons of Josiah are named (Johanan, Jehoiakim, Zedekiah and Shallum), is not clear and seems to have derived the name of Shallum from the present passage. Disregarding this, two views are before us. According to the former it is assumed that the Shallum named here had really another name, as cases of double names were, as is well-known, not uncommon among the Jews, especially in this period. (Comp. Uzziah-Azariah, Eliakim-Jehoiakim, Mattaniah-Zedekiah. Comp. SIMONIS, *Onomast.,* p. 20; MOVERS, *Chronik, S.* 156 sqq.; THENIUS, on 2 Kings xiv. 21). But only the possibility of Jehoahaz and Shallum being the same, not the actual case, is admitted. According to the other view the name Shallum is a *nomen reale* (HENGSTENBERG) *i. e.* a symbolical name. The ancients (JEROME and many of the older Rabbins) have taken the word in the sense of *consummatio,* completio, referring it to the destruction of the kingdom, and understanding by Shallum either Zedekiah or Jehoiakim. This explanation is however contrary to the clear purport of ver. 10.—שִׁלֻּם may mean *recompense* (so GESENIUS), *recompenser* (FUERST, comp. שִׁלֻּם וְחַן), "and to whom it is recompensed" (HENGSTENBERG). But in none of these meanings will the word exactly suit as a prophetic name. "Recompenser" is certainly not appropriate. But "recompense" and "to whom it is recompensed" are such general ideas, that the name might be ascribed as well to any other wicked king, who was visited by the divine judgment. The turn also, that the name may have been given *per analogiam*, in remembrance of the Israelitish Shallum, who reigned only a month (2 Ki. xv. 13) is not satisfactory. For then it must first have been evident that every king in general, whose reign was numbered by months, was called Shallum. Why otherwise should Jehoahaz only be so named, since Jehoiachin also reigned only three months? It is thus seen that both these modes of explanation have difficulties. I should decide in preference for the former, in the sense that Jeremiah, of the two names borne by the immediate successor of Josiah, retained the earlier, as the simple personal name, without regard to its meaning, since the other, the royal name (יְהוֹאָחָז, Jehovah holds, sustains) contradicted the historical, as also Jeremiah never calls the successor of Jehoiakim Jehoiachin, but only by his original personal name of Jeconiah or Coniah. Comp. ver. 24.—**King of Judah** is in apposition to Shallum, since it was only this name which needed further definition.—**Who reigned,** *etc.* Jehoahaz, although the younger son (comp. 2 Ki. xxiii. 31 with 36), was raised to the throne by the people (ver. 30), his elder brother Eliakim being passed over, and the rights of the primogeniture disregarded, most probably on account of Eliakim's character, which Jeremiah afterwards portrays in such dark colors. Eliakim does not seem to have submitted with a good will. He threw himself into the arms of the Egyptians. By the favor of Pharaoh Necho he became king in his brother's place, which position however he had to purchase by a tribute, which was very oppressive to the people (2 Ki. xxiii. 33-35). In Riblah Jehoahaz was taken prisoner, whether enticed thither, or in some other way, must remain undecided. He was then taken to Egypt and from that time nothing more is known of him. Comp. 2 Chron. xxxvi. 1 sqq.; Ezek. xix. 3, 4.—On Pharaoh Necho comp. the Encyclopædias.

---

c. Prophecy, respecting the person of Jehoiakim.

XXII. 13-19.

13 Woe unto him that buildeth his house by injustice,
    And his upper chambers by unrighteousness;
    Who uses his neighbor's service for nothing,
    And payeth him not his wages![1]
14 Who saith: I will build me a wide house,[2]
    And roomy upper chambers![3]
    And breaks out himself windows,[4]
    Ceils it with cedar and paints it with vermillion.[5]
15 Wilt thou be a king, because thou makest a show with cedars?
    Thy father, did he not eat and drink,
    And execute justice and righteousness?
    Then it was well with him.
16 He procured justice for the poor and the humble,
    Then it was well with him.
    Was not this[6] the fruit of knowing me? saith Jehovah.
17 For thine eyes and thy heart are directed only to thy advantage,
    And to the blood of the innocent, to shed it,
    And to oppression and violence,[7] to practise them.
18 Therefore thus saith Jehovah concerning Jehoiakim,
    The son of Josiah, king of Judah.
    They shall not mourn for him (saying),
    Alas! my brother! Alas! sister!
    They shall not mourn for him (saying),
    Alas! Lord! Alas! his majesty!
19 With the burial of an ass shall he be buried;
    Dragged and cast out far from the gates of Jerusalem.

TEXTUAL AND GRAMMATICAL.

[1] Ver. 13.—פְּעֻלָּה-פָּעַל, wages (Lev. xix. 13; Ps. cix. 20; Isa. xl. 10; xlix. 4). Comp. Job vii. 2.

[2] Ver. 14.—בֵּית מִדּוֹת Comp. אַנְשֵׁי מִדּוֹת (Numb. xiii. 2), or מִדָּה (Isa. xlv. 14) [literally: a house of extensions].

[3] Ver. 14.—מְרֻוָּחִים. This verbal form here only. The Kal of this *verb. denomin.,* 1 Sam. xvi. 23; Job xxxii. 20, is the sense of "to be airy, light." Airy chambers=lofty, roomy.

4 Ver. 14.—The form חַלּוֹנָי (Kamets on account of the pause) is not sufficiently accounted for either as plural (GESEN.), or as dual termination (Ew., § 177, a ; GES., ed. ROEDIGER, § 88, 1, Anm. 1, coll. § 87, 1, c), or as an adjective form (comp. בֵּילַי, Isa. xxxii. 5, 7, BÖTTICHER). As a suffix form it does not give a satisfactory meaning. OLSHAUSEN, § 111, c. Anm., is of opinion that חַלּוֹנִים is to be restored. But it is more natural, with J. D. MICHAELIS, HITZIG, GAAB, MEIER, to connect the following וְ with the word and to read חַלּוֹנָי.—Instead of סָפוּן we must then read כָּפוּן, corresponding to the following מָשׁוֹחַ. Comp. NAEGELSB. Gr., § 93, e. The manner of writing סָפוּן might arise the more easily, as in the six passages where the word occurs in the Old Testament five have the passive part. in Kal. (Deut. xxxiii. 21; 1 Ki. vii. 3, 7; Hagg. i. 4, and the text), and of these again there are two which contain the words וְכָפֻן בָּאָרֶז (1 Ki. vii. 3, 7). As Jeremiah evidently alludes to the erections of Solomon, it was natural to seek also this literal agreement. The radical signification of כָּפַן [comp. צָפַן and שָׂפַן, Deut. xxxiii. 19; סְפִינָה, Jon. i. 5, a ship with a deck in distinction from an open boat ; סִפֻּן, ceiling, 1 Ki. vi. 15, in distinction from קַרְקַע, floor; בָּתִּים סְפוּנִים, ceiled houses, as opposed to פֵּית הַרֵב, Hagg. i. 4] is certainly to cover; yet whether merely the roofing is meant, or also the clothing of the walls with cedar-wood (which is also a covering) appears to me doubtful.

5 Ver. 14.—שָׁשַׁר is found also in Ezek. xxiii. 14. According to the Vulgate, sinopis, i. e. rubrica Sinopensis; LXX., μίλτος=red, vermillion; KIMCHI, cinnabaris, minium.

6 Ver. 16.—On the neuter rendering of הִיא, which besides appears here to be attracted by דַּעַת, comp. NAEGELSB. Gr., § 60, 6, b.

7 Ver. 17.—מְרוּצָה, from רָצָה-רוּץ, crushing [comp. OLSH., S. 386], occurs in this sense here only. It is not to be confounded with כְּרוּצָה, cursus, viii. 6; xxiii. 10; 2 Sam. xviii. 27.

EXEGETICAL AND CRITICAL.

The prophet cries, Woe to Jehoiakim, the king of Judah, who unlike his father Josiah, ruled despotically and oppressed the people, especially in behalf of his fine architecture (vers. 13, 14). Is the kingdom of heaven founded on cedar-beams? asks Jeremiah. Josiah knew a better foundation. He ate and drank indeed, but he practised justice and righteousness. Then it was well, and it was evident that to know the Lord was true prosperity (vers. 15, 16). Jehoiakim, a genuine despot, had only his own advantage in view, and to this end practised violence and the shedding of innocent blood (ver. 17). Therefore he will perish miserably, unwept, dragged and cast out like an ass, his corpse will lie far from Jerusalem (vers. 18, 19).—This declaration must have been addressed to Jehoiakim as the reigning king, for he is not only called king (ver. 18), but Josiah's reign is referred to as past and the end of Jehoiakim's as future. Thus this prophecy pertains to the reign of Jehoiakim, and since there is no mention of the Chaldeans, and Jehoiakim appears to be in full and undisturbed exercise of his despotism, to the beginning of it, i. e., before the crisis of the fourth year (chap. xxv.).

Vers. 13 and 14. **Woe unto him . . . with vermillion.** Comp. Hab. ii. 12; Mic. iii. 10.—**Who useth,** etc. Comp. xxv. 14; xxvii. 7; xxx. 8, etc.—**And breaks out,** etc. קָרַע is to tear to pieces, to cut up of garments (Gen. xxxvii. 29, 34) of bodies (by wild beasts, Hos. xiii. 8) of a book (Jer. xxxvi. 23). In Jer. iv. 30 it is used of the paint which makes the eyes look as if they were torn open, i. e., larger. In the sense of tearing open, it seems to be used here, only that the tearing seems to be effected not by painting, but by breaking through.

Vers. 15, 16. **Wilt thou be a king . . . saith Jehovah.** The prophet tells the king that not splendid buildings are the foundation of a kingdom, but righteousness, and proves this to him by the example of his father Josiah. Comp. Prov. xiv. 34; xvi. 12; xx. 28; xxv. 5; xxix. 14.—**Makest a show,** etc. (כִּתְחַרֶה בָאֶרֶז. On the verbal form. Comp. OLSH., § 255, a). The words have been strangely declared by many to be meaningless. But the meaning which the word has in xii. 5 (where alone it occurs), is equally appropriate here. There it is undoubtedly æmulari, to vie, (to heat one's self, to be zealous, from חָרָה to glow. Comp. Neh. iii. 20), and is connected with אֶת = with, for the designation of the relation to a rival. Here it is not said, with whom Jehoiakim vies. That is a matter of course: He vies with all those who have also built cedar palaces, whether they were prior, contemporaneous, or subsequent to him. It is however said, whereby he seeks to surpass them, in בָאָרֶז, **cedar,** being taken generally, as in ver. 14.—**Did he not eat,** etc. Josiah enjoyed life also, he was no ascetic. But he did not sacrifice his duty and conscience to the pleasures of life, but practised the highest duty of a ruler, righteousness, in a manner pleasing to God. Thus he laid a secure foundation, and his rule was a prosperous one.—**Was not this the fruit** refers not **to procured justice, but to it was well with him.** For that the knowledge of Jehovah (the True) includes the practice of righteousness, Jehoiakim did not probably deny. But he did deny, if not in thesi, yet in praxi, that the true living knowledge of Jehovah ensures the desired satisfaction to a prince. Accordingly הִיא, **this,** is predicate, הֲלוֹא דַעַת אֹתִי **knowing,** subject.

Vers. 17-19. **For thine eyes . . . gates of Jerusalem.** For refers to a thought to be supplied : Not so thou, for, etc.—**Blood of the innocent.** Comp. Deut. xix. 13; 2 Kings xxiv. 4.—**Alas! my brother,** etc. The prophet quotes the verba ipsissima of the usual wail for the dead. Hence the apparently unsuitable **Alas! Sister!** He distinguishes the wail of the relatives (comp. 1 Kings xiii. 30), and that of the subjects (comp. xxxiv. 5) הוֹד of the highest royal majesty, comp. Ps. cxlviii. 13; 1 Chron. xxix. 25.

Ver. 19. **Dragged.** Comp. xv. 3.—**Far from,** etc. כַּנְבֵלָה as a collective idea, is the accusative governed by הַשְׁלֵךְ. The place of casting away is, according to a well-known idiom, designated as one presenting itself from far beyond the gates of Jerusalem. Comp. EXEG. rems. on xx. 17; NAEGELSB. *Gr.*, § 112, 5 *d.*—As to the fulfilment of the prophecy, it should first be remarked, that the latter is repeated in other words in xxxvi. 30. The historical accounts touching the end of Jehoiakim are very scanty. In 2 Kings xxiv. 6 we read only, "So Jehoiakim slept with his fathers." This expression indicates nothing concerning the burial, which is the more surprising, as the book of Kings elsewhere always designates the place particularly. We are not justified in casting doubt on the statement in 2 Chron. xxxvi. 6, that Nebuchadnezzar bound Jehoiakim with two chains to take him to Babylon, on the ground that the Chronicler transferred what from ver. 6 onwards relates to Jehoiachin, to his predecessor (GRAF). For this statement does not contradict that of the book of Kings. According to this also (xxiv. 1), Nebuchadnezzar went up against Jehoiakim. The book of Kings does not expressly say that at this time he carried away the vessels from the temple, but the case, as related in Chronicles, is in itself probable. It is here said that Nebuchadnezzar carried off simply "the vessels of the house," *etc.*, while in connection with Jehoiachin, he carried off "the goodly vessels," *etc.* If then the account in Chronicles is not inauthentic, it affords sufficient data for the fulfilment of the prophecy in the text. Since Chronicles does not state that Jehoiakim was brought to Babylon, but only that Nebuchadnezzar bound him to take him thither, it is quite possible that he died on the way, and endured the sad fate prophesied in the text. We need not then assume either that Jehoiakim was taken from his grave, after the capture of the city under Jehoiachin, dragged through the gate and cast out, or that having died on the way, his body was delivered up by the Chaldeans for sepulture (VAIHINGER in HERZOG, *R.-Enc.* VI., *S.* 790).

---

d. The consequences to the people.

XXII. 20–23.

20   Go up to Lebanon and cry,[1]
    And in Bashan lift up thy voice and cry from Abarim,
    That all thy lovers are broken in pieces.
21 I spoke to thee in thy prosperity,—
    Thou saidst, I will not hear.
    This was thy manner from thy youth,
    That thou heardest not my voice.
22 The wind shall depasture all thy pastors,
    And thy lovers shall go into captivity;
    Then shalt thou be put to shame,[2]
    And confounded for all thy wickedness.
23 Thou that sittest on Lebanon,
    That nestlest in cedars,[3]
    How dost thou groan[4] when pains come upon thee,
    Pangs[5] as of a parturient!

TEXTUAL AND GRAMMATICAL.

[1] Ver. 20.—On the form וְצַעֲקִי, comp. OLSH., § 65 *b*, and § 234, *e*.

[2] Ver. 22.—אן תֵבֹשִׁי׳ is pleonastic. Comp. ii. 35; NAEGELSB. *Gr.*, § 109, 1 *a*.

[3] Ver. 23.—On the forms יֹשַׁבְתְּ and מְקֻנַּנְתְּ, comp. rems. on x. 17. Yet it should be observed that in the latter passage the Keri reads יֹשֶׁבֶת, while in this place we must read מְקֻנַּנְתְּ, יֹשֶׁבֶת. The latter forms are not impossible (comp. יָרְדָה, Gen. xvi. 11; Jud. xiii. 5, 7, certainly in a standing formula), but are called forth here only by the proximately standing נֶחֱנַתְּ, which, however, should not be confounded, as 2 P. Sing. Fem. Perf., with those participial forms.

[4] Ver. 23.—נֶחֱנַתְּ. On the termination, comp. rems. on ii. 20; iii. 5. The form, as it stands, is Niph. of חָנַן (comp. OLSH. *S.* 593). But since a Niphal of חָנַן *to be kind, gracious*, nowhere else occurs, most modern commentators suppose that it is written for נֶאֱנַחַתְּ, and this for נֶאֱנַחְתְּ (from אָנַח *to sigh, to groan*). Yet FUERST is of opinion that a root חָנַן may be assumed, parallel to the Arabic *hanna, to groan, to sigh*, from which תַּחֲנוֹת, Job xix. 17 and our נֶחֱנַתְּ are derived. The latter plan would certainly be more simple than the assumption of a double change of consonants. The decision is still to be expected.

[5] Ver. 23.—חִיל וְ. Comp. vi. 24.

EXEGETICAL AND CRITICAL.

The people are next addressed,—after the king. They have harmonized too well with their pastors in worldly lust and pride, they must then share their fate. It is evidently this thought of the agreement of the people with such princes as Jehoiakim, which is prominent. Dwelling on Lebanon and making nests among cedars (ver. 23) pleased them, however displeasing the service might be to those who were compelled to render it (vers. 13-15). The passage is thus connected with the preceding, (comp. vers. 20 and 23, with vers. 6, 7 and vers. 13-15). The train of thought is as follows:—The people of Israel are required to announce from the highest summits of the mountains, bordering on their country, the fall of their lovers (ver. 20). For he who will not hear must feel. Thus it must be with Israel, who from his youth has never listened to the voice of the Lord (ver. 21). When then the pastors of Israel are blown away by the storm and their lovers are gone into captivity, Israel will expiate his wickedness in deep shame (ver. 22), and groan for his pride in profound anguish, like a woman in travail (ver. 23).

Vers. 20, 21. **Go up ... my voice.** Lebanon, Bashan and Abarim, are named as the highest summits of the mountains bordering on Palestine.—**Go up on Lebanon** forms an ironical antithesis to **that sittest on Lebanon.** The people now proudly dwelling in cedars on Lebanon shall in the future mount on Lebanon (in the proper sense) to lament—an ascent which is really a descent. Bashan stands for the mountain of Bashan (Ps. lxviii. 15), *i. e.,* Hermon. On Abarim with Mt. Nebo, comp. Numb. xxi. 11; xxvii. 12; Deut. xxxii. 49; RAUMER, *Paläst., S.* 72. Israel is to raise his cry of lamentation from the bordering mountains that his shame and the conqueror's glory might be widely manifest as a terror to others.—**All thy lovers** must, according to the connection, mean the kings. For 1, it is inconceivable that **thy pastors** in ver. 22, are not the same as **thy lovers.** *ibid.* The former, however, are unquestionably the kings (xxiii. 1-8). 2. The very punishment inflicted on the kings, affected the people themselves immediately. Hence the humiliating lament to which they are summoned in vers. 20-23. 3. The punishment of the pastors and lovers is the same which was announced to Jehoiakim in vers. 18, 19. To the objection that a similar use of the word "lovers," cannot be produced, it may be replied that it is an unjustifiable demand, to require a proof of every special application of a meaning admitted in itself. מְאַהֵב means *the lover;* this is sufficient. It cannot be doubted that this in and of itself, might be said of kings, in reference to their people. The only question is, whether this mode of expression can be shown to be appropriate in particular cases. This is, however, the case here. For here the prophet (comp. ver. 2) announces the judgment to the people, because they sympathize with the sin of the king, both suffering and promoting it. When there is such concert in wickedness between prince and people, the prince may be named the paramour, unchaste lover (and this is the specific meaning of מְאַהֵב. Comp. Ezek. xvi. 33, 36, 37; xxiii. 5, 9, 22; Hos. ii. 7, 9, 12, 14, 15), of his people. Comp. besides Lam. i. 19.—**Prosperity.** The plural שַׁלְוֹת is found here only. Since the singular=*felicitas, rerum status securus atque secundus* (comp. Ps. cxxii. 7; Prov. i. 32; xvii. 1, *etc.*), the plural is=*res secundæ,* prosperous, quiet, secure relations. So long as these lasted, Israel would know nothing of obedience to the voice of his God. Comp. ii. 25-28.—**This was thy manner,** *etc.* Comp. ii. 2, 23, 33, 36; Ezek. xxiii. 8.

Vers. 22, 23. **The wind ... of a parturient.** The pastors are the leaders of the people, especially the princes. In this sense is רֹעִים also found in x. 21; xxiii. 1-8; l. 6. As the pastor is behind his flock to drive it, so the storm is behind the pastors to sweep them away. Comp. iv. 11, 12; xiii. 24; Hos. iv. 19.—**Thy wickedness.** Comp. ii. 19, iii. 2; iv. 18: xi. 15.—According to the sense, ver. 23 is a further development of **thou shalt be put to shame,** ver. 22. For the shame of the people will appear the more distinctly, the more proudly and securely they now live as on Lebanon. This is evidently intended in a double sense; (*a*) as an emblem of proud, unapproachable exaltation (comp. remarks on ver. 6); (*b*) as an allusion to the cedar-houses, into which they had brought the "glory of Lebanon" (Isa. lx. 13), so that Jerusalem, in a certain respect, is like Lebanon. For as on this mountain the birds make their nests in the cedars, so the princes of Judah built their nests of the cedars of Lebanon.

e. Prophecy relating to the person of Jehoiachin.

a. **Before the Deportation.**

XXII. 24–27.

24 As I live, saith Jehovah, though Coniah,[1]
 The son of Jehoiakim, king of Judah,
 Were the signet ring upon my right hand,
 Yet would I pluck thee thence.[2]
25 And I give thee into the hand of them that seek thy life,
 And into the hand of those before whom thou fearest,
 Even into the hand of Nebuchadrezzar, king of Babylon,
 And into the hand of the Chaldeans.
26 And I cast thee forth, and thy mother that bare thee,
 Into another country,[3] where ye were not born;
 And there ye shall die.
27 But to the land whither their soul desires to return,[4]
 Thither shall they not return.

TEXTUAL AND GRAMMATICAL.

[1] Ver. 24.—The abbreviation יְהָנְיָ is found in Jeremiah here and in xxxvii. 1 only. HENGSTENBERG is of opinion that by striking out the י the word takes a future meaning. But this is contained not merely in the י but in the vowel also: Perf. כָּ, Imperf. יִכָּוּ (Job xxxi. 15) from which, in a double closed syllable and with the accent moved on, is formed יְכִ. The meaning of the perfect (Jehovah stands fast) also would be no less comforting than that of the future: Jehovah will stand fast.

[2] Ver. 24.—On the form אֶתְּקֶנְךָ, comp. OLSH., § 68 d. coll. 97, a; EW. § 250, b. [GESEN. Gr., § 103, b.—S. R. A.]

[3] Ver. 26.—If the twice repeated עַל־הָאָרֶץ (vers. 27 and 28) has not occasioned the article before אֶרֶץ, the case is analogous to the הַגֶּפֶן נָכְרִיָּה, which see. Comp. also xvi. 13.

[4] Ver. 27.—וּמְנַשְּׂאִים. Comp. xliv. 14; Deut. xxiv. 15.

EXEGETICAL AND CRITICAL.

Jehovah swears by His life, that though Jehoiachin, the king of Judah, were the signet-ring on His right hand, yet He would tear it off (ver. 24); give him into the hands of Nebuchadnezzar (ver. 25), and hurl him forth, together with his mother, into a foreign land. There they shall die (ver. 26) and never return to the home for which they have so longing a desire (ver. 27). It is evident that this utterance is addressed to Jehoiachin during his reign. He is addressed as king; Nebuchadnezzar stands menacingly in the vicinity; the captivity is still future.

Ver. 24. **As I live ... thence.** King Jehoiachin, Jehoiakim's son and successor, who however reigned only three months (2 Kings xxiv. 8; three months and ten days, 2 Chron. xxxvi. 9), appears under the name of Jeconiah also in xxiv. 1; xxvii. 20; xxviii. 4; xxix. 2; 1 Chron. iii. 16, 17; comp. Esth. iii. 6. I believe that the abbreviation here denotes a disparaging treatment of the royal name. Somewhat of the feeling expressed in ver. 28 may be traced in it: "Is not this man Coniah a despised broken vessel?"—Since moreover Jeremiah never calls this king Jehoiachin (יְהוֹיָכִין, he is so called only in lii. 31), it is possible that Jeconiah was his proper, original name, and Jehoiachin only supplementary, assumed during his brief reign. Although Jeremiah acknowledges him as king, he guards against using a name expressing a false arbitrary hope, as he also retains the original personal name Shallum, instead of the inappropriately chosen royal name of Jehoahaz (xxii. 11). —**Though Coniah ... were**, etc. If it were not for יְהִי (imperfect) I should be disposed to render in the sense of *although he is*. But אִם with the imperfect cannot possibly be taken otherwise than in the sense of a conditional sentence. I do not think that we can regard the signet-ring here as a symbol of power, *i. e.* as a sign of investiture with royal authority. (Comp. Gen. xli. 42; Esth. iii. 10; viii. 2). For in this sense Jeconiah was really a signet-ring. But the signet is here only a jewel, a costly valuable ornament (Song of Sol. viii. 6). The Lord would therefore say: As I would pluck away the denrest jewel from which I had never parted hitherto, were it become bad, useless, therefore unworthy of me, so must I reject Jeconiah, as one who is despicable, useless, unworthy, even though he were the signet-ring on my right hand, which he is not. אִם is here as in Ps. cxxxix. 8, 9; Am. ix. 2–4; Isa. x. 22; Ob. 4.

CHAP. XXII. 28-30.

Vers. 25-27. **And I give thee unto the hand ... they not return.** Comp. xix. 7; xxi. 7; xxxiv. 20, 21.—**And thy mother.** She was Nehushta, the daughter of Elnathan, 2 Ki. xxiv. 8. Comp. xiii. 18.

β. **After the Deportation.**

XXII. 28-30.

28 Is then this man Coniah a despised broken vessel?
   Or a vessel wherein is no pleasure?
   Why are they then hurled forth, he and his seed?
   And cast into the land which they know not?
29 O land, land, land, hear Jehovah's word!
30 Thus saith Jehovah: Write ye this man childless,
   As one who has no prosperity in the days of his life;
   For not one of his seed shall succeed
   To sit upon the throne of David and rule again over Judah.

EXEGETICAL AND CRITICAL.

These words were spoken after Jeconiah had been carried away captive. Compare "I cast thee forth," ver. 26, with "hurled forth" and "cast" in ver. 28. Hence Jeconiah himself is not addressed, but the prophet speaks of him to others. He first sets forth how in the fate of Jeconiah the divine judgment of his unworthiness is manifested. The antithesis is here plainly felt to the "signet-ring on my right hand," ver. 24, and that in this comparison there was a cutting irony (ver. 28). Thereupon the prophet addresses the land directly, solemnly repeating ארץ thrice (ver. 29), to announce concerning it the fatal declaration of Jehovah, that no descendant of Jehoiachin will any more sit on the throne of David.

Vers. 28-30. **Is then ... over Judah.** To the question of ver. 28 an affirmative answer is expected. Comp. rems. on vii. 9; xii. 9; coll. ii. 14. On the abbreviated name Coniah, the object of which comes out here with especial distinctness, comp. rems. on ver. 24.—**Childless.** Jeconiah was eighteen years old when he became king (2 Kings xxiv. 8), and it is expressly stated that he had wives. That he had some offspring is therefore not impossible, and is not even excluded by ver. 30. But even if he had no children, there was other "royal seed" (Dan. i. 3).—**Into the land.** Comp. ver. 26; xvi. 13. The article is explained by the circumstance that this unknown land is the same time hovered before the prophet as one often mentioned and definitely designated.—The repetition of **land** is to call attention to the fact that the prophet has somewhat unusually important to say with respect to the country. This is the announcement that none of the offspring of Jeconiah should possess the throne of David, by which it is at the same time indicated that an important change would take place in the throne itself, i. e. that it would cease and give place to the throne of a universal empire.—**Write.** The prophet has evidently in view those who are entrusted with the keeping of the family record (comp. SAALSCHÜETZ, Mos. Recht. S. 61; Ezek. xiii. 9; coll. Jer. xvii. 13; Ps. lxix. 29; Isai. iv. 3). When it is said that they are to write him as childless, it is said only that he is to pass for such, not that he was really so. In 1 Chron. iii. 17, 18, his sons are at least mentioned. Whether they were natural offspring (observe the phrase כָּנָיהָ אֲסִיר, the imprisoned Jeconiah [A. V.: Jeconiah, Assir, etc.—S. R. A.]) or only legal (by a Levirate marriage), is doubtful, comp. EHRARD, Kritik der ev. Gesch. S. 201, sqq.—**As one,** etc. This sentence is subordinate to the preceding, as explanation and more exact definition: Jeconiah is called childless, because his whole life through he will be an unprosperous man. This will be manifest, in that he will have seed, but no successor. None of his descendants will succeed to his throne. Zedekiah was Jeconiah's uncle and the last king of Judah of the family of David. The text accordingly rather favors than opposes the hypothesis that Jeconiah had natural offspring.—**Shall succeed to sit** (יִצְלַח־יֵשֵׁב)—he will not have success or prosperity, as sitting, etc. We should say: he will not have the good fortune to sit, etc.

f. Conclusion and Consolation, in a glance at the just and the justifier

XXIII. 1-8.

1   Wo, pastors,[1] who destroy and scatter the sheep of my pasture,[2] saith Jehovah!
2 Therefore thus saith Jehovah, the God of Israel, concerning the pastors,[3] that pasture my people:
Ye have scattered my flock, and dispersed and not visited them.
Behold I visit[4] upon you the evil of your doings, saith Jehovah.
3 And I will gather the remnant of my flock
Out of all the countries whither I have dispersed them,
And bring them back to their field;[5] and they shall be fruitful and increase.
4 And I awaken over them pastors who shall pasture them.
And they shall fear no more nor be dismayed;[6]
Neither shall they be missing,[7] saith Jehovah.
5 Behold the days are coming, saith Jehovah,
That I awake unto David a righteous scion,
Who shall reign as king and shall prosper,[8]
And exercise judgment and righteousness in the land.
6 In his days will Judah be saved,
And Israel dwell securely;
And this will be the name by which they will call[9] him [Israel],
Jehovah our righteousness.
7 Therefore, behold, the days are coming that they shall no more say,
As Jehovah liveth, who brought the children of Israel out of the land of Egypt,
8 But, as Jehovah liveth, who brought and led the seed of the house of Israel out
of the north country,
And out of all lands, whither I had dispersed them;
And they shall dwell in their own land.

TEXTUAL AND GRAMMATICAL.

[1] Ver. 1.—There is nothing remarkable in the absence of the article with רֹעִים, for this is generally the case with הוֹי. It occurs with the article in seven places only: Isa. v. 20; x. 1; xxix. 15; xxxi. 1; Am. v. 18; vi. 1; Hab. ii. 6. Of these places, the first six have the plural, one the singular, but in a collective signification.

[2] Ver. 1.—מַרְעִיתִי may designate both the act (Hos. xiii. 6) the place (Isa. xlix. 9), and the object (Jer. x. 21; xxv. 36) of the pasturing. Hence צֹאן־מַרְעִיתִי (comp. Ezek. xxxiv. 31; Ps. lxxiv. 1; lxxix. 13; c. 3) may mean both: the flock which I pasture (as chief shepherd), and: the flock which feeds on my pasturage. The sense is essentially the same.

[3] Ver. 2.—Here רֹעִים has the article, because the shepherds already mentioned (ver. 1) are meant.

[4] Ver. 2.—פָּקַד is here used for the sake of a paronomasia *in bonam* (comp. Ps. viii. 5; Exod. iii. 16) and *in malam partem* (comp. v. 9; xxv. 12; xxvii. 8; Hos. i. 4) comp. Zech. x. 3.

[5] Ver. 3.—נְוֵהֶן. Sing. Comp. Olsh., ¿ 165, *f*. Since it is sheep which are spoken of, נָוֶה here as in 2 Sam. vii. 8; Isa. lxv. 10; Jer. xxxiii. 12; Ezek. xxv. 5 = *pascuum*, place of pasturage, field. The fem. suffix is remarkable. Comp. Gen. xxx. 30; Naegelsb. *Gr.*, ¿ 60, 4.

[6] Ver. 4.—יֵחָתּוּ. Comp. xvii. 18.

[7] Ver. 4.—יִפָּקֵדוּ. This word is frequently used of *missing*, scattered or robbed sheep, 1 Sam. xxv. 7, 15, 21; comp. 1 Sam. xx. 18.

[8] Ver. 5.—וְהִשְׂכִּיל is best taken here in a double sense: *rem bene, i. e., prudenter et feliciter geret.* Comp. rems. on x. 21; Isa. lii. 13.

[9] Ver. 6.—The reading יִקְרְאוֹ which is found in some Codd. is occasioned by the endeavor to obtain a designation of the subject, perhaps also by the rarer form of suffix. With respect to the former point the well-known idiom may be referred to, according to which the subject is usually wanting with קָרָא in the meaning "they call." Comp. Naegelsb. *Gr.*, ¿ 101, 2, *b*. With respect to the latter comp. Hos. viii. 3; Ps. xxxv. 8; Eccles. iv. 12; Olsh., ¿ 231, *c*.

EXEGETICAL AND CRITICAL.

This passage is in general suitably connected with the entirety of the previous context, since in relation to the previous specifications (xxii. 10-30), it may be regarded as a comprehensive conclusion. But originally it formed a connected whole only with xxii. 1-9; 13-23, since xxii. 10-12 must have been inserted afterwards. Going down into the house of the king, who can have been no other than Jehoiakim, Jeremiah first, in xxii. 1-9, addressed an alternative to him, the purport of which was such that servants and people were also obliged *pro rata* to apply it to themselves. For in vers. 13-19 he turned to the king alone with an incisive speech of rebuke and menace, to which was appended a singular one addressed to the people (vers. 20-23). Finally, in a grand survey, he contrasts with the deep decline, effectuated by the wicked pastors (xxiii. 1, 2), the other extreme, the salvation to be imparted to the re-assembled people, in the distant future, by the Messiah. The remnant restored to their home shall again become a numerous people (ver. 3). This people shall be fed in blessing by shepherds appointed by the Lord (ver. 4). In particular a "righteous scion," sprung from the stock of David, shall rule as king with wisdom and righteousness, to the prosperity of Judah and Israel,—a king, whose deepest significance for his people is expressed in the wonderful name given to the people—**Jehovah our Righteousness** (vers. 5-6). Oaths will then no longer be taken by the name of Jehovah, who brought Israel out of Egypt, but by the name of Jehovah, who brought back Israel from the north country to his native land (vers. 7, 8). The same antithesis, between deepest impending ruin and highest glory to be expected in the distant future, was found also in ch. iii.

Vers. 1, 2. **Wo, Pastors ... saith Jehovah.** As the sections xxii. 1-9; 13-23; xxiii. 1-8 contain the discourse delivered in the house of the king, this section is immediately attached to xxii. 13-23. Both sections begin with הוֹי. After the alternative in xxii. 3-9 also the prophet pronounces a double woe: first on the shepherds, *i. e.* on the person of the king then reigning, then on all which may be called bad shepherding. That the kings are to be understood by the shepherds follows: 1. from the previously stated connection of the discourse of which this passage forms a part; 2. from the description of the conduct of the bad shepherds (who destroy and scatter the flock, etc., vers. 1, 2) which appears to produce so much effect, both extensively and intensively, that we can recognize it only as the action of those who occupy the highest, most influential positions; 3. from the antithesis of the good shepherd, ver. 4, and of the righteous scion of David, ver. 5, in particular. For that beneficial influence (ver. 4) can only be that of the chief, and in ver. 5 the "righteous scion" is directly designated as king. They first corrupt the people morally, and thus effect the external destruction which culminates in their dispersion, comp. 2 Kings vii. 21-23; xxi. 10-12; xxiii. 26, 27; Jer. xv. 4.

Vers. 3, 4. **And I will gather ..... saith Jehovah.** Comp. xxix. 14; xxxi. 8-10; Mic. ii. 12; Ezek. xxxiv. 12.—**The remnant,** *etc.* On this HENGSTENBERG remarks: "The gathering being promised only to the remnant (comp. Is. x. 20; Rom. ix. 27) indicates that justice accompanies mercy."—**And they shall be fruitful,** *etc.* Comp. rems. on iii. 16. In the following verse it should first of all be observed that the prophet has in view two older prophecies: First the foundation-prophecy of the future glory of the Davidic house in 2 Sam. vii. 12, where we read the words, "I will set thy seed after thee." The prophet's choice of this particular utterance here and in ver. 5, could not have been without the object of a double allusion to the passage above quoted, and to the name of Jehoiakim. Since this name (as well as the name יוֹיָכִין) is chosen undoubtedly with reference to the passage mentioned, it was natural that the prophet, thinking in joyful hope of that prophecy, should at the same time remember the contradiction, which prevailed between the present and the promised Jehoiakim. The second passage, to which Jeremiah more plainly alludes, is his own utterance in iii. 15. He must have been reminded of this the more readily that it relates to the same future period.

Ver. 5. **Behold the days ... in the land.** The connection of this verse with the previous one is formed by **behold the days.** This expression does not refer to the difference in time. It does not declare that what is spoken of in ver. 5 will take place after the events of ver. 4, but is antithetic only to the present.—**Pastors,** *etc.*, in ver. 4 is a figurative expression, which is explained in ver. 5 in proper language. On the question as to the relation of the singulars צֶמַח, **scion,** מֶלֶךְ, **king,** *etc.*, to the plural רֹעִים, **pastors,** there are three views. According to one רֹעִים is to be taken as a generic plural, which does not exclude the possibility of *one* shepherd being intended. Thus HENGSTENBERG. On the other hand it is rightly objected that elsewhere Jeremiah presents the prospect of a multiplicity of rulers of the seed of David for the time of the great restoration: xxxiii. 17, 18—

"There shall not be wanting to David a man, Sitting on the throne of the house of Judah .. And to the priests and levites shall not be wanting a man, Offering burnt-offerings," *etc.*
Ibid. ver. 22. "As the host of heaven cannot be numbered
Nor the sand of the sea measured;
So will I multiply the seed of David my servant, And the Levites that minister to me."
Ibid. ver. 26. "If I have not appointed the laws of heaven and earth;
Then also may I reject the seed of Jacob
And David my servant,
That I should not take of his seed to be rulers (מֹשְׁלִים)
To the seed of Abraham, Isaac, and Jacob."

According to the second view the passages just quoted are regarded as forming the measure of this, and accordingly the singular צֶמַח, **scion,** is taken in a collective sense. GRAF, who adopts this view, appeals (*a*) to the idiom, according to which it always has a collective meaning (Gen. xix. 25; Ps. lxv. 11; Ezek. xvi. 7; Isai. lxi 11); (*b*) to the idiom according to which דָּוִד, **David,** and עַבְדִּי דָּוִד as much designate the descendants of David, as יַעֲקֹב **Jacob,** and עַבְדִּי יַעֲקֹב, the descendants of Jacob: Jer. xxx. 9; Hos. iii. 5; Ezek. xxiv. 23, 24; xxxvii. 24, 25; xlv. 8; xlvi. 16, coll. Jer.

xxx. 10; xlvi. 27, 28; Isai. xliv. 1; xlv. 4; xlviii. 20, etc.—To this view it may be objected that this entirely ignores the fact that the Jews expected ONE great deliverer and restorer of their State, the MESSIAH. Comp. the article "Messias," by OEHLER in HERZOG, R.-Enc. We can only treat here of two points: 1. How is this passage related to the expectation of a *single* great son of David? 2. If it is based on this idea, how is it to be reconciled with the other that a number of princes of David's line will rule over Israel? As to the first question, I am of opinion that this passage declares the unity of the Messiah, notwithstanding that pastors preceding (ver. 4) intimates a multiplicity. I therefore propose a third view, taking רֹעִים in a plural sense, but צֶמַח, etc., notwithstanding in the sense of unity. The reasons for this are as follows: 1. If Jeremiah wished to set forth a multiplicity, why did he not continue in the plural? Why does he not say "Who shall reign as kings?" צֶמַח has, in the comparatively few passages where it occurs, a collective sense. But not necessarily. It is *germen, proles* in general, and may accordingly designate as well a single individual as a number. If the prophet wished it to be taken in the latter sense, and therefore as absolutely identical with רֹעִים, he must have indicated this by the plural. 2. Ezekiel and Zechariah, who, as is acknowledged, refer to this passage, evidently understood it in the sense of unity. Ezekiel says expressly in xxxiv. 23, "And I will set up *one* shepherd over them."—And Zechariah in iii. 8, and vi. 12, used צֶמַח as a proper name, saying (iii. 8): "For I bring my servant Zemach" [The Branch]—and (vi. 12): "Behold a man, Zemach his name, under whom it shall sprout." As to the second question, previously raised, the subjective conception of the prophet is to be distinguished from the objective reality of the fulfilment. To the prophets the pictures of the future, which came within the circle of their vision, contained by no means always sharply circumscribed and distinctly impressed forms (comp. 1 Pet. i. 11). These forms were as little born entirely of the future, severed from the present. Rather were they eternal ideas, which had derived their body from the present. Of this kind are most of the Messianic prophecies. In reality Christ is a different king, priest and prophet, from what the authors of Ps. ii.; cx.; Deut. xviii. conceived, and yet His advent is the true fulfilment of those prophecies. Thus Jeremiah also sees together with the one grand form of the archshepherd, many others, whom he recognizes as His seed. If the prophet conceived among his offspring of a successor, in the sense in which successors of a no longer reigning prince are spoken of, this must have been a point which remained obscure to the subjective perception of the prophet,—in a similar manner, as it may have been dark to the prophet, how he could live so long, of whom it was said that He gave His soul an offering for sin (Isai. liii. 10). Objectively considered, from JEROME and THEODORET understood the apostles by the many רֹעִים— an interpretation which is certainly exposed to the objection of too great limitation. It would be more appropriate, to consider, with others, that we, so far as we are ἐν Χριστῷ, are not only Abraham's seed (Gal. iii. 29) but also David's. We are indeed a royal priesthood (1 Pet. ii. 9); and He has made us not only priests but kings ἐποίησας αὐτοὺς βασιλείαν καὶ ἱερεῖς, καὶ βασιλεύουσιν ἐπὶ τῆς γῆς, Rev. v. 10, coll. i. 6). [HENDERSON: "By the better shepherds whom Jehovah promises to place over His restored people, I understand Zerubbabel, Ezra, Nehemiah, the Maccabees, etc., under whose superintendence and rule they were re-instated in their possessions, and enjoyed protection against both internal and foreign enemies."—S. R. A.] If now the inquiry is made, how the prophet came to choose the expression צֶמַח, it was long ago pointed out by the Comm. that he had in mind Isai. xi. 2; liii. 2. As there the sprouting forth of a scion, from the apparently withered root of the house of David, is announced, so here the growth of a scion in the midst of a people, gathered again after a long dispersion, and thus about to enter upon a new national existence. This conception appears also to form the basis of the translation of the LXX., which translates צֶמַח here as in Zech. iii. 8; vi. 12, ἀνατολή. Comp. especially καὶ ὑποκάτωθεν αὐτοῦ ἀνατελεῖ, in the passage last mentioned.—Justice or righteousness is the chief quality of a good king according to the Old Testament doctrine. Comp. Ps. xlv. 5, 7, 8; lxxii. 1-4, 12-14; lxxxii. 2-4; ci. 1-8.— Hence righteous scion, of which the confirmation in fact is declared in shall exercise judgment. Comp. Ps. cxlvi. 7; ciii. 6, and the remarks on vii. 5, 6; ix. 23.

Ver. 6. In his days . . . . our righteousness. Comp. Deut. xxxiii. 28, 29.—Repetition of our passage, xxxiii. 16 —Judah is fem. as in iii. 7; xiv. 2; xxxiii. 16; Lam. i. 3; Nah. ii. 1; Mal. ii. 11. It is then equivalent to daughter of Judah, Lam. ii. 2, 5. Comp. NAEGELSB., *Gr.* lx. 4.—They will call him. According to the explanation prevalent even from antiquity, this refers to righteous scion. But as Jeremiah is his own best interpreter, the name must be referred to Israel. For in the parallel passage, xxxiii. 16, where instead of "and Israel dwell securely," we read "Jerusalem shall dwell securely," the word he, in the latter clause of the verse ("and this is the name by which *he* shall be called") can refer to no other than Jerusalem. Jehovah our Righteousness is not then the name of the scion of David, but of the nation. It is a symbolical surname, which is distinguished from other names, in that it serves not for real use, but only for objective characterization, an ideal inscription, as it were. Hence this name is also ascribed to an object, which already has a name. For the nation is already called Israel, but nevertheless it is to be called "Jehovah, etc." The prophet does not mean that the old name is to be changed into a new one; for the name does not recur (except in the repetition of this passage, xxxiii. 16) and the nation appears as before under its old name, which is also a sacred, God-given name. (Gen. xxxii. 28.) Jerusalem elsewhere receives other names which are likewise not intended for daily use: in Ezek. xlviii. 35, the name יְהוָה שָׁמָּה (The Lord is there) is attributed to the city. In Isai. lx. 14 we read "they shall call thee The city of Jehovah, the Zion of the Holy One of Israel." In a similar manner Nathan gives his pupil Solomon the name Jedidiah, which he never bore in reality. With respect to the name Emmanuel (Isai. vii. 14; viii. 8-10) the case appears to be the same.—Similar in form are the names Jehovah-nissi (Exod. xvii. 15), Jehovah-shalom (Jud. vi. 24), Jehovah-jireh (Gen. xxii. 14). The LXX. makes a proper name of it, 'Ιωσεδέκ. I suppose with HERMANN (*Gött. Weihn. Progr.* 1752, comp. J. D. MICHAELIS, *Observ. S.* 189) that it referred the passage to the post-exilic restoration, and understood by 'Ιωσεδέκ its representative, the high-priest Joshua, the son of Jozedek, which it always pronounces 'Ιωσεδέκ (Hagg. i. 1, 12; Ezr. iii. 2, 8; v. 2; Neh. xii. 26). In favor also of this view is the Jewish interpretation of the passage concerning Zerubbabel, combated by THEODORET and EUSEBIUS (*Dem. Ev.*, vii. 9), which seems to be supported by the LXX. The strange expression ἐν τοῖς προφήταις (THEODORET: αὐτὸς ἐν τ. πρ., perhaps a trace of the final syllable ט, which is wanting in 'Ιωσεδέκ: EUSED. 'Ιωσεδεκίμ) is also in its favor. It is indeed transferred from ver. 9, where it stands as a title, but it is not impossible that the Alexandrian translators perceived in it a reference to the post-exilic prophets, under whose co-operation Joshua and Zerubbabel labored. The Syriac and SYMMACHUS, moreover, read צדקנו, for they translate δικαίωσον ἡμᾶς.—If it is not the name of the Messiah, but of the people, then of course all the deductions are futile, which have been drawn from it in support of the deity of the Messiah. Only one thought remains, that Israel will be a nation, that will have no other righteousness than Jehovah's. Some would take צדק exclusively in the sense of "salvation" (GRAF). Without denying that it may have this meaning (comp. Rems. on vii. 5; ix. 23; Isa. xlvi. 12, etc.), I do not think that here בְּרָכָה תְּשׁוּעָה יֵשַׁע or any similar word would have done as well. The prophet certainly chose צדק not without reason, *i. e.* not without regard to its specific meaning. We are therefore justified in taking it in the entire fulness of its verbal significance as expressing the thought that Jehovah is His people's righteousness and therefore their salvation. The expression is thus one of those which contain more than the prophet himself imagines, and we may therefore find in it also an antithesis to personal righteousness, which Israel thought to obtain by the works of the law (Rom. ix. 31, 32; xi. 7), but did not succeed. It has been further correctly remarked (*Vide* HENGSTENBERG, *Christology ad h. l.*) that Zedekiah changed his former name into this with reference to this passage. Compelled by Nebuchadnezzar to assume another name (2 Ki. xxiv. 17, comp. KEIL on xxiii. 34) he chose this, which may very well signify "Jehovah my Righteousness," and by which he expressed the presumptuous hope, that Jeremiah's glorious promise would find in him the beginning of its fulfilment—in which he expressed rather an irony than a glorification of himself.

Vers. 7, 8. **Therefore . . . in their own land**. These two verses are repeated with unessential alterations from xvi. 14, 15. They stand in both places in a suitable connection, and Jeremiah himself may here, as frequently, have reproduced his own words spoken before. The omission of these verses here by the LXX., and their supplementation at the end of the chapter, whereas ver. 6 closes with the words: 'Ιωσεδέκ ἐν τοῖς προφήταις, I cannot, with HITZIG and GRAF, regard as a proof that the two verses were wanting in the Hebrew original of the Translator. The admitted capricious arbitrariness of this translator deprives his testimony of all demonstrative force. The occasion of the transposition may have been the circumstance that the verses have in xvi. 14, 15 a minatory, here a friendly, meaning, which led him to think that they must be introduced in the same connection as in ch. xvi. This end he attained by placing them at the close of the minatory prophecy against the prophets. It should further be remarked that both verses, in the positive part of their relative clauses, agree in part *verbatim* with ver. 3, and in so far might be regarded as superfluous in this place. But the main emphasis is to be laid on the main proposition, "they shall no more say, As Jehovah liveth, etc., but: As Jehovah liveth," etc., and in this sense they have the significance of a concluding doxology. The reduction of Israel from the later exile will furnish a more glorious substratum to the oath by the name of Jehovah.

---

2. *Against the False Prophets* (xxiii. 9–40.).

a. The Blind Leaders of the Blind.

XXIII. 9-15.

9   Against the Prophets:—
    Broken is my heart in my breast, all my bones quake,[1]
    I am become like a drunken man, and a man whom wine has overcome,
    Because of Jehovah and because of his holy words.
10 For the land is full of adulterers.
    (For on account of the curse[2] the land mourns,
14

The pastures of the desert are dried up:)
And their course is become evil and their might not right.
11 For both prophet and priest are profane,
Even in my house have I found their wickedness, saith Jehovah.
12 Therefore their way shall be to them as slippery places in the dark;
They shall be driven³ ṭ ... they fall therein;
For I shall bring calamity upon them in the year of their visitation,
Saith Jehovah.
13 Also in the prophets of Samaria have I seen perversity.⁴
They prophesied⁵ by Baal and led my people Israel astray.
14 But in the prophets of Jerusalem I saw what is horrible;
Adultery and dealing in falsehood,—
They strengthened the hands of the evil-doers,
That they did not turn⁶ every one from his wickedness.
They are all become to me like Sodom,
And their inhabitants like Gomorrah.
15 Therefore saith Jehovah Zebaoth thus concerning the prophets:
Behold, I feed them with absinthe [wormwood],
And give them poison-water to drink,
For from the prophets of Jerusalem profanation has gone out over the whole land.

TEXTUAL AND GRAMMATICAL.

¹ Ver. 9.—רחפו. Kal here only. Elsewhere Piel only occurs; Gen. i. 2; Deut. xxxii. 11. The radical meaning seems to be *flaccidus, debilis, mollis fuit*. Comp. the Arabic *rachapha*=*mollis, tenuis fuit*, and רחה.

² Ver. 10.—The LXX., Syriac, and Arab. read אלה instead of אלה. So also Hitzig and Meier. אלה, however, merely designates the effect as indirect, occasioned by the curse, with reference to Deut. xxviii. 15–68; xxix. 19–28.

³ Ver. 12.—וּדְחוּ from דחה, comp. Olshausen, § 265 e.

⁴ Ver. 13.—תפלה, *insulsum, insipidum* [unsavoriness]. Besides only in Job i. 22; xxiv. 12.

⁵ Ver. 13.—הנבאו. Comp. Naegelsb. *Gr.*, § 23, *Anm.* 9; Ezek. xxxvii. 10.

⁶ Ver. 14.—לבלתי שבו. This construction is found besides only in xxvii. 18; Ezek. xiii. 3. In Ezek. xiii. 22, where these words are quoted, we read לבלתי־שוב, but we are not therefore to assume an error here. The finite verb is admissible, because a condition, which actually existed, is to be designated.

EXEGETICAL AND CRITICAL.

The prophet begins by describing his feelings at the reception of this revelation. His sensations were those of a man of broken heart, or of a drunken man (ver. 9). By this introduction we obtain a standard, by which to measure the importance of the following passage. First the moral condition of the people is described as very bad, especially from the prevalence of adultery. (Punishment of this the prevalent drought) (ver. 10). How could it be otherwise when the spiritual leaders of the people, prophets and priests were themselves profane men, who even desecrated the sanctuary with their crimes? (ver. 11). Therefore in the corresponding period punishment must come upon them also (ver. 12). Even the prophets in Samaria had led the people of Israel astray by their scandalous behaviour (ver. 13). The prophets of Jerusalem, however, had in the point of popular seduction, accomplished something truly horrible. Not only had they gone before with their example of wickedness, but had actually strengthened the evil-doers in their wickedness and restrained them from conversion, so that the nation had become to the Lord like Sodom and Gomorrah (ver. 14). Therefore, as the profaners of the land, they must be given poison to drink and be fed with bitterness (ver. 15).

Ver. 9. **Against the prophets . . . holy words.** To connect, as indicated by the accents, **broken with against the prophets**, is not grammatically impossible (coup. *ex. gr.* xxxi. 20), but not altogether appropriate in meaning. For a broken heart does not signify anger or indignation (which is the only state of mind Jeremiah could be supposed to be in towards the false prophets), but humiliation, anxiety, care. Comp. Ps. xxxiv. 19; li. 19; lx. 19; Isa. lxi. 1. But it becomes perfectly clear that we have here a superscription before us, when we observe that evidently the whole section, xxiii. 9–40, as relating to the prophets, is opposed to the preceding as relating to the kings, that the title consequently states the main purport, not only of the next verses, but of the whole following discourse. Such superscriptions are moreover common in the book of this prophet: xlvi. 2; xlviii. 1; xlix. 1, 7, 23, 28.—By **holy words** are meant the revelation contained in what follows. What shocked the prophet to such an unusual degree was doubtless a glance granted him into the depths of human depravity and on the other hand of the divine wrath. Comp. iv. 19; viii. 18 sqq.

Vers. 10–12. **For the land is full . . . visitation, saith Jehovah.—For** is causal. But since the reason of the prophet's great shock is not expressed in the next sentence only, but in the whole of what follows also, **For** is to be referred to the entire following discourse.—**Adul-**

terers. That this crime prevailed most extensively is evident from v. 7, 8; ix. 1; xxix. 23. Where, however, אכן in this respect is not discovered, it is difficult to find it in other respects, and especially in relation to God. Comp. rems. on v. 1.—**For on account**, *etc.* This sentence to **dried up** is to be regarded as a parenthesis. From the general calamity of drought may be argued the presence of a general guiltiness. Moreover, both the indication of the drought, which looks like a *demonstratio ad oculos* and the leading back to the false prophets (ver. 11), reminds us very strongly of xiv. 2, 13-18.—**And their course** is connected with "full of adulterers." Their thought and endeavor generally (their walking and running, comp. viii. 6; Prov. i. 16; Isa. lix. 7; Rom. ix. 16) is directed to evil, therefore itself evil; they are strong only for that which is not right. Comp. rems. on viii. 6.—**For both prophet,** *etc.* This sentence states the reason why the moral corruption is so general: it cannot be otherwise, since the teachers and leaders of the people are not only themselves profane and godless, but practise their ungodliness even in the sanctuary, the most influential centre of theocratic life. Therefore the prophet says directly in ver. 15, From the prophets of Jerusalem is gone forth profanation over the whole land. Evidently **profanation** is there used with reference to **profane** here. On the subject comp. xxxii. 34; Ezek. viii. 3 sqq. The priests are moreover mentioned only incidentally; in the whole subsequent part of the discourse Jeremiah speaks only of the prophets. Perhaps the juxtaposition of the two is only a reminiscence from xiv. 18, where alone the expression occurs.—**In the dark**. Comp. Ps. xxxv. 6 [THOMSON, *The Land and the Book*, I., p. 106].—**Year of visitation**. Comp. xi. 23. It is apparent from this expression that **the visitation is still in the indefinite future.**

Vers. 13-15. **Also in the prophets of Samaria . . . over the whole land.** In these verses it is more particularly shown *how* the corruption extended from the prophets over the whole country. At the same time its merited punishment is announced to them.—The 1 here (**Also**) and at the beginning of ver. 14 (**But**) correspond, but the whole sentences are not parallel, for it could not be said: *Both* in the prophets of Samaria I see perversity, *and* in the prophets of Jerusalem what is horrible, the latter clause containing a climax. The expression is founded on a mingling of two ways of speaking, "both in the prophets of Samaria I see what is bad, *and* in the prophets of Jerusalem," and "in the prophets of Samaria I see תפלה, but in the prophets of Jerusalem *even* שערורה." Both are confounded in the sentence: both in the prophets of Samaria I see what is bad, and in the prophets of Jerusalem what is horrible.—We cannot well render these modes of expression word for word. Comp. the parallel, equally unfavorable for Judah, in iii. 6-10.—**By Baal**. Comp. rems. on ii. 8.—**Led astray**. In this leading astray by means of prophecy in the name of idols is the point of connection between vers. 10 and 11.—**Horrible**. Comp. v. 30.—**Strengthened,** *etc.* They thus not only seduced the people into wickedness by their example, but sustained them therein by the authority of their example and detained them from repentance.—The subject of **are become** is the prophets, while **their** must refer to Jerusalem —The comparison with Sodom and Gomorrah is here as in Zeph. ii. 9, yet with this difference, that they are here the emblem of moral corruption, there of outward desolation.—**Poison-water**. Comp. viii. 14; ix. 14.—**Profanation**. Comp. iii. 9. In this last causal sentence (for from the prophets of Jerusalem has profanation gone out), the fundamental thought of the strophe again comes out clearly.

υ. Warning against deception by the Prophets.

XXIII. 16-22.

16 Thus saith Jehovah Zebaoth,
    Listen not to the words of the prophets who prophesy to you;
    They deceive you.[1]
    They speak their own heart's vision, not from the mouth of Jehovah.
17 They say continually to my despisers:
    Jehovah hath spoken,[2] "There shall be peace to you;"
    And wherever one walketh[3] in the hardness of his heart,
    There they say: no evil shall come upon you.
18 For he who hath stood in the counsel of Jehovah,
    Let him perceive[4] and hear his word,
    Let him who hath marked my word[5] proclaim it.[6]
19 Behold, a storm-wind of Jehovah!
    Fury is gone forth[7] and whirling storm—
    Upon the head of the ungodly it will be rolled.

20 The anger of Jehovah will not turn back,
Till he execute and carry out the plans of his heart.
At the end of days ye will become aware of this.
21 I sent not the prophets, yet they ran,
I spake not to them, yet they prophesied.
22 But had they stood in my counsel,
Then they would have proclaimed my words to my people,
And have brought them back from their wicked way,
And from the wickedness of their deeds.

TEXTUAL AND GRAMMATICAL.

¹ Ver. 16.—מהבלים, Hiph. here only. The Kal in ii. 5; 2 Ki. xvii. 15; Ps. lxii. 11; Job xxvii. 12. He who renders another frivolous, so that his mind is directed to what is frivolous, has led him astray, deceived him. Comp. xiv. 14; Ezek. xiii. 2, 3.

² Ver. 17.—אמרים אמור ונו׳. On the construction comp. NAEGELSB. Gr., § 97, 1, a, Anm.—Instead of דָּבָר the LXX. and Syriac, according to the view of some, read דִּבֶּר. But they might have taken דָּבָר itself as a subst.—דָּבָר, as in Hos. i. 2; Jer. v. 13. The LXX. also connect the word with the preceding: τοῖς ἀπωθουμένοις λόγον κυρίου, while the Syriac translates: dicunt iis, qui me exasperant; ex oraculo Domini pax erit vobis. דָּבָר certainly never stands as an introductory formula (= כֹּה אָמַר): it most prevalently stands after אֲשֶׁר or כַּאֲשֶׁר. But as Jeremiah was quoting the words of the Pseudo-prophets he may have purposely avoided the current formula of the true prophets. As the more difficult reading then דִּבֶּר deserves the preference.

³ Ver. 17.—וְכֹל הֹלֵךְ. The construction is not to be explained by the effect of the לְ before יֹצֵא סְנַאי, but the participle is used absolutely as it is frequently, especially after כֹּל. Comp. NAEGELSB. Gr., § 97, 2 b.

⁴ Ver. 18.—יֵרֶא. Jussive apodosis. On the Vau comp. NAEGELSB. Gr., § 111, 1 b.

⁵ Ver. 18.—דְּבָרִי. The Masoretes unnecessarily alter into דְבָרוֹ הקשיב with the accus. in Job xiii. 6; Ps. xvii. 1; lxi. 2.

⁶ Ver. 18.—If we take כִּי, as we have done, as a relative pronoun, and read וַיַשְׁמֵעַ, the apodosis is wanting to the second clause. From this reading it appears that the Masoretes took כִּי for an interrogative. By comparison with ix. 11, and with ver. 22 below, it is thus seen that we are to punctuate וְיַשְׁמַע (comp. Jud. xviii. 25), he may cause to hear, may proclaim.

⁷ Ver. 19.—הִנֵּה is in explicative apposition. יָצְאָה is to be taken as a perfect: the hurricane has already burst forth.

EXEGETICAL AND CRITICAL.

The main thought is: warning against false prophets who deceive the people and proclaim what comes not from the mouth of the Lord but from their own heart (ver. 16). Thus they proclaim peace to the despisers of the Lord, and impunity to those who go about in the hardness of their heart (ver. 17). Thus too they betray themselves. For to whom is granted the honor of receiving information concerning the counsel of the Lord, cannot do otherwise than proclaim the Lord's word as he received it (ver. 18). But the word of the Lord never proclaims impunity to the despisers. Rather concerning these is to be expected a tempest of anger from the Lord, who will not rest till He has carried out all His plans. In the end of days this will indeed be marked (vers. 19, 20). Thus they are not sent or commissioned by the Lord (ver. 21). But even had they, without receiving any express commission, only assisted as witnesses to the counsel of the Lord they would have proclaimed the word of the Lord to the people, and have turned them from their wicked way (ver. 22). The warning against the false prophets is thus occasioned by the admission of the double fact, that the Lord has not sent them, and that they have not been present at the counsel of the Lord or received information thereof. That the Lord has not sent them will be proved by His doing just the contrary of what they predicted. But that they have not at all entered into the counsel of the Lord is seen from this, that what they proclaimed to the people does not agree with the genuine word of the Lord, and that they have not labored to turn the people from their wicked way.

Ver. 18. **For he who hath stood . . . proclaim it.** There are two modes of explanation: 1. He who has stood in the counsel of God, he sees and hears my word, he who has marked my word let him proclaim it (GRAF). 2. For who has stood in the counsel of the Lord? etc. The latter explanation would however either have the meaning, that no one had stood in the counsel of the Lord, which a prophet could not say, or we must take עָמַד בְּסוֹד in the sense of privately, without calling, assisting in the counsel of the Lord—which would be arbitrary and require before ver. 18 the supplementation of the double thought: "such things have I not said to them, and they cannot have heard them in my counsel (quasi me invito).'' Hence כִּי can be taken in the sense of quisquis only according to the first mode of interpretation. (Comp. NAEGELSB. Gr., § 79, 6). The connection is then as follows: Listen not to the prophets, they deceive you, for they proclaim their own thoughts, not my commissions, promising impunity to my despisers. For he who has stood in the counsel of the Lord, must proclaim the Lord's word, which cannot possibly be favorable to His despisers. The point of the thought is therefore contained in ver. 17: the despisers of the service of Jehovah were well-known people. If prophets, who pretended to speak in the name of Jehovah, promised such impunity, they thus proved themselves indisputably to be deceivers.—To stand in the counsel is not to sit in the counsel (Ps. i. 1). The latter designates assistance with an advisory voice.—Such an one is called עֲצַת אִישׁ Isa. xl. 13. Comp. Rom. xi. 34. Standing in the counsel of the Lord, *i. e.* as hearers, is declared in the proper sense of prophets: Isa. vi. 1-8; 1 Ki. xxii. 19-23.—Yet we shall not err, if we assume that Jeremiah wishes the expression here to be taken in a wider sense, in which sense Am. iii. 7 גָּלָה סוֹדוֹ is used. Comp. Ps. xxv. 14. For we cannot suppose that all the prophets received all their revelations in the form in which, according to the passages cited, Micah and Isaiah received those mentioned.—**Let him perceive** [see]. How can the word of the Lord be seen? A reference to ii. 31; Eccles. i. 16 does not seem to me satisfactory. Certainly the divine revelation might partly be *seen* in vision (comp. הֲזוֹן לָבָּם ver. 16; i. 11, 13; xxiv. 1), partly heard (1 Sam. iii. 9, 10); it could be received by the organ of the eye or the ear.—The effect of the seeing and hearing is indicated by "mark:" he who *gives heed* to my word, hears it not only with the outer but the inner ear, he may, *etc.*

Vers. 19, 20. **Behold, a storm-wind... aware of this.** In antithesis to ver. 17 it is here set forth, what the true intention of Jehovah is with respect to the people. Both verses are repeated xxx. 23, 24.—**A storm-wind of Jehovah, not physical but spiritual; an outburst of divine wrath is proclaimed by the prophet.—Upon the head.** Comp. 2 Sam. iii. 29.—**Will not turn back.** The storm will produce not merely a slight passing effect but a thoroughly destructive one. It will not cease till the will of the holy and just God is completely accomplished. Comp. Isa. xlv. 23; Ps. cxxxii. 11.—**At the end of days,** *etc.* Comp. Gen. xlix. 1; Numb. xxiv. 14; Deut. iv. 30; xxxi. 29; Isa. ii. 2; Jer. xlviii. 47; xlix. 39. A contrast to the present is here involved: you do not now regard it as possible; at the end of days, however, *i. e.* at the conclusion of this section of history in which we live, you will indeed perceive it, *viz.,* that it can and must be thus. **End of days,** therefore, expresses a relative idea. Comp. ver. 12.

Vers. 21, 22. **I sent not... their deeds.** A new and perfectly clear reason for the desolation in ver. 16. How could those be true prophets whom the Lord sent not, to whom He spoke not? If, however, they should allege, that if not *rite* officially and *de jure* yet actually they had received information of the divine counsel, they must at least proclaim the word of Jehovah in its severity as hostile to the wicked and urging them to repentance. But since this is not the case they are irrefutably demonstrated to be false prophets and deceivers.

---

c. The Criminal Mingling of Man's word and God's Word.

XXIII. 23–32.

23 Am I a God at hand? saith Jehovah,
  And not a God at a distance?¹
24 If a man conceal himself in a hiding place,
  Shall I not see him? saith Jehovah.
  Am I not he, who filleth heaven and earth? saith Jehovah.
25 I have heard what the prophets say,
  Who prophesy falsely in my name;
  "I have dreamed, I have dreamed."
26 How long still is the fire in the heart of **the prophets,**
  Who prophesy falsehood,—
  The prophets of the deceit of their own heart?
27 Who make the endeavor² to cause my people
  To forget³ my name by their dreams,
  Which they relate one to another,
  As their fathers forgot my name through Baal.
28 Let the prophet, to whom a dream came, relate **the dream,**
  Let him to whom my word came, relate my word truly.⁴
  What has the straw to do with the grain? saith Jehovah.
29 Is not my word just like the fire? saith Jehovah,
  And like the hammer, which breaketh rocks in pieces?
30 Therefore behold, I am against the prophets, saith Jehovah,
  Who steal my words one from another!
31 Behold, I am against the prophets, saith Jehovah,

Who take their tongue and pronounce oracles.[5]
32 Behold, I am against them, who prophesy false dreams, saith Jehovah,
And relate them and lead my people astray,
By their falsehood and by their boasting.[6]
I had not sent them nor commissioned them,
They can also be of no profit to this people, saith Jehovah.

TEXTUAL AND GRAMMATICAL.

[1] Ver. 23.—On the construction, comp. NAEGELSB. *Gr.*, § 63, 4 *e*
[2] Ver. 27.—הַהֹשְׁבִים in apposition to נְבִאִים in ver. 26.
[3] Ver. 27.—לְהַשְׁכִּיחַ. Hiphil, here only.
[4] Ver. 28.—אָכָה, *Accus. adverb.* Comp. x. 10; NAEGELSB. *Gr.*, § 70, *k.*
[5] Ver. 31.—יְנָאֲמוּ. Of the whole verb, besides this single form, we find only נְאֻם.
[6] Ver. 32.—פַּחֲזוּת is ἅπαξ λεγ. The meaning (comp. Jud. ix. 4; Zeph. iii. 4; Gen. xlix. 4)=*insolentia*, impudent boasting.

EXEGETICAL AND CRITICAL.

As though the exalted (ver. 23) and omniscient God, who fills heaven and earth would know nothing of it (ver. 24), the false prophets dared to give forth their dreams as the word of God (ver. 25). How long will this unreason, which is at the same time deception and self-deception, last? (ver. 26). How long will they seek by their dreams to bring Jehovah into oblivion among the people, as their fathers forgot Him for Baal? (ver. 27). With this is associated a second mischief, that they give out the dream not as *their* dream, but as Jehovah's word is to be proclaimed *as such*, connect this with their productions, though they have no more relation than the straw has to the grain (ver. 28), or to the fire, or the rock-crushing hammer (ver. 29). Hence the prophet finally formulates a triple charge against the prophets: 1. They steal God's words (ver. 31); 2. They ape the form of genuine prophecy; 3. They lead the people astray by their lying dreams.

Vers. 23, 24. **Am I a God ... saith Jehovah.** The audacity of the false prophets, who did not fear to cover themselves with the name of Jehovah, is founded on the delusion that He was not in a condition to perceive their presumption. They regard the Lord as a God, who is only able to behold that which is near, *i. e.* can overlook only a limited domain. In opposition to this the Lord calls Himself אֱלֹהֵי מֵרָחֹק, *i. e.* a God who takes note of that which occurs even in the remotest distance, who from His throne in heaven overlooks also the earth, because as filling heaven and earth He is present in both. Comp. Am. ix. 2-4; Job xi. 8, 9; Ps. cxxxix. 7-12.

Ver. 25. **I have heard ... dreamed.** This is the main charge, the sin which stands first in view of the omnipresent and omniscient God. Dreams were in themselves an acknowledged and legitimate medium of divine revelation. Comp. Numb. xii. 6; 1 Sam. xxviii. 6, 15; Joel iii. 1; Dan. vii. 1. But they occupy a low stage among the forms of divine communication. Comp. KNOBEL, *Proph. d. Hebr.*, I, S. 174 sqq. HERZOG, *Real-Enc.*, XVI., S. 207 ff.; DELITZSCH, *Psychologie, Kap.* IV., § 14.—These false prophets always speak only of their dreams as the media of their divine illumination. Of course

For the dream is most withdrawn from the control of other men. Nothing is easier than to say, Last night I dreamed this or that. Who can refute it? The prophets thus make an immoderate and in itself suspicious use of dreams. They are dreamers, and it is remarkable that in Deut. xiii. 1, 3, 5 נָבִיא, by which there a *false* prophet is always meant, is regularly distinguished also as חֹלֵם חֲלֹם, a dreamer of dreams. ["Although it pleased God to reveal Himself sometimes in dreams to His faithful people of old, yet when false prophets arose, who opposed the true, such revelations were rare. We have no instance of them in Isaiah, Jeremiah, or Ezekiel, or other prophets who were opposed by false prophets." WORDSWORTH.—S. R. A.]

Vers. 26, 27. **How long ... through Baal.** By how long the Lord makes known that the conduct of these prophets, which is more particularly described in these two verses, is intolerable to Him. Great difficulty is caused by הֲיֵשׁ. The ancient translations coolly omit the הֲ and make it otherwise convenient to themselves. Vulg. and Chald.: *usque quo istud est in corde, etc.* LXX.: ἕως πότε ἔσται ἐν καρδίᾳ, etc. Syr.: *quousque erunt in ore falsorum prophetarum prophetice falsa?*—The interpretations which adhere to the text are three: 1. The question is asked by a double interrogative הֲ and כָּת, which, however, amounts to this that the latter is quite superfluous. HITZIG appeals indeed to xlviii. 27 and Mic. vi. 10. But in neither of these places is there a double interrogative. Besides the subject is wanting, and the thought: How long have they still the material for dreams? is certainly strange. 2. נִבָּא and נְבִיא are rendered according to the construction יָחֶל נֹחַ אִישׁ הָאֲדָמָה Gen. ix. 20. Comp. EWALD, § 298 *b.* NAEGELSB. *Gr.*, § 95, *g, Anm.* Thus EWALD and MEIER. But apart from this that both ignore the interrogative *He*, the construction with שׁ is without a precedent, forced and feeble in sense, for it seems as though the Lord expected an alteration in these prophets, though He had previously represented them as incurably corrupt (comp. vers. 11, 14), and according to ver. 27, expects nothing from them but the endeavor to bring Him into forgetfulness among the people. Is the thought suitable in this connection: "How long do the prophets purpose to be false prophets?" (MEIER). 3. The interpretation is most satisfactory which was first offered by LUDWIG DE DIEU and adopted by SEB. SCHMIDT, CHR. B. MICHAELIS, ROSENMUELLER, UMBREIT, GRAF and others, according to which עד כתי is to be rendered as an independent sentence (=how long still will this last?) הֲיֵשׁ בְּלֵב to be taken as = have in mind? and הַהֹשְׁבִים, ver. 27, to be regarded as a resumption of the question interrupted by the words following בלב: have in mind the prophets, who .... think they, to make my people forget? Although this interpretation gives a sense which is tolerably satisfactory, it is opposed by the grammatical difficulty, that הֵם should stand after הַהֹשְׁבִים as a recapitulation of the subject, which could not be absent after the interruption and the removal thereby effected of the proper subject. If then this interpretation also is not perfectly satisfactory, it is natural to suppose that the text is faulty. Should we not read הָאֵשׁ instead of הֲיֵשׁ? Jeremiah had above, xx. 9, compared the irresistible impulse to proclaim the word of the Lord, to a fire burning in his heart. Could not he who loves to quote himself, and who knows how to wield the weapon of irony against his opponents, in order to set forth incisively the difference between the true and false prophets, ironically presuppose in the latter what, as he well knew, was possessed only by the true prophets? He, staggering under the burden of persecution, had said (xx. 9): " I will not speak any more in His name," but he was obliged to do so. Those who ought not compelled themselves to prophesy in the name of Jehovah. Did then such a fire burn also in their hearts? And if so, how long will it continue? Every one is summoned by these questions to make the comparison, but every one will also be obliged to confess that the miserable little flame of human egotism is not to be compared with the high and noble flame of divine inspiration, which burned in the prophet's breast.—**The prophets of the deceit**, *etc.* They deceive others, after and because they have deceived themselves. Comp. xiv. 14; Ezek. xiii. 2.—**Cause to forget.** On the subject-matter comp. ii. 32; iii. 21; xiii. 25; xviii. 15; 1. 6.—**One to another.** Not every one to his colleagues, but every one to his fellow. For they have corrupted the people by their lies. Comp. ver 32; xiv. 13 sqq.; xxiii. 14 sqq.; l. 6. —**Through Baal.** Comp. ii. 8. It is apparent that these false prophets did not prophesy in the name of an idol, but in the name of Jehovah, but they proclaimed in His name not His word but the deceit of their own heart.

Vers. 28, 29. **Let the prophet . . . rocks in pieces.** The Lord does not object if the prophets relate *their own* dreams *as such.* But they are not to mix them with the true word of God, and on the ground of this mingling utter them as a divine revelation. As the dreams are to be related *as such,* so also the real revelation of God is to be handed down purely, *i. e.* without addition or subtraction. It is clear that the connection requires this meaning for אֵמֶת. Comp. ii. 21; Prov. xi. 18. A mixture of the two elements is just as unsuitable as a mingling of empty straw with grain. The straw cannot be used with the grain, nor the grain with the straw. This comparison, and the following one of the hammer and "who steal," ver. 30, shows that Jeremiah here, *i. e.* from ver. 25, has in view not the presentation of the products of human subjectivity as the products of divine objectivity, but the mingling of the two elements. He censures the former in vers. 25-27. As merchants often sell wholly sham goods, or those which are partly sham and partly genuine, as genuine, so do these prophets. Both are certainly שֶׁקֶר.— **Is not my word like a fire?** *etc.* A point in the comparison with straw is further developed. The straw is not only false ware, when found (as chopped straw) among the bread-corn, but simply as straw it has no strength, and is useless for defence or offence. So is also the word of the false prophets. In opposition to this, God's word is like the all-conquering fire (comp. Song of Sol. viii. 6, 7), or like the hammer crushing the hardest rock (Heb. iv. 12; Eccles. xii. 11). How despicable does the word of the pseudo-prophets appear in these comparisons and what a disgraceful mesalliance do they cause by their mingling! I do not think that the prevalent minatory and punitive import of the genuine prophecies was meant, for the Gospel is the most intensive force (1 Cor. i. 18-24; ii. 4; Rom. i. 16).

Vers. 30-32. **Therefore behold . . . saith Jehovah.** These three similarly opening verses recapitulate the main thoughts of the section in reverse order, in such wise also, that a point latent in the foregoing context (ver. 31), is now plainly set forth. Ver. 30 evidently corresponds to ver. 28. They steal the genuine words of God, not directly every one from his colleague (ver. 27), but every one from his fellow as he pleases, thus in part at first hand from true prophets, in part at second hand from false prophets, or wheresoever they can find them. Unmixed falsehood betrays itself too easily and is insipid. But falsehood mingled with truth is powerful error, and the beauty of truth serves as an ornamental covering to its deformity. The second **Behold**, *etc.*, ver. 31, corresponds to "who prophesy falsely in my name." vers. 25, 26. For thereby it is implicitly declared that they proclaimed their lies in the same form as the true prophets, as oracles of Jehovah. But how cheaply they hold these! All they needed was to set their tongues to work. How dear on the other hand did Jeremiah account the honor of being Jehovah's true prophet! Comp. xx. 7-9.—The third **Behold**, *etc.*, corresponds to vers. 25-27, the import of which it plainly repeats.

d. The criminal use of the word "burden."

XXIII. 33–40.

33 And when this people, or the prophets[1] or priests,
Ask thee, What is the burden of Jehovah?
Thou shalt tell them what the burden of Jehovah is;[2]
Namely, "I reject you,"[3] saith Jehovah.
34 And the prophet, the priest, or the people
That say, "Burden of Jehovah;"
On such a man and his house will I visit it.
35 Thus shall ye say, every one to his neighbour and every one to[4] his brother:
What hath Jehovah answered? or What hath Jehovah spoken?
36 But "burden of Jehovah" ye shall no more take into your mouth;
For the burden will be to each his own word;
Because ye have perverted the words of the living God,
Jehovah Zebaoth, our God.
37 Thus shalt thou say to the prophet:
What has Jehovah answered thee?
Or, What has Jehovah spoken?
38 But if ye say, "Burden of Jehovah,"
On this account saith Jehovah thus:
Because ye say this word, "Burden of Jehovah,"
And I had sent unto you a message of this purport,
"Ye shall not say, 'Burden of Jehovah,'"—
39 Therefore, behold, I burden you[5] and thrust you,
And this city which I gave to you and your fathers,
Away from my presence;
40 And lay upon you everlasting reproach,
And everlasting shame, that shall not be forgotten.

TEXTUAL AND GRAMMATICAL.

[1] Ver. 33.—The article is general, and נָבִא expresses the idea of species. Comp. NAEGELSB. *Gr.*, § 71, 4, *a*.

[2] Ver. 33.—אֶת־מַה־מַשָּׂא. Many modern commentators follow the LXX. and Vulg. which read אַתֶּם הַמַּשָּׂא, but incorrectly. In His answer the Lord purposely uses the words of the question: *Verba retorquet*. The arrow directed against him must, being reversed, strike those insolent questioners. It should indeed properly read אֶת אֲשֶׁר כְּשָׂא. But the necessity of retaining the words of the question justified this grammatical license, which moreover (Comp. NAEGELSB. *Gr.*, § 79, 6) is not altogether without precedent. אֶת depends on וְאָמַרְתָּ. Comp. xiv. 17, *etc*. The construction is therefore by no means so artificial and clumsy as EWALD supposes.

[3] Ver. 33.—וְנָטַשְׁתִּי is not co-ordinated with וְאָמַרְתָּ, as is apparent from נְאֻם. It rather expresses the purport of that which Jeremiah is to proclaim as the "burden," *etc*. is therefore=and indeed. It should only be remarked that here in this meaning stands before a whole sentence, which, however, on account of its brevity is not thereby rendered less easily intelligible.

[4] Ver. 35.—On the interchange of עַל and אֶל, comp. rems. on x. 1.

[5] Ver. 39.—וְנָשִׁיתִי. The paronomasia requires us to read נָשִׁיתִי, as the LXX, Vulg., Syr., and some Codd. and editions really do. It is not necessary to assume the Piel form נִשִּׁיתִי, since forms like כְּלֹאתִי Ps. cxix. 102; כְּלֹתְנִי 1 Sam. xxv. 33; צָמַת Ruth ii. 9, justify the assumption of also in the Kal according to the analogy of the לה verbs. Comp. OLSH., § 223, *a*, *Anm*.—The reading נָשִׂיתִי, which does not afford any satisfactory sense, but may be translated "I forget," or "I heard not," is doubtless occasioned by the unusual punctuation (נָשִׁיתִי). A proof that the latter is the original is found in the Inf. נָשֹׁא, the א of which is likewise abnormal and therefore a sure trace of the original נָשָׁא. כְּלִמַּת ἅπ. λεγ. and perhaps to be read כְּלִמַּת, after xx. 11.

EXEGETICAL AND CRITICAL.

The word of double meaning מַשָּׂא, which signifies both "saying" and "burden," was mis-

used by the Jews, who were accustomed to ask the prophets mockingly what sort of a מַשָּׂא they had. Jeremiah is to tell those who thus ask, what sort of a burden threatens them, *viz.*, that they shall be rejected (ver. 33), and each who thus asks shall, for this derision, be subjected to a special visitation (ver. 34). If any wish to ask the prophets, he is to make use of the expression, What has the Lord answered or spoken? (ver. 35). But the expression מַשָּׂא (burden and saying) is no more to be used, for this perversion of a divine word will be avenged, such insolent words falling back like a heavy burden on the head of their authors (ver. 36). The inquiry is to be made thus: What has the Lord answered or spoken? (ver. 37). If, notwithstanding, the forbidden word is used (ver. 38), the Lord will carry away the people like a burden (ver. 39), and give them up to everlasting shame (ver. 40).

Vers. 33, 34. **And when this people ... visit it.—What burden?** It appears to have been the custom, whenever the prophets made their appearance in public to ask them if they had received any new revelation. There can be no doubt that מַשָּׂא means "saying, utterance," as well as "burden." Comp. the thorough demonstration in GRAF, S. 315. The passages from which it evidently follows that מַשָּׂא signifies *effatum*, any utterance, besides those where the verb נָשָׂא is used in the sense *vocem proferre* with and without קוֹל, voice (Isa. iii. 7; xlii. 2, 11 coll. Exod. xx. 7; xxiii. 1; Numb. xxiii. 7; Ps. cxxxix. 20, *etc.*), are especially the following: Isa. xiv. 28; Lam. ii. 14; 2 Ki. ix. 25; Prov. xxx. 1; xxxi. 1. HENGSTENBERG and RUECKERT, following the example of JONATHAN, AQUILA, the Syriac, JEROME and LUTHER, would take the word exclusively in the sense of "burden." We have translated "burden" above, but only because we have no expression, which without forcing unites both meanings. Of the many attempts to unite them by DE WETTE, EWALD, FUERST, MEIER, none are really satisfactory. DE WETTE's translation is most so. [*Wehsagung: utterance of woe.*—S. R. A.]. At all events the opposers emphasized the idea of burden. They wished to say that every declaration of Jehovah was only a new burden, that only what was burdensome, not what was pleasing, came from this God. In so far the question was one of blasphemous derision. It is implied by the word namely that what follows is a quotation. The passage to which Jeremiah refers is doubtless xii. 7, "rejected mine inheritance." The significance of this passage is clear from the fact that it is reproduced in a comprehensive survey in 2 Ki. xxi. 14.—**Will I visit it.** Besides the judgment announced to the people generally on account of their sins, those who make use of the expression "burden" in a wicked manner, shall receive special punishment.

Vers. 35-37. **Thus shall ye say ... Jehovah spoken.—For the burden will be,** *etc.* Even the insolent words will be to him who utters them a crushing burden, though the utterance of Jehovah, with respect to which he uses the term, is not in itself a burden at all.—These words are a parenthesis, and hence **because ye have perverted,** *etc.*, is connected with **ye shall no more take into your mouth** and declare the result of using the forbidden word. —**Living God.** Comp. x. 10.

III. APPENDIX.

(Chap. XXIV.)

POSTSCRIPT TO XXII. 13-30. *The Fourth King.*

XXIV. 1-10.

1 The LORD [Jehovah] shewed me, and behold, two baskets[1] of figs *were* set[2] before the temple of the LORD [Jehovah] after that Nebuchadrezzar, king of Babylon, had carried away captive Jeconiah the son of Jehoiakim king of Judah, and the princes of Judah, with the carpenters and smiths, from Jerusalem and had
2 brought them to Babylon. One basket had[3] very good figs, like the figs first ripe,[4] and the other basket had very naughty [bad] figs, which could not be eaten,[5] they
3 were so bad. Then said the LORD [Jehovah] unto me, What seest thou, Jeremiah? And I said, Figs; the good figs very good, and the evil [bad] very evil [bad], that cannot be eaten, they are so evil [bad].
4 Again the word of the LORD [Jehovah] came unto me, saying:
5 Thus saith the LORD [Jehovah], the God of Israel:
 Like these good figs, so the captives of Judah,
 Whom I have sent away from this place into the land of the Chaldeans,
 Will I regard[6] for good;
6 And will set mine eye upon them for good,
 And will bring them back into this land;

And will build them and not pull them down,
And plant them and not pluck them up;
7 And will give them a heart to know me, that I am Jehovah,
And they shall be my people;
I however will be their God,
When they return to me with their whole heart.
8 But like the bad figs, which cannot be eaten they are so bad,
—Thus saith Jehovah: I will make Zedekiah,
The king of Judah and his princes,
And the residue of Jerusalem, that are left in this land,
And those that dwell in the land of Egypt.
9 And I will make them a horror,
A calamity for all the kingdoms of the earth,
A shame and a proverb, a taunt and a curse,
In all places whither I shall drive them.
10 And I will send among them the sword,
The famine and the pestilence;
Till they be entirely extirpated from the land,
Which I gave to them and their fathers.

TEXTUAL AND GRAMMATICAL.

¹ Ver. 1.—הוּרְדִים. This plural form is found in this sense here only (in another sense Gen. xxx. 14). It is to be derived from a sing. דּוּד. Comp. Olsh. § 216, d. Elsewhere the plural of דּוּד is דּוּדִים and דּוּדִים, 2 Chron. xxxv. 13; 2 Ki. x. 7.

² Ver. 1.—יָעַד is to determine, appoint. The Hiph. is *diem dixit, in jus vocavit aliquem* (Job ix. 19; Jer. xlix. 19; l. 44). The Hoph. cannot therefore mean simply *positum, collocatum esse*. Seb. Schmidt: *duo calathi singulariter a Deo ante templum propositi, ut prophetia inde sumeretur*. Graf: The baskets were appointed; they would not have stood there, if God had not had a special object in it. I also believe that in מוּעָדִים is implied the idea of *ex mandato*. Yet it seems less probable to me that a *mandatum speciale* is meant, than that the prophet had in view that *mandatum generale*, of which we read in Exod. xxiii. 19; xxxiv. 26; Deut. xxvi. 2 sqq. The latter passage is particularly important.

³ Ver. 2.—אֶחָת. Comp. Naegelsb. *Gr.*, § 82, 4.—Observe the tropical use of the nominative: *continens pro contento*. Comp. Fürard, *Dogma r. h. A. M.* [Doctrine of the Lord's Supper] I. S. 14.

⁴ Ver. 2.—הַבַּכֻּרוֹת ἅπ. λεγ. On account of הָאֵן it is to be regarded as the subject: *ficus præcocitatum*. The early figs are the nicest. Comp. Isai. xxviii. 4; Hos. ix. 10; Mic. vii. 1.

⁵ Ver. 2.—תֵּאָכַלְנָה. The Imperf. here as in vers. 3 and 8, might certainly be taken as a simple future:—which are not eaten. The prophet then expresses the certainty, that no one will be in a condition to eat these figs. But the sentence may also be taken with אֲשֶׁר in the sense of a general declaration; אֲשֶׁר is then = *quales*, which kind of figs cannot be eaten. The Imperf. is then used to designate the permanent quality. Comp. Naegelsb. *Gr.*, § 87, d.

⁶ Ver. 5.—הִכִּיר = to recognize, with the collateral idea of approval, allowal. Comp. Ruth ii. 10, 19; and the expression הַכִּיר פָּנִים in Deut. i. 17; xvi. 19; Prov. xxiv. 23.

EXEGETICAL AND CRITICAL.

After the carrying away of Jehoiachin the prophet beholds in vision two baskets of figs placed before the temple (ver. 1). The figs of one basket were very good, those of the other very bad (ver. 2). The prophet, when asked, affirms that he has perceived this correctly (ver. 3). Thereupon the Lord Himself interprets the vision: the good figs signify the portion of the people already carried away. The Lord will recognize them as good, bring them back, build and plant, inwardly renew them; He will be their God, they shall be His people (vers. 4–7). The bad figs signify the people left in Palestine with Zedekiah, and those who had already emigrated to Egypt (ver. 8). These shall be to all nations an object of horror and scorn (ver. 9), for the Lord will send among them the sword, famine and pestilence, till they are exterminated from the land (ver. 10). The date of this passage may be learned exactly from ver. 1. It was the time immediately subsequent to the carrying away of Jeconiah (2 Ki. xxiv. 10–12). Hitzig correctly remarks, that the expression אַחֲרֵי הַגְלוֹת, after ... carried away, ver. 1, without further distinction, does not permit us to think of another epoch than that immediately subsequent to the deportation. The prophecy is also best explained by the situation at that period. For, as Graf remarks, those who remained may have triumphed over the others, and extolled their good fortune. On this feeling the prophet places a damper by the declaration, that the lot of the captives would be preferable to that of the others (comp. xx. 10). At all events the prophecy was delivered before the sending of that letter to the captives, which is treated of in ch. xxix. On the relation of this passage to the previous chapters consult the introduction to the Eighth Discourse.

Vers. 1, 2. **The Lord . . they were so bad.** The opening is like that of Amos vii. 1, 4, 7; viii. 1. Comp. Jer. i. 11, 13.—**Shewed me.** This distinguishes the subjective act of vision from the object seen, and designates the former as caused by Jehovah. This distinction with respect to physical vision is found times innumerable, (comp. the mode of expression in Gen. xiii. 10; xviii. 2; xxii. 4, 13, etc.), but has only a rhetorical significance. In passages like this and the above from Amos, to which may be added Zech. i. 8; ii. 1, etc., it cannot be a seeing with the outward eye which is spoken of. This is apparent, 1, from the object of vision; it is not supposable that baskets of bad and good figs were in reality placed before the temple; 2, from the question, What seest thou? The question evidently has a proper meaning, when there is a possibility of seeing incorrectly. On the point whether this is supposable in visions in a subjective and objective respect comp. the remarks on i. 11; 3, from the general character of the state in which the prophet must have been while talking with God. Such a conversation as is here reported can only have taken place ἐν πνεύματι. For man cannot see and hear God with the bodily senses. But if as talking with God he is ἐν πνεύματι, then he must also see what God shows him ἐν πνεύματι. For it is not supposable that in such a case there would be a duplicity of perception. The case being thus, KÖHLER is right in his remark (on Zech. i. 7) "wherever the description of a prophetic vision is introduced with the words רָאִיתִי or וָאֶרְאֶה (here הִרְאַנִי) followed by הִנֵּה the prophet thus declares that as רָאָה or הָיָה he has beheld a vision, or had a vision, Isai. xxx. 10." As to the way in which the Lord opens the inner sense so that it can behold spiritual things, comp. 2 Ki. vi. 17.—Carpenters and smiths. According to 2 Ki. xxiv. 14-16, Nebuchadnezzar carried away beside the king, his mother and his wives, the princes, the officers, the mighty of the land, the strong and apt for war, and then the craftsmen and smiths. These were all the mighty men of valor, and only the poorest sort of the people were left. Nebuchadnezzar evidently wished to remove all who were fit for war, as well as those who were skilled in the preparation of warlike instruments. The smiths had once before been carried off for a similar purpose by the Philistines (1 Sam. xiii. 19). So far all is clear. But who now especially are the מַסְגֵּר? The word occurs only in the accounts of this occurrence: xxix. 2; 2 Ki. xxiv. 14, 16. Besides with the meaning of "custody, prison," in Isai. xxiv. 22; xlii. 7; Ps. cxlii. 8. The ancient translations greatly differ from each other. The LXX. have here δεσμώτας (comp. Bar. i. 9) in 2 Ki. xxiv. 14 and 16, τὸν συγκλείοντα: Syr. milites, satellites; Chald. janitores (so also RASCHI): Arab. mancipia (comp. the interpretation of HITZIG) [who translates "hod-carriers," and refers the term to the descendants of the aborigines, who were condemned to be wood-splitters and water-carriers in Israel (Deut. xxix. 10; comp Jos. ix. 21) deriving it from סַג socager, and גֵּר stranger.—S. R. A.] If we derive the word, which is certainly most natural, from סָגַר, we have either the primitive meaning clausor, shutter, gate-shutter, or the derived: he who prepares what is necessary for shutting, shutting in, i. e., either locksmith; or if we derive from סָנַר, those who prepare siege-works. engineers (EWALD). EWALD would certainly also allow the word to be taken in the sense of "purveyor," by which he under-

stands people "who procure for the king the supplies of his kingdom." But he omits any further proof. HITZIG, THENIUS, who are followed by GRAF and (as it seems also) by MEIER, who translates "daily laborer," compose the word of כַּס tribute-service and גֵּר sojourner, and understand by it common laborers, or hod-carriers, in contrast to skilled artizans. For this interpretation however we find, 1, no analogy in the language, for neither הִכְקֵל which alone is adduced by HITZIG, nor כָּס עָבַד (Josh. xvi. 10) suit here; 2. that in 2 Ki. xxiv. 14 it is expressly stated that דַּלַּת עַם־הָאָרֶץ, the common people, remained, and to these must have necessarily belonged those classes of the people, who were כַּס and גֵּר. Compare the connection of the passage (2 Ki. xxiv. 13-16) and it will be found that HITZIG'S explanation does not agree with it. Since then, grammatically, the derivation from סָנַר claudere is most natural, as there is further a מַסְגֵּר which signifies "custody," etc., and consequently the meaning of shutting or of employment in that which serves to shut, or shut up (ex. gr., the bolts of gates, Deut. iii. 5; 1 Ki. iv. 13; Neh. iii. 3, 6, 13, etc.), which is the best founded etymologically, I understand, with most recent Comm. the locksmith, the workman, who makes what serves for shutting up in custody. What may be the relation of מַסְגֵּר to חָרָשׁ (carpenters), is certainly obscure. GRAF is meanwhile wrong in supposing that something more general is here to be designated. It may just as well be intended to set forth only a kind of artificer.

Vers. 3-7. **Then said the Lord . . . with their whole heart.** The construction is: as I acknowledge these good figs (am pleased with them), so I acknowledge the captives . . .—**for good,** i. e., to render them good. Comp. xiv. 11; Ps. lxxxvi. 17; Neh. v. 19; xiii. 31.—The tertium comparationis is: as one is pleased with good figs and retains them, but throws the bad away, so shall I be pleased with the captives of Judah and retain them, but reject those who remain.—**And I will set,** etc. Comp. xxi. 10. —**and will bring them back.** Comp. rems. on iii. 14-17.—**and will build,** etc. Comp. i. 10.— **And they shall be my,** etc. Comp. rems. on xi. 4.—**When they,** etc. Not "if" but "when." In accordance with the opening words of the verse the thought cannot be expressed hypothetically. Comp. moreover iii. 14-17; iv. 1-4.

Vers. 8-10. **But like the bad. . . . their fathers.—Thus saith Jehovah** is a parenthesis. The כִּי is phonastic at the beginning of a direct sentence (comp. NAEGELSB. Gr. § 109, 1, 4), so that the verbum dicendi to be supplied is to be borrowed from ver. 5, to which the כִּי refers. It is as though the prophet would say, I have already said, I repeat it, that, etc. As to the Jews then already living in Egypt, reference may not be made to xxii. 11. For those who were carried away with Jehoahaz are certainly included under the promised blessing, vers. 5-7, not under the curse. But it is to be supposed that since the invasion of Nebuchadnezzar, after the battle of Carchemish, many Jews fled from Egypt to the king conquered in this battle as to their natural ally, as they also did afterwards (ch. xlii. sqq.).—**A horror**, comp. remarks on xv. 4.—**A calamity.** This after the example of the LXX. is struck out by HITZIG, EWALD, UMBREIT, GRAF. But why should not the prophet wish to say that the Jews should not merely be given up themselves to destruction but should be the cause of destruction to others also? Has not the Jewish people, sighing under the curse, even to the most recent times developed the bad elements of its native peculiarity in many ways, to the destruction of the nations among whom it has been driven?—**A proverb**, comp. xxix. 18, 22; Deut. xxviii. 37.—**And I will send**, comp. xxix. 17-22, where Jeremiah repeats the main thoughts of ch. xxiv.

DOCTRINAL AND ETHICAL.

1. On xxi. 2. "King Zedekiah sends word to Jeremiah, that *the Lord is to do according to all His miracles, that Nebuchadnezzar may withdraw.* A demand rather cavalierly made in such evil circumstances. But the noble are so unfortunate! It is indeed as though it only depended on them to arrange matters with God; as if He were only waiting for them, as if it were a point of honor not to be over-hasty, but first to await a little extremity. . . . . . . It is a very necessary observance for a servant of the Lord, that he try his superiors, whether there is any trace remaining in them of having been once baptized, well brought up and instructed in the fear of the Lord. If he observe anything of this kind, he must insist upon it and especially not allow them to deal too familiarly with the Judge of all the earth, but plainly demonstrate to them their insufficiency and nothingness, if they measure themselves by Him. Though Zedekiah had spoken so superficially, Jeremiah answered him without hesitation, definitely and positively, and accustomed him to a different manner of dealing with the Lord." ZINZENDORF. "When the ungodly desire God's help, they commonly appeal not to His saving power to heal them, but to His miraculous power to save them, while they persist in their impenitence." STARKE.

2. On xxi. 8. "It is pure grace on the part of God, when He leaves to man the choice between the good and the evil; not that it is permitted him to choose the evil, but that he may choose freely the good, which he is under obligation to do, Deut. xxx. 19." STARKE. "God lays before us the way of life and the way of death. The way of life is however always contrary to human reason, and that on which it sees merely death and shame. . . . If thou wilt save thyself thou must leave the false Jerusalem, fallen under the judgment, and seek thy life where there seems to be only death. He who would save his life must lose it, and he who devotes it for the sake of the truth will save it." DIEDRICH.

3. On xxi. 11-19. "To be such a king is to be an abomination to the Lord, and severe judgment will follow. God appoints magistrates for His service and for the use of men: he who only seeks his own enjoyment in office, is lost. Jerusalem, situated on rocks in the midst of a plain, looks secure; but against God neither rocks avail nor aught else. The fire will break out even in them, and consume all around, together with the forest of cedar-houses in the city. The corruption is seated within, and therefore proceeds from within outwards, so that nothing of the former stock can remain. What shall a government do which no longer bears the sword of justice? What shall a church do which is no longer founded on God's truth as its only power?" DIEDRICH. Comp. moreover on the whole of ch. xxiv. the extended moral reflections of CYRILLUS ALEX. περὶ τῆς ἐν πνεύματι καὶ ἀληθ. προσκυνήσεως. Lib. I.

4. On xxii. 1. "Jeremiah is to deliver a sermon at court, in which he reminds the king of his office of magistrate, in which he is to administer justice to every man." CRAMER.

It was no easy task for Jeremiah to go into the lions' den and deliver such an uncourtly message to him. We are reminded of the prophet Jonah. But Jeremiah did not flee as he did.

5. On xxii. 1-3. ["But we ought the more carefully to notice this passage, that we may learn to strengthen ourselves against bad examples, lest the impiety of men should overturn our faith; when we see in God's church things in such disorder, that those who glory in the name of God are become like robbers, we must beware lest we become on this account alienated from true religion. We must, indeed, desert such monsters, but we must take care lest God's word, through men's wickedness, should lose its value in our esteem. We ought then to remember the admonition of Christ, to hear the Scribes and Pharisees who sat in Moses' seat (Matt. xxiii. 2)." CALVIN.—S. R. A.]

6. On xxii. 10. [" Dying saints may be justly envied, while living sinners are justly pitied. And so dismal perhaps the prospect of the times may be, that tears even for a Josiah, even for a Jesus, must be restrained, that they may be reserved for ourselves and our children (Luke xxiii. 28)." HENRY.—S. R. A.]

"*Nequaquam gentilis plangendus est atque Judæus, qui in ecclesia non fuerunt et simul mortui sunt, de quibus Salvator dicit: dimitte mortuos sepelire mortuos suos* (Matt. viii. 22). *Sed eos plange, qui per scelera atque peccata egrediuntur de ecclesia et nolunt ultra reverti ad eam damnatione vitiorum.*" HIERON. *Epist.* 46 *ad Rusticum.* "*Nolite flere mortuum, sed plorate raptorem avarum, pecuniæ sitientem et inexplebilem auri cupidinem. Cur mortuos inutiliter ploramus? Eos ploremus, qui in melius mutari possunt.*" BASILIUS SELEUCENSIS. Comp. BASIL, MAGN. *Homil.* 4 *de Gratiarum actione post dimid.*—GHISLERUS.

7. On xxii. 6-9. "God does not spare even the authorities. For though He has said that they are gods, when they do not rightly administer their office they must die like men (Ps. lxxxii. 6) . . . No cedars are too high for God, no splendor too mighty; He can destroy all at once, and overturn, and overturn, and overturn. Ezek. xxi. 27." CRAMER.

Another passage from which it is seen how perverse and unjustifiable is the illusion that God's election is a surety against His anger, and a permit to any wilfulness. The individual representatives of the objects of divine election should never forget that God can march over their carcases, and the ruins of their glory, to the fulfilment of His promise, and that He can rebuild on a higher stage, what He has destroyed on a lower. Comp. remarks on ver. 24.

8. On xxii. 13-19. It is blasphemy to imagine that God will be *frère et compagnon* to all princes as such, and that He has a predilection for them as of His own kind. Does He not say to his majesty the king of Judah, with whom, in respect of the eminence of his dynasty and throne no other prince of earth could compare, that he should be buried like an ass, dragged and cast out before the gates of Jerusalem? This Jehoiakim was however an aristocrat, a heartless, selfish tyrant, who for his own pleasure trampled divine and human rights under foot. If such things were done in the green tree, what shall be done in the dry?

"He who builds his house with other people's property, collects stones for his grave." CRAMER.

9. On xxii. 14. ["It was a proof of luxury when men began to indulge in superfluities. In old times the windows were small; for use only was regarded by frugal men; but afterwards a sort of madness possessed the minds of many, so that they sought to be suspended as it were in the air. And hence they began to have wider windows. The thing in itself, as I have said, is not what God condemns; but we must ever remember, that men never go to excesses in external things, except when their hearts are infected with pride, so that they do not regard what is useful, what is becoming, but are carried away by fondness for excess." CALVIN.—S. R. A.]

10. On xxii. 15. "God may grant the great lords a preference in eating and drinking and the splendor of royal courts, but it is not His will that these be regarded as the main things, but that true religion, right and justice must have the precedence;—this is the Lord's work. But cursed is he who does the Lord's work remissly. Jer. xlviii. 10." CRAMER.

11. On xxii. 17. "Description of haughty, proud, magnificent, merciless and tyrannical lords and rulers, who are accomplices of thieves." CRAMER.

12. On xxii. 19. ["God would have burial a proof to distinguish us from brute animals even after death, as we in life excel them, and as our condition is much nobler than that of the brute creation. Burial is also a pledge as it were of immortality; for when man's body is laid hid in the earth, it is as it were a mirror of a future life. Since then burial is an evidence of God's grace and favor towards mankind, it is on the other hand a sign of a curse, when burial is denied." CALVIN.—S. R. A.]

13. On xxii. 24. "Great lords often imagine that they not only sit in the bosom of God, but that they are a pearl in His crown; or as the prophet says here, God's signet-ring. Therefore, it is impossible that they should not succeed in their designs. But God looks not on the person of the princes, and knows the magnificent no more than the poor. Job xxxiv. 19." CRAMER.

14. On xxii. 28. ["What is idolized will, first or last, be *despised and broken*, what is unjustly honored will be justly contemned, and rivals with God will be the scorn of man. Whatever we idolize we shall be disappointed in, and then shall despise." HENRY.—S. R. A.]

"The compliment is a very poor one for a king, who thinks somewhat of himself, and to whom it in a certain measure pertains that he be honored..... But here it is the word of the LORD, and in consideration of these words it is declared in 2 Chron. xxxvi. 12, to be evil on the part of Zedekiah, that he did not humble himself before Jeremiah. Teachers must be much on their guard against assuming such purely prophetic, that is, extraordinary acts. It cost the servants of the Lord many a death, who were obliged thus to employ themselves, and when it is easy for one to ape it without a divine calling he thus betrays his frivolity and incompetence, if not his pride and delusion." ZINZENDORF.

15. On xxii. 28-30. IRENÆUS (*Adv. Hær.* III. 30) uses this passage to prove that the Lord could not have been Joseph's natural son, for otherwise he would have fallen under the curse of this passage, and appear as one not entitled to dominion ("*qui eum dicunt ex Joseph generatum et in eo habere spem, abdicatos se faciunt a regno, sub maledictione et increpatione decidentes, quæ erga Jechoniam et in semen ejus est*"). BASIL the Great (*Epist. ad Amphilochium*) endeavors to show that this passage, with its declaration that none of Jeconiah's descendants should sit on David's throne, is not in contradiction to the prophecy of Jacob (Gen. xlix. 10), that a ruler should not be lacking from Judah, till He came for whom the nations were hoping. BASIL distinguishes in this relation between dominion and royal dignity.—The former continued, the latter ceased, and this period of, so to speak, latent royalty, was the bridge to the present, in which Christ rules in an invisible manner, but yet in real power and glory as royal priest, and at the same time represents Himself as the fulfilment of the hope of the nations. In like manner John of Damascus concludes that according to this passage there could be no prospect of the fulfilment of the promise in Gen. xlix. 10, if Mary had not *virgineo modo* borne the scion of David, who however was not to occupy the visible throne of David. (*Orat.* 11. *in Nativ. B. Mariæ p. med.*) —AMBROSE finally (*Comment. in Ev. Luc. L.* III. *cap. ult.*) raises the question how Jeremiah could say, that *ex semine Jechoniæ neminem regnaturum esse*, since Christ was of the seed of Jeconiah and reigned? He answers: "*Illic* (Jer. xxii. 30) *futuros ex semine Jechoniæ posteros non negatur et ideo de semine ejus est Christus* (comp. Matt. i. 11), *et quod regnavit Christus, non contra prophetiam est, non enim seculari honore regnavit, nec in Jechoniæ sedibus sedit, sed regnavit in sede David.*" GHISLERUS.

16. On xxiii. 2. "*Nonnulli præsules gregis quosdam pro peccato a communione ejiciunt, ut pæniteant, sed quali sorte vivere debeant ad melius exhortando non visitant. Quibus congrue increpans sermo divinus comminatur: pastores, qui pascunt populum meum, vos dispersistis gregem meum, ejecistis et non visitastis eum.*" ISIDOR. HISP. *de summo bono sive LL. sentt. Cap.* 46. GHISLERUS.

17. On xxiii. 5, 6. EUSEBIUS (*Dem. Ev.* VII. 9) remarks that Christ among all the descendants of David is the only one, who rules over

the whole earth, and everywhere not only preaches justice and righteousness by His doctrine but is Himself also the author of the rising [of the Sun] of righteousness for all, according to Ps. lxxii. 7: ἀνατελεῖ ἐν ταῖς ἡμέραις αὐτοῦ δικαιοσύνη, καὶ πλῆθος εἰρήνης ἕως οὐ ἀνταναιρεθῇ ἡ σελήνη (LXX.) CYRIL of Alex. (*Glaphyr. in Gen.* l. p. 133) explains Ἰωσεδὲκ as *justitia Dei*, in so far as we are made righteous in Him, not for the sake of the works of righteousness that we have done, but according to His great mercy. Rom. iii. 24; Tit. iii. 5.

18. On xxiii. 6. ["If we regard God in Himself, He is indeed righteous, but not our righteousness. If we desire to have God as our righteousness, we must seek Christ; for this cannot be found except in Him. . . . Paul says that He has been given or made to us righteousness,—for what end? that we might be made the righteousness of God in Him. (1 Cor. i. 30). Since, then, Christ is made our righteousness, and we are counted the righteousness of God in Him, we hence learn how properly and fitly it has been said that He would be *Jehovah*, not only that the power of His divinity might defend us, but also that we might become righteous in Him, for He is not only righteous for Himself, but He is our righteousness." CALVIN. See also a long note in WORDSWORTH, to show that JEHOVAH OUR RIGHTEOUSNESS refers to Christ.—S. R. A.]

"The character of a true church is when the Lytrum, the ransom-money of Jesus Christ, is known and valued by all, and when they have written this secret, foolish and absolutely inscrutable to reason, in the heart with the finger of the living God; that Jesus by His blood has taken away the sins of the world. 'O let it ne'er escape my thought, at what a price my soul was bought.' This is the evening and morning prayer of every church, which is a true sister from above." ZINZENDORF.

19 On xxiii. 5-8. "The return under Ezra was also a fulfilment of this promise, but inferior and preliminary: not all came, and those who did come brought their sins back with them. They were still under the Law and had to wait for Righteousness; still in their return they had a pledge that the Messiah was yet to come and prepare the true city of peace. Now, however, all has been long fulfilled and we can enjoy it perfectly, if we have the mind for it. We have now a country of which no tyrant can rob us; our walk and citizenship is in heaven. We have been delivered from all our suffering, when we sit down at the feet of Jesus to hear His word. Then there is a power of resurrection within us, so that we can fly with our souls beyond the world and laugh at all our foes. For Christ has made us righteous by His daily forgiveness, so that we may also bring ourselves daily into heaven. Yea verily, the kingdom of heaven is come very nigh unto us! Jeremiah then longed to see and hear this more nearly, and now we can have it." DIEDRICH.

20. On xxiii. 9. "Great love renders God's servant so ardent, that he deals powerful blows on the seducers. He does not think that he has struck a wasp's nest and embittered his life here forever, for he has a higher life and gives the lower one willingly for love. Yet all the world will hold him for an incorrigible and mad enthusiast, who spares no one. He says himself that he is as it were drunk with God and His word, when he on the other hand contemplates the country." DIEDRICH.

21. On xxiii. 11. "*They are rogues.* They know how to find subterfuges, and I would like to see him who accuses a false and unfaithful teacher, and manages his own case so that he does not himself come into the dilemma." ZINZENDORF.

22. On xxiii. 13, 14. "*In the prophets of Samaria I see folly.* This is the character which the Lord gives to error, false religion, heterodoxy. *But in the prophets of Jerusalem I find abomination.* This is the description of the orthodox, when they apply their doctrine, so that either the wicked are strengthened or no one is converted." ZINZENDORF.

23. On xxiii. 15. "*From the prophets of Jerusalem hypocrisy goes forth into all the land.* This is the natural consequence of the superiority, which the consistories, academies, ministers, etc., have and in due measure ought to have, that when they become corrupt they communicate their corruption to the whole region, and it is apparent in the whole land what sort of theologians sit at the helm." ZINZENDORF.

24. On xxiii. 16. *Listen not to the words of the prophets, they deceive you.* LUTHER says (*Altenb. Tom.* 11. p. 330): "But a Christian has so much power that he may and ought to come forward even among Christians and teach, where he sees that the teacher himself is wanting," etc.; and "The hearers altogether have the right to judge and decide concerning all doctrine. Therefore the priests and liveried Christians have snatched this office to themselves; because, if this office remained in the church, the aforesaid could retain nothing for their own." (*Altenb. Tom.* 11. p. 508). —The exercise of this right on the part of members of the church has its difficulties. May not misunderstanding, ignorance, even wickedness cause this to be a heavy and unjust pressure on the ministers of the word, and thus mediately tend to the injury of the church? Certainly. Still it is better for the church to exercise this right than not to do so. The former is a sign of spiritual life, the latter of spiritual death. It will be easier to find a corrective for some extravagances than to save a church become religiously indifferent from the fate of Laodicea (Rev. iii. 19).

25. On xxiii. 16. ["But here a question may be raised. How can the common people understand that some speak from God's mouth, and that others propound their own glosses? I answer, That the doctrine of the Law was then sufficient to guide the minds of the people, provided they closed not their eyes: and if the Law was sufficient at that time, God does now most surely give us a clearer light by His prophets, and especially by His Gospel." CALVIN.—S. R. A.]

26. On xxiii. 17. "The pastors, who are welcome and gladly seen at a rich man's table, wish him in fact long life, good health, and all prosperity. What they wish they prophesy. This is not unnatural; but he who is softened by it is ill-advised." ZINZENDORF.

27. On xxiii. 21. ["There is a twofold call; one is internal, the other belongs to order, and

may therefore be called external or ecclesiastical. But the external call is never legitimate, except it be preceded by the internal; for it does not belong to us to create prophets, or apostles, or pastors, as this is the special work of the Holy Spirit. . . . But it often happens that the call of God is sufficient, especially for a time. For when there is no church, there is no remedy for the evil, except God raise up extraordinary teachers." CALVIN.—S. R. A.]

28. On xxiii. 22. "If I knew that my teacher was a most abominable miscreant, personally, and in heart the worst enemy of God in his parish ; so long as, for any reason, he preaches, expounds, develops, inculcates the word of God ; even though he should betray here and there in his expressions, that this word was not dwelling in him ; if only he does not *ex professo* at one time throw down what at another time he teaches of good and true *quasi aliud agendo :* I assure you before the Lord that I should fear to censure his preaching." ZINZENDORF.

29. On xxiii. 23. "God's essential attribute is Omnipresence. For He is higher than heaven, what canst thou do? deeper than hell, what canst thou know? Longer than the earth and broader than the sea (Job iv. 8). And He is not far from every one of us (Acts xvii. 27)." CRAMER.— " We often think God is quite far from us, when He is yet near to us, has us in His arms, presses us to His heart and kisses us." LUTHER.— " When we think the Sun of righteousness, Jesus, is not risen, and is still behind the mountain, and will not come to us, He is yet nearest to us. The LORD is nigh unto them that are of a broken heart. (Ps. xxxiv. 19)"—"*Deus et omni et nullo loco*"—" *Cuncta Deus replens molem se fundit in omnem.*" MS. notes to my copy of CRAMER's *Bibel.*—" *Si vis peccare, O homo, quære tibi locum, ubi Deus non videat.*" AUGUSTINE.

30. On xxiii. 28. [" When any one rejects the wheat because it is covered with chaff, and who will pity him who says that he has indeed wheat on his floor, but that it is mixed with chaff, and therefore not fit for food? . . . If we be negligent, and think that it is a sufficient excuse for despising the Word of God, because Satan brings in his fallacies, we shall perish in our sloth like him who neglects to cleanse his wheat that he might turn it to bread." CALVIN.—S. R. A.]

He who cannot restrain his mouth or his ink let him expectorate. But let him say openly and honestly that they are his own dreams, which he preaches. The false prophets certainly know that mere falsehood is empty straw. They therefore always mingle some of the genuine word of God amongst it. An unavailing mixture! It is in this mingling that Satan's highest art is displayed, so that he at the same time furthers his own work and testifies against himself. Comp. Gen. iii.

31. On xxiii. 29. God's word is the highest reality, life and power, while the dreams of the false prophets are pretence, death and weakness. God's word is therefore compared to a fire which burns, warms, and enlightens, so that it burns up the hardest flint, melts the thickest ice, illuminates the deepest obscurities. It is compared further to a hammer which crushes the hardest rocks into sand.—He who mingles God's wheat among his straw, will find that the wheat will become fire and burn up the straw (1 Cor. iii. 12-15). He who handles the word of the Lord purely, let him not despair if he sees before him hearts of adamant (Zech. vii. 12). He who seeks peace is not ashamed to bow beneath the hammer of the word. For the destructive power of the word applies to that in us which is opposed to God, while the God-related elements are loosed and set free by those very crushing blows.—He, however, to whom the peace of God is an object of derision, may feed on the straw of this world. But how will it be when finally the day comes that God will come upon him with fire and hammer? What then remains to him as the result of his straw-diet, which is in a condition to withstand the blows of the hammer and the fire?

Help, Lord, against Thy scornful foes,
Who seek our souls to lead astray ;
Whose mockeries at mortal woes
Will end in terrible dismay!
Grant that Thy holy word may root
Deep in our hearts, and richer fruit
May ever bear to endless day.

"God's word converts, all other doctrine befools." LUTHER.

32. On xxiii. 29. "God's word in general is like a fire : the more it is urged the more widely and brightly it extends. God has caused His word to be proclaimed to the world as a matter, which they can dispense with as little as fire. Fire often smoulders long in secret before it breaks out, thus the power of the divine word operates in its time. God's word can make people as warm as if glowing coals lay upon them; it shines as brightly upon them, as if a lamp were held under their eyes; it tells every one the truth and purifies from all vices. He who deals evilly with God's word burns himself by it, he who opposes it is consumed by it. But the word of God is as little to blame as a lamp or a fire when an unskilful person is burned by it. Yet it happens that often it will not be suffered in the world, then there is fire in all the streets. That is the unhappy fire of persecution, which is kindled incidentally in the world by the preaching of the Gospel." JOS. CONN. SCHALLER, Pastor at Cautendorf, *Sermons on the Gospels*, 1742.

33. On xxiii. 30. "Teachers and preachers are not to steal their sermons from other books, but take them from the Bible, and testify that which they speak from their inward experience (John iii. 11). False teachers steal God's word, inventing a foreign meaning for it, and using this for the palliation of their errors." STARKE.— "*Hinc illi ζῆλοι* at auctions, who can obtain this or that good book, this or that manuscript? Here they are thus declared to be *plagiarios ;* and they are necessarily so because they are not taught of God. But I would rather they would steal from true men of God than from each other."—ZINZENDORF.

34. On xxiii. 33-40. "When the word of God becomes intolerable to men, then men in their turn become intolerable to our Lord God ; yea, they are no more than *inutile pondus terræ*, which the land can no more bear, therefore they must be winnowed out, Jer. xv. 17." CRAMER.

35. On xxiv. 5-7. "He who willingly and readily resigns himself to the will of God even to

the cross, may escape misfortune. But he who opposes himself to the hand of God cannot escape." CRAMER.—" The captives are dearest to God. By the first greater affliction He prepares their souls for repentance and radical conversion, so that He has in them again His people and inheritance. O the gracious God, that He allows even those who on account of sin must be so deeply degraded and rendered slaves, even in such humiliation to be His people! The captives are forgiven their opposition to God; they are separated from the number of nations existing in the world, politically they are dead and banished to the interior. Now, God will show them what His love can do; they shall return, and in true nearness to God be His true Israel." DIEDRICH. 36. On xxiv. 7. ["Since He affirms that He would give them a heart to understand, we hence learn that men are by nature blind, and also that when they are blinded by the devil they cannot return to the right way, and that they cannot be otherwise capable of light than by having God to illuminate them by His Spirit. . . . This passage also shows, that we cannot really turn to God until we acknowledge Him to be the Judge; for until the sinner sets himself before God's tribunal he will never be touched with the feeling of true repentance. . . . Though God rules the whole world, He yet declares that He is the God of the Church; and the faithful whom He has adopted He favors with this high distinction, that they are His people; and He does this that they may be persuaded that there is safety in Him, according to what is said by Habakkuk, 'Thou art our God, we shall not die' (Hab. i. 12). And of this sentence Christ Himself is the best interpreter, when He says, that He is not the God of the dead, but of the living (Luke xx. 38)." CALVIN.—S. R. A.]

HOMILETICAL AND PRACTICAL.

1. On xxi. 8. This text may be used on all occasions when an important decision is to be made or on the entrance on a new section of life, as, e. g., at synods, diets, New Years, beginning of the church-year, at confirmations, weddings, installations, etc. *What the present day demands and promises:* I. It demands from us an important choice. II. It promises us, according as we choose, life or death.

2. On xxii. 2–9. *In how far the divine election is conditional and unconditional.* I. It is conditional with respect to individual elected men, places, things. For 1, these become partakers of the salvation promised by the election only by behaviour well-pleasing to God; 2, if they behave in a manner displeasing to God, the election does not protect them from destruction. II. The election is unconditional with respect to the eternal ideas lying at the foundation of the single appearances, and their absolute realizations.

3. On xxii. 24. [PAYSON:—"The punishment of the impenitent inevitable and justifiable. I. To mention some awful instances in which God has verified this declaration: (a), the apostate angels; (b) our first parents; (c) destruction of mankind by the flood; (d) the children of Israel; (e) Moses, David, the disobedient prophet, Christ. II. Some of the reasons for such a declaration. Not a disposition to give pain or desire for revenge. It is the nature and tendency of sin to produce misery."—S. R. A.]

4. On xxiii. 5, 6. *The Son of David.* What the prophet declares of Him is fourfold: 1. He will Himself be righteous; 2. He will rule well as king and execute judgment and righteousness; 3. He will be our righteousness; 4. Under Him shall Judah be helped and Israel dwell safely.

5. On xxiii. 14. [LATHROP: "The horrible guilt of those who strengthen the hands of the wicked. 1. All sin is horrible in its nature. 2. This is to oppose the government of the Almighty. 3. It directly tends to the misery of mankind. 4. It supports the cause of the Evil Spirit. 5. It is to become partakers of their sins. 6. It is horrible as directly contrary to the command of God, and marked with His peculiar abhorrence."—S. R. A.]

6. On xxiii. 23, 24. *The Omnipresence of God.* 1. What it means. God is everywhere present. (a). He fills heaven and earth; (b) there is no removal from Him in space; (c) nothing is hidden from Him. 2. There is in this for us (a) a glorious consolation, (b) an earnest admonition. [CHARNOCK, JORTIN, and WESLEY have sermons on this text, all of very similar outline. The following are JORTIN's practical conclusions: "This doctrine 1. Should lead us to seek to resemble God's perfections. 2. Should deter us from sin. 3. Should teach us humility. 4. Should encourage us to reliance and contentment, to faith and hope."—S. R. A.]

7. On xxiii. 29, 30. *God's Word and man's word.* 1. The former is life and power (wheat, fire, hammer). The latter pretence and weakness (dream, straw). 2. The two are not to be mixed with each other. [CECIL: This shows 1. The vanity of all human imaginations in religion. (a). What do they afford to man? (b). How much do they hinder? 2. The energy of spiritual truth. Let us entreat God that our estimate may be practical.—S. R. A.]

8. On xxiv. 1–10. *The good and bad figs an emblem of humanity well-pleasing and displeasing to God.* 1. The prisoners and broken-hearted are, like the good figs, well-pleasing to God. For (a) they know the Lord and turn to Him; (b) He is their God and they are His people. 2. Those who dwell proudly and securely are displeasing to God, like the bad figs. For (x) they live on in foolish blindness; (b) they challenge the judgment of God.

CHAP. XXV. 1-11.

9. NINTH DISCOURSE.

(CHAP. XXV.)

WITH THREE HISTORICAL APPENDICES (CHAPS. XXVI.—XXIX.)

The superscription, xxv. 1, *to which a similar one follows first in* xxx. 1, *shows that the compiler of the book regarded* chh. xxv.—xxix. *as a connected group. The motive of this arrangement may be recognized. First, the connection of* ch. xxvii. *with* ch. xxv. *is perfectly clear, the figurative discourse of the cup of wrath, which Jeremiah is to offer the heathen nations* (xxv. 15 sqq.), *having a practical commentary in the yokes, which, according to* xxvii. 2-12, *the prophet is to send to those nations.* Ch. xxviii. *is however based directly on* ch. xxvii., *since here the false prophet Hananiah breaks the yoke, which Jeremiah, according to* ch. xxvii., *had hung upon his neck, and Jeremiah replaces this wooden yoke by an iron one. In subject then these three chapters are closely connected.* Ch. xxix., *moreover, stands in intimate topical connection with* chh. xxvii. *and* xxviii., *since it is directed against the false prophets, who contradicted the prophecy of Jeremiah with respect to their position in Babylon. Though* ch. xxv. *and* chs. xxvii.—xxix. *belong to very different periods (on which point see the particular chapters), yet their connection in fact is beyond a doubt.* Ch. xxvi. *is not indeed related to* ch. xxv. *topically, but it is chronologically, for it belongs to the beginning of the reign of Jehoiakim. This chapter is, however, intimately connected with the following, in that it likewise has for its subject the conflict of the true prophet with the false prophets, and with the people as favoring the latter* (comp. xxvi. 7, 8, 11, 16 *with* xxvii. 9, 14, 16). *As* ch. xxvi. *is thus related in subject to* chh. xxvii.-xxix., *and in date to* ch. xxv., *it stands between them. Comp. my art. on Jeremiah in* HERZOG, *Real-Enc.*, VI., S. 486, 7.—*The position of the group*, chh. xxv.-xxix., *here seems to be due primarily to chronological reasons.* Ch. xxv., *the basis of the section, belongs to the* 4th *year of Jehoiakim. The main trunk of the preceding section*, chh. xxi.-xxiv., *belongs to the beginning of the reign of this king, prior to his fourth year* (comp. Introd. *to the Eighth Discourse). All the portions following* ch. xxix., *belong mainly to the times of Zedekiah, or to the later period of Jehoiakim's reign* (comp. ch. xxxvi.). *Accordingly*, ch. xxv. *with its appendix is in the right place. It concurs with this, though without design, that with respect to its subject also this chapter is rightly placed; for its position in the middle of the book corresponds exactly to the central significance, which pertains to it in the collection of Jeremiah's prophecies.*

We first then consider ch. xxv., *the central prophecy, by itself. It may be divided into three sections:*—
1. Vers. 1-11.—*The Judgment on Judah.*
2. Vers. 12-29.—*The Judgment on Judah and the kingdoms of the world.*
3. Vers. 30-38.—*The Judgment of the world.*

A. THE CENTRAL PROPHECY AND PROGRAMME (CHAP. XXV.).

1. *The Judgment on Judah.*

XXV. 1-11.

1 The word which came to[1] Jeremiah concerning all the people of Judah in the first year of Jehoiakim, the son of Josiah, king of Judah, that [the same] was the first
2 year of Nebuchadnezzar, king of Babylon; the which Jeremiah the prophet spake
3 unto all the people of Judah and to all the inhabitants of Jerusalem, saying, From the thirteenth year of Josiah, the son of Amon, king of Judah, even unto this day, this[2] is the three and twentieth year [these 23 years], the word of the LORD [Jehovah] hath come unto me, and I have spoken unto you, rising early[3] and speak-
4 ing, but ye have not hearkened. And the LORD [Jehovah] hath sent unto you all his servants the prophets, rising early and sending them; but ye have not hearkened,
5 nor inclined your ear to hear. They said [saying], Turn ye again now every one from his evil way, and from the evil of your doings, and [ye shall] dwell[4] in the land that the LORD [Jehovah] hath given unto you and to your fathers for ever
6 and ever: And go not after other gods to serve them and to worship them, and provoke me not to anger with the works of your hands; and I will do you no hurt.
7 Yet ye have not hearkened unto me, saith the LORD [Jehovah]; that ye might
8 provoke me to anger[5] with the works of your hands to your own hurt. Therefore thus saith the LORD of hosts [Jehovah Zebaoth]: Because ye have not heard my
15

9 words, Behold, I will send and take all the families of the north, saith the LORD [Jehovah] and [even to][6] Nebuchadrezzar, the king of Babylon, my servant, and will bring them against this land, and against the inhabitants thereof, and against all these[7] nations round about, and will utterly destroy them,[8] and make them an
10 astonishment and an hissing and perpetual desolations. Moreover I will take from them the voice of mirth, and the voice of gladness, the voice of the bridegroom, and the voice of the bride, the sound of the millstones, and the light of the candle.
11 And this whole land shall become a desolation, and an astonishment;[9] and these nations shall serve the king of Babylon seventy years.

TEXTUAL AND GRAMMATICAL.

[1] Ver. 1.—On גַּי, which is twice used here as synonymous with אֶל, Comp. rems. on x. 1.

[2] Ver. 3.—On the adverbial use of זֶה. Comp. NAEGELSB. Gr., § 79, 2 [GESEN. Gr., § 100, 2 e.].

[3] Ver. 3.—אַשְׁכֵּים is possibly an Aramaism (comp. OLSH. § 191, g; 255, b), and is possibly on account of the rarer י in the final syllable (הַשְׁכֵּים is found only in xliv. 4, and Prov. xxvii. 14), as an addition to אָרֹב, written purposely as 1 Pers. Imperf.; yet more probably it is a mere oversight and, therefore, according to the Keri, and related passages (vii. 13; xxv., xi. 7; xxvi. 4; xxvi. 5; xxix. 19; xxxii. 33; xxxv. 14,15; xliv. 4), to be read הַשְׁכֵּם.

[4] Ver. 5.—וּשְׁבוּ. On the construction, comp. NAEGELSD. Gr., § 90, 2.

[5] Ver. 7.—הַכְעִסוּנִי. The Chethibh must be pronounced הַכְעִסֻנִי, as in viii. 19, but does not suit the connection. The Keri הַכְעִיסֻנִי is according to the analogy of vii. 18; xxxii. 29; 2 Chron. xxxiv. 25 coll. Jer. xi. 17; xxxii. 32; xliv. 3, 8; 1 Kings xiv. 9; xvi. 2. It seems to me more probable that הַכְעִסוּן is the true reading, since this form might pass more easily into הַכְעִיסוּן, and is moreover recommended by the shortly preceding תִּכְעִיסוּ (ver. 6), but was not preferred by the Masoretes, because the Inf. הַכְעִיס after ל, or לְמַעַן is alone used in this sense and connection. The prophet seems, moreover, to have Deut. xxxi. 29 in view. Comp. xxxii. 30; vii. 6.

[6] Ver. 9.—אֶל. It is certainly easy, with the Vulgate and Chald. (the Syr. is doubtful), and some MSS. to read אֶת, or at least, as is also done by some MSS. to omit ן before אֶל. But there is no necessity for this. For וְאֶל is by no means without sense, and may be justified grammatically. It must not then be rendered as depending on שָׁלַח. For then the intermediate sentence, וְלָקַחְתִּי, etc., is intolerably harsh. But אֶל depends on לָקַחְתִּי. Then ן before אֶל—and indeed, as not seldom in Jeremiah (vi. 2; xvii. 10; xix. 12. Comp. besides Gen. iv. 4; 2 Sam. xiii. 20; Isa. lvii. 11; Am. iii. 11; iv. 10; Ps. lxviii. 10). אֶל is used here as ex.gr., in Levit. xviii. 18 in the sentence וְאִשָּׁה אֶל־אֲחֹתָהּ לֹא תִקָּח thou shalt not take a wife to her sister. Comp. Ezek. xliv. 7; Lam. iii. 41. Even in the verse of the present 26th chapter we find אֶל in this sense: all the kings of the north, the near and far, אִישׁ אֶל־אָחִיו, that is, one to the other—one with another. The prophet therefore says: behold, I send and take (or fetch) all the families of the North, and indeed to Nebuchadnezzar.

[7] Ver. 9.—The pronoun הָאֵלֶּה stands δεικτικῶς: we must suppose a corresponding gesture of the hand.

[8] Ver. 9.—וְהַחֲרַמְתִּים. The word is found frequently in the books of Deut. and Joshua (x. gr., Deut. ii. 34; iii. 6; vii. 2; xx. 17, etc.; Josh. viii. 26; x. 28, 35, 40, etc.), in Jeremiah, elsewhere only in l. 21, 26; li. 3.

[9] Ver. 11.—לְשַׁמָּה וְגוֹ. Comp. vers. 11, 12, 18; xviii. 16; xix. 8; xxix. 18; xlix. 13, etc.

EXEGETICAL AND CRITICAL.

In the fourth year of Jehoiakim, which was the first of king Nebuchadnezzar of Babylon (ver. 1), Jeremiah addresses to the whole of Judah and Jerusalem a prophecy of the following import (ver. 2): After Jeremiah had spoken to the people for 23 years, from the 13th year of king Josiah (ver. 3), after other prophets also had unceasingly held forth to the people (ver. 4), that in case of their conversion they would remain quietly in the land (ver. 5), but in case of their apostasy to idols they would experience the Lord's anger (ver. 6); and finally the people not having regarded these exhortations and threatenings, it is solemnly declared (vers. 7 and 8), that the tribes of the North under the leadership of Nebuchadnezzar, king of Babylon, would invade the land of Judea and the neighboring nations, lay everything desolate, and render these countries tributary to the king of Babylon for seventy years (vers. 9-11).—The pre-eminent signifi-cance of this prophecy is clear from the following data: 1. From the special detail of the introduction, which apart from the date, is distinguished from all other introductory formulas in Jeremiah, in that in vers. 1 and 2 it lays special emphasis on the object and address of the discourse. 2. From the date in ver. 1. It is the first time in which a date is prefixed to a prophecy of this seer. Only general indications of time are found in the earlier prophecies, and these only rarely (iii. 6; xiv. 1). We find exact chronological statements only on the entrance of the great catastrophe and the principal stages of its course; (xxviii. 1; xxxii. 1; xxxvi. 1; xxxix. 1, and the following chh.). 3. Here in ver. 2 Jeremiah calls himself for the first time נָבִיא (comp. the Introd. to the Seventh Discourse, chh. xviii.-xx.). It is as though he had renounced this title, till he could announce the beginning of the fulfilment of his minatory prophecy (comp. Deut. xviii. 21, 22). 4. The prophet casts a comprehensive glance at his whole previous ministry of 23 years, admits the fact that the people had paid no attention to his prophetic exhortations and threatenings, and announces the immediate infliction of the punitive judgment promised in such a case. Hence it is evident that he regards the present moment as forming a decisive crisis. The reason for this it is not difficult to perceive. While Jeremiah in all his previous prophecies speaks indefinitely of the judgment as one menacing from the north, he here for the first time names Nebuchadnezzar, the king of the Chaldeans, as he who would inflict it, at the head of all the "nationalities of the North" (ver. 9). The victory of Nebuchadnezzar at Carchemish (comp. xlvi. 2) and his ascension of the throne were the historic facts, in which the divinely inspired glance of the seer perceived the most important crisis in the history of the world. It was at once clear to him that the victor of Carchemish was the great divinely chosen instrument to inflict judgment on the theocracy and the other nations, and so in a certain sense to found the first universal empire. As his predictions of calamity at once attained concrete definiteness by this fact, so did his predictions of deliverance. He perceived and predicted with the same definiteness that the empire of the Chaldeans would last only 70 years, and that at the close of it would begin the redemption of the holy nation. It was hidden from him into how many stages and of what duration the fulfilment of these prophecies would be resolved. 5. In the same year Jeremiah, in obedience to the divine command, began to *write out* his prophecies (xxxvii. 1, 2). He did this, according to xxxvi. 3, 7, in the hope even at the eleventh hour of moving the hearts of the people by the total impression of his prophetic discourses, which at the same time intimates that a moment of conclusive and irrevocable decision had come.

Vers. 1, 2. **The word ... saying.** Why the fourth year of Jehoiakim is the right moment for this important prophecy is clear from the additional clause: the same was the first year of Nebuchadnezzar, king of Babylon. Nebuchadnezzar had this year become king by the death of his father. As this circumstance is emphasized, it is highly probable that Jeremiah received the impulse to this prophetic discourse on the news of Nebuchadnezzar's accession. There is no contradiction in this to our previous designation of the battle of Carchemish as the occasion. The news of his father's death must have come to Nebuchadnezzar soon after that victory. The prophet mentions here merely the ascent of the throne, because he might presuppose that it was enough to mention the later fact to remind also of the earlier and not less important one. With respect to the chronological date, the statement of our passage that Jehoiakim's fourth year was the first of Nebuchadnezzar agrees with the statements in 2 Kings xxiv. 12; xxv. 8; Jer. lii. 12; xxxii. 1. It is generally admitted that this year was B. C., 605 or 604. Comp. HOFMANN, *ägypt. u. israelit, Zeitrechnung, S.* 54; BUNSEN, *Biblework,* 1. S., cxxi., cccx.; NIEBUHR, *Ass. u. Babel, S.* 371; DUNCKER, *Gesch. d. Altesth* 1, *S.* 825, 3 *te Aufl.* ["The precise dates of the events of this period cannot be determined. Dr. Pusey (p 309) supposes that Josiah died in the spring of B. C., 609. Jehoahaz or Shallum, reigned three months. Then Jehoiakim's reign would have begun in the summer of 609, and his fourth year would have begun in the summer of B. C., 606." WORDSWORTH.—S., R. A.]—The native form of the name נְבוּכַדְרֶאצַּר appears on the Babylonian monuments to have been Nabu-kudur-uzur, or Nabu-kudurr-usur [or Nabu-kudari-utsur] (OPPERT, *Exp. en. Mesop., T.* 11., p. 259 *sqq.*). From this the various transformations are derived. Comp. NIEBUHR, *Ass. u. Bab., S.* 41.—On the meaning of name comp. SCHERENZER in the *Zeitschrift d. morgenl. Gessellsch. Bd.* XVI., *S.* 487, and RÖSCH. in the same *Journal, Bd.* XV., *S.* 505. [RAWLINSON. *Herodotus* I., p. 511-16. *Ancient Monarchies,* III., pp. 489, 528. SMITH's *Bible Dict.*, s. v.—S. R. A.]

Vers. 3, 4. **From the thirteenth year ... to hear.** Josiah, according to 2 Kings xxii. 1, reigned 31 years. According to i. 2 also Jeremiah's prophetic ministry began in his 13th year. He had therefore labored 18 years [or 19 years, according to PUSEY and WORDSWORTH] under Josiah and four under Jehoiakim, and was then, especially if we reckon in the three months of Jehoahaz, in the 23d year of his ministry.—The words from **but ye have not to hear** (ver. 4) are, on account of the following **saying,** which belongs to **sending,** to be regarded as a parenthesis.

Vers. 5-7. **Saying, Turn ye ... to your own hurt.—Turn ye now.** Comp. xviii. 11; xxxv. 15.—**In the land.** Comp. Exod. xx. 12; Deut. v. 16.—**For ever and ever** is to be regarded as depending on **turn,** for the consolation consists, not in God's having appointed the land for an everlasting habitation, but in that it will be really such.—**And provoke me not,** *etc.*, and **I will do you no hurt,** are sentences which express a purpose paratactically: comp. NAEGELSB. *Gr.,* § 109, 2.—On the subject-matter comp. vii. 6, 7.

Vers. 8-11. **Therefore thus saith ... seventy years.** These verses contain the consequence necessarily resulting from the premises. —**All the families of the north.** A reference to the announcement often repeated since the commencement of his prophetic ministry, and now again appearing in the form which it had in i. 15, viz., that the enemy coming from the north is designated as "*all* the families of the north," an expression which is evidently not to be taken literally, but as the designation of an extended empire—**And [even to] Nebuchadnezzar.** [Comp. TEXTUAL NOTES]. Previously northern nations only were spoken of, here we learn that they are first to be brought to the king of the Chaldeans and then (of course under his command) into the land. Since this explanation is grammatically possible, I give the reading in the text the preference, as the more difficult. HITZIG and GRAF indeed maintain that the name of Nebuchadnezzar was inserted afterwards. HITZIG finds the mention of this name so altogether "frank" that he sees in it "a glossation of the gloss in ver. 12," and an impertinence, after the indefinite phrase "a horde from midnight" purposely left that name to be guessed. GRAF, however, finds the mention of the name in no way compatible with the construction, for neither אֶל (which he makes dependent on

שלח) nor אֶל nor אֵת gives a satisfactory sense, the last because then Nebuchadnezzar would appear only as "supplementary." The latter objection disappears of itself in our explanation. Hitzig's arguments, however, emanate too evidently from the objection which he has to any special and exactly fulfilled prophecy, to need serious refutation. We say: after the victory at Carchemish, Nebuchadnezzar's mission and its result were so fully made out to the prophet that there could be neither indistinctness nor hesitation with respect to the mention of his name.— The Lord calls Nebuchadnezzar his servant (עַבְדִּי, ver. 9) as in xxvii. 6; xliii. 10, the performer of His commands. He is to come with his hosts "over all *these* nations round about."— **The voice of the bridegroom,** *etc.* Comp. vii. 34; xvi. 9—[**The millstones and the light of the candle.** "The one the sound of those who prepare daily food by grinding the hand-mill, see Exod. xi. 5 and Matt. xxiv. 41; the other the evidence of domestic habitation. Both emblems are combined in the Apocalypse (xviii. 22, 23."—WORDSWORTH. Comp. also THOMSON, *The Land and the Book*, II., 275.—S. R. A.]— Ver. 11. **This whole land.** Since the prophet, from ver. 9 onward, has in view not only Judah but all the neighboring nations, "this land" is to be referred not only to Palestine but to the whole of the territory inhabited by those nations. —**And these nations shall serve.** HITZIG was the first to cast doubt on the genuineness of these words. DE WETTE (*Einl. S.* 330) and GRAF (*S.* 322, 326) concur with him. On the other hand compare especially HAEVERNICK, (*Einl.* II., 2, *S.* 225 sqq.).—What appears especially to offend HITZIG is the circumstance that the seventy years here would prove to be right within two years, nay, that if Darius the Mede is an historical personage, they would prove so exactly. "Such coincidence of history with prophecy would be a surprising accident; or else Jeremiah knew beforehand the number of years, which the dependence on Babylon would last." To this may be added the point, which GRAF renders prominent, that a prediction of destruction addressed to Babylon at the same moment when it is described as a power divinely commissioned to execute judgment, is somewhat unsuitable and improbable. But the seventy years here and in ver. 12 are regarded as an interpolation and *vaticinium ex eventu*, which does not very well agree with the statement, that it is transposed hither from xxix. 10, which passage is acknowledged to be genuine. For even if the sending of the letter in ch. xxix. occurred a decennium later, the promise of a liberation after seventy years, contained in ver. 10, is not by a hair less than xxv. 11, 12, either a genuine prophecy or a statement which happened to prove true. For the difference of ten years, in view of the many possibilities of longer or shorter periods is not so important that a general agreement may not be spoken of. We can of course enter into no controversy here with those who deny altogether any foreknowledge of future things on the basis of divine revelation, but if any is offended that the prophet here mentions a definite number, let him consider that without this definiteness the prediction would cease to be a prophecy in the true sense. That the dominion of the Chaldeans would not stretch *in infinitum* does not need to be prophesied. The chief source of consolation for Israel also is contained in this definite number. (Comp. Dan. ix. 2). ["Thus a safeguard was provided against the dangers to which God's captive people, Israel, were exposed in Babylonia, from the seductions of Chaldean idolatry; and a hope of restoration to their own land was cherished in their heart till the time of their chastisement was past."—WORDSWORTH.—S. R. A.] "Prophetic analogy" also is not wanting for him, who in Gen. xv. 13-16 and Dan. ix. 24-26 sees anything but *vaticinium ex eventu*. Whoever finally maintains that this was not the right moment to pronounce a prophecy of the overthrow of Babylon mistakes both the nature of that historical event and the meaning and object of prophecy. We have already seen that the Babylonian empire was determined by the victory at Carchemish, and was not this a suitable moment to present a prophetic programme of the divine world-policy? Or should merely the subjection of Judah and other nations be spoken of and not the judgment upon Babylon? Let it be observed that in ch. xxv. the prophet presents three stages of the divine judgment; the judgment on Judah, on the nations forming the Babylonian empire, and finally on all the nations of the earth. In this general view of the divine judgments that on Babylon could not of course be omitted, if the prophet was not to give a false representation. Observe, moreover, that the prophet speaks of the overthrow of Babylon only in brief hints. He says of it only so much as is necessary on the one hand for the completeness of the picture, and on the other hand in order not to encourage Israel to obstinate resistance, while not altogether dispiriting them. For this reason almost all the minatory predictions conclude with a consolatory outlook. (Comp. iii. 12 sqq.; x. 23 sqq.; xii. 14 sqq.; xxiii. 3 sqq.; yea, even the prophecies against the heathen nations, xlvi. 26; xlviii. 47; xlix. 6, 39). There is then no reason, why the second half of ver. 11 should be declared spurious. On the contrary, the words, like the related ones in xxvii. 7, are entirely in place.—As concerns the numbering of the seventy years thus much is certain, that Jeremiah would say: In seventy years from *this time* Babylon will be visited. For, as shown above, he has placed the date, contrary to his former custom, at the head of the chapter, simply because this fourth year of Jehoiakim is at the same time the year of the battle of Carchemish and the first of Nebuchadnezzar, and because Nebuchadnezzar's victory and accession to the throne were the symptoms of a crisis in universal history, which germinally included all the other successes of the Chaldean king. From the moment when Jeremiah received the news of the victory at Carchemish, it was for him decided that Nebuchadnezzar would exercise universal dominion and that Judah, as well as the rest of the nations, would be subject to him; in xxvii. 6 indeed he represents this, by his categorical נָתַתִּי, as accomplished, though in reality it was still waiting fulfilment. Hence also in xxix. 10 he does not alter the number, though this prophecy is of a later date. The seventy years have become to him a fixed measure of time, which at any rate has its point of commencement in that fourth year of Jehoiakim. Its final point is less clear. (Comp. on the different modes of reckoning, ROSENMUELLER on xxv. 11 and the literature there quoted). If we take the year of the battle of Carchemish as the beginning of the Chaldean empire, this corresponds best to the conquest of Babylon by Cyrus. As that first fact germinally involved the captivity, so did the second the deliverance therefrom. The dates are, as is well known, not yet determined with certainty. According to the reckoning approved by most, the battle of Carchemish took place in the year B. C. 605-4, the conquest of Babylon in the year 538. Between these two dates lies a period of sixty-seven years. [The Canon of PTOLEMY, confirmed by RAWLINSON, makes the reigns of Babylonian kings from Nebuchadnezzar to the end of Belshazzar cover sixty-six years. Comp. COWLES ad loc.—S. R. A.]. Aside from the possibility that a more exact agreement might result on more accurate knowledge, this number may suffice as a round sum. Comp. NIEBUHR. Assur u. Babel, S. 7. ["These seventy years begin with B. C. 606, the fourth year of Jehoiakim, and the first year of Nebuchadnezzar, when he made his first attack on Jerusalem, and end with the capture of Babylon in the first year of Cyrus, and the restoration of the Jews, B. C. 536. Comp. DAVISON, on Prophecy, p. 225; PUSEY, on Daniel, p. 267, who justly condemns the theory of some, who allege that *seventy years* is here either a mere approximative number or a symbolical one, signifying a long time." WORDSWORTH.—S. R. A.]

2. *The judgment on Judah and the kingdoms of the world.*

XXV. 12-29.

12 And it shall come to pass, when seventy years are accomplished,[1] that I will punish the king of Babylon and that nation,[2] saith the LORD [Jehovah], for their iniquity, and the land of the Chaldeans, and will make it perpetual desolations.
13 And I will bring upon that land all my words, which I have pronounced against it, all that is written in this book, which Jeremiah hath prophesied against all
14 the nations. For [of them, even these] many nations and great kings shall serve themselves of them also [exact service]: and I will recompense them according to
15 their deeds and according to the works of their own hands. For thus saith [hath said] the LORD [Jehovah the] God of Israel unto me, Take the wine-cup [the cup of the wine] of this fury at my hand, and cause [give] all the nations, to whom I
16 send thee, to drink [of] it. And they shall drink and be moved [stagger] and be mad [stunned], because of the sword that I will send among them.
17 Then took I the cup at the LORD's [Jehovah's] hand, and made all the nations
18 to drink, unto whom the LORD [Jehovah] had sent me: Jerusalem and the cities of Judah and the kings thereof, and the princes thereof, to make them[3] a desola-
19 tion, an astonishment, an hissing and a curse; as it is this day ; Pharaoh, king of
20 Egypt, and his servants and his princes, and all his people ; and all the mingled [allied][4] people and all the kings of the land of Uz and all the kings of the land of the Philistines and Ashkelon [Askalon] and Azzah [Gaza] and Ekron and the
21 [whole] remnant of Ashdod, Edom, and Moab and the children of Ammon,—
22 and all the kings of Tyrus and all the kings of Zidon, and the kings of the isles
23 [coast-land] which are beyond the sea, Dedan and Tema and Buz and all that are
24 in the utmost corners [cut short the hair], and all the kings of Arabia, and all the
25 kings of the mingled people, that dwell in the desert, and all the kings of Zimri
26 and all the kings of Elam and all the kings of the Medes [Media], and all the kings of the north, far and near, one with another, and all the kingdoms of the world,[5] which are upon the face of the earth :—and the king of Sheshach shall drink after them.
27 Therefore [And] thou shalt say unto them, Thus saith the LORD of hosts [Jehovah Zebaoth], the God of Israel, Drink ye and be drunken and spue[6] and fall
28 and rise no more, because of the word which I will send among you. And it shall be, if they refuse to take the cup at thine hand to drink, then shalt thou say unto them . Thus saith the LORD of hosts [Jehovah Zebaoth] : Ye shall certainly [and

29 must] drink. For, lo, I begin to bring [do] evil on the city which is called by [bears] my name, and should ye be utterly unpunished? Ye shall not be unpunished, for I will call for a sword upon all the inhabitants of the earth, saith the LORD of hosts [Jehovah Zebaoth].

TEXTUAL AND GRAMMATICAL.

[1] Ver. 12.—HITZIG would find an intimation of spuriousness in the reading כִּמְלֹאוָה. These forms are certainly prevalent in the later writings, but there are also instances of them in the earlier. Comp. Jud. vii. 1; Ps. xxv. 7; Mic. i. 5; Jer. xv. 13, etc. Comp. besides OLSH., § S. 299, 344; 534.—The LXX. translates ver. 12, ἐκδικήσω τὸ ἔθνος ἐκεῖνο καὶ θήσομαι αὐτοὺς εἰς ἀφανισμὸν αἰώνιον, thus omitting עַל מֶלֶךְ בָּ and נְאֻם־ to סְשָׁדַיִם. But such an omission in the LXX. has no authority. The position of הַ־נְאֻם (HITZIG finds it, as in ver. 9, too far back in the sentence) has nothing objectionable in it, if we consider that a double more remote object is connected with אֶפְקֹד by means of the preposition עַל. Comp. v. 15; xiii. 11; xvi 5, etc.

[2] Ver. 12.—וְיָעַל־הֶגְוִי הַהוּא. הוּא is perfectly regular here (comp. NAEGELSB. Gr., § 79, 3), as a pronoun referring to something more remote in opposition to what is said δεικτικῶς, הָאָרֶץ הַזֹּאת הַגּוֹיִם הָאֵלֶּה, vers. 9 and 11. There is no rule, as MOVERS supposes, why אֶת־עֲוֹנָם should not be separated from אֶפְקֹד by נְאֻם. There is good reason for the subsequent position of וְיָעַל־אֶרֶץ כַּשְׂדִּים, in that guilt cannot be ascribed to the land as to the king and the people. The use of אֹתָהּ finally is explained thus, that the prophet does not refer it to אֶרֶץ only (though this also is of common gender), but also to גּוֹי, as in ver. 9 also he refers וְנוּ לְשַׁמָּה וְשָׁכָחְתִּי to the preceding גּוֹיִם and הָאָרֶץ. These reasons would not therefore determine me to believe in the unauthenticity of ver. 12. But there are other reasons, which afford important testimony against the authenticity not only of this verse, but of the two following verses. Comp. EXEGETICAL NOTES.

[3] Ver. 13.—אֹתָם is construed like וְיָתֵן in ver. 12, and the suffixes of the verbs in ver. 9 b.

[4] Ver. 20.—וְאֵת כָּל־הָעֵרֶב. The expression is found also in Exod. xii. 38, where it is said that עֵרֶב רַב went with the Israelites out of Egypt; Neh. xiii. 3 (in both these places punctuated עֶרֶב), where it is said that after hearing the Torah they separated from themselves כָּל־עֵרֶב; Jer. l. 37, where it is predicted that the sword will come also אֶל כָּל־הָעֵרֶב אֲשֶׁר כְּתוּב בְּכָל; Ezek. xxx. 5, where in a prophecy against Egypt, among those who are to perish by the sword, together with Cush, Phut, etc., כָּל־הָעֵרֶב is mentioned. In all these places the meaning is easily perceived. They are σύμμικτοί, i. e. strangers who are mingled with a nation as μέτοικοι, allies, vassals, mercenaries. This meaning corresponds exactly to the root עָרַב, which in Chald. and Syr. denotes miscere, in Hebrew however is found only in the subst. עֶרֶב, the woof in weaving (Levit. xiii. 48-59), and in Hithpael הִתְעָרֵב (to mix one's self in anything, Prov. xiv. 10, to enter into company with any one, Ps. cvi. 35; Prov. xx. 19; xxiv. 21; in the marriage relation, Ezr. ix. 2) only reveals this meaning.

[5] Ver. 26.—אָרֶץ כָּל־הַמַּמְלְכוֹת. The article before מַמְלְכוֹת is contrary to rule (comp. NAEGELSB. Gr., § 71, 5), and therefore GRAF supposes, with reference to xv. 4; xxiv. 9, etc., and not incorrectly, that הָאָרֶץ, which is besides superfluous, has crept in by mistake.

[6] Ver. 27.—קִיץ, ἅπ. λεγ. It is the other form of קוּץ (Lev. xviii. 28). Comp. קִיא. Isa. xxviii. 8, etc.

EXEGETICAL AND CRITICAL.

Leaving aside vers. 12-14 for the present, let us first take into view the relation of vers. 15-29 to the foregoing context. The prophet has been prophesying the judgment on Judah and the neighboring nations, to be executed by Nebuchadnezzar ("all these nations round about," ver. 9). In ver. 11 b he had intimated that the supremacy of Babylon over these will come to an end after 70 years. He had thus erected the bridge by which to pass to the prediction of a second and more comprehensive stage of divine judgment, viz., that it will also involve Babylon itself. How is this conceivable? Vers. 15-29 explain this. The Lord purposes to hold judgment over all the nations of the then known world, which also represent the aggregate of the subsequent Babylonian empire. He will begin with Judah. On this and the nations, only hinted at before in ver. 9 sqq., but enumerated in ver. 19 sqq., and several others, which cannot be numbered among those meant in ver. 9 (comp. vers. 25, 26), Babylon will itself be an instrument of execution. Was it however to be itself spared? Was it better than the nations subjugated by it? No, it will only drink the cup of wrath last. For if the chosen people is not spared, no other nation can expect that its of-

fence (עָוֹן, ver. 12) will remain unrecompensed. We see that this passage presupposes the previous one, being its necessary supplement. For while in the first part, neighboring nations beside Judah are mentioned without being particularly designated, the second part gives a complete and orderly catalogue of nations, beginning with Judah and ending with Babylon, thus presenting a considerably extended circle before our eyes. While, however, in the second part, objects of punitive judgment only (and Babylon indeed as such) are mentioned, we learn from the first that Babylon will be the executor of the Divine will on the whole series of nations mentioned before it (vers. 18-26 a).

Vers. 12-14. **And it shall come to pass.. their own hands.** The following reasons favor the unauthenticity, not only of ver. 12, but of the two following verses. 1. The whole passage, xxv. 12-14, is directed against Babylon. Now it has been already intimated in ver. 11, and will likewise be below in ver. 26, that Babylon herself will not be spared from the judgment of the Lord. But how briefly and obscurely are these intimations given! If **Sheshach** is really to be explained by the Atbash, and in this form to be regarded as a genuine word of Jeremiah's, this mysterious name would certainly be suitable for the purpose of speaking obscurely of the destruction of Babylon at this moment

And there was reason for this. For the Jews were so little disposed in accordance with the will of Jehovah, to subject themselves to the Babylonian king, that all needed to be avoided, which would confirm them in this obstinacy. Is it then, in view of this, credible that the prophet, in the fourth year of Jehoiakim, after the battle of Carchemish, spoke in so detailed and emphatic a manner of the destruction of Babylon, as is done in vers. 12-14? I think not. 2. Vers. 12 and 13 presuppose the existence of the prophecy against Babylon (chh. l. li.) For (*a*) the expression שִׁמְמוֹת עוֹלָם, **perpetual desolations**, is an evident quotation from this prophecy. It not only occurs exclusively in this prophecy (li. 26 and 62, and besides only as שִׁמְמוֹת עוֹלָם, Ezek. xxxv. 9), but in li. 62 it is significantly treated in a certain measure as its pith and token, so that the employment of this expression in the text is to be regarded as an intentional reference to chh. l. li. (*b*). The words "and I will bring upon that land all My words which I have pronounced against it, all that is written in this book," in ver. 13, point likewise with all possible definiteness to the prophecy against Babylon as one in existence. Now since this, according to li. 59 was first composed in the fourth year of Zedekiah, it is thus already shown that vers. 12 and 13, so far as they presuppose the prophecy against Babylon, cannot possibly have been written in the fourth year of Jehoiakim. 3. The second half of ver. 13 presupposes also the existence of the other prophecies against the nations, and this too as one *Sepher*. Now though most of these prophecies are certainly older than the battle of Carchemish (comp. on xlvi. 2 and the Introd. to chh. xlvi.–li.), it is yet evident from the opposition in which the second half of ver. 13 stands to the first, that here that *Sepher* against the nations is meant, which contains the prophecy against Babylon. This *Sepher* however cannot, as we have said, have been in existence before the fourth year of Zedekiah. We might assume that Jeremiah himself, after the completion of the *Sepher* against the nations, subjoined here the words of ver. 13. The striking addition " which Jeremiah hath prophesied," etc., is however opposed to this. For is it credible that Jeremiah himself put these words in the mouth of the Lord? Every one will feel that these words offend not only against rhetorical concinnity, but against religious feeling. 4. The demonstrative הָיָּה, this, after הַסֵּפֶר the book, evidently presupposes that he who wrote it regarded the present passage, *i. e.*, ch. xxv., as belonging to the *Sepher* against the nations. For in any other case the demonstrative would be incorrect. Now it may certainly be proved that the prophecies against the nations must once have stood in immediate connection with ch. xxv. The LXX. still has it in this place, so that, omitting ver. 14, the prophecy against Elam (xlix. 34-39, Heb.) follows directly on ver. 13. Then the others come in the following order: against Egypt (ch. xlvi.), against Babylon (chh. l. and li.), against Philistia, Tyrus and Sidon (xlvii. 1-7), against Edom (xlix. 7-22), against Ammon (xlix. 1-5), against Kedar (xlix. 28-33), against Damascus (xlix.

23-27), against Moab (ch. xlviii.). Then follows xxv. 15-38 as a comprehensive conclusion. This arrangement is certainly, as regards the order of sequence, not the original one, but it still bears, as a whole, unmistakable traces of the original connection. In and of itself indeed the circumstance that the LXX. brings the *Sepher* against the nations into connection with ch. xxv., inserting it between vers. 13 and 15 of this chapter, is not of any great weight, for it might be due to pure arbitrariness on the part of the translator. But there is another circumstance, which evidently cannot have sprung from arbitrariness, and hence lends great importance to that connection. The prophecy against Elam has in the LXX. a superscription (τὰ Αἰλάμ) and a postscript. This postscript is however nothing else but the first verse of ch. xxvii., which is wanting in the LXX. For the details concerning this see xxvii. 1, xlix. 34 and the Introd. to chh. xlvi.–li. It is hence plain that the prophecies against the nations must once have had their place directly before xxvii. 1, and that the prophecy against Elam must have formed their conclusion. Chap. xxv. however was reckoned as part of the immediately following *Sepher* against the nations. Therefore the author could say with perfect correctness of ver. 13: **in this book**. Thus then ver. 13 was inserted in the text at a time, when the *Sepher* against the nations had its place immediately after this chapter, as a whole, which included it. It is not probable, for the reason adduced above, that the prophet himself inserted it. As to ver. 14 finally, the first half is taken almost verbally from xxvii. 7, and in such wise that the perfect וְעָבְדוּ, shall serve, which is incorrect here though it corresponds perfectly with the context there, is retained. In xxvii. 7 וְעָבְדוּ is used quite regularly in the sense of the future, after the preceding statement of time עַד־בֹּא עֵת אַרְצוֹ. Comp. NAEGELSB. *Gr.*, § 84, *o*. In the present passage, however, none of the conditions are fulfilled on which the rendering of the perfect as future depends, while the perfect or present signification contradicts the context throughout. The second half of the verse, which HITZIG regards as the genuine supplement of ver. 11, strongly reminds us of l. 29; li. 24. On **according to the works of their own hands**, comp. vers. 6 and 7. In itself then the passage contains nothing which Jeremiah might not have written. But it is clear that if the preceding sentences are to be critically suspected this single little sentence is all the less able to maintain its position, as standing isolated it would disturb the connection. In conclusion we give a brief synopsis of the different critical views respecting this passage, omitting those which consider it wholly original, or only subsequently supplied by Jeremiah. 1. Ver. 11 *b*-14 inauthentic (GRAF). 2. Ver. 11 *b*-14 *a* inauthentic (HITZIG). 3. Vers. 12-14 a later addition (NAEGELSBACH). 4. Vers. 13 *b*-14, inauthentic (BERTHOLD). 5. Ver. 13 *f*, inauthentic (VENEMA, SCHNURRER). 6. Ver. 13, the words אֲשֶׁר נִבָּא יִרְמְיָהוּ עַל־כָּל־ inauthentic (HENSLER).

Vers. 15 and 16. **For thus saith ... will send among them.**—For introduces the proof of the sentence pronounced in ver. 12, that even Babylon, called according to vers. 9-11 to universal dominion, will be punished in its time. It might seem strange that in the same breath, as it were, conquest and destruction are predicted of the Babylonians. The prophet explains how this will be in the following verses, to ver. 26. He says that all the nations will have to empty the cup of wrath, but Babylon *last*. In this it is implied that Babylon will first be the instrument of accomplishing the judgment on the other nations, but at last will itself be subject to judgment. Those who declare vers. 11 *b*–14 and ver. 26 *b* to be unauthentic, act therefore with perfect consistency. But it is wrong to reject a thought here, which is one of the foundation pillars of Jeremiah's prophecy (comp. especially li. 20-24), without which it must be regarded as partial, and which ought least of all to be wanting here in the prophet's great programme.—The figure of the "cup of fury" and "cup of trembling" is frequent in the Scriptures: Isai. li. 17, 22; Hab. ii. 16; Jer. xlix. 12; li. 7; Lam. iv. 21; Ezek. xxiii. 31 sqq.; Ps. lx. 5; lxxv. 9. The drinking of the cup is emblematic of suffering punishment, the effect of the drinking, intoxication and reeling, is the emblem of shattered forces and of lost hold and self-command.—**I send thee.** The sending is to be regarded in general as merely imaginary. Comp. i. 10. It was afterwards, at any rate, partially real. Comp. xxvii. 2 sqq. It is evident from הִנֵּה אָֽנֹכִי and especially from ver. 17 that the prophet describes an inward experience.—**Because of the sword.** Observe the transition from the figurative to the ordinary mode of speech.

Vers. 17 and 18. **Then took I . . . this day.** The prophet begins with Jerusalem. Why he does so is seen from ver. 29. We may conclude from this that the entire *Sepher against the nations* (chh. xlvi.-51) followed this present prophecy.— **The kings thereof.** The plural here, since Nebuchadnezzar, as is well known, caused three Jewish kings in succession to feel his supremacy, may be taken in the proper sense. It may also however be the general plural and in what follows, when the number of the conquered kings could neither be known to the prophet, nor is any check possible on our part, the plural *must* be taken as general. Comp. rems. on xix. 3.—**To make them a desolation.** Comp. vers. 9, 11; xxiv. 9; xlii. 18; xliv. 8, 22; xlix. 13.—**As it is this day.** The explanations "truly and certainly," or "as it is impending," or "as we have begun to experience," are grammatically impossible. The LXX. omit these words. They are at any rate a later addition, whether by the prophet or some other can scarcely be decided. Comp. xi. 5; xxxii. 20; xliv. 6, 22, 23.

Vers. 19-21. **Pharaoh . . . children of Ammon.** In this enumeration of the nations the prophet evidently proceeds in general from South to North, beginning with Egypt and concluding with the kings of the North (ver. 26). From Egypt he goes up to the South-West (Philistia), and South-East (Uz), then to the East (Edom, Moab, Ammon), and West (Phoenicia), of the holy land. The Phoenicia are connected the islands of the remote West, whereupon the prophet leaps over to the far East (Arabian nations), in order to get by the North-East (Elam, Media), to the North (ver. 26), when his view loses itself in the remote distance.—**Mingled people.** As to Egypt in particular we know exactly what Jeremiah understands by עֶרֶב which he attributes to this country. They are without doubt foreign mercenaries (ch. xlvi. 21); primarily those Ionians, Carians and Phoenicians whom Psammetichus took into his service, and to whom he afterwards assigned residences in Egypt (HEROD. II., 152, 154; DUNCKER, *Gesch. d. Alterth. 3te Aufl.* I., *S.* 922);—but then also strangers from other nations, which Jeremiah (xlvi. 9) and Ezekiel (xxx. 5) mention.—The case appears to be different with the **mingled people** in ver. 24, of which below.—**The land of Uz.** (אֶרֶץ הָעוּץ). The passages of the Old Testament where Uz is mentioned are Gen. x. 23; xxii. 21; xxxvi. 28; Job i. 1; Lam. iv. 21, and the present passage.— DELITZSCH (HERZ. *R.-Enc.*, VI. *S.* 112) remarks that we can still say nothing more definite with respect to the situation of this country than that, as we are told in the addition at the close of the book of Job in the LXX., it lay ἐπὶ τοῖς ὁρίοις τῆς Ἰδουμαίας καὶ Ἀραβίας. This is favored by the present passage, which includes the country in its catalogue directly after Egypt and before Philistia, (the latter corresponding to the South-eastern border-land), but especially by Lam. iv. 21 (daughter of Edom, that dwellest in the land of Uz), and the origin of Eliphaz in Teman (Job ii. 11), which is an Edomite city (according to Jer. xlix. 7). Uz is not thus identified with Edom, in which case alone GRAF's remark that Uz needed not to be specially mentioned together with Edom, would be justified. Comp. however the articles on Uz and Esau by Dr. SPRENGER in the Journal of the Germ. Oriental Society (*Zeitsch d. d.-Morgenl. Gesell.*, 1863, *S.* 373), who seeks to prove the identity of Uz and Esau from Oriental sources.—In opposition to FRIES (*Stud. u. Krit.,* 1854, 2) DELITZSCH correctly remarks that he seeks for the country too far to the North, (in the province of El-Tellul, west of the Haurau mountains).—**The Philistines,** *etc.* Of the five cities of the Philistines Gath only is wanting (Josh. xiii. 3; 1 Sam. vi. 17). It was deprived of its walls by Uzziah (2 Chron. xxvi. 6) and lost its importance (comp. Am. vi. 2). For the same reason it seems to be passed over in Am. i. 6 sqq.; Zeph. ii. 4; Zech. ix. 5 sqq. Comp. KÖHLER on the last passage.—Why Jeremiah speaks only of a "remnant of Ashdod" is explained by history. Psammetichus had after a siege of 29 years taken the city and destroyed it. (HEROD. II. 157). [RAWLINSON, *Herodotus*, II. p. 242.—S. R. A.]

Vers. 22-24. **And all the kings of Tyrus . . that dwell in the desert.—Kings of the isles** (הָאִי). The singular only in Isa. xx. 6; xxiii. 2, 6; Jer. xlvii. 4. All sea-washed land, whether continent or island, is called אִי. Here the collective אִי, as elsewhere the plural אִיִּים (Isa. xl. 15; xli. 1; xlii. 4, 10, *etc.*), denotes not merely the continental Phoenician colonies, but all the coast-lands, and thus also the islands of the Mediterranean.—In vers. 23 and 24 Arabian races are enumerated, which are in opposition to אִי and in relation to Edom, Moab and Ammon, represent the remote east.—**Dedan** (דְּדָן), comp.

CHAP. XXV. 12–29.   231

Gen. x. 7; 1 Chron. i. 9 with Gen. xxv. 3; I Chron. i. 32 coll. Isa. xxi. 13; Ezek. xxv. 13; xxvii. 15 20; xxxviii. 13; Jer. xlix. 8. Both the statements of Genesis as to their derivation, and the geographical statements as to the position of their country, lead to a double Dedan; a southern situated on the Persian gulf, and a northern bordering on Edom. It has been sought to connect the two by the supposition of colonization. Comp. ARNOLD in HERZOG, R.-Enc., I. S. 462.—**Tema**, (תימא), comp. Gen. xxv. 15; 1 Chron. i. 30; Job vi. 19; Isa. xxi. 14. This name is also borne by two different localities. The biblical Tema is "the most northern of all Arabian places," the second chief place in Djöf, three days journey from the territory of Damascus. Comp. HERZ. R.-Enc., XV., S. 706 [RITTER, Erdkunde, XII. 159; XIII. 384, etc.].—**Buz** (בוז), is mentioned in Gen. xxii. 21 as a son of Nachor and brother of Uz. Elihu (Job xxxii. 2) is a Buzite. It is at all events an Arabic tribe, but no further particulars are known. Comp. WINER, R.-W.-B., s. v., Buz.—**All in the utmost corners** (קצוצי־פאה). comp. Comm. on ix. 25; xlix. 32.—**Arabia** (ערב). It is well known that this word, which occurs first in Isaiah (xiii. 20; xxi. 13) designates, not the whole of the now so-called Arabia, but only a part bordering on Palestine (GESENIUS supposes the territory of the Ishmaelites. Comp. Thes., pp. 1066 and 1441; coll. Gen. xxv. 18). So also **the mingled people that dwell in the desert** designates Arabian peoples, of which we know nothing further. The expression **all the kings of Arabia**, occurs besides only in 1 Kings x. 15, where it is said that Solomon received 666 talents of gold beside what he had of the merchantmen and all the kings of the mixed peoples [Eng. Vers. Arabia] and the governors of the country. Comp. KEIL on the passage.—The עֶרֶב of this passage and the book of Kings, were probably mixed states of various tribes, which for the sake of protection were tributary to some neighboring power. Such little unions seem to have been formed in the Arabian desert near the borders of Palestine, of which, however, the remembrance was lost in a comparatively brief period. The author of the book of Chronicles, at least, did not know what he was to understand by the מַלְכֵי עֶרֶב (1 Kings x. 15). He therefore wrote for it simply מַלְכֵי עֲרָב (2 Chron. ix. 14). As to the fulfilment of these prophecies respecting the Arabian tribes, we are left, in the absence of all positive statements, to conjectures. Comp. NIEBUHR. Ass. u. Babel., S. 209. 10; DUNCKER, Gesch. d. Alterth., I. S. 827, and what is subsequently remarked on ver. 26 a.

Vers. 25 and 26. **And all the kings of Zimri . . . drink after them.** The LXX. omits the kings of Zimri. AQUILA has Ζαμρί (MONTFAUCON, p. 221); Vulg., Zambre (Zambri); Syr. Samron; THEODORET, Ζαμβρή. He says παρὰ τῷ Ἑβραίῳ καὶ τῷ Σύρῳ Ζεμβρᾶν εὑρήκαμεν. τῆς δὲ Χετοίρας οὗτος υἱός. Accordingly most expositors have taken Zimri (the name does not occur elsewhere as a gentilicium) for the nation descended from Simran (Gen. xxv. 2). But where this nation is to be sought for is very uncertain. To think of the Ethiopic Zimiris (PLIN. Hist. Nat., 36, 16, 25), or the Σεμβρῖται (STRABO, XVII. 1, 786) is forbidden by the connection.—Zabra also, the urbs regia between Mecca and Medina, of which GESENIUS reminds us (Thes., p. 421), will not suit. WINER (R.-W.-B., II., p. 465, 3d Ed.), mentions Zimara on the upper Euphrates in Lesser Armenia, and the city of the same name in Greater Armenia, and Zimura in Asia. Comp. RUETSCHI, in HERZ. R.-Enc. XIV., S. 409.—None of these views are satisfactory. The matter must remain in suspenso.—**Elam**, the Medes (עֵילָם, מָדַי). These two are also mentioned together in Isa. xxi. 2. As to Elam, it appears in the primæval period as an independent country with its own princes (Gen. xiv. 1, 9). It is maintained by many that Elam includes Persia, and therefore in the older period, stands for what was known in later times as פָּרָס (comp. DRECHSLER on Isa. xxi. 2), but this is denied by others (comp. VAIHINGER, HERZ. R.-Enc., III. S. 747). As to its position this much is certain, that it lay to the east of the Tigris, and, moreover, of its mouths. But the greatest uncertainty prevails with respect to its boundaries and extent. Comp. VAIHINGER, with KIEPERT'S Atlas of the Ancient World, and M. NIEBUHR, Ass. u. Babel., S. 384.—Media, situated to the north of Elam, forms the transition to the kingdoms of the north, of which Jeremiah mentions none by name. He speaks only of the near and the distant (comp. xlviii. 24). In chh. l. and li. "an assembly of great nations from the north country," is mentioned as the executors of the destined punishment on Babylon (l. 3, 9, 41 · li. 48). Some are then called by name to accomplish this,—Ararat, Minni, Ashchenaz (li. 27), and Media [the Medes], (li. 28). From this we see that the Medes are reckoned among the northern nations, which does not contradict the present passage and might well be so, for Media extends certainly from the northeast to the north of Babylon.—**One with another.** Comp. rems. on ver. 9.—As to the fulfilment of this prophecy, thus much only is ascertained with certainty, that Nebuchadnezzar subjugated the lands west of the Tigris down to Egypt and the borders of Lydia. Whether he also subjugated the lands lying east, or the Median kingdom, is disputed. NIEBUHR (Ass. u. Bab.) maintains that Nebuchadnezzar held his kingdom as a fief of Media, but without paying tribute. But after the death of Cyaxares, he ended victoriously a great war with Media (Ib., S. 211 sqq). DUNCKER, on the other hand (I., S. 798, 844, etc.), combats both the dependence of Babylon on Media, and the victory over it. This controversy is of no importance for us. The prophet does not mean to say that God had given to Nebuchadnezzar all the five parts of the world, with all the beasts therein (xxvii. 6), and the men, for an actual possession, nor can this be maintained for all the lands here expressly mentioned by name. After the victory at Carchemish and Nebuchadnezzar's accession to the throne, the prophet recognizes this star, which has ascended the political horizon, as the sun which is to shine over all. In the grand prophetic view of history (which rests on the essential and regards the collateral as non-existent), since there has been any history at all, one nation always stands at the head of all the rest. This nation is that which rules the world, i. e., which dominates all the other nations, if not really, ideally or *de jure*, and is the representative worldly kingdom in antithesis to the kingdom of God. This is the sense of this passage, and of the later one, xxvii. 5 sqq. It may then well be said that this passage (xxv. 15-26) involves two judicial acts; one by which the Chaldean empire is founded, and a second by which it is judged (ver. 26 b).—**The king of Sheshach** (וּמֶלֶךְ שֵׁשַׁךְ) It seems indubitable from the context here and from li. 41, where the two ideas correspond in the parallelism, that **Sheshach** is Babylon, and this is acknowledged by all the expositors. MANSHAM is the only exception, who takes שֵׁשַׁךְ as equivalent to שׁוּשַׁן (Shushan). Comp. GES. *Thes.*, p. 1486. But we are very much in the dark as to the origin, the etymology and the meaning of the word. It is easily understood that Jeremiah here used a word for Babylon which somewhat veiled the idea. He may have done this for the sake of his countrymen. For the object of his prophecy requires that the impression of terror, which the name of Babylon must have made on their minds, should not be weakened. Hence with the exception of chh. 1., li., he says nothing against Babylon, and these chapters, as is clear from the mode of publication, were intended much more for the future than for the present. That regard for the Chaldeans was his motive for such concealment, I do not believe. It might be said that he was afraid, as indeed many, JEROME at their head, have supposed. Jeremiah, however, surely feared the Chaldeans no more than his own countrymen. What other motive he had for concealing the name of Babylon from the Chaldeans, we cannot conceive. What had the Chaldeans to do with him? If they received information of the prophecy, yet it was not written for them. In the only passage where שֵׁשַׁךְ occurs besides this (li. 44), the need of change has evidently occasioned the expression. Jeremiah namely, in connection with chh. 1. and li., never uses the word Babylon in the two parallel members of a verse, except li. 49, where the antithesis requires it. Elsewhere he uses as parallel with Babylon either Chaldeans (l. 8, 35, 45; li. 24, 35, 54), or **land of Babylon**, (li. 29), or a figurative expression like **hammer** (פַּטִּישׁ, l. 23), or **heart of my insurgents** (לֵב־קָמָי, li. 1). He also twice uses instead of Babylon figurative expressions, as in li. 21. In li. 41 the name of Babylon occurs in the second clause. Accordingly it is quite in order that this name should not be used in the first clause of the sentence. Instead of it we have two synonymous expressions, of which one "the praise of the whole earth" is evidently of a figurative nature. The other is our שֵׁשַׁךְ. We see then that Jeremiah uses this expression in the one case for concealment, in the other for variety. Whence did he obtain it? Is it to be explained by the Atbash? Is it a species of Cabbalistic *Temura* or anagram which is either simple (*ex. gr.* כְּלָאֲבִי, Exod. xxiii. 28=כְּבָאֲלִי), or elaborate?

The latter consists in turning the Alphabet round and beginning at the end (ת for א, שׁ for ב, etc., hence Atbash), or in the middle (ל for כ, מ for ל, hence Albam). Comp. BUXTORF, *Lex. Chald.*, p. 248. 9; HERZOG, *R.-Enc.*, VII. 205 [GESENIUS denies that the Atbash was in use in Jeremiah's time, and HITZIG accordingly attributes the anagram to a later period, when fear of Babylon furnished a motive for its use.—S. R. A.].—Has Jeremiah really made use here of such a play upon words? Many maintain this. It is said, if a prophet can make alphabetically arranged songs, he can make use of the Atbash. It may be that the two things are related, and hence I will not dispute the possibility. But I make this admission unwillingly and would rather say, with many of the elder theologians (*ex. gr.*, SELDEN, *De Diis Syr. Synt.*, II., *Cap.* 13): *vix risum hic fortasse teneas*. As regards the signification of the word, it is certainly most natural to think of the *radix* שֶׁכַךְ, coll. שָׁחַח, שׁוּחַ, שָׁכַב, שָׁבַן, שָׁקַע (Isa. xli. 64), and thence derive the meaning *demissio, submersio*, sinking down (HENGSTENBERG), humbling (GRAF). HENGSTENBERG remarks in opposition to my view (in *Jer. u. Bab., S.* 131), that the reason of its use is rhetorical, the prophet wishing to deprive of their terror the names Babylon and Casdim, which had a most terrible sound in the Israelitish ear, pointing by a slight alteration at the ruin hidden behind the greatness of Babylon; to which it may be replied, that these names were certainly not of terrible sound at the moment when destruction was being predicted to their bearers. This is however the case in xxv. 26, and in chh. l. and li. And why should Babylon be mentioned so frequently as the instrument of Israel's chastisement, without the "fearful sound" of the name being mitigated by the pleasant שֵׁשַׁךְ? The meaning "*demissio, submersio*" does not appear to suit at all in li. 41. For there it stands parallel with "praise of the whole earth." Others, therefore, have interpreted the name otherwise: CHR. D. MICHAELIS, *urbs bellatrix* from the Arabic *shaka=fortitudinem in bello ostendit*; J. D. MICHAELIS χαλκόπυλον, from the Arabic *sakka=ferro obduxit portam*; BOHLEN, *atrium regis*, from an analogy in modern Persian. But all this is dubious. I believe that the whole matter must be left still *in suspenso*. Perhaps the Assyrian Babylonian monuments will throw light on it. At least RÖDIGER (in GES. *Thes.*, p. 2486), refers to a discovery which RAWLINSON has made (comp. *Journal of the Asiat. Soc.*, XII., p. 478) according to which שֵׁשַׁךְ was the name of a Babylonian deity. I have not been able anywhere to find a confirmation of this statement [" Sir H. RAWLINSON has observed that the name of the moon-god, which was identical, or nearly so, with that of the city of Abraham, Ur (or Hur), might have been read in one of the ancient dialects of Babylon as *Shishaki*, and that consequently a possible explanation is thus obtained of the Sheshach of Scripture,(RAWLINSON'S Herodotus, I., p. 616). Sheshach may stand for Ur. Ur itself, the old capital, being taken (as Babel the new capital was constantly) to represent the country." SMITH'S *Bible Dictionary*.—S. R. A.].

Vers. 27-29. **Therefore thou shalt say**

the **Lord of hosts**. These verses, containing the figure of the cup, express the immutability of the divine counsel.—**Which is called by** **my name**. Ver. 29. Comp. Comm. on ver. 18 and vii. 10.—**Ye shall not be unpunished**. Comp. xlix. 12, after which passage ours is formed.

---

3. *The Judgment of the World.*

XXV. 30-38.

30 But do thou prophesy against them all these words,
And say unto them:
Jehovah roareth from on high,[1]
And utters his voice from his holy habitation:
He roareth against his pasture;
With a clear cry, like the vintagers, he answers the inhabitants of the land.
31 Tumult reacheth to the extremity of the earth;
For Jehovah hath a controversy with the nations;[2]
He pleadeth[3] with all flesh:
The godless—he giveth them a prey to the sword, saith Jehovah.
32 Thus saith Jehovah Zebaoth:
Behold, evil goeth forth from nation to nation,
And a great tempest riseth from the ends of the earth.
33 And the slain of Jehovah shall on that day lie
From one end of the earth to the other end of the earth:
They shall not be lamented nor gathered nor buried;
They shall become dung on the face of the earth.
34 Howl, O ye shepherds and cry aloud,
And wallow, ye strong ones of the flock:
For your days for slaughter are accomplished;[4]
And I scatter you,[5] that ye shall fall like an elegant vessel.
35 And the refuge shall vanish from the shepherds,
And deliverance from the strong ones of the flock.
36 Hark! Crying of the shepherds and howling[6] of the strong ones of the flock;
For Jehovah devastates their pasture.
37 The fields of peace are desolated[7] before the fury of Jehovah's anger.
38 He hath quitted, like a lion, his covert,
For their land is become waste before the fury of the destroyer,[8]
And before the fury of his anger.

TEXTUAL AND GRAMMATICAL.

[1] Ver. 30.—יְהוָה מִמָּרוֹם יִשְׁאָג. These words to קוֹלוֹ are a quotation from Joel iv. 16; Am. i. 2, only that instead of בְּצִיּוֹן there, we have מִמָּרוֹם, and קָדְשׁוֹ מִמְּעוֹן instead of מִירוּשָׁלַיִם.

[2] Ver. 31.—רִיב, with בְּ, as in Gen. xxxi. 36; Jud. vi. 32; Hos. ii. 4.

[3] Ver. 31.—נִשְׁפָּט (to have a suit at law, *litigare*. Comp. ii. 25) with לְ here only.

[4] Ver. 34.—וּנ כִּי מְלֹאוּ. The construction (*constr. praegnans*. Comp. NAEGELSB. *Gr.*, § 112, 7) is as in Gen. xxv. 24.

[5] Ver. 34.—וּתְפוֹצוֹתִיכֶם. The Masoretes would have this word pronounced תְּפוֹצוֹתִיכֶם. Many MSS. and Edd. however read תְּפֽוֹצֹתֵיכֶם. So also AQUILA, THEOD., SYMM. (οἱ σκορπισμοὶ ὑμῶν); JEROME, *dissipationes vestrae* [A. V.: your dispersions]. Now whether we connect this idea with the foregoing context ("your days are accomplished and your scatterings," as RASHI, EWALD in his *Crit. Gr.*, *S.* 186, MAURER, UMBREIT read), or with the following ("and as to your scatterings—," as KIMCHI and others; "and your scatterings will take place," as CHR. B. MICHAELIS), the construction is still artificial or faulty and the sense feeble. The Masoretes would have the form regarded as a verb. But since תְּפוּצוֹתֵיכֶם is a monstrous form, HITZIG and GRAF would read וַהֲפִצוֹתִיכֶם as Hiph., with strengthened ה, like תְּחִרָה, xii. 5; xxii. 75 coll. תִּרְגַּל Hos. xi. 3. The ת has given occasion to regard the form as a substantive; since, however, there are no substantives of the form תְּקִימָה, תְּפוּצוֹת has been made from תָּפוּץ, I also adopt this view. As to the meaning of the word, however, I hold that of "scattering" to be correct. For 1. the Hiph. occurs only in this sense, never that of *breaking*; 2. *breaking* in relation to the preceding context would be tautological, while it is very suitable to say that a part of the flock shall be slaughtered, another part scattered, but in such wise that the scattered also shall be overthrown and

broken, like fine delicate vessels (כְּלִי הֶמְדָּה Hos. xiii. 15; 2 Chron. xxxii. 27; xxxvi. 10; Neh. ii. 10; Dan. xi. 8); 3. The mention of the כָּנוּם and of the פְּלֵיטָה ver. 35 (comp. פָּלִיט, the escaped) applies better to scattered fugitives than to broken vessels.
⁶ Ver. 36.—On the form וְיִלְלַת comp. Olsh., § 39 b; 78 e.

⁷ Ver. 37.—Since there is no utterance transporting the reader to the future, וְנָרְכוּ is to be taken either as præterite or present (comp. Comm. on xviii. 4; xix. 4, 5). The latter is to be preferred, since נָרְכוּ is evidently parallel to שָׁדַד, which expresses the present (ver. 36). The participle נִדְּכִים should be taken as præterite. (Comp. NAEGELSB. Gr., § 96, 2).
⁸ Ver. 38.—וְנָהּ [destroyer, from נָהָה, to be violent] does not occur elsewhere as an independent substantive. It stands objectively after חֶרֶב, Jer. xlvi. 16; l. 16, after עִיר, Zeph. iii. 1. More frequently it is not found. On the other hand, חָרוֹן stands only before ֻ אַף. The word does not occur in any other connection. The hypothesis of HITZIG, EWALD, GRAF is therefore well-founded, that with the LXX. and Chald. we are to read חֶרֶב הַיּוֹנָה.

EXEGETICAL AND CRITICAL.

While in the previous section a long series of nations was adduced by name as the object of judgments, in such wise, however, that the enumeration ended indefinitely (ver. 26), in what follows no nation is mentioned by name, but the limits of the territory to be reached by the judgment are strictly defined in the words **all the inhabitants of the earth** (ver. 30), **all flesh** (ver. 31), **from one end,** etc. (ver. 33). From this it follows that the prophet here beholds the judicial act of God in its last and highest stage. After having, in vers. 1-11, described the judgment of the kingdom of God in the world, in vers. 12-29 the judgment of *the kingdom of the world* (i. e. that kingdom which represents the culminating point of history), he now describes the world-judgment, i. e. the judgment of all nations of the earth absolutely, without regard to their greater or less historical importance. We thus perceive here the same appearance, which not rarely occurs elsewhere (comp. ez. gr. Joel i. 15; ii. 1, 2 coll. iii. 4 sqq.; Isa. xiii. 9 sqq.; Zeph. i. 2-18; Matt. xxiv), viz., that single temporal acts of divine judgment are designated as types and preludes of the last and highest judgment.—The passage includes four sections: 1. vers. 30, 31, prediction of the judgment in general, declaration as to *who* is the judge, from whence the judge proceeds, how far the judgment will extend; 2. vers. 32, 33, more special description of that which the judge does; the storm rolls from nation to nation, till the whole surface of the earth is covered with the slain; 3. vers. 34 and 35, address to the judged; they are to howl and wallow, for the day of slaughter is come and there is no possibility of escaping it; 4. vers. 36-38, the judgment is in course of execution, the cry of the oppressed is heard;—afterwards all becomes quiet, the lion has desolated the land.

Vers. 30, 31. **But do thou prophesy . . . saith Jehovah.** The person of Jehovah is evidently presented in these two verses as the judge. His appearance is described in its terribleness, as at the conclusion of His judicial acts.—**But do thou prophesy.** With these words the Lord, having dismissed those who protest against the cup (vers. 28 and 29), turns to the prophet, in order to put into his mouth, not a more moderate, but on the contrary a more emphatic threatening of judgment. We see that the prophet plainly wishes to represent the judgment as proceeding from the upper sanctuary. He was the only obliged to do this as the earthly sanctuary

was itself to be an object of the judgment. Comp. **his pasture,** directly afterwards. The roaring is immediately explained by the synonymous **utters his voice,** which in Old Testament usage is frequently a designation of the thunder (Ps. xviii. 1; xxix. 3 sqq.; xlvi. 7; lxviii. 34; Joel ii. 11).—**Against his pasture.** The holy land, of course including Jerusalem and the temple. Here, as in ver. 18 coll. מָחוֹל ver. 29, the prophet names these sacred places first. On נָוֶה, pasture, comp. x. 25; Ps. lxxix. 7; Exod. xv. 13.—**With a clear cry,** etc. Nature in uproar! Thunder, lightning and tempest! The thunder roars, the tempest howls, hisses, whistles. This is the הֵידָד the hillo, heigh-ho, of the vintager (comp. הִלּוּלִים, Jud. ix. 27), who, however, here wades in human blood instead of the blood of the grape; for in the words like **the treaders,** an allusion has, doubtless correctly, been found to the comparison of a bloody conqueror with a treader of the wine-press. הֵידָד is found also in xlviii. 33; li. 14; Isa. xvi. 9, 10, and everywhere in a sense similar to that of this passage.—**He answers.** Comp. li. 14; Ps. xxxii. 18; cxix. 172.—**Tumult reacheth,** etc. Description of the whole tumult and its extent.—**For Jehovah,** etc. The LORD disputes not with individuals but with all. Therefore the noise is so fearful.—**To the sword.** Comp. xv. 9.

Vers. 32, 33. **Thus saith Jehovah Zebaoth . . . face of the earth.** The *person* of the judge retires; what He *does* is brought into the foreground and is described as proceeding from the ends of the earth, from nation to nation, a destructive tempest (ver. 32), especially as a universal dying, in consequence of which the earth will be full of unburied corpses (ver. 33). —**Goeth forth.** Comp. ix. 2; xxiii. 19.—**Ariseth.** Comp. vi. 22.—**Pleadeth,** etc. Comp. Isa. lxvi. 16.—**Shall not be lamented,** etc. A quotation from viii. 2; xvi. 4. Observe, moreover, the Old Testament coloring of this description. The prophet's gaze remains fixed on the earth. Comp., on the other hand, Matt. xxiv. 30 sqq.; xxv. 31 sqq.; 1 Thess. iv. 16 sqq.

Vers. 34, 35. **Howl . . . strong ones of the flock.** The prophet turns to the judged themselves, chiefly to the shepherds and the strong ones of the flock. Since the judgment of the world appears generally in Holy Scripture as the overthrow of worldly empires by the kingdom of God (comp. Ps. ii. 8 sqq.; cx. 1 sqq.; Dan. ii. 44; vii. 27; 1 Cor. xv. 24 sqq.; Heb. xii. 26 sqq.; Rev. xi. 15), by which it is proved that the first shall be last, and the last first, and that God has chosen the foolish and weak things of the world to confound the strong;—we have here to understand by the shepherds and strong ones of the flock primarily the kings and princes (comp. "the kings thereof," etc., ver. 18), as the most eminent bearers and representatives of worldly power. Still a limitation and an extension are in place; a limitation, in so far that by shepherds are most usually meant the kings of kings, *i. e.* the rulers of the world in general, here primarily Babylon,—an extension, in so far as the **strong ones of the flock** doubtless denote all that is great, strong and glorious in the world. Comp. Deut. xxxii. 15; Ps. xxii. 13; Jer. l. 11; Ezek. xxxix. 17 sqq.—**Wallow.** Wallowing in dust and ashes is also elsewhere an expression of anxious supplication in the greatest distress. Comp. vi. 26; Mic. i. 10; Ezek. xxvii. 30.

Vers. 36-38. **Hark ... his anger.** The prophet describes here both the judgment in its course (ver. 36) and the appearance of the earth after its accomplishment. The cry of the mighty and the strong is heard, for the Lord is devastating their pasturage. Here also only the shepherds and the strong ones of the flock, the fat rams, the strong steers, the wild stallions, are mentioned, for the Lord has chosen the weak ones of the world.—**The fields of peace,** the pastures hitherto peaceful.—**Before the fury.** Comp. iv. 26.—**Like a lion.** Comp. Hos. v. 14; Ps. x. 9.—**For their land,** *etc.* We might perhaps expect **therefore.** But then the following reason **before the fury,** *etc.*, would be dragging tautology. The sentence with פִּי simply explains the figure used:—because the land, in consequence of the divine anger, is devastated by the sword, it may be said that it looks like a pasturage visited by a lion.

DOCTRINAL AND ETHICAL.

1. On vers. 3-7. " God is a long-suffering God, who desireth not the death of a sinner, but that he may turn and live, Ezek. xxxiii. 11. Therefore He gives the first world 120 years time for repentance, Gen. vi. 3. Lot preaches to Sodom and Gomorrah more than twenty-five years, Gen. xiii. 13 and xix. 14. Christ preaches repentance three and a half years, the apostles forty years, before the destruction of Jerusalem. But dost thou not know that the goodness of God leadeth thee to repentance? Rom. ii. 4." CRAMER.

2. How is it that those to whom the Lord has chiefly revealed His goodness and truth and whom He has made the bearers and medium of His promises: how is it, we ask, that it is just these men who are the most hardened in impenitence? The people of Nineveh, says the Lord, in Matt. xii. 41, will rise at the last judgment with this generation and will condemn it; for they repented at the preaching of Jonah and behold a greater than Jonah is here. He cries, Woe to Chorazin and Bethsaida, for had such mighty works been done in Tyre and Sidon as were done in them, they would have repented long ago in sackcloth and ashes. And in like manner He says to Capernaum, which was exalted to heaven, that it shall be brought down to hell, for if such mighty works had been done in Sodom it would have remained to this day (Matt. xi. 21-23). The key is contained in the words " temple of Jehovah, temple of Jehovah," vii. 4. Israel does not hear the "if" in the words of his calling and election. They regard themselves as chosen unconditionally, and on this account as better than all others, being such as need no repentance. Thus grace has become a snare to them, and so it is to all who use their privileges as a lever of their wickedness. (1 Pet. ii. 16). [The election to gracious privileges not being necessarily election to eternal life.—S. R. A.]

3. [" **Nebuchadnezzar my servant.** It is remarkable that the Holy Spirit gives to Nebuchadnezzar by Jeremiah (xxv. 9; xxvii. 6; xliii. 10) the same title that Isaiah gives even to the Messiah Himself: namely, 'My Servant.' And inasmuch as the Chaldean king was appointed and empowered by God to conquer the nations, such as Ammon, Edom, Moab (which were types of the enemies of Christ and His Church,) we need not scruple to say that in these victories He foreshadowed the conquests of Christ, who made Himself a servant to do His Father's will." WORDSWORTH.—S. R. A.]

4. On ver. 12. "*Deus uti consuevit impiorum opera quoad malum pœnæ. Malum vero culpæ minime prodit, sed eos ipsos propter illud gravissime punit, præsertim si modum excesserint* (Zech. i. 15). *Solet istud illustrari apposita similitudine a virga, quam pater in castiganda sobole usurpat, usurpatum vero mox in ignem conjicit.*" FÖRSTER.

5. On ver. 12. "*Verbum Domini est veracissimum tum in comminationibus, de quibus hic et 2 Reg.* x. 16, *tum in promissionibus, de quibus Ps.* xxiii. 14. *Unde scite* AUGUSTINUS (*de Civ. D.* 22, 3)*: 'venient hæc quoque sicut ista venerunt; idem enim Deus utraque promisit, utraque ventura esse prædixit.'—Per quod quis peccat, per idem punitur et ipse.*" FÖRSTER.

6. On ver. 20. "*Verissimum est illud* CLEMENTIS ALEXANDRINI: *proximus Deo plenissimus flagellis* (the nearer God, the nearer trouble, the better Christian, the greater the cross: it meets him first who is nearest to God). *Contra vero* BERNHARDUS: *Qui hic non in laboribus hominum, illic erunt in laboribus dæmonum.*" FÖRSTER.

7. On ver. 30 sqq. "The strict judgment of God sounds much stronger and clearer than we can bear. Hence the 600,000 men were so terrified when they heard the voice of God, that they said: let not God speak with us, lest we die (Exod. xx. 19). It is well that we do not refuse to hear, or stop our ears against the sweet sound of God's voice in the sacred office of the preacher, because we can have it (Ps. xcv. 8), or the time will come, when we shall be obliged to hear its awful roaring, which God forbid. For when the lion roars, who shall not be afraid? (Am. iii. 8.)" CRAMER.

HOMILETICAL AND PRACTICAL.

The entire chapter treats of the divine judgments and affords occasion to speak of them (in a series of sermons) in various relations. We can thus speak, I. of the judicial acts of God according to the conditions of their manifestation. They are (1) required by the sins of men (vers. 5 and 6); (2) deferred by the love of God (vers. 5-6); (3) driven to accomplishment by the impenitence of mankind (ver. 7 sqq.).—II. Of the judicial acts of God according to the stages of their manifestation. (1) The preliminary. (a) in the life of individuals, (b) in the life of nations. God judges continually here below both single individuals and entire nations (vers. 9-29). (2) The final judgment: (a) in so far as it has already begun (vers. 9-11, 29 coll. 1 Pet. iv. 17; Matt. xxiv.). The theocracy in its outer relations is already judged; in this sense the universal judgment has begun at the house of God; (b) in so far as it is still future (single empires have already been destroyed, as well as single men, but the judgment of the world as a whole is still impending, ver. 30 sqq.). —III. The judicial acts of God differently represented in the Old and New Testaments. (1) In the Old Testament they are (a) represented in figures (vers. 30, 31 sqq., 38), (b) limited to the earth (vers. 30, 33): (2) In the New Testament they are represented (a) in their full superterrestrial reality, (b) as extended over heaven and earth. (Comp. in contrast to this passage Matt. xxv.; 1 Cor. xv.; 1 Thess. iv.: 2 Pet. iii.). —IV. The judicial acts of God differently felt, according to the different inward conditions of men—(1) As destruction on the part of the godless (ver. 7 sqq.); (2) As deliverance on the part of the pious (vers. 11 and 12).

B. The Three Historical Append-ces.

THE PROPHET OF THE LORD AND THE FALSE PROPHETS.

CHAPTERS XXVI. to XXIX.

[*It has been already shown in the introduction to the ninth discourse that these chapters stand here together, because their common topic is the conflict of the true prophet with the false prophets. Their position just here, however, is occasioned by the close historical connection of chh. xxvii., xxviii., with ch. xxv. There is thus a double connection, (1) that of chh. xxvii., xxviii., with ch. xxv. (Cup of wrath and yoke); (2) that of chh. xxvi.-xxix. with each other (false prophets). Before ch. xxvii., however, stands ch. xxvi., and thus separates the connected passages, ch. xxv., and chh. xxvii., xxviii., because it is the oldest in time. It comes before the fourth year of Jehoiakim. Perhaps also the four chapters were found in this order, and transposed here as a whole. Chh. xxvii., xxviii. belong to the fourth year of Zedekiah (Comp. Comm. on xxvii. 1). Ch. xxix. is somewhat earlier in date (Comp. the Introd. to this chapter). The arrangement of these four chapters is thus not consistently chronological. Perhaps first, the struggle of the prophet with the false prophets in their home (ch. xxvi.-xxviii.), then his struggle with those who had emigrated to Babylon is represented. ["Jeremiah goes back here from the mention of the fourth year of Jehoiakim to the beginning of that king's reign, in order to suggest to his readers an evidence, a fortiori, of God's mercy and forbearance to Jerusalem. God gave solemn denunciations to Jehoiakim and Jerusalem in Jehoiakim's fourth year. But He did more than this: He had sent a prophetic message of warning to him even at the beginning of his reign. Such considerations as these will suggest the reasons for which Jeremiah's prophecies are not placed in chronological order." WORDSWORTH.—S. R. A.]*

1. *The conflict of Jeremiah with the false prophets before the fourth year of Jehoiakim.*

XXVI. 1-24.

1 In the beginning of the reign of Jehoiakim the son of Josiah, king of Judah,
2 came this word from the LORD [Jehovah] *saying*, Thus saith the LORD [Jehovah]: Stand in the court of the LORD'S [Jehovah's] house and speak unto all the cities of Judah, which come to worship in the LORD's house, all the words that I command
3 thee to speak unto them; diminish [omit] not a word. If so be [perhaps] they will hearken, and turn every man from his evil way, that I may repent me of the evil,
4 which I purpose to do unto them because of the evil of their doings. And thou shalt say unto them: Thus saith the LORD [Jehovah]: If ye will not hearken to
5 me, to walk in my law, which I have set before you, to hearken to the words of my servants the prophets, whom I sent unto you, both[1] rising up early, and sending
6 them, but ye have not hearkened: then will I make this house like Shiloh, and
7 will make this[2] city a curse to all the nations of the earth. So the priests and prophets and all the people heard Jeremiah speaking these words in the house of the
8 LORD [Jehovah]. Now it came to pass, when Jeremiah had made an end of speak-

ing all that the Lord had commanded him to speak unto all the people, that the priests and the prophets, and all the people took him, saying, Thou shalt surely die.
9 Why hast thou prophesied in the name of the Lord [Jehovah] saying, This house shall be like Shiloh, and this city shall be desolate without an inhabitant? And all the people were gathered against Jeremiah in the house of the Lord [Jeho-
10 vah]. When the princes of Judah heard those things, then they came up from the king's house into the house of the Lord [Jehovah] and sat down in the entry of the
11 new gate³ of the Lord's [Jehovah's] house. Then spake the priests and the pro-
12 phets unto the princes and to all the people, saying, this man is worthy to die; for he hath prophesied against this city, as ye have heard with your ears. Then spake Jeremiah unto all the princes and to all the people, saying, The Lord [Jehovah] sent me to prophesy against this house and against this city all the words that ye
13 have heard. Therefore now amend your ways and your doings, and obey the voice of the Lord [Jehovah] your God, and the Lord will repent him of the evil that
14 he hath pronounced against you. As for me, behold, I am in your hand: do with
15 me as seemeth good and meet unto you. But know ye for certain, that if ye put me to death, ye shall surely bring innocent blood upon yourselves, and upon this city and upon the inhabitants thereof: for of a truth the Lord hath sent me unto you to speak all these words in your ears.
16 Then said the princes and all the people unto the priests and unto the prophets: This man is not worthy to die: for he hath spoken to us in the name of the Lord
17 [Jehovah] our God. Then rose up certain of the elders of the land, and spake to
18 all the assembly of the people, saying, Micah⁴ the Morasthite prophesied in the days of Hezekiah, king of Judah, and spake to all the people of Judah, saying,
Thus saith Jehovah Zebaoth:
Zion shall be plowed as a field,
Jerusalem shall become a heap of stones,
And the mountain of the house woody heights.
19 Did Hezekiah, king of Judah, and all Judah put him at all to death? did he not fear the Lord [Jehovah] and besought [propitiated]⁵ the Lord [Jehovah] and the Lord [Jehovah] repented him of the evil which he had pronounced against them. Thus might we procure great evil [We however are about to commit great wicked-
20 ness] against our [own] souls. And there was also a man that prophesied in the name of the Lord [Jehovah], Urijah the son of Shemaiah of Kirjath-jearim, who prophesied against the city and against the land, according to all the words of
21 Jeremiah. And [when] Jehoiakim, the king, with all his mighty men [warriors] and all the princes, heard his words [and], the king sought to put him to death: but [when] Urijah heard of it [and] he was afraid and fled, and went into Egypt.
22 And Jehoiakim, the king, sent men into Egypt, Elnathan, the son of Achbor, and
23 certain men with him into Egypt. And they fetched forth Urijah out of Egypt, and brought him unto Jehoiakim the king; who slew him with the sword, and
24 cast his dead body into the graves of the common [sons of the] people. Nevertheless [But] the hand of Ahikam the son of Shaphan was with Jeremiah, that they should [did] not give him into the hands of the people to put him to death.

TEXTUAL AND GRAMMATICAL.

¹ Ver. 5.—The ן before הַשְׁכֵּם=and, moreover, comp. NAEGELSB. *Gr.*, § 111, 1.
² Ver. 6.—הֲאִתָה. This form is found here only in the Chethibh. It is not a scriptural error, the ה being the so-called paragogic. Comp. OLSH. § 101, e, and § 133, S. 254.
³ Ver. 10.—[*Targum*: The east gate.]
⁴ Ver. 18.—The Masoretes alter מִיכָיְה into מִיכָה, not because they regard the former as correct, but to bring out clearly the identity of this Micah with him whose book is included in the canon (comp. CASPARI, *Micha der Morasehtite*, S. 12).—The passage quoted is found verbatim in Mic. iii. 12, except that there we read יַעַר instead of עִיִּים. (Comp. OLSH., *S.* 207, 288.)
⁵ Ver. 19.—[Literally: Soothed by prayer the face of the Lord.—S. R. A.]

EXEGETICAL AND CRITICAL.

It has been shown above that this chapter is not immediately connected with chap. xxv., but mediately through chh. xxvii., xxviii. The assertion of GRAF that "the narrative of this occurrence has no connection either with the preceding or with the following context" is incomprehensible. For if we do not agree with EWALD that each of the three supplements concludes with a glance at those prophets, who either prophesied what was directly false or did not defend the truth with becoming steadfastness (*Proph. d. A. B.*, II., S. 137), it is yet indisputable that all these four chapters treat of the conflict of the prophet with false prophets, that they follow each other in chronological order, and that chh. xxvi.-xxix. presuppose ch. xxv. as their basis. This explains the position of ch. xxvi. here. I cannot accept the statement of GRAF that as a record of personal experiences it ought to have stood before ch. xxxvi.: for here the narrative would stand quite isolated topically, and chh. xxxiv.-xliv., are not the only place for the prophet's personal experiences, for they are inserted elsewhere, according to the connection of facts. Comp. chh. xx. and xxx. And this is the case with chh. xxvi.-xxix. We might rather expect that, on account of the relation of the facts, it would come after ch. xxiii. But on the one hand it would disturb the plan of that group (against kings and prophets) by partial details, and on the other the principal matter of chh. xxvii. and xxviii. has too close an historical connection with ch. xxv. to be separated from it, or even only to be placed before it. The reason why this chapter does not stand after chh. vii. sqq., where it properly belongs in historical connection, is that the series of great discourses was not to be interrupted by a long historical section. As far as ch. xviii. are discourses only. From this point onwards the historical element is successively brought forward. Although thus separated in position, this ch. xxvi. refers back to the great discourse in chh. vii.-x., and describes the almost fatal consequences, which it had with respect to the person of the prophet (vers. 1-19). At the same time, however, the opportunity is afforded for the narrative concerning another prophet, Urijah, the son of Shemaiah, who had no such courageous patron as Ahikam, and really fell a sacrifice to his fidelity to his calling at the command of the ungodly king Jehoiakim.

Vers. 1-6. **In the beginning . . . all the nations of the earth.** In the beginning of the reign of Jehoiakim, at any rate before the battle of Carchemish, since there is no mention made of the Chaldeans, Jeremiah receives the command to stand in the fore-court of the temple (comp. xix. 4, and EXEG. on vii. 2), and proclaim a revelation he has received to all the Jews who have come up to the feast. What feast this was we know not (comp. Comm. on vii. 2). The introductory formula in vii. 1 is: Go into the gate and proclaim as follows. Here it is said: Stand in the fore-court and proclaim all that I have commanded thee, without omitting anything. There the command to go into the gate precedes the revelation. Here the order is reversed. For here the words **which I command thee, and omit not a word,** point back to the revelation as one previously received. The latter especially would have no sense, if what is to be delivered by the prophet had not been already communicated. Still, however, in ver. 4 sqq., the chief contents of the discourse follow in a brief and pregnant recapitulation. There is no contradiction in this. It may have been that the prophet received the revelation of the great discourse in chh. vii.-x., at the same time with the command to deliver it in the temple, and that afterwards,

when the moment of performance came, the command was repeated with a reference on the one hand to the revelation received (xxvi. 2), and on the other with a brief recapitulation of its main import (xxvi. 4-6).—**Omit not a word** reminds us of Deut. iv. 2; xiii. 1 coll. Rev. xxii. 19.—**If so be they will hearken,** ver. 3. It is apparent that the assembly to the feast must have appeared a specially favorable opportunity for a decisive attempt.—**Repent me of the evil.** Comp. xviii. 8; אל as in vers. 13 and 19; xlii. 10; Jud. xxi. 6; 2 Sam. xxiv. 16.—**rising early.** Comp. vii. 13, 25; xxv. 3, 4.—**But ye have not hearkened,** retained as a reminiscence of the passage vii. 13, is to be regarded as a parenthesis; since the apodosis begins with ver. 6.—**Like Shiloh.** In these words the prophet reproduces most distinctly the main threatening of the great discourse in chap. vii. (comp. vers. 12 and 14, and the rems. thereon).—**A curse.** Comp. xxiv. 9; xxv. 18.

Vers. 7-11. **So the priests . . . have heard with your ears.** The priests and prophets here appear as the real opponents of Jeremiah. Very probably most of the false prophets were themselves priests. Comp. Comm. on xx. 6.—The people allow themselves to be carried away, though on the speech of the princes they are disposed to espouse the cause of Jeremiah against the priests and prophets (ver. 16), and in other circumstances would be ready to execute the sentence of death on him (ver. 24). The princes are not yet filled with that blood-thirsty hatred towards Jeremiah, which they afterwards manifest (ch. xxxvii. sqq.).—In the words **like Shiloh** they allude to vii. 12, 14, as in the following **without an inheritance** to ix. 10.—On **gate of the Lord's house,** comp. rems. on xx. 2.—**Worthy to die.** This expression (משפט מות) occurs also in Deut. xix. 6; xxi. 22. As the first word in itself signifies judgment or condemnation, the phrase may from the connection denote judgment or condemnation to death. The expression in ver. 11 and Deut. xix. 6, may be taken in the first, in ver. 16 and Deut. xxi. 22 in the second sense.

Vers. 12-19. **Then spake Jeremiah . . . our souls.** In the words **amend your ways** the prophet repeats the chief requisition of his discourse in vii. 3, 5. It is thus to be seen that he is neither terrified nor evilly disposed towards his people. On this condition, but on this condition only, does he promise salvation. If they do not like this they may do with him as they will. They are, however, at the same time to know that in killing him they would bring upon themselves the guilt of shedding innocent blood. This answer of Jeremiah's, short and simple but firm and decided, appears to have made a deep impression on the judges and the people. For Jeremiah is acquitted. Some of the elders of the people (זקני הארץ), **elders of the land,** ver. 17, are distinguished from the שרים, **princes,** ver. 10, who are in the king's house, at court and members of the government, while the former represent the local magistrates throughout the country, comp. xxxvii. 15; xxxviii. 5, 25 sqq.) support this sentence by reference to a former occurrence. The prophet Micah, [of Moresheth, near Eleutheropolis, in Philistia. EU-SEB., JEROME], had not been punished by Heze kiah on account of a similar utterance.—On the point, that the passage iii. 12 forms the climax of the minatory prophecies of Micah, and that Jeremiah quotes the book of Micah especially in the discourse in chh. vii.-ix. comp. CASPARI, *passim*. From the last mentioned circumstance it follows that Jeremiah himself reminds his hearers of Micah, and institutes a comparison between himself and this prophet. CASPARI however errs in attributing the discourse in chh. vii.-ix. to the reign of Josiah. [On the fulfilment of the prophecy of Micah and Jeremiah, comp. THOMSON, *The Land and the Book*, II., 475.—S. R. A.]

Vers. 20-24. **And there was also a man ... to put him to death.** That this narrative about Urijah does not continue the words of Jeremiah's friends, is clear from the circumstance that in this case a precedent would be referred to unfavorable to Jeremiah. It is evident that they are not the words of his opponents from the absence of any introductory formula. Others affirm that this story must have related to a later period than the commencement of Jehoiakim's reign. This however depends on how far we extend the commencement. Apart then from the question, whether this occurred earlier or later, which it will be difficult to decide, I think, with GROTIUS, SCHNURRER, ROSENMUELLER and others, that Jeremiah himself adds this story in order to show in how great danger he then was of his life. At all events the events narrated had happened when Jeremiah wrote his book, which he did the first time in the 4th and 5th years of Je-

hoiakim (xxxvi. 1 sqq. ; 9 sqq.), and the second time immediately after the destruction of the first book in the 9th month of the 5th year of Jehoiakim (xxxvi. 28 sqq.) The events might have occurred up to this time ; and even if they belong to a later period, the possibility is not excluded that they were inserted here by Jeremiah himself. Yet it is easier to explain the phrases **this city** and **this land**, in ver. 20, if we suppose that the prophet had these expressions, which strictly taken presuppose an oral address, still in remembrance from the preceding conversation. Nothing further is known either of Urijah, or his father Shemaiah.—Elnathan the son of Achbor is also mentioned in xxxvi. 12, 25 among the princes favorable to Jeremiah. Jehoiakim appears to have been his son-in-law, for Nehushta, the mother of Jehoiachin was, according to 2 Ki. xxiv. 8, a daughter of Elnathan. Achbor is mentioned in 2 Ki. xxii. 12 as one of the princes, who were in personal attendance on Josiah.—The graves of the common people (ver. 23) appear elsewhere as an unhallowed place (2 Ki. xxiii. 6). On the expression "sons of the people" comp. Comm. on xvii. 19.—Ver. 24. **But the hand of Ahikam.** The particle אַךְ, *only, but*, presupposes a thought, which easily flows from the previous context, *so would it have been with Jeremiah*. From the mention of Ahikam alone it is plain that it was he who caused the decision to be favorable to Jeremiah, (ver. 16 sqq.) He is also mentioned in 2 Ki. xxii. 12-14, together with Achbor, and according to xxxix. 14; xl. 5, and other passages, he was the father of the governor Gedaliah.

---

2. *The conflict of Jeremiah with the false prophets in the fourth year of Zedekiah.*

CHAPTERS XXVII. AND XXVIII.

XXVII. 1-22.

1 In the beginning of the reign of Jehoiakim [Zedekiah], the son of Josiah, king
2 of Judah, came this word unto Jeremiah from the Lord saying, Thus saith the
3 Lord to me, Make thee bonds and yokes and put them upon thy neck, and send them to the king of Edom and to the king of Moab, and to the king of the Ammonites, and to the king of Tyrus, and to the king of Zidon, by the hand of the mes-
4 sengers which came to Jerusalem unto Zedekiah, king of Judah. And command them to say unto their masters, Thus saith the Lord of hosts [Jehovah Zebaoth]
5 the God of Israel, Thus shall ye say unto your masters; I have made the earth, the man and the beast that *are* upon the ground, by my great power and by my
6 out-stretched arm, and have given it to whom it seemed meet unto me. And now have I given all these lands into the hand of Nebuchadnezzar, king of Babylon,
7 my servant; and the beasts of the field have I given him also to serve him. And all nations shall serve him, and his son, and his son's son, until the very time of his land come: and then many nations and great kings shall serve themselves of
8 him. And it shall come to pass, that the nation and kingdom which will not serve the same Nebuchadnezzar, the king of Babylon, and that¹ will not put their neck under the yoke of the king of Babylon, that nation will I punish, saith the Lord [Jehovah] with the sword, and with the famine, and with the pestilence, until I

9 have consumed² them by his hand. Therefore hearken not ye to your priests, nor to your diviners, nor to your dreamers, nor to your enchanters, nor to your sorcer-
10 ers, which speak unto you, saying, Ye shall not serve the king of Babylon For they prophesy a lie unto you, to remove you far from your land ; and that I should
11 drive you out, and ye should perish. But the nations that bring their neck under the yoke of the king of Babylon, those will I let remain still in their own land,
12 saith the Lord; and they shall till it and dwell therein. I spake also to Zede-
kiah, king of Judah, according to all those words, saying, Bring your necks under
13 the yoke of the king of Babylon, and serve him and his people, and live.³ Why will ye die, thou and thy people, by the sword, by the famine, and by the pestilence, as the Lord hath spoken against the nation that will not serve the king of
14 Babylon? Therefore hearken not unto the words of the prophets that speak unto you, saying, Ye shall not serve the king of Babylon ; for they prophesy a lie unto
15 you. For I have not sent them, saith the Lord, [Jehovah] yet they prophesy a lie in my name; that I might drive you out, and that ye might perish, ye and the
16 priests that prophesy unto you. Also I spake to the priests and to all this people, saying, Thus saith the Lord [Jehovah] ; Hearken not to the words of your prophets that prophesy unto you, saying, Behold the vessels of the Lord's house shall now shortly be brought again from Babylon ; for they prophesy a lie unto you.
17 Hearken not unto them ; serve the king of Babylon, and live : wherefore should
18 this city be laid waste? But if they be prophets, and if the word of the Lord be with them, let them now make intercession to the Lord of hosts [Jehovah Zebaoth] that the vessels which are left in the house of the Lord, and in the house of the king of Judah, and at Jerusalem, go⁴ not to Babylon.
19 For thus saith the Lord of hosts concerning the pillars, and concerning the sea, and concerning the bases, and concerning the residue of the vessels that remain in
29 the city, which Nebuchadnezzar king of Babylon took not, when he carried away captive⁵ Jeconiah the son of Jehoiakim king of Judah from Jerusalem to Babylon,
21 and all the nobles of Judah and Jerusalem ; Yea, thus saith the Lord of hosts, the God of Israel, concerning the vessels that remain in the house of the Lord
22 [Jehovah] and in the house of the king of Judah and of Jerusalem ; they shall be carried to Babylon, and there shall they be until the day that I visit them, saith the Lord ; then will I bring them up, and restore them to this place.

XXVIII. 1-17.

1 And it came to pass the same year, in the beginning of the reign of Zedekiah king of Judah, in the fourth year,⁶ and in the fifth month, that Hananiah the son of Azur the prophet, which was of Gibeon, spake unto me in the presence of the
2 priests, and of all the people, saying, Thus speaketh the Lord of hosts, the God of
3 Israel, saying, I have broken the yoke of the king of Babylon. Within two full years⁷ will I bring again into this place all the vessels of the Lord's house, that Nebuchadnezzar king of Babylon took away from this place, and carried them to
4 Babylon : And I will bring again to this place Jeconiah the son of Jehoiakim king of Judah, with all the captives of Judah, that went into Babylon, saith the Lord, for I will break the yoke of the king of Babylon.
5 Then the prophet Jeremiah said unto the prophet Hananiah in the presence of the priests, and in the presence of all the people that stood in the house of the
6 Lord [Jehovah]. Even the prophet Jeremiah said, Amen :⁸ the Lord do so : the Lord perform thy words which thou hast prophesied, to bring again the vessels of the Lord's house, and all that is carried away captive, from Babylon into this
7 place. Nevertheless hear thou now the word that I speak in thine ears, and in the
8 ears of all the people ; the prophets that have been before me and before thee of old prophesied both against many countries, and against great kingdoms, of war,
9 and of evil, and of pestilence.⁹ The prophet which prophesieth of peace, when the word of the prophet shall come to pass, then shall the prophet be known, that the Lord hath truly sent him.
10 Then Hananiah the prophet took the yoke from off the prophet Jeremiah's neck,

11 and brake it.[10] And Hananiah spake in the presence of all the people, saying, Thus saith the Lord; even so will I break the yoke of Nebuchadnezzar king of Babylon from the neck of all nations within the space of two full years. And the
12 prophet Jeremiah went his way. Then the word of the Lord came to Jeremiah, after that Hananiah the prophet had broken the yoke from off the neck of the
13 prophet Jeremiah, saying, Go and tell Hananiah, saying, Thus saith the Lord; Thou hast broken the yokes of wood, but thou shalt make for them yokes of iron.
14 For thus saith the Lord of hosts, the God of Israel; I have put a yoke of iron upon the neck of all these nations, that they may serve Nebuchadnezzar, king of Babylon; and they shall serve him: and I have given him the beasts of the field also.
15 Then said the prophet Jeremiah unto Hananiah the prophet, Hear now Hananiah; The Lord hath not sent thee; but thou makest this people to trust in a lie.
16 Therefore thus saith the Lord, Behold, I will cast[11] thee from off the face of the earth; this year thou shalt die, because thou hast taught rebellion against the
17 Lord. So Hananiah the prophet died the same year in the seventh month.

TEXTUAL AND GRAMMATICAL.

[1] XXVII. 8.—The construction here is not an anacoluthon, but הגוי is accusative, and את אשר is not co-ordinate to the first אשר but to הגוי: as to the nation which will not serve, and as to that which will not bow the neck, etc. Hence the singular יתן stands properly also in the second relative clause. The sign of the accusative stands before the second אשר to distinguish it as an accusative from the first, which is nominative, (comp. EWALD, § 277 d, 2, and Gen. xlvii 21; 2 Ki. viii. 31), and thus at the same time to indicate that אשר does not stand parallel to הגוי.

[2] Ver. 8.—יעבדו־הכי. תכם in a transitive sense, as in Ps. lxiv. 7.

[3] Ver. 12.—ורחו. Comp. TEXTUAL NOTE on xxv. 5.

[4] Ver. 18.—לבלתי באו. The form באו as a perfect is abnormal. In 1. 5 it is to be taken as imperative. It is therefore not improbable, as HITZIG, OLSHAUSEN and GRAF suppose, that we are to read לבלת יבאו.

[5] Ver. 20.—בגלותו. Comp. Exod. xiii. 21; Isa. xxiii. 11; Ps. lxxviii. 17; OLSH. § 78, c.

[6] XXVIII. 1.—Instead of בשנת הרביעית as the Chethibh is to be read, the Masoretes would here have בשנה הי as in xxxii. 1. The reading of the Chethibh is found unimpeached by the Masoretes in xlvi. 2; 11. 59. Probably the Masoretes wished, here as in xxxii. 1, the same punctuation for the word occurring twice in the verse, while in xlvi. 2 and li. 59, no occasion was given for such an effort at conformity. On the St. const. in this connection, comp. NAEGELSB. Gr., § 65, 2, c.

[7] Ver. 3.—שנתים ימים. On the construction comp. NAEGELSB. Gr., § 70, g. Comp. besides Gen. xli. 1; 1 Sam. xiii 23, etc.

[8] Ver. 6.—אמן occurs besides in Jeremiah, only in xi. 5.

[9] Ver. 8.—On the construction in this verse, comp. NAEGELSB. Gr., § 88, 7; 111, 1, b, 10.

[10] Ver. 10.—The masc. suffix in וישברהו refers to the idea of על. Comp. NAEGELSB. Gr., § 60, 4.

[11] Ver. 16.—The word משלח, I cast thee off, must, as HITZIG has remarked, contain an allusion to שלחך, in ver. 15.

EXEGETICAL AND CRITICAL.

The two chh. xxvii. and xxviii. are so evidently parts of a whole that we do not seem to be justified in separating them. The occurrence here narrated is based entirely on ch. xxv. The sending of the yoke to the neighboring nations can indeed be regarded as the fulfilment of the commission received by the prophet in xxv. 15 only in so far as it may be understood in a double sense; in the sense of proclamation and the sense of the execution of the divine sentence.—The command to acknowledge Nebuchadnezzar as a world-ruler appointed by God is supplemented by the warning not to allow the deceptive promises of the false prophets to deter them from yielding in subjection to him (xxvii. 9-22). Notwithstanding this, one of the false prophets, Hananiah, the son of Azur, dares to give the prophet of Jehovah the lie and by breaking the wooden yoke, which the latter bore on his neck, to symbolize his liberation from the dominion of Nebuchadnezzar. Thereupon Jeremiah receives the command to replace the wooden yoke by an iron one, and to predict Hananiah's speedy death in the course of the year. Hananiah really died two months afterwards. The date of the whole occurrence is the fourth year of Zedekiah (xxviii. 1), since the statement in xxvii. 1 (beginning of the reign of Jehoiakim) is at any rate, and the other in xxviii. 1 (beginning of the reign of Zedekiah) is very probably incorrect. Further particulars on this point below.

XXVII. 1-11. **In the beginning ... dwell therein.** There are weighty critical suspicions with respect to the first verse. In the first place the name **Jehoiakim** has long been a stumbling-block. How could the prophet receive a commission in the beginning of the reign of Jehoiakim to the ambassadors who had come to Zedekiah, (ver. 3)? And how could the prophet execute the same commission to Zedekiah (ver. 12), and say in xxviii. 1 that in the same year, in the beginning of the reign of Zedekiah, Hananiah contradicted his prediction? HAEVERNICK indeed [II., 2, S. 217) says "the words הבאים (ver. 3) pertain to the compilation of the chapter,—to show how Zedekiah should fulfil that older prophecy of the time of Jehoiakim, and should behave towards the nations which were his allies." But this would presuppose that Jeremiah received a message to ambassadors who did not come to Jerusalem till from eleven to fifteen years afterwards. Further, according to this the name of Nebuchadnezzar and the Chaldeans would have been mentioned in the beginning of the reign of Jehoiakim, while we have demonstrated that before the battle of Carchemish, in the fourth year of Jehoiakim, Jeremiah did not yet know that the enemies coming from the north would be the Chaldeans under Nebuchadnezzar. Add to this that the compiler must have proceeded very inconsiderately, to substitute the time of receiving the commission for that of its execution. We ought to have read in that case: In the time of Jehoiakim Jeremiah received the commission to declare the following to foreign ambassadors who should come. These ambassadors came in the beginning of the reign of Zedekiah and unto them spake Jeremiah, etc. Instead of this we have: In the beginning of Jehoiakim's reign Jeremiah received the command to deliver this message to the ambassadors, who are come to Zedekiah, etc. To attribute to the supposed compiler such a violent treatment of the text is truly much worse than to assume an oversight of the copyist. It is, moreover, a wonder to me that, as far as my knowledge extends, no commentator has hit on the idea of taking הַבָּאִים in the sense of the Fut., or Fut. exacti.: who come or will have come. There is unquestionably grammatical authority for this. For the participle, which in itself has no tense, may be taken according to the connection as present, past or future. Comp. NAEGELSB., Gr., § 97; EWALD, § 335, b. Compare especially the same word in Isa. xxvii. 6=temporibus futuris, Eccles. ii. 16, הַיָּמִים הַבָּאִים diebus venturis, etc.—Whatever we have already urged is certainly opposed to this rendering of the word, viz. 1, the improbability of the communication of a message not to be delivered for fifteen years; 2, above and the entirely unhistorical mention of Nebuchadnezzar and the Chaldeans in the beginning of the reign of Jehoiakim. The objections to the reading **Jehoiakim** are of ancient date. JEROME helps himself out of the difficulty by connecting the verse with the previous chapter. It does not disturb him that thus ch. xxvi. begins and ends with a similar date; yet he supposes that it was this circumstance, which led the Seventy to omit the verse. The Syriac and the unprinted *Arabs Oxoniensis* read "Zedekiah." Likewise the Cod. Regiomont., II. KENNICOTT in his *Diss. super ratione text. Hebr. V. T., I., p. 503; II., p. 346, Ed.* TELLER, decidedly favors the view that a copyist who had forgotten that Zedekiah was also a son of Josiah was moved by xxvi. 1 to alter the name of Zedekiah into Jehoiakim. I also hold the view that xxvi 1 affected the rendering of xxvii. 1, for as we shall see below at xlix. 34, chapter xxvii. has lost its original superscription by the oversight of a diaskenast who added this verse of the prophecy against Elam as a postscript. Hence xxvii. 1 is still wanting in the LXX.; on the other hand the prophecy against Elam has in the LXX. a superscription and a postscript, in the Hebrew text a superscription which does not correspond to the general purport, and ch. xxvii. has obtained in the Hebrew a new beginning which was formed after xxvi. 1, while the original text of xxvii. 1, is to be sought nowhere else but in xlix. 34 (with the omission of אֶל־עֵילָם). So MOVERS and HITZIG, with whom on this point I feel obliged to agree. From xxviii. 1 it is evident that by the beginning of Zedekiah's reign we are to understand his fourth year. This appears to be entirely suitable in point of fact. For it is not to be imagined that Zedekiah undertook revolutionary projects immediately after his ascension of the throne. As to the mode of expression, "beginning" is a relative idea, and the first half of a period may be designated as the beginning, the latter half as its close. From the words **Thus saith Jehovah unto thee**, it is moreover apparent that from ver. 2 onward the prophet communicates the words as he spoke them to the people. Comp. "saith Jehovah," ver. 11 and ver. 16. The introductory formula in ver. 1 b, is then not to be referred specially to the moment of revelation, but it has this sense, that all the actions and speeches related in what follows are the result of a revelation to the prophet.

Ver. 2. **Bonds** i. e. cords (ii. 20; v. 5; xxx. 8), not to hold together the wooden parts of the yokes, for such yokes there are none, but to fix the yoke to the body, are what Jeremiah is to prepare. So with מֹטוֹת. The word (מוֹט, tottering above, crooked, broken from the branch, the bough, piece of wood) is in both these chapters used in a material sense, while עֹל always denotes the yoke in a figurative sense (xxvii. 8, 11, 12; xxviii. 2, 4, 11, 14 coll. xxviii. 10 sqq.). Jeremiah is to put these yokes on his neck and send them by the messengers to their master. As certainly as the prophet should put a yoke upon his neck, and has really put it on (xxviii. 10 sqq. coll. Isa. xx. 2; Hos. i. 2 sqq.: Ezek. xii. 3 sqq.), so certainly should he really give the yoke to the messengers. This corresponded to oriental customs. If the messengers would not take the yoke with them, that was their affair. The four neighboring nations here mentioned (Edom, Moab, Ammon, Sidon) are named in the same order in xxv. 1, 2. NIEBUHR (*Ass. u. Bab., S.* 211) connects this consultation with the diversion, which resulted from Nebuchadnezzar's pretended expedition against Media after the death of Cyaxares in B. C. 594 (*Vid. sup.*, xxv. 26). But this connection is altogether uncertain, and we must be content to be ignorant why that epoch was considered adapted for a revolt. At all events the words of the prophet made an impression on the king. For in the same year (593) we find him on a journey to Babylon (li. 59), which can have had no other object than renewed homage. When DUNCKER (*S.* 834, etc.) says the Phœnicians were then left to their fate and subjugated by Nebuchadnezzar, the first part of the statement is correct. But I doubt whether they then immediately revolted on their own account, and were again subjugated. For when Sidon (Ezek. xxxii. 29) is mentioned among the nations which had fallen before the sword of Nebuchadnezzar, before the twentieth year of this king (Ezek. xxxii. 17), therefore before B. C., 586, it does not seem at all necessary to assume that the Phœnicians revolted sooner than Zedekiah himself, who was moved to open revolt by Hophra

CHAP. XXVII. 1-22.—XXVIII. 1-17.

the new king of Egypt, in B. C. 589. When also after the destruction of Jerusalem (586) only Tyrus among the Phœnician cities was still to be subdued, the conquest of the rest may have well taken place immediately before the attack on Judah and Jerusalem (588). The Edomites, Moabites and Ammonites, who are mentioned in 2 Kings xxiv. 2 as Chaldean allies against Judah, appear according to our passage in their love of freedom to have momentarily forgotten their ancient enmity towards Judah, as well as their fear of the Chaldeans. But they can scarcely have revolted. According to Ps. cxxxvii. 7 coll. Lam. iv. 21, 22; Ezek. xxxvi. 5 the Edomites were zealous co-operators at the destruction of Jerusalem.
Ver. 5. **I have made,** *etc.* The Creator has the right to dispose of His creatures. — **As seemed meet unto me.** Comp. xviii. 4.—Ver. 6. **And the beasts of the field.** Nebuchadnezzar is declared universal governor *de jure divino.*— Ver. 7. This verse is wanting in the LXX. MOVERS and HITZIG regard it as interpolated. Comp. on the other hand GRAF, S. 348, *Anm.* An interpolator would certainly not have interpolated so incorrectly. For Nebuchadnezzar was succeeded only by his son Evilmerodach, who was murdered by Neriglissar, his father-in-law. He was succeeded by his son Labosoarchad, a child who was killed after a reign of nine months, to make place for Nabonnet, one of the conspirators. The latter was Babylon's last king. On the contrary the LXX. omitted the verse because it seemed so inaccurate. The prophet does not, however, intend to be exact. The phrase "his son and his son's son" is to denote an indefinite but brief period (Exod. **xx.** 5; xxxiv. 7; Deut. v. 9). The chronicler seems to refer to this passage in 2 Chron. xxxvi. 20.—**Shall serve themselves of him.** Comp. xxv. 14. The expressions **many nations,** *etc.,* remind us of 1. 9, 41. When we remember that this passage originated at the same time with chh. 1. and li., this relationship may well have its foundation in the mind of the prophet.—Ver. 8. **The nation which . . . that will not,** *etc.* At first it seems natural to take the second sentence as the correction of the first: he who will not serve, or rather, he who will not voluntarily submit himself. For all, indeed, will serve. He who has to be compelled may expect the extremity of distress, while he who voluntarily submits will retain at least his land and his life. But unfortunately it is not grammatically allowable to take 1 in the meaning of "or rather." We must therefore make this distinction between "serve" and "put their neck under the yoke," that the former refers to the nations already subject to the Babylonian dominion, the latter to the others. In warning the heathen nations of their diviners, sorcerers, *etc.,* the prophet puts the false prophets of the Jews afterwards mentioned in the same category with them.—Ver. 10. **To remove.** The consequence is represented as the object. Comp. ver. 15.—**And that I should drive.** Observe the return of the discourse from the secondary to the main form. Comp. NAEGELSB. *Gr.,* § 99, 3.—vers. 15 and 22.
Vers. 12-15. **I spake also to Zedekiah . . . prophesy unto you.** As in ver. 2, the prophet

here and in ver. 16 sqq. gives an account, not of the reception, but the execution of the divine commission. Comp. EXEG. rems. on xxvi. 2.—**By the sword,** *etc.* Comp. ver. 8.
Vers. 16-22. **Also I spake to the priests . . . restore them to this place.** Jeremiah speaks to the king of political subjection, to the priests and the people of the vessels which were the ornaments of the temple and its worship. These vessels carried away by Nebuchadnezzar (2 Kings xxiv. 13) are according to the words of the false prophets to be brought back in a very brief period. In opposition to this Jeremiah makes the requisition on the false prophets to prove their authority by preventing through their intercession (יִפְגְּעוּ). Comp. vii. 16) the deportation of the vessels still in their possession.—The pillars (1 Kings vii. 15-22), sea (Ib. 23-26), and bases (ver. 27 sqq.), were the largest and heaviest vessels, which were not therefore carried away the first time. Comp. EXEG. rems. on lii. 17.—**All the nobles.** Comp. Is. xxxiv. 12; Jer. xxxix. 6 and xxix. 2; 2 Kings xxiv. 11 sqq.—The refutation of MOVERS' and HITZIG's assertion that vers. 16-21 are interpolated, may be seen in GRAF, S. 351. He has also on pp. 344, 345 shown that the abbreviated name-ending, which prevails in chh. xxvii.-xxix. (יְ instead of יָה) is not to be regarded as the sign of a later date of composition.

XXVIII. 1-4. **And it came to pass . . . the yoke of the king of Babylon.** In the same year, doubtless shortly after the occurrences narrated in ch. xxvii. came Hananiah from Gibeon (a city of priests, Josh. xxi. 17) and, therefore, probably himself a priest, in opposition to Jeremiah prophesying that in two years time the Lord will break the yoke of Nebuchadnezzar, and bring back the sacred vessels and king Jehoiachin, together with the other captives from Babylon. On the date "in the beginning" comp. Comm. on xxvii. 1. The month is mentioned on account of the statement in ver. 17.—The deceptive promise of Hananiah is directly opposed to what Jeremiah has said in xxii. 26, 27; xxvii. 16.
Vers. 6-9. **Then the prophet Jeremiah said . . . truly sent him.** Jeremiah replies: would that thou wert right! But only prophecies of calamity have the presumption of truth in their favor, for they are connected with danger to their author. Prophecies of good fortune may be flattery. We must, therefore, wait for their result.—On ver. 9 comp. Deut. xviii. 21, 22.
Vers. 10 and 11. **Then Hananiah . . . went his way.** Hananiah has the audacity to answer Jeremiah's speech by taking the yoke from his neck and breaking it, at the same time repeating his previous prediction (vers. 3 and 4). Jeremiah goes away for the time without uttering a word in reply. On מוֹטָה and עַל comp. EXEG. rems. on xxvii. 2.
Vers. 12-17. **Then the word . . . seventh month.** After some time Jeremiah received from the Lord a double message to Hananiah: 1. By the breaking of the wooden yoke all that he has effected is that an iron one takes its place, for iron will be the yoke, which Nebuchadnezzar will put upon the nations, according to the will of God; 2. Hananiah, who misuses the name of

God and has misled the people into vain confidence, is to die this year. This also came to pass, for he died two months afterwards.—**Yokes of wood.** The plural is generic, as was remarked on xxvii. 2. Comp. NAEGELSB. *Gr.*, § 61, 2 *d.*—**Yoke of iron.** The prophet appears to have had Deut. xxviii. 48 in mind. On ver. 14 comp. xxvii. 6.—**Rebellion** (הָּרְס֣) comp. xxix. 32. It is=revolt, rebellion, on account of the following אֵל־.—**In the seventh month** corresponds to fifth month, ver. 1.

---

3. The conflict of Jeremiah with the false prophets in Babylon.

CHAPTER XXIX.

1. The Letter to the Exiles.

XXIX. 1-23.

1 Now these are the words of the letter that Jeremiah the prophet sent from Jerusalem unto the residue of the elders which were carried away captives, and to the priests, and to the prophets, and to all the people whom Nebuchadnezzar car-
2 ried away captive from Jerusalem to Babylon (after that Jeconiah the king, and the queen, and the eunuchs, the princes of Judah and Jerusalem, and the carpen-
3 ters and the smiths, were departed from Jerusalem); By the hand of Elasah the son of Shaphan, and Gemariah the son of Hilkiah (whom Zedekiah the king of Judah sent unto Babylon to Nebuchadnezzar, king of Babylon), saying,
4 Thus saith the Lord of hosts [Jehovah Zebaoth], the God of Israel, unto all that are carried away captives, whom I have caused to be carried away from Jerusalem
5 unto Babylon: Build ye houses and dwell in them, and plant gardens and eat the
6 fruit of them; Take ye wives, and beget sons and daughters; and take wives for your sons, and give your daughters to husbands, that they may bear sons and
7 daughters; that ye may be increased there and not diminished. And seek the peace of the city whither I have caused you to be carried away captive, and pray unto the Lord [Jehovah] for it: for in the peace thereof shall ye have peace.
8 For thus saith the Lord of hosts, the God of Israel: Let not your prophets and your diviners, that *be* in the midst of you, deceive you, neither hearken to your
9 dreams which ye cause to be dreamed[1] For they prophesy falsely unto you in my
10 name: I have not sent them, saith the Lord. For thus saith the Lord, That after seventy years be accomplished at Babylon I will visit you, and perform my good
11 word toward you, in causing you to return to this place. For I know the thoughts that I think toward you, saith the Lord, thoughts of peace and not of evil, to give
12 you an expected end. Then shall ye call upon me, and ye shall go and pray unto me,
13 and I will hearken unto you. And ye shall seek me, and find *me*, when ye shall
14 search for me with all your heart. And I will be found of you, saith the Lord: and I will turn away your captivity,[2] and I will gather you from all the nations, and from all the places whither I have driven you, saith the Lord; and I will bring you again into the place whence I caused you to be carried away captive.
15,16 Because[3] ye have said, The Lord hath raised us up prophets in Babylon; *Know* that thus saith the Lord of[4] the king that sitteth upon the throne[5] of David, and of all the people that dwelleth in the city, *and* of your brethren that are not gone
17 forth with you into captivity; Thus saith the Lord of hosts: Behold, I will send upon them the sword, the famine, and the pestilence, and will make them like vile[6]
18 figs, that cannot be eaten, they are so evil. And I will persecute them with the sword, with the famine, and with the pestilence, and will deliver them to be removed to all the kingdoms of the earth, to be a curse, and an astonishment, and an
19 hissing, and a reproach, among all the nations whither I have driven them: Because they have not hearkened to my words, saith the Lord, which I sent[7] unto them by my servants the prophets, rising up early and sending *them;* but ye would not hear, saith the Lord [Jehovah].

20   Hear ye therefore the word of the Lord, all ye of the captivity, whom I have
21 sent from Jerusalem to Babylon: Thus saith the Lord of hosts, the God of Israel,
of Ahab the son of Kolaiah, and of Zedekiah the son of Maaseiah, which prophesy a
lie unto you in my name: Behold, I will deliver them into the hand of Nebuchad-
22 nezzar, king of Babylon; and he shall slay them before your eyes; And of them shall
be taken up a curse by all the captivity of Judah which *are* in Babylon, saying, The
Lord make thee like Zedekiah and like Ahab,⁸ whom the king of Babylon roasted
23 in the fire; Because they have committed villany in Israel, and have committed
adultery with their neighbours' wives, and have spoken lying words in my name,
which I have not commanded them: even I know⁹ and *am* a witness, saith the Lord.

TEXTUAL AND GRAMMATICAL.

¹ Ver. 8.—מַחֲלֹמִים. Hiph. from חלם occurs only in Isa. xxxviii. 16 and here; Part. Hiph. here only. The causative conjugation would not inappropriately intimate the self-made character of those dreams (HITZIG). The form is not without analogies. Comp. כִּינוֹרִים, 2 Chron. xxviii. 23, כְּחֻצְרִים (Keri) 1 Chron. xv. 24. But comp. OLSH., § 258 *a*, S. 580.

² Ver. 14.—שׁוּב in this connection is used transitively. That שְׁבוּת cannot be taken as accusative of the object (I turn myself *to the* captivity) is evident from the circumstance, that, where the connection requires the imperfect we have אָשִׁיב; xxxii. 44; xxxiii. 11, 26 (Keri); xlix. 6, 39 (Keri); in Ezek. xxxix. 25; xxxiii. 7 we have even the perfect Hiphil.

³ Ver. 15.—'בְּ. Comp. NAEGELSB. *Gr.*, § 109, 1 *a*. Since the pleonastic בְּ requires a *verbum dicendi* to be supplied before it, we must here supply: thus I say; thus I declare to you. בְּ before אֲמָרְתֶם=when, or as to this that—as almost all the commentators admit. The perfect is used (comp. the imperf. ver. 13), because the fact supposed is real.

⁴ Ver. 16.—אֶל־הַמֶּלֶךְ, ver. 16. אֶל=*in respect to, of*, as frequently elsewhere: ver. 21; xxii. 11. Comp. NAEGELSB. *Gr.*, § 112, 5, *b*.

⁵ Ver. 16.—אֶל־כִּסֵּא. אֶל for עַל, as frequently in Jeremiah. Comp. rems. on x. 1.

⁶ Ver. 17.—שֹׁעֵר (probably from שָׂעַר) here only—meaning *horridus, abominandus*. Comp. שַׁעֲרוּרָה.

⁷ Ver. 19.—אֲשֶׁר־שָׁלַחְתִּי. On the construction with a double accusative comp. NAEGELSB. *Gr.*, § 69, 2 *c*.

⁸ Ver. 22.—כְּאָחָב. In consequence of the elision of the א, patahh must, according to the well-known rule, pass over into Segol.

⁹ Ver. 23.—On the reading הַיּוֹדֵעַ comp. TEXTUAL NOTES on xvii. 23.

EXEGETICAL AND CRITICAL.

Jeremiah did not limit himself to contending against the perverse nationalism of the Jews in their own home, for those who had already been carried away captive were in constant communication with home, and the accounts of the views and expectations prevailing among the former at all events influenced the conclusions of the latter. If they adapted themselves to their state of exile and described it as tolerable, when they saw its inevitable necessity, and admonished their countrymen to bow to this necessity, this was at any rate a powerful auxiliary to Jeremiah's preaching. Hence Jeremiah seeks to move the captives to humble submission to their lot, presenting before them on the one hand the true consolation of a deliverance to be hoped for after seventy years, and on the other hand most emphatically warning them against the false consolation of a deliverance in a shorter period, which the false prophets set before them. Jeremiah thus avails himself of the opportunity afforded by an embassy, despatched by Zedekiah to Babylon (xxix. 3), to send a letter to those who had been already deported. We know nothing further either of the object of the embassy or of the persons of the ambassadors. As to the time of the composition and despatch of the letter HITZIG has correctly remarked that all the data we have point to the period between the first and the fourth years of Zedekiah. The deportation under Jeconiah had taken place (xxix. 1, 2). The deportation appears to be that event on which the sending of the letter leans; there seems to be nothing more important as the occasion of it. Add to this that the counsel which Jeremiah gives suits the commencement of the exile. How are the exiles to arrange matters? Are they to compose themselves for a brief or lengthened sojourn? Jeremiah tells them they are to do the latter. It is incredible that he delayed this advice for years, the more so since of the seventy years of exile, for those who were carried away with Jeconiah, eight were already past. Besides this, it is not probable that Zedekiah in his fourth year, when he himself went to Babylon (li. 59), would send an embassy thither. I therefore agree with HITZIG, who ascribes the epistle to the first or second year after the deportation. The vision, of which ch. xxiv. relates, must have preceded this letter, not only because from its purport it must have followed immediately after the deportation of Jeconiah, while our letter presupposes the arrival of the captives in Babylon, but also because in several places in the letter reference is made to it (comp. ver. 10 with xxiv. 6; ver. 17 with xxiv. 2, 8; ver. 18 with xxiv. 9).—It is true many commentators regard vers. 16-20 as inauthentic, but incorrectly as we shall see.—The question, whether we have a true copy of the letter or only a later reproduction, or account of it, is variously answered. The last view has in its favor: 1. that the writing has not the form of a letter; 2. the apparently unconnected position of vers. 15-20. But what is the Hebrew form of a letter? From the few examples which the Old Testament affords (comp. 2 Sam. xi. 14; 1 Ki. xxi. 8; 2 Ki. x. 1-6; 2 Chron. xxx. 6; Ezr. iv. 8; Neh. vi. 5), we cannot derive any set form, and as to the absence of connection we shall hereafter show (on ver. 15 sqq.) that such an absence does not exist. I find therefore no reason for doubting the agreement of our letter with the original. It contains four parts: 1. vers. 4-7, the positive command to arrange for a longer sojourn in Babylon; 2. Warning against being deceived by the false prophets, since Jehovah promises deliverance and return only after seventy years; 3. vers. 15-20, Warning against trusting in the false prophets, especially in reference to that part of the people which had remained in Jerusalem, since it is devoted to destruction; 4. vers. 21-23, prediction of the severe punishment of two false prophets.

Vers. 1-7. **Now these are the words . . . shall ye have peace.** After the words of historical introduction, which give information concerning the receivers and bearers of the letter, follows the first part of the letter (vers. 4-7). As the command of God (ver. 4), Jeremiah proclaims to the exiles that they should build houses and lay out gardens (ver. 5), marry and give their children in marriage (ver. 6), and seek the welfare of the place assigned them as a residence as a condition of their own (ver. 7). HITZIG regards vers. 1-3 as showing traces of a later hand in the abbreviated forms of the names, the mention of Nebuchadnezzar, which name is omitted by the LXX., and in the remark that Jeremiah was a prophet. But comp. on the other hand GRAF, S. 342 sqq.—**The residue of the elders.** The explanation of HITZIG and GRAF that these were the elders who were not at the same time priests or prophets, cannot possibly be correct. For then this phrase must have come after, since those priests and prophets who were not elders, can be no others than those straightway mentioned. The supposition that the deceased elders must have been already replaced by others, so that the council of elders could not appear to the prophet as merely a *residue*, is unfounded. How could Jeremiah assume an organized community, when in his letter he exhorts them to enter into such relations. He will of course address those elders only who are alive. —Does the date in ver. 2 refer to "sent" or "carried away?" Manifestly to the latter, for if referred to "sent" it would declare that Jeremiah wrote immediately after the surrender, which is not to be imagined. The sentence "after that," *etc*., is therefore to be referred to "carried away" and the sense is: "which Nebuchadnezzar carried away after that, in accordance with the required condition, Jehoiachin, with those afterwards named, surrendered himself. For אָצָי is used of the surrendering of besieged persons (2 Ki. xxiv. 12 sqq.; 1 Sam. xi. 3, 10; 1 Ki. xx. 31; Isa. xxxvi. 16; Jer. xxi. 9; xxxviii. 2, 21).—**The queen.** Comp. xiii. 18; 2 Ki. xxiv. 8, 12, 15.—**The eunuchs, the princes.** The two terms appear to be in apposition, but the princes of Judah were certainly not eunuchs. Either then is סָרִים to be taken in the sense of chamberlain, courtier (of which use there is certain proof. Comp. 2 Ki. xxiv. 14, 15. GESEN. *Thes*., p. 973), or else ן, **and**, is wanting before שָׂרֵי, **princes.—On carpenters,** *etc*., comp. rems. on xxiv. 1.—The Lord designates the captives as carried away by *him:* vers. 4, 7, 14, 20.—**Increased there.** This ancient theocratic blessing (Gen. xiii. 16; xv. 5; xvii. 2; Jer. iii. 16, 19) is thus to be preserved to the people even in captivity.

Vers. 8-14. **For thus . . . carried away captive.** The direction in vers. 5-7 is given by the prophet for two reasons, a negative and a positive. The negative reason is, the expectation of a speedy liberation, which false prophets sought to produce in the people and which is an illusion of their own dreams, a nonentity, by which they are not to allow themselves to be deceived (vers. 8 and 9). The positive reason is that not till after **seventy years** will the Lord verify His promise of grace. Then will the people call upon their God and seek Him, and He will hear and be found of them and turn away their captivity and bring them home from all the places where they have been dispersed (vers. 10-14).—Ver. 10. **Seventy years.** Comp. xxv. 11. The prophet does not calculate from the present, but he has in mind the absolute period of duration appointed to the Babylonian empire. Observe also, that he does not say: when the years of your exile are ended. The seventy years represent primarily the years of the Babylonian empire and only secondarily those of the captivity. The more justified are we in dating the seventy years from the siege of Carchemish. It should further be observed that the prophet opposes the arbitrary unfounded thesis of the false prophets, not in a harsh and severe but mild and consolatory antithesis, in which even the severest point, the seventy years' duration of the exile, is expressed in the most forbearing manner. The Lord evidently wishes to soften and win their hearts, which had been rendered obstinate by false consolation, by presenting the true. Hence also the gracious thoughts of ver. 11. I still know my thoughts, says the Lord, *i. e.* I have not forgotten them or let them pass from my view. אַחֲרִית corresponds to our English "future" (to "have a future," *etc*.). Comp. Prov. xxiii. 18; xxiv. 14, 20; Ps. xxxvii. 37; Jer. xxxi. 17. The Lord, however, sets before the people not merely a future of outward prosperity, but above all a future of internal welfare, without which the former would be altogether inconceivable.—**Ye shall go** (והלכתם), ver. 12, is best taken of going to a place of worship. So that **ye shall call and pray** are distinguished as private and public worship (comp. 1 Ki. viii. 20, 29, 30, 35, *etc*.). If the sentences of ver. 13 and "I will be found of you," ver. 14, are not tautological, we must regard them as two sentences with two clauses each, the second forming the basis of the former; כִּי is not "when" but "for," or "because:" ye will seek me and find me; because ye shall seek me with all your heart, I will be found of you.—**Turn away your captivity.** The expression is rooted in Deut. (xxx. 3), as generally in our whole passage this chapter hovered before the mind of the prophet. The expression is found with special frequency in Jeremiah, and chiefly in chs. xxx.-xxxiii. and xlvii.-xlix. To turn the captivity stands, however, for *restitutio in integrum* generally (Job xlii. 10; Jer. xxx. 18). The return from exile was only a weak beginning of the fulfilment of our prophecy. Comp. rems. on iii. 12 sqq.

Vers. 15-19. **Because ye have said ... saith Jehovah.** Not only has ver. 15 been declared to be transposed hither from its first place, but the whole passage, vers. 16-20, has been pronounced spurious (HITZIG), which is thought to be the more justified, because the passage is wanting in the LXX. It seems to me that two things have been overlooked here. 1. Jerusalem with its remaining population and the theocratic king at their head naturally still continued to be the exiles to be the sun of their happiness and their hope. So long as Jerusalem and the temple were standing, the main foundation of the theocracy was unshaken and the hope existed that the present temporary adversity might be followed any moment by a turn for the better. Hence also the prophecies of the false prophets dwelt above all on the continuance of Jerusalem. Even the present misfortune, the partial deportation of the people and the sacred vessels, although they had not predicted it, they could explain as a mere episode, which did not refute the main tenor of their promises, so long as Jerusalem and the temple were standing, and there were people in Jerusalem. Hence Jeremiah takes away the ground from under the feet of those false prophets, by predicting in vers. 16-20 the total destruction of the present population of Jerusalem, together with their king. We are not then to say that these words, vers. 16-20, apply to the population of Jerusalem. They certainly do so, but only secondarily. Primarily they are to overthrow the basis on which the false prophets of the captivity are standing. I can then regard the words only as necessary parts of the genuine letter, written by Jeremiah to the exiles, and cannot assume with GRAF that we have in this chapter only a report of the letter. 2. In its grammatical relations the יִכּ in the beginning of ver. 16 has given the greatest trouble to the commentators. They have taken it mostly in the causal signification, which it certainly usually has in this formula, which however affords no sense, whether we connect ver. 16 with ver. 15 or ver. 14. It is here rather the pleonastic יִכּ which so frequently introduces a direct statement. We have had it already in ver. 10. Comp. ii. 35; xxii. 22; and TEXTUAL NOTE.—**Hath raised,** etc. Jeremiah supposes a reply to vers. 8, 9. You despise our prophets; we however assure you that Jehovah raises up prophets not only in Jerusalem, but He has extended the inspiring influence of His Spirit even to Babylon. Hence the local form בָּבֶלָה.—**The sword.** Comp. ix. 15; xxiv. 10; xxvii. 8, 13.—**Figs.** The prophet has xxiv. 2 in view. That the exiles were acquainted with the vision in ch. xxiv. is possible but not necessary. This passage is intelligible to those who had no knowledge of ch. xxiv.—**Ye would not hear.** The 2 pers. plur. proceeds doubtless simply from the circumstance that the prophet quotes entire a frequent saying there: vii. 13; xxv. 3, 4, 7, 8; xxvi. 5. On ver. 20 comp. xxiv. 5.

Vers. 20-23. **Hear ye therefore ... witness, saith Jehovah.** In conclusion the prophet predicts the punishment of two of those false prophets for their presumption and blasphemy generally by a terrible death. Nothing further is known of this Ahab and Zedekiah.—**Slay them.** It is very natural to suppose that Nebuchadnezzar feared the exciting preaching of such prophets and that he wished to terrify others by inflicting death in a terrible manner.—Ver. 22 a. Comp. xxiv. 9; xxv. 18; xxvi. 6 coll. Isa. lxv. 15.—**Roasted.** Comp. Dan. iii.6.—**Villany,** (נְבָלָה) a deed of shame, *facinus rationi legique divinæ repugnans* (FUERST). Comp. Gen. xxxiv. 7; Deut. xxii. 21; Josh. vii. 15.—The Lord calls Himself a knower and witness, because He not only knows the truth, but brings it also to light. Comp. Mal. iii. 5. Levit. v. 1 may in general have been hovering before the mind of the prophet.

---

2. *The Consequences of the Letter.*

XXIX. 24-32.

24, 25 Thus shalt thou also speak to Shemaiah the Nehelamite, saying, Thus speaketh the Lord of hosts, the God of Israel, saying, Because thou hast sent letters in thy name unto all the people that *are* at Jerusalem, and to Zephaniah, the son of Maa-
26 seiah the priest, and to all the priests, saying, The Lord hath made thee priest in the stead of Jehoiada the priest, that ye should be officers in the house of the Lord, for every man *that is* mad[1] and maketh himself a prophet, that thou shouldest put
27 him in prison, and in the stocks.[2] Now therefore why hast thou not reproved[3] Je-
28 remiah of Anathoth, which maketh himself a prophet to you? For therefore[4] he sent [a letter] unto us *in* Babylon, saying, this *captivity is* [will continue] long:[5] build ye houses, and dwell *in them;* and plant gardens, and eat the fruit of them.
29 And Zephaniah the priest read this letter in the ears of Jeremiah the prophet.
30, 31 Then came the word of the Lord unto Jeremiah, saying, Send to all them of

the captivity [a message] saying, Thus saith the Lord concerning Shemaiah the Nehelamite; Because that Shemaiah hath prophesied unto you, and I sent him
32 not [without my having sent him] and he caused you to trust⁶ in a lie : Therefore thus saith the Lord: Behold, I will punish Shemaiah the Nehelamite, and his seed: he shall not have a man to dwell among this people; neither shall he behold⁷ the good that I will do for my people, saith the Lord ; because he hath taught rebellion against the Lord.

TEXTUAL AND GRAMMATICAL.

¹ Ver. 26.—כְּשֵׁנָא. Only the Part. Pual and Part. and Inf. Hiphil of this word are found. The radical meaning is *to be astray*. (Comp. שָׁנָא, שָׁנָה, שָׁנָה). The Hiphil is used of raving in general, 1 Sam. xxi. 15, 16 ; כְּשֻׁנָּע likewise in Deut. xxviii. 34 and 1 Sam. xxi. 16 ; elsewhere only of prophets and always in a bad sense: Hos. ix. 7 ; 2 Ki. iv. 11.
² Ver. 26.—צִינֹק. The word is ἅπ. λεγ. The root צָנַק also does not occur elsewhere in Hebrew. From the dialects the most suitable comparison is afforded by the Arabic *zinág*, collar, ring (Hitzig). According to the older Rabbis in Kimchi צִינִים = לִידִים מִסְגֵּר כְּלִי as כְּהֻפֶּכֶת = לֹאוָאר מִסְגֵּר. Symm.: μόχλος lever, pole, bar. Ges. *Thes.*, p. 1175. Hitzig rightly supposes that both instruments formed the complete instrument of torture, one serving to confine the neck, the other the hands and feet.
³ Ver. 27.—גָּעַרְתָּ. Properly to chide (comp. Gen. xxxvii. 10) then to interfere, to stop any one (Ruth ii. 16; Mal. iii. 11).
⁴ Ver. 28.—כִּי־עַל־כֵּן. In itself these particles might be taken in the most natural sense ; for on this account (*viz.*, on account of defective control); but elsewhere they always designate the reason supposed as the object or result; xxxvii. 4; Gen. xviii. 5 ; xix. 8; xxxiii. 10; xxxviii. 26. Comp. Rendler, *lexical. Erörterungen. Stud. u. Krit.*, 1811, S. 983 sqq.
⁵ Ver. 28.—אֲרֻכָּה, of extension in time (2 Sam. iii. 1), and in space (Job xi. 9). On the neuter signification of the feminine, comp. Naegelsb. *Gr.*, § 60, 6 *b*.
⁶ Ver. 31.—On וַיַּבְטַח comp. xxviii. 15.
⁷ Ver. 32.—רָאָה with בְּ. Comp. Naegelsb. *Gr.*, § 112, 5, *a*; Ps. xxxvii. 34; liv. 9; cxviii. 7.

EXEGETICAL AND CRITICAL.

The letter, xxix. 4-23, caused great exasperation among the false prophets at Babylon. One of them, Shemaiah, complains to the overseer of the temple in Jerusalem that he did not interfere against the conduct of the mad Jeremiah. Jeremiah gets information of this letter and receives the command to announce to Shemaiah that his family shall become extinct, and that he himself will not see the salvation of Israel. The arrangement of the sentences in this passage is very irregular. In the first place all explanation concerning the proximate occasion of this utterance is passed over. Yet this may be accounted for by the fact that this may be learned from the tenor of the passage itself. The beginning will then be made with the command to make an announcement to Shemaiah. This announcement does begin in ver. 25, and takes its regular course to the close of ver. 28, so that in vers. 26-28 the letter is communicated *verbatim*, which gave the occasion for the announcement to Shemaiah. Here the address to Shemaiah breaks off without a conclusion. Instead of this, after the prophet has suddenly sprung back from the point of the communication *by* him to the point of the communication *to* him, the conclusion is given in the form of an address to the exiles, in which Shemaiah is spoken of in the third person (vers. 30-32). Here accordingly two announcements seem to have been made (comp. vers. 24, 25 with vers. 30, 31), which on account of their identical tenor the prophet allows to combine in the course of his narrative.

Vers. 24-28. **Thus shalt thou ... eat the fruit of them.** We might indeed translate אֵל here, as in vers. 16 and 21, *of* [Shemaiah] instead of *to*, but ver. 25 contains a direct address to Shemaiah. Neither he nor his birth-place is mentioned elsewhere.—The letter, communicated in vers. 26-28, is addressed specially to the priest Zephaniah. When notwithstanding, in ver. 25, letters are spoken of which were addressed to all the prophets and all the priests besides Zephaniah, this may be explained in two ways ; either there really were letters with the three addresses mentioned, the principal letter only being communicated to Zephaniah; or this letter was the only one, but designated in ver. 25 as intended to be communicated to a wider circle. Both explanations are grammatically possible. For **letters** (סְפָרִים) may be a general plural. (Comp. כְּלֻבֹּת, **yokes**, xxviii. 13 and Isa. xxxvii. 14; xxxix. 1).—Zephaniah, the son of Maaseiah, was כֹּהֵן מִשְׁנֶה, **second priest**, lii. 24. Comp. xxi. 1 and xxxvii. 3.—**Officers** (פְּקִדִים). This also might in itself be a general plural, if the mention of the predecessor did not require us to refer it to both officers.—**That is mad.** Here the expression involves an insult to Jeremiah. Zephaniah was not to restrain all those who prophesied, but only those who were deranged and presumed to prophesy, and Jeremiah is reckoned among these.—**In prison.** Comp. xxx. 2.—**This is long.** By this the 70 years are meant (ver. 10), which, in comparison with the time predicted by the false prophets, would be a very long period.

Vers. 29-32. **And Zephaniah ... against Jehovah.** The words of ver. 29 do not clearly indicate whether Zephaniah read the letter of Jeremiah alone or in the presence of others. We may conclude from the two embassies (xxi. 1 ; xxxvii. 3) that he was probably not personally hostile towards Jeremiah. We also find no indication that Shemaiah's letter was at that time of any injury to Jeremiah. It is indeed possible that Zephaniah, though unable to keep the purport of the letter altogether secret, yet acted with the utmost possible consideration toward the prophet. At any rate Jeremiah was not intimidated. Shemaiah receives a reproving answer from the Lord's prophet: his race shall be extirpated (the phrase "dwelling among his people" signifies a peaceful, secure existence, 2 Ki. iv. 13) and he himself will not have his eyes gladdened by the prosperity of his people.

DOCTRINAL AND ETHICAL.

1. On xxvi. 3. ["See how God *waits to be gracious*, waits till we are duly qualified, till we are fit for Him to be gracious to, and in the meantime tries a variety of methods to bring us to be so." HENRY—S. R. A.]
2. On xxvi. 6. "*Deus nulli loco præcise alligatus est ita, ut ecclesiam suam et doctrinam cœlestem inde dimovere nequeat propter hominum ingratitudinem. Vehementer igitur errant Romanenses, dum ex auctoritate urbis Romæ suæ ecclesiæ ac religionis auctoritatem evincere satagunt. Multo rectius Hieronymus in hoc memorabili dicto, quod etiam allegatur in Jure Canon. Dist.* 19: *Non facile est stare loco Pauli et tenere gradum Petri cum Christo regnantium. Non enim Sanctorum filii sunt, qui tenent loca Sanctorum, sed qui exercent opera eorum.*" FÖRSTER.
3. On xxvi. 8 sqq. "Scarcely has Jeremiah done speaking than they take him to task, and threaten his life. What does Jeremiah do? Instead of vindicating himself he says: 'Reform your life, and hearken to the voice of the Lord, and it will be better for you,' ver. 13. You do not wish me to thunder away at you; reform then and I can let it alone. This preaching was seasonable, and produced an admirable effect. The priests and elders contradicted the priests, the parrhesia [free-spokenness, Acts iv. 13] of the man filled them with astonishment. 'He is not worthy of death,' ver. 16. A brief illustration of the saying 'We need not our senses lose, when our enemies accuse.' Jeremiah has to thank his honesty for this presence of mind, his profound meditation, his constrained calling, the necessity, the ardor, which urged him to preach, for no personal inclination had any share in it. I know in more recent times a man, who has unaffectedly practised Jeremiah's behavior, a pastor, a teacher, I might say a prophet of many thousand people. Whenever he had to vindicate himself (which happened now and then) he preached, he repeated to the commissioners the very things of which he was accused, confessed and denied not, but pressed them on their hearts, and showed *aliud agendo* his innocence, his mind, his steadfastness, and all at the same time so plainly that they always returned with full conviction and knew not whether they had gone forth to see a prophet or were sent to examine a culprit? 'Never man,' they said, 'spake like this man.' That cannot be counterfeited. One must be just as full of the matter, as absorbed in the subject, as pressed at heart, kindled with the same ardor in order to explain himself with the same indifference, repose and plainness, when there is a knife at his throat." ZINZENDORF.

4. On xxvi. 12 sqq. "*Si injuriam deposueris penes Deum, ultor est; si damnum, restitutor est; si dolorem, medicus est; si mortem, resuscitator est.*" TERTULLIAN. ["Those that persecute God's ministers hurt not them so much as themselves." HENRY.—S. R. A.]
5. On xxvi. 7, 8, 11, 16. "*Auctores persecutionis plerumque esse solent ii, qui in ordine ecclesiastico eminent.*" FÖRSTER. "Especially are the priests and men-pleasing prophets mad with Jeremiah, for if he is right they have lied." DIEDRICH.
6. On xxvi. 18. ["By this it appears that a man may be a true prophet of the Lord and yet may prophesy the destruction of Zion and Jerusalem. When we threaten secure sinners with the taking away of the Spirit of God, and declining churches with the removal of the candlestick, we say no more than what has been said many a time, and what we have warrant from the word of God to say." HENRY.—S. R. A.]
7. On xxvi. 20 sqq. "Urias, a true prophet, preached like Jeremiah, therefore the king wished to kill him, so he fled to Egypt but could not escape. Jeremiah did not flee and was spared ... Our running and anxiety are of no use. The wickedness of the world must for its judgment be displayed on God's servants, and these must yield to it; but on whom it is to come first God has in His own hand; and we may spare ourselves all our care and flight." DIEDRICH. ["Nothing more is known of Urijah than is here related; but this incident suggests that God mercifully strove with His people by the ministry of many prophets whom He sent, rising up early and sending them (ver. 5) whose names are written in the Book of Life and are canonized in God's Martyrology, but do not appear in the pages of any earthly history." WORDSWORTH.—S. R. A.]
8. On xxvi. 24. "*Monemur hic, Deum servis suis fidelibus subinde largiri quosdam patronos, ut Jeremiæ hic Achikamum et infra cap.* 38 *Ebedmelechum, Eliæ et prophetis* συγχρόνοις *Obadiam* 1 *Reg.* 18, *Luthero Electores Saxoniæ Fridericum sapientem, Johannem pium, Johannem-Fridericum constantem.*" FÖRSTER.
9. On xxvii. 2-11. Historical times are preceded by a long series of centuries which present themselves to us as altogether obscure or only in the dubious twilight of tradition. Accredited history also comprises only a relatively small portion of the human race, for the nations which are added as ciphers to the factors of history form the majority. A universal ruler in the biblical sense is not one whose dominion actually extends over the entire globe—for there is none such—but he who represents the leader in the concert of history. This part is here given to Nebuchadnezzar. Among all the universal monarchies that represented by him appears richest in noble capacity. It is therefore compared to the golden head of the image in Dan. ii. Comp. AUBERLEN, *der Prophet Daniel, S.* 41 sqq.
10. On xxvii. 5 sqq. ["The things of the world are not the best things, for God often gives the largest share of them to bad men, that are rivals with him and rebels against him. Dominion is not founded in grace. Those that have not any colorable title to eternal happiness may yet have a justifiable title to their temporal good things." HENRY.—S. R. A.] "Great lords sit

indeed on high thrones, but not firmly, for they are only God's vassals. And when they do not please Him and act accordingly, he can easily transfer the fief to another; Dan. ii. 21; iv. 14, 22." CRAMER.

11. On xxvii. 12. ["The conduct of Jeremiah, counselling Zedekiah and Jerusalem to submit to Nebuchadnezzar, has been represented as an act of political prudence to be imitated by Statesmen and Ecclesiastics, who are thereby justified in making large concessions of national rights and national independence in times of public emergency (STANLEY, Lect. 534).

But was it not rather one of religious duty? God had revealed to the prophet that He had given the Nation into the hand of Nebuchadnezzar, '*His servant*,' on account of their sins, and they must submit to Him as the Minister and Vicegerent of God." WORDSWORTH. "Many might have prevented destroying providences by humbling themselves under humbling providences. It is better to take up a lighter cross in our way, than pull a heavier on our own head." HENRY.—S. R. A.]

12. On xxvii. 14. "It is one sign of our depraved nature that we are more ready to believe lies than the truth. For when Jeremiah and his colleagues preached, no one believed. But no sooner did the false prophet come and open their mouths, than all their discourses must be spoken directly from heaven, and what they said, must pass current on earth (Ps. lxxiii. 9). But not what Jeremiah said. Take for example our mother Eve; what God said was of no account, but what the serpent said was something purely excellent." CRAMER.

13. On xxvii. 18. "True prayer is a certain sign of Godliness and a fruit of faith and the Holy Ghost, which cries in our hearts: Abba, dear Father. Therefore he who cannot or will not pray is not a good Christian." CRAMER.

14. On xxvii. 18. "*If they be prophets let them supplicate the Lord.* This was the great demonstration of Elias, to which Jeremiah adheres. It is infallibly the case that a false teacher has no heart for the Saviour, and goes out of His way. A heretic, who has a heart to pray (and that too in secret) is certainly not far from the truth." ZINZENDORF.

15. On xxvii. 22. ["We are apt to set our clock before God's dial, and then to quarrel because they do not agree, but the Lord is a God of judgment, and it is fit that we should wait for Him." HENRY.—S. R. A.]

16. On xxviii. 1 sqq. "Wherever the dear Lord builds His church, the devil has a chapel near by." CRAMER. This **Hananiah** (comp. xxviii. 2, 11) shows us plainly what it is to lie or deceive in the name of God.

"O Lord, and must Thy glorious name
Thus be a cover to their shame?" FÖRSTER.

17. On xxviii. 6. "*Amen! the Lord do so.* Quite a different attitude of the prophet from the preceding. A false prophet, a miserable comforter disputes with him, brings good news and appeals to an oracle, a voice which he had perhaps heard more lately than Jeremiah. Jeremiah without getting warm about it, says I shall be heartily glad if it be so: but take care that you have understood it correctly. His opponent is encouraged and goes further, he breaks off the prophetic yoke from Jeremiah's neck. Jeremiah, with the same indifference, which he has shown from the beginning, goes his way . . . I dare not speak of anything, says Paul, which Christ hath not wrought by me (Rom. xv. 18)." ZINZENDORF.

18. On xxviii. 10, 11. "*Chananias hic præbet exemplum impudentiæ Jesuiticæ, cujus magistrum non abs re appellaveris Eumundum Campianum* (1580) *qui epistola quadam Theologos Angliæ provocare non erubuit, ponens inter alia verba hæc fere thrasonica: Si præstitero cœlos esse, divos esse, Christum esse, fidem esse, causam obtinui: hic non animosus ero? Occidi quidem possum, superari non possum. Pari impudentia Jesuwitas ante Colloquium Ratisbonense scriptitasse legimus*: The Prædicantes should come, if they had a heart in their body, they would catch them alive; if they would bring a syllogism, which is in Bocardo, they would throw it at one's head and say it was in Bocallo." FÖRSTER.

19. On xxix. 7. "*Monemur hic, orandum esse pro magistratibus et non tantum iis, qui nostræ religioni addicti et veræ ecclesiæ membra, sed etiam pro iis, qui extra ecclesiam adeoque gentiles ut Nebuchadnezzar et Nero tyrannus* (2 Tim. ii. 2). *Nam ex salute reipublicæ etiam salus et incolumitas ecclesiæ constat. Et Lutherus pereleganter: Politia, inquit, servit ecclesiæ. ecclesia servat politiam.*" FÖRSTER. "*Quod pastori hoc et ovibus.*" The symbol of the Emperor Charles the Bald.

20. On xxix. 11. "God always has compassion, and His heart breaks for us (Jer. xxxi. 20), for he exercises guardianship over His elect (Wisd. iv. 15). And he knows how, in all that he does, to mitigate His justice with His mercy, so that we may see how richly His mercy is diffused over all His works; that even when He punishes, He straightway has mercy again according to His great goodness, and causes His mercy to be the more richly dispensed, because He knows our frame (Ps. ciii. 14), *viz.*, that we are flesh, a wind which passeth away and returneth not again (Ps. lxxviii. 40). CRAMER.

21. On xxix. 10, 11. "The waiting of the righteous has always something to depend upon, namely, the promise, and it is a duty to God to believe the promises, but an insult and dishonor to the name of the Lord when no faith is put in them. Is it not enough that ye injure men, will ye also insult the Lord my God? (Isa. vii. 13)." ZINZENDORF.

22. On xxix. 11. "God gives a happy ending; He also tells us beforehand, that we may honor Him by hoping; but He deals with us according to His wisdom and His righteousness, so that He chastens us as long as we need it. We cannot, therefore, do otherwise than place ourselves in His hands." DIEDRICH.

23. On xxix. 12. "Let this be firmly established among the brethren, that there is no sham about the hearing of prayer. I remember that once a great minister said across the table: My pastor wrote me that he had settled it with the dear Lord that my wife should live; I should be comforted. My wife died. Now my pastor congratulates me and says, I could now indeed see that she lived. No wonder. The Bible has a

nose of wax; and gentlemen also can explain their own words. . . . Is it then to be in vain that the Lord Jesus has said; whatever ye ask believing that ye shall receive, shall be given unto you (Mark xi. 24; John xvi. 23; Matt. vii. 7; Jas. iv. 4)? . . . Test it as often as it is necessary; ask however in faith, and doubt not. I know most assuredly that you will be heard. But I regard it as a matter for consideration, *whether* one is to ask." ZINZENDORF.

24. On xxix. 15, 16. "A heavy cross often frees us from a heavier, which would otherwise have come upon us. The best way, therefore, is to be satisfied with God's ways, who can bring good out of evil (1 Pet. iv. 19; Gen. l. 20)." STARKE.

25. On xxix. 24-32. "Those who seek their own consolation without God must be eternally deprived of the true consolation, which God grants to those who at this time humble themselves under Him. Those who preach false consolation confirm the resistance of men to the divine guidance and thus preach revolt, though intending to act conservatively. But in their blindness, they do not see what sort of a time it is." DIEDRICH.

HOMILETICAL AND PRACTICAL.

1. On xxvi. 1-24. A sermon in rebuke of the corruptions of Zion. 1. Its purport (vers. 4-6); 2. How it is received (vers. 7-11); 3. How the preacher must defend himself (vers. 12-15); 4. What the fate of the preacher will be (*a*), in the most favorable case (vers. 16-19, 24) (*b*), in the most unfavorable case (vers. 20-23).

2. On xxvii. 1-22. How the Lord's servants are to treat Politics.—1. They are to point out to the people that it is the Lord who raises and overthrows the kingdoms of this world (vers. 2-8). 2. They are to admonish the people to do what the Lord commands (vers. 12, 13). 3. They are to warn against those who speak their own thoughts to the people (vers. 9-11, 14-17). 4. They are to admonish to prayer and intercession (ver. 18 sqq).

3. On xxviii. 1-17. Of false and true prophets. 1. False prophets, (*a*) publish on their own responsibility what the people like to hear (vers. 2-4); (*b*) boldly contradict the true word of God (vers. 10 and 11); (*c*) come to shame, by the non-fulfilment of their predictions (vers. 8 and 9) and by their personal destruction (vers. 15-17). 2. True prophets (*a*) proclaim faithfully the true word of God, (*b*) fearlessly oppose the lusts of men and the lies of the false prophets; (*c*) They are honored (*α*) by the fulfilment of their prophecies, (*β*) by martyrdom, *i.e.*, honor with God and posterity.

4. On xxviii. [**This year thou shalt die.** DWIGHT:—A Sermon on the New Year.—S. R. A.]

5. On xxix. 7. The best Christians the best citizens: 1. They know that the prosperity of the whole is their own prosperity (they do not, therefore, seek selfishly their own personal advantage); 2. They actually labor with all diligence for the furtherance of the common good; 3. They employ for this end the power of Christian prayer. [A. FULLER:—Christian patriotism, or the duty of religious people towards their country. Christianity a religion of peace.—S. R. A.]

6. On xxix. 11. The thoughts of the Lord concerning us. 1. They are thoughts of peace and not of evil: 2, we must *wait* for their realization, for the Lord *delays* this, but he does not *forget* it.

7. On xxix. 11. Sermon at the funeral service of the Grand Hereditary Prince of Russia, delivered by Prof. Christiani, in Dorpat, 14 April, 1865: 1. Of the thoughts of peace which the Lord has had in this death; 2. Of the fruits and effects of these thoughts of peace.

8. On xxix. 11-14. Whereupon is our hope of peace based? 1. Objectively upon this, that the Lord Himself has thoughts of peace concerning us. 2. Subjectively on this, that we (*a*) call upon and seek the Lord with all our hearts, (*b*) patiently wait for the time of hearing.

---

10. The Book of Consolation.

A. THE TENTH DISCOURSE.

CHAPTERS XXX. and XXXI.

The close of the prophetic discourses referring to the entire Theocracy is formed by two prophecies of exclusively consolatory purport, of which, at least, the first (chh. xxx. and xxxi.) was intended to be preserved as a special writing (and only as such. Comp. rems. on xxx. 1). It is quite natural that these consolatory prophecies should form the close of the discourses; for salvation and peace will in reality be the end of God's ways.

The first of these consolatory prophecies is also the earlier in date. It is indeed one of the oldest parts of the whole book. The absence of any mention of the Chaldeans (the general "north country" occurs in xxxi. 8) is a sure sign of its composition before the fourth year of Jehoiakim. This discourse moreover is so closely related in its subject-matter to the second discourse (chh. iii.-vi.), the consolatory part (iii. 11-25), that we cannot but attribute it to the same period. We may indeed say that it is only a further development of the consolatory section mentioned. The relationship is seen both in general and in particulars. With respect to the first it may be remarked that Israel and Ju-

dah, here as there, form the ground of the division of the discourse, for as in iii. 6-10 *a comparison is instituted between Judah and Israel in reference to the past, and in* iii. 11-17 *to the future, first of Israel, then (with a gradual transition) of Judah, and in* iii. 18-25 *the future return of both is described, so in* ch. xxx. *the prophet directs his attention first to entire Israel, in* xxxi. 1-22 *to Ephraim alone, in* xxxi. 23-26 *to Judah, in* xxxi. 27-40 *again to both. Though Jeremiah elsewhere also (Comp. rems. on* xxx. 4) *in single intimations views the nation according to its two divisions, yet he does this nowhere in so marked a manner as in* chh. iii. *and* xxx.-xxxi.—*Further, as in* iii. 14-20 *the return of the two halves of the nation into the holy land is the basis of all further prosperity, so also in* chh. xxx. *and* xxxi. *Compare* xxx. 3, 10, 18; xxxi. 2, 8, 12, 16, 21, 23.—*As further in* iii. 21 sqq. *the return is represented as the consequence of an honest inward turning, so also in* xxxi. 18 *the sincere penitence of the people is the reason of the return graciously permitted them. It should here be especially observed that in the section* xxx. 16-22 *the prophet gives variations of the idea of* שוב *in the same way as he did in ch.* iii. *Comp.* EXEG. *rems. on* xxxi. 22. *The way also in which the penitential return is described in* xxxi. 9, 18, 19 *reminds us at many points of* iii. 21. *A series of expressions further may be specified which occur only in* chh. xxx., xxxi. *and* iii.-vi.: עשה כלה *only in* xxx. 11 and iv. 27; v. 10, 18, *and besides in* xlvi. 28, *as a quotation from* xxx. 11.—תערי *only in* xxxi. 4 *and* iv. 30. בכי ותחנונים *only in* xxxi. 9 *and* iii. 21. אב *used of Jehovah in reference to Israel only in* xxxi. 9 and iii. 19.—כיעם *only in* xxxi. 20 and iv. 19. ערב *in the sense of to be sweet only in* xxxi. 26 and vi. 20.—עצמו *of sins only in* xxx. 14, 15 and v. 6. תמררים *only in* xxxi. 15 and vi. 26.—בעל *to rule only in* xxxi. 32 and iii. 14. *We meet besides with expressions and utterances which are taken from* chh. i. and ii., *which also belong to that initial period. Thus above all* xxxi. 28 coll. i. 10, 12; xxxi. 3 coll. ii. 2; xxxi. 10 אים coll. ii. 10 (*the plural is found only in these two clauses*)—מנע *only in* xxxi. 16 and ii. 25.—*There are further many points of contact with* chh. xxii. and xxiii., *which are, however, to be explained by the use of this chapter there. For as the prophet had occasion in* xxiii. 3-8 *to deliver a glorious Messianic prophecy, it was natural that he should be thus reminded of the earlier one of similar purport. In the main point, indeed, the words referring to the person of the Messiah* (xxx. 9, 10, 21 coll. xxiii. 5, 6), *the similarity is only topical. With respect to expression, both prophecies retain their own individuality. Still in the less important points there is an agreement in expression:* xxx. 13 coll. xxii. 16; xxx. 14 coll. xxii. 20, 22; xxx. 16 coll. xxii. 22; xxx. 5, 6 coll. xxii. 23.—*With respect to the verses* xxx. 28, 24, *consult the Exposition.*
On account of the undeniable specific relationship, which exists between the present chapters and the second discourse (chh. iii.-vi.), especially the consolatory portion (ch. iii.), *I am convinced that* chh. xxx. and xxxi. *owe their origin to the same time, the reign of Josiah* (comp. iii. 6).
With the exception of xxx. 22-24, *I cannot discover any spurious elements in these chapters.* MOVERS and HITZIG *have thought they could repeatedly recognize the hand of the assumed Isaiah II., but have been so satisfactorily refuted by* GRAF, *that I now only refer to him.* GRAF *himself regards* xxxi. 35-40 *as a latter addition. I think, however, that I have shown in the Exposition that these verses fit into the connection as integral parts, and that therefore, as the diction betrays no foreign traces, they are to be recognized as genuine and original.*
The articulation of the discourse is as follows:—
The glorious Future of the People Israel at the end of days.
I. THE THEME, xxx. 1-3.
II. THE DELIVERANCE OF ENTIRE ISRAEL, xxx. 4-22.
1. *The great day of judgment of the world and deliverance of Israel,* xxx. 4-11.
2. *The turn of affairs: The Lord for the chastised, against the chastiser,* xxx. 12-17.
3. *The consummation of salvation,* xxx. 18-22.
III. THE SPECIAL DISTRIBUTION OF SALVATION TO THE TWO HALVES OF THE NATION, xxxi. 1-26.
   a. Ephraim's share, xxxi. 1-22.
   1. *The decree of restoration,* xxxi. 1-6.
   2. *Its execution,* xxxi. 7-14.
   3. *The threefold turn,* xxxi. 15-22.
   b. Judah's share.
   The blessing of the sanctuary, xxxi. 23-26.
IV. THE ENTIRE RENEWAL, xxxi. 27-40.
1. *The new life,* xxxi. 27-30.
2. *The new covenant,* xxxi. 31-40.

The Glorious Future of the People Israel at the End of Days.

I. The Theme.

XXX. 1-3.

1, 2   The word that came to Jeremiah from the Lord [Jehovah] saying, Thus speaketh the Lord [Jehovah] God of Israel, saying, Write thee all the words that I

3 have spoken unto thee in a book. For [Namely] lo, the days come, saith the Lord [Jehovah], that I will bring again the captivity of my people Israel, and Judah, saith the Lord [Jehovah]; and will cause them to return to the land that I gave to their fathers, and they shall possess it.

EXEGETICAL AND CRITICAL.

The superscription is one of the greater sort. It pertains to chh. xxx. and xxxi., a similar one not recurring till xxxii. 1. Jeremiah had certainly received this prophecy before, as follows from the words that I have spoken in ver. 2. Nevertheless ver. 1 is not merely the announcement of what is said in vers. 2 and 3, as Hitzig su; poses, but the superscription of the oracle, for such superscriptions always stand as the introduction to the larger sections. As it here introduces the command to write and what is to be written directly follows (ver. 4 sqq.), the superscription refers to both. J. D. MICHAELIS is of opinion that we have here the *expressum mandatum* to collect the prophecies into a book, and that this is the first book, which closes with ch. xxxii. The Paralipomena, collected after the dea h of Jeremiah, form the second book. It is plain, however, that this view is altogether untenable, for this, apart from other reasons, that in vers. 2, 3 and 4 the command to write is referred to the next following prophecy, as SCHNURRER has already proved against MICHAELIS. These chapters also cannot be parts of that book which Jeremiah was caused to write in the fourth year of Jehoiakim (xxxvi. 2). For this book, according to xxxvi. 6 sqq., was intended to be read to the people, that they might hear "all the evil which the Lord purposed to do with them, that they might return every man from his evil way and the Lord might forgive them," so that it appears merely to have contained an exhortation and threatening. This also explains the great displeasure occasioned by it. It was cut into pieces from the first to the last leaf and cast into the fire (xxxvi. 23), which was certainly not the case with these chapters. Even ROSENMUELLER calls attention to the circumstance that Jeremiah here (xxx. 2) receives the command, "*non, ut ante concionem habere et quæ ab eo sint annuntianda ad populum per sermonem deferre, sed libro inscribere.*" This prophecy was not to be delivered orally, but merely committed to writing, just as the prophecy against Babylon (li. 60 sqq.). The people were not then in the mood to hear these great booming predictions of salvation. These were to be bequeathed as written documents, that on the one hand they might serve to encourage the people in their deepest distress, and on the other hand it might be evident that the Lord and no other had brought about this favorable turn in their affairs (Isa. xlviii. 5), but also, that the Lord had not afterwards altered His purpose, but already in the times of the deepest decline, when the people were receiving only threatening words from the mouth of the prophet, He had conceived and made known the plan of salvation. Comp. Isa. xxx. 8; Job ii. 2. The prophecy was thus presented separately and only afterwards incorporated into the entire collection. It does not seem probable to me, as

GRAF thinks, that it was included in the second enlarged book (xxxvi. 32). The words in xxxvi. 27 sqq. make throughout the impression that the second book in relation to the first contained only a heightened repetition. Nor can we see why, if these chapters are portions of a larger book, they alone should bear at their head the special command to write them down. This command must either be found before all the single portions or only where the origin of the whole is mentioned. The special command to commit to writing which we find here (xxx. 2) shows that here also we have to do with a special independent writing.

Ver. 3. **For lo.** The construction seems to require כִּי to be taken in a causal sense, for it would be somewhat harsh to take it in the sense of "that," or "namely," on account of the following הִנֵּה and ׳ נְאֻם, which seems rather to require לֵאמֹר before it. On the other hand, the causal rendering also has its difficulties. For then in ver. 3 the main point is not expressed in the statement of the reason, *viz.*: the Lord wishes that when the good days come He may be able to point to the documentary evidence of His purpose of salvation, as a proof of His being the author of the present prosperity. This thought would have still to be supplied, while the words as they stand evidently state only the purport of *the words,* ver. 2. It will therefore be correct here to take כִּי = "that" or "namely," in the sense in which לֵאמֹר, saying, occurs elsewhere. This latter word would not be suitable after in **a book,** because it would have meant that the purport of what was to be written in the book was to be stated, whereas it is the tenor of the words already spoken which is to be quoted summarily. This was necessary in order to define the general phrase **all the words,** which was liable to be misunderstood. Hence I think that כִּי is to be taken here as introducing the direct statement, which radically also is used only for the more common לֵאמֹר. Comp. NAEGELSB. *Gr.,* § 1:19, 1 *a*. The original act of speaking itself is certainly not related here, but the purport of a discourse already delivered is quoted, by which the כִּי obtains the somewhat modified (explicative) meaning of *namely*. The words from הִנֵּה to וִירֻשָׁה are therefore to be regarded as a quotation. Hence הִנֵּה and ׳ נְאֻם. They are not found *verbatim* as a whole in the following chapters or anywhere in Jeremiah; but they are an accurate synopsis of the words and thoughts which form the heads of the following promise of prosperity. For in ver. 18 sqq : xxxi 27-32, the return of the whole people of Israel to their home is represented as the close of the mournful past and the basis of a new and glorious future. Comp iii. 14-18.—On **bring again the captivity** comp. Comm. on xxix. 14.—["The four following chapters display a beautiful contrast to the former denunciations of judgment and captivity for sin are here succeeded by promises of mercy and restoration to Jerusalem—promises to be fulfilled in the bringing back of all true Israelites to God by the Divine Deliverer and Redeemer, JESUS CHRIST. The joyful transition is marked by a sudden change from grave and mournful accents in solemn prose, to a jubilant outburst of poetic ecstasy." WORDSWORTH.—S. R. A.]

II. The Deliverance of Entire Israel (xxx. 4-22).

1. *The great day of judgment of the world and deliverance of Israel.*

XXX. 4-11.

4 And these are the words which Jehovah hath spoken concerning[1] Israel and concerning Judah:
5 For thus saith Jehovah:
 We have heard a cry of terror,[2]
 Fear and no deliverance.
6 Ask ye now and see if a male is parturient?
 Why do I then see every man with his hands on his hips like a parturient,
 And all faces turned into paleness?[3]
7 Alas! for great is that day, with none like it,[4]
 And it will be a time of trouble to Jacob,
 But—he shall be delivered from it.
8 And it shall come to pass on that day, saith Jehovah Zebaoth,
 I will break his yoke off from thy neck,
 And I will tear asunder thy bonds,
 And strangers shall no longer enslave him :[5]
9 But they shall serve Jehovah their God,
 And David their king, whom I will raise up[6] for them.
10 But fear thou not, my servant Jacob, saith Jehovah,
 And be not dismayed, O Israel.
 For behold, I will deliver thee from afar,
 And thy seed from the land of their captivity ;
 And Jacob shall return and rest,
 And be tranquil and undisturbed.
11 For I am with thee to deliver thee, saith Jehovah.
 Though I make a full end[7] of all the nations,
 Whither I have scattered them,
 I will not make an end of thee ;
 But I will chastise thee according to justice,
 And not leave thee unpunished.

TEXTUAL AND GRAMMATICAL.

[1] Ver. 4.—אֶל=in reference to, of, concerning, as in xxix. 16, 21; xxii. 11.

[2] Ver. 5.—קוֹל חֲרָדָה. חֲרָדָה is found here only in Jeremiah. The terror is not occasioned by the sound of war, but the apprehension of judgment. Comp. Luke xxi. 25, 26.

[3] Ver. 6.—לְיֵרָקוֹן. Abstr. for concrete. Comp. NAEGELSB. *Gr.*, § 59, 1. The expression is found here only.

[4] Ver. 7.—כְּאַיִן. Comp. rems. on x. 6, 7; NAEGELSB. *Gr.*, § 106, 5.

[5] Ver. 8.—The words from וְהָיָה to וְאָרַךְ are a quotation almost verbatim from Isa. x. 27 coll. xiv. 25. This explains the suffix in עֻלּוֹ, which, as the passage in Isaiah, is to be referred to the inimical tyrants. If, with GNAF, we refer it to יַעֲקֹב, ver. 7, וְאֵת immediately afterwards is intolerably harsh. It is true the person changes in בּוֹ יַעַבְדוּ, yet this is at least a new sentence, in which case the change has nothing surprising in it. Comp. NAEGELSB. *Gr.*, § 101, 2, *Anm.*

[6] Ver. 9.—אָקִים is used here in the same sense as in vi. 17; xxiii. 4, etc.

7 Ver. 11.—אִישׁ כָּלֹה. This expression is found in Jeromiah (besides in xlvi. 28, as a quotation from this passage) only in iv. 27; v. 10, 18. The construction with the accus. is the prevailing and original construction: Nah. i. 8, 9; Zeph. i. 18; Ezek. xi. 13; xx. 17; Neh. ix. 31. With בְּ it is found here only. It appears to signify in this connection: to cause destruction among, etc.

EXEGETICAL AND CRITICAL.

What was summarily comprised in ver. 2 is now set forth in detail (ver. 4). Cry of terror, fear without a possibility of deliverance (ver. 5); all the men have their hands on their thighs like women in travail, all faces have become pale (ver. 6), for the great day of the Lord, a day with none like it, is breaking, a day which will be a time of dread even for Jacob, but yet at the same time the day of redemption (ver. 6), for on this day an end is to be put to Israel's servitude (ver. 8). Israel is from thenceforward to serve only his God and his king David (ver. 9), Judah and Israel are then to be brought back from the lands of their captivity to a peaceful habitation of their home (ver. 10), for while the Lord will execute on all the Gentiles a judgment of destruction, He will indeed chastise Israel so as not to leave him unpunished, but will not destroy him.

Vers. 4-7. **And these ... delivered from it.** Apart from some brief intimations (ix. 25; xi. 10-17; xiii. 11; xxiii. 6; l. 4) the prophet makes Israel and Judah, the two great halves of the Israelitish nation, the subject of his longer discourses, only here (ver. 3; xxxi. 27), and in the second discourse (chs. iii.-vi.), which belongs to the time of Josiah.—Ver. 5. This **for,** which is logically indeed superfluous but not incorrect (ver. 4 announces the *entirety* of the following discourse as God's word and כִּי, ver. 5, introduces the particulars), has rhetorically the character of a certain solemn breadth. With dramatic vividness the prophet transports us into the midst of the future, which he describes, causing those who are concerned to be the speakers together with himself. It is clear that the day of terror which he describes cannot be the day of Jerusalem (Ps. cxxxvii. 7). For (1) the day of the destruction of Jerusalem by the Chaldeans cannot be represented as at the same time a day of salvation for all Israel; (2) "the great day of the Lord like which there is no other" always designates the divine judgment in its highest and most comprehensive sense. For even when Joel, who is the first to speak of the great and fearful days (ii. 11), understands by it primarily the day of the devastation by locusts, he yet beholds in this special act only the first act of the great drama of judgments (iii. 4), with which he first connects the idea of the redemption and restoration of Israel (iv. 1, 7). After him Hosea speaks of the great day of Jezreel (ii. 2), on which Judah and Israel will return again united under their common head. Afterwards the judicial activity of God is mirrored before the eyes of Isaiah in the judgment on Babylon (xiii. 6), the return of the whole people being again connected with it (xiv. 1 sqq.). Next before Jeremiah finally, the idea of the "day of the Lord" forms the central point of Zephaniah's prophecy, and if he also understands primarily by the "great day" (i. 14) the day of the judgment of Jerusalem, yet he also regards all the judicial acts of God as elements or stages of the whole, and to him also the consummation of the judgment is the turning-point of the deliverance and restoration of all Israel (iii. 10 sqq.; 20). After Jeremiah there is Malachi only who speaks in express words of "the great and dreadful day of the Lord" (iv. 5).—**No deliverance.** Comp. vi. 14; viii. 11; Ezek. vii. 25; xiii. 10, 16.—**Ask now,** *etc.* Comp. xviii. 13. The prophet portrays with drastic vividness the effects of the terror by saying that he saw men behaving like women in the pangs of childbirth—pressing their hands on their loins. Comp. Isa. xxi. 3; Jer. vi. 24; xxii. 28; xlix. 24; l. 43.—**That day.** From that (הַהוּא) we see (1) that the prophet means a day not immediately impending, but (2) the same as was spoken of in vers. 5 and 6.—**And it will be a time of trouble,** *etc.* Israel also is not unaffected by the sufferings of that time (comp. Matth. xxiv. 21, 22); but for them it is only a crisis, which leads to salvation.

Vers. 8 and 9. **And it shall come to pass ... raise up for them.** The deliverance announced in the concluding words of ver. 7 is described more particularly. It has its negative and its positive side. The nation will no longer serve strangers (ver. 8) but their God alone, the King graciously given by God, the Messiah (ver. 9).—**Thy bonds.** Comp. ii. 20; v. 5.—**Enslave.** Comp. xxvii. 7; xxv. 14.—**Serve Jehovah.** For Israel to serve his God is at the same time his first duty and the fundamental condition of salvation. This salvation is to be communicated by the anointed of the Lord, the second David. The Messiah is called David, not merely as a descendant of David still called by his name, but as a real David in the highest degree. As David was the founder of the earthly throne of David, so the Messiah as the fulfiller is the founder and occupant of the eternal throne of David. Jeremiah supports himself here chiefly on Hos. iii. 5, coll. Isa. lv. 3, while after him Ezekiel (xxxiv. 23, 24; xxxvii. 24, 25) leans on his predecessors, especially Jeremiah. The conception of the second David is analogous to that of the second Adam (1 Cor. xv. 45 sqq.) It is therefore altogether different from the Rabbinical doctrine of a double Messiah, Ben Joseph and Ben David, (comp. OEHLER in HERZOG, *Real.-Enc.,* IX. *S.* 440; BUXTORF *Lex.,* p. 1273) with which HAEVERNICK seems (*Comm. on Ezek., S.* 557) to confound the Christian conception. It is accordingly clear that we must protest against the lower view, that Jeremiah is here speaking of a Davidic dynasty (SANCTIUS), or of Zerubbabel (GNOTIUS; *is David vocatur et hic et Ezech.* xxxiv. 23; xxxvii. 24, *nimirum sicut a Ptolemæo orti Ptolemæi, a Cæsare Cæsares*), or indeed of a personally resuscitated David (V. AMMON, *Fortd. d. Chr.* I., *S.* 178; STRAUSS, *Glaubensl.* II., *S.* 80). This latter conception is imputed by HITZIG to Ezekiel (*ad loc. S.* 245) as having thus interpreted the אָקִים of Jeremiah. As to the rest comp. Comm. on ver. 21 and xxiii. 5; HENGSTENBERG, *Christol.* [*Eng. Tr.* II., p. 413 sqq.]

Vers. 10 and 11. **But fear thou not .. unpunished.** GRAF has called attention to the circumstance that these words are addressed to the people living in exile " in opposition to those delivered in ver. 9." More strictly we should say, that vers. 8 and 9 announce the salvation objectively (whence also Israel is spoken of predominantly in the 3d person), but in ver. 10 the subjective application follows in the exhortation to be comforted and not to fear, but yet with a repetition of the objective basis. It is not however to be denied that the adversative rendering "thou however" is not appropriate. MEIER translates "so fear thou nothing," evidently not accurately, but in the correct feeling that the connection requires an inferential rather than an adversative sentence. Comp. Isa. xliv. 1, 2, which passage certainly occurred to the prophet, the words " fear not my servant Jacob " being taken from it verbatim, and we are thus led to think that instead of וְאַתָּה here we should read יַעֲקֹב) with which the passage in Isa. commences. The latter certainly would correspond better with the connection. HITZIG and MOVERS find in these two verses the idiom of Isaiah II., and would therefore regard it as an interpolation by him. GRAF however has satisfactorily shown that with the exception of the expression עבדי יעקב (I say, with the exception of " אל־תירא) all the rest betrays the older, and specifically Jeremiah's, idiom. Why should not that evident quotation from Isa. xliv. 2 be just as good an instance for the priority of the alleged Isaiah II. in relation to the genuine Jeremiah? The union of Judah and Israel, which is here spoken of from ver. 3 onwards, may have reminded the prophet of that passage in Isaiah, which declares this union. Other declarations of Isaiah, as li. 7, may also have been in the mind of our prophet. Perhaps also passages like xlix. 12; lx. 4, 9.—**Rest and be tranquil.** Comp. xlviii. 11.—**Undisturbed.** Comp. rems. on vii. 33.—**For I am with thee.** Comp. xv. 20; xlii. 11.—**Chastise thee.** The expression is found in x. 24 in the same sense. Whether in Isa. xxviii. 26 also is disputable. On ל comp. NAEGELSB. *Gr.*, § 112, 5, *b*.—**And not leave thee,** *etc.* From Exod. xxxiv. 7; the expression is found in Numb. xiv. 18. in Nah. i. 3. and here.—Comp. further xlvi. 27, 28, where these two verses are reproduced.

---

2. *The turn of affairs: the Lord for the chastised and against the chastiser.*

XXX. 12–17.

12 For thus saith Jehovah, thy wound is incurable,[1]
Mortal thy stroke.
13 There is no one who undertaketh thy case,
For thy wound thou hast no remedies of bandages.[2]
14 All thy lovers have forgotten thee;
They ask not after thee;
For I have smitten them with the stroke of an enemy,
With cruel chastisement for the greatness of thy guilt;
Because thy sins are innumerable.[3]
15 Why criest thou over thy wound,
That thy sorrow is incurable?[4]
Because of the greatness of thy guilt,
Because thy sins are innumerable, I have done this.
16 Therefore all who devour thee shall be devoured,
And all thy oppressors shall go awa꜡ together into captivity.
And they that spoil thee[5] shall be a spoil,
And all thy plunderers will I give up to plunder.
17 For I will restore health unto thee,
And I will heal thee of thy wounds, saith Jehovah;
For they call thee " Outcast,"
" Zion, which no man asketh after."

TEXTUAL AND GRAMMATICAL.

[1] Ver. 12.—The construction of אָנוּשׁ with ל is found here only. Perhaps Nah. iii. 19 was in the prophet's mind. The thought lying at the basis of this construction is: *insanabile vulneri tuo*, or more exactly: incurable is the predicate which belongs to your wound.

[2] Ver. 13.—As כִּי does not agree with הֵינָךְ, I refer it, with GRAF, to what follows, in the sense of *rubtus* (that which is wrapped in bandages, as in Hos. v. 13, רְפֻאוֹת תְּעָלָה = *medicamenta ligaminis*, dressings. Comp. xlvi. 11; Ezek.

CHAP. XXX. 18-24.

xxx. 21. [A. V.: There is none to plead thy cause, that thou mayest be bound up. Others render: for thy cure thou hast, etc. HENDERSON: "I take רְפֻאוֹת to be a nominative absolute; as for medicines."—S. R. A.]
² Ver. 14.—Here as afterwards in ver. 15, a whole sentence is twice dependent on כִּי. (Comp. NAEGELSB. Gr., § 112, 9).
⁴ Ver. 15.—[A. V.: Why criest thou for thine affliction? Thy sorrow is incurable. WORDSWORTH after EWALD, UMBREIT, GRAF: Why criest thou for thine affliction, that thy sorrow is incurable.—S. R. A.]
⁵ Ver. 16.—שֹׁאסָיִךְ. The Chethibh is to be punctuated שֹׁאֲסַיִךְ. Since the root שׁאס does not occur in Hebrew, this form is to be explained as an Aramaism for שׁכב, Keri שֹׁסַיִךְ (I. 11; Isa. xvii. 14).

EXEGETICAL AND CRITICAL.

This whole strophe is most closely connected with ver. 11, and explains the three thoughts expressed in this verse: that Zion is chastised according to its deserts, but is not to be destroyed, while destruction shall be the lot of its enemies. Thus vers. 12-15 are a commentary on the words "chastise thee according to justice" in ver. 11. For it is here set forth that Israel is given over to severe sickness without a protector and physician (vers. 12 and 13), that all friends have forsaken the people so severely chastised by God, (ver. 14), which people moreover have no right to complain of such treatment, for the Lord has done this on account of their sins (ver. 15). The sentence therefore, etc. (ver. 16), refers back to the declaration in the 11th verse that the Lord will make an utter end of the nations, among whom He scattered Israel. The right of retribution is to be exercised on them in the fullest measure. Ver. 17 finally is connected with the third point in ver. 11, viz., that Israel is to be healed of his wounds after he has been apparently outcast and forgotten.

Vers. 12-15. For thus saith Jehovah ... I have done this.—For introduces the proof that Israel will not really be left unpunished, but will be severely chastised, so that he will only not be utterly destroyed.—Mortal thy stroke. Comp. x. 19; xiv. 17. Ver. 13. There is no one, etc. Comp. v. 28; xxii. 16.—Thy lovers. Comp. xxii. 20, 22.—For ... stroke of an enemy. When a man is forsaken by God his fellow-men also forsake him.—For the greatness, etc. In these and the following words to the end of ver. 15 lies the confirmation of according to justice, ver. 11—v. 6; xiii. 22.—Why criest thou? Israel has no right to complain of severe treatment. The Lord deals with him "according to justice," ver. 11.

Ver. 16. Therefore all .. give up to plunder.—Therefore has no sense if we refer it to

what immediately precedes. For it cannot be said that the enemies are to be destroyed, because the Lord has punished His people according to the greatness of their guilt. For if only strict justice prevailed, Israel deserved the same punishment as, or even severer punishment than the heathen. Comp. ii. 10 sqq. I therefore refer Therefore to ver. 11, to which this whole passage is only a corollary, and particularly to the words Though I make a full end of all the nations, etc. Israel's guilt is in the past, and cause of the present calamity, hence for in ver. 12. The destruction of the heathen is future, and the effect of the judgment pronounced by God in ver. 11, hence therefore, ver. 16.—All who devour thee. Comp. rems. on ii. 3; x. 25.—Go away together, etc. Comp. xxii. 22.—Shall be a spoil. Comp. Zeph. i. 13; 2 Ki. xxi. 14.—To plunder. Comp. ii. 14.

Ver. 17. For I will restore ... asketh after. This sentence also refers to ver. 11, and to the words Will not make an end of thee. The Lord will not utterly destroy Israel, for He has in mind to heal the people of the blows to which they have been exposed.—I will restore, etc. Comp. rems. on viii. 22.—For they call. The statement of the reason refers here to the thought that Israel needed healing.—Outcast. Comp. Isa. xvi. 3, 4; Mic. iv. 6; Zeph. iii. 19.—Zion, etc., a sentence of the object, dependent on a verbum dicendi contained in call.—Which no man asketh after = ea, quam nemo curat.

[Vers. 12-15. "So desperate were the circumstances of the Jews in Babylon while enduring the punishment God had inflicted upon them for their crimes, that no human interposition which they would naturally expect, could avail for their deliverance. Egypt, Syria, Tyre, etc., which had formerly been their confederates, were all laid prostrate by the same haughty conqueror whose chains they themselves wore. They are accordingly represented under the metaphor of a body full of wounds, left entirely destitute of medical aid." HENDERSON.—S. R. A.]

3. *The consummation of Salvation.*

XXX. 18-24.

18 Thus saith Jehovah,
   Behold, I will turn the captivity of Jacob's tents[1]
   And have mercy on his dwelling-places;
   And [the] city[2] shall be built on its own heap,[3] [of ruins]
   And the palace shall be inhabited according to its right.[4]
19 And out of them shall proceed thanksgiving,

And the voice of them that rejoice;
And I will increase them, and they shall not be diminished,
And honor them, and they shall not be small.
20 Their children also shall be as aforetime,
And their congregation shall be established before me;
And I will punish all their oppressors.
21 And their ruler shall be of themselves,
And their prince shall proceed from the midst of them;
And I will bring him near and he shall approach me,
For who is he, who would have pledged his heart to approach me? saith Jehovah.
22 And ye shall be my people,
And I will be your God.
23 Behold, a tempest of Jehovah, fury is loose,
Whirl-winds[5]—it will roll on the head of the ungodly.
24 The fierceness of Jehovah's anger will not return,
Till he do and execute the plans of his heart.
In the end of days ye will consider it.

TEXTUAL AND GRAMMATICAL.

[1] Ver. 18.—אֹהֶל, poetical for house. Comp. iv. 20; 1 Kings viii. 66; Job xxi. 8.

[2] Ver. 18.—עִיר, without the article, therefore not the city κατ᾽ ἐξοχήν, i. e., Jerusalem, but the city generally, that is, any city.

[3] Ver. 18.—עַל־תִּלָּהּ. The prophet has evidently Deut. xiii. 16 in view, where it is said of a city on which a curse is laid, that it shall be burned and shall be עוֹלָם תֵּל, *it shall not be built again*. Comp. Josh. viii. 28; xi. 13; Jer. xlix. 2. We see from this that תֵּל is the heap of rubbish formed by the ruined city.

[4] Ver. 18.—יַל־מִשְׁפָּטוֹ יֵשֵׁב. Hitzig: The palace will stand in its proper place. Graf [and Henderson]: shall be inhabited in its proper place. Both say that *after an appropriate manner* would be כְּמִשְׁפָּטוֹ. But the phrase may also mean *according to its right.* Comp. Deut. xvii. 11.—יֵשֵׁב is more than stand. It is here used intransitively as in xvii. 6, 25; Isa. xiii. 20; Ezek. xxvi. 20; Zech. vii. 7 (comp. Nägelsb. *Gr.*, § 69, 1), but the meaning of *inhabit* remains. If, however, we take the phrase *upon, in its place*, then the idea of *inhabit* is superfluous, as Hitzig has rightly felt. I therefore consider "it will be inhabited as becomes it," as the correct rendering. A palace will not be inhabited as a beggar's hut. The prophet wrote עַל, through occasion of עַל־תִּלָּהּ, but the second עַל must not therefore be regarded as being as local in signification as the first.

[5] Ver. 23.—Instead of כְּתְחוֹלֵל, xxiii. 9, we read here כְּתְגוֹרֵר by which the paronomasia with יָתְגַּל is destroyed. The forcible בִּינָה at the close is also wanting. As to מִתְגּוֹרֵר, this Hithp. occurs only here and in Hos. vii. 14 and 1 Kings xvii. 20. In Hosea the meaning "to alarm one's self," is most recommended, in 1 Kings xvii. that of "*commorari*" is necessarily required by the connection. In this passage the commentators vacillate greatly; *an abiding storm* (Hengstenberg); *a rolling storm* from גָּרַר, *gurgarisare* (Meier); *turbo cuncta abripiens* from גָּרַר, *rapere*, (Gesen. *Thes.*, p. 306); a whirling storm, from נָגַר—גָלַל *volvere*. The last meaning would come nearest the original כְּתְחוֹלֵל. Comp. Fuerst, s. v., גּוּר, III. and גָּרַר.

EXEGETICAL AND CRITICAL.

The restored nation will in every respect present the picture of a flourishing commonwealth. The ruined dwellings will be rebuilt (ver. 18), praise and rejoicing will be heard from them, the number of the inhabitants and the honor of the State will be great (ver. 19); the latter will regain its former importance and preserve it, but all its oppressors shall be chastised (ver. 20); the ruler of the State shall no more be a stranger, but a native, who will at the same time stand in the closest relation to Jehovah (ver. 21); the people will be God's people, and the Lord his people's God (ver. 22). All this, however, applies only to the Israel which submits to the Lord. The day of the Lord will break upon the ungodly (vers. 5–7) like a tempest and destroy them (vers. 23 and 24).

Vers. 18–20. **Thus saith Jehovah . . . oppressors.** It is evident that the phrase **turn the captivity** may be taken here in a figurative sense, from its application to the ruined buildings. Comp. rems. on xxix. 4.—Graf refers **out of them**, ver. 19, to the allies, Hitzig to the palaces, but in the sense that he regards the Israelites as the subject of the egression, in the sense of xxxi. 4, 13; xxxiii. 10, 11.—The latter could not well be excluded. But why should not the sound of sacred joy be heard from the dwellings of Israel in any sense, and therefore in the sense, that it proceeds from those who are within? This is at the same time a further adornment of the houses themselves, to which, in a collective sense, **out of them** is to be referred. These thus become, as it were, instruments of sacred music.—Isa. li. 3.—**Of them that rejoice.** Comp. xv. 17; xxxi. 4.—**Diminished.** Comp. xxix. 6.—**As aforetime.** As formerly "*sub Davide et Salomone rerum statu florentissimo.*" Rosenmueller. Comp. Ps. lxxiv. 2; Lam. v. 21.—**Their congregation.** Comp. 2 Sam. vii. 10; Ps. cii. 29; Prov. xvi. 12; 1 Kings ii. 12.

Vers. 21 and 22. **And their ruler . . . your**

God. The description of the glorious future is crowned by the declaration of the relation of the prince to Jehovah. He is called מֶלֶךְ, king, in ver. 9, here אַדִּיר, ruler, and מֹשֵׁל, prince. This is not a low predicate, as J. D. MICHAELIS supposes, but a high one. For not every king may be thus called. There are counterfeit kings (Eccles. iv. 13; x. 16). This king, however, is a אַדִּיר, a predicate which is given to the King of all kings (Ps. viii. 2, 10; xciii. 4), and מֹשֵׁל for the מִשְׂרָה is on his shoulder (Isa. ix. 5), and the key of David (Isa. xxii. 22), that he may open and no man shut, and shut and no man open. Comp. Mic. v. 1. This powerful ruler is of Israel's flesh and blood, no foreigner, no representative of the empire hostile to God's people. And not merely is this declared, but also that proceeding from the midst of the people, he may approach unto Jehovah. The mediatorial position of the king is here announced.—**Him** after **bring** refers to the king. HITZIG has correctly remarked that altogether too little would be said of the king if his Israelitish origin merely were set forth, but besides this negative reason, we have also in our rendering of מִכְּנוּ **from themselves**, and מִקִּרְבּוֹ **from their midst**, a positive necessity of referring the suffix to the king. Ὁ μεσίτης ἑνὸς οὐκ ἐστιν, Gal. iii. 20. He proceeds from the midst of the people and approaches God. An intimation has been rightly found in **bring near** and **approach** of priestly attributes (Exod. xxiv. 2; Numb. xvi. 5). The sentence with **For** states the reason why the Lord leads the prince to Himself. The reason is a negative one; there is no other who would be capable of entering into this relation of nearness and communion to God. All here depends especially on the correct understanding of the expression עָרַב אֶת־לִבּוֹ, **pledge his heart**. The verb עָרַב, with the accusative, may signify two things only. Either "to stand, be a surety for some one, to vouch, guarantee" (comp. Gen. xliii. 9 coll. xliv. 32. עָרַב זָר *spopondit pro alieno*, Prov. xi. 15; xx. 16; xxvii. 13 coll. Job xvii. 3; Isa. xxxviii. 14), or "to pledge something." For the latter meaning we can appeal only to Neh. v. 3. The meanings "*applicare* (Vulg.), *convertere* (Syr.), *lubentem reddere* (so in sense the LXX., Chald. and others), *accommodare, formare* (CALVIN)," have no grammatical basis, and are all occasioned by לִבּוֹ. If we adhere to the two meanings which are proved, the second, as we have shown, rests only in the authority of one passage in the book of Nehemiah. It is not, however, to be used directly, but the meaning must first be derived from it "to stake, risk, venture." לֵב **heart**, must then be taken as=נֶפֶשׁ, soul, life. GRAF has adduced analogies in favor of this (iv. 18 coll. iv. 10; Exod. ix. 14; Ps. lxxxiv. 3 coll. xvi. 9; xxxi. 10; lxiii. 2), but of these only the first is of consequence, and even these passages only prove that the *physical* heart may also be designated as the him of the sword which is threatening the life. There may be other cases where the connection allows *the heart* to be set for *the life*, but this is not the case here. Every one feels that here to say "heart" for "life," would be harsh. I therefore think that we must take עָרַב in the sense of "to be bail, to stand for another." We should then have to translate: for who stands bail for his heart, to approach to me? Ought we to take לֵב in the sense of "courage" as HITZIG does? There are passages where it gets this meaning from the context (Gen. xlii. 28; 1 Sam. xvii. 32; 2 Sam. vii. 27; xvii. 10; Job xli. 15), but this is not its direct meaning. I think then that it must be taken here in its general sense as the seat of *moral volition*. The prophet wishes to say: Who can stand for his heart, that it approach me? and this can certainly be taken in the sense; that it has the will, the power, the courage, to approach me? The point of the thought is evidently in the antithesis, *bring him* and *pledge his heart, i. e.*, between the divine causality and human spontaneity. No man can undertake to be a mediator between God and man in his own strength. For if one should even have the courage to begin this difficult undertaking, he cannot vouch for himself that he will have the power to carry it out. The nearer the man came to the glory of God, the lower would his courage fall. God alone confers the power to approach him, and he will confer it on him whom he has chosen to be a mediator. In so far now as approaching God is represented as something unattainable by human strength, it is clear that the prophet has not the ordinary priests' approaching to God in mind. The answer to the question: Who is he who would give his heart as surety, to approach me?—must evidently be: No one. Now not every Israelite indeed, but every normally created member of the priestly or high priestly family would be justified and authorized to approach God as a priest in the sense of the Mosaic law. Even these, however, are excluded by the *no one*, which the question requires as answer. Consequently the promised mediator can only be an extraordinary personage. Our text gives no further information, as to *how* the divine causality renders it possible for him to approach God, for this may be done in different ways, from without or from within, in a mechanical or an organic way.

Ver. 22. **And ye**, etc. The thought certainly accords well with ver. 21, since the inward communion between God and the people, which is predicted in ver. 22, is not otherwise possible, even in view of the question, **For who is he?** *etc.*, than by a mediator; it is however the necessary glorious result of his ministry (comp. Heb. viii). Since, however, vers. 23 and 24 are decidedly to be regarded as a late addition (*Vid. infra,*) the thought of our verse appears to be repeated immediately afterwards in xxxi. 1. Such a repetition of these words in immediate sequence is indeed surprising, but not impossible. Since in both instances the words are highly appropriate, in the first as the close of the prophecy relating to the whole, in the second as the beginning of that relating to the first main division, and since further in xxxi. 1 the inversion of the clauses of the sentence is designed to avoid monotony, I regard it as probable that the words are authentic in both instances. If they are to be accounted spurious in one case, I would vindicate the genuineness of xxxi. 1, since here they occur in a characteristic setting. Observe the words **to all the families of Israel**, which evidently correspond to **concerning Israel and concerning Judah**, xxxi. 4, and give xxxi. 1 the appearance of being a superscription to the following section.

Vers. 23 and 24. **Behold, a tempest ... consider it.** The words are repeated with slight variations from xxiii. 19, 20. As chh. xxx. and xxxi. belong to the reign of Josiah (iii. G. Comp. *Introd.*), and the prophecy, xxiii. 9-40, from which our verses are taken, cannot have originated before the first four years of Jehoiakim, it is clear that verses 23 and 24 cannot have stood originally in this place. Did then Jeremiah himself add them subsequently? I do not regard this as probable, since the words do not corresspond to the general character of these chapters. These contain only a prediction of salvation; they represent the brightest and most joyful, we might say, the only untroubled moment in Jeremiah's life (comp. on xxxi. 26). The verses 23 and 24 accordingly have the effect of a dissonance. Whence, in such a time as the prophet describes, are רְשָׁעִים **whirl-winds** to come (comp. xxxi. 18, 19)? And what thoughts of anger is Jehovah to carry out at a time when He has already turned the captivity of His people? I regard it as not impossible that some later writer thought himself compelled to separate the essentially equivalent words in xxx. 22 and xxxi. 1 by sentences which he deemed appropriate.

III. The Special Distribution of Salvation to the Two Halves of the Nation
(xxxi. 1-26).

a. EPHRAIM'S SHARE (xxxi. 1-22).

1. *The Decree of Restoration.*

XXXI. 1-6.

1 At that time, saith Jehovah, I will be God to all the families of Israel,
  And they shall be my people.
2 Thus saith Jehovah; the people left of the sword has found grace in the desert.
  Up![1] to bring him to rest,[2] even Israel.
3 Jehovah appeared unto me from afar.
  And I love thee with everlasting love,
  Therefore have I in loving-kindness respited thee.[3]
4 Again will I build thee and thou shalt be built, Virgin Israel;
  Again shalt thou adorn thyself with thy tabrets,
  And go forth in the dance of those that make merry.
5 Again shalt thou plant vineyards on the mountains of Samaria;
  The planters shall plant and enjoy the fruit.
6 For there is a day when the watchmen cry on Mount Ephraim,
  Arise and let us go up towards Zion, to Jehovah our God.

TEXTUAL AND GRAMMATICAL.

[1] Ver. 2.—הָלוֹךְ. The infinitive absolute is to be taken as an imperative, in the sense of a summons to one's self. Comp. NAEGELSB. *Gr.*, § 92, 2, *b*.

[2] Ver. 2.—לְהַרְגִּיעוֹ the prophet evidently alludes to Deut. xxviii. 65. This Hiphil denotes *quietem agere*, to make a rest (comp. NAEGELSB. *Gr.*, § 18, 3). There is indeed no further instance to adduce in favor of the meaning *quietum facere*, yet, apart from its grammatical admissibility, it rests on a good foundation, partly in the etymology (comp. מַרְגּוֹעַ, Jer. vi. 16; מַרְגֵּעָה Isa. xxviii. 12) partly in the connection.—On the anticipation of the object by the suffix, Comp. NAEGELSB. *Gr.*, § 77, 2 and rems. on ix. 14.

[3] Ver. 3.—מְשַׁכְתִּיךְ חֶסֶד in the sense of *prolongare gratiam* is found in Ps. xxxvi. 11; cix. 12 coll. lxxxv. 6. The sense would also be perfectly appropriate. Then the suffix would have to be taken in the sense of the dative. This use of the suffix is however proved only in the 1st person (י), and the similar case of the third pers. masc. (ו). For such a use in the 2d pers. we have only the uncertain instance of Isa. lxv. 5. Comp. NAEGELSB. *Gr.*, § 78.—I therefore take מְשַׁךְ with HITZIG and FUERST in the sense of "respite" (Eccles. ii. 3). חֶסֶד is the Accus. Instr. Comp. NAEGELSB. *Gr.*, § 70, *i*.

EXEGETICAL AND CRITICAL.

According to xxx. 4 the prophet has in the previous passage been addressing Israel and Judah. Now he turns to Israel alone, as far as xxxi. 22, then in vers. 23-26 to Judah alone, finally in vers. 27-40 to the entire Israelitish nation. After the comprehensive promise (ver. 1), which now allots the consolation, assured in xxx. 22 to the entire nation, especially to the ten tribes; he announces that the residue of Israel has found grace, and that the Lord arises to bring it to rest (ver. 2). The people see the Lord approaching from a distance, and telling them that he loves them with an everlasting love, of which the previous respite was a proof (ver. 3). Then follows the consolatory promise that the Virgin Israel shall be rebuilt, that she shall again go forth in cheerful dances (ver. 4), that vineyards shall again be planted in Samaria, and those who have planted shall enjoy the fruit (ver. 5). And not only this. Israel will also again have recourse to the national Sanctuary, and go up for worship to Jerusalem.

Ver. 1. **At that time . . . my people.** The section begins as the previous one had closed. That glorious consolation is again proclaimed specially to the ten tribes, the most ruined and almost lost portions of the people. The alterations and extensions occasioned by its position in the beginning and the inversion mark at the same time the distinction in reference to xxx. 22. Vers. 2-6. **Thus saith Jehovah . . . our God.** It is impossible that there can be a reference here to those who were delivered from the captivity in Egypt. Apart from particular objections, the ten tribes did not then obtain a special deliverance, and the whole description relates to the future, as is clear from **up! to bring,** etc., and still more plainly from vers. 4-6. The declarations of these latter verses only particularize what was said in vers. 2 and 3. The perfects in vers. 2 and 3 are also *prophetical.*—**Has found grace.** Israel had fallen into disfavor, now he has again found favor. In the desert the Lord finds the remnant spared by the sword of the enemy. It is certain that the prophet means the north-eastern desert situated between Palestine and the Euphrates. For the **escaped of the sword,** mentioned in li. 50 are not those which Jer. here has in mind. There he is speaking of Jews, here of those pertaining to the ten tribes. The prophet is thinking of them as they were during the period of their disfavor, oppressed and persecuted by enemies and driven out into the desert. There, in their deepest distress, the Lord finds them. We have however no right to deny that this prophetic picture of the future has its corresponding historical reality in an external, literal sense. Ver. 3. A dramatic change of persons! The people speak. They see the Lord appear from afar. For He had kept Himself afar off, He had indeed quite disappeared from the sight of the people. Now He is again visible, of course from Zion. Comp. Ps. xiv. 7; Isa. xlix. 9 sqq.—**And I love.** The connection of what Jehovah says with what the people say by means of Van, **and** (HITZIG appropriately compares 1 Ki. xx. 34) makes the impression that the Lord at once agrees to what is said, confirms it, makes indeed glorious additions to it. Van therefore = *and indeed* (comp. NAEGELSB. *Gr.,* § 111, 1, *a*) is connected with a collateral causal significance (comp. NAEGELSB. *Gr.,* § 110, 1, *c*), since that eternal love is the only ground of the appearance.—On the subject-matter comp. Deut. vii. 13; Isa. liv. 7, 8; 1 Ki. x. 9.—**Build,** etc. Build here is to be taken not merely in the sense of building walls, but of *restitutio in integrum.* Comp. Ps. xxviii. 5; cii. 17; Jer. xii. 16. ["This metaphor, which may appear harsh in English, is to be explained from the use of the Hebrew word *banah,* to *build,* as applied to the building up a family of sons (*banim*) and daughters (*banoth*) who are like living stones of the household, built up from the mother, wedded as a Virgin Bride to her husband." WORDSWORTH.—S. R. A.]—**Adorn thyself,** etc. Comp. iv. 30. The kettle-drum, [or timbrel] is here designated as pertaining to the ornaments of a woman who appears in festal apparel.—Comp. xxxi. 19.—To the rebuilt cities and the restored commonwealth, it is also necessary in order that the people may be happy, that there be agriculture, especially the culture of the vine, the fruit of which rejoiceth the heart of man.—**Mountains of Samaria** (comp. 1 Ki. xvi. 24) are the mountains of the northern kingdom generally, in so far as they permitted the culture of the vine. Comp. Jud. ix. 27.—Hos. ii. 17.—**Enjoy the fruit.** Jeremiah here refers to the legal enactment, Lev. xix. 13-25, that the fruit of newly planted trees should not be eaten at all in the first three years, and in the fourth year they should be holy unto the Lord; not until the fifth year should they be enjoyed *ad libitum* (comp. SAALSCHUETZ, *Mos. Recht. S.* 168, 9). This appropriation permitted from the 5th year onwards is designated by the expression הִלֵּל *profanare, in usum profanum convertere.* He who has planted a vineyard and has not yet enjoyed the fruit of it is free from service in war, Deut. xx. 6. It is also one of the punishments threatened to the ungodly man that he shall plant a vineyard but another shall make it common (Deut. xxviii. 30). In antithesis to this passage it is here promised as an element of blessing that the planter shall also be the profaner or partaker. (כִּחֵל). Comp. Isa. lxv. 21.—**For there is a day,** *etc.* All this blessing promised to Israel in vers. 4 and 5 shall and will be imparted to them on this account, that the people themselves will return to the service of Jehovah as of old. *כִּי* **For,** ver. 6, thus gives the reason of Jehovah's action (vers. 4 and 5) in the behavior of Israel.—**Watchmen.** There were not only watchmen stationed on lofty eminences (comp. 1 Ki. xvii. 9; xviii. 8) to announce danger from enemies (iv. 6, 19; vi. 1, *etc.*) but also to announce the new moons and feasts. Comp. SAALSCHUETZ, *Mos. Recht., S.* 387, 401.—The cry then, up to Jerusalem to worship Jehovah! sounds again as before the separation. Israel and Judah are again united in the Lord.

2. The Execution.

XXXI. 7-14.

7 For thus saith Jehovah, Shout joyfully over[1] Jacob,
   And exult[2] over the head of the nations! Sing praises[3] aloud and say:
   Deliver, O Jehovah, thy people, the remnant of Israel.
8 Behold, I bring them from the North country,
   And collect them from the ends of the earth.
   Among them are the blind and lame,
   The pregnant and the parturient together;
   A great assemblage shall they return hither.
9 With weeping shall they come, and with supplication.
   I conduct them;[4] I lead them to water-brooks,
   By a straight way in which they shall not stumble:
   For I am Israel's father,
   And Ephraim is my first-born son.
10 Hear Jehovah's word, ye nations,
   And proclaim it to the isles afar off,[5] and say:
   He that scattered Israel will collect him,
   And guard him as a shepherd his flock.
11 For Jehovah has redeemed Jacob,
   And liberated him from the hand of him who was too strong for him.
12 And they will come and shout on the summit of Zion,
   And stream hither to the blessing[6] of Jehovah,
   For the corn and the new wine and the oil,
   And for young lambs and calves:
   And their soul shall be as a watered garden;
   And they shall not languish any more.[7]
13 Then will the virgin rejoice in the dance,
   And young men with the aged together;
   And I will turn their mourning into joy,
   And comfort them after their sorrow.
14 And I will satiate the soul of the priests with fat,
   And my people shall be full of the blessing, saith Jehovah.

TEXTUAL AND GRAMMATICAL.

[1] Ver. 7.—לְ רִנּוּ לְ as in Ps. xxii. 31; lxix. 6, 27. Comp. NAEGELSB. *Gr.*, S. 227.—The accus. הַכָּה עִם שִׂמְחָה ls ver. 3.

[2] Ver. 7.—וְצַהֲלוּ. Comp. Isa. x. 30; xii. 6; Jer. v. 8; l. 11. The construction with בְּ, as in Isa. xxiv. 14.

[3] Ver. 7.—On the construction הַשְׁמִיעוּ הַלְלוּ, comp. rems. on iv. 5; xiii. 18.

[4] Ver. 9.—HITZIG would connect אוֹבִילֵם with what follows because it does not agree with תַּחֲנוּנִים, which does not signify *miseratio, clementia*. But we need not use the word in this sense. [Comp. EXEG. rems. which, however, do not accord with the rendering given by NAEGELSBACH in the text. HENDERSON and NOYES adhere to the A. V.: and with supplications will I lead them.—S. R. A.]

[5] Ver. 10.—בְּמֶרְחָק. On the construction comp. NAEGELSB. *Gr.*, § 112, 5, d.

[6] Ver. 12.—אֶל־טוּב. On אֶל and its interchange with עַל comp. rems. on x. 1.—טוּב, in distinction from טוֹב, is never used of moral, but always of material good. Comp. ii. 7; Hos. iii. 5.

[7] Ver. 12.—לְדַאֲבָה עוֹד. Comp. ver. 25, and OLSHAUSEN, S. 532.

EXEGETICAL AND CRITICAL.

After in the previous strophe the Lord has made known His purpose to liberate and restore Israel, the present strophe goes a step farther. It contains a summons at the head of each of its two halves. The first (ver. 7) is addressed to the Israelites themselves, and exhorts them, after the Lord in the foregoing verses, 1-6, has made known His gracious determination, to approach Him now with petitions for its *actual execution*.

It is also at once promised that the Lord will respond to these petitions (vers. 8 and 9), for in these verses it is described how they will accomplish their journey from the North country and the most remote lands, a journey which will set in the most glorious light the filial relation of Israel to his God. At the head of the second half (vers. 10-14) is a summons to all nations to hear and proclaim the decree which God has formed with respect to His people, that, namely, they shall be liberated (vers. 10, 11) and be brought home to a glorious life in joy and abundance on their native soil (vers. 12-14).
Vers. 7-9. **For thus saith ... first-born son.—For** refers not merely to ver. 7 but to all that follows. All that is subsequently said of the realization of the divine intentions is a proof of the truth of the promise given in vers. 1-6. The summons to exult joyfully is addressed to the individual members of the holy nation. Who else will then supplicate for Israel? The antithesis to ver. 10 also favors this view. There the heathen are summoned not to pray for Israel but to proclaim the purpose which the Lord has formed on this account. Israel is called the head of the nations. The prophet depends in this expression on those passages in the Pentateuch where Israel is called the holy nation, the **treasure above all people,** (Ex. xix. 5, 6; Lev. xx. 24, 26; Deut. vii. 6; xiv. 2; xxvi. 18), the great nation, to which the Deity approaches (Deut. iv. 7, 8), the people of inheritance (Deut. iv. 20), the highest above all nations (Deut. xxvi. 19); further on prophetic passages which designate the nation as **chief of the nations** (Am. vi. 1 coll. iii. 2) as **one nation in the earth** (2 Sam. vii. 23 coll. Numb. xxiii. 9; Deut. xxxiii. 28).—**Deliver,** etc. It is evident that this is meant as an earnest petition from the nation accusative *thy people.* By His promise in vers. 1-6 the Lord has given the Israelites the right and the courage to supplicate in comfort and in joy for the redemption of their nation. There is, it is true, an assonance in this word to the words of praise הוֹשִׁיעָה נָּא [Hosanna. A.V.: save now. Comp. Matth. xxi. 9] (Ps. cxviii. 25) which are however not merely words of praise, but according to their verbal significance, are at the same time a petition, and in so far as they are that form of petition which is sure of being heard are at the same time praise. Vers. 8 and 9 then contain the comforting promise that the petition will be heard. It is as if the Lord in ver. 7 had only provoked the petition, in order to announce His readiness to realize the promise given in vers. 2-6.—**From the North country.** As the שָׁבִים came from the North, the שָׁבִי must also be brought back from the North country. Comp. iii. 12, 18; xvi. 15.—**Ends of the earth.** Comp. vi. 22; xxv. 32; l. 41.—**Among them,** etc. The deliverance is to comprise the whole people. The weak and frail will then not be excluded, but be conducted in a manner suited to their circumstances. With tears of joy and contrition, with prayer and supplication to the Lord their God will they retrace their way. Comp. iii. 21; l. 4. As in Ps. xlv. 15; Isa. lv. 12, a

being led forth with gladness and with peace is spoken of, so here it is said that the Lord will lead Israel with supplication, *i. e.,* in the continued spirit and practice of prayer. Only thus is the symmetry of the construction preserved, according to which a more particular definition is to be given to each verb by means of a prepositional expression.—To water-brooks, in a level and comfortable path, are they to be brought. Comp. Isa. xlviii. 21.—This careful guidance is truly paternal. No wonder; for Jehovah is Israel's father (comp. Deut. xxxii. 6; Isa. lxiii. 16; Jer. iii. 19; Henzog, *R.-Enc.,* XVII. *S.* 252), and Ephraim is His first-born son. This predicate is ascribed to the whole nation. Exod. iv. 22 coll. Deut. xiv. 1. Here however Ephraim is purposely designated as first-born, in allusion to the preference, which Jacob awarded to the sons of Joseph (Gen. xlix. 22 coll. 4), and which is distinctly defined in 1 Chron. v. 2, where it is said that Judah obtained the dignity of chief ruler (נָגִיד), but Joseph the birthright (בְּכֹרָה). Comp. Delitzsch on Gen. xlix. 3, 4; Henzog, *R.- Enc.* XIV., *S.* 769.
Vers. 10-14. **Hear ... saith Jehovah.** The nations themselves which held Israel captive and mocked at his expulsion (xv. 4; xxiv. 9; xxix. 18), must proclaim the purpose of God to liberate His people. We are here reminded of the edict of Cyrus (Ezr. i. 1 sqq.). This proclamation by those hitherto in power is itself a new and important step towards the realization of the promise given in vers. 1-6.—**Isles.** Comp. Exeg rems. on ii. 10; xxv. 22.—**Scattered.** Comp. xv. 7-xxiii. 3; xxix. 14.—Observe that the prophet, as in vers. 8 and 9 he had described the glory of the return, so now he portrays the glory of the arrival and the prosperity to be expected afterwards.—**For the corn.** Comp. Deut. xxviii. 51; Joel i. 10; ii. 19, *etc.*—**Watered garden.** Isa. lviii. 11.—**Then will the virgin,** *etc.* Comp. ver. 4. The dances of virgins with men according to our custom are not to be thought of, for such dancing was not practised by the ancients generally and especially not by the Hebrews. (Comp. Henzog, *R.-Enc.* XV., *S.* 414 sqq.). Men's dances also occur (comp. Jud. ix. 27; 2 Sam. vi. 14), but in general dancing was regarded as something particularly appropriated to women and especially virgins. (Comp. Exod. xv. 20; Jud. xxi. 21; xi. 34; 1 Sam. xviii. 6; Winer, *R.-W.-B. s. v.* Tanz). Hence the joy in the dance is to be referred to the virgin alone. When it is further said that youths and old men would rejoice with each other, this is to express the general diffusion of the joy. Not only youth, the period addicted to joyousness, but even age shall be infected by the joy, so that all ages and sexes will participate in it. And every rank also! Hence the priests are rendered especially prominent, their share in the sacrifices (Lev. vii. 32-34; ix. 21) being set forth as particularly fat, *i. e.* ample and dainty (the eating of fat being strictly forbidden, Lev. vii. 23-25).

3. *The threefold Turn.*

XXXI. 15-22.

15   Thus saith Jehovah : A voice is heard in Ramah,
Lamentation and most bitter crying ;
Rachel weeps for her children,
Refusing[1] to be comforted for her children, for they are no more.[2]
16 Thus saith Jehovah : Restrain thy voice from weeping,
And thine eyes from tears :
For there is reward for thy work, saith Jehovah ;
And they shall return from the land of the enemy.
17 There is also hope for thy future, saith Jehovah ;
And children[3] shall return to their border.
18 I have surely heard Ephraim bemoaning himself ;
Thou hast chastised me,
And I allowed myself to be chastised like an untrained bullock :
Turn thou me again, that I may turn ;
For thou art Jehovah my God.
19 For after my revolt,[4] I repent ;
And after I have learned to know myself,[5] I smite on the thigh :
I blush, I am also ashamed
That I have borne the reproach of my youth.
20 Is then Ephraim a favourite[6] son to me or a bosom-child,[7]
That whenever I speak against him I must still remember him ?
Therefore my bowels heave towards him ;
I must have pity on him, saith Jehovah.
21 Erect for thyself signals, set up for thyself poles,[8]
Turn thy mind to the highway, the way thou wentest!
Return, O virgin Israel,
Return to these thy cities.
22 How long wilt thou turn hither and thither,[9] thou backsliding daughter ?[10]
For Jehovah has created a new thing on earth :—
The woman shall turn the man.

TEXTUAL AND GRAMMATICAL.

[1] Ver. 15.—מְאָנָה. Comp. lii. 3; v. 3; viii. 5; xv. 18.
[2] Ver. 15.—כִּי אֵינֶנּוּ. As in xi. 4 the plural pronoun is referred to a singular, regarded collectively, so here, the case being reversed, the singular pronoun is referred to a plural, regarded as a unity. Comp. NAEGELSB. *Gr.*, § 61, 1 ; Ps. v. 9 ; Job xxiv. 24 ; בָּלָה, viii. 6, *etc.*
[3] Ver. 17.—The article is wanting before בָּנִים, comp. NAEGELSB, *Gr.*, § 71, 3.
[4] Ver. 19.—אַחֲרֵי שׁוּבִי. This שׁוּב has been commonly taken in the same sense as in ver. 18 [A. V.: Surely after that I was turned], which has given rise to great obscurity and to arbitrary attempts to avoid it, as *e. g.* by VENEMA, who takes שׁוּב at once for לִי, *i. e.* after I had come again to myself. The only correct rendering is that of HITZIG and GRAF. They take שׁוּב in the sense of *se avertere a Jove*. They are justified in this by כְּשׁוּבָה (iii. 6, 8, 11, 12, *etc.*), שׁוֹבָב (iii. 14, 22), שׁוֹבֵבָה (viii. 5 ; xxxi. 22), and by the expression שׁוּב מֵאַחֲרֵי (iii. 19), which does not indeed occur without the מֵאַחֲרֵי in viii. 4, but it does in Josh. xxiii. 12. It seems as though the prophet, here also as well as in ch. iii., were endeavoring to bring the idea of שׁוּב into application in as great a variety of meanings as possible.
[5] Ver. 19.—הִוָּדְעִי. Many commentators take this word in the sense of the passive of יָדַע, *edocere*—to be made wise, to be instructed. But Niph. is only the reflexive or passive of Kal. It means therefore only to be acknowledged or to be known, one's self. The latter signification, in which it moreover appears to be used in no other passage of the Old Testament but this, corresponds perfectly to the connection.
[6] Ver. 20.—יַקִּיר. Hebrew here only ; Chald. Ezr. iv. 10; Dan. ii. 11. It denotes, like יָקָר (xv. 19 ; Lam. iv. 2, *etc.*) and יְקָר (xx. 5), what is precious, a jewel.
[7] Ver. 20.—שַׁעֲשֻׁעִים. Comp. שַׁעֲשׁוּעַ יֵצֶר, Isa. v. 7 coll. Prov. viii. 30, 31

⁸ Ver. 21.—תְּמרוּרִים from תָּמַר, *prominuit*, related to תֹּמֶר, *palmae truncus*, x. 5, and תִּמרָה, *columna*, Joel iii. 3, occurs here only. All other preparations are comprised in the brief phrase שִׁתִי לִבֵּךְ וגו. Comp. Exod. vii. 23; Ps. xlviii. 14.

⁹ Ver. 22.—הִתְחַמֵּק. The verb is found only in Cant. v. 6 and connected with עָבַר. The connection requires the meaning of "to turn one's self away," with which the only noun derived from it חָמוּק (Cant. vii. 2) accords. This can only signify "winding, rounding" (DELITZSCH: the swinging of thy loins). According to the etymology then the Hithp. must have the sense of turning one's self hither and thither.

¹⁰ Ver. 22.—הֲבַת הַשּׁוֹבֵבָה. Observe that it is שׁוֹבֵבָה, not שׁוֹבָבָה, as in iii. 14, 22; Isa. lvii. 17. The passive form has doubtless the meaning of "turned away, alienated." The active form must primarily have an active meaning. The Piel from שׁוּב is primarily objective causative and signifies to make some one or something return, bring back (1. 19), restore (Ps. lx. 3; xxiii. 3), to render alienated (Isa. xlvii. 10). It may also have a subjective causative meaning: to make a turn, back or away, *i. e.* to turn one's self back, to desert. Hiphil has primarily this signification. (Comp. NAEGELSB. *Gr.*, § 18, 3; 1 Ki. viii. 47). But the Piel forms also have it (EW., § 120, c). As now it is decided by the connection in what sense the verb שׁוֹבֵב is to be taken, the meaning of the *N. verbale* is also thus decided. It may then mean one who brings back, restores, alienates, and also one who turns, deserts. It has the latter meaning in xlix. 4 and Mic. ii. 4.—The Pilel of hollow roots includes also the significance of the Piel (EWALD, § 121 a, coll. § 120). Especially does this word seem to me to involve the idea of שׁוּב in the causative sense, which corresponds to the following הָשׁוֹבֵב, *i. e.* in the sense of *reducens* (comp. כְּשׁוֹבֵב, Isa. lviii. 12; OLSH., S. 552).

EXEGETICAL AND CRITICAL.

This strophe causes the return of Israel, set forth before us in prospect, to be seen from another side, *viz.* as at the same time an inward return to God, or conversion. In a wonderfully touching picture the prophet represents Rachel, the mother of the house of Joseph, as raising a lamentation at Ramah over the tracks of those who are going into exile, as though they were dead (ver. 15). Jehovah Himself, however, comforts her; a reward is still to be hoped for her work and comfort for the future, for the return of her children is promised (vers. 16 and 17). But is this possible? Yes, for Israel will turn inwardly to the Lord and thus fulfil that condition, which the outward return as a necessary consequence thereof must have. The prophet does this by introducing Ephraim as speaking and causing him to make an honest and hearty confession (vers. 18 and 19). On this Jehovah gives us to understand in touching words that His love for Ephraim is deeply rooted and invincible (ver. 20). Ephraim consequently receives the command to make all the preparations for return. Thus at the same time the (according to iii. 1) entirely new and unheard of case is now realized, that a woman, rejected and shared by other men, brings back her first husband (vers. 21 and 22).

Ver. 15. **Thus saith Jehovah . . . they are no more.** With respect to Ramah and the grave of Rachel the greatest obscurity still prevails. My view is as follows: 1. The tomb of Rachel was near Ramah. This definitely follows from this passage and 1 Sam. x. 2. DELITZSCH remarks (*Comm. on Genesis*, 2te *Aufl.* 2ter Thl./., S. 53) that Rachel's weeping is heard in Ramah not because her tomb is in the neighborhood, but because, according to Jer. xl. 1, the exiles assembled there, but to this it is opposed (*a*) that according to 1 Sam. x. 2 the tomb of Rachel was positively near Ramah; and (*b*) that Rachel's weeping does not refer to the exiles mentioned in xl. 1; for these were Jews, while according to the whole connection of this passage, Rachel bewails the exile of the Ephraimites. 2. Ramah, near which was Rachel's tomb and where Samuel dwelt (1 Sam. x. 2) was in Benjamin, in the vicinity of Gibeah, north of Jerusalem. This is seen from Jud. xix. 13; Isa. x. 29; Hos. v. 8. In Josh. xviii. 25 it is expressly said that Ramah was in Benjamin. The original and complete name is Ramathaim Zophim (רָמָתַיִם צוֹפִים), 1 Sam. i. 1 coll. ver. 19. The statement that Ramah was situated on the mountains of Ephraim (Jud. iv. 5; 1 Sam. i. 1) is not in contradiction to this, for the southern slopes of the mountains of Ephraim extended thus far. (Comp. HENZOG, *R.-Enc.* XII., S. 515 [ROBINSON, *Bibl. Researches*, II., 315-317; 331-334; THOMSON, *The Land and the Book*, II., 503.—S. R. A.]). It has been objected to the identity of the Ramah of Samuel and the Ramah near Gibeah that Saul in seeking the she-asses took three days in going from Gibeah to Ramah (1 Sam. ix. 20), and that David fleeing from Gibeah took refuge in Ramah (1 Sam. xix. 18). Even RAUMER (*Paläst. S.* 219) lays some weight on these objections. [Comp. also SMITH, *Bible Dict.*, s. v. Ramah.—S. R. A.]. As to the first, however, it is clear from 1 Sam. ix. 4, 5 that Saul did not follow the direct road, but seeking or pursuing the track of the asses, reached Ramah by a very circuitous route. With respect to the second RUETSCHI (HERZ. *R.-Enc.*, *ut sup.*) has replied that David did not seek (temporary) protection from the city of Ramah but from Samuel. 3. There is also a Ramah in Gilead (Ramoth, Ramah Mizpeh, Josh. xiii. 26; xx. 8; xxi. 38, *etc.*); another south-west from Jerusalem, west of the mountains of Judea (Ramathlebi, Jud. xv. 17—Eleutheropolis. Comp. RAUMER, *Paläst.*, S. 185, 6); a third in Naphtali (Josh. xix. 36); a fourth in Asher (Josh. xix. 29). A fifth place, which sometimes occurs under this name is Ramlah, a city which is not mentioned at all in the Old Testament (unless perhaps in Neh. xi. 33), of later origin, and very probably identical with Arimathea, and situated to the west of Jerusalem in the plain of Saron near Lydia (Diospolis). Comp. RAUMER, *Paläst.*, *S.* 217, 8, 448. There is then no Ramah in the vicinity of Bethlehem! 4. Bethlehem is doubtless also called Ephrath or Ephratah (Mic. v. 1; Ruth i. 2; 1 Sam. xvii. 12). Now if Rachel's tomb is in the neighborhood of Ramah it cannot be near Bethlehem, and the Ephratah near which (Gen. xxxvi. 16, 19 coll. xlviii. 7) Rachel bore Benjamin and was buried, cannot be Bethlehem.

Now we read in 2 Chron. xiii. 19 of a place in the neighborhood of Bethel, the name of which according to the Chethibh is עֶפְרוֹן, but according to the Keri עֶפְרָיִן. The latter reminds us of 'Εφραίμ or 'Εφρέμ, a little town, which, according to JEROME, lay 20 m. p. north from Jerusalem, where Christ remained for some time after the resurrection of Lazarus (John xi. 54). JOSEPHUS also relates (*B. Jud.* IV., 9, 9) that Vespasian destroyed Βηθηλᾶ τε καὶ 'Εφραὶμ πολίχνια, and then rode to Jerusalem. In Josh. xviii. 23 עָפְרָה is mentioned among the cities of Benjamin. The same name recurs in 1 Sam. xiii. 17. EUSEBIUS in his *Onomast., s. v.* Aphra, says: "*est et hodie vicus Effrem in quinto milliario Bethelis ad Orientem respiciens.*" The distances given point to the identity of Ephraim (Ephron) and Ophra. (Comp. ROBINSON, II., *S.* 333 sqq. [III., 124]; RAUMER, *S.* 189 and 216). Now it is remarkable that the Alexandrian translators in 1 Sam. xiii. 17 render the name עָפְרָה by Γοφερά, and on the other hand in Josh. xviii. 23 by 'Εφραθά (Cod. Alex. 'Αφρά). From this it seems to follow that even in very ancient times עָפְרָה and אֶפְרָת were interchanged, and that hence not only the הוּא בֵית לָהֶם, Gen. xxxv. 19; xlviii. 7, but also the name אֶפְרָתָה, xxxv. 16, 19; xlviii. 7, is to be regarded as a corruption of the original reading. I had reached this result before GRAF's treatise on the situation of Bethel and Rama (*Stud. u. Krit.,* 1854, IV., *S.* 868) became known to me.—The prophet goes back in spirit to the time when the inhabitants of the kingdom of the ten tribes were led away to Assyria into captivity. Since that time, he says, making use of figurative language, may be heard in Ramah, the greater city near Rachel's tomb (1 Sam. xx. 2), nightly wailing and bitter weeping (vi. 26). It is Rachel who is weeping for her children. The inhabitants of the kingdom of the ten tribes may be designated children of Rachel, because at their head stands the tribe of Ephraim, which is frequently mentioned as a representative of the kingdom of Israel, Isa. vii. 2-5, 8, 9, 17; xi. 13; Hos. iv. 17, etc.; Jer. vii. 15; xxxi. 9, 18, 20. The mother of the ruling tribe appears thus as the personification of the kingdom ruled by it. The spirit of Rachel is the genius of the kingdom of the ten tribes, whom the prophet represents by a bold poetical figure as rising from her tomb by night and bewailing the misery of her children.—**Are no more.** Comp. Isa. xvii. 14; Gen. xxxvi. 21.

Vers. 16 and 17. **Thus saith Jehovah . . . their border.** The Lord comforts Rachel by promising her a glorious reward for her maternal labor and care, (on **restrain thy voice** comp. **guard thy foot,** ii. 25. On **there is reward** comp. 2 Chron. xv. 7) *viz.* her children shall be redeemed from the land of captivity—and by setting before her the consolatory hope for the future, that the children will also return to their native land. On **there is also hope** comp. xxxi. 11.

Vers. 18 and 19. **I have surely . . . of my youth.** These verses give the inner reason of that joyful change: Israel will fulfil the condition required of him by the Lord (iii. 13 sqq.).

First the people express their acknowledgment that the chastisement was necessary for them, for they were like an untamed and untrained bullock (the prophet evidently has in mind Hos. x. 11), but they have also let themselves be chastened and accepted the chastening (v. 3). As Jeremiah here generally moves in the same circle of thought as in ch. iii., so especially in what follows, where also as there the idea of turning forms the central point or pivot of his representation.—**Turn thou me,** *etc.* The knowledge gained as the result of the chastisement produces a double effect: a positive and a negative. The positive effect consists in the desire to return to Jehovah. Meanwhile the people are well aware that willing is not performing. They therefore pray the Lord that He Himself will turn their hearts to Him, who alone is Israel's God. (This is the sense of the causal sentence. **For thou art,** *etc.*). Then only will they really return. The bodily return is connected with the spiritual in the closest causal relation. Comp. Rems. on שׁוּבִי, ver. 19, and Lam. v. 21. —Lam. iii. 40; Ps. lxxx. 4, 8, 20.—The negative effect, which on their part forms the psychological condition of the positive, and is therefore introduced by **for,** is the inner turning and cutting loose from all that which had allured Israel, but had yet only brought them to hurt and shame. —The smiting on the side (יָרֵךְ) יְרֵכַיִם *duo femina cum natibus,* comp. Ezek. xxi. 17) was a sign of mourning. Comp. WINER and HERZOG, *R. Enc., s. v. Trauer.*—**I blush,** *etc.* Comp. Isa. xlv. 16, 17.—The connection of this passage is then as follows: Ephraim has taken the chastening to heart. In consequence he addresses the prayer for power to return to Jehovah, for he has now learned to repent of his turning away from Him, and to be ashamed of the consequences.

Vers. 20-22. **Is then Ephraim . . . the man.** Jehovah grants the moving petition. Astonished at surprising Himself, as it were, in such tender feelings towards Ephraim, Jehovah asks Himself if then Ephraim is his favorite son, his darling child (*enfant gâté*), since often as he has been obliged to bring the severe judgment of rejection upon him, he has yet never been able to forget him.—**Speak against.** We may compare 2 Chron. xxii. 10, where it is said of Athaliah that she arose and וַתְּדַבֵּר all the seed royal. But apart from דָּבַר being here construed with a single accusative, we have in the parallel passage (2 Kings. xi. 1) וַתְּאַבֵּד so that it is easy to suspect a mistake. Now דִּבֵּר and נִדְבַּר in the sense of "speak," are frequently connected with בְּ in different meanings: *loqui per aliquem* (Num. xii. 2), *de aliquo* (Deut. vi. 7; 1 Sam. xix. 3; Ps. cxix. 46 coll. 23), *ad aliquem* (Numb. xii. 8; Hab. ii. 1; Zech. i. 9, *etc.,* Numb. xii. 2, *etc.,* 1 Sam. xxv. 39; Caut. viii. 8). But it also signifies *loqui contra aliquem,* Numb. xxi. 7 coll. ver. 5; Ps. l. 20; lxxviii. 19. This last meaning corresponds perfectly to the connection here:—Often as I מִדֵּי as in 1 Sam. xviii. 30; 1 Kings xiv. 28) speak against him, *i. e.,* cast him from me by a sentence of reprobation, yet I cannot forget him. I am always reminded of him again, and then the old feelings of love and pity are excited anew.—**My**

bowels. DRECHSLER correctly remarks on Isa. xvi. 5, that בְּנֵי עַם does not like σπλάγχνα, viscera, include the nobler entrails (the heart). The word does not therefore designate the innermost source of the feelings, but only a place of the external organism where these make themselves specially noticeable. Comp. Cant. v. 4; Job xxx. 27; Lam. i. 20; ii. 11; Isa. lxiii. 15; Jer. iv. 19.—The immediate effect of this excitation of love, is that Israel receives directions to make preparations for the journey homewards. Thus persons are to be sent in advance to set up stone pillars as way marks for the coming train, צִיּוּן *cippus, monumentum;* comp. 2 Kings xxiii. 17; Ezek. xxxix. 15.—Israel's returning by the same road which he came is comforting in two respects, first in itself, second because it is known and easier to retrace.—The word **these**, before **thy cities**, shows unquestionably that the author has his point of view in Palestine, and not in the lands of the captivity. Comp. GRAF, *S.* 387, *Anm.* **Turn hither and thither.** HITZIG finds in this not incorrectly the collateral idea of delay. This accords well with **how long?** which expresses a certain degree of impatience. Israel does not respond quickly enough to the invitation to return. The Lord has to drive him. The expression **backsliding daughter**, occurs besides only in a much later passage, of the people of the Ammonites.—It is surprising, that the Lord in the midst of this assurance of His tenderest love, and after Israel in vers. 18 and 19, has manifested such sincere and deep penitence, should utter another word of harsh censure. In this passage there appears to me to be a play upon words. In the section iii. 1–iv. 2 namely, to which this discourse is most closely related in matter as well as in form, the prophet gives as many variations of the theme שׁוּב as possible, sometimes applying the idea to Israel and Judah in a physical, at others in a spiritual sense. A similar variation though in abbreviated measure is found in viii. 4, 5. In this passage also from ver. 19 onwards, the idea of שׁוּב forms the main thought. It is, however, variously modified: in vers. 16 and 17 the word is referred to bodily return, in ver. 18 to spiritual and bodily turning, and in ver. 19 to spiritual alienation, in ver. 21 again to bodily conditioned by spiritual turning. Now when the prophet in ver. 22 calls Israel שׁוֹבֵבָה, would he not thus wish to say that Israel is a person, who makes much of turning, who applies the idea of שׁוּב in every possible way? It appears to me that the prophet with the following sentence goes back again to the conceptions of ch. iii. In the beginning of this chapter he designates it as a crime profaning the land that a man return to his rejected wife, who has meanwhile been another's. Notwithstanding that Israel is such a wife, Jehovah yet calls her back to Himself. This is the repentance of which our passage speaks. For when the Lord does something which, according to His own law, has been hitherto regarded as inadmissible, this is certainly an exception to the rule, therefore something new and extraordinary. If now we ask how the Lord comes to make such an exception? —the answer is given in xxxi. 20. Israel has done this to the Lord, he is His darling child, whom he cannot forget. Israel is like a magnet which irresistibly attracts the Lord. Israel, the woman, here mentioned by the specific name of the sex נְקֵבָה, causes the Lord to turn to herself, who is also antithetically designated by the word גֶּבֶר which sets forth the specific distinction of the male sex. Thus the weak is victorious over the strong. It is not only a new thing that the Lord returns to his desecrated wife, but that this power to bring back proceeds from the weak, so that the strong succumbs to the weak. I therefore take תְּסוֹבֵב in the sense of "to turn round," to cause to turn back." Although no passage can be shown where סוֹבֵב is really used in this sense (everywhere where it occurs, it means either *circuire*, Ps. xxvi. 6; lv. 11; lix. 7, 15; Cant. iii. 2, or *circumdare;* Deut. xxxii. 10; Ps. vii. 8; xxxii. 7, 10; Jon. ii. 4, 6), this is only accidental, for there is nothing in the radical meaning which excludes this sense. The root סב which is radically related to שׁוּב has the meaning of turning or returning in the widest sense. And that it may also stand for *reverti* is shown by the passage, Ps. lxxi. 20, 21, where the verb is interchanged with שׁוּב. It cannot then be denied that תְּסוֹבֵב may mean *reducit.* תְּשׁוֹבֵב would certainly be more suitable, especially as corresponding more exactly to שׁוֹבֵבָה, and it is not indeed impossible that the prophet did originally write תְּשׁוּבָה. Neither the שׁוּבָה, nor in general the importance of the idea שׁוּב for the explanation of the whole passage, and particularly the reference to iii. 1 being understood, may have occasioned the change into תְּסוֹבֵב, unless indeed it is an error of the copyist. It is not, however, at all necessary to alter the reading, since even this, as we have shown, gives the sense required by the connection. It is exceedingly difficult to give the play upon words in the translation, since we have no corresponding word with the same variety of meanings. I know no better rendering now than "thou turn-coat daughter," though the phrase is not particularly suitable as applied to a nation. This explanation is not a new one. It is essentially that of most of the Rabbins: *"Proinde Hebræi hunc locum sic legendum contendunt: femina reducet virum, et hoc est novum in terra, ut mulier, quæ passim aliis viris se prostituit, veteris mariti cupida, illum iterum sui amantem obtineat."* MUENSTER. My explanation of שׁוֹבֵבָה only is new, so far as I know, for all the commentators take the word as simply equivalent to שׁוֹבֵבָה. The other explanations of the passage whose number is legion, all do violence either to the language or the connection. To mention only the principal ones—the old orthodox explanation, which refer the words "a woman shall compass," etc., to the birth of the Saviour from a virgin, must take נְקֵבָה in the sense of virgin, a meaning which the word never has nor can have. ABARBANEL explains *"feminæ viros circumdabunt, i. e., superabunt,"* understanding by the women the weak Israelites, by the men their strong enemies. But neither is this a *new thing,* nor has סוֹבֵב this meaning. *"Femina vertetur in virum"* is the translation of ABULMALID, R. TANCHUM, who are followed by LUTHER (in the first edit.ous of his Bible till 1538) and by EWALD among the moderns. The alteration of הְכוֹבֵב into תְּסוֹבֵב, however, or the rendering of the former in a passive sense is forced: the sense also must be such as to agree with the context. The explanation proposed by SCHNURRER, which is adopted by many modern commentators, is "the woman will protect the man,"—but neither corresponds to the connection, nor is it satisfactory in itself. When women protect men, either the men are become women and the women men, or there is no need of any protection.—The explanation given by HITZIG, "femina ambibit virum," which is found also in CASTALIO and CLERICUS (Vid. GRAF, S. 350) is not inappropriate in meaning, but cannot be justified grammatically. HENGSTENBERG, to whom GRAF attaches himself for want of a better, takes סבב in the sense of "to keep one's self near, to persist in dependence, seeking protection" (Christology, Eng. Tr., II., p. 429). But this rendering is developed from the idea of "surrounding" which cannot be declared of a single person with respect to another. The sense thus obtained is also the reverse of the primary meaning of the words, on which the rendering is based. Radically the explanation of HENGSTENBERG is no other than that the man will surround the woman with his protection, as MEIER also actually renders the words in his translation. Besides the larger commentaries, there are many monographs on this passage. Lists of them are found in SEB. SCHMIDT, STARKE, J. D. MICHAELIS, Observ. in Jer., p. 248; ROSENMUELLER; DIETELMAIR in the Engl. Biblework, Tom. IX., S. 543. I add ANDR. DAN. HABICHHORST, Diss. de femina circumdante virum, 1670 and 1677.

[Of English and American commentators, BLAYNEY renders "a woman shall put to the rout a strong man." HENDERSON: "Woman shall encompass man," following however BLAYNEY and CALVIN in his explanation, "Jehovah would make the feeblest of them more than a match for the most powerful of their foes." WORDSWORTH retains the interpretation of the words, which refers them to the miraculous conception of the Virgin, quoting in favor of this view S. JEROME and JACKSON and PEARSON on the Creed, with references also to JUSTIN MARTYR, CYPRIAN, AUGUSTINE, LUTHER, ŒCOLAMPADIUS, CHEMNITZ, GALATINUS, CALOVIUS, HUETIUS, etc. NOYES translates "the woman shall protect the man," with the note, "there shall be a state of peace and security, so that those who are regarded as feeble and defenceless, and unfit for war, shall be competent to the defence of the country." COWLES agrees most closely with NAEGELSBACH, referring "the woman" to the Virgin Israel, the people of God, who "instead of perpetually going about after other lovers, will go about (in the sense of seeking to win the love of) her own divine Lord."—S. R. A.]

---

§. THE SHARE OF JUDAH.

The Blessing of the Sanctuary.

XXXI. 23-26.

23   Thus saith Jehovah Zebaoth, the God of Israel:
     Yet will they speak this word in the land of Judah,
     And in its cities, when I turn their captivity:
     Jehovah bless thee, dwelling-place of salvation [or justice][1]
     Mountain of the sanctuary!
24   And Judah shall dwell therein and all its cities together,
     As husbandmen and those who go forth with flocks.[2]
25   For I refresh the panting soul,
     And every languishing[3] soul I satisfy.
26   Upon this I awoke and looked up;
     And my sleep had been sweet unto me.

TEXTUAL AND GRAMMATICAL.

[1] Ver. 23.—On נְוֵה. Comp. Prov. iii. 33; xxiv. 15; for צֶדֶק comp. rems. on vii. 5; ix. 23.

[2] Ver. 24.—וְנָסְעוּ בָעֵדֶר. Supply אֲשֶׁר before נָסְעוּ. This verb is the technical term for the nomadic mode of life. Comp. Gen. xxxiii. 12; xxxv. 21; xlvi. 1, etc.—On בְּ=in medio, i. e., cum. Comp. NAEGELSB. Gr., ₴ 112, 5 a.

[3] Ver. 25.—דָאֲבָה. Comp. ver. 12. I do not see why this word should necessarily be a participial form. It may be a finite verb with אֲשֶׁר wanting. Comp. xiv. 4; Isa. ii. 1; Ps. vii. 16.

EXEGETICAL AND CRITICAL.

After the prophet had promised the ten tribes spiritual and material prosperity in richest measure, he now does the same with respect to Judah. Judah will also return to his country; the sanctuary, the central point and source of all blessing is again saluted with benedictions (ver. 23). The whole land is again inhabited: agriculture and cattle-breeding again flourish (ver. 24). For the Lord is disposed to afford help in every distress, satisfaction for every need (ver. 25). The prophet received this revelation in a dream. Its joyful import was the cause of his feeling on awaking that his sleep had been sweet (ver. 26). He remarks this specially because with no other revelation in a dream had he had a similar experience.

Vers. 23-25. **Thus saith Jehovah . . . satisfy.—When I turn.** Comp. on xxix. 14.—**Jehovah bless thee.** The words may mean either Jehovah will bless thee, or, Jehovah bless thee. The former bears more of the priestly character. the latter is more appropriate as spoken by the congregation. We find such a benediction specified in Ps. cxxii. 6-9.—**Dwelling-place,** etc. Comp. 1. 7, where Jehovah himself is so-called.—**Mountain,** etc., may be in apposition to **dwelling-place,** etc., and then the expression may either be a designation of the temple alone, or of the whole city of Jerusalem (comp. Isa. lxvi. 20; Zech. viii. 3). It may also be taken as an asyndeton, so that then the former will designate the holy city, the latter the temple. Finally the double phrase may designate both at the same time, i. e., the city including the temple, and as there is no reason for excluding either of the two, this may well be the correct rendering. Comp. Ps. ii. 6; xlviii. 2 sqq.; Isa. xi. 9; Joel iv. 17.—Ver. 25. **Therein,** i. e., the land, ver. 23.—**Judah and all its cities.** The expression cannot designate Jerusalem and the provincial cities (comp. xi. 12), nor the whole and the single parts of the nation, because such a distinction can be made only *in abstracto.* I therefore think that the prophet really distinguishes the people and the cities. Both sit, dwell, lie in the land. Comp. יָשַׁב, xxx. 18; Zech. ii. 8; xii. 6; xiv. 10.—Ver. 25. **For I refresh.** The perfect is the prophetical perfect. It represents the future fact as already accomplished. **For** denotes that all that has been previously mentioned is only the realization of the purpose of Jehovah to relieve every distress and need, wherefore the satisfaction of hunger and thirst spoken of in ver. 25 is only to be understood as *instar omnium.* עָיֵף of the thirsty. Comp. Ps. lxiii. 2; cxliii. 6; Prov. xxv. 25; Job xxii. 7; Isai. xxxii. 2.

Ver. 26. **Upon this . . . sweet unto me.**

If we take these words, with CHR. B. MICHAELIS, ROSENMUELLER, UMBREIT and others, as the words of God, we have the altogether crooked sense that Jehovah designates the time, when He was acting as a severe judge, as a time of sweet sleep. If we understand the people as awaking, then we have again the contradictory thought that the time of visitation is compared with a sweet sleep. The explanations of EWALD (quotation from a well-known song, which is to show that then they will have no more bad dreams), and of GRAF (therefore will it then be said, I awake, *etc.*), are too artificial, for they require the supplementation of introductory formulas which by no means offer themselves. As the words stand they can be understood only of the prophet. But is it a question, whether it is a real physical sleep or an ecstatic condition resembling sleep, which is spoken of. It is difficult to decide. HENGSTENBERG has declared in favor of the latter (*Christology,* Eng. Tr. II., 426). But in Zech. iv. 1, to which passage HENGSTENBERG appeals, the prophet is awakened *to* an ecstatic vision. I do not think, moreover, that the ecstatic condition is anywhere directly called sleep, and that he who awakes from it has the feeling of having slept. It cannot be doubted that dreams generally served as the physical means of divine revelation. Comp. rems. on xxiii. 25 and Numb. xii. 6; Joel iii. 1; 1 Ki. iii. 5 : ix. 2. Jeremiah never tells us elsewhere in what bodily condition he was when he received his revelation, but of this he tells us that he received it in sleep. Why here only such a remark on the outward form of the revelation and the feeling which he had in connection with it? Let us remember that this prophecy is the only uninterruptedly consolatory one in the whole book. Is it not then very intelligible that that moment was never forgotten when, awaking after the reception of this revelation, he had the feeling of an exceedingly sweet and refreshing sleep? I therefore perceive in this brief remark an indication that Jeremiah himself regarded the moment of the reception of this revelation as a point of light in his otherwise rough and laborious prophetic career (comp. xx. 7 sqq.). We may indeed truly say that here we stand at the most comforting and brightest point in the prophecies of Jeremiah.—**Upon this.** עַל־זֹאת may well mean "upon this," combining the local and causal senses (comp. iv. 28).—**Looked up.** The prophet mentions that he opened his eyes and saw, to intimate that he was really and fully awake, and that in a fully awake and self-conscious state he had the feeling that his sleep had been sweet. There is, as we know, a half-awaking, which is only apparent and therefore deceptive.—**Sweet unto me.** Comp. Prov. iii 24; Jer. vi. 20.

IV. The Entire Renovation.

1. *The New Life.*

XXXI. 27-30.

27 Behold, the days are coming, saith Jehovah,
When I will sow the house of Israel and the house of Judah,
With the seed of man and with the seed of beast.
28 And it shall be that as I have been wakeful over them,
To pluck up and to root out,
To pull down, to destroy and to afflict,
So I will be wakeful over them,
To build and to plant, saith Jehovah.
29 In those days it shall no more be said,
The fathers have eaten sour grapes,
And the teeth of the children are blunted.
30 But every one shall die for his own iniquity:—
Every man who eats sour grapes,
His teeth shall be blunted.

EXEGETICAL AND CRITICAL.

Whether Jeremiah fell asleep again at once or whether the following revelation was separated by a longer interval from the previous one is a question which must remain undecided. Both cases are possible. At any rate there is a close logical connection. This and the quotation from i. 10 indicate that this passage by no means takes its origin from a sensibly later period. The prophet who, in ch. xxx., had treated of Judah and Israel, in xxxi. 1-22 only of Israel, and in xxxi. 23-26 only of Judah, now again directs his prophetic gaze on both (comp. iii. 18; v. 11). He promises the old theocratic blessing of great fruitfulness both of the men and the cattle (ver. 27), the absence of all that is destructive or afflictive, and on the other hand growth and progress on all sides (ver. 28). Entering more deeply into the ground of the previous destructive judgment, he sets before them so lofty a position and such energy of general morality that common guilt and solidaric implication of the following generations shall no more be spoken of. But the transgressions would he only exceptional cases, which would hence be no longer injurious to the whole, but only to the single individual (vers. 29 and 30).

Vers. 27 and 28. **Behold the days... saith Jehovah.** On the promise of fruitfulness, comp. rems. on xxix. 6.—**I will sow.** Comp. Gen. xlvii. 23.—**I have been wakeful.** Comp. rems. on i. 12, 10; xviii. 7, 9.

Vers. 29 and 30. **In those days ... be blunted.** The proverb of the sour grapes and blunted teeth, here mentioned for the first time, may have a double meaning. It may mean the fathers have *begun* to eat sour grapes, but it is the sons only who have had their teeth blunted, *i. e.* the punishment does not always come immediately on the *first* who are guilty, but on those of the second, third and fourth generations. It may also mean that the punishment does not always come on the guilty *father*, but often only on the *innocent* son or grandchild. In the latter sense Ezekiel, chap. xviii., combats the proverb as a blasphemy of God's justice. In the former sense however the proverb involves no blasphemy, but expresses only what the law itself declares in the words, I am a jealous God, visiting the sins of the fathers on the children, to the third and fourth generation of them that hate me (Exod. xx. 5; xxxiv. 7: Numb. xiv. 18; Deut. v. 9; Jer. xxxii. 18; Lam. v. 7). This canon of the divine justice rests on the hypothesis that sin is not only an individual but a corporate sin, a sin of families, races, generations, nations, states. Of course every such sin, common to many, has its history. It unfolds like every other germ, till it has attained its widest extent and fullest maturity. When the point of maturity is reached the judgment comes. Those who are then living have their teeth blunted, possibly indeed as the less guilty (think of Louis XVI., of France)—always, however, as the children of their fathers in the same sense as the expression is used in Matt. xxiii. 31, 32, *i. e.* as the apple falling not far from the trunk, as the organic continuation and perfection of the moral tendency adopted by the fathers. According to those who understand the proverb only in a bad sense, Jeremiah only declares in this passage "that Jehovah will not then as now be accused of unrighteousness in an ungodly proverb, but it will be perceived that each one has to suffer for his own guilt (GRAF)." Appeal is made in favor of this explanation to Deut. xxiv. 16. To which I make the following objections: 1. The non-employment of the proverb (in the false sense) proves certainly a correct knowledge of the justice of God, but only elementary, merely negative knowledge. It is not a symptom of greatly advanced knowledge to perceive that God does not punish any innocent person; while according to the whole connection of this passage a period of the highest prosperity of theocratic life is to be here described, an essential basis of which is a corresponding stage of religious and moral perfection. Comp. vers. 18 and 19.—2. The passage Deut. xxiv. 16 is to be regarded not as the norm of divine, but only of human punitive justice. By this declaration that savage custom of the heathen merely was to be guarded against, according to which *ob noxam unius omnis propinquitas* was to perish. (Comp. Jud. xv. 6; HAEVERNICK on Ezek., S. 286). Comp. also 2 Ki. xiv. 6; 2 Chron. xxv. 4.—I accordingly do not supply they shall say after but, ver. 30, but I regard ver. 30 as the declaration of the prophet. The moral level will be so high that only individual transgressions will occur as isolated exceptions from the rule. In general, and as a whole, Israel will be a holy congregation in which the power of the prevailing spirit will not allow the evil proceeding from individuals to extend itself. This will be restricted to the individual author and lead to the ruin of himself alone. Comp. Isa. lx. 18, 20. I find here the same view of the moral condition, which the kingdom of God is to attain as the highest stage of its earthly perfection, which lies at the basis of the Sermon on the Mount, and which found its certainly only precursory and passing realization in the apostolic church at Jerusalem. For in Matt. v. 21 sqq., the Lord tells us what will be the prevailing spirit in His Church, and according to what standard any contravention by individuals will be punished, to which Acts v. furnishes a practical commentary. In this view of the passage its connection with what follows is also clear, this passage being a preparation for what the prophet says of the Lord's new covenant with the Church, and that being an elucidation of the present passage.

---

2. *The New Covenant.*

XXXI. 31-40.

31 Behold, the days are coming, saith Jehovah,
   When I will make a new covenant with the house of Israel and the house of Judah:
32 Not like the covenant which I made with their fathers
   In the day that I took them by their hand,[1]
   To lead them forth out of the land of Egypt;
   Which my covenant they broke;
   And yet I was their husband, saith Jehovah.
33 But this is the covenant which I will make
   With the house of Israel after those days, saith Jehovah:
   I will put my law within them, and write it on their heart,
   And I will be their God and they shall be my people.
34 And a man will no more teach his neighbor,
   Nor a man his brother, saying, Know Jehovah!
   For all will know me from[2] the least to the greatest, saith Jehovah:
   For I will forgive their sin,
   And their iniquity I will remember no more.
35 Thus saith Jehovah, who giveth the sun for light by day,
   And the laws of the moon and stars for light by night,
   Who exciteth the sea so that its waves roar,
   Jehovah Zebaoth is his name:
36 If these laws perish before me, saith Jehovah,
   The seed of Israel will also cease to be a nation before me forever.
37 Thus saith Jehovah, When the heavens above are measured,
   And the foundations of the earth searched out beneath,
   Then will I also reject the whole seed of Israel
   For all that they have done, saith Jehovah.
38 Behold, the days are coming,[3] saith Jehovah,
   When the city shall be built for Jehovah,
   From the tower of Hananeel to the corner-gate.

39 And the measuring-line⁴ shall go forth further,
Straight out to the hill Gareb and turn towards Goath.
40 And the whole valley of the dead bodies and of the ashes,
And all the land⁵ to the brook Kedron,
To the corner of the horse-gate towards the east,
Shall be holy unto Jehovah,
And shall no more be devastated nor destroyed forever.

TEXTUAL AND GRAMMATICAL.

1 Ver. 32.—On the punctuation of הֶחֳיִ֫קָ comp. OLSHAUSEN, § 192 *f.*

2 Ver. 34.—On לְכִי comp. rems. on vii. 7, 25.

3 Ver. 38.—בָּאִים which is wanting in the Chethibh, but is supplied by the Keri, is nowhere else lacking in the formula, so frequent in Jeremiah. There is probably then a scriptural error.

4 Ver. 39.—Instead of קַוְה the Masoretes would read קָו (here as in 1 Ki. vii. 23; Zech. i. 16). Although קַו is the usual form, the form קַוְה (comp. עֵדָה) is however not to be discredited.

5 Ver. 40.—A word שְׁרֵכָה does not occur, nor is a root שָׁרֵך to be found. We are therefore obliged to read with the Masoretes שְׁדֵמוֹת. (Comp. Isa. xxxvii. 27; xvi. 8; Hab. iii. 17; Deut. xxxii. 32; 2 Ki. xxiii. 4).

EXEGETICAL AND CRITICAL.

This prophecy reaches its acme in the promise of a new covenant (ver. 31). This new covenant is the foundation of the moral condition set before us in vers. 29 and 30. For the essence of the new covenant, in distinction from the old, which was broken (ver. 32), will be an inward central union with God (ver. 33), the *consequence* of which will be, that on the part of men, outward instruction will be superfluous, the *ground* of which, on the part of God, is His forgiving love (ver. 34). This covenant has two further characteristics: 1. it will be eternal, as the eternal ordinances of nature (vers. 35-37); 2. it will also have in its train the penetration of the natural sphere with the elements of holy life. Jerusalem will be inwardly so holy to the Lord that even the unholy places, which the city has hitherto had, like all other cities, in its suburbs, will now, as being sanctified, be reckoned to the city itself (vers. 38-40).

Vers. 31, 32. **Behold ... Jehovah.** Here also the prophet's discourse extends to both halves of the nation. The Lord will conclude a new covenant with the whole of Israel (xxxii. 40; l. 5; Isa lv. 3). This new covenant stands in contrast to the old, which the Lord made with the fathers of the Israelites "in the day when He took them by the hand to lead them out of the land of Egypt." Wrong as it would be to understand by this "day" the stay at Sinai, equally so would it be to restrict it to the day of the exodus (Exod. xii. 51; xiii. 3, 4). Two things pertain to the conclusion of a covenant, a performance and a condition or requirement; the concluding of the covenant between Jehovah and the people Israel then lasted through the whole period of the Mosaic legislation, just as long as the bringing forth out of Egypt lasted. The manuduction ends only with the promised land, and from the day of the exodus to the day of his death Moses did not cease to give laws to the people (Exod. xii. to Deut. xxxii.). Since now there is no grammatical necessity of taking "day" in a literal sense (comp. Isa. xi. 16; 2 Sam. xxi. 12; xxii. 1), we are justified in understanding by the covenant of ver. 32 that covenant which Jehovah concluded through the mediation of Moses in different acts (Deut. xxix. 1; comp. KURTZ, *Gersch. d. A. B.* II., S. 522 [*History of the Old Covenant*] with the people Israel, and required as its condition the keeping of the Torah (comp. בְּחוּצְרָאל Deut. xxix. 24; xxviii. 1 sqq., 13 sqq.).—**Which my covenant. Which** is at any rate to be referred to **my covenant**, since this is also the main conception in the previous clause of the sentence.—**They** is emphatic: *they* broke the covenant, not *I*. It was the weak side of this covenant that it could be broken, and had God made this only, there might have been a doubt either as to His omniscience or His holy love. The first covenant, however, was only preliminary, preparatory and typical.—**And yet I was their husband.** The LXX., which translates iii. 14 κατακυριεύσω ὑμῶν, here has ἠμέλησα αὐτῶν. So likewise in Heb. viii. 9. From the context we should certainly expect an idea corresponding to **broke**, *i. e.* a word by which Jehovah's relation to the covenant-breakers would be designated. Meanwhile grammatical considerations require us to take בָּעַל in the meaning, which it has everywhere else, namely =to possess, and indeed (predominantly) as spouse. But we cannot, with HENGSTENBERG, take the sentence **and yet I**, *etc.*, as a promise (I will marry them), for that would be an anticipation of the turn of thought beginning with **But**, in ver. 33; for we must rather, with EWALD, regard it as an antithetical statement of a fact: and yet I was (or: while I was their husband). Thus the emphasis rests on the idea of husband; and the sense is: it is not a covenant concluded *inter pares*, which each of the contracting parties may renounce, which they have broken, but a marriage alliance in which they represent the woman, who is never justified in desiring the dissolution of the matrimonial connection, or in effecting it. [" Probably the true rendering is, *and therefore I rejected them* (from *bâal*, to refuse, to loathe). See the Syriac, POCOCKE (*Port. Mosis*, pp. 5-10, GESENIUS, 130, and Mr. TURPIE'S valuable work, '*The Old Testament in the New,*' pp 251, 252)." WORDSWORTH.—S. R. A.].

Vers. 33 and 34. **But this is ... remember no more.** 'כִּי is "for," but in the sense of "but," because it corresponds to **not**, in ver. 32. Comp. NAEGELSB. *Gr.*, § 110. 4.—**Those days.** It is not said **these**, for this would be the days of the present, while the word used refers to more distant days, to those namely, which will precede the turn to good, the שׁוּב שְׁבוּת (ver. 16 sqq.).—**I will put**, *etc.* The prophet evidently has in view the stone tables of the Law, on which the ten "words," the kernel of the Torah, were written. This law of commandments (Eph. ii. 15; Col. ii. 14) externally imposed on men by a subordinate mediator (Gal. iii. 19), was ἀσθενὴς καὶ ἀνωφελής (Heb. vii. 19), wherefore it is also said of it οὐδὲν ἐτελείωσεν (Heb. vii. 19). It was only to render men conscious how far the human subject in and of himself was in a condition to satisfy the demands of a holy God, *i. e* the law was to produce conviction of sin (Rom. iii. 20). Only a heart in which the law has been livingly written and in which it dwells, *i. e.* only a human will, which has become one with the divine will, and thus free, can continue in covenant with God (xxxii. 40; xxiv. 7; Ezek. xi. 19; 2 Cor. iii. 3). Only where this takes place is God truly the man's God, and the people God's people. To be God is to be the most exalted being, therefore the highest good, the source and end of life. Only where God is thus for man, is He truly his God. And a people only which stands in this relation to God, is truly God's people (comp. vii. 23).—HENGSTENBERG is of opinion that between the old and new covenants there is only a quantitative not a qualitative difference. "Parallel to the passage under consideration is the promise of God of the pouring out of the Spirit, Joel iii. 1, 2 (ii. 28, 29), so that what we remarked on that passage is applicable here also ... As under the New Covenant generally in its relation to the Old there is nowhere an absolutely new beginning but always a completion only ... so in reference to the communication of the Spirit, Joel puts only abundance in the place of scarcity, many in the place of few" [*Christology, Eng. Tr.* II., p. 439]. It is true no legal enactment of the Old Covenant is declared false in the New (Matth. v. 17-19); it is true that men knew even under the Old Covenant that the law, in order to be fulfilled must not be merely externally before the eyes, or merely in the head, but that it must be in the heart (Deut. xxx. 6; Ps. xl. 9; Prov. iii. 1-3). But this Old Testament having-in-the-heart, which is spoken of in the passages cited, is quite a different thing from that which Jeremiah means in this passage. There were many God-fearing Jews who had the law at heart, and in their heart, and who loved the Lord with all *their* strength, but was one of them justified by this observance of the law? We shall recur to this again directly.

Ver. 34. **No more teach**, *etc.* THEODORET says, τῶν δὲ ῥητῶν τούτων τέ τέλος ὁ μέλλων δώσεται βίος. We have however no intimation that the prophecy of ver. 34 will be fulfilled at another time than that which is spoken of before and afterwards. No passage can be shown in which the Old Testament prophets make predictions concerning the heavenly state. The prophet therefore sets before his hearers a period of terrestrial development in which the illumination of the Spirit (Joel iii. 1, 2; John vi. 45) will lead each of himself to the essentially correct knowledge of God. Reciprocal furtherance is certainly not thus denied.—**For all will**, *etc.* In these words the prophet indicates the proper basis of the gifts of grace previously named. So also the author of the Epistle to the Hebrews understands the passage, quoting x. 16 sqq. (in distinction from viii. 7 sqq.) so that after διδοὺς νόμους μου ἐπὶ καρδίας αὐτῶν καὶ ἐπὶ τὴν διάνοιαν αὐτῶν ἐπιγράψω αὐτούς he directly adds the concluding words of ver. 34, καὶ τῶν ἁμαρτιῶν αὐτῶν καὶ ἀνομιῶν αὐτῶν οὐ μὴ μνησθήσομαι ἔτι. Only where the real (not merely ideal and hypothetical) forgiveness of sins conditioned by the true atoning sacrifice is imparted (comp. Heb. x. 1-4), can there be the communication of the spirit of adoption (Gal. iii. 2, 5), and thus true knowledge, and the true walk according to God's will. And herein also consists the most radical objective difference between the Old Covenant and the New, in the former all is shadow and type, the latter only has the essence of the good things itself (Heb. x. 1). Not till the sacrifice was offered on the cross was the veil of the temple rent, and the way of access to God actually opened. Now even if Moses and Elias be pointed to (Matth. xvii. 3), it is certain that no one received the knowledge of the "mystery of godliness" (1 Tim. iii. 16) before the death and resurrection of our Lord. John was more than a prophet, and yet the least in the kingdom of heaven is greater than he (Matth. xi. 9 sqq.) The **for** before **I will forgive** is therefore to be well observed. Here also we learn the meaning of בְּרִיתִי. It is without doubt incorrect to take it in the sense of "*constituere*, to establish, make arrangements," for everywhere else it signifies to conclude a covenant. But where God concludes a covenant it is always at the same time He who works the will and the execution, whence also in this passage *gifts* of God only are mentioned. At the same time we are neither justified nor in a condition to give a definite historical date for the conclusion of the New Covenant. If we should designate the day of the crucifixion as on the part of God the moment when He entered into the New Covenant relation, yet on the part of mankind there would then be no corresponding date of acceptance. In the fact that the Covenant is in the most exalted sense *granted*, lies also the necessity of its acceptance. God does not give His Son for an uncertainty. The taking is included in the giving. In fact the measure of the covenant members becomes full by the successive accession of individual believers.

Vers. 35-37. **Thus saith ... Jehovah.** Not only by its inwardness, but, also, closely connected with this by its eternal duration, is the New Covenant distinguished from the Old. The Old was broken by Israel and the nation therefore rejected by Jehovah. This will no more take place under the New Covenant. This will be as it were a second ordinance of nature. It will be as immovable as the great laws of nature. Gen. i. 14 in view. Comp. Ps. cxxxvi. 8. The expression **and the laws**, *etc.*, seems to be a reminiscence of Job xxxviii. 33, which comes out more plainly in xxxiii. 25.—**Who exciteth the sea**, *etc.*, is taken from Isai. li. 15. There the *might* of the Lord, as it has been displayed in the wonders of history and of nature in general, is set forth for the comfort of Israel. Here all the emphasis lies on the idea of the fixedness and stability of the ordinances of nature, which God has created. That God can excite the mighty ocean is rather a proof of His power than an instance of the inviolate order of nature, and it is hence probable that the expression originated with Isaiah.—Ver. 36. **If these laws**, *etc.* As certainly as the laws of nature are inviolable, so certainly shall Israel everlastingly continue as a nation before the Lord (xxxiii. 20-26; Ps. lxxxix. 37, 38). The question is natural here: why then has Jehovah raised the eternal continuance of the people of Israel as it were to the rank of a law of nature? The answer is given in ver. 37, (which does not feebly hobble after, as GRAF supposes), not however with a solution of the problem, but with the declaration that the ground of the historical fact is as secret as the heavens above us are immeasurable, and the earth beneath us in its profoundest depths is unsearchable. Comp. xxxiii. 22. 26.

Vers. 38-40. **Behold the days . . . forever.**—**Tower of Hananeel.** This tower designates, as is acknowledged, the North-East corner of Jerusalem. It is also mentioned in Zech. xiv. 10; Neh. iii. 1; xii. 39. The corner-gate (comp. 2 Ki. xiv. 13; 2 Chron. xxvi. 9, and also שַׁעַר הַפִּנִּים Zech. xiv. 10) designates the North-West corner. *Vid.* RAUMER, *Paläst. S.* 290. By these two points then the northern limit of the city is defined. As the tower of Hananeel and the corner tower were part of the fortifications of the city, there seems to be no further extension on this side.—**Straight out**, נֶגְדּוֹ accus. of motion to the question *whither?* To its opposite, *i. e.*, straight out. Comp. Am. iv. 3; Josh. vi. 5, 20. —Gareb occurs here only as the name of a place, as the name of a person in 2 Sam. xxiii. 38; 1 Chron. xi. 40. The meaning of the word must according to גָּרַב *scabies*, (Lev. xxi. 20; xxii. 22) be "scabby, leprous." In accordance with the other localizations, this must mean, as GRAF has shown, the South-West corner. What Goath

(גֹּעָה) is, is quite uncertain. The word occurs here only. The Chald. has בְּרֵכַת עֶגְלָא (cowpond), the Syr. *tormeto*, *i. e.*, rocky hill, by which it seems to have understood the projecting rock of the castle Antonia (HITZIG, FUERST). VITRINGA and HENGSTENBERG take it as = גַּל נוּעָתָה, *i. e.*, Golgotha. But both the etymology and topography are very uncertain. The valley of corpses and ashes is without doubt the vale of Hinnom in the South, for that was the place where all the refuse of the city ran or was carried. (Comp. Comm. on xix. 2). פֶּגֶר is the unburied *cadaver* of men and beasts (xli. 9; Gen. xv. 11), דֶּשֶׁן is especially the ashes of burnt fat (Lev. i. 16; iv. 1). It is better to regard it as the ashes of the offal, burned without the camp, than of the sacrifices burned on the altar (flesh, skin, dung, Lev. iv. 11, 12; vii. 17, 19; viii. 17, 32; ix. 11;

xvi. 27; xix. 6) and clothing (Lev. xiii. 52, 55, 57). The horse-gate was on the East of the city by the temple (Neh. iii. 18; xii. 39, 40). So far as we can perceive in general from these local determinations, the subject is not primarily, as in Ezek. xlviii. 15 sqq. an extension of the city. For the gain in space according to the boundaries mentioned is relatively insignificant. Only in the South-West, South, and at any rate in the South-East, are some small portions added to the city. The main point is that by this extension the places which were unholy will be rendered holy. They were the purlieus of the city. If even these places are added to the city, it shows that the city no longer needs such places. It is in itself so thoroughly holy to the Lord that it will have nothing unholy to cast out. Nothing unclean will enter (Rev. xxi. 27), therefore nothing unclean will proceed from it. It will be thoroughly sanctified and enlightened, therefore safe from destruction to all eternity.

DOCTRINAL AND ETHICAL.

1. JOH. CONR. SCHALLER, pastor at Cautendorf, says in his *Gospel Sermons*, (Hof. 1742, *S.* 628), " These chapters are like a sky in which sparkle many brilliant stars of strong and consolatory declarations, a paradise and pleasure-garden in which a believing soul is refreshed with delightsome flowers of instruction, and solaced with sweetly flavored apples of gracious promise."

2. On xxx. 1-3. The people of Israel were not then capable of bearing such a prophecy, brimming over with happiness and glory. They would have misused it, hearing to the end what was promised them, and then only the more certainly postponing what was the only thing then necessary—sincere repentance. Hence they are not yet to hear this gloriously consolatory address. It is to be written, that it may in due time be perceived that the Lord, even at the time when He was obliged to threaten most severely, had thoughts of peace concerning the people, and that thus the period of prosperity has not come by chance, nor in consequence of a change of mind, but in consequence of a plan conceived from the beginning and executed accordingly.

3. On xxx. 7. The great and terrible day of the Lord (Joel iii. 4) has not the dimensions of a human day. It has long sent out its heralds in advance. Yea, it has itself already dawned. For since by the total destruction of the external theocracy judgment is begun at the house of God (1 Pet. iv. 17), we stand in the midst of the day of God, in the midst of the judgment of the world. Then the time of trouble for Jacob has begun (ver. 7), from which he is to be delivered, when the fulness of the Gentiles is come in (Rom. xi.)

4. On xxx. 9. Christ is David in his highest potency, and He is also still more. For if we represent all the typical points in David's life as a circle, and draw a line from each of these points, the great circle thus formed would comprise only a part of the πλήρωμα given in Christ. Nevertheless Christ is the true David, who was not chosen like Saul for his bodily stature, but only for his inward relation to God (comp. Ps. i., 7), whose kingdom also does not cease after a short period of glory, but endures forever; who will

CHAP. XXX. 1—XXXI. 40.

not like Saul succumb to his enemies, but will conquer them all, and will give to his kingdom the widest extent promised; all this however not without, like David, having gone through the bitterest trials.

5. On xxx. 11. "*Modus paternæ castigationis accommodatus et quasi appensus ad stateram judicii Dei adeoque non immensus sed dimensus.*" "*Christus ecclesiam crucis suæ hæredem constituit.* GREGON. M." FÖRSTER.

6. On xxx. 14. "*Cum virlutem patientiæ nostræ flagella transcunt, valde metuendum est, ne peccatis nostris exigentibus non jam quasi filii a patre, sed quasi hostes a Domino feriamur.* GREGON. M. *Moral.* XIV. 20, on Job xix. 11." GHISLER.

7. On xxx. 17. "*Providentia Dei mortalibus salutifera, antequam percutiat, pharmaca medendi gratiâ componit, et gladium iræ suæ φιλανθρωπίᾳ acuit.* EVAGR. *Hist. Eccl.* iv. 6."—"*Quando incidis in tentationem, crede, quod nisi cognovisset te posse illam evadere, non permisisset te in illam incidere.* THEOPHYL. *in cap.* xviii Joh." FÖRSTER.—"*Feriam prius et sanabo melius.* THEOPHYL. *in* Hos. xi." GHISLER.

8. On xxx. 21. "This church of God will own a Prince from its midst—Jesus, of our flesh and blood through the virgin Mary, and He approaches God, as no other can, for He is God's image, God's Son, and at the same time the perfect, holy in all His sufferings, only obedient son of man. This king is mediator and reconciler with God; He is also high-priest and fulfilled all righteousness, as was necessary for our propitiation. What glory to have such a king, who brings us nigh unto God, and this is our glory!" DIEDRICH.

9. On xxxi. 1. "There is no greater promise than this: I will be thy God. For if He is our God we are His creatures, His redeemed, His sanctified, according to all the three articles of the Christian faith." CRAMER.

10. On xxxi. 2. "The rough heap had to be sifted by the sword, but those who survived, though afflicted in the desert of this life, found favor with God, and these, the true Israel, God leads into His rest." DIEDRICH.

11. On xxxi. 3. "The love of God towards us comes from love and has no other cause above or beside itself, but is in God and remains in God, so that Christ who is in God is its centre. So herein is love, not that we loved God, but that He loved us (1 John iv. 10)." CRAMER. "*Totum gratiæ imputatur, non nostris meritis.* AUGUSTINE *in Ps.* xxxi." FÖRSTER. "Before I had done anything good Thou hadst already moved towards me. Let these words be written on your hearts with the pen of the living God, that they may light you like flames of fire on the day of the marriage. It is your certificate of birth, your testimonial. Let me never lose sight of how much it has cost Thee to redeem me." ZINZENDORF. "God says: My chastisement even was pure love, though then you did not understand it; you shall learn it afterwards." DIEDRICH. ["I incline to the construction given in the English version, both because the suffix to the verb is more naturally, 'I have drawn *thee*,' than 'I have drawn out *toward* thee,' and because there seems to be a tacit allusion to Hos. xi. 4, 'With loving-kindness have I drawn thee.'—A great moral truth lies in this passage so construed, *viz.*, that the main power which humbles man's pride, softens his hard heart and makes him recoil in shame and sorrow from sinning, comes through his apprehension of God's love as manifested in Christ and His cross. It is love that draws the fearful or stubborn soul to the feet of divine mercy." COWLES.—S. R. A.]

12. On xxxi. 6. "It is well: the watchmen on Mount Ephraim had to go to Zion. They received however another visit from the Jewish priests, which they could not have expected at the great reformation, introduced by John, and which had its seat among other places on Mount Ephraim. The Samaritans were not far distant, and Mount Ephraim had even this honor that when the Lord came to His temple He took His seat as a teacher there." ZINZENDORF. ["God's grace loves to triumph over the most inveterate prejudices. . . No words could represent a greater and more benign change in national feeling than these: Samaria saying through her spiritual watchmen, 'Let us go up to Zion to worship, for our God is there.'" COWLES. "'*Ascendamus in Sion, hoc est in Ecclesiam*' says S. JEROME. According to this view, the watchmen here mentioned are the Preachers of the Gospel." WORDSWORTH.—S. R. A.]

13. On xxxi. 9. "**I will lead them.** It is an old sighing couplet, but full of wisdom and solid truth:—

'Lord Jesus, while I live on earth, O guide me,
Let me not, self-led, wander from beside Thee.'"
—ZINZENDORF.

14. On xxxi. 10. "He who has scattered Israel will also collect it. Why? He is the Shepherd. It is no wolf-scattering. He interposes His hand, then they go asunder, and directly come together again more orderly." ZINZENDORF.

15. On xxxi. 12-14. "*Gaudebunt electi, quando videbunt supra se, intra se, juxta se, infra se.* AUGUSTINE."—"*Præmia cœlestia erunt tam magna, ut non possint mensurari, tam multa, ut non possint numerari, tam copiosa, ut non possint terminari, tam pretiosa, ut non possint æstimari.* BERNHARD." FÖRSTER.

16. On xxxi. 15. "Because at all times there is a similar state of things in the church of God, the lament of Rachel is a common one. For as this lament is over the carrying away captive and oppressions of Babylon, so is it also a lament over the tyranny of Herod in slaughtering the innocent children (Matt. ii. 1-7.)" CRAMER. "*Premuntur justi in ecclesia ut clament, clamantes exaudiuntur, exauditi glorificent Deum.* AUGUSTIN." FÖRSTER.—With respect to this, that Rachel's lament may be regarded as a type of maternal lamentation over lost children, FÖRSTER quotes this sentence of CYPRIAN: *non amisimus, sed præmisimus* (2 Sam. xii. 23). [On the application of this verse to the murder of the innocents consult W. L. ALEXANDER, *Connexion of the Old and New Testament,* p. 54, and W. H. MILL in WORDSWORTH'S Note in *loc.*—S. R. A.]

17. On xxxi. 18. The conversion of man must always be a product of two factors. A conversion which man alone should bring about, without God, would be an empty pretence of conversion; a conversion, which God should produce, without man, would be a compulsory, manufactured affair, without any moral value. The merit and the praise is, however, always on God's side.

He gives the will and the execution. Did He not discipline us, we should never learn discipline. Did He not lead back our thoughts to our Father's house which we have left (Luke xv.) we should never think of returning.

18. On xxxi. 19. "The children of God are ashamed their life long, they cannot raise their heads for humiliation. For their sins always seem great to them, and the grace of God always remains something incomprehensible to them." ZINZENDORF. The farther the Christian advances in his consciousness of sonship and in sanctification, the more brilliantly rises the light of grace, the more distinctly does he perceive in this light, how black is the night of his sins from which God has delivered him. ["It is the ripest and fullest ears of grain which hang their heads the lowest."—S. R. A.]

19. On xxxi. 19. "The use of the dear cross is to make us blush (Dan. ix. 8) and not regard ourselves as innocent (Jer. xxx. 11). And as it pleases a father when a child soon blushes, so also is this tincture a flower of virtue well-pleasing to God." CRAMER. "*Deus oleum miserationis suæ non nisi in vas contritum et contribulatum infundit.* BERNHARD." FÖRSTER.

20. On xxxi. 19. **The reproach of my youth.** "The sins of youth are not easily to be forgotten (Ps. xxv. 7; Job xxxi. 18). Therefore we ought to be careful so to act in our youth as not to have to chew the cud of bitter reflection in our old age. It is a comfort that past sins of youth will not injure the truly penitent. *Non nocent peccata præterita, cum non placent præsentia.* AUGUSTINE. To transgress no more is the best sign of repentance." CRAMER.

21. On xxxi. 20. "Comforting and weighty words, which each one should lay to heart. God loves and caresses us as a mother her good child. He remembers His promise. His heart yearns and breaks, and it is His pleasure to do us good." CRAMER. "*Ipsius proprium est, misereri semper et parcere.*" AUGUSTINE.—"*Major est Dei misericordia quam omnium hominum miseria.*" IDEM.

22. On xxxi. 23. **The Lord bless thee, thou dwelling-place of righteousness, thou holy mountain.** "Certainly no greater honor was ever done to the Jewish mountains than that the woman's seed prayed and wept on them, was transfigured, killed and ascended above all heavens." ZINZENDORF. "It cannot be denied that a church sanctifies a whole place..... Members of Jesus are real guardian angels, who do not exist in the imagination, but are founded on God's promise (Matt. xxv. 40)." IDEM.

23. On xxxi. 29, 30. "The so-called family curse has no influence on the servants of God; one may sleep calmly nevertheless. This does not mean that we should continue in the track of our predecessors, *ex. gr.*, when our ancestors have gained much wealth by sinful trade, that we should continue this trade with this wealth with the hope of the divine blessing. . . . . If this or that property, house, right, condition be afflicted with a curse, the children of God may soon by prudent separation deliver themselves from these unsafe circumstances. For nothing attaches to their persons, when they have been baptized with the blood of Jesus and are blessed by Him." ZINZENDORF.

24. On xxxi. 29, 30. "*In testamento novo per sanguinem mediatoris deleto paterno chirographo incipit homo paternis debitis non esse obnoxius renascendo, quibus nascendo fuerat obligatus, ipso Mediatore dicente: Ne vobis patrem dicatis in terra* (Matt. xxiii 9). *Secundum hoc utique, quod alios nutales, quibus non patri succederemus, sed cum patre semper viveremus, invenimus.*" AUGUSTINE, contra *Julian*, VI. 12, in GHISLER.

25. On xxxi. 31. "*In veteribus libris aut nusquam aut difficile præter hunc propheticum locum legitur facta commemoratio testamenti novi, ut omnino ipso nomine appellaretur. Nam multis locis hoc significatur et prænuntiatur futurum, sed non ita ut etiam nomen legatur expressum.*" AUGUSTINE, *de Spir. et Lit. ad Marcellin*, Cap. 19 (where to Cap. 29 there is a detailed discussion of this passage) in GHISLER.—"In the whole of the Old Testament there is no passage, in which the view is so clearly and distinctly expressed as here that the law is only παιδαγωγός. And though some commentators have supposed that the passage contains only a censure of the Israelites and not of the Old Covenant, they only show thus that they have not understood the simple meaning of the words." EBRARD, *Comm. zum Hebräerbr. S.* 275.

26. On xxxi. 31, sqq. "*Propter veterem hominis nozum, quæ per literam jubentem et minantem minime sanabatur, dicitur illud testamentum vetus; hoc autem novum propter novitatem spiritus, quæ hominem novum sanat a vitio vetustatis.*" AUGUSTINE, *c. Lit. Cap.* 19.

27. On xxxi. 33. "*Quid sunt ergo leges Dei ab ipso Deo scriptæ in cordibus, nisi ipsa præsentia Spiritus sancti, qui est digitus Dei, quo præsente diffunditur charitas in cordibus nostrio, quæ plenitudo legis est et præcepti finis?*" AUGUSTINE, *l. c. Cap.* 20.

28. On xxxi. 34. "*Quomodo tempus est novi testamenti, de quo propheta dixit: et non docebit unusquisque civem suum, etc. nisi quia ejusdem testamenti novi æternam mercedem, id est ipsius Dei beatissimam contemplationem promittendo conjunxit?*" AUGUSTINE, *l. c. Cap.* 24.

29. On xxxi. 33, 34. "This is the blessed difference between law and Gospel, between form and substance. Therefore are the great and small alike, and the youths like the elders, the pupils more learned than their teachers, and the young wiser than the ancients (1 John ii. 20 sqq.). Here is the cause:—For I will forgive their iniquities. This is the occasion of the above: no one can effect this without it. Forgiveness of sins makes the scales fall from people's eyes, and gives them a cheerful temper, clear conceptions, a clear head." ZINZENDORF.

30. On xxxi. 35-37. "*Etsi particulares ecclesiæ in totum deficere possunt, ecclesia tamen catholica nunquam deficit aut deficiet. Obstant enim Dei amplissimæ promissiones, inter quas non ultimum locum sibi vindicat quæ hic habetur* Jer. xxxi. 37." FÖRSTER.

31. On xxxi. 38-40. "Jerusalem will one day be much greater than it has ever been. This is not to be understood literally but spiritually. Jerusalem will be wherever there are believing souls, its circle will be without end and comprise all that has been hitherto impure and lost. This it is of which the prophet is teaching, and which he presents in figures, which were intelligible to the people in his time. The hill Gareb, probably the residence of the lepers, the emblem of the

sinner unmasked and smitten by God, and the cursed valley of Ben-Hinnom will be taken up into the holy city. God's grace will one day effect all this, and Israel will thus be manifested as much more glorious than ever before." DIEDRICH.

HOMILETICAL AND PRACTICAL.

1. On xxx. 5-9. Sermon on one of the last Sundays after Trinity or the second in Advent. The day of the judgment of the world a great day. For it is, (1) a day of anxiety and terror for all the world; (2) a day of deliverance from all distress for the church of the Lord; (3) a day of realization of all the happiness set in prospect before it.
2. On xxx. 10-12. Consolation of the church in great trial. 1. It has well deserved the trial (ver. 12); 2. it is therefore chastised, but with moderation; 3. it will not perish but again enjoy peace.
3. On xxx. 17. ["The Restorer of mankind. 1. Faith in the Christian Sacrament and its attendant revelation of divine character alone answer the demand of the heart and reason of man for a higher state of moral perfection. 2. Christianity offers to maintain a communication between this world and that eternal world of holiness and truth. 3. It commends itself to our wants in the confirmation and direction of that principle of hope, which even in our daily and worldly life, we are perpetually forced to substitute for happiness, and 4. By the adorable object, which it presents to our affections." ARCHER BUTLER.—S. R. A.]
4. On xxxi. 1, 2. *Gesetz and Zeugniss* (Law and Testimony) 1864, *Heft.* 1. Funeral sermon of AHLFELD.
5. On xxxi. 2-4. *Ib.* 1865. *Heft* 1. Funeral sermon of BESSER, S. 32 ff.
6. On xxxi. 3. C. Fr. HARTMANN (Wedding, School, Catechism and Birth-day sermons, ed. C. CHR. EBERH. EHEMANN. Tüb. 1865). Wedding sermon. 1. A grateful revival in the love of God already received. 2. Earnest endeavor after a daily enjoyment of this love. 3. Daily nourishment of hope.
7. On xxxi. 3. FLOREY. *Comfort and warning at graves.* 1. *Bändchen, S.* 253. On the attractions of God's love towards His own children. They are, 1. innumerable and yet so frequently overlooked; 2. powerful and yet so frequently resisted; 3. rich in blessing and yet so frequently unemployed. [For practical remarks on this text see also THOLUCK, *Stunden der Andacht*, No. 11.—S. R. A.]
8. On xxxi. 9. Confessional sermon by Dekan V. BIARKOWSKY in Erlangen (in PALMER's *Evang. Casual-Reden*, 2 *te Folge*, 1 *Band*. Stuttgart, 1850.) Every partaking of the Lord's supper is a return to the Lord in the promised land, and every one who is a guest at the supper rises and comes. 1. How are we to come? (weeping and praying). 2. What shall we find? (Salvation and blessing, power and life, grace and help).
9. On xxxi. 18-20. Comparison of conversion with the course of the earth and the sun. 1. The man who has fallen away is like the planet in its distance from the sun; he flees from God as far as he can. 2. Love however does not release him: *a.* he is chastened (winter, cold, long nights, short days); *b.* he accepts the chastening and returns to proximity to the sun (summer, warmth, light, life). Comp. BRANDT, *Altes und Neues in extemporirbaren Entwürfen*. Nüremberg, 1829, II.
5. [The stubborn sinner submitting himself to God. I. A description of the feelings and conduct of an obstinate, impenitent sinner, while smarting under the rod of affliction: He is rebellious—till subdued. II. The new views and feelings produced by affliction through divine grace: (*a*) convinced of guilt and sinfulness; (*b*) praying; (*c*) reflecting on the effects of divine grace in his conversion. III. A correcting but compassionate God, watching the result, *etc.*, (*a*) as a tender father mindful of his penitent child; (*b*) listening to his complaints, confessions and petitions; (*c*) declaring His determination to pardon. PAYSON.—S. R. A.]
10. On xxxi. 31-34. Sermon on 1 Sunday in Advent by Pastor DIECHERT in Gröningen, S. STERN *aus Jakob*. I. Stuttg. 1867.
11. On xxxi. 33, 34. Do we belong to the people of God? 1. Have we holiness? 2. Have we knowledge? 3. Have we the peace promised to this people? (CASPARI in *Predigtbuch von* DITTMAR, Erlangen, 1845).
12. On xxxi. 33, 34. By the new covenant in the bath of holy baptism all becomes new. 1. What was dead becomes alive. 2. What was obscure becomes clear. 3. What was cold becomes warm. 4. What was bound becomes free (FLOREY, 1862).

B. THE ELEVENTH DISCOURSE.

CHAPTERS XXXII.—XXXIII.

WITH AN APPENDIX (CHAP. XXXIV. 1-7).

The thirty-third chapter contains a revelation of somewhat later date than ch. xxxii. *In* xxxiii. 1 *it is expressly stated that the contents of this chapter were communicated to the prophet separately, and subsequently to the revelation contained in* ch. xxxii. *The word* **second** (שֵׁנִית) xxxiii. 1, *however, designates this chapter as the second part or continuation of* ch. xxxii., *which also accords with its very similar purport. As* ch. xxxii. *shows us that the occupation of the Israelitish country by the northern foes does not prevent the Lord from commanding the prophet to purchase a piece of this very land, as a pledge that the time will come when the land can be bought and sold and inhabited and tilled in peace, so in* ch. xxxiii., *in connection with the destruction of many houses in the city of Jerusalem for the purposes of defence it is predicted that the city apparently devoted to entire devastation shall be rebuilt, that joy and rejoicing shall again prevail in it, that in the country breeding of cattle shall again be followed with blessing, and especially that from the house of David a "righteous sprout" shall proceed, by whom righteousness and salvation shall be diffused through the land. The throne of Israel shall no more lack a prince of the house of David, nor the worship Levitical priests. This covenant shall stand everlastingly as the laws of nature; innumerable as the stars of heaven or the sand of the sea shore shall be the seed of David and Levi. In the midst of the present mourning the prophet makes known these promises, for—and this is the formal basis, which* ch. xxxiii. *has in common with* ch. xxxii.—*the Lord has the power to do this; nothing is too wonderful for Him* (comp. xxxiii. 2, 3 with xxxii. 17, 27). *Without doubt these prophecies, proceeding from the court of the prison, are among the grandest which the prophet uttered. We shall see what a depth of misery this court of the prison involved for the prophet and for Israel. And in the very midst of this prophecy the abused prophet raises his voice in the most glorious prediction, that the wonder-working power of God may be recognized and praised, and faith, which rests not on the seen, but on the unseen* (2 Cor. iv. 18), *may be thus confirmed and encouraged. The fulfilment of this prophecy runs through all the stages of development, from that first feeble beginning, which was made after the return from exile, to the consummation of the βασιλεία τῶν οὐρανῶν which the future æon will bring us.*

From what has been said, it is evident that the present discourse forms a parallel to the earlier consolatory discourse, chh. xxx. and xxxi., *and that both, being placed purposely at the close of the collection, may with propriety be called the Book of Consolation. Though the general purport of the two discourses is similar, some differences are also noticeable. While the first* (chh. xxx. and xxxi.) *may be compared to a picture which beams with light and color, and in which the shading is indicated only by a few though powerful strokes* (comp xxx. 5-7, 11; xxxi. 15, 16, 18, 19), *the second seems like a picture, in which the deepest shades and the brightest light are equally divided and displayed in vivid contrast. Not only does the promise in the second discourse rise from present distressing circumstances, but the guilt of Israel, which is the cause of this distress, is portrayed with a strong hand* (xxxii. 29-35). *Still as the shade is stronger in the second discourse than in the first, so is the light. That which may be called the crown of all theocratic promise, viz., the Messianic kingdom, together with the priesthood standing inseparably by its side as a necessary supplement, is in the second discourse set forth much more clearly, much more comprehensively, and in much more various relations. While in the first discourse the Messianic king is spoken of in a few words only, and with no special emphasis,* xxx. 9, 21, *in the second the most prominent passage is occupied in detail with the Messianic king and priesthood. The passage* xxxiii. 14-26, *which is evidently to form the crowning close of the whole discourse, is entirely devoted to that most important subject of Messianic prediction.*

The time of the composition of chh. xxxii. and xxxiii. *is stated in the text. In* xxxii. 1 *it is expressly mentioned that the events there narrated took place in the tenth year of Zedekiah, the eighteenth of Nebuchadnezzar* (i. e., B. C., 587), *during the siege by the Chaldeans, and while Jeremiah was a prisoner in the court of the gaol. Only a little later followed, as a continuation and completion of the consolatory prediction, the revelation communicated to us in the thirty-third chapter* (comp. xxxiii. 1). MOVERS, DE WETTE and HITZIG *regard* ch. xxxiii. *as worked over by the author of Isa.* xl.-lxvi. *This view has been so thoroughly refuted by* GRAF *that it will suffice to refer to him* (comp. GRAF, S. 369, 415). —J. D. MICHAELIS (Orient. Bibl., XVII., S. 172 sqq.), JAHN (Vatt. Messian., P. II., S. 112 sqq.) *and* HITZIG *dispute the genuineness of* xxxiii. 14-26. MOVERS (de utr. Rec., etc., S. 41) *declares that vers.* 18, 21 b-25 *at least, are an interpolation. He may also appeal to* GRAF *for the refutation of this view* (S. 369, 370, *and his exposition of the passages in question). For a valuation of the circumstance that the section mentioned is wanting in the* LXX, *comp.* GRAF, Einleitung, pag. XLVIII. GRAF *himself however regards* xxxiii. 2, 3 *as interpolated. I refer on the other hand to my exposition of this passage.*

Since both chapters are so far of similar import, that ch. xxxiii. *may be regarded as a continuation and extension of* ch. xxxii., *the two together may consequently be regarded as* ONE *prophetic discourse. They are not so, however, in a logical and rhetorical sense, since they did not originate contemporaneously. We shall therefore treat the two halves separately.*

I. CHAPTER XXXII.

The most glorious future warranted in the midst of the most gloomy present by the purchase of a piece of ground in the enemy's hands.
1. *The transaction of the purchase.* xxxii. 1-15.
2. *A prayer of praise and inquiry,* xxxii. 16-25.
3. *Nothing is impossible to the Lord,* xxxii. 26-44.

II. CHAPTER XXXIII.

Promise of the most glorious future, given at the moment when the destruction of Jerusalem was already begun by its own inhabitants in the interest of defence.
1. *Brief transition: summons to new prayer in the sense of* xxxii. 16-25, *and promise of a hearing,* xxxiii. 1-3.
2. *Destruction in the present. Glorious internal and external rebuilding in the future notwithstanding,* xxxiii. 4-9.
3. *The glorious city-life of the future,* xxxiii. 10, 11.
4. *The glorious country-life of the future,* xxxiii. 12, 13.
5. *The glorious kingdom and priesthood of the future,* xxxiii. 14-18.
6. *The kingdom and priesthood of the future eternal,* xxxiii. 19-26.

---

1. CHAPTER XXXII.

The most glorious future warranted in the midst of the most gloomy present by the purchase of a piece of ground in the hands of the enemy.

1. *The transaction of the Purchase.*

XXXII. 1-15.

1 The word that came to Jeremiah from the Lord in the tenth year of Zedekiah,
2 king of Judah, which was the eighteenth year of Nebuchadrezzar. For then the king of Babylon's army besieged Jerusalem: and Jeremiah the prophet was shut up in the court of the prison [or guard] which was in the king of Judah's house.
3 For Zedekiah king of Judah had shut him up,¹ saying, Wherefore dost thou prophesy, and say, Thus saith the Lord, Behold, I will give this city into the hand
4 of the king of Babylon, and he shall take it; And Zedekiah king of Judah shall not escape out of the hand of the Chaldeans, but shall surely be delivered into the hand of the king of Babylon, and shall speak with him mouth to mouth, and his
5 eyes shall behold his eyes; And he shall lead Zedekiah to Babylon, and there shall he be until I visit him, saith the Lord : though ye fight with the Chaldeans, ye
6 shall not prosper. And Jeremiah said, The word of the Lord came unto me, say-
7 ing, Behold, Hanameel the son of Shallum thine uncle shall come unto thee, saying, Buy thee my field that *is* in Anathoth: for the right of redemption *is* thine to
8 buy *it*. So Hanameel mine uncle's son came to me in the court of the prison according to the word of the Lord, and said unto me, Buy my field, I pray thee, that *is* in Anathoth, which *is* in the country of Benjamin: for the right of inheritance *is* thine, and the redemption *is* thine; buy *it* for thyself. Then I knew that
9 this *was* the word of the Lord. And I bought the field of Hanameel my uncle's son, that *was* in Anathoth, and weighed him the money, *even* seventeen shekels of
10 silver.² And I subscribed the evidence [deed],³ and sealed *it*, and took wit-
11 nesses, and weighed *him* the money in the balances. So I took the evidence [deed] of the purchase, *both* that which was sealed *according* to the law and custom [*or*
12 (containing) the assignment and limitation], and that which was open: And I gave the evidence [deed] of the purchase unto Baruch, the son of Neriah, the son of Maaseiah, in the sight of Hanameel mine uncle's *son.* and in the presence of the witnesses that subscribed the book of the purchase, before all⁴ the Jews that sat in

13, 14 the court of the prison. And I charged Baruch before them, saying, Thus saith the LORD of hosts, the God of Israel; Take these evidences, this evidence of the purchase, both⁵ which is sealed, and this evidence which is open; and put them
15 in an earthen vessel, that they may continue many days. For thus saith the LORD of hosts, the God of Israel; Houses and fields and vineyards shall be possessed again in this land.

TEXTUAL AND GRAMMATICAL.

¹ Ver. 3.—אשר כלאו. The *Nota relationis* is to be regarded as in the accusative. Comp. NAEGELSB. *Gr.*, § 70, *b*; Num. xiii. 27; Isa. lxiv. 10; Ps. lxxxiv. 4.
² Ver. 9.—On the accus. הבכף. Comp. NAEGELSB. *Gr.*, § 70, *g*.—On the article. *Ib.* 71, 4 *a.*
³ Ver. 10.—The article in בכפר is again general. NAEGELSB. *Gr.*, § 71, 4 *a.*
⁴ Ver. 12.—לעיני כל. Misled by the Atnach, many suppose that ו is wanting here. But this לעיני does not belong to ואתן, *init. ver.*, but to הפתבים.
⁵ Ver. 11.—ואת—את. The two Vaus here as in ver. 20=both, and also comp. v. 24. NAEGELSB. *Gr.*, § 110, 3. The construction would certainly be simpler and clearer, if את were wanting before החתם, and it would certainly not be impossible that, as GRAF thinks, this ואת may have been repeated from ver. 11 by an oversight. A certain solemn breadth may, however, also have been intended. Then first the quantitative multiplicity or duplicity of the deeds may be generally set forth, then their qualitative unity (they form together only one deed of sale. Comp. vers. 11 and 12); finally the multiplicity is specified: there are two deeds, one sealed, the other open. The הגלוה and גלוי can then both be referred at the same time to החתם.

EXEGETICAL AND CRITICAL.

In the tenth year of king Zedekiah, during the siege of Jerusalem by the Chaldeans, at a time when all hope of deliverance had vanished and the overthrow of the kingdom was certain to all those who were not blinded, Jeremiah, who was then on account of his prophecy of inevitable ruin held a prisoner in the prison court, received a divine revelation, which announced that the lot of ground of his uncle Shallum at Anathoth would be offered him for sale on account of his right of redemption. Hanameel, the son of Shallum, really came with this offer to Jeremiah. The latter recognizing the Lord's will, buys the lot, carefully observing all the formalities, as a sign that "houses, fields and vineyards will again be bought in the land of Judah."

Vers. 1-5. **The word ... shall not prosper.** The superscription is again of the larger kind. It dominates chh. xxxii. and xxxiii. The word of Jehovah which it announces, is not merely the next following brief revelation of ver. 7, but all the revealed contents of both chapters. Comp. rems. on xxx. 1.—**In the tenth**, *etc.* Comp. rems. on xxviii. 1. The numerical statements are in entire agreement with xxxix. 1; xxv. 1; lii. 12.—**Besieged.** Comp. xxi. 4; xxxvii. 5; xxxix. 1; Deut. xx. 12, *etc.*—**Court of the prison.** According to xxxvii. 15, Jeremiah was incarcerated by the princes in בית האסור [prison, *literally:* house of bonds]. When the king had him brought out for an audience, he besought that he might not be taken back to that prison. The king granted his request and had him kept in the **court of the guard**, חצר המטרה, xxxvii. 21 coll. xxxviii. 6, 13, 28; xxxix. 14, 15). Accordingly this must have been at any rate a more tolerable place. The expression occurs, besides the passages mentioned, only in xxxiii. 1; Neh. iii. 25; xii. 39. מטרה is *custodia* and may mean watch as well as custody. As his detention here afforded him relief, as he received visits and was supported from without (xxxvii. 21), we may with the greater probability suppose that it was the closed court in which the palace-watch was stationed.—**Wherefore dost thou prophesy.** Comp. xxi. 4 sqq.; xxxiv. 2 sqq.; xxxvii. 17. The words from **I will give** to **Zedekiah to Babylon** agree almost *verbatim* with xxxiv. 2, 3. From the slight differences we may infer that we have here two independent records, of which the passage xxxiv. 2-5 is so far to be regarded as the more complete, as it gives the particulars of Zedekiah's fate after his captivity, while in xxxii. 5 all that relates to this is comprised in the words, "and there shall he be until I visit him." If we compare xxxiv. 4, 5 with xxxix. 7; lii. 11, we shall see that in the first passage the fate of the king is portrayed from its favorable, in the latter passages from its unfavorable side. The representations are by no means contradictory. In xxxiv. 4, 5 it is merely stated that the king will not die by a violent, but in peace by a natural death, and after his death will receive an honorable interment. This by no means excludes the cruel treatment, which he received according to xxxvii. 7; lii. 11. The indefiniteness of the expression **visit** and the prospective, leaving it open either to deliverance or death, was perceived even by Jerome, who says "*visitatio et consolationem significat et supplicum.*" It should also be not unobserved that the expression "die in peace," xxxiv. 5, admits of this double meaning.—**Though ye fight,** *etc.* These words are not found in the record, ch. xxxiv. Coming after the positive prediction of calamity they do not make the impression of being intended for an admonition, but appear to have the meaning of a statement of reason: if you fight with the Chaldeans it certainly cannot result otherwise; ye cannot then prosper. The prophet does not want to call forth a subjective volition, but merely to present the objective *nexus rerum*. On the subject-matter, comp. xxi. 9; xxvii. 8 sqq., as well as the introduction to xxxiv. 1-7, and the remarks on xxxiv. 1-5.

Vers. 6 and 7. **And Jeremiah ... to buy it.** After that in vers. 1-5 the general situation had been portrayed in which the following event took place, ver. 6 begins the narrative of the event itself. This narrative is given as the report of a third person. From **the word** in ver. 6, to the close of the prayer in ver. 25, it is Jeremiah who speaks. It is, however, a third person who tells us that Jeremiah spoke all these things, as is seen from the words **and Jeremiah said,** ver. 6. This form of presentation is not unusual in this book. Comp. xix. 14, 15; xxvi. 7-9; xxviii. 5-7 coll. ver. 1; ch. xxxvii. etc.—**Son of Shallum thine uncle.** That the uncle was named Shallum is seen from vers. 8 and 9. Though Hanameel is also designated דוֹד, uncle, this is explained by the possibility of using this word in the wider sense. The meaning of *"patruus"* is the innermost of a series of concentric circles, which represent a progress from general to particulars. From the Canticles we unquestionably obtain the radical meaning of *"caritas, amor"* (i. 2, 4, *etc.*). From this is derived the meaning of *"carus, amicus"* (*abstr. pro concreto* as in מוֹדַעַת), comp. Isa. v. 1; Cant. i. 13, 14, 16, *etc.* Now though the father's brother is especially called the dear one, the friend of the family, this is an honorable distinction, which may of course in certain circumstances be transferred to another relative, as is doubtless the case here for the sake of brevity with respect to the son of the דוֹד.—**Right of redemption.** According to Lev. xxv. 25 in the case of an impoverished Israelite wishing to sell his piece of ground, his nearest of kin have the right of purchase. Comp. SAALSCHUETZ, *Mos. Recht.*, S. 147 sqq.; 483, 808 sqq.—The members of the tribe of Levi also, according to Numb. xxxv. 2 coll. Josh. xxi. owned real estate, *viz.*, so much as was included in the precincts of the cities allotted to them (כְּרֵי, comp. 1 Chron. vi. 40, 41). The statement in Lev. xxv. 34, that this real estate could not be sold appears simply to mean that the sale of priests' property to those who are not priests was forbidden. Among the family the sale must have been possible, otherwise an illegal act would have been demanded of Jeremiah, not only by his cousin but by the Lord Himself. The right of redemption (גְּאֻלָּה) had moreover its two sides. Towards **the seller** it was a duty, towards the more distantly related it was a right. Comp. Ruth iv.

Vers. 8-10. **So Hanameel ... in the balances.** The right of inheritance was generally and especially among the priests the basis of the right of redemption. For it was indeed the sense of the whole institution, that the real estate should remain in the family. Accordingly it was always the next heir who was in the first place entitled and obligated to the גְּאֻלָּה. We find no intimation in the Law what the relation of the גֹּאֵל was to the מֶכֶר (comp. SAALSCHUTZ, *Mos. R. S.* 811). After all it appears to me that this was left to the friendly understanding of the two relatives, and the loyal disposition of the *goel* was reckoned upon. From the fact that the visit announced to him by revelation was really received, Jeremiah knew that the proposal, which his visitor made him, and of which the Lord had not yet said anything, was also an expression of the divine will.—The price seems small. This has been explained by supposing that the seller was driven to the sale by urgent need and that the property was depreciated by the war. Both may be correct, but I do not think that the small price is thus explained. This would have been unworthy of the prophet. Could Jeremiah buy as a speculator? LIVY relates (XXVI. 11) that when Hannibal was before the gates of Rome the very field on which his camp stood was sold, *"nihil ob id diminuto pretio."* Comp. FLORUS, II. 6 (*Parva res dictu, sed ad magnanimitatem populi Romani probandum satis efficax, quod illis ipsis quibus obsidebatur diebus ager, quem Hannibal castris insederat, venalis Romæ fuit hastæque subjectus invenit emtorem*).—Can the proud assurance of the Romans have produced a greater effect than the trust reposed by our prophet on the divine promise? I therefore think that seventeen shekels was the nominal price. Its smallness may be explained, apart from the possible smallness of the object purchased, by the nearness of the jubilee year. Though we have no data by which to determine how far distant the jubilee was from the time of sale, it may be safely assumed that the provisions of the law, Lev. xxv. 15, 16, were not unobserved. The year of *manumissio*, spoken of in ch. xxxiv., was not a jubilee. Comp. rems. on xxxiv. 14 and HERZOG, *R.-Enc.* XIII., *S.* 212. Seventeen shekels in our money was little more than ten dollars. Comp. HERZ. *R.-Enc.*, IV., *S.* 764.—Whence did Jeremiah obtain the money? Had he, the prisoner, for whom a daily scanty subsistence was furnished (xxxvii. 21), pecuniary means at command? His silence on this point shows that he regarded it as of little moment. There was probably more money than bread in the city. Baruch also might have procured him the funds.—After the account of the purchase and the price in ver. 9, the particulars of the transaction are specially enumerated in ver. 10. First the writing and sealing. From what follows we see that the deed of purchase was written in duplicate. One copy remained open, the other was closed with seals. *"Quæ emtionum consuetudo hucusque servatur, ut quod intrinsecus clausum signaculo continent, hoc legere cupientibus apertum volumen exhibeat,"* JEROME on ver. 14. Whether the open copy also bore a seal cannot be definitely ascertained from the text. The object of the writing in duplicate appears to me to have been twofold. First, that which duplicates generally have, *viz.*, to have a second copy in case the first is lost; secondly (and this is especially the destination of the sealed deed), in case of injury or defacement, which the open deed might suffer either by accident or design, to have an intact original. The circumstance that Jeremiah does not mention the witnesses till after the sealing is not to be explained, with HITZIG, as though the contents of the closed deed and the price were concealed from them. Evidently the prophet does not wish to confuse the three points in ver. 10. He therefore relates first of the **deed** (סֵפֶר), then of the witnesses, then of the weighing of the money. The order of subjects then prevails, not however excluding the order of time, since the weighing out the money at any rate came last. If we should argue as HITZIG does, we should come to the conclusion that the witnesses had nothing at all to do with the documents. This, however, is contradicted by ver. 12, where it is expressly stated that the witnesses "subscribed the book of the purchase." As now in ver. 11, ver. 12 init., ver. 14 סֵפֶר הַמִּקְנָה appears to be a general conception, to which the specifications given in the second half of the verse are subordinate, the word may in ver. 12 also designate both documents; they may therefore have both been subscribed by the witnesses.

Vers. 11 and 12. **So I took ... of the prison.** The words הַמִּצְוָה וְהַחֻקִּים in ver. 11, are difficult. Those explanations do violence both to grammar and context which (*a*) assume an accusative of the norm; *according to the law and customs*, for which no instance can be adduced; (*b*) consider these words to indicate the contents of a third סֵפֶר. The enumeration in ver. 14 is opposed to this, and the difficulty of perceiving what laws and customs were observed in a third deed, and why this was drawn. Only one explanation is grammatically possible and in agreement with the context, *viz.*, that which takes the words as in apposition to הַחְתֻמִים. Then the question arises, what are we to understand by the words themselves? The respective definitions of the Mosaic law (comp. *ex. gr.* Deut. v. 28)? But why should these be written out in detail and be designated as the main contents of the הַחְתֻמִים? It is better then to take מִצְוָה in the sense of *statutum*, establishing, settling, and חֻקִּים in the sense of stipulation. The main thing established, *i. e.* the object of the purchase and the price, as well as the special stipulations or conditions of sale were then fully contained

only in the חָתוּם. Yet I confess that this explanation also is not perfectly satisfactory. We must wait for further illumination.—Baruch is here mentioned for the first time. Hence the more exact statement of his lineage. Josephus (*Antt.* X. 9, 1) calls him ἐξ ἐπισήμου σφόδρα οἰκίας ὄντα καὶ τῇ πατρῴᾳ γλώττῃ διασεσηκότως πεπαιδευμένου. The high position of his brother Serainh at court (li. 59) seems to prove that he was of a respectable house.—**Before all the Jews.** The prophet intimates that two circles of witnesses are to be imagined surrounding the central point, formed by Jeremiah and Baruch, a narrower and a wider. The wider circle testifies to the witness of the narrower.

Vers. 13-15. **And I charged ... in this land.—In an earthen vessel.** To keep the deeds from damp, moths or dirt. Can the earthen vessel have survived the abomination of destruction? It matters not. The main thing was the establishment of the fact that the Lord in the midst of their dread of destruction, at a moment when all hope for the future seemed to have fled, gave the promise of a glorious restoration, as indicated in ver. 15. The object of this promise was on the one hand to comfort those who were involved in the present ruin, and on the other hand to prove that the Lord had forewilled, foreknown and foretold the predicted favorable turn of affairs. Comp. rems. on xxx. 1. To attain the latter object the transaction had certainly to be brought to the knowledge of posterity in an authentic manner. For this purpose the documents themselves relating to the purchase, which would hardly contain any account of the accompanying circumstances, would be less useful than on the one hand oral tradition based on the declaration of many eye and ear witnesses, and on the other hand the written report of the prophet.

---

2. *A Prayer of Praise and Inquiry.*

XXXII. 16-25.

16 Now when I had delivered the evidence of the purchase unto Baruch the son of
17 Neriah, I prayed unto the LORD, saying, Ah LORD God! behold, thou hast made the heaven and the earth by thy great power and stretched out arm, *and* there is
18 nothing too hard for thee [hid from thee]:[1] Thou shewest loving-kindness unto thousands, and recompensest the iniquity of the fathers into the bosom[2] of their children after them: the Great, the Mighty God, the LORD of hosts [Jehovah
19 Zebaoth] *is* his name. Great in counsel, and mighty in work[3]: for thine eyes *are* open upon all the ways of the sons of men : to give every one according to his ways,
20 and according to the fruit of his doings. Which [who][4] hast set signs and wonders in the land of Egypt, *even* unto this day, and in Israel, and among *other* men; and
21 hast made thee a name, as at this day ; And hast brought forth thy people Israel out of the land of Egypt with signs, and with wonders, and with a strong hand
22 and with a stretched out arm, and with great terror; And hast given them this land, which thou didst swear to their fathers to give them, a land flowing with milk
23 and honey; And they came in, and possessed it; but they obeyed not thy voice, neither walked in thy law[5]; they have done nothing of all that thou commandedst

24 them to do: therefore thou hast caused all this evil to come upon them.⁴ Behold the mounts [ramparts], they are come unto the city to take it: and the city is given into the hand of the Chaldeans, that fight against it, because of [οἱ in consequence of] the sword and the famine and of the pestilence: and what thou hast 25 spoken is come to pass; and, behold thou seest it. And thou hast said unto me, O LORD GOD, Buy thee the field for money, and take witnesses; for [and yet]⁷ the city is given into the hands of the Chaldeans.

TEXTUAL AND GRAMMATICAL.

¹ Ver. 17.—לֹא יִפָּלֵא. Comp. Gen. xviii. 14; Deut. xvii. 8; Zech. viii. 6; NAEGELSB. *Gr.*, § 75, 2, 4.

² Ver. 18.—Instead of חֵיק אֶל we find in Deut. vii. 10, פָּנִים אֶל. Comp. besides Isa. lxv. 6, 7; Ps. lxxix. 12.

³ Ver. 19.—The form עֲלִילִיָּה is found here only.

⁴ Ver. 20.—The construction in the sentence שֶׁכֵּת אֲשֶׁר הַזֶּה הַיּוֹם עַד, is as in xi. 7. In both cases עַד is to be regarded as depending on the idea latent in the verb of "stretching, lasting." It is accordingly a *constructio prægnans*. Comp. NAEGELSB. *Gr.*, § 112, 7.

⁵ Ver. 23.—וּבַתְרוּתָךְ. The reading of the Chethibh which is תְּרוּתָהּ (xxxviii. 22; comp. NAEGELSB. *Gr.*, § 44, 4, *Anm.*) is probably to be explained by a mere oversight of the ו. Comp. rems. on xvii. 23.

⁶ Ver. 23.—וַתִּקְרָא. Hiphil here only. Comp. Deut. xxxi. 29.

⁷ Ver. 25.—וְהָעִיר. To obtain the meaning: although the city, as spoken by Jehovah, we should have to read גַם כִּי. On the ו comp. EWALD, § 341 *a*; NAEGELSB. *Gr.*, § 110, 4.

EXEGETICAL AND CRITICAL.

The main thought of this prayer is praise of the omnipotence, justice and grace of God. It consists of three parts: 1. Vers. 17-19; 2, vers. 20-23; 3, vers. 24 and 25. In the first part God's omnipotence is shown from the creation (ver. 17), then His justice from His providence in history (vers. 18, 19). In the second part God's omnipotence is shown from His leading of the people of Israel, as it was especially glorified in the deliverance from Egyptian bondage (vers. 20-22), then His justice from the terrible calamity which has now come upon the disobedient nation (ver. 23). In the third part, which is least in extent, but the most important, a problem or unsolved riddle appears to be proposed. It is said that the Lord sees this calamity, and yet commands the prophet to buy the lot of ground (ver. 24). All however which has been previously said of the Lord's omnipotence, especially "nothing is too hard for thee," in union with that which must be extolled of the Lord's grace towards Israel (ver. 21 sqq.), gives the key for the solution of that riddle.

Vers. 16-19. **Now when ... fruit of his doings.** On ver. 17 comp. xxvii. 5; Deut. xxix. 9.—**Thou shewest loving-kindness,** *etc.* Comp. Exod. xx. 6; xxxiv. 7; Deut. v. 10. For לַאֲלָפִים we find in Deut. vii. 9 דּוֹר לְאֶלֶף. If we compare with this the phrase in the parallel clause שִׁלֵּשִׁים רִבֵּעִים (Exod. xx 5; xxxiv. 7; Numb. xiv. 18; Deut. v. 9) which can only signify the offspring of the third and fourth generation, it is clear that the phrase in the text is taken in such a general signification that the idea of "thousands, belonging to the thousandth generation" is included.—**And recompensest,** *etc.* Comp. rems. on xxxi. 29, 30.—**The mighty God.** Comp. Deut. x. 17.—**Jehovah Zebaoth.** Comp. x. 16; xxxi. 35, *etc.*—**Great in counsel,** *etc.* Comp. Isa. xxviii. 29; Ps. lxvi. 5.—**To give every one,** *etc.* Comp. xvii. 10.

Vers. 20-23. **Who hast set ... evil to come upon them.** It is as though it were said, thou who in Egypt didst set in operation a wonder-working power, which continues to operate until this day.—The antithesis of *Israel* and *other men*, as in Isai. xliii. 4; Ps. lxxiii. 5.—**As at this day.** Comp. xxv. 18.—**With signs.** Comp. Deut. iv. 34; xxvi. 8.—**Which thou didst swear.** Comp. Gen. xii. 7; rems. on xi. 5.

Vers. 24, 25. **Behold the ramparts ... the Chaldeans.** הַסֹּלְלוֹת are ramparts set up by the besiegers. Comp. xxxiii. 4; vi. 6.—**Given,** *etc.* The Chaldeans are indeed still without the city, but according to the prophet's idea this is as good as surrendered, and on the fall of the chief city naturally follows the exile and the impossibility of further cultivation of the soil.—**In consequence of** depends on **given.** Sword, famine and pestilence, bring the city into the hands of the enemies. Comp. xiv. 12; xxv. 16, 27; xxxviii. 9. The Lord sees the condition of the city and yet He commands the prophet to buy a field. The fact that the prayer closes with this paradox must be regarded as an expression of the most tormenting uncertainty and helplessness, if the prophet had not himself in the previous context accumulated the most ample material to dispel such doubts. This apparently unsatisfactory conclusion is thus in the highest degree skilful and elevated. He leaves it to the reader to find the solution of the problem, after giving him all the aid that he needs. The concluding sentence, **and the city,** *etc.*, ver. 25 *b*, viewed as spoken by the prophet, appears at first sight a tautological repetition. We might therefore be tempted to take it as spoken by Jehovah; buy the field although the city, *etc* But although is not suitable in the mouth of Jehovah, for whom, in fact, the apparent contradiction is non-existent. The sentence is then spoken by the prophet; but it is not co-ordinate with **buy thee,** but an exclamation, in which the main point in the apparent contradiction is expressly repeated from ver. 24. Comp. the translation and TEXTUAL NOTES.

3. *Nothing is impossible to the Lord.*

XXXII. 26–44.

26, 27 Then came the word of the LORD unto Jeremiah, saying, Behold, I am the
28 LORD, the God of all flesh : is there anything too hard for Me? Therefore thus
saith the LORD : Behold, I will give this city into the hand of the Chaldeans, and
29 into the hand of Nebuchadrezzar, king of Babylon, and he shall take it: and the
Chaldeans that fight against this city shall come and set fire on [to] this city, and
burn it with the houses, upon whose roofs they have offered incense unto Baal and
30 poured out drink offerings unto other gods, to provoke Me to anger. For the children of Israel and the children of Judah have only done evil before Me from their
youth ;[1] for the children of Israel have only provoked Me to anger with the work
31 of their hands, saith the LORD. For this city hath been to Me as a provocation of
Mine anger [*or* for My anger] and of my fury from the day that they built it even
32 to this day ; that I should remove it from before my face,[2] because of all the evil
of the children of Israel and the children of Judah, which they have done to provoke Me to anger, they, their kings, their princes, their priests, and their prophets,
33 and the men of Judah and the inhabitants of Jerusalem. And they have turned
unto Me the back [neck] and not the face: though I taught them, rising up early
34 and teaching them, yet they have not hearkened to receive instruction. But they
35 set their abominations in the house, which is called by My name, to defile it. And
they built the high places of Baal, which are in the valley of the son of Hinnom
[*or* valley of Ben-Hinnom] to cause their sons and their daughters to pass through
the fire unto Molech ; which I commanded not, neither came it into My mind, that
they should do this abomination, to cause Judah to sin.[3]
36 And now therefore thus saith the LORD, the God of Israel, concerning this city,
whereof ye say, It shall be delivered into the hand of the king of Babylon by the
37 sword, and by the famine, and by the pestilence; behold I will gather them out
of all countries, whither I have driven them in Mine anger, and in My fury, and in
great wrath; and I will bring them again unto this place, and I will cause them to
38, 39 dwell safely ; and they shall be My people, and I will be their God : And I
will give them one heart,[4] and one way, that they may fear me forever, for the good
40 of them, and of their children after them : And I will make an everlasting covenant
with them,[5] that I will not turn away from [*lit.*, behind] them, to do them good;
41 but I will put my fear in their hearts, and they shall not depart from me. Yea, I
will rejoice over them to do them good, and I will plant them in this land as-
42 suredly [*or* in truth] with my whole heart and with my whole soul. For thus
saith the LORD : Like as I have brought all this great evil upon this people, so will
43 I bring upon them all the good that I have promised them. And fields[6] shall be
bought in this land, whereof ye say, *It is* desolate without[7] man or beast; it is
44 given into the hand of the Chaldeans. Men shall buy fields for money, and subscribe evidences [deeds][8] and seal them, and take witness in the land of Benjamin, and in the places about Jerusalem, and in the cities of Judah, and in the cities
of the mountains, and in the cities of the valley, and in the cities of the South : for
I will cause their captivity to return, saith the LORD.

TEXTUAL AND GRAMMATICAL.

[1] Ver. 30.—On מִנְּעֻרֹתֵיהֶם (the fem. form here only). Comp. iii. 24, 25 ; xxii. 21.

[2] Ver. 31.—The עַל is less surprising (since this preposition is frequently interchanged with אֶל. [comp. rems. on x. 1, Isai. xxix. 11, 14], and even ל [comp. עַל־רְצוֹן Isai. lx. 7 with לְרָצוֹן lvi. 7; Jer. vi. 20]) than the suffix in the following ל. Accordingly the construction, which takes עַל in the causal sense and makes לְהָכִירָה depend immediately

on הָיְתָה, on account of the pregnant sense in which הָיְתָה must then be taken, and on account of the suffix in הַסִּירָה is still more difficult. This latter word forms the transition to the special grounds of the judgments, of which vers. 32–35 treat. In ver. 32 first follows a specification of the subjects. Comp. ii. 26; xvii. 25. Then in vers. 33–35 a specification of the predicates.

³ Ver. 35 —On the form חָהְטִי comp. Olsh., § 38, c.: 192, f. Olshausen supposes a clerical error, which may certainly, as Graf thinks, have been occasioned by the following א. Comp. xix. 15.
⁴ Ver. 39.—On the infinitive יִרְאָה comp. Ewald § 238, a; Olsh. § 245, d.
⁵ Ver. 40.—The construction with ל as in Isa. lv. 3; lxi. 8; Ezek. xxxiv. 25; xxxvii. 26; Ps. lxxxix. 4.—אֲשֶׁר here is evidently a conjunction = that. Comp. Naegelsb. Gr., § 109, 1 b.
⁶ Ver. 43.—הַשָּׂדֶה. The article is generic. Comp. rems. on ver. 9.
⁷ Ver. 43.—בָאָרֶץ. Comp. ii. 15; iv. 7; ix. 9-12; Naegelsb. Gr., § 106, 5.
⁸ Ver. 44.—וְכָתוֹב. Comp. Naegelsb. Gr., § 92, 2, a.

EXEGETICAL AND CRITICAL.

At the head of this discourse, the limpid but diffuse style of which is peculiar to the prophet's later period, and is notably distinguished from that of the preceding discourse, we again find the thought, which the prophet has once before made the basis of a prayer (ver. 17): can anything be too wonderful for the Lord? (ver. 27). The answer is, No! Therefore Jerusalem shall indeed be destroyed by the Chaldeans (vers. 28, 29), as a well deserved punishment for the manifold abominations, by which Judah and Israel had provoked the Lord from the first (vers. 30–35), but therefore also a re-assembling and bringing back of the people to their own country shall take place (vers. 36, 37). Then will Israel be Jehovah's people and Jehovah be Israel's God (ver. 38); they will with unanimity serve the Lord to their own eternal welfare (ver. 39); the Lord will conclude an everlasting covenant with them, in consequence of which neither will He ever cease to do them good, nor will they ever again depart from the Lord (ver. 40); it will be a joy to the Lord to do them good, and with all His heart He promises them that from this time forward they shall be firmly planted and rooted in their land (ver. 41). With these two colors does the prophet paint the future of his nation, for (ver. 42) this is the very proof of His omnipotence, to which nothing is impossible, that as certainly as He has now brought destruction on Jerusalem, He will one day also perform His promise of blessing to the people (ver. 42). Then will fields again be bought in the country, which is now called a desert (ver. 43); yea, with all the usual formalities will purchases be made, deeds drawn, sealed and witnessed in all parts of the country (ver. 44). The passage thus seems to be closely connected with the historical basis of Jeremiah's purchase of a field (ver. 7 sqq.), as well as to be a logical exposition of the main thought of ver. 27 b:—nothing is impossible to the Lord, therefore He destroys Jerusalem and restores it again. It is because He is almighty that He can do both.

Vers. 26-29. **Then came the word ... provoke me to anger.—God of all flesh.** The expression reminds us of Numb. xvi. 22; xxvii. 16, where God is called the God of the spirits of all flesh.—**Is there anything,** etc. Comp. ver. 17.—**Therefore.** The blinded Israelites thought it impossible that the chosen place of the sanctuary could be destroyed (comp. rems. on vii. 4; xxi. 13). They did not reflect that to the Lord nothing is impossible.—**Set fire.** Comp. xvii. 27; xxi. 10, 14; xxxiv. 22; xxxvii. 8.—**Offered incense,** etc. Comp. vii. 9; xix. 4, 13.

Vers. 30-35. **For the children ... Judah to sin.** These six verses express the reason of the punitive judgment announced in vers. 28, 29. Verses 30, 31 give the general reason, vers. 32–35 the special. In vers. 30, 31 we find three causal sentences beginning with **for**. In what relation do these stand to each other and to the preceding context? The first **for** might refer (1) to the acts of the Chaldeans, or (2) to **offered incense,** etc., and **poured out.** etc., or (3) to **to provoke me**. It is not probable that it can refer to (2), for no one expects a reason in this connection for the Jews having offered incense to their idols, but for the Lord's giving up the place of the sanctuary to destruction. (Comp. on **therefore** ver. 28). This **for** may then refer either to (1) or (3). Regarded according to the subject both amount to the same, for what produced the anger of the Lord also brought about the destruction. The ground of the one is also the ground of the other. Add to this that a special ground of the **to provoke me** is expressed in the sentence immediately preceding. We shall thus have to refer the first causal sentence, ver. 30, essentially to the prediction of destruction in vers. 28, 29. This will accordingly have for its motive the objective fact of the habitual sinfulness of the Jews and Israelites, since **done evil** further strengthened by **only** expresses the habitual state. The second and third causal sentences set forth more the subjective element of the Divine anger; Jerusalem must be destroyed, for they have provoked Jehovah. It must not however be overlooked that the words **have only provoked me to anger by the work of their hands** look back to ver. 29 b. For (1) **provoked** is only a confirmation of **to provoke**; (2) the work of their hands is not their moral conduct in general (this would be only a tautological repetition of the first half of the verse), but the idol images are to be understood by it in a concrete sense, to which according to ver. 29 b incense was burned. Comp. i. 16; Deut. iv. 28; xxvii. 15. The prophet appears also to have had Deut. xxxi. 29 generally in view.—The third causal sentence forms a climax with the second. He no longer uses the expression **to provoke** but the cumulative and stronger expressions **for My anger and for My fury**. Jerusalem has filled the measure of the divine anger, hence the total destruction announced in vers. 28, 29. The expression **this city has been to Me, for My ang r and for My fury** (on which the passages lii. 3; 2 Ki.

xxiv. 3, 20 seem to be founded) is unusual. The sense can only be that the city became an object of anger to Me. On ver. 33 comp. ii. 27; vii. 13, 25; xxv. 3, 4. On vers. 34, 35 comp. vii. 30, 31; xix. 5.—In ver. 35 the sentence **neither came it**, *etc.*, does not depend on **which**, but is to be regarded as a new and independent sentence. Both sentences however, from **which** to **abomination**, are parentheses, and **to cause . . . to sin** is connected with **cause . . . to pass.** Vers. 36-41. **And now therefore . . . my whole soul.** By **and now** Jeremiah designates the joyful present in contrast with the mournful past, which he described in the previous context. This is indeed not yet real but ideal, yet none the less certain; for this ideal present is based on the word of Divine promise. **Therefore,** as already remarked, corresponds to **therefore** in ver. 28, and now draws the second inference from the proposition that nothing is too wonderful for God. As from this followed the destruction which appeared impossible to the Jews, so also follows the apparently equally impossible restoration.—אל העיר with respect to this city, comp. xxii. 11; xxviii. 8, 9; xxix. 16, 21.—**By the sword.** Comp. *because of the sword,* ver. 24.—**Behold I will gather them** refers to the idea of "inhabitants, citizens" contained implicitly in *the city,* to which in the widest sense all those enumerated in ver. 32 belong. On the subject-matter comp. Deut. xxx. 3 sqq.; Jer. iii. 18-20; xxiii. 3; xxix. 14; xxxi. 8, 10.—**Cause them to dwell safely.** Comp. Hos. xi. 11; Ezek. xxxvi. 11, 33.—Ver. 38. **And they shall be,** *etc.* Comp. rems. on xxx. 32.—Ver. 39. **And I will give,** *etc.* The restoration and return must necessarily be at the same time spiritual (comp. xxxi. 18-20.) An essential element of this spiritual return is also the cessation of all enmity and discord among the members of the people, consequently the prevalence of a spirit of love and concord among them. Comp. Ezek. xi. 19; Jer. xxiv. 7; xxxi. 34.—**One way.** An allusion to the division introduced by Jeroboam I. between Judah and Israel. Comp. x. 2; Am. viii. 14.—**That they may fear me.** In this the unity of the way is manifested that they fear the Lord with one mind. The sentence is taken verbatim from Deut. iv. 10.—**For the good of them.** A reminiscence from Deut. vi. 24 coll. x. 13; xxx. 9, 10.—Ver. 40. **And I will make,** *etc.* Comp. rems. on xxxi. 31, 32; l. 5. According to the stipulations of the covenant the Lord promises two things: (1) that He will no more turn away behind the people in respect of doing them good, *i. e.*, that as a faith-

ful shepherd to His people He will always follow them with His protective and blessed guardianship; (2) that He will also give the people themselves the power no longer to turn away from Him. We see that the Lord takes the *priestanda* entirely upon Himself. Hence also the construction ל ברית כרת, which does not occur elsewhere in Jeremiah.—**That they shall not,** *etc.* Comp. Deut. xvii. 20, Josh. xxiii. 6.—**Yea, I will rejoice,** *etc.* Comp. Deut. xxviii. 63; xxx. 9; Isai. lxii. 5.—**I will plant,** *etc.* This נטע is the opposite of נתש. Comp. i. 10; xviii. 7 sqq.; xxxi. 28.—**In truth** is explained in the following words. The first planting had been imperfect (comp. ii. 21) as much so as the first covenant, (xxxi. 32). Because this was only hypothetical (vii. 5-7) and because the Lord knew that the condition would not be kept, He could not be in it with His whole heart. Now He knows (for He has Himself promised, ver. 40 *b*), that the condition will be fulfilled; therefore He can designate the planting as done in truth (*i. e.*, without the reservation that it is only for a short time), and also as one which He performs with a full and undivided heart. Comp. 2 Sam. vii. 10.

Vers. 42-44. **For thus saith . . . Jehovah.** From ver. 27 onwards a double inference is drawn from the general proposition that nothing is impossible to the Lord (vers. 28-35, and vers. 36-41). From ver. 42 onwards the argument is different. It is to demonstrate the certainty of the promise, vers. 36-41. This is done by pointing to the fulfilment of the minatory prophecy, which was indeed regarded as impossible by blinded Israel. As certainly as the Lord has brought great calamity on us, and so verified His word on the one hand, so certainly will He verify it on the other hand. Comp. xxxi. 28.—Ver. 43. **And fields,** *etc.* Return to the historical point of departure. Comp. ver. 15.—**In the land of Benjamin.** Comp. xvii. 26; xxxiii. 13. Benjamin is mentioned not because Anathoth belonged to this tribe, but because the tribes of Benjamin and Judah constituted the Jewish kingdom. Benjamin as the smaller part of this kingdom is named only in general, while Judah as the main part is characterized according to its chief constituents, as they are also enumerated elsewhere. (Comp. besides *loc. cit.* Josh. x. 40; Jud. i. 40). ["The New Testament mentions the sale of lands in Judea in Apostolic times, when Jerusalem was about to be destroyed, and the church was to be planted in all the world (Acts iv. 34; v. 4)." WORDSWORTH.—S. R. A.]

II. CHAPTER XXXIII.

Promise of the most glorious future given at a moment when the destruction of Jerusalem by its own inhabitants in the interest of defence was already begun.

1. *Brief transition: Summons to new prayer in the sense of* xxxii. 16–25, *and Promise of a Hearing.*

XXXIII. 1–3.

1 Moreover the word of the LORD came unto Jeremiah the second time, while he was yet shut up in the court of the prison, saying,
2 Thus saith Jehovah, who does it,
   Jehovah, who prepares it, to complete it,—Jehovah is His Name,
3 Call upon Me, and I will answer thee,
   And will announce to thee great and hidden things that thou knewest not.

EXEGETICAL AND CRITICAL.

The prophet, still in the court of the prison, receives a second time a revelation of an exceedingly comforting character. It is introduced by some words of Jehovah, which set forth His power to carry out his thoughts (ver. 2), as well as His readiness to afford the prophet on his request a glimpse into the great facts of the future, which the Lord intends to accomplish, notwithstanding that they are now regarded as impossible (ver. 3). Some would consider these words a later addition, because they cannot distinguish Jeremiah's style in them (GRAF). But GRAF himself has shown in opposition to MOVERS and HITZIG that the style of the alleged Isaiah II. is not seen in these verses, that rather the main elements (קְרָא הָכִין, of calling upon God, יהוה שְׁמוֹ) accord well with the style of Jeremiah. I add that יָצַר, in the sense of "forming thoughts," is found parallel with חשב מחשבה in Jer. xviii. 11. The expression עָשָׂה, as far as the meaning of the verb goes, has nothing specific about it, and the neutral signification of the feminine suffix is not foreign to the style of Jeremiah, iv. 28; xiii. 17.—On גְּדֹלוֹת, *etc., vid. infra.*—What might most make the impression of a style differing from that of Jeremiah is this Introduction in itself, and especially the peculiar turn of ver. 8: Call upon me, and I will answer, *etc.*—But we must here well observe that these words are occasioned by the prayer of the prophet in xxxii. 16–25. The prophet had indeed already received an answer to this prayer in xxxii. 26–44. But he is here admonished to approach the Lord more frequently with such petitions. The God, who has the power to carry out His determinations, is ready and willing to afford him a glance into His great thoughts of the future. A proof of this immediately follows. Consequently the verses, xxxiii. 1–3, form a bridge of connection between chh. xxxii. and xxxiii. In the admonition to pray more frequently they point back to the previous context and prepare by the promise **I will announce,** *etc.*, for the following disclosures.

Vers. 1–3. **Moreover the word ... knewest not.—Who does it.** This passage both in the thought and the words reminds us of Isa. xlvi. 11.—**Jehovah is his name.** Comp. x. 16; xxxi. 35; xxxii. 18. In the name of Jehovah lies the guarantee of His action. For what He is called He is.—**And I will announce.** It might here be asked whether the prophet is promised an insight into the inner connection of the divine arrangements (in the same sense as הִגִּיד is used of the solution of riddles, Jud. xiv. 12–14), or only a view of facts. I believe that the two are to be connected. The innermost grounds of the divine action are a secret to the prophet as to the angels (1 Pet. i. 11, 12). When however the Lord shows the prophet a chain of facts, it can not only be evident to him what will happen, but also how one thing follows from another. This may have taken place in only a limited degree, yet it furnished the prophet with a bridge of connection between the past and the present.

Hidden things, בְצֻרוֹת. In Isa. xlviii. 6 we read יְדַעְתָּם וְלֹא נְצֻרוֹת. The resemblance is unmistakable. The whole connection of the passage renders it incredible that the words in Isaiah are a quotation, they must therefore be so here. The reading here, בְּצֻרוֹת, may be due to a critical error (ב for נ), especially as the word does not occur elsewhere in this altered sense. It is always used elsewhere of walls or cities (Num. xiii. 28; Deut. i. 28; ix. 1; Josh. xiv. 12, *etc.*). Meanwhile it is also conceivable that the prophet may have written בְּצֻרוֹת. He frequently modifies the words which he quotes. This might take place the more easily as the related passage, Isa. xxxvii. 26, may at the same time have hovered before his mind. בְּצֻרוֹת is not in itself inappropriate, as it may signify "secluded, separate, inaccessible."

2. Destruction in the Present. Nevertheless glorious Internal and External Rebuilding in the Future.

XXXIII. 4–9.

4   For thus saith Jehovah, the God of Israel,
Concerning the houses of this city,
And concerning the houses of the kings of Judah,
Which were thrown down against the ramparts and against the sword,
5 Which are come to fight against the Chaldeans,[1]
And to fill them with the dead bodies of men,
Whom I have slain in my anger and in my fury,
And for all whose wickedness I have hid my face from this city:
6   Behold, I bring it health[2] and cure, and heal them,
And reveal[3] unto them an abundance[4] of peace and truth.
7 And I turn the captivity of Judah and the captivity of Israel,
And build them as in the beginning.
8 And I cleanse them from all their guilt, with which they have sinned against me,
And pardon all their transgressions, with which they have sinned and transgressed[5]
against me.
9 And it [the city] shall be to me a name of joy,
A praise and an honor before[6] all the nations of the earth,
Who shall hear all the good that I do unto them;[7]
And shall tremble and quake on account of all the goodness,
And on account of all the prosperity, that I procure unto it.

TEXTUAL AND GRAMMATICAL.

[1] Ver. 5.—באים להלחם וגו׳. This passage is a difficult one. MOVERS and HITZIG strike out בָּאִים entirely, after the example of the LXX., by which the sense certainly becomes easy. But how can this difficult word have got into the text? EWALD emends בָּאִים חֶרֶב into הַחֲרָבִים, which he takes, after Ezek. xxvi. 9, in the sense of "heavy siege weapons, artillery." But the plural of חֶרֶב is never חֲרָבִים. MEIER reads בָּאִים הֶחָרֵד, and translates "and against the desolation of the invaders." Both this use of the infinitive, however, and the mode of expression (the ramparts are erected by the invaders not for the purpose of hindering the desolation of the invaders) render the alteration suspicious. If we adhere to the text the question is, To what does בָּאִים refer? It has been referred to the Chaldeans (venient ad pugnandum Chaldaei, DE DIEU, SCHNURRER, ROSENMUELLER). In this case, however, אֵת would be nota nominativi, which is impossible. Comp. NAEGELSB. Gr., § 69, 1, Anm. 1.—Others refer it to the Jews. So JEROME, Chald., Syr., SEB. SCHMIDT, VENEMA, J. D. MICHAELIS, and these translate either veniunt or venientium, referring בָּא to the persons implied in the city. In the first case there is no subject designated, and in the second the connection with בָּתֵּי הָעִיר וגו׳ is very harsh, apart from the circumstance that the expression בָּאִים is not appropriate to the inhabitants of the city, and that לְכִלְאָם presents great difficulty with regard both to the suffix and the prefix. As the text now stands, we can take בָּאִים only as co-ordinate with הַנְּתֻצִים in second apposition to בָּתֵּי. The absence of the article is certainly not normal, but yet not without analogy. Comp. ii. 27; x. 12, 23; Ps. civ. 2-4; cxxxv. 7; Zech. xii. 1; NAEGELSB. Gr., § 97, 2 a.

[2] Ver. 6.—On אֲרֻכָה comp. Comm. on viii. 22. The suffixes in רְפָאתִים and לָהֶם refer to the same object as the suffix in לָהּ, i. e. to the holy city. It is the same constructio ad sensum as in בָּאִים. See rems. on this.

[3] Ver. 6.—וְגִלֵּיתִי. In itself there is nothing to hinder this word from being derived from גָּלָה, to reveal. Yet comparison with גָּלִיתִי, xi. 20; xx. 12, leads us to think that the form may be traced to גָּלַל, to roll (HITZIG), or with FUERST to גלה II., synonymous with גלל. Comp. Am. v. 24; Isa. xlviii. 18; lxvi. 12.

[4] Ver. 6.—עֲתֶרֶת is ἅπ. λεγ. For the verb comp. Prov. xxvii. 6; Ezek. xxxv. 13.

[5] Ver. 8.—פָּשַׁע radically means: to break, from which is developed the meaning: to revolt. It is stronger than חָטָא. אֲשֶׁר is the accusative of the instrument. Comp. NAEGELSB. Gr., § 70, i.

[6] Ver. 9.—לְכֹל. The preposition as in לְעֵינֵי, xxviii. 1, 5, 11; xxxii. 12. Comp. NAEGELSB. Gr., § 112, 5, b. e.

[7] Ver. 9.—אוֹתָהּ may stand for אֹתָהּ (i. 16), but it may also be the accusative of the object. Comp. NAEGELSB. Gr., § 69, 2 d.

EXEGETICAL AND CRITICAL.

In connection with the view which the city of Jerusalem then afforded, with many houses thrown down in the interest of defence (vers. 4, 5), the prophet promises the city healing and peace (ver. 6), the return of all the exiles, restoration (ver. 7) and forgiveness of all sin (ver. 8). Jehovah will again make Jerusalem the ob-

CHAP. XXXIII. 4-9.

ject of His joy and His glory in view of all the nations of the earth, who will be most powerfully impressed by this marvel of restoration to peace and prosperity (ver. 9).

Vers. 4, 5. **For thus saith Jehovah . . . from this city.** By for at the beginning of ver. 4 the prophet introduces the specification of the great and wonderful facts of redemption promised in general in vers. 2, 3. This כִּי is thus the key of the whole chapter.—**Concerning the houses.** From Isa. xxii. 10 we see that houses were thrown down in sieges, to repair or strengthen the walls. It was natural that those houses should be used for this purpose which were nearest the walls, whether private or royal property, and it is unnecessary, with Hitzig, to explain the prominence of the royal houses from the greater ease in obtaining them or the superiority of their materials. It is clear that we cannot render *for* ramparts and *for* sword, for in the first place, as has been repeatedly remarked, the Hebrew does not signify ramparts of defence but of attack (comp. xxxii. 24; vi. 6; 2 Sam. xx. 15; 2 Ki. xix. 32; Ezek. iv. 2; xvii. 17; xxi. 27; xxvi. 8; Dan. xi. 15), and in the second place, *for sword* would not be appropriate. We are not justified in rendering this singular in any other than the usual sense, especially as it is not at all certain that the plural חֲרָבוֹת, Ezek. xxvi. 9, has any other than the usual meaning. Comp. HAEVERNICK, *in loc.*—To take אֶל for לְ and to attribute a causal meaning to it so that it is equivalent to *through*, is altogether arbitrary. It cannot be urged that the prophet here speaks of all the houses of Jerusalem as being destroyed. Jeremiah only takes occasion, in a view of the houses destroyed in behalf of the defence, to set over against this gloomy picture of the present, which certainly was the prelude of entire destruction, the most glorious picture of the future restored city. אֶל is here therefore=against.—**Sword** is evidently used by synecdoche for all manual weapons, while the ramparts also include the machines erected upon them, so that these two words comprise the totality of the implements of attack. Comp. Ezek. xxi. 24, 25.—**Which are come,** etc. Comp. TEXTUAL NOTES. As the text now stands it is declared of the houses that they are come (1) to fight with the Chaldeans, (2) to fill them (*viz.*, the houses) with corpses. Now though the first may be said, in so far as by a bold hyperbole, the houses thrown down would be designated as moved forward into line of battle and taking part in the fray, still the second is in the highest degree surprising. For how can the houses come to fill *them* with corpses? This "them" must either denote *themselves*, which would be grammatically and logically incorrect, or it must be referred to the other houses, which would be doing violence to it, seeing that the other houses have not been previously mentioned. Then also the *filling*, *etc.*, must be regarded as the unintended result, which seems forced. Since, then, the present text proves to be incapable of giving us a satisfactory sense, nothing further is left us but to resort to an emendation. We have mentioned in the TEXTUAL NOTES attempts already made, none of which, however, meet with our approval. Perhaps it would be better to read *Jerusalem* (xxxvii. 10), or *to Jerusalem* (xxxiv. 1-7 coll. xxxii. 24, 29) instead of *the Chaldeans*. Then the words *are come* would refer to *ramparts* and *sword*. The circumstance that these substantives are feminine is of no account. For the masculine **come** may be referred κατὰ σύνεσιν to the persons, to whom the ramparts and sword serve as implements. (Comp. NAEGELSB. *Gr.*, § 60, 4).—**Them** after **fill** would then be referred to the idea of **houses**, which is prominent enough in ver. 4 to justify such a construction. Perhaps also we might read **to fill it** (comp. לָהּ ver. 6). The alteration into **the Chaldeans** might be explained by the difficulty of understanding *are come* of the ramparts and sword, and by the idea that it might refer to the *houses of the city* or their inhabitants. Perhaps also the remembrance of xxxii. 5 may have assisted in this. Meanwhile I confess that I perceive the difficulties attending this conjecture also, and therefore will gladly receive better instruction.

Vers. 6, 7. **Behold I bring . . . as in the beginning.** In opposition to *tearing down* in ver. 4 the prophet promises *bandages* or *healing*, instead of *filling with corpses* he promises *cure*. —**Peace and truth**, *i. e.* genuine, lasting prosperity. Comp. xiv. 13; Ps. lxxxv. 11.—**Build them.** Comp. xxiv. 6; xxxi. 4. The expression is chosen with reference to the occasion of the prophecy, ver. 4. Yet the idea is not to be taken merely in the narrower sense.—**As in the beginning.** The phrase is used proleptically, comp. ver. 11. It is not the building which is compared with the building of the beginning, but the result of the building is compared with the original state of things. Comp. besides Isa. i. 26; 1 Ki. xiii. 6.

Vers. 8, 9. **And I cleanse . . . procure unto it.** In ver. 8 the internal, heart-restoration is described. Comp. xxxi. 18-20, 34.— **Which they have sinned.** Comp. Zeph. iii. 11.—Ver. 9. **And it shall be.** The subject is the city. Comp. לָהּ ver. 6.—**A name of joy.** שֵׁם שָׂשׂוֹן, which reminds us of שֵׁכֶר שִׂישִׂי (Ps. xlv 8; Isa. lxi. 3), is joyful renown, renown which brings joy. On the subject-matter comp. xiii. 11; Zeph. iii. 19, 20; Deut. xxvi. 19.—**Before all the nations.** How far Jerusalem will extend the Lord's glory among the nations is declared in the following clause. The view of all the good which the Lord is preparing for Jerusalem will fill them with dread. At any rate with a wholesome fear, for after they have in their terror perceived that they have neglected the almighty and benevolent God for vain idols, they will turn again to the former. Comp. Num. xiv. 13-15; Deut. xxix. 24; Isa. ii. 2-4; xi. 10; xix. 17.

8. The glorious City-life of the Future.

XXXIII. 10, 11.

10 Thus saith Jehovah, Again shall be heard in this place,
Of which ye say, It is desolate without man and beast—
In the cities of Judah and in the streets of Jerusalem, which are desolate,
Without man, without inhabitant and without beast—
11 The voice of joy and the voice of gladness,
The voice of the bridegroom and the voice of the bride,
The voice of those who say, Praise Jehovah Zebaoth,
For Jehovah is good, for his mercy endureth forever!—
Who bring thank-offerings into the house of Jehovah.
For I will reverse the captivity of the land as at the beginning, saith Jehovah.

EXEGETICAL AND CRITICAL.

After, in the previous context, the restoration in general, viz. of the city and the state, had been promised on the basis of inward purification, the prophet now becomes more specific; city and country are again to be peopled and to become the theatre of joyous civil and religious life.

Vers. 10, 11. **Thus saith . . . Jehovah.** The subject of shall be heard is **the voice of joy,** etc., ver. 11.—**This place is the land** (comp. ver. 12; xxiv. 5; xvi. 3; vii. 7) as is seen from the following "in the cities of Judah," etc.—**Of which ye say.** Comp. xxxii. 36, 43. **Without man,** etc. Comp. vers. 32, 43.—**The voice,** etc. Comp. vii. 34; xvi. 9; xxv. 10; Zech. viii. 4, 5.—**Praise Jehovah.** A frequent liturgical formula of thanksgiving in the later period. Ps. cvi. 1; cvii. 1; cxviii. 1-3; cxxxvi. 1-3; Ezr. iii. 11; 2 Chron. v. 13; vii. 3, etc.— **Who bring,** etc. Comp. rems. on xvii. 26; Ps. lvi. 13.—**For I will reverse,** etc. Comp. rems on xxix. 14.

---

4. The Glorious Country-life of the Future.

XXXIII. 12-13.

12 Thus saith Jehovah Zebaoth, Again will there be in this place,
Which is desolate, without man and beast,[1]
And in all its cities a habitation [or pasture]
Of shepherds causing their flocks to lie down.
13 In the cities of the mountain, in the cities of the plain,
And in the cities of the south and in the land of Benjamin,
And in the environs of Jerusalem and in the cities of Judah,
The sheep will again pass under the hands of him that numbereth them, saith Jehovah.

TEXTUAL AND GRAMMATICAL.

[1] Ver. 12.—כִּאֵין אָדָם וְעַד־בְּהֵמָה. The construction here is instead of וּמֵאֵין in ver. 10. עַד expresses the idea of an all-embracing completeness, even to the extremest limits (comp. Gen. vi. 7; vii. 23; Num. viii. 4). עַד requires the supplementation of a corresponding verbal idea: ex. gr. 1 Sam. xviii. 4 הַרְבוּ, וַיַּךְ et ita percussit usque ad, etc.—Where כִּי־יֵעַד occurs there is a confounding of two constructions. Comp. NAEGELSB. Gr., § 111, 1.—In the passage under consideration יַעַד seems to have arisen from the כִּי in כְּאֵין, which reminds us of the כִּי in constructions like וְעַד מִקְטוֹן נָדוֹל.

EXEGETICAL AND CRITICAL.

The prophet passes from the relations of the city to those of the country, the breeding of cattle will again flourish throughout the land.—**This place** Comp rems. on ver. 10.—**Habitation of shepherds.** Comp. rems. on xxxii. 3 —On ver. 13. Comp. xxxii. 44.—**Under the hands.** The expression designates the relation of the Lord, invested with full authority, to the person or thing given into His power, which is represented as *on* or *in* His hand, so that He can do with it according to His own pleasure. Comp. v. 31; xviii. 21; Job xvi. 11; 1 Chron. xxv. 2; iii. 6. So also here. The sheep pass or enter past, "on the hands," *i. e.*, as objects of which the numberer is bound to take notice. We are not to understand it as meaning guidance and protection in general. The expression **numbereth** (מוֹנֶה) which occurs here only in this sense (comp. besides Ps. cxlvii. 4), is not used by chance, and therefore not to be identified with רֹעֶה. It is to be emphasized that the sheep will *have necessarily* to be numbered. When there are a few sheep only, so that they can be surveyed with a glance, this is unnecessary The whole connection of this passage forbids us to suppose that the prophet here, as in xxiii. 3, 4, makes use of figurative language to portray the prosperity of Israel as Jehovah's flock. He describes the joyful future as including all mental and spiritual well-being (comp. xxxii. 38-40; xxxiii. 8), but always on a corporeal and realistic basis. Comp. Deut. xxviii. 3-5; xxx. 9. [So also WORDSWORTH, who refers to Job x. 3 and 3 John 14, "Greet the friends by name." HITZIG however says "Literally, after the hand, acknowledging each by a movement. They were numbered to control the shepherd, regularly and doubtless twice (VIRG. *Eclog.*, iii. 34), on being driven out and on returning home."—S. R. A.]

---

5. *The Glorious Kingdom and Priesthood of the Future.*

XXXIII. 14-18.

14 Behold the days are coming, saith Jehovah, that I will fulfil
    The good word that I have spoken of the house of Israel and the house of Judah.
15 In those days and that time will I cause[1]
    The sprout of righteousness to spring to David,
    And he shall execute[2] justice and righteousness in the land.
16 In those days will Judah be saved and Jerusalem dwell safely,
    And this will be her name, Jehovah our Righteousness.[3]
17 For thus saith Jehovah, a man shall never be wanting to David,
    Who may sit upon the throne of the house of Israel.
18 And to the priests, the Levites, a man shall not be wanting before me,
    Who may offer burnt-offerings and kindle meat-offerings,
    And offer sacrifices continually.

TEXTUAL AND GRAMMATICAL.

[1] Ver. 15.—אַצְמִיחַ. In xxiii. 5 we find וַהֲקִמֹתִי. The former corresponds better with the following צֶמַח while the reading in xxiii. 5 is occasioned by the preceding וַהֲקִמֹתִי, ver. 4. Instead of צַדִּיק we have here צְדָקָה, but the meaning is the same. The change shows in this case, as in that of most other differences, merely that the prophet quotes freely from memory.

[2] Ver. 15.—וְעָשָׂה. Before these words וּמָלַךְ מֶלֶךְ וְהִשְׂכִּיל is omitted. No essential alteration of the sense is thus produced, for the royal nature of the צֶמַח is clear even, besides this passage, from vers. 17, 21, 26.

[3] Ver. 16.—The divergence of this passage from xxiii. 6, which is very troublesome to many of the old expositors, they seek either to paralyze by taking הֹן as a nominative referring to יִקְרָא—and he who will call it (the *Ecclesia*, *New Testament*) is Jehovah, our righteousness (FÖRSTER)—or by supplying הוּא after הֹן and taking יִקְרָא as passive and לָהּ as לְ auctoris, and he is the one who the city of Jerusalem will be called: the Lord, who is our righteousness (CRAMER).

EXEGETICAL AND CRITICAL.

Passing from the general to the particular, the circumference to the centre, the prophet further declares with respect to the happy future, that in it the promise previously announced will be fulfilled (ver. 4), a sprout of righteousness shall spring from the stock of David, who will restore justice and righteousness in the land (ver. 15), and by whom Judah and Jerusalem will be raised to such a height of prosperity that the latter will actually bear the name "Jehovah our Righteousness" (ver. 16). The race of David shall never die out (ver. 17), nor the priestly tribe of Levi and the priestly service ever cease.

Vers. 14-16. **Behold, the days . . . our Righteousness.** What is "the good word" in ver. 14? The expression occurs besides in Jeremiah only in xxix. 10. There it refers, as is evident from the mention of the seventy years, to xxv. 11. If the expression is to be taken there in a special sense, so also here. For here we have a still plainer reference to a former promise (xxiii. 5, 6). The reference to the general salvation, i. e., to the most universal manifestation of salvation is thus not excluded. Though this view is favored by the circumstance that the prophet, as already remarked, proceeds in this chapter from the general to the special, yet the special salvation, to which ver. 15 sqq. refer, is the central point comprising all that has been said hitherto, being a condition of all salvation in the widest sense. HENGSTENBERG incorrectly accentuates the two prepositions אֶל and עַל. According to the usage of our prophet they are so like each other in signification, that one frequently stands for the other (comp. xxv. 1 coll.; vii. 1; xi. 1, etc.; xxvi. 15), or by the side of the other with absolutely identical meaning (xi. 2; xviii. 11; xxiii. 35; xxv. 2; xxxvii. 19; xliv. 20).—Ver. 15. **In those days,** etc. In these words the chronological statement in ver. 14 is resumed after the interruption, so that in sense this beginning coincides with that in xxiii. 5. The addition **and that time** here as in l. 4, 20 possesses a merely rhetorical significance. It serves to render the declaration more solemn. The alteration from **in his days** (xxiii. 6) is unimportant. It is however important to note the change of Israel into Jerusalem, this being founded in the connection of the chapter. While the general object of the prophet, as is seen in ver. 14, is to show that the comforting prophecy given in former times, still holds good, notwithstanding the comfortless circumstances in which Jerusalem then was, being sorely pressed by the Chaldeans, yet he cannot avoid somewhat modifying the prophecy in accordance with the present occasion. This occasion according to ver. 4 is the sight of the houses thrown down in defence. In view of this mournful spectacle he had in vers. 6, 7 to promise healing of wounds, rebuilding of the city. He has also here the city of Jerusalem especially in view, though he does not by any means forget Israel, but on the contrary diligently sets forth its share in the promise given to Judah (ver. 14). Hence the alteration to *Jerusalem.*—With this it is also connected that the last clause states the name which Jerusalem will bear as a significant symbolical inscription. Comp. rems. on xxiii. 6.

Vers. 17, 18. **For thus saith Jehovah . . . continually.** The principal statement refers neither to ver. 15 nor to ver. 16 exclusively, but to both. Improbable as it must then have appeared at the time of Zedekiah that the house of David, which was reduced so low both inwardly and outwardly, should send forth so excellent and glorious a scion, equally so must the happy condition promised to the people in ver. 16 have appeared. Both however are shown to be possible by the announcement in ver. 17 of the everlasting continuance of the house of David and of its dominion over Israel. Observe, moreover, that it is not said *on the throne of David* nor *on his throne* (ver. 21; xiii. 13; xxii. 4), but *on the throne of the house of Israel.* The house of Israel is evidently here the whole of Israel, and the eternal duration of David's rule over it involves both the inner and outer rejuvenescence of the Davidic race, and the welfare of the people, which essentially depends thereon, since it may be subjected not to foreign rulers, but to their own native royal family.—**A man shall never.** etc. Comp. xxxv. 19. The sense of the expression is not, *none* shall ever be extirpated, but *every one* shall never be extirpated, so that none will be left. Herein is thus primarily contained only the promise of succession of rulers extending *in perpetuum.* HENGSTENBERG, however, calls attention to the circumstance (*Christol.*, S. 516) [Eng. Tr., II., p. 461] that we are not to suppose a "perfectly uninterrupted succession," but only one that is not broken off entirely. The prophet moreover reproduces almost verbatim the ancient promise given to the house of David, as it is repeated on the basis of 1 Sam. vii. 16, by David in his parting words to Solomon (1 Kings ii. 4), and afterwards by the latter himself at his dedication of the temple (1 Kings viii. 25), and finally by the Lord Himself in His renewed promise to Solomon (1 Kings ix. 5).—**And to the priests,** etc. A second pillar on which rests the redemption and secure continuance of Israel (ver. 16) is the normal permanence of the national priesthood. This is the Levitic.—**The Levites** is therefore in apposition (comp. Deut. xvii. 9, 18; Josh. iii. 3; Ezek. xliv. 15 coll. Deut. xxi. 5). The descendants of Levi, who according to the Mosaic law were alone eligible to the priesthood (Num. iii. 10; xvi. 40; xviii. 7), will be opposed to others who might possibly assume the priesthood to themselves. The question may here arise how this promise of the eternal continuance of the Levitic priesthood is related to other declarations, especially of the Epistle to the Hebrews, according to which this Levitical priesthood as only an inferior stage is to give way to a higher priesthood, *viz.*, that after the order of Melchizedek (Heb. vii.-ix. coll. Jer. iii. 16; Ps. cx. 4). I believe that this question must be decided according to the standard of Matt. v. 17, 18. As not a tittle of the law is absolutely abrogated, and thrown aside as worthless, but is kept by being fulfilled and thus being elevated to a higher potency, so also the Levitical priesthood being absorbed by a higher, is lost in its outward, temporal and local form, but in its ideal character is now first established. Hence the expressions of this passage (as well as the related ones in Ezek. xl.-xlii.) neither contradict former declarations of Jeremiah (as iii. 16; xxxi. 31-33), nor the doctrine of the Epistle to the Hebrews. Comp. rems. on ver. 22 and my review of "BALMER-RINCK, *The Prophet Ezekiel's vision of the Temple*" in REUTER'S *Repertorium*, 1860, *Heft. III.*, S. 152.—**Who may offer,** etc. Comp. Exod. xxix. 18; Lev. i. 9, 17; ix. 10; Num. xviii. 17, etc.—The three species of offerings are mentioned also in xvii. 26; Num. xv. 3, 4.

6. The Kingdom and Priesthood of the Future eternal.

XXXIII. 19-26.

19, 20   And the word of Jehovah came to Jeremiah, saying, Thus saith Jehovah:
If ye will break my covenant[1] of the day and my covenant of the night,
So that[2] there shall not be day[3] nor night in their season;
21   My covenant with David my servant shall also be broken,
So that he shall have[4] no son to be king on his throne,—
And with the Levites, the priests, who serve[5] me.
22   As[6] the host of heaven cannot be numbered,
Nor the sand of the sea measured,
So will I multiply the seed of David, my servant,
And the Levites who serve me.[7]
23   Moreover the word of Jehovah came to Jeremiah, saying:
24   Hast thou not seen,[8] what this people saith,
"The two families which Jehovah had chosen he has rejected?"[9]
And thus despise my people, that they are no more a nation before them [in their sight.]
25   Thus saith Jehovah, If my covenant continue not day and night,
And I have not appointed the ordinances[10] of heaven and earth;
26   Then will I reject the seed of Jacob, and David my servant,
That I will not take of his seed rulers over the seed of Abraham, Isaac and Jacob:
For I will reverse their captivity[11] and have mercy on them.

TEXTUAL AND GRAMMATICAL.

[1] Ver. 20.—The י— at the end of בְּרִיתִי is a suffix. Comp. NAEGELSB. Gr., § 63, 4 g.

[2] Ver. 20.—The ו before לְבִלְתִּי =and indeed. Comp. NAEGELSB. Gr., § 111, a, and Jer. vi. 2; xvii. 10; xix. 12; xxv. 9; xxvi. 5.

[3] Ver. 20.—יוֹמָם is used as a substantive in the sense of יוֹם here and in ver. 25 only. In Ezek. xxx. 16 it =quotidie. Comp. קְלָלַת חִנָּם, Prov. xxvi. 2. HAEVERNICK on Ezek., S. 515, 6.—Since יוֹמָם according to all analogies is an old nominal form (comp. OLSH. § 222, b), it is possible that for the sake of solemnity Jeremiah made use of this old form without regard to the adverbial signification which had become usual.

[4] Ver. 21.—כִּהְיוֹת. Comp. NAEGELSB. Gr., § 106, 6.

[5] Ver. 22.—מְשָׁרְתֵי. שָׁרֵת is the technical term for the ministration of the Levites and priests. Num. iii. 6; 1 Sam. ii. 11; Joel i. 9; ii. 17; 2 Chron. xiii. 10, etc. Comp. HERZOG, R.-Enc., XII, § 175, 6.

[6] Ver. 22.—אֲשֶׁר is here used accusatively, i. e., adverbially for בַּאֲשֶׁר. Comp. Isa. liv. 9.

[7] Ver. 22.—מְשָׁרְתֵי אֹתִי. Comp. EWALD, § 288, a; NAEGELSB. Gr., § 64, 5 c.

[8] Ver. 24.—הֲלֹא רָאִיתָ. In Ezekiel this idiom is frequent, viz. 12, 15, 17 coll. ver. 6; xlvii. 6. Comp. also Jer. iii. 6 coll. vii. 17. This use of רָאָה by synecdoche, is like that in v. 12; Lam. iii. 1; Gen. xlii. 1, coll. 2.

[9] Ver. 24.—וַיִּמְאָסֵם. Comp. vi. 19; NAEGELSB. Gr., § 88, 7 e.

[10] Ver. 25.—חֻקּוֹת. In xxxi 36, חֻקִּים. Comp. xxxii. 11. The former is more usual in Jeremiah,—v. 24; x. 3; xxxi. 35; xliv. 10, 23.

[11] Ver. 26.—אָשׁוּב. Only in xl. 39 besides do we find in Jeremiah the imperfect Kal in this formula. It also occurs in Joel iv. 1. Elsewhere, where the thought is expressed in the imperfect, we find the imperfect Hiphil. (N. B. The Perf. Hiph. occurs also xxxiii. 7), xxxii. 44; xxxiii. 11; xlix. 6; Ezek. xxxix. 25. The Masoretes would therefore, and probably not incorrectly, read אָשִׁיב in these three places also.

EXEGETICAL AND CRITICAL.

The preceding section concluded with the word "continually." The idea thus briefly intimated, of a perpetual duration of the promised blessing, forms the main thought in what follows. As it does not lie within the power of man to break the covenant of the Lord, which ensures the change of day and night, so also the covenant is not to be broken which guarantees the perpetual succession of Davidic kings and Levitical priests (vers. 19-21). A natural guarantee of this duration will be given by the innumerable increase of the royal and priestly seed (ver. 22). In opposition to the presumptuous speech that Jehovah had chosen Judah and Israel and yet afterwards rejected them, which contains both a complaint against the Lord and a despising of the people (vers. 23 and 24), the assurance is again given that so long as day and night, and the fundamental laws of heaven and earth continue, so long also will kings of Jacob's and David's race rule over the seed of Abraham, Isaac and Jacob. Their rejection is only temporary. The Lord will turn the captivity of the people (vers. 25, 26). From this table of contents it is clear, that vers. 19-26 are related to vers. 14 18, just as in ch. xxxv. vers. 35-37, are to vers. 31-34. In form and character the section fully accords with th: character of the prophet, as will be seen from a consideration of the particulars. HITZIG'S view, which attributes the section to Ezekiel, is deficient in any solid basis. We may indeed infer from the introductory formulas (vers. 19 and 23), that the prophet received these revelations separately, but not that they are disconnected later additions, seeing that these formulas stand in the middle between the large (comp. xxxii. 1), and the small divisions (**thus saith Jehovah**). Moreover this formula with **to Jeremiah**, is found all along from ch. xxviii.; xxviii. 12; xxix. 30; xxxii. 26; xxxiii. 1, 19, 23; xxxiv. 12; xxxv. 12; xxxvi. 27; xxxvii. 6; xlii. 7; xliii. 8. Previously we find **to me**; i. 4, 11; ii. 1; xiii. 3, 8; xvi. 1; xviii. 5; xxiv. 4.

Vers. 19-22. **And the word ... who serve me.** To break the covenant on which the changes of day and night are founded, is not in the power of man. For according to the divine promise (Gen. viii. 22) in no circumstances, not even in the case of an apostasy similar to that which occasioned the flood, will any change take place in the laws of nature, *so long as the earth stands.* In these words it is certainly declared that the earth will one day cease to exist, but it will then according to the teaching of the Scriptures only pass to a higher stage of existence (Isa. lxv. 17; lxvi. 22; 2 Pet. iii. 13; Rev. xxi. 1), and this transition is not an annulling of the promise given to David, but only leads to a corresponding transition to a higher stage of realization.—**My covenant of the day** is the covenant which I have concluded with respect to the day, whose object is the day.—**David my servant.** Comp. 2 Sam. iii. 18; vii. 5, 8; Ezek. xxxiv. 24, *etc.*—These verses express substantially the same thought as xxxi. 32-37.—**As the host,** *etc.* The reference to the promise given to the patriarchs, Gen. xv. 5; xxii. 17; xxxii. 13 is evident, and corresponds with the mention of the same in ver. 26. HENGSTENBERG has pointed out with perfect justice that Jeremiah here by no means prophesies an unlimited increase of the royal and priestly posterity which, as JAHN remarks, would be only a burden on the people. But in perfect accordance with the declaration of the Lord, that all Israel shall be a "kingdom of priests" (Exod. xix. 6), and with the prophetic utterances (Isa. lxi. 6, "and ye shall be named the priests of Jehovah: men shall call you the Ministers of our God;" lxvi. 20, 21, "and I will also take of them to be priests and Levites [Levitic priests]"). Jeremiah here declares that the threefold promise of 1. innumerable increase; 2. the priestly and royal character of the whole people; 3. the everlasting continuance of kingdom and priesthood, will form a grand harmonious chord. If, as cannot be denied, Jeremiah has in view that time, in which all that is ideal will be real,

his words cannot (whether he was conscious of it or not, is a matter of indifference), express anything else but this; the priestly and royal seed will be innumerable, because the whole nation having now become innumerable, will consist according to its original and essential idea of priests and kings. The innumerousness of the people, which was never actual even in the times of the highest prosperity (comp. 2 Sam. xxiv. 9) rests on the inclusion of the whole of regenerate humanity (Isa. lxvi. 20).

Vers. 23-26. **Moreover the word ... have mercy on them.** In the preceding verses (20-22) was positively declared the eternal duration of the covenant which Jehovah has concluded with the theocratic kingdom and priesthood: in the following verses this declaration is defended against a malicious attack.—It is altogether wrong to understand by "this people," foreign nations (SCHNURRER understands Egypt, JAHN Chaldean warriors, MOVERS Samaritans, HITZIG the neighbors of the Jews and of Ezekiel on the Chaboras). It was surely not worth the trouble to rebut such an assertion, if it were made by the heathen. Their judgment had no weight in such a case. But when Israelites, who ought to know the relation of their nation to the Lord, subscribed to such pessimism, a counter-testimony was in place.—It is evident that Judah and Israel are meant by the two families. It is clear both from the following phrase "my people," and "seed of Jacob," and "seed of Abraham, *etc.*," ver. 26. מִשְׁפָּחָה is often used in Jeremiah of national races; i. 15; x. 25; xxv. 9—**And thus despise,** וְאָן is here "*cum irrisione spernere,*" as in general the idea of rejection, rejection with disdain, is related to that of contempt. Comp. xiv. 21 where תִּנְבַּז is used as synonymous with תִּתְאַץ. These Jews thus pronounce on their own responsibility, without any occasion on the part of the Lord, a sentence of rejection upon their nation, thus on the one hand insulting God, as though He were inconsistent, on the other their nation, as though it were only good enough to be the foot-ball of its Lord's caprice.—**A nation before them.** From xxxi. 36 coll. xxxv. 19 we see that 1, "to be a nation" signifies national existence in opposition to division and scattering of the constituents of the nation; 2. that "before them" is not to be taken in a temporal but a physical sense; *i. e.,* they maintain that they will no longer be witnesses of that national existence, that their eyes will no longer be gratified by the sight of such prosperity.—**If my covenant,** *etc.* Comp. xxxi. 35, 37. The charge is rebutted by an appeal to the guarantee involved in the order of nature. Is this more firmly established than the order of salvation? To supplement if by the following **have appointed,** as in 2 Sam. xxiii. 5, seems to me forced. If we do not wish to take לֹא according to Job vi. 21 as a substantive, it is sufficient to regard it as a negative particle; if my covenant is not daily and nightly, *i. e.,* has no real, permanent existence.—**Then will I reject the seed,** *etc.* Observe that the charge in ver. 24 involved the rejection of both tribes. With a view to this, "seed of Jacob" is placed first as the main conception, "and David my servant" is inserted, because if the charge were well-founded, the promise in vers. 17, 18 would also fall to the ground. Since now, however, the seed of Jacob is to remain in possession of his promise, the basis is thus given for the preservation of the seed of David. The priests are no longer spoken of specially, being included in the seed of Jacob. The prophet lays special emphasis on the seed of David, because in ver. 15 he started with this idea as the security and central point of the theocracy. He then connects this idea with that of the seed of Jacob by saying that there shall never fail a descendant of David to rule over the seed of Abraham, Isaac and Jacob. In naming the three patriarchs he throws new weight into the scale in favor of the nation. Not only Jacob, but Isaac and Abraham also must have lost favor in the sight of God, if He reject their seed. They, however, are dear for the fathers' sake (Rom. xi. 28, 29 coll. i. 2, 16). Comp. Exod. ii. 24, 25; xxxii. 13; Lev. xxvi. 42; 2 Kings xiii. 23; Ps. cv. 8-10; Isa. xli. 8.

DOCTRINAL AND ETHICAL.

1. On xxxii. 3. "An effect of anger and a procedure almost like that of Ahab with the prophet Micah. The same spirit prevails now-a-days. For without entering on an investigation, with what right or reason men are found who often in pretty general expressions in a call to repentance, borrow from the prophet all sorts of judicial threatening and point to this or that city, we cannot avoid seeing why they are always put in arrest, viz.: for this cause, 'Why dost thou prophesy what we do not like to hear?' When one is sure of his cause, a noble disdain of such people would be the best means to use against them. But men cannot bear a bad conscience and threatenings of all sorts together, and the fear that it may be true has the foolish effect, that they cause the bearers of such unpleasant tidings to come to a bad end, in order to affright others from coming with similar messages." ZINZENDORF.

2. On xxxii. 7 sqq. "Fundatur in hoc textu locus classicus de contractibus emtionis et venditionis, quos improbant Anabaptistæ, probat Scriptura, sicut ostendunt hæc quæ jam sequuntur documenta: Prov. xxxi. 14; Matt. xiii. 8." FÖRSTER.

3. On xxxii. 15. "The prophet had often enough declared the land lost to the Chaldeans. Here, however, he must testify that it is not lost forever: his purchase was to restore confidence in the future to other troubled souls. Thus the most afflicted servant of God must again be the most hopeful."—"When we are outwardly prosperous, we think no one can take our prosperity from us, and when trouble comes upon us, we again think that no one can help us. Both courses are, however, equally ungodly. Therefore God's servants must contradict both those who are at ease, and those who are in despair. The reverse is always right. In good days humble thyself, and in bad days let thyself be exalted, for then it is a great thing to do." DIEDRICH.

4. On xxxii. 9, 16, 24, 25. "Jeremiah also contends, but as a servant of the Lord. First he obeys and afterwards speaks about it. This is a noble way, by which every teacher, who knows the Lord, may prove himself. As soon as he observes that the Lord wishes this or that, it is not the time to expostulate, but to act, not to call anything in question, but to set to work. If then any hesitation is left, or one and another scruple, it is time afterwards to consult with the Lord about it, when one has first shown obedience." ZINZENDORF. [" Though we are bound to follow God with an implicit obedience, yet we should endeavor that it may be more and more intelligent obedience. We must never dispute God's statutes and judgments, but we may and must inquire, What mean these statutes and judgments? Deut. vi. 20." HENRY.—S. R. A.]

5. On xxxii. 25. TERTULLIAN (c. Marc., L. IV., c. 40) sees in the words "Buy thee the field for money," the prophetic passage to which Matt. xxvii. 9 refers, regarding the reading 'Ιερεμίου as correct. Comp. EUSEB. Demonstr. Ev., L. X., c. 4; AUGUSTIN, De consensu Evang., L. III., c. 7.

6. On xxxii. 27. To God there is no wonder [miracle]. There are wonders only on the lower stage of existence. Every higher stage is a wonder to the lower. Or is there only one stage of existence, and accordingly only one order of nature? When the North American savages cruelly murdered one of their number who had been on a visit to the Great Father in Washington, and told them of the wonders of civilization, as a demoniacally possessed liar, were they less in the right than our highly civilized savages, to whom it is a fundamental axiom, that there is no other world, but that which they can reach with their five senses? It is certainly not proved that there is a living, personal, omnipotent God. But this is not to be proved, it is to be felt from the heart. He who is born of God heareth His voice. To him also miracles cease to be aught irrational. He knows well how to distinguish between true and false miracles, but the former come to him like a voice from the higher world, in which he feels truly at home. For the stages of existence and orders of nature are not hermetically sealed towards each other, but the higher break through in order to lift the lower up to themselves.

7. On xxxii. 36 sqq. On the fulfilment of this prophecy comp. the Comm. on xiii. 14, and the Doctrinal notes on iii. 18-25, No. 8. As the threatening that Israel should be dispersed among all nations from one end of the earth to the other (Deut. xxviii. 64-66) has been literally fulfilled, why should not this promise also be literally fulfilled, that they shall be collected from all lands whither the Lord has cast them out? Why cannot this people be destroyed? Why do they retain their peculiarities with such tenacity, that neither the most raging fanaticism, nor the most humane cosmopolitanism, which is much more dangerous than the former, can mingle them with other nations; so that we can follow the course of their national stream through the sea of nations, as it is said of the Rhine that its water flows unmingled through the lake of Constance? Assuredly this people must yet have a future. Only thus much is correct, that the real kernel of these prophecies is offered to us in a shell which the prophets prepared from contemporary events, but it is difficult to determine where the

shell ceases and the kernel begins. Comp. RINCK, *The Scripturalness of the doctrine of the Millennial reign defended against* HENGSTENBERG. Eberfeld, 1866, *S.* 45 sqq.

8. On xxxii. 36 sqq. "Is the consummation of the redemptive work possible while Israel is rejected as a nation? According to the Old Testament this question must be unconditionally negatived. This knows only a temporary rejection of Israel, which at the same time has this result, that Israel does not perish as a nation, but is preserved for future restoration. Is this law annulled since Israel despised the gracious visitation of the Messiah, the kingdom of God taken from them and given to a people which bring forth the fruits thereof? Are thus the predictions of the prophets, which treat of a glorification of Israel in the latter days, eternally abrogated on account of the nation's sin? Or can their fulfilment be found only in a spiritual manner in the Christian church, the main trunk of which was formed by a chosen few from Israel? These questions are answered in the affirmative by BERTHEAU (*Old Testament prophecy of Israel's national glory in their own land. Jahrb. f. deutsche Theol.*, 1859 and 1860) in accordance with the older protestant theology (comp. especially HOLLAZ, *Exam. theolog. ed. Teller*, p. 1264 sqq.) as decidedly as according to our conviction they must, on the ground of Rom. i. 25 sqq., be negatived. It seems to us to be irrefragably established that when the times of the world-nations are full (Luke xxi. 24), Israel will obey the gospel call, and thus be prepared to welcome the Messiah (Matt. xxiii. 39); that for this reason in its dispersion among the nations of the earth it has never been absorbed by them, but preserved in separate existence for its final destination, because God's gifts of grace and calling are ἀμεταμέλητα." OEHLER in HERZOG, *R.-Enc.*, XVII., *S.* 658, 9.

9. On xxxiii. 3. "This is the Lord's declaration to His obedient servant Jeremiah. My dear child, He says, thou hast acted according to my will, without knowing why. Thou hast done well. But I will make it clear to thee, so that thou wilt wonder no more; I will tell thee that and yet more, so that thou wilt at last say, 'Yes, let it be so.' We find such connections a few times elsewhere in the Scriptures. The Lord says, 'How can I hide from Abraham the thing that I do?' (Gen. xviii. 17.) And the same Lord declares to His disciples, whence comes this inclination or predisposition to tell something new to His disciples, 'Henceforth I call you not servants, for the servant knoweth not what his Lord doeth, but I have called you friends, for all things that I have heard of my Father, I have made known unto you.' (John xv. 15). So also is it here with Jeremiah." ZINZENDORF.

10. On xxxiii. 6. Healing, restoration, joy and permanent prosperity are promised by the prophet to Jerusalem at a time when all seemed lost, and it seemed impossible to regain them. How desolate must it have then appeared in Jerusalem when one house after another was thrown down to furnish means of defence! How wildly raged the tumult of war, and how comfortless was the condition of the city shut in by the enemy and completely cut off from the rest of the country! To the mind of him, who then thought of Jerusalem in the future, pictures of destruction alone presented themselves. Jeremiah, however, whose sight was sharpened by the divine anointing, sees beyond the present abomination of desolation in the far distant future pictures of peace and, moreover, of everlasting peace, such as no eye has ever seen, nor hath it entered into the heart of man. There was the patience and faith of the saints (Rev. xiii. 10). 'Impossible' is a word, which does not occur in God's language.

11. On xxxiii. 8. "After the stubborn race has been partly annihilated and partly humbled, God will turn the captivity of the nation, as a whole. Israel cannot perish eternally. God will purify the people from their sins, by forgiveness, the only way in which men can be really freed from sin. Grace and forgiveness are the only ground on which we stand as Christians. This seems nothing to the world, and yet it is more than heaven and earth." DIEDRICH.

12. On xxxiii. 7–13. "An important doctrine meets us in these words, that it is not the gifts of God which we should seek to apprehend, but the love of God which is manifested in that He imputes not our sin to us. Otherwise we treat the Divine benefits like the fishes which swallow the hook with the bait." HEIM and HOFMANN. *The major prophets expounded for edification*, 1839, *S.* 509.

13. On xxxiii. 14–17. "All God's promises are at the same time fulfilled by the true man, the Son of Man, the pure sprout of David. He will be a King, in whom we have perfect protection from all destructive agencies, for He will help us from sin, procuring and executing on earth justice and righteousness for all mankind. As we all together inherited sin and death from Adam, so Jesus by His righteousness has brought justification of life for all men, if we would now only take it with joy. Jerusalem will itself bear the King's name, as he was called in xxiii. 6: Jehovah our Righteousness, *i. e.*, that Jehovah bestows on us the righteousness, which is the bond, which at the same time unites us to the citizens of His celestial city." DIEDRICH.

14. On xxxiii. 15, 16. [*The Lord our righteousness.* "This is to be explained by the union of the Church with Christ (see Rom. xii. 4, 5; 1 Cor. x. 17; xii. 12; Eph. i. 22; iv. 12, 15, 16, 25; vi. 23, 30; Col. i. 18, 24) so that what belongs to Him is communicated to her (CALVIN, PISCATOR, MUENSTER).—Thus, by virtue of her mystical union with Christ, and by the imputation of His merits, and the infusion of His Spirit, the Name of the Church may be said to be 'The Lord our righteousness:' she hides herself in Him, and is seen by God as in Him; she is clothed with Christ the Sun of righteousness (see Rev. xii. 1) and is accepted in the Beloved (Eph. i. 6)." WORDSWORTH.—S. R. A.]

15. On xxxiii. 17. [" When the First-begotten was brought into the world it was declared concerning Him, *The Lord God shall give unto Him the throne of His Father David*, Luke i. 32." HENRY.—S. R. A.]

16. On xxxiii. 13–22. [" Four words, each of them full of meaning, comprise the conceptions which we attribute to the Paradisaical state. They are these: Innocence, Love, Rural Life,

Piety; and it is towards these conditions of earthly happiness that the human mind reverts, as often as it turns, sickened and disappointed, from the pursuit of whatever else it may have ever labored to acquire. The *innocence* we here think of is not virtue recovered, that has passed through its season of trial, but it is Moral Perfectness, darkened by no thought or knowledge of the contrary. This Paradisaical *love* is conjugal fondness, free from sensuous taint. This *Rural Life* is the constant flow of summer days, spent in gardens and afield, exempt from our exacted toil. This *piety* of Paradise is the grateful approach of the finite being to the Infinite,—a correspondence that is neither clouded, nor is apprehensive of a cloud." ISAAC TAYLOR, *Spirit of Hebrew Poetry.*—S. R. A.]

17. On xxxiii. 19-22. [" The richest promises are confirmed by the strongest assurances." COWLES.—S. R. A.] "As God's arrangements in nature do not fail, still less can His word fail in His kingdom of grace, and all His word refers to the divine Son of David and His eternal kingdom of grace. Yea, the whole innumerable Israel, Abraham's spiritual posterity, shall become Davids and Levites, *i. e.*, priests and kings, as was designed even at the beginning of Israel. (Exod. xix. 6; 1 Pet. ii. 9; Rev. v. 5)." DIEDRICH.

18. On xxxiii. 18-22. [WORDSWORTH rejects HENGSTENBERG'S explanation that these words are to be applied to all Christians indiscriminately, and approves of the argument derived by the ancient Christian fathers from the passage in favor of the *threefold order* of ministers in the Christian church. He adds "The Gospel of Christ and the Church of Christ possess the spiritual essence of whatever was commanded in the Levitical dispensations. Whatever was local and personal in those dispensations has passed away. The Tabernacle, the Temple, their Sacrifices, their Sabbaths, their Annual Festivals, their threefold Ministry, all these have been spiritualized in the Gospel. Sinai is perpetuated in Zion. The glory of the Law has been absorbed into that of the Gospel. See Ps. lxviii. 17, the great Pentecostal Psalm."—S. R. A.]

19. On xxxiii. 23-26. " In the first place they will not be warned, and afterwards they will not be comforted. The true prophet however announces death to sinners according to the law, but afterwards grace for renovation and for life. Despair is blasphemy. God's kingdom stands and will be perfected, but the fainthearted will not enter it. God answers: so long as heaven and earth are preserved by Me, it is for the sake of *My* kingdom, and as a pledge that it will not fail. Israel yet, what is the same thing, David's seed shall be a royal seed, and the captivity which the people must now endure is transient. It is however impossible for the worldly to comprehend this, who persist in carnal repose as though no God could punish them, and again in affliction are so despondent, as though there were no God to help them any more." DIEDRICH. [" Deep security commonly ends in deep despair: whereas those that keep up a holy fear at all times have a good hope to support themselves in the worst of times." HENRY.—S R. A.]

HOMILETICAL AND PRACTICAL.

1. On xxxii. 16. [" Before Jeremiah went to prayer he delivered the deeds that concerned his new purchase to Baruch, which may intimate to us, that when we are going to worship God we should get our minds as clear as may be from the cares and encumbrances of this world.—*Note,* Prayer is the salve of every sore." HENRY.—S. R. A.]

2. On xxxii. 17-25. *The Divine promises our best consolation in every affliction.* 1. There are promises of Divine help for every kind of distress in human life. 2. These promises often sound very wonderful (vers. 24 and 25). 3. Their fulfilment on the part of God is guaranteed by the perfection of the Divine nature (vers. 17-19). 4. Their fulfilment is on our part conditioned by faith.

3. On xxxii. 18, 19. Harvest [Thanksgiving-day] Sermon. "To what should our admiration of the power and grace of God in the present harvest lead us? 1. To thank God. 2. To trust all to Him, that He has promised us. 3. To obey His voice." JENTSCH., *Gesetz and Zeugniss*, 1853.

4. On xxxii. 19. " The very serious and important truth, the eyes of the Lord are open to all the paths of the children of men. This should 1, shake us and awake us from our security, if some of our ways are sinful and such as the Lord must certainly disapprove; 2, humble us, if we are indeed under the discipline of God's Spirit, and yet turn to our own self-made courses, and have not yet allowed a fixed and sure heart to be imparted to us; 3, be for our comfort and encouragement, when we are often led in dark and difficult paths." J. M. MUELLER, *Zeugnisse v. Christo*. [*Witnesses to Christ*]. *Neues Predigtbuch.*, Stuttgart, 1866, S. 757.

5. On xxxii. 19. [" The greatness of God's wisdom and the abundance of His power. Proved from His nature. Rem. 1. God hath the power of making the deepest affliction of His children produce their highest happiness. 2. The contrivances of tyrants to oppress the church procure its establishment. 3. The triumphs of Satan turn to the destruction of his empire." SAURIN. —S. R. A]

6. On xxxii. 39. Wedding-sermon, " The promise which the Lord gives to God-fearing couples. 1. One heart. 2. One way. 3. One blessing, which shall extend to their children." FLOREY, 1862.

7. On xxxii. 40. Wedding-sermon. The nature and fruit of a true marriage. 1. Its nature: it is a covenant which a man and a woman conclude in the Lord, and with the Lord (put My fear in their hearts;—not depart from Me;— everlasting covenant). 2. Its fruit: good from the Lord without ceasing.

8. On xxxii. 40. [" Teachers may put good things into our heads, but it is God only that can work them into our hearts, that can work in us *both to will and to do.*" HENRY.—S. R. A.]

9. On xxxii. 39-41. " The greatest and dearest of all the promises of God to a marriage in the highest degree happy and delightful." G. CONR. RIEGER.

10. On xxxii. 40, 41. Baptismal Sermon. " The

gracious promises of God, which He gives to a child of man in holy baptism." FLOREY, 1862.
11. On xxxii. 42. "In communion of suffering of pious Christians is also a blessed fellowship of consolation, since 1, when we as Christians bear with one another, we can also with each other and by each other obtain composure with respect to whatever has befallen us; 2, our heart is revived by what remains, viz., love on earth and hope in heaven; 3, we become strong for whatever duty is laid upon us, viz., labor and courage." FLOREY, 1863
12. On xxxiii. 1. ["No confinement can deprive God's people of His presence; no locks or bars can shut out His gracious visits; nay, oftentimes *as their afflictions abound their consolations much more abound*, and they have the most reviving communications of His favor then when the world frowns on them Paul's sweetest Epistles were those that bare date out of a prison." HENRY.—S. R. A.]
13. On xxxiii. 6. "The disease of our times is no other than a rebellious spirit, and the cause of this is no other than a want of reverence for God and His law." Discourse on the Birth-day of the king by Deacon HAUBER in Tübingen. PALMER, *Ev Casualreden, 2te Folge*, 1, 1850.
14. On xxxiii. 14-16. "Jesus Christ a King. 1. From what a noble royal stock did He proceed! (Raised by God, descending from David, both by His deity and humanity heir of the throne). 2. How well has He exercised His rule with judgment and righteousness (He Himself is the Lord, who is our righteousness). 3. How far does His dominion extend! (From Jerusalem to the ends of the earth). 4. How safely does His people dwell by His help in peace!" NAUMANN, in *Gesetz u. Zeugn.*, 1860, March.
15. On xxxiii. 14-16. "Who is He announced to-day? 1. The long promised—with reference to His historical appearance. 2. The Son of David and at the same time God's Son—this is His personal significance. 3. The Lord, who is our righteousness—this relates to His holy office and work." ANACKER, in *Gesetz u. Zeugn.*, 1860, March.

C. Historical Appendix to xxxii. 1-5.

(CHAP. XXXIV. 1-7).

From the introductory words to chh. xxxii. and xxxiii. we perceive that the event, which is here narrated (xxxiv. 1-7), falls in the 10th year of Zedekiah, since the conference, in consequence of which Jeremiah was confined in the court of the prison (xxxii. 3), must be that of which we have an account in this passage. Both passages agree almost verbatim in the announcement of the fate impending on the king and the city (comp. xxxii. 3-5 with xxxiv. 2, 3); especially is the phrase "thy mouth shall speak to His mouth, thine eyes shall see His eyes" peculiar to both. What is said in xxxiv. 4, 5 of the fate of Zedekiah is found in a condensed form in xxxii. 5 in the words, "and there shall he be until I visit him." The concluding words of xxxii. 5 "though ye fight, etc.," are not found in ch. xxxiv. (comp. rems. on xxxii. 1-5).—XXXIV. 1-7 is therefore evidently the special report, written by Jeremiah himself of his conference with Zedekiah. In consequence of this conference he was thrown back into the court, notwithstanding his favorable announcement to Zedekiah, xxxiv. 4, 5. The king might have expected something better from the prophet, as he approached when not called for. It was after this return to the court that Jeremiah received the revelation contained in chh. xxxii. and xxxiii. The event narrated in xxxiv. 1-7 also precedes these two chapters in the order of time. The report of it, perhaps written by the prophet immediately after the interview, is however, as a brief isolated passage, added as an appendix. It is evident that the conversation with Zedekiah did not long precede the facts related in chh xxxii., xxxiii., from the circumstance that the confinement of Jeremiah in the court, which is spoken of in xxxii. 3 as a consequence of the conversation, was properly a remanding to prison. If then the first confinement, as appears from xxxvii. 17-21, especially ver. 21, falls in the last period of the siege, after the return of the Chaldeans from their diversion against the Egyptians (B. C. 687), the second incarceration cannot be placed earlier, but must be ascribed to a somewhat later date of the same year

XXXIV. 1-7.

1 The word which came unto Jeremiah from the LORD [Jehovah] when [or while] Nebuchadnezzar king of Babylon, and all his army, and all the kingdoms of the¹ earth, of [subject to, *lit.*, the dominion of His hand] His dominion, and all the peo-
2 ple, fought against Jerusalem. and against all the cities thereof, saying, Thus saith the LORD, the God of Israel: Go and speak to Zedekiah king of Judah, and tell him, Thus saith the LORD; Behold, I will give this city into the hand of the king of Ba-
3 bylon, and he shall burn it with fire: And thou shalt not escape out of his hand, but shalt surely be taken, and delivered into his hand; and thine eyes shall behold the eyes of the king of Babylon, and he shall speak with thee mouth to mouth,² and

CHAP. XXXIV. 1-7.   801

4 thou shalt go to Babylon. Yet [only] hear the word of the LORD, O Zedekiah king
5 of Judah; Thus saith the LORD of thee, Thou shalt not die by the sword : But thou
shalt die in peace ; and with the burnings[3] of thy fathers the former kings which
were before thee, so shall they burn odors[4] for thee; and they will lament thee,
saying, Ah [alas] lord! for I have pronounced the word [spoken a word], saith
6 the LORD. Then Jeremiah the prophet spake all these words unto Zedekiah king
7 of Judah in Jerusalem. When [while] the king of Babylon's army [power] fought
against Jerusalem, and against all the cities of Judah that were left, against Lachish,
and against Azekah : for these defenced cities remained of the cities of Judah.

TEXTUAL AND GRAMMATICAL.

[1] Ver. 1.—The article is wanting before אֶרֶץ, as in lii. 2; xiv. 18.
[2] Ver. 3.—[Literally: thy mouth shall speak with his mouth].
[3] Ver. 5.—HENDERSON says twenty-eight MSS., with the LXX., Arab., Syr., Vulg., read like the burnings.—S. R. A.]
[4] Ver. 5.—[Some render : light the funeral fire, but comp. EXEG. rems.—S. R. A.]

EXEGETICAL AND CRITICAL.

During the siege (ver. 1) Jeremiah receives command to go and announce to king Zedekiah that the city will be given into the hands of the king of Babylon and burned (ver. 2). Zedekiah himself will be captured, brought before the king, and carried to Babylon (ver. 3). Yet he will not perish by the sword (ver. 4), but die in peace and be interred with royal honors, after the traditional manner (ver. 5). Jeremiah executed this commission punctually (ver. 6) at the time when Jerusalem and the still uncaptured fortified cities of Lachish and Azekah were being besieged (ver. 7).

Vers. 1-5. **The word ... saith Jehovah.** The style in vers. 1, 2 bears the character of great diffuseness, such as is peculiar to Jeremiah in the later period of his ministry. Hence such phrases as **all the people,** ver. 1, and **tell him,** ver. 2, which strictly taken are superfluous, need not surprise us.—**Of the dominion of his hand.** This addition is a restriction and definition of **the earth** ; not all kingdoms of the earth, but of the earth in so far as it was the "dominion of his hand." Comp. li. 28; 1 Ki. ix. 19.—**Go,** etc. Two questions here present themselves which it is not easy to answer. How is the conference with Zedekiah here narrated connected with the other mentioned in xxxii. 3; xxxvii. 17? 2. What relation does that bear which is said in vers. 4, 5 of Zedekiah's end, to the other declarations concerning it (xxxix. 5-7; lii. 9-11 ; 2 Ki. xxv. 6, 7)? These two questions seem to be heterogeneous. There is, however, a close connection between them, for which reason we investigate the second question here instead of at vers. 4, 5.
Are the words of the prophet in vers. 2-5 to be understood in a good sense for Zedekiah, or as a menace? All depends on the understanding of the sentence **yet hear,** etc., ver. 4. VENEMA, CHR. B. MICHAELIS, HITZIG and GRAF are of opinion that this sentence proposes an exceptional case, viz., in case Zedekiah obeys the command to give himself up to the Chaldeans the threatening pronounced against him in ver. 3 will not be fulfilled, but he will die in quiet possession of his throne. The reasons urged for this explanation are: The pleasant prospect, which in vers. 4, 5 is placed before Zedekiah,

would contradict the elsewhere constantly repeated exhortation to surrender himself; it would also be otherwise too favorable. Here it is presupposed that ver. 5 can be understood only of the quiet possession of the throne and of a peaceful end and honorable interment, which Zedekiah will receive as the reigning king. Aside from ver. 4 a, this explanation would certainly be possible. It is, however, also possible to understand ver. 5 as an antithesis to "thou shalt not die by the sword," not a violent death in battle, but a natural, peaceful end. This might be, even if Zedekiah died a prisoner (comp. lii. 11), as imprisonment is not necessarily a hinderance to the usual funeral obsequies. The Jews were generally well treated while in captivity,—many of them enjoyed the favor of the rulers, and excited the envy of the natives by their preferment, and most of them were undesirous of returning to their native land.—Jehoiachin was elevated to royal honors after twenty-seven years' confinement (lii. 31). Why may not Zedekiah have been kept in mild imprisonment and permission have been given to the Jews after his death to bury their king according to the custom of their country ? This appears to be the only possible explanation, as the sentence "Thus saith the Lord of thee," ver. 4 b, cannot be other than a summary of the word of God, which, according to ver. 4 a, Zedekiah is to hear. I leave out of account that the other explanation would require "Listen to" or "Heed" the word, and also a designation of the divine word to which Zedekiah is to listen. But it would be indispensable that "hear the word," etc., should be plainly designated as a condition, and what follows as a consequence of the condition's being fulfilled. As the words now read ver. 4 b can be taken only as the word which Zedekiah is to hear. Ver. 4 a then expresses no condition, but in vers. 4 and 5 a restriction or more exact definition (not a continuation, as HITZIG supposes), is added to ver. 3. In ver. 3 it was said that Zedekiah should be captured and taken to Babylon. Vers. 4 and 5 mitigate this harsh sentence, adding that he shall not die by violence there, but in peace and be buried with royal honors. Thus rendered, the passage harmonizes with the other intimations, which are given with respect to the end of the king: xxxii. 7; xxxix. 5-7; lii. 9-11 ; 2 Ki. xxv. 6, 7. Is then this declaration adapted to excite the anger of the king? Though the first part of it is gloomy, the second presents some points of comfort. The terrible fate which befel the tyrant Jehoiakim (the words "will lament thee," ver. 5, are in evident contrast to xxii. 18) will not be Zedekiah's. His fate, when the severest crisis is past, will take a (relatively) better turn; he will at least enjoy a respectful treatment as a prisoner, and indeed again receive honor after death. Zedekiah is thus relatively favored. Should he for this have the prophet confined, as must have been the case if the conference reported here be identical with that mentioned in xxxii. 3? According to chh. xxxvii. and xxxviii., where the whole history of the relations between Zedekiah and the prophet is related according to its main features, the former confined the latter in the court only with benevolent intentions. In the first instance the court of the guard was assigned as a mitigation in contrast to the terrible detention he had suffered in the prison of Jonathan, the Scribe (xxxvii. 20). Afterwards the court of the guard was again assigned him out of kindness, after his still more terrible confinement in the pit (xxxviii. 13). Chh. xxxvi. and xxxvii. make the general impression that Zedekiah kept the prophet in custody only on account of the princes. Had it not been for these he would have given him his entire freedom (comp. xxxviii. 5). It should, moreover, be observed that according to xxxiv. 2 Jeremiah seeks the king freely, while according to chh. xxxvii. sq. this scarcely seems possible. Then we have reports of two conferences of Jeremiah with the king. On the first he is brought from strict confinement in the house of Jonathan (xxxvii. 17), on the second he is brought after his deliverance from the pit (xxxviii. 14). The fear, which Jeremiah expresses on this latter occasion, shows that he had no desire to present himself before the king. Thus it appears as if the different accounts of Jeremiah's conferences with Zedekiah would not agree, especially does a confinement in the court of the guard as a punishment, according to xxxii. 3, seem to agree neither with chh. xxxvii. and xxxviii. nor with xxxiv. 2-5. Meanwhile as the apparent want of agreement itself excludes the idea of an interpolation, and as there is nothing in the language which betrays a strange hand, we are forced to the hypothesis that in xxxii. 1-5 and xxxiv. 1-5 we have an account of a conference of Zedekiah with Jeremiah which is distinct from the two narrated in. xxxvii. 17-20 and xxxviii. 14-16. From the words "wilt thou not certainly put me to death," xxxviii. 15, it is clear that Jeremiah did not expect a very kindly disposition on the part of the king. It is conceivable that the court was assigned him as a place of punishment, when after a voluntary visit to the king (comp. xxii. 1), he was dismissed with the ungracious words "back into the court!" Although, as we have shown, the words in xxxiv. 4, 5 are relatively favorable to the king, yet he may have expected something better of the prophet when he appeared uncalled for and have accordingly become indignant at the essentially invariable prediction of the capture of the city and his own imprisonment If it is asked what was the object of this address to the king, not occasioned by the king but com-

manded by God, it is surprising that the prophet does not say what the fate of the city will be in case of voluntary submission (comp. xxxviii. 17). He does not, however, say fully what will be the fate of the king in case of stubborn refusal to surrender. Nothing is here said of Zedekiah's children together with the princes of Israel being killed before his eyes, of his own eyes being put out (lii. 10), or of his wives being given to the Babylonian princes (xxxviii. 21-23). This lack of an alternative distinguishes the present passage from xxi. 9; xxxviii. 2, 17. This passage reads like an unconditional sentence, in which, however, it is expressly remarked that this still severe sentence is yet to be regarded as a mitigation. (Comp. vers. 4 and 5 with xxii. 18). It accordingly seems probable that this passage, together with the prophecy closely connected with it in chh. xxxii. and xxxiii . belongs to the period indicated in xxxviii. 23, *i. e.* to the period after the last exhortation which the prophet addressed to Zedekiah *conditionally*. Now a simple announcement is made to him of what will take place. The possibility that Zedekiah may yet tread the path of deliverance so often pointed out to him, is no longer thought of. It is still a great favor that the full terrible reality is not yet disclosed to him. He doubtless owed this as well as the relative mildness of his sentence to the good-will he had manifested towards the prophet. It certainly seems, as remarked above, that this announcement of his sentence, by the prophet who comes before him uncalled-for, first irritated him towards the latter, on which supposition the words, "Wherefore dost thou prophesy?" in xxxii. 3, would be explained.

And with the burnings of thy fathers. The burning of the dead was not a Jewish custom. Burning alive only occurs as a punishment, Lev. xx. 14; xxi. 9 coll. Isa. vii. 25—and there is a trace of burning corpses in time of pestilence in Am. vi. 10 (if משרפו=מסרפו). At any rate in the present passage it is the burning of spices which is meant, 2 Chron. xvi 14; xxi. 19. With this also will agree the dative of the pronoun and the form of the verb. Comp. the verb with the accusative of the thing and the dative of the person for whom the sacrifice is burned. Exod. xxx. 20; Lev. vii. 5; 2 Chron. xiii. 11. [CALVIN says, that to prevent putrefaction, the bodies of the dead were dried by a slow fire, but only at the burial of kings.—S. R. A.]

For I have spoken a word. Not merely breath, but a word which is spirit, life, power has the Lord uttered. (Comp. Deut. xxii. 47; Ps. xxxiii. 4; xxxv. 100; Prov. xxx. 5; Isa. xl. 8; lv. 10, 11 ; Jer. xxiii. 29). The expression "I have spoken," without "word," is found with special frequency in Ezekiel, v. 13, 15, 17; xvii. 21, 24, *etc.*

Vers. 6, 7. **Then Jeremiah ... cities of Judah.** The performance of the task is mentioned as a proof that Jeremiah had the courage to appear before the king with a message, which was by no means such as he wished to hear in a time of severe affliction.—Lachish and Azekah were both situated in the Sephela, the low country in the south-western part of the tribe of Judah (Jer. xv. 33, 35, 39). They were both fortified by Rehoboam (2 Chron. xi. 9). Lachish was besieged by Sennacherib (2 Ki. xviii. 14, 17; xix. 8; Isa. xxxvi. 2; xxxvii. 8). ["This celebrated siege is supposed by Layard to be depicted on certain slabs disinterred from the ruins of Nineveh."—COWLES].—**Fortified cities** cannot well be taken as in apposition to **cities of Judah**, because this addition would either be superfluous or would give the wrong thought that unfortified cities were still left. It cannot also well be attached as a definition to **remained**: *nam hæc oppida ex oppidis Judæ munita supererant* (ROSENMUELLER). It is not credible that there were no other fortified cities besides these. It can only be in apposition to **these**; these, as fortified cities, were still left. The reason of their remaining is thus expressed, and this reason was the strength of their fortifications.

---

11. Historical Appendix to the Collection of Discourses.

(CHAP. XXXIV. 8-22 and CHAP. XXXV.)

At the close of the collected discourses we find two portions which may be regarded as an appendix, inasmuch as they afford a glaring instance of Israel's disobedience towards Jehovah, in contrast with the obedience of a non-Israelitish tribe towards the command of their ancestor. The history of the discharge of servants, ordered in the pressure of distress but taken back when the danger seemed to be past, is a proof how lightly obedience to Jehovah's law sat on the hearts of the Israelites, while the obedience of the Rechabites to their ancestral ordinances was deeply rooted and impregnable. Although the two portions are chronologically far apart, the first belonging to the tenth year of Zedekiah (more exactly to the time of the temporary suspension of the siege), the second to the reign of Jehoiakim (more exactly when the first invasion of the Chaldeans under Nebuchadnezzar was expected); yet it is quite appropriate that they should stand side by side, since, as remarked above, the second serves as a foil to the first.
The reason for placing the older portion last may be that the following chapter (xxxvi.) belongs to the same period, viz., the fourth year of Jehoiakim.
The division into two parts is very clear and simple. The facts are narrated in xxxiv. 8-11. Then in vers. 12-16 the facts are recapitulated by the prophet with reference to the legal enactments, finally in vers. 17-22 the divine sentence is pronounced on the covenant-breaking Israelites.—Chap. xxxv. is plainly divisible into two halves. In the first (vers. 1-11) the facts are again related, in the second the parallel is drawn between the behaviour of the Rechabites and of Israel, and corresponding recompense announced to both.

A. THE DISOBEDIENCE OF THE ISRAELITES SHOWN IN THEIR BEHAVIOUR IN SETTING FREE THEIR SERVANTS.

XXXIV. 8-22.

8 *This is* the word that came unto Jeremiah, from the LORD, after that the king Zedekiah had made a covenant with all the people which *were* at Jerusalem, to
9 proclaim liberty unto them;[1] That every man should let his man-servant, and every man his maid-servant, *being* an Hebrew or an Hebrewess, go free; that none should
10 serve himself of them,[2] *to wit,* of a Jew his brother. Now when all the princes, and all the people, which had entered into the covenant, heard that every one should let his man-servant, and every one his maid-servant, go free, that none should serve themselves of them any more, then they obeyed, and let *them* go.
11 But afterward they turned, and caused the servants and the handmaids, whom they had let go free, to return, and brought them into subjection for [*or* compelled
12 them to be][3] servants and for handmaids.[4] Therefore the word of the LORD came
13 to Jeremiah from the LORD, saying, Thus saith the LORD, the God of Israel; I made a covenant with your fathers in the day that I brought them forth out of
14 the land of Egypt, out of the house of bondmen, saying, At the end of seven years let ye go every man his brother an Hebrew, which hath been sold [*or* who hath sold himself] unto thee; and when he hath served thee six years, thou shalt let him go free from thee: but your fathers hearkened not unto me, neither inclined
15 their ear, And ye were now [to-day] turned, and had done right in my sight, in proclaiming liberty every man to his neighbor; and ye had made a covenant before me in the house which is called by my name [whereupon my name is called]:

16 but ye turned and polluted my name, and caused every man his servant, and every man his handmaid, whom he had set at liberty at their pleasure, to return, and brought them into subjection [compelled them], to be unto you for servants and for handmaids.
17 Therefore thus saith the LORD [Jehovah], Ye have not hearkened unto me, in proclaiming liberty, every one to his brother, and every man to his neighbor: behold, I proclaim a liberty for you, saith the LORD [Jehovah], to the sword, to the pestilence, and to the famine; and I will make you to be removed[5] into all the
18 kingdoms of the earth. And I will give[6] [or deliver] the men that have transgressed my covenant, which [who] have not performed the words of the covenant which they had made before me, when they cut the calf in twain, and passed be-
19 tween the parts thereof, the princes of Judah, and the princes of Jerusalem, the eunuchs, and the priests, and all the people of the land, which passed between the
20 parts of the calf; I will even give them into the hands of their enemies, and into the hands of them that seek their life: and their dead bodies shall be for meat
21 unto the fowls of the heaven, and to the beasts of the earth. And Zedekiah, king of Judah, and his princes will I give into the hand of their enemies, and into the hand of them that seek their life, and into the hand of the king of Babylon's
22 army, which are gone up from you. Behold, I will command, saith the LORD, and cause them to return to this city; and they shall fight against it, and take it, and burn it with fire; and I will make the cities of Judah a desolation without an inhabitant.

TEXTUAL AND GRAMMATICAL.

1 Ver. 8.—The construction is *ad sensum*, and very common in Hebrew. Comp. 2 Ki. x. 24; NAEGELSB. *Gr.*, § 95, 2.
2 Ver. 9.—בָּם רָבַד. Comp. xxii. 13; xxv. 14; xxx. 8.
3 Ver. 11.—וַיָּשׁוּבוּ. The Hiphil does not occur elsewhere. The Masorytes therefore read Kal (ver. 10; 2 Chron. xxviii. 10).
4 Ver. 11.—On the construction ן לַעֲבָדִים comp. NAEGELSB. *Gr.*, § 95 *g.*, *Anm.* 5.
5 Ver. 17.—[A. V. marg.: for a removing; NAEGELSB.: for a horror; HENDERSON: give you up to agitation.—S. R. A.]
6 Ver. 18.—[NAEGELSB., HITZIG, WORDSWORTH: I will make the men who . . . . the calf which they cut; *i. e. like* the calf, etc.—Comp. NAEGELSB. *Gr.*, § 69, 3.—S. R. A.]

EXEGETICAL AND CRITICAL.

Vers. 8-11. **This is the word . . . for servants and for handmaids.** Though the expression "to make a covenant" generally means that two persons pledge themselves to a mutual performance, which accrues to the advantage of both parties, the expression here denotes a performance which all do in common in the interest of a third, from which, however, advantage is expected for all. For the setting free was chiefly for the advantage of those set free. It was, however, also hoped that it would be for the general good, account being taken partly of the gratitude of the freedmen and their increased activity in the defence, partly perhaps also of the favor of Jehovah thus to be procured. It is clear that the word "covenant" is thus employed in essentially the same sense as usual.—**To proclaim liberty unto them.** The expression is found in this sense besides only in Lev. xxv. 10; Isa. lxi. 1; Ezek. xlvi. 17. **Them** of course refers to the servants mentioned afterwards. The law on this point is found in Exod. xxi. 1 sqq.; Lev. xxv. 39-41; Deut. xv. 12. Every servant of Hebrew origin was to be set free after six years' service (without respect to the Sabbatical year), according to Lev. xxv. this was to be done in the year of jubilee. This involves no contradiction, for in Lev. xxv. it is the law of the jubilee year which is given. The former enactment is merely supplemented from this point of view, the jubilee year is to end the service unconditionally, wherefore the price was to be determined by the time intervening before the jubilee (ver. 50 sqq. where it is the sale of Israelitish servants to heathen inhabitants which is spoken of, but there is no reason to doubt the application of this rule to the purchase by Israelites). Comp. SAALSCHUETZ, *Mos. Recht. Kap.*, 14 and 101, § 3.—These legal prescriptions had, like so many others, remained unobserved. The reformation under Josiah may have revived the knowledge, but not the observance of them. The pressure of the siege aroused the thought that the observance of this law might be of use in both the ways above indicated. They therefore pledged themselves on the king's demand by mutual agreement to set free the Hebrew servants and maids, and as appears from ver. 9, all of them, even those who had not served six years. The supererogation with regard to some was outweighed by their short-comings with respect to the others. But—and this is a striking instance of false conversion, springing from bad motives,—when the danger seemed over on the withdrawal of the Chaldeans, they brought the servants again under the yoke.
Vers. 12-16. **Therefore the word . . . for handmaids.—In the day.** Comp. vii. 22; xi. 4; xxxi. 32.—**House of bondmen.** Themselves delivered from oppressive servitude, Israel should be kind towards their servants, which is expressly designated in Deut. xv. 15 as the motive of the law of manumission.—**At the end of seven years** cannot mean at the end of every

CHAP. XXXIV. 8–22.

seven years. This would contradict what follows, "after he has served six years," and the similar legal enactments (Exod. xxi. 2; Deut. xv. 12). It can only signify at the close of a *septennium*. The preposition מִן then retains its proper signification;—from the close, *i. e.*, when the close of the *septennium*, the seventh year, has begun. Comp. similar expressions in Deut. xv. 1; xiv. 28 coll. xxxi. 10.—**Who hath sold himself.** These words are a quotation from memory from Deut. xv. 12.—**Turned,** vers. 15 and 16. The meaning of the verb is the same in both cases, only the *termini a quo* and *in quem* are opposite.—**Called by my name.** Every transgression of the divine commands, but especially a breach of a covenant sworn in His name, is a desecration thereof (comp. Lev. xix. 12; xx. 3).—**At their pleasure.** The expression occurs also in Deut. xxi. 14. It is there used of the captive woman, married but afterwards disapproved. Here the antithesis is evidently not property or family, so that the sense would be, what she possesses belongs to her, but thou shalt set her *person* at liberty. But the antithesis is the unfreedom of the sold, who must go wherever his master sends him, and the freedom of the dismissed, to go wherever he wishes. The word then=according to, *or* at, their pleasure, נַפְשָׁם being regarded as the seat of desire, as in the expression "if it be your mind," Gen. xxiii. 8; 2 Kings ix. 15.

Vers. 17–22. **Therefore . . . without an inhabitant.**—Liberty is used the second time in ver. 17 ironically; because ye did not proclaim liberty (that which is taken back again directly is as good as none), liberty shall be proclaimed to you, but a liberty of which you will be the victims. [I set you, whom I have hitherto regarded as my servants, free, deliver you over, to your fate, to the sword, *etc.*—HITZIG].—**The calf.** Ver. 18 seems to me better connected with **I will give [make],** in which we are grammatically fully justified (comp. NAEGELSB. *Gr.*, § 69, 3). So also LUTHER and others. The symbolical meaning of the rite here alluded to appears then immediately applied, in order to present before the covenant breakers the threatening punishment. They themselves are to be the calf cut in two. On this rite comp. Gen. xv. 10, and DELITZSCH thereupon. According to the other explanation, "the calf" is in opposition to "the covenant." Then, however, the similarity in the fate of the transgressor to that of the calf, is only implicitly hinted at, not expressed. The late and anacoluthic resumption "I will give," in ver. 21, is then also troublesome.—In ver. 19 chiefs of tribes, city-chiefs (elders of the city), courtiers, priests and common people, are distinguished. When afterwards, verse 21, his princes are again mentioned with the king, we must attribute this to Jeremiah's diffuseness, and emphasize it the less, as it is very common to mention the king and princes together (xxiv. 8; xxv. 19, *etc.*).

DOCTRINAL AND ETHICAL.

1. On xxxiv. 8–11. "The peculiar difference between hypocritical repentance and true conversion. The hypocrites when they do penance, do it (1.) not from faith, but from fear of distress and danger, in which they are at the time; (2.) they do not make a change in all points of disobedience, but only in the ethical, as here with the jubilee year, as if there were nothing more to be altered; (3.) they do such things as make a show for the people and have a high regard, as the manumission, letting loose the rabble, would have a great noise and show, but meanwhile there were few thoughts of faith, love, fear of God, hope and thanksgiving; (4.) such penitence does not last long, but as soon as the distress finds a hole, the devotion goes with it." CRAMER.

2. On ver. 12. "*Qua locutione mystica (verbum Jovæ factum esse a Jova) qualis etiam*, Gen. xix. 24, *innuitur mysterium Trinitatis juxta regulam Lutheri commendatam nobis in aureo scripto de ultimis verbis Davidis. Insinuatur enim hic et similibus loquendi formulis pluralitas personarum, ut hic Filii et Spiritus sancti.*" FÖRSTER.

3. On xxxiv. 15, 16. "Converted, but not rightly; friendship made when the foot is on the neck, Pharisaic repentance. Yet thus, there is often an interval, a period of rest and of refreshment for the kingdom of Christ. And God has this in view when He extorts conversions of this kind." ZINZENDORF.

4. On xxxiv. 15, 16, 18–22. The Jews thus committed a double sin: 1. They did not keep the promise made to each other and to the servants; 2. They desecrated the name of God by their disobedience and breach of the oath sworn in God's name and house.

HOMILETICAL AND PRACTICAL.

True repentance in distinction from false. 1. The occasion may be the same in both; external distress (comp. *ex. gr.*, Isa. xxviii. 19; 1 Cor. xi. 32; Tit. ii. 12). 2. In false penitence the inward disposition remains unchanged; in true penitence man turns inwardly with pain and sorrow from evil and to God. 3. False penitence lasts as long only as the outward need; true penitence is a permanent condition of the heart, and notwithstanding single backslidings, advances to a more complete subjugation of the old man (the old Adam in us is to be drowned and perish by daily sorrow and repentance).

B. THE COUNTERPART TO THE DISOBEDIENCE OF THE ISRAELITES: THE OBEDIENCE OF THE RECHABITES (CHAP. XXXV.).

1. *The Fact.*

XXXV. 1-11.

1 The word which came unto Jeremiah from the LORD in the days of Jehoiakim
2 the son of Josiah king of Judah, saying, Go unto the house of the Rechabites, and speak unto them, and bring them into the house of the Lord, into one of the cham-
3 bers, and give them wine to drink. Then I took Jaazaniah the son of Jeremiah, the son of Habaziniah, and his brethren, and all his sons, and the whole house
4 of the Rechabites; And I brought them into the house of the LORD, into the chamber of the sons of Hanan, the son of Igdaliah, a man of God, which was by the chamber of the princes, which was above the chamber of Maaseiah the son of
5 Shallum, the keeper of the door [*or*, threshold]. And I set before the sons of the house of the Rechabites pots¹ full of wine, and cups, and I said unto them, Drink
6 ye wine. But they said, We will drink no wine: for Jonadab the son of Rechab our father commanded us, saying, Ye shall drink no wine, *neither* ye, nor your sons
7 for ever: Neither shall ye build house, nor sow seed, nor plant vineyard, nor have *any:* but all your days ye shall dwell in tents: that ye may live many days in the
8 land where ye *be* strangers. Thus have we obeyed the voice of Jonadab the son of Rechab our father in all that he hath charged us, to drink no wine all our days,
9 we, our wives, our sons, nor our daughters; nor to build houses for us to dwell in:
10 neither have we vineyard, nor field, nor seed: but we have dwelt in tents, and have obeyed, and done according to all that Jonadab our father commanded us.
11 But it came to pass, when Nebuchadrezzar king of Babylon came up into the land, that we said, Come, and let us go to Jerusalem for fear of the army of the Chaldeans, and for fear of the army of the Syrians: so we dwell at Jerusalem.

TEXTUAL AND GRAMMATICAL.

¹ Ver. 5.—גְּבִיעַ, related to גֶּבַע, גִּבְעָה, hill, designates here a larger round vessel (*crater*), from which the cups were filled. Comp. Gen. xliv. 2, 5, 12.

EXEGETICAL AND CRITICAL.

Vers. 1-5. **The word . . . Drink ye wine.** As the Rechabites did not live in houses, **the house of the Rechabites** must be taken in a gentilic sense. The Rechabites were a branch of that tribe of Kenites, which springing from Hobab, the brother-in-law of Moses (Num. x. 29), migrated with the Israelites from the desert to Canaan, and were therefore closely connected with them politically, as well as religiously (comp. Jud. i. 16; iv. 11; 1 Sam. xv. 6; xxvii. 10; xxx. 29). To what an extent this, especially the latter, was the case may be learned from what is said of Jonadab, the ancestor and lawgiver of the Rechabites, in the book of Kings (2 Kings x. 15, 23). The injunctions which, according to vers. 6, 7, Jonadab laid on his descendants, were doubtless for the purpose of preserving their nomadic state and avoiding the evils of stationary and agricultural life. Jonadab appears to have forbidden the drinking of wine, not merely for the sake of the immediate conse-quences, which it might easily have, but also that the love of wine might not be the occasion of their becoming settled. The conscientiousness with which the Rechabites after three centuries still followed the commands of their ancestor, is a testimony that they held him in high honor. That he deserved this honor, and that it was shown him by others during his life-time, is seen in the respect with which Jehu treated him, taking him as a witness of his zeal in the service of Jehovah. Comp. KEIL on 2 Kings x. 12-17.—

The לִשְׁכוֹת were rooms in the buildings enclosing the fore-courts, appropriated to various uses (1 Chron. xxviii. 12 coll. ix. 26; Jer. xxxvi. 10, 12, 20, 21; Ezr. x. 6; Neh. x. 38). One of these rooms, which must have been a hall corresponding to the number of the persons, was named after "the sons of Hanan, the son of Igdaliah, the man of God." It is not known who this Hanan was. From the designation "man of Elohim," we may infer that he was a prophet (comp. Deut. xxxiii. 1; Josh. xiv. 8; 1 Sam. ii. 26; ix. 8, 10, *etc.*), and from "sons" (comp. 1 Kings. xx. 35; 2

Kings ii. 3, 5, 7, 15, *etc.*), that the room was a place of assemblage used by him and his pupils and adherents. Maaseiah, the threshold-keeper (of which there were three, lii. 24; 2 Kings xxv. 18, and who stood in rank immediately after the כֹּהֵן מִשְׁנֶה. Comp. 2 Kings xxiii. 4) is probably identical with the Maaseiah, whose son Zephaniah was a "second priest" (lii. 24; xxxvii. 3; xxix. 25, xxi. 1).—Of the region inhabited by the Rechabites we have no further indication than the brief notice, 1 Chron. ii. 55, from which we learn merely that they dwelt in the tribe of Judah. Jud. i. 16 agrees with this, where it is said of the Kenites, that they settled in the wilderness of Judah, which lies south of Arad (near the wilderness of Kadesh to the south of Hebron, RAUMER, *Paläst.*, S. 172). As they were Nomads, they needed land suited to this mode of life. There is no objection to their southern position from the approach of the enemies from the North. For they might justly fear an inundation of the whole land, and therefore sought refuge in Jerusalem betimes, before they were cut off. Ver. 11. **Army of the Syrians.** Aram is Syria in the more restricted sense. Before B. C., when it became an Assyrian province, it played an important part among the foes of the Israelites (2 Sam. viii. 3 sqq., *etc.*), and afterwards it still appears among their number in the train of Assyria (Isa. ix. 11), as here in that of Babylon (comp. 2 Kings xxiv. 2).

2. *The Application.*

XXXV. 12-19.

12, 13 Then came the word of the LORD unto Jeremiah, saying, Thus saith the LORD of hosts [Jehovah Zebaoth], the God of Israel; Go and tell the men of Judah and the inhabitants of Jerusalem, Will ye not receive instruction to hearken
14 to my words? saith the LORD. The words[1] of Jonadab the son of Rechab, that he commanded his sons not to drink wine, are performed; for unto this day they drink none, but obey their father's commandment: notwithstanding I have spoken unto you, rising early and speaking [*i. e.*, zealously and unceasingly[2]]; but ye
15 hearkened not unto me. I have sent also unto all my servants the prophets, rising up early and sending[3] them, saying Return ye now every man from his evil way, and amend your doings, and go not after other gods to serve them, and ye shall dwell in the land[4] which I have given to you and to your fathers: but ye have
16 not inclined your ear, nor hearkened unto me. Because the sons of Jonadab the son of Rechab have performed the commandment of their father, which he com-
17 manded them; but this people hath not hearkened unto me: Therefore thus saith the LORD God of hosts, the God of Israel; Behold, I will bring upon Judah, and upon all the inhabitants of Jerusalem all the evil that I have pronounced against them: because I have spoken unto them, but they have not heard; and I have
18 called unto them, but they have not answered. And Jeremiah said unto the house of the Rechabites, Thus saith the LORD of hosts, the God of Israel; Because ye have obeyed the commandment of Jonadab your father, and kept all his precepts,
19 and done according unto all that he hath commanded you: Therefore thus saith the LORD of hosts, the God of Israel; Jonadab the son of Rechab shall not want a man to stand before me for ever.

TEXTUAL AND GRAMMATICAL.

[1] Ver. 14.—הוּקַם אֶת־דִּבְרֵי. On the construction. Comp. NAEGELSB. *Gr.*, § 100, 2.

[2] Ver. 14.—Comp. vii. 13.

[3] Ver. 15.—הַשְׁכֵּם וְשָׁלֹחַ. Comp. vii. 25; xxv. 4.

[4] Ver. 15.—וַיֵּשְׁבוּ אֶל־הָאֲדָמָה. Comp. xxv. 5. אֶל for עַל. Comp. Comm. on x. 1, as also אֶל־יְהוּדָה, ver. 17, and the reverse in עַל־מִצְוַת, ver. 18.

EXEGETICAL AND CRITICAL.

The commands of Jonadab, the Rechabite, have been kept centuries after his death by his people who are not descendants of Abraham, and who consequently participate in the covenant of promise only mediately, and in the second line. Israel, however, has not obeyed the commands of Jehovah, the God of hosts, though they have been presented and inculcated unceasingly by prophets. Therefore all the threatenings pronounced by the Lord on Israel shall be fulfilled. But to the Rechabites it is promised, that Jonadab shall not want a man to stand before Jehovah.

Vers. 12–15. **Then came . . . hearkened unto me.** From "go," ver. 13, we see that Jeremiah was to speak these words, not in the "chamber," but outside, to the people.—**Instruction.** Comp. ii. 30; xxxii. 33.—**Return ye now,** etc. Comp. xxv. 5.

Vers. 16–19. **Because the sons . . . forever.—Shall not want a man.** Comp. rems. on xxxiii. 17.—**To stand before me.** As this expression involves the idea of service (comp. Comm. on vii. 10), and according to the connection that of the priestly service or worship (comp. Comm. on xv. 19), it is not merely the continuance of the Rechabite family, but its perseverance in the worship of Jehovah. It is said that there are still Rechabites in Asia. WOLFF, the missionary to the Jews, met them in Mesopotamia and Yemen. WOLFF designates the desert of Yemen near Senaar, as the proper residence of these Rechabites, who still assert their origin from Hobab, the brother-in-law of Moses. Comp. Dr. JOSEPH WOLFF'S *Travels*.

DOCTRINAL AND ETHICAL.

1. As the Lord says to the Jews of His time, Luke xi. 31, 32, that the queen of the South and the people of Nineveh will rise up in the judgment against the people of this generation, and will condemn them, for a greater than Solomon or Jonah is here, so might Jeremiah say to his contemporaries that the Rechabites would rise up against them, and condemn them, for a greater than Jonadab is here.

2. The Rechabites' obedience to their ancestor's command is in itself praiseworthy and exemplary. It is in perfect accordance with the fourth Commandment. Comp. Ecclus. iii. Were the Rechabites equally conscientious in their observance of the Divine commands! Would not a custom contrary to the divine command have been retained with equal tenacity on the authority of their chief? The family feeling and national spirit are natural. They do not mortify our flesh. They may, for the sake of the honor and interest of our family, which is mediately our own personal honor and interest, impel us to the most difficult performances. I have heard of children, on whom the inculcation of the divine commands made little impression; but when they were told, it is the King's will, they did what was desired of them. Comp. Mark vii. 8 sqq.

3. "All families could not pursue Rechab's mode of life, nor should they. God gives many different callings; happy are they who can feel content in the most simple, and who constantly preserve the feeling of being pilgrims in this world. It is also not contrary to God's ordering that distinct families, ranks and callings, are formed, or that special plans are adopted for the exercise of partnerships in certain times and circumstances, just as the church at Jerusalem introduced a kind of community of goods. We are only not to perceive any special sanctity in such arrangements; they are only practices, and all depends on the mind in which they are undertaken." DIEDRICH.

4. "*Abuti consueverunt hac narratione de Rechabitis Monachi ad stabiliendam vitam monasticam, quemadmodum Bellarminus ex hoc capite causam eorum agere conatur (De Mon. II., cap. 5), hunc in modum scribens: 'Habemus etiam* Jer. xxxv. *insignem commendationem nepotum Rechab, qui, cum iis pater sive avus praecepisset, ut domus non aedificarent, agros non seminarent, vineas non plantarent, vinum nunquam biberent, vitam durissimam quasi extra mundum agerent, omnia diligentissime observarunt, quos etiam monachorum nostrorum figuram gessisse scribit Hieronymus in Epist. ad Paulin.*' *Cf. Hieron. in Exod. cap.* 21." FÖRSTER.

HOMILETICAL AND PRACTICAL.

True obedience shown in the example of Israel and the Rechabites. 1. The Rechabites put Israel to shame, in so far as they obey the command of their earthly ancestor, while the latter does not obey the Lord's command. 2. The obedience of the Rechabites to the command of their earthly ancestor is however no pledge of their obedience to the commands of God. 3. Obedience to God's commands is guaranteed only among the spiritual Israel, *i. e.*, among those, who by the Holy Spirit have become members of a higher order of nature, in which the will of God is written in the hearts of all, and has consequently become the innermost principle of life.—Or, 1. In respect to legal obedience the Jews are surpassed by the Rechabites (the difference between the two). 2. The obedience of the Rechabites to their ancestor does not guarantee their obedience to God (equality of the two). 3. Only spiritual Israel bears in itself the guarantee of obedience to God's command (the higher third).

SECOND DIVISION.

Historical Presentation of the most important Events from the fourth year of Jehoiakim to the close of the Prophet's ministry.

(B. C. 605—570).

CHAPTERS XXXVI.—XLIV.

To the collection of discourses and its appendices are now added historical sections. These contain, with the exception of the beginning and the conclusion, a continuous historical narrative. The beginning is formed by a single but highly important event of the fourth and fifth years of Jehoiakim's reign—the writing out of the prophecies (ch. xxxvi.) *The conclusion* (ch. xliv.) *is formed by a portion, which, after a pause embracing 16-18 years, gives an account of Jeremiah's last appearance, in the midst of the people even in Egypt still devoted to idolatry. From* ch. xxxvii. *to* ch. xliii. *the events are continuously narrated, which occurred from the beginning of Zedekiah's reign up to the arrival of the fugitive remnant in Egypt. It should be remarked that the presentation begins indeed with the beginning of Zedekiah's reign, but hurries rapidly over the first ten years* (xxxvii. 1, 2) *and begins the connected narrative with the imprisonment of the prophet, which took place in the tenth year of this king. The thread on which the events are hung is the personal experience of the prophet; the behaviour of the people towards the Lord's servant being both the ground and consequence of the fate which befel them. The single portions of this section may be arranged as follows:*

A. The events before the capture of Jerusalem, chh. xxxvi.-xxxviii.

I. *The writing out of the prophecies in the fourth year of Jehoiakim*, ch. **xxxvi.**

1. *The command and first writing*, xxxvi. 1-8.
2. *The reading to the people*, xxxvi. 9-18.
3. *The reading to the king*, xxxvi. 19-26.
4. *The prediction of punishment to Jehoiakim and the second writing*, xxxvi. 27-32.

II. *The events in the tenth and eleventh years of Zedekiah*, chh. xxxvii. and xxxviii.

1. *The embassy of the king and the imprisonment of the prophet in its first and second stages*, ch. xxxvii.
2. *Jeremiah in the pit (third stage of imprisonment), his conference with the king and confinement in the court of the guard (fourth stage of imprisonment)*, ch. xxxviii.

B. The events after the capture of Jerusalem, chh. xxxix.-xliv.

1. *Jeremiah liberated from the court of the guard, and delivered to Gedaliah*, xxxviii. 28 b—xxxix. 14.
2. *Appendix to* xxxix. 1-14; *the promise made to Ebed-melech the Cushite*, xxxix. 15-18.
3. *Jeremiah liberated in Ramah and delivered the second time to Gedaliah*, xl. 1-6.
4. *The gathering of the people under Gedaliah*, xl. 7-16.
5. *The murder of Gedaliah and its consequences*, ch. xli.
6. *The hypocritical inquiry*, xlii. 1-6.
7. *The unwelcome answer*, xlii. 7-22.
8. *The flight to Egypt*, xliii. 1-7.
9. *Jeremiah in Tahpanhes*, xliii. 8-13.
10. *Jeremiah at the festival of the Queen of Heaven in Pathros. The last act of his prophetic ministry*, ch. xliv.

    a. *The charge against the obstinately idolatrous people*, xliv. 1-14.
    b. *The replication of the people*, xliv. 15-19.
    c. *The recapitulation of the prophet*, xliv. 20-30.

        α. *The refutation of the people's assertions*, xliv. 20-23.
        β. *The positive prediction of severest punishment*, xliv. 24-30.

A. The events before the capture of Jerusalem, (chh. xxxvi.—xxxviii.)

I. The writing out of the prophecies in the fourth year of Jehoiakim (ch. xxxvi.)

1. *The Command and the first writing.*

XXXVI. 1-8.

1 And it came to pass in the fourth year of Jehoiakim the son of Josiah king of
2 Judah, *that* this word came unto Jeremiah from the LORD, saying, Take thee a roll of a book, and write therein[1] all the words that I have spoken unto thee against Israel, and against Judah, and against all the nations, from the day I spake unto
3 thee, from the days of Josiah, even unto this day. It may be that the house of Judah will hear all the evil which I purpose to do unto them; that they may return
4 every man from his evil way; that I may forgive their iniquity and their sin. Then Jeremiah called Baruch the son of Neriah: and Baruch wrote from the mouth of Jeremiah all the words of the LORD, which he had spoken unto him, upon a roll of
5 a book. And Jeremiah commanded Baruch, saying, I *am* shut up [hindered]; I
6 cannot go into the house of the LORD. Therefore go thou, and read in the roll, which thou hast written from my mouth, the words of the LORD in the ears of the people in the LORD's house upon the fasting day: and also thou shalt read them in
7 the ears of all Judah that come out of their cities. It may be they will present their supplication[2] before the LORD, and will return every one from his evil way: for great *is* the anger and the fury that the LORD hath pronounced against this
8 people. And Baruch the son of Neriah did according to all that Jeremiah the prophet commanded him, reading in the book the words of the LORD in the LORD's [Jehovah's] house.

TEXTUAL AND GRAMMATICAL.

[1] Ver. 2.—אֶל for עַל (comp. rems. on x. 1) as is evident from vers. 4 and 29. In עַל יִשְׂרָאֵל however עַל has the meaning of "against," as we see from ver. 3, "all the evil."

[2] Ver. 7.—[NAEGELSB.: Their supplication will come (prevail) before Jehovah.]

EXEGETICAL AND CRITICAL.

In the fourth year of Jehoiakim's reign Jeremiah receives the command to commit to writing the prophecies delivered by him from the beginning of his prophetic ministry (therefore for twenty-three years). The fourth year of Jehoiakim, as frequently shown already, was a turning-point both in the political world and in Jeremiah's ministry. It was then that in consequence of the battle of Carchemish both the call of Nebuchadnezzar to universal dominion was decided, and also the question, who were to be the northern executers of the judgment on Judah, so often predicted by the prophet. It was now clear that they would be the Chaldeans under Nebuchadnezzar. The way to Palestine and beyond was open to them. Their arrival was to be expected after a very brief interval. It was the last moment when Israel could still propitiate the Lord by sincere penitence, and avert the threatening danger. To determine Israel to make use of the last gracious respite thus granted a last attempt was to be made by the presentation of Jeremiah's prophecies as a whole. They were now to hear at once, and in a concentrated form, what they had been hearing piece-meal in the course of twenty-three years, and that a powerful effect might be expected from the total impression, is seen from ver. 16. Jeremiah now, to discharge his exalted commission, dictates the words of Jehovah to his faithful Baruch, and commands him to read what he has written to the assembled people on the occasion of a fast-day, since he himself, Jeremiah, is hindered from being present.

Vers. 1-3. **And it came to pass ... their sin.** From the period before the fourth year of Jehoiakim, we find in the book of our prophet as we have it at present, chh. ii.; iii.-vi.; vii.-x.; xi.-xiii.; xiv.-xvii.; xviii.; xxi. 11-14; xxii. 1-23; xxiii.; xxvi. Chh. **xxv.** and xlvi. 1-12; xlvii.–xlix. 33 are also to be reckoned in here, since they certainly precede the writing, which extended into the fifth year of Jehoiakim (xxxvi. 9). Chh. xxx. and xxxi. also belong here chronologically, but in subject they form a כֵפֶר by itself (comp. xxx. 2), and cannot have been a part of the book here meant, which consisted only of minatory prophecies. The first writing however did not, according to ver. 32, contain all these passages, at least not in their present extent. The view of HITZIG, that Jeremiah was not to write out the discourses for the first time, but only from the scattered leaves to compile them into a book, because the former would not have been possible even for the most retentive memory, has been well refuted by GRAF from HITZIG'S own point of view. From my own point of view I remark that the same supernatural factor which operated in the production of the prophecies must have acted also in their reproduction (comp. John xiv. 26). Here neither the much nor the little enters into consideration, nor must we lay too much weight on the similarity of the prophecies, for even the variations of the theme have their specific object and occasion, and could not be arbitrarily altered.

It is remarkable that the expression מְגִלָּה, apart from Ps. xl. 8, occurs only in Jeremiah and later writers (Ezek. ii. 9; iii. 1; Zech. v. 1, 2). Ps. xl., however, as is well known, is ascribed by many to Jeremiah. But comp. Isai. xxxiv. 4. HENGSTENBERG, *Beiträge* II., *S.* 494 sqq.—LEYRER in HERZ. *R.-Enc.*, XIV., *S.* 18.—Ver. 3. **It may be**, *etc.* It is not expressly said, but may be understood, that the words of Jehovah were to be read after being written, as the effects mentioned could not be attributed to the mere writing, and so Jeremiah understood it, vers. 6-8.—**That before they may return is** difficult. We should expect **and they will return**, (comp. xxvi. 3). The prophet however distinguishes a nearer and a more remote object. The first is that they hear, not in a physical sense, for that was not problematic, but in a spiritual sense, *i. e.*, in the sense of marking, observing, taking to heart. Comp. vii. 13; xxv. 3, 4, *etc.* The more remote and properly main object, to which the proclaiming and the marking were related only as means, was that they should be converted.

Vers. 4-8. **Then Jeremiah ... in Jehovah's house.** Respecting Baruch comp. xxxii. 12. The reason why Jeremiah did not write himself is not necessarily that he could not. From xxxii. 10; li. 60 on the contrary it seems to follow that Jeremiah was well able to write. At least it is not apparent why in these passages it should not be said that Jeremiah dictated, since such a minute statement would well accord with the particularity of his style elsewhere. It may however easily be conceived that in the discharge of so great a task, the aid of a writer to take the mechanical part, was a necessity to the prophet. As the reading, according to ver. 9, did not take place till the ninth month of the fifth year of Jehoiakim, the writing occupied nearly a year.—**Shut up** (עָצוּר). As, according to vers. 19 and 26, Jeremiah and Baruch were able to hide themselves, this cannot mean "imprisoned" as it may well do in xxxiii. 1; xxxix. 15. Jeremiah was therefore only detained or hindered. By what we have no means of ascertaining.—**And read in the roll.** Comp. Deut. xvii. 19; Neh. viii. 8, 18.—**Upon the fasting day.** The prophet does not mean either the regular yearly fast, which was observed in the seventh month (Lev xvi. 29; xxiii. 27), nor does he expect in the ninth month several (extraordinary) fasts, so that we should translate "on *a* fast-day." The absence of the article is no more emphatic here than in iii. 2; vi. 16, *etc.*—Were the ordinary fast meant in ver. 6, and an extraordinary fast-day in ver. 9, as many of the older commentators suppose, we cannot conceive why only the second reading had results, but the first passed away without a trace.—Ver. 7. **They will present.** Comp. xxxvii. 20; xlii. 2 coll. xxxviii. 26; xlii. 9; Dan. ix. 18, 20, where we find the Hiphil. The expression is evidently a stronger form of "come before thee" (Ps. lxxix. 11; lxxxviii. 3; cxix. 170 coll. Job xxxiv. 28) in so far as it involves the idea of *humble* petitioning, and at the same time the collateral idea of prevailing, being heard. For that which *falls down* before one, can as little remain unobserved as that which *comes* before one.—**And will return.** The prophet presupposes that the words of Jehovah will render clear to the people above all the necessity of repentance, and that accordingly their prayer will above all have reference to power for the fulfilment of this indispensable condition. He also hopes that this effect will be produced by the reading, as by this the greatness of God's anger will be brought vividly before the minds of the people, and must produce a wholesome fear in them. In ver. 8 the accomplishment of the task is reported in general. The particulars follow. Comp. HITZIG *in loc.*

2. *The reading to the people.*

XXXVI. 9-18.

9 And it came to pass in the fifth year of Jehoiakim the son of Josiah king of Judah, in the ninth month, *that* they proclaimed a fast before the LORD to all the peo-
10 ple in Jerusalem and to all the people that came from the cities of Judah unto Jerusalem. Then read Baruch in the book the words of Jeremiah in the house of the LORD, in the chamber [cell] of Gemariah, the son of Shaphan the scribe, in the higher court, at the entry of the new gate of the LORD'S house, in the ears of
11 all the people. When Michaiah the son of Gemariah, the son of Shaphan, had
12 heard out of the book all the words of the LORD. Then he went down into the king's house, into the scribe's chamber:[1] and, lo, all the princes sat there, *even* Elishama the scribe, and Delaiah the son of Shemaiah, and Elnathan the son of

312   THE PROPHET JEREMIAH.

Achbor, and Gemariah the son of Shaphan, and Zedekiah the son of Hananiah,
13 and all the princes. Then Michaiah declared unto them all the words that he had
    heard when Baruch read the book in the ears of the people.
14 Therefore all the princes sent Jehudi the son of Nethaniah, the son of Shelemiah,
    the son of Cushi, unto Baruch, saying, Take in thine hand the roll wherein thou
    hast read in the ears of the people, and come.² So Baruch the son of Neriah took
15 the roll in his hand, and came unto them. And they said unto him, Sit down now
16 and read it in our ears. Now it came to pass, when they had heard all the words,
    they were afraid both one and other,³ and said unto Baruch, We will surely tell the
17 king of all these words. And they asked Baruch, saying, Tell us now, How didst
18 thou write all these words at his mouth?⁴ Then Baruch answered them, He pro-
    nounced⁵ all these words unto me with his mouth, and I wrote them with ink⁶ in
    the book.

TEXTUAL AND GRAMMATICAL.

¹ Ver. 12.—[NAEGELSBACH: *Chancery* chamber or *chancellor's* room, according to the original Roman use of the word *chancellor* for chief notary or scribe, or according to the Scripture use for master of decrees, or president of the council, Ezra iv.—S. R. A.]

² Ver. 14.—According to our idiom the expression designates removal from the speaker. In Hebrew it merely designates the leaving of the former position on the part of the person addressed, the *terminus in quem* being inferred from the
context. Comp. 1 Sam. ix. 9; xi. 14.

³ Ver. 16.—פחדו איש אל־רעהו. On the construction comp. NAEGELSB. *Gr.*, § 112, 7; Gen. xlii. 28.

⁴ Ver. 17.—כי. The LXX. omit the word. So also EWALD. Others take it as = המה as it must be according to
their understanding of the question. [See EXEGET.]

⁵ Ver. 18.—יקרא. The Imperf. designates duration in the past, wherefore also the part. כתב corresponds to it. Comp.
NAEGELSB. *Gr.*, § 87, *f*—xiii. 7; xv. 6.

⁶ Ver. 18.—דיו. The word is ἅπ. λεγ. It implies that Baruch only performed the mechanical work. Comp. WINER,
H.-W.-B. Art. Schreibekunst; HERZOG, *R.-Enc., Art. Schriftzeichen und Schreibekunst*, S. 19, [SMITH, *Dict.* III., 1802].

EXEGETICAL AND CRITICAL.

In the fifth year of Jehoiakim and the ninth
month Baruch on occasion of a public fast reads
to the assembled people in the temple the discourses of Jeremiah, written down by him (vers.
9, 10). Michaiah, the son of Gemariah, gives
notice of this to the princes assembled in the
royal chancery, among whom was his father
(vers. 11-13). Thereupon the princes cause
Baruch to be brought with his roll, and commanded him to read it to them (vers. 14, 15).
What he reads fills them with terror. They declare to Baruch that they must inform the king
and inquire as to the particular circumstances
of the writing (vers. 16, 17). Baruch replies
simply that Jeremiah dictated the words to him
and he wrote them down (ver. 18).

Vers. 9, 10. **And it came to pass . . . all
the people.** The rendering of the "ninth
month" of the fifth year of Jehoiakim as the
ninth month of the civil year, *i. e.* about December, is favored especially by the circumstance
that the statement of the months and days
(comp. xxxix. 2), without a previous exact statement of the day and month of the beginning of
the reign, would be unintelligible and purposeless, while, if we understand the months and
days of the civil year, the matter is clear, provided that the fragments of the initial and concluding years are reckoned as full years.—**Proclaimed a fast.** It was at any rate an extraordinary fast, such as was not infrequently appointed
in times of distress (comp. Joel i. 14; ii. 15; 1
Ki. xxi. 9, 12; 2 Chron. xx. 3), then probably
occasioned by the danger threatening from the
Chaldeans (comp. ver. 29). It is therefore very
probable, that Nebuchadnezzar then (in December of the fifth year of Jehoiakim) had not yet
retired from Jerusalem. This is opposed to those
who make the battle of Carchemish immediately
precede the siege of Jerusalem ("only a few
weeks." Comp. GUSTAV RÖSCH, Art. *Bibl. Zeitrechnung* [Bibl. Chronology] in HERZOG, *R.-Enc.,*
XVIII., *S.* 464). The subject, proclaiming the
fast, appears (as in Jon. iii. 5 coll. Joel i. 14;
ii. 15) to be the whole people. Elsewhere it is
the presiding officers who proclaim the fast (1
Ki. xxi. 9, 12; 2 Chron. xx. 3; Ezr. viii. 21).
Whether by the former mode of expression anything is intimated concerning the suggestion of
the appointment, or a rite in proclamations unknown to us, is not clear. EWALD, as it seems to
me incorrectly, after the Vulg., connects "all the
people" with "fast" as a genitive [*jejunium
omni populo*].—**In the chamber of Gemariah,**
ver. 10. Comp. rems. on xxxv. 2, 4.—This
Gemariah is named immediately afterwards as
one of the princes assembled in the royal chancery. He had, it seems, as scribe a room in the
temple, and also took part in the official transactions in the scribe's chamber in the king's
house. (Comp. *infra* on ver. 12). His father
appears to have been scribe under Josiah (2 Ki.
xxii. 3 sqq.). Possibly the family was a priestly
one. (Comp. 2 Ki. xxii. 3 with 1 Chron. ix. 11,
12). His brother Ahikam is mentioned as a
protector of Jeremiah, xxvi. 24. On the upper
fore-court and new gate comp. comm. on xx. 2;
xxvi. 10. The room was situated not *in* the
entry but *at* the entry, so that it might probably
be entered directly from the gateway. At any
rate it was a very frequented spot. As the
higher court was that of the priests (comp.
HERZ. *R.-Enc.* XV., *S.* 509), which the people

might not enter, it is possible that the new gate led from the higher into the outer (Ezek. xl. 17), or great court (2 Chron. iv. 9), and that accordingly the room, from its elevated position, afforded a view over the great court. Comp. Hitzig, *in loc.*

Vers. 11-18. **When Michaiah . . . in the book.** Michaiah, the son of that Gemariah in whose temple-chamber Baruch held his lecture, who was probably present in the chamber, thought himself called upon to inform his father. He found him in the royal chancery (so Luther). According to ver. 20, the princes go from the chancery into the court of the palace, to the presence of the king. Accordingly, the chancery appears to have been placed more on the outer side of the palace, probably for the sake of accessibility. The "scribe" Gemariah appears to have had the ecclesiastical department (ver. 10, minister of worship), and the "scribe" Elishama the political. The latter was thus chancellor, or Secretary of State. Comp. Herzog, *R.-Enc.* XIV., *S.* 2. On the general meaning of "princes" comp. the list of Solomon's princes, 1 Ki. iv. 2 sqq.—If Elishama is identical with the one mentioned in xli. 1 and 2 Ki. xxv. 15, which is not impossible, he was a prince of the royal family. Comp. on xli. 1.—Elnathan, the son of Achbor, was mentioned before in xxvi. 22.—**Jehudi,** *etc.* The name of his ancestor leads us to conclude that he was of Cushite descent. It is not probable that the name Jehudi was given with reference to the injunction in Deut. xxiii. 8, for there it is merely said that the descendants of the *Edomites* and *Egyptians* are not to enter the congregation of the Lord till the third generation. With respect to the other nations (with the exception of still more strictly excluded Canaanites, Ammonites and Moabites) there was no such limitation. They might be naturalized in the first generation on fulfilment of the conditions. Comp. Saalschuetz, *Mos. Recht, Kap.* 92, § 3; *Kap.* 100, § 2. Moreover, both the father and grandfather bear Israelitish names, and Jehudi is a family, not a national name. The feminine, Judith, appears, even in ancient times, as a proper name among the Hittites (Gen. xxvi. 34). Comp. Fuerst *s. v.*—**Sit down now.** They are evidently friendlily disposed. Comp. vers. 19 and 25.—I do not believe that they were terrified merely in the interest of Jeremiah and Baruch. It was possible to protect them. Without doubt the concentration of the threatenings did not fail of its intended object in their case.—It was clear that after the public reading in the temple, the matter could not be kept concealed from the king. Purposed concealment might be dangerous to those whose duty it was to report.—Rosenmueller, Hitzig, Graf understand the question in ver. 17 as if the princes wished to know whether Baruch had not compiled the book against the will and knowledge of Jeremiah, from memory or written documents. But then the reading would have been different. [See Textual Notes]. As the words stand, they seem to me simply to express the curious desire for a peep, as it were, into the prophet's workshop. They supposed that Baruch must have been a witness of secret transactions, and they, therefore, wish to know how the dictation, on the part of the prophet, was given, whether, *ex. gr.*, consciously or in a state of ecstasy. Baruch answers that Jeremiah simply pronounced the words and he as simply wrote them down with ink. There was nothing wonderful about it. How Hitzig can say that קרא cannot mean speaking, but only reading to another, I do not understand. Dictation requires no less an elevation of the voice than reading aloud, and may therefore be designated as "calling." The phrase "with his mouth" also seems to imply just the opposite of reading from a book. Comp. ver. 4 with vers. 6 and 10.

---

3. *The Reading before the King.*

XXXVI. 19-26.

19 Then said the princes unto Baruch, Go, hide thee, thou and Jeremiah; and let
20 no man know where ye be. And they went in to the king, into the court, but they laid up[1] the roll in the chamber of Elishama the scribe, and told all the words in
21 the ears of the king. So the king sent Jehudi to fetch the roll: and he took it out of Elishama the scribe's chamber. And Jehudi read it in the ears of the king,
22 and in the ears of all the princes which stood beside [before] the king. Now the king sat in the winter house, in the ninth month; and *there was a fire* on the hearth,
23 burning before him [the pot[2] kindled before him]. And it came to pass, that when Jehudi had read three or four leaves [columns], he cut it with the penknife, and cast it into the fire that was on the hearth [in the pot], until all the roll was con-
24 sumed in the fire that was on the hearth [in the pot]. Yet they were not afraid, nor rent their garments, the king nor any of his servants that heard all these words.
25 Nevertheless[3] [And even though] Elnathan and Delaiah and Gemariah had made intercession to [prayed] the king that he would not burn the roll: but [yet] he

26 would not hear them. But the king commanded Jerahmeel, the son of Hamme-lech [the king], and Seraiah, the son of Azriel, and Shelemaiah, the son of Abdeel, to take [fetch] Baruch the scribe and Jeremiah the prophet: but the LORD [Jehovah] hid them.

TEXTUAL AND GRAMMATICAL.

¹ Ver. 20.—On הפקידו comp. xxxvii. 21; xl. 7.

² Ver. 22.—ואת־האח. ואת is not here—and indeed with. It is an emphasizing of the subject, which we might paraphrase by "and as to," but which the Hebrews express by the accusative. Comp. 2 Ki. vi. 5; EWALD, § 277, d; GESEN., § 117. 2.

³ Ver. 25.—Observe the paratactic construction, since נם according to the connection belongs to רא שמים. Comp. NAEGELSB. Gr., 2, 111, 1 Anm.

EXEGETICAL AND CRITICAL.

The princes command Baruch, together with Jeremiah, to hide themselves (ver. 19). Thereupon they give the king personally notice of what has occurred (ver. 20). The king has the roll brought, read, cut and thrown into the fire, notwithstanding the intercession of three princes (vers. 21-25). He also wishes Baruch and Jeremiah to be taken into custody, but the Lord had hid them (ver. 26).

Vers. 19, 20. **Then said . . . ears of the king.** It is noteworthy that under the despotic and ungodly Jehoiakim the princes were friendly to Jeremiah, while under the weak but kindly-disposed Zedekiah they were hostile to him. The reason for this may be partly the outward circumstances, partly the personality of the king. Under Jehoiakim the danger was not so near, and Jeremiah's continual exhortation to submit did not make so much the impression of treachery and of a laming influence (xxxviii. 4). Add to this, that Jehoiakim's annoyance provoked opposition, as Zedekiah's weakness did insolence.—The proper dwelling-house of the king (doubtless identical with the winter house) stood in a court of its own, "which, regarded from the entrance, formed the hinder court of the whole citadel" (KEIL on 1 Ki. vii. 8).—They did not take the roll with them, in order as much as in them lay, to withdraw it from the eyes and fury of the despotic king. If the king himself had it fetched, they were not responsible for what he did with it.

Vers. 21-24. **So the king . . . these words.** —**Beside the king.** The king sat on the floor, those who were standing were therefore above him. Comp. Gen. xviii. 8; Jud. iii. 19; 2 Sam. xx. 11.—On the winter-house (Am. iii. 15) and the fire-pot comp. WINER, R.-W.-B. s. v. Häuser, near the end. ["In common parlance, the lower apartments are simply él beit—the house; the upper is the 'allíyeh, which is the summer-house. Every respectable dwelling has both, and they are familiarly called beit shetawy and beit seify—winter and summer house. If these are on the same story, then the external and airy apartment is the summer house, and that for winter is the interior or more sheltered room." THOMSON, The Land and the Book, 1. p. 478.—" The Orientals still use pots made of burnt earthenware for warming, instead of fire-places. These pots have the form of a large pitcher, and are usually placed in a hollow place in the middle of the room. When the fire is out, a frame like a table is put over them, and is covered with a carpet, and thus the warmth is kept in them. See also NIEBUHR and TAVERNIER in WINER, R.-W.-B. 1., 468; STANLEY, Lect. 536-538." WORDSWORTH. —S. R. A.].—The ninth month corresponds nearly to our December. It was therefore the cold and rainy season of the year.—Ver. 23. **And it came to pass,** etc. It is unequivocally evident from the words "until all the roll was consumed" that the book did not consist of many leaves, but only of one roll. The roll must also have been written on one side only or the whole could not have been read. That Jehudi did read the whole is evident (1) from the imperfect קרעה: If Jehudi, after reading some sections, had cut them off and at the same time thrown them with the rest into the fire, we should have had the perfect.—It would then be a matter of indifference whether Jehudi threw the rest into the fire entire or after successive abscissions, for the latter is in itself a perfectly unessential circumstance. It is only of account if the successive reading was connected with it. Only in the latter case is the imperfect, expressing repetition in the past, in place (compare remarks on קרא, ver. 18).—(2) From the words "till all the roll was consumed" and the preceding words, Had Jehudi thrown all at once into the coals, it could at most be said that they looked on and waited till the entire roll was burned up. But as it is said, that Jehudi cut and threw into the fire till the whole roll was consumed, there must evidently have been a repeated cutting and throwing. Such a course, however, presupposes also a successive reading of the whole, for if he did not wish to read it, why should he not throw it all at once into the fire. With this also agrees the prefix כ before קרא, which designates the coincidence (comp. Gen. xviii. 1; xxxix. 18; Deut. xvi. 6; 1 Kings i. 21), and accordingly is repeated actions must assume the meaning of "as often as." How GRAF can deny this, is as inconceivable as the assertion, that the successive reading and cutting would be unnatural or indeed trifling. As to the first, the tenor was interesting and exciting enough to render the king desirous of knowing the whole; as to the second, it was the subservient Jehudi who would not wait till the end, to execute punishment on the hateful book. If the דלתות were not single leaves, they were columns, the lines of which ran parallel with the margin of the roll. The expression *doors*, which occurs nowhere else in this sense, is easily explained by the square shape of the columns, which were probably also enclosed in lines. Jehudi's cutting the roll with his penknife, and not tearing it with his hands, is explained by the character of the material. Even if it were a papyrus roll, cutting was to be preferred to tearing, because in this latter way he would be sure to injure the next columns. It is, moreover, questionable whether they would have burned a leather or parchment roll.—**Rent their garments.** On this custom comp. WINER, *R.-W.-B.*, Art. *Trauer*. By the servants of the king who "heard all these words," are here evidently to be understood those who heard them here for the first time, not those who had already heard them in the secretary's office. Their petition shows the respect which they entertained for the words of the Lord.

Vers. 25, 26. **And even though . . . hid them.—Jerahmeel, the king's son.** As according to 2 Kings xxiii. 36, Jehoiakim came to the throne when twenty-five, and was then in the fifth year of his reign, at most thirty years of age, he could not have had a grown-up son, such as this Jerahmeel must have been. "Son of the king" is, therefore, here a prince royal. Comp. xxxviii. 6 with xli. 1; Dan. i. 3.—Who Seraiah, the son of Azriel, Shelemiah, the son of Abdeel were, we do not know, but the messengers, judging from the rank of the first, appear to have been very respectable. Jehoiakim thus at least honored the prophet of the Lord, sending men of the highest rank to apprehend him. According to ver. 19 the kindly-disposed princes commanded Jeremiah and Baruch to hide themselves. They had obeyed. We are now informed that the Lord Himself had guided them in the choice of a hiding-place, and thus guarded against their discovery.

4. *The Prediction of Punishment to Jehoiakim and the Second Writing.*

XXXVI. 27–32.

27 Then the word of the LORD [Jehovah] came to Jeremiah, after that the king had burned the roll, and the words which Baruch wrote at the mouth of Jeremiah, say-
28 ing, Take thee again another roll, and write in it all the former words that were
29 in the first roll, which Jehoiakim the king of Judah hath burned. And thou shalt say to¹ Jehoiakim, king of Judah, Thus saith the LORD [Jehovah]; Thou hast burned this roll, saying, Why hast thou written therein, saying, The king of Babylon shall certainly come and destroy this land, and shall cause to cease [exterminate] from thence man and beast?
30 Therefore thus saith the LORD [Jehovah] of [against]¹ Jehoiakim, king of Judah, He shall have none to sit upon the throne of David: and his dead body shall
31 be cast out in the day to the heat, and in the night to the frost [cold]. And I will punish² him and his seed and his servants for their iniquity; and I will bring upon them, and upon the inhabitants of Jerusalem, and upon the men of Judah, all the evil that I have pronounced against them; but they hearkened not.
32 Then took Jeremiah another roll, and gave it to Baruch the scribe, the son of Neriah, who wrote therein from the mouth of Jeremiah all the words of the book which Jehoiakim king of Judah had burned in the fire: and there were added besides unto them many like³ words.

TEXTUAL AND GRAMMATICAL.

¹ Vers. 29, 30.—עַל after אָמַר has the meaning of "over, concerning," though from the connection in a hostile sense. Ot. ver. 31, where after הֵבֵאתִי the third time we find אֶל, comp. remarks on x. 1.

² Ver. 31.—[Literally: I will visit upon.—S. R. A.]

³ Ver. 32.—[Or, as many more; literally: as many as they.—S. R. A.]

EXEGETICAL AND CRITICAL.

Jehoiakim could, indeed, burn the roll, bu not the living word of God present in the mind of the prophet. He, therefore, gained nothing by his act. On the contrary he thus increased both his guilt and the number of the prophecies predicting calamity in the new roll.

Vers. 27-32. **Then the word ... like words.** The direct address to Jehoiakim in ver. 29 passes over into the indirect in ver. 30. But as the former is not to be conceived of as to the king in bodily presence, and as it was interrupted by the question put into the mouth of Jehoiakim, "Why hast thou written," *etc.*, the transition to the third person is easily explained. Comp. NAEGELSB. *Gr.*, § 101, 2, *Anm.*—Ver. 30. **He shall have none,** *etc.* The successor of Jehoiakim was his son Jehoiachin (2 Kings, xxiv

6). But the reign of the latter was so brief (it lasted only three months) that it does not come into consideration. On what is said of his corpse comp. rems. on xxii. 19.—**Like words.** In itself בְּהֵמָה may certainly be referred to "words," and the similar import of the additions to be thus declared. Then, however, it would stand better after "words." Its position after "many," seems to be to indicate that it is to be referred to this word, and that thus the quantitative similarity is to be declared. Accordingly the new collection must have been about double the size of the previous one.

HOMILETICAL AND PRACTICAL.

1. On ver. 2. The object of the writing was not only that "*litera scripta manet*" (CRAMER: "the mouth speaks only to those who are present, but the pen to the absent; the mouth speaks only to the present hours and times, the pen many hundred years afterwards also." Comp. Exod. xxxiv. 27; Deut. x. 4, 5; xvii. 18; Isa. xxx. 8; Hab. ii. 2). but also to collect all the single lightning strokes into one grand prophetic tempest. Moreover, it is a matter of course that the written word was of special use, not only to posterity, but also to the contemporaries in so far as it rendered possible continued study, repeated quiet contemplation, and careful comparison. Jeremiah certainly prevented no one from taking copies of his book.

2. On ver. 4. Did Jeremiah hold such a relation to the Spirit of God as Baruch to Jeremiah when dictating? Then it was a matter of indifference to whom the dictation was made. Then a Saul would do as well as a Samuel, if he could only write. The best writer would be the most chosen instrument. There was no mingling of the individuality of the prophet except in the MS., and that is lost to us with the original. All prophetic writings must have the same type as to form and purport, which, as is well known, is so little the case that according to the saying of BUFFON, *le style c'est l'homme*, the portrait of a prophet might almost be drawn from his style.

3. On ver. 5. "God's word is not bound; 2 Tim. ii. 9. Paul for example wrote his most beautiful epistles from prison, as those to the Galatians, the Ephesians, the Philippians, the Colossians, to Philemon, and the second to Timothy." CRAMER.

4. On ver. 14. "It is a good state of things when rulers ask for God's Word, and cannot be answered or helped promptly and quickly enough to the fulfilment of their purpose. So it was a joy to Paul that he could tell Agrippa what the Lord had done for his soul, and his heart yearned after Agrippa, Festus and all those around them." ZINZENDORF.

5. On ver. 16. "When a true servant of God gets his superiors so far that they hear him, he may surely not doubt, that he will also bring them to obedience. It is then not his, but the Lord's affair." ZINZENDORF.

6. On ver. 23. "The higher the enemies of God are, the more dangerous; the greater, the more bitterly opposed to the work of the Lord, and the general patience with respect to the wickedness and unrighteousness of men, has certainly given something special to the δόξαις. *Procul a Jove procul a fulmine.*" ZINZENDORF.

7. On ver. 23. "*Locus maxime principalis in præsenti hoc textu est de combustione sacrorum librorum, quale fatum illi experti sunt non tantum* Jer. xxxvi., *verum etiam* 1 Macc. i. 59 *sub Antiocho Epiphane; nec non tempore Diocletiani, qui et ipse multa bibliorum sacrorum exemplaria undiquaque conquisita comburi jussit; quorum vestigiis insistere non dubitarunt Pontifices romani et præsertim Leo X. qui anno* 1520 *binos legatos emisit ad Fridericum Sapientem, postulantes ab ipso, ut libros Lutheri combureret . . . Quid hodie Jesuitæ de librorum combustione, qui a Lutheranis eduntur, sentiant, peculiari scripto Gretserus aperuit, quod de hoc argumento consarcinavit (de jure et more prohibendi, expurgandi et abolendi libros hæreticos et noxios. Ingolst.* 1603, 4º)." FÖRSTER.

8. On ver. 25. "When John's head was in question, Herod did not understand how he could resist his magnates. When Daniel is to go into the lions' den, Darius has not the heart to refuse his princes. When Jeremiah is to be delivered up, Zedekiah says with great modesty to his princes: 'the king can do nothing against you' (xxxviii. 5). But when anything evil is to be done, the rulers can insist on having their own way. Here we have an instance: he hearkened not unto them." ZINZENDORF.

9. On ver. 26. "*Dominus eos abscondidisse dicitur, qua ratione olim Eliam* (1 *Reg.* xvii. 2 *sqq. et* xviii. 12), *nec non Elisæum* (2 *Reg.* vi.), *itemque Athanasium et Augustinum et nostro tempore Lutherum abscondidit.*" FÖRSTER.

10. On ver. 27. ["Here is a sublime specimen of the triumph of God's Word, when repressed by the power, and burnt by the rage of this world, whether it be in the suppression of the Scriptures, or in preventing their circulation, or in casting copies of them into the fire, or in the imprisonment and martyrdom of God's preachers. That Word rises more gloriously out of all its persecutions." WORDSWORTH.—S. R. A.]

HOMILETICAL AND PRACTICAL.

1. On vers. 2, 3. Sermon at a *Bible Society Anniversary. The blessing of the written word.* 1. That which it has in common with the spoken word (ver. 3): preparation of the heart for the reception of salvation. 2. That which it brings in distinction from the written Word: (*a*) it is present for every one; (*b*) it is present at every time and at every place· (*c*) it is present in all its parts (comparison).

2. On vers. 21–32. *The majesty of the Word.* 1. The power, which the word exercises. 2. The independence, which it maintains. 3. The self-verification which it continually effects. *Sermons in Berlin* by FR. WILH. KRUMMACHER. Berlin, 1849.

3. On ver. 24. ["The guilt of indifference to the divine threatenings. It involves: 1, contempt of God; 2, unbelief, making God a liar; 3, extreme hardness of heart." PAYSON.—S. R. A.]

II. The Events in the Tenth and Eleventh year of Zedekiah.

(CHAP. XXXVII. and XXXVIII.)

1. *The embassy of the King and the Imprisonment of the Prophet in its First and Second Stage.*

CHAP. XXXVII.

1 And king Zedekiah the son of Josiah reigned[1] instead of Coniah, the son of Jehoiakim, whom Nebuchadrezzar king of Babylon made king[2] in the land of Judah.
2 But neither he, nor his servants, nor the people of the land, did hearken unto the words of the LORD [Jehovah], which he spake by the prophet Jeremiah.
3 And Zedekiah the king sent Jehucal the son of Shelemiah and Zephaniah the
4 son of Maaseiah the priest to the prophet Jeremiah, saying, Pray now unto the LORD [Jehovah] our God for us. Now Jeremiah came in and went out among
5 the people: for they had not put him into prison.[3] Then Pharaoh's army was come forth out of Egypt, and when the Chaldeans that besieged Jerusalem heard tidings of them, they departed from Jerusalem.
6 Then came the word of the LORD [Jehovah] unto the prophet Jeremiah, saying,
7 Thus saith the LORD, the God of Israel; Thus shall ye say to the king of Judah, that sent you unto me to inquire of me; Behold, Pharaoh's army, which is come
8 forth to help you, shall return [is returning][4] to Egypt into their own land. The Chaldeans shall come again, and fight against this city, and take it, and burn it
9 with fire. Thus saith the LORD; Deceive not yourselves,[5] saying, The Chaldeans
10 shall surely depart from us: for they shall not depart. For though ye had smitten the whole army of the Chaldeans that fight against you, and there remained *but* wounded men among them, *yet* should they rise up every man[6] in his tent, and burn
11 this city with fire. And it came to pass,[7] that when the army of the Chaldeans was
12 broken up [had retired] from Jerusalem for fear of [before] Pharaoh's army, Then Jeremiah went forth out of Jerusalem to go into the land of Benjamin, to separate
13 himself thence [to raise an inheritance there] in the midst of the people. And when he was in the gate of Benjamin, a captain of the ward [watch] *was* there, whose name *was* Irijah, the son of Shelemiah, the son of Hananiah; and he took [seized] Jeremiah the prophet, saying, Thou fallest away [art going over] to the
14 Chaldeans. Then said Jeremiah, *It is* false [a lie]: I fall not away [am not going
15 over] to the Chaldeans. But he hearkened not to him: so Irijah took Jeremiah, and smote him, and put him in prison in the house of Jonathan the scribe: for
16 they had made that the prison. When[8] Jeremiah was entered into the dungeon,
17 and into the cabins,[9] and Jeremiah had remained there many days; Then Zedekiah the king sent, and took him out: and the king asked him secretly in his house, and said, Is there *any* word from the LORD? And Jeremiah said, There is: for, said
18 he, thou shalt be delivered into the hand of the king of Babylon. Moreover Jeremiah said unto king Zedekiah, What have I offended against thee, or against thy
19 servants, or against this people, that ye have put me in prison? Where *are* now[10] your prophets which prophesied unto you, saying, The king of Babylon shall not
20 come against you, nor against this land? Therefore hear now, I pray thee, O my lord the king: let my supplication, I pray thee, be accepted[11] before thee; that thou cause me not to return to the house of Jonathan the scribe, lest I die there.
21 Then Zedekiah the king commanded that they should commit Jeremiah into the court of the prison, and that they should give [and they gave him] him daily a piece of bread out of the bakers' street, until all the bread in the city were spent. Thus Jeremiah remained in the court of the prison [*or* guard.]

TEXTUAL AND GRAMMATICAL

1 Ver. 1.—NAEGELSB.: And Zedekiah became king. The phrase וַיִּמְלָךְ־מֶלֶךְ (instead of the simple וַיִּמְלֹךְ), as is especially common in the book of Kings. Comp. 1 Ki. xi. 43; xii. 17; xiv. 20, 31, etc.), does not occur except in xxiii. 5 where, however, there is more reason for the כֶּלֶךְ. We must not, however, find a parallel, as Kimchi does, with such expressions as בְּנֵי גֵּר נֵדֵר נֵדֶר, where the noun stands in the accusative, nor with Hitzig attract צִדְקִיָּהוּ מֶלֶךְ, and translate: and a king. Zedekiah, came to the government, etc., for Zedekiah was not king when he came to the government. מֶלֶךְ is rather to be taken as more exact definition of the predicate: and Zedekiah came to the government as king, etc. The pleonasm seems to accord with Jeremiah's more diffuse style.

2 Ver. 1.—אֲשֶׁר before הִמְלִיךְ is accus., and to be referred to Zedekiah. Comp. 2 Ki. xxiv. 17.

3 Ver. 4.—בֵּית הַכְּלִיא. Here, as in lii. 31, in which passages alone the word occurs, the Masoretes would alter without any necessity to כֶּלֶא. Comp. GESEN., § 84, 13, etc.

4 Ver. 7.—שָׁב לְאַרְצוֹ. The participle, having itself no tense can, from the context, signify only that they are in the act of returning.

5 Ver. 9.—[Literally: your souls.—S. R. A.]

6 Ver. 10.—Hitzig correctly remarks that אֲנָשִׁים, in antithesis to כָּל־חַיִל denotes individuals, and that therefore it is more correct to connect בְּאָהֳלוֹ אִישׁ with what follows, as the punctuation denotes, since it is evidently intended to express that these individuals, without any previous agreement, would arise, moved by a divine impulse, to perform the work of destruction.

7 Ver. 11.—וְהָיָה. This form stands here, a trace of the later usage, for וַיְהִי. Comp. iii. 9; xxxviii. 28 b; EWALD, § 345 b; NAEGELSB. Gr., § 88, 7, Anm.

8 Ver. 16.—בְּ at the beginning of the verse is surprising. Neither its causal nor its temporal signification is suitable here. The LXX. translate καὶ ἦλθεν, HITZIG, EWALD, GRAF and others read וַיָּבֹא with reference to 1 Sam. ii. 21, and 2 Ki. xx. 12 coll. Isai. xxxix. 1.

9 Ver. 16.—[Or: cells; NAEGELSBACH has: vaults. "Some suppose it to mean *bent bars*, by which the prisoner was confined, and in which he sat as in a cage in a distorted position, (GESEN., GRAF)." WORDSWORTH.—S. R. A.]

10 Ver. 19.—With respect to the form אֵין, the question is, how the Chethibh is to be pronounced אֵיוֹ or אַיִן. Usually the former is adopted, an obscuration of the suffix-meaning being maintained as in חֲזוֹ. FUERST on the other hand (*Vid.* H. W. B. S. 66) is of opinion that we are to read אִיָּו, which stands for אַיִן with the old plural termination, the traces of which are preserved in verbs and particles (Comp. OLSH., § 16, b). The decision is difficult, as the form is a solitary one with either punctuation.

11 Ver. 20.—[Literally: fall].

EXEGETICAL AND CRITICAL.

This chapter consists of two parts, reporting two events, which had their course or beginning in the pause occasioned by the departure of the Chaldeans. In the first part (vers. 1-10) it is related that Jeremiah replied to an embassy of king Zedekiah, which he sent to the prophet with the request for his intercession (vers. 1-5):—The army of Pharaoh which has come out to your assistance will return again to their own country, the Chaldeans however will resume the siege of Jerusalem and capture the city and burn it (vers. 6-8). Therefore deceive not yourselves! Even were the Egyptians to smite the entire Chaldean army, and there were only a few wounded men left, these would rise from their tents and burn Jerusalem (vers. 9, 10).—In the second part the imprisonment of the prophet is described, in vers. 10-16 its occasion and first stage, and then in vers. 17-21, the (by the favor of Zedekiah) less severe second stage.—Jeremiah had wished, during the pause caused by the temporary withdrawal of the Chaldeans, to leave Jerusalem and go into the land of Benjamin to attend to a little business of inheritance (vers. 11, 12). He was however detained at the gate by the commander of the watch, as he entertained the suspicion that Jeremiah wished to go over to the enemy (ver. 13). Jeremiah's assurance that he had no such intention was of no avail. He was brought before the princes, who caused him to be beaten and closely imprisoned in a dungeon, where he languished for some time (vers. 14-16). From this prison Zedekiah had him secretly brought one day, to inquire whether there was any word from the Lord. Jeremiah could answer in the affirmative, but could only give a revelation of the same tenor as before, Thou wilt be given into the hands of the Chaldeans. Still at the earnest petition of the prophet Zedekiah does not send him back to the prison, but has him confined in the court of the guard, and scantily supplied with bread (vers. 17-21).

Vers. 1, 2. **And king Zedekiah . . . the prophet Jeremiah.** With respect to Coniah comp. rems. on xxii. 24.—**People of the land.** Comp. rems. on i. 18.—**Did not hearken.** Comp. xxxvi. 31.

Vers. 3-5. **And Zedekiah . . . from Jerusalem.** Jehucal, the son of Shelemiah, is also mentioned among the "princes" in xxxviii. 1 coll. 4. Zephaniah, the son of Maaseiah, was, according to lii. 24 coll. xxi. 1; xxix. 25 a priest of the second order. The messengers were thus very respectable.—**Pray now.** The prophet is not merely to inquire, but to intercede. Comp. **to inquire of me,** ver. 7. From this it is apparent that notwithstanding the withdrawal of the Chaldeans the state of mind was not one of perfect confidence. The result of the conflict between the rival forces had still to be expected.—**Came in and went out.** This is emphasized in antithesis to the subsequent imprisonment and also to the statement in xxxvi. 26, that Jeremiah and Baruch had to hide themselves. The freedom in which Jeremiah lived accorded with the respect which the king showed him, and explains at the same time how Jeremiah could think of a journey. Both verses 4 and 5 are to be regarded as a parenthetical and explanatory sentence (EWALD, § 341).—**Pharaoh's army.** This Pharaoh was Pharaoh Hophra (xliv. 30), successor of Psammuthis, and ascended the throne B. C. 588. In the first, or at least the second year of his reign, seventeen years after the battle of Carchemish, he undertook to make war on Nebuchadnezzar, occasioned probably by the embassy of Zedekiah (Ezek. xvii. 15). Hophra was slain (comp. Ezek. xxix. 1-16; chh. xxx.-xxxii.) and the hopes excited in the Israelites by the withdrawal of the Chaldeans were shown to be nugatory.

Vers. 6-10. **Then came the word ... with fire.** Jeremiah does not cease to demonstrate the vanity of their hopes. He might have insinuated himself into the favor of the king and great men by a prophecy correspondent to their wishes, but he does not. With inflexible fidelity he proclaims the word of the Lord as he has received it.—**Deceive not your souls.** Comp. xxix. 8; 2 Ki. xviii. 29 coll. 2 Chron. xxxii. 15. The prophet warns against self-deception. On this meaning of נָשָׁא comp. NAEGELSB. *Gr.*, § 81, 2.

Vers. 11-16. **And it came to pass .. many days.** Jeremiah wishes to use the time, while the ways are free, to do some business in the land of Benjamin, (probably from לַחֲלֹק in Anathoth). —**To separate**, *etc.* This is a difficult passage. LXX. translates τοῦ ἀγοράσαι ἐκεῖθεν ἐν μέσῳ τοῦ λαοῦ, which THEODORET explains by πρίασθαι ἄρτους. The other ancient translations all express the idea of division of inheritance, in which they are followed by most of the commentators. The different explanations are as follows : ABARBANEL takes הֶחֱלִיק in the sense of *demulcere* (to smooth. Comp. Prov. xxix. 5) and refers it to the people of Anathoth who were inimical to Jeremiah : *Ad demulcendum eos blandis verbis, ut amarent ipsum et inter illos inveniretur, si abirent in exilium.* KIMCHI, SANCTIUS : *Ad dividendum se et separandum ab Hierosolymis, in quibus fuit in medio populi.* LYRANUS : *Ut agrum emtum* (cap. xxxii.) *separaret ab aliis.* LUTHER : To till fields [*Aecker zu bestellen*]. HITZIG : To separate his own from the portions of land which had become common property in the Sabbatical year (which HITZIG regards as B. C. 588, on the basis of xxxiv. 8 sqq.) TREMELLIUS, PISCATOR, ROSENMUELLER : *Ad lubrificandum se ipsum, i. e., ad subducendum se.* SEB. SCHMIDT : *Ut divideret cum populo relicta Chaldæorum spolia, partemque sibi acciperet et in urbem secum sumeret.* L. DE DIEU : *Ut partitim commoraretur nunc hic nunc illic.* All these explanations are manifestly forced or grammatically incorrect. The ancient interpretation alone, which understands לַחֲלִיק of a division of inheritance, appears admissible according to the present form of the text. The form of the word is like לִשְׁכֹּר Isai. xxiii. 11. Comp. OLSH., § 78, *c.* **In the midst of the people** declares that the prophet had no secret purpose, but wished to transact his business with the usual amount of publicity. Comp. Ruth iv. In this explanation however some points must still be considered unsatisfactory. 1. That הֶחֱלִיק must be taken in the specific meaning "to divide inheritance" in which it nowhere else occurs; though חֵלֶק, חֶלְקָה may mean *patrimonium* (Num. xviii. 20); 2. That to the Hiphil, in order to be able to connect it with שָׁם, must be specially also attributed the meaning of *fetching,* since primarily it contains only the idea of *parting*. Meanwhile, as said above, the text as it stands does not afford a satisfactory meaning. It has been attempted to alter the text. J. D. MICHAELIS would read לְהַחְלִיקָם שָׁם or שָׁם לְחַלְּקוּ. This however would not be good Hebrew. The *scriptio defectiva* לַחֲלֹק, as well as the similarity of ק and ף renders it easier to read מִשָּׁם חֲלֹף.—חָלַף means *to change*, which meaning appears with various modifications. For not only all kinds of change of place are designated by it (comp. *transiit,* Job ix. 11 ; *transgressus est,* Isai. xxiv. 5 ; *abiit,* Cant. ii. 11 ; *perrexit,* 1 Sam. x. 3 ; *pertransivit,* Jud. v. 26 ; *periit,* Isai. ii. 18, in which meanings it is for the most part synonymous with עָבַר) but *change of material* (comp. *renovari, revivescere,* Hab. i. 11 ; Ps. xc. 5) and *of form* (comp. Piel., Gen. xli. 14 ; Hiph., Gen. xxxi. 7, 41 ; xxxv. 2 ; further חֲלִיפוֹת and חֵלֶף). It might then be declared that the prophet's going to Benjamin had for its object a change of residence. מִשָּׁם might very suitably be referred to Jerusalem. It might however also according to well-known usage (comp. NAEGELSB. *Gr.*, § 112, 5, *d*) signify "in that direction, thither" (comp. Isai. xvii. 13). It might thus be intimated to us that the prophet had no intention of going over to the Chaldeans, or of fleeing to secure his personal safety, but simply of returning to his native place, because he knew that a residence in Jerusalem no longer afforded him any safety, and because he deposited his ministry there as ended. (Comp. STARKE. *ad h. l.*) It is however declared by the words "in the midst of the people" that he did not take this step alone and secretly, but publicly and in company with many others, perhaps of those who believed in his prophetic utterances. From this as well as from מִשָּׁם (because it indicates that the prophet took his way not to the army of the Chaldeans, but in the opposite direction) it would be clear how unjustifiable the imprisonment of the prophet was. In this however I merely express my own supposition.—On the gate of Benjamin comp. xxxviii. 7, and rems. on xx. 2.—**Thou fallest away to the Chaldeans.** The expression נָפַל appears to be an allusion to the answer, which Jeremiah, according to xxi. 9, gave a former embassy of Zedekiah. I say a former. For at the time, to which ch. xxi. belongs, Jerusalem was besieged by the Chaldeans, but the prophet was at liberty (comp. xxi. 1, 2, and xxxvii. 3, with xxxvii. 17). After his imprisonment, related in xxxvii. 13, however, Jeremiah was not again set at liberty. Chap. xxi. must therefore be placed before the retirement of the Chaldeans related in xxxvii. 5.

—The princes, before whom Jeremiah was brought, were, as GRAF correctly remarks, not the same as those, who had so warmly espoused his cause under Jehoiakim (chh. xxvi. xxxvi.) These had probably been carried away with Jeholachin into captivity (xxiv. 1; xxix. 2) comp. rems. on xxviii. 1.—The house of the secretary Jonathan, of which we have no further knowledge, was used as a prison, because there were parts of it adapted for such a purpose. These are designated (1) by the word בּוֹר. This word does not necessarily everywhere mean a pit, though it certainly does in xxxviii. 6, 7, 9, as is shown by passages like Gen. xl. 15: Exod. xii. 29. It is at any rate a subterranean cavity, and בֵּית־הַבּוֹר is a house where there are such cavities, for the word may be taken collectively. Such places are (2) designated as חֲנֻיֹת. The word occurs here only. In the dialects, according to the radical meaning, it is "to let one's-self down, to encamp, to turn in," and " a camp, a place to put up at, a booth, a cell." (FUERST). Here it is evidently the cell or dungeon of a prison. (Comp. ROSENMUELLER *ad h. l.*)

Vers. 17-21. **Then Zedekiah ... court of the guard.** The second stage of imprisonment! The weak king, dependent on his nobles, has the prophet secretly brought from his prison to ask him, whether there is not a word from the Lord which in their desperate condition would give them some light and comfort. From the scarcity of means of subsistence (ver. 21) it is seen that the city was again blockaded. Jeremiah's prophecy (ver. 8) was thus already fulfilled. This was doubtless the circumstance which filled Zedekiah with so much solicitude, that he determined to have the prophet called, a step which involved humiliation to himself (comp. ver. 19), and it might also compromise him with the princes (comp. "secretly," ver. 17).—From the circumstance that Zedekiah has the prophet brought from the prison in the house of Jonathan, it is plainly seen that we have not before us the same conference, as that spoken of in xxxii. 3-5 and xxxiv. 2-5. For in this Jeremiah took part voluntarily, and for this as a punishment he was confined in the court of the guard, (xxxii. 3). For the conference here recorded he was brought from the prison, and afterwards as a favor assigned to the court of the guard. Since now the other conference at all events belongs to the last stage of the siege, as was shown above on xxxiv. 1-5, which entire stage Jeremiah spent partly in prison and partly in the guard-court, the conference recorded here must be the earlier of the two.—It is accordingly also clear that the prophecy " thou shalt be delivered into the hand of the king of Babylon" cannot be, as GRAF supposes, identical with that contained in xxxii. 4, 5; xxxiv. 2-5, *i. e.*, it is so in subject but not in time. Jeremiah boldly tells the king the truth; but he also uses the opportunity to promote his own personal interest. He does this by giving expression on the one hand to the consciousness of his innocence, which was exhibited with eclat in the shaming of the false prophets (vers. 18, 19), and on the other by beseeching earnestly that he may not be taken back to the dungeon (ver. 20).—**On let my supplication,** *etc.*, comp. xxxv. 7.—On **court of the guard,** comp. xxxii. 2.—On **piece of bread** and **bakers' street,** comp. the articles " *Backen*" and " *Brod* " in HERZOG, *R.-Encycl.* [SMITH, *Dict.* I., 227].

---

2. *Jeremiah in the Pit (third stage of his imprisonment), his Conference with the King and Confinement in the court of the guard (fourth stage of imprisonment).*

CHAP. XXXVIII.

1 Then Shephatiah the son of Mattan, and Gedaliah the son of Pashur, and Jucal the son of Shelemiah, and Pashur the son of Malchiah, heard the words that Jere-
2 miah had spoken unto all the people, saying, Thus saith the LORD [Jehovah]: He that remaineth in this city¹ shall die by the sword, by the famine, and by the pestilence: but he that goeth forth to the Chaldeans shall live; for he shall have his
3 life for a prey, and shall live. Thus saith the LORD, This city shall surely [or must] be given into the hand of the king of Babylon's army, which shall take it.
4 Therefore the princes said unto the king. We beseech thee, let this man be put to death;² for thus³ he weakeneth⁴ the hands of the men of war that remain in this city, and the hands of all the people, in speaking such words⁵ unto them: for this
5 man seeketh not the welfare [*lit.* peace]⁶ of this people, but the hurt. Then Zedekiah the king said, Behold, he *is* in your hand: for the king *is* not *he that* can
6 do *any* thing [the king can do nothing]⁷ against you. Then took they Jeremiah, and cast him into the dungeon [pit, *or* cistern]⁸ of Malchiah the son of Hammelech [the king] that *was* in the court of the prison: and they let down Jeremiah with cords. And in the dungeon *there was* no water, but mire: so Jeremiah sunk in the
7 mire. Now when Ebed-melech the Ethiopian, one of the eunuchs which [who]

was in the king's house, heard that they had put Jeremiah in the dungeon; the
8 king then sitting in the gate of Benjamin; Ebed-melech went forth out of the
9 king's house, and spake to the king, saying, My lord the king, these men have done evil in all that they have done to Jeremiah the prophet, whom they have cast into the dungeon: and he is like to [or must; *lit.:* is dead] die for hunger in the
10 place where he is⁹: for *there is* no more bread in the city. Then the king commanded Ebed-melech the Ethiopian, saying, Take from hence thirty¹⁰ men with
11 thee,¹¹ and take up Jeremiah the prophet out of the dungeon, before he die. So Ebed-melech took the men with him, and went into the house of the king under the treasury, and took thence old cast clouts,¹² and old rotten rags [rags of tattered and worn out clothes], and let them down by cords into the dungeon to Jeremiah.
12 And Ebed-melech the Ethiopian said unto Jeremiah, Put now *these* old cast clouts and rotten rags under thine armholes¹³ under the cords. And Jeremiah did so.
13 So they drew up Jeremiah with cords, and took him up out of the dungeon: and
14 Jeremiah remained in the court of the prison [guard]. Then Zedekiah the king sent, and took Jeremiah the prophet unto him into the third [or principal] entry¹⁴ that *is* in [to] the house of the LORD [Jehovah]: and the king said unto Jeremiah,
15 I will ask thee a thing;¹⁵ hide nothing¹⁶ from me. Then Jeremiah said unto Zedekiah, If I declare it unto thee, wilt thou not surely put me to death? and if I
16 give thee counsel wilt thou not hearken unto me? So Zedekiah the king swore secretly unto Jeremiah, saying, *As* the LORD [Jehovah] liveth, that¹⁷ made us this soul, I will not put thee to death, neither will I give thee into the hand of these men that seek thy life.
17 Then said Jeremiah unto Zedekiah, Thus saith the LORD [Jehovah], the God of hosts, the God of Israel: If thou wilt assuredly go forth unto the king of Babylon's princes, then thy soul shall live, and this city shall not be burned with fire;
18 and thou shalt live, and thine house: but if thou wilt not go forth to the king of Babylon's princes, then shall this city be given into the hand of the Chaldeans,
19 and they shall burn it with fire, and thou shalt not escape out of their hand. And Zedekiah the king said unto Jeremiah, I am afraid¹⁸ of the Jews that are fallen to the Chaldeans, lest they deliver me into their hand, and they mock me.¹⁹
20 But Jeremiah said, They shall not deliver *thee*. Obey, I beseech thee, the voice
21 of the LORD [Jehovah], which²⁰ I speak unto thee: so it shall be²¹ well unto thee, and thy soul shall live.²¹ But if thou refuse to go forth, this is the word that the
22 LORD [Jehovah] hath showed me: And, behold, all the women that are left in the king of Judah's house *shall be* brought forth to the king of Babylon's princes, and those *women* [they] shall say, Thy friends [men of thy place]²² have set thee on [over-persuaded] and have prevailed against thee:²³ thy feet are sunk in the
23 mire,²⁴ *and* they are turned away back. So they²⁵ shall bring out all thy wives and thy children to the Chaldeans: and thou shalt not escape out of their hand, but shalt be taken by the hand of the king of Babylon: and thou shalt cause this city to be burned with fire.
24 Then said Zedekiah unto Jeremiah, Let no man know²⁶ of these words, and thou
25 shalt not die. But if the princes hear that I have talked with thee, and they come unto thee, and say unto thee, Declare unto us now what thou hast said unto the king, hide it not from us, and we will not put thee to death; also what the king
26 said unto thee: then thou shalt say unto them, I presented my supplication before the king, that he would not cause me to return to Jonathan's house, to die there.²⁷
27 Then came all the princes unto Jeremiah, and asked him: and he told them according to all these words that the king had commanded. So they left off speaking²⁸
28 with him [*lit.:* were silent from him]; for the matter was not perceived. So Jeremiah abode in the court of the prison [guard] until the day that Jerusalem was taken.

TEXTUAL AND GRAMMATICAL.

¹ Ver. 2.—The same words as in xxi. 9. Only here וְנָפַל and הַצָּרִים עֲלֵיכֶם are wanting, and instead we have at the close a repeated חָיָה. The Chethibh וְחָיָה is here as in xxi. 9 the more correct reading, agreeing better with the order of the sentence (נְבִיא). חָיָה, in sense superfluous, but in accordance with the verbose style of the prophet, is construed like Deut. iv. 42 coll. xix. 4; Ezek. xviii. 13; xx. 11; NAEGELSB., *Gr.*, § 84, *t*. On the form comp. OLSH., *S.* 480, 482, 460.
21

² Ver. 4.—וֹ) יוֹכַה־נָא אֶת הָאִישׁ. Comp. NAEGELSB. *Gr.*, § 100, 2.

³ Ver. 4.—On כִּי יַל־כֵּן. Comp. rems. on xxix. 28.

⁴ Ver. 4.—כַּרְפָּא for כַּרְפֶּה. Comp. OLSH., § 249, a; NAEGELSB. *Gr.*, § 39 *Anm.*

⁵ Ver. 4.—לָרְבַע. Comp. NAEGELSB. *Gr.*, § 95, e.

⁶ Ver. 4.—The construction with לְ, as in Job x. 6; Deut. xii. 30; 1 Chron. xxii. 19; 2 Chron. xv. 13; xvii. 4, *etc.*

⁷ Ver. 5.—Since אֶתְכֶם can be only the *nota Acc.* with suffix (not on account of the meaning, but the form), יוּכַל must be taken in the meaning "overpower" (comp. Ps. xiii. 5), אֵין as purely adverbial with emphatic significance (comp. Job xxxv. 15; 1 Sam. xxi. 9; NAEGELSB. *Gr.*, § 106, 3), דָּבָר as accusative of more exact definition: the king can not go beyond you in any matter.

⁸ Ver. 6.—On the article's position in כִּי הַבּוֹר comp. NAEGELSB. *Gr.*, § 71, 5 *Anm.* 1, *b*.

⁹ Ver. 9.—יְ.הָתַח. The preposition is to be taken in its original meaning as a substantive, and as accusative of place: in its underspace, *i. e.* as we say, on the spot. Comp. 2 Sam. ii. 23; Exod. x. 23; xvi. 29; Jud. vii. 21; 1 Sam. xiv. 9; 2 Sam. 19; 1 Chron. xvii. 9.

¹⁰ Ver. 10.—HITZIG (and after him EWALD, GRAF, MEIER) would read שְׁלשָׁה, because thirty men is too many and אֲנָשִׁים is contrary to the syntax, and also in 2 Sam. xxiii. 13 the same correction is made by the Keri. This alteration does not appear to me to be necessary. Zedekiah might not have ordered the larger number for the sake of the drawing up (for which four men would suffice, as HITZIG reckons), but for greater security and to hinder any resistance. The text is corrupt in many places. Comp. NAEGELSB. *Gr.*, § 76, 4; GESEN. § 120, 2; 2 Sam. iii. 20; 2 Kl. ii. 16 coll. 17.—In 2 Sam. xxiii. the text is corrupt in many places.

¹¹ Ver. 10.—בְּיָדְךָ. Comp. Gen. xxx. 35; xxxii. 17; Numb. xxxi. 49; Jud. ix. 29.

¹² Ver. 11.—בְּלוֹיִם from בְּלוֹי, *vetustate tritum* (comp. Josh. ix. 4, 5), occurs here only. Comp. OLSH., § 173, 9. So also כְּחָבוֹת from כָּחַב, to rend, to tear (xv. 3; xxii. 19; xlix. 20). They are shreds, tatters, rags. The article, which the Keri exscinds, is abnormal and probably occasioned by הַכְּחָבוֹת, ver. 12. מְלָחִים also is not found elsewhere. The root מָלַח is found only in Isa. li. 6, in the meaning of *diffluere*, unless we assume another כָּלַח, synonymous with כָּרַח (Isa. xxxviii. 21; Lev. xxi. 20), to rub, rub away, and כָּרַךְ, to rub, polish (xlvi. 4; Lev. vi. 21; 2 Chron. iv. 16).

¹³ Ver. 12.—From the connection this must be the meaning [not knuckles of the fingers]. Comp. Ezek. xli. 8, the only place where אַצִּילָה occurs besides. In Ezek. xiii. 18 we find יְדֵי אַצִּילֵי in a related meaning as to both words, for the latter is used by Ezekiel also in the wider sense, as is seen from ver. 20, where זְרוֹעוֹת stands for it. Comp. Zech. xiii. 6; Isa. xxv. 11 and the analogous use of רֶגֶל in the sense of leg. Isa. vii. 20; xxxvi. 12 Keri; Deut. xxviii. 57.

¹⁴ Ver. 14.—On the construction comp. NAEGELSB. *Gr.*, § 73, 2 *Anm.* [The LXX. render: εἰς οἰκίαν Ἀσελεισηλ, regarding it as a proper name, but this is no authority for a punctuation הַשְּׁלִישִׁי, entry of the τρισστάτα.—HITZIG.]

¹⁵ Ver. 14.—The sense is the same as in the former question, xxxvii. 17. The Part. אֵל is to be taken as future: *quæsiturus sum*. Comp. NAFGELSN. *Gr.*, § 97, 1 *a*.

¹⁶ Ver. 14.—The second דָּבָר (observe that הַכְחֵד does not stand simply with a suffix) belongs to the negation, in the sense of *ne quid*. Comp. NAEGELSB. *Gr.*, § 82, 2.

¹⁷ Ver. 16.—אֶת אֲשֶׁר. If the Chethibh is correct, which is favored by the greater difficulty of the reading, these words simply *eum qui*. The relative frequently includes the idea of the demonstrative pronoun (comp. vi. 18; NAEGELSB. *Gr.*, § 80, 5). Since now יְהוָֹה is in the accusative, the pronoun relating to it must also be in the accusative; since, however, אֲשֶׁר must at the same time be the nominative to עָשָׂה, it evidently involves the double conception of *eum qui*, which is only rendered possible by the אֶת. In Latin it would be impossible to say *quem* in such a case.

¹⁸ Ver. 19.—דָּאַב. Comp. xvii. 8; xlii. 16.

¹⁹ Ver. 19.—וְהִתְעַלְּלוּ בִי. Comp. Num. xxii. 29; Jud. xix. 25; 1 Sam. xxxi. 4 coll. Lam. i. 22; ii. 20; iii. 51. In the Hithp. the meanings of "to gratify, indulge one's self" and "to mock" appear to be united, the LXX. usually rendering the word by ἐμπαίζω, in this place, however, by καταμωκάομαι.

²⁰ Ver. 20.—לַאֲשֶׁר. לְ=in respect to. Comp. NAEGELSB. *Gr.*, *S.* 227; Gen. xvii. 20; xxvii. 8.

²¹ Ver. 20.—וְיִתַּח. יָטַב are Jussives with the signification of intended effect. Comp. NAEGELSB. *Gr.*, § 89, 3, *b*, 2.

²² Ver. 22.—Comp. xx. 10; Ps. xli. 10.

²³ Ver. 22.—Comp. xliii. 3; Isa. xxxvi. 18. The two verbs together express the idea of successful seduction.

²⁴ Ver. 22.—בֹּץ ἅπ. λεγ. Comp. בִּצָּה Job viii. 11; xl. 21.—The form רַגְלֶךָ is indeed irregular, but not without analogy. Comp. NAFGELSN. *Gr.*, § 44, 4 *Anm.*

²⁵ Ver. 23.—On the absence of a subject comp. NAEGELSB. *Gr.*, § 97, 2, *b*.

²⁶ Ver. 24.—Comp. Gen. xix. 33, 35; 1 Sam. xxii. 15; Job xxxv. 15. This also seems to be a pregnant construction, the prefix בְּ accordingly being dependent on the idea of penetrating latent in יָדַע. That it would be regarded as partitive I cannot believe. We should then expect כִּי.

²⁷ Ver. 27.—This inf. (לְמוֹת) depends on הִשְׁבִּיעַנִי, and לְ, לְבִלְתִּי designates here not the subjective purpose, but the objective result. Comp. Gen. xix. 21; Num. xi. 11.

²⁸ Ver. 27.—On the construction comp. rems. on ver. 23.

EXEGETICAL AND CRITICAL.

The chapter consists of two parts. In the first part (vers. 1-13) it is narrated how the princes prevailed on Zedekiah to give up Jeremiah to them, on account of his continual exhortations to surrender, that they might render him harmless (vers. 1-5). They then lower him down into a pit of mud, from which however the king has him drawn up, on the petition of the Cushite Ebed-melech (vers. 6-13). In the second part (14-28) it is recorded how the king has the prophet brought from the court of the guard, to

CHAP. XXXVIII. 1-28.   323

which he had returned from the pit, for a secret conference (vers. 14, 15). The king desires that Jeremiah disclose the future to him without reserve, and promises him with an oath that his life shall be spared and protected. Jeremiah has, however, nothing else to say to the king, but that surrender is the only way of escape (vers. 16-23). Then the king forbids the prophet to communicate the purport of this conference. In accordance with the king's command, Jeremiah tells the princes, who really come to inquire from him about the conversation, that he only petitioned the king that he might not be taken back to the house of Jonathan, the secretary. The princes have to depart with this answer. Jeremiah, however, remains in the court of the guard till the capture of the city (vers. 24-28).

Vers. 1-6. **Then Shephatiah . . . in the mire.** Jeremiah, brought back into the court of the guard, has further opportunity of intercourse with the people, and uses it again and again to counsel voluntary surrender as the only means of escape.—Of the four princes, who hear the prophet's discourse, Shephatiah, son of Mattan, and Gedaliah, son of Pashur, are not further mentioned; Jucal, son of Shelemiah, is evidently identical with Jehucal, son of Shelemiah, xxxvii. 3. Pashur son of Malchiah, has been mentioned in xxi. 1. Pashur was of sacerdotal (comp. rems. on xxi. 1), Jucal of Levitic descent (comp. 1 Chron. xxvi. 1, 2, 9, 14). These "princes" were thus neither "raised from a lower rank," as GRAF supposes (on xxxvii. 15), nor do their former relations to the prophet lead us to conclude that they were inimically disposed towards him. We do not send, to present petitions, as is the case in xxi. 1, 2; xxxvii. 3, *personas ingratas*. The intended departure of Jeremiah (xxxvii. 12) seems thus to have awakened suspicion against him.—On ver. 3 comp. xxi. 10. —**Seeketh not the welfare.** On the subject-matter comp. xxix. 7; Deut. xxiii. 7; Ezr. ix. 12. —The charge against the prophet is unjust. He has the true welfare of the people in view, *viz.* that which is in accordance with the divine will, and the confidence which he seeks to break, is not a fully satisfied heroic courage, founded on genuine trust in God, but carnal obstinacy, which must lead to destruction. It is inconceivable how any one can fail to see this and take the part of the prophet's opponents. Comp. DUNCKER, I. *S.* 831. The king, fearing on the one hand the higher power supporting the prophet, and on the other not having the courage openly to oppose the princes standing *in corpore* before him, delivers the prophet into their hands. That he expected the prophet would be merely taken back to the house of Jonathan (GRAF) I do not believe. The princes had decisively demanded Jeremiah's death (ver. 4). Their not having him executed at once, but thrown into a pit, where his escape would appear possible only by a miracle, may have been due either to their wickedness or to a certain fear of shedding the blood of the prophet. Comp. Gen. xxxvii. 22-24.

Jeremiah is now thrown into a cistern, which bears the name of an otherwise unknown prince, Malkiah (comp. rems. on xxxvi. 26), probably because he had it dug. The pit may have been often used as the severest imprisonment. The princes in letting down Jeremiah into it may have intended either his most painful death, or an evasion on their part, that they had not shed his blood, but only thrown him into a prison appropriate to such traitors. If he perished there the guilt would not be theirs. In the central point of the theocracy, opposed to prophets and priests who are filled with diabolical hatred and a weak king led by them, this solitary "servant of Jehovah" is at the lowest stage of humiliation and of suffering. All the hatred of Jerusalem, "that killest the prophets and stonest them that are sent unto thee" (Matt. xxiii. 37), culminates at this time in this behaviour towards Jeremiah, by which the measure of guilt was fulfilled and the sentence of destruction was pronounced over the unhappy city. The fulfilling and completing antitype of this historical event is certainly not what happened to John the Baptist (as HENGSTENBERG supposes, *Christol.*, II. *S.* 400 [Eng. Tr., II., 403]), but what our Lord Himself suffered, who was also the object of the most intense hatred on the part of carnal Israel, as being the prophet of its final overthrow (Matt. xxiii. and xxiv.).—Comp. Ps. lxix.

Vers. 7-13. **Now when Ebed-melech . . . court of the guard.** The expression "one of the eunuchs" (comp. lii. 25) seems to intimate that a real eunuch is here meant. As the Mosaic law forbade such mutilation (comp. Deut. xxiii. 1) and, on the other hand, it is not improbable that eunuchs were then employed in the service of the harem (2 Ki. xxiv. 15), it is not very strange to find a foreign eunuch in the service of a Jewish king, with whom, as we infer from vers. 22, 23, the harem occupied an important position. That Ethiopians were preferred for such service seems to be indicated by some traces (comp. Dan. xi. 43; TERENT. *Eun.*, I. 2, 85), as at the present day most of these people come from upper Egypt. (Comp. WINER, *R.- W.-B.* s. v., *Verschnittene.* [SMITH's *Dict.*, I. 590]). Ebed-melech [servant of the king] (N. B. not הַמֶּלֶךְ) is the proper name of the man, chosen with reference to his function. This name is so purely Hebrew and in accordance with the man's position at the Jewish court, that it is not to be conceived how FUERST could come to suppose that it is a Hebraized from an Ethiopic name. Comp. *H.-W.-B.*, *S.* 583.—This Ebed-melech is moreover a proof that the called are not always the chosen, that on the contrary the last are often the first. A stranger, a heathen, a Moor feels compassion for the prophet and horror at the crime committed on him, while in Israel not a hand or tongue is moved in his favor. Comp. Luke iv. 25; xix. 40; Matt. viii. 10.—**Who was in the king's house.** A relative sentence which expresses that Ebed-melech received the news, while he was present in the palace, but the king was absent, sitting in the gate of Benjamin. Comp. xxxvii. 13.—**Have done evil,** ver. 9. Comp. xliv. 5; Mic. iii. 4; 2 Ki. xxi. 11.—וַיָּמָת תַּחְתָּיו. This may certainly mean grammatically, "and he had died," *etc.* But Ebed-melech does not wish to blame them, that instead of death by famine, which he would have suffered without this, they had inflicted on him another death, but that they had placed him in a position in which he must die at any rate, but must inevitably before all succumb to the famine. As is well known the Imperfect with Vau consecutive may represent any action which is not really past, but only represented as such, while in reality it is present or future, or even merely the wish, command, or assumed possibility of it. So here, that is related as an accomplished fact which is merely undoubtedly to be expected. Comp. NAEGELSB. Gr., § 88, 5; Jer. viii. 16; ix. 2; xx. 17.—Ebed-melech pre-supposes two things, (1) That the detention in the pit is not in itself absolutely fatal; (2) but that Jeremiah must at all events die of hunger in the pit. The latter pre-supposition is evidently founded on this fact, that in the general scarcity of means of subsistence one who was thrown into a pit might least of all expect to be provided for.

Vers. 14-16. **Then Zedekiah ... seek thy life.** How long after the liberation from the pit the following conference took place, is not stated. HITZIG supposes that Zedekiah sent for the prophet very soon after his liberation, perhaps on the same day, since otherwise the evasion in ver. 26 would have lost all probability, for "days or weeks later, being let alone in the meantime, Jeremiah must have been set at rest with respect to the king's designs." But with a king of so weak and vacillating character Jeremiah could not, even after weeks, be safe from cruel measures towards his person. All that can be said is, that immediately after showing a favor a contrary treatment was less to be feared than some time afterwards. Nothing more exact can be determined. At all events, in the interval between the deliverance from the pit and the conference no remarkable event occurred.—**Third entry.** What entrance to the temple this was is unknown. At any rate, it must have afforded a suitable place for a secret conference. —HITZIG, by the use of 2 Ki. xvi. 18; xxiii. 11; 1 Chron. xxvi. 18, has attempted a clever combination, which is, however, based on too insecure premises to be satisfactory. [The outer entrance ("the king's entry without," 1 Ki. xvi. 18) leading from the citadel and there at the time of Ahaz from the temple into the προάστειον, where there was the cell of a royal eunuch, 2 Ki. xxiii. 11.—S. R. A.]—From the prophet's answer we see that he neither trusted the king with respect to his own person, in spite of the favors he had received from him, nor with respect to the subject in hand did he expect any receptivity to the divine communications. Proudly and boldly he at first declines to answer the question. But the king swears to him that he will neither put him to death himself nor surrender him to his enemies. —Zedekiah swears by the God of life that he will preserve the prophet's life. Comp. xvi. 14, 15.

Vers. 17-23. **Then said Jeremiah ... to be burned with fire.** Jeremiah again offers the king the alternative which had been so frequently presented before, either voluntary surrender to the Chaldean generals (שָׂרֵי, comp. xxxix. 3, 13, Nebuchadnezzar himself was in Riblah, xxxix. 5) and at least the safety of his life and preservation of the city, or continued resistance and destruction of the city and the endangering of his own person. Observe the negative expression, "thou shalt not escape," in ver. 18. Comp. xxxii. 4, 5; xxxiv. 2-5. Zedekiah, however, cannot make up his mind to follow the advice of the prophet. He alleges that he fears ill-treatment from the Jews who had already gone over to the Chaldeans. It can scarcely be supposed that this fear was seriously intended, though those *transfugæ* might represent a party, which was discontented with the government of Zedekiah and ascribed all the calamities of the State to him. For even the quieting assurance of Jeremiah, ver. 20, makes no impression, which would have been the case if the king had had no other reason. There was really no reason to distrust the prophet's assurance.—In case Zedekiah, from fear of the insults of his fugitive subjects, refuses to follow the admonition of the prophet, the prospect of insult to his wives is set before him. —**This is the word that Jehovah hath showed me.** This does not logically follow as apodosis to the protasis **if thou refuse**, *etc.* A middle clause is wanting expressing the thought, thus shalt thou know, or I have to announce to thee as follows. Further, וְהִנֵּה is the standing formula with which the subject of the vision is introduced, xxiv. 1; Am. vii. 1, 4-7; viii. 1. Accordingly ver. 21 *b* seems to be contracted from "hear now the word which I speak in thine ears, which Jehovah," *etc.* (xxviii. 7). It is not, however, denied that the expression in itself is admissible as it stands. Comp. Ezek. xi. 25.— The prophet's setting before the king the prospect of the deportation of all his remaining wives, seems to intimate that these were a specially esteemed part of his household, in other words, that he had a large and to him very dear harem. The expression "the women that are left in the king of Judah's house," in distinction from "thy wives" in ver. 23, indicates that there were still wives of former kings as fixtures in the royal household (comp. 2 Sam. xii. 8; MICHAELIS, *Mos. Recht.*, I. S. 207; SAALSCHUETZ, *Mos. Recht.*, S. 85), and that even the deportation under Jehoiachin (2 Ki. xxiv. 15), had by no means exhausted the supply of these fixtures. I do not think that by the "women that are left," are to be understood the maidens, as distinguished from the wives, as GRAF supposes. For their being taken forth to the princes, points to higher rank and estimation. A satirical speech is placed in the mouths of these women, the first part of which is found verbatim (with the exception of הַשִּׁיאוּךָ instead of הִסִּיתוּךָ) in the prophecy of Obadiah (ver. 7). On the indications that Jeremiah borrowed from Obadiah, and not the reverse, comp. CASPARI, *Obadja*, S. 8, and the article *Obadja* in HERZOG, *R.-Enc.*—**Turned away back.** Comp. xlvi. 5; Isa. xlii. 17; Ps. xxxv. 4; xl. 15; cxxix. 5. As in the first clause, so also in the second two verbs are employed to express the thought, of which the second expresses the result of the first. The warrior sinking in the mire must fall back. The words are characteristic of Zedekiah. They represent him distinctly as a weak man, dependent on the influence of others. No wonder then that instead of a victor's pœan, with which the women usually receive a conqueror (1 Sam. xviii. 7), a song of mockery awaits him. Observe also, that this satirical song is not put into the mouths of Zedekiah's own wives, for these (in ver. 23) are evidently distinguished from the other occupants of the royal harem.—**Taken by the hand.** As תָּפַשׂ signifies only "to seize," the words can mean only: thou wilt be taken *by* the hand, or *into* the hand of the king, *etc*. The former would be a mode of expression foreign to the style of the prophet (comp. xx. 4; xxi. 7; xxvii. 6; xxix. 21; xxxii. 3. 4; xxxiv. 3, *etc*. The second construction (*Constr. præguans*. Comp. NAEGELSB. *Gr*., § 112, 7) is frequent in Jer. iv. 31; xi. 7; xiv. 2; xxv. 34; xxxii. 20; comp. also *infra*, vers. 24 and 27. The sentence is to be regarded as the contraction of two thoughts into one, according to the example of xxxiv. 3.—The following sentence is also strange. For Jeremiah to say to Zedekiah, Thou wilt burn the city, although correct in a certain sense, is contrary to his usual mode of expressing himself. The LXX., Syr., Chald., read תִּשָּׂרֵף. The punctuation תִּשְׂרֹף may be occasioned by אֵת. The latter is, however, not seldom used to emphasize an antithetical new conception, for which we should say: *but as to, etc*. Comp. EWALD, § 277, *d*, and especially the passages Ezek. xvii. 21; xliv. 3; Jer. xxxvi. 22; 2 Ki. vi. 5. So EWALD, HITZIG, GRAF, MEIER and others.

Vers. 24-28. **Then said Zedekiah ... was taken.** The king feared that if the import of his conversation with Jeremiah were known, he would be regarded as vacillating and be suspected of inclining to the view of the prophet. Though he knew that the fact of the conversation could not remain concealed, he wished, however, that it might be represented as occasioned by Jeremiah himself, and as relating purely to his personal interests.—**And thou shalt not die,** may be regarded as a threat on the part of the king, but at the same time also as a reference to the danger threatening from the princes. For the king would say: I will have you put to death if you betray me, and the princes will kill you if they learn that you have summoned me again to surrender. In the supposed inquiry of the princes, ver. 25, the words **hide it not from us, and we will not put thee to death,** are a parenthesis, the latter expressing the threat, which Zedekiah presupposes in case the prophet should refuse to make a satisfactory statement. —**I presented,** *etc*. Comp. rems. on xxxvi. 7. The pit is not mentioned here. Zedekiah seems thus to presuppose that Jeremiah need not fear a taking back to the pit, from which he had been liberated at the king's command, but that a return to the prison of Jonathan (xxxvii. 15), to avert which he had already offered a petition, might he regarded as possible. The latter seems to have been an ordinary place of confinement, while the pit was only an extraordinary one.— The princes really come to Jeremiah. The fact of the conference thus did not remain concealed, but concerning the import of it, nothing had become known (**the matter was not perceived**). They must have regarded the declaration of Jeremiah made in accordance with the king's command as probable, for they do not urge the prophet further, but withdraw in silence. After this Jeremiah remained in the court of the guard till the capture of the city. On that which further occurred between Jeremiah and Zedekiah during this last stage of his confinement comp. rems. on xxxii. 2-5; xxxiv. 1-5.

DOCTRINAL AND ETHICAL.

1. On xxxvii. 2, 3. The Lord's words Zedekiah did not care to hear, but the help of the Lord he would have liked to have. This seeking for help then did not proceed from a truly believing heart. It was merely an experiment, as in time of need one tries everything. Hence Zedekiah did not venture to come to the Lord himself, but Jeremiah was to intercede for him. "It is, however, in vain for intercession to be made for him, and he himself does not help to pray. Take the example of Pharaoh, Exod. viii. 29; ix. 28; x. 17." CRAMER.

2. On xxxvii. 5-10. Nothing is more bitter than in time of greatest need to see apparent help again disappear. Raised from the depths, one is then cast back into a still profounder deep. The Jews had invoked the aid of the Egyptians on their own responsibility. It was a triumph of worldly policy. The Lord disappoints their calculations. He is not to be so easily put out. The Chaldeans withdraw, but only to defeat the Egyptians, and then return. And Jeremiah must be the prophet of this disappointed hope. A few mortally wounded men, he must proclaim, would suffice to execute the Lord's decree on Jerusalem. Comp. 2 Sam. v. 6.

3. On xxxvii. 10. This passage is also adduced as an instance of the so-called *scientia media* or *de futuro conditionato* (*Vide* BUDDE, *Inst Dogm*., *pag*. 228), together with 1 Sam..xxiii. 11, 12; Jer. xxxviii. 17; Ezek. iii. 6; Matt. xi. 21, 22; xxiv. 22; Acts xxvii. 31. STARKE.

4. On xxxvii. 11, 12. If Jeremiah really wished to leave Jerusalem, because in the city he no longer hoped to secure safety or any success to his ministry (comp. STARKE: "It appears that the prophet would betake himself to the country-people, because he hoped from them better results in penitence and the averting of the divine judgments, since hitherto he had been mostly hindered in his office by the priests and the court"), he was in error and took an arbitrary step. For in the first place the servant of God, who is at his post, is under divine protection, and in the second, he had to proclaim the will of God again and again to the stubborn people. There was then still the possibility of their obedient submission to the divine will. Jeremiah did afterwards repeatedly show that deliverance was still possible on the condition of submission (xxxviii. 2, 3, 17), and also, as he had to proclaim ruin unconditionally (xxxii. 3-5; xxxiv. 2-5), this testimony was necessary, partly as a proof of the inviolability of the divine counsel, partly to cut off all excuse for the Jews afterwards, partly as a foil to the glorious Messianic prophecies (chh. xxxii. and xxxiii.) which pertain to this last stage before the destruction of the city. If then Jeremiah really had the purpose at that time to leave the city, it was an arbitrary step, which was not to succeed, and for which his arrest and what followed was a just

punishment. In this sense DIEDRICH also says (*S*. 120), "The saints also err, and God deals with them punctiliously, so they also must be docile under the divine chastisements."

5. On xxxvii. 15. "Jeremiah's prophecies applied to the whole situation (political), and he thus could not avoid the appearance, which his disposition to recommend to the king the surrender of the city occasioned. God be praised! our Lord's kingdom is not of this world. His servants may renounce the matters, which pertain thereto, with full freedom, and this the more because the Lord raises the instruments who are to labor for the amelioration of the State and the circumstances of mankind also from this kingdom, but gives the prophets of the New Testament a complete dispensation therefrom; of which we have a living example in Jesus and all His Apostles, who did not meddle by a word in any of the civil matters of the authorities, under whom they taught. Justice and chastity were Paul's themes with the procurator Felix, which were matters of the interior, and that is enough." ZINZENDORF.

6. On xxxvii. 17. "The king was commanded to put the book of the law before him, and always have it with him, Deut. xvii. 19. As now he did not do this, he must be in awe even of his own servants: sometimes he must look at his counsellors through his fingers and let them do as they will, and though he might have been a master, he must be a servant. For God poureth contempt upon princes and looseth the covenant of the mighty (Job xii. 21)." CRAMER.

7. On xxxvii. 18-20. In the consciousness of his official dignity the prophet proudly appears before the king, saying, Although it has come out clearly that I was right and your prophets wrong, you have done me injustice. Nevertheless he applies with humble and earnest petition to the king in behalf of his person, that he may not be taken back again to the dreadful prison. "After Jeremiah's example, one may well petition tyrannical magistrates for a mitigation of persecution, but not speak to please them for the sake of the mitigation." CRAMER.

8. On xxxviii. 1-4. Jeremiah is like a running spring, which has an abundance of water. The mouth of the tube may be stopped. But no sooner is a slight temporary opening afforded, than the water breaks forth with full power. Although he knew what was before him, he was not silent. For he could not be silent (xx. 9). Even if they had beaten him to death on the spot with clubs, yet dying he would have cried : **he that goeth forth shall live.** Jeremiah was, however, no arch-traitor, but the truest patriot in all Israel. Is not this proved by the courage, with which he inflexibly repeated his apparently so unpatriotic counsel? Certainly his opponents regard him as the most dangerous man among the people, just as Ahab accused Elijah of troubling Israel (1 Kings xviii. 18), Amaziah Amos (vii. 10), the Jews Paul (Acts xvi. 20).

9. On xxxviii. 5 Legal right to carry out their will, in opposition to that of the king, the princes had none. Zedekiah's speech, therefore, displays only his individual weakness. He also shows by it how little he was subject to God. For had he been faithful to God, he would

have found means to compel the obedience of his princes. He who has the right, has also the Lord on his side. If this was manifest in the case of the poor priest Jeremiah, how much more so in that of the king. But this king was no Jeremiah.

10. On xxxviii. 6. No prophet was ever maltreated so pitiably as Jeremiah. He represents the culminating point in the humiliation of the servant of Jehovah, but also the extreme point in the alienation from God of the theocracy, which was immediately followed as a merited punishment by the deepest outward decline. Therefore in Jeremiah also must "Christ's resurrection become visible (DIEDRICH)."

11. On xxxviii. 7-13. A Moor, a heathen, must have compassion and raise his voice against the enormity, while all Israel was silent. Thus is completed the testimony to Israel's decline, and the guilt appears to be a common one.

12. On xxxviii. 14, 15. This seems to be the manner of princes. They say: I wish to hear the truth, the truth only, the whole truth. And when one tells them the truth, he draws upon himself their highest displeasure. For these lords, accustomed to a Homeric life of the gods (θεοὶ ῥεῖα ζώοντες), do not like to be disturbed in this their bliss. Nothing, however, affects them more rudely than the truth. Zedekiah even does not seem to have been in earnest with his "pray, hide nothing from me," for otherwise he would at least have done what he could to follow the prophet's counsel.

13. On xxxviii. 19-23. Zedekiah gives as a pretext his dread of mocking and maltreatment from the fugitive Jews. For these, the malcontents, who attributed all the blame to his government and had therefore fled, might possibly have him delivered over to them, and then take their revenge on him. Jeremiah assures him that he has no insult to fear from them. But he will be exposed to the most sensible insults from a quarter where he would least expect it, *viz*., from the women of his own harem. To be received by his own wives with insulting songs, instead of songs of victory—what greater disgrace could be conceived for a man and a prince? *Incidit in Scyllam qui vult vitare Charybdim.*

14. On xxxviii. 24-27. Did Jeremiah participate in a prevarication, or not? The opinions on this point are divided. FÖRSTER says: *Non quidem disertis verbis mentitus est Jeremias ; interim tamen hoc ejus factum speciem quandam mendacii habet, vel certe est dissimulatio, quæ non omni ex parte excusanda.* Others on the other hand call attention to two points: 1. Although in vers. 15-17, no such request is mentioned as, according to ver. 26, Jeremiah is said to have made, it is yet implied, both in the words of the prophet in ver. 15, and in the answer of the king, ver. 16. It follows from what is said by both of them, that Jeremiah wished that he might neither be put to death nor brought into such a condition as would inevitably involve his death. Consequently, he at any rate, cherished the same wish, which he expressed to the king in xxxviii. 20. 2. If then the declaration of ver. 26 does not contain the whole truth, it contains no untruth. The princes, however, had no right to demand the whole truth from Jeremiah. For they were simply murder-

ers. No one, however, is bound to a murderer to expose himself to his knife, by the confession of the truth. This latter view may well be the correct one. [Comp. WORDSWORTH and STANLEY, *Jewish Church*, p. 524.—S. R. A.]

HOMILETICAL AND PRACTICAL.

1. On xxxvii. 3. To supplicate the Lord or to intercede with the Lord is indeed right, but it is useless and wrong to desire the help, but not the Lord Himself. [Sinners contradict their prayers, and thus render them unsuccessful, by their lives. LATHROP.—S. R. A.]

2. On xxxvii. 5-10. Instructive example of the difference between man's help and God's help. Man's help self-sought, self-made, shows at first indeed a joyous hopeful countenance, but it is hollow and vacuous, and confidence therein is self-deception. In due course it shows itself perfectly powerless, indeed it turns to the contrary, to destruction. God's help on the other hand is announced at first under gloomy aspects and hard conditions (surrender to the Chaldeans), but these hard conditions are wholesome chastisement, from which proceed life and salvation.

3. On xxxvii. 11-13. "It is the manner of God's enemies, that they shamefully misinterpret the acts of His servants, when these indeed justify themselves, but when they find no hearing they suffer and are silent; only from the confession of the truth they will not forbear." *The Major Prophets*, by HEIM and HOFFMANN.

4. On xxxviii. 4. "Worldly people are still disposed to reproach the preachers of the Gospel with the injury which they inflict on the commonwealth, because they seek to hinder the God-forgotten course of the commonwealth, as the worldly people wish it to be. One must not be put out by this, but go on." HEIM and HOFFMANN.

5. On xxxviii. 4-13. As at the time of Christ the external theocracy was approaching its final overthrow, so at the time of Jeremiah it was its precursory overthrow. Christ was the prophet of the former, Jeremiah of the latter. As Christ was accused of being an arch-traitor and corrupter of the people (John xi. 48, 50), so also Jeremiah. The true ground here, as there, was diabolical hatred to the divine truth and carnal dependence on outward supports and their own excellence. The princes, who threw Jeremiah into the pit, correspond to the rulers of the people at the time of Christ, the weak Zedekiah to the weak Pontius Pilate, Ebed-melech to those believers from the heathen (the ruler of Capernaum, the Cannanitish woman. the Samaritans) who put Israel to shame by their faith. And as Jeremiah is delivered from the pit, so Christ after three days rises from the grave.

6. On xxxviii. 19-23. *Our ways and God's ways.*
1. Our ways: (a) preserve us not from that which we feared (ver. 22): (b) they lead to destruction (ver. 23). God's ways: (a) preserve us from that which we feared (vers. 19, 20): (b) they lead to safety and life (ver. 20)

B. **The Events subsequent to the Capture of Jerusalem** (chh. xxxix.–xliv).

1. *Jeremiah liberated from the court of the guard and given in charge to Gedaliah.*

XXXVIII. 28 b—XXXIX. 14.

28 b. And he was there¹ [And it came to pass] when Jerusalem was taken,
XXXIX. 1 (In the ninth year of Zedekiah king of Judah, in the tenth month, came Nebuchadrezzar king of Babylon and all his army against Jerusalem, and they be-
2 sieged it. *And* in the eleventh year of Zedekiah, in the fourth month, the ninth day
3 of the month, the city was broken up. And [that] all the princes of the king of Babylon came in, and sat in the middle gate, *even* Nergal-sharezer, Samgar-nebo, Sarsechim, Rab-saris, [*or* the chief of the eunuchs] Nergal-sharezer, Rab-mag [*or* the chief of the Magi], with all the residue of the princes of the king of Babylon.
4 And it came to pass, *that* when Zedekiah the king of Judah saw them, and all the men-of-war [*or* and all the men-of-war saw them], then they fled and went out of the city by night, by the way of [to] the king's garden, and the gate betwixt the
5 two walls: and he went out the way of the plain. But the Chaldeans' army pursued [hastened] after them, and overtook Zedekiah in the plains of Jericho: and when they had taken him [and took him] they [and] brought him up to Nebuchadnezzar king of Babylon to Riblah in the land of Hamath, where he gave
6 [held]² judgment upon him. Then the king of Babylon slew the sons of Zedekiah in Riblah before his eyes: also the king of Babylon slew all the nobles of Judah.
7 Moreover he put out Zedekiah's eyes, and bound him with chains [a double chain],
8 to carry [take] him to Babylon. And the Chaldeans burned the king's house, and the houses of the people, with fire, and brake down the walls of Jerusalem.

9 Then Nebuzar-adan the captain of the guard [halberdiers, *lit.*: executioners\
    carried away captive into Babylon the remnant of the people that remained in the
    city, and those that fell away, that fell to him [the deserters, who had gone over to
10 him], with the rest of the people that remained. But Nebuzar-adan the captain
    of the guard left of the poor of the people, which had nothing, in the land of Ju-
11 dah, and gave them vineyards and fields³ at the same time. Now Nebuchadrezzar
    king of Babylon gave charge concerning Jeremiah to Nebuzar-adan the captain
12 of the guard, saying, Take him, and look well to him, [set thine eyes upon him]
13 and do him no harm; but do unto him even as he shall say unto thee. So Ne-
    buzar-adan the captain of the guard sent, and Nebushasban, Rab-saris [chief of
    the eunuchs] and Nergal-sharezer, Rab-mag [chief of the Magi], and all the king
14 of Babylon's princes: Even they sent, and took Jeremiah out of the court of the
    prison [guard], and committed him unto Gedaliah the son of Ahikam the son of
    Shaphan, that he should carry him home [into the house]: so he dwelt among the
    people.

TEXTUAL AND GRAMMATICAL.

¹ Ver. 28 *b*.—These words cannot either logically or grammatically be connected with the previous context. The **Vulg.** and Chald. translate ungrammatically: *cf. factum est, ut aperiretur Hierosolyma*. The Syr. omits the words altogether. The LXX. translate merely וַיְהִי, connecting it immediately with xxxix. 1. On the other hand, an entirely appropriate sense and connection is furnished, if the words are connected with ver. 3. On וַיְהִי, comp. rems. on xxxvii. 11. The Masoretes, moreover, objected to the present division of the text, as may be seen from their פְּסוּקָא בְּאֶמְצַע בָּקְעָה (*lacuna in medio versu*). Comp. GESEN.: *Lehrgeb*., S. 124; HUPFELD, *Stud. u. Krit*., 1837, S. 835. Similar cases are found in Gen. xxxv. 22; Num. xxv. 19; Josh. iv. 1; Ezek. iii. 16, *etc.* Comp. FUERST, *Propylaei Mosora*, § 29 in the *Concordance*, p. 1369.—In ver. 1, בְּעָשׂוֹר לַחֹדֶשׁ is wanting in our text, possibly through the oversight of the transcriber; אָז is likewise wanting before וַיִּצְרוּ עָלֶיהָ וַיִּבְנוּ עָלֶיהָ דָּיֵק is contracted from the longer sentence "and pitched against it, and built forts against it round about, so the city was besieged." Finally הָעִיר הָבְקְעָה is contracted from "the famine prevailed (was sore) in the city, and there was no bread for the people of the land, and the city was broken up." It is evident that the author of this text was concerned only to present the main thoughts.

² Ver. 5.—The expression מִשְׁפָּטִים אֶת דִּבֶּר for "to hold judgment," occurs only in Jeremiah: i. 16; iv. 12; xii. 1. The present account also has the form here only, while in 2 Ki. xxv. 6 we find שָׁפַט. Moreover the expression is not found elsewhere with the following אֶת and with the meaning "*litigare*, hold judgment," but it signifies elsewhere (Ps. xxxvii. 30; Isa. xxxii. 7) simply "to speak justice."—This is a point which would favor the Jeremian origin of ch. lii. (comp. HAEVERNICK, *Einl*., II. 3, S. 233), if this grammatical agreement might not be due to other causes.

³ Ver. 10.—וִיגֵבִים is ἅπ. λεγ.

EXEGETICAL AND CRITICAL.

The text of this chapter is interwoven with portions from chap. lii. (2 Ki. xxv.). Immediately after the opening words an abridged account is interpolated from lii. 4-7 (2 Ki. xxv. 1-4), of the capture of the city mentioned in these words (vers. 1 and 2). Then after ver. 3, vers. 4-10 a similarly abridged account of the flight, capture and punishment of the king, and of the burning of the city and deportation of the people is added from lii. 7-16 (2 Ki. xxv. 4-12). What further follows (vers. 11-14) is not derived from elsewhere, but with xxxviii. 28 *b*, and xxxix. 3, forms the only independent portion of this section, xxxix. 1-14. The question, whether the statements in vers. 11-13, agree with ver. 3, will be treated in the *Exeg. Rems.* Here it may simply be observed that after the excision thus made the original constituents of the section are occupied purely with the person of the prophet, informing us that by order of Nebuchadnezzar, the captain of dragoons Nebuzar-adan has the prophet brought out of the court of the guard and given in charge to Gedaliah, son of Ahikam, after which Jeremiah remained "among the people."

XXXVIII. 28 *b*.—xxxix. 2. **And it came to pass ... broken up.** As the verses 1, 2 cannot in any way be grammatically connected with the preceding and following context, they may be regarded as a parenthesis. The mention of the capture of Jerusalem in xxxviii. 28 *b* occasioned the insertion of this chronological notice relating thereto. It is evident that this insertion was not made by the prophet himself, but proceeded from a later source. Even KEIL acknowledges that the account of the destruction of Jerusalem, which is contained in two recensions, Jer. lii. and 2 Ki. xxiv 18—xxv. 4, cannot have proceeded from the hand of the prophet (comp. *Commentar zu den BB. d. Könige*, 1865, S. 10, 11 with which, however, what is said in *S*. 378 *Anm.*, does not quite agree). Since now vers. xxxix. 1, 2 are taken from that account of the destruction of Jerusalem which we find in Jer. lii. and 2 Ki. xxv., and this account (comp. the narrative of Jehoiachin's end, Jer. lii. 31-34), must necessarily be of later date than Jeremiah, the extract from that account cannot have been made by Jeremiah. These verses are, therefore, to be regarded as a gloss, which probably came into the text, not by the will of the author, but by the fault of the transcriber. Once having entered the text, they pressed back also those words at the close of the previous chapter, since the parenthesis was doubtless then found to be too long and disjointed, and the connection of the words with ver. 3 impracticable. What means the oldest commentators took to fit the words to the previous context, we have already seen. Ver. 3 **That all the princes . . king of Babylon.** These words attach themselves as we have shown to xxxviii. 28 b. How long after the capture of the city this event took place, the words themselves do not inform us. For the connection of the sentence, xxxviii. 28 b, may designate both an immediate chronological sequence, or a longer interval. Let us first regard more particularly the place and object of the assembly, and the persons assembled. The place is called the gate of the middle. As is well known, David had first conquered and fortified (2 Sam v. 7, 9) Mount Zion, the city of David, which Josephus (*Antiq* V., 2, 2) calls the καθύπερθεν πόλις in distinction from the κάτω πόλις. The expression seems to denote one of the gates in the wall separating this upper and lower city. It does not occur elsewhere. Perhaps, however, עִיר הַתִּיכֹנָה (Keri הַתִּיכָנָה) 2 Ki. xx. 4 is connected with it. ARNOLD (HERZ.: *R.-Enc.* XVIII., S. 629) [SMITH, *Dict.*, I. 1027] supposes that the middle gate is to be sought in the middle of the north wall of Mt. Zion. If the gate of the middle is then to be sought, not in the outer city-wall, but in the interior of the city, perhaps as the main entrance to the upper city, it appears to be a central point quite favorable for the commander's purpose. At the same time the sitting of the commander in this gate, as the central point of the city-life (comp. on the significance of the gate in this regard, HERZOG's *R.-Enc.* XIV., S. 721) may have been the signal of the formal and solemn taking possession. In taking their places where the rulers and elders of Jerusalem were accustomed to discharge their office, the Chaldean princes gave it to be understood that they were now masters of the city. That they had "taken up their quarters" in the gate, as GRAF supposes, I do not think. For a gate is no place for living in, least of all for princes. As we perceive from 2 Ki. xxv. 1 (Jer. lii. 4), Nebuchadnezzar himself began the siege, but left its continuation to his generals, he himself being at the time of the capture in Riblah (2 Ki. xxv. 6; Jer. xxv. 9; xxxix. 5). These generals are now enumerated. HITZIG has made the ingenious conjecture, that the four names which we here read, are to be reduced to three, of which each is followed by an official title. Thus Nergal-sharezer bears the title Samgar, which in the Persian signifies "he who has the cup," so that it is equivalent to Rabshakeh (Isa. xxxvi. 2) the cup-bearer. Nebo, which in compound names never occurs in the last place (which is certainly correct), is to be connected with the following name. Sar-sechim is identical with Rab-saris (for ככ from סכה, or שכה secare, from which שְׂפִין knife, is equivalent to eunuch). This idle, sportive accumulation of designations of a man has now after Nebo supplanted the second half of the old name, Shasban (ver. 13). We thus obtain three names, each with a title: 1. Nergal-sharezer, cup-bearer; 2. Nebushasban, chief-eunuch; 3. Nergal-sharezer, chief-magian. This conjecture, on which GRAF has bestowed his approbation, is very plausible, especially as Rabsaris is certainly called Nebushasban in ver. 13, and we cannot conceive why the chief-eunuch, of which there cannot well have been more than one, bears a different name in ver. 3, from that in ver. 13. According to HITZIG the last two names in ver. 13 agree with the corresponding ones in ver. 3, the only difference being in the first name, which is however fully explained by the circumstance, that during the interval which had elapsed between ver. 3 and ver. 15, Nebuzar-adan, who was highest in rank of all the princes, had arrived, and is therefore named first in the latter passage instead of the Nergal-sharezer of ver. 3. The sense and connection are thus in favor of HITZIG's conjecture, but it still lacks a secure etymological basis. That Samgar means cup-bearer, and Sar-sechim is equivalent to Rab-saris, is not yet sufficiently proved. On the name Nergal-sharezer comp. NIEBUHR, *Ass. u. Bab.*, S. 37, 42, 43, *Anm.* [On the identification of Nergal-sharezer with Neriglissat, son-in-law of Nebuchadnezzar, see RAWLINSON, *Ancient Monarchies*, III., 232, 528, and SMITH's *Bible Dictionary*, *s. v.*—S. R. A.] On Nebo also, *Ib.* S. 30, 34.

Vers. 4–10. **And it came to pass . . at the same time.** This passage is, as already remarked, taken with abbreviations from lii. 7-16 (2 Ki. xxv. 4-12). The object is evidently to give, in a compressed picture of the general distress, a background for the original representation, relating merely to the fate of the prophet. That this was necessary, together with ch. lii., must be doubted. For what author will unnecessarily write the same thing twice over? Or would not the author of ch. xxxix. expect that the reader could himself derive the necessary elucidation of this narrative from ch lii.? xxxix. 4–10 is however taken from ch. lii., not from 2 Ki. xxv. For if we compare xxxix. 4 with lii. 7; xxxix. 5 with lii. 8, 9; xxxix. 6 with lii. 10 (N. B.: the slaughter of the princes is not mentioned in 2 Ki. xxv.) and xxxix. 7 with lii. 11, we shall find that the present passage contains all which distinguishes the narrative of ch. lii. from that in 2 Ki. xxv., while in no point does it agree with 2 Ki. xxv., in opposition to ch. lii. In the verses xxxix. 8-10 the narrative in relation both to ch. lii. and 2 Ki. xxv. is so much abbreviated, that any special relationship with one of the two passages is not perceptible. They differ in this section however only in single words, which have no bearing on the essential import, so that we may say that the present text is related to ch. lii., as well as to 2 Ki. xxv., as extract and elucidation. On this more below. If, now, xxxix. 4-10 is indisputably of later date than ch. lii., so as to presuppose this chapter, we cannot avoid regarding the text as originally a marginal gloss, which was gradually by the fault of the transcriber incorporated into the text. As regards particular points, the words " And it came to pass that when Zedekiah," ver. 4, may be recognized as a skillfully added connecting gloss, for 1, the original text contains nothing of this; but lets the flight follow immediately on the breaking in of the Chaldeans, lii. 7; 2 Ki. xxv. 4; 2, it is

also in itself improbable, that Zedekiah deferred his flight till the Chaldean princes had taken their post in the middle gate. The flight was effectuated in a direction opposite to that in which the enemies came from the North approached, viz., by the exit to the South "on the way to the garden of the king through the gate between the double wall." This garden of the king is mentioned only in Neh. iii. 15, where it borders on the pool of Siloah. Comp. ARNOLD in HERZOG, R.-Enc., XVIII., S. 680 v. 635; LEYRER in the same, XIV. S. 371. [SMITH, Dict., I., 653]. According to ARNOLD this garden of the king is probably identical with the garden of Uzza (2 Ki. xxi. 18, 26). The gate between the double walls also is mentioned only here and in the parallel passages. It is to be sought for in the exit of the Tyropœon, and is probably identical with the gate of the fountain (Neh. ii. 14 ; iii. 15 ; xii. 37). Comp. ARNOLD, S. 629 et pass.; THENIUS, BB. d. Könige, S. 456; ROBINSON, Pal. II., S. 142.—The double-wall mentioned besides here (and parallel passages) only in Isa. xxii. 11, appears to have been a double connection between Zion and Ophel. But concerning this there are various views. Comp. THENIUS, The graves of the kings of Judah in ILLGRU'S Zeitschr. f. hist. Theol., 1844, 1. S. 18 sqq.; HERZOG, R.-Enc., V. S. 157; XIV. S. 374 ; XVIII. S. 633 ; KEIL, BB. d. Kön., S. 381.
From this southern exit Zedekiah turned eastward to the עֲרָבָה. This is the general term for the plain or vale of the Jordan, both on its eastern (comp. Deut. i. 1 ; iii. 17 ; iv. 49 ; Josh. xii. 1) and its western shore (comp. Josh. viii. 14; xi. 2, 16; 2 Sam. ii. 29). Yet it seems as though Arabah is not only to be taken in a narrower and wider sense, (in the wider it comprises the entire depression of the lake Gennesaret to the Elamitic gulf, of which the southern half, from the southern end of the Dead Sea, is still called Wady el Araba) but to be generally of a fluctuating character. For in Deut. xi. 30 for instance the region of Sichem, where Mts. Ebal and Gerizim are situated, is reckoned to the Arabah. Zedekiah is overtaken in the עַרְבוֹת יְרֵחוֹ. This is a part of the Arabah, the enlargement of the Jordan-valley, three leagues wide, near Jericho, watered by the brook of Elisha.
The captured king is taken to Riblah, the northern boundary city of Palestine, at the source of the Orontes, (Numb. xxxiv. 11) the point of juncture for the roads eastward into the Euphrates, southward to Damascus and the Jordan, and westward to Phœnicia, which had previously been the head-quarters of Pharaoh Necho (2 Ki. xxiii. 33). Here Nebuchadnezzar held judgment over him. Nebuchadnezzar had made him king (2 Ki. xxiv. 17); Zedekiah was therefore a rebel against him (lii. 3; 2 Ki. xxiv. 20).
The punishment which Zedekiah had to suffer for his revolt was a cruel one : his children were slain before his eyes, likewise all the great men of Judah (הָרֵי for שָׂרֵי lii. 10 probably as a reminiscence from xxvii. 30); he himself was blinded and carried in chains to Babylon. From **to carry**, ver. 7, onwards, the abridgement is great and in so far unfortunate that one main point is omitted, viz., the circumstance that Nebuchadnezzar on the news of the capture of Jerusalem

sent the captain of his body-guard, Nebuzar-adan, to Jerusalem, who arrived there four weeks after the capture. The mention of this circumstance was important, because without it the appearance of Nebuzar-adan, from xxxix. 9 onwards, is wholly unaccounted for. One consequence of this omission is also that in ver. 8 it is not Nebuzar-adan who burns the city, but the Chaldeans. Why the temple is not mentioned among the objects burned is not clear In ver. 4 the obscure and superfluous words "the poor of the people," found in lii. 15, are omitted, and instead of "that fell to the king of Babylon," we have simply "that fell to him," עָלָיו (2 Ki. xxv. 11, עַל מֶלֶךְ בָּ, almost the only point in which ch. xxxix. approaches more nearly to 2 Ki. xxv. than ch. lii.). Since the king of Babylon has not been named just before (comp ver. 6 fin.) "to him" can refer only to the Nebuzar adan mentioned in the following verse; a reference which cannot be historically justified, since by the deserters mentioned are to be understood such only as went over before the conquest. After the deserters our text mentions besides "the remnant of the people." In antithesis to the "remnant of the people that remained in the city" can be understood only the inhabitants remaining in the *country*. In the place of the second הָעָם we find in 2 Ki. xxv. 11 הֶהָמוֹן, in Jer. lii. 15 הָאָמוֹן. The former denotes "tumult, multitude of people " (comp. Isai. xiii. 4; xvii. 12) and our text takes the latter doubtless in the same sense. Whether correctly is another question. Comp. rems. on lii. 15. Nebuzar-adan, the "captain of the guard," is here named for the first time. Sent by the king to Jerusalem on receipt of the news that Jerusalem is taken (comp. lii. 12; 2 Ki. xxv. 8), he immediately assumes the chief command, as is evident from this passage, and the following (xxxix. 10-12; xl. 1-5). The nature of his office, as well as the expression "who stood before the king" in lii. 12, indicate that he took precedence of all other princes.— The tenth verse, in this differing from the rest, contains an extension of the original text, the expression "the poor" being explained by the addition "which had nothing," wanting in ch. lii. and 2 Ki. xxv. The author evidently held it to be desirable (though unnecessary), to call attention to the fact that דַּל is not here to be taken in the sense of "*afflictus, miser.*" The brief phrase "for vine-dressers and for husbandmen " in lii. 16 ; 2 Ki. xxv. 12 (Keri) he extends into a sentence.—The words "at the same time" (in the same day) are to mark the difference in time between what was last narrated and what follows. It might otherwise have seemed as if the events narrated in ver. 11 occurred contemporaneously with those in vers. 9, 10.

Vers. 11-14. **Now Nebuchadnezzar . . . among the people.** STRUENSEE, MOVERS, GRAF, MEIER, dispute the genuineness of vers. 11-13, HITZIG only of ver. 13. The objections to the authenticity appear to be the following: 1. The commission given to Nebuzar-adan, according to xl. 1, not executed. Only in Rama (xl. 1) does Nebuzar-adan (comp. xl. 4) what according to xxxix. 11, 12 he was commanded to do. 2. If Nebuzar-adan, who according to lii. 12 came to Jerusalem four weeks after its capture, first ordered the liberation of Jeremiah from the court of the guard, Jeremiah had remained there four weeks after the capture, which is in contradiction to xxxviii. 28. 3. The three vers. are wanting in the LXX. 4. As to ver. 13 in particular, it is a mere connecting clause, rendered necessary by the insertion of vers. 11, 12. For ver. 14 could not be connected directly with ver. 12; for the subject of "sent" would then be obscure. By the mention of Nebuzar-adan the connection with ver. 12 and the previous context, and by the mention of the other princes the connection with ver. 13 is established. I do not think that these arguments are conclusive. As to the first point, Nebuzar-adan certainly made the necessary arrangements for the execution of his commission. He liberated the prophet from the court of the guard, and entrusted him to Gedaliah for his further maintenance. But he seems not to have been in a condition to keep the prophet specially in view, so that he might be preserved from any personal malignity. In the confusion which was necessarily connected with the destruction of the city, the prophet, who voluntarily or involuntarily had been included in the multitude of the people, was treated like the rest. He was bound like the others. It was only in Ramah, where probably the first halt was made, and the arrangement of the caravan was definitely adjusted, that the captain of the halberdiers remembered his commission with respect to the prophet. There he liberated him from the chains, which he had borne "among all that were carried away captive" (xl. 1) and committed him the second time to Gedaliah (xl. 6). With regard to the second point it should first of all be remarked that "day," xxxviii. 28, must not necessarily be understood in the most restricted sense. This word, as is well known, frequently designates the period of an historical event in general, without any thought of a day of twenty-four hours. Comp. vii. 25; xi. 7; Jud. xviii. 30, etc. If now we consider that the princes who, according to xxxix. 3, sat down in the middle gate, thus took possession of Jerusalem in the name of the Chaldean king, but could not undertake further measures with respect to the fate of the city till they had heard from him, it cannot truly be surprising that for four weeks, till the arrival of Nebuzar-adan (lii. 12) things remained essentially as before, and that thus Jeremiah could not be removed from the court of the guard. The absence of the vers. 11-13 in the LXX. (which moreover omits the whole section 4-13, while it has vers. 1, 2) is of no significance, the reasons for it being apparent. The translator wished by the omission of vers. 11, 12 to avoid an apparent contradiction, by the omission of ver. 13 a repetition. As to the fourth argument it falls to pieces of itself, in so far that ver. 13 seems necessary in any case, whether we regard vers. 11, 12 as genuine or not. The names of the princes might indeed be named together after וַיִּשְׁלְחוּ. But we see that the author's thoughts (after vers. 11, 12) were so much occupied with Nebuzar-adan that he names him first and as the chief personage (hence וַיִּשְׁלַח ver. 13), adding the rest only by way of supplement. When now after the long series of names and titles he repeated the principal verb once more, and in the plural, this is evidently done purely in the interest of perspicuity. We cannot then regard the arguments against the genuineness of vers. 11-13 as valid. On the other hand the following positively favor the genuineness: 1. In point of idiom there is nothing which is foreign to the prophet's usage. It is worth notice that in ver. 11 the name of the Chaldean king is Nebuchadrezzar (as Jeremiah is always accustomed to write it) while in ver. 5 we read Nebuchadnezzar. The expression בְּיַד is one current in Jeremiah. It is found thirty-eight times, more frequently than in any of the other prophets. The expression שִׂים עַיִן is found besides here and xl. 4 only in Gen. xliv. 21. The phrase "do him no harm" (on the Dag. f. in עַיִן comp. OLSH. § 83, f.) is not indeed specifically Jeremian, but by no means as GRAF asserts, an unnecessary explanatory addition. Could it have been unnecessary to enjoin on Nebuzar-adan that no harm should be done to Jeremiah? Was this beyond the reach of possibility? The actual fate of the prophet gives the answer to this question. Or could the עַיִן be omitted? Then we should have an ambiguous expression. For, strictly taken, the sentence without עַיִן would make it Nebuzar-adan's duty to behave indifferently towards Jeremiah. 2. It is in favor of the authenticity that the passage (vers. 11-13) is shown to be neither a foreign property, borrowed from elsewhere (like vers. 1, 2; 4-10), nor an interruption of the connection, but on the contrary as necessary to furnish a perfectly clear picture of the occurrences. That the passage is not borrowed is acknowledged by all. That the course of Nebuzar-adan, as it is related in xl. 1-6 presupposes a commission of Nebuchadnezzar is involved in the nature of the case. For how could Nebuzar-adan dare to distinguish a single person with such favors if he had not been sure of the approval of his master? And is it then improbable that this approval was assured to him by a positive commission? Must an interpolator have invented this commission when Nebuchadnezzar may have heard a thousand times from the mouth of deserters that there was a prophet in Jerusalem who incessantly and with constant danger to his life had designated Nebuchadnezzar as an instrument in the hand of the Lord and submission to him as the only way of escape? And if Nebuchadnezzar had heard this, is there any reason for regarding the commission as the idle, unhistorical conjecture of a later editor? I believe that the narrative in ver. 11-14, in most intimate connection with ver. 3, presents us with the events in a perfectly natural manner, both as to form and contents. It is not at all necessary to take וַיְצַו, ver. 11, as pluperfect. For this command was actually given after the event related in ver. 3, which we have regarded above as the act of solemn taking possession. After Nebuchadnezzar had received the news of the capture of Jerusalem he sent Nebuzar-adan with his further orders. Among these was one respecting the person of the prophet. This alone is here mentioned, as the subject of the verses xxxix. 3,

11-14, is simply the personal experiences of Jeremiah. In the execution of this commission, the princes, at whose head no longer stood Nergal-sharezer but Nebuzar-adan, had the prophet taken out of the court of the guard. This could not be done before, because till the arrival of Nebuchadnezzar all had to remain in general the same as it had been at the capture of the city. Jeremiah was now given in charge to Gedaliah, the son of Ahikam. This Ahikam, of a noble family (comp. 2 Ki. xxii. 12, 14), had already favored the prophet (xxvi. 24). Gedaliah evidently belonged to that small party, who having taken Jeremiah's prophecies as the rule of their political course, had gone over to the Chaldeans (xxxviii. 19). Gedaliah was to bring the prophet from the court of the guard אֶל־הַבָּיִת. By this some have understood the temple (HITZIG), others the king's house (GRAF, et al.). But according to lii. 13 (2 Ki. xxv. 9), both these were burned down by Nebuzar-adan, together with the other houses of Jerusalem, directly on his arrival. And assuredly those large public buildings were not the last to which the Chaldeans applied the destroying hand. It is credible that some private dwellings might be preserved to the last, to afford shelter to some privileged persons. "Into the house" may thus designate the genus, private dwelling in general, in contrast to "quarters at the public expense," such as the court afforded, it thus remaining undecided whether the private dwelling in which Jeremiah was taken were Gedaliah's own house, or some other. In this private dwelling Jeremiah was not placed under confinement. He could freely go in and out. And so he had intercourse with the people, doubtless warning and comforting them with his prophetic words, and was thus in the vast confusion of the destruction, plundering and deportation, treated by the soldiers who had charge of the details like the mass of the populace, i. e., bound in chains, and placed in the trains of captives. Nebuchadnezzar's order thus remained unobeyed, without any fault of Nebuzar-adan and Gedaliah, till they reached the station of Ramah.

2. *Appendix to* xxxix. 1-14.—*The Promise made to the Cushite Ebed-melech.*

XXXIX. 15-18.

15 Now the word of the LORD came unto Jeremiah, while he was shut up in the court
16 of the prison [guard], saying, Go and speak to Ebed-melech the Ethiopian, saying, Thus saith the LORD of hosts [Jehovah Zebaoth], the God of Israel; Behold, I will bring¹ my words upon this city for evil, and not for good; and they shall be² ac-
17 complished in that day before thee. But I will deliver thee in that day, saith the
18 LORD [Jehovah]: and thou shalt not be given into the hand of the men of whom thou *art* afraid. For I will surely deliver thee, and thou shalt not fall by the sword, but thy life shall be for a prey unto thee: because thou hast put thy trust in me, saith the LORD [Jehovah].

TEXTUAL AND GRAMMATICAL.

¹ Ver. 16.—On מֵבִיא. Comp. OLSH., *S.* 69, 332, 581.

² Ver. 16.—הָיָה is evidently used here in a pregnant sense=to be realized, to attain to a real existence. Comp. Isa. vii. 7; xiv. 24.

EXEGETICAL AND CRITICAL.

The Cushite Ebed-melech, to whom the words of our Lord may be applied (Luke xix. 40), "if these should hold their peace, the stones would cry out," is here honored by a special consolatory promise. In the nature of the case this falls into the period after the occurrence related in xxxvii. 7-13. The expression shut up, etc., is found besides only in xxxiii. 1 (comp. xxxii. 2). As we know from other grounds that chh. xxxii. and xxxiii. pertain to the last stage of the confinement in the court of the guard (xxxvii. 28, comp. on xxxvii. 17), we may place our brief passage in the same period as that great consolatory discourse. This portion might, therefore, be attached to those chapters. It is, however, evident that the contents are too trifling in comparison with the importance of that great theocratic book of consolation, and that the historical connection seems better preserved in this place. After the prophet had related his own experiences till the capture of the city, he appends this brief prophecy uttered shortly before that epoch. In connection with ch. xlv. it would have been neither historically nor topically in the right place.

Vers. 15-18. Now the word . . . saith Jehovah. Two thoughts lie at the foundation of ver. 16: 1. The fulfilment of my threatenings against Jerusalem shall take place *before thine eyes*. Ebed-melech is to *see* what he before believed. This is, as it were, the immanent reward of faith, its crown and corroboration. 2. Notwithstanding that all Jerusalem with all the people therein perishes the person of Ebed-melech shall remain unimperilled. This is the second physical and palpable reward of faith.—As the import of God's word cannot be conceived of as indifferent, admitting of fulfilment either in a good or a bad sense, "for evil" must be regarded as dependent on "words." Comp. xxi. 10.—**In that day**, ver. 16, refers necessarily to the point of time in "I will bring," and expresses that the moment of fulfilment will be at the same time the moment of visible perception. There may be a fulfilment which takes place invisibly. Compare what is said under xxv. 11 of the invisible reality of the beginning of the exile. In the same day Ebed-melech is to experience the power and grace of God in the deliverance of his own person. For he is not to be given into the hand of the men of whom he is afraid (ver. 17). It might be asked whether the Chaldeans are meant, or the Jews who were hostile to him on Jeremiah's account. The expressions used in the following verse **thou shalt not fall by the sword**, and especially the contrast to the general destruction, involved in **thou shalt have thy life for a prey** (comp. xxi. 9: xxxviii. 2; xlv. 5), favor the former. Ebed-melech believed and trusted in the Lord. He held the word of the Lord, which Jeremiah proclaimed, to be true, he dared to oppose Jeremiah's enemies; he consequently did not set his hope on the means of escape, on which these foolishly trusted, but on the Lord. In the words **put thy trust**, then, there is a double point of applause and of confidence.

DOCTRINAL AND ETHICAL.

1. On xxxix. 11, 12. "*Elucet inde veritas illius Salomonis* (Prov. xxi. 1): *Cor regis in manu Dei, quo vult illud inclinat.*" FÖRSTER.

2. On xxxix. 11-14. "Nebuchadnezzar the king and Ebed-melech the Ethiopian enhanced the guilt of the Jews. For these, although they were heathens, were not shy of the prophet. The Jews, however, who had grown up with the prophetic words, paid no regard to the divine word, but on the contrary subjected the prophet to manifold maltreatment." THEODORET.

3. On xxxix. 11-14. "*Deus ex iisdem hominibus diversa singulis disponit præmia, qui ex iisdem elementis pro meritorum qualitate electis et reprobis diversas impendit remunerationes. Nam aqua maris rubri, quæ cultores Dei illæsos servabat Israelitas, eadem interfecit Ægyptios idololatras. Similiter flamma camini, quæ regis Babylonis juxta furnacem atroces interfecit ministros, eadem laudantes et benedicentes Dominum in medio ignis conservavit pueros, unde vir sapiens in laudibus Dei ait: creatura enim tibi factori deserviens excandescit in tormentum adversus injustos et lenior fit ad benefaciendum pro his, qui in te confidunt* (Sap. 16, 24)." RHABANUS MAURUS in GHISLER.

4. On xxxix. 15-18. "Well for him, whose help is the God of Jacob, whose hope is in the Lord his God (Ps. cxlvi. 5). Well for the people, whose God is the Lord (Ps. cxliv. 15). For of what avail was it to Zedekiah that he was king? And of what injury was it to Ebed-melech that he was a servant? For the former had to endure all on account of his ungodliness, while the latter on account of his piety suffered no evil." THEODORET.

5. On xxxix. 15-18. "*Ecce principes, qui Jeremiam expetiverunt ad carceris pœnam, Chaldaicæ captivitatis perpessi sunt vindictam. Hic autem Eunuchus, qui prophetam liberavit de carcere, Domino remunerante perfecta potitus est libertate.*" RHABANUS MAURUS in GHISLER.

6. On xxxix. 15-18. "This pious courtier had interceded for the prophet with the king, but the prophet had again interceded for him with God the Lord. Ebed-melech had drawn him out of the pit, but Jeremiah draws him by his prayer from the jaws of all Chaldean war-vortices. Those who receive a prophet shall receive a prophet's reward (Matt. x. 41). Preachers do their patrons more good than they get from them." CRAMER.

HOMILETICAL AND PRACTICAL.

1. On xxxix. 11-14. *Jeremiah's deliverance an example of how wonderfully the Lord helps His own.* 1. While in Jerusalem his fellow believers hate and persecute him, the heathen king in Riblah thinks of him, and commands to liberate him. 2. While the city of Jerusalem with all its population perishes, he is protected and brought into safety.

2. On xxxix. 15-18. *What can we learn from the example of the believing Ebed-melech?* 1. That faith is not connected with limits of any external communion; 2, that assent and confidence pertain to its nature (ver. 18); 3, that there is an internal (ver. 16) and external (ver. 17) reward of faith.

3. Jeremiah liberated in Ramah and committed the second time to Gedaliah.

XL. 1–6.

1 The word that came to Jeremiah from the LORD, after that Nebuzar-adan the captain of the guard had let him go from Ramah, when[1] he had taken him being bound in chains[2] among all that were carried away captive of Jerusalem and Ju-
2 dah, which were carried away captive unto Babylon. And the captain of the guard took[3] Jeremiah, and said unto him, The LORD [Jehovah] thy God hath pro-
3 nounced this evil upon this place. Now the LORD [Jehovah] hath brought it,[4] and done according as he hath said: because ye have [had] sinned against the LORD [Jehovah], and have not obeyed his voice, therefore this thing is come upon you.
4 And now, behold, I loose thee this day from the chains which *were* upon thine hand. If it seem good unto thee to come with me into Babylon, come; and I will look well unto thee: but if it seem ill unto thee to come with me into Babylon, forbear: behold, all the land *is* before thee: whither it seemeth good and convenient
5 [right] for thee to go, thither go. Now while he was not yet gone back [answered],[5] *he said*, Go back also to Gedaliah the son of Ahikam the son of Shaphan, whom the king of Babylon hath made governor over the cities of Judah, and dwell with him among the people: or go wheresoever it seemeth convenient unto thee to go. So the captain of the guard gave him victuals and a reward [present], and let him
6 go. Then went Jeremiah unto Gedaliah the son of Ahikam to Mizpah; and dwelt with him among the people that were left in the land.

TEXTUAL AND GRAMMATICAL.

[1] Ver. 1.—כִּ is here causal. Comp. 2 Chron. xvi. 7; xxviii. 6.

[2] Ver. 1.—בְּאזִקִּים. The form with א only here and in ver. 4. Besides זִקִּים in Job xxxvi. 8; Isa. xlv. 14; Nah. iii. 10. From יָדְךָ, ver. 4, we see that hand-fetters are meant.

[3] Ver. 3.—The construction of לִקְחוֹ with לְ is an Aramaism. Comp. EWALD, § 277, e.

[4] Ver. 3.—The pronominal object of וַיָּבֵא is to be supplied from the foregoing context. Comp. NAEGELSB. *Gr.*, § 78, 2, Anm. The absence of the article before דָּבָר to which the Masoretes object, is no rare occurrence. Comp. xxxii. 14; xxxviii. 14; 1. 16; NAEGELSB. *Gr.*, 72, 2, *Anm.*

[5] Ver. 4.—וְעוֹדֶנּוּ, ver. 4, may be taken both grammatically (comp. NAEGELSB. *Gr.*, § 44, 4, *Anm.*), and according to the sense either as singular or plural. On אַל־טֻב. Comp. EWALD, § 335, a.

[6] Ver. 5.—[NAEGELSB.: Place, however, he had not yet answered. See EXEG. AND CRIT. "So J. D. MICHAELIS, DAHLER, UMBREIT, NEUMANN. But Jeremiah never uses the verb שׁוּב in this sense, but always in the sense of *returning*." WORDSWORTH.—S. R. A.]

EXEGETICAL AND CRITICAL.

In the unavoidable confusion Jeremiah, contrary to the command of the king (xxxix. 11-14), is included among the captives, and bound with chains. This error is first remarked in Ramah. The captain of the halberdiers has him immediately liberated, and gives him the choice to go with them to Babylon or remain in the country. As Jeremiah, as it appears, hesitated in answering, the captain of halberdiers, guessing the wish of the prophet, decides himself that he is to remain. Provided with a supply of food and presents, Jeremiah hereupon betakes himself to Gedaliah, who was appointed by Nebuchadnezzar governor over the country, in Mizpah.

Ver. 1. **The word . . . unto Babylon.** The superscription is of the larger kind. It extends over the four chh. xl.-xliii., for a similar one recurs only in xliv. 1. Since the formula, "the word that came," etc., appears constantly as the superscription to the longer sections (comp. vii. 1; xi. 1 [xiv. 1]; xviii. 1; xxi. 1, *etc.*), it has gradually assumed a double character. It is primarily, according to the meaning of the words, the announcement of a word of God spoken to the prophet. Since, however, these words represent at the same time the main sections of the prophetic book, historical narrative being annexed only as introductory or supplementary commentary, the formula has gradually become the superscription of a main section, even where historical narrative predominates. This is certainly nowhere to so great an extent the case as here. In a less degree it is found also in xxi. 1-3 (comp. "And Jeremiah said," ver. 3). The formula is certainly never found as a superscription of a purely historical section. Nor are chh. xl.-xliii. such. For in xlii. 7-22 we have an account of a revelation made to the prophet, to which all the previous and subsequent context is related as historical background. In xliii. 8-13 is a second oracle, from which it again follows, that we are to regard the formula in this verse as a comprehensive title of a section, which may refer not only to other matter besides a revelation, but also to more than one revelation. Moreover the superscription here is related also to i. 3. For there the narrative of the events till the deportation in the fifth month of the eleventh year of Zedekiah is announced. Our section, being written at a later date, records the events immediately after this date, and till the arrival in Egypt.—**When he had taken him.** This is to explain why a liberation of Jeremiah can be spoken of, after what is narrated in xxxix. 11-14. Nebuzar-adan had to liberate the prophet in Ramah, because he had taken him captive (by a misunderstanding. Comp. rems. on xxxix. 11-13), and bound him with chains. — **Being bound**, etc., more particularly describes in what condition Jeremiah was in consequence of being taken, and when he was liberated by Nebuzar-adan.—**Among all**, etc. This addition also is evidently to contribute to the explanation of Jeremiah's being bound. Jeremiah standing alone would not have suffered this indignity. It was only in consequence of his remaining "among the people" (xxxix. 14), and was contrary to the purpose of the general. It has been already remarked above that Ramah, being the first station after Jerusalem, served as the place of assembly and final arrangement of the caravan, (in reference to its position. Comp. rems. on xxxi. 15).

Vers. 2-4. **And the captain . . . thither go.** What Nebuzar-adan here says to Jeremiah presupposes that he was well acquainted with the purport of his prophecies, and that he acknowledged their fulfilment as a manifestation of the power of the God in whose name they had been pronounced. It could not be difficult for a heathen to admit that the national deity of the Jews, enraged because this people preferred other deities to Him, had given them up to their enemies. Nebuzar-adan may also have spoken Hebrew, though the mode of expression betrays that Jeremiah gives only the sense, not the precise words of his speech. Comp. xvi. 10; xix. 15; xxxii. 42; xxxvi. 31; xxxix 16.; xliv. 2.

Vers. 5, 6. **Now while . . . in the land.** The words וְעֹדֶנּוּ לֹא יָשׁוּב mock at every attempt to explain them according to the grammar and lexicon. For 1. It is contrary to rule to take עוֹדֶ as simply equivalent to עוֹד, since it is a complete sentence (and he is still), and either requires no predicate or it can have one only in the form of a participle or adjective. It must be וְעוֹד הוּא לֹא יָשׁוּב, or וְעוֹד לֹא יָשׁוּב, or וְעוֹדֶנּוּ שָׁב לֹא, or כְּשִׁיב, or something like this. 2. The connection with the following שָׁבָה by the mere ו is likewise abnormal. We should expect, since in sense וְשָׁבָה cannot simply continue the speech interrupted by a parenthesis—as a contradiction would thus be produced—some connective formula like וַיֹּאמֶר. 3. The meaning of יָשׁוּב is enigmatical. For whomsoever we take as the subject, Jeremiah or the king of Judah or Gedaliah, or (with SEB. SCHMIDT) the inhabitants of the place of residence selected by Jeremiah, or an indefinite "they," no satisfactory meaning is obtained. The ancient translators therefore rendered with arbitrary freedom, LXX. εἰ δὲ μή, ἀπότρεχε, ἀνάστρεψον πρὸς τὸν Γοδολίαν. Vulg.: *et mecum noli venire, sed habita apud Godoljam.* Syr.: *dixit etiam ad eum: si maneas, commorare in medio populi apud Gedaljam.* Chald.: *et si tu non vis reverti, revertere ad Gedaljam.* I consider the text corrupt. Since in ver. 4 Nebuzar-adan leaves it to Jeremiah to go wherever he wishes, but ver. 4 says distinctly that he must return to Gedaliah, there must have stood between the two a sentence reporting the preference, which Jeremiah somehow intimated, to remain in the country. How this sentence read is no longer to be ascertained. Since from Jeremiah's not returning it could not be concluded that he wished to return, while from his not answering this conclusion might easily be drawn, since more honor would be done to the Chaldeans if Jeremiah preferred a residence in their country to one in his desolated home, I am of opinion, that originally some form of שׁוּב stood here, involving the idea of answering.— Nebuzar-adan now dismisses the prophet with a supply of food (אֲרֻחָה) comp. lii. 34; Prov. xv. 17) and presents (מַשְׂאֵת, literally load, what is carried away, *i. e.* presents. Comp. Esth. ii. 18; Am. v. 11). Jeremiah, following the advice given him, betakes himself to Gedaliah in Mizpah, doubtless that city among the five of this name which was situated in Benjamin, and is named together with Gibeon and Ramah in Josh. xviii. 25, 26; comp. 1 Sam. vii. 16; x. 17; 1 Ki. xv. 22; 1 Macc. iii. 46; RAUMER, *Paläst.*, S. 213. [This Ramah is supposed to have been about six miles north of Jerusalem, on the road to Bethel. Comp. SMITH, *Dict.*—S. R. A.]

4. *The gathering of the people under Gedaliah.*

XL. 7–16.

7   Now when all the captains of the forces[1] which *were* in the fields, *even* they and their men, heard that the king of Babylon had made Gedaliah the son of Ahikam governor in the land, and had committed unto[2] him men, and women, and children, and of the poor[3] of the land, of them that were not carried away captive to Baby-
8   lon; then they came to Gedaliah to Mizpah, even[4] Ishmael the son of Nethaniah, and Johanan and Jonathan[5] the sons of Kareah, and Seraiah the son of Tanhumeth, and the sons of Ephai the Netophathite, and Jezaniah the son of a [the] Maacha-
9   thite, they and their men. And Gedaliah the son of Ahikam the son of Shaphan sware unto them and to their men, saying, Fear not to serve the Chaldeans: dwell
10 in the land, and serve the king of Babylon, and it shall be well with you. As for me, behold, I will dwell at Mizpah, to serve the Chaldeans,[6] which will come unto us: but ye, gather ye wine, and summer fruits, and oil, and put *them* in your
11 vessels, and dwell in your cities that ye have taken. Likewise when all the Jews that *were* in Moab, and among the Ammonites, and in Edom, and that *were* in all countries, heard that the king of Babylon had left a remnant[7] of Judah, and that
12 he had set over them Gedaliah the son of Ahikam the son of Shaphan; Even all the Jews returned out of all the places whither they were driven, and came to the land of Judah, to Gedaliah, unto Mizpah, and gathered wine and summer fruits
13 very much. Moreover Johanan the son of Kareah, and all the captains of the
14 forces that *were* in the fields, came to Gedaliah to Mizpah, and said unto him, Dost thou certainly know that Baalis the king of the Ammonites hath sent Ishmael the son of Nethaniah to slay thee?[8] But Gedaliah the son of Ahikam be-
15 lieved them not. Then Johanan the son of Kareah spake to Gedaliah in Mizpah secretly, saying, Let me go, I pray thee, and I will slay Ishmael the son of Nethaniah, and no man shall know *it;* wherefore should he slay thee, that all the Jews which are gathered unto thee should be scattered and the remnant in Judah
16 perish? But Gedaliah the son of Ahikam said unto Johanan the son of Kareah, Thou shalt not do this thing:[9] for thou speakest falsely of Ishmael.

TEXTUAL AND GRAMMATICAL.

[1] Ver. 7.—חֲיָלִים. The word is found in the sense of "riches" in Isa. xxx. 6. In the sense of "forces, bands," it occurs only in Jeremiah (xl. 13; xli. 11, 13, 16; xlii. 1, 8; xliii. 4, 5), and in later books (1 Ki. xv. 20; 2 Ki. xxv. 23, 26; Eccl. x. 10; 1 Chron. vii. 5–7; Dan. xi. 10). By the addition of אֲשֶׁר בַּשָּׂדֶה these bands are distinguished from the main forces of the regular army in the capital.

[2] Ver. 7.—הִפְקִיד אִתּוֹ. This Hiphil denotes not only *inspicientem*, but also *inspiciendum facere:* xli. 10; xxxvi. 20; xxxvii. 21; Ps. xxxi. 6; Isa. x. 28; 2 Chron. xii. 10, in which case he to whom the *inspectio* is committed is designated in various ways by לְ, by אֵת, by בְּיַד or עַל יַד.

[3] Ver. 7.—וּמִדַּלַּת. Comp. xxxix. 10; 2 Ki. xxv. 12. The partitive מִן expresses that not all the "poor of the land" were left behind, which also follows from lii. 15 coll. 16. In the following כִּי before אֲשֶׁר there is a sort of attraction, and it is therefore not to be emphasized, as it would then signify that Gedaliah was not set as inspector over all the remaining people.

[4] Ver. 8.—The Van is explicative—and indeed. Comp. NAEGELSB. *Gr.*, § 111, 1.

[5] Ver. 8.—2 Ki. xxv. 23 has only "Johanan son of Kareah." The words "and the sons of Ephai" are also omitted, so that "the Netophathite" is referred to Tanhumeth. Instead of יוֹנָי finally we read there יֵאזַנְיָהוּ. From these alterations it follows that the present text is the original. For the similarity of the names Johanan and Jonathan, which appears more in writing than in speaking, as well as the obscurity of the name עֵיפַי (which according to the Chethibh is to be spoken עוֹפַי, according to the Keri עֵיפָי. Comp. עֵיפָה, Gen. xxv. 4; Isa. lx. 6; 1 Chron. ii. 46, 47) well explains the omission of these words, while their insertion in the text appears in the highest degree improbable.

[6] Ver. 10.—[" Literally, *to stand at the face of the Chaldeans:* to be their representative, and to do their will, and also to mediate with them on your behalf (HITZIG)." WORDSWORTH.—S. R. A.]

[7] Ver. 11.—שְׁאֵרִית נָתַן. Comp. xliv. 7; Gen. xlv. 7; 2 Sam. xiv. 7.

CHAP. XLI. 1-18.   337

⁸ Ver. 14.—נַפְשֵׁךְ לְהָכֹתְךָ. Comp. Gen. xxxvii. 21; Deut. xix. 6, 11; xxvii. 25; NAEGELSD. *Gr.*, § 70, *f.*
⁹ Ver. 16.—אֶל־הֶעָשִׂיט. The Keri would read הֶעָשֻׁיט (comp. on this form OLSH., § 240, *a Anm.*), unnecessarily. Comp. xxxix. 12; Gen. xxii. 12; Job xiii. 20.

EXEGETICAL AND CRITICAL.

The leaders of the scattered bands roving through the country, who had managed to escape the Chaldean forces, assembled to Gedaliah in Mizpah on the news that he had been set by Nebuchadnezzar over the country (vers. 7, 8). Gedaliah, after promising them on oath on his part protection and support, urges them to collect whatever the land contains of the necessaries of life and willingly to serve the Chaldeans (vers. 9, 10). The dispersed Jews from the neighboring countries also gathered about Gedaliah (vers. 11, 12). It however came to be rumored that one of those band-leaders, Ishmael, the son of Nethaniah, of the royal stock, had been incited by Baalis, king of the Ammonites, to murder Gedaliah. The rest of the band-leaders, therefore, warned Gedaliah of Ishmael, but Gedaliah believed them not (vers. 13, 14). One of the leaders, Johanan the son of Kareah, even offered to murder Ishmael secretly. Gedaliah, however, would not permit it, declaring the suspicion prevailing against Ishmael to be based on a lie (vers. 15, 16).

Vers. 7, 8. **Now when all . . . their men.** These two verses are also found in 2 Ki. xxv. 23 in an abridged form.—This Ishmael was, according to xli. 1, of royal lineage, which partly explains his enmity to Gedaliah. The other persons named are otherwise altogether unknown.—Who the sons of the Netophathite were (the place belonged to Bethlehem, comp. 1 Chron. ii. 54; ix. 16; Neh. vii. 26; Ezr. ii. 22) is as little known as what the proper name of the Maachathite was (Maachah a province of Syria on the northeastern borders of Palestine, Deut. iii. 14; Josh. xii. 5 coll. 2 Sam. x. 6, 8; RAUMER, *Paläst.*, *S.* 226, 7). Comp. rems. on xlii. 1.

Vers. 9-12. **And Gedaliah . . . fruits very much.** Ver. 9 is also found in 2 Ki. xxv. 24, reproduced with the noteworthy alteration, "to be the servants of the Chaldeans" instead of "to serve the Chaldeans." The former expression however (we should expect at least "servants of the king of the Chaldeans") corresponds neither to the usage of the prophets, nor the connection of the passage. Remarkably also the LXX. translate here: μὴ φοβηθῆτε ἀπὸ προσώπου τῶν παίδων τῶν Χαλδαίων, while in 2 Ki. xxv. 24 they have μὴ φοβεῖσθε πάροδον τῶν Χαλδαίων.— What Gedaliah has sworn to them is, according to ver. 10 *a*, that he would stand in Mizpah before the Chaldeans, who would come to them. He means by this that he would be the medium of intercourse with the Chaldean ambassadors, officers, soldiers, *etc.*, and would represent the interest of the country with them (comp. xv. 1). The Jews on their part are to care for their sustenance by collecting the fruits still to be found in the country (it was now autumn, comp. lii. 12; xli. 1). In the desolated and plundered land this was naturally a matter of the highest importance. The collected supplies they were to preserve in the cities which, according to their own choice, they had taken into their possession. On the news that Nebuchadnezzar had left of the Jewish people, as it were a remnant of root in their land, and over this feeble remnant had appointed Gedaliah overseer, the dispersed Jews also returned from the neighboring lands, in order to gather around Gedaliah in Mizpah, who must thus have been a *persona grata*.

Vers. 13-16. **Moreover Johanan . . . of Ishmael.** Whether Baalis, king of the Ammonites, had any special hatred towards the person of Gedaliah, or whether he wished to destroy the Jews' last point of cohesion and crystallization, is uncertain. His making use of Ishmael may have been due to the personal jealousy of this man, who as a prince royal (xli. 1) regarded Gedaliah's post of honor as properly belonging to him. The plan became known. The captains came to Mizpah (**in the fields** is not a thoughtless repetition from ver. 7, but indicates that the bands were still essentially the same, namely, free corps roving through the country) to warn Gedaliah. He, however, did not believe them. And when Johanan alone in secret conference offered to kill Ishmael, he directly forbade him, declaring the accusation to be a lie.

---

5. *The murder of Gedaliah and its consequences.*

CHAP. XLI.

1 Now it came to pass in the seventh month, *that* Ishmael the son of Nethaniah the son of Elishama, of the seed royal, and the princes of the king, even ten men with him, came unto Gedaliah, the son of Ahikam to Mizpah; and there they did
2 eat bread together in Mizpah. Then arose Ishmael the son of Nethaniah, and the ten men that were with him, and smote Gedaliah the son of Ahikam the son of Shaphan with the sword, and slew him, whom the king of Babylon had made
3 governor over the land. Ishmael also slew all the Jews that were with him, *even* with Gedaliah, at Mizpah, and the Chaldeans that were found there, the men of war.

22

4   And it came to pass the second day after he had slain Gedaliah, and no man
5   knew it, that there came certain [men] from Shechem, from Shiloh, and from
    Samaria, *even* fourscore [eighty] men, having their beards shaven and their clothes
    rent, and having cut themselves [their bodies], with offerings and incense in their
6   hand, to bring *them* to the house of the LORD [Jehovah]. And Ishmael the son of
    Nethaniah went forth from Mizpah to meet them, weeping all along as he went:
    And it came to pass, as he met them, he said unto them, Come to Gedaliah the son
7   of Ahikam. And it was so, when they came into the midst of the city, that
    Ishmael the son of Nethaniah slew them *and cast them* into the midst of the pit
8   [slew them into the cistern],[1] he, and the men that were with him. But ten men
    were found among them that said unto Ishmael, Slay us not: for we have treasures
    in the field, of wheat, and of barley, and of oil, and of honey. So he forbare, and
9   slew them not among their brethren. Now the pit [cistern] wherein Ishmael had
    cast all the dead bodies of the men, whom he had slain because [by the hand] of[2]
    Gedaliah, was it [that] which Asa the king had made for fear[3] of Baasha king of
    Israel: *and Ishmael the son of Nethaniah filled it with them that were* [the] slain.
10 Then Ishmael carried away captive all the residue of the people that *were* in
    Mizpah, *even* the king's daughters, and all the people that remained in Mizpah,
    whom Nebuzar-adan the captain of the guard [halberdiers] had committed to
    Gedaliah the son of Ahikam: and Ishmael the son of Nethaniah carried them
    away captive, and departed to go over to the Ammonites.
11 But when Johanan the son of Kareah, and all the captains of the forces that
    were with him, heard of all the evil that Ishmael the son of Nethaniah had done,
12 then they took all the men, and went to fight with Ishmael the son of Nethaniah,
13 and found him by the waters that *are* in Gibeon. Now it came to pass, *that* when
    all the people which *were* with Ishmael saw Johanan the son of Kareah, and all
14 the captains of the forces that *were* with him, then they were glad. So all the
    people that Ishmael had carried away captive from Mizpah cast about and returned,
15 and went unto Johanan the son of Kareah. But Ishmael the son of Nethaniah
    escaped from Johanan with eight men, and went to the Ammonites.
16 Then took Johanan the son of Kareah, and all the captains of the forces that
    were with him, all the remnant of the people whom he had recovered from Ishmael
    the son of Nethaniah, from Mizpah, after *that* he had slain Gedaliah the son of
    Ahikam, even mighty men of war,[4] and the women, and the children, and the
17 eunuchs, whom he had brought again from Gibeon: and they departed, and dwelt
    in the habitation of Chimham,[5] which is by Beth-lehem, to go to enter into Egypt,
18 because of the Chaldeans: for they were afraid of them, because Ishmael the son
    of Nethaniah had slain Gedaliah the son of Ahikam, whom the king of Babylon
    made governor in the land.

TEXTUAL AND GRAMMATICAL.

[1] Ver. 7.—Pregnant construction. Comp. NAEGELSB. *Gr.*, § 112, 7 ; 2 Ki. x. 14 ; 1 Macc. vii. 19.

[2] Ver. 9.—בְּיַד. J. D. MICHAELIS conjectures בְּיָד (comp. vi. 7 Keri), which reading is said to be found in one Codex of DE ROSSI (comp. ROSENMUELLER *ad l.*). The LXX. translate φρέαρ μέγα τοῦτό ἐστιν, as if they had read הוּא הַגָּדוֹל בּוֹר, which reading is adopted by DAHLER, MOVERS, HITZIG, GRAF. It would afford a good meaning. But the reading is not to be altered unnecessarily.

[3] Ver. 9.—מִפְּנֵי, *before*, properly "on account of," but used here in the sense of "against." Comp. Jud. ix. 21 ; 1 Chron. xii. 1.

[4] Ver. 10.—אַנְשֵׁי הַמִּלְחָמָה is in apposition to גְּבָרִים and is to express that the latter is not to be taken in the sense of *mares* generally, in which even the children might be included, but in the sense of "fighting men."

[5] Ver. 17.—בְּכְהָם גֵּרוּת (Keri). The Chethibh seems to require the pronunciation בִּכְיוֹתָם. The meaning of the word is not apparent. The old translators all express, though with great want of clearness and agreement among themselves, a proper name. Only JOSEPHUS (*Antiq*. X., 9, § 5) says : εἴς τινα τόπον μάνδραν λεγόμενον. He evidently read גְּדֵרָה (wall, protection, hurdle. Comp. Zeph. ii. 6).—גֵּרוּת is ἅπ. λεγ., but from its etymology must mean *hospitium, diversorium*.

EXEGETICAL AND CRITICAL.

The suspicion against Ishmael was only too well-founded. He really murders Gedaliah and his retinue, consisting of Jews and Chaldeans (vers. 1–3) also seventy Israelites who were bringing offerings to the destroyed sanctuary (vers. 4–9). The rest of the people he leads away captive from Mizpah, but is overtaken by Johanan and the other band-leaders. The captives immediately leave him, and he escapes with eight

CHAP. XLI. 1-18.   339

men to the Ammonites (vers. 10-15). Thereupon the leaders assemble the whole people in the neighborhood of Bethlehem, to prepare for removal to Egypt, for in consequence of the murder of Gedaliah they think that they will be liable to the extreme vengeance of the Chaldeans if they remain longer in the country.

Vers. 1-3. **Now it came to pass ... men of war.** There is a brief extract from these verses in 2 Ki. xxv. 25. The event took place in the seventh month, therefore three months after the capture of the city (xxxix. 2), and two after the destruction and deportation by Nebuzar-adan (lii. 12; 2 Ki. xxv. 8). Ishmael was of the royal, therefore David's seed. Neither he nor his father Nethaniah (1 Chron. xxvi. 2, 12; 2 Chron. xvii. 8, Levites are thus named) are mentioned elsewhere. Nethaniah is called the son of Elishama. Whether this person is identical with the "scribe" mentioned in xxxvi. 12, 20, 21, or the Elishama named in 2 Sam. v. 16; 1 Chron. iii. 6 (SI: xiv. 7 as a son of David is meant, is not apparent. Both cases are possible. In the latter Elishama would be the ancestor of the family, "son" being used according to a well known idiom, in the wider sense. Ishmael would then belong to a collateral branch of the royal family.—**Princes of the king.** It is clear that the king of Judah is meant. Not so clear the grammatical connection. It may be referred to "royal seed." HITZIG in opposition to this correctly remarks that the "princes" did not form an hereditary caste. It is therefore, according to some, governed by "of." Is it not however a matter of course that Ishmael as a prince belonged to the רַבִּים, especially as this word by no means designates a definite category of greatness? Further, is it probable that Ishmael with ten men could overpower the entire Jewish retinue of Gedaliah, together with the Chaldean soldiers (ver. 3), eighty men (ver. 7), who if not provided with arms were with legs, and then lend away captive against their will the whole population of Mizpah (ver. 14)? We are thus recommended to take רַבִּי as a nominative = and great men of the king. It would then be declared that Ishmael and other Jewish nobles (doubtless each with his own retinue), and ten men who formed the personal retinue of the former, accomplished the deed. The passage lii. 10 would not contradict this. For since even the Chaldeans could not kill any one whom they did not have, that passage states only that the Chaldeans took the life of all the princes who fell into their power. Now besides here רַב never occurs in Jeremiah of the great men of the Hebrews, but only of the Chaldean grandees in general (xxxix. 13), and of the principal court-officers in particular. Comp. Rab-Mag., etc., xxxix. 3, 13, etc.—It is then natural to suppose that the words "and the princes of the king" are a gloss, occasioned by the difficulty of crediting such deeds to a little band of eleven men.

Slew him. These words expressly set forth that though several smote Gedaliah with their swords, Ishmael was the real murderer, upon whom rested the immense responsibility of having killed the Chaldean king's chief officer in the country. I therefore do not think that, as HIT-ZIG and GRAF propose, we must read "smote" also in the singular (וַיַּכֵּן). That by "all the Jews that were with Gedaliah at Mizpah" we are not to understand the whole population of the city, is apparent from ver. 10. It is rather the armed men, who were at the disposal of Gedaliah as governor, who are intended and who, whether permanently or temporarily, were strengthened by Chaldean soldiers.

Vers. 4-9. **And it came to pass ... with the slain.** Ishmael knew how to guard against the murder of Gedaliah being known immediately outside the city. He evidently intended to use Mizpah as a trap. So it happened that on the second day the approach of a troop of men was announced, who from a distance presented the appearance of a peaceful caravan, and from the burdens they bore one promising booty. They came from Shechem, Shiloh and Samaria. The LXX. read Σαλήμ, and HITZIG, as well as GRAF, is disposed to give this reading the preference, since thus a more correct order (according to geographical position we should have Shiloh, Shechem, Samaria) and vicinage of the cities is obtained. Salem would then be the place mentioned in Gen. xxxiii. 18, 19 as near Shechem (comp. HENZON, R.-Enc., XIII. S. 326). But the authority of the LXX. is, as is well known, unreliable. Shiloh also lies so near the road that travellers proceeding from it might meet with those coming from Samaria and Shechem. As to the order, as this in itself was a matter of indifference, a more external circumstance may well have suggested it: the word of one syllable is placed first, then that of two syllables, and of these again that of five consonants after that of three.

From 2 Chron. xxxiv. 9 it is apparent, that at the time of Josiah there was still in the cities of the ten tribes a "remnant of Israel," which contributed to the house of the Lord in Jerusalem, which appears as a resumption and continuance of the co-operation, which even in the reign of Hezekiah the pious Israelites had afforded in establishing the worship of Jehovah in Jerusalem (2 Chron. xxx. and xxxi.) These men came as mourners over the destruction of the sanctuary (comp. on xvi. ℓ: xlvii. 5; xlviii. 37) with gifts of meat and incense offerings, as the beasts necessary for burnt offerings could not well be brought from so great a distance. Doubtless the feast of Tabernacles, occurring in the Seventh month (Lev. xxiii. 34; Numb. xxix. 12; Deut. xvi. 13) was the occasion of their coming. Although they could not hope to find altar and priests in the holy place, they would still deposit their gifts there in order at least to manifest their devotion. GROTIUS calls attention here to the expression of Papinian (Instit. de rerum divisione, § Sacrae): "Locus, in quo ædes sacræ sunt ædificatæ etiam diruto ædificio sacer adhuc manet."

What was the motive of Ishmael's act? It is supposed by some that he feared to be betrayed, and therefore killed those strangers whom he could not drag away with him. But he only needed them not to admit them into Mizpah. GRAF sees in the deed an act of revenge which Ishmael took on these Israelites for the murder of his relatives and associates in rank (lii. 10), because these, living with heathens, had for a long time been Assyrian and Chaldean subjects. But these Israelites, coming with all the tokens of deepest sorrow, had shown themselves to be well-disposed towards the Jews, and it is inconceivable how Ishmael could have chosen them for the objects of his vengeance. I think he had simple robbery in view. For after this Ishmael, who was evidently a rough and wild man, had from personal jealousy, to the disadvantage of his people and in the political interest of his Ammonitish protection, assassinated the noble Gedaliah, he must either attempt to maintain himself in the latter's position or flee. When he quickly, before the matter has become known, murders a peaceful caravan of temple pilgrims, and spares only a few of them, who offer him treasures, and at last drags with him as captives the whole *turba imbellis* from Mizpah into slavery, he shows himself to be simply a robber.

Ver. 6. **Weeping all along as he went** [lit.: in going and weeping]. LXX.: αὐτοὶ ἐπορεύοντο καὶ ἔκλαιον. They then refer the words to the eighty. HITZIG and GRAF find this reference quite in order. Why should Ishmael weep? We might suppose it to be perfectly clear that Ishmael wept to deceive those people, in order to present the appearance of a person who from internal grief was not thinking of worldly things at all, much less of robbery and murder. HITZIG and GRAF however deny that Ishmael wept at all, because he had no ostensible reason for doing so. HITZIG says he would not weep for the fate of the temple, since he did not in them meet again old friends for the first time since its destruction, he did not go to meet them in ceremony as notorious temple-pilgrims, nor was he himself on the way to Jerusalem. GRAF says if he had wept like the pilgrims over Jerusalem, this would have been unnatural behaviour for one who was sojourning in the vicinity of the city. But are these reasons? It is scarcely credible that they can be intended seriously. If in those days of the most tremendous national calamity a train of Jewish pilgrims, bearing themselves all the signs of grief, meet another Jew weeping, about what will they suppose that he is weeping? Will they not most naturally suppose that he accords with the general mourning of the country? There can be no doubt this was the supposition which Ishmael wished to produce in the pilgrims' minds. There may have been one and another among them who regarded the weeping comer as not a partaker in the general grief, it sufficed for Ishmael that he was generally regarded as such. Murder and robbery are not expected from such a person. Ishmael tried in this way to deceive them. If they had mistrusted him his project must have failed or be must have tried other expedients. HITZIG and GRAF fail to convince us that they would have more readily believed a person who was not mourning, but who invited them to Gedaliah in a tone usual at other times. GRAF also urges that it was not necessary for Ishmael to shed tears the whole way, even though it was a short one, which however is implied in the grammatical construction (comp. on this point NAEGELSB *Gr.*, § 93, *b*, *Anm.*) To this it may be replied that Ishmael could not know how sharp-sighted any one of the eighty might be, so that he would rather begin to weep too early than too late, and consequently traversed the greatest part of the distance, perhaps the whole way from the gate, weeping. **Come to Gedaliah**. Why Gedaliah invites them he does not say. Many reasons might be imagined: Gedaliah might wish to show them hospitality, or to accompany them, or to impart some injunction or warning in his gubernatorial capacity. At any rate he was a powerful man, whose requisition was not to be ignored. They therefore followed. But in the midst of the city, at any rate in a place where eleven men sufficed to close up both their advance and their retreat, in some narrow lane, Ishmael fell upon them. Ten of them evidently perceived at once why this was done. They saw that it was robbery on which he was intent. They therefore promise him מַטְמֹנִים, *i. e.*, *promptuaria subterranea* (from טָמַן *abscondidit*), such being used from the earliest times in many countries of Asia and Africa for the concealment and preservation of the fruits of the earth. Comp. ROSENMUELLER *ad. l.*, and GESENIUS *Thesaurus*, s. v.: WINER, *R.-W.-B.*, s. v. *Ernte*,—**By the hand of Gedaliah**. The words are difficult. The explanations: by the fault of Gedaliah, on Gedaliah's account, (*i. e.*, as friends of Gedaliah); *coram Gedalja*, *i. e.*, together with Gedaliah, *una cum Gedalja*, *in potestate Gedalja* (*i. e.*, as *imperio G. subjectos*) are all ungrammatical. The normal significance of the words seems to me to afford an appropriate meaning. Ishmael had made use of Gedaliah's name, to allure them to destruction. He had called to them: Come to Gedaliah (ver. 6), and on the authority of this name they had followed him. Thus we may well say that Ishmael killed them by means of Gedaliah. Of course the person of Gedaliah was not the instrument of execution, but his name was the means by which their wills were determined in the intended direction.—**Was that which Asa**, etc. We read in 1 Ki. xv. 22 that king Asa, with the material of which Baasha had fortified Ramah built Geba-Benjamin and Mizpah. This pit appears to have been part of these works of fortification, but as to its destination we are not informed. Was it a cistern, a ditch, or a mere pit, which might defend a narrow approach, and in ordinary times was bridged over? HITZIG assumes the latter. But as GRAF remarks, the pit appears according to ver. 7 to have been situated in the interior of the city. It cannot have been a ditch, such never being called בּוֹר. It was then probably a large and deep cistern (Comp. ROSENMUELLER on ver. 7), which was built to afford water to the fort, and which accordingly might be reckoned among the means of defence, with which Asa provided the city for fear of Baasha. Whether the pit, which is here spoken of, is identical with the great *bore* that is in Sechu, 1 Sam xix. 21, and with the ὄρεαρ μέγα 1 Macc. vii. 19, must be left undecided.

Vers. 10-15. **Then Ishmael .. to the Ammonites**. The intimidated, and probably in addition unarmed people, among them the king's daughters (probably in the wider sense of princesses, as "king's son," xxxvi. 26; xxxviii. 6),

Ishmael carried away captive, either to use them as slaves or to sell them. Meanwhile however the Jewish band-captains had received intelligence of the events in Mizpah. They hasten thither with their people, and encounter Ishmael by the "great water" near Gibeon. Gibeon is only half a league distant from Mizpah in a northeasterly direction. Till Ishmael had done with the eighty pilgrims and the gathering of the rest of the population prior to their departure, so much time might pass that the captains could hurry up and almost reach him in Mizpah. The "great waters" of Gibeon are a pond. Comp. 2 Sam. ii. 13. ROBINSON (II. 351, 2) recognizes Gibeon in the village El-Jib. [Comp. THOMSON. *The Land and the Book*, II., p. 546.—S. R. A.] At the east of the village he found a beautiful fountain and the remains of a large water-tank. All Ishmael's prisoners left him at once to attach themselves to Johanan. Ishmael escaped with eight men. It seems then that there was a fight, in which he lost two of his ten men.

Vers. 16-18. **Then took Johanan . . . in the land**. It cannot be denied that there is some difficulty in the relative sentence from **whom he had recovered** to **son of Ahikam**. Especially troublesome is **from Mizpah**. Also the singular הֵשִׁיב as well as the sentence after **he had slain**, *etc.* (we should expect: after they had driven Ishmael off) are striking: so too the relative sentences **whom he had recovered from Ishmael** and **whom he had brought again from Gibeon**, as they both state the same fact. HITZIG supposes that "whom Ishmael carried away captive" should be read after ver. 14. Certainly the connection thus becomes clear and intelligible. And as the sentence **whom he had recovered from Ishmael** stands directly between **whom Ishmael carried away captive from Mizpah**, ver. 14, and **whom he had brought again from Gibeon**, *fin.* ver. 16, it is quite conceivable that an exchange may have taken place.—**Mighty men of war**. It is evident from these words that the great mass of the Jewish people still left were assembled in Mizpah, comp. xl. 7-11.—It is the more strange that Ishmael could take all these captive with ten men. Were they unarmed? Were they surprised? Did Ishmael terrify them with threats, by making a false show of Ammonitish help at hand?—However this may be, Johanan betakes himself with all these to a more southern *rendezvous* on the road to Egypt. This according to the Keri is called the "habitation (hospice, caravanserai) of Chimham [Kimham]," who according to 2 Sam. xix. 37-40 was the son of the Barzillai who purveyed so well for David and his army on their flight. Why did an inn or caravanserai in the vicinity of Bethlehem bear the name of Chimham? We do not know.—This point was to serve as a meeting-place. There were still single bands or individuals scattered through the country. Preparations had also to be made for the march through the desert. The vengeance of the Chaldeans, in spite of the surely provable innocence of the Jews, appeared however so certain, and the fear of it was so great, that the resolution to flee to Egypt was already fixed, before they asked the prophet's advice. Hence this act was a mere farce.

6. *The hypocritical inquiry.*

XLII. 1-6.

1   Then all the captains of the forces, and[1] Johanan the son of Kareah, and Jezaniah the son of Hoshaiah, and all the people from the least unto the greatest, came
2   near, and said unto Jeremiah the prophet, Let, we beseech thee, our supplication be accepted before thee, and pray for us unto the LORD [Jehovah] thy God, *even* for all this remnant; (for we are left *but* a few of many,[2] as thine eyes do behold us):
3   that the LORD [Jehovah] thy God may shew us the way wherein we may walk, and the thing that we may do.
4   Then Jeremiah the prophet said unto them, I have heard[3] *you;* behold, I will pray unto the LORD [Jehovah] your God according to your words; and it shall come to pass, *that* whatever thing the LORD [Jehovah] shall answer you, I will de-
5   clare *it* unto you; I will keep nothing back from you. Then they said to Jeremiah, The LORD be a true[4] and faithful witness between us, if we do not even according to
6   all things for the which the LORD thy God shall send[5] thee to us. Whether *it be* good, or whether *it be* evil[6] we will obey the voice of the LORD our God, to whom we[7] send thee; that it may be well with us, when[8] we obey the voice of the LORD our God.

TEXTUAL AND GRAMMATICAL.

[1] Ver. 1.—The וְ before יוֹחָנָן as in xl. 8 [=even].

[2] Ver. 2.—On הַרְבֵּה comp. OLSH., S. 358 and 583.

⁴ Ver. 4.—שְׁמַע־נָא involves the sense of hearing and granting, and is at the same time the token of the acceptance and approval of the petition. It corresponds nearly to the German "*Gut!*" [Eng.: good!]
⁵ Ver. 5.—The expression יָד אֶת כֹּה is found besides only in Prov. xiv. 25 coll. ver. 5, עַר נֶאֱמָן Ps. lxxxix. 38; Isal. viii. 2.
⁵ Ver. 5.—On שָׁלַח with a double accusative, comp. NAEGELSB. *Gr.*, § 6ʹ, 2, c.
⁶ Ver. 6.—To אִם טוֹב וְאִם רָע we are not to supply הַדָּבָר for then we must have הוּא after רָע. Much rather is the whole sentence in apposition to the following קוֹל, as in Eccles. xii. 14 to the preceding יַעֲשֶׂה.
⁷ Ver. 6.—וַאֲנַ֫חְנוּ. The form occurs only here in the Old Testament. Comp. OLSH., § 93, *b*, 5. It is indeed possible that it was not incorrectly put into the mouth of the people, for the form usual in post-biblical Hebrew may have been a popular expression even at that time.
⁸ Ver. 6.—כִּי is here necessarily *because*, not *if*. For there is no question about their obeying. They will obey, but expect prosperity from this obedience as such, apart from the immediate result of the step commanded them. Comp xxiv. 7.

EXEGETICAL AND CRITICAL.

The people request the prophet to inquire of the Lord what is to be done (vers. 1-3); Jeremiah promises to do so (ver. 4). The people therefore solemnly promise punctual obedience to all that the prophet shall disclose to them as the commands of their God (vers. 5, 6).

Vers. 1-3. **Then all ... that we may do**. Jezaniah is here called the son of Hoshaiah; in xl. 8 he is called the son of the Maachathite, in xliii. 2 Azariah is named as the son of Hoshaiah. There must then have either been two Jezaniahs and two Hoshaiahs, or there is an error in the text. The LXX. has in xli. 1 and xliii. 2 Ἀζαρίος υἱὸς Μαασαίου. There is thus the possibility that here Jezaniah is written by mistake for Azariah.—These leaders and the whole people with them address to the prophet the humble petition (comp. rems. ou xxxvi. 7; xxxvii. 20), that he will address to Jehovah in their behalf, the small remnant of the great nation, a prayer for instruction concerning the path to be taken.

Vers. 4-6. **Then Jeremiah ... our God**. When the people express their readiness to submit to the direction of Jehovah, however this may turn out, but afterwards (xliii. 2-7) rebel so decidedly against this direction, their declaration here must be explained either as hypocrisy or on the supposition that the question was not of remaining in the country, but there was doubt only as to the direction of their flight. They appeal to the Lord to appear as a true and faithful witness against them, if they do not submit to the divine indication expected through the prophet. The Lord however is, as is presupposed in every oath, at the same time Witness and Judge.

7. *The unwelcome answer*.

XLII. 7-22.

7 And it came to pass after ten days, that [*or* that after ten days] the word of the
8 Lord [Jehovah] came unto Jeremiah. Then called he Johanan the son of Kareah, and all the captains of the forces [band-leaders] which *were* with him, and all the
9 people from the least even to the greatest, and said unto them, Thus saith the Lord [Jehovah] the God of Israel, unto whom ye sent me to present your suppli-
10 cation before him; If ye will still abide¹ in this land, then will I build you, and not pull *you* down; and I will plant you, and not pluck *you* up: for I repeat me
11 of the evil that I have done unto you. Be not afraid of the king of Babylon, of whom ye are afraid; be not afraid of him, saith the Lord: for I *am* with you to
12 save you, and to deliver you from his hand. And I will shew mercies unto [prepare pity for]² you, that he may have mercy upon you, and cause you to return³
13 to your own land But if ye say, We will not dwell in this land, neither obey the
14 voice of the Lord your God, Saying, No; but we will go into the land of Egypt, where [that]⁴ we shall see no war, nor hear the sound of the trumpet, nor have
15 hunger of [for]⁵ bread; and there will we dwell: and now⁶ therefore hear the word of the Lord, ye remnant of Judah; Thus saith the Lord of hosts [Jehovah Zebaoth] the God of Israel; If ye wholly set your faces to enter into Egypt,
16 and go to sojourn there; then it shall come to pass *that* the sword, which ye feared, shall overtake you there in the land of Egypt; and the famine, whereof ye were
17 afraid, shall follow close after you there in Egypt; and there ye shall die. So shall it be with all the men that set their faces to go into Egypt to sojourn there; they shall die by the sword, by the famine, and by the pestilence: and none of them

CHAP. XLII. 7-22.   343

18 shall remain or escape from the evil that I will bring upon them. For thus saith the LORD of hosts [Jehovah Zebaoth] the God of Israel; As mine anger and my fury hath been poured forth upon the inhabitants of Jerusalem; so shall my fury be poured forth upon you, when ye shall enter into Egypt; and ye shall be an execration, and an astonishment [horror] and a curse, and a reproach; and ye shall
19 see this place no more. The LORD hath said concerning you [Jehovah hath spoken to you] O ye remnant of Judah; Go ye not into Egypt: know certainly that I
20 have admonished [warned]⁶ you this day. For ye dissembled in your hearts [deceived yourselves],⁹ when¹⁰ ye sent me unto the Lord your God, saying, Pray for us unto the LORD our God; and according unto all that the LORD our God shall
21 say, so declare unto us and we will do it. And now I have this day declared it to you; but ye have not obeyed the voice of the LORD your God, nor any thing¹¹
22 for the which he hath sent me unto you. Now therefore know certainly that ye shall die by the sword, by the famine, and by the pestilence, in the place whither ye desire to go and to sojourn.

TEXTUAL AND GRAMMATICAL.

¹ Ver. 10.—שׁוּב is evidently abbreviated from יָשׁוֹב, since the sense renders the derivation from שׁוּב impossible. CHB. D. MICHAELIS and ROSENMUELLER indeed translate, si revertendo illuc mansneritis in hac terra. But then the Inf. abs. would be placed after the finite verb. Comp. NAEGELSB. Gr., § 93, e.—This apocopation of ו is certainly unexampled in this form, but most readily assumed in a verb פ׳׳י according to the analogy of the Inf. constr. and Imperfect Comp. besides OLSN., § 89; 170, a, Anm.; 245, h, Anm.
² Ver. 12.—From the following sentence it is evident that רִי נָתַן here does not mean "to show compassion," but "to prepare pity, to procure it on the part of another." Comp. Gen. xliii. 14.
³ Ver. 12.—וְהֵשִׁיב. LXX., Vulg., Syr., J. D. MICHAELIS, HITZIG, EWALD, GRAF, would read, הוֹשִׁיב, but this would not agree with the following אֶל. Comp. also EXEG. and CRIT. rems. [BLAYNEY: would settle you in, etc.—S. R. A.]
⁴ Ver. 14.—אֲשֶׁר = that. Comp. Gen. xi. 7; Exod. xx. 23; Deut. iv. 40; vi. 3.
⁵ Ver. 14.—לִלְחֹם. From Am. viii. 11 we perceive that the meaning of the expression is, to hunger for or after bread.
⁶ Ver. 15.—With וְעַתָּה begins the apodosis (paratactically introduced. Comp. NAEGELSB. Gr., § 110, 2) to וְאִם in ver. 13.
⁷ Ver. 16.—וְהָיְתָה has this form by attraction, as well as וִיהִי ver. 17. Comp. EWALD, § 345, b.
⁸ Ver. 19.—הֵעִיד, literally to bring in witnesses, then to adduce testimony (according to the directly causative mode of speaking, on which comp. NAEGELSB. Gr., § 18, 3). From the idea of giving testimony is developed that of earnest solemn address, admonition, warning. Comp. Ps. l. 7; Deut. viii. 19; Jer. xi. 7.
⁹ Ver. 20.—הִתְעָה is also to be regarded as directly causative = errationem fecit (GESEN.) Comp. Prov. x. 17. It is therefore doubtful whether בְּ indicates the object or the place. The word is at least not found elsewhere with בְּ of the person. The prophet might well say, ye have erred in your souls, i. e., in your volition and thought, and have thus taken a false direction, while ye supposed ye were on the right track. The Chethibh הִתְעֵתֶם is evidently a mistake. The Keri is correct הִתְעֵיתֶם. [NOYES strangely renders, "ye err to your ruin."—S. R. A.]
¹⁰ Ver. 20.—כִּי = when. Comp. Jud. ii. 18; Ps. xxxii. 3; Ezek. iii. 19.
¹¹ Ver. 21.—וּלְכֹל may mean, and indeed with respect to all, etc. Since, however, only one point is treated of, the emphatic expression of a multiplicity of points is remarkable. I therefore think that the word stands in simple parallelism to the first clause, while שָׁמַע is construed only with לְ instead of with בְּ, a construction which (apart from לִקְוֹל שָׁמַע, Gen. iii. 17; Jud. ii. 20; Ps. lviii. 6) is peculiar to the later idiom: Neh. ix. 29; xiii. 27; 2 Chron. x. 16; Dan. i. 14; Lev. xxvi. 21. A double disobedience is thus declared against Jehovah and against the prophet.

EXEGETICAL AND CRITICAL.

After ten days the prophet receives answer from the Lord, which he immediately communicates to the leaders, and to the whole people (vers. 7, 8). If they remain in the country they shall have nothing to fear from the Chaldeans, but the Lord will so direct the heart of the king that he will aid in their restoration (vers. 9-12). If, however, they do not remain in the country, but from fear of the Chaldeans flee to Egypt, they shall perish there by the same calamities, which they thought to escape by flight (vers. 13-18). Finally the prophet urgently admonishes them not to despise this warning, although he knows only too well, that it was pure self-deception when they inquired of the Lord by Him, since they had already resolved not to obey the Lord's command. Well, they shall also know, that they will come to their ruin in the country, whither their desires lead them (vers. 19-22.)

Vers. 7-12. **And it came to pass . . . your own land.** The opinion of HITZIG and GRAF, that Jeremiah used the ten days in procuring information and arriving at a clear and firm conviction, is in accordance with modern science but not with history. The prophet really received the answer to his prayer for divine direction (comp. ver. 4; xxxii. 16) not until after ten days. It is significant that he received it on the tenth day (comp. Ezek. iii. 16), although we cannot stop here to investigate the ground of this signification (comp. [on symbolical numbers] HERZOG. *Real-Enc.*, XVIII., *S.* 381). **On to present,** etc comp. xxxviii. 26.—**On for I repent,** etc. comp.

xxvi. 3.—**Cause you to return.** When we consider, that the prophet has in view not only the return of those who had been already carried away into exile, but may also with perfect correctness regard those as such who have assembled at Bethlehem and prepared to leave their home, turning their back upon it, the alteration [cause to dwell] proposed in the text seems unnecessary. It was not unpatriotic policy, nor indolence, nor selfishness, nor any view based on human foresight, which caused the prophet to speak thus. For, humanly considered, there was nothing left for the Jews but flight. The hope for further indulgence on the part of the Chaldean king must seem like madness. The prophet, however, does not reckon alone with human factors. He is the organ of God, to whom nothing is impossible (xxxii. 26 sqq.), and who especially has the hearts of kings in His hand, and turns them whithersoever He will (Prov. xxi. 1).

Vers. 13-18. **But if ye say ... this place no more.** The words from **neither obey**, ver. 13, to **dwell**, ver. 14, are a parenthesis.—**Sound of the trumpet.** Comp. iv. 19, 21.—**Remnant,** etc. Comp. xli. 16; xlii. 2, 19; xliii. 5.—**Wholly set your faces.** Comp. ver. 17; xliv. 12; 2 Kings xii. 18.—By sword, famine and pestilence (comp. xiv. 12; xxi. 9; xxvii. 8, 13; xxix. 18; xxxii. 3 b; xxxviii. 2; xliv. 13), will the disobedient perish in Egypt, and not a single individual will escape (comp. xliv. 14; Lam. ii. 22; Josh. viii. 22). As on Jerusalem, so also on them will the fury of the Lord be poured out (vii. 20; 2 Chron. xxxiv. 21); they shall become an object of cursing, horror and derision (comp. xxiv. 9; xxv. 18; xliv. 22, etc.), and never return to their native land (comp. rems. on vii. 3).

Vers. 19-22. **Jehovah hath ... to sojourn.** In a very earnest closing speech the prophet sets forth that the Lord Himself has spoken to the people. Then he reminds them that they have been warned. They cannot then have the excuse of ignorance. In the third place the prophet discovers to them their self-delusion. They perhaps imagined that they honestly desired the right, when they commissioned him to present their petition before God. What, however, is opposed to this honest intention easily appears to them to be incorrect, and therefore justifying them in resistance. The prophet therefore desires to convince them that they did not honestly wish to do the right. It was self-deception, when they declared themselves ready to obey unconditionally the divine command.—In the fourth place, the prophet tells them before they had opened their mouth to reply, what was now passing in their minds, viz., that they had formed the fixed resolution not to obey the faithfully reported direction of Jehovah, in spite of their solemn declaration given in vers. 5, 6.—In the fifth place, finally, he proclaims to them, that the very place, to which an irresistible longing attracts them, will be their destruction. He announces this apodictically, because he knows that they will inevitably do what will bring them to this.

---

8. *The Flight to Egypt.*

XLIII. 1-7.

1 And it came to pass, *that* when Jeremiah had made an end[1] of speaking unto all
   the people all the words of the LORD their God, for which the LORD their God had
2 sent him to them, *even* all these words, Then spake Azariah the son of Hoshaiah,
   and Johanan the son of Kareah, and all the proud[2] men, saying[3] unto Jeremiah,
   Thou speakest falsely: the LORD our God hath not sent thee to say, Go not into
3 Egypt to sojourn there: but Baruch the son of Neriah setteth thee on [has excited
   thee][4] against us, for to deliver us into the hand of the Chaldeans, that they might
4 put us to death, and carry us away captives into Babylon. So Johanan the son of
   Kareah, and all the captains of the forces [band-leaders], and all the people,
5 obeyed not the voice of the LORD, to dwell in the land of Judah. But Johanan
   the son of Kareah, and all the captains of the forces, took all the remnant of Judah,
   that were returned from all nations, whither they had been driven, to dwell in the
6 land of Judah; *even* men, and women, and children, and the king's daughters,
   and every person that Nebuzar-adan the captain of the guard [halberdiers] had
   left with Gedaliah the son of Ahikam the son of Shaphan, and Jeremiah the pro-
7 phet, and Baruch the son of Neriah. So they came into the land of Egypt: for
   they obeyed not the voice of the LORD: thus came they *even* to Tahpanhes.

TEXTUAL AND GRAMMATICAL.

[1] Ver. 1.—כְּכַלּוֹת as in xxvi. 8.

[2] Ver. 2.—הַזֵּדִים. The word occurs here only in Jeremiah. The LXX. omits it, and reads instead καὶ πάντες οἱ ἀλλογενεῖς, xliii. 17, reading הַזָּרִים for הַזֵּדִים. The reverse in xviii. 14; li. 2.

CHAP. XLIII. 8-13.   345

* Ver. 2.—אֹמְרִים. Instead of לֵאמֹר, because the words spoken do not follow immediately. Comp. xiv. 15; xxiii. 17.
4 Ver. 3.—מסית. Comp. xxxviii. 22; Isa. xxxvi. 18.

EXEGETICAL AND CRITICAL.

On the communication, which Jeremiah made in the name of Jehovah to the Jews, these declared, that they regard it, not as a message from their God, but as the result of incitement by Baruch, who is friendly to the Chaldeans (vers. 1-3). Thereupon they, with the whole mass of the remaining population, including Jeremiah and Baruch, commence their journey to Egypt, where, on their arrival, they settle first in Tahpanhes (vers. 4-7).

Vers. 1-3. **And it came to pass ... into Babylon.** The phrase all these words indicates that the words written in ch. xlii. are an exact rendering of the prophet's verbal communication. Comp. li. 60.—On Azariah, the son of Hoshaiah. Comp. rems. on xlii. 1.—On what facts this charge against Baruch was supported, it is difficult to perceive. From this book we learn only that Baruch was a faithful adherent and servant of the prophet. It was doubtless merely the circumstance that Baruch, to the envy of many, was the most intimate of all the Jews with Jeremiah, which gave a handle to the accusation.

Vers. 4-7. **So Johanan ... Tahpanhes.—All the remnant of Judah.** Those who had returned from the dispersion are mentioned first, probably because among them there were few or none of the "poor of the land" (xl. 7). It seems surprising that in ver. 6 a specification follows which, on account of the mention of the **king's daughter**, does not correspond to the general statement in ver. 5 b. But the specification concludes with **children**, and with king's daughters commences the description of the second division of the remnant of Judah. Besides, those who had returned, viz., the king's daughters and all the other souls are mentioned. If we consider that in ver. 5 a, the heads of those who had remained in the country are named as the subjects of the deportation, it is intelligible that besides these the princesses were the most eminent personages in this category (comp. xli. 10).—**Every person.** Comp. Josh. x. 28. The expression is so general that it comprehends all the other members of the remnant of Judah (comp. xli. 16). —On Tahpanhes comp. rems. on ver. 8.

9. Jeremiah in Tahpanhes.

XLIII. 8-13.

8, 9 Then came the word of the LORD unto Jeremiah in Tahpanhes, saying, Take great stones in thine hand, and hide them in the clay [mortar]¹ in the brick-kiln, which *is* at the entry of Pharaoh's house in Tahpanhes, in the sight of the men of
10 Judah; and say unto them, Thus saith the LORD of hosts [Jehovah Zebaoth], the God of Israel; Behold, I will send and take Nebuchadrezzar, the king of Babylon, my servant, and will set his throne upon these stones that I have hid; and he shall
11 spread his royal pavilion² over them. And when he cometh,³ he shall [he shall come and] unite the land of Egypt, *and deliver* such as *are* for death to death; and such as *are* for captivity to captivity: and such as *are* for the sword to the sword.
12 And I will kindle a fire in the houses of the gods of Egypt; and he shall burn them, and carry them away captives: and he shall array himself with the land of Egypt, as a shepherd putteth on his garment; and he shall go forth from thence
13 in peace. He shall break also the images [statues] of Bethshemesh [the house of the sun], that is in the land of Egypt; and the houses of the gods of the Egyptians shall be burned with fire.

TEXTUAL AND GRAMMATICAL.

1 Ver. 9.—מֶלֶט is ἅπ. λεγ. The analogies milát, molto (Syr.), μάλθα, malta, are vouchers for the meaning of "mortar, cement, clay."
2 Ver. 10.—The meaning of שַׁפְרִיר is doubtful. The word occurs here only. HITZIG, with J. D. MICHAELIS, refers to *suphra* (Arab. for *corium orbiculare, quod solo insternitur*), which agrees with *nat'* (Arab. the leathern veil of the judge of life and death). According to the text the throne is to be first placed on the stones, and then the שַׁפְרִיר stretched above it. Is a veil spread over a throne? And is not שָׁטַח the technical term for the spreading of a tent? The meaning "pavilion," seems then most suitable, it being, however, still doubtful whether it be so named *a splendore* (שָׁבַר, *nituit*, שִׁפְרָה, שִׁפְרָה, *splendor, pulchritudo*), or *a cavitate* (comp. שׁוֹפָר, *tuba*, שִׁפְרָה, Pi. Job xxvi. 13?) ["The Keri proposes שַׁפְרִיר as the proper form

which is, indeed, that in which nouns, with the third radical germinated, most frequently appear. Comp. סָגְרִיר, Prov.
xxvii. 15." HENDERSON.—S. R. A.]
³ Ver. 11.—וּבָאָה). Chethibh וּבָאָה. The Keri would unnecessarily strike out the suffix. Comp. rems. on xi. 15; xxvii. 8; xxxi. 2; xli. 3; xlviii. 44.

EXEGETICAL AND CRITICAL.

In Tahpanhes Jeremiah receives the command to hide great stones in the clay of a brick-kiln, opposite the royal palace in the sight of the Jews, and to tell them that the Lord will bring king Nebuchadnezzar to Egypt, and that he will erect his throne and stretch his tent on these stones (vers. 8-10). Then will Nebuchadnezzar visit the land of Egypt with all the terrors of war, burn the idol-temples, subjugate the land completely to his sway, and depart in peace (vers. 11 and 12). It is especially emphasized at the close that Nebuchadnezzar will break in pieces the statues of Beth-shemesh and burn up the idol-temples (ver. 13).

Vers. 8, 9. **Then came . . . men of Judah.** When we compare the larger superscriptions, xl. 1 and xliv. 1, it is evident that the first introduces the events after the deportation, the second the occurrences in Egypt. Hence it might seem as if this passage were not in place, or as if the superscription, which stands in xliv. 1, belonged in this place, xliii. 8. But it is evident from xliv. 1 that the passage, which begins with this superscription, is to narrate what happened to the Jews already established in Egypt (**who dwelt in the land**), while the event related here is, as it were, a part of the journey. For Tahpanhes (comp. ii. 16) is the eastern boundary city of Egypt, situated on the Pelusian branch of the Nile. Here Jeremiah, by a symbolical act, was to set before the eyes of the Jews, how impossible it is to escape from the Lord (comp. the prophet Jonah), and that by their removal from Egypt they had only come from bad to worse. Thus clear as is the meaning of the symbolical act in general, the definition of the details is still difficult. The word **brick-kiln** (כִּלְבֵּן) occurs, besides here, only twice in the Old Testament: 2 Sam. xii. 31, and Nah. iii. 14. In the first passage it is related that David caused them to pass under saws, harrows and axes of iron. It then continues, "and made them pass through the brick-kiln" (the Chethibh has, doubtless incorrectly, כְּלְבֵּן, which is no word). When we recall the frequently occurring phrase "made his son to pass through the fire" (comp. 2 Ki. xvi. 3; xxi. 6, etc.), we cannot doubt that a similar cruel mode of death is spoken of here also. As such also appears the putting into heated brick-ovens (לִבְנָה, brick, from which the denominative verb לָבַן, to make bricks, Exod. v. 7, 14). In the second passage, Nah. iii. 14, the Assyrians are ironically called upon to "repair the fortifications, go into the mud and tread the mortar, and repair the brick-kiln." EICHHORN, HITZIG and GRAF think it incredible that a brick-kiln can have stood immediately opposite the royal palace. Hence HITZIG takes the word in the sense of a projection of tiles or brick-work under the threshold, a stone-floor probably cemented over. Besides the analogies in Arabic, the meanings of כִּלְבֵּן in later Hebrew (*area, massa, tabula, quadrata.* Comp. BUXTORF, *Lex. Chald.*, p. 1120) favor this rendering. On the other hand, as GRAF himself correctly remarks, it is equally incredible that Jeremiah could have torn up the pavement before the gate of the king's palace, and inserted large stones. I am now quite of NEUMANN's opinion that we are to regard this brick-kiln not as permanently, but only temporarily, present.

The brick-yard need not have been in the court of the royal palace and directly before the doors of the building. It may have been situated opposite the gate of the outer court or avenue to the palace. The place may have been designated to the prophet on account of this position, and perhaps also because it was the place, from which the material was taken for the extension of the palace now building, as NEUMANN [comp. also HENDERSON] supposes. In this case the thought would be expressed that Egypt, to whose protection the Jews had fled, was only weak, fragile clay. Since the prophet was to *hide* the stones *in the clay*, it is evident, that he did not place them visibly on the surface, and therefore set them up on the walls of the brick-kiln. **Brick-kiln** must be, therefore, understood as *pars pro toto.* The whole place is called כִּלְבֵּן, not merely the oven. Jeremiah is to hide the large stones in clay belonging to this kiln. He is to lay the foundation for a future ideal building. In place of the weak clay, which signifies Egypt, the Lord lays the foundation stones of a power, which He intends to found, the bearer of which will be His servant (ver. 10), or the organ of His will. It is a fact, still hidden in the womb of the future, that Egypt will groan under the foot of the Babylonian conqueror; but the stones guarantee this fact. Men of Judah were present as witnesses (ver. 9), when they were laid. The significance of the stones is disclosed to these witnesses. The memory remained; the word of the Lord was pledged. On the fulfilment comp. the remarks on xliv. 29, 30.

Vers. 10-13. **And say unto them . . . burn with fire.** On **Behold, I will send**, etc., comp. xxv. 9.—The Lord Himself has hidden the stones, and in so far the prophet was only an instrument. On these stones Nebuchadnezzar shall one day erect his throne and stretch his tent.—HITZIG thinks that the erection of a tent would not be threatening, or dangerous; on the contrary, it would be only a matter of curiosity. It seems to me, however, that Nebuchadnezzar's tent, erected before the royal palace in Tahpanhes, is dangerous enough, signifying neither more nor less than the conquest of Egypt by Nebuchadnezzar. — **Such as are for death.** Comp. rems. on xv. 2. The sense of the expression is, that not only one kind of destruction will come upon Egypt, but many, and that each one

CHAP. XLIII. 8-13.   347

will also really devour the victims apportioned to it.—**Away captives**, *viz.*, the idols. Comp. rems. on xlviii. 7.—**And he shall array**, *etc.* Commentators have frequently, and as it seems to me, quite unnecessarily, stumbled over this expression. How does a shepherd put on his garment? In general like any other person, but there is this difference, that in doing so the shepherd has regard to no one, because no one sees him. He therefore puts on his garment entirely at his own whim and convenience. So according to his own pleasure, without the slightest regard to others, will Nebuchadnezzar deal with conquered Egypt. After he has thus made Egypt his own property, he will depart in peace, without any one being able to detain or harass him or rob him of his booty.—Ver. 13 is surprising. The discourse seemed to have concluded with ver. 12. For what is there to report of Nebuchadnezzar's doings in Egypt, when his departure is already announced? Further, the second clause of the verse is tautological. Comp. **burn them**, ver. 12. Finally the addition **that is in the land of Egypt** is very surprising, for did Jeremiah, writing in Egypt, need to say this? Hence not merely three words (in the original text), but the whole verse, might be suspected. If, however, these words originated with the rest, then by Beth-shemesh must be meant not the temple of the sun at Heliopolis, but this city itself. The images of Beth-shemesh are above all the obelisks, of which there was an unlimited number in the city. Of the oldest, which however were not the largest (comp. Herod II., 111), one still remains in its place. Comp. Herzog, *R.-Enc.*, X., S. 610 sqq.

[The fulfilment of this prophecy is confirmed by Josephus (*Ant.* X., 9, 7). "It is also probable, that during the thirteen years in which some of Nebuchadnezzar's forces were engaged in the blockade of Tyre, he extended his campaign into Egypt; and there is a confirmation of this opinion in the narrative of Megasthenes in Strabo, XVI., 687. Joseph. *Ant.* X., 11, 1; *c. Apion.* I., 20. Abulfeda, *Hist. Ante-islam*, p. 102." Wordsworth.—S. R. A.]

DOCTRINAL AND ETHICAL.

1. On xl. 1-3. "Although the calamity, which has come upon Jerusalem, is great and terrible, God does not allow such evil to befal it that good will not result from it, as the Chaldean captain not obscurely intimates, that he has made a fair beginning in the knowledge of the true God. For he confesses, first, that the God of the prophet is a lord ; secondly, that He knows future things ; thirdly, that He causes His servants to proclaim these beforehand ; fourthly, that God has conducted the war and done everything ; fifthly, that He was displeased with the sinful manners of the people (among which idolatry was the worst); sixthly, that He has punished their disobedience to His word." Cramer.

2. On xl. 4. "The friendliness, shown to the prophet, appears to proceed from men, but it comes from God. For God's works are all made so that they are hidden among the creatures; for as He conceals His wisdom in the creation of heaven and earth, as He hides His kindness in the fruits of the earth, so also He disguises His help in the king of Babylon. For God executes His works now by rational and anon by irrational creatures. As when He fed Elijah by the widow and by the ravens and by the angels (1 Ki. xvii. 3 sqq.; 14 sqq. and xix. 5). For all are His instruments." Cramer.

3. On xl. 2, 3. "*Nebusaradan attestatione sua comprobat et confirmat veritatem ac certitudinem prædictionum prophetæ. Unde haud inscite colligi conjicique potest, quod Satrapa ille Babylonicus præditus fuerit agnitione veri Dei eâque salvatus. Et sic Deus subinde aliquos ex Magnatibus ad sui agnitionem et æternam salutem traducit* (Ps. lxviii.). *Potest istud exemplum ἐλεγκτικῶς obverti absoluto Calvinianorum decreto.*" Förster.

4. On xl. 5. "In this, that Jeremiah preferred remaining in the country to going to Babylon, it strikes me further—that 'a discreet man, who knows the world and his heart and the true interest of God's cause—is as much as possible contented, and does not think to better himself by going further. He is willing to remain at court unknown, and at any rate he would rather be taken away than go away.—The advice, which Solomon gives, is verified, 'Stand not in the place of great men.' We are a generation of the cross, and our symbol is 'an evil name and little understood.'" Zinzendorf.

5. On xl. 5. In Babylonia honor and a comfortable life invited the prophet, in Judea danger, dishonor and need in the desolated country. In Babylonia a respectable field of labor was opened to him among the great mass of his people, in Judea he had only rabble and *condottieri* about him. Jeremiah, however, was not a bad patriot, as many accused him of being. By remaining in Judea he showed that the import of his prophecies, apparently friendly to the Chaldeans and hostile to the Jews, had proceeded from the purest love to his people and his fatherland. Thus he imitated Moses, of whom it is written in Heb. xi. 25, that he chose rather to suffer affliction with the people of God than to enjoy the pleasures of sin for a season. The holy ground of the fatherland bound him to it, and in addition—if he went, who was to take spiritual oversight of the poor forsaken remnant, to proclaim the word of God and bestow on them consolation and admonition? Those who were in Babylon had Ezekiel. And could not the Lord raise up other prophets for them? So he remained with the sheep, who had no shepherd. Jeremiah had not sought his own through his whole life, nor did he here.

6. On xl. 7 sqq. "Human reason, and indeed nature shows, that in worldly government men cannot be without a head. For as the bees cannot be without a queen, or the sheep without a shepherd, so no large number of people can exist without a head and government. God has wisely ordered it, and we should be thankful for the authorities." Cramer.

7. On xl. 11 sqq. We may well perceive in this "remnant of Judah" a fulfilment of the prophecy in Isa. vi. 11 sqq.: "Then said I, Lord, how long? And he answered, Until the cities be wasted without inhabitant, and the houses without man, and the land be utterly desolate, and Jehovah have removed men far away, and

great is the forsaking in the midst of the land. And if a tenth remains in it, this again must be removed. Yet as the terebinth and the oak, in which when they are felled, a ground-stock still remains, so is its stock a holy scion."

8. On xl. 13 sqq. Gedaliah, in whom not only Nebuchadnezzar, but also his people, had confidence, must have been a noble man, to whom it was difficult to think evil of his neighbor. "Those who are of a pious disposition, cannot believe so much evil, as is told of people. But we must not trust too much, for the world is full of falseness (Wisd. xxxvii. 3). He who believes too easily, will be often deceived, and he who believes no one is also deceived. Therefore is he indeed a happy man, who can preserve the golden mean." CRAMER.

9. On xl. 13 sqq. "Misfortune is like the waves of the sea; when one is broken another follows, and the end of one trouble is the beginning of others." CRAMER.

10. On xli. 1-3. "Judas's kiss and Jacob's brethren are very common in the world and take after their grandfather Cain, who spake kindly to Abel and yet had blood-thirsty thoughts (Gen. iv. 8). Yea, they take after their father, the devil, who is a murderous spirit (John viii. 44), and disguises himself as an angel of light (2 Cor. xi. 14)." CRAMER.

11. On xli. 1 sqq. "*Similia perfidiæ exempla* (*simulatæ fraternitatis*): 2 Sam. xiii. 24; xx. 9 sq. *Quadrat etiam huc historia nuptiarum Parisiensium celebratum* 1572 *mense Augusto.*" FÖRSTER.

12. On xli. 4 sqq.

"Murder and avarice love to go with each other,
And one crime is often a prolific mother."—CRAMER.

13. On xli. 10 sqq. It is very remarkable that even this last centre and rendezvous of the unfortunate people must be destroyed. It might be supposed that with the destruction of the city and deportation of the people the judgments would have terminated. It seems as if the deed of Ishmael and the removal of the remnant to Egypt transcended the measure of punishment fixed by Jehovah, for the Lord did not send Ishmael, and the removal to Egypt He directly forbade. And yet it seems that only by Ishmael's act and the flight to Egypt could the land obtain its Sabbath rest, which is spoken of in Lev. xxvi. 34, 35.

14. On xlii. 1-6. "Had not Johanan and his people asked for advice, but gone directly to Egypt, their sin would not have been so great. They feigned, however, submission to the will of God, while they yet adhered to their own will. It is a common fault for people to ask advice while they are firmly resolved what they will do. For they inquire not to learn what is right, but only to receive encouragement to do what they wish. If we advise them according to their inclination they take our advice, if not, they reject it.—We must be on our guard when we appeal to God's decision, that we do not previously decide for ourselves. For thus we fall into hypocrisy, which is the most fatal intoxication and blindness." HEIM and HOFFMAN, *The Major Prophets*. [" Those will justly lose their comfort in real fears, that excuse themselves in sin with pretended fears." HENRY.—S. R. A.]

15. On xlii. 7. After the murder of Gedaliah the anger of Nebuchadnezzar seemed inevitable. But the Lord, to whom nothing is impossible (xxxii. 17), promises to perform a miracle, and restore Israel to new prosperity in their land if they will give Him the honor and trust in Him. Nebuchadnezzar's heart is indeed in His hand. If this is not acknowledged and Nebuchadnezzar more feared than the Lord, their sin is then against the first commandment.

16. On xlii. 13 sqq. "God reminds His people of the favor with which He adopted them as His people, which was the most sacred obligation to obedience; that Egypt was to them a land of destruction, a forbidden land, as indeed all confidence in human aid is forbidden to those who would live by faith, which was known to them from the history of their fathers and all the prophets. It is a great sin to deem one's self safer under the protection of man than under that of God. It is incomprehensible, how blind unbelief makes people, so that the Jews have not yet learned the truth in the destruction of Jerusalem and the temple of God." HEIM and HOFFMAN. "*Fides futurorum certa est ex præcedentibus.*" TERTULL. "*Venient hæc quoque sicut ista venerunt.*" AUGUSTIN.—FÖRSTER.

17. On xliii. 2 sqq. "Hypocrites forsooth do not wish to be regarded as rejecting and setting themselves in opposition to God's word, or accusing God of falsehood. For then is all the world pious, and no one refuses to be submissive to the dear Lord. God is truly God and remains so. It is only against this parson Jeremiah that they must act· he lies, he is not sent, his ruling and preaching cannot be endured." CRAMER.

18. On xliii. 3. "Observe the old diabolical trick: when preachers practice God's word and their office with zeal, the world understands how to baptize it with another name and call it *personal interest*, as even here Baruch must bear the blame, as if he only wished to vent his anger on them and be contrary." CRAMER.

19. On xliii. 6. The ancients here examine the question why Jeremiah accompanied the people to Egypt and take occasion to discuss the 1 *Comm. de fuga ministrorum* with reference to AUGUSTIN. *Epist.* 150 *ad Honorar.* With respect to Jeremiah, it is clear that he did all in his power to avert the journey to Egypt. After the whole people, however, were once on their way it was impossible for him and Baruch to remain alone in the deserted country. They were obliged to go with their flock. The more these were wandering, the more need they had of the shepherds. Thus, even if they were not compelled, they had to go with them. It seems, however, to follow from the expression וַיִּקַּח, ver. 5, that no choice was given them. The people wished to have the prophet with them. In no case can we say that Jeremiah fled, for according to his own prophecy, he knew that he was going to meet ruin in Egypt.

20. On xliii. 8-13. At the present day when we wish to convey to posterity the account of some accomplished fact, or the prediction of some fact to be accomplished (*ex. gr.* a last testament), we take paper and ink, write it down, seal it, have it subscribed by witnesses and preserve it in the registrar's or recorder's office

In ancient times they took a simpler and surer way. Jacob and Laban simply erected a heap of stones (Gen. xxxi.), the two and a half tribes (Josh. xxii.) built an altar on the bank of the Jordan. As long as the heap and the altar were standing, the record was transmitted from generation to generation for what object these stone witnesses were set up, and thus, that which it was desired to convey to posterity lived in the memory of men. Jeremiah also knows how to use ink and pen (ch. xxxii.), but here he returns once more to the old manner of preserving archives. He simply places great stones in the clay, declaring what they signify, viz., that here, on this spot, Nebuchadnezzar's tent shall stand. Whether the Egyptians and Jews then believed him or not, is of no consequence. The record of these stones and their meaning at any rate remained alive, and the Lord's word was thus safely preserved till the day of its fulfilment.

HOMILETICAL AND PRACTICAL.

1. On ch. xl. 1-12; xli. 1-3; xlii. 1-16. Israel, the chosen nation, is in its destinies a type of human life in general. Consider only the exodus from Egypt. So also *the destinies of the people of Israel, after the destruction of Jerusalem by Nebuchadnezzar, are pretypical.* For 1. The deportation of the whole people in chains and fetters is a type of our universal human misery, from which no one (not even Jeremiah) is free. 2. The fate of Gedaliah and the journey to Egypt is a type of the insufficiency of all mere human help. 3. As the Jews after Gedaliah's murder, so men at all times, find protection and deliverance in the Lord alone.

2. On xl. 1-6. The Christian in the tumult of the world. 1. He is regarded externally like others. 2. The eye of the Lord watches with special care over him, so that (a) not a hair of his head is bent, (b) all his wants are provided for. 3. He, however, on his part directs all his efforts to the kingdom of God and His righteousness, and will not be turned aside from this either by the violence or the friendliness of the world.

3. On xl. 7-xli. 3. Gedaliah's fate an example of what befals even the most noble in times of deep corruption. 1. They enjoy general confidence. 2. They are incapable of attributing extreme wickedness to men. 3. They become a sacrifice to their confidence. 4. They are therefore not in a condition to stay the divine judgments.

4. On xlii. 1-16. What is the surest way of coming to the right conclusion in difficult cases? 1. To inquire of the Lord. 2. To obey unconditionally the direction which the Lord communicates. ["We must still in faith pray to be guided by a *spirit of wisdom* in our hearts, and the hints of Providence." HENRY.—S. R. A.]

5. On xliii. 1-7. Characteristic example of the artfulness of the human heart: the Jews inquire of the Lord and promise to obey His direction (xlii. 20). But when the direction does not accord with their wish, they at once declare it to be supposititious, not from the Lord. The prophet must be a liar, an alleged enemy has incited him. But what was long previously determined in the heart is obstinately brought to execution. ["Those that are resolved to contradict the great ends of the ministry, are industrious to bring a bad name upon it. It is well for persons who are thus misrepresented that their *witness is in heaven*, and their *record on high*." HENRY. —S. R. A.]

6. On xliii. 8-13. The ways of the Lord are wonderful. Israel flees before Nebuchadnezzar far away to Egypt. But there they are not safe. The Lord causes it to be proclaimed to them that at the entrance of the king's palace at Tahpanhes Nebuchadnezzar's tent shall stand. Now indeed there is a brick-kiln there, in the clay of which Jeremiah is to place stones, the foundation stones, as it were, for the Chaldean king's pavilion. Thus the Lord lays the germs of future events, and whatever He prepares in secret He reveals in His own time to the glory of His wisdom, omniscience and omnipotence.

---

10. *Jeremiah at the Festival of the Queen of Heaven in Pathros. The Last Act of his Prophetic Ministry.*

a. The charge against the stubbornly idolatrous people.

XLIV. 1-14.

1 The word that came to Jeremiah concerning [for, to] all the Jews which dwell [who dwelt] in the land of Egypt, which dwell at Migdol, and at Tahpanhes, and
2 at Noph, and in the country of Pathros, saying, Thus saith the LORD of hosts, the God of Israel: Ye have seen all the evil that I have brought upon Jerusalem, and upon all the cities of Judah; and, behold, this day they *are* a desolation, and no
3 man dwelleth therein; because of their wickedness which they have committed to¹ provoke me to anger, in that they went to burn incense, *and* to serve other
4 gods, whom they knew not, *neither* they,² ye, nor your fathers. Howbeit I sent unto you all my servants the prophets, rising early and sending *them*, saying, O,

5 do not this abominable thing² that I hate. But they hearkened not, nor inclined
6 their ear to turn from their wickedness, to burn no incense unto other gods. Wherefore my fury and mine anger was poured forth, and was kindled in the cities of Judah and in the streets of Jerusalem: and they are wasted *and* desolate, as at
7 this day. Therefore now thus saith the LORD, the God of hosts, the God of Israel: Wherefore commit ye *this* great evil against your souls,⁴ to cut off from you man
8 and woman, child and suckling, out of Judah, to leave you none to remain: In that ye provoke me unto wrath with the works of your hands, burning incense⁵ unto other gods in the land of Egypt, whither ye be gone to dwell, that ye might cut yourselves⁶ off, and that ye might be a curse and a reproach among all
9 the nations of the earth? Have you forgotten the wickedness [evil]⁷ of your fathers, and the wickedness of the kings of Judah, and the wickedness of their [his]⁸ wives, and your own wickedness, and the wickedness of your wives, which they⁹ have committed in the land of Judah, and in the streets of Jerusalem?
10 They are not humbled *even* unto this day, neither have they feared, nor walked in
11 my law, nor in my statutes, that I set before you and before your fathers. Therefore thus saith the LORD of hosts, the God of Israel: Behold, I will set my face
12 against you for evil, and to cut off all Judah. And I will take the remnant of Judah, that have set their faces to go into the land of Egypt to sojourn there, and they shall all¹⁰ be consumed, *and* fall in the land of Egypt; they shall *even* be consumed by the sword *and* by the famine: they shall die, from the least even unto the greatest, by the sword and by the famine: and they shall be an execration, *and*
13 an astonishment, and a curse, and a reproach. For I will punish them that dwell in the land of Egypt, as I have punished Jerusalem, by the sword, by the famine,
14 and by the pestilence: So that none [there shall be none escaped or remaining] of the remnant of Judah, which are gone into the land of Egypt to sojourn there, shall escape or remain, that they should return [and then to return] into the land of Judah, to the which they have a desire to return to dwell there: for none shall return but such as shall escape.¹¹

TEXTUAL AND GRAMMATICAL.

¹ Ver. 3.—In לָלֶכֶת לְהַכְעִסֵנִי and לָלֶכֶת the לְ is the gerundial (comp. NAEGELSB. *Gr.*, § 95, *e*), in לִקְטֹר לַעֲבֹד it is the supinal (*Ib.*, § 95, *f.*). Comp. xi. 17; xxxii. 32.

² Ver. 3.—הֻכָּה is not to be regarded as accusative, since this has been already expressed by the suffix in יָדְעוּם, but as nominative. The third person stands in close connection with the preceding, the הֻכָּה with the sudden change of person (comp. *infra* vers. 5 and 10 and NAEGELSB. *Gr.*, § 101 *Anm.*) is however explained by י׳ אִתָּם, with which a return is made to the second person used in the beginning of the sentence (ver. 2).

³ Ver. 4.—דָּבָר as in Jud. xix. 24.

⁴ Ver. 7.—רָעָה must here have the same sense as רָעוֹת, ver. 9. For the connection is: the רָעָה that ye now do can only be explained, by your having forgotten the רָעוֹת of the past. Since now רָעוֹת must necessarily be taken in a double sense, so must also רָעָה in this passage. י׳ לְהַכְרִית is a gerundial infinitive. On נַפְשֹׁות comp. NAEGELSB. *Gr.*, § ⁶¹. l c.

⁵ Ver. 8.—לְקַטֵּר לְהַכְעִיסֵנִי and are also gerundial infinitives (comp. ver. 3).

⁶ Ver. 8.—In ver. 7 הַכְרֵית has a definitely expressed object. Many would supply this here. Others take לָכֶם for אֶתְכֶם, according to the analogy of xl. 2. הַכְרֵית may, however, also be taken in a directly causative sense—prepare extermination, so that the dative would have nothing abnormal in it. Comp. הָרֵעַ Jer. l. 34; הֹכִיחַ Isa. ii. 4; הַצְדִּיק Isa. li. 11 with לְ; NAEGELSB. *Gr.*, § 69, 1 *Anm.* 2.

⁷ Ver. 9.—From אֲשֶׁר עָשׂוּ it would follow that רָעוֹת is to be taken in a moral sense. But can it be said of those who are censured on account of their persistence in these sins: Have you forgotten your sins? J. D. MICHAELIS is therefore disposed to read הִשְׁפַּחְתֶּם, with a marginal reading of a Königsberg Codex: *majus peccando memoriam peccatorum ante commissorum obliterastis*. But this reading is not sufficiently authenticated. We must therefore take רָעוֹת, as in ver. 7, in a double sense, so as to designate at the same time the *mala poenae* and the *mala culpae* (comp. Gen. l. 15). Their forgetfulness of the sufferings which they had drawn on them by their sins is the cause of their obstinate persistence in the latter.

⁸ Ver. 9.—רָשָׁיו נָשָׁיו Both the introduction of the "wives" and the singular suffix are surprising. The LXX. read τῶν ἀρχόντων ὑμῶν, שָׂרֵיכֶם or נְשֵׁיאֲכֶם would certainly correspond better to the connection, as well as to the usage of the prophet elsewhere (comp. vers. 17, 21; i. 18; ii. 26; xxiv. 8; xxv. 18; xxxii. 32; xxxiv. 21). But the more difficult reading is to be preferred. The singular suffix is not to be referred to Judah, since the expression "wives of Judah" is neither used elsewhere nor suitable to the connection, but to the king of the time. Comp. Hos. iv. 8; Zech. xiv. 12; NAEGELSB. *Gr.*, § 105, 7 *Anm.* 2.

CHAP. XLIV. 1–14.

⁹ Ver. 9.—אֲשֶׁר עָשׂוּ. Change of person as in vers. 3, 5. Comp. NAEGELSB. *Gr.*, § 101, 2, *Anm.*
¹⁰ Ver. 12.—וְתֹמּוּ כֹל. According to the accents the sentence is to be construed as in the translation. On כֹּל comp. Isa. xxx. 5; EWALD, 286, e.
¹¹ Ver. 14.—כִּי אִם פְּלֵטִים. Strictly taken these words form a direct contradiction to the beginning of the verse, which declares that there shall be a פָּלִיט or שָׂרִיד, and the words כִּי לֹא יָשׁוּבוּ are no other than the confirmation of this statement. It is therefore natural to regard the words as a later addition, as HITZIG does. The brevity of the previous sentence, and its apparent contradiction of ver. 28 seemed to require this supplementation. In ver. 28 it is expressly stated that some, having escaped, will return, and it is hence evident that the declaration here, ver. 14, is not to be taken with absolute literalness.

EXEGETICAL AND CRITICAL.

The word of the Lord is communicated through Jeremiah to the Israelites dwelling in Egypt; ye have seen how I have punished Judah and Jerusalem for their idolatry (vers. 1-6). Why then do you continually commit the same wickedness? Have ye forgotten the lecture? It appears so, for they have not humbled themselves, nor endeavored to keep the law of God (vers. 7-10). Therefore shall the remnant of Judah in Egypt, even like unto Judah and Jerusalem, be destroyed by sword, famine and pestilence, and at most single fugitives shall return home (vers. 11-14).

Ver. 1. **The word . . . saying.** We have here the last document of Jeremiah's prophetic ministry. Far from home, after terrible judgments, he has still the same thing to say to the Jews as at first. They have not become wiser or better. From Tahpanhes they had spread abroad in the land. What occasion had brought them together in so large an assembly, is not indeed stated in the superscription, which is of the greater sort (comp. xl. 1; xxxvi. 1; xxxv. 1; xxxiv. 1, etc.), but is evident enough from what follows.—**Dwelt.** The fugitives have already established themselves in fixed abodes. Comp. rems. on xliii. 8.—**Migdol** (comp. xlvi. 14; Ezek. xxix. 10; xxx. 6 coll. Exod. xiv. 2; Num. xxxiii. 7) was one of the north-eastern boundary points of Egypt [near Syene]. In Herodotus (II. 159) and the LXX. the place is called Μάγδωλον; according to the *Itiner. Anton.* (p. 171) it was twelve Roman miles from Pelusium.—On **Tahpanhes** comp. rems. on xliii. 8.—**Noph** is Memphis, the ancient capital of lower Egypt. Comp. rems. on ii. 16.—**Pathros** (comp. ver. 15; Isa. xi. 11; Ezek. xxix. 14; xxx. 14) is upper Egypt. Comp. HERZOG, *R.-Enc.*, I. *S.* 149. The assembly was held, according to ver. 15, in Pathros. A considerable time must have elapsed since the migration, because we find the colony already dispersed and settled in different places. On the other hand the meeting cannot have occurred so long after the migration that those who are addressed by Jeremiah can belong to the second generation. They were the Jews who had come into the country (ver. 8), and the longing for home was still strong in them. Comp. rems. on vers. 29, 30.

Vers. 2-6. **Thus saith . . . as at this day.** The prophet presents before the Jews first the great catastrophe, portraying its genesis in the order of its elements.—**Whom they know not.** Comp. xix. 4.—**I sent,** *etc.* Comp. vii. 13, 25; xxix. 19.—**This abominable thing.** Comp. xxxii. 35.—**Was poured forth.** Comp. xlii. 18.—**In the cities of Judah.** Comp. vers. 9, 17, 21; vii. 17; xi. 6; xxxiii. 10.—**As at this day.** Comp. vers. 2, 22, 23; xi. 5.

Vers. 7-10. **Therefore now thus . . . before your fathers.** After the Jews had just learned in a different manner how fearfully Jehovah avenges apostasy from Him, how can they now again, to their unendurable shame and ruin, commit the same sins? It appears as if they had forgotten the lesson and not yet learned to bow in obedience to the divine law.—**Man and woman.** Comp. 1 Sam. xv. 3; xxii. 19; Lam. ii. 11.—**The works of your hands.** From i. 16 coll. xxv. 14 it is evident that the prophet wishes the expression to be understood in a physical sense of the idol images.—**Burning incense** in the wider sense. Comp. rems. on i. 16.—**That ye might be,** *etc.* Comp. xlii. 18; Zech. viii. 13.—**Have ye forgotten,** *etc.* The present unlawful conduct of the people is explained only by their forgetfulness of the former calamities occasioned by their idolatry.—HITZIG well calls attention to the fact, that the royal wives played an important part in the history of Jewish idolatry. Comp. the wives of Solomon (1 Ki. xi. 1 sqq.) Maachah, the mother of Asa (xv. 13) and Athaliah (xi. 1).

Ver. 10. **They are not humbled.** Comp. Isa. lvii. 15. How unwillingly does the prophet turn away and address his discourse concerning these, to whom he has hitherto spoken, to others. Comp. Mic. i. 2; Jer. l. 8.—**Nor walked.** Comp. ix. 12; xxvi. 4.

Vers. 11-14. **Therefore . . . shall escape.** Because the Jews, notwithstanding they had experienced the fearful severity of God's punitive justice, again committed the same sins, therefore (לָכֵן ver. 11) will the Lord set his face against them, the last remnant of Judah, and by the destruction of this utterly exterminate the nation. Comp. ver. 7.—**And I will take.** The expression involves an antithesis to **set their faces to go.** They thought in their own power to take a path which would lead them away from the punitive hand. But the Lord seizes them as He once did the prophet Jonah.—**Shall be an execration.** Comp. rems. on xlii. 18.—**Them that dwell.** Comp. ix. 24, 25; xlvi. 25.—**None escaped.** The Jews had gone to Egypt to remain there temporarily, and then return home. On **which are gone** then depends not only **to sojourn there** but also **and to return with** the following relative sentence.—**To the which.** Comp. xxii. 27.—**But such as shall escape.** Comp. TEXTUAL NOTE.

b. The Replication of the People.

XLIV. 15-19.

15 Then all the men which knew that their wives had burned incense unto other gods, and all the women that stood by a [there in the] great multitude [assembly], even all the people that dwelt in the land of Egypt, in Pathros answered Jere-
16 miah, saying, *As for* the word[1] that thou hast spoken unto us in the name of the
17 Lord, we will not hearken unto thee. But we will certainly do whatsoever thing [word] goeth forth [has gone forth] out of our own mouth, to burn incense unto the queen of heaven, and to pour out drink offerings unto her, as we have done, we, and our fathers, our kings, and our princes, in the cities of Judah, and in the streets of Jerusalem: for *then* had we plenty of victuals, and were well,[2] and saw
18 no evil. But since we left off to burn incense to the queen of heaven, and to pour out drink offerings unto her, we have wanted all *things*, and have been consumed[3]
19 by the sword and by the famine. And when we burned incense to the queen of heaven, and poured out drink offerings unto her, did we make her cakes to worship her,[4] and pour out drink offerings unto her, without our men?

TEXTUAL AND GRAMMATICAL.

[1] Ver. 16.—הַדָּבָר is to be regarded as accusative of restriction. Not generally, but only with respect to this particular word, do they declare that they will not obey the prophet. Comp. NAEGELSB. *Gr.*, § 70, *f*.
[2] Ver. 17.—טוֹבִים *felices*. Comp. Isa. iii. 10, and DELITZSCH *ad loc*.
[3] Ver. 18.—On the form וַכֻּנּוּ, which is found only in the root כבה, comp. OLSH., S. 483, *f*.
[4] Ver. 19.—לְהַעֲצִבָה. The Hiph. here only. The Piel only in Job x. 8 decidedly in the meaning of "to form, shape." Compare further עָצָב, עֲצָבִים (Jer. xxii. 28), so the meaning of the Hiph. in this place cannot be other than "to form, copy," with reference to the moon-shaped form of the cakes. Comp. rems. on vii 18. The circumstance that the ה is written without Mappik (which however is found in some MSS.) does not stand in the way of this. (Comp. OLSH., § 96, *e* ; Isai. xxi. 2; xxiii. 17, 18). [We must then render : make her cakes to copy her.—S. R. A.]

EXEGETICAL AND CRITICAL.

From the purport of this passage it is manifest that the people had come together to celebrate a festival in honor of the queen of heaven, and to perform the vows they had made. The assembly consisted principally of women. Hence they were the chief speakers. They now declare to the prophet that they will not obey his words (ver. 16), but perform their vows, and make their offerings to the queen of heaven, as they had also done at home. It was then well with them (ver. 17), only since they neglected her worship, has it gone badly with them (ver. 18). In addition, they (the women) had devoted themselves to the service of this goddess only with the concurrence of their husbands.

Ver. 15. **Then all ... saying**. The assembly consisted (1) of men, who well knew that their wives offered incense to other gods (comp. rems. on ver. 3); (2) of women, who were a **great multitude**. From the circumstance that the "great assembly" is designated as consisting of women, it has been rightly concluded that they formed the majority, which explains the emphasis laid on the women in vers. 24, 25.— The Jewish women thus appear to have come together from all parts of Egypt to a festival of the queen of heaven, which was held in a place of upper Egypt (Pathros), not more particularly designated, in order there to perform their vows made to this goddess. The men seem to have been both those who lived in the neighborhood and those who had come from a distance as husbands of a part of the women mentioned. The assembly consisted (3) of representatives of all the people, who were settled in Egypt, among whom we must suppose individuals, who were neither husbands nor wives.—**In Pathros** accordingly designates the place of meeting, and is not to be connected with **lived** but with **answered**. The prophet had endeavored by his discourse, vers. 2-14, to hinder the observance of this idolatrous festival, but was not successful.

Vers. 16-19. **As for the word ... without our men.—We will not hearken**. Comp. vii. 16.—The expression **whatsoever word has gone forth out of our mouth** indicates vows that had been made (comp. Num. xxx. 3, 13; x.:xii. 24; Jud. xi. 36). On the queen of heaven comp. rems. on vii 18.—**And when we burned**. According to the apodosis this ought properly to be in the feminine instead of the masculine, as in ver. 15 (מְקַטְּרוֹת). The masculine form has not only a general justification, as being the chief form, and frequently occurring for the feminine (comp. NAEGELSB. *Gr.*, § 60, 5, 4), but also a special, since the speakers had in view the entire number who took part in the offering. According to Num. xxx. 7 sqq., the women were responsible for the observance of their vows only when approved by their husbands (or fathers, comp. ver. 4). Hence they now declare, that in consequence of having obtained the concurrence of their husbands they are at any rate free from all personal responsibility. On cakes comp. rems. on vii. 18. It is evident from the latter passage, that this cult was not first adopted in Egypt, but imported from home.

c. The Rejoinder of the Prophet (xliv. 20-30).

a. Refutation of the Popular Assertions.

XLIV. 20-23.

20 Then Jeremiah said unto[1] all the people, to the men, and to the women, and to
21 all the people which had given him *that* answer, saying, Is it not so? The incense[2] that ye burned in the cities of Judah, and in the streets of Jerusalem, ye, and your fathers, your kings, and your princes, and the people of the land, did not the LORD remember them, and came it *not* into his mind? [Jehovah remembered
22 it,[3] and it came into his mind].[4] So that the LORD [Jehovah] could no longer bear[5] because of the evil of your doings,[6] *and* because of the abominations which ye have committed; therefore is your land a desolation,[7] and an astonishment [a waste] and
23 a curse, without an inhabitant,[8] as at this day. Because ye have burned incense, and because ye have sinned against the LORD, and have not obeyed the voice of the LORD, nor walked in his law, nor in his statutes, nor in his testimonies; therefore this evil is happened[9] unto you, as at this day.

TEXTUAL AND GRAMMATICAL.

[1] Ver. 20.—On the interchange of עַל and אֶל comp. rems. on x. 1.

[2] Ver. 21.—The Piel form קִטֵּר, which occurs here only (comp. OLSH. § 182, e) corresponds to the German "Geräucher" [fumigating, incensing]. Observe also the emphatic position of the word at the beginning of the sentence [the incensing that ye did].

[3] Ver. 21.—The plural suffix in אֹתָם refers to the plural idea contained in the intensive form. Compare remarks on xi. 4.

[4] Ver. 21.—Comp. rems. on iii. 16.

[5] Ver. 22.—וְלֹא יוּכַל. The imperf. is evidently used here in an aoristic sense, but since the fact in question is removed from all objective human perception, it is consequently founded, notwithstanding its undoubted correctness, on a subjective conception. Comp. Isa. xxxvii. 4; 1 Ki. viii. 5.

[6] Ver. 22.—לָשֵׂאת. With מִפְּנֵי following, here only. It seems to be used in the absolute sense of "endure, hold out," also in Isa. i. 4; Prov. xxx. 21—וְתַן. Comp. iv. 4; xxi. 12; xxiii. 2, 22; xxiv. 2 sqq.; xxvi. 3.

[7] Ver. 22.—לְחָרְבָּה. Comp. vers. 6, 12.

[8] Ver. 22.—מֵאֵין יוֹשֵׁב. Comp. rems. on ii. 15.

[9] Ver. 23.—קָרָאת. Comp. OLSH., S. 449, 478.—GES., § 74, Anm. 1; EWALD, § 194, b.

EXEGETICAL AND CRITICAL.

To the assertion of the people that it had gone well with them so long as they had served the queen of heaven, and that their misfortunes dated from their cessation of this service, the prophet answers with a *non post hoc sed propter hoc*. It was precisely on account of this idolatrous cult (ver. 21) which Jehovah could no longer suffer, that their misfortunes had come upon them (ver. 22). And for the sake of emphasis Jeremiah repeats this bitter truth once more (ver. 23).

β. The Positive Announcement of Severest Punishment.

XLIV. 24-30.

24 Moreover Jeremiah said unto all the people, and to all the women, Hear the
25 word of the LORD [Jehovah's word] all Judah that *are* in the land of Egypt. Thus
saith the LORD of hosts [Jehovah Zebaoth] the God of Israel, saying : Ye and
your wives have both¹ spoken with your mouths, and fulfilled with your hand, saying, We will surely perform our vows that we have vowed, to burn incense to the
queen of heaven, and to pour out drink offerings unto her; ye will surely accom-
26 plish² your vows, and surely perform your vows. Therefore hear ye the word of
the LORD [Jehovah's word] all Judah that dwell in the land of Egypt; Behold, I
have sworn by my great name, saith the LORD, that my name shall no more be
named in the mouth of any man of Judah in all the land of Egypt, saying, The
27 LORD God [Adonai Jehovah] liveth. Behold, I will watch over them for evil, and
not for good ; and all the men of Judah that *are* in the land of Egypt shall be con-
28 sumed by the sword and by the famine, until there be an end of them. Yet a
small number that escape³ the sword shall return out of the land of Egypt into
the land of Judah, and all the remnant of Judah, that are gone into the land of
29 Egypt to sojourn there, shall know whose words shall stand, mine, or theirs.⁴ And
this *shall be* a sign unto you, saith the LORD, that I will punish⁵ you in this place,
30 that ye may know that my words shall surely stand against you for evil : Thus
saith the LORD: Behold, I will give Pharaoh-hophra, king of Egypt, into the hand
of his enemies, and into the hand of them that seek his life; as I gave Zedekiah,
king of Judah, into the hand of Nebuchadrezzar, king of Babylon, his enemy, and
that sought his life.

TEXTUAL AND GRAMMATICAL.

¹ Ver. 25.—On the Vau consecutive comp. NAEGELSB. *Gr.*, § 88, 7, and Jer. iii. 9; vi. 19; xxxiii. 24.
² Ver. 25.—On the form תָּקֵמְנָה comp. OLSH., S 579; EWALD, § 196, c; GES., § 72, 5, *Anm.*
³ Ver. 28.—פְּלִיטֵי חֶרֶב comp. Ezek. vi. 8 : NAEGELSB. *Gr.*, § 64, 5, c.
⁴ Ver. 28.—The construction מִכֶּנִי וּמֵהֶם (comp. analogies in GRAF) is found in this form here only. The two pronouns analyze the idea שְׁנֵי. Since, however, both members of the disjunctive question were to be distinctly expressed,
the only way was either to say דְּבָרַי וְאִם דִּבְרֵיכֶם אִם (comp. Joel i. 2), or as there are no independent possessive pronouns, to use the personal pronouns, which, however, could be employed only in the form of suffixes to the partitive prepositions.
⁵ Ver. 29.—פֹּקֵד with עַל as in ver. 13.

EXEGETICAL AND CRITICAL.

As that which the land and people of Judah
had experienced from the Chaldeans, was a punishment for their previous wickedness, so in the
future also new calamities will be the recompense of their newly-repeated offences. The
Jews persist in performing their idolatrous vows.
Well, they shall do so (ver. 26). But they shall
also hear, that there will soon be no longer a Jew
in Egypt, who may even take the name of Jehovah into his mouth (ver. 26). For they shall be
exterminated by sword and famine (ver. 27), and
only a few shall return into the land of Judah,
that this stubborn people may learn who is in a
position to execute his will, Jehovah or they?
(ver. 28). And this may serve for a token, that
the Lord will make good His word, that Hophra,
king of Egypt, will be given into the hand of his

mortal enemies, just as Zedekiah was given into
the hand of his enemy, the king of Babylon
(vers. 29, 30).

Vers. 24, 25. **Moreover Jeremiah . . your
vows.** The women are here also expressly mentioned (see rems. on ver. 15). In ver. 25 even
the predicate to ye and your wives, as well as
the predicates in the concluding sentence of the
verse has the feminine form.—The sentence **and
fulfilled with your hand** is to be regarded as
a parenthesis, occasioned by the circumstance,
that the discharge of the vows was already in
progress at the very moment the prophet was
speaking. We may conclude from this, that
the words in vers. 24 sqq. were spoken later
than the preceding context, *viz.*, towards the close
of the meeting.

Vers. 26-28. **Therefore hear . . . or theirs.**
As you obstinately carry out your will, hear
what the Lord will do to effect His. He has

sworn by His great Name (comp. xxii. 5; xlix. 13; li. 14), that a time will yet come, when no Jew in Egypt will any more take the name of Jehovah into his mouth as an oath (comp. iv. 2; v. 2; xii. 16), simply for this reason, that there will be none there (ver. 27). "In the form of asseveration the name of Jehovah would be still retained, although they had long since become devoted to the service of other gods. But Jehovah, who is an אֵל קַנָּא [jealous God], rejects honor and acknowledgment which He must share with others; and so His name shall no longer be heard from the mouth of any Jews in Egypt." HITZIG.—In **Behold, I will watch**, there is evidently a reminiscence of i. 12, so that the close of the prophecies is thus connected with the beginning.—Only a few individuals will escape the sword and return home (comp. rems. on ver. 14).—**A small number.** Comp. Gen. xxxiv. 30; Deut. iv. 27; Ps. cv. 12.—And thus Israel shall learn by this fact, whose word will stand (כִּי דְבַר. Comp. viii. 9; Gen. xxiv. 23; קוּם, Isa. xiv. 24; vii. 7; xlvi. 10), theirs (vers. 17, 18) or Jehovah's.

Vers. 29, 30. **And this shall be a sign ... sought his life.** The Jews might think that in Egypt they were out of sight of their God, whose throne was in Jerusalem. To expel this delusion the prophet announces to them a sign, that the Lord has them well in view. When they see this sign it will be a pledge that the punishments threatened in vers. 26–28 will really overtake them. The sign will consist in this, that Hophra, the Egyptian king, will be given into the hands of his enemies, as Zedekiah was into the hands of Nebuchadnezzar. Now Herodotus certainly relates (II., 161 sqq.) that Apries [Manetho, Οὐάφρις, LXX., Οὐαφρῆ], (i. e., Hophra) whom he calls after Psammetichus the most fortunate of the earlier kings, in consequence of an unsuccessful battle with the Cyrenians, had to experience a revolt of the Egyptians. Amasis, who was sent to treat with them, himself went over to the rebels, and Apries was compelled to fignt the Egyptians under Amasis with an army consisting only of foreign auxiliaries. He was so presumptuous as to think, says Herodotus, that no God could cast him from his throne, so firmly was he seated upon it. He was, however, vanquished and taken captive. Amasis now indeed treated him very well in the palace, but the Egyptians took it ill that he was so indulgent to his and their greatest enemy. Therefore Amasis delivered Apries up to the Egyptians, who strangled him (II., 169). If we compare this narrative with the passage under consideration, we find that they agree perfectly, not only in speaking of a "surrender of Hophra into the hands of those who sought his life" (comp. וַיְבַקְשׁוּ and בְּקֵשׁ, ver. 30 a, with the singular in hemistich b) but also in this, that the circumstance of the surrender of the king being predicted as a sign, appears to be thus well accounted for, in Apries having by his obstinate arrogance challenged the divine Nemesis. But how about the chronology? It has been assumed that the surrender of Apries occurred at too late a date for it to have served as a sign, or that Jeremiah could have lived to any proximate period. The death of Apries must certainly be placed in B. C., 570 (comp. DUSCKEN, S. 930; M. NIEBUHR, Ass. u. Bab., S. 217). We have remarked above on ver. 1, that the Jews are still designated as having come into the country (vers. 8, 12, 14), and therefore not as born in it, and a strong longing for the land of their fathers is still ascribed to them (ver. 14). But does this prevent us from supposing that they have been already about sixteen years in the country? There is nothing opposed to this in the text. This simply records that they had settled down at different places, and were now assembled for a festival in Upper Egypt. This might happen as well after sixteen years as after two, but better then, than in the first year. A longing for home is not yet altogether extinguished in the Jews even at the present day. Comp. Ps. cxxxvii.—As to the age of Jeremiah—if he was a נַעַר, about twenty, in the thirteenth year of Josiah (comp. i. 2, 6), he must have been about seventy-six or seventy-seven in the year B. C., 570. This is not impossible. What object could the subsequent insertion of this verse as a vaticinium post eventum, alleged by HITZIG and GRAF, have had? There was no need for it (as there perhaps was for פְּלִיטִים, כִּי אִם, ver. 14), and if it was not Jeremiah's custom to offer tokens, this would all the more have deterred from such an interpolation. Even if we grant that there are no other tokens of this kind to be found in Jeremiah, this does not involve the impossibility of his ever having given such a one. He might have a special reason for doing so here. I think I can perceive such a reason in the presumptuous declaration on the part of the king, recorded by Herodotus. This prediction of the fate impending over the king was the answer of the true God to this provocation. The point of the prediction is evidently directed against this latter. That which Jeremiah loudly proclaimed in an open assembly of the Jewish people could not remain hid. The king could and should hear it, even though he held the old Jewish soothsayer in disdain. Only thus is it explained why Jeremiah gave a token just now, and why he gave just this. He was obliged to predict his fate to the king, in order that when this came, the hand of God might be recognized in it, and at the same time this prediction was to be a pledge to the Jewish people for the fulfilment of the judgment threatened to him. Let us remember how the mighty hand of the Lord was once displayed through Moses on Egypt and its king, in order that they might perceive that He was the Lord, and His the earth (Exod. vii. 5, 17; viii. 22; ix. 14, 29; x. 2). After the lapse of a thousand years the last remnant of the theocratic nation return as fugitives to the same Egypt, from which the Lord had so gloriously conducted them. Israel had failed of the high goal, appointed for it—but the Lord had remained the same, and His last prophet like His first was commissioned to be the medium of announcement to the proud empires of the just judgments of the only true God, who does not allow Himself to be despised with impunity.

How now was the threatening fulfilled that the remnant of Judah in Egypt should perish by sword and famine, except a few who should return home (ver. 28), and none should be left in Egypt who could take the name of Jehovah for an oath on his lips (ver. 26)? In the first place it may here be mentioned, that it is a matter of indifference to this question, whether Nebuchadnezzar really came to Egypt and fulfilled the prophecy in xliii. 8–14, or not. I leave entirely out of account the fabulous record of Megasthenes (in STRABO, XVI., p. 687, a; JOSEPH., *Antiqq.*, X., 11, 1; c. *Ap.*, I., 20), that Nebuchadnezzar subjugated not only Egypt, but also Lybia and Iberia, and came to the pillars of Hercules, yea even to Thrace and the Pontus (comp. HAEVERNICK, *Comm.* on Ezek., S. 496 sqq., and the narratives confirming the conquest of Egypt in Arabian authors: AUULFEDA, *Hist. ante-Islam*, p. 102. FLEISCHER, *Abdollatif, Rel. de l'Egyp.*, p. 184, 247; ed. DE SACY). But JOSEPHUS, as is well known, relates also (*Antiqq.*, X., 9, 7) that Nebuchadnezzar in the fifth year after the capture of Jerusalem himself led an army to Cœlo-Syria, and after the conquest of this country, made war also on the Ammonites and Moabites, and invaded Egypt. On this occasion he killed the king then reigning in Egypt, set up another in his stead, and again led Jews away captive to Babylonia. Now if whatever in this account relates to the Egyptian king be decidedly erroneous (Comp. M. NIEBUHR, *Ass. u. Bab.*, S. 215, *Anm.* 3), it is, however, still possible that Nebuchadnezzar, during the thirteen years siege or blockade of Tyre, which began directly after the conquest of Jerusalem, had the desire and the leisure to make an expedition through Cœlo-Syria and the East-Jordanic countries to Egypt. It would make no essential difference if he entrusted this expedition to one of his generals. The prophecy in xliii. 8–14, may then have been fulfilled. Captive Jews and Egyptians may also have been really carried away on this occasion. Comp. lii. 30; M. NIEBUHR, S. 215, *et passim*. But, as we have said, the question, what happened to the Jews still living in Egypt B. C., 570, is not affected by an expedition of the Chaldæans to Egypt ten or twelve years earlier.

It is surprising that in ch. xliv. the extermination of the Jews living in Egypt is so definitely prophesied, while some centuries later we find the Jews in Egypt very numerous, and Egypt a centre of the Jewish diaspora (comp. HERZOG, *R.-Enc.*, XVII. S. 285.) Alexander the Great finds so many Jews in Egypt, that he peoples the city founded by him, and named after him, chiefly with them (comp. HERZOG, *R.-Enc.*, I., S. 235). How did these Jews come into Egypt? Till the time of Nehemiah (about B. C., 441), Judea was so thinly populated, that it certainly could not afford to send out colonists. The many Persian expeditions to Egypt (B. C., 525, 484, 460, 458, 373), may indeed have carried many single Jews with them. The same may also be said of the brief occupation of Palestine by Tachos, king of Egypt (B. C., 361). It is related of Ochus, that in his expedition, undertaken B. C., 350 for the reconquest of Egypt, he dragged many Jews with him to Egypt. It is, however, added that he afterwards took part of them back to Babylon, and part of them he banished to Hyrcania. Comp. HERZFELD, *Gesch. d. V. Isr.*, etc., [History

of the Israelitish nation from the completion of the Second Temple to Simon Maccabeus], I., S. 118. It is recorded of Alexander the Great himself that on his expedition to Egypt he incorporated many Jews and Samaritans in his army (comp. HERZFELD, S. 120, *et pass.*), but it is scarcely probable that he left all these warriors behind in Egypt. When in Babylon, he wished to rebuild the temple of Belus, he had Jews in his army, as is related by Hecatæus in JOSEPH., *c. Ap.*, I., 22 (p. 1186 sqq., ed. OBERTHUER). Whence then the great number of Jews that Alexander found already in Egypt? I believe we must seek them for the most part in the descendants of those who immigrated with Jeremiah. But then the prophecy was not fulfilled. May we not assume that the idolatrous practices ceased among the exiled Jews in Egypt, as well as among those in Babylon? And if this was the case, how can it be a question, what turning-point we must suppose between the idolatrous period, in which we still see them in Jer. xliv., and the later one of fidelity to Jehovah? May not the powerful words of the aged and venerable Jeremiah, and the literal fulfilment of the prophecy uttered by him respecting the king (xliv. 29, 30) have produced an overpowering impression on their minds? According to tradition (HIERON., *adv. Jovin.*, 2, 37; TERTULLIAN, *Scorp.* 8; EPIPHAN. περὶ τῶν προφητῶν, *Opp.*, II., p. 239) Jeremiah was stoned by his countrymen in Tahpanhes. But this legend is surely without foundation. If they stoned him, they must have done it after the discourse in ch. xliv., which was not delivered in Tahpanhes (xliv. 15). It is, however, also possible that the idolatrous inclination in them, as in their countrymen in Babylonia, was now exhausted, and that the Lord in view of their repentance, repented Him of the evil, which He had spoken against them (xxvi. 13, 18).

DOCTRINAL AND ETHICAL.

1. "*Obfirment animum suum ministri ecclesiæ hujus capitis meditatione, ne pertinacia auditorum se territuri patiantur, sed ut potius dehortando, objurgando, comminando intrepide instent ex præcepto apostoli* 2 Tim. iv. 2." FÖRSTER.

2. On xliv. 2–13. A mirror of the stubborn heart of man! For centuries unceasingly warned by the prophets—and how warned! Not by sentimental talk, but by words of thunder and strokes of power,—think only of Elijah, Elisha, Hosea, Isaiah, etc.!—yet Judah bowed not his stubborn neck. Then at last when long-suffering love was exhausted, the judgment of just love was executed. And yet in the wretched remnant the old root of unbelief and disobedience remains still unbroken.

3. On xliv. 9. "Though thou shouldest bray a fool in a mortar with a pestle as vetches, yet will his foolishness not depart from him (Prov. xxvii. 22). And he that sings songs to a heavy heart, it is like a torn garment in winter, and vinegar on nitre (Prov. xxv. 20)." CRAMER.

4. On xliv. 15. "*Hoc loco imaginem quandam conspicere licet seditionis, de qua Ethnicus: ἐν τῇ στάσει πᾶσα ἰδέα κακοῦ ἔνεστιν,—itemque confusionis plus quam cyclopicæ, de qua notum est illud tritum: οὐδεὶς οὐδενὸς οὐδὲν ἀκούει.*" FÜRSTER.

CHAP. XLIV. 24–30. 351

5. On xliv. 16. "Ungodliness continually extends and even goes beyond itself. In the foregoing chapter they wish it to be considered as having to do only with Jeremiah's private person, but now they are become bolder so that they contradict him officially and thus God Himself, not considering that they know what he says to be spoken not on his own, but on God's account, which is a great blasphemy of God." CRAMER.

6. On xliv. 17. "The ungodly are blind. For they ascribe all their good fortune to their idolatry. When, however, a misfortune comes God and His word must be to blame, and they say: It is vain to serve God (Mal. iii. 14). The charge of the Papists is used again now-a-days. when times are dear and the country suffers such like chastisements, that it is the fault of the Gospel; since on the other hand their mass is regarded as a regular Egyptian Meleket, by which they think to obtain temporal and eternal blessings both for the living and the dead." CRAMER.

7. On xliv. 17. "*Non ovum ovo tam simile est atque huic Judæorum orationi nostrorum hominum vox contendentium, sub papatu aureum fuisse sæculum, cum tamen contrarium testentur historiæ de bellis, peste et fame in papatu, præsertim ea, quæ incidit in annum Christi* 1315, *quo tempore,fere tertia pars Germaniæ partim fame, partim peste extincta. Hinc versus: Ut lateat nullum tempus famis, ecce cucullum.*" FÖRSTER.

8. On xliv. 17. "*Non mirum, quod urbes peste vexentur, cum Æsculapius et Dii ab iis procul absint, nam ex quo Jesus colitur, nihil jam utilitatis a Diis consequimur.* PORPHYRIUS." MS. note in my copy of CRAMER's *Bible*.

9. On xliv. 19. "There is no doubt that the inconstant, frivolous women were the first to be seduced into idolatry, as Eve (2 Cor. xi. 3). When these are taken captive, he then proceeds farther, and knows how to bring in the Adam also. Therefore keep the doors of thy mouth from her that lieth in thy bosom (Mic. vii. 5)." CRAMER.

10. On xliv. 19. "The harmony and complaisance of married people is never more easily secured than when it is against the Lord, and it is nothing unusual for domestic peace to be adduced as the cause of a lack of zeal in religion. It is an ancient custom; Ahab, Abaziah and Solomon only followed Adam. The wife had to be deceived by a subtle serpent; the man was bound to keep peace in the family; she gave him and he ate." ZINZENDORF.

11. On xliv. 20. "God remembers the good and the evil; the good that He may reward it, the evil that He may punish it." CRAMER. ["God will have the last word. The prophets may be run down, but God cannot." HENRY.—S. R. A.]

12. On xliv. 26. "This is the severest punishment of all, that God takes away His holy name and word, as He says in Deut. xxxii. 20: I will hide my face from them, I will see what their end shall be. And this is the famine, not of bread, but of the word of God which they seek and yet do not find (Am. viii. 11)." CRAMER.

13. On xliv. 29, 30. Between Moses and Jeremiah, between the exodus from Egypt and the return thither of the remnant, there lies a period of almost a thousand years, and what a history! But the Pharaoh, under whom Israel made the exodus, Menephthes (comp. LEPSIUS in HERZ., *R.-Enc*, I., S. 146) is described by Herodotus as an arrogant and ungodly man (II., 111), just like Hophra. And at both times Israel was a poor despised heap in the land of Egypt. But the heathen were to know that the God of this despised heap is the only true God, and that their idols were naught, as also Nebuchadnezzar, Belshazzar and Darius the Mede had also to learn (Dan. ii.-vi.).

HOMILETICAL AND PRACTICAL.

1. On xliv. 1-14. The holy love of God: 1. long-suffering; 2. just.

2. On xliv. 9-14. How ruinous a course it is to forget the chastisements of the Lord. This will be shown, if we ponder that this forgetfulness 1. implies chastisement already suffered, 2. proves its want of good results, 3. calls forth severer chastisements from God.

3. On xliv. 15-18. The utmost alienation of a people from their God, shown in the example of the Jews in Egypt. 1. They place the benefits received to the account of their idols. 2. The evils suffered they place to the account of the Lord. 3. They renounce their obedience to the Lord. 4. They vow their service to their idols.

4. On xliv. 26, 27. The severest punishment which the Lord can bring upon a people, who have hitherto served Him. 1. It consists in this, that the Lord removes the candlestick of His word from among this people, *i. e.* that by depriving them of the means of grace, He brings Himself into forgetfulness among the people. 2. It is founded in this, that this people on their part have striven to forget the Lord. 3. It has the effect, that this people is given up to the powers of evil to their complete destruction.

Appendix to the Prophecies Relating to the Entire Theocracy.

THE PROMISE GIVEN TO BARUCH (CHAP. XLV).

While in the fourth year of Jehoiakim, according to ch. xxxvi., *Jeremiah was dictating to his true friend and servant, Baruch, the revelations hitherto received, the latter appears to have been quite overpowered by a feeling of deep sorrow and anguish. Then Jeremiah receives a commission to address to him some words of consolation. This brief address doubtless formed the conclusion of the whole, of the original writing of which an account is given in* ch. xxxvi. *For it is incredible that Baruch was overcome with grief, when he had written the prophecies against the heathen, so far as these were extant in the fourth year of Jehoiakim, in their original position after* ch. xxv. *and before* ch. xxvii. *(comp. rems. on* xxv. 12-14 *and the Introd. to* chh. xlvi.-li.); *these being of relatively consolatory import to the Israelites (comp. especially* xlix. 1 sqq.). *But when he could survey at a glance the entirety of the threatening words pronounced against the theocracy, this may have been the moment when he broke out into the utterance recorded in* xlv. 3. *The word* בִּכְתֹבוֹ, *ver.* 1, *is not opposed to this. For it is not necessary to take the prefix in the sense of " whilst." It merely expresses that Baruch received the revelation at a time when he was at work as amanuensis, neither before nor after; but does not determine whether he received it at the beginning, in the midst, or at the end of this time. Even when the prophet had dictated to him his last words his work was not done : he had still to look over and revise what he had written. It is therefore not credible, that the great main work was interrupted by this personal communication. The present chapter is thus an appendix to the entire collection of Jeremiah's prophecies. Its position at the close corresponds to the dignity and importance of Baruch, who as the faithful friend and amanuensis of the prophet was closely connected with the book as a whole, while Ebed-melech, for whom a similar word of promise is found in* xxxix. 15-18, *came into contact with Jeremiah only at a single epoch. The revelation concerning him was therefore inserted at the corresponding place in the narrative.*

XLV. 1-5.

1 The word that Jeremiah the prophet spake unto Baruch the son of Neriah, when he had written [was writing] these words in a book at the mouth of Jeremiah, in the fourth year of Jehoiakim the son of Josiah, king of Judah, saying,
2, 3 Thus saith the LORD [Jehovah], the God of Israel, unto thee,¹ O Baruch: Thou didst say, Woe is me now! for the LORD hath added grief to my sorrow; I fainted
4 [am weary]² in my sighing, and I find no rest   Thus shalt thou say unto him, The LORD saith thus: Behold, *that* which I have built will I break down, and that
5 which I have planted I will pluck up, even this whole land.³ And seekest thou great things for thyself? seek *them* not: for, behold, I will bring evil upon all flesh, saith the LORD; but thy life will I give unto thee for a prey in all places whither thou goest.

TEXTUAL AND GRAMMATICAL.

¹ Ver. 2.—On עָלֶיךָ in עָלֶיךָ comp. rems. on x. 1.

² Ver. 3.—The verb יָגַע is found besides in Jeremiah only in li. 58.

³ Ver. 4.—As to the construction here, many are of opinion that the article is wanting before הִיא, as *ex. gr.* Gen. xxxii. 23. But we should then have אֵת. Others would take אֵת in the emasculated sense, in which it " approaches to " לְ=in respect to, as to (EWALD, § 277, d). But in the connection of this passage אֵת appears plainly as the sign of the accusative, governed by the preceding transitive verb. I therefore think that הִיא is used here simply with an emphatic significance, which we may express by inserting the word " even :" even the whole land, *even this!* Comp. Num. xviii. 23 ; Isa. vii. 14. This is also the case with הִיא after a personal pronoun: אָנֹכִי עָנָה הוּא, Isa. xliii. 25 ; Jer. xlix. 12, *etc.*

EXEGETICAL AND CRITICAL.

In the fourth year of Jehoiakim, when Baruch, the son of Neriah, was writing out the prophecies of Jeremiah at his dictation (vers. 1 and 2), the proclamation is made to him, in answer to his expression of sorrow (ver. 3): that the Lord is intending to desolate the whole land (ver. 4), but he, Baruch, without laying claim to greater things, should accept, as a reward of distinguished grace, that whithersoever he might be cast, he should everywhere escape with his life (ver. 5).

CHAP. XLV. 1–5.   359

Vers. 1-3. **The word ... find no rest.**
After Baruch (comp. rems. on xxxii. 12) had finished writing what was dictated to him, Jeremiah receives the command to address a prophecy to him, concerning only his own person.
—Baruch was evidently powerfully affected by the total impression made by the prophecies upon him (comp. rems. on xxxvi. 1, 16). In addition to the sorrow, which he must have felt with every other Israelite, at the present disturbed condition of his native land, was the anxiety for the future, which had been awakened by the minatory predictions he had heard.—**Grief** Comp. viii. 18; xx. 18; xxxi. 13.—**I faint.** The same thought as in Lam. v. 5.
Vers. 4, 5. **Thus shalt thou ... thou goest.** Two things are involved in these words:
1. Although the theocracy is the Lord's creation, it is yet His fixed determination to destroy His work. With respect to the expression, comp. i. 10; xviii. 7, 9; xxxi. 28.—**Even this whole land.** If we compare xxv. 15-26, we shall perceive that this determination to destroy is to be understood in a twofold degree, and accordingly אָרֶץ is to be taken in the double sense of land and earth. The whole earth and the existence of all nations upon it is the Lord's work, but the Lord will cause His judgment to issue on all this, His work. But Israel's land and people is especially His sanctuary, the first fruits of His increase (ii. 3), His precious inheritance (iii. 19; Ezek. xx. 6, 15), and of course Baruch's sorrow relates above all to the ruin threatening his own, the chosen nation. It is thus declared by the words, "this whole land," that it is not a partial visitation, but a total devastation of the country, which is impending.—2. If now the whole (comp. xii. 12; xxv. 31) is under sentence of total destruction, no single individual can claim a high degree of positive earthly prosperity. Even the best must be content, if only mere earthly existence, bare life, is guaranteed him. This is done here with respect to Baruch. Thus a measure is given of the degree and extent of the calamity relating to the whole. Comp. xxi. 9; xxxviii. 2, 17.

DOCTRINAL AND ETHICAL.

1. Baruch did not act as secretary for hire but for love. He esteemed it an honor and a happiness, that by his skill he could serve the Lord, to whom he owed it. Therefore a glorious reward is imparted to him unsought, so that his name and remembrance are immortalized in the sacred record by an oracle addressed specially to him. This honor is to be esteemed still higher than the assurance, that this wretched mortal life should not be taken by violence before its time.

2. On xlv. 3. "*Non Stoicos nos esse convenit, qui ἀπάθειαν commendare atque asserere soliti, qualis etiam fuit Münzerus ejusque progenies Anabaptistæ.*"
FÖRSTER.
3 On xlv. 4. Compare the remarks on vii. 4. There is no delusion more ruinous than to suppose that the Lord cannot destroy His own work again. The destruction will certainly only come upon the bad. But it is the bad on the earth, among the chosen people, in the church and on the throne, who imagine themselves to be secure, in spite of their badness, by the fact of the divine appointment or choice, whereby they make God the servant of sin. God has created the earth. He will destroy it by fire. But a new earth and a new heaven will proceed from the conflagration. He has thrown down the holy city and temple and scattered the people of Israel. But the Ἰσραήλ κατὰ πνεῦμα still lives and will one day permeate the Ἰσραήλ κατὰ σάρκα with new life again (Rom. xi.). The Christian Church in the East has been devastated by Islam, and what guarantee then have Rome, Geneva and Wittenberg that it will not be with them as with Jerusalem? Princes too are not to understand the divine right of legitimacy as that God can appoint princes but cannot depose them. Yet even if all present Christian churches were to be destroyed and all thrones overthrown, neither the Church of the Lord would cease to be, nor the magistracy, which is ordained of God (Matt. xvi.; Rom. xiii.).

4. On xlv. 5. "*Felices frustra nobis promittimus annos semper enim curæ tristitiæque premunt.*" Quotation by FÖRSTER.

5. On xlv. 5. Endeavor not after high things. Is it then not a great thing in this world, laden as it is with a curse (Gen. iii. 17-19), if one has sustenance and clothing? (1 Tim. vi. 8). And is it not the greatest thing of all, if one knows that his soul is saved in heaven, even if he must take the place there, with which the prodigal son would have been content in his father's house? (Luke xv.).

HOMILETICAL AND PRACTICAL.

1. On xlv. 2-5. A word of consolation and exhortation for all the tried children of God. 1. Let no one be surprised at the heat, which he encounters, as though something strange had happened to him. 2. Let every one be satisfied with the one thing needful: (*a*) for his body, (*b*) for his spirit.
2. On xlv. 4. God's own institutions. We must distinguish in these: 1. the temporary form (not secured against decay and outward ruin); 2. the everlasting kernel (this is indestructible and bears in itself the guarantee of eternal duration and ever more glorious development).

III. SECOND MAIN DIVISION.

The Prophecies Against Foreign Nations.

(CHAPP. XLVI.—LI.)

The prophets of Israel could not avoid bringing the heathen nations also within the sphere of their predictions. They were compelled to this, partly even from their theocratic and particularistic point of view, in so far as the interests of the theocracy were essentially affected by the standing or falling of their heathen neighbors, and partly in a general view, as they represented the idea of the all-embracing divine love and providence. Hence we find declarations concerning heathen nations in most of the prophetic books. We find these prophecies relating to heathen nations, comprising larger groups, in Isaiah, chh. xiii.-xxiii., in Ezekiel chh. xxv.-xxxii., and here also in Jeremiah xlvi.-li.
The main trunk of these prophecies is formed by a Sepher, which according to its principal part, owes its origin to the period immediately before the battle of Carchemish (comp. rems. on xlvi. 2). As Amos makes his way through a cycle of seven nations to his main goal, the kingdom of Israel (i. 3—ii. 5), and as Ezekiel predicts a judgment on seven nations, so our Sepher also contains declarations against seven nations: Egypt, Philistia, Moab, Ammon, Edom, Damascus, and Elam. This arrangement is evidently intentional; proceeding from Egypt the prophet advances to the Philistines; from these he springs across to their eastern neighbors and concludes with Elam, as representing the distant East and North. It is evident that these seven utterances form the main trunk, of the Sepher against the nations, from two circumstances. First, that in none of them is Nebuchadnezzar or the Chaldeans mentioned. This is the certain and constantly observed sign of composition before the battle of Carchemish. Secondly, that five of them (or six, comp. infra, rems. on xlix. 34-39) have a similar commencement, viz.
לְמוֹאָב לְמִצְרַיִם, *etc. This grammatical form is closely connected with the common superscription,* **The word of Jehovah which came to Jeremiah against the nations, xlvi. 1.**
The prefix לְ, *viz. expresses the comprehension of the following special prophecies under this general title (comp.* NAEGELSB. *Gr.,* § 112, 5, b). *On this point, however, two things are to be remarked. 1. The prophecy against the Philistines (ch. xlvii.) bears a superscription according to a different formula, and provided with a special date. We shall show, on xlvii. 1, that this prophecy is older than the six others of the Sepher against the Nations, that it is indeed the oldest of all the prophecies of Jeremiah against heathen nations. It was therefore already extant, when the Sepher was formed, and was therefore included in it, just as it was. 2. The prophecy against Elam (xlix. 34-38) likewise bears a title differing both in form and purport, by which the utterance is assigned to the fourth year of Zedekiah. With this superscription the case is quite peculiar. In the* LXX., *viz. ch. xxv. continues after ver. 13:* Ἃ ἐπροφήτευσεν Ἱερεμίας ἐπὶ τὰ ἔθνη τὰ Αἰλάμ. *Hereupon follows the prophecy which we read in the Hebrew text* xlix. 35-38. *At the close of this, however, we find the words:* Ἐν ἀρχῇ βασιλεύοντος Σεδεκίου βασιλέως ἐγένετο ὁ λόγος οὗτος περὶ Ἀλλάμ. *The prophecy against Elam in the* LXX. *thus has no superscription and a postscript, which is unexampled in Jeremiah. Now, however, the double circumstance comes in, that in the* LXX. *the superscription of ch.* xxvii. *is wanting, the same which in the Hebrew text contains the evidently and admittedly false name Jehoiakim, and that in the Hebrew text the prophecy against Elam is in* xlix. 34 *assigned to the fourth year of Zedekiah, though Nebuchadnezzar and the Chaldeans are not mentioned, as they usually are in prophecies subsequent to the battle of Carchemish. From this state of the case I draw the following conclusions: 1. The prophecy against Elam must originally have had the superscription* לְעֵילָם, *in conformity to the superscriptions of the prophecies against Egypt I., Moab, Ammon, Edom and Damascus. For only thus is the abrupt* τὰ Αἰλάμ *in the superscription of the prophecy in the* LXX. *explicable. The article* τὰ *proceeds from the circumstance that they connected* Αἰλάμ *grammatically with* τὰ ἔθνη, *to which neither grammar nor criticism give any justification, for they arbitrarily separated* אֲשֶׁר
בָּא יִרְמְיָהוּ עַל־הַגּוֹיִם, xxv. 13, *from the previous context, and made it the superscription, then arbitrarily placed* לְעֵילָם *as if in apposition to* הַגּוֹיִם, *and finally, with equal arbitrariness, transposed the whole prophecy hither, for it stood originally in another place. From the postscript, viz. we see that 2. the prophecy must originally have stood, as it still does in the Hebrew text, at the close of the Sepher against the nations, but immediately before* ch. xxvii., *this postscript being evidently no other than the first verse of* ch. xxvii. *(modified according to circumstances), which is entirely wanting in the* LXX., *and in the Hebrew contains the wrong name of a king. How did this prophecy come by a postscript, since no other prophecy in Jeremiah has such an one? Whence came it that* xxvii. 1 *is entirely wanting in the* LXX.? *To say nothing of the circumstance, that the date* ἐν ἀρχῇ βασιλεύοντος Σεδεκίου *in the prophecy against Elam is as incorrect as* xxvii. 1 *is undoubtedly alone correct (comp. rems. on* xxvii. 1 *and* xlix. 34). *But how now does verse 1 of* ch. xxvii. *come to be the postscript, in the*

Hebrew the superscription to the prophecy against Elam? Evidently the prophecies against the nations must once have had their place after ch. xxv. and before ch. xxvii. 1. They were, however, taken away from this place, and xxvii. 1 went with them, whether it was that it was really taken for the postscript of the prophecy, or by an unintentional error. If this view is correct it is thus determined that the Sepher against the nations then concluded with the prophecy against Elam. Whether the subsequently added prophecies against Egypt II., against the Arabians and against Babylon were then incorporated in the Sepher cannot be ascertained. Where, however, did the Sepher begin, or rather on what portion of our book did it follow? Chapter xxv. cannot have preceded it, for it is quite out of the question, that it can ever have had place between chh. xxvi. and xxvii. Since that detached verse (xxvii. 1) is found at the close, or at the beginning of the prophecy against Elam, and not at the close of the passage xxv. 15-38, it necessarily follows that this passage did not follow, but preceded the Sepher against the nations. Thus the Sepher cannot have been attached to xxv. 14, 13 or 12. It can, therefore, have had its place only between xxvii. 1 and xxv. 38. Both the present form of the text in the LXX., and the purport of xxv. 13 b, show that it must have been placed in the immediate neighborhood of this verse. For what reason? The verses 12, 13 and 14 of ch. xxv.. are directed against Babylon. They treat of the ruin of Babylon with an emphasis and a detail, which do not correspond at all to the historical fact to which ch. xxv. owes its origin. The first half of xxv. 13 decidedly presupposes the prophecy against Babylon, pertaining to the fourth year of Zedekiah (comp. li. 59). From this it follows, that the Sepher against the nations can have been transposed from its original place between xxv. 38 and xxvii. 1 to that before xxv. 15, only with the prophecy against Babylon, therefore after its becoming known. We shall not err if we suppose that the words in xxv. 11, "and these nations shall serve the king of Babylon seventy years," gave occasion both to the more extended portrayal of the visitation of Babylon only implicitly, intimated as we have it in the verses xxv. 12-14, and also the transposition hither of the Sepher against the nations now extended by the prophecy against Babylon. The LXX. version flowed from a recension affording this form of the text. For omitting ver. 14, it is connected with ver. 13, and then gives, though in a different order from the Masoretic text, the prophecies against the nations and as a comprehensive conclusion follows the passage xxv. 15-38 in ch. xxxii. From ch. xxxiii. onward the remaining chapters follow in the same order as in the Masoretic text, only that a chapter is not devoted to the prophecy for Baruch, this appearing in the LXX. merely as the conclusion of ch. li. Another diaskeuast (who it was it would be impossible to determine) now found it more to the purpose to separate the prophecies against the nations from the passages relating to the theocracy. And thus they were then, without making any alteration in vers. xxv. 12-14, transposed to the place, where we now find them in the Masoretic text.—The prophecy against Babylon was, however, the only addition to the original Sepher against the nations. Two new portions were inserted at appropriate places between the original ones, viz.: 1, a second prophecy against Egypt (xlvi. 13-26) which expressly mentions the name Nebuchadnezzar; 2. a prophecy against the northern Arabian kingdom (xlix. 28-33), in which at any rate Nebuchadnezzar's name is mentioned in vers. 28 and 30. The insertion of the second prophecy against Egypt after the first, and that against the Arabians after that against Damascus, and before that against Elam, cannot be regarded as other than appropriate.

1. THE SUPERSCRIPTION.

XLVI. 1.

1   The word of the LORD [Jehovah] which came to Jeremiah the prophet against the Gentiles [THE NATIONS].

This superscription extends over the whole of the prophecies here brought together and forming a ספר. It thus forms the heading to chh. xlvi.-li., and introduces the second main division of the Book. The form is the same as in xiv. 1; xlvii. 1; xlix. 34. On the grammar, comp. rems. on xiv. 1

2. THE FIRST PROPHECY AGAINST EGYPT

XLVI. 2-12.

2   Against [concerning] Egypt, against the army of Pharaoh-necho king of Egypt, which was by the river Euphrates in Carchemish, which Nebuchadrezzar king of Babylon smote in the fourth year of Jehoiakim the son of Josiah king of Judah.
3   Prepare ye the buckler and the shield,
    And move ye on to the battle.
4   Harness the horses, and mount ye horsemen,
    And stand forth with your helmets,
    Furbish[1] the spears, put on coats of mail.[2]
5   Why, (as) I see, are they dismayed—retreat?
    And their heroes are dashed to pieces;
    They flee in haste, and turn not again?[3]
    Fear round about![4] saith Jehovah.

6 Let not the swift flee away;[5]
  Nor let the mighty escape!
  Northwards, by the margin of the river Euphrates, they totter, they fall.
7 Who is he who riseth up like the Nile,
  His waters roll along like the streams?[6]
8 Egypt riseth up like the Nile,
  His waters roll along like the streams;
  And he said, I will up, cover the land,
  Destroy[7] the city and them that dwell therein.
9 Mount ye[8] the horses, and rage, ye chariots;
  And let the mighty warriors go forth:
  Cush and Phut, who handle the shield,
  And Lydians, that handle and tread the bow.[9]
10 And that day is a day of vengeance for the LORD, Jehovah Zebaoth,
  That he may avenge himself on his enemies;
  And the sword shall devour[10] and be satiate,[11]
  And be drunken with their blood:
  For a slain offering has the LORD, Jehovah Zebaoth,
  In the land of the North by the river Euphrates.
11 Go up towards Gilead and fetch balm, Virgin daughter of Egypt![12]
  In vain takest thou many medicines;
  There is no plaster[13] for thee.
12 Nations hear of thy shame,
  And with thy crying the earth is filled,
  For one warrior threw down another,
  They are both of them fallen together.[14]

TEXTUAL AND GRAMMATICAL.

[1] Ver. 4.—מרק. Comp. Lev. vi. 21; 2 Chron. iv. 16. The meaning is to clean, polish by rubbing.

[2] Ver. 4.—סריון only here and in li. 3, for שריון.

[3] Ver. 5.—יבהת. Comp. Mic. i. 7; Job iv. 20; OLSH., § 261.—נסוג. Comp. Lev. xxvi. 36; NAEGELSB. Gr., § 93, d, Anm.—הפנה Hiph. in direct causative signification—make a turn. Comp. ver. 21; xlvii. 3; xlix. 24; NAEGELSB. Gr., § 18, 3.

[4] Ver. 5.—כנור מסביב. Comp. vi. 25; xx. 3, 10; xlix. 29.

[5] Ver. 6.—אל־ינוס. If it were not the unabbreviated form, the words might be taken as the divine command. As it is אל must be taken in the feebler senso לא. Comp. 2 Kings vi. 27; Ps. xxxiv. 6; xli. 3; Job v. 22, etc.

[6] Ver. 7.—יאור, a word of Egyptian origin, signifies as an appellative "ditch, canal," Isa. xxxiii. 21; Job xxviii. 10, as a proper name the Nile only, Am. viii. 8; ix. 5: Isa. xix. 8; xxiii. 10, etc.—נהרות is also an Egyptian reminiscence, in so far as it is used of the arms or canals of the Nile, Exod. vii. 19; viii. 1; Ezek. xxxii. 2, 14.

[7] Ver. 8.—אבידה, comp. GESEN., § 68, 2, Anm. 1; OLSH., § 237 b.—עיר. Comp. viii. 16; xlvii. 2.

[8] Ver. 9.—הרכב, vocative. Comp. NAEGELSB. Gr., § 71, 5, Anm. 4.

[9] Ver. 9.—On תפשי רכבי קשת. Comp. קשת רמי, Ps. lxxviii. 9; NAEGELSB. Gr., § 63, 4, e.

[10] Ver. 10.—ואכלה ונו. As was remarked on ver. 1, these perfects with the Vau conversive can be taken in a future sense only. Nothing in the context transposes us into the past. All previous verbs relate to the future, and if the day were to be designated as past this would have to be done either disertis verbis, or by ואכל. Except on a false interpretation of ver. 2, we obtain the impression from vers. 7-9 that it is the future which is being described, and if the day (ver. 10) is recognized as future, the following verbs can only be so rendered. Comp. NAEGELSB. Gr., § 84, o.

[11] Ver. 10.—ושביעה ונו. Comp. Isa. xxxiv. 5 sqq.

[12] Ver. 11.—On בתולת בת מי. Comp. NAEGELSB. Gr., § 64, 4.

[13] Ver. 11.—תעלה. Comp. xxx. 13. The word occurs only in these two passages in Jeremiah, and in these only with the meaning of "something laid on, bandage, plaster."

[14] Ver. 12.—גבור בגבור. The prefix ב is to be taken in its proper, instrumental signification: One stumbles by another, because one throws another over the heap. Comp. Lev. xxvi. 37.

EXEGETICAL AND CRITICAL.

After the double, viz., general and special title (vers. 1, 2), two pictures are presented before us. The first (vers. 3-6) is the more general and indefinite; warriors are admonished to equip themselves for battle (vers. 3, 4). Then, however, directly follows a description of the defeat and terrible flight, with a statement as to the place of the battle (vers. 5, 6). In the second picture not only is Egypt mentioned as the army addressed by the prophet, but it is also portrayed in colors taken from specially Egyptian relations. That we have, moreover, two pictures before us, is seen from the circumstance, that in vers. 7-12

CHAP. XLVI. 2-12.   365

the whole course of the struggle from beginning to end is described in its main features: the prophet sees the Egyptian host approaching like the overflow of the Nile (vers. 7, 8); he then summons horses, chariots and all warriors (among them the neighboring nations, forming part of the host), to the fight (ver. 9). But the fight does not end well for Egypt: it is a day of the vengeance of Jehovah on Egypt, a sacrificial feast, in which Egypt is the slaughtered victim (ver. 10). The consequences of the lost battle are so fatal to Egypt, that it cannot recover, and the report of its overthrow fills the world (vers. 11, 12).—Does this passage contain a prophecy of the battle, or does it presuppose the battle as already fought? I think the former. For according to ver. 10 (וְאָכְלָה וגו׳), the battle is evidently still future. But the prophet felt himself moved to this prophecy, not during the advance of the Egyptian host from its country, but when it had already taken up a position on the Euphrates and the decisive conflict was there to be expected. This follows clearly from ver. 2 in connection with ver. 6 b, and ver. 10 b, as will be further seen in the exposition of these passages. The prophetic and poetical prediction of the approaching battle comes into the foreground, but this does not exclude brief significant hints with respect to the consequences of the battle for the whole future of Egypt.

Ver. 2. **Against Egypt . . . of Judah.** לְמִצְרַיִם, comp. xxiii. 9; xlviii. 1; xlix. 1, 7, 23, 28. The prefix לְ restricts the general idea expressed in the main superscription to a special part. Comp. xix. 13; Ezek. xliv. 9; Lev. xii. 6, 7. Pharaoh-necho (נְכֹה, 2 Ki. xxiii. 29-35) was the sixth king of the twenty-sixth dynasty. He reigned after his father, the great Psammetichus, from B. C., 610-595. Comp. DUNCKER, I., S. 817, 925; HERZOG, R.-Enc. X., S. 257.—He came from Egypt by sea, landed to the north of Carmel in the bay of Acco, and defeated Josiah at Megiddo (608). Jehoiakim was his creature (comp. 2 Ki. xxiii. 34). He was thus at the time de facto ruler of Judah. After the battle at Megiddo, it must have been easy for him to subjugate Phœnicia and Syria, for who was there to offer him any resistance? The power of the Assyrians, Medes and Babylonians, was concentrated in and around Nineveh. Nineveh fell B. C., 606. Now first did the Babylonian army advance under the leadership of Nebuchadnezzar. It met the Egyptians at Carchemish. The city was situated at the confluence of the Chaboras [Chebar or Khaboor], and the Euphrates, on a peninsula formed by the two rivers. Here was the principal passage across the Euphrates (comp. NIEBUHR, S. 205, 369; HERZOG, Real-Enc. VII., S. 379), and here as "the extreme line of defence of his new province" (NIEBUHR, S. 369), Necho took up his position. He must have lain here for some time, whether because the siege of the city occupied much time, or because it was a part of his plan not to advance further, but here in a favorable position to await the enemy. Observe in the text the double relative sentence **which was,** etc., and **which Nebuchadnezzar,** etc. It is doubtless not by accident that by the first of the two, the first mentioned stay of Necho at Carchemish is especially set forth. If the chief emphasis lay on the battle, that first sentence would have been quite superfluous. It would have been enough to say: "which Nebuchadnezzar smote by the Euphrates in Carchemish." From the emphasis on the stay by the Euphrates it is clear to me that this, and not the battle, was the occasion of the prophecy. When Jeremiah learned that the Egyptian army had taken up a position at Carchemish, he recognized at once the importance of the situation. He knew, that now a collision between the southern and northern empires was inevitable, that there on the Euphrates the destinies of the world would be decided for the proximate future. Egypt on the Euphrates! This was the fatal juncture which summoned him to prophetic utterance. Observe, also, that in the prophecy itself he does not yet mention Nebuchadnezzar (he names him, as I have frequently shown, only after the battle), but he twice mentions in a significant manner the position on the Euphrates (ver. 6 and ver. 7); an evident proof that it was this, which led him to speak. He foresees that it would eventuate in a battle. And with equal definiteness, he sees what the result will be (vers. 5, 6; ver. 10 sqq.). The entire superscription (ver. 2) was added subsequently by the prophet on the writing of the prophecy. In the first relative sentence he indicates the occasion, in the second he declares that the fulfilment followed very speedily in the fourth year of Jehoiakim (B. C. 605-4). The date refers primarily to "smote," but it does not follow that the prophecy may not have been made the same year, or sooner. The particulars here are not to be determined, but it is possible that the news of the establishment of the Egyptians on the Euphrates, did not reach Jerusalem before the fourth year of Jehoiakim. NIEBUHR is of opinion that the battle had already taken place in the third year of Jehoiakim (Ass. u. Bab., S. 50, 86, 370), and that hence the date here refers to the composition of the poem, not to the historical event of the battle. The chronological relations are not to be investigated here, but exegetically it seems to me as impossible to put a point after smote (NIEBUHR, S. 86, Anm.), as to refer **in the fourth year to the word,** etc., ver. 1, as GRAF proposes. Apart from their being so far removed from each other, ver. 1 is a general title referring to all the following chapters, including ch. li. The construction too, would then be obscure and forced. We should then have to take לְמִצְרַיִם as a more particular definition: with respect to Egypt, however, in the fourth year; which would give the sense that only this prophecy was uttered against Egypt, in the fourth year of Jehoiakim, which is incorrect.

Vers. 3-6. **Prepare ye . . . the fall.** The first battle-picture commences with the call to the warriors to prepare buckler and shield (the Egyptian monuments show two kinds of shields, a larger [צִנָּה] and a smaller. Comp. NEUMANN, II., S. 383), to harness the horses (to the chariots) and to mount. פָּרָשִׁים designates the horses for riding in distinction from carriage-horses in 2 Sam. i. 6; 1 Kings v. 6; Joel ii. 4;

Ezek. xxvii. 14. This usage being established, and the parallelism favoring the meaning "*equi*," I believe that הפרשים is to be translated not in the vocative, but as in the text: and mount ye riders. Of the other expressions in ver. 4, the first, after horses and riders, must refer to the footmen, the rest, as in ver. 3, to all species of arms.—In the second act of the first picture, the prophet sees the army defeated: **Why, I see, are they dismayed?** Comp. xxx. 6. As הכה (they) is the nominative and ראה requires the accusative after it in a still higher degree than היה, our passage cannot, as GRAF supposes, be explained by Ezek. xxxvii. 19 coll. Gen. vi. 17, but **I see** must be taken as a parenthetical sentence.—The description closes significantly with two perfects, the prophet sees the tottering and falling as accomplished facts. Comp. ver. 12.

Vers. 7-12. **Who is he . . . fallen together.** The second battle picture is more in detail, more concrete, and as it were painted with specifically Egyptian colors. The prophet sees the Egyptian army approaching like the overflowing Nile. The immediate preparations for the battle are described in ver. 9, as in ver. 4, only still more concretely. Cavalry, chariots and footmen are equally distinguished. I am therefore of opinion that we must render עלו ו here as in ver. 4 "mount the horses."—The chariots are to rage (comp. Nah. ii. 5), the mighty warriors to go forth on foot. Egypt's neighboring nations accompany the expedition, and the Ethiopians and Lybians are described as shield-bearers, and therefore masters of close combat (*cominus*), the Lybians (comp. Gen. x. 13 coll. 22; Isa. lxvi. 19; Ezek. xxvii. 10) as archers. The three nations stand together, as here, as Egyptian auxiliaries in Ezek. xxx. 5 coll. Nah. iii. 9. On **Lydians** לוד, comp. ARNOLD in HERZOG, *Real.-Enc.*, VIII., S. 510.

All these preparations, however, do not ensure the victory, it being ordained that the day of battle shall be a day of vengeance for Jehovah, and a bloody sacrificial festival. Egypt both in ancient and more recent times has injured the theocracy, and now stands opposed to the chosen instrument of the Lord, Nebuchadnezzar, and must therefore be subdued.—**Day of vengeance.** Comp. li. 6; Isa. xxxiv. 8; lxi. 2; lxiii. 4.—**Sacrifice.** A slain offering, where the original meaning of the verb (comp. Numb. xxii. 40; 1 Ki. i. 19) comes into the foreground, but the word must not be taken in its literal signification. Comp. Isa. xxxiv. 6; Zeph. i. 7. In the last two verses the *consequences* of the lost battle are described. Egypt is ironically called upon to fetch balm from Gilead (comp. rems. on viii. 22). But the blow was fatal. Therefore remedies are of no avail, to however great extent applied. The fearful defeat cannot of course remain hidden. The nations must learn the shame of Egypt, since the cry of the stricken ones fills the world (xiv. 2 coll. Isa. xlii. 11). Ver. 12 *b* contains a step backwards, an additional statement of reason. This is occasioned by the evident endeavor to close the second picture in correspondence to the first.

3. THE SECOND PROPHECY AGAINST EGYPT.

XLVI. 13-26.

With an Appendix, xlvi. 27, 28.

13   The word that the LORD [Jehovah] spake to Jeremiah the prophet, how [concerning the coming of] Nebuchadnezzar, king of Babylon, should come and [to] smite the land of Egypt.
14   Proclaim ye it in Egypt and publish it in Migdol,
    Publish it also in Noph and Tahpanhes.
    Say ye, Stand fast[1] and prepare thyself;[2]
    For the sword hath devoured thy neighbors.
15   Wherefore is thy bull[3] dragged away?
    He stood not, for Jehovah thrust him away
16   He causeth many to totter;
    One also falleth upon another:
    And they say, Up! let us return to our own people,
    And to the land of our birth, from the murderous sword.
17   There they cry:[4] Pharaoh, king of Egypt, is lost;[5]
    He hath lost the time through neglect!
18   As truly as I live, saith the king,
    Jehovah Zebaoth is his Name;

As Tabor among the mountains,
And as Carmel by the sea, shall he come.
Make thyself preparations [apparatus] for journeying,
Thou inhabitant, daughter of Egypt;
19 For Noph shall become a wilderness,
And destroyed without an inhabitant.
20 A finely formed heifer is Egypt;
A gad-fly[6] from the north is coming, is coming.[1]
21 Her hirelings also in her midst are like fatted calves
For they also turn and flee away together.
They stand not, for the day of their destruction is come upon them,—
The time of their visitation.
22 Her sound[8] goeth like the sound of serpents;
For with power they advance,
And are come to her with axes as hewers of wood.
23 They have cut down her forest, saith Jehovah.
For it is not to be searched;
For they are many, more than the locusts,
And of them there is no number.
24 The daughter of Egypt has been put to shame,
Delivered into the hand of a people from the North.
25 Saith Jehovah Zebaoth, the God of Israel,
Behold, I visit the Amon of No,
And Pharaoh and Egypt, and its gods and its kings,
And Pharaoh and those that trust in him.
26 And I give them into the hand of those that seek their lives,
And into the hand of Nebuchadnezzar, the king of Babylon,
And into the hand of his servants:
And afterwards it shall be inhabited[9]
As in the days of old, saith Jehovah.

TEXTUAL AND GRAMMATICAL.

[1] Ver. 14.—הִתְיַצֵּב comp. ver. 4.

[2] Ver. 14.—וְהָכֵן לָךְ. Comp. Ezek. xxxviii. 7. It is a direct causative Hiphil: make preparation, equipment for thy self. NAEGELSB. *Gr.*, § 69, 1, *Anm.* 2.

[8] Ver. 15.—Jeremiah uses the plural אַבִּירִים elsewhere only in the meaning of "strong horses" (viii. 16; xlvii. 3; L 11). But neither this meaning nor that of "strong men, heroes" גִּבּוֹרִים suits the connection. For apart from נִסְחַף (besides here in Prov. xxviii. 3 only) which as a fore-going predicate may certainly stand in the singular, the singulars עָבַד and הָדְפוֹ show that אַבִּירֶיךָ is to be taken as singular. Then, however, nothing is more natural than, with the LXX., to think of the Apis. This is the LXX. translation: διατί ἔφυγεν ἀπό σου ὁ Ἆπις; ὁ μόσχος ὁ ἐκλεκτός σου οὐκ ἔμεινεν. אָבִּיר both in the singular and plural is frequently used for bulls: Isa. xxxiv. 7; Ps. xxii. 13; 1. 13; lxviii. 31. But who but Apis is the bull of Egypt? The plural suffix has been explained as an abnormal pausal pronunciation (comp. תְּהִלָּתֶיךָ Ps. ix. 15; שְׁנָאתֶיךָ Ezek. xxxv. 11—כִּי־נֶיךָ [Gen. xvi. 5; 1 Ki. xv. 19] which GRAF adduces, does not belong here), comp. OLSH., § 39, c, *Anm.*; § 131, k, but this is unnecessary. אַבִּיר (observe that Jehovah also is called אֲבִיר יִשְׂרָאֵל or אֲבִיר יַעֲקֹב Isa. i. 24; xlix. 26, etc.) stands in the plural as a name of God, according to the analogy of בַּעַל אָדוֹן, תְּרָפִים, קְדֹשִׁים, which again themselves follow the analogy of אֱלֹהִים. Comp. NAEGELSB. *Gr.*, § 61, 2, *Anm.*; OLSH., § 122, g; GESEN., § 108, 2, *Anm.*, b.

[4] Ver. 17.—קָרְאוּ שָׁם. LXX., Vulg., Syr., and after them many modern commentators read these words קִרְאוּ שֵׁם (comp. xx. 3; Isa. viii. 3; xx. 7), but, as it appears to me, unnecessarily. The nominative of קָרְאוּ is not the auxiliaries, and שָׁם need not be referred to their home. It may very well be referred to the place where Apis was maltreated, and the warriors were killed, thus generally to the place of the previously described defeat. It might even be referred to the time, for שָׁם has also a temporal signification. Comp. Ps. xiv. 5; liii. 5; Job xxxv. 12; Hos. ii. 17; Jer. l. 9. The subject of קָרְאוּ may be an indefinite number:—*they* call. Comp. iii. 16, 17; NAEGELSB. *Gr.*, § 101, 2, a.

[5] Ver. 17.—The meaning of שָׁאוֹן is *strepitus, tumultus* (Isa. v. 14; xiii. 14; Jer. xxv. 31; xlviii. 45; li. 55, etc.). With the idea of tumult and confusion is connected that of destruction and ruin (comp. בּוֹר שָׁאוֹן, Ps. xl. 3). The word would then be used as *abstr. pro concreto:* Pharaoh is ruin, *i. e.*, ruined, (Comp. NAEGELSB. *Gr.*, § 59, 1) and there is no need to read שֵׁאוֹן with MAURER. We know not why the prophet chose this particular word, but there is probably an allusion in

It to some Egyptian word unknown to us. Why Pharaoh is ruined the prophet proceeds to tell us. כוּעֵר is the appointed season (Gen. i. 14; xvii. 21; xxi. 2, etc.) עָבַר of passing over a time is quite usual (comp. ex. gr., viii. 20; Job xxx. 15).

⁶ Ver. 20.—קֶרֶץ. The word occurs here only. The root קָרַץ signifies "to pinch, press together" (of the eyes Prov vi. 13; x. 11; xxxv. 19, of the lips Prov. xvi. 30) then "to pinch off" (Job xxxiii. 6). קָרַץ is then pinching, pinching off or that which pinches. The old translations are vacillating: LXX. ἀπόσπασμα; Chald. קָטְלִין יָכְמִין populi interfectores; Syr. exercitus; Vulg. stimulator. Attaching himself to the last ROSENMUELLER translates *tabulus*; COCCEIUS, SCHULTENS, EICHHORN, HITZIG, GRAF, MAIER, gad-fly; Bremsel, comparing the Arabic quarsa, *papagil* pulex, quarls, *insectum cimici simile*, or quirs, a kind of small fly. Much more unsuitably EWALD adduces quarsa, and understands by it a great, fearful monster. The meaning *excidium*, which the Rabbis, GESENIUS, UMBREIT and others attribute to the word, does not correspond very exactly to the specific radical signification. Following this and the Arabic analogies I regard the meaning gad-fly as correct, which suits the connection admirably. Comp. Exod. xxiii. 28; Deut. i. 44; vii. 20; Isa. vii. 18; Ps. cxviii. 12. [BLAYNEY translates "breeze" though he admits the radical meaning and the Arabic analogies: NOTES has "destruction" as the A. V., NEUMANN, FUERST, etc.—S. R. A.]

⁷ Ver. 20.—The reading בָּהּ אַף in the LXX., Chald., Syr., Arab., and many codd. of KENNICOTT and DE ROSSI is only a weak correction.

⁸ Ver. 22.—I do not approve of the reading קוֹלָם followed by the ancient translators and by HITZIG. קוֹלָהּ refers to Egypt. The feminine suffix (comp. בְּקִרְבָהּ שְׂכִירֶיהָ ver. 21) is to be referred, if not to עָנְלָה, yet to בַּת מִצְרַיִם (ver. 19). The construction of the sentence is as I. 9; Nah. ii. 5. Comp. NAEGELSB. *Gr.*, § 65, 3, *Anm.* There is, it is true, no passage in which דֶּרֶךְ is used expressly of the voice; but why may not the voice be described as going? לִשְׁוֹנָם תַּהֲלֹךְ Ps. lxxiii. 9 is at least related. If we take יֵלֵךְ as a relative sentence (like a serpent, which goes) the expression is very feeble, and the meaning "creeps," which GRAF substitutes, either declares nothing, or must have an artificial meaning to it.

⁹ Ver. 26.—שָׁכַן is used here in the neutral sense, as in Isa. xiii. 20; Jer. xvii. 6, 25; xxx. 18; l. 13, 39.

EXEGETICAL AND CRITICAL.

This prophecy cannot be regarded as an immediate contemporaneous continuation of the previous one. 1. The title announces it as an independent passage. There is not the slightest ground for regarding this as a later addition, for it contains nothing which Jeremiah could not himself have written. 2. In ver. 26 Nebuchadnezzar is mentioned by name. Jeremiah never does this before the battle of Carchemish. As now we must assign the passage xlvi. 1-12 to the period immediately before that battle, it follows that the present passage must have originated at a later period. 3. If the superscription in ver. 13 expresses nothing with regard to the time of composition, but only states the main purport of the passage, it is yet clear that a prophecy concerning the coming of Nebuchadnezzar more probably originated at a time in which Jeremiah demonstrably expected this coming than at a time of which we have no trace that the prophet cherished this expectation. The prophet does not express the definite expectation that Nebuchadnezzar will come to Egypt, before xliii. 8-13. Previously, indeed, we have a general declaration, that Egypt will succumb to him (xxv. 19; xlvi. 11, 12), but none purporting that he will himself enter the country. It is therefore much more probable that this passage is contemporaneous with xliii. 8-13 than that it belongs to the time of xlvi. 3-12. The reason, which GRAF urges against this hypothesis, that Jeremiah there prophesies the conquest of Moab, Edom, Ammon, *etc.*, in consequence of the battle of Carchemish, but with respect to Egypt, had contented himself with a song of triumph over its defeat, is not of weight; for evidently Egypt is the most important of all the countries, against which chh. xlvi.-xlix. contain prophecies. It is hence no matter of surprise, if we have *two* prophecies against it, of which the first (xlvi. 3-12) treats of the defeat and destruction of Egypt *in general* (xlvi. 11, 12), the second specially of the latter.

This prophecy, like the preceding one, evidently consists of two halves. In the first the Egyptian cities are summoned to equip themselves against the approaching enemy (ver. 14); then the thought is expressed, that all, which is great in Egypt, Apis (ver. 15) the foreign auxiliaries (ver. 16), Pharaoh (ver. 17) must bow before the greatness of the Chaldean prince, who approaches like Tabor among the mountains and Carmel in the sea, in order to carry away the Egyptians into captivity (vers. 18, 19). In the second half the *quantitative* conception seems to prevail. Egypt is a fair, fat cow, but a gad-fly from the North brings destruction to it (ver. 20). Their mercenaries also, who are here compared to fatted calves, flee (ver. 21). Egypt is further compared to a forest, in which stand innumerable trees. Yet there is only a hissing like a snake in a thicket, while the enemies proceed to cut down the trees (vers. 22, 23). Finally it is proclaimed in blunt words, without a figure, that Egypt with its gods, its kings, and all who trust in them, must be given into the hand of Nebuchadnezzar, but that a time will come, in which Egypt will be inhabited as quietly and undisturbed as of old (vers. 24-26). The two halves are distinguished thus: 1. The Egyptian power is described from its intensive and qualitative, in the second from its intensive or quantitative side. 2. The first half closes with the prospect of exile, the second with a consolatory outlook into a distant but happy future.

Ver. 13. **The word ... Egypt.** The superscription is of the larger kind, but in the form which occurs besides only in xlv. 1 and l. 1. It is indubitable that such a superscription introduces a specifically new passage. The only question is, Who composed this, the prophet himself or a later writer, who had no right to do it? No reasons can be urged against its composition by the prophet, either general or special. The form לָבוֹא, both alone and with a second infinitive depending on it, is very common in Jeremiah; it is found more frequently in him than in any other book of the Old Testament. (Comp. xxxvi. 5; xl. 4; xli. 17; xlii. 15, 17, 22; xliv 12; xlviii. 16). לְ also after a verb. dicendi is Jeremiah. Comp. xxviii. 8, 9.

Ver. 14. **Proclaim . . . thy neighbors.** Egypt is alarmed, before all the boundary-cities. On Migdol, Noph and Tahpanhes, comp. rems. on ii. 16; xliv. 1.—Immediate preparations are necessary, since the surrounding countries, the neighbors, have already been devastated by the hostile sword. Comp. xxi. 14; xlviii. 17, 39; xlix. 5.

Vers. 15-19. **Wherefore . . . without an inhabitant.** The three heads of Egypt are Apis, the army consisting of foreigners, and the king. The overthrow of this triad is here described. With respect to the form it is noteworthy that the transition is made with the same turn from the summons to prepare and the description of the defeat as in ver. 5.—The Apis, which had hitherto in divine majesty enjoyed most undisturbed existence in his temple, is now dragged away like a common ox to the slaughter, and can make no resistance, for it is Jehovah who thrusts him on, as it were, from behind. Numb. xxxv. 20; Ezek. xxxiv. 21. It is Jehovah, likewise, who causes great defeat among those upon whom the power of Egypt in war depended. Since the time of Psammetichus foreign mercenaries (עָרֶב xxv. 20; Ezek. xxx. 5) composed the main strength of the Egyptian forces. (Comp. DUNCKER, 1., S. 922); but they are unable to resist the enemy whom God sends against them. They therefore flee to their homes.— **Falleth upon another.** Comp. xxix. 9, 26.— **Murderous sword.** Comp. rems. on xxv. 38. —The king himself finally, whom the Egyptians adored as an incarnation of the deity (comp. DUNCKER, I., S. 150, "The Egyptians went further in their exaltation of their rulers than any other nation, even according divine worship to their despots") becomes an object of ridicule.— **Lost the time.** These words signify that he has allowed the time to pass by. What time? The gracious respite appointed by Jehovah? Not impossibly. The prophet then places the confession in the mouth of the Egyptians, 'that they have not followed the advice given them in xxv. 15 coll. xxvii. 8. In contrast to this humiliation of the Egyptian king the prophet exalts (verse 18) the greatness of the true king, the King of all kings, the Lord of hosts, Jehovah, and for of His chosen servant and instrument (xxv. 9; xxvii. 6), the king of Babylon, Jehovah, who is called king also in xlviii. 15; li. 57, swears solemnly by Himself (xxii. 5, 24; xliv. 26), that he, who is not indeed here mentioned by name, but is plainly recognized from the connection, viz. the king of Babylon, will on his expedition to the other kings be as Tabor to the mountains rising to the north of it (comp. RAUMER, Pal. S. 37) and will present himself as Carmel seen from the sea, for this "looks like a watch-tower westward over the Mediterranean" (RAUMER, S. 45). In such circumstances should it fare better with Egypt than with Judah? No, the former also cannot escape captivity. He is therefore called upon to prepare himself for this.

—כְּלֵי גוֹלָה (comp. Ezek. xii. 3 sqq.) are a very necessary equipment, such as exiles are allowed to take with them. As the capital of Judah was not spared, so the capital of Egypt, Memphis, shall be destroyed (comp. ii. 15).

Vers. 20-23. **A finely formed heifer . . . no number.** In a new double picture Egypt's destruction is here portrayed. These pictures refer, as already remarked, more to the extent and quantity of the Egyptian forces, the first setting forth their volume, the second their numerical strength. Accordingly Egypt is first compared to a state-cow, which is of course to be regarded as well kept. We are involuntarily reminded of Pharaoh's fat kine in Gen. xli. 18. עֶגְלָה is moreover a *young* cow, but one which has attained its full vigor, for it may be three years old (xlviii. 34; Isa. xv. 5; Gen. xv. 9), give milk (Isa. vii. 21, 22), be already trained (Hos. x. 11), draw the plough (Jud. xiv. 18), but also may still rejoice in the untamed wildness of its life (xxxi. 18).—This cow is to be attacked by a gad-fly coming from the north, from whence Jeremiah is accustomed to see the Chaldeans coming (comp. i. 14, etc). [BLAYNEY and WORDSWORTH find here a probable allusion to the legend of Io, who was transformed into a heifer, and driven by a gad-fly into Egypt, where she was worshipped as Isis. Comp VIRG. Georg., III., 147; OVID, Metam. Lib., I.—S. R. A.]

The double **is coming** portrays the vehemence of the assault. Comp. Ezek. vii. 6; Ps. xcvi. 13. The same fulness and breadth are seen in the well-kept mercenaries as in Egypt itself. (Comp. HEROD., II. 158; DUNCKER, I., S. 922). They are fatted calves, and consequently lazy, as is seen in their fleeing instead of fighting.—**Turn.** Comp. rems. on ver. 5.— **Day of destruction.** Comp. Deut. xxxii. 35; Jer. xviii. 17.—**Time of visitation.** Comp. x. 15; 1. 27.—In a second picture it is described how the forces of the Egyptians, though so great in number, are overcome. Egypt is in this behalf compared to a forest, which serves for the abode of a serpent. The serpent has retired into a thicket. It is only heard to hiss. Thus the ancient power of Egypt, which led Ezekiel to compare it to a crocodile (xxix. 3; xxxii. 2), is come to an end. It is only a serpent hissing with impotent rage in a thicket. It no longer attacks nor bites, for it is afraid. There is also reason for this. For the enemies rush upon it with power (בְּחַיִל, comp. Zech. iv. 6); they come upon it with axes (comp. xlix. 9) as hewers of wood. Whether this figure is occasioned by the circumstance that the Persians, Massagetes, and Scythians made use of battle-axes, as GRAF supposes, or whether it has no connection with this, must be left undecided.— Ver. 23. With their axes the enemies hew down the forest, i. e. they kill the warriors, destroy the fortifications and supplies. This forest is not to be otherwise described, for it is unsearchable, impenetrable. A thin forest may be taken possession of by going through it, but a thick, impenetrable one must be cut down tree by tree. The enemies can do this, for they are more numerous than the locusts.—**Not to be searched**

(יָקָק) I would not refer to the enemies, 1. on account of the sing. number; 2. because then the same thought would be expressed three times.—In the following context the thought of Egypt's subjugation is expressed without a figure.

Vers. 24-26. **The daughter ... saith Jehovah.—Put to shame.** Comp. ii. 26; vi. 15; xlviii. 1; l. 2, *etc.*—The God of Israel, who is more powerful than the gods of the Egyptians, declares that He will visit the Amon of No (the highest deity of the Egyptians, comp. HERZOG, *R.-Enc.* I., *S.* 286, which had its seat in Thebes, hence called אָמוֹן מִנֹּא, Nah. iii. 8; comp. *Ib.* X., *S.* 392), Pharaoh and the land itself, and further all the other kings (*i. e.* those entitled to be so) and gods, and finally Pharaoh and the entire mass of those who trust in him as a god. (Comp. rems. on ver. 17). The style is here very broad and verbose, in order to express the completeness of the destruction. All those shall fall into the hands of those who seek their life (comp. rems. on xliv. 30), and be given into the hand of Nebuchadnezzar and his servants.—**And afterwards**, *etc.* If we compare on the one hand ver. 19, and on the other passages like xlviii. 47; xlix. 6; xlix. 39, it appears in the highest degree probable, that here at the close a favorable prospect is to be opened up to the Egyptians. In the days of old, ancient Thebes, of which no one knows when it was built, was peaceful, unassailed and prosperous. A remembrancer of this condition can be understood only as a word of blessed promise.

Appendix to the Prophecies against Egypt; a Consolatory Declaration to Israel.

XLVI. 27, 28.

27 But fear thou not, my servant Jacob,
 And be thou not dismayed, O Israel;
 For behold, I will save thee from afar
 And thy seed from the land of their captivity,
 And Jacob shall return and be at rest,
 And quiet, and none shall make him afraid.
28 Fear thou not, my servant Jacob,
 Saith Jehovah, for I am with thee.
 For I will make a full end of the nations,
 Whither I have dispersed thee:
 But I will not make a full end of thee,
 I will correct thee in measure and not leave thee unpunished.

TEXTUAL AND GRAMMATICAL.

This brief consolatory passage is reproduced here from xxx. 10, 11. The discrepancies are slight. In ver 27 נְאֻם is wanting after עֲבְדִּי יַעֲקֹב. In ver. 28 the initial words of ver. 27 are repeated to יַעֲקֹב with נְאֻם appended, which is not the case in xxx. 11. Further, in xxx. 11 לְהוֹשִׁיעֶךָ נְאֻם stand after כִּי אִתְּךָ אָנִי; instead of הֲבִאתִיךָ we find in xxx. 11 הֲפִיצוֹתִיךָ; finally, in the latter place אַךְ אֹתְךָ stands for וְאֹתְךָ.

EXEGETICAL AND CRITICAL.

It is acknowledged that these words stand in the original and suitable connection in ch. xxx., as well as that they are not necessary to ch. xlvi., and would not be missed if they were omitted. Still it may be said that every injury befalling the enemies of the theocracy is a corroboration of the latter, and that it cannot be unsuitable also to express in words this mutual relation founded in the nature of the case, the two going constantly hand in hand in chh. l., li. (Comp. l. 4-6, 17-19, 28, 33; li. 5, 6, 10, 35, 45, 50). But the overthrow of the Babylonian kingdom by Cyrus bore the deliverance of Judah immediately in its womb. This can be said of the conquest of Egypt no more than of that of the other small nations against which chh. xlvii.-xlix. are directed. Hence in these three chapters there is no trace of that mutual relation. Why then just here? And how does it agree with the fact that elsewhere in Egypt Jeremiah pronounces only the severest threatenings against the Israelites (chh. xlii.-xliv.)? There is much then that is opposed to the genuineness of the passage, while on the other hand it is easy to suppose that a later seer saw fit to oppose this light to the former shadow. Moreover, as we have said, the words are not absolutely unsuitable here, and how can we cannot therefore deny the possibility, that Jeremiah, who, as is well known, is very fond of quoting himself, himself felt the need of causing the light of Israel to shine

DOCTRINAL AND ETHICAL.

1. FÖRSTER states four reasons why the prophets had to proclaim judgment on the heathen nations also. The first is διδασκαλικός: it is to be known that the prosperity of the heathen is not lasting, but that heathendom has no basis of true prosperity. The second reason is παρηγορικός: the pious are not to fear that the heathen will get the upper hand and suppress the church. The third is ἐπανορθωτικός: God's people are to guard against forming alliances with the heathen and trusting in their help. The fourth is ἐλεγκτικός: a conclusion is to be drawn *a minori ad majus*: if God does not spare the heathen who are deprived of His light, how much less will He spare His people, if they despise the light of His word.

2. " Jeremiah's God is also the Lord of all the heathen and makes their destinies. They find it so according to their words and especially their posture towards the chosen people Israel. They haste to their destruction, for one nation only is eternal; this, however, is the nation which has been passed through a thousand sieves and in comparison with others is no nation. That which is in Israel, as in other nations, passes away, and only that which it has above other nations remains eternal. Jeremiah prophesies most against Egypt, Moab and Babylon, in which the wealth, the jealous, scoffing manner of the mean world, and the cavalier spirit of great states is rebuked. .... He who rightly understands this sees here not sermous addressed to generations long since passed away, but to the natural humanity streaming through this world, as it is continually presented with new names and yet always with the same carnal impulses and based on the same unreason. To him, who thus understands Jeremiah, he is again alive, and the Jewish legend is fulfilled, that Jeremiah must come again before the Messianic kingdom can bloom up again in glory. Yea, let Jeremiah rise truly for thee to mourn, and Christ, with the hosannas of His eternal hosts of disciples, will not longer be hidden from thee, and in Him thou wilt have all things." DIEDRICH.

3. On xlvi. 6. "The race is not to the swift. Eccles. ix. 11. Therefore let not the strong man glory in his strength. Jer. ix. 22 Also are horses and chariots and such like things of no avail: for to those who have not God on their side, all is lost." CRAMER.

4. On xlvi. 10. "God may long delay His reckoning. This Pharaoh-necho had killed the pious Josiah, conquered his son Jehoahaz and laid the land of Judah under tribute. But guilt rusts not, however old, and though God comes slowly He comes surely." CRAMER.

5. On xlvi. 10. "Although the ungodly go free for a long time and rejoice with timbrel and harp and are glad with pipes and spend their days in wealth (Job xxi. 12), yet he lets them go free like sheep for the slaughter, and spares them for the day of slaughter (Jer. xii. 3)." CRAMER.

6. On xlvi. 25. "*Bonum confidere in Domino et non in principibus* (Ps. cxlvi.). When their help is most needed they lie down and die." FÖRSTER.

7. On vers. 27, 28. "When God turns things upside down and takes care that neither root nor branch remains, His little flock must be preserved. The punishments which redound to the destruction of the ungodly redound to the amelioration of the godly. For from these He takes the eternal punishment, and the temporal must also redound to their advantage, but the ungodly drink it to the dregs." CRAMER.

HOMILETICAL AND PRACTICAL.

1. On xlvi. 1-12. The power of God in contrast to human power. 1. Human power confides in its strength ; (*a*) in a qualitative (vers. 3, 4, 7) ; (*b*) in a quantitative respect (ver. 8). 2. The divine power strikes it down, whereby (*a*) arrogance is chastised (vers. 5, 6, 11); (*b*) the righteousness of God is satisfied (ver. 10).

---

4. PROPHECY AGAINST THE PHILISTINES.

CHAP. XLVII.

1 The word of Jehovah, which came to Jeremiah, the prophet, against the Philistines, before Pharaoh had smitten Gaza.
2 Thus saith Jehovah :
  Behold, waters rise out of the North,
  And become an overflowing torrent,
  And overflow the land and whatever is therein,
  The city and those that dwell therein ;
  And the men shall cry aloud,[1]
  And all the inhabitants of the country shall howl,
3 Before the thundering hoof-beat[2] of his horses,[3]
  Before the rattling of his chariots,[4] the rumbling of his wheels.
  Fathers, for feebleness[5] of hands, turn not for their children,

24

370   THE PROPHET JEREMIAH.

4 Because of the day that cometh to extirpate all the Philistines,
   To exterminate from Tyre and Sidon every escaped one that might help;
   For Jehovah extirpates the Philistines,
   The remnant of the coasts of Caphtor.
5 Baldness is come upon Gaza,
   Ashkelon is struck dumb,[7] the remnant of their valley.
   How long wilt thou still wound thyself by cutting?
6 Alas! sword of Jehovah, how long ere thou wilt rest?
   Back[8] into thy sheath, rest and be still!
7 How canst thou rest? Jehovah has given it a charge
   Against Ashkelon and against the sea-shore—
   Thither[9] has he appointed it.

TEXTUAL AND GRAMMATICAL.

[1] Ver. 2.—In regard to the construction, there are only two principal verbs from 2 b to 4 a:—וְקַקֹּ֫ב and הַפְנִ֔י. Evidently whatever comes before the latter depends on the former, and what follows on the latter.

[2] Ver. 3.— שַׁעֲטָה ἅπ. λεγ. From analogies like לוּן and לֵעַ, בּוּס and בּוּז, קוּם and קֻם (Samar.), גֻּל and בֻּעַל (comp. FUERST, H.-W.-B., s. v. גֻּל) there can be no doubt that the radix is identical with שׁוּט, which appears to me, according to שׁוּט, flagellum, שָׁט (Ezek. xxvii. 8, remiges, remigare=remis percutere), שׁוּט (strike out, discurrere), to have the radical signification of "beating."

[3] Ver. 3.—אַבִּירָיו. Comp. rems. on xlvi. 15.

[4] Ver. 3.—רַעַשׁ לִרְכֻבּוֹ. The construction with ל seems to proceed here from a striving after change. Otherwise in ver. 6. Comp. NAEGELSB. Gr., § 67, 2.

[5] Ver. 3.—רִפְיוֹן is ἅπ. λεγ.

[6] Ver. 4.—לְהַכְרִית. Comp. xliv. 7. We should expect כָּל־עֹזֵר שָׂרִיד. But the radical meaning of שָׂרִיד is not reliquus, but elapsus. Hence the meaning of the expression is not "every helper remaining," but "every escaped one that might help," i. e. even the weakest, separated, ineffective helper.

[7] Ver. 5.—If we should take נִדְמְתָה in the sense of "being destroyed," the prophet must have suddenly dropped his figure. I therefore take דָּמָה, with GRAF, in its original meaning=דָּכָה (comp. Ps. xlix. 13), and regard this being made dumb as a lower grade, or preliminary, of destruction, for Philistia still supplicates and according to ver. 7 b the enemy has still to take Ashkelon and the sea-coast.

[8] Ver. 6.—הֵאָסְפִי, put up thyself. Comp. Ezek. xxi. 35.

[9] Ver. 7.—The emphatic repetition of the object by שָׁם is the reverse of the anticipatory construction, which occurs more frequently in Jeremiah. Comp. ix. 14; xi. 15; xli. 3; li. 56, etc.

EXEGETICAL AND CRITICAL.

From the North the prophet sees the hostile hosts approaching like great water-floods against the Philistines. Terror will seize these to such a degree, that fathers will not once look round after their children. Then will the Philistines be extirpated even to the last remnant, and the last helper be taken from the Phœnicians (vers. 2-4). Gaza and Ashkelon will fall, for the consideration that the sword of the Lord has already had enough bloody work, and will now stand still before the last of these cities, does not hold good (vers. 5-7).
Ver. 1. **The word . . . smitten Gaza.** According to history Jeremiah lived to see one, and possibly two conquests of Gaza by Pharaoh, for Herodotus relates (II., 159): Σίροισι πεζῇ ὁ Νεκὼς συμβαλὼν ἐν Μαγδώλῳ ἐνίκησε· μετὰ δὲ τὴν μάχην Κάδυτιν πόλιν τῆς Συρίης ἐοῦσαν μεγάλην εἷλε. Thus after the battle of Megiddo (for this is admitted to be Μάγδολος) Pharaoh-necho conquered Gaza. That Κάδυτις is Gaza (according to the Egyptian Katatu; comp. BRUGSCH, I., S. 342, 818) is now generally acknowledged. Comp. M. NIEBUHR, Ass. u. Bab., S. 369; ARNOLD in HERZOG, R.-Enc. IV., S. 672; GRAF ad h. loc., S. 523; DUNCKER, etc.—Possibly Gaza had also been conquered by Psammetichus. He took Ashdod, according to Herodotus (II., 157), after a twenty years' siege. DUNCKER is correctly of opinion "that the siege of Ashdod could not well be undertaken, before Gaza and Ashkelon had been captured" (S. 816, Anm.). Jeremiah must have survived the capture of Ashdod, for he speaks in xxv. 20 of the **remnant of Ashdod.** This must also have occurred in the second decennium of his prophetic labors, since Psammetichus cannot have commenced his expeditions against the Philistines before B. C., 640 (comp. DUNCKER, S. 816). If then Jeremiah did witness a conquest of Gaza in consequence of the undertaking against Ashdod, it was yet an event of relatively small importance. Gaza appears by no means to have been destroyed, for in the same passage, where Jeremiah speaks of the remnant of Ashdod (xxv. 20), he speaks of Ashkelon, Gaza and Ekron, as cities still intact. It is inconceivable that this capture of Gaza, which if it took place, was of secondary importance, could be the occasion of this prophecy, since the words "before Pharaoh smote Gaza," can be understood only of a celebrated, well-known conquest of Gaza. Any other must have required a more particular designation. Add to this, that when Jeremiah prophesies the visitation of Philistia, and mentions the cities to be destroyed by name, he could not have left Ashdod unmentioned, if the great and celebrated siege of this city was then in progress. From his not mentioning it, we may with safety conclude that the capture of this city

was already a fact in the past. From all which it follows that the superscription must refer to the capture of Gaza by Pharaoh-necho, which, Herodotus says, took place after the battle of Magdolos or Megiddo. Two points are now to be observed:—

1. This capture took place before the fourth year of Jehoiakim, the battle of Megiddo occurring in B. C., 608 (comp. DUNCKER, S. 817). It is perfectly intelligible that Necho, who, as we have seen above, landed with his army in the bay of Acco, sought to keep his retreat open by subjugating the large fortified cities of Philistia, especially Gaza, the key of the road to Egypt. He would have been lost after the battle of Carchemish, if he had not taken these precautionary measures. Accordingly the present prophecy belongs not to those which Jeremiah published in the year 604, after the battle of Carchemish, but is older. It agrees with this, that in this chapter the Chaldeans and Nebuchadnezzar are not mentioned, but an enemy from the north is spoken of generally.

2. If now the waters rising from the north (ver. 2) are the Chaldeans, as according to Jeremiah's constant usage they must be, this superscription has not the sense that it asserts the fulfilment of the prophecy by the conquest of Gaza which soon followed on the part of Necho, but on the contrary it is to declare, that Jeremiah prophesied destruction to the Philistines by an enemy from the north, at a time when conquest by an enemy from the south was impending. It might indeed be alleged that Jeremiah understood by the "waters from the north" the Egyptians, because they were then making their attack on Philistia from the north. This, however, was only an accidental circumstance which Jeremiah would certainly have designated as such. It was natural that at a time when the Egyptian forces, after the battle of Megiddo, were turned against Philistia, Jeremiah should find occasion for a prophecy against this country, but that at this time he should designate its destruction as the work of a *northern* enemy, corresponds perfectly to the character of that prophet who buys land which is in possession of the enemy (ch. xxxii.), and proclaims to the Jews in Tahpanhes, that the throne of the Chaldean king will stand before the gates of the royal palace (ch. xliii.) I do not think that the capture of Gaza was made by the army of the Egyptians returning defeated from Carchemish. I lay no great weight on Herodotus' placing it immediately after the battle of Magdolos, yet it is in itself improbable that Necho could have deferred the capture of "the key to Egypt" so long, or have accomplished it with his defeated army.

Vers. 2-4. **Thus saith . . . coasts of Caphtor.** The figure of an overflowing stream is frequently used of armies. Comp. *ex. gr.,* Isa. viii. 7; Jer. xlvi. 7.—**From the north.** Comp. i. 13-17.—**And overflow.** Comp. viii. 16.—**The city,** *etc.* Comp. xlvi. 5.—**On turn not.** Comp. xlvi. 5. The exhaustion caused by the terror of that day will hinder even parents from going to the help of their children. A similar expression, but in a different sense, is found in Mal. iii. 24; Luke i. 17.—**The** prediction of ver. 4 was soon afterwards fulfilled. The Phœnicians in the distress caused by the Chaldeans which followed the destruction of Jerusalem, must have grievously missed the aid of their Philistine neighbors.— **The remnant,** *etc.* Comp. Am. ix. 7; Gen. x. 14; Deut. ii. 23; Ezek. xxv. 16; Zeph. ii. 5. It is certain that a part of the Philistines originated from Caphtor, but not whether by Caphtor we are to understand Creta or the coast of the Egyptian delta (so STARKE, *Gaza, S.* 76). Comp. HERZ. *R.-Enc.,* the articles "Philistia," "Creta," and "Caphtor."

Vers. 5-7. **Baldness . . . appointed it.** While in the previous context the catastrophe is designated as still future, it appears here in great part to have occurred. The prophet in spirit sees the country already in the hands of the enemy. Gaza, the strong southern fortification, the key of the country is, as it were, a head shaven bare (comp. ii. 16); Ashkelon, the seaport, the mouth of the stream of traffic, is a mouth struck dumb. It is not yet, indeed, destroyed like Gaza, but its gates are closed. No one any more goes in or out, for the enemy is before them.—**Remnant of their valley.** In the topography of Philistia a hilly country (in the east), and a low country may be distinguished. Comp. VAIHINGER'S art., *Philistia* in HERZ. *R.-Enc.* XI., *S.* 553. Although the proper name of this low land is שְׁפֵלָה, it is yet possible that עֵמֶק also may be put for it (comp. 1 Sam. xxxi. 7). It must further be admitted that Ashkelon and Gaza are not inappropriately termed the remnant of the valley, for they were the strongest cities: the enemy coming from the north through Judea, has beset the hill region (אֶרֶץ, Josh. x. 40; xii. 8. Comp. VAIHINGER, *ut sup.*): in the low country Gaza and Ashkelon resist the longest; when these are fallen, the last remnant of the low lands, consequently the whole land, is in the power of the enemy.—**Their** and the following sentence **how long,** *etc.,* refer to the whole Philistia. These self-woundings were a heathen custom in conjunction with earnest supplication of their deities (comp. 1 Ki. xviii. 28; HERZ. *R.-Enc.,* Art. *Baal*). The prophet then represents the Philistines here as humbling themselves. They perceive that it is the God of Israel, who is bringing his judgment upon them (comp. 1 Sam. v.), they therefore appeal to Him after their manner for grace. The prophet tells them, however, that this can no longer help them, the judgment having already begun with the facts intimated in ver. 5, *a.* This explanation appears satisfactory. I cannot, therefore, conclude to read with GESENIUS (*Thes. s. v.,* עֵמֶק), HITZIG and GRAF after the LXX., עֲנָקִים (Anakim), much as this reading has in its favor, affording, as it does, a suitable supplementation to "remnant of the coasts of Caphtor," ver. 4, and an appropriate allusion to Gath, the chief residence of the last of these giants (1 Sam. xvii. 4; 1 Chron. xx. 5-8). Alterations of the reading are to be permitted only in cases of extreme necessity. The words of ver. 6 contain the import of the supplications accompanying the self-woundings. There seems to me to be an intimation that these were the words of the Philistines in the expression of **Jehovah** (לַיהוָה), for though not bad

Hebrew, it has a foreign sound and makes the impression that the speakers attribute the sword raging against them only unwillingly and hesitatingly to Jehovah. In vi. 25; xii. 12, the construction is different.—In ver. 7 the prophet answers the petition of ver. 6. In the first clause attaching himself closely to the question, a change of person is thus occasioned, as so often in Jeremiah. Comp. v. 14; xii. 13; xvii. 13; xxi. 12 (Chethibh), xxxvi. 29, 30; xlvi. 3, 9.—**The seashore** is used in Ezek. xxv. 16 also of Philistia, but it is not impossible that, as GRAF supposes, it may refer also to the Phœnicians of ver. 4. It also intimates that the enemy will advance from the East. Comp. xxiii. 19, 20; xlviii. 10; Isa. lv. 10.

DOCTRINAL AND ETHICAL.

Among all the neighboring nations the Philistines were those who showed enmity to the Israelites longest and with most success. For from the times of Shamgar (Jud. iii. 31) down to Hezekiah (2 Ki. xviii. 8), they were both hostile (comp. אֵיבַת עוֹלָם, Ezek. xxv. 15), and dangerous neighbors. Even Israel's great heroic and victorious period, the time of Samuel, Saul and David, did not result in rendering these opponents perfectly innoxious (comp. 1 Ki. xv. 27; xvi. 15; 2 Chron. xxi. 16, 17; xxviii. 18). Ezekiel even mentions them among those who delighted with malicious joy in the fall of Jerusalem. Since now it is perfectly natural that the theocratic prophecy should include the Philistines and reckon the destruction of these old enemies among the bright points in Israel's future (comp. Isa. xi. 14; xiv. 28, 29; Obad. 19; Am. i. 6; Zeph. ii. 4; Ezek. xxv. 15), our prophecy is probably the earliest of Jeremiah's predictions against foreign nations. As, however, Jeremiah in ver. 6 predicts a humbling of the Philistines, so Zechariah their complete conversion to the Lord and their reception into Israel (ix. 7).

HOMILETICAL AND PRACTICAL.

1. On xlvii. 1. The inviolable majesty of the divine word has nothing to fear from an apparent momentary violation. Jeremiah predicts too the Philistines' destruction by an enemy from the north, at the moment when an enemy from the south was about successfully to assail them.

2. On xlvii. 3. A noble picture of extreme despair! Comp. Isa. xlix. 15. Yet it has occurred that women have killed and eaten their children; 2 Kings vi. 28, 29. Comp. Deut. xxviii. 53-57; Lam. ii. 20; iv. 10.

3. On xlvii. 6. "The terribly pathetic discourse which the prophet here holds with God's sword, should remind us; 1, that no calamity comes, but by the Lord's will; 2, that it goes no further than God will; 3, that it will not cease before God will." CRAMER.

---

5. PROPHECY AGAINST MOAB (CHAP. XLVIII).

Although Israel had received the command by Moses, not to oppress or make war on the Moabites (Deut. ii. 9), the Moabites on their part acted in a most hostile manner towards Israel, and according to Balaam's counsel (Num. xxxi. 17), did them greater injury by seducing them to idolatry, than they could have done with weapons of war. In consequence of the command given by Moses, the Israelites took possession of none of the country of the Moabites, but the Arnon, which had formed the boundary line between the Moabites and Ammonites (Num. xxi. 13; Jud. xi. 18), now formed that between Moab and Reuben (Deut. ii. 36; Josh. xiii. 9). From this time the history of the relations between Israel and Moab falls into two periods. The first extends from the occupation of the transjordanic country to the subjugation of the Moabites by David (2 Sam. viii. 2). During this period many struggles took place between the two nations with varying success (Jud. iii. 12 sqq.; 28 sqq.; 1 Sam. xiv. 47). The second period embraces the subjection of the Moabites under David and his successors (after the division under the kings of Israel) to their revolt after the death of Ahab (2 Ki. i. 1; iii. 4, 5). The third period again is one of hostility with varying success (2 Ki. iii. 6-27; xiii. 20), but closes with the occupation of the region to the north of the Arnon by the Moabites in consequence of the deportation of the East-jordanic Israelites by Tiglath Pileser (2 Ki. xv. 29; 1 Chron. v. 6, 26). The fourth period embraces their entire subsequent history. In this the only account we have of wars between the two nations is, that Moabitish troops were sent against Jehoiakim after his revolt from the Chaldeans (2 Ki. xxiv. 2). Under Zedekiah we see the Moabites in league with Israel against the common enemy, the Chaldeans (Jer. xxvii. 1-3), of which Josephus (Ant. X., 9, 7) records that Nebuchadnezzar in the fifth year after the destruction of Jerusalem subjugated the Ammonites and Moabites. In this fourth period fall the other prophecies against Moab, with the exception of the brief oracle, Am. ii. 1-3, viz., those of Isaiah (chh. xv. and xvi. coll. xxv. 16-19) Zephaniah (ii. 8-11), Jeremiah (ch. xlviii.), Ezekiel (xxv. 8-11).

No proof is needed that Jeremiah had occasion to direct a prophecy against this old hereditary foe. The account in 2 Ki. xxiv. 2 shows that even specially at that time the disposition of the Moabites was hostile to Judah; for this prophecy certainly belongs to the time of Jehoiakim and before the fourth year, the Chaldeans and Nebuchadnezzar not being mentioned. The form of the superscription favors its contemporaneousness with the first prophecy against Egypt (xlvi. 1, 2). Comp. rems. on that pas-

sage.—Jeremiah's object in this prophecy was evidently to reanimate, as it were, the former declarations of similar purport, and comprise them together for the sake of a powerful total effect. From ver. 29 onwards, *there is a constant, more or less free, use of older utterances. Of special importance appeared to our prophet the prophecy of Isaiah, itself reproducing an older oracle* (Isa. xvi. 13). *He makes very extensive use of it, particularly of* vers. 29-38. *Amos also* (comp. בְּשָׁאוֹן, ver. 45, and הַקְּרִיוֹת, vers. 24 and 41, with Am. ii. 2). *Zephaniah* (comp. הִגְדִיל, vers. 26 and 42, with Zeph. ii. 8, 10) *and even older utterances of the Pentateuch* (comp. vers. 45, 46 with Num. xxi. 28, 29; xxiv. 17) *have not been left unemployed. Thus the prophecy has not only become very long, but many unevennesses have been produced by the introduction of foreign matters.* MOVERS *and* HITZIG *have thus been misled to assume various interpolations.* GRAF, *however, has satisfactorily rebutted these attacks on the integrity of our text. As regards the structure of the discourse, it consists, according to the peculiarity of Jeremiah's style, in pictures of various extent, of which we number eleven. The first five are predominantly occupied with the description of the punitive judgment breaking in upon Moab* (vers. 1-25), *while the four following* (vers. 26-42) *have the reasons of this judgment for their subject. The last two pictures* (vers. 43, 44, and vers. 45, 46) *are related to the two main divisions as supplements, in so far as they contain nothing new, but draw only on two older sources, viz.:* 1, *a drastic passage by Isaiah, which moreover has nothing to do with Moab;* 2, *some declarations of the book of Numbers referring to Moab. The last verse is a consolatory glance forming a conclusion to the whole.*

1. The Description of the Punitive Judgment (XLVIII. 1-25.)

1. *The Devastation Proceeding from City to City.*

XLVIII. 1-5.

1 AGAINST MOAB.
Thus saith Jehovah Zebaoth, the God of Israel:
Woe unto Nebo, for it is laid waste!
Confounded and taken is Kiriathaim!
Confounded and broken to pieces is the citadel [Misgab].
2 The glory of Moab is departed.
In *Heshbon* they have *spun* evil against her.
"Up! and let us cut her off from being a nation!"[1]
Thou also, *O Madmen*, art made *mad* [feeble]:[2]
Behind thee cometh the sword.
3 Hark! Crying from Choronaim—
Desolation and great ruin.
4 Broken in pieces is Moab!
They cry aloud towards Zoar.[3]
5 For the ascent of Luhith is ascended with weeping, with weeping.[4]
For on the descent of Choronaim are heard the oppressors'[5] of the cry of woe.

TEXTUAL AND GRAMMATICAL.

[1] Ver. 2.—מִנּוֹי. Comp. NAEGELSB. *Gr.*, § 106, 6.

[2] Ver. 2.—Whether תִּדֹּמִּי is Kal or Niphal, is doubtful. Both are possible. The Niphal meaning would correspond best to the connection. Comp. OLSH., § 243 *d*, with EWALD, § 140 *b*.

[3] Ver. 3.—I concur with GRAF in reading צֹעֲרָה, following the LXX., instead of צְעִירֶיהָ. In Isa. xv. 5, which passage the prophet had in view here, the fugitives of Moab flee עַד צֹעַר, and in ver. 34 of this chapter. צֹעַר is mentioned with Choronaim. The reading צְעִירֶיהָ which appears also to have led the LXX. astray, so that they write Ζογόρα instead of Σηγώρ, as they elsewhere render צֹעַר (Gen. xiv. 2; xix. 22 sqq.; Isa. xv. 5) seems to have arisen in a similar manner with שׁוּבִי הוֹאֵשׁ יָאֹ, etc. Comp. rems. on xvii. 23. The analogy of xiv. 3 finally produced the alteration into צְעוּרֶיהָ.

[4] Ver. 5.—יַעֲלֶה is a paronomasia with מַעֲלֵה; grammatically it is the third person singular impersonal. Comp. NAEGELSB. *Gr.*, § 101, 2 *b*. Instead of the second בְּכִי, we have בוֹ in the passage in Isaiah. It is natural to suppose that here בְּכִי arose from a blending of the following בְּ with the preceding בְּ, in consequence of indistinct or defective writing of the vowel. DELITZSCH also (*Jes., S.* 207) attributes the reading to a mistake. It is not, however, to be denied that Jeremiah may possibly have written בְּכִי. Then it would be more advisable to take the second as an emphatic rhetorical repetition of the first with omission of the preposition (comp. NAEGELSB., *Gr.*, § 112, 8), than to give it the part of the subject. For, when we compare cases like שָׁנָה בְשָׁנָה, בְּעֵין יָעֵן, we must not forget that here the immediate juxtaposition of the two assonant words is essential.

[5] Ver. 5.—Comp. נצ with accus., and following עַל as a designation of the *term. ad quem*; Jud. ix. 31; Isa. xxix. 3, and on the construct state, as a substitute for the preposition, NAEGELSB. *Gr.*, § 64, 5 *c*. In accordance with the exegesis of

this passage, as given below, we neither to take צָרִי as an abstraction=*angustia*, nor with Hitzig to read צָרִי (אֲרָא), and regard this as the literal name, and connect it as a gloss with עָבַר, meaning the same, nor with GRAF to take צָרִי (which does not once occur in old Hebrew) in connection with צְעָקָה=cry of murder.

EXEGETICAL AND CRITICAL.

The prophet proclaims destruction to Moab by, as it were, sketching a great picture, in which we not only perceive the abomination of desolation embracing and, as it were, enveloping the whole country, but also distinguish particular points marked by glaring colors. In the enumeration of the cities there is a general progress from north to south.

Against Moab. The superscription leans for support on xlvi. 2. Comp. the introduction to chh. xlvi.–li.

Ver. 1. **Thus saith . . . citadel.** That the mountain Nebo is not meant, is seen from the verb, both in its sense and form (fem.). The city of Nebo (comp. ver. 22; Num. xxxii. 3, 38) was situated, according to the *Onomasticon* of JEROME, eight Roman miles south of Heshbon, while Mt. Nebo was six miles west of this city. Comp. RAUMER, *Paläst.*, *S.* 265.—Kiriathaim (comp. ver. 23; Gen. xiv. 5; Num. xxxii. 37; Josh. xiii. 19; Ezek. xxv. 9) is one of the oldest cities of the East-Jordanic district. BURKHARDT (*Travels in Syria*, II., *S.* 626) found ruins of a place called Et-Taim, half an hour west of Medaba, which, however, does not well harmonize with the statement of JEROME, who places Καριάθα (Koroiatha, Kiriathaim), ten Roman miles west of Medaba. Comp. RAUMER, *S.* 263, 4 *et pass.*; HERZ. *R.-Enc.*, VII., *S.* 710.

The **citadel [Misgab].** It is very probable from the context that a definite locality is meant, for otherwise either the citadel of the last mentioned city must be intended, or the citadels of Moab generally. In both cases, however, we should expect the word to have a suffix. Hence the chief fortress of the Moabites, Kir-Moab, or Kir-heres (comp. vers. 31 and 36; Isa. xv. 1; xvi. 7, 11; 2 Ki. iii. 25) has been correctly understood. No appeal can be made in behalf of this view to Isa. xxv. 12, since it is extremely questionable whether a definite locality is there intended. Comp. DRECHSLER on Isa. xxv. 12. On Kir-Moab, comp. HERZ. *R.-Enc.* VII., *S.* 558 sqq.

Ver. 2. **The glory . . . the sword.** From vers. 29, 30, we see that the Moabites were inclined to proud self-praise, but we cannot here take the word translated **glory** in the subjective sense, as the whole strophe has for its subject the destruction of real objects. It is, therefore, here as in Deut. xxvi. 19; Jer. xiii. 11; li. 4, the subject of their glory.—The name of the city Heshbon gives occasion for a play upon words. We translate "spun" after the example of MEIER. Heshbon was then in the possession of the Ammonites (xlix. 3). On arriving at the boundary the enemy projects his plan of attack. Comp. rems. on ver. 45. After the deportation of the East-Jordanic tribes by Tiglath-Pileser (2 Ki. xv. 29; 1 Chron. v. 26), the Moabites appear to have taken possession of their territory. Hence Isaiah (xv. 4; xvi. 8, 9) mentions Heshbon among the Moabitish cities. The Ammonites must have come subsequently into possession of the city. Comp. GRAF, *S.* 554; VON RAUMER, *S.* 262 and 269, 270.—A place called Madmen, in Moab, is not expressly mentioned elsewhere, but there seems to be a trace of it in the figure of the dung-pit (Isa. xxv. 10), to the choice of which Isaiah may have been occasioned by the existence of such a place, as JOSEPH KIMCHI supposed. Besides a כַּרְכֻּנָּה is mentioned in Benjamin, Isa. x. 31; a מַדְמֵנָה in Judah, Josh. xv. 31; a דִּמְנָה in Zebulon, Josh. xxi. 35. Hence מַדְמֵן here also is not to be taken as an appellative, as some modern commentators would do, following the LXX., Vulg. and Syr., but as a proper noun.

Vers. 3–5. **Hark . . . cry of woe.** From Choronaim (comp. Isa. xv. 5) a loud cry is heard, and at the same time the noise of the city falling into ruins. Comp. iv. 6; vi. 1; l. 22; Is. lix. 7; lx. 18.—GRAF has made it very probable that by Moab in ver. 14 is to be understood, not the country, but the city (Num. xxi. 28; Isa. xv. 1; Num. xxii. 36). The mention of several cities in connection, and the feminine gender of the verb (comp., however, the masculine in ver. 11) favor this. I refer also to Num. xxi. 15, where עָר alone seems to be given as the name of the city.—The first hemistich of ver. 5 is taken almost *verbatim* from Isa. xv. 5, there being a difference only in the last words. As we have Luhith in Isaiah, without any difference in reading, we are justified in following the Keri, which has the same here. From the other reading (לִשְׂחוֹת=tables, boards) a suitable sense can be wrung only with difficulty. "*Est usque hodie vicus inter Areopolin (i. e., Ar-Moab) et Zoarum nomine Luitha,*" says JEROME in the *Onomasticon*. By **For** the declaration of the preceding verse, that the inhabitants of Ar-Moab cry **towards** Zoar, is explained, *viz.*, the ascent of Luhith, which is on the road designated, they are seen to ascend weeping.—In the second half of the verse we find a much altered copy of the second half of the verse in Isa. xv. 5. Instead of "in the way of Horonaim" it is in Jeremiah, "in the descent of Horonaim." The present form of the text appears to me to betray an effort after greater distinctness and closer correspondence to the topography. Hence the ascent of Luhith is opposed to the descent of Horonaim. He who would go from Ar-Moab to Zoar, would have to go down a declivity at Horonaim, and ascend an elevation at Luhith. Similarly VITRINGA on Isa. xv. 5, only that he makes Luhith come first after Ar-Moab and Horonaim afterward, which, however, evidently contradicts the connection. In Isaiah it reads "they raise a cry of destruction," and here it ought to be objected, how could those who go up by Luhith weep, because they raise a cry at Horonaim? When the ascent of Luhith is taking place, the descent of Horonaim lying in the rear is vacant. Or are the people of Horonaim supposed to have remained behind, when the stream of fugitives passed through from Ar-Moab? How could this stream raise a cry at Horonaim while ascending Luhith? They might,

CHAP. XLVIII. 6-10.

however, be anxious when they heard the oppressors behind them at Horonaim. I therefore think that 'עָר, which has given the commentators so much trouble, and produced so many curiosities of exegesis, is quite correct. צָר is the oppressor; for עָר is *premere, urgere aliquem hostili modo*. The genitive is to be taken in that wider and freer sense, which the construct state so frequently has. The oppressors of the cry of woe are those who cause the cry by their oppressions.

2. Summons to flight, which yet will not secure safety.

XLVIII. 6-10.

6 Flee, save your lives!
But they shall be[1] like a forsaken one[2] in the wilderness.
7 For on account of thy confidence in thy bungling work[3]
And in thy treasures shalt thou also be taken,
And Chemosh shall go into captivity,
His priests and his princes together.[4]
8 And the spoiler shall come upon every city,
And the city shall not be delivered;
The valley also shall perish,
And the plains shall be devastated—as[5] Jehovah hath spoken.
9 Give wings[6] unto Moab, for it will flee forth.
But its cities shall be desolation
Without any to dwell therein.
10 Cursed be he who doeth Jehovah's work remissly,
And cursed be he who keepeth back his sword from blood.

TEXTUAL AND GRAMMATICAL.

[1] Ver. 6.—וְתִהְיֶינָה. If the condition to be expected as a consequence of the flight were to be designated, יִהְיוּ or תִּהְיֶינָה would be grammatically more correct. Hence I take ו in the adversative sense, and the Imperf. as a simple announcement. The plural of the third person refers to the ideal plural contained in the collective נַפְשְׁכֶם.

[2] Ver. 6.—It has been with reason supposed that כַּעֲרוֹעֵר is to be read instead of כַּעֲרוֹעֵר, according to the analogy of xvii. 6. The opinion that the strange word was also the name of a city, and indeed of the well-known Aroer, may easily have given occasion to the reading of the text. The ancient translations vacillate: the LXX. translate ὄνος ἄγριος (עָרוֹד).

Vulg.: *myrica* (*virgultum humile et spinosum*); Syrus: *truncus arboris, stips*. All these renderings lack proper etymological foundation. GESENIUS (*Commentary* on Isa. vii. 2), and in his *Thesaurus* (S. 10, 74), fixes the meaning of *rudera, ruinæ*, on עֲרוֹעֵר itself, but for this there is also no etymological basis.

[3] Ver. 7.—The meaning of מַעֲשִׂים is doubtful—bulwark, bungling work (idol images), property—the latter according to passages like Exod. xxiii. 16; 1 Sam. xxv. 2. But in these passages מַעֲשֶׂה denotes only the pursuit of agriculture and its products. An emphasis on this appears to be superfluous with אוֹצְרוֹת. Since immediately afterwards the disgraceful carrying away of the principal idol of Moab is expressly mentioned, the mention of these manufactured idols as vain supports is more suitable to the connection (i. 16; x. 3, 9; xxv. 6, 7. Comp. xlix. 4).

[4] Ver. 7.—יַחַד (Chethibh) does not occur elsewhere in Jeremiah. In the parallel passages, also, we find יַחְדָּו.

[5] Ver. 8.—אֲשֶׁר אָמַר. This אֲשֶׁר, whether we take it as=as, because, or which, is quite contrary to the usage of Jeremiah, since he always inserts יְ אָכֵן alone (vi. 15; xxx. 3; xxxiii. 11, 13; xlix. 2, 18). J. D. MICHAELIS supposes it is *ortum ex repetitione finalium literarum præcedentis*, כַּאֲשֶׁר. It is also wanting, according to him, in Cod. 72.

[6] Ver. 9.—צִיץ from the radical meaning *micare, promicare*, has also the meanings of "forehead-plate" (of the high-priest, Exod. xxviii. 36-38), "flower," and "wing," in which last it occurs here. In Chaldee it is used for *ala*, Ps. cxxxix. 9; for fin Lev. xi. 9. Comp. BUXTORF's *Lex. Chald.*, p. 1907. The choice both of this word and the following נָצָא seems to have been occasioned by an effort at paronomasia. For נָצָא also (properly נָצָה. Comp. נָצָה, wing; Ezek. xvii. 3, 7; Job xxxix. 13—the א for the sake of uniformity with צִיץ. Comp. NAEGELSB. *Gr.*, § 93 *d, Anm.*), is ἅπαξ λεγόμενον.

EXEGETICAL AND CRITICAL.

This strophe portrays the destruction threatening Moab by summoning the people to flight, but at the same time distinctly declaring that this would not avail. This summons is made in a double gradation: 1. Moab is simply called upon to flee (ver. 6 *a*), but it is directly remarked that Moab would only barely escape and then be recaptured (vers. 6 b–7 a), and that in consequence the entire people, idols, priests and princes at their head, would be carried into captivity, while all remaining immovable property would be destroyed (vers. 7 b, 8). 2. The means of flight are offered to Moab in a figure (9 a) but, as the second half of the verse briefly intimates, the end will yet be the same, namely, devastation (ver. 9 b). It cannot also possibly be otherwise, for the Lord makes known His fixed resolution to destroy Moab, by threatening remissness or forbearance in the work of destruction with His curse (ver. 10).

Vers. 6–8. **Flee . . . hath spoken.** The call to flee is evidently intended ironically, for the announcement directly follows that the condition of the fugitives will be an extremely wretched one, that they will indeed be again taken.—**Like a forsaken one,**—like Aroer. Three Aroers are known: in Judah (1 Sam. xxx. 26), in Gad (Num. xxxii. 34; Josh. xiii. 25; Jud. xi. 33; 2 Sam. xxiv. 5), and in Reuben (Deut. ii. 36; iii. 12; iv. 18; Josh. xii. 2; xiii. 9; Jud. xi. 26). The first cannot possibly be meant. How one of the two others, whether that on the Arnon, or that further to the north, in the vicinity of Rabbath-Ammon, can be called "Aroer in the wilderness," it is difficult to perceive. For if even on the basis of Isa. xvii. 2, the city be supposed to be then destroyed, it is yet strange that a destroyed city should be designated as situated " in the wilderness," since this expression by no means involves the idea of destruction. Hence I have adopted the alternate reading proposed, which is favored by what follows. Neither a city, nor a tree, nor ruins, can flee and be taken, but this may easily happen to one *nudatus et desertus* in the wilderness. The causal sentence, ver. 7, has then the sense: thy flight will no longer procure thee protection, an one forsaken in the desert finds out, for thou also (like other nations) wilt be taken. And this will be the punishment of Moab for having founded its happiness on false supports.—Chemosh (the Chethibh כְּמִישׁ is perfectly unique) was the national god of the Moabites and Ammonites (1 Ki. xi. 7; 2 Ki. xxiii. 13; Jud. xi. 24). Moab is, therefore, called the people of Chemosh (ver. 46; Num. xxi. 29); accordingly here, also, his princes are called princes of Chemosh. The idol goes into captivity when his image is carried away. Comp. xlix. 3; Am. i. 15; Hos. x. 5, 6. The passage Am. i. 15 seems to have been in the prophet's mind here, as in xlix. 3.—Ver. 8 describes the destruction of the immovable property; cities, valleys (all river-valleys in antithesis to elevated plains and mountains), and plains (כִּישׁוֹר the plateau of Rabbath-Ammon, south as far as the Arnon. Comp. Deut. iii. 10; iv. 43; Josh. xiii. 9, 16, 17, 21; xx. 8; Raumer, *Pal. S.* 71 ff.)

Ver. 9. **Give wings . . . therein.** In comparison with ver. 6 there is evidently a progress here; there it is a mere call to flight, here the call is to afford Moab the only still imaginable means for this, *viz.*, wings. The one call is as ironical as the other. There is a strengthening of the irony in the word "for," which designates the fleeing away as the object not of the speaker, but of Moab. Comp. Isa. xvi. 2.—The second half of the verse corresponds as a brief synopsis to all that has been mentioned from ver. 6 b to ver. 8, as the result of the first summons (ver. 6 a). The expression is as in xlvi. 19; xlix. 17; li. 43; iv. 9, *etc.*

Ver. 10. **Cursed . . . from blood.** These words are the foil to the foregoing description. On this background the irony appears in its full strength. From these words we perceive what was the true meaning of the summons to flight, and how much more bitter the severity is rendered by these contrasting announcements (ver. 6 b–ver. 8; ver. 9 b). Moab's destruction is designated as the work of the Lord, because this is no more than the execution of a decree of judgment pronounced by Him. Comp. xxv. 31; xlvi. 10; li. 6.—**Remissly.** Comp. Prov. x. 4; xii. 27.

---

3. *The Transfusion.*

XLVIII. 11–13.

11 Moab hath been at ease from his youth,
    And he lay still on his lees,
    And was not drawn off from one vessel to another,[1]
    Neither hath he gone into exile:
    Therefore hath his taste remained in him,
    And his fragrance hath not changed.
12 Therefore behold, the days are coming, saith Jehovah,
    That I will send unto him tilters, who shall tilt him up
    And empty his vessels and dash his dishes in pieces.
13 And Moab shall be put to shame by Chemosh,
    As the house of Israel was put to shame by Bethel, their confidence.

TEXTUAL AND GRAMMATICAL.

[1] Ver. 11.—On אֶל for עַל comp. rems. on x. 1.

[2] Ver. 12.—צִעָה, *inclinare*, only here and li. 20 in Jeremiah. In ף צָעִים the object is Moab, or the wine representing it; since it is to be mentioned what is made empty there must be another object to יְרִיקוּ, and as נֶבֶל (originally a leathern bottle, and then *cadus, urceus;* comp. xiii. 12; Lam. iv. 2; Isa. xxx. 14) offered itself as a paronomasia [alliteration] to נִפֵּץ, it is given as the third object, though really the object remains the same. In order to render the alliteration we have translated, after LUTHER, [BLAYNEY, NOYES, WORDSWORTH] "tiltors" and "tilted;" [COWLES: emptyers; and the former after MEIER, render "dash" and "dishes."—S. R. A.]

EXEGETICAL AND CRITICAL.

In a very palpable figure the prophet compares Moab with wine, which has never been drawn off into another cask and has therefore retained its taste and scent unchanged (ver. 11). The Lord will transfuse Moab and cause his old cask to be broken in pieces (ver. 12), and then, like Israel, he will be put to shame by his idols.

Vers. 11-13. **Moab . . . their confidence.** Since the Moabites took the land from the original inhabitants, the Emims (Deut. ii. 10), they had generally remained in quiet possession of it. They had never been carried into captivity, as had been the case with Israel in their stay in Egypt and the deportation of the ten tribes. That this is the meaning of the figure is expressly declared in ver. 11, by the words **neither hath he gone into exile.** It seems to me doubtful whether Jeremiah has reference to Isa. xxv. 6; at any rate, on account of the difference in the main thoughts, the reference can be only cursory and verbal. Essentially the same thought, however, is expressed in the same words in Zeph. i. 12, whence it is probable that Jeremiah had this passage in mind. Four points are distinguished: 1. As a basis the fact that Moab has never been transfused. 2. The primary consequence that its taste and odor have remained. So far as this refers to the outward *status rerum*, a great degree of national prosperity is thus designated. In so far, however, as the words refer to the inward *habitus*, or to their relation to God and connected with this to His people, they express a sense unfavorable to Moab. They declare that Moab has never been thoroughly purified, never been freed from its enmity to the Lord and His people. 3. As a secondary consequence, it is mentioned, that a time of visitation is impending on Moab, since it cannot possibly be privileged against such a season. The instruments of the visitation are designated, in accordance with the figure in ver. 11, as coopers, who are to tilt up the old casks, empty and then break them in pieces. 4. As the final result it is mentioned that Moab will be put to shame by Chemosh as Israel by Bethel. The long undisturbed quiet was physically considered a benefit to Moab, but spiritually a gracious opportunity which it did not make use of. Hence Moab must become wise, like Israel, by loss and suffering (comp. 1 Ki. xii. 28-33).

---

4. The Vanity of Human Glory.

XLVIII. 14-17.

14 How can ye say, we are heroes
And strong men for the war?
15 Desolated is Moab and his cities go up,[1]
And his best young men go down to the slaughter,
Saith the King, Jehovah Zebaoth is his name.
16 Moab's destruction is near approaching,
And his calamity hastens on apace.[2]
17 Bemoan him, all his neighbors,
All ye, who know his name,
Say, how is the mighty stem broken,
The splendid rod!

TEXTUAL AND GRAMMATICAL.

[1] Ver. 15.—The singular עָלָה is certainly surprising, but the alteration of the text to שֹׁדֵד (the spoiler of Moab and his cities goes up) [as J. D. MICH., EWALD, GRAF, BLAYNEY], seems to me unnecessary. I believe that Jeremiah had in view the passage in Jud. xx. 40 (וְהִנֵּה עָלָה כְלִיל־הָעִיר הַשָּׁמַיְמָה), and that thus the sing. masc. is explained, which moreover in the principle of the ideal number (the entirety of the cities regarded as a unit. Comp. NAEGELSB. *Gr.*, § 105, 4 *a*) has a grammatical support.

[2] Ver. 16.—Comp. Isa. xiii. 22; lvi. 1; NAEGELSB. *Gr.*, § 95, 3 *b*.

EXEGETICAL AND CRITICAL.

All human glory is turned to shame, whether one glorify himself, as, according to ver. 14, Moab had done, to which the destruction of all his warlike power stands in strong contrast (ver. 15), or good friends and neighbors praise us. These may soon and easily find occasion (ver. 16) to turn their song of praise into a lamentation.
Vers. 14, 15. **How can ... his name.** In opposition to Moab's boastful glorying in his warlike strength, desolation is announced in general and destruction according to a just Nemesis of the main objects of his glorying: the fortified cities, which seemed to rest immovably on their foundations, must fly away in smoke; the strong youths, who aimed high, must go down to slaughter.—**Go down,** etc. Comp. Isa. xxxiv. 6, 7; Jer. l. 27; li. 40.—**Saith,** etc. Comp. xlvi. 18; li. 57.
Vers. 16, 17. **Moab's destruction ... splendid rod.** So near and certain is the destruction of Moab that his neighbors and friends are called upon to bemoan the overthrow of this power so highly extolled hitherto by themselves.—**Bemoan him.** Comp. xv. 5; xvi. 5; xxii. 10.—**Neighbors** (comp. xlvi. 14; xlviii. 39; xlix. 5), literally those round about him, therefore most intimately acquainted with him, ye **who know his name,** being the more distant acquaintances. (Comp. the related expressions in Ps. lxxxvii. 4; Job xix. 13; xlii. 11; Ps. lvi. 14; lxxxviii. 9, 19).—**The mighty stem.** Comp. Ps. cx. 2; Ezek. xix. 12, 14.

6. *Message to the Fugitives on the Arnon.*

XLVIII. 18-25.

18   Come down from thy glory and seat thyself in the thirsty,[1]
     Thou inhabitant daughter of Dibon ![2]
     For the spoiler of Moab is advancing against thee,
     He destroyeth thy strongholds.
19   Place thyself by the wayside and look out,
     Thou inhabitress of Aroer;
     Ask of the fugitive and her who is escaped ![3]
     Say, What hath been done ?[4]
20   "Moab is confounded, for she is broken down.[5]
     Howl and cry ![6]
     Proclaim it on the Arnon, that Moab is destroyed;
21   And judgment has come on the land of the plain,
     On Holon and on Jahazah, and on Mephaath,
22   And on Dibon, Nebo and Beth-diblathaim,
23   And on Kiriathaim, Beth-gamul and Beth-meon,
24   And on Kerioth and Bozrah,
     And on all the cities of the land of Moab, far or near.
25   The horn of Moab is broken off,
     And his arm is shattered "—saith Jehovah.

TEXTUAL AND GRAMMATICAL.

[1] Ver. 18.—Judging from the parallel passage (Isa. xlvii. 1) we must read with the Keri צְמָא‎, צָמָא‎ everywhere else signifies thirst. "To seat one's self in the thirst," however, sounds very strange. We must then either punctuate אָצְמָ‎, or regard צָמָא‎ as a collateral form of צָמֵא‎ (comp. רָכָב‎ with רֹכֵב‎, Gen. xlix. 12; חָלָב‎ with חָלֵב‎, Exod. xxiii. 19). In Latin also *silentia* is used for *regiones aridæ*. Comp. Plin. *Hist.*, N X. 73; XII. 28; XXV. 11.
[2] Ver. 18.—יֹשֶׁבֶת בַּת־דִּיבוֹן‎. This form of expression is found besides here only in xlvi. 19. The construction is as in בְּתוּלַת בַּת צִיּוֹן‎, Isa. xxxvii. 22. Comp. NAEGELSB. *Gr.*, § 64, 4.
[3] Ver. 19.—נָס וְנִמְלָטָה‎. The different gender is to express the variety. On the irregular accentuation of נִמְלָטָה‎ comp. OLSH., S. 233 and 363.
[4] Ver. 19.—On נִהְיָתָה‎ and its difference from the masc. (the idea of multiplicity involved in the feminine) comp. NAEGELSB. *Gr.*, § 60, 6 *b*.
[5] Ver. 20.—The fem. חַתָּה‎ can only be referred to Moab, in spite of the immediately preceding הֹבִישׁ‎. It is the same change in gender as in ver. 9, ver. 11, ver. 15 שֻׁדַּד כִּי וְעָרֶיהָ‎, and then again בַּחוּרָיו‎, vers. 38 and 39. Observe besides that הֹבִישׁ‎ precedes as שֻׁדַּד‎ does.

CHAP. XLVIII. 18–25.

* **Ver. 20.**—The alteration of the Keri (to accord with the following הֵן־דִּי) is unnecessary, since the fem. form of the **imporf.** evidently attaches itself to the preceding עָרְכִי, etc. Accordingly it is Aroer, which is addressed, not Moab.

EXEGETICAL AND CRITICAL.

An animated picture! First some concrete forms of cities are directly addressed: Dibon is to go down, Aroer to question the fugitives (vers. 18, 19). The answer of the latter is sad enough. Arrived on the Arnon, where Aroer is situated, and thus on the borders of the *mishor*, they proclaim that it is at an end with Moab, for all the cities of the northern half of the country are taken (vers. 20-24). From this it follows as the total result, that the power of Moab is broken (ver. 25).

Ver. 18. **Come down . . . thy strongholds.** Isa. xlvii. 1 was here in the prophet's mind, "Come down and sit in the dust, O virgin daughter of Babylon."—On Dibon, which, as we conclude from **thy strongholds**, was a fortified city and was situate a league north of the Arnon, comp. Num. xxxii. 3, 34 ; Josh. xiii. 9, 17; Isa. xv. 2; RAUMER, *Pal. S.* 261.

Ver. 19. **Place thyself . . . done.** To the inhabitants of Aroer, the southern boundary city of the מִישׁוֹר (comp. rems. on ver. 8) the sad summons is addressed to go out into the street, to spy out (comp. Nah. ii. 2) and then to make inquiries from the approaching train of the fugitives.

Vers. 20-25. **Moab . . . saith Jehovah.** These verses contain the answer of the escaped. —**Judgment.** The choice of the expression is occasioned by the *mishor, plain,* which signifies not merely *plain,* but *æquitas, justitia.* Comp. Ps. xxix. 11; xlv. 7; lxvii. 5. Judgment is thus to come upon the land, whose name also signifies "land of righteousness." The cities mentioned afterwards are all in the Mishor. Holon (different from another in Judah, Josh. xv. 51) is mentioned here only. Jahaza (Comp. Isa. xv. 4; Num. xxi. 23; Josh. xiii. 18; Jud. xi. 20) lay, according to EUSEBIUS and JEROME, in the vicinity of Medaba. Comp. RAUMER, *S.* 263. —**Mephaath** is elsewhere called מֵפָעַת (Josh. xiii. 18) or מֵיפַעַת (Josh. xxi. 37; 1 Chron. vi. 64). According to the passages cited from the book of Joshua it belongs to the tribe of Reuben and to the *Mishor*.—**Dibon.** Comp. rems on ver. 18.—**Nebo.** Comp. rems. on ver. 1.— **Beth-diblathaim is not mentioned elsewhere** in the Old Testament. Its position is clear from the statement of JEROME, that Jahaza was situated between Medaba and Diblathaim. (*Vid. Onomasticon s. v.* Jaffa).—**Kiriathaim.** Comp. rems. on ver. 1.—**Beth-gamul** occurs here only. If PORTER is correct in recognizing Bozrah, Kerioth and Beth-gamul in the present ruined cities of the Hauran, Bosra, Kureiyeh and El Jemal, we have here three cities not in Moab, but separated from it by the entire territory of the Ammonites. Comp. RAUMER, *Pal. S.* 251, 2. This hypothesis is, however, improbable, since real Moabitish cities can be shown for Bozrah and Kerioth. See below.—**Beth-meon** was named in full Beth-baal-meon (Josh. xiii. 17); elsewhere Baal-meon (Num. xxxii. 38), and is designated among the other places as belonging to the Mishor and to the tribe of Reuben. Comp. RAUMER, *S.* 259 and 264.—**Kerioth.** Comp. ver. 41 and Am. ii. 2. SEETZEN found a place on Mt. Attarus (comp. עֲטָרֹת Num. xxxii. 34, 35) called El-Karriât, which he decidedly regards as Kerioth not Kiriathaim. Comp. RAUMER, *S.* 251, 2.—**Bozrah.** There is a Bozrah mentioned as in Edom (comp. rems. on xlix. 13) and one as in the Hauran, but the latter not in the Bible. It was the Bostra of the Romans, the birthplace of Philippus Arabs. Immense ruins still testify to the importance of the city. Comp. RAUMER, *S.* 244. Since, however, a place בְּצֶר in the *Mishor* is expressly mentioned (Deut. iv. 43; Josh. xx. 8; xxi. 36), and since the LXX. always render this name by Βόσορ, we do not hesitate to recognize בְּצְרָה in this בָּצְרָ.—**And on all the cities,** etc. From the context it can only be the cities to the north of Aroer which are meant, for according to ver. 19 sqq., the fugitives announce to the people of Aroer that both the cities further to the north, and also those more to the south in the vicinity of Aroer were already taken. From this it follows that the whole northern half of the country was in the hands of the enemy, and consequently Moab's horn and arm (the biblical types of dominion and strength, comp. Ps. lxxv. 5, 11, 1 Sam. ii. 31; Ps. x. 15) are broken.

[On the Moabitic stone recently discovered, which confirms many of the names here mentioned, see *Bibliotheca Sacra,* Oct. 1870. Andover. —S. R. A.]

II. The Reasons of the Punitive Judgment (XLVIII. 26-42.)

1. *Moab's Pride and his Punishment in General.*

XLVIII. 26-30.

26 Make ye him drunken, for against Jehovah hath he magnified himself!
    And Moab may wallow[1] in his vomit,
    And he also may become a derision!
27 Or[2] was not Israel a derision[3] unto thee,
    When he was found[4] among the thieves?
    Yea, for at each of thy words concerning him thou shookest thyself.
28 Leave the cities and dwell in the rock, ye inhabitants of Moab,
    And be as the dove that maketh her nest on the walls of the yawning ravine.
29 We have heard the arrogance of Moab, the very arrogant,[5]
    His loftiness, and his arrogance and his pride and the haughtiness of his heart
30 I know, saith Jehovah, his insolence
    And the nothingness of his boastings; nothing have they effected.[6]

TEXTUAL AND GRAMMATICAL.

[1] Ver. 26.—סָפַק an onomatopoëtic word, denotes originally "to spank, to clap." Comp. סָפַקְתִּי עַל יָרֵךְ, xxxi. 19. Then it is frequently used of striking hands: Num. xxiv. 10; Job xxxiv. 37; Lam. ii. 15.—שָׂפַק is used in part for סָפַק (Job xxvii. 23), and in part as an independent root with meaning *sufficere*. In the latter signification it occurs, however, in the Hebrew of the Old Testament only in the imperfect יִשְׂפֹּק (1 Ki. xx. 10), and (perhaps) in the Hiphil (Isa. ii. 6), and besides (perhaps) the substantive שֶׂפֶק (Job xxxvi. 18). Yet in consequence of the interchange of the related radical סָפַק occurs in Job xx. 22, as also in the Aramaic סְפַק and סְפִיקָא in the sense of sufficiency and superfluity. Here it is evident that the rendering "that Moab had superfluity in his vomit" (MEIER) is feeble, and moreover unsafe, since the prefix בְּ is striking, and it is not proved that the meanings of sufficiency (of the things) and of having a superfluity (of the persons) are united in the verb. The common radical meaning of סָפַק to strike, to clap, gives a perfectly satisfactory sense. Comp. Isa. xix 11.

[2] Ver. 27.—וְאִם=or? Comp. NAEGELSB. *Gr.*, § 107, 4. In the second clause of the disjunctive question הֲ (with a following Dag. *forte*. Comp. NAEGELSB. *Gr.*, § 53, 3 *Anm.*) is repeated as in Gen. xvii. 17; Ps. xciv. 9.

[3] Ver. 27.—שְׂחֹק=object of derision as in Job xii. 4.

[4] Ver. 27.—The fem. נִמְצָאָה is unjustly suspected by the Masoretes. Comp. rems. on חָתְתָה, ver. 20.

[5] Ver. 29.—גֵּאֶה is an adjective (Comp. Isa. ii. 12; Ps. xciv. 2), and to be referred to Moab.

[6] Ver. 30.—Isa. xvi. 6 concludes with בַּדָּיו לֹא־כֵן. Here the words לֹא כֵן עָשׂוּ, also are added. And the Masoretes punctuate so as to connect בַּדָּיו with עָשׂוּ as its subject. We cannot, however, doubt that בַּדָּיו, in accordance with the fundamental passage, belongs to לֹא־כֵן. It would then be "the nothingness (comp. 2 Ki. xvii. 9; Prov. xv. 7) of his boastings (Isa. xliv. 25; Job xi. 3)," while the words לֹא־כֵן עָשׂוּ seem to declare the nothingness of his *deeds*.

EXEGETICAL AND CRITICAL.

To ver. 42 the prophet describes specially the judgment of God on the criminal arrogance of Moab, which he manifested particularly towards Israel and Israel's God. First, generally, (vers. 26-30) the disgraceful fate of a drunken man, who falls into his own vomit (ver. 26), is announced as a just punishment for the scorn, with which they always treated Israel when chastised by his God (ver. 27), and further, the fate of the dove driven into the fearful clefts of the rock (ver. 28) as a punishment for his insolent and false arrogance (vers. 29, 30).

Vers. 26, 27. **Make ye him . . . shookest thyself.** A man, who is beastly intoxicated, falls into his own vomit, and how does he provoke to its full extent the derisive laughter of the beholder! So shall it be to Moab for his boasting against Jehovah. This making drunk reminds us of the figure of the cup of wrath (xxv. 15 coll. xiii. 13). As there, those who make drunk are those whom the Lord has appointed His agents in executing the punishment.—**Magnified himself.** Comp. ver. 42. The expression seems to be taken from Zeph. ii. 8, 10, an older prophecy against Moab. Comp. also Joel ii. 20.—The objection on the part of Moab that this is too severe a punishment is met with the intimation that Moab had done the same to the Israelites.—**When he was found**, *etc.* This is usually also taken as a question. But was not Israel really often caught in thievery and punished for it? Jeremiah expressly affirms this in ii. 26. What reason would Moab otherwise have had for scorning Israel? I therefore regard אִם as a particle of time=when, as often as (Num. xxi. 9; Gen. xxxviii. 9). It is then thus admitted that Israel had been more than once caught in criminal conduct and punished, but observe that it is said among *thieves*. In this there is an allusion to the fact that Israel was only seduced by others, and that the principal thieves, to which Moab belonged, were his heathen neighbors.—**Yea. for**, *etc.* This is the answer to the question. We supply **Yea.**—כִּי=*pro sufficientia, pro ratione* (Isa. lxvi. 23; Zech. xiv. 16), comp. xxxi. 20. From the latter passage we see also that (בוֹ) him is to be referred to **thy words.**—**Shookest thyself.** This may be shaking of the head (comp. xviii. 16) or shrugging of the shoulders, but equally in either case is it an expression of scorn.

Ver. 28. **Leave... yawning ravine.** The preceding figure was adapted to humble Moab's national pride, the present relates to his warlike pride. They boasted greatly of their valor in war (ver. 14), and doubtless also of their excellent fortifications (comp. ver. 18). They are now told that they will be driven from their bulwarks and into the rocky mountains, there like a wild pigeon to pass a troubled, ever threatened existence.— **On the walls.** The word is found besides only in Isa. vii. 20, where it undoubtedly signifies beyond. עָבַר, however, signifies not merely the side beyond, but the side generally. (Comp. xlix. 32; 1 Ki. v. 4; Exod. xxxii. 15). On the doves in Palestine comp. Henzog, *Real-Enc.*, XV. S. 425.

Vers. 29, 30. **We have heard ... effected.** These two verses are no more than a reproduction, extended by a few additions, of Isa. xvi. 6 in accord with Zeph. ii. 10. In this quotation the prophet expresses the thought, which is expected as a foundation to vers. 26-28, viz., an answer to the question, whence comes on the one hand Moab's scorn towards Jehovah and His people, on the other, the particularly severe punishment of the same? Answer: to the pride of Moab corresponds both his scorn against Israel and the chastisement, which he receives on the part of Jehovah. Hence the prophet labors by an accumulation of terms to describe the arrogance of the Moabites as surpassing all bounds.

2. *Moab utterly Destroyed.*

XLVIII. 31-35.

31   Therefore I howl over Moab,
   And over Moab, the whole of it, I cry.
   Over the men of Kir-heres there is sighing.[1]
32 My tears over Jazer flow even to thee, thou vine of Sibmah:
   Thy shoots are gone over the sea,
   Even to the sea of Jazer they did reach.
   On thy fruit harvest and thy vintage is the spoiler fallen ;
33 And joy and gladness is taken from the fruit fields and the land of Moab;
   And I cause the wine to fail from the wine presses ;
   They will not tread with shouting,—
   With a shouting that is no shouting.
34 From the cry of Heshbon even to Elealeh,
   Unto Jahaz they raise their voice:
   From Zoar to Horonaim, the three year old heifer,[2]
   For even the waters of Nimrim shall be desolations.[3]
35 And I destroy Moab, saith Jehovah,
   Him who ascends[4] the high places and burns incense to his gods.

TEXTUAL AND GRAMMATICAL.

[1] Ver. 31.—The correction אֶהֱגֶה, which MEIER allows himself, is unnecessary and not sufficiently authorized by the examples adduced by him (Mic. vi. 10, אִשׁ for יֵשׁ, ver. 11, אֻכָּה יֹפְכֶה for דוֹאֵר for הוֹיִן).

[2] Ver. 34.—עֶגְלַת is used of nations in xlvi. 20; l. 11; Hos. iv. 16; x. 11. The genitive עֶגְלַת is explained by analogies like שְׁנַת הָרְבִעִית, *anno quarti, i. e., numeri* (Jer. xlvi. 2; Ii. 59; 2 Ki. xvii. 6), מִשְׁפַּט אֶחָד (Lev. xxiv. 22), אָרוֹן אֶחָד (2 Ki. xii. 10).

[3] Ver. 34.—We have adopted the translation of MEIER [German]—.*Nimrim nimmer rinnen* [Nimrim will never run, which expresses the alliteration of the Hebrew, but is rather a free rendering]. The כִּי at the beginning of the verse is transferred

from Isaiah, where it is fully in place. In the present passage it can only introduce a single point in corroboration of the main proposition (ver. 31).

Ver. 35.—Is מַעֲלֶה a participle or a substantive? Grammatically the latter is the easier (comp. ver. 5), but the discrepancy with בְּקֹטִיר is disturbing. We may take it then in the direct causative meaning (*ascensum faciens*. Comp. on xlviii. 5, 2), and observe the remark of GRAF that correspondence with this word occasioned the choice of the Hiphil participle.

EXEGETICAL AND CRITICAL.

After the reason and manner of the judgment on Moab have been set forth in general, the latter is now described more in particular. This is done by the prophet's first expressing (ver. 31 *a*) what feeling he has in consequence of his knowledge of the destruction threatening *all* Moab (*i. e.*, no longer merely the northern half as in vers. 18-25), and then turns to single places of the *whole* land, with special emphasis on the destruction which is impending on the vine and fruit culture of Moab (vers. 32, 33), as well as the worship of the idols connected therewith (ver. 35).

Ver. 31. **Therefore . . . there is sighing.** This verse begins with a free rendering of Isa. xvi. 7. While there the third person is used, here Jeremiah speaks in the first person, being evidently himself shocked by the fearful import of the message which he has to deliver. Comp. Isa. xv. 5; xvi. 9, 11; xxi. 3 and DRECHSLER *ad loc.*—In the words, **the whole of it**, he declares that here he has not merely the northern half of the country, the Mishor, but the whole country in view, mentioning a series of cities from the north to the extreme south (ver. 34).—**Over the men**, *etc.* In the original passage it reads "over the raisin-cakes of Kir-hareseth will ye sigh, deeply troubled." There is no need of seeking aid from indistinctly written MSS., it being quite in Jeremiah's manner to substitute for a marked and strange expression, one softer and more usual. He has evidently omitted the concluding words and substituted אֲנָשֵׁי (men) for אֲשִׁישֵׁי (grapes, raisin-cakes). The second person plural would be in too strong a contrast to the first person in the hemistich, and therefore the third person singular masculine is chosen, which is to be taken in its impersonal sense.

Vers. 32, 33. **My tears . . . no shouting.** In Isa. xvi. 9 it reads "Therefore I will bewail with the weeping of Jazer." If we take בְּכִי of the text in the sense of a comparison the connection in meaning with the original would disappear, and then no good ground for the comparative is apparent. Jaazer, according to the *Onomast.* (s. v. Azer and Jazer), was 15 m. p., Sibmah only five hundred paces from Heshbon. They were, therefore, neighboring towns in a fertile district abounding in fruit and wine. Since then they were thus, as it were, sisters, the centres of agriculture closely connected by solidarity of interest, and the blow which strikes one affects the other also, one is not to be bewailed alone, but both at the same time. This is essentially the meaning of בְּבְכִי (in the weeping over Jaazer is contained also that over Sibmah) and of בְּכִי (Sibmah participates in the tears which flow over Jaazer).—The district of Salt, in the vicinity of which Jaazer must have been situated (comp. RAUMER, *S.* 262, 3) is still very rich in vines. Comp. HERZOG, *R.-Enc.*, XVII. *S* 611. The elements of the two following sentences also are found in Isa. xvi. 8, "branches" only instead of "shoots" and "sea," being wanting before Jazer. The sea of Jazer may denote only a pond or great basin. That the term may be so used is shown by the "sea" in the temple (1 Ki. vii. 23). "The sea of Jazer was probably some celebrated large pond, like the ponds of Heshbon, in which the water of the Wady (Nahr) Sir, which springs near by, was collected. SEETZEN found some ponds there still." DELITZSCH, *Jes.*, *S.* 211 [Eng. Tr., p. 384]. RAUMER, *Pal.*, *S.* 263, *Anm.* The hypothesis that the repetition of the word *sea* is based on a scriptural error is therefore unnecessary. The widely extended (even according to Isa. xvi. 7, 8, over the Dead Sea) wine-culture of Moab is poetically represented under the figure of a single vine. Comp. DRECHSLER [and ALEXANDER] on Isa. xvi. 8.—**On thy fruit-harvest,** *etc.* Comp. xl. 10, 12. Instead of **vintage**, which suits the connection better, we find in Isa. xvi. 9 "harvest," and instead of **spoiler** the more forcible but less distinct. "shouting."—**And joy**, *etc.*, from Isa. xvi. 10. Comp. Joel ii. 20; iv. 15. Carmel (fruit-fields) cannot possibly be a proper noun here. For what occasion had the prophet to make such a spring? In Isa. xvi. 10, also stands מִן הַכַּרְמֶל, but there without the following **and the land of Moab**, and hence evidently in an appellative significance. The prophet would say: joy and gladness having vanished from the vineyards they have departed from the whole country.—**And I cause**, *etc.* These words are altered from Isa. xvi. 10 *b*, in a peculiar manner. Instead of **they will not tread with shouting**, we read in Isaiah "the treaders shall tread out no wine in their presses." The following words contain the justification of the rendering given. It is emphasized that the treading will be altogether without shouting. A shouting will indeed be heard, not, however, such as pertains to the treading of grapes (xxv. 30), but another, a warlike shouting. The word is elsewhere only applied to war-cries, li. 14.

Ver. 34. **From the cry . . be desolations.** These words to **their voice** are taken, with modifications from Isa. xv. 4. The cry of Heshbon, as it is called in Jeremiah, represents at the same time a place, and consequently serves as a *terminus a quo*. On Heshbon comp. rems. on ver. 2. Elealeh (now El Al) lies only half an hour from Heshbon. Comp. Numb. xxxii. 37; Isa. xvi. 19; RAUMER, *S.* 261. Jahaz (identical with Jahza, ver. 21) must, according to Numb. xxi. 23 have lain to the south-east, towards the desert. Zoar (comp. ver. 4) and Horonaim (ver. 3) represent the south country of the Moabites. We distinctly meet here the idea of the *whole* of Moab (ver. 31) in contrast to the limitation, in which Moab is spoken of in vers. 18-25. The individual elements are taken from Isa. xv. 5. There Eglath-shalishiyah appears to stand in apposition to Zoar. In the present passage it is as formally co-ordinated with the name Horonaim. Both are possible only if Eglath, etc., is either a place near both the cities in question, or a predicate equally applicable to both. The latter view is favored by the grammatical structure, for in the former case we should expect לְ *unto* or עַד (comp. on **Jahaz**, ver. 21, *etc.*) In what sense, however, are these cities called Eglath-shalishiyah? Küsren (*Stud. u. Krit.*, 1862, 1., S. 113 ff.) perceives herein a topographical definition. Egla was a Tripolis, and "Egla of the third part" is equivalent to the third part of Egla. Egla is the principal name, Zoar and Horonaim the names of the two other parts. It is however surprising that of this group of cities, which must certainly have been of some importance, we find no trace elsewhere. We should also expect the reverse order. Shalishah-Eglath, and if Egla, Zoar and Horonaim form *one* city, what is the cry from Zoar to Horonaim to mean? DELITZSCH (on Isa. S. 206) [Eng. Tr., p. 336] attaches himself to GESENIUS and his predecessors (Vulg., Targ.) taking the words to signify "*juvenca tertii, i. e. anni*" = *indomita, jugoque non assueta*. Yet he does not refer the predicate to Moab (which can be done in Isaiah only with great harshness, and in Jeremiah not at all) but to Zoar "the beautiful, fortified, hitherto unconquered city." Although the reason why Zoar should be so called is not very transparent, the language compels us to give this exegesis the preference. Whether Horonaim deserved the predicate in the same degree as Zoar is a question of minor importance, for the transference to Horonaim, which is mentioned only one line after in Isa. xv. 5, can be only accidental.—**For even**, *etc.* Comp. Isa. xv. 6. If by מֵי נִמְרִים we are to understand Beth-Nimrah, we shall thus be carried into the extreme north-west of the country, not inappropriately to the purport of the strophe. (Comp. **the whole**, ver. 31). The name and character of Beth-Nimrah favor the identity, for this place at the mouth of the Wady Shaib or Shoêb in the plain of the Jordan is still celebrated for its wealth of springs. Comp. WINER, *R.-W.-B.*, *s. v.* Bethnimra. Yet it must be confessed, that according to the connection, a place in the South, as the ruined Numêre with the spring Moyet Numêre (DELITZSCH, *S.* 207) [Eng. Tr., p. 327], might be meant.

Ver. 35. **And I destroy ... to his gods.** The prophet has Isa. xv. 2 and xvi. 12 in mind. What he means by the words מְעָלֵה בַכָּה is not perfectly clear. They may mean, who erects the high places, throws them up (HITZIG) or, who offers on the height (literally: offerers of the height), or who ascends to the height; or, finally, the ascending to the height. Each of these renderings has its light and its shadow. In Isa. xvi. 12, however, the idea of going up to the sanctuary is expressed. Hence I give those explanations the preference which take מְעָלֵה in the sense of ascending.

---

3. *The Lamentation for the Dead.*

XLVIII. 36–38.

36 Therefore my heart sighs over Moab like flutes.
 And my heart sighs like flutes over the men of Kir-heres ;
 Because the remnant¹ of what was gained has perished.
37 For every head is bald, and every beard cut short,
 Upon all hands cuttings, and on the loins sackcloth !
38 On all the roofs of Moab and in his streets all is lamentation :²
 For I have broken Moab like a vessel
 Wherein there is no more pleasure, saith Jehovah.

TEXTUAL AND GRAMMATICAL.

¹ Ver. 36.—On the construct state of יִתְרַת עָשָׂה comp. NAEGELSB. *Gr.*, § 65, 2, 3.
² Ver. 38.—In regard to the construction, the abstract stands for the concrete. Comp. NAEGELSB. *Gr.*, § 59, 1.

EXEGETICAL AND CRITICAL.

The prophet feels his heart to be, as it were, a mourning flute in view of the great loss of Moab (ver. 36) and this all the more that he perceives in Moab itself on every hand lamentation for the dead (vers. 37, 38 a). This is also warranted, for the Lord has broken Moab like a vessel which has become worthless (ver. 38 b.)

Ver. 36. **Therefore .. perished.** This verse is parallel to ver. 31. For 1, both begin with **therefore**; 2, in both the object of the utterance of feeling is designated as Moab (hardly Ar Moab ver. 4, on account of "whole," ver. 31—and why should Jeremiah have constantly omitted the עָר?) and Kir-heres; in both cases an analogous thought is introduced by the particle "therefore;" there the expression of howling and crying, here the sighing of the heart compared with the tone of a funeral flute. "Therefore" in ver. 36 then refers not to the special calamities enumerated immediately before, but to that general description, which we have read in vers. 25-30. Moreover here also the single elements of the discourse are taken primarily from Isa. xv. This employment of foreign property explains much of the unevenness in the arrangement of the sentences. Isa. xvi. 11 and xv. 5 are in the prophet's mind, but he changes the harp, spoken of in Isa. xxi. 11 into the flute, as is correctly remarked, because the flute is the instrument used in mourning, and thus conformity is obtained with the funeral customs afterwards described. On the use of the flute in mournings for the dead comp. Matth. ix. 23. Joseph. *Bell. Jud.* III., 9, 5; Ovid *Fast.* VI., 656; Herzog, *R.-Enc.*, XVI. S. 364.—**Because**, *etc.* The words are from Isa. xv. 7, but there they are the object of the following verb (שָׂאוּם) instead of which we here find *perished*. The words **remnant**, *etc.*, must therefore be the subject of the verb, since אָבַד never means "to lose" but only "to be lost, to perish." The plural of the predicate is explained by the collective meaning of the subject.—עַל־כֵּן is also here taken from Isa. xv. 7, but it cannot possibly signify "therefore" as it does there. So unless we assume an error there is nothing left but to take it as equivalent to עַל־כֵּן אֲשֶׁר, a meaning which is certainly not proved, since this very passage is adduced as the strongest evidence (comp. Gesen., *Thes. pag.* 669). A double reason is then given for the mourning of the prophet in ver. 36: 1. a mediate, ver. 36 *b;* 2. an immediate, vers. 37, 38 *a*. Whence dost thou know that all is lost? From the fact that all mourns.

Vers. 37, 38. **For every head . . Jehovah**. Isa. xv. 2, 3 is the original passage. On **Bald** comp. vii. 20; xvi. 6. Instead of **cut short** (גְּרֻעָה) Isaiah has "cut off" (גְּדֻעָה) *cæsa*. In the latter passage however the editions vary. Comp. Delitzsch, S. 205 [Eng. Tr., p. 325].—**Cuttings**. Comp. xvi. 6; xli. 5.—**Sackcloth**. Comp. iv. 8; vi. 26; Joel i. 8.—**Roofs**. Comp. Isa xxii, 1; Herzog, *R.-Enc.* XVI., S. 363.—**All is lamentation**. In Isaiah "everything wails, melting into tears."—**For I have broken**, *etc.* The ground of the facts which cause the lamentation is, that (not chance, or any human or demoniac power, but) Jehovah has broken Moab. In **like a vessel**, *etc.*, Jeremiah quotes himself, xxii. 28.

4. *Pride comes before a Fall.*

XLVIII. 39-42

39 How is she broken! How do they howl!
How has Moab turned the back shamefully!
And Moab shall become a derision
And a horror to all his neighbors.
40 For thus saith Jehovah: Behold like an eagle he flies,
And spreads his wings over Moab.
41 Taken are the cities,[1]
And the fortresses captured,[2]
And the heart of the heroes of Moab in that day
Shall be like the heart of a parturient woman.[3]
42 And Moab shall be destroyed from being a nation,
For against Jehovah hath he magnified himself.

TEXTUAL AND GRAMMATICAL.

[1] Ver. 41.—קְרִיּוֹת cannot here as in ver. 14, be a proper name on account of the following מְעָדוֹת. The plural קְרִיּוֹת does not indeed occur in an appellative sense elsewhere, but this forms no objection, since the prophet may have chosen this form with reference to the names of the Moabitish cities. Comp. Olsh., § 146 *d*; 152 *a*.

[2] Ver. 41.—On the singular נִתְפָּשָׂה comp. Naegelsb. *Gr.*, § 105, 4, *b*; Ewald, § 317, *a*.

[3] Ver. 41.—The expression אִשָּׁה מְצֵרָה (*mulier uterum comprimens*) occurs here and in xlix. 22 only. On the subject-matter comp. iv. 31.

EXEGETICAL AND CRITICAL.

With ver. 38 the quotations from Isa. xv. and xvi. cease; the beginning of ver. 39 reminds us of the beginning of vers. 31 and 26; vers. 39 and 41 are evidently closely related, reproducing, as it were, the fundamental thought of vers. 26, 27 that Moab is to become a derision, because he has magnified himself against the Lord. I therefore take vers. 39-41 as *one* strophe. This begins with an exclamation: how is Moab broken, given up to shameful flight, and thus become an object of ridicule and horror (ver. 39)! This effect corresponds exactly to the cause, for a powerful enemy, comparable to a powerful eagle, is to come upon Moab (ver. 40). In consequence the fortified places are taken, the courage of all the warriors broken (ver. 41), and Moab stricken from the roll of nations. This is his punishment for having magnified himself against Jehovah.

Ver. 39. **How is she ... his neighbors.** Moab is here again conceived of as feminine. Comp. rems. on ver. 20. Since this passage was generally in the prophet's mind, הָיָה also must be taken in the meaning which it has there, viz., of being broken. (Comp. Isa. vii. 8). The first result of this being broken is howling. We however take הֵילִילוּ as 3d pers. perf., since the imperative here, as afterwards in בֹּשׁוּ, does not suit the connection. The further consequence is shameful flight (בּוֹשׁ to be regarded as in the accusative. Comp. Mic. i. 11). From all this it follows lastly that Moab is become two things, a derision (vers. 26, 27) and a terror (xvii. 17) to all his neighbors.

Ver. 40. **For thus saith ... over Moab.**

—**For** is argumentative. The effect corresponds to the cause. The choice of figures is founded on Deut. xxviii. 49, where the people of Israel are assured in case of apostasy of severe judgment, to be executed by a nation coming from afar. In iv. 13 also there was an echo of this passage. It is possible that Isa. xlvi. 11 was in the mind of the prophet, even as this present passage lay before the prophet Ezekiel, when in xvii. 3 he used the same figure of Nebuchadnezzar. Who the eagle is here the prophet does not say. If what we have said in the introduction concerning the date of composition of this and the contemporary prophecies against the Nations is correct, the present passage is in so far dissimilar to xlvi. 18 in that there Nebuchadnezzar is mentioned just before (ver. 13). Here the non-mention is due to the circumstance that the prophet did not yet know who was the chosen instrument for the execution of the judgment.—**And spreads,** *etc.* Here also a passage from Deuteronomy (xxxii. 11) seems to have hovered before the prophet's mind. This however applies only to the expression, for here the spreading of wings is intended in an exactly opposite sense. Comp. also Job xxxix. 26. A repetition of this passage and of the following verse is found in xlix. 22.

Vers. 41, 42. **Taken ... magnified himself.** The prophet here passes into the literal style of discourse.—**From being,** *etc.* Comp. ver. 2 and Isa. vii. 8.—**For against Jehovah,** *etc.* This points back to ver. 26, and here as there is to be regarded as a reminiscence from Zeph. ii. 8, 10. The prophet here brings to a close that part of his prophecy, which has the pride of Moab especially for its object.

III. Two Appendices with a Concluding Word (xlvii.. 43–47).

1. *Application to Moab of a passage from Isaiah.*

XLVIII. 43, 44.

43 Terror[1] and ditch [pit] and trap[2] on thee,
    Thou inhabitant of Moab,[3] saith Jehovah.
44 He that fleeth[4] from the terror shall fall into the ditch,
    And he that riseth from the ditch shall be taken in the trap;
    For I bring upon them, upon Moab,[5]
    The year of their punishment, saith Jehovah.

TEXTUAL AND GRAMMATICAL.

[1] Ver. 43.—פַּחַד fear, terror, is found besides in Jeremiah only in xxx. 5 and xlix. 5.

[2] Ver. 43.—פַּחַת pit, only in ver. 28. פַּח snare, only in the plural, xviii. 22. [The rendering ditch for pit and trap for snare is given to express the alliteration of the original pa'hadh, pa'hath, pa'h.—S. R. A.]

[3] Ver. 43.—יֹשֵׁב מוֹאָב. This expression is entirely contrary to the usage of Jeremiah, as he never uses the singular in this connection. Isaiah however uses the singular in a similar connection.

[4] Ver. 44.—The Chethibh הַנָּס (comp. FUERST, *Concord*, N. 691, 1365) is a form which does not occur elsewhere, so the Keri would read הַנָּס after Isaiah. An echo of this passage is found in Lam. iii. 47.

6 Ver. 44.—אֱלִיה אֶל־כּוֹאָב. Comp. ix. 14; xi. 15; xxvii. 8, etc. NAEGELSB. Gr., § 77, 2. ["אֱלִיה is anticipative of אֶל־מוֹאָב as the pronominal suffixes frequently are in the Aramaic dialects." HENDERSON.—S. R. A.

EXEGETICAL AND CRITICAL.

Application of a passage from Isaiah (xxiv. 17, 18). That Jeremiah is the original here, and at most took the remote analogy of Am. v. 19 for his model, appears to me an entirely unwarranted assertion. This pithy drastic play upon words corresponds as much more to the Old Testament master of such word-play, Isaiah, as it is contrary to the softer and more fluent style of our prophet. In addition it is inconceivable that at the close of his discourse, where he has evidently already exhausted himself and has for some time been speaking only in quotations, he should suddenly make such a pithy original utterance. Comp. DELITZSCH in DRECHSLER'S *Comm. zu Jes.* III., S. 405, 6, and in his own *Comm. on Isaiah,* S. 271 [Eng. Tr., pp. 431, 2].

---

2. *The Testimony of the Book of Numbers concerning Moab, and concluding word.*

XLVIII. 45–47.

45   In the shade of Heshbon the fugitives stand powerless;[1]
   For fire[2] goes forth from Heshbon,
   And flame from the midst of Sihon,
   And it devoured the side of Moab
   And the crown (of the head) of the sons of tumult.[3]
46 Woe unto thee, Moab!
   Destroyed is the people of Chemosh,
   For thy sons are led away into prison,
   And thy daughters into captivity.[4]
47 And I turn the captivity of Moab at the end of days, saith Jehovah.
   —Thus far the judgment on Moab.

TEXTUAL AND GRAMMATICAL.

[1] Ver. 45.—On the privative מִן in מִכֹּחַ comp. NAEGELSB. Gr., § 112, 5, d; Jer. x. 14.

[2] Ver. 45.—אֵשׁ is used in Numbers as feminine, as it usually is, but here as masculine, as in Ps. civ. 4. (In Job xx. 26 פֻּחָה regarded as neuter is in apposition. Comp. NAEGELSB. Gr., § 60, 4 coll. Jer. xx. 9).

[3] Ver. 45.—קָרְקַר, Numb. xxiv. 17, not being appropriate to the present passages (it signifies *suffodit, radicitus evertit* from קוּר *fodit*) we cannot say that קָדְקֹד is the original reading, although it seems to suit the passage in Numbers better, and is really the reading of Cod. Samarit. Jeremiah, dealing very freely after his manner with the text of his sources, may have substituted a word of similar form. שְׁאוֹן is of like meaning with שֵׁת, as the latter stands for מְאֵת, Lam. iii. 47 (as שֵׁת Job xli. 16 for שְׂאֵת, שְׂאֵת xiii. 11) and this for שְׁאֵת. Comp. OLSH., § 153.

[4] Ver. 46.—The form שְׁבִיָה is found in Jeremiah here only. Since he uses שִׁבְיָה (שְׁבוּה) only in the connection of שְׁבִי שָׁבָה he was obliged, in order to have a corresponding word to שָׁב, to choose either שְׁבִיה or שְׁבִיָה, which latter occurs more rarely than the former, since it is found only in Isa. lii. 2.

EXEGETICAL AND CRITICAL.

With the exception of ver. 45 a, the verses are a free reproduction of Num. xxi. 28, 29; xxiv. 17. The prophet who already in the previous context has brought into use old prophecies against Moab, does the same here with some passages of the book of Numbers. It is only natural that Jeremiah should not leave unemployed those ancient utterances occasioned by the first conflict between Israel and Moab. This use is evidently the main intention, and no emphasis is therefore to be laid on the less strict connection of the words with the previous context, and with each other. GRAF has, therefore, rightly rejected the hypothesis of MOVERS and HITZIG, that these verses are a later gloss.

Vers. 45, 46. **In the shade . . . captivity.** As the passage to be used speaks of a going forth of the fire from Heshbon upon the Moabites (Num. xxi. 28), the Moabites must be represented as having come into the district of Heshbon. This is done by assuming a flight of the Moabites in that direction (doubtless also with a reference to "he that fleeth," ver. 44). It has indeed been correctly remarked that as the enemy is approaching from the north, the flight could not be

CHAP. XLVIII. 45–47.

towards Heshbon (comp. rems. on ver. 19 sqq.), but all that concerns the prophet is to show that the ancient sentence will be verified anew in this judgment on Moab. It is assuredly not his meaning that this will take place literally in the form chosen by him (for which Isa. xxx. 2, 3, also was, perhaps, in his mind). Ver. 45 *a* is thus a mere connecting clause, of which the expressions are not to be emphasized.—**Powerless** declares that the fugitives, who for protection had betaken themselves to the shade of Heshbon, receive from thence no strength but the contrary. The following בְּ which is also taken from Num. xxi. 28, need not then be taken in an adversative sense (but).—**From the midst of Sihon.** In Num. xxi. 28 it reads, "from the city of Sihon." Heshbon is called in xxi 26 the city of Sihon the king of the Amorites. Owing to the omission of city here, I would neither alter the text with J. D. MICHAELIS, EWALD and MEIER (מִבֵּן for מִבֵּין) so as to read, from the *house* of Sihon, nor with GRAF, conceive an ideal presence of Sihon (with reference to Gen. xlix. 10), but as in ver. 4, and more frequently according to GRAF, Moab stands for Ar-Moab, and elsewhere usually Shechem for city of Shechem (Gen. xxxiii. 18), so here also the name of Lord of the city stands for the city itself. The sense of **from the midst,** is that fire breaks forth from between the openings of the city (*i. e.*, the gates of the walls and towers).—**The side of Moab.** Num. xxiv. 17, "and a sceptre shall rise out of Israel, and shall smite the borders of Moab." As here the subject is a staff which smites, the borders can mean only the sides of the body. Accordingly in this passage also it is more natural to think of the *side* (MEIER) as burnt or roasted by the fire, than the end of the beard [HENDERSON: corner of the beard], which would inflict no material injury.—**And the crown,** *etc.* Num. xxiv. 17, "and destroy all the children of Sheth." Sheth has also the meaning of tumult. The children of tumult are *homines tumultuosi.* The designation corresponds on the one hand to the arrogant character of the Moabites mentioned in vers. 26-30, and on the other hand there seems to be an allusion to Am. ii. 2, where it reads "and Moab shall die with tumult."—**Woe unto thee,** *etc.*, from Num. xxi. 29. Moab is called the people of Chemosh (comp. ver. 7) as Israel the people of Jehovah (Num. xi. 29; xvii. 6; Jud. v. 11).—**For thy sons,** *etc.*, Num. xxi. 29: he gives his sons up as fugitives, and his daughters into captivity. It is apparent that the original is softened down. Comp. Gen. xii. 15.

Ver. 47. **And I turn ... on Moab.**—Close of the chapter. Comp. xlvi. 26; xlix. 6, 89.—**I turn.** Comp. xxx. 3, 18; xxxiii. 7, 11.—**At the end of days.** Comp. rems. on xxiii. 20. The expression points to that final period in which the heathen also will be converted to the God of Israel. Comp. iii. 17; Isa. xxiv. 13-16; xxv. 6; Hagg. ii. 7.—**Thus far the judgment.** Comp. ver. 21; li. 64. With the exception of the latter passage (on which comp. the exeg. rem.s.) this formula is not found in Jeremiah. It appears to be a later addition.

DOCTRINAL AND ETHICAL.

1. "Because the destruction of the Moabites is of no service to us except for penitence, we must note well what particular sins are specified, of which they were guilty, and for which such heavy punishments were heaped upon them, *viz.*: 1. *Disdain,* in that they gave no one a good word, were unfriendly and only blustered and boasted with every one, Ps. lii. 3 (1). 2. *Confidence* in their fortifications, in their power, money and riches, 2 Chron. xxxii. 8; Isa. xl. 6. 3. *Security,* all being prosperous and peaceful, which was the sin of their sister Sodom, Ezek. xvi. 49; Zeph. ii. 9. 4. *Talking great things,* and thrasonic self-praise. But although Goliath was such a mighty fellow he had yet to bite the grass, 1 Sam. xvii. 50. 5. *Pride* and *Arrogance.* These never do well, but act with violence and injustice. By violence, injustice and avarice, however, a kingdom passes from one people to another, *Sir.* 10, 8." CRAMER.

2. On ver. 10. "*His verbis duo peccata severissime prohibentur* 1. *negligentia in operibus vocationis, cui oppositum cap.* 39 *Sir.;* 2. *misericordia intempestiva* (2 Tim. iv. 2)." FÖRSTER.

3. On ver. 10. *Est ex ore Dei maledictus et impius est hic Qui Domini curat corde dolosus opus.* (MS. marginal note in my copy of the CRAMER *Bible*).

4. On ver. 10. God glorifies Himself in such judgments over the malignant and proud powers of the world. He who knows Him is also made strong, as to see the world perish and yet be able to sing praises to God thereon." DIEDRICH.

5. On ver. 11. "Moab retained its old character; being far from the traffic of the great world it was well pleased to keep to itself. Yet things cannot continue thus in this world forever, every family and every nation is at some time rudely terrified from its rest, for what is peculiar, natural or national is not in itself the good. This comes here only through conflict and tribulation, and by God's word among men. One's own way is full of idolatry, and all idols will in like manner come to shame: the golden calf of the Israelites certainly first, but afterwards Kamosh." DIEDRICH.

6. On ver. 11. "*Hic notetur, quod hac allegoria Jeremiæ nefarie et fanatice abusus circa annum Christi* 1564 *quidam Martinus Steinbuch, rector vinarius sive doliarius Selecrstadiensis, qui se esse dictitavit spiritum sanctum incarnatum uti Christus filius incarnatus est, hæreseos suæ fundamentum statuens hoc præsens Jeremiæ dictum. Cumque sibi asseclas fecisset circiter viginti ex plebe, obiit et se post mortem appariturum splendore luminis affirmavit. Vide Theatr. Zwingeri Vol.V., L.* 4, *F.* 1328." FÖRSTER.

7. On vers. 26, 27. Proud men rejoice with malicious pleasure when they can treat one, whom they do not like, as a caught thief. But it may happen to them that notwithstanding their age, rank and high dignity, they may yet fall in a truly beastly manner into that which they have themselves vomited, and thus become a laughing stock to the street gamins.

8. On ver. 39. "It also comes about that the natural man hangs his head, and at this time believers commonly look up and raise their heads, because their redemption draweth nigh." ZINZENDORF.

HOMILETICAL AND PRACTICAL.

1. "How many are still like the Moabites?

For how many are there of those who depend on their power and violence, their fortified cities and buildings, riches, money and property, and set all their hope and confidence thereupon! How many are there of those who, when they have been some time at peace, become secure and think there is no more trouble from the rising to the setting of the sun! How many of those who rely on their own strength and say, let the enemy come, they are a match for him! How many who, when they surpass others in bodily and mental gifts or in perishable goods, become proud and despise, ridicule and treat badly their inferiors, as if they had found such among thieves, as God the Lord here says! Not to mention that even the dear God is not exempted. For although all good and perfect gifts come only from above, from the Father of light (Jas. i. 17), yet many will not acknowledge this, but ascribe them to their own wisdom and skill, do not thank God for them, and thus make themselves and the outward means, by which they obtain one and another thing, the idol which they serve." *Bibl. Summarien,* Halle, 1848.

2. On ver. 10. *Remissness in the work of the Lord.* 1. Wherein it consists (in not doing or doing ill that which is commanded. Comp. Saul in 1 Sam. xv., and doing that which is forbidden). 2. Its causes (**Selfishness, Pride, Unbelief, Cowardice,** Indolence, worldly interests). 3. Its punishment (to be cursed).

[JEREMY TAYLOR: 1. He that serves God with the body, without the soul, serves God deceitfully. 2. He that serves God with the soul, without the body, when both can be conjoined, doth the work of the Lord deceitfully. 3. They are deceitful in the Lord's work that reserve one faculty for sin, or one sin for themselves, or one action to please their appetite and many for religion. 4. And they who think God sufficiently served with abstaining from evil, and converse not in the acquisition and pursuit of holy charity and religion.—S. R. A.]

3. On ver. 42. *The world's boldness towards God.* 1. Whereon it is supported (on the one hand on the *real* [material] powers apparently standing at its behest alone; on the other hand, on the apparent powerlessness of God's servants, who have only truth and right on their side). 2. What its end will be (Destruction, or termination of national existence). [COWLES: "If all the historians who record the ultimate extinction of nations were inspired of God to give the true reasons of their fall, we should often meet this testimony, 'Perished of national pride, producing contempt of God and of fundamental morality.'" —S. R. A.]

---

6. Prophecy against the Ammonites.

XLIX. 1-6.

The Ammonites also, the brother nation of the Moabites, (Gen. xix. 37) *after centuries of various conflict* (comp. Jud. iii. 13; x. 7 sqq.; xi. 32: 1 Sam. xi.; 2 Sam. x., xi., xii. 26; 2 Chron. xx.; xxvi. 8; xxvii. 5) *in consequence of the deportation of the East-Jordanic tribes have appropriated a part of their territory. This fact forms the point of departure for the present prophecy. Older prophecies against Ammon are extant only by Amos* (i. 13-15) *and Zephaniah* (*in consequence of a declaration against Moab,* (ii. 9, 10). *Of these Jeremiah has made considerable use of the prophecy of Amos. Comp. the exposition. There is at most an echo of the brief utterance of Zephaniah in the expression* **desoiation**, ver. 2. coll. Zeph. ii. 9. *Since Nebuchadnezzar and the Chaldeans are not named, the prophecy must be older than the battle of Carchemish, and since the beginning agrees in form with the beginning of the first prophecy against Egypt* (xlvi. 2), *and the prophecies against Moab* (xlviii. 1), *Edom* (xlix. 7) *and Damascus* (xlix. 23), *the supposition is natural that the date of its origin is the same as that of these prophecies.*

1 AGAINST THE CHILDREN OF AMMON.
Thus saith Jehovah: Has then Israel no children, or has he no heir?
Why then does Malcom inherit Gad and his people dwell in his cities?
2 Therefore behold, the days come, saith Jehovah,
That I cause the war-shout to be heard against Rabbah of the children of Ammon;
And she shall become a desolated heap,
And her daughter shall be burned with fire :
And Israel shall be heir to his heirs, saith Jehovah.
3 Howl Heshbon, for devastated is Ai!
Cry, ye daughters of Rabbah, gird on sackcloth;
Lament and run to and fro' on the walls;
For Malcom must go into captivity,
His priests and his princes together.

4 Why boastest² thou of the valleys?
Thy valley is flowing away,³ thou rebellious daughter,
Who trusted in her treasures;—" Who will come to me?"
5 Behold, I bring fear upon thee, saith the Lord, Jehovah Zebaoth,
From all thy neighbors;
And ye shall be driven away, each one before him;
And there shall be no gatherer of the fugitives.
6 But nevertheless I will turn the captivity of the children of Ammon,
Saith Jehovah.

TEXTUAL AND GRAMMATICAL.

¹ Ver. 3.—התשוטט. On the form comp. OLSH., § 67, Anm., 272, a.

² Ver. 4.—התהלל invariably denotes to boast, to brag. The object of the boasting is most frequently connected by
בְּ. Comp. iv. 2; ix. 22, 23; Ps. xlix. 7, etc.

³ Ver. 4.—זָב עִמְקֵךְ. The explanation of EWALD and GRAF, " of the luxuriance, the superfluity of thy valley " would
suit the connection, but the abstract rendering of זָב is an objection, since this form (קֹם) elsewhere is used almost wholly
in the formation of participles, very rarely of substantives of concrete meaning, as עָב people, עֵר city. זָב occurs (in the
masc. form) only of a man with emission of seed (Lev. xv. 4), in the fem. of a woman with emission of blood (Lev. xv. 19),
and of Canaan as a land flowing with milk and honey (Exod. iii. 8, 17; Lev. xx. 24; Num. xiii. 27, etc.) Hence the explanation: thy valley flows away, passes away, or redundat sanguine confessorum, does not correspond to the use of the word
elsewhere. I would, therefore, explain with SCHLEUSSNER: quid gloriaris vallibus tuis? (quod scilicet) fœcunda sit vallis
tua? Thus one idea is expressed independently of the preposition.

EXEGETICAL AND CRITICAL.

Four parts may be plainly distinguished. In the first (vers. 1, 2) the prophet alludes to the fact, from the theocratic point of view regarded as improper, that the Ammonites had taken possession of the Gadite territory (ver. 1), and declares that this cannot remain so. Ammon must be involved in war, the capital with the neighboring cities destroyed, and Israel again put into possession of his country (ver. 2). In the second part (ver. 3) a brief specification follows, in the third (vers. 4, 5) a reason for the punitive judgment, with express indication, that the recompense would correspond exactly to the inculpation. In the fourth part (ver. 6) the prophet concludes with a consolatory outlook into the future.

Vers. 1, 2. Against ... saith Jehovah.—
The prophet here presupposes the possession of the Gadite territory by the Ammonites in consequence of the deportation of the East-Jordanic tribes by Tiglath-Pileser (2 Ki. xv. 29; 1 Chron. v. 6, 26. Comp. Introd. to ch. xlviii.). Amos refers to former attempts by the Ammonites for the same object (i. 13).—Malcom. Jeremiah has Am. i. 15 in view. In this passage Malcom appears to me to be used in a double sense. Why should the king be mentioned only with the people of the Ammonites? Why does Amos say of Damascus (ver. 5) and Philistia (ver. 8), "him that holdeth the sceptre," and of Moab (ii. 3) "the judge?" Did he not wish it to be understood that the expression used only of Ammon, wes to be taken here in a special sense? I believe, then, that Malcom (Am. i. 16) refers primarily to the King, but in such wise that an allusion to the God is also intended. This allusion was all the plainer, if the Ammonites really, as MOVERS supposes (Phœnic., 1., S. 323. Comp. HERZOG, Real-Enc., IX., S. 714), called the god מַלְכָּם, i. e., our king. With reference to this he

might fitly, when the Ammonites were spoken of, be called מַלְכָּם by the Israelites. It is, therefore, unnecessary here, and in ver. 3 to read מִלְכֹּם, as EWALD, GRAF and MEIER would do, after the example of the LXX. and Syr. Since we cannot express the specific meaning of the word by the translation, we have retained Malcom as if it were a proper name.—The war-shout, etc., is a reminiscence from Am. i. 14.—Rabbah Beni Ammon. This was the complete name of the city (comp. Deut. iii. 11; 2 Sam. xi. 1; xii. 26 sqq). It was called Rabbah, the great, the capital, in contrast to the neighboring cities. Comp. HERZ., R.-Enc. XII., S. 469.—A desolate heap, literally hill of desolation, therefore, heap of ruins. Comp. Josh. viii. 28 and Zeph. ii. 9.—Burned with fire. This also reminds us of Am. i. 14 (comp. OLSH., § 242 b).

Ver. 3. Howl Heshbon ... princes together. The immediate consequences of the war-shout being heard are specified. Heshbon is to howl. It was then an Ammonitish city. Comp. rems. on xlviii. 2, 45. It is given as a reason that Ai is destroyed. What city this was is not to be ascertained. VENEMA'S and EWALD'S explanation (Rabba ita vastata est, ut jam sit tumulus ruderum) is forced. GRAF would read עִי with reference to Rabbah. But Rabbah could be called עִי only in the appellative sense, and then it must have the article. To suppose that Ai is transferred hither from Josh. viii. 28, because there alone the expression "heap of desolation" occurs, is to attribute to the prophet either ignorance or carelessness. Many commentators therefore (J. D. MICHAELIS, HITZIG, comp. V. RAUMER, S. 168, Anm. 150) are disposed to assume an East-Jordanic Ai, which expedient seems to me thus far the best.—There is no reason for taking daughters of Rabbah in a different sense here from ver. 2.—Sackcloth. Comp. rems. on xlviii. 37.—On the walls. I do not see why these should be regarded as the walls of a sheep-fold, as many would do. What is more natural in a city, against which the enemy is advancing, than to run up and down on the walls to take measures for defence? That the city walls may be meant is evident from Ps. lxxxix. 41; Ezek. xlii. 12.—**For Malcom**, etc. These words are taken from Am. i. 15. Only in the present passage we have **his priests for "he,"** which is evidently not from misunderstanding, but to emphasize more plainly the intended meaning of Malcom. Comp. rems. on xlviii. 7.

Vers. 4, 5. **Why boastest thou .... fugitives.** Reason of the primitive judgment. The pride, the stubbornness, the security of Ammon must be correspondingly punished. Comp. xlviii. 26, 30.—**Rebellious daughter.** Comp.

xxxi. 22.—**Who will come to me?** The Ammonites' boast, Who will come to us? The Lord tells them, the enemies will come *upon* them, and that from all sides, yea, even behind them, so that the Ammonites will be driven straight before them, and because the enemies come from all sides will be so scattered that no one will be in a condition to collect the fugitives again.—Fear. Comp. xlviii. 43, 44.—**Each one before him.** Comp. ''every man straight before him,'' Josh. vi. 5, 20; v. 13.—**Gatherer.** Comp. Isa. xiii. 14; lvi. 8; Nah. iii. 18.

Ver. 6. **But nevertheless .... Jehovah.** Ammon also is to share in the salvation of the future, which is to issue from Israel unto all nations. Comp. rems. on xlviii. 47 and xlix. 39.

---

7. Prophecy against Edom (xlix. 7-22).

On account of their relationship to the Israelites, the Edomites, in consequence of an express divine command, were not treated as enemies on the journey to Canaan (Deut. ii. 4; xxiii. 7). *Saul, however, conquered them* (1 Sam. xiv. 47). *David subjected them entirely* (2 Sam. viii. 14). *In this state of dependence they remained after Hadad's attempt at revolution had failed* (1 Ki. xi. 14-22) *till the reign of Joram, when they revolted* (2 Ki. viii. 20-22; 2 Chron. xxi. 8). *Amaziah and Uzziah indeed made by no means unsuccessful attempts to bring them again into subjection* (2 Ki. xiv. 7, 22), *but their success was not lasting. In the reign of Ahaz the Edomites again invaded Judea* (2 Chron. xxviii. 17), *and in the time of the Chaldeans we also find their ambassadors among those who came to Zedekiah to consult concerning means to be taken in common* (Jer. xxvii. 3); *but at the destruction of Jerusalem they are on the side of the Chaldeans, greeting the destruction of the long hostile city* (comp. אֵיבַת עוֹלָם, Ezek. xxxv. 5) *with scornful triumph* (Lam. iv. 21; Ezek. xxxv. 15; xxxvi. 5; Ps. cxxxvii. 7).

As regards the date of our prophecy, the construction of the superscription (לֶאֱדוֹם), *as well as the non-mention of the Chaldeans, point to the same date at which the other portions with similar superscription, at the head of which is the first against Egypt* (xlvi. 1-12), *originated, i. e., the time immediately before the battle of Carchemish. Comp. rems. on* xlvi. 1, 2, *and Introd. to the Prophecies against the Nations.*

Of special importance for our prophecy is its relation to the prophecy of Obadiah directed against Edom. They correspond to each other as follows:

Jer. xlix. 7 and Obad. 8.
  "   "   9   "   "   5.
  "   "   10   "   "   6, 7.
  "   "   14   "   "   1.
  "   "   15   "   "   2.
  "   "   16   "   "   3, 4.

That Jeremiah drew from Obadiah, and not vice versâ, has been shown by CASPARI (*Der Proph. Obadja ausgel.* Leipzig, 1842) *in such an exhaustive manner that there can be no further question on this point. The quotations then from Obadiah extend only to ver. 8 of his prophecy. On the other hand, the following context* (Obad. 9 sqq.) *has frequent points of contact with Joel, which is not the case in the previous context, and it is just in these verses that the indubitable references to the capture of Jerusalem by the Chaldeans are found* (comp. Obad. 10, 16). *Hence recently either the old theory has been retained* (*held by* AUGUSTI, KRAHMER, EWALD, MEIER *in* ZELLER'S *Jahrb.* I. 3, *S.* 526) *of the use of an older source in common on the part of Jeremiah and Obadiah* (comp. MEIER, *die proph. BB. d. A. T. übersetzt u. erk.*, *S.* 368 [*The proph. Books of the O. T. transl. and explained*]), *or it is supposed that Obad.* 9-21 *was a later addition, composed after the Chaldean catastrophe. This it not the place to enter into this difficult investigation specially or with the precision which it requires. I content myself therefore with putting two questions:* 1. *Is it then so decidedly demonstrated that Obadiah quotes Joel and not Joel Obadiah?* 2. *How is it, that in vers.* 12-14 *Edom is only warned against committing hostilities against Judah* "*in the day of their calamity?*" *Such hostilities had certainly been already committed* (vers. 10, 11, 15, 16). *But is it not clear from the turn which the*

discourse takes (with וְאַל*) in ver.* 12 *that the prophet distinguishes two points of time, a past and a future? Once already have the Edomites greeted the calamity of Jerusalem with malicious joy. When now they are warned against doing this again, is it not presupposed that Jerusalem is still by no means wholly destroyed, but that the really great day of calamity is still impending (observe the* בְּיוֹם וִי *repeated eight times in vers.* 12-14)? *Would it not accordingly be exegetically more exact to suppose that the prophet, finding occasion in the hostility displayed by the Edomites in a transient occupation of Jerusalem, warns them from a repetition on the great day of Jerusalem, which he foresees as inevitable, and on the presupposition that this warning will not avail, threatened them with a just recompense?*
Of the other older prophecies against Edom (Isa. xxxiv. 5-17; Am. i. 11, 12; Joel iv. 19) *Jeremiah has made no use.*
The whole prophecy is plainly to be discriminated into three parts. The first (vers. 7-13) *has for its topic the judgment to be executed on Edom according to the elements of its outward appearance* (vers. 7-10) *and its objective inward ground, which is the decree of Jehovah. The second part* (vers. 14-18) *is predominantly occupied with the statement of the* subjective *ground of the visitation, i. e., with the guilt of Edom. The third part* (vers. 19-22) *brings before us the subject of the destination, that is, the instrument thereof, chosen by Jehovah.*

1. *The judgment on Edom in its external appearance and objective reason.*

XLIX. 7-13.

7 AGAINST EDOM. Thus saith Jehovah Zebaoth:
   Is there no longer wisdom in Teman?
   Hath counsel vanished from the intelligent?[1]
   Is their wisdom expended?[2]
8 Flee, turn, bow low,[3] ye inhabitants of Dedan!
   For the destruction of Esau I bring upon him,
   The time, when I visit him.
9 If vintagers come to thee they will leave no gleanings,
   If thieves by night they destroy their fill.
10 For I have stript Esau bare, discovered his hiding places,
   And he cannot hide himself.[4]
   His seed is destroyed and his brethren and his neighbors,
   And he is no more.
11 Leave[5] thy orphans, I will preserve their life,
   And let thy widows confide[6] in me.
12 For thus saith Jehovah, Behold,
   They, whose rule it was not to drink the cup, must drink it,
   And art thou[7] to remain unpunished?
   No, but thou shalt drink.
13 For I have sworn by myself, saith Jehovah,
   That Bozrah shall become a desolation,
   A reproach, a desert[8] and a curse;
   And all her cities shall become desolate for ever.

TEXTUAL AND GRAMMATICAL.

[1] Ver. 7.—מִבָּנִים Part. Kal from בִּין instead of the more usual Part. Niph. נְבֹנִים (Gen. xli. 33, 39, *etc.*). The form does not occur elsewhere.

[2] Ver. 7.—סָרַח is to overflow, overhang. So **Exod.** xxvi. 12 of the overhanging curtain; Ezek. xvii. 6, גֶּפֶן סֹרַחַת, *vitis patula, late effusa*. Part. Pual סָרוּחַ, poured out, stretched out on the couch, Am. vi. 4, 7. סְרוּחֵי טְבוּלִים, Ezek. xxiii. 15, *redundantes mitris d. i. gestantes mitras longe dependentes*. Hence Niph. (which occurs here only), *profusum, effusum esse*, נִסְרַח from בָּקַק, Isa. xix. 3 coll. Jer. xix. 7.

[3] Ver. 8.—As נֻסוּ can only be Imperative, הֶעְמִיקוּ and הָפְנוּ must also be taken as such. The former (on the construction with the Inf. comp. NAEGELSB. *Gr.*, § 95, *e*) is also used in ver. 30 as an Imperative. Other instances, וְהַחֲשׁוּ, 2 Ki. ii. 3, 5; וְהָאתִי, Jer. xii. 19; comp. OLSH., § 256, *a, b*. הָפְנוּ is likewise a rare form, but not impossible or without analogy. Comp. הַשְׁבְּבָה, Ezek. xxxii. 19; הַשְׁפִּי, Job xxi. 5; OLSH., § 260, coll. *S.* 631.

[4] Ver. 10.—וְנֶחְבָּה לֹא for לְהֵיאָ, comp. OLSH., § 263, *b*. The perfect would have to be translated: and does he hide himself, he cannot, which is forced. We should expect at least וְלֹא. EWALD and GRAF would punctuate נֶחְבָּה, comp.

forms like נִקְרָא, גִּדְכָה, נָהֲתוֹם (OLSH., § 266, c), and as regards the construction, ver. 23. This expedient removes at least the great grammatical difficulties which נֶחְפָּה affords.

[5] Ver. 11.—On the Imperative form comp. OLSHAUSEN, § 234, a.
[6] Ver. 11.—הֲכִבוּ. Comp. Ezek. xxxvii. 7. Except in connection with suffixes, we find only this and הָיְא as examples of the abnormal affirmative. Comp. OLSH., S. 452, 3.
[7] Ver. 12.—אֹתָה הוּא. Thou, such an one! xiv. 22; Ps. xliv. 5, comp. NAEGELSB. Gr., § 79, 3.
[8] Ver. 13.—Instead of חֹרֶב we find חָרְבָּה in the parallel passages.

EXEGETICAL AND CRITICAL.

The destruction of Edom is described, 1. as it appears outwardly, 2. according to its inner reason in the divine decree. First the irresistible nature of the attack is set forth, in opposition to which all the renowned wisdom of Edom will be unavailing (ver. 7). The Dedanites, the neighbors and commercial allies of Edom, are warned to consult their own safety (ver. 8). The enemies will come, and, like vintagers or thieves, make a clean sweep (ver. 9). It will turn out that Edom's material means of defence, his rock fortresses regarded as impregnable, together with his own and his allied offensive forces, cannot avert destruction (ver. 10). This must be so, because it is the will of Jehovah. This is seen in Jehovah's taking charge, as it were, of the widows and children of the Edomites, which presupposes the death of their guardians (ver. 11). Jehovah must permit their death, as without being unjust, He cannot spare Edom the cup which Israel had to drink. Edom must therefore drain it irrevocably (ver. 12) for Jehovah (in accordance with the imperative demands of His justice) has sworn, that Edom will be a prey to everlasting desolation (ver. 13). Thus the strophe concludes, and from the similarity of this conclusion with ver. 18 it is seen, that in both cases we have a larger section of the discourse.

Ver. 7. **Against Edom . . . expended.** Wisdom and intelligence are necessary in carrying on war (Prov. xxiv. 6) and where these fail, all is lost. This lack is observable in Edom. This is the more striking since the wisdom of Edom and especially of Teman was celebrated from of old. Comp. Ob. 8; Job ii. 11 (Teman was the home of Eliphaz); Baruch iii. 22, 23. On Teman comp. HERZ., R.-Enc., III., S. 650. [COWLES on this verse.—S. R. A.]

Ver. 8. **Flee . . visit him.** On Dedan comp. rems. on xxv. 23. They were not Edomites but neighbors (Ezek. xxv. 13), and at all events connected with them by mercantile intercourse (comp. Isa. xxi. 13). Hence they are also threatened by the tempest which is breaking over Edom. They are therefore admonished to look to their own safety.—**For,** etc. Comp. ver. 32; xlvi. 21; vi. 15.

Vers. 9, 10. **If vintagers . . . no more.** Ver. 9 is taken from Obad. 5. The sense is clear. It could not be so if we should render the sentence interrogatively, as many do, in too servile adherence to the passage in Obadiah. Ver. 10 re-

minds us of Obad. 6, though there we read "searched out" and "sought up" for **stript bare and discovered.** These terms applied to Esau refer to the uncommonly strong fortress-dwellings, occupied by the Edomites. Comp. rems. on ver. 16.—**His seed is destroyed,** etc. "Both the real Edomites and the descendants of related and other nations, which were mingled with them, as the Amalekites, Gen. xxxvi. 12; Horites, Gen. xxxvi. 20; Simeonites, 1 Chron. iv. 42 and neighboring tribes, as Dedan, ver. 8. Tema and Buz, Jer. xxv. 23 " are to be destroyed says GRAF. He also justly remarks that the expression **his brethren and his neighbors** appears to have been occasioned by "men of thy confederacy" and "men of thy peace" in Obad. 7.—**And he is no more.** Comp. Isa. xix. 7.

Vers. 11-13. **Leave thy orphans . . . desolate forever.** HITZIG sees in ver. 11 a preliminary conclusion parallel to ver. 6 and xlviii. 47. But ver. 11 is no conclusion, being followed by two sentences with **for,** vers. 12, 13, of such a purport that no inference favorable to Edom can possibly be drawn from them. I therefore take ver. 11 with THEODORET, NEUMANN and others, as irony. The Edomites are called upon, the men, namely, to leave their widows and orphans. Observe that it is not said, wives and children. The death of the men is presupposed. When Jehovah immediately adds that He will care for the survivors, this is a poor consolation for the Edomites who do not believe in Jehovah. For what other care but such as slaves receive, can be expected from Him, who announces as his unalterable determination so total a destruction of Edom, as in vers. 13, 17, 18, 20, 21?—**I will preserve,** etc. Comp. Exod. i. 17, 18; 2 Sam. xii. 3; 1 Ki. xviii. 5; Isa. vii. 21. We see from these passages that the meaning of the word is primarily negative: not kill, but secondarily positive: do what is necessary for the preservation of life.—**Whose rule it was not,** etc. It was an abnormal thing for Israel, the chosen people, to be obliged to drink the cup of wrath. I therefore take מִשְׁפָּט in the sense of norm, law, rule. Comp. xxx. 11; viii. 7.—**The cup.** Comp. xxv. 15 sqq.—**Unpunished.** Comp. xxv. 29.—**Have sworn,** etc. Comp. xxii. 5.—**A desolation.** Comp. xxv. 11, 18; xliv. 6, 22.—**Bozrah** (Isa. xxxiv. 6; lxiii. 1; Am. i. 11, 12) was one of the most important cities of Edom (comp. xlviii. 24) of which there are still remains under the name of Besseyrn, i. e., Little Bozrah. Comp. RAUMER, Pal., S. 278.—**Desolate for ever.** Comp. xxv. 9.

2. The Judgment on Edom according to its subjective reason.

XLIX. 14–18.

14 I have heard a report from Jehovah,
And a messenger is sent among the nations:
"Assemble yourselves and come up against her,
And rise ye for the war."
15 For behold, I make thee small among the nations;
Despised among men.
16 Thy object of horror[1] deceived thee,
The pride of thy heart,
Thou that dwellest in the clefts of the rock,
Thou that occupiest the height of the hill.
Even though, like an eagle, thou buildest thy nest high,
I will bring thee down from thence, saith Jehovah.
17 And Edom shall become a wilderness;
Every one that passeth by shall be horrified,
And jeer on account of all her strokes.
18 As in the overthrow of Sodom and Gomorrah,
And their neighboring cities, saith Jehovah,
No man will dwell there,
Nor a son of man sojourn in her.

TEXTUAL AND GRAMMATICAL.

[1] Ver. 16.—תִּפְלַצְתְּ does not occur elsewhere. It is usually taken in the sense of *terror* = פַּלָּצוּת (Jer. xxi. 4) and understood to mean the terror which Edom inspires. But because the following verb is in the masc. some have thought it necessary to separate תִּפְלַצְתְּךָ from it and regard it as an isolated exclamation (comp. הַפְּכְכֶם, Isa. xxix. 16), which SCHLEUSNER renders *O arrogantiam tuam*; HITZIG, "fear to thee;" GRAF, "horror at thee." But this exclamation appears somewhat exaggerated. Why should a people, who are deceived by pride, be especially inspired with fear? Is not this very common? Was the pride of Edom greater than that of Moab (xlviii. 29)? Or was it threatened with a worse fate? I find it more suitable to take תִּפְלַצְתְּ in the sense of מִפְלֶצֶת. The latter word in 1 Ki. xv. 13; 2 Chron. xv. 16 designates an idol, an idol-image. This is called a terror, an object of holy horror, as frequently פַּחַד, Gen. xxxi. 42; מוֹרָא, Isa. viii. 13; אֵימִים, Jer. l. 38 are used in an analogous sense. The LXX. may have the same idea, translating ἡ παιγνία σου, *i.e.*, *risus*, *jocus tuus*. According to SCHLEUSNER, they had Priapus in mind, for which also JEROME holds מִפְלֶצֶת in 1 Ki. xv. and 2 Ki. xv. Rabbis also, according to KIMCHI's testimony, have understood the word of עֲבוֹדָה זָרָה, *i.e.*, idolatry. Among the moderns, J. D. MICHAELIS and MEIER adopt this view. The gender of the verb is no hinderance, for the prophet could properly use the masc. when thinking of the person of the idol. Comp. NAEGELSB. *Gr.*, § 60, 4.

EXEGETICAL AND CRITICAL.

Jeremiah proclaims in the words of Obadiah, that nations will be summoned to make war upon Edom, to make her small and despised (vers. 14, 15). To such a procedure has Edom given occasion by her idolatrous abominations and her pride. This pride is now to be punished (ver. 16) and Edom is now to become a horrible waste and like Sodom and Gomorrah (vers. 17, 18). These verses are taken with modifications from Obadiah 1-4. The main thought is evidently expressed in ver. 16; the statement of the subjective cause of the punitive judgment, impending over Edom.

Vers. 14, 15. **I have heard .. among men.** Hemistich 1 is taken from Obad. 1 only with the alteration of "we have heard" (Israel) to "I have heard," and "arise ye" to "assemble yourselves." The report which the prophet bears directly from the Lord and the message (צִיר *viator, nuntius*, Prov. xiii. 17; xxv. 13; Isa. xviii. 2; lvii. 9) which is sent among the nations are of the same purport. We must regard the report however as expressing not only the command itself, but also that it has been issued. Hemist. 2 is extended in Jeremiah. It reads in Obadiah "Arise ye, and let us rise up against her in battle." Ver. 15, taken from Obad. 2, states the object of the war, for the attainment of which the nations are summoned. The words correspond to vers. 11-13, expressing the decree of Jehovah concerning Edom, the execution of which is the object of the war. "For" is wanting in Obadiah. In **small and despised** there is evidently an antithesis to Edom's pride (ver. 16). Hemist. 2 reads in Obadiah, "thou art greatly despised."

Ver. 16. **Thy object of horror... saith Jehovah.** We evidently have here the kernel of the strophe, that by which it is distinguished from the context, viz., the guilt of Edom is here stated, the *subjective* reason of her destruction. While Obadiah mentions as this reason only "the pride of thine heart" (ver. 3), Jeremiah mentions also the "being a terror," or, as I understand the word, the horror, *i. e.*, the idol. We may well conceive that wishing to extend the text of his source the prophet would insert a word which would state the ground of Edom's moral corruption. Whence does arise the moral pollution of the heathen world? According to Rom. i. from idolatry. Here also Jeremiah would say that it was really the idol which deceived Edom, pride being involved in idolatry.—**The pride of thy heart** is then in apposition to **horror.** It is in accordance with this that inaccessible rock-castles are designated as the ground of pride, for, were not all heathen idols local deities? Was not then the idol who had built these rocks and continually protected them the real lord on whom their proud confidence was founded? —**Clefts of the rocks,** *etc.* It appears to me beyond doubt that Jeremiah had here in view the peculiar character of the Edomite cities, especially the capital, which was called Sela (2 Ki. xiv. 7; Isa. xvi. 1). Comp. the remarks on Bozrah, ver. 13. The second hemistich is abbreviated from Obad. 4. Comp. Am. ix. 2.

[" The descriptive points in this verse are wonderfully accurate. Petra, the ancient capital of Edom, for ages the main thoroughfare of the great trade and travel between India and Mesopotamia on the East, and Egypt and North Africa on the South-West; the seat therefore of wealth and art, perhaps of wisdom also, and culture, held a position of great military strength. It was built in a vast ravine, partly on the broad area inclosed by lofty precipitous walls of rock, which by some of nature's mighty convulsions had been rent asunder, and partly in those very fronts of lofty rock, chiseled out with immense labor, so that the pillars of the temples and the apartments of its tombs and dwellings were wholly cut from the solid, eternal rock. Here—her nests built high in these crags like the eagle's—old Petra sat in her pride and her strength, cherishing the vain fancy that no power could ever bring her down. But the Almighty spake and it was done! —The site of ancient Petra, for ages unknown, has been brought to light during the present century. A number of travelers have visited and explored it. Laborde, Dr. Robinson and others, have given full and precise statements of its wonderful ruins, placing Petra in the front rank of those ancient witnesses who bear their silent but resistless testimony to the precision of the old prophetic descriptions, and to the marvellous correspondence in the most minute details between prophecy and history—the prophecy of twenty centuries ago and the history of to-day." COWLES.—S. R. A.]

Vers. 17, 18. **And Edom ... sojourn in her.** These verses do not contain any reminiscences from Obadiah, but they do from Jeremiah himself and from other writings.—**And Edom,** *etc.*, is formed after xxv. 11, 38. Comp. l. 13.—**Every one that passeth.** Comp. xix. 8.—**As in the overthrow,** *etc.* Comp. ver. 22. Comp. Isa. xiii. 19; Jer. l. 40. The expression **neighboring cities** points to Deut. xxix. 22, where Admah and Zeboim are mentioned with Sodom and Gomorrah. Comp. Hos. xi. 8.—**No man will dwell,** *etc.* Comp. ver. 33; l. 40; li. 43.

---

3. *The instrument chosen by Jehovah for the destruction of Edom.*

XLIX. 19–22.

19 Behold, as a lion he cometh up
 From the pride of Jordan to the evergreen pasturage,
 For in a twinkling I drive him (Edom) from thence.[1]
 And who is chosen?[2] Him will I set over him.
 For who is like me? And who will appoint me the time?
 And who is the shepherd that would stand before me?
20 Therefore hear the counsel of Jehovah which He hath counselled against Edom,
 And His thoughts, which he has thought concerning the inhabitants of Teman:
 Verily they will be dragged along, the feeble little sheep;
 Verily their pasturage will be astounded[3] at them.
21 At the sound of their fall[4] the earth trembles.
 Crying![5] The sound of it[6] is heard on the Red Sea.
22 Behold, as an eagle he ascends and flies,
 And extends his wings over Bozrah;
 And the heart of the heroes of Edom on that day
 Will be as the heart of a woman in anguish.

TEXTUAL AND GRAMMATICAL.

[1] Ver. 19.—The construction as in Zeph. iii. 7 coll. Prov. xii. 19. Comp. NAEGELSB. Gr., § 95 g, Anm.—מֵעָלֶיהָ is undoubtedly to be referred to נָוֶה, although this word is elsewhere used as a masc. (Isa. xxvii. 10; xxxiii. 20), since the idea of "country" lies at its basis. Comp. rems. on תִּפְלֶצֶת ver. 16.
[2] Ver. 19.—כִּי is used as e. g. in Exod. xxiv. 14. Comp. NAEGELSB. Gr., § 79, 6.—אֵלֶיהָ for עָלֶיהָ. Comp. remarks on x. 1.
[3] Ver. 20.—יַשִּׁים Hiphil (on the form comp. OLSH., S. 577, 8; Numb. xxi. 30) is to be taken as the direct causative: *stuporem efficere*, to produce astonishment and horror not in others, but in one's self, i. e., to be horrified. Comp. NAEGELSB. Gr., § 18, 3. ["אִם־לֹא *if not*, a strong mode of asseveration for the purpose of expressing the certainty of any event." HENDERSON—S. R. A.]
[4] Ver. 20.—נִפְלָם is infinitive. Comp. 2 Sam. i. 10; OLSHAUSEN, § 245 b.
[5] Ver. 21.—עֵצָקָה the main idea placed emphatically in advance, which is more accurately defined in the following context. Comp. EWALD, § 309, b.
[6] Ver. 21.—["For צֹעֲלָה which refers to צְעָקָה, we find the less appropriate reading קוֹלָם in eighty-four MSS.: it has been originally in fourteen more; it is in three by correction, and is in the text of twenty-one printed editions. The only version which supports it is the Targum." HENDERSON. Hitzig however approves of this reading as the more difficult, referring it to הָאָרֶץ, the land, i. e. the population thereof.—S. R. A.]

EXEGETICAL AND CRITICAL.

This strophe also describes the destruction of Edom, but in such wise that the instrument in the hand of the Lord is prominent, without being mentioned by name. As a lion from the reed thickets of the Jordan falls upon a flock, which is pasturing on the luxuriant, ever-green meadows of the Gor, so shall Edom be surprised in his rock-dwelling and be driven away in a twinkling. So shall a new shepherd, chosen *ad hoc* by the Lord Himself, be set over Edom, for the previous shepherds of Edom have no prerogative to maintain their position in spite of the Lord (ver. 19). The new Shepherd, however, will not pasture the flock in the old way peaceably, but will drag them away, so that their pasturage will be astounded at the disappearance of the flock (ver. 20). Thus the fall of Edom will be a violent one, so much so that the sound of it will be heard afar (ver. 20). Again, in conclusion, the one who is called to the destruction of Edom is compared with an eagle (after Deut. xxviii. 49), who will extend his wings over Bozrah, which is fortified indeed, but powerless against such an enemy, so that on that day even the heroes of Edom will be as faint-hearted as parturient women.

Ver. 19. **Behold as a lion . . . before me.** As in xlvi. 18 with Carmel, and in xlviii. 40 with an eagle, so here the instrument of the Lord is compared with a lion, one who lurks in the reedy margin of the Jordan (the pride of Jordan, "the luxuriant bushes and reeds growing on its banks, by which it is enclosed as by a green garland." KÖHLER on Zech. xi. 3 *coll.* Jer. xii. 5; RAUMER, *Pal. S.* 58; HERZOG, *R.-Enc.*, VII., S. 8) and from thence makes his inroads on the flocks pasturing on the luxuriant evergreen meadows of the Jordan valley. For the Gor, though in general arid and infertile, where brooks flow down from the mountains to the Jordan has oases, which under the influence of the tropical climate are exceedingly fertile. Comp. ARNOLD in HERZOG, *R.-Enc., S.* 10, etc. I am therefore of opinion that נְוֵה אֵיתָן does not directly signify the land of Edom, and thus is neither to be taken as " rock-dwelling" nor as " evergreen pasturage " with sole reference to the undisturbed possession of the land for centuries. I take it in the latter meaning, but I think that the expression is chosen because it admits of a double reference, to the oases of the Jordanic valley and to Edom itself, which may be thus designated both as the ancient residence of the Edomite nation, and with reference to the strength and indestructibility of its national defences (comp. Num. xxiv. 21; Mic. vi. 2). In referring the expression at the same time to Edom, a transition is formed from the comparison to the thing compared.—**For in a twinkling.** From the "For" we see that the prophet has in view the suddenness of the attack as a *tertium comparationis*. From the thickets of the Jordan lions could easily fall upon herds feeding near the bank (comp. HERZOG, *R-Enc*. XI. *S.* 29). In like manner shall Edom be suddenly assailed and driven away from his pasturage.—**And who is chosen?** We see from this expression that the prophet had no definite person in view. He does not yet know who the chosen one is, but only that there will be one. Whoever it is will really obtain the supremacy over Edom, appointed to him. (xv. 3; li. 27). The older commentators understood Nebuchadnezzar, or even (*interprete Luthero*, as Förster says) Alexander the Great.—**For who is like me?** Edom's princes of ancient and illustrious descent (Gen. xxxvi.) might well be caught in the delusion of inviolable security. Here they are told that they have a higher power above them, who can remove them, and set others more pleasing to him in their place.—Jehovah, namely, who has none like unto Him, (Comp. CASPARI, *Micha der Morast*, *S.* 14 sqq.; Exod. xv. 11), whom no one can bring to an account (Job ix 19), whom no earthly national shepherd (x. 21; xxv. 34; xxiii. 1) can defy. [" To 'appoint one the time' is the ancient phrase for a legal indictment and summons. Who shall prosecute me before the court for this proceeding, *i. e.*, set himself against me as an opponent, or an antagonist." COWLES—S. R. A.]

Vers. 20, 21. **Therefore hear . . . Red Sea.** As it is, therefore, undeniable that the Lord has power over all kingdoms of the nations, it is solemnly made known to all the world as the decree of the highest Majesty; the Edomites shal' suffer the same fate from Him, who shall attack them like a lion, as the lion brings upon the weaker animals, i. e., they shall be dragged away (xv. 3; xxii. 19)—carried into captivity. Thus will the land be desolated, as the prophet poetically expresses it in the words, the land will be horrified at the sudden stillness and desolation. There is a similar personification in Job vii. 10, (Ps. ciii. 16). From this it follows 1. that the entire representation of these two verses is based on a figure of a place of pasturage; 2. that by the *new* shepherd, a conqueror is understood who will desolate the land and carry the people into captivity; 3. that the sentence with **therefore**, occasioned by the emphatic causal sentence of three clauses, ver. 19, b, contains no more than an emphatically repeated inference (A, then B, therefore A), consequently the same thought in substance, which was already expressed in **I will drive him from thence**. On ver. 20a comp. ver. 30; xviii. 11; xxix. 11; Isa. xiv. 26, 27; xix. 12 —**Teman**, comp. ver. 7. The city lay according to Jerome, five, according to Eusebius, fifteen Roman miles from Petra, comp. RAUMER, *Pal. S.* 279.

The little sheep. Comp. xiv. 3; xlviii. 4. The "smallest of the flock" are the weakest, most helpless, who are least adapted for flight or resistance, and most for being dragged away.— [HENDERSON adheres to the A. V., making "the smallest of the flock" the nomi native.—S. R. A.] —**At the sound**, &c., immediate effect of the overthrow of the power of Edom. Comp. Ezek. xxvi. 15; xxxi. 16; Isa. xiii. 13; Jer. li. 29.—The whole passage, vers. 19-21, is repeated and applied to Babylon (l. 44-46).
Ver. 22. **Behold . . . in anguish.** That which is in ver. 19 declared by means of a figure taken from a lion, is here repeated in the form of a figure derived from an eagle. The first half of the verse is taken from xlviii. 40, the second from xlviii. 41. The reason of the assailer of Bozrah appearing here as an eagle may be that the "castellated rock" of this city is designated as accessible only to an eagle. Comp. RAUMER, *Pal.* S. 278; SCHUBERT, *Reise in das Morgenland, II.* S. 426.

8. Prophecy against Damascus.

XLIX. 23-27.

Out of a large number of small kingdoms (thirty-two are mentioned in 1 Ki. xxi. 1, 16) with which the Israelites after the period of the Judges had to endure many conflicts, (Jud. iii. 3; 1 Sam. xiv. 47: 2 Sam. viii. and x.), a large one was formed after David's death by Rezon, with Damascus for its capital (1 Ki. xi. 23, 24). With this great Syrian kingdom also the two kingdoms of Israel had to endure many and severe conflicts, (1 Ki. xv. 18 sqq.; xx. 1 sqq.; xxii. 1 sqq.; 2 Ki. v. 1 sqq.; vi. 8 sqq.; viii. 28, 29; x. 32, 33; xii. 17; xiii. 3; xiv. 25; xv. 37; xvi. 5, 6), till at last the Assyrians, solicited by Ahaz of Judah, (2 Ki. xvi. 7-10), fell upon Syria and brought the country permanently under their dominion (2 Ki. xvi. 9). We need not seek the fulfilment of Jeremiah's prophecy of the destruction of Damascus in a particular "conquest and devastation of the country by Nebuchadnezzar." (GRAF). For even if Nebuchadnezzar did seize Syria and Damascus and treat them with a certain degree of hostility (whether as an Assyrian province or as an Egyptian tributary) yet the prophet's perspective extends over the whole future of Damascus (comp. the Introd. to chh. l. li.). He sees in one picture what in the fulfilment will be divided into many stages, comp. HERZOG *R.-Enc. III.,* S. 260.
As regards the date of the prophecy both the superscription and the purport of it indicate that it formed part of that Sepher, beginning with xlvi. 1, which owes its origin to the period before the battle of Carchemish. Comp. Introd. to the Prophecies against the Nations.

23 AGAINST DAMASCUS.
   Ashamed are Hamath and Arpad,
   For a bad report have they heard: they are dissolved.[1]
   In the sea there is terror,[2] it cannot rest.
24 Enfeebled is Damascus, she turns to flee,
   And terror[3] seizes her,[4]
   Anguish and sorrow lay hold on her like a parturient.
25 How! Is not the city of renown abandoned,
   The place of my delight?
26 Hence her youths fall in the streets,
   And all men of war shall perish on that day, saith Jehovah Zebaoth.
27 And I kindle a fire in the wall of Damascus,
   Which shall devour the palaces of Benhadad.

TEXTUAL AND GRAMMATICAL.

¹ Ver. 23.—נְמֹג used frequently of the effect of fear in loosening the *compagines corporis*; Exod. xv. 15; Josh. ii. 9, 24; Ps. lxxv. 4; Isa. xiv. 31.
² Ver. 23.—רָאֲנָה בַּיָּם Since the following words הַשְׁקֵט לֹא יוּכַל are taken verbatim from Isa. lvii. 20, the previous words in Isaiah may rule the previous words here. There we read שׁ נִגְרָשׁ בַּיָּם וְהָרְשָׁעִים. It would now be certainly most convenient to read בָּיָּם in the present passage instead of בַּיָּם. Jeremiah however does not quote the last words accurately as a whole. And בָּיָּם also is not without difficulty. We should expect it to be in the construct state. I therefore think that the reading in the text is the correct one.—דְּאָגָה is fear, terror, unrest. Comp. Josh. xxii. 24; Prov. xii. 25; Ezek. iv. 16; xii. 18, 19. The subst. in Jeremiah here only; the verb in xvii. 8; xxxviii. 19; xli. 16.
³ Ver. 24.—רֶטֶט ἀπ. λεγ. a Syrian word, without doubt chosen purposely. Comp. רָהָה, Hos. xiii. 1.
⁴ Ver. 24.—הָחֱזִיקָה is so punctuated by the Masoretes that it is evident they took Damascus for the subject (*terrorem prehendit*) having in view passages like Isa. xiii. 8; Job xviii. 20; xxi. 6. But the punctuation הֶחֱזִיקָה would correspond better to Jeremiah's usage. Comp. vi. 24; viii. 21; l. 43.

EXEGETICAL AND CRITICAL.

An enemy coming from the north threatens first Hamath and Arpad, which are thus thrown into commotion, like a tempestuous sea (ver. 23). This agitation reaches also Damascus, hence discouragement, anxiety, in part flight (ver. 24). The city is not abandoned by all the troops (ver. 25), hence a great blood-bath and destruction of the army in the streets (ver. 26) and destruction of the city by fire (ver. 27).

Ver. 23. **Against Damascus . . . cannot rest.** The superscription is as in xlvi. 2; xlviii. 1; xlix. 1, 7. I cannot at all discover that the superscription is too limited, as GRAF supposes, for in fact this brief utterance is occupied only with Damascus, the cities Hamath and Arpad being mentioned only to designate the successive advance of the calamity and the direction in which the enemy comes. It is a matter of course that the fall of the capital involves that of the kingdom, hence the superscription is incorrect neither in itself nor in relation to the purport of the passage. According to Num. xxxiv. 8 Hamath is to be the northern limit of the land to be occupied by Israel. The boundaries were also really extended thus far at times. Comp. 2 Ki. xiv. 28 with 2 Chron. viii. 4. The city was situated on the Orontes to the North of Damascus, and was afterwards called Epiphania by the Greeks. Comp. JEROME on Am. vi. 2, 14. Arpad, which is always named together with Hamath (Isa. x. 9, comp. DELITZSCH on the passage; xxxvi. 19; xxxvii. 13), must have been situated in the neighborhood of this city. We thus see that the prophet expects the enemy from the North, as it was natural that the army of the Egyptians then in northern Syria should turn his gaze in that direction. Hamath and Arpad stand confounded in consequence of the evil tidings. They flow away, dissolve, pass away with anguish.—The following words are taken verbatim from Isa. lvii. 20. Jeremiah has doubtless from this passage the idea of the sea in general in his mind. The expression נָבֹגוּ had directed his thoughts to that passage and still exerts some influence. He thus imagines these cities as a wildly agitated sea. In the swaying hither and thither of the waves is mirrored the inward unrest and anguish. It is not then the real sea that is meant (HITZIG), but the human multitude compared to a sea. (Comp. Isa. xvii. 12; viii. 7, 8).

Vers. 24-27. **Enfeebled . . . Benhadad.** The bad report reaches even the capital, and this in consequence falls into critical agitation. Despair seizes on the inhabitants. A part turns to flight. (Comp. rems. on xlvi. 5, 21). Anguish takes hold upon them.—**How? Is not**, *etc.* We are not justified in regarding the negative as a strong affirmation, or taking **abandoned** in the sense of, left free, spared. Rather does the prophet say really: how then is the city not forsaken? (Comp. 2 Sam. i. 14). He is astonished and complains, that it has not been abandoned. This would have been better for the Syrians. For just because it has not been, their youths fall in their streets and their whole army is destroyed. Flight might have saved them.— **City of renown**, *etc.* Comp. li. 41; Isa. lx. 18; lxi. 7.—**My** refers to the prophet and there is no irony in it. He lamented that the city was not abandoned. He has a human pity for the destroyed city as he has a human joy in its beauty. Comp. rems. on xlviii. 31. [The Vulg., Syr., Chald., omit *my*. BOOTHROYD maintains that this omission is necessary to make good sense!—S. R. A.].—**The youths**. Comp. ix. 20.—Ver. 27. **And I kindle**. The whole verse in its main constituents is taken from Am. i. and ii. Comp. Am. i. 4, 7, 10, 12, 14; ii. 2, 5.—**In the wall**, not *on* the wall, for the wall itself does not burn, but *within* the wall, so that all which the wall includes is consumed by the fire. The palaces of Benhadad are the royal palaces, since Benhadad (there were three of them, 1 Ki. xv. 18, 20; xx. 1-3; 2 Ki. vi. 24; viii. 7, 9; xiii. 3, 24, 25) was the best known name of Syrian kings.

9. Prophecy against Kedar and the Kingdoms of Hazor.

XLIX. 28–33.

From Damascus the prophet turns his gaze eastward to the bordering Arabians, comprised in the designation of the title. In xxv. 23, 24 Jeremiah mentions among the populations to be subdued by Nebuchadnezzar several Arabian tribes. We feel impelled to suppose that the limits of the Arabian conquests of Nebuchadnezzar were undefined in the mind of the prophet, for we shall be obliged to distinguish a real and ideal dominion of that ruler, though the boundary line between the two is a vague one. It is unnecessary to inquire after a special occasion for this prophecy. Nebuchadnezzar being now universal ruler, the Arabs, being the immediate southern neighbors of his native country, cannot possibly be omitted from subjection to his power. Moreover, the Arabs had enough to do with the Israelites from the time of Gideon (comp. Jud. vi.–viii.; 2 Chron. xvii. 11; xxi. 16, 17; xxvi. 7).— As regards the date of this prophecy we have in the mention of Nebuchadnezzar's name a sure proof that it was written later than most of its sisters in chh. xlvi.–xlix., for only a single one of these (the second against Egypt, xlvi. 13-28) mentions Nebuchadnezzar. If his expedition against the Arabian tribes were really the first, which he made after his ascension to the throne (comp. the exeg. rems. on vers. 28, 29) this prophecy might be ascribed most fitly to the time in which he was preparing for the undertaking.

28 Against KEDAR and the kingdoms of HAZOR, which Nebuchadnezzar[1] the king of Babylon smote,
Thus saith Jehovah:
Arise, go up against Kedar,
And spoil ye the sons of the east.[2]
29 Their tents and their flocks shall they take,
Their curtains and all their utensils;
And their camels shall they take for themselves,[3]
And shall cry over them, "Terror round about."
30 Flee, run apace, stoop, ye inhabitants of Hazor, saith Jehovah,
For Nebuchadnezzar king of Babylon hath planned a plan against you,
And hath had thoughts against you.
31 Up! Move against a nation at ease,[4]
That dwelleth securely, saith Jehovah.
They have neither doors[5] nor bolts,
They dwell apart by themselves.
32 And their camels shall become a prey,
And the multitude of their flocks a plunder;
And I scatter to all (the four) winds, those with cropped hair-corners,
And from all sides I bring their destruction, saith Jehovah.
33 And Hazor shall become a habitation for jackals,
A desolation in perpetuity:
Not a man shall dwell there,
Nor a son of man sojourn therein.

TEXTUAL AND GRAMMATICAL.

[1] Ver. 28.—The ו with which the king's name is written in the Chethibh is due to a scriptural error occasioned by the word הָעֹצֵר standing just before.

[2] Ver. 28.—וּשְׁדֻדוּ. On the singular imperative form comp. OLSH. § 235, 6.

[3] Ver. 29.—לָהֶם יִשְׂאוּ. The pronoun is grammatically more correctly referred to the enemies of the Arabs (comp. Num. xvi. 6; Deut. ii. 35; iii. 7; NAEGELSB. Gr., § 81, 1 b) since the reference to the Arabs must have been expressed by מֵהֶם.

[4] Ver. 31.—The form שְׁלֵי formed like עֵיר (comp. OLSH. § 180, Anm.) is found here only. Elsewhere שָׁלֵו (Job xvi. 12; xx. 20) or שָׁלֵיו (Job xxi. 23).

[5] Ver. 31.—לֹא דְלָתַיִם by this are meant not house-doors, but city gates. Comp. Deut. iii. 5; 1 Sam. xxiii. 7.

EXEGETICAL AND CRITICAL.

Plunder, desolation and dispersion by Nebuchadnezzar are proclaimed to the pastoral tribes living in Arabia to the East of Palestine. First the enemies are called upon to advance, and with war-cries to fall upon the Arabs and spoil them (vers. 28, 29). The Arabs, however, are admonished to flee and hide themselves,, to escape the plans formed against them (ver. 30). Hereupon the enemies are summoned anew to the attack, and are told, as if to allure them, that they have to deal with a people at peace and not intrenched behind bulwarks (ver. 31). Rich booty is placed before them in prospect. Dispersion on all sides will be the result, corresponding to the attack on all sides (ver. 32). The lan l shall be devastated and cease to be a habitation for man (ver. 33).

Vers. 28, 29. **Against Kedar . . . terror round about.** Kedar is named in Gen. xxv. 13 as the second son of Ishmael, with which the Arabian tradition agrees. Comp. HERZOG, *R.- Enc.* I. *S.* 463. [Comp. KEIL and DELITZSCH, *Comm. on the Pentateuch* (Eng. Ed) Vol. I. p. 264]. They lived "in the desert between Arabia Petræa and Babylonia" (KNOBEL, *Gen. S.* 212), and are frequently mentioned as rich in flocks, living in tents (Song of Sol. i. 5; Ps. cxx. 5; Isa. xlii. 11; lx. 7; Ezek. xxvii. 21) and celebrated for their skill in archery (Isa. xxi. 16, 17). Comp. rems. on ii. 10.—**Hazor**, different from the localities of this name in Palestine (Josh. xi. 1-3; xii. 19; xix. 36; Jud. iv. and v ; I Ki. ix. 15; xv. 29—Josh. xv. 23, 25—Neh. xi. 33), is mentioned here only as a district in Arabia. According to NIEBUHR (*Ass. u. Bab.*, *S.* 210 coll. 428), Hazor is "the present Hadshar, a district which occupies the whole north-eastern corner of Nedshed, and to which in the wider sense the coast lands of Lachsa also belong." This corner is formed by the southern course of the Euphrates and the Persian Gulf. With regard to the meaning of the name it is natural to think of Isa. xlii. 11 and to suppose that חָצֹור denotes the inhabitants of the הַצֵּרִים, *i. e.* villages without walls and gates (comp. Gen. xxv. 16). DELITZSCH remarks on Isa. xlii. 11, "the settled Arabs are still called *Hadarije* in distinction from *Wabarije*, the tent Arabs; *hadar*, חָצֵר is the fixed dwelling-place in contrast to *bedû*, the steppe, where the tents are erected temporarily now here and now there." Accordingly קֵדָר and חָצֹור are related not as opposites, but only as the more limited and more extended idea, and Jeremiah would address his words to Kedar and to all other Arabs dwelling in חֲצֵרִים. With this would accord not only the Chaldean incursion generally, which it is easier to regard as directed against a settled people than against nomads, but especially the description of the devastation in ver. 23, which seems to presuppose not the pasturage of a passing horde but the abiding-place of men who build houses. It seems opposed to this, however, that in ver. 29 the tents and curtains of the attacked are spoken of, according to which part of them at least were tent-dwellers. It is also surprising that in Isa. xlii. 11 the Kedarenes are inhabitants of הַצֵּרִים, while elsewhere (comp. the passages cited) they are described as tent-dwellers. I believe that all may be united in the hypothesis that there were some Kedarenes living in tents and some in villages, and that the text has in view both these and also the other tribes settled in villages of northern Arabia.—**Which Nebuchadnezzar**, *etc.* These words appear to be a later addition, as otherwise the prophecy characterizes itself as a *vaticinium post eventum*. Yet even HITZIG remarks, the addition is "contained in the LXX. and preserving the older form of the proper name as in xliv. 30 is relatively very old, and probably genuine and certainly contains historical truth, which is not handed down elsewhere." NIEBUHR (*Ass. u. Bab.*, *S.* 209, 10) and DUNCKER (*Genh. des. Alterth.*, I. *S.* 827) are of opinion that Nebuchadnezzar, after returning from the victory of Carchemish, had strengthened his internal dominion, first taking into consideration "the extension of his dominion over the Arabs on the lower Euphrates, in North Arabia and the Syrian desert" (DUNCKER). It is to be remarked in this connection, that according to CTESIAS, whose statement DUNCKER regards as credible (*S.* 804, 806 *Anm.* 2, *etc.*), the Babylonians had already brought Arabs with them to the siege of Nineveh.—"The expression "sons of the East" is the "general designation of the Arabs, especially the nomad tribes of northern Arabia" (ARNOLD in HERZ., *R.-Enc.* I. *S.* 460). Comp. Jud. vi. 3, 33; vii. 12; viii. 10; I Ki. v. 10; Job i. 3; Isa. xi. 14; Ezek. xxv. 4, 10.—**Curtains** are the mats or canvas of which the tents consist. Comp. iv. 20; x. 20; xlvi. 5. *Major missabib.* Comp. vi. 15; xx. 3, 10; xlvi. 5. Vers. 30-33. **Flee . . . therein.** On flee, *etc.*, comp. ver. 8. On **planned a plan** comp. ver. 20 ; xviii. 11.—**At ease.** Comp. Jud. xviii. 7.—**Apart by themselves.** Comp. xv. 17; Numb. xxiii. 9; Deut. xxxiii. 28.—**And I scatter**, *etc.* Comp. Ezek. v. 12; xii. 14.—**Cropped hair-corners.** Comp. rems. on ix. 25; xxv. 23.—**From all sides.** Comp. rems. on xlviii. 28; 1 Ki. v. 4—vor. 8; xlvi. 21.—**Shall become**, *etc.*, ver. 33. Comp. ver. 18; ix. 10; x. 22; li. 37; l. 40.

10. Prophecy against Elam.

XLIX. 34-39.

Elam is mentioned in the Old Testament in Gen. x. 22; xiv. 1, 9; Isa. xi. 11; xxi. 2; xxii. 6; Jer. xxv. 25; Ezek. xxxii. 24; Dan. viii. 2; Ezra iv. 9. *Comp. supra ad* xxv. 25. *It is here mentioned as the representative of the more remote populations, beyond the Tigris, all those who are enumerated in the catalogue of nations beyond the Tigris in* xxv. 25, 26. M. NIEBUHR *assumes as certain a victorious war of Nebuchadnezzar with Elam between the ninth and twentieth years of his reign (Ass. u. Bab. S.* 212). *In this, however, he relies not on positive historical testimony but only on inferences, the correctness of which may be disputed. We are further in no need of an actual overthrow of Elam by Nebuchadnezzar. The kernel of the prophecy is an idea which retains its truth even if Nebuchadnezzar had never made war on Elam.*
Why Jeremiah chose Elam as the representative of the eastern nations is not apparent. The supposition of EWALD *(Proph. d. A. B., II. S.* 130), *that "the wild warlike Elamites had acted as auxiliaries shortly before in the deportation of Jehoiachin and the first great deportation of the people, and in this had shown themselves particularly cruel," does not appear to be well-founded. For* 1. *if the Elamites already served in the army of Nebuchadnezzar they needed not to be subjugated ;* 2. *the superscription affords no sure criterion of the date. For it is highly probable that it is placed here by mistake, as we shall show on ver.* 34. *The prophecy does not mention Nebuchadnezzar by name, and we must therefore regard it as of the same date as the others in* chh. xlvi.-xlix. *against the nations (except* xlvi. 13 sqq. *and* xlix. 28-33).

34 The word of Jehovah which came to Jeremiah the prophet with respect to Elam, in the beginning of the reign of Zedekiah, king of Judah, saying,
35 Thus saith Jehovah Zebaoth:
Behold, I will break the bow of Elam,
The chief part of their strength.
36 And I will bring upon Elam four winds from the four corners of heaven,
And will scatter them to all those winds;
And there shall be no nation whither the dispersed of Elam[1] shall not come.
37 And I will terrify[2] Elam before their enemies,
And before those who seek their life;
And I will bring calamity upon them,
The fierceness of my anger, saith Jehovah;
And I will send the sword after them,
Until I have utterly consumed them.
38 And I will set my throne in Elam,
And destroy king and prince from thence, saith Jehovah.
39 And it shall be at the end of days,
I will turn the captivity of Elam, saith Jehovah.

TEXTUAL AND GRAMMATICAL.

[1] Ver. 36.—עוֹלָם in the Chethibh has expressions such as ver. 13; xxv. 12; li. 26, 62, *etc.*, in view.
[2] Ver. 37.—On הַחְתַּתִּי comp. OLSH., *S.* 563, 4,—xlvi. 26; ix. 15.

EXEGETICAL AND CRITICAL.

The bow of the Elamites, wherein their strength consists, shall be broken (ver. 35). They shall be attacked and scattered on all sides (ver. 36), and be pursued to destruction (ver. 37). The country itself the Lord will hold strict judgment and exterminate all the rulers (ver. 38). Yet in the distant future Elam also shall be liberated and obtain salvation (ver. 39).

Ver. 34. **The word ... Judah.** There are well-founded doubts as to the authenticity of this superscription. We have hitherto found without an exception, that in all prophecies which are older than the battle of Carchemish, Jeremiah never mentions Nebuchadnezzar and the Chaldeans, while in all the oracles subsequent to this catastrophe he knows and names Nebuchadnezzar as the Lord's chosen instrument. If now this prophecy really dates from the beginning of Zedekiah's reign, why is not Nebuchadnezzar mentioned? Why are the agents of the punishment spoken of in as general a manner as in the older prophecies? Or must not Nebuchadnezzar be necessarily regarded as the agent, as GRAF supposes (S. 576)? I hold it quite impossible for Jeremiah in the beginning of the reign of Zedekiah to have thought of any other than Nebuchadnezzar as an instrument of the execution, or to have left this point even *in suspense*. Compare only xxvii. 5 sqq., where the whole earth, with all that is thereon, is given over without exception or reserve to the Chaldean king. Add to this an external circumstance. Unreliable as the Alexandrian translation in general is, yet in some circumstances it may serve to indicate the original form of the text (comp. GRAF, *Einl. S.* LVII.). This is here the case. As is well-known the prophecies against the nations have in the LXX. their place immediately after that indication of a Sopher, containing them, in xxv. 13, and this prophecy against Elam is at their head. It is introduced with the words: ἃ ἐπροφήτευσεν Ἰερεμίας ἐπὶ τὰ ἔθνη τὰ Αἰλάμ. It further closes with the words: ἐν ἀρχῇ βασιλεύοντος Σεδεκίου βασιλέως ἐγένετο ὁ λόγος οὗτος περὶ Αἰλάμ, and these words form in addition the beginning of ch. xxvi. However severely we may judge the arbitrariness of this translator, it must be admitted that this exceeds the customary degree thereof, which is substantially confined to abridgement (comp. GRAF, *Einl., S.* XLIII.). What could have induced him to invent this postscript, since the brief oracle was sufficiently characterized by the prefixed words τὰ Αἰλάμ (evidently corresponding to the Hebrew לְעֵילָם, but on account of its brevity added as in apposition to the preceding ἐπὶ τὰ ἔθνη? Whence now that postscript? It is remarkable that in the LXX. the first verse of ch. xxvii. (Heb.) is wanting. It is the verse with the undoubtedly false name of Jehoiakim! Now ch. xxvii. stands in the closest topical relation to ch. xxv. In the symbolic sending of the yoke it forms an actual commentary to the symbol of the cup of wrath, xxv. 15 sqq. Ch. xxvi. on the other hand belongs to a much earlier date, and is merely inserted here, because it likewise (as ch. xxvii.) has for its subject the conflict with the false prophets, and bears as date the beginning of the reign of Jehoiakim. Compare the Introduction to the Ninth Discourse (ch. xxv.), and the rems. on xxvii. 1. This postscript now which the LXX. subjoins to the oracle against Elam suits exactly (only with the omission of the words περὶ Αἰλάμ) in the place of the verse wanting at the beginning of ch. xxvii., and, which is a matter of importance, it contains the right king's name, *viz.,* that of Zedekiah. The supposition is thus pressed upon us that the prophecies against the nations originally had place immediately after ch. xxv., that ch. xxvii. was connected directly therewith (without the intervention of ch. xxvi.), that the prophecy against Elam formed the conclusion of the oracle against the nations, and that by mistake the Diaskeuast who altered that original order, removed xxvii. 1, and attached it, as a postscript, to the oracle against Elam. In this behalf the words "against Elam," had to be inserted. This alteration must have been made in very early times, for it makes itself felt in both the Hebrew text and in the LXX. only with this difference.

that in the text, on which the LXX. was based, the misplaced words still stood at the close of the word directed against Elam, so that this had a superscription and a postscript, while in our Masoretic recension the postscript is made into the title by the assumption into it of the words אֶל־עֵילָם. For this purpose the form of the sentences must also have been altered, so that it was in correspondence with the superscription, xlvi. 1 and xlvii. 1, while in the Greek text (xxvi. 1) the old form is still perceptible. Thus substantially MOVERS and HITZIG, with whom I feel compelled to agree in the main.

Vers. 35–39. **Thus saith ... saith Jehovah.** It seems to me far-fetched to take קֶשֶׁת in the sense of *viri fortes* as HITZIG and GRAF would do, after the example of the Targum and several Rabbis. This meaning also does not seem to me to be proved. For in Isa. xxi. 17 the word is to be understood peculiarly (comp. DELITZSCH, *ad loc.*). In 1 Sam. ii. 4 and Hos. i. 5, it stands by synecdoche for all the means of attack and defence. And it is thus to be rendered here the rather as we know from history, that the Elamites were really celebrated as archers (comp. Isa. xxii. 6; Livy XXXVII. 27; HERZOG, *R.-Enc.*, III. *S.* 748). The bow was the chief part of their strength (comp. ii. 3; Am. vi. 1, 6). When HITZIG inquires "why limit the breaking to the bow?" the answer is, because it was the main element of their power. To break their bow was to render them defenceless. When this is done, the advance is made upon them positively; from the four corners of the heaven are the four winds to rage against them and drive them one to another, *i. e.,* the four winds shall scatter them to the four winds (comp. ver. 32; Zech. ii. 10; vi. 5). Without a figure, they shall be attacked on all sides and scattered on all sides, so that there will be no nation in which such Elamites are not to be found. That this is the sense is clear from ver. 37, where the same thing is expressed without a figure.—In the country itself will the Lord erect His throne (comp. the related but not identical expression, i. 15 and xliii. 10), *i. e.,* He will sit in judgment, and the heads of the people must appear to receive their sentences. But Elam also at the end of days shall share in the salvation which the Lord shall then bring to all nations by the Messiah (comp. xlix. 6; xlviii. 47). It is also not to be doubted that this word of consolation applies not to Elam alone, but to all the nations before mentioned.

DOCTRINAL AND ETHICAL.

1. On xlix. 1. Has then Israel no heir? So the prophet tells the Ammonites. But to Israel himself he speaks differently; I will cast you out from my presence, as I cast out all your brethren, the whole seed of Ephraim (vii. 15). Thus the Ammonites have no right in Israel, and Israel, although he has forfeited his claim with respect to Jehovah, still has a right to his country with respect to the Ammonites, which he will one day, through God's grace, make good again. "Israel will one day possess and rule his possessors and rulers. This is Israel's eternal calling, which, in spite of every sin, must again be manifested,

and is fulfilled in the Christian church to which all nations are given as a possession. Even now Jeremiah by God's word, of which he is the bearer, has power over Ammon as over all the heathen world. He surveys their whole character, and already holds judgment. In him is Israel's majesty and triumph even though on this account he is most mocked by the Jews." (DIEDRICH). As then the servants of Malcom occupied the territory of Israel, so since then have the servants of Mohammed occupied the territory of the Christian church in Asia and Europe. In both cases it was a judgment on the latter without conferring any right on the former. A time, however, will come when the restoration of Israel and of Christianity to their country, and their right will take place at the same time.

2. On vers. 4, 5. "The real confidence of the world is always on Mammon. They would satisfy the deity with their dead self-devised works, but with desire and the tension of all their powers does the world serve material interests, as they are now-a-days called? Soon, however, Ammon's corn-fields are overflowed by enemies, then even their confidence gives way to despair." DIEDRICH.

3. On ver. 7. "We see here, how God puts to shame those who depend on their wisdom and craftiness, so that we may ask: is there no more wisdom or counsel among the wise? Is their wisdom come to naught? Paul also writes of this (1 Cor. i. 19, 20) from the prophet Isaiah (xxix. 14 coll. Jer. ix. 23, 24). *Biblische Summarien, etc.*

4. On ver. 7 sqq. "Although Edom was the nation nearest to Israel both in relationship and acquaintance, it is thus only a precursor of Antichrist, who endeavors to hide a worldly character in Christian forms. Edom is irritated by the existence of Israel, the presence of the pure word of God is always a thorn in his conscience. From Edom came Herod who wanted to murder the child Jesus, and who also mocked the suffering Saviour. Edom was celebrated for wise proverbs; it possessed high mental endowments; but are not even these put to shame, when not accompanied by the fear of God?" DIEDRICH.

5. On ver. 12. Israel was the chosen nation, the son of the house (comp. Exod. iv. 22; Jer. xxxi. 9), and yet he was severely chastised. Further, there were in Israel many just and pious men, who did not share the sins of their people, but zealously contended against them. But even these also had to bear the severe chastening. "Prophets and priests were also carried away to Babylon; Daniel, Ezekiel and pious men like Ananiah, Azariah, Mishael, and probably very many others," says Theodoret. How then could another nation expect to be treated differently? Comp. Prov. xi. 31; 1 Pet. iv. 17, 18. There will, however, be a similarity also in this that finally the chastisement of both, the chosen nation and the other, will redound to their eternal welfare. Comp. ver. 39. "*Justus est Dominus et rectum omne judicium ejus! Quæ etiam erat confessio Mauritii imperatoris, quum ederet, cum videret sanctum suum uxorem gladio feriri paulo post feriendus et ipse.*" FÖRSTER. Pss. cxix., cxxxvii.

6. On ver. 16. "Fortifications may be constructed and made due use of, but they must not be depended upon. For no fortification is too strong or too high when God is angry, and will punish. And he has various ways of bringing them into the hands of the enemies as, He can cause provisions to fail; or a spark to fall in a powder-magazine; water may be wanting; there may be pestilence or the dysentery or mutiny among the soldiers, or bribes may be used as scaling ladders. Then all is in vain." CRAMER. "What the world calls protection, cannot protect against God's judgment; death mounts over all rocks." DIEDRICH.

7. On ver. 19. "God gives all authority and respect, and takes it all away. For He it is, who poureth contempt upon princes, Job xii. 21; Ps. cvii. 40; Isa. xl. 23." CRAMER. ["We need not be surprised by such a searching question as that in the present passage concerning CHRIST, when we remember that Edom is the prophetical type of Christ's enemies," *etc.* WORDSWORTH.— S. R. A.]

8. On ver. 25. "God can suffer moderate joyousness, but to be joyous from security and in an Epicurean manner, is commonly a preliminary to destruction, Matt. xxiv. 39." CRAMER.

9. On ver. 30. "*Non est quo fugias a Deo irato, nisi ad Deum placatum*, AUGUSTIN in *Ps.* lxxiv."— FÖRSTER.

10. On ver. 38. Where judgment is held there is the Lord's throne. For even the idea of judgment is divine, and all judges are the lower representatives of the highest judge. Woe to those judges who proceed so as to efface the idea which they represent. Well for us that there is a superior tribunal which will reverse all unjust judgments, and in all points bring true justice to the light, before which also *summum jus* will not be *summa injuria*.

11. On ver. 39. "*In promissione spondetur Persis vocatio ad regnum Christi, cujus primitiæ fuerunt Magi* (Matt. ii.), *qui et ob id a Chrysostomo Patriarchæ gentium appellantur.*" FÖRSTER. [The fulfilment of this prophecy was seen, in part, when the Magi came to our Lord at Bethlehem; and still more on the day of Pentecost, when 'Parthians, Medes and *Elamites*' listened to the preaching of St. Peter at Jerusalem, and were received into the Christian church (Acts ii. 9, 14)." WORDSWORTH.—S. R. A.],

HOMILETICAL AND PRACTICAL.

1. On vers. 1, 2. Lament and hope of the church with respect to lost territory. 1. The lament (ver. 1). 2. The hope (*a*) with respect to the overcoming of opponents; (*b*) with respect to the reacquisition of the lost.

2. On vers. 4, 5. Warning against arrogance. 1. Whereon it depends (ver. 4, trusted in her treasures, *etc.*). 2. What its end will be (destruction of its sources of help, fear, flight).

3. On ver. 7. The insufficiency of human wisdom. 1. Its strength (the renowned wisdom of the Edomites was not unfounded). 2. Its weakness (it must fail before the strokes of the Lord).

4. 3. On ver. 11. A word of comfort for widows and orphans. 1. They have lost their human protectors and supporters. 2. Their shield is the Lord, if they trust in him.—"How blessed is God's kind promise to widows and orphans 1.

It calms the heart of every dying father: 2. It comforts the heart of all who are left orphans; 3. It encourages us all to trust ourselves with our children more faithfully to God. FLOREY, *Biblisch. Wegweiser für geistl. Grabredner*, 1861, S. 101.
5. On ver. 12. The justice of the Lord. 1. It directs its strokes with strict impartiality against the children of the house and against strangers.

2. It always has in view the true welfare of those who are smitten. 6. On vers. 15, 16. The folly of those who would contend against God. 1. The ground of it (pride, earthly power). 2. Its fate (overthrow and destruction by divine omnipotence) 7. On vers. 38, 39. The Lord's judgments. They are 1, irresistible; 2, directed not to complete destruction, but to amelioration and true well-being.

11. Prophecy against Babylon (chh. l., li.).

INTRODUCTION.

1. Before the battle of Carchemish Jeremiah predicted to his people a severe visitation by a people coming from the north, whom he afterwards recognized as the Chaldeans, and then constantly proclaimed that Israel and the other nations would be saved from complete destruction only by subjection to Nebuchadnezzar. It may, therefore, be said that during part of his ministry he spoke of the Chaldeans unknowingly in a manner favorable to them. There is no contradiction, however, as many suppose, in his here predicting the destruction of Babylon itself, and in the same manner by a people coming from the north (l. 3, 9, 41; li. 48). For Jeremiah would only say that for the present, in the proximate future, Babylon is the instrument of judgment on all nations (l. 23; li. 20 sqq.), but the time is coming when Babylon itself must drain the cup of wrath, in punishment for the sins which it has incurred in the execution of its mission (l. 11, 24, 28, 32; li. 6, 11, 24, 36, 56). Jeremiah's declarations for and against Babylon are thus related to each other, as in xxv. 27 the brief declaration, "and the king of Sheshach shall drink after them," is to the previous announcements that Babylon shall offer the cup of wrath. It is not strange to find a prophecy against Babylon in Jeremiah, but must be regarded as perfectly natural.

2. Prophecy against Babylon has a history. First, Isaiah, probably moved by the embassy, which Merodach-Baladan sent to Hezekiah (Isa. xxxix.; 2 Ki. xx. 12 sqq.) proclaimed the judgment of destruction on Babylon (Isa. chh. xiii., xiv., xxi.; xliii. 14; xlvi. 1-2; xlvii.; xlviii. 14 sqq.). He is followed by Micah, who, in a brief declaration, comprises all which Jeremiah has said in his whole book for and against Babylon, "thou shalt dwell in the field, and thou shalt go to Babylon; there shalt thou be delivered; there the Lord shall redeem thee from the hand of thy enemies." Mic. iv. 10. Habakkuk then, the cotemporary of Jeremiah, prophesied before him, but after the battle of Carchemish, against Babylon, characterizing it not only in the narrower sense as a power hostile to the people of Israel, but also in a higher and more comprehensive sense as a worldly power, self-deifying, and the enemy of God. Jeremiah finally appropriates his predecessors' ¥ represents the acme of Old Testament prophecy against Babylon. He thus forms the main foundation for the prophecy of the Apocalypse concerning the Babylon of the final period. It is, however, to be observed that he gives relatively less prominence than Habakkuk to the ideal significance of Babylon as a type of ungodly, self-deifying, worldly powers. The latter does this in brief but wondrously profound and significant utterances. "For, lo, I raise up the Chaldeans, that powerful and irrepressible nation, which goes as far as the earth extends, to occupy dwellings which are not. Terrible and fearful are they: from themselves proceed their judgment and their dignity" (i. 6, 7). "Then he overflows with courage and transgresses and becomes guilty; this his power is unto his God" (i. 11). "Lo, inflated, not upright is his soul within him, but the just by faith shall live" (ii. 4). "Yea also because wine stultifies a man, who is arrogant and is not contented, who enlargeth his desire as hell, and is like death and cannot be satisfied, but draweth to himself all nations and gathereth to himself all nations" (ii. 5).—Jeremiah by no means passes over this element, but he rather intimates it only in single words, in those significant names which he gives to Babylon when he calls it Double defiance (l. 21), Pride (as personification in l. 31, 32), Heart of my opponents (li. 1), Golden cup making the whole earth drunk (li. 7). We may then say that of the two contemporary prophets, who lived to see the culmination of the Babylonian power, Jeremiah draws the grandest and most complete picture of the destruction menacing Babylon, but in such wise that he only intimates the ideal element which represents Babylon as the centre and type of all worldly enmity to God, while Habakkuk, who, notwithstanding the external insignificance of his little book, has a powerful and profound mind, gives us deeper glances into the inner life of the Babylonian empire.

3. It is not, however, the prophets who first stamped Babylon as a centre and type of ungodly empire. This character was impressed upon it from the earliest period. It was the locality of the first earthly princedom. That Nimrod, whose memory is preserved to the present day by the ruined tower of the Birs Nimrud, and who still lives in the traditions of the East as a great

criminal and enemy of God, had, according to Gen. x. 8 sqq., Babylon as the beginning of his dominion. The first aristocrat, hero of the chase and of war, conqueror, and despot, proceeded from Babylon. Add to this, that the Babylonian tower-structure is, according to its most essential nature, to be regarded as an undertaking of human pride begun without God and in man's own strength. The tower was to be a memorial of a period of gigantic effort and aspiration towards the political concentration of the human race into one irresistible power. Thus we see that the ideas of earthly power and glory were from the first native to the soil of Babylon. Comp. NAEGELSB., *Jer. u. Bab.*, S. 5 sqq.; PERIZONIUS, *Origg. Babylonicæ*, Cap. 10-12; JAHN, *Archæology* I., 1. S. 30, *coll.* DEYLING, *Observ. Sacræ.*, P. III., p. 19 ff.—BRIAN WALTON in his *Polyglott*, Lond., *Prolegg.* 1., *pag.* 3; HETZEL, *Gedanken über den babylonischen Thurmbau*, Hildb., 1775; GÖRRES, *Die Völkertafel des Pent.*, Regensburg, 1845,1, S.51. The seed sowed in that primitive period reached its full bloom in Nebuchadnezzar. By him Babylon was really made the first "all-devouring" universal monarchy, by which I mean that his power was greater than that of the Assyrians before him, or the Persians and Romans after him. But he also devoured the theocracy, *i. e.*, the only point on this earth where the kingdom of God was represented in the form of a human popular and civil life. Since that time the kingdom of God *as such* has had no place on earth. It is still as the church in the embrace of worldly power. Babylon, however, the first worldly power which brought the kingdom of God into this condition, appears from that time in the Scriptures as the worldly power, κατ' ἐξοχήν, so that not only what the Old Testament prophets declare of the different representatives of worldly dominion, of Egypt (Rev. xi. 8), Tyre (Rev. xviii. 11 *coll.* Ezek. xxvii.), Nineveh (Rev. xviii. 3, 5 *coll.* Nah. iii. 4; Jon. i. 2), is transferred in the New Testament to Babylon, but even the name of Babylon itself is attributed to the final form of the worldly power, antichristian Rome. Comp. Rev. xvii. 9, 18. See in general Rev. xiv. 8; xvi. 9, and especially chh. xvii., xviii. This subject is treated more in detail in NAEGELSB. *Jer. u. Bab.*

4. With regard to the etymology of the name Babylon there have been two opposite views. According to one, which was first broached by STEPHANUS BYZANTINUS and the *Etymologicon Magn, s. v.* Βαβυλών, the name, designates Bel as the founder of the city. EICHHORN (*Biblioth. d. bibl. Litt.* III., S. 1001) accordingly explains בָּבֶל as arising from Bâb Bel, *i. e.*, *porta* or *aula Beli*. GESENIUS (*Thesaur., pag.* 212), TUCH and others modify this view, in so far that they translate בָּבֶל *domus Beli*, since the word is written in Arabic bâbel, and bâ is frequently used in Arabic names of cities for bî, bêt. KNOBEL (*Gen.*, S. 128) derives Babel from Bar-bel, *i. e., arz* (βᾶρις, בִּירָה) *Beli*. It is opposed however to these explanations that they are supported on partly much too recent and partly altogether insecure linguistic analogies. The other explanation is founded on Gen. xi. 7, 9 (נָבְלָה שְׂפָתָם) ver. 7 and

(כִּי שָׁם בָּלַל יְיָ שְׂפַת כָּל־הָאָרֶץ). According to this arose from בַּלְבֵּל. The punctuation of the first syllable is to be explained after the annalogy of כּוֹכָב for כָּכְבָא, טוֹטָפוֹת for טְפָטֹת (Ew. § 158, c; OLSH. § 74, § 189, a). For the Segol of the second syllable appeal might be made to כְּרַם (DELITZSCH on Gen. xi. 9). The meaning would be *confusio*. Comp. Exod. xxix. 2, 40; Lev. ii. 4-6; further, בְּלִיל, *farrago*; תֵּבֵל, troubling, blemish (Lev. xxi. 20). These explanations are also favored by the ancient translations. ONKELOS translates נָבְלָה, Gen. xi. 7, by נְבַלְבֵּל, ver. 9, by בִּלְבֵּל, *confudit*. Comp. BUXTORF, *Lex. Rabb. et Talm., pag.* 309. The Peshito version has in xi. 9 balbel (comp. CASTELLI, *Lex., pag.* 100); SAADIAH balbala *confudit*.—Comp. GADLER, *Urgeschichte* II. 2, S. 228. HAEVERNICK, *Einleit. i. A. T.*, 1., S. 147, 8.—The Babylonian monuments lead to still another etymology. According to OPPERT, namely (*Exp. en. Mesop.* II. S. 46), the word reads on the monuments Babi-ilu, Babilu. Bab is the Shemitic בַּב door, Ilu the Ἴλος in Diodorus, the Κρόνος of the Greeks, Saturn, the god of the deluge. The meaning of the name would then be *Porta Dei diluvii*. Coup. Ib., S. 67, 157, 259.—Which of these explanations is the correct one is by no means decided, for even the cuneiform inscriptions, presupposing that they are correctly deciphered, represent a late date in relation to the origin of the name, and it is a question whether the Babylonian scholars themselves knew the correct etymology of the word. [Comp. also SMITH's *Dictionary of the Bible. s. v.*, Babel, Babylon; RAWLINSON, *Ancient Monarchies*, I., p. 149; ID., *Herodotus*, II., p. 574; DR. PUSEY, *Lectures on Daniel*, p. 271, *n*, quoted in WORDSWORTH *ad loc.*—S. R. A.]

5. The genuineness of this prophecy has been shown by me in detail in my work *Jeremia und Babylon*, S. 69 ff. GRAF also acknowledges it (S. 580 ff.). Only EWALD and MEIER, so far as I know, still persist in maintaining its unauthenticity. "This portion evidently belongs to the last period of the exile, and cannot therefore proceed from Jeremiah," says the latter (*Die prophet. Bücher d. A. T.*, S. 350, 2). I myself formerly regarded the passage l. 41-46 as a gloss, but I have now retracted this opinion. But after repeated investigation I cannot regard the passage li. 15-19 as original. Consult the exegesis. In respect to the word שֵׁשָׁךְ, li. 41, also, my suspicions have not yet been removed.

6. In what manner the prophecy is related to its fulfilment has been fully shown in NAEGELSB. *Jer. u. Bab.*, S. 135. I add to the remark there, that according to THEODORET Jews were the last inhabitants of the destroyed city of Babylon, the following notice from OPPERT (*Exp.* 1., S. 135): "Hillah fut fondée par Seifeddaulet vers l'an 1100 à la place de l'antique ville de Babylone, τὸ ἄστυ. Jusque-là, des Juifs avaient habité seuls la ville ou plutôt les ruines de Babylone; en 1030 après Jesus-Christ ils quittèrent ces lieux." Many later witnesses thus corroborate the statement of THEODORET, that the people of Israel

could not separate themselves from the corpse of the city, which had destroyed Jerusalem and the temple.

7. In regard to the division of the portion, I am no longer of opinion that the whole is to be discriminated into three main sections with thirteen subdivisions. I still think that three chronological stages may be distinguished, in so far as the destruction of Babylon is represented partly as future, now in the stage of preparation (comp. l. 9, 21, 26, 41) partly as present, in the process of execution (comp. l. 14, 24, 35, 43, etc.; li. 1, 11, 27), partly as already accomplished (comp. l. 2, 15, 46; li. 39, 41, 46, 57). And these three stages are so distributed that the first is chiefly in the beginning, the second chiefly in the middle, the third towards the close; but not so sharply defined that l. 21—li. 33 may be regarded as the second and the foregoing and following as the first and third divisions. The single tableaux or pictures, of which, according to the peculiar style of Jeremiah, the discourse consists, are more distinct. I find nineteen of these, exclusive of the superscription and the historical close. The exegesis will exhibit these in detail.

1. *The Superscription.*

L. 1.

1 The word which Jehovah spoke against Babylon, against the land of the Chaldeans, by Jeremiah the prophet.

EXEGETICAL AND CRITICAL.

The form of the superscription is like those in xlv. 1; xlvi. 13. The expression בְּיַד is not found in any other superscription of Jeremiah's. It occurs in this sense only in xxxvii. 2. In my work, *Jer. u. Bab.*, S. 22, I have proposed the hypothesis that there is in this an intimation that this prophecy, according to li. 59 sqq., was given only by the hand, not by the mouth of the prophet. אֶל־אֶרֶץ defines more particularly the idea of בָּבֶל and guards against too narrow a rendering. Comp. l. 8, 45; li. 54.

2. *The cord broken; Israel free* (PS. cxxiv. 7).

2 Declare it among the nations,
Publish it and erect a signal;
Publish it, conceal it not.
Say "Babylon is taken, with shame stands Bel,
Merodach is thrown down, with shame stand her images,
Thrown down are her idols."
3 For a nation cometh against her from the north,
And will make her land desolate,
That no inhabitant shall be therein
From man down to beast they flee; up, away!
4 In those days and at that time, saith Jehovah,
The children of Israel shall come,
They and the children of Judah together;
Weeping shall they come
And seek Jehovah their God.
5 After Zion shall they inquire,
Their faces turned thitherward:
"Come, let us join ourselves[1] to Jehovah.
In a perpetual covenant[2] that shall not be forgotten."

TEXTUAL AND GRAMMATICAL.

¹ Ver. 5.—וְנִגְלוּ בֹּאוּ. Both forms are Imperative, and there is no need either to take בֹּאוּ as Perf. or to alter נִגְלוּ into נְלִיָה (Graf.). Comp. Ewald, §226, b; Olsh. §264; Joel iv. 11; Isa. xliii. 9.

² Ver. 5. בְּרִית עוֹלָם. Accus. modalis. Comp Naegelsb. Gr., §70, i; xxxi. 31, 32; xxxii. 40.

EXEGETICAL AND CRITICAL.

The prophet in the first two verses goes to work analytically, first (ver. 2) causing the destruction of Babylon to be proclaimed aloud to all nations, and then (ver. 3) saying, how and by whom this destruction will be accomplished. This analytic description serves him, however, only as a basis for a promise important to him above all, viz., that in those days the captives of Israel and Judah being liberated, will come home and be united to their God in an eternal and unforgetable covenant (vers. 4, 5).

Vers. 2, 3. **Declare it . . . up, away.** The importance of the matter is shown in the grandeur and animation of the opening, in which the summons to proclaim and the declaration of the destruction are five times repeated. Comp. iv. 5, 6; v. 20; xxxi. 7; xlvi. 14.—**Erect a signal,** i. e., for the rapid spread of the tidings. Comp. li. 12, 27; iv. 6; vi. 1; Isa. v. 26; xiii. 2.—**Conceal it not.** The address seems to be to the friends of Babylon, who might be disposed to withhold this Job's post.—**Taken.** Comp. viii. 9; x. 14; xlviii. 24; xlviii. 1.—Bel and Merodach are not different deities, but one and the same (comp. Delitzsch on Isa. xlvi. 1). The temple of Belus (comp. Herod. I. 181, 2) was also the temple of Marduk, as he is called on the monuments. Here he was worshipped as the Bilu rabu (רַב בֵּל) as deus augurationis and protective deity of Babylonia. "Toute la dynastie Babylonienne (says Oppert, Exp. en Mesop., Tom. II., p. 272) le met (Merodach) à la tête des Dieux, et l'inscription de Borsippa le nomme le roi du ciel et de la terre. Nebo prend la seconde place et les autres divinités ne paraissent que rarement." Comp. Tom. 1, p. 178, 9.—That he is not Mars, as I formerly supposed and Hauf in Drechsler's Jesaja on xxxi. 1 (II., 2, S. 212) directly maintains, is decidedly affirmed by Oppert (p. 271).—The purport of the proclamation is expressed in vers. 2 b and 3 only. From ver. 4 we have the words of the prophet, who predicts in what manner these results will be attained. This is seen from the imperfects יִהְיֶה, שָׁעִיר, etc.—**A nation from the north.** Comp. ver. 9. The destroyers of Babylon are to come from the north, and in li. 27, 28 nations to the north and north-east of Babylonia are mentioned. Comp. the map in Niebuhr's Ass. u. Bab., and S. 135, Anm. 1; 427, 8.—Moreover, the remarkable parallelism should be noticed, Babylon, once the nation from the north, menacing Israel, is now attacked by such a nation. Comp. ii. 15; iv. 7; ix. 9; xxxiii. 12; li. 62.

Vers. 4, 5. **In those days . . . . forgotten.** The destruction of Babylon is immediately followed by the redemption. The prophets so regard it as to comprise all the stages of its fulfilment through several thousand years in one picture. To this picture belongs above all the reunion of the tribes of the northern and southern kingdom (comp. iii. 14-16) and then their honest conversion to the Lord (comp. ii. 21; xxxi. 9-19; Hos. iii. 5), the return to Zion (xxxi. 8), the conclusion of a covenant with Jehovah, which shall not be broken and forgotten like the first (comp. Gen. xvii. 10; Lev. xix. 5-7; Deut. xxix. and xxx.). Comp. also Jer. xx. 11; xxiii. 40.

---

3. The Chastisement of the Chastiser.

L. 6-13.

6   A lost herd[1] was[2] my people:
Their shepherds had led them astray on seductive mountains,[3]
From mountain to hill they went,
Forgat their fold.
7   Whoever found them devoured them,
And their oppressors said: We incur no guilt,
Because they have sinned against Jehovah,
The true pasturage and their fathers' hope, Jehovah.
8   Flee out of Babylon and—
Let them go[4] forth out of the land of the Chaldeans,
And be as the rams before the sheep!
9   For behold, I raise and lead[5] against Babylon
An assembly of great nations from the north country;

CHAP. L. 6-13.   407

They equip themselves against her, there⁶ she is taken—
Their arrows⁷ like those of a successful⁸ hero, who returneth not empty,
10 And Chaldea shall become a prey;
All that plunder her shall be satisfied, saith Jehovah.
11 For thou rejoicedst,⁹ for thou exultedst, robber of my heritage,
For thou skippedst like a thrashing¹⁰ calf
And neighedst like the strong steeds.
12 Your mother is put to great shame,
She that bare you blushes.
" Behold the last of the nations, wilderness, waste, and steppe,"
13 Because of the wrath of Jehovah it shall be uninhabited,
And shall be wholly a desolation :
Whoever passeth by Babylon is amazed,
And mocks her on account of all her strokes.

TEXTUAL AND GRAMMATICAL.

Ver. 6.—The plural אֲבָדוֹת depends on the ideal plural in צֹאן. Comp. NAEGELSB. *Gr.*, § 105, 3; Gen. xxx. 38; Jer. xxxiii. 13; Job i. 14.
² Ver. 6.—The Chethibh הָיָה is referred to the subject as *e.g.*, in Gen. xxxi. 8. The Keri is therefore unnecessary.
³ Ver. 6.—הרים שׁובבים. The Chethibh is usually read שׁובָבִים (iii. 14, 22) the Ker שׁובְבִים. I think, however, that we must read the Chethibh שׁובְבִים (comp. xxxi. 8; xlix. 4), and understand it in the meaning of "alienating, seductive mountains." We then take the word in the same sense as those who follow the Keri, and find our support like them in passages like Isa. xlvii. 10. Comp. rems. on xxxi. 8.
⁴ Ver. 8.—Chethibh יָצָא. This sudden change of person is not uncommon. (Comp. v. 14; xli. 13; xvii. 13; xxi. 12 Chethibh); xxxi. 3; xxxvi. 29, 30; xliv. 3-6; xlvii. 7. NAEGELSD. *Gr.*, § 101, 2, *Anm.*
⁵ Ver. 9.—מֵעִיר וּמֵעֲלָה. Observe the paronomasia and compare li. 1, 11; Isal. xliii. 17.
⁶ Ver. 9.—מִשָּׁם. If this word is regarded as local, it is difficult after עָרְכוּ לָהּ to find a suitable *terminus a quo*. I therefore prefer to understand it with ROSENMUELLER, DE WETTE, UMBREIT, of time. Comp. Hos. ii. 17; Job xxxv. 12.
⁷ Ver. 9.—הִצָּיו. The suffix is to be referred to the entirety of those nations regarded as *one* male person.
⁸ Ver. 9.—מַשְׂכִּיל. Comp. x. 21; xxiii. 5.
⁹ Ver. 11.—The Keri תִּשְׂמְחִי, *etc.* is occasioned by כִּי שָׂמֵחַ, but is unnecessary, for the prophet conceives the Chaldean nation as *one* female individual, as in חָזָק the enemies as one male. Comp. *c. g.,* iii. 8-10, and אֹיְבָם in ver. 12.
¹⁰ Ver. 11.—דָּשָׁא. Part. from דּוּשׁ to thrash (Hos. x. 11), א for ה as *e.g.*, Lam. iii. 12; comp. OLSH. § 108, *e, Anm.* 164, *b*.

EXEGETICAL AND CRITICAL.

Israel has certainly sinned greatly by idolatry (ver. 6), and has therefore been deservedly chastised by his enemies (ver. 7). But now the hour of deliverance strikes (ver. 8), for the Lord sends against Babylon great hosts of nations from the north, who will attack it successfully (ver. 9). In consequence Babylon itself shall become a prey (ver. 10), and receive the punishment for having discharged its office as punisher of Israel with arrogant and malicious joy (ver. 11). It shall thus be the last of nations, and the country be a horrible wilderness (vers. 12, 13).

Vers. 6, 7. **A lost herd . . . hope, Jehovah.** Comp. Ezek. xxxiv. 4, 16; Ps. cxix. 176; Luke xv. 4, 6.—**Their shepherds.** Comp. x. 21; xii. 10; xxiii. 1 sqq.—**Seductive.** The mountains may well be thus called, which by means of the worship of high-places practised upon them, exerted such an irresistible charm on the heart of carnal Israel. Comp. ii. 20; iii. 2; vi. 23; xvii. 2.—**Whoever found them.** Comp. ii. 3; x. 25; xxx. 16. In this expression there is evidently an intimation that Israel has been often devoured. The enemies had a certain degree of justification in this, but in yielding to the illusion that they could not sin against Israel, forsaken by his God, and could therefore do any thing to him, they incurred great guilt, as is seen in what follows.—**True pasturage.** Zion is called נְוֵה־צֶדֶק in xxxi. 23. Here Jehovah Himself is so called, as elsewhere a fortress (Ps. xviii. 3) sun, shield (Ps. lxxxiv. 11), shade (Ps. cxxi. 5).—**Father's hope.** Comp. xiv. 8; xvii. 13.

Vers. 8-10. **Flee . . . saith Jehovah.** The tables are turned. Babylon must now suffer the punishment of injustice. The hour of deliverance has struck for Israel and the other nations held in bondage. Hence the summons is made to Israel to flee. Comp. Isa. xlviii. 20; lii. 11; Zech. ii. 10.—**As the rams,** *etc.* The sense is not both that Israel is to press forward in order to save himself before all, but rather that it is to go before all (comp. ver. 16) as an example and leader in the flight.—**North.** Comp. rems. on ver. 3.—**Like those,** *etc.* Comp. iv. 31; xlvi. 22; NAEGELSB. *Gr.*, § 65, 3 *Anm.*—**Who returneth,** *etc.* Comp. 2 Sam. i. 22.—**Chaldea.** Kasdim as the name of the country, as in li. 24, 35; Ezek. xi. 24.—**A prey.** Comp. xlix. 32.

Vers. 11-13. **For thou rejoicedst . . . stroke.**—I take כִּי simply as "for," so that ver 11 gives the reason why Chaldea is to become a prey. The imperfects then designate the action as continuing in the past. Comp. NAEGELSB. *Gr.*, § 87 f.: Jer. xv. 9; xxxvi. 18.—Vers. 12, 13 conclude the discourse with a lively description, sketched in a few powerful strokes of the condition of Babylon after the attack predicted in vers. 9, 10. The prophet beholds this as though it had been produced in his presence. Hence the perfects **is put to shame, and blushes** (xv. 9). Observe that the prophet here addresses the single individuals of the nation. Hence **your** mother and *last of the nations.* Comp. Ps. cxxxix. 9; Am. ix. 1; Jer. xxxi. 7.—**Waste** (הִיָּה). Comp. li. 43.—**Uninhabited**. Comp. Isa. xiii. 20; Jer. xvii. 6, 25; xxx. 18.—**Whoever passeth**. Comp. xviii. 16; xix. 8; xlix. 17.

4. *The Vengeance of Jehovah.*

L. 14-16.

14 Array yourselves against Babylon round about, all ye archers,
    Shoot¹ at her, spare not² the arrows,
    For against Jehovah hath she sinned.
15 Cry against her round about!
    She stretches forth³ her hand;
    Fallen are her bastions,⁴
    Thrown down are her walls.
    For Jehovah's vengeance it is.
    Avenge yourselves on her!
    As she hath done, do also unto her.
16 Exterminate the sower from Babylon,
    And him that handleth the sickle at the time of harvest.
    Before the destroying sword let every one turn to his people,
    And every one flee into his own land.

TEXTUAL AND GRAMMATICAL.

¹ Ver. 14.—ידוּ. The Kal here only. Elsewhere Piel only occurs; Joel iv. 3; Obad. 11; Nah. iii. 10; Lam. iii. 53, Zech. ii. 4.

² Ver. 14.—חָמַל with אֶל, as in li. 3; Isa. ix. 18.

³ Ver. 15.—Owing to the animation of style, the perfects are without the connecting Vau. Comp. Josh. vi. 5, 10, 16, 20; 1 Sam. xvii. 20.

⁴ Ver. 15.—אֲשׁוּיֹתֶיהָ or אָשְׁיֹתֶיהָ (Chethibh) occurs here only. Likewise the form of the Keri אָשְׁיֹתֶיהָ. The root appears to be אָשָׁה, from which at most in Hebrew the proper name אַשְׁיָה is derived. Related, however, is וֻּשָׁשׁ, to be strong, firm (Arab. assa) from which אָשִׁישׁ (Isa. xvi. 7) the foundation-walls and the Aram. אֻשִּׁין plur. אֻשִּׁין (Ezr. iv. 12; v. 16; vi. 3), which the prophet chose purposely. Comp. ver. 23. From the radical meaning "to be strong," may also be derived that of fortification, defence, bastion.

EXEGETICAL AND CRITICAL.

This picture is a supplement to the foregoing, and a further delineation of particular features. (a) The attack is described more in detail (vers. 14. 15 a); (b) the connection between the fall of Babylon and its malignant pride (ver. 11) traced through the idea of recompense and vengeance of Jehovah (vers. 14 b, 15 b); and (c) the desolation of Babylon, described generally in vers. 12, 13, is rendered more palpable in ver. 16 by the setting forth of single characteristic features.

Vers. 14, 15. **Array ... unto her.**—Array evidently refers to **equip** (עִרְכוּ), ver. 9, but as the attack was only ordered there in general, the manner of it is here more specially designated. Comp. ver. 29; xlvi. 9.—Both these verses correspond exactly in their structure. Each begins with a summons to attack, and closes with a causal sentence of the purport that this warlike proceeding is an act of Jehovah's vengeance. Yet there is a gradation in the two, for while in ver. 14 the attack is described in only its first stage, ver. 15 brings before us the last decisive storm in the words **Cry against her**, which has the surrender for its immediate consequence. That the words are to be understood in this sense, seems to me clear from **round about**. Comp. ver. 14. The triumphant cry sounds not from the environs, but from within the city.—**Stretches forth her hand**. This is a token of subjection. *Det manus vincique se patiatur*. CICERO, *De Amic. Cap. 26 fin*. Comp. 2 Chron. xxx. 8; Lam. v. 6.—**For Jehovah's**, *etc.* This point also is here expressed more strongly than in ver. 14 b, and thus forms the transition from ver. 14 to the threatening of judgment. Babylon has called forth the vengeance of Jehovah by its malicious pleasure and arrogant violence. Comp. ver. 28; li. 6, 11, 36; xlvi. 10.—**As she hath done**. Comp. ver. 29; Ps. cxxxvii. 8; Rev. xviii. 6, 7.

Ver. 16. **Exterminate ... his own land**. This verse also specializes a general idea expressed in the previous context, *viz.*, that of desolation, and this from two points of view. It is first said that what had hitherto been an ornament of the city, and had increased their power of resistance, viz., the fields inside the walls (Diod. Sic., II. 9; Curt. v. 4; Plin. Hist. Nat., XVIII. 17), will be given up to desolation for lack of men. It is evident that the prophet had these fields within the city in view from the fact that he is describing the siege of the *city* of Babylon throughout. Then, however, he predicts the flight of all who are not Babylonians (for the Babylonians will fall by the sword), Israel at their head (ver. 8). Comp. xlvi. 16; Isa. xiii. 14.

—**Destroying sword.** Comp. xxv. 38; xlvi. 16. In the latter passage the LXX. translates as here, μάχαιρα ἑλληνική, which Theodoret explains: πρὸ τῆς Βαβυλῶνος Λυδοὺς ὁ Κῦρος κατεστρέψατο καὶ Ἴωνας καὶ Αἰολίας. Another explanation is given by WALTON (*Polyglott*, Lond., Tom. 1., pag. 47. Introd.): *Ira columbae* (xxv. 38), *gladius columbae designant iram et gladium Chaldæorum, in quorum labaro erat columba argentea pennis inauratis Semiramidem repræsentans.*

---

5. *The Happy Turn.*

L. 17-20.

17 A scattered sheep is Israel, which the lions chased.[1]
 First the king of Assyria devoured him,
 And last this Nebuchadnezzar king of Babylon hath broken his bones.[2]
18 Therefore thus saith Jehovah Zebaoth, the God of Israel;
 Behold, I visit the king of Babylon and his land
 As I have visited the king of Assyria.
19 And I bring Israel home to his pasturage,
 To pasture on Carmel and Bashan,
 And on mount Ephraim and Gilead his soul shall be satisfied.
20 In those days, at that time, saith Jehovah,
 The iniquity of Israel shall be sought for,[3]—and it is gone!
 And the sins of Judah—but thou findest them not.[4]
 For I will pardon him whom I reserve.

TEXTUAL AND GRAMMATICAL.

[1] Ver. 17.—This is to be regarded as a relative sentence with אֲשֶׁר understood. Comp. NAEGELSB. *Gr.*, § 80, 6.

[2] Ver. 17.—עִצְּמוֹ here only. It is formed like דִּשֵּׁן, denominative from עֶצֶם. As this signifies "to strip off, to gnaw off" (Num. xxiv. 8; Ezek. xxiii. 34), so the former means "to bone, to destroy the bones."

[3] Ver. 20.—וגו׳ יְבֻקַּשׁ אֶת־עֲוֹן. Comp. xxxi. 34; xxxiii. 8; xxxvi. 3. In regard to the construction comp. NAEGELSB. *Gr.*, § 100, 2.

[4] Ver. 20.—תִּמָּצֶאנָה. Comp. OLSH., § 265, c.

EXEGETICAL AND CRITICAL.

Hitherto Israel has been a poor frightened sheep, driven and devoured by two mighty wild animals, Assyria and Babylon (ver. 17); but the tables are to be turned. Assyria has already received its chastisement. That of Babylon will not be deferred (ver. 18). Then will Israel again feed peaceably on his own pasture (ver. 19). The reason of this wonderful change consists in this, that the Lord will show kindness to His people and forgive them all their iniquity (ver. 20).

Vers. 17-19. **A scattered . . . be satisfied.** Assyria destroyed the northern, Babylon the southern kingdom. In both cases the destruction was complete, and consequently represented by the figure of devouring, only with this difference that as a still higher degree the breaking of the bones is mentioned in the second case. After the destruction of the kingdom of the ten tribes the kingdom of Judah still remained as the skeleton of the theocracy. In destroying Jerusalem and the temple Nebuchadnezzar, as it were, broke its bones.—**As I have visited.** Comp. xlvi. 25. The then already long past destruction of Nineveh is thus the type and place of the destruction of Babylon.—**Bring Israel home.** Comp. Ezek. xxxviii. 4; xxxix. 2.—**Pasturage.** Comp. xxiii. 3; xxii. 6; Mic. vii. 14; Isa. xxxiii. 9; Nah. i. 4; Ezek. xxxiv. 13, 14.

Ver. 20. **In those days . . . reserve.** Comp. ver. 4. As in the mention of Assyria and Babylon, vers. 17, 18, there was a reference to the community of the two halves of the theocratic nation in misfortune, so here their union in prosperity is expressly set forth. Comp. rems. on ver. 4. The reason of their restoration to prosperity is here mentioned; Jehovah's grace which will grant forgiveness to the survivors, and cause their guilt to disappear without a trace.

6. One Hammer crushed by the Other.

L. 21-23.

21 Against the land of DOUBLE-DEFIANCE;[1]
    Go up against it and against the inhabitants of VISITATION!
    Slay[2] and burn after them, saith Jehovah,
    And do according to all that I commanded thee!
22 Cry of war in the land and great ruin!
23 How is the hammer of the whole earth crushed and broken!
    How is Babylon become a horror of desolation among the nations!

TEXTUAL AND GRAMMATICAL.

[1] Ver. 21.—EWALD has well remarked that the word כְּרָתַיִם is used in antithesis to אֲרַם־נַהֲרַיִם, Mesopotamia. Not Double-river, but Double-defiance (comp. Zweibrücken [*Bipontes*] in Germany) was to be Babylon's title. For similar names comp. *e. g.*, Mic. i. 10. The word does not occur elsewhere. It may be derived from כְּרִי, although the mention of Israel by this name (Ezek. ii. 7; xliv. 6) may be regarded as analogous to, or an imitation of (comp. פְּקוֹד, ver. 21, and Ezek. xxiii. 23) this expression. A singular כָּרָה from מְרָה, *rebellis fuit*, also does not occur. כְּרָתַיִם is a new form made by the prophet. FUERST would derive it from כָּרָה, to which he ascribes the meaning of "lordship." But the analogies מוֹרָה (Job xxxvi. 22; Aram. בָּרָא, כַּר), כְּרֹתִים (Mic. i. 12) are very uncertain, and admit of another explanation. The word כָּרָה, *rebellis fuit*, is always used elsewhere of Israel, but this limitation of the use is not necessarily founded in the radical signification. There is no reason then why a word formed from the root, new and specially *ad hoc*, should not be applied in another case. In regard to the dual it is ungrammatical to attribute to it the significance of a climax, which it never has elsewhere.

[2] Ver. 21.—חֲרֹב a denominative from חֶרֶב. Comp. ver. 27; 2 Ki. iii. 23.

EXEGETICAL AND CRITICAL.

A complete picture, the specific element of which is the prophet's showing how the Lord sends a chosen instrument to crush Babylon, which has hitherto served Him as such in the chastisement of mankind. In brief but powerful lines be described the summons to the instrument (ver. 21), the execution of the commission (ver. 22), the result (ver. 23).

Vers. 21-23. **Against the land ... among the nations.** What is meant by the *double* defiance it is difficult to say. We may regard it not inappropriately as the double visitation of the theocratic nation by Assyria and Babylon (vers. 17, 18). The name, however, is given only to Babylon, which according to this view represents only half the defiance. The connection seems to require an interpretation according to which Babylon itself receives the whole reproach, and here, as it seems to me, two points may be observed: 1. The defiance which Babylon manifested both towards man and God, in revolting against the king of Assyria its master, and in sinning against Jehovah by its arrogant demeanor towards Israel. 2. The double defiance, which Babylon manifested in the earliest period in the erection of the tower of Babel and the founding of the first worldly kingdom (Gen. x. 8 sqq.), and in later times by its behaviour towards the theocracy. I formerly inclined to the latter view, but now give the former the preference, because it is more natural and presents more clearly the element of doubleness. For the sin of Babylon against the Lord in earlier and more recent times is too entirely one and the same for it to be represented as a double one.—**Against it.** Comp. ver. 3. The singular appears to me to be due to a different reason from that in ver. 3, for there we find גּוֹי, nation, which according to what follows is to be taken as collective. Here, however, the subject is left indefinite. This is the more surprising, as previously the enemies of Babylon are always called upon in the plural (vers. 14-16). When then in the following ver. 23 Babylon is designated as the crushed hammer, *i. e.* as the instrument of Jehovah, which He Himself has destroyed, is it not most natural to regard as the subject of the imperative in ver. 21 the instrument of which the Lord will make use in the destruction of His former instrument? Then, however, it is natural to place over against the Babylonian *hammer* (פַּטִּישׁ, comp. GROTIUS *ad loc.*), *viz.*, Nebuchadnezzar, another *hammer*, *i. e.* over against the already known and mentioned (ver. 17) representative of the first empire, the representative (certainly only sometimes present in idea) of the other empire called to its destruction. Comp. li. 20.—**Visitation** is also a name formed *ad hoc*, and given to Babylon in antithesis to its double-defiance, which deserves visitation. Thus the former name designates Babylon's guilt, the latter its punishment. Comp. vers. 18 and 31 and Ezek. xxiii. 23, which passage is based on this. Comp. HAEVERNICK on the passage.—**Burn.** Comp. xxv. 9.—**Cry of war**, *etc.* Comp. iv. 6; vi. 1; xiv. 17; xlviii. 3; li. 54.—**How**, *etc.* Comp. Isa. xiv. 12; Jer li. 20, 41.

7. *Babylon surprised and destroyed, Israel liberated.*

L. 24–28.

24 I have placed¹ a net for thee and thou art also taken,
  O Babylon, and thou knowest it not.
  Thou art found and also caught,
  For against Jehovah hast thou striven.²
25 Jehovah hath opened his arsenal,
  And brought forth the weapons of his wrath ;
  For the LORD Jehovah Zebaoth hath a work in the land of the Chaldeans.
26 Come hither even the last, open her storehouses,³
  Cast it up as heaps of rubbish and burn it,⁴
  Let there be nothing left of it.
27 Slay all her bullocks,
  Down with them to the slaughter-house!
  Woe unto them, for their day is come,
  The time of their visitation.
28 Hark! the fleeing and escaped from the land of Babylon,
  To proclaim in Zion the vengeance of Jehovah, our God,
  The vengeance of his sanctuary.

TEXTUAL AND GRAMMATICAL.

¹ Ver. 24.—The verb יקשׁ is not found elsewhere in Jeremiah. But compare נוֹקָשׁ, v. 26.
² Ver. 24.—הִתְגָּרִית. This word does not occur elsewhere in Jeremiah. Comp. Deut. ii. 5, 19, 24 ; Prov. xxviii. 4
³ Ver. 26.—כָּאֳבֻסֶיהָ. This word is ἅπ. λεγ.
⁴ Ver. 26.—The suffix in כְּלוּהָ and הַחֲרִימֻהָ may be referred to the land or more fitly to the contents of the storehouses. Comp. xxxiii. 2, 3 ; NAEGELSB. *Gr.*, § 60, 6, b.

EXEGETICAL AND CRITICAL.

In this picture the element of secrecy and surprise as excluding all resistance, which will prevail at the capture of Babylon, is made prominent (ver. 24). This mode of capture is rendered possible by the Lord's having opened His armory and brought into use all the means of attack which it affords. He has done this because He would manage the business with Babylon as a matter of the highest importance (ver. 25). As now, however, the Lord has emptied His arsenal *against* Babylon, so also shall all store-houses in Babylon be emptied and all living and dead treasures contained therein be destroyed (vers. 26, 27). The escaped of Zion, however, shall bring home the joyful tidings of Jehovah's vengeance (ver. 28). We see that these verses also furnish a complete picture progressing from the beginning to the close with special prominence of single specific elements.

Ver. 24. **I have placed . . . striven.** In this placing of a net or snare lies the element of commencement on account of which we regard this verse as the commencement of a new picture. This must be so the rather as ver. 23 evidently contains a conclusion. The prophet in spirit sees Babylon unexpectedly caught in a net or snare. How literally this would be fulfilled Jeremiah himself might have no idea (comp. 1 Pet. i. 11). Twice was Babylon taken by stratagem, and both times so that the city was in the power of its enemies, before it was aware. Herodotus says (I. 191), with reference to the capture by Cyrus, that if the Babylonians had known or observed his plan (the diversion of the Euphrates) they could have inflicted great injury on the Persians. But these came upon them quite unexpectedly (ἐξ ἀπροσδοκήτου σφι παρίστησαν οἱ Πέρσαι), the outer parts of the city being already taken before those who dwelt in the central parts had observed what was going on (τοὺς τὸ μέσον οἰκέοντος οὐ μανθάνειν ἑαλωκότας). With reference to the capture by Darius Hystaspis, however, he says (III. 158) that a part of the Babylonians, who saw the entrance of the Persians through the gate opened by Zopyrus, fled, the rest remaining every one in his place till they also perceived that they were betrayed (ἐς ὃ δὴ καὶ οὗτοι ἔμαθον προδεδομένοι).

Vers. 25-28. **Jehovah . . . sanctuary.** The capture of a city like Babylon by an overwhelming surprise is not possible without great means. Such are now provided by Jehovah, for He opens His arsenal (comp. x. 13 ; li. 16) to take from it all necessary implements of war (comp. Isa. xiii. 5). This He does because He has a מְלָאכָה, a business in the land of the Chaldeans

A business or work of Jehovah is always a great and important matter, and is therefore not to be performed negligently (xlviii. 10). To the execution of this work He now summons His servants and instruments (ver. 26), who are to come מִקֵּץ. If we refer this to the city (attacked from the end, not from the middle) the meaning is feeble and unsuitable, for a city can only be attacked from without and thus from the ends of it. If it be rendered "from all ends" (round about, vers. 15, 29) we miss the word for "all." Hence it is best to take it with EWALD and GRAF =*ad unum omnes*. If the outermost come, all come. Comp. Gen. xix. 4; xlvii. 2; Isa. lvi. 11; Ezek. xxxiii. 2. To the opening of the arsenal of Jehovah is to correspond the violent breaking open and emptying of the storehouses of Babylon.—**Slay all**, *etc*. The bullocks are the representatives and chief personages of the human population. Comp. Isa. xxxiv. 6, 7; Jer. xlviii. 15; li. 40.—**The time**, *etc*. Comp. xlvi. 21.—**Fleeing**. Comp. vers. 4, 8.—**Vengeance**. Comp. ver. 15; li. 11.

8. *The Punishment of Pride.*

L. 29–32.

29 Call against Babylon archers ;[1]
   All ye that bend the bow camp against it round about ![2]
   No escape! Recompense her according to her work,
   Just as she hath done, do ye also unto her,
   For against Jehovah was she proud,
   Against the Holy One of Israel.
30 Therefore shall her young men fall in her streets,
   And all her warriors shall be cut off in that day, saith Jehovah.
31 Behold I come to thee, O Pride, saith the Lord, Jehovah Zebaoth.
   For come is thy day, the time of thy visitation.
32 Then Pride totters and falls,
   And none helps him up ;
   And I kindle a fire in his cities,
   Which shall devour all round about.

TEXTUAL AND GRAMMATICAL.

[1] Ver. 29.—רָבִים. As there is no substantive here as in ver. 41; xvi. 16, the meaning appears to be different. Derived from רָבַב (Gen. xlix. 23; Ps. xviii. 15 *coll.* רָבָה Gen. xxi. 20) רָב is found with the meaning of "archer," also in Job xvi. 13; Prov. xxvi. 10.
[2] Ver. 29.—וְאֶל־יְהִי. The Keri unnecessarily adds ה) from ver. 26.

EXEGETICAL AND CRITICAL.

Warriors are summoned to recompense Babylon for the pride which it has manifested towards Jehovah (ver. 20). Its men shall perish (ver. 31). Thus will the Lord on the day of recompense bring their pride to totter and fall; no one will raise it up, fire will consume all its power (vers. 31, 32).
Ver. 29. **Call . . . of Israel**. *Convocatio militum initium belli*. Comp. ver. 14. הַשְׁמִיעוּ is taken by most commentators and translators in the sense of *vocare, convocare*, as in li. 27 ; 1 Ki. xv. 22 *coll.* 1 Sam. xv. 4.—**All ye**, *etc*. Comp. ver. 14.—**Recompense**, *etc*. Comp. ver. 15; xxv. 14.—**Proud**. Deserved humiliation of the pride of Babylon is predicted by earlier prophets: Isa. xiii. 11; xiv. 13 sqq.; xlvii. 7, 8; Hab. ii. 5, 8.—**Holy One of Israel**. Comp. li. 5. This expression is peculiar to Isaiah. "All Isaiah's prophecies bear this name of God as their peculiar stamp. It occurs twelve times in chh. i.-xxxix., seventeen times in chh. xl.-lxvi." DELITZSCH on Isa. vi. 3.
Vers. 30–32. **Therefore . . . round about.** Ver. 30 is repeated almost verbatim from xlix. 26. The only difference is that here we have **her warriors** for *the* warriors. The verse is not necessary, but rather disturbing, for ver. 31 is closely connected by **Pride** with ver. 29 (proud). It may have been a gloss.—**Behold I come**, *etc*. Comp. xxi. 13; xxiii. 30 sqq.; li. 25.—**Pride**. "*In nominis proprii formam transiit*." J. D. MICHAELIS.—**Thy day**. Comp. ver. 27; xlix. 8.—**Totters**, *etc*. Comp. Isa. xxxi. 3; Jer. xlvi. 6.—**I kindle**, *etc*. Comp. xxi. 14; xvii. 27; xlix. 27.—**Him** in ver. 32 refers to **Pride**.—Babylon is regarded as the metropolis. Comp. ver. 12; li. 43; ix. 10, *etc*.

9. *Israel Free, the Sword upon Babylon.*

L. 33-40.

33 Thus saith Jehovah Zebaoth:
Oppressed are the children of Israel and the children of Judah together,
And all their captors hold them fast,
They refuse to let them go.
34 Their Redeemer is strong, Jehovah Zebaoth is his name.
He will well prosecute their cause,
That he may give rest[1] to the land,
And procure disquiet to the inhabitants of Babylon.
35 A sword upon the Chaldeans, saith Jehovah,
And upon the inhabitants of Babylon,
And upon her princes and upon her wise men.
36 A sword upon the coxcombs, that they become fools,
A sword upon her heroes, that they be dismayed.
37 A sword upon their horses and their chariots,
And upon all her auxiliaries in her midst, that they become as women,
A sword upon her treasures, that they be plundered.
38 Drought[2] upon her waters, that they dry up;
For it is a land of idols,
And on objects of horror[3] they foolishly trust.
39 Therefore shall wild-beasts[4] dwell there with the jackals,[4]
And the daughters of the ostrich shall dwell there;
And never more will it be inhabited further,
Nor dwelt in from generation to generation.
40 As God overthrew Sodom and Gomorrah and their neighbors, saith Jehovah,
A man shall not dwell there,
Nor a son of man sojourn in her.

TEXTUAL AND GRAMMATICAL.

[1] Ver. 34.—On the Infinitive form הַרְגִּיעַ comp. OLSH., § 192 f.; EWALD, § 238 d.

[2] Ver. 38.—The Masoretes read בְּחָרֶב evidently because חֶרֶב, sword, does not apply to water. The idea of a sword may, however, be used by synecdoche for war (comp. xi. 6) or חֶרֶב may have a double meaning. Not a few exegetes assume for Deut. xxviii. 22 a word, חֹרֶב, derived from חָרֵב, with the meaning "drought, dryness." Comp. FUERST s. v. חֹרֶב.

[3] Ver. 38.—אֵימִים is used for "idols" here only. Comp. Gen. xiv. 5; Deut. ii. 10, 11; Ps. lxxxviii. 16; Job xx. 25. [In Ps. lxxxviii. 16 the word is translated "terrors."]

[4] Ver. 39.—צִיִּים (in Jeremiah here only, comp. besides Ps. lxxii. 9; Dan. xi. 30) from צִי, *desertum*, are inhabitants of the desert, especially wild beasts. אִיִּים from אִי (אִיָּה to *howl*, comp. DELITZSCH on Isa. xiii. 21) are jackals. Ibn-Awi is the Arabic name for jackal. Our translation "Stuhlen and Uhus" [horned owls], is based on formal grounds. [UMBREIT and BLAYNEY read "wild-cats and jackals" or "wild-dogs." HITZIG as in the text.—S. R. A.]

EXEGETICAL AND CRITICAL.

Proceeding from the condition of bondage in which Judah and Israel are found (ver. 33), the prophet predicts deliverance by the strong hand of Jehovah (ver. 34), which to Babylon signifies destruction of all that supports its power and glory: the inevitable fate of an idolatrous people (vers. 35-38). In consequence of this Babylonia will become a deserted and horrible waste (vers. 39, 40).

Vers. 33, 34. **Thus saith ... inhabitants of Babylon.** The prophet, who knows the exile of Israel as an accomplished fact and has predicted for years the exile of Judah as impending, may well describe Judah and Israel as oppressed, held fast by their captors (שֹׁבִים, *captivatores*, Isa. xiv. 2; 1 Ki. viii. 46 sqq.; Ps. cxxxvii. 3). It is the same thought which lies at the foundation of the summons to flight (ver. 8 coll. vers. 4 and 28).—**They refuse,** etc. As Pharaoh, Exod. vii. 14-27; ix. 2.—The strong captor is, however, opposed by a still stronger deliverer of Israel,—Jehovah. With the exception of the words "Jehovah Zebaoth is His name" (x. 16; xxxi. 35; xxxii. 18; xxxiii. 2), the first half of ver. 34 is taken from Prov

xxiii. 11 coll. xxii. 23; Isa. xlvii. 4; xlviii. 20. —That he may give rest, etc. Since it may be appropriately declared of Babylon, as the "hammer of the whole earth," ver. 23, that it has disquieted the earth (Isa. xiv. 16), and that consequently its disquieting must contribute to the peace of the earth, I agree with those who take הַרְגִּיעַ in its usual meaning, "to make rest, quiet" (Deut. xxviii. 65; Isa. xxxiv. 14; li. 4; Jer. xxxi. 2).

Vers. 35-38. A sword ... foolishly trust. In these verses it is specially shown how the Lord will conduct His cause with Babylon an I bring disquiet upon it. The sword is as it were cited to exercise the office of avenger, both in general and in particular. For as its objects are designated: 1. the Chaldeans in general; 2. the inhabitants of the capital, with the resident princes, wise men (counsellors of the king), Magians (בַּדִּים, "talk, chattering," xlviii. 30; Isa. xvi. 6; Job xi. 3; here personally the lying prophets, astrologers, Isa. xlv. 25, comp. DELITZSCH ad loc.; xlvii. 13, xix. 13) and warriors; 3. horses, chariots and auxiliaries (xxv. 20; comp. NIEBUHR, Ass. u. Bab., S. 206 Anm. 2 and the article "Griechen" in the Register S. 519; li. 30); 4. treasures and water, on which last the power and safety of Babylon in great measure depended. (Comp. li. 13, 36; Isa. xxi. 1 and DELITZSCH ad loc.).—For it is a land, etc. This sentence corresponds to ver. 34. As there the positive reason of the destruction breaking over Babylon is stated, so here the negative. The positive ground is the strength of Jehovah (הָזָק, ver. 34), the negative is the powerlessness of the idols. Comp. li. 47, 52.—Foolishly trust. The prefix בְּ [on] may designate either the means and instrument, or the supporting or moving reason. The former yields the conception that the idol-images served as the instruments of mad behaviour, the latter that they were the ground thereof. Without doubt the latter is the more correct. The senseless, inflated, arrogant behaviour of the Babylonians was supported by their belief in idols. Comp. נָבָא with בְּ in ii. 8 and the Greek μαίνεσθαι ὑπὸ τοῦ θεοῦ. HEROD. IV. 79.

Vers. 39, 40. Therefore shall ... sojourn in her. The first half of ver. 39 is composed of reminiscences from Isaiah (Isa. xiii. 21, 22; xxxiv. 14). The second half of the verse is taken verbatim from Isa. xiii. 20. Comp. ver. 13; xvii. 6. Ver. 40 is a repetition of xlix. 18, but taken originally from Isa. xiii. 19 coll. Am. iv. 11. The original passage on which all these prophetic utterances are based is Deut. xxix. 22.—Comp. xlix. 33; li. 43.

10. *Non tu, sed tibi.*

L. 41-46.

41 Behold, a people cometh from the north,
And a great host and many kings break up from the ends of the earth.
42 Bow and lance they bear,
Cruel are they[1] and without compassion.
Their sound roareth like the sea,
And on horses they ride equipped like a man for the battle
Against thee, thou daughter of Babylon.
43 The king of Babylon hath heard the report of them,
And his hands are feeble;
Anguish hath seized him, trembling as a parturient.
44 Behold, like a lion he ascends
From the pride of Jordan to the evergreen pasturage,
For in a twinkling I drive her[2] from thence,
And—who is chosen? Him I set over her.
For who is like me, and who will order me?
And who is the shepherd who may stand before me?
45 Therefore hear the counsel of Jehovah that he hath counselled against Babylon,
And his thoughts which he hath thought against the land of the Chaldeans:
Yea, they will be dragged away, the weak little sheep,
Yea, the pasturage will be amazed concerning them.
46 With the cry, "Babylon is taken," the earth trembles,
And a crying is heard[3] among the nations.

TEXTUAL AND GRAMMATICAL.

[1] Ver. 42.—אֵבוּרִי הֵכֵה. Comp. NAEGELSN. *Gr.*, § 105, 4, *b*, 2.
[2] Ver. 44.—אֱרֹצָם is probably only a mistake, and is therefore to be read with the Keri אֱרִיצָם (comp. אַצְרִיגוּ xlix. 19).
[3] Ver. 46.—נִשְׁמַע) is occasioned by xlix. 21, and moreover comp. NAEGELSN. *Gr.*, § 60, 4.

EXEGETICAL AND CRITICAL.

This entire passage consists of quotations, vers. 41-43 being taken from vi. 22-24, vers. 44-46 from xlix. 19-21. As the prophet has already repeatedly designated the enemy as one coming from the north, it was natural to apply the former prophecy of the enemy threatening Judah from the north to Babylon, and it must also be admitted that the prophet would find it appropriate to transfer the prophecy of the chosen instrument for the destruction of Edom (xlix. 19-21) to the similarly chosen instrument of the destruction of Babylon. Although thus the quotations here are accumulated to a degree greater than heretofore, I am yet convinced (contrary to my former view in *Der proph. Jer. u. Bab.*, *S*. 128 ff.) that the passage is genuine and original. The idea of the unity of God's judgments and of just recompense was to be represented here. This would receive no detriment, even if every single feature of the former prophecies did not seem adapted to be applied to Babylon. This, however, is not the case, for we find in the text such modifications as the application to Babylon required; daughter of Babylon, ver. 42; King of Babylon, ver. 43; against Babylon and the land of the Chaldeans, ver. 45; Babylon is taken, ver. 46; among the nations, for, in the Red Sea, ver. 46. What is not altered is not then opposed, according to the author's judgment, to its application to Babylon. The figure in ver. 44 *a* is therefore not inappropriate. The pride of Jordan and evergreen pasturage belong to the picture. The lion, which, from the reed-thickets on the Jordan, falls upon the flocks feeding near the bank (comp. rems. on xlix. 19), is a figure which may be applied to any case of overpowering hostile attack. Likewise the description of the northern people (vi. 23) is by no means so special that it may not be applied to any people advancing with warlike impetuosity. Moreover, Jeremiah, when he wrote vi. 22-24, neither had the Chaldeans specially in view, nor are they so very different from their neighbors, the Medes.

The addition **and many kings** in ver. 41 is thus explained, that in the conception of the prophet the picture was present of a host of enemies, composed of many different elements (comp. li. 27, 28).

---

11. *The Heart of the insurgents, the Fanners and the Inviduate.*

LI. 1-6.

1 Thus saith Jehovah:
 Behold, I raise up against Babylon,
 And against the inmates of the heart of my insurgents
 A destroying wind.[1]
2 And I sent unto Babylon fanners,[2]
 Who shall fan it and empty out its land,
 For upon it are they from all sides in the day of calamity.
3 Against him that bendeth let the archer bend his bow,
 And against him who lifteth himself up[3] in his harness,[4]
 And spare ye not her young men,
 Banish ye the entire host.
4 That the slain fall in the land of the Chaldeans,
 And the pierced through in her streets.
5 For Israel and Judah are not widows[5] from their God,[6] Jehovah Zebaoth,
 But their land is full of guilt on account of the Holy One of Israel.
6 Flee out of Babylon, and let every man deliver his soul;
 Let not destruction come upon you through their sin.
 For it is a time of vengeance for Jehovah,
 He rendereth recompense unto her.

TEXTUAL AND GRAMMATICAL.

1 Ver. 1.—רֻחַ as masc. also in Exod. x. 13; Ps. li. 12; Eccles. i. 6, מַשְׁחִית, comp. ver. 25; li. 30; v. 26.

2 Ver. 2.—זָרִים. The analogy of xlviii. 12 seems to require the punctuation זָרִים. זָרִים is very troublesome. Although violence by strangers is spoken of in many places (comp. ver. 51), this idea does not at all suit this connection, and the frequent occurrence of זָרִים while זָרִים is not found elsewhere (only זֵרוּ occurs in Ruth iii. 2), may indeed have occasioned the Masoretic punctuation, unless זָרִים itself may be taken as Part. Kal. after the analogy of הָרָה הָרָה, יָרֵא, מָלֵא, etc. (comp. Olsn., §245, a).

3 Ver. 3.—וְאַל־יִתְעַל. This is the main difficulty in ver. 3. For, 1. this Hithp. form does not occur elsewhere, 2. the abbreviated Imperfect form, if the word comes from עָלָה, is surprising. According to the laws of the Hebrew language, however, יִתְעַל can come only from עָלָה (comp. Olsn., §269, d). It must then signify "lift one's self up." Then the abbreviated form is strange, which might be in place after אַל, but not after אֶל. I do not think, however, that we need be so scrupulous in the matter. As in Jeremiah (and elsewhere) the full form stands where we should expect the abbreviated (comp. iii. 7; Ew., §224, c), so may the latter stand where we should expect the former. Comp. Jer. xvii. 8, Chethibh; Ewald, §224, c, Anm.; Ges., §123, 2, Anm. Then the rest, according to the reading of the Chethibh, affords no difficulty. With respect to the absence of the nota relationis, comp. 1 Chron. xv. 12; Naegelsb. Gr., § 80, 6, 2, a.

4 Ver. 3.—כְּרִי. Comp. xlvi. 4; Ewald, § 49, d.

5 Ver. 5.—The masc. אַלְמָן here only—to be regarded as neuter. Comp. שָׁדוּד, iv. 30.

6 Ver. 5.—מֵאֱלֹהָיו. Pregnant construction. Comp. Naegelsb. Gr., § 112, 7.

EXEGETICAL AND CRITICAL.

Babylon, the heart of Jehovah's opponents, shall be fanned like chaff (vers. 1, 2). Without a figure; a strong, warlike power shall cast down Babylon (vers. 3, 4). For Israel and Judah are not forsaken widows; rather shall they be delivered and Jehovah's vengeance executed on Babylon (vers. 5, 6).—The passage thus consists of two halves: vers. 1-4, and vers. 5, 6. In the first half the judgment on Babylon is announced, (a) under the figure of fanning, vers. 1, 2; (b) in unfigurative language, vers. 3, 4. The second half is related to the first as a statement of the reason (**For**, ver. 5). The judgment, namely, is impending, because the Lord will show Himself a faithful husband with respect to Israel, a righteous recompenser with respect to Babylon.

Vers. 1, 2. **Thus saith ...... calamity.** Whether קָמַי לֵב [heart of my insurgents] is to be explained by the Atbash [or principle of alphabetical inversion, according to which it is equivalent to Casdim, the Chaldeans] is doubtful, for the expression might be used by the prophet without any reference to that permutation of letters. As he called Babylon Double-defiance and Visitation in l. 21 and Pride in l. 31, so might he call it Heart-of-my-insurgents. This designation was a natural one. It is founded in the significance which the idea of Babylon has in the consciousness of the entire Old and New Testament prophecy. For though it is only in the Apocalypse that Babylon is distinctly set forth as the comprehensive centre of all and every hostility to the Lord and His kingdom (comp. Naegelsb. Jer. u. Bab., S. 10 ff.), this representation is rooted in the views of the Old Testament prophets concerning Babylon, and we shall not err if we regard this passage as the chief basis of this conception of Babylon by the New Testament revelator, according to which it is declared to be the "Mother of harlots and abominations of the earth" (Rev. xvii. 5). Still it is remarkable that the name כַּשְׂדִּים should form,

according to the Cabbalistic play upon words, an expression with a suitable meaning (comp. Buxtorf, Lex. Chald., p. 248, 9; Herzog, Real-Enc., VII., S. 205). The expression הֵעִיר רוּחַ signifies indeed everywhere else (ver. 11; Hagg. i. 14; Ezr. i. 1, 5; 1 Chron. v. 26; 2 Chron. xxi. 16; xxxvi. 22) "to awaken, excite the spirit." But the expression is not necessarily restricted to this meaning. In this passage where fanning is spoken of, the context requires the meaning "wind." It seems that the expression first began to come into use in the time of Jeremiah, for previously it does not occur. It is however quite natural that a mode of expression still in its formative state should at first waver in its signification. Only when it has become fixed by long usage in a definite sense can it no longer be taken in another sense without misapprehension.—**Who shall fan.** Comp. xlix. 32, 36.—**And empty.** Comp. xix. 1, 7; Isa. xxiv. 1; Nah. ii. 3. Here the prophet passes from the figurative to the literal mode of speech, for the fanning will consist in just this, that the land will be emptied, men and property being carried away.—**For upon it,** etc. Comp. iv. 17; xvii. 17, 18.

Vers. 3-6. **Against him ..... unto her—Spare not,** etc. Comp. Isa. xiii. 18; Jer. l. 14.—Fall, etc. Comp. vers. 47, 49, 52; xxxvii. 10; Isa. xiii. 15.—**Not widows,** etc. Comp. Isa. l. 1; liv. 4-6; Lam. i. 1.—**Their** is to be referred to Babylon. The sense of this half of the verse is: it might appear as if the Lord were better disposed towards Babylon than Israel, because the latter is a captive in the power of the former. It is not so. Babylonia is laden with guilt with respect to Jehovah, and is therefore under the curse of the Holy One of Israel. I do not see what there is unlike Jeremiah in this verse. That אָשָׁם for guilt does not occur elsewhere in Jeremiah is nothing to the point. The occurrence of the expression **Holy One of Israel** here, as in l. 29, is not strange in view of the frequent quotations from Isaiah. With respect to the connection with the preceding and following contexts, however, it should be mentioned that ver. 5 in an exceedingly appropriate manner gives a double reason for the announcement contained in vers. 1-4: 1. a negative one (Israel is not rejected); 2. a positive one (Babylon is full of guilt). Ver. 5 is also connected with ver. 6 in two ways: 1. as an integral part of the entire discourse, vers. 1-5, in so far that ver. 6 draws the inference from all that has gone before (vers. 1-5); 2. specially by the words, "Let not destruction come upon you through their sin," which apparently refer to "their land is full of guilt."—**Flee**, *etc.* Comp. Isa. xiii. 14; xlviii. 20; Jer. xlviii. 6; 1. 8.—**Let not**, *etc.* Comp. xlix. 26; l. 30—Gen. xix. 15.—**For it is a time**, *etc.* Comp. Isa. xxxiv. 8; Jer. xlvi. 10; l. 15, 28; li. 11—Rev. xviii. 4.—**Vengeance**, *etc.* Comp. Joel iv. 4; Isa. lix. 18; lxvi. 6; Prov. xix. 17; Ps. cxxxvii. 8.

12. *The golden Cup broken.*

LI. 7-10.

7   A golden cup was Babylon in the hand of Jehovah,
    Which made all the earth drunken:
    Of its wine have nations drunk,
    And nations have become mad.
8   Suddenly is Babylon fallen and shattered!
    Howl over her, take balsam for her pain,
    If so be she may be healed.
9   We have healed[1] Babylon, but she was not healed:
    Forsake her and let us go each into his own country:
    For her judgment reacheth[2] unto heaven,
    And towers up even to the clouds.
10 "Jehovah hath brought forth our righteous works:
    Come and let us declare in Zion the work of Jehovah, our God."

TEXTUAL AND GRAMMATICAL.

[1] Ver. 9.—The perf. רְפָאנוּ is to be understood *de conatu.* Comp. NAEGELSB. *Gr.*, § 100, 4, *Anm.* 2.

[2] Ver. 9.—On נָגַע specially comp. iv. 10, 18.

EXEGETICAL AND CRITICAL.

These verses also contain a picture complete in itself. For the prophet shows us first Babylon at the height of its power, when it was like a golden cup, in which Jehovah gave the nations the wine of His wrath to drink (ver. 7). Now the parts are changed. Babylon is itself "a sick man," and the prophet therefore calls upon the nations that have become tributary to him to give him medicine (ver. 8). These answer that they had tried this in vain, and mutually expect each other to flee from the common prison (ver. 9). Israel is one among these nations, and therefore calls upon those who belong to it to journey home, and in their home declare the mighty acts of the Lord in the deliverance and justification of His people (ver. 10). We see that the discourse is dramatically arranged, and as to its purport, proceeds from the height and greatness of Babylon to its fall.

Vers. 7, 8. **A golden cup ... be healed.** The prophet had here xxv. 15 in mind. That which in l. 23 and li. 20 is expressed by the figure of the hammer is expressed here by the figure of the cup, except that in the hammer the element of irresistible power, in the golden cup that of pride and glory, is more prominent. The cup, however, is "in the hand of Jehovah." It is therefore Jehovah's instrument, and what it bestows is the gift of Jehovah. From the effect of this gift we see that its object was punishment. The nations are intoxicated by it, and become like mad (comp. xxv. 16). This figure portrays the overwhelming fulness of destructive effect which they were obliged to receive.—Comp. Rev. xvii. 2, 4.—[Babylon, "like a fair harlot, has bewitched thee with the love potions of her idolatries." WORDSWORTH. The same image is used in the Apocalypse. Comp. also DOCTRINAL NOTE No. 17.—S. R. A.]—Now Babylon itself is thrown down, shattered, sick unto death. The expression "**Babylon is fallen**" seems to be taken from Isa. xxi. 9. Comp. Rev. xiv. 8; xviii. 2. The figure of the cup is abandoned gradually. It is still perceived in the word **shattered**, but the balsam and the pain presuppose a living organism. Those who are called upon must be the same who afterwards speak, vers. 9, 10. It is the nations conquered and held in captivity by Babylon which speak, among them Israel. They are the same who were spoken of in l. 8, 16. These are summoned to heal Babylon, because they are now his servants, and thus obligated to render him assistance.—**Balsam.** Comp. xlvi. 11, viii. 22.

Vers. 9, 10. **We have healed .. our God.**

Those who are called upon do not refuse to render the service. but this is shown to be in vain. They express this after having made the attempt, and hence the perfect tense—vi. 14; xv. 18; xvii. 14. They thus express that in the service of Babylon they have honestly done what they could for its deliverance. As all their attempts have proved vain, they think of their own safety by flight into their native lands. Comp. Isaiah xiii. 14; Jer. xlvi. 16.—The reason why Babylon was not to be helped lies in the immensurable greatness of the evil which has come upon it. The punitive judgment advances upon them so overpoweringly that it reaches even to the sky. Comp. Ps. xxxvi. 6; vii. 11; cviii. 5.—Israel, who is especially benefited by the breaking of the prison, rejoices above all that his honor is saved, that he has not everlastingly disappeared and perished as something entirely bad, but is still preserved as good for something. We might be tempted to take righteous works (תִּקְצָה) in the sense of "salvation" (comp. Isa. lxii. 1), but the plural is opposed to such a rendering. For though the "righteousnesses of Jehovah" are spoken of in the sense of "saving acts" (comp. Jud. v. 11; Ps. ciii. 6) the righteousness of Israel, which the Lord has brought to light, cannot well be other than such facts as render manifest that Israel is still worthy the honor of being the people of Jehovah (comp. Is. lxii. 2). Comp. Ps. xxxvii. 6; Jer. l. 20.

---

13. *The triple Threatening.*

LI. 11–14.

11 Sharpen[1] the arrows, fill the shields![2]
Jehovah hath awakened the spirit of the kings of Media,
For his mind is against Babylon to destroy it;
For the vengeance of Jehovah it is,
The vengeance of his sanctuary.
12 Against the walls of Babylon raise standards,
Strengthen the watch, appoint watchmen,
Lay the ambush!
For as Jehovah hath thought so also hath he done—
All that he hath spoken against the inhabitants of Babylon.
13 O thou that dwellest on great waters, on greatness of treasures!
Thine end is come, the ell of thy section.[3]
14 Sworn hath Jehovah Zebaoth by himself:[4]
"Have I filled thee with men as with grasshoppers,
So shall they sing over thee the song of the vintage."

TEXTUAL AND GRAMMATICAL.

[1] Ver. 11.—הָבֵרוּ is properly to *polish*, but arrows are polished by being sharpened. The word is thus rendered by the Chaldee and Vulgate.

[2] Ver. 11.—שְׁלָטִים. The meaning is doubtful. It may be quiver, arrow, or shield. ROEDIGER, in *Ges. Thes.*, p. 1418, decides for the last, and I also think that both the parallel passages (comp. Song of Sol. iv. 4 with 2 Chron. xxiii. 9; Ezek. xxvii. 11; 1 Chron. xviii. 7) and the use of the word in Aramaic favor the meaning "shield." To fill the shields is a phrase like *brachia implere*. Comp. שֶׁת קְלָא, Zech. ix. 13, and KOEHLER thereon. [WORDSWORTH prefers the translation *quivers* as given by the Vulg., Syriac, and Targum. COWLES: "The Hebrew word means primarily to *fill*. GESENIUS supposes it means here, Fill the shields with the soldiers' own body, *i.e.*, put them on; while MAURER suggests the sense, 'Fill them with oil, anoint them as a preparation for service, arguing that this is in harmony with the preceding clause, 'Polish the arrows,' and corresponds with Isaiah xxi. 5, 'Anoint the shields.'"—S. R. A.]

[3] Ver. 13.—According to this rendering [A. V.: measure of thy covetousness], בִּצְעֵךְ is inf. Kal from בָּצַע (comp. בְּתַחֲךָ, xlviii. 7; OLSH., § 245, *b*) meaning to *strike off, cut off*, etc.

[4] Ver. 4.—בְּנַפְשׁוֹ. Comp. Am. vi. 8.

EXEGETICAL AND CRITICAL.

A triple call of threatening against Babylon forming a climax; first (ver. 11 *a*) a general summons to war, with mention of the warlike power thus called upon, then (ver. 12 *a*) an immediate attack on the walls of the city is commanded, and in the third place (ver. 13), its approaching end is announced. Each of the calls is, however, followed by a statement of reasons, in which also a climax may be perceived. For ver. 11 *b* announces the decree of Jehovah and its cause; ver. 12 *b* contains the assurance that with the Lord purposing and acting are the same thing. Ver. 14 strengthens the threatening of ver. 13 by reference to a solemn oath of Jehovah.

Ver. 11. **Sharpen . . . sanctuary.**—Hath

awakened, *etc.* Comp. rems. on ver. 1. This passage is taken from Isa. xiii. 17, from which we see that the definition of the enemies, threatening from the north (l. 9, 41), as the Medes is older than Jeremiah. Comp. ver. 28. In this sentence the prophet informs us to whom the summons of the preceding clause is addressed. The second half of the verse contains a double statement of cause, first the proximate and immediate, then the remote and mediate, but at the same time deepest ground of the summons. Comp. l. 15, 28.

Ver. 12. **Against the walls** . . . **of Babylon**. The military signals are to precede the attack on the walls of Babylon. On account of **against the walls**, הַנֵּס **standards**, seems here to be not the mere general signal of convocation or message, but a military sign indicating a particular point of attack. The word also denotes the flags of ships (Isa. xxxiii. 23; Ezek. xxvii. 7). Comp. WINER, *R.-W.-B.*, *s. v.* "*Fahnen*" and "*Schiffe*." The **watch** and **watchmen** appear to be related to each other as defensive and offensive (comp. 2 Sam. xi. 16, and HITZIG).—**Ambush**. Comp. Josh. viii. 14-16; Jud. xx. 33-35.—**For**, *etc.* To wish and to do are to be shown to be identical with Jehovah. Comp. iv. 28; Lam. ii. 17; Zech. i. 6; viii. 14, 15.

Vers. 13, 14. **O thou that dwellest** . . . **vintage**. The greatest supports of the power of Babylon were the waters surrounding it (comp. vers 32 and 36; l. 38; Isa. xxi. 1; Ps. cxxxvii. 1), and the great riches which Nebuchadnezzar accumulated (comp. Βαβυλὼν ἡ πολύχρυσος, Æsch. *Pers.* 52, and OPPERT, *Exped. en Mésop.* I. p. 175), and which rendered it possible for him to erect his immense buildings. DUNCKER says in reference to this: "Nebuchadnezzar had no need to fear that he would exhaust the subjects of his native land by the cost of his buildings. The immense booty of Nineveh, the greater part of which accrued to the Babylonians, the plunder of Jerusalem, the tributes of Syria and the Phœnician cities furnished the greatest means. The fruitfulness of the Babylonian territory, the produce of the fields depended on the overflowing of the Euphrates. By an extensive system of dams, canals and conduits, Nebuchadnezzar succeeded both in conducting the water of the Euphrates to every point of the Babylonian plain, and in draining the marshes and averting the violent inundations, which were not infrequent" (*Gesch. d. Alterth.*, I., S. 846). Add to this that these water-courses were of the greatest importance for the defence of the country. "Their object was primarily irrigation and navigation: but they afforded at the same time strong lines of defence against the enemy," says NIEBUHR (*Ass. u Bab.*, S. 229).—On a cylinder in the possession of Mr. Thomas Phillips, which has been deciphered by Grotefend, Nebuchadnezzar says (according to OPPERT, p. 231): "*Tout autour je fis couler de l'eau dans cette digue immense de terre. A travers ces grandes eaux comparables aux abimes de la mer, je fis faire un conduit.*" Comp. *Ib.*, p. 234.—**Their end is come**. Comp. Gen. vi. 13.—**Ell of thy section**. There are two renderings of this, "measure, end of thy fury, avarice, gain." So GROTIUS, CAPELLE, CHR. B. MICHAELIS, ROSENMUELLER, EWALD, HITZIG. But אַמָּה is the ell or yard measure, and does not involve the idea of full measure, or end. Hence the other rendering is to be preferred, which, after the example of Jerome (*pedalis præcisionis tuæ*), is adopted by VENEMA, J. D. MICHAELIS, EICHHORN, DE WETTE, GESENIUS, BÖTTCHER (*Proben altestam. Schrifterkl.*, S. 289, *Anm. m*), MAURER, GRAF. The idea lying at the foundation of the expression "the ell of the cutting thee off," is that the thread of life is measured, and when a definite number of yards is reached, will be cut off. Comp. Isa. xxxviii. 12; Job vi. 9.—**Have I, כִּי אִם**, are not here particles of asseveration, as in 2 Sam. xv. 21; 2 Ki. v. 20, but conditional, *if* I have filled thee with men as with grasshoppers (comp. xlvi. 23), this was only in order to be able to tread the more abundant vintage (הֵידָד. Comp. rems. on xxv. 30). Hence even the song of the treaders is a sign of their work yielding abundant returns.

Passage inserted from x. 12-16.

LI. 15–19.

15 Who maketh the earth by his power,
   Establisheth the globe by his wisdom,
   And by his understanding stretched out the heavens.
16 At the sound of his voice, throng of waters in the **heavens**,
   And vapors he bringeth up from the ends of the **earth;**
   He maketh lightnings to the rain,
   And bringeth the wind out of his chambers.
17 All men stand there mute, without understanding;
   All the founders of idol images are put to shame,
   For a lie is their molten work, no spirit is therein.
18 They are vapor, turned to ridicule;
   At the time of their visitation they perish.

19 Not so the portion of Jacob;
   For he formeth all things and the rod of his inheritance.
   Jehovah Zebaoth is his name.

EXEGETICAL AND CRITICAL.

This whole passage is a quotation from x. 12–16. It interrupts the connection in a disturbing manner. For even if the words in vers. 15, 16 may be regarded as suitable to support the thought that Jehovah, who has sworn in ver. 14 to destroy Babylon, has also the power to realize this threat, the following exposition of the vanity of idols is a superfluous appendage to the present prophecy. There is no point either in the following or previous context which requires such an exposition. It is a mere digression. Add to this, that in ver. 19 the words וְיִשְׂרָאֵל are omitted before שֶׁבֶט (comp. x. 16). If this omission is not due to a mere oversight, it betrays the hand of an emendator, who, to honor the tribe of Judah, wishes to remove the appearance as though only the Israel of the ten tribes were the stock of Jehovah's inheritance. Comp. NAEGELSB. *Jer. u. Bab.*, S. 131 *ff.*; GRAF, S 590, 1.

14. *How the Lord punishes His own Hammer.*

LI. 20–24.

20 A hammer[1] art thou to me, weapons of war,
   And with thee I break nations in pieces,
   And with thee I overthrow kingdoms.
21 And with thee I break in pieces the horse and his rider,
   And with thee I break in pieces the chariot and its driver.
22 And with thee I break in pieces man and woman,
   And with thee I break in pieces old man and boy,
   And with thee I break in pieces young man and maiden,
23 And with thee I break in pieces the shepherd and his flock,
   And with thee I break in pieces the husbandman and his team,
   And with thee I break in pieces magistrates and rulers.[2]
24 And I recompense to Babylon and all the inhabitants of Chaldea all the evil,
   Which they have done to Zion before your eyes, saith Jehovah.

TEXTUAL AND GRAMMATICAL.

[1] Ver. 20.—כַּפָּץ (a participial form derived from the Hiphil. Comp. *e.g.*, מַכְנֵר, and as a related synonym מֵפִיץ, Prov. xxv. 18) does not occur elsewhere.

[2] Ver. 23.—פַּחוֹת. Comp. vers. 28, 57; Ezek. xxiii. 6, 23; 1 Kl. x. 15; Neh. ii. 7; Ezr. viii. 36; Esth. viii. 9. According to BENFEY (*Monatsnamen*, S. 195), the word comes from the Sanscrit (Pakscha, *socius*, *amicus*), and is certainly related to the Arabic Pascha. Comp. GESEN., *Thes.*, *pag.* 1100.—סְגָנִים, which occurs only in the plural (Isa. xli. 25; Ezr. ix. 2; Neh. ii. 16, *etc.*), are likewise *præfecti provinciarum*. On the different derivations comp. GESEN. *Thes.*, *pag.* 937.

EXEGETICAL AND CRITICAL.

A picture very clearly complete in itself. The prophet sees in spirit a large number of persons before him who are to serve the Lord for a hammer, in order therewith to dash to pieces nations and kingdoms, especially, however, Babylon in all its parts, and thus to recompense to it what it has inflicted on Zion.

Vers. 20-24. **A hammer ... saith Jehovah.** In l. 23 Babylon was called "the hammer of the whole earth," and it might certainly be addressed again in the same way here. Many expositors, the LXX., JEROME, THEODORET at their head, are of opinion that it is so. But I, it should be observed that another word and, indeed, one formed *ad hoc* is chosen. Comp. TEXTUAL NOTE 1. May not the prophet have intended to indicate by using another word, specially formed for the occasion, that he meant another hammer than that spoken of before in l. 23? 2. The perfects with the Vau consecutive may, indeed, be taken in a past sense (comp. xviii. 4; xix. 4, 5; xxxvii. 11), but this construction is not normal. The imperfect would be more correct. 3. וְשִׁלַּמְתִּי, ver. 24, must at any rate be taken in a future sense. Since, however, this word is a perfectly similar form to the previous perfects and similarly construed, there is a presumption that the perfects are also to be rendered as futures. 4. In l. 21 we found an ideal person addressed, of which the Lord would make use as His instrument in the chastisement of Babylon. It is to the same that the prophet here turns. That he referred in thought to l. 21, 22, is evident from בָּבֶל, which he opposes to מַשְׁחִית there used. He here, however, extends the task appointed to the hammer, for it is not to visit Babylon only, as in l. 21, but many nations and kingdoms. Who this chosen instrument was to be the prophet was ignorant.—To take בְּלִי weapon, as singular for כְּלִי, with HITZIG and GRAF, appears to me unnecessary. The former is not a single weapon, but comprehends all weapons of war. The objects enumerated as to be broken form in a certain measure a circle, proceeding from the great and strong to the small and weak, and then rising from the young man and maiden again to the great and strong.—Chaldea. Kasdim as the name of the country, as in l. 10 coll. li 35.—Before your eyes, is to be referred to I recompense, since it would be superfluous referred to have done, and expresses the thought that those who now hear of the destruction of Babylon will also see it, and thus be convinced by ocular demonstration of the truth of Jeremiah's prediction.

15. *The Destroying Mountain.*

LI. 25, 26.

25 Behold, I come to thee, thou destroying mountain,
  Saith Jehovah, which destroyed the whole world;
  And I stretch forth my hand over thee,
  And roll thee from the rocks and make thee a burnt mountain.
26 And they shall take no stone of thee for a corner,
  Nor a stone for foundations,
  But thou shalt be perpetual ruins, saith Jehovah.

EXEGETICAL AND CRITICAL.

Babylon is here compared to a mountain, which has a widely destroying influence. This can refer only to a volcano, and with this it agrees that the mountain, after being laid bare to its rocky heart, is said to be a burnt-out mountain (ver. 25). So much, however, has it suffered by the destroying energies that its stones are not even available for building material.—We see that these two verses afford a picture perfectly complete in itself. [COWLES: "This blending of the figures of the volcano and the avalanche may not conform to the nicest rules of rhetoric, but none can say the conceptions are not grand and their significance both clear and strong."—S. R. A.]

Vers. 25, 26. **Behold, I come ... saith Jehovah.**—Behold, *etc*. Comp. xxi. 13; xxiii. 30-32; l. 31.—The expression destroying mountain [הַר הַמַּשְׁחִית], occurs besides only in 2 Ki. xxiii. 13, where the mount of Olives (or the southern peak thereof, the *mons scandali* or *offensionis* of ecclesiastical tradition; comp. KEIL on Kings, *S.* 362), is so called [A. V. "Mountain of corruption"]." The Mount of Olives evidently received this appellation from the corrupting influence which proceeded from it in religious matters. May not Babylon also be called a destroying mountain in spiritual relations? If then we remember that the name of Babylon is connected even in primæval traditions with defiant worldly power and idolatry (comp. l. 29-32, and NAEGELSB. *Jer. u. Bab.*, *S.* 5 ff.), we may well suppose that the prophet also had the corrupting spiritual influence of Babylon in mind (comp. also l. 38; li. 1, 44). We are not, however, justified in restricting his view to this single point, the element of destructiveness in a physical sense being also quite natural. It is repeatedly expressed in this prophecy. Comp. the hammer, l. 23, and the cup, li. 7 coll. li. 15-17.—We may then assume that Babylon is designated as a destroying mountain in a spiritual and physical reference. Perhaps in the term "mountain," there is also a hint at the tower which was widely visible, and corresponded to the widely extended influence. As to the picture in itself the question arises, What sort of a mountain had the prophet in mind? How must a (natural) mountain be constituted so as to be fitly designated a widely destroying mountain? I am of opinion that this designation can be given only to a volcano, for men seek the vicinity of mountains because these afford protection to their habitations and agriculture. Even the vicinity of volcanoes is not shunned, because these become dangerous only from time to time, and the general advantage of their vicinity outweighs the temporary disadvantage. The following description seems also to point to a volcano. How otherwise can we explain the words "roll thee from the rocks," than of a volcanic eruption? The mountain is to be laid bare, the overlying strata are to be thrown down so that nothing will remain but the skeleton,—the masses of stone which form its interior. All this can be said only of volcanoes. And when finally the result of this process is designated by the words שְׂרֵפָה לְהַר וּנְתַתִּיךָ, is not this a good conclusion to the figure drawn from a volcano? שְׂרֵפָה is *combustio, exustio.* Comp. Isa. ix. 4; lxiv. 10. A *mons combustionis* or *exustionis* is either one from which the *combustio* issues, or one which suffers or has suffered combustion. In the former case it would be difficult to perceive how this could be a punishment. In the latter case the question arises, whether the mount of combustion is to be understood as burning or burnt out. If we regard the previous and following context, we cannot doubt that the words "make thee a mountain of combustion," designate the result of the process, which is further described in ver. 26. The mountain is so burnt out that its stones are not even available for building materials. To GRAF's remark that "this latter point in itself doubtful was hardly so established in the experience of a Jew, that he could make use of it as a figure which would commend itself to his countrymen," I reply, that it did not need much experience to know that stones cracked or vitrified by fire, are bad building material, and that, moreover, here at the close the discourse evidently passes from figure to reality. The prophet has certainly the burnt-up city in view, the stones of which could not be used for building purposes. [COWLES: "In fact, large building stones *were never there.* Her immense structures were built of brick, either sun-dried or kiln-burnt. Hence the great mass of these materials lie to this day more or less decomposed in the mountains of rubbish which mark the site of that once magnificent city."—S. R. A.] —**But thou shalt,** *etc.* Comp. ver. 62; xxv. 9.

---

16. *War against the Threshing-floor of Babylon.*

LI. 27–33.

27 Raise ye a standard in the land,
    Blow the trumpet among the nations,
    Consecrate nations against her,
    Call upon her the kingdoms of Ararat, Minni and Ashkenaz;
    Appoint a captain against her,
    Bring up horses like bristly locusts.
28 Consecrate nations against her,
    The kings of Media with her satraps and all her governors,
    And the whole land of their dominion.
29 Then the earth quakes[1] and trembles,
    For the thoughts of Jehovah are being fulfilled[2] on Babylon,
    To make the land of Babylon a waste without an inhabitant.
30 The heroes of Babylon have ceased to fight,
    They sit in their strongholds;
    Dried up[3] is their strength,
    They are become women;
    They have burned her dwellings,
    Her bars are broken.
31 Courier runneth against courier, messenger against messenger,
    To announce to the king of Babylon
    That his city is taken to its utmost end,
32 The passages occupied, the ponds burned with fire, the men of war confounded.
33 For thus saith Jehovah Zebaoth, the God of Israel,
    "The daughter of Babylon is like a threshing floor,
    Now they tread her,[4]
    Yet a little and the time of harvest will come to her."

TEXTUAL AND GRAMMATICAL.

[1] Ver. 29.—וַתִּרְעַשׁ. The Imperf. with Vau consec. is used here because the prophet transports himself so vividly to the future that he regards it as already past. Comp. NAEGELSB. *Gr.*, § 88, 5. There is therefore no necessity of reading וְתִרְעַשׁ with MEIER.

[2] Ver. 29.—קָמָה. Comp. xliv. 28, 29. On the singular comp. NAEGELSB. *Gr.*, 105, 4 *b*.

[3] Ver. 30.—The form נָשְׁתָה is probably to be derived from שׁתת *eraruit.* This root occurs only in two passages elsewhere: Isa. xix. 5, וְנִשְּׁתוּ, and xli. 17, נָשָׁתָּה. The latter form may have stood for נָשַׁתָּה with *Dag. f. euphon.* Comp.

CHAP. LI. 27-33.   423

OLSH., § 83 b and 232 e; DELITZSCH on Isa. xix. 5. Others would derive the forms from שָׁתָה, שָׁתָה or נָשָׁה. Comp.
FUERST s. v. שָׁתָה, GESEN., Thes. s. v. שָׁכָן. At any rate a play upon words with לָבֻשׁ appears to be intended.
⁴ Ver. 33.—דָּרַךְ = הַדְרִיךְ, facere. Comp. HITZIG ad loc.—With regard to the construction, it is not necessary to assume an irregular infinitive form, but simply to supply אֲשֶׁר. Comp. ver. 3 and NAEGELSB. Gr., § 80, 6.

EXEGETICAL AND CRITICAL.

A very animated picture! Three main groups may be plainly distinguished, and a conclusion. The first group (vers. 27-29) shows us the enemies of Babylon, the Medes with the nations subject to their dominion advancing against Babylon with so great an army that the earth trembles. The second group is composed of the Babylonian warriors, who, overwhelmed by the success of the enemy, let their hands fall in powerless and spiritless dismay (ver. 30). In the third group we perceive the king of Babylon, who, sitting in his castle, receives from all sides the news of the capture of the city (vers. 31, 32). In the closing words the prophet expresses the thought that all which is now being done to render the city splendid and glorious is no more than the preparation of the threshing-floor, on which in a short time the harvest will be piled. These verses are clearly distinguished from those which precede and follow, and exhibit a clear and connected picture.

Vers. 27-29. **Raise ye . . . inhabitant.** Ver. 27 evidently contains a new beginning, for it summons to that which has to be done in the beginning of a warlike expedition. Comp. ver. 12; 1. 2.—**Consecrate,** etc. It was the custom to commence every war with sacred rites (comp. HERZ., R.-Enc., and WINER, R.-B.-W., s. v. "Krieg"); but here, as in Isa. xiii. 3, the war appears to be designated as a holy one, because it has to do with a "work of Jehovah" (l. 25) and "the vengeance of His sanctuary" (l. 28). Comp. vi. 4; xxii. 7; Joel iv. 9; Mic. iii. 5.—**Call.** Comp. l. 2, 29.—**Ararat.** Comp. Gen. viii. 4. [COWLES: "The name *Ararat* is Sanskrit, meaning 'the holy land,' a name probably due to traditions of Noah's ark."—S. R. A.].— In Isaiah (xxxvii. 38 coll. 2 Ki. xix. 37) a land of Ararat is spoken of. THEODORET says on the present passage, Ἀραρὰτ τὴν Ἀρμενίαν καλεῖ. According to Moses of Chorene (*Hist. Armen.* p. 361) Ararat was the chief district of Armenia and divided into twenty circuits. Comp. DELITZSCH on Isa. xxxvii. 38.—**Minni** also, which occurs here only, Ps. xlv. 9 being doubtful, belongs to Armenia; it was, according to NIEBUHR (*Ass. u. Bab. S.* 427 coll. 136), the second chief state of this country.—**Ashkenaz** must be sought for at any rate in the neighborhood of Armenia, since Togarmah is the brother of Ashkenaz according to Gen. x. 3, and "the country on the Pontus, Ararat and Caucasus is in general the home of the children of Japheth" (NIEBUHR *ut sup.*). KNOBEL (*Völkertafel* and on Gen. x. 3) regards Ashkenaz as the *Asorum genus* and says in reference to this passage: "The Ashkenaz mentioned in Jer. li. 27 appears to be a remnant of the Asi nation in Asia." [Comp. also KEIL and DELITZSCH on Gen. x. 3, *Tr.* 1. p. 163.—S. R. A.]. In general these three peoples here mentioned correspond to the "nations from the north" which are spoken of in l. 3, 9.—**Appoint a captain**—טִפְסָר. The word occurs besides only in Nah. iii. 17. The meaning is doubtful. All we learn from the context is that something hostile to Babylon is intended. The words against her follow four times in vers. 27, 28, and cannot be taken in another sense the third time from the other three. It is therefore not a measure *within* Babylon but *against* Babylon which is spoken of. **Appoint** is then used as in xv. 3. I do not think that number, multitude can be the point of comparison between this and the parallel **horses** (it is certainly not so with כֶּנֶי in Nah. iii. 17), and that therefore the word designates "troops" of any kind (GRAF, MEIER). It is admitted by most commentators that it is an Assyrian word. (Comp. STRAUSS on Nahum, *S.* 123). In the inscription of Bisutun, the Assyrian text of which has been rendered in Hebrew letters by OPPERT, (*Exp. en Mésop*, II. p. 238), the word כַּר occurs times innumerable in the sense of "King," as a title of Darius. Comp. also STRAUSS, *S.* 124 *Anm., etc.;* BRANDIS, *Gewinn, etc., S.* 101, 2. טִפְסָר might thus be a compound of סַר. The circumstance that the different nations have their leaders in their "kings" is no ground against this hypothesis, for the multifarious host would still need a common head. I therefore adhere provisionally to the meaning "captain."—**Like bristly locusts.** Comp. ver. 14. The comparison is very graphic, both with respect to the number and also the form and movements of the animals. Comp. CREDNER on Joel i. 4.—**Consecrate nations** is repeated as a sign that the prophet will yet make new and important additions to the nations already mentioned.—**Kings of Media.** The plural is no more to be regarded as an absolutely indifferent matter than as depending on distinct historical knowledge. It simply leaves open the possibility of a plurality. A great war with Babylon would certainly occupy the whole royal family of Media and might occupy several Median kings in succession. For an analogous case comp. xvii. 20; xix. 3.—Jeremiah's mention of the Medes is significant for two reasons: 1. because at that time, in the fourth year of Zedekiah (155 Nabon.=B. C. 593), Nebuchadnezzar was in all probability at war with Media. His father-in-law, Cyaxares, had died the year before, B. C. 594. This was a favorable epoch to cast off the previous supremacy of Media. "We think that we may unhesitatingly assume that Nabukudrussur had to undertake a great war with Media in the years 154 and 155," says NIEBUHR (*Ass. u. Bab., S.* 212, 3 and on his reasons for this view *Ib. S.* 211 and *S.* 284),— 2. because in the mention of the Medes there is a strong argument against those who assert that this prophecy was composed *post eventum*, during the captivity, for at this time the Persians and not the Medes would have been designated as the conquerors of Babylon. Comp. ver. 11.—

Her satraps. Comp. vers. 23 and 57.—**To make,** *etc.* Comp. Isa. xiii. 9; Jer. ii. 15; iv. 7; ix. 10; xlvi. 19; l. 3; li. 47.

Ver. 30. **The heroes of Babylon . . . broken.**—**Become women.** Comp. l. 37; Nah. iii. 13.—**They have burned.** The subject is the enemies.—**Bars are broken.** Comp. Am. i. 5; Isa. xlv. 2; Lam. ii. 9.—As only the capture of the city is described, the burning of the dwellings must not be referred to a burning of the whole city, presupposing the capture. It must rather be intended as a parallel to the breaking of the bars. The sentence discloses that the enemies had begun their work by setting the dwellings on fire. [Compare the account of the siege of Babylon in XENOPHON as given by WORDSWORTH.—S. R. A.]

Vers. 31, 32. **Courier . . . confounded.** The prophet conceives of the king as in the midst of the city, in his citadel. When the city is taken "from the end thereof" (comp. l. 26) the messengers hastening to inform the king would meet each other. This is a sad meeting, an accumulation of calamities which reminds us of the Job's posts (Job i. 13 sqq.).—**Passages.** כָּרֻבוֹת, are passages. Forts may be meant, but also bridges or tunnels, or even the stations of the messenger or ferries, since on account of the walls a landing could not be made at pleasure. Concerning the bridges which connected the two banks of the river in the middle of the city and the tunnel under the Euphrates, which connected the two royal castles, comp. OPPERT, I. *S.* 192, *etc.* The Euphrates, moreover, had no fords, and the article forbids us to think of the bed of the Euphrates, laid dry by the diversion of the stream (*Herod.*, I. 191), as it denotes that definite and well-known points of transition are meant. The expression may well be referred to the bridge, the ferry-stations and perhaps also to the tunnel. Both this sentence and the following parts of ver. 33 belong to the announcements spoken of in ver. 31.—**The ponds burned with fire.** This sentence is enigmatical. The view that the burning is not to be understood literally, but merely to be taken as figurative for drying up, for which an appeal is strangely made to 1 Ki. xviii. 38, seems to me as untenable as that, according to which the burning is to be referred merely to the sedge. The former view is opposed by the formal reason that the figure would be an unsuitably exaggerated one, the latter by the material reason that the burning of the sedge seems purposeless. But are the great waterworks of Nebuchadnezzar to be conceived of as having no wood-work about them? Did not the flood-gates at least consist of wood? The great basin of Sepharvaim, *e. g.*, might be opened and closed by flood-gates (comp. DUNCKER, *Gesch. d. Alterth.* I. *S.* 849). If the Euphrates were dried up and it was wished to complete the act of demolition, the destruction of the sluices by fire might be an appropriate way of accomplishing this. I do not mean to say that I perceive a special prediction in these words. Jeremiah paints the picture of the destruction of Babylon in colors, which in general betray a correct knowledge of Babylonian circumstances. This picture could not be applied to the capture of any city at pleasure, but the coloring is nowhere so specific that we must say it is either a mantic prediction or a *raticinium post eventum.* Jeremiah's mind was occupied only with the great theme,—Babylon will fall and be destroyed, and Israel will be delivered. He greatly varies this theme, and here and there a feature finds a surprisingly accurate fulfilment, but there may be here a deeply hidden connection between cause and effect, which we cannot fathom or demonstrate, and the prophet had no foreknowledge of this agreement of his words with the future reality. Comp. l. 24 and the rems. on li. 39. KUEPER in the *Beweis des Glaubens,* February and March, 1867.—**Are confounded.** Comp. Isa. xiii. 8. The words as the purport of the message correspond exactly to what was reported as a fact in ver. 30. [Comp. HEROD., I. 181; ARISTOT., *Polit.* III. c. 1; RAWLINSON, *Anc. Mon.* III. 363; and PUSEY, on *Daniel,* p. 268, in WORDSWORTH and his note on the fulfilment of this prophecy.—S. R. A.]

Ver. 33. **For thus saith . . . to her. For** attaches these words closely to the previous verse. What follows is separated by its specific contents, and thus the statement of reason forms a conclusion. When Jeremiah wrote Babylon stood at the zenith of its bloom. The rejoinder might then be made to him, How canst thou, contrary to all appearances, speak of such an enfeebling of this glorious army and of the capture and destruction of those impregnable bulwarks? Jeremiah replies, Babylon is a threshing-floor. All that is now done to render her great and glorious is no more than a preparation of the floor by treading. In a short time, however, the season of harvest will come to her. Jeremiah here leans back upon l. 26. The glorious city shall one day serve only as a threshing-floor for all the treasures harvested by her enemies.

17. Babylon's Misdeed, Israel's Complaint, Jehovah's Sentence.

LI. 34–40.

34 Nebuchadrezzar, king of Babylon, devoured us, he crushed us,
   He put us away as an empty vessel,
   He swallowed us like a dragon,
   He filled his belly[1] with my best and cast us out.[2]
35 " My wrong and my flesh be on Babylon," say the inhabitress of Zion,
   " My blood on the inhabitants of Chaldea," say Jerusalem.
36 Therefore thus saith Jehovah:
   Behold, I fight thy battle, and execute thy vengeance,
   And cause her sea to dry up and seal up her spring.
37 And Babylon shall become ruins, the abode of jackals,
   A terror and an object of scorn, which is bare of inhabitants.
38 They will roar one with another like young lions,
   They will growl[4] like the young of the lioness.
39 For *their* intoxication I prepare them a drinking-bout,
   And make them drunken that they may rejoice,
   Fall asleep to a perpetual sleep
   And never awake, saith Jehovah.
40 I will bring them down like lambs to the slaughter,
   Like rams with he-goats.

TEXTUAL AND GRAMMATICAL.

[1] Ver. 34.—בְּרֵשׂ, belly, is ἅπ. λεγ.

[2] Ver. 34.—יְדִיחָנוּ. The singular suffix has induced the Masoretes to make the previous verbs conformable to this, but this change of number is by no means rare. Comp. ix. 7; x. 4; xiii. 20; xliv. 9; NÄGELSB. *Gr.*, § 105, 7 *Anm.* 2. Some commentators would attach the word to the following, and read וַהֲדִיחֻנוּ because the Hiph. of נדח signifies to wash, rinse away (Isa. iv. 4; Ezek. xl. 38; 2 Chron. iv. 6), and does not occur elsewhere in Jeremiah, while הדיח is very common with him (viii. 3; xvi. 15; xxiii. 3, 8; xxvii. 10, 15, *etc.*). The meaning of rinsing, however, lies at the foundation of that casting away (" the Hiph. of נדח is to cast away, wash away," DELITZSCH on Isa. iv. 4, S. 59), and the brevity of the second half of the verse is not without analogy. Comp. l. 26; li. 28.

[3] Ver. 35.—שְׁבַח. Comp. Isa. xii. 6. The expression occurs only in these two places.

[4] Ver. 38.—נָעַר, snarl, growl, is an ἅπ. λεγ.

EXEGETICAL AND CRITICAL.

Nebuchadnezzar has devoured Israel, emptied his land and caused it to stand like an empty vessel, having cast out the people (ver. 34). For this Israel invokes the vengeance of Jehovah (ver. 35). To this desire the Lord declares Himself willing to respond; as Babylon has emptied Israel, so shall it become an empty unwatered desert; as Nebuchadnezzar has devoured Israel like a dragon, so shall the Chaldeans roar like lions; as they have revelled in Israel's flesh and blood, so shall they empty the cup of wrath even to fatal drunkenness, and be brought as sheep to the slaughter (vers. 36–40). Three main thoughts are thus plainly distinguishable, the *expositio facti*, the complaint and the sentence.

Ver. 34. **Nebuchadrezzar . . . cast us out.** Nebuchadnezzar has devoured (l. 7, 17) and crushed (literally *disturbavit*, Ex. xiv. 25; xxiii. 27; Josh. x. 10; 2 Chr. xv. 6) Israel; and then let the land stand like an empty vessel. HITZIG regards the words **he put us away**, as spoken by the land, but this view is opposed by the plural pronoun. It is better to regard the people and land as speaking together. Then the first clause refers to the persons, the second to the land, the third to the particular things, which the enemy took with him as plunder out of the country.—Dragon, תַּנִּין, is 1, *bellua maritima*, κῆτος, (Gen. i. 21; Job vii. 12; Ps. clviii. 7). 2. Serpent (Ex. vii. 9, 10, 12; Deut. xxxii. 33; Ps. xci. 13). 3. Crocodile (Isa. xxvii. 1; li. 9; Ezek. xxix. 3; xxxii. 2; Ps. lxxiv. 13). In this place it is usually translated dragon, this being viewed as a modification of the second meaning. It is really a matter of indifference what great animal is intended, and it therefore suffices to render the word by a general term.

Ver. 35. **My wrong . . . Jerusalem.** After the representation of the condition of things, Israel here appears as a plaintiff, and demands as his right the punishment of the oppressor.—

My wrong. Comp. Gen. xvi. 5.—**My flesh and my blood** point back to **devoured,** ver. 34.—**Inhabitants of Chaldea.** Comp. ver. 24; l. 10. ["By **my flesh** we are here to understand the blood-relations of the inhabitants of Jerusalem, or the Jews throughout the country, who were killed or carried captive to Babylon." HENDERSON.—S. R. A.]

Vers. 36-40. **Therefore thus ... with he-goats.** The Lord receives the complaint of Israel. He declares himself ready to execute the punishment desired. The close connection of the words with ver. 35 is clear from **therefore,** and from its whole purport.—**I fight,** *etc.* Comp. l. 34; li. 6, 11, 56; l. 15, 28.—**Cause to dry up,** *etc.* The abundance of water, to which the land of Babylon owes its fertility and power, the Lord will dry up and even seal up the springs. Comp. l. 38.—**Her sea.** Comp. rems. on ver. 13. "The main land, on which Babylon stands, is ... a large ... plain, which is so broken up with marshes and lakes by the Euphrates, that it floats, as it were, in the sea. The low land on the lower Euphrates is, as it were, wrung from the sea; for before Semiramis erected the dikes, the Euphrates used to overflow it all (πελαγίζειν, Herod., l., 184); Abydenus (in EUSEB. *Prœp.,* IX., 41), even says that at first it was all water, and was also called θάλασσα." DELITZSCH on Isa. xxi. 1.—**Become ruins.** Comp. ix. 10; xviii. 16; xix. 8; xxv. 9, 18; xxix. 18; li. 29. According to the theory of recompense which the Lord has presented in ver. 36 (comp. ver. 6) the desolation and evacuation here predicted corresponds to the emptying, which Israel, according to ver. 34, had experienced from Babylon.—In ver. 38 it is not an element of the punishment, but on the contrary the revelling of the Babylonians in the enjoyment of their plunder, which is described (comp. ii. 15; Am. iii. 4).—Ver. 39. While now they are in the heart of their greedy enjoyment (comp. Hos. vii. 4-7) the Lord will prepare them a banquet of his own kind. He will pour them out a full cup, but of wrath (xxv. 15-27). Of this excitement and sleep will be the consequence—the excitement of anguish and the sleep of death (ver. 57).—**That they may rejoice,** is therefore intended ironically. Comp. Isa. xxi. 5, and DELITZSCH, *ad loc.*—The remarkable fulfilment of these words in the surprise of the Chaldeans while feasting (Dan. v. 1 sqq.; HEROD., I., 191; CYROP., VII., 23) is no more to be traced to special prediction, than the fulfilment of vers. 31, 32; l. 24. The prophet has no expectation that his picture of wild carousal, and the exchange of this for another ironically so-called, would correspond so literally to the facts. That this was the case was not, however, due to a coincidence, but to divine Providence. Comp. rems. on vers. 31, 32.—**I will bring them,** *etc.* Comp. xlviii. 15; l. 27. Lambs, rams, he-goats! All classes of the population are to fall a sacrifice to the butcher's knife. Comp. Isa. xxxiv. 6; Ezek. xxxix. 18; Jer. l. 8. —This description also, from ver. 38 onwards, stands in evident contrast to the devouring of Israel by the Chaldeans, in ver. 34.

---

18. *The Demolition of the Prison, the Liberation of the Captives.*

LI. 41-46.

41 How is Sheshach taken,
   And the praise of the whole earth captured!
   How is Babylon become a horrid waste[1] among the nations!
42 The sea is come up over Babylon,
   With the multitude of its waves is she covered.
43 Her cities are become a desolation,
   A land of aridity and steppe,
   A land wherein no man will dwell,
   Which no son of man will pass through.
44 And I visit Bel in Babylon,
   And take from his mouth what he hath devoured,
   And no more shall the nations flow to him:
   The wall also of Babylon is fallen.
45 Go out from the midst of her, my people,
   And let every one save his soul from the fury of Jehovah's anger.
46 And let not your heart faint,[2]
   Nor fear on account of the rumor which is heard in the land,
   For in that year the rumor comes[3] and the year after[4] another,
   And feud in the land, ruler against ruler.

TEXTUAL AND GRAMMATICAL

¹ Ver. 41.—שִׁפָּה is *stupor* in v. 30; viii. 21. As in the verbal root, so also in the noun, the idea of being rigid and confused is connected with that of horrible desolation. Comp. ii. 15; iv. 7; 1. 3, 23, *etc.*
² Ver. 46.—וְיֵרָךְ וּבֵן. Comp. Deut. xx. 4; Isa. vii. 4.—אַל=פֶּן as frequently. EWALD, § 337, *b*.
³ Ver. 46.—אֲבָל וְגוּ. The construction is as, *e g.*, in xxvii. 10. Comp. NAEGELSB. *Gr.*, § 99, 3.
⁴ Ver. 46.—אַחֲרָיו is to be regarded as neuter. Comp. NAEGELSB. *Gr.*, § 60, 4.

EXEGETICAL AND CRITICAL.

A double picture! As in vers. l. 1-5, on the background of Babylon destroyed the prophet sees Jerusalem delivered. He thus first shows us Babylon taken and desolated (vers. 41-43), the gods robbed of all ability to retain plunder or attract worshippers, and even the strong, proud walls thrown down (ver. 44). He then summons Israel to flee from the abomination of desolation (ver. 45), and not to be afraid at the alarm of war (ver. 46).
Vers. 41-44. **How is Sheshach ... is fallen.** Comp. l. 2.—**Sheshach.** Comp. rems. on xxv. 26. If it is to be derived from שָׁבַב to stoop down, and taken in the sense of "humiliation, submission," the idea does not accord with the following "praise of the whole earth." It must wait further illumination.—**Praise**, *etc.* Comp. xlviii. 2; xlix. 25. Herodotus says of Babylon, ἐκεκόσμητο ὡς οὐδὲν ἄλλο πόλισμα τῶν ἡμεῖς ἴδμεν (I., 178).—**The sea**, *etc.* We might think here of the sea of nations (comp. Isa. viii. 7, 8; xvii. 12; Jer. xlvi. 7, 8), especially since in ver. 36 and ver. 43, the contrary is expressed. It is, however, possible that the prophet would really say both, *viz.*, that Babylon will be exposed to horrible aridity and fearful inundations. The Euphrates, when left to itself, has at some times too much, and at others too little water. Nebuchadnezzar's great water-works were to regulate the supply, and when those are destroyed (comp. ver. 32) Babylon incurs the double danger.—**Her cities**, *etc.* Comp. ix. 10.—**Land of aridity,** *etc.* Comp. ii. 6; l. 12.—**No man**, *etc.* Comp. ix. 9-11; xlix. 18, 33; l. 40.—**Bel** (comp. rems. on l. 2) is here mentioned as Babylon's highest deity, and accordingly as the shield of its power and glory. Whoever conquers and plunders Babylon, conquers and plunders Bel, and whatever Babylon retains of plundered property in its hand, that has Bel. He has, as it were, swallowed all (comp. ver. 34; l. 17). Israel then with all the plunder of Jerusalem (comp. Dan. i. 2) may be represented as "devoured by Bel," and this he is to restore. He is also no longer to have the renown of being a powerful protector. Foreigners shall no longer stream thither to commend themselves to his protection and be amazed at his glory. On the expression, comp. Isa. ii. 2.—The mention of the wall of Babylon (comp. ver. 58; l. 15) again as by way of supplement, may seem surprising. The walls of Babylon, however, seem here to be regarded as a sanctuary of Bel. This is intimated in their names; Imgur-Bel, *i. e.*, Bel protect, was the name of the outer wall comprising 480 stadia, Nivitti-Bel, *i. e.*, residence of Bel, was the name of the inner wall, 360 stadia long. Comp. OPPERT, I., *S.* 227. [The name of the king also was Belshazzar. — S. R. A.]
Vers. 45, 46. **Go out ... ruler.** That which, according to vers. 41-44 is to come upon Babylon, is the effect of Jehovah's wrath. In order that this may not fall upon the Israelites also, they are to flee. Comp. ver. 6; l. 8.—**From the fury,** *etc.* Comp. iv. 8, 26; xii. 13; xxv. 37, 38; xxx. 24.—**Feud,** *etc.* Comp. xxx. 21; xxxiii. 26.—The prophet evidently presupposes a great war. Comp. rems. on ver. 28. This passage reminds us of Matt. xxiv. 6; Luke xxi. 28. [Comp. RAWLINSON, *Anc. Mon.*, III., p. 515, as quoted in WORDSWORTH.—S. R. A.].

---

19. Babylon's fall an Occasion of Joy to Heaven and Earth, but especially to Israel.

LI. 47-52.

47 Therefore behold, the days come that I visit the idols of Babylon,
And her whole land shall be put to shame,
And her wounded ones shall all fall in the midst of her.
48 But heaven and earth, and all therein, shall rejoice over Babylon,
For from the north come¹ the destroyers, saith Jehovah.
49 As Babylon caused² the slain³ of Israel to fall,
So at Babylon are fallen the slain of the whole land.
50 Ye that have escaped the sword,
Go on,⁴ stand not still:
Remember Jehovah from afar,
And let Jerusalem come into your hearts.

51 "We are ashamed, for we have heard reproach,
Shame covers our face, for strangers are come into the sanctuaries of Jehovah's house."
52 Wherefore behold, the days come, saith Jehovah, that I punish her idols;
And in her whole land groan[5] the slain.

TEXTUAL AND GRAMMATICAL.

[1] Ver. 48.—The singular בוֹא stands here as an anticipated predicate. Comp. NAEGELSB. *Gr.*, § 105, 4, 6, 3.

[2] Ver. 49.—Before לִנְפֹּל should be supplied הָיְתָה. The sense of the connection is then Babylon tended to, occasioned, the fall. Comp. NAEGELSB. *Gr.*, § 95, 3 *b*.

[3] Ver. 49 —וְ הַלְלִי need not be taken as vocative. It is the construction of a sentence in which the infinitive represents the predicate, and the subject is implied in a substantive, depending on a preposition. Comp. v. 26; vi. 7; xvii. 2; xxxiv. 9; NAEGELSB. *Gr.*, § 95, 2.—If we take it as voc. (HITZIG, EWALD, GRAF, *etc.*), the two clauses of the disjunctive sentence either contain the same thought, or we must take לְ as the לְ *auctoris*, which is harsh. The Perf. נָפְלוּ is according to this interpretation the prophetic perfect. The prophet sees the *strages* of the Babylonians as something which has already happened. Hence he addresses the Israelites as having escaped from the overthrow.

[4] Ver. 50.—הָלְכִי. This imperative occurs here only. The choice of the expression is, however, explained by the circumstance, that הָלַךְ here does not signify to go away, but as is clear from the antithesis הַעֲמֹד (comp. Gen. xix. 17; Jer. iv 6) to go on, and is thus used with a certain emphasis. Hence it is also unnecessary with the LXX. to connect the ה with the previous word, and read הַחֲרָבָה or חָרְבָּה.—Comp., moreover, ver. 45; I. 8, 28.

[5] Ver. 52.—אָנַק in Jeremiah here only. Comp. Ezek. xxvi. 15.

EXEGETICAL AND CRITICAL.

We may observe in this passage that it gradually exhausts itself, and hastens to the conclusion. We may also perceive the effort to revert to the commencement. Hence the great similarity of these verses to l. 3–5. Babylon's idols are to be visited, the land confounded, and filled with the slain (ver. 47), to the joy of heaven and earth. The destroyers coming from the north are to accomplish this (ver. 48). Thus will be recompensed to Babylon what it has done to Israel (ver. 49). The Israelites, however, are encouraged to go home comforted (ver. 50). They seem not to understand the call, for they answer with complaining words, from which it is seen that no other feeling could find place in their hearts, than that of the disgrace they had suffered (ver. 51). But the prophet comforts them by skilfully repeating the opening words of the picture, indicating that even for their disgrace the promised visitation of the idols and of their country would procure satisfaction (ver. 52). If our division is correct, and ver. 52 is really the close of the strophe beginning at ver. 47, and if, as cannot be doubted (see the proof in detail below), these verses reproduce in a certain measure the beginning of the whole prophecy, l. 2–5, an artificial arrangement is here noticeable, of which a trace also recurs in the last picture, for ver. 58 also in its purport refers back to ver. 53.

Vers. 17, 48. **Therefore behold . . . saith Jehovah.**—**Therefore** draws a further special conclusion from the premises stated in the previous context. The main purport of this picture follows from all which has been previously stated as the decree of Jehovah concerning Babylon.—**Behold, the day.** Comp. ix. 24. This formula is found fourteen times in Jeremiah, vii. 32; xvi. 14; xix. 6, *etc.*—**The idols**, *etc.* Generalization of what is said in ver. 44 of Bel alone. In l. 2 also the confusion of Bel, Merodach and the idols generally is spoken of. Comp. ver. 52.

—**Put to shame.** Comp. xlviii. 13.—**Her wounded.** Comp. ver. 4.—If we render "slain," we get no suitable meaning from the sentence, even if the emphasis be laid on "in the midst of her," we must, therefore, take the word in the sense of wounded, as in Ps. lxix. 26; Job xxiv. 12. All the wounded will fall, *i. e.*, all their wounds will be mortal.—Ver. 48. **Shall rejoice**, *etc.* These words express the main thought of the first part (vers. 47, 48) and at the same time the only new element. Heaven and earth certainly must rejoice when once again the justice, wisdom and power of the Lord celebrate a triumph, and it is anew evident that He, and not the devil, is Lord in the world. Comp. Isa. xliv. 23; xlix. 13; Ps. xcvi. 10, 11.—The sentence gains much in clearness if we regard it as a parenthesis, and refer the following causal sentence to ver. 47. According to the logical sequence the destroyers are the first cause, and the destruction of Babylon the second cause of the rejoicing. If we do not take the imperative sentence as a parenthesis, we must at least refer the causal sentence to all the foregoing context, so that the destroyers appear as the ground both of the fall and the rejoicing. The words **for from the north**, also remind us of l. 3 *coll.* l. 9, 41, standing here in the same connection as there.—**Destroyers.** Comp. ver. 53.

Vers. 49-52. **As Babylon . . . the slain.** In this second part of the picture the prophet expresses substantially the same thought as in the first, but with special application to Israel and emphasis on the idea of recompense. The sin of Babylon against Israel shall be recompensed, and Israel, at first unable to receive the joyful tidings, is greatly comforted by the repeated solemn proclamation of judgment on the destroyers. —**Remember**, *etc.* These words remind us vividly of l. 4, 5.—**From afar.** Jehovah is still always considered as dwelling in Zion. Comp. xli. 5.—**Come**, *etc.* Comp. iii. 16; xliv. 21.— The Israelites answer the call, but with words of grief. They cannot receive the joyful tidings. Their minds are still full of the feeling of the disgrace they have suffered. It is as though they would say, What is the thought of Jehovah and Jerusalem for us? Have we not from thence recollections only of the deepest shame and reproach? We are put to shame and we are ashamed (comp. ix. 18), for we have heard reproach, scorn and ridicule as the part of the heathen (vi. 10; xxiv. 9), the consequence of which is that shame covered our face (Ps. lxix. 8; xxxv. 26; lxxi. 13). This scorn which has come upon us refers however to the fact that strangers (comp. v. 19; xxx. 8; Isa. i. 7) have come into the sanctuaries (i. e., into all parts, even those forbidden to profane feet) of Jehovah's house. It must appear surprising that the Israelites respond to the joyful call of the prophet, ver. 50, with words of grief. The strophe cannot therefore possibly be concluded here, or it would end in a harsh dissonance. We therefore attach ver. 52 to it. Even on this account, says Jeremiah, skilfully repeating the opening words of the picture, shall the idols be visited and their land filled with the slain. The prophet speaks very appropriately of the visitation of the idols, for just this is the recompense for the disgrace inflicted on the house of Jehovah.

20. *No wall is a defence against the Lord.*

LI. 53–58.

53 "Even though Babylon should mount up to heaven,
 And tower up¹ his defences² to a precipitous height,
 From me will destroyers come to her," saith Jehovah.
54 A loud crying from Babylon
 And great ruin from the land of the Chaldeans!
55 For Jehovah destroyeth Babylon,
 And extirpates from her the loud noise.
 And her waves roar like mighty waters,
 The noise of their calling resounds.
56 For there is coming upon her, upon Babylon, a destroyer,
 And her heroes are taken, their bows broken ;³
 For a God of recompense is Jehovah,
 Who well requiteth.
57 "And I make drunk her princes and her wise men,
 Her counts, her dukes and her heroes,
 That they may sleep a perpetual sleep,
 And never awake," saith the King:
 Jehovah Zebaoth is his name.
58 Thus saith Jehovah Zebaoth,
 "Babylon's broad wall⁴ is laid bare,⁵
 And her high gates burn⁶ in the fire!
 Thus then have peoples labored in vain,
 And nations wearied themselves⁷ for the fire."

TEXTUAL AND GRAMMATICAL.

¹ Ver. 53.—The Piel בצר denotes to cut off, to separate sharply. This is used in the sense of fortifying, like Kal in בְּצוּרָה, Isa. ii. 15; xxxvii. 26 *coll.* מִבְצָר, because fortifications are sharply separated from their surroundings. Comp. Isa. xxii. 10.

² Ver. 53.—עֹז is here as in עֹז כִגְדַּל, Jud. ix. 51; Ps. lxi. 4; Prov. xviii. 10; עֹז צוּר, Ps. lxii. 4; עִיר or עֹז קִרְיַת עֹז, Isa. xxvi. 1; Prov. x. 12; xviii. 11, a strong bulwark for defence or protection.

³ Ver. 56.—חִתְּתָה=to make חַת, i. e., to make cracked. Comp. פָּחַד, Isa. xlviii. 8; lx. 11; פָּחַד, Isa. ii. 13; and with respect to the meaning "broken," 1 Sam. ii. 4; on the singular, comp. NAEGELSB. *Gr.*, § 105, 4, *b*.

⁴ Ver. 58.—הֹמוֹת is construed as sing. here only. Evidently the totality of the walls, which, in a certain aspect, was a six-fold line of circumvallation (comp. OPPERT, p. 228, *etc.*), is regarded as a unit. Comp. EWALD, § 318, *a*.

⁵ Ver. 58.—עָרְעֵר. Inf. abs. Pilpel. (comp. OLSH., § 253, *Anm.*) with Hithpalp. from עָרָה, to strip one's self, *i. e.*, thrown down, discovered to their foundations. Comp. עָרָה, Hab. iii. 13; Psalm cxxxvii. 7; and Isaiah xxiii. 13; Ezek. xiii. 14.

⁶ Ver. 58.—יִצַּתּוּ. Comp. xlix. 2; Isa. xxxiii. 12; OLSH., § 242, *b*.

⁷ Ver. 58.—Regarding these words as original to Habakkuk, we may also regard וְיִעֵפוּ as a scriptural error, it being easy to write this instead of יִיעָפוּ. Comp. NAEGELSB. *Jer. u. Bab.*, S. 97.

EXEGETICAL AND CRITICAL.

The main thought of the picture is that no dead or living wall can save Babylon, for the Lord, the righteous recompenser, has determined upon its fall. The dead wall of Babylon will not avail, because the Lord will send destroyers, as first expressed in ver. 53. In the following verses the fulfilment of this declaration is exhibited: great noise is heard from Babylon (ver. 54). Whence comes this? Hence, that the Lord has begun the work of destruction on Babylon—destroying both the great masses (ver. 55) and the élite of the population. His justice requires this (ver. 56). Substantially the same thought closes the discourse as began it, and both the beginning and conclusion appear as the *verba ipsissima* of Jehovah, so that in form also the end reverts to the beginning. The princes and wise men of Babylon may be designated as its living wall. They shall be made drunk with the cup of Jehovah's wrath, and sleep an everlasting sleep (ver. 57). The dead wall, with its lofty gates, shall be subjected to fire, so that it will be made manifest that the immense work, the fruit of the labor of many nations, was achieved in vain, to be consumed by fire (ver. 58).

Ver. 53. **Even though . . saith Jehovah.** In the opening words there appears to be a double allusion : 1. to the tower of Babel, Gen. xi. 4 ; 2. to the high walls with which Babylon was surrounded. Their height must have been very great. Even if the statements of 200 yards (HERODOTUS) and 250 yards (OROSIUS) are to be considered exaggerated, the lowest estimates of the ancients (PHILOSTR., Apoll. Tyan., 25) speak of three and a half plethra, *i. e.*, 150 feet (OPPERT, *Exp.*, I., p. 224, 5).—Comp. Ob. 4 ; Hab. ii. 9 ; Jer. xlix. 16.—**Destroyers**. Comp. ver. 48. [WORDSWORTH: "We may compare also the words of Nebuchadnezzar still extant on this cylinder: 'In Babylon is the tower of my abode. . . . To make more difficult the attack of an enemy against *Imgour-Bel*, the indestructible Wall of Babylon, I constructed a bulwark like a mountain,'" *etc.*—S. R. A.]

Vers. 54-56. **A loud crying . . requiteth.** That ver. 54 describes the execution of what is threatened in ver. 53, the work therefore of the destroyers (comp. l. 22, 46; xlviii. 3) is seen from vers. 55, 56. It is at the same time clear from the connection that the loud noise spoken of in ver. 54 is the united consequence of a double operation directed to the two main portions of the Babylonian population. At one time the work of the destroyers is against the great mass of the people. This is the sense of **loud noise** and **her waves**. The sentence **And her waves**, *etc.* expresses the result. The destruction of Babylon and the extirpation of the great tumult of nations cannot take place without bringing the masses of the people into wild and noisy excitement, for, as was remarked on ver. 42, masses of people may certainly, as here, be compared with masses of water.—**Roar**. Comp. v. 22; xxxi. 35; Jer. li. 15—Jer. vi. 23.—Afterwards, however, the work of the destroyers is against the élite of the people, the heroes, *i. e.*, the brave men and warriors (ver. 30; l. 36) and their weapons.—**For a God of recompense,** *etc.* The causal particle refers of course not only to the immediate, but all the previous context. The object of *recompense* is here stated as the ground of Jehovah's procedure against Babylon, as in l. 15, 28; li. 6, 11, 36. Comp. 2 Sam. xix. 37; Isa. lix. 18.

Vers. 57, 58. **And I make . . . for the fire.** These verses also contain, like ver. 53, the *verba ipsissima* of Jehovah, and ver. 58 also treats of the dead wall. When, in ver. 57, it is said of the princes, wise men and warriors (comp. l. 35, 36; li. 23, 28), that the Lord will make them drunk and cause them to sleep a perpetual sleep (comp. rems. on ver. 39, whence these words are taken, and xxv. 15, 16, 27), it is evidently to be thus intimated that the Lord will paralyze all the forces which might be able in any way to delay the fall. It may then be said that the prophet treats in ver. 57 of the destruction of the living, in ver. 58 of the dead stone defences. I may be allowed here to insert a passage relating to the building of the walls from the cylinder-inscription already mentioned, as given by OPPERT (*Exp.*, l., p. 230). "Babylon is the refuge of the God Merodach ; I have finished (observe that Nebuchadnezzar is the speaker) Imgur-Bel, his great enclosure. In the thresholds of the great gates I have adjusted folding-doors in brass, very strong railings and gratings (?), I have dug its ditches, I have reached the bottom of the waters, I have constructed the banks of the trench with bitumen and bricks. Wishing to preserve the pyramid more efficaciously and to defend it from the enemy and the attacks which might be made on Babylon the imperishable, I caused to be constructed in masonry in the extremities of Babylon a (second) great enclosure, the boulevard of the Rising Sun, which no king had made before me. I had the ditches made dry, and caused the banks to be constructed on barrels." Here follow the words quoted above in ver. 13.—The walls of Babylon, however, were not the work of Nebuchadnezzar alone. According to an inscription, now at Aberdeen, some share in the glory of this work is due to Assarhaddon, the son of Sanherib. He says (OPPERT, p. 227, *etc.*), "Babylon is the city of laws, Imgur-Bel is its enclosure, Nivitti-Bel its rampart; from the foundation to the battlements I founded, continued, enlarged them." OPPERT is of opinion that these words express too much, and that Nabopolassar, and especially Nebuchadnezzar, are to be regarded as at least the completers of the work. As to the destruction of the wall, OPPERT says (p. 225, *etc.*), " It is to be presumed that the outer wall, encroached upon by Cyrus, spoiled by Darius, filled with breaches by Xerxes, did not exist at the commencement of the fourth century of the vulgar era. The ditches had been filled—and at least in the greater part the wall had disappeared which was so imposing to the enemies of Babylon, and which inspired Jeremiah with the words recorded in li. 53, 58."
—**Thus then have peoples,** *etc.* These words are found with slight alteration (transposition of in vain and for the fire) in Hab. ii. 13. Habakkuk was the contemporary of Jeremiah, and also prophesied the punitive judgment to be executed on Judah by the Chaldeans. As in i. 6 Habakkuk expressly mentions the Chaldeans,

he cannot have prophesied before the battle of Carchemish, for it is inconceivable that the appointment of this nation was disclosed to him earlier than to Jeremiah. It is possible that he wrote in the reign of Zedekiah, for we see from chap. i. that the dominion of the Chaldeans had then lasted for some time. If now the words "Behold, is it not of the Lord of hosts?" which in Hab. ii. 13 immediately precede the words common to this passage, are to be regarded as a formula of quotation, it is not impossible that this is the passage which he quotes, although, of course, it cannot be denied that both may have drawn from a common source. It is, however, grammatically more correct to take נֶאֻם in the sense of command or determination (as in Josh. xi. 20; Ezek. xxxiii. 30), and to translate (with EWALD, MEIER) "it is decreed of the Lord that the nations," etc., and then it is more probable that the words are original to Habakkuk. They suit the context admirably. For Habakkuk wishes to show that a building erected with blood and injustice cannot endure, from which in passing we may derive the important information that Nebuchadnezzar did not execute his immense works without despotic violence.—**Labored** and **wearied themselves** are synonymous expressions, comp. Isa. xl. 38 sqq.; so that if we render **and wearied themselves** (as required by the text here, but not in Hab. ii. 13), we must understand this in an enhanced signification, as **exhausted themselves**, or *are sinking*, which it is doubtful if the word will bear. Nor is it in accordance with the sense and connection of the original passage to attribute to the nations, who were compelled to build the wall, a sinking when the wall falls! It is for them rather a victory than a defeat. This long discourse, as EWALD remarks, "very suitably closes with this sentence of Habakkuk, which is here quite appropriate." בְּדֵי־רִיק (**to a sufficiency in vain**), involves a certain irony. The great wall will be good enough to satisfy the lust of the all-devouring annihilation, or of the fire. It is therefore stronger than לָרִיק. Isa. xlix. 4; lxv. 23. Comp. Nah. ii. 13.

21. *Historical conclusion.*

LI. 59-64.

59 The word which Jeremiah the prophet commanded Seraiah the son of Neriah, the son of Maaseiah, when he went with Zedekiah the king of Judah into Babylon in the fourth year of his reign. And *this* Seraiah *was* a quiet prince [caravan-
60 marshall]. So Jeremiah wrote in a book all the evil that should come¹ upon Ba-
61 bylon, *even* all these words that are written against Babylon. And Jeremiah said to Seraiah, When thou comest to Babylon, and shalt see, and shalt [see that thou]²
62 read all these words; then shalt thou say, O LORD [and say, O Jehovah], thou hast spoken against this place, to cut it off, that none shall remain in it, neither
63 man nor beast, but that it shall be desolate for ever. And it shall be, when thou hast made an end of reading this book, *that* thou shalt bind a stone to it, and cast
64 it into the midst of Euphrates: And thou shalt say, Thus shall Babylon sink,³ and shall not rise from [because of] the evil that I will bring upon her : and they shall be weary [exhausted].⁴ Thus far *are* the words of Jeremiah.

TEXTUAL AND GRAMMATICAL.

¹ Ver. 60.—On the sense of the Imperfect תָּבֹא comp. NAEGELSB. *Gr.*, ? 87, 1.

² Ver. 61.—וְרָאִיתָ. This word cannot mean "and when thou seest it (for the first time)." The suffix would certainly not be wanting in th t case. Nor can we see why the reading should take place at the first sight of the city. Both time and place might then be very unfavorable. It is rather the apodosis; then see to it. It is inculcated upon him that he discharge his commission with circumspection. Comp. 1 Ki. xii. 16; Ps. xxxvii. 37; Isa. xxii. 11.

³ Ver. 64.—שָׁקַע, *demergi, desidere,* in Jeremiah here only. Comp. Am. viii. 8; ix. 5.

⁴ Ver. 64.—If the word וְיָעֵפוּ is not genuine, it can have come here only through the transposition of the following words, "Thus far," *etc.*, with which the copyist, through carelessness or of purpose, connected this. This, however, involves the inauthenticity of vers. 59-64 or their original position before l. 1. HITZIG says the passage "bears some marks of genuineness, none of the contrary, and it is incredible that it stood before l. 1, since it would then appear that this great prophecy was only of secondary importance. If, then, vers. 59-64 are genuine and in their original position, the same must be said of the concluding words, since they could never have had their position before ver. 59. A copyist could not have added וְיָעֵפוּ by mistake. Jeremiah, then, must have done it. His object probably was to give a token of identity to the sinking prophecy by an unmistakable quotation from it. The ancient translations, with the exception of the LXX., which is of no authority, all express the word. Comp. NAEGELSB. *Jer. u. Bab* , *S.* 96.

EXEGETICAL AND CRITICAL.

When King Zedekiah, in the fourth year of his reign, made a journey to Babylon, Jeremiah gave to Seraiah, the brother of Baruch, the marshall, the prophecy against Babylon to take with him and read in Babylon, and then with prayer to the Lord to cast it into the Euphrates.

Ver. 59. **The word . . . caravan-marshall.** The commission which Seraiah receives really forms the chief part of this section. For after ver. 60, in which the restoration of the roll forming the basis of this commission is described, all the rest contains only the words in which Jeremiah imparts the commission.—Seraiah, according to xxxii. 13, must be a brother of Baruch, the friend and assistant of our prophet, which explains why the commission was given to him. Other persons named Seraiah are mentioned in this book, xxxvi. 26; xl. 8; lii. 24. It seems to have been a common name among the priests. Comp. 1 Chron. vii. 6, 14; Ezr. vii. 1, 4; Neh. x. 2; xi. 11; xii. 1, 12.—It is not perfectly clear why Zedekiah went to Babylon. His fourth year is the same in which the envoys of the neighboring nations met in Jerusalem, to treat concerning a defensive alliance against the Chaldean power. Comp. rems. on xxvii. 1 and xxviii. 1. NIEBUHR thinks that the diversion then made by Nebuchadnezzar's war with Media was the occasion of this meeting (*Ass. u. Bab.*, S. 211). The journey to Babylon shows that nothing came of the project, whether that the reports from the East caused the matter to appear too dangerous, or that the warnings of Jeremiah made some impression.—**A quiet prince** (שַׂר־מְנוּחָה). This expression has been interpreted in the most various and strangest ways, concerning which comp. ROSENMUELLER and J. D. MICHAELIS *ad loc.* The latter was the first to give the substantially correct rendering in his *Translation of the Old Testament*, 1778, Leader of the caravan. MAURER first proposed "Reisemarschall," marshall of the journey. Literally it denotes "Prince of the resting-place." Comp. Numb. x. 33.

Vers. 60-64. **So Jeremiah wrote . . . exhausted.** We may assume that this journey of Zedekiah was the occasion of the prophecy against Babylon. For homage, if not the only object, was certainly one of the objects, of the journey, and it therefore involved a deep disgrace to the theocracy. How fitting it was that the prophet should make use of this journey to furnish the medal with an appropriate reverse. While the king of Judah, in view of all, was casting himself in homage before the throne of the Chaldean king, Seraiah was to cast a roll in the Euphrates, on which was recorded as a divine decree the destruction of Babylon and deliverance of Israel. —That Jeremiah copied the prophecy from the book-roll mentioned in xxxvi. 32 (GRAF) is only supposable, in case Jeremiah successively increased that collection of writings begun in the fifth year of Jehoiakim, first inserting the present prophecy in it, and thus giving Seraiah a copy, a confirmation of which hypothesis may be found in the expression **in a** [אֶחָד, one] **book.** It is, however, possible that Jeremiah would thus intimate that he purposely wrote the prophecy upon *one* roll, in antithesis to the many rolls forming the main collection. The reason of the prophet's care to write the whole on *one* roll, would then doubtless be that *one* could be handled more easily and safely than two.—The reading was evidently for a threefold purpose: 1. With respect to the city of Babylon it was an announcement of judgment (ΗΙΤΖΙΟ), which appears the more significant, as the announcers were not in a condition to make a declaration against Babylon, coming, as they did in all humility, to do homage. 2. With respect to God, it was to be affirmed that the people of Israel had taken solemn notice of the divine promise. Hence after the reading the Lord is to be expressly addressed and reminded of the word of His promise in its main features (comp. ver. 62 with l. 3; li. 26). He is thus, as it were, to be taken at His word and pledged. 3. To the Israelites there was naturally a great comfort in all this, which must have been of special value to them in that moment of deep shame.—The sinking of the roll in the Euphrates is added to the reading as supplementary and confirming the words by a visible symbolic action. The roll being compelled to sink by the stone and thus outwardly given up to destruction, suggests the thought that this external part was no longer necessary after, by the reading, the purport had been received into the living spiritual archives of the consciousness. At the same time, as is expressly stated in ver. 64, the sinking by the weight of the stone is to represent symbolically the ruin of Babylon.—**Shall not rise,** as the roll with the stone will not.—**From the evil** does not designate the element in which Babylon is to sink, but the figure is here forsaken and the transition made to literal speech. **מִפְּנֵי** then =in consequence of [because of, the evil].— **Shall be weary.** These words might certainly be dispensed with, as they rather injure than promote the clearness of the sense. As is well understood, however, the easier reading is by no means always the more correct. The question depends on whether the finer and more hidden sense which may be contained in the words is able to balance the formal reasons which favor their spuriousness. Comp. the TEXTUAL remarks.

Thus far the words of Jeremiah. These words, which I cannot regard as misplaced (comp. rems. on ver. 64) have simply the object of indicating that ch. lii. does not proceed from Jeremiah himself, but is the addition made by another person.

DOCTRINAL AND ETHICAL.

1. "Daniel's Babylonian empire resumes, as it were, the thread which was broken off with the tower-erection and kingdom of Nimrod. In the Babylonian tower-building the whole of the then existing humanity was united against God; with the Babylonian kingdom began the period of the universal monarchies, which again aspired after an atheistical union of entire humanity. Babylon has since and even to the Revelation (ch. xviii) remained the standing type of this world." AUBERLEN, *Der proph. Daniel, S.* 230.

2. For what reason does Babylon appear as a type of the world? Why not Nineveh, or Persepolis, or Tyre, or Memphis, or Rome? Certainly not because Babylon was greater, more glorious, more powerful or prouder and more ungodly than those cities and kingdoms. Nineveh especially was still greater than Babylon (comp. DUNCKER, *Gesch. d. Alterth. I. S.* 474, 5), and Assyria was not less hostile to the theocracy, having carried away into captivity the northern and larger half of the people of Israel. Babylon is qualified for this representation in two ways: 1. because it is the home of worldly princedom and titanic arrogance (Gen. x. 8; xi. 1-4); 2. because Babylon destroyed the centre of the theocracy, Jerusalem, the temple and the theocratic kingdom, and first assumed to be the single supreme power of the globe.

3. "When God has used a superstitious, wicked and tyrannical nation long enough as His rod, He breaks it in pieces and finally throws it into the fire. For even those whom He formerly used as His chosen anointed instruments He then regards as but the dust in the streets or as chaff before the wind." CRAMER.

4. "No monarch is too rich, too wicked, too strong for God the Lord. And He can soon enlist and engage soldiers whom He can use against His declared enemies." CRAMER.

5. "Israel was founded on everlasting foundations, even God's word and promise. The sins of the people brought about that it was laid low in the dust, but not without hope of a better resurrection. Babylon, on the other hand, must perish forever, for in it is the empire of evil come to its highest bloom. Jeremiah owns the nothingness of all worldly kingdoms, since they are all under this national order to serve only for a time. We are to be subject to them and seek their welfare for the sake of the souls of men, whom God is educating therein; a Christian however cannot be enthusiastic for them after the manner of the ancient heathen nor of current Israel, for here we have no abiding city, our citizenship is in heaven. The kingdoms of this world are no sanctuaries for us and we supplicate their continuance only with the daily bread of the fourth petition. Jeremiah applies many words and figures to Babylon which he has already used in the judgments on other nations, thus to intimate that in Babylon all the heathenism of the world culminates, and that here also must be the greatest anguish. What, however, is here declared of Babylon must be fulfilled again on all earthly powers in so far as, treading in its footprints, they take flesh for their arm and regard the material of this world as power, whether they be called states or churches." DIEDRICH.

6. On l. 2. In putting into the mouth of Israel, returning from Babylon, the call to an everlasting covenant with Jehovah, the prophet causes them 1. to confess that they have forgotten the first covenant; 2. he shows us that the time of the new covenant begins with the redemption from the Babylonish captivity. He was far, however, from supposing that this redemption would be only a weak beginning, that the appearance of the Saviour would be deferred for centuries, that Israel would sink still deeper as an external πολιτεία, and that finally the Israel of the new covenant would itself appear as a μυστήριον, εἰς ὃ ἐπιθυμοῦσιν ἄγγελοι παρακύψαι (1 Pet. i. 9-12).

7. From what Jeremiah has already said in xxxi. 31-34 of the new covenant we see that its nature and its difference from the old is not unknown to him. Yet he knows the new covenant only in general. He knows that it will be deeply spiritual and eternal, but *how* and *why* it will be so is still to him part of the μυστήριον.

8. On l. 6. Jeremiah here points back to ch. xxiii. Priests, kings and prophets, who should discharge the office of shepherds, prove to be wolves. Yea, they are the worst of wolves, who go about in official clothing. There is therefore no more dangerous doctrine than that of an infallible office. Jer. xiv. 14; Matt. vii. 15; xxiii. 2-12.

9. On l. 7. It is the worst condition into which a church of God can come, when the enemies who desolate it can maintain that they are in the right in doing so. It is, however, a just nemesis when those who will not hear the regular messengers of God must be told by the extraordinary messengers of God what they should have done. Comp. xl. 2, 3.

10. On l. 8. "Babylon is opened, and it must be abandoned not clung to, for the captivity is a temporary chastisement, not the divine arrangement for the children of God. God's people must in the general redemption go like rams before the herd of the nations, that these may also attach themselves to Israel, as this was fulfilled at the time of Christ in the first churches and the apostles, who now draw the whole heathen world after them to eternal life. Here the prophet recognizes the new humanity, which proceeds from the ruins of the old, in which also ancient Israel takes the way; thus all, who follow it, become Israel." DIEDRICH.—"The heathen felt somewhat of the divine punishment when they overcame so easily the usually so strongly protected nation. But Jeremiah shows them still how they deceived themselves in thinking that God had wholly rejected His people, for of the eternal covenant of grace they certainly understood nothing." HEIM and HOFFMANN on the Major Prophets.

11. On l. 18. "The great powers of the world form indeed the history of the world, but they have no future. Israel, however, always returns home to the dear and glorious land. The Jews might as a token of this return under Cyrus; the case is however this, that the true Holy One in Israel, Christ, guides us back to Paradise, when we flee to His hand from the Babylon of this world and let it be crucified for us." DIEDRICH.

12. On l. 23. "Although the Chaldeans were called of God for the purpose of making war on the Jewish nation on account of their multitudinous sins, yet they are punished because they did it not as God with a pure intention, namely, to punish the wrong in them and keep them for reformation; for they were themselves greater sinners than the Jews and continued with impenitence in their sins. Therefore they could not go scot-free and remain unpunished. Moreover, they acted too roughly and dealt with the

Jews more harshly than God had commanded, for which He therefore fairly punished them. As God the Lord Himself says (Isa. xlvii. 6): When I was angry with My people I gave them into thine hands; but thou shewedst them no mercy. Therefore it is not enough that God's will be accomplished, but there must be the good intention in it, which God had, otherwise such a work may be a sin and call down the divine punishment upon it." *Würtemb. Summ.*

13. On l. 31-34. "God calls Babylon Thou Pride, for pride was their inward force and impulse in all their actions. But worldly pride makes a Babylon and brings on a Babylon's fate. . . . Pride must fall, for it is in itself a lie against God, and all its might must perish in the fire; thus will the humble and meek remain in possession of the earth: this has a wide application through all times, even to eternity." DIEDRICH.

14. On ver. 33. "Israel is indeed weak and must suffer in a time of tyranny; it cannot help itself, nor needs it to do so, for its Redeemer is strong, His name The Lord Zebaoth—and He is now, having assumed our flesh, among us and conducts our cause so that the world trembles." DIEDRICH.

15. On l. 45. "An emblem of the destruction of anti-christian Babylon, which was also the true hammer of the whole world. This has God also broken and must and will do it still more. And this will the shepherd-boys do, as is said here in ver. 45 (according to LUTHER's translation), that is, all true teachers and preachers." CRAMER.

16. On ch. li. "The doctrines accord in all points with the previous chapter. And the prophet Jeremiah both in this and the previous chapter does nothing else but make out for the Babylonians their final discharge and passport, because they behaved so valiantly and well against the people of Judah, that they might know they would not go unrecompensed. For payment is according to service. And had they done better it would have gone better with them. It is well that when tyrants succeed in their evil undertakings they should not suppose they are God's dearest children and lean on His bosom, since they will yet receive the recompense on their crown, whatever they have earned." CRAMER.

17. ["Though in the hand of Babylon is a golden cup; she chooses such a cup, in order that men's eyes may be dazzled with the glitter of the gold, and may not inquire what it contains. But mark well, in the golden cup of Babylon is the poison of idolatry, the poison of false doctrines, which destroy the souls of men. I have often seen such a golden cup, in fair speeches of seductive eloquence: and when I have examined the venomous ingredients of the golden chalice, I have recognized the cup of Babylon." ORIGEN in WORDSWORTH.—S. R. A.]

"The seat and throne of Anti-christ is expressly named Babylon, namely, the city of Rome, built on the seven hills (Rev. xvii. 9). Just as Babylon brought so many lands and kingdoms under its sway and ruled them with great pomp and pride (the golden cup, which made all the world drunk, was Babylon in the hand of the Lord (li. 7), and all the heathen drank of the wine and became mad)—so has the spiritual Babylon a cup in its hand, full of the abomination and uncleanness of its whoredom, of which the kings of the earth and all who dwell on the earth have been made drunk. As it is said of Babylon that she dwells by great waters and has great treasures, so writes John of the Romish Babylon, that it is clothed in silk and purple and scarlet and adorned with gold, precious stones and pearls (Rev. xviii. 12). Of Babylon it is said that the slain in Israel were smitten by her; so also the spiritual Babylon is become drunk with the blood of the saints (Rev. xvii. 6). Just, however, as the Chaldean Babylon is a type of the spiritual in its pride and despotism, so also is it a type of the destruction which will come upon it. Many wished to heal Babylon but she would not be healed; so many endeavor to support the ruinous anti-christian Babylon, but all in vain. For as Babylon was at last so destroyed as to be a heap of stones and abode of dragons, so will it be with anti-christian Babylon. Of this it is written in Rev. xiv. 8: She is fallen, fallen, that great city, for she has made all nations drink of the wine of her fornication. And again, Babylon the great is fallen, and is become the habitation of devils and is hold of all foul and hateful birds (Rev. xviii. 2). As the inhabitants of Babylon were admonished to flee from her, that every man might deliver his soul (li. 6)—and again, My people, go ye out from the midst of her and deliver every man his soul, etc. (li. 45)—so the Holy Spirit admonishes Christians almost in the same words to go out from the spiritual Babylon, that they be not polluted by her sins and at the same time share in her punishment. For thus it is written in Rev. xviii. 4, I heard, says John, a voice from heaven saying, Go ye out of her, My people, that ye be not partakers of her sins and that ye receive not of her plagues, for her sins reach unto heaven and God remembers her iniquities." *Würtemb. Summarien.*

18. On li. 5. "A monarch can sooner make an end of half a continent than draw a nail from a hut which the Lord protects.—And if it is true that Kaiser Rudolph, when he revoked the toleration of the Picards and the same day lost one of his principal forts, said, 'I thought it would be so, for I grasped at God's sceptre' (WEISMANNI, *Hist. Eccl. Tom.* II. p. 320)—this was a sage remark, a supplement to the words of the wise." ZINZENDORF.

19. On li. 9. **We heal Babylon, but she will not be healed.** Babylon is an outwardly beautiful but inwardly worm-eaten apple. Hence sooner or later the foulness must become noticeable. So is it with all whose heart and centre is not God. All is inwardly hollow and vain. When this internal vacuity begins to render itself externally palpable, when here and there a rent or foul spot becomes visible, then certainly come the friends and admirers of the unholy form and would improve, cover up, sew up, heal. But it does not avail. When once there is death in the body no physician can effect a cure.

20. On li. 17, 19, 20. "The children of God have three causes why they may venture on *Him*. 1. All men are fools, *their* treasure is it not; 2. The Lord is their hammer; He breaks through

CHAP. LI. 59–64.

everything, and 3, they are an instrument in His hand, a heritage; in this there is happiness." ZINZENDORF.

21. On li. 41-44. "How was Sheshach thus won, the city renowned in all the world thus taken? No one would have thought it possible. but God does it. He rules with wonders and with wonders He makes His church free. Babylon is a wonder no longer for its power, but for its weakness. We are to know the world's weakness even where it still appears strong. A sea of hostile nations has covered Babylon. Her land is now a desolation. God takes Bel, the principal idol of Babylon, symbolizing its whole civil powers in hand, and snatches his prey from his teeth. Our God is stronger than all worldly forces, and never leaves us to them." DIEDRICH.

22. On li. 58. "Yea, so it is with all walls and towers, in which God's word is not the vital force, even though they be entitled churches and cathedrals . . God's church alone possesses permanence through His pure word." DIEDRICH.

23. On li. 60-64. When we wish to preserve an archive safely, we deposit it in a record-office where it is kept in a dry place that no moisture may get to it. Seraiah throws his book-roll into the waters of the Euphrates, which must wash it away, dissolve and destroy it. But this was of no account. The main point was that he, Seraiah, as representative of the holy nation had taken solemn stock of the word of God against Babylon, and as it were taken God at His word, and reminded Him of it. In this manner the matter was laid up in the most enduring and safest archive that could be imagined; it was made a case of honor with the omniscient and omnipotent God. Such matters can, however, neither be forgotten, nor remain in dead silence, nor be neglected. They must be brought to such an end as the honor of God requires.

HOMILETICAL AND PRACTICAL.

1. On l. 2. This text may be used on the feast of the Reformation, or any other occasion with reference to a *rem bene gestam*. The Triumph of the Good Cause, 1. over what enemies it is gained; 2. to what it should impel us; (*a*) to the avoidance of that over which we new triumph; (*b*) to the grateful proclamation of what the Lord has done for us, by word and by deed.

2. On l. 4-8. The deliverance of Israel from the Babylonian captivity a type of the deliverance of the Church. 1. The Church must humbly acknowledge the captivity suffered as a just judgment of God. 2. She must turn like Israel inwardly with an upright heart unto the Lord; 3. She must become like Israel to all men a pattern and leader to freedom.

3. On l. 5. A confirmation sermon. "What is the hour of confirmation? 1. An hour which calls to separation; 2. an hour which leads to new connections; 3. an hour which fixes forever the old covenant with the soul's friend." FLOREY, 1863.

4. On l. 18-20. Assyria and Babylon the types of all the spiritual enemies of the church as of individual Christians. Every one has his Assyria and his Babylon. Sin is the destruction of men. Forgiveness of sins is the condition of life, for only where forgiveness of sins is, is there life and blessedness. In Christ we find the forgiveness of sins. He destroys the handwriting. He washes us clean. He is also the good shepherd who leads our souls into green pastures, to the spiritual Carmel.

5. On l. 31, 32. Warning against pride. Babylon was very strong and powerful, rich and splendid. It seemed invincible by nature and by art. Had it not then a certain justification in being proud, at least towards men? No; for no one has to contend only with men. Every one who contends has the Lord either for his friend or his enemy. It is the Lord from whom cometh victory (Prov. xxi. 31). He it is who teacheth our hands to fight (Ps. xviii. 35; cxliv. 1). His strength is made perfect in weakness (2 Cor. xii. 9). He can make the lame (Isa. xxxiii. 23; Mic. iv. 7) and mortally wounded (Jer. xxxvii. 10) so strong that they overmaster the sound (comp. ver. 45). He can make one man put to flight a thousand (Deut. xxxii. 30; Isa. xxx. 17). With him can one dash in pieces a troop and leap over a wall (Ps. xviii. 29). No one accordingly should be proud. The word of the Lord, "I am against thee, thou proud one!" is a terrible word which no one should conjure up against himself.

6. On l. 33, 34. The consolation of the Church in persecution. 1. It suffers violence and injustice. 2. Its redeemer is strong.

7. On li. 5. God the Lord manifests such favor to Israel as to declare Himself her husband (ii. 2; iii. 1). But now that Israel and Judah are in exile, it seems as if they were rejected or widowed women. This, however, is only appearance. Israel's husband does not die. He may well bring a period of chastisement, of purification and trial on His people, but when this period is over, the Lord turns the handle, and smites those through whom He chastised Israel, when they had forgotten that they were not to satisfy their own desire, but only to accomplish the Lord's will on Israel.

8. On li. 6. A time may come when it is well to separate one's self. For although it is said in Prov. xviii. 1; he who separateth himself, seeketh that which pleaseth *him* and opposeth all that is good—and therefore separation, as the antipodes of churchliness, *i. e.*, of churchly communion and humble subjection to the law of the co-operation of members (1 Cor. xii. 25 sqq.) is to be repudiated, yet there may come moments in the life of the church, when it will be a duty to leave the community and separate one's self. Such a moment is come when the community has become a Babylon. It should, however, be noted that one should not be too ready with such a decision. For even the life of the church is subject to many vacillations. There are periods of decay, obscurations, as it were, comparable to eclipses of the stars, but to these, so long as the foundations only subsist, must always follow a restoration and return to the original brightness. No one is to consider the church a Babylon on account of a passing state of disease. It is this only when it has withheld the objective divine foundations, the means of grace, the word and sacrament, altogether and permanently in their saving efficacy. Then, when the soul can no longer find in the church the pure and divine

bread of life; it is well "to deliver the soul that it perish not in the iniquity of the church." From this separation *from* the church is, however, to be carefully distinguished the separation *within* the church, from all that which is opposed to the healthy life of the church, and is therefore to be regarded as a diseased part of the ecclesiastical body. Such separation is the *daily* duty of the Christian. He has to perform it with respect to his private life in all the manifold relations, indicated to us in Matt. xviii. 17; Rom. xvi. 17; 1 Cor. v. 9 sqq.; 2 Thess. iii. 6; Tit. iii. 10; 2 John 10, 11.—Comp. the article on *Sects*, by PALMER in HERZOG, *R.-Enc.*, XXI., S. 21. 22.

9. On li. 10. The righteousness which avails before God. 1. Its origin (not our work or merit, but God's grace in Christ); 2. Its fruit, praise of that which the Lord has wrought in us (*a*) by words, (*b*) by works.

10. On li. 50. This text may be used at the sending out of missionaries or the departure of emigrants. Occasion may be taken to speak 1, of the gracious help and deliverance, which the Lord has hitherto shown to the departing; 2, they may be admonished to remain united to their distant land with their brethren at home by (*a*) remembering the Lord, *i. e.*, ever remaining sincerely devoted to the Lord as the common shield of salvation; (*b*) faithfuly serving Jerusalem, *i. e.*, the common mother of us all (Gal. iv. 26), the church, with all our powers in the proper place and measure, and ever keeping her in our hearts.

IV. Conclusion.

HISTORICAL APPENDIX, CONTAINING A BRIEF SURVEY OF THE EVENTS FROM THE BEGINNING OF THE REIGN OF ZEDEKIAH, TO THE DEATH OF JEHOIACHIN (ch. lii.).

By *the concluding words of* li. 64 (*Thus far, etc.*) *the final editor of the book evidently wished to indicate that the words of Jeremiah cease with* ch. li., *and that, therefore, what follows is not from him, but some other. We are thus expressly warned by those concluding words against the mistake of attributing* chap. lii. *to the prophet. Nevertheless the chapter has been considered by* D. KIMCHI, ABARBANEL *and many others, as a work of Jeremiah.* SEB. SCHMIDT, *e. g., in opposition to the opinion of* ABARBANEL, *says that the men of the great synagogue took the history of the destruction of Jerusalem from the Book of Kings and inserted it here,* "*ne forte erremus in eo, quod supra scriptum est.*" *And afterwards* "*Contrarium potius statuimus, scripta hæc esse a Jeremia propheta et transsumta in librum Regum, sicut in eum historia Hiskiæ ex Jesaja translata est, cum aliquo tamen variatione, ut appareat, utrumque scriptorem habere quod sibi proprium et a Spiritu sancto inspiratum.*" *All orthodox commentators of the older period do not however adopt this view. The strict Lutheran* FÖRSTER, *e. g., says in his Commentary, which appeared in* 1672, "*Hucusque fuit prophetia Jeremiæ. Caput istud ultimum ab alio quodam viro pio et sancto ἐπεισάγματος quasi loco superadditum fuit vel huc transcriptum ex II. Reg. c. 25.*"—*Among the more modern authors* HAEVERNICK *adopts the view that Jeremiah wrote the history of Jehoiachin and Zedekiah just as Isaiah wrote that of Hezekiah. He then, as editor of the Book of Kings allotted its natural place to this description in* 2 Ki. xxv. (*Einl. II.*, S. 172) *while* Jer. lii. *was added to these by the collectors of the prophecies. He afterwards* (*II.* 2, S. 248) *modifies this view, at least declaring* vers. 31-34 *to be a subsequently added notice, which, however, passed naturally and probably at the same time to* 2 Ki. xxv.—KEIL (*Einl. II.*, *Aufl.*, S. 261; *Comm. über die proph. Geschichtsbücher des A. T., III. Bd.*, 1865, S. 378, 9) *is of opinion that an extended history of the last times of the kingdom of Judah, composed* "*perhaps by Jeremiah or Baruch*" (*in the Einl., etc., it is* "*either by Jeremiah or by Baruch*"), *was in existence. The two narratives of* Jer. lii. *and* 2 Ki. xxv. *were brief extracts from this. Most commentators, however, are of opinion that the present passage belonged originally to the Book of Kings, and was inserted by a later hand with several lesser and one great modification* (*the insertion of* Jer. lii. 28-30, *in the place of* 2 Ki. xxv. 22-26). *I also adopt this view in substance, for the following reasons:* 1. *The introduction of the passage* (lii. 1, 2) *contains the standing formula of the Book of Kings, with which the succession of a new king is usually recorded. This introduction is thus undoubtedly original in the Book of Kings. For whoever composed it, and from whatever source it may have been drawn, it was at any rate, as it now reads, written originally for the Book of Kings, and in* Jer. lii. *is only a transposition from thence.* 2. *The rest also is so composed that it cannot be said there is anything contained in it contrary in form or purport to the usual character of the Books of the Kings.* 3. *There is, therefore, a strong presumption that the narrative also thus introduced was originally written for the Book of Kings, to which it is essential and indispensable, and which, without it, would be so much mutilated, while the Book of Jeremiah receives in it a conclusion however useful, yet essentially foreign.* 4. *The transference from the Book of Kings is made purposely and with consideration. This is evident from the fact that the brief section,* vers. 28-30, *was inserted instead of the narrative concerning the fate of the Jews remaining in the country, which is only a brief extract from Jeremiah,* chh. xxxix.-xliii., *and therefore in the Book of Jeremiah would have been an unnecessary repetition.* 5. *As the form of the text the relation is as follows:* (*a*) *in* vers. 1-5, Jer. lii. *has some traces of an older form of the text, not*

CHAP. LII. 1-11.   437

yet purified from roughnesses. Comp. וְהִגִּידָה עַד־הַשְׁלִיכוֹ, ver. 3, *with* 2 Ki. xxiv. 20. *Likewise the older form* נְכוּבְרוּ *ver.* 4, *with* 2 Ki. xxv. 1. *On the other hand* וַיְהִי *ib. betrays the hand of an emendator.* (*b*) *In vers.* 6-11, *the text of* Jer. lii. *is in general, especially as regards completeness and correctness much better;* ver. 6 *contains the indispensable statement of the month, which is strangely lacking in* 2 Ki. xxv. 3; *so also* Jer. lii. 7 *contains the verbs indispensable to the sense,* יִבְרְחוּ וַיֵּצְאוּ וי. Ver. 10 *b contains the statement concerning princes of Judah,* ver. 11 *a similar one concerning the imprisonment of Zedekiah, which are both wanting in* 2 Ki. xxv. *The text of* 2 Ki. xxv. *thus appears here to be more than contracted (comp. also* אֹתוֹ, 2 Ki. xxv. 5 *with* אֶת־צִדְקִיָּהוּ Jer. lii. 8, *whereby the harshness occasioned in* 2 Ki. xxv. 7 *by a change of subjects is removed*). *The absence of those essential parts of speech in vers.* 3, 4, *can be the result only of the transformations which the text has suffered. Thus also the other wants of the text may be explained, and there is no necessity for assuming the common use of a third source.* (*c*). *From vers.* 12-23 *the Book of Kings shows in vers.* 8-17 *a text variously emended and purged from real or apparent offences. In ver.* 8 Nebuchadnezzar, *ib.* עֶבֶד *for* עָבַד, *and* יְרוּשָׁלִַם *for* בּ״י, *in* ver. 9 כָּל־בֵּית־נָדוֹל *for the more difficult* הַגָּדוֹל. *In ver.* 10 *the superfluous* כֹּל *is absent before* חוֹמֹת; *in ver.* 11 *for the same reason is wanting* וּמִדַּלּוֹת הָעָם; *the rare word* הָאָמוֹן *is altered into the more current* הֶהָמוֹן, *in ver.* 12 *we read* דַּלַת *for* דַּלּוֹת, *which does not occur elsewhere; ib. the name Nebuzaradan seemed superfluous; ib.* נָבִים *Chethibh for* נְבִים, *not occurring elsewhere; in* ver. 14 מִזְרָקוֹת, *and likewise in ver.* 15 סִפִּים *and* סִירוֹת, *because otherwise these names would be mentioned twice, also in* ver. 15 *the two neighboring words to the two last mentioned have disappeared; in ver.* 16 *with perfect justice the statement concerning the twelve oxen is absent; ib. we find the easier* לִנְחֹשֶׁת; *in* ver. 17 *the apparently superfluous* וְהָעַמּוּדִים *is wanting in the beginning, then all from* חוּט, *perhaps because these statements were already to be found in* 1 Ki. vii. 15, 16; *in* ver. 17 אַחַת *is wanting after* הַכֹּתֶרֶת; *ib.* שָׁלֹשׁ *is an evident mistake; after* ver. 17 *that is entirely wanting which forms* Jer. lii. 23, *perhaps because its main import had been already expressed in* 1 Kings vii. 20. — (*d*). *In verses* 24-27 *again the text of* Jeremiah lii. *shows itself to have been emended, but not happily; in* ver. 24 הַמִּשְׁנֶה *is only an apparent improvement; in* ver. 25 אֲשֶׁר הָיָה *is certainly plainer; ib.* שִׁבְעָה *is doubtful; the absence of the article before* סֹפֵר *seems to proceed from ignorance.* (*e*). *In the concluding section, vers.* 31-34, *again the text of the book of Kings betrays the hand of the emendator; in* ver. 27 (2 Ki. xxv.) הַמִּשָּׁה *is obscure, but* וַיּוֹצֵא אֹתוֹ *seemed evidently superfluous; instead of the rarer form* כִּלְאָ *stands the more usual* כֶּלֶא, בְּבֵית כֶּלֶא *is a simplification;* שְׁנָא *in ver.* 29 *is a later Aramaic form; in ver.* 30 בְּבֶל *is wanting as superfluous, for the same reason also* עַד יוֹם מוֹתוֹ.

From all this it seems to follow that Jer. lii. *is certainly a transposition of* 2 Ki. xxv. *but that in the former passage we have a better text, neither disfigured by needless correction nor by other injuries. Whether the author of the book of Kings is Jeremiah himself, or whether especially at the close of his history he made use of this prophet's writings, I leave undecided. This much, however, is certain, that this chapter neither stood originally in this place, nor is it an extract made by another person from the same source, from which* 2 Ki. xxiv. 18-25, 30 *was derived. Whatever opinion, however, may be held regarding the sources,* Jer. lii. *was not drawn therefrom by another person, but transposed from the book of Kings, and yet has preserved the text more pure than the original passage.*

The object of the transposition was evidently first to furnish the reader of the prophecies with the necessary historical guidance. The object may also have been prominent to show how completely and exactly the threatenings of the prophet against the stiff-necked people were fulfilled.

1. *The capture of the city, together with the circumstances immediately previous and subsequent thereto.*

LII. 1-11.

1 Zedekiah *was* one and twenty years old when he began to reign, and he reigned eleven years in Jerusalem. And his mother's name *was* Hamutal the daughter
2 of Jeremiah of Libnah. And he did *that which was* evil in the eyes of the LORD,
3 according to all that Jehoiakim had done. For¹ through the anger of the LORD [For so] it came to pass in Jerusalem and Judah [that Jehovah was angry] till he had cast them out from his presence, that [And] Zedekiah rebelled against the king
4 of Babylon. And it came to pass in the ninth year of his reign, in the tenth month,² in the tenth *day* of the month, *that* Nebuchadrezzar king of Babylon came, he and all his army, against Jerusalem, and pitched against it, and built forts [a rampart]³

5 against it round about. So the city was besieged¹ unto the eleventh year of king
6 Zedekiah. And in the fourth month, in the ninth *day* of the month, the famine
  was sore in the city, so that there was no bread for the people of the land [the
7 common people]. Then the city was broken up [through], and all the men of war
  fled, and went forth out of the city by night by the way of the gate between the
  two walls, which w·s by the king's garden ; (now the Chaldeans *were* by the city
8 round about ;) and they went² by the way of [to] the plain. But the army of the
  Chaldeans pursued after the king, and overtook Zedekiah in the plains of Jericho;
9 and all his army was scattered from him. Then they took the king, and carried
  him up unto the king of Babylon to Riblah in the land of Hamath ; where he gave
10 judgment upon him. And the king of Babylon slew the sons of Zedekiah before
11 his eyes: he slew also all the princes of Judah in Riblah. Then he put out the
   eyes of Zedekiah ; and the king of Babylon bound him in chains [a double
   chain], and carried him to Babylon, and put him in prison till the day of his
   death.

TEXTUAL AND GRAMMATICAL.

¹ Ver. 3.—הִשְׁלִיכוּ, if there be no mistake in the writing, is an abnormal form of the infinitive. Comp. OLSH., § 191, *b*, *f*; EWALD, § 238, *d*. On the neuter meaning of the fem. verb הָיְתָה comp. NAEGELSB. *Gr.*, § 60, 6, *b*; Isaiah xi. 20; 2 Kings xxiv. 3.

² Ver. 4.—The differences between the text here and in 2 Kings xxv. 1, 2 are as follows: 1. Instead of הְ בְּשָׁנָה here בִּשְׁנַת הַתְּשִׁיעִית there. The latter mode of expression (*anno noni, i. e., numeri,* comp. NAEGELSB. *Gr.*, § 65, 2, *a*) is found in Jer. also in xxviii. 1, Chethibh ; xxxii. 1, Chethibh ; xlvi. 2 ; li. 59. Besides also in lii. 28 ; xxix. 30. 2. 2 Kings has the later form in Heb., Nebuchadnezzar (comp. xxi. 2-7 ; xxiv. 1 ; xxxii, 1 ; xxxv. 11 ; xxxix. 11 ; xliii. 10 ; xliv. 30 ; xlvi. 2 ; l. 17 with xxvii. 6, 20; xxviii. 3; xxxix. 5; Hitzig on xxiv. 1). 3. יִחַן, 2 Kings, instead of וַיְּחַן, which is required by וַיָּבֹן.

³ Ver. 4.—The word רִיק occurs, besides here and in the parallel passages, only in Ezek. iv. 2; xvii. 17 ; xxi. 27 ; xxvi. 8. It is thus a later word. The root רוק does not occur in Hebrew, but is very common in the Chaldee, Syriac and Samaritan, where it has the meaning, *speculari, inspicere, circumspicere,* רִיק is therefore *specula,* the watch-tower, from which the besieged city may be watched and assailed. With this agrees what Isa. xxiii. 13, where the בַּחוּנִים of the Chaldeans are spoken of. It is surprising that the word never occurs in the plural, as we should expect, if it designated only the single towers. We may therefore suppose that it signifies the whole line of circumvallation, including the towers, and is thus a *potiori*, a collective designation. As the Chaldeans were celebrated for their skill in sieges (comp. HERZOG, *Real-Enc.,* IV., S. 394), the word may have passed from their language into the Hebrew. Comp. KEIL on 2 Ki. xxv. 1 ; HAEVERNICK on Ezek. iv. 2, S. 49 ; GESEN., *Thes.*, p. 330.

⁴ Ver. 5.—בְּצוּר is primarily *coarctatio* in general and then specially *coarctatio* by means of *obsidio*, hence it assumes the latter meaning in connections like עִיר בָּצוּר (Ps. xxxi. 22 ; lx. 11), בָּנָה כִּי (Deut. xx. 20), נָתַן מִי עַל (Ezek. iv. 2), בּוֹא פֶּה (2 Kings xxiv. 10 ; xxv. 2), without involving a complete suppression of the radical signification. Comp. x. 17 ; xix. 9.

⁵ Ver. 7.—Instead of וַיֵּלְכוּ we find in 2 Ki. the manifestly less correct form, וַיֵּלֶךְ.

EXEGETICAL AND CRITICAL.

Vers. 1-3. **Zedekiah . . . king of Babylon.**
These three verses are of the same purport with 2 Ki. xxiv. 18-20, with only two unessential differences. In the latter passage, ver. 20, we find וּבִיהוּדָה for בִיהוּדָה, and עַד־הִשְׁלִיכוֹ for עַד־הִשְׁלִיכוּ, in both cases an easier and more correct reading, of which it is more natural to suppose that it arose out of the other, than the reverse. The present passage then has the presumption of originality in its favor. Comp., moreover, 2 Chron. xxxvi. 11-13.—**For through the anger,** *etc.* The reason for Jehovah's anger is punishment, in ver. 2, however, to which the for refers, it is sin, not punishment, which is spoken of. Accordingly the words are not to be taken as causal, but as was shown on xxxii. 31 (p. 287) עַל is used here as frequently elsewhere for אֶל or לְ, and אַף־עַל is the statement of the

effect: it came to pass that Jehovah was angered —which may be said of what happened *in* Jerusalem, as well as *against* it.
Vers. 4, 5. **And it came to pass . . . Zedekiah.** These words are found almost exactly the same in 2 Ki. xxv. 1, and in an abridged extract in xxxix. 1. Compare also Ezek. xxiv. 1. For the exposition of the parts reproduced in ch. xxxix., see there the differences between this text and that of the Book of Kings. Comp. the TEXTUAL NOTES.
Vers. 6, 7. **And in the fourth month . . . the plain.** These opening words, found also in xxxix. 2, are wanting in 2 Kings, although the statement of the day without that of the month, makes no sense, and also the words **and went out of the city**, though thus the sentence loses its predicate. KEIL (on 2 Ki. xxv. 4) supposes that not only the predicate has fallen out after **all the men of war**, but also still more before these words, in 2 Ki. and Jer. lii., namely, the words found in xxxix. 3, "and it came to pass, when Zedekiah the king of Judah saw them," because

the king (according to 2 Ki. xxv. 5; Jer. lii. 8; xxxix. 5) was among the fugitives, and because the words "and all the men of war," have no proper connection with the previous context and could not form an adverbial sentence. But if Keil were right, the whole verse xxxix. 3 must have dropped out, since **them** refers to the persons mentioned in it. We have already shown on ch. xxxix. that vers. 1, 2, 4-10 are only an abridged extract from ch. lii. and that the words quoted above are only a connecting clause between the original and genuine ver. 3, and the following verses derived from ch. lii. These words are therefore of later date than ch. lii., and cannot have been omitted before "and all the men," etc. The previous mention of the king is not necessary, since he is included; the sentence moreover is not adverbial, but a narrative of a by no means unusual construction (comp. Ewald, § 346, b).

Vers. 8-11. **But the army . . of his death.** The Book of Kings reads "him" instead of **Zedekiah.** It is plain that the former could be more easily derived from the latter than the reverse.—**In the land of Hamath** is wanting in 2 Ki. xxv. 6, while it is found ib. ver. 21 (comp. 2 Ki. xxiii. 33).—**He gave judgment.** 2 Ki. xxv. 6, has "they gave," etc., on which comp. rems. on xxxix. 5.—The first half of ver. 10 agrees with xxxix. 6, even to the there added words, "in Riblah." In 2 Ki. xxv. 7 it reads, "and they slew the sons," etc., the Chaldeans of ver. 5 being still the subject. The second half of ver. 10 is entirely wanting in 2 Kings. The blinding and binding in chains of king Zedekiah is narrated in both places in the same way, but in 2 Ki. the singulars **put out** (יְעַוֵּר) and **bound him** (וַיַּאַסְרֵהוּ) are the more surprising, as the sentence is contained in the plural **carried him** (וַיְבִאֻהוּ). 2 Ki. xxv. is entirely silent on the confinement of Zedekiah in Babylon. Hitzig justly calls attention to the fact that בֵּית־הַפְּקֻדֹּת is not simply a prison, this being always otherwise expressed (comp., e. g., ver. 31). Jeremiah, who is not blinded, is put into prison; but Zedekiah, the more guilty, is blinded and put into the house of correction. Comp. Simson on Jud. xvi. 21. The LXX. also has εἰς οἰκίαν μυλῶνος. Yet it appears that towards the end his confinement was less rigorous, and that an honorable interment was granted him after his death, for this is the purport of the promise made to him through Jeremiah in xxxiv. 1-5.

---

2. *The Destruction of the City and Deportation of the People.*

LII. 12-16.

12 Now in the fifth month, in the tenth day of the month, which was the nineteenth
    year of Nebuchadrezzar king of Babylon, came Nebuzar-adan, captain of the guard
    [of the halberdiers], who served [stood before][1] the king of Babylon, into Jerusalem.
13 And burned the house of the LORD [Jehovah] and the king's house; and all the
    houses of Jerusalem, and all the houses of the great men [every great house],[2] burned
14 he with fire. And all the army of the Chaldeans, that were with the captain of
15 the guard, brake down all the walls of Jerusalem, round about. Then Nebuzaradan captain of the guard [halberdiers] carried away captive *certain* of the poor
    [a part of the lowest] of the people, and the residue of the people that remained in
    the city, and those that fell away, that fell to the king of Babylon, and the rest of
16 the multitude [work-people].[3] But Nebuzar-adan the captain of the guard left
    certain of the poor [part of the meanest][4] of the land for vinedressers and for
    husbandmen.[5]

TEXTUAL AND GRAMMATICAL.

[1] Ver. 12.—For עָמַד לִפְנֵי, of which words the former owes its punctuation to the erroneous connection with יְרוּשָׁלַםִ (hence also רָב), 2 Kings reads עָבַר as a correction, and יְרִי without בְּ. He ought doubtless to read עָבַד. Comp. xxxv. 19; Jud. xx. 28.

[2] Ver. 13.—Before גָּדוֹל the article is wanting in 2 Ki. according to rule. Comp. Naegelsb. *Gr.*, § 82, 6. But the construct state of בֵּית is surprising in both cases. Probably it read originally, as Hitzig supposes, בֵּית גָּדוֹל. A mistake (comp. the בֵּית twice before) caused בֵּית, from which came בֵּית הַגָּדוֹל. This can be taken only in the sense of rhetorical emphasis, הַגָּדוֹל being collective for "the great" (2 Ki. iv. 8; v. 1). Then certainly the constr. state is perfectly normal, but in 2 Ki. the traces of an older form of the text are to be recognized. Before חוֹמֹת ver. 14 is wanting in 2 Ki. the certainly unnecessary כָּל, before רַב־טַ however the grammatically necessary אֶת.

[3] Ver. 15.—Instead of יֶתֶר הָאָמוֹן, 2 Ki. has הֶהָמוֹן. The word אָמוֹן must have seemed obscure even to the authors

of the text of 2 Ki. xxv. and Jer. xxxix., the one rendering it as above, the other by הָעָם הַנִּשְׁאָרִים. In Prov. viii. 36 אֹמְוּ‎ and in Song of Sol. vii. 1 אָמוֹן certainly has the sense of work-man, and accordingly we may take the word here as a collective designation of the חָרָשׁ and כַּסְגָּר, whose deportation is spoken of in xxiv. 1 and xxix. 2. Thus HITZIG, GRAF, MEIER. KEIL, on the other hand, appeals to xxxix. 9. But this passage, as well as 2 Ki. xxv. 11, proves only that to both authors the word אָמוֹן appeared strange. Whether they interpreted it correctly is another question. If it should be alleged that it is a word appertaining only to a higher style, we reply that it would not be an easy alteration from הָכִין.

⁴ Ver. 16.—Instead of כְּדַלּוֹת 2 Ki. has כְּדַלַּת. This also betrays the hand of the corrector, since דַלּוֹת does not occur elsewhere either as plural or singular (EWALD, §185, c). It is the plural of דָלָה (xl. 7; 2 Ki. xxiv. 14; xxv. 12)—*tenuitates*, insignificances.

⁵ Ver. 16.—The name Nebuzar-adan appeared superfluous to the author of 2 Ki. xxv., having been mentioned in ver. 12. The word יֹגְבִים, which does not occur elsewhere, he altered into יֹגְבִים (from גּוּב, *fodit, aravit*). Comp. remarks on xxxix. 10.

EXEGETICAL AND CRITICAL.

Vers. 12-14. **Now in the fifth ... round about.** Instead of the tenth day, 2 Kings (as also Bar. i. 2) mentions the seventh, as the same text also states three cubits instead of the five in ver. 23, and five men instead of the seven in ver. 25. HITZIG, THENIUS, GRAF, KEIL [BLAYNEY, HENDERSON] rightly suppose that these differences arose from the interchange of the letters of the older alphabet used as numerals. Which statements are correct is not ascertainable. THENIUS [comp. also WORDSWORTH] declares the statement here made to be the correct one, because the Jews afterward kept the ninth day as a fast. But on the other hand comp. KEIL on 2 Ki. xxv. 8.

Vers. 15, 16. **Then Nebuzar-adan .... husbandmen.—The poor of the people**, which is wanting in 2 Ki., has come here either by mistake from ver. 16, where it also begins the sentence, or it is to express the thought that the poor people did not all remain behind, but were partly carried away. The latter is probably the correct view.—**Multitude** [work-people]. It is difficult to decide which is the correct rendering. Both suit the sense, for a remnant of work-people might just as well be spoken of as a remnant of the masses of the people (either in antithesis to the warriors or the population of the city). I prefer to take the word in the sense in which it undoubtedly occurs in Prov. viii. 30 [then was I as a workman with him], and Song of Sol. vii. 1.

3. *The Carrying away of the sacred Vessels.*

LII. 17-23.

17 Also the pillars of brass that *were* in [belonged to]¹ the house of the LORD, and the bases, and the brazen sea that *was* in the house of the LORD [Jehovah] the
18 Chaldeans brake, and carried all² the brass of them to Babylon. The caldrons [pots] also, and the shovels, and the snuffers, and the bowls, and the spoons, and
19 all the vessels of brass wherewith they ministered, took they away. And the basins,³ and the firepans,⁴ and the bowls, and the caldrons [pots], and the candlesticks, and the spoons, and the cups ;⁵ *that* which *was* of gold *in* gold, and *that* which *was* of silver *in* silver [which were entirely of gold or silver]⁶ took the captain of
20 the guard [halberdiers] away. The⁷ two pillars, one⁸ sea, and twelve brazen bulls that *were* under⁹ the bases, which king Solomon had made to [for] the house
21 of the LORD [Jehovah]; the brass¹⁰ of all these vessels was without weight. And *concerning* the pillars, the height¹¹ of one pillar *was* eighteen cubits; and a fillet of twelve cubits did compass it; and the thickness thereof *was* four fingers; *it was*
22 hollow.¹² And a chapiter of brass *was* upon it; and the height of one chapiter *was* five cubits, with network¹³ and pomegranates upon the chapiter, round about, all
23 *of* brass. The second pillar also and the pomegranates¹⁴ *were* like unto these. And there were ninety and six pomegranates on a side; *and* all the pomegranates upon the network *were* a hundred round about [round about were a hundred].

TEXTUAL AND GRAMMATICAL.

¹ Ver. 17.—Instead of אֲשֶׁר לְבֵית we read in 2 Ki. xxv. 13 בֵּית. אֲשֶׁר בֵּית. The latter—which were in the house of Jehovah, the former—which belonged to the house, etc.

² Ver. 17.—In 2 Kl. כֹּל is wanting before נְחֹשְׁתָּם as in ver. 14 before חֹמוֹת.
³ Ver. 19.—סִפִּים (1 Kl. vii. 50; 2 Kl. xii. 14, סִפּוֹת, 2 Sam. xvii. 28, סַפּוֹת) from סַף, basin, bowl (Ex. xii. 22; Zechariah xii. 2) not to be confounded with סַף, threshhold (ver. 24). סִפּוֹת כֶּסֶף are expressly mentioned in 2 Kings xii. 14.
⁴ Ver. 19.—מַחְתּוֹת (from חָתָה, to hold, seize, specially used of bringing fire, Isa. xxx. 14; Prov. vi. 27) are vessels for carrying burning substances, whether coals (Lev. xvi. 13) or lighted incense (Num. xvi. 17 sqq.).
⁵ Ver. 19.—מִזְרָקוֹת are mentioned besides only in Ex. xxv. 29; xxxvii. 16; Num. iv. 7, and in all these places among the utensils of the shew-bread-table (comp. rems. on כַּפּוֹת, ver. 18) and as pertaining to libation, (אֲשֶׁר יֻסַּךְ בָּהֵן). In Ex. xxv. 29 these vessels are expressly designated as to be made of gold.
⁶ Ver. 19.—The double position of זָהָב and כֶּסֶף has the sense of "only" or "wholly" (massive). Comp. NAEGELSB. Gr., § 22 b.—The words וְאֶת הַסִּפִּים and וְאֶת הַסִּירוֹת to מִזְרָקוֹת are wanting in 2 Kings. It is noteworthy that thus (a) the repetition of סִירוֹת and כַּפּוֹת, and (b) the plural סִפִּים, which occurs nowhere else in the sense of "basins" are avoided; (c) that the words following סִירוֹת and כַּפּוֹת are also removed.
⁷ Ver. 20.—With respect to the construction of ver. 20 we are to regard the substantives set first absolutely as in the accusative: as to the pillars, etc., their brass was not to be weighed. The verse is to express that it was those large pieces which raised the weight of the brass to such a degree.
⁸ Ver. 20.—Instead of הָאֶחָד the Keri would have read (not in 2 Ki.) merely אֶחָד, probably because both numbers stand before and afterwards without the article. Grammatically both are possible. Comp. NAEGELSB. Gr., § 73, 2 Anm.
⁹ Ver. 20.—The explanation of תַּחַת in the sense of "instead" is as forced as the assumption that the text originally read וַחֲפִצְכוֹת is arbitrary.
¹⁰ Ver. 20.—Instead of לִנְחֻשְׁתָּה (the suffix by anticipation, comp. NAEGELSB. Gr., § 77, 2; Jer. li. 56 and on xlviii. 44) we find in 2 Ki. xxv. 16 simply לִנְחֻשְׁתָּן.
¹¹ Ver. 21.—The Keri קוֹמַת, with which the Chethibh in 2 Ki. xxv. 17 and 1 Ki. vii. 14 accords, is unnecessary, for קֹמָה may be regarded as the accusative of measure (comp. NAEGELSB. Gr., § 70, g): eighteen cubits was a pillar as to height.
¹² Ver. 21.—On the construction comp. NAEGELSB. Gr., § 97, 2 a and Anm. 1.
¹³ Ver. 22.—בְּבֹכֶךָ from שָׁבָךְ, nectere, plectere inus (comp. סְבָךְ Nah. i. 10; Job viii. 13; סָבַךְ, thicket, Gen. xxii. 13, etc.), is opus reticulatum, network. Comp. 1 Ki. vii. 17 sqq.; 2 Ki. i. 2; 2 Chron. iv. 12, 13; Job xviii. 8.
¹⁴ Ver. 22.—רִמֹּנִים at the close of ver. 22 is wanting in 2 Ki. xxv. 17, and we find instead עַל-הַשְּׂבָכָה. This makes the impression that this expression seemed unsuitable to the author of Jer. lii. (it must denote together with the network), both on account of the עַל and because the pomegranates were also named after the network, and that, in order besides the general וְאֵלֶּה to set forth a special part, he chose in preference the last mentioned, the רִמֹּנִים.

EXEGETICAL AND CRITICAL.

Vers. 17-20. Also the pillars ... weight.
Concerning the brazen pillars of Solomon's temple comp. 1 Ki. vii. 15-22; 2 Chron. iii. 15 sqq.; WINER, R.-W.-B., s. v. Jachin und Boas; HERZOG, R.-Enc. VI. S. 366, 7. [WORDSWORTH, ad loc., and SMITH's Dict. s. v.].—The מְכֹנוֹת, bases (comp. 1 Ki. vii. 27 sqq.), were pedestals or stands, four cubits long, four broad and three high, to serve as supports for the ten basins required in washing the flesh of the sacrifices (2 Chron. iv. 6). Comp. KEIL on the Books of Kings.—The brazen sea (comp. 1 Ki. vii. 23-26; 1 Chron. xviii. 8; 2 Chron. iv. 2-6) served for the priests' washing (comp. Exod. xxx. 18 sqq.). WINER, R.-W.-B. s. v.—HERZ., R.-Enc. IX. S. 236 sqq. [Comp. WORDSWORTH and SMITH's Dict.].—Of the smaller vessels are mentioned סִירוֹת, pots for carrying away the ashes from the altar; יָעִים, shovels for removing the ashes; מְזַמְּרוֹת, not to be confounded with כְּמָרוֹת, a vine-dresser's knife, occurring in three places only besides this: 1 Ki. vii. 50; 2 Ki. xii. 14; 2 Chron. iv. 22, and always with מִזְרָקוֹת, of uncertain meaning: Vulg., etc., psalteria; LUTHER, etc., knife; GESENIUS, etc., scissors, lamp-scissors, at any rate an instrument so-called a carpendo; מְזָרֵקוֹת, which is wanting in 2 Ki., probably that it might not occur twice, from זָרַק, sparsit, therefore vas unde spargitur, bowls, mentioned in Exod. xxvii. 3; xxxviii. 3; Num. iv. 14 among the altar-utensils, therefore used for sprinkling the blood of the sacrifices, but comp. also Am. vi. 6; כַּפּוֹת, likewise of uncertain meaning, LXX. κεράγρα, flesh-fork, flesh-hook, the moderns—spoons, pans, bowls, on account of their resemblance to the bent hand. Comp. KEIL on Kings. In Exod. xxv. 29 these appear among the utensils of the table of shew-bread, comp. Num. vii. 14, 20, 26, etc. WINER, R.-W.-B. and HERZ., Real-Enc. s. v. Schaubrodtisch. All these vessels were of brass [HENDERSON, copper]. In the following verse the golden and silver vessels are also enumerated, which the Chaldeans carried away. HITZIG has unjustly attacked ver. 19 as spurious, for it does not interrupt the connection, since evidently in vers. 18, 19 all the smaller vessels are to be enumerated, the larger ones having been mentioned in ver. 17. These latter could, of course, be only of brass, but the total amount of the brass plundered was so great that it seemed to merit the special emphasis given to it in ver. 20. The golden and silver vessels are not there mentioned, because it was only the brazen ones which were of such immense weight. The pots, sprinkling cups and spoons are mentioned a second time in ver. 19, simply because there were such utensils both of brass and of gold and silver. HITZIG's

opinion that *all* the golden and silver vessels had already been carried away at Jehoiachin's deportation, certainly finds some support in 2 Ki. xxiv. 13 ("all the vessels of gold"). From the circumstance, however, that only golden vessels are spoken of, we may conclude that the cream only was then removed, *i. e.* the most valuable. The golden vessels of low value as well as all the silver remained for the thorough evacuation made by Nebuzar-adan.—The words **and twelve brazen bulls which were under** are rightly wanting in 2 Ki. xxv. 16. For they contain a double error: 1. the twelve bulls were not under the bases, but under the sea, according to 1 Ki. vii. 25; 2 Ki. xvi. 17. 2. In 2 Ki. xvi. 17 it is expressly related that Ahaz had already taken away the twelve bulls and replaced them by a substructure of stone. Whither they went is not indeed stated, but no more is it recorded that they were restored to their original position. I therefore, in opposition to KEIL (*Comm. on Kings*), agree with those who regard the words in question as the arbitrary addition of some one, whose mind was not clear about the "bases," and who had forgotten the passage in 2 Ki. xvi. 17. [Comp. WORDSWORTH].

Vers. 21-23. **And the pillars ... a hundred.** Supplementary and more particular description of the pillars.—**And the pillars** wanting in 2 Ki. The height is also stated at eighteen cubits in 1 Ki. vii. 15. The description there given is in general the basis of this.—**And a fillet,** *etc.*, to the end of the verse, is also wanting in 2 Ki.—If the pillars were twelve cubits in circumference, the diameter (comp. WINER, *R.-W.-B.* s. v. *Jachin und Boas*) was about four cubits, which gives a perfectly correct proportion. The thickness of the brass was four fingers. Thus the pillars were hollow, as indeed is remarked.—**A chapiter.** This is the capital, *coronamentum* of the pillar. Comp. 1 Ki. vii. 16; 2 Chron. iv. 12, 13.—Instead of *five* cubits 2 Ki. xxv. 17 has *three*. The number five is the correct one according to 1 Ki. vii. 16.—**Of one** is unnecessary, but not incorrect, since of course it is understood not of a second capital, but the capital of the second pillar. It is evidently based on 1 Ki. vii. 16.—The pomegranates were also an ornamentation on the hem of the priest's ephod, or surplice (Ex. xxviii. 33, 34). A figure of it may be seen in THENIUS, *Comm. on Kings*, Taf. III. Fig. 2 *bb.*—Ver. 23 is entirely wanting in 2 Kings. Ninety-six pomegranates on each pillar were placed רוּחָה, *i. e.* towards the wind, towards the four winds or sides [HENDERSON after HITZIG, towards the air, the outside of the capitals]. The expression is found here only. Comp. Ezek. xxxvii. 9. It is clear that this is the meaning from the statement that the entire number of the pomegranates attached to the network was a hundred. There must then have been also a pomegranate at each corner.

---

4. *The Execution of the Representatives of the People and Statement of the Number of the Captives.*

LII. 24-30.

24 And the captain of the guard [halberdiers] took Seraiah the chief priest, and
25 Zephaniah the second priest, and the three keepers of the door: He took also out of the city a eunuch [court officer], which had the charge [was[1] overseer] of the men of war; and seven men of them that were near the king's person, which were found in the city; and the principal scribe[2] of the host [the scribe, the prince of the host], who mustered the people of the land; and three-score men of the people
26 of the land, that were found in the midst of the city. So Nebuzar-adan the captain of the guard took them and brought them to the king of Babylon to Riblah.
27 And the king of Babylon smote them, and put them to death in Riblah in the land
28 of Hamath. Thus Judah was carried away captive out of his own land. This *is* the people whom Nebuchadrezzar carried away captive: in the seventh year three
29 thousand Jews and three and twenty: In the eighteenth year of Nebuchadrezzar he carried away captive from Jerusalem eight hundred and thirty and two per-
30 sons: In the three and twentieth year of Nebuchadrezzar Nebuzar-adan the captain of the guard carried away captive of the Jews seven hundred forty and five persons: all the persons *were* four thousand and six hundred.

TEXTUAL AND GRAMMATICAL.

[1] Ver. 25.—In 2 Ki. xxv. we find הָיָה for הָיָה. The former does not necessarily, as HITZIG asserts, signify "which is." הָיָה takes the place of the copula generally, without reference to time. Comp. EWALD, § 297 *b*.

[2] Ver. 25.—וְאֵת כֹּפֵר. In 2 Ki. xxv. הַסֹּפֵר, which I regard as the more correct reading.

EXEGETICAL AND CRITICAL.

Vers. 24-27. **And the captain ... out of his own land.** These verses differ from the corresponding verses in 2 Ki. xxv., with the exception of some trifling variations in language, only in the statement of a number (seven instead of five in ver. 25), of which hereafter. It is related that representatives of all classes of the people, priests, officials and simple citizens had to suffer death, evidently in token that Nebuchadnezzar held not only the king but the people guilty of rebellion. At the head of those executed stands the high-priest Seraiah, who is nowhere mentioned in the book of Jeremiah. According to 1 Chron. v. 40 he was the son of Azariah and grandson of Hilkiah ; according to Ezr. vii. 1, Ezra was descended from him.—After Seraiah is mentioned Zephaniah, doubtless the same who is mentioned in xxi. 1; xxix. 25, 29; xxxvii. 3 as priest simply and son of Maaseiah. Here he is called **the second priest**, but in 2 Ki. xxv. **second priest** only without the article. As according to 2 Ki. xxiii. 4 (where as here three grades of priests are enumerated) there were several second priests, the reading of the Book of Kings is probably the correct one. Comp. OEHLER in HERZOG, *R.-Enc.* VI. *S.* 203, 4.—The **keepers of the door** [or threshold] are also mentioned in 2 Ki. xii. 10; xxii. 4; xxiii. 4; Jer. xxxv. 4. As only three of them are mentioned, we must regard these as the superiors of the four thousand Levitical שֹׁעֲרִים (1 Chron. xxiii. 5). For further details consult OEHLER in HERZ., *R.-Enc.* VIII. *S.* 354-6.—In the second category of those executed are mentioned certain inhabitants of Jerusalem, who held offices at court, especially in the war-department. The city here seems to stand in antithesis both to the temple (ver. 24) and to the country (ver. 25 *b*). The one סָרִיס (court-officer, but possibly at the same time eunuch, comp. rems. on xxix. 2) was not *the* overseer, but only *an* overseer, etc. He was therefore one of the generals, perhaps commander of the city garrison.—**And seven men.** In 2 Ki. xxv. we read *five* men, whether correctly or incorrectly cannot here be decided as in vers. 12 and 22. The analogy of these cases however favors our text.—**That were near the king's person**, literally, "that saw the king's face," *viz.* in the sense of a daily custom, is a designation of high, yea, highest position (Esth. i. 14; comp. Matt. xviii. 10). These were therefore officials of high rank, and as it is not said that they were endued with military functions, they may be regarded as representatives of the civil authorities.—**Scribe, the prince of the host.** Scribe is not a writer in our sense. The title belongs not only, as GRAF supposes, to the "people of the pen," but is given to the highest officers of State. Comp. 2 Sam. viii. 7 ; xx. 25; 2 Ki. xii. 11; 1 Chr. xviii. 16; xxvii. 32. And in 2 Chr. xxvi. 11 it is expressly recorded that Uzziah's army went out "by the hand of Jeiel the scribe." This Sopher was not the leader of the host, but chief of the war-department, minister or secretary of war. Comp. SAALSCHUETZ, *Mos. Recht. S.* 63.—**And threescore men.**

These sixty men appear as the third class of persons executed, and representatives of the country population, as is indicated by their number and the remark that they were found **in the midst of the city** (2 Kings xxv. 19 "in the city"). This remark would be altogether superfluous, if the object was not to set forth that these men did not originally belong to the city.—**On Riblah** comp. rems. on xxxix. 5.—The words, **Thus Judah was carried away captive out of his land**, are found in both texts and in both places are appropriate. For in Jeremiah they form the transition to the numbering of the deported, and in 2 Kings they lead to the account of what happened in the country after the deportation. They therefore furnish no data for the solution of the question which of the two recensions is the original. Moreover, there seems to be an allusion in them to i. 3.

Vers. 28-30. **This is the people ... four thousand and six hundred.** This section is entirely wanting in 2 Kings. It is difficult to bring it into harmony with the other statements respecting the deportations. The differences are as follows: 1. This section speaks of three deportations, while according to the other testimonies of the Old Testament there were only two (under Jehoiakim and Zedekiah). 2. The section follows a divergent chronology, stating that the deportations took place in the seventh, eighteenth and twenty-third years of Nebuchadnezzar, while this very chapter (ver. 12) and 2 Ki. xxiv. 12; xxv. 8 have the eighth and nineteenth years of Nebuchadnezzar as the dates of the deportation, but know nothing of any in the twenty-third year of this king. 3. According to this passage three thousand and twenty-three were carried away the first time, eight hundred and thirty-two the second time, seven hundred and forty-five the third time, total four thousand six hundred, which sum is expressly given at the close of ver. 30. According to 2 Ki. xxiv. 14-16, however, eighteen thousand souls were carried away at the first deportation alone. There are no counter-statements with regard to the other numbers, but their smallness is surprising; of this hereafter. On these points we make the following remarks: 1. By the seventh year in ver. 28, we are certainly to understand the seventh year of Nebuchadnezzar, since both the other deportations are dated in years of this monarch. 2. These statements are not necessarily erroneous, but may possibly follow another reckoning of the years, and perhaps the same as Josephus follows (*Antiqq.* X., 8, 5; *C. Ap.* I., 21), though evidently only on the basis of this passage. Comp. NIEBUHR, *Ass. u. Bab., S.* 58 sqq. 3. Ver. 29 mentioning the eighteenth year after ver. 12 has stated the nineteenth as the date of the same fact, shows that we have here another author. 4. The view of EWALD (*Gesch. d. V. Isr.*, III., 1 *S* 435) which GRAF also adopts, that in ver. 29 we are to read שְׁבַע עֶשְׂרֵה, that accordingly *one year before* the last capture of Jerusalem three thousand and twenty-three were carried captive from the *country* (hence הָאָרֶץ), *after* the capture eight hundred and thirty-two from the *city* (hence מִירוּשָׁלָיִם, ver. 29), and finally five years later from the land already somewhat repopulated seven hundred and forty-five, has much in its favor, but is yet not perfectly satisfactory. For the circumstance that the difference between the eighth and nineteenth, and the seventh and eighteenth years of Nebuchadnezzar is the same, does not authorize us to supply a word עֲשִׂרָה fallen out after שָׁבַע. Then, too, the deportation of the *mass* of the people *during* the war, at a time when the Egyptian army was to be feared (comp. xxxvii. 5), is scarcely probable. Finally the assumption of a deportation five years after the capture of the city is pure hypothesis, for which there is no positive testimony. It is also not to be supposed that five years after the destruction, admitting the return of a few scattered individuals, an almost equally great number could be carried away as after the destruction of the capital. Would not these have rather again betaken themselves to flight? 5. Even if we grant that the strikingly small numbers of the exiles are to be judged from a specific point of view, and therefore do not necessarily imply an error, any more than the number of the years of Nebuchadnezzar's reign, yet the differences between vers. 12 and 28 still remain, with the exceedingly obscure third deportation, as irremovable stones of stumbling, and I therefore agree with Niebuhr, when he says, "it cannot be a subject of doubt that vers. 28-30 in the fifty-second chapter of Jeremiah are a gloss."

5. *The Favorable turn in the Fate of Jehoiachin.*

LII. 31-34.

31 ¹ And it came to pass in the seven and thirtieth year of the captivity of Jehoiachin king of Judah, in the twelfth month, in the five and twentieth *day* of the month, *that* Evil-merodach king of Babylon, in the *first* year of his reign, lifted up
32 the head of Jehoiachin king of Judah, and brought him forth out of prison, and spake kindly unto him, and set his throne above the throne of the kings that were
33 with him in Babylon, and changed² his prison-garments: and he did continually
34 eat bread before him all the days of his life. And *for* his diet, there was a continual diet given him of the king of Babylon, every day a portion [the day's requirements] until the day of his death, all the days of his life.

TEXTUAL AND GRAMMATICAL.

¹ Ver. 31.—2 Kings xxv. for כָּלְכָתוֹ has כִּלְאוֹ; וַיֵּצֵא אֹתוֹ is wanting; for הַכְּלִיא it reads כְּלָא, instead of לְכֶסֶא כִּסֵּא בְּכֵל more simply בְּסֵא; כְּעַל further שְׁנָא for שָׁנָה (ver. 33); לִפְנֵי תָּכִיד the same words reversed, for הַפְּלֶךְ (ver. 34) merely הַפְּלֶךְ; the words עַד יוֹם מוֹתוֹ are entirely wanting in 2 Kings. All these alterations indicate that the author of 2 Ki. xxv. endeavored to give an, in his opinion, improved text.

² Ver. 33.—שָׁנָה is the Hebrew, שְׁנָא (2 Ki. xxv.) the later Aramaic form. Comp. Olsh., § 233, Anm., and § 246, b. Anm.

EXEGETICAL AND CRITICAL.

To this section there is an almost exactly corresponding one in 2 Ki. xxv. (27-30). The differences are unessential: instead of the twenty-fifth day, 2 Ki. xxv. 31 has the twenty-seventh (comp ver. 25, where the reverse is the case), so that one is tempted to think that one of the two authors has interchanged these two passages; (comp. also rems. on ver. 12). For other differences comp. the TEXTUAL NOTES.—The expression to lift up the head, is found also in Gen. xl. 13 coll. 19 and 20, and designates the elevation of one who is prostrate. Comp. the expression in another sense in Ex. xxx. 12; Num. i. 2, *etc.*; Ps. lxxxiii. 3.—In the first year of his reign. It was evidently an act of grace, which Evil-merodach performed on the occasion of his ascending the throne. May not the influence of Daniel and other highly esteemed Jews at the Babylonian court have operated in favor of the imprisoned king?—Out of prison. Comp. rems. on xxxvii. 4.—Above the throne. This expression does not mean that Jehoiachin received a seat on the same level, but surpassing the others in height, but that his seat stood higher up than the others, *i. e.*, that he could sit nearer to the king. Whether the others were princes constantly or transiently present, may be left undecided. Perhaps both.—His diet, אֲרֻחָה (comp. xl. 5), evidently comprehends all that Jehoiachin needed for himself and household, besides the food which he had at the royal table. The accumulation of expressions, indicating that Jehoiachin continued without interruption to the end of his life to enjoy royal honors, shows that this fact gave great satisfaction to the author.—On the chronological relations, comp. NIEBUHR, *Ass. u. Babel.*, *S.* 87 sqq.; DUNCKER, *Gesch. d. Alterth*, I., *S.* 864, 5.

—The ascension of the throne by Evil-merodach occurred in the year B. C., 561. It is not absolutely impossible that Jeremiah was still alive at this time. Supposing that he began his ministry at the age of twenty, he would be then about eighty-six. Comp. the dates in xxiii. 3, and lii. 31. It is also not impossible that he received in Egypt the news of Jehoiachin's exaltation. But this notice includes not only the liberation of the ex-king, but his death (vers. 33, 34). Thus vanishes all probability of Jeremiah's being its author, as well as from the consideration that the notice, if proceeding from Jeremiah, must have been found in another place, and not at the close of this supplement, evidently compiled by a later hand.

DOCTRINAL AND ETHICAL.

1. "*Docemur hoc capite, quod comminationes divinæ non sint de pelvi fulgura, quodque Deus pro misericordia sua infinita calamitates a se immissas mitigare plerumque soleat, si seria interveniat pœnitentia.*" FÖRSTER.

2. On vers. 1-3. "From this we see why God sometimes places ungodly rulers over a country, who cast it to destruction. It is done on account of the rulers' and the people's sins, that they may draw down the well merited punishment, as Sirach says. On account of violence, injustice and avarice, a kingdom passes from one nation to another (x. 8). So also says king Solomon. Because of the sins of a nation occur many changes of rulers, but for the sake of the people who are intelligent and reasonable, the State is prolonged (Prov. xxviii. 2)." *Wurtemb. Summarien.*

3. On ver. 4. "God allows many slight and mild punishments to come as warnings, till at last comes the finishing stroke. This is a witness to the divine long-suffering (Rom. ii. 4)." CRAMER.

4. On ver. 6. "The fact that in this siege compassionate women had to kill and eat their own children (Lam. iv. 10) is a reminder that by bodily hunger God would punish; 1. satiation and disgust towards His holy word and soul-food; 2. the terrible offering up of children to Moloch; 3. the loose discipline of children." CRAMER.

5 On ver. 7. "No fortress can protect the ungodly, even though they had their nest in the clouds." CRAMER.

6. On ver. 8. "An example of faithless, perjured men of war. But as Zedekiah broke his oath to the king at Babylon, he was paid back in the same coin." CRAMER. "His people forsook the poor king Zedekiah on his flight and he was captured, from which we see that great men cannot depend on their body-guard; these flee in time of need, and leave their masters in the lurch. The surest and best protection is when we have the holy angels for our guard . . . This angelic protection is, however, to be obtained and preserved by faith and godliness, but is lost by unbelief and ungodly conduct." *Wurtemb. Summ.*

7. On vers. 9-11. The punishment of perjury. "*Ubi monemur, quod fides hosti, etiam barbaro, qualis hodie Turca, a Christianis data, minime violanda.*" FÖRSTER.

8. On ver. 9. sqq. "God had shown Zedekiah by Jeremiah a way in which he could escape the calamity. But because he forsook the Lord and would not follow it, the others were only leaky cisterns (Jer. ii. 13). For woe to the rebellious who take counsel without the Lord (Isa. xxx. 1). This is useful for an instance against the holy by works, who reject God's way of escaping the Devil; when they devise other ways for themselves they are caught by the Chaldeans of hell." CRAMER.

9. On ver. 12 sqq. "Holy places, external ceremonies and *opus operatum* do not avail for hypocrites . . . If God punished His own institution so severely, how shall human institutions remain unpunished?" CRAMER.

10. On ver. 12. "*Quale fatum, ne et nostris obtingat templis . . . caveamus, ne profanemus templa ulterius tum externa vel materialia, tum interna vel spiritualia in cordibus nostris, de quibus* 1 Cor. iii. 16 sqq.; vi. 19 sqq." FÖRSTER.

11. On ver. 15. "It is another work of mercy that some of Judah were preserved. For God's grace is always to be found in His punishments." CRAMER.

12. On ver. 15. "He who will not serve God and his neighbor at home and in quiet, must learn to do it in a strange land in affliction and distress." CRAMER.

13 On ver. 24 sqq. "As teachers are often to blame for their behaviour that sin gets the upper hand in a community, it is exceedingly just when God brings such for an example into great punitive judgment (1 Sam. ii. 27-34)." STARKE.

14. On ver. 24. "The priests are caught and slain; 1. because they could not believe the truth for themselves; 2. because they led others astray; 3. because they appealed to the temple of the Lord; 4. because they persecuted the true prophets: 5. because they troubled the whole church of God. But he who troubleth shall bear his judgment, whosoever he be (Gal. v. 10)." CRAMER.

15. On ver. 31 sqq. "*Sane omnino verisimile videtur judicio Philippi Melanchthonis in Chron. part, I fol. 33 Evilmeroduchum amplexum esse doctrinam Danielis de Vero Deo, quam et pater publico edicto professus est, eamque ob causam clementiam exercuisse erga regem Jechoniam.*" FÖRSTER. — "*Narrant Hebræi hujusmodi fabulam: Evilmerodach, qui patre suo Nabuchodonosor vivente per septem annos inter bestias, ante regnaverat, postquam ille restitutus in regno est, usque ad mortem patris cum Joakim rege Judæ in vinculis fuit; quo mortuo, quum rursus in regnum succederet, et non susciperetur a principibus, qui metuebant, ne viveret qui dicebatur extinctus, ut fidem patris mortui faceret, aperuit sepulcrum et cadaver ejus unco et funibus traxit.*" JEROME on Jer. xiv. 18. 19. JOSEPHUS *speaks of it as follows*: "Ἀβιλμαρώδοχος εὐθὺς τὸν Ἰεχονίαν τῶν δεσμῶν ἀφεὶς ἐν τοῖς ἀναγκαιοτάτοις φίλοις εἶχε . . . Ὁ γὰρ πατὴρ αὐτοῦ τὴν πίστιν οὐκ ἐφύλαξε τῷ Ἰεχονίᾳ, παραδόντι μετὰ γυναικῶν καὶ τέκνων καὶ τῆς συγγενείας ὑλῆς ἑκουσίως ἑαυτὸν ὑπὲρ τῆς πατρίδος, ὡς ἂν μὴ κατασκαφείη ληφθεῖσα τῇ πολιορκίᾳ." (*Antiqq.,* X. 11, 21.)

16. On ver. 31 sqq. "*Ceterum potest hoc exemplo, quod Jechonias rex dignitati suæ in exilio Babylonico restitutus, refutari exceptio Judæorum contra vaticinium Jacobi* (Gen. xlix. 10) *de Messia jamdudum exhibito, nonquam per Romanos sceptrum de Juda ablatum ad quod τεκμήριον Messiæ jamjam nascituri esse debuit.*" FÖRSTER.

17. On ver. 31 sqq. "No one should despair in misfortune, for the right hand of the Highest can change all (Ps. lxxvii. 10) and Christ rules even in the midst of His enemies (Ps cx. 2). For His are the praise, the glory and the power from everlasting to everlasting. Amen." CRAMER.

HOMILETICAL AND PRACTICAL.

1. On vers. 1-11. The truth of the word "What a man soweth, that shall he also reap," exhibited in the example of the Jewish State under Zedekiah. 1. The seed (ver. 2); 2. The crop (*a*) the siege, (*b*) the famine, (*c*) the capture of the city and flight of the king, (*d*) the punishment of the king and his princes, (*e*) the fate of the people (ver. 3). 2. On vers. 12-20. The rejection of Judah appears at first sight a contradiction. For Jerusalem is the holy city (Matt. iv. 5; Neh. xi. 1, 18), the city of God (Ps. xlvi. 5; xlviii. 2, 9; lxxviii. 3); the temple is the house of Jehovah (Jer. vii. 2, *etc.*); God's service rests on divine authority (Ex. chh. xxv.-xxvii., xxx., xxxi). But God cannot contradict Himself. We have, therefore, to show "the unity of the divine thoughts in the choice and rejection of Jerusalem." 1. The rejection was a conditional one (vii. 3 sqq). Hence notwithstanding the election the rejection involved nothing contradictory, but was a necessary consequence of the unfulfilled condition.—

2. The election remains (*a*) objectively notwithstanding the rejection; it is (*b*) subjectively brought to its realization by the rejection, the latter as a means of discipline operating to produce the disposition, from which alone the fulfil ment of this condition can proceed. Comp. rems. on xxxii. 41, p. 288.
3. On vers. 24-27. "That great lords sometimes make an example of gross miscreants, promotes righteousness, only it must not be done on the innocent, or with such severity that there is no proportion between the crime and its punishment (Josh. vii. 25)." STARKE.
4. On vers. 31-34. The deliverance of Jehoiachin. 1. It shows us that the Lord can help (*a*) out of great distress (grievous imprisonment of thirty-seven years), (*b*) in a glorious manner. 2. It admonishes us (*a*) to steadfast patience, (*b*) to believing hope, Ps. xiii. ["It was a prelude and pledge of the liberation and exaltation of the Jewish Nation, when it had been humbled and purified by the discipline of suffering; and of its return to its own land; and a joyful pre-announcement of that far more glorious future restoration which the prophets in the Old Testament, and the Apostles in the New foretell—of Israel to God in Christ; to whom, with the FATHER and HOLY GHOST, be ascribed all honor, glory, dominion, adoration and praise, now and forever. Amen." WORDSWORTH.—S. R. A.].

www.ingramcontent.com/pod-product-compliance
Lightning Source LLC
Chambersburg PA
CBHW022135300426
44115CB00006B/200